the human past

World Prehistory & the Development of Human Societies

Edited by Chris Scarre

With 753 illustrations, 211 in colour

Thames & Hudson

Half-title Neolithic figurine of a seated man, from Cernavoda, Romania, late 4th millennium BC.
Title page Stonehenge, in southern Britain, a megalithic monument dating in its final phase to around 2500 BC.

First published in the United Kingdom in 2005 by
Thames & Hudson Ltd, 181A High Holborn, London WC1V 7QX

www.thamesandhudson.com

British Library Cataloguing-in-Publication Data
A catalogue record for this book is available from the British Library

ISBN-13: 978-0-500-28531-2
ISBN-10: 0-500-28531-4

Picture research by Sally Nicholls

Printed and bound in Slovenia by MKT PRINT d.d.

the human past

BRIEF CONTENTS

CONTRIBUTORS 17
PREFACE 19
TIMELINE 22

1 INTRODUCTION:
THE STUDY OF THE HUMAN PAST 24

PART I THE EVOLUTION OF
HUMANITY *6 million to 11,500 years ago* 44

2 AFRICAN ORIGINS 46

3 HOMININ DISPERSALS IN THE
OLD WORLD 84

4 THE RISE OF MODERN HUMANS 124

PART II AFTER THE ICE
11,500 years ago to the Early Civilizations 174

5 THE WORLD TRANSFORMED:
FROM FORAGERS AND FARMERS
TO STATES AND EMPIRES 176

6 FROM FORAGERS TO COMPLEX
SOCIETIES IN SOUTHWEST ASIA 200

7 EAST ASIAN AGRICULTURE AND
ITS IMPACT 234

8 AUSTRALIA AND THE AUSTRONESIANS
264

9 ORIGINS OF FOOD-PRODUCING
ECONOMIES IN THE AMERICAS 306

10 HOLOCENE AFRICA 350

11 HOLOCENE EUROPE 392

12 THE RISE OF CIVILIZATION IN
SOUTHWEST ASIA 432

13 THE MEDITERRANEAN WORLD 472

14 SOUTH ASIA: FROM EARLY VILLAGES
TO BUDDHISM 518

15 COMPLEX SOCIETIES OF EAST AND
SOUTHEAST ASIA 552

16 MESOAMERICAN CIVILIZATION 594

17 FROM VILLAGE TO EMPIRE IN SOUTH
AMERICA 640

18 COMPLEX SOCIETIES OF NORTH
AMERICA 678

19 THE HUMAN PAST: RETROSPECT
AND PROSPECT 716

GLOSSARY 721
BIBLIOGRAPHY 726
SOURCES OF ILLUSTRATIONS 759
INDEX 762

CONTENTS

CONTRIBUTORS 17

PREFACE 19

TIMELINE 22

1 INTRODUCTION:
THE STUDY OF THE HUMAN PAST 24
Chris Scarre, University of Cambridge

What is Archaeology? 25
Prehistory vs. History 26

The Relevance of World Archaeology 27

The Origins of Archaeology 28
Renaissance Beginnings 28
Advances in the 17th and 18th Centuries 30
Developments in the 19th Century 31

Social Evolution 32

Developments in Methodology and Techniques 33

Explaining Change: Archaeological Theories 35
Cultural Ecology and Agency Theory 35
Mechanisms and Patterns of Change 36
• *Innovation, Diffusion, Emulation, and Migration* 36
• *Linear and Cyclical Patterns* 37
Processual and Postprocessual Archaeology 38

Humans in Long-term Perspective 39
Humans and the Environment 40
Demographic Growth 40
Symbols and Cognition 41

Summary and Conclusions 43

Further Reading and Suggested Websites 43

PART I THE EVOLUTION OF
HUMANITY 6 million to 11,500 years ago 44

2 AFRICAN ORIGINS 46
Nicholas Toth and Kathy Schick, Indiana University

Evolution and Human Origins 47
Models of Evolutionary Change 48
The Human Evolutionary Record 49

The Primate Ancestors of Apes and Humans 49
What is a Primate? 49
Overview of Primate Evolution 50

• *Early Anthropoid Features* 51
• *Old World Monkeys and Apes* 51
Our Ape Ancestry: The Comparative Anatomical and Genetic Evidence 51
• *Anatomical Evidence* 52
● KEY CONTROVERSY Classifying the Primates 52
• *Genetic Evidence* 53

The Environmental Background 55
● KEY METHOD Reconstructing Paleoenvironments 56
Climate Change and Early Hominin Evolution 56

The Rise of the Earliest Hominins 57
The Australopithecines 57
● KEY DISCOVERY Discovering the "Ape Men" 59
● KEY SITES Hadar and Laetoli: "Lucy," the "First Family," and Fossil Footsteps 60
The Emergence of Homo 61

The First Stone Tools and the Oldowan 61
Technology 66
● KEY SITE Olduvai Gorge: The Grand Canyon of Prehistory 67
Who Made the Oldowan Tools? 68
● KEY CONTROVERSY Modern Apes as Oldowan Toolmakers? 69
The Nature of the Sites 70
● KEY SITES Regional Overview of Major Oldowan Sites 71
● KEY METHOD Dating Early Hominins and their Archaeology 74

Food Procurement and Diet 74
Hunters or Scavengers? 75
● KEY DISCOVERY What were Oldowan Tools Used For? 76
Food for Thought: Diet and Encephalization 77

The Behavior of Oldowan Hominins 78
Social Organization 78
Diet 78
Technology 78
Fire 79
Site Modification 79
Art, Ritual, and Language 79

Recent Trends in Approaches to the Oldowan 80
Experiments in Site Formation Processes 80
Isotopic Studies 82
Landscape Archaeology 82

Summary and Conclusions 82

Further Reading and Suggested Websites 83

3 HOMININ DISPERSALS IN THE OLD WORLD 84
Richard G. Klein, Stanford University

Homo ergaster 85
  Anatomy 85
    • *The Turkana Boy* 86
    • *Human Evolution and the Inferences of the Turkana Boy* 88
    ● KEY DISCOVERY The Discovery of the Turkana Boy 89
  The Relationship of Homo ergaster *to Other Hominins* 92

The Acheulean 93
  The Acheulean Hand Axe Tradition 93
  ● KEY DISCOVERY The Acheulean Hand Axe Tradition 94
  Hand Axe Function 95
  Variation within the Acheulean Tradition 96

Homo erectus 97
  The Discovery and Dating of Homo erectus *in Java* 97
  ● KEY CONTROVERSY The Dating of Javan *Homo erectus* 98
  The Discovery and Dating of Homo erectus *in China* 99
  The Archaeology of Chinese Homo erectus 100

The Dispersion of *Homo ergaster* and the Fate of *Homo erectus* 101
  ● KEY CONTROVERSY Did *Homo ergaster* Disperse Partly by Boat? 102
  The Initial Expansion of Homo ergaster *from Africa* 102
  The Expansion of Homo ergaster *to Eurasia: The Dmanisi Discoveries* 102
    • *Dating the Dmanisi Fossils* 103
    • *Evidence that* Homo ergaster *Persisted to 1 Million Years Ago or Later* 104
  The Persistence of Homo erectus *in Java* 105

Homo heidelbergensis and the Earliest Occupation of Europe 106
  ● KEY METHOD Electron Spin Resonance Dating 107
  ● KEY SITE The Gran Dolina TD6 and the History of Cannibalism 108
  Unsuccessful European Colonizers: Homo antecessor *and the Ceprano Skull* 108
  Brain Expansion and Change within the Hand Axe Tradition 110
  The Evolution of the Neanderthals in Europe 110
  ● KEY METHOD Uranium-Series Dating 111

Evidence for Early Human Behaviour apart from Stone Artifacts 112
  Raw Materials besides Stone 112
  ● KEY CONTROVERSY How did Human Fossils Reach the Sima de los Huesos? 113
  Site Modification 114

  Fire 116
  Art 117
  Diet and Food Procurement 118
    • *Plant Foods: Foraging* 118
    • *Animal Foods: Hunting and Scavenging* 119
  ● KEY METHOD Luminescence Dating 119

Summary and Conclusions 121
  ● KEY CONTROVERSY Acheulean Big-Game Hunters? 122

Further Reading and Suggested Websites 123

4 THE RISE OF MODERN HUMANS 124
Paul Pettitt, University of Sheffield

The Climatic Background 125

Competing Hypotheses for the Origin of *Homo sapiens* 127
  The Multi-regional Evolution Hypothesis 128
  The Out of Africa Hypothesis 128
  Other Hypotheses and Attempts at Consensus 128
  ● KEY CONTROVERSY Multi-regional Evolution and Modern Human Emergence in Asia and Australasia 130

The Anatomy of *Homo sapiens* 130

Evolution in Low Latitudes: Evidence for the Rise of Modern Humans in Africa 132
  Earliest Homo sapiens 133
  Transitional Homo sapiens 134
  Anatomically Modern Humans 137

Genetic Keys to the Origins of Modern Humans 137
  Mitochondrial DNA and the Theory of an Early African "Coalescence" 138
  Other Theories and Potential Consensus 139
  Mitochondrial DNA and the Evolution of Homo neanderthalensis 140

Archaeology and the Emergence of "Modern" Behavior in Middle Stone Age Africa 140
  Artifactual Evidence 141
  ● KEY SITE Katanda and the Earliest Harpoons 142
  Hunting and Dietary Evidence 142
  Evidence of Site Modification and Art 143
  ● KEY SITE Klasies River Mouth: Middle Stone Age Hunters? 144
  ● KEY CONTROVERSY The Evolution of Language 146

Evolution in High Latitudes: The Neanderthals 146
  The Anatomy of Homo neanderthalensis 146
  Exploitation of Resources: Hunting, Gathering, and Scavenging 149
  The Mousterian Lithic Industry 150
  Neanderthal Behavior 151

CONTENTS

Early Dispersals of *Homo sapiens* into the Levantine Corridor 152

The Colonization of East Asia and Australia 154
● KEY CONTROVERSY *Homo floresiensis*: A Small-bodied Hominin from Indonesia 155

The Colonization of Europe, and the Middle to Upper Paleolithic Transition 156
● KEY METHOD Radiocarbon Dating 157
The Aurignacian 157
Neanderthal "Transitional" Industries 158
Relations between Neanderthals and Incoming Homo sapiens? 159
● KEY SITES The "Three Cs" of Upper Paleolithic Art: Cosquer, Chauvet, and Côa 160

Developments in Modern Behavior: The European Upper Paleolithic 161
The Gravettian 161
Gravettian Behavior 162
The Magdalenian 163
● KEY CONTROVERSY The Meaning of "Venus" Figurines 164

Late Pleistocene Dispersals: Colonization of the Americas 166
Possible Source Populations 166
• *Archaeology and Human Remains* 166
• *Linguistic and Genetic Evidence* 166
● KEY CONTROVERSY Kennewick Man 168
The Archaeological Evidence for Pre-Clovis Sites 168
• *Interpreting the Evidence* 169
● KEY SITE Monte Verde, Chile 170
The Clovis Phenomenon 171

Summary and Conclusions 172
● KEY CONTROVERSY Big-Game Extinctions in North America 172

Further Reading and Suggested Websites 173

PART II AFTER THE ICE *11,500 years ago to the Early Civilizations* 174

5 THE WORLD TRANSFORMED: FROM FORAGERS AND FARMERS TO STATES AND EMPIRES 176
Chris Scarre, University of Cambridge

Climate Change and Faunal Extinction at the End of the Pleistocene 177

The Early Holocene Environment 179
Coasts and Islands 179

Forests and Deserts 181
Hunter-Gatherer Adaptations to the Holocene 181
A Note on Terminology 182

The Beginnings of Agriculture 183
What is Agriculture? 183
Domestication by Hunter-Gatherer Groups 183
The Development of Domesticates 184
The Geography of Domestication 184
● KEY METHOD DNA and Domestication 185
Why Agriculture? 186

The Spread of Agriculture 187
● KEY CONTROVERSY Explaining Agriculture 188

The Consequences of Agriculture 190
Settlement 190
Social Complexity 191
Material Culture 191
Warfare 192
Agricultural Intensification 192

Cities, States, and Empires 193
The Development of States 194
• *The Geography of State Formation* 195
• *Archaeological Features of States* 195
● KEY CONTROVERSY Cities, States, and Civilizations Defined and Explained 196
Toward History: The Adoption of Writing 196
States and Empires 198

Summary and Conclusions 198

Further Reading and Suggested Websites 199

6 FROM FORAGERS TO COMPLEX SOCIETIES IN SOUTHWEST ASIA 200
Trevor Watkins, University of Edinburgh

The Environmental Setting 201

New Strategies of Settlement and Subsistence: Epipaleolithic Hunter-Gatherers 204
The Early Epipaleolithic in the Levant, c. 18,000–12,000 BC 205
• *Ohalo II and Neve David* 206
● KEY SITE Ohalo II: Epipaleolithic Lifeways in the Levant 207
The Late Epipaleolithic in the Levant, c. 12,000–9600 BC 208
• *The Discovery of the Natufians* 208
• *Evidence for Natufian Lifeways* 208
The Late Epipaleolithic Beyond the Levant 209
● KEY SITE Eynan 210
An Epipaleolithic Summary 212

Culture Change in the Aceramic Neolithic,
c. **9600–6900** BC 212
New Stoneworking Technologies 213
Innovations in Art and Ideas 213
● KEY SITE Abu Hureyra: The Transition from Foraging to Farming 214
The First Large Settlements: Jericho and Çatalhöyük 216
• *Jericho* 216
• *Çatalhöyük* 217
Social Organization 217
Communal Buildings and Rituals 218
● KEY SITE Jerf el Ahmar: A Neolithic Village 218
Burials and Skull Caching 221
● KEY SITE 'Ain Ghazal 222
● KEY SITE Çatalhöyük 224

The Beginning of Cultivation and Plant and Animal Domestication 226
Plant Domestication 226
Hunting and Herding 227
Mixed Farming Economies 228
• *The Evidence of Ali Kosh* 228
● KEY DISCOVERY The Colonization of Cyprus 229
Social Exchange and Networking 230

Transformation and the Ceramic Neolithic,
c. **6900–6000** BC 231
The Levant 231
Syria and Turkey 231
Iraq and Iran 232

Summary and Conclusions 232

Further Reading and Suggested Websites 233

7 EAST ASIAN AGRICULTURE AND ITS IMPACT 234
Charles Higham, University of Otago

The Transition to Agriculture in East Asia 235
The Origins of Millet Cultivation: The Yellow River Valley 237
• *Hunter-Gatherer Sites from before c. 7500 BC* 238
• *Agricultural Sites from after c. 6000 BC* 238
● KEY SITE Cishan: The Transition to Agriculture in the Yellow River Valley 239
The Origins of Rice Cultivation: The Yangzi River Valley 240
• *Gathering Wild Rice: Yuchan and Zhangnao* 241
• *The Transition from Wild to Cultivated Rice: Diaotonghuan and Xianrendong* 241
The Development of Permanent Villages in the Yangzi Valley 242
● KEY CONTROVERSY The Origins of Rice Cultivation 243
● KEY SITE Bashidang: An Early Agricultural Village 244

The Growth of Agricultural Communities 245
Neolithic Cultures in the Yellow River Valley 245
• *The Yangshao Culture* 245
• *The Dawenkou Culture* 245
Neolithic Cultures in the Yangzi River Valley 246
• *The Daxi Culture* 246
• *Hemudu* 246
● KEY SITE Hemudu 247
• *The Majiabang, Songze, and Chengbeixi Cultures* 247

The Expansion of Rice Farmers into Southeast Asia 248
Initial Dispersal into Southern China 248
From Southern China into Vietnam 249
The Khorat Plateau, Thailand 250
• *Early Rice Farmers in Thailand* 250
Cambodia and the Mekong Delta 252
The Bangkok Plain 252
• *Khok Phanom Di and Ban Kao* 252
• *Khok Charoen, Non Pai Wai, and Tha Kae* 254
● KEY SITE Khok Phanom Di: Sedentary Hunter-Fishers 254

The Expansion of Rice Farmers into Korea and Japan 256
Korea 256
Japan 258
• *Jomon Antecedents* 258
• *Yayoi Rice Farmers* 259
● KEY DISCOVERY Sedentism without Agriculture 260

The Linguistic Evidence 261

Summary and Conclusions 263

Further Reading and Suggested Websites 263

8 AUSTRALIA AND THE AUSTRONESIANS 264
Peter Bellwood and Peter Hiscock, Australian National University

Australia 265
Early Foragers in a Changing Landscape 266
Technology in Uncertain Times 268
● KEY SITE Kenniff Cave 269
● KEY CONTROVERSY Explaining Technological Change in Australia 270
Changing Life in Tasmania 270
Changes in Aboriginal Perceptions of the Landscape 271
● KEY CONTROVERSY Why Did the Tasmanians Stop Eating Fish? 272
The Growth of Trade Networks 273
Population and Settlement Change 273
The Effects of Historic Foreign Contacts 274

● **KEY SITE** Barlambidj: Aboriginal Contact with Southeast Asia 275

The Islands of Southeast Asia and Oceania 275
Early Human Settlers in Island Southeast Asia 277
Early Agriculturalists in New Guinea 277
● **KEY DISCOVERY** Early Farming in the New Guinea Highlands 278

The Austronesian Dispersal 279
Who Are the Austronesians? 279
A Basic History of the Austronesian Languages 280
● **KEY CONTROVERSY** The Origins of the Austronesians 282
The Archaeology of Early Austronesian Dispersal 283
  • *Taiwan* 283
  • *Dispersals to Southeast Asia and Madagascar* 284
● **KEY SITE** Beinan 286
The Colonization of Oceania 287
Lapita Economy 288
● **KEY CONTROVERSY** The Origins of Lapita 289
The Settlement of Polynesia 290
  • *Eastern Polynesia* 290
● **KEY SITE** Talepakemalai 291
● **KEY CONTROVERSY** Expert Navigation or Sheer Good Luck? 292
  • *Why Migrate?* 294

The Austronesian World After Colonization 294
Polynesian Complex Societies: Easter Island and Elsewhere 294
● **KEY CONTROVERSY** Causes of Landscape Change 296
● **KEY CONTROVERSY** Easter Island and South America 297
Hawai'i and New Zealand: Varying Social Responses to Environmental Constraints 298
The Chiefdoms of Polynesia: Comparative Ethnographic Perspectives 299
  • *Theories of Social Evolution* 301

Sea-borne Trade and the Transformation of Tribal Society in Southeast Asia 301

Summary and Conclusions 304

Further Reading and Suggested Websites 305

9 ORIGINS OF FOOD-PRODUCING ECONOMIES IN THE AMERICAS 306
David L. Browman, Gayle J. Fritz, Patty Jo Watson, Washington University
The Late Paleoindian Period David J. Meltzer, Southern Methodist University

The Late Paleoindian Period 307
The Plains 307

West of the Rocky Mountains 311
The Eastern Forests 311
Central and South America 312
Changes to Come 313

The Archaic Period, c. 9500 BC onward 313

The Mexican Archaic and the Origins of Mesoamerican Agriculture, c. 9500–2500 BC 313
The Earliest Cultigens 314
● **KEY CONTROVERSY** The Domestication of Maize 316

Southwest North America 317
The Archaic Period 317
Agricultural Beginnings 317
  • *Models of Agricultural Adoption and Dispersal* 319
Later Agricultural Developments and Systems 319

Eastern North America 321
Early to Middle Archaic, c. 9500–4000 BC 322
The Beginnings of Agriculture in the Middle and Late Archaic 323
● **KEY SITE** Koster: An Archaic Camp in Illinois 324
● **KEY DISCOVERY** The Archaic Dog 326
Late Archaic Sites and Lifeways 326
  • *Bacon Bend and Iddins, Tennessee* 326
  • *The Carlston Annis Shell Mound in West Central Kentucky, and the Rockshelters of Arkansas and Eastern Kentucky* 326
  • *Horr's Island, Florida* 327
  • *The Earliest Pottery* 327
Early Woodland Period, c. 1000–200 BC 328
● **KEY SITES** Watson Brake and Poverty Point, Louisiana 328
Later Agricultural Developments 330
  • *Tobacco* 330

Western North America: Alternatives to Agriculture 330
Great Plains Bison Hunting 331
The Pacific Northwest Maritime Cultures 331
The Great Basin Desert Archaic 332
The Archaic Period in California 333

The South American Pacific Lowlands 334
The North Pacific Coast 334
The Peruvian Coast 334
The Chilean Coast 336
● **KEY SITES** La Paloma and Chilca: Archaic Villages of the Peruvian Coast 337
● **KEY DISCOVERY** The Chinchorro Mummies 338
Southern Chile and Southern Argentina 338

The Andean Highlands 338
The Northern Andes 339
The Central Andes 340

• *Northern Peru* 340
• *Central Peru* 341
• *Southern Peru* 341
The Southern Andes 342
● KEY SITE Asana: Base Camp and Herding Residence 343
Andean Animal and Plant Domestication 343
● KEY SITE Caral: The Rise of Socio-political Complexity 345

The Amazonian Lowlands 346

The Atlantic Lowlands 347

Summary and Conclusions 348

Further Reading and Suggested Websites 349

10   HOLOCENE AFRICA 350
     Graham Connah, Australian National University

The Environmental Setting 351

Intensification of Hunting, Gathering, and Fishing 354
Southern and Central Africa 355
• *Southern African Rock Art* 356
Northern, Eastern, and Western Africa 356
• *North Africa and the Sahara* 356
● KEY CONTROVERSY Symbolism in Southern African Rock Art 358
• *East Africa* 359
• *West Africa* 359
● KEY CONTROVERSY A Green Sahara? 360

The Beginnings of Farming 361
The Sahara 361
● KEY CONTROVERSY The Domestication of Cattle in the Sahara 362
The Nile Valley 363
West Africa 363
Northeast and East Africa 364

Ironworking Societies and the Adoption of Farming South of the Equator 365
Movements of Bantu-speaking Peoples 366
Ironworking Farmers 367
● KEY CONTROVERSY The Origins of African Ironworking 368
Domesticated Plants and Animals 369
Interaction Between Hunter-Gatherers and Farmers 369

Urbanization and the Growth of Social Complexity in Ancient Egypt 370
The Predynastic Period 371
The Early Dynastic Period 373
The Old Kingdom 374

● KEY CONTROVERSY How "African" was Ancient Egypt? 375
● KEY DISCOVERY New Insights from the Pyramids 376
The First and Second Intermediate Periods and the Middle Kingdom 376
The New Kingdom and After 377

Urbanization and State Formation in the Rest of Africa 380
Nubia and Ethiopia 380
• *Kerma* 380
• *Napata and Meroë* 381
• *Aksum* 382
North and West Africa 383
● KEY SITE Jenné-jeno: Origins of Urbanism in West Africa 383
Eastern, Southern, and Central Africa 384
• *The Zimbabwe Plateau* 385
• *Remoter Parts of Central Africa* 385
● KEY SITE Great Zimbabwe 386

Africa and the Outside World 387
The Mediterranean, Southwest Asia, and the Red Sea 387
The Indian Ocean 388
● KEY CONTROVERSY Did External Trade Cause African State Formation? 389
The Atlantic Coast 389
● KEY SITE Igbo-Ukwu 390

Summary and Conclusions 390

Further Reading and Suggested Websites 391

11   HOLOCENE EUROPE 392
     Chris Scarre, University of Cambridge

From Foraging to Farming 393
After the Ice: Europe Transformed 394
● KEY SITE Star Carr: a Mesolithic Campsite in Northeast England 396
Farming Comes to Europe 397
● KEY CONTROVERSY Replacement or Continuity? Population Genetics and the First European Farmers 398

Southeastern Europe 400
Neolithic Settlements 400
Figurines and Evidence for Social Complexity 401
The Introduction of Metals 402

The Mediterranean Zone 402
● KEY SITE The Varna Cemetery 403
Neolithic Settlements 404
The Emergence of Social Complexity 405

Central Europe 406
The Bandkeramik Culture 407

CONTENTS

Later Regional Groups 408
● KEY DISCOVERY The "Iceman" 408

Atlantic Europe 410
Mesolithic Settlements 410
● KEY SITE The Talheim Death Pit 411
● KEY SITE The Bandkeramik Settlements at Langweiler, Germany 412
Megalithic Monuments: The Neolithic Transition 413

Northern Europe 415
The Ertebølle-Ellerbek and Later Cultures 415
● KEY CONTROVERSY Stonehenge and Megalithic Astronomy 416
Neolithic Burial Practices 418

Toward Complexity: Europe from 2500 BC to the Roman Empire 419

Later Prehistoric Societies in Central and Western Europe 420
Beaker Pottery and Metalwork 420
Small-scale Settlement and Long-distance Contact 422
• *"Princely Centers"* 423

Later Prehistoric Societies in Eastern Europe 424
Urnfields 425
The Fortified Site of Biskupin 425

European Society at the Dawn of History 426
● KEY CONTROVERSY Rock Art – Representation of Myth or Reality? 426
European Societies Beyond the Mediterranean 427
The So-called "Celtic" Societies 428
• *Bog Bodies* 428
• *The Expansion of Roman Control* 429

Summary and Conclusions 429
● KEY CONTROVERSY Who Were the Celts? 430

Further Reading 431

12 THE RISE OF CIVILIZATION IN SOUTHWEST ASIA 432
Roger Matthews, University College London

Farmers of the Early Chalcolithic: The Halaf and Ubaid Periods, c. 6000–4200 BC 433
The Halaf Period, c. 6000–5400 BC 433
• *Hunting and Warfare* 436
• *Religion and Society* 436
The Ubaid Period, c. 5900–4200 BC 436
• *Eridu* 436
• *Ubaid Sites Beyond Lower Mesopotamia* 437

Urban Communities of the Late Chalcolithic: The Uruk Period, c. 4200–3000 BC 438
The Lower Mesopotamian Site of Uruk 438

The Invention of Writing 440
• *Cylinder Seals* 441
Uruk Expansion and Trade 442

City-States, Kingdoms, and Empires of the Early Bronze Age, c. 3000–2000 BC 443
Sumerian City-States 443
Upper Mesopotamian, Iranian, and Anatolian Cultures 445
Kingdoms and Empires of the Later 3rd Millennium BC 445
● KEY SITE Tepe Yahya 446
● KEY CONTROVERSY The End of the Early Bronze Age 448

Commerce and Conflict in the Middle Bronze Age 448
Lower Mesopotamia and the Persian Gulf 449
Upper Mesopotamia and the Levant 450
● KEY SITE Troy 450
● KEY SITE Ebla 452
Upper Mesopotamia and Anatolia 453

Empires and States at War and Peace: The Late Bronze Age 453
Anatolia and the Hittites 454
● KEY SITE Hattusa, Capital of the Hittites 455
The Levant in the Late Bronze Age 456
• *Ugarit* 457
Upper Mesopotamia and Syria: Hurrian Mittani 458
● KEY SITE The Uluburun Shipwreck 459
The Rise of Assyria 460
Lower Mesopotamia: Kassite Babylonia 461
Elam 462
The End of the Late Bronze Age 463

New and Resurgent Powers of the Iron Age 463
The Levant: Philistines, Phoenicians, Neo-Hittites 463
• *The Philistines* 463
• *The Phoenicians* 464
• *The Neo-Hittites* 464
The Levant: Israel and Judah 465
The Assyrian Empire 465
● KEY CONTROVERSY The Old Testament and Archaeology 466
Anatolian States 467
Babylonia 468
The Achaemenid Empire and the Conquest of Southwest Asia 469

Summary and Conclusions 469
● KEY CONTROVERSY Who Owns the Past? 470

Further Reading and Suggested Websites 471

13 THE MEDITERRANEAN WORLD 472
Susan E. Alcock and John F. Cherry
University of Michigan

Defining the Mediterranean, Redefining its Study 473

The Bronze Age 476
• *Neolithic and Copper Age Settlement* 477
The Aegean Early Bronze Age 477
● KEY CONTROVERSY Early Cycladic Marble Figures 479
• *The Cyclades* 479
• *The Greek Mainland and Troy* 479
Minoan Crete: The Palace Period 480
• *Features and Functions of the Minoan Palace* 480
• *Life Outside the Palaces* 481
• *The End of the Minoan Palaces* 482
Mycenaean Greece 482
• *Mycenae* 482
● KEY DISCOVERY Linear B 484
• *Other Mycenaean Palaces* 485
• *Mycenaean Society and Overseas Influence* 485
• *The End of the Aegean Bronze Age* 486

Cultural Variety in the 1st Millennium BC 486
Greece and the Aegean 486
• *The Dark Age* 486
• *The Archaic Period* 486
• *The Classical Period* 487
Greek Colonization 488
● KEY SITE The Necropolis at Metapontum 489
The Phoenicians and Phoenician Expansion 490
The Etruscans and the Italian Peninsula 491
● KEY CONTROVERSY Who Were the Etruscans? 493
The Structure of the Archaic and Classical Greek Polis 494
• *The Hinterland: The Economic Foundation of the City* 494
● KEY DISCOVERY The Parthenon 494
• *Outside the City Walls: The Cemetery* 496
• *Life Within the City Walls* 496
● KEY CONTROVERSY The Silent Greek Countryside 498
• *The Commonality of Greek Culture* 499

Growing Powers, Growing Territories 500
Alexander and the East 500
• *The Conquests of Alexander* 500
• *The Hellenistic World* 501
● KEY SITE Alexandria-by-Egypt 502
Carthage and the Carthaginian Empire 503
The Rise of Rome 504
● KEY SITE The Tophet: Child Sacrifice at Carthage 505
• *Roman Expansion* 506

A Mediterranean Empire 507
Rome, Center of the World 508
The Provinces and Frontiers 509

● KEY CONTROVERSY Pompeii – All Problems Solved? 510
• *Reactions to Roman Annexation* 511
● KEY SITE The Mahdia Shipwreck 512
• *The Roman Army* 514
• *A Multiplicity of Gods* 515
The Later Empire 515

Summary and Conclusions 516

Further Reading and Suggested Websites 517

14 SOUTH ASIA: FROM EARLY VILLAGES TO BUDDHISM 518
Robin Coningham, University of Bradford

Land and Language 519

The Foundations: c. 26,000–6500 BC 522
Western India 522
The Ganges Plain 522
Central India 522
Sri Lanka 523
Seasonality and Mobility 523

Early Neolithic Villages: The First Food Producers 524
Western Pakistan 524
● KEY SITE Mehrgarh: An Early Farming Community 524
Kashmir and the Swat Valley 526
The Ganges Basin 527
Peninsular India 527

An Era of Regionalization: Early Harappan Proto-Urban Forms 528
● KEY CONTROVERSY Foreign Contact and State Formation 1: The Indus Cities 529
Kot Diji and Early Pointers Toward the Indus Civilization 530

An Era of Integration: The Indus Civilization, c. 2600–1900 BC 532
● KEY CONTROVERSY The Decipherment of the Indus Script 532
A Hierarchy of Settlement Forms 533
• *Urban Settlements* 533
• *Second Tier of Settlements* 533
● KEY SITES Mohenjo-daro and Harappa 534
• *Third Tier of Settlements* 535
• *Fourth Tier of Settlements* 535
Character of the Indus Civilization 536
Subsistence and Trade 536
The Western Borderlands 536

An Era of Localization: The Eclipse of the Indus Civilization, c. 1900 BC 536

CONTENTS

● **KEY CONTROVERSY** The Social Organization of the
Indus Civilization 537
The Core Cities 537
● **KEY CONTROVERSY** The End of the Indus Cities 538
Peripheral Areas 539
• *Gandharan Grave Culture* 539
• *The Ganges-Yamuna Doab* 539
• *The Western Deccan* 540

The Re-emergence of Regionalized Complexity,
c. 1200–500 BC 540
Developments in the Northwest and East 540
● **KEY CONTROVERSY** Foreign Contact and State
Formation 2: The Early Historic Cities 541
● **KEY CONTROVERSY** Dating the Historical Buddha 542
• *Painted Gray Ware* 543
• *"Great Territories"* 543
Southern India and Sri Lanka 544
● **KEY SITE** Taxila 544

Reintegration: The Early Historic Empires,
c. 500 BC–AD 320 546
The Mauryan Empire 547
Post-Mauryan Dynasties 548
The Kushan, Satavahana, and Later Dynasties 549
● **KEY CONTROVERSY** Roman Contact and the Origins of
Indian Ocean Trade 550

Summary and Conclusions 551

Further Reading and Suggested Website 551

15 COMPLEX SOCIETIES OF EAST AND
SOUTHEAST ASIA 552
Charles Higham, University of Otago

China 553
The Rise of Complex Societies 553
• *The Liangzhu Culture* 553
• *The Hongshan Culture* 554
The Longshan Culture 555
The Lower Xiajiadian Culture 556
The Xia Dynasty, c. 1700–1500 BC 557
The Shang Dynasty, c. 1500–1045 BC 558
● **KEY DISCOVERY** The Origins of Chinese Writing 558
● **KEY SITE** Zhengzhou: A Shang Capital 561
● **KEY DISCOVERY** Southern Rivals to Shang Culture 562
The Changjiang Culture 562
The Western Zhou Dynasty, 1045–771 BC 563
● **KEY SITE** Sanxingdui 564
• *Western Zhou Bronzeworking* 565
The Eastern Zhou Dynasty, 770–221 BC 566
● **KEY DISCOVERY** Confucianism 567
The Qin Dynasty, 221–207 BC 568
The Han Dynasty, 206 BC–AD 220 569

• *Administration* 569
• *Agriculture* 570
● **KEY SITE** Tonglushan: A Copper-Mining Site 571
• *Religious Beliefs* 571
● **KEY SITE** Mawangdui 572

Korea 574
Koguryo 574
Kaya 574
Paekche 575
Silla 575
Great Silla, AD 668–918 577

Japan 568
Early Yamato 568
The Growth of Yamato Power 578
Decline and Civil War 580
The Asuka Enlightenment 580
● **KEY DISCOVERY** The Origins of Chinese Metallurgy
582
The Transition from Yamato to Nara 582

The Central Asian Silk Road 583
Khotan 583
Shanshan 584

The Southeast Asian Maritime Silk Road 585
● **KEY CONTROVERSY** The Origins of Southeast Asian
Indianized States 585
Funana, the Mekong Delta 586
Angkor, Cambodia 586
● **KEY SITE** Angkor: Capital City of the Khmer 587
The Arakan Coast, Burma 590
The Pyu of Burma 590
The Dvaravati of Thailand 590
The Cham of Vietnam 591

Summary and Conclusions 593

Further Reading 593

16 MESOAMERICAN CIVILIZATION 594
*David Webster and Susan Toby Evans,
The Pennsylvania State University*

The Landscape and its Peoples 595

The Spread of Agriculture and the Rise of Complex
Societies in Preclassic Mesoamerica 598
● **KEY DISCOVERY** The Mesoamerican Ball Game 599
The First Agricultural Communities 600
● **KEY SITE** Paso de la Amada and the Emergence of Social
Complexity 601

The Olmecs, *c.* 1200–400 BC (Early to Middle
Preclassic) 602
San Lorenzo and La Venta 602
The Olmecs as a "Mother Culture"? 604

West Mexican Polities, c. 1500 BC–AD 400 604
● KEY CONTROVERSY Were the Olmecs Mesoamerica's "Mother Culture"? 605

Late Preclassic Mesoamerica 606
Calendars and Writing 606
● KEY DISCOVERY The Mesoamerican Calendar 606
● KEY CONTROVERSY Who Invented Mesoamerican Writing? 608
● KEY CONTROVERSY Metallurgy in Mesoamerica 610
Kings, Courts, and Cities 610
• Monte Albán 612
• Teotihuacán 613
● KEY SITE Teotihuacán 614

The Classic Period: Teotihuacán and its Neighbors 616
Teotihuacán's Wider Influence: The Middle Horizon 616
● KEY CONTROVERSY The Teotihuacán Writing System 617
● KEY SITE Classic Monte Albán 618
Cholula, Cantona and the Teuchitlan Cultural Tradition – Independent Polities? 620
The Demise of Teotihuacán 620

Epiclassic Mesoamerica, AD 600–900 621

The Classic Maya 623
Kingdoms and Capitals 624
Maya Society 625
• Royalty 625
• Lords and Officials 625
• Commoners 626
• Warfare 627
● KEY SITE Tikal 626

Postclassic Mesoamerica 627
● KEY CONTROVERSY Mesoamerican Urbanism 628
The Rise of the Toltecs 628
● KEY CONTROVERSY The Collapse of Maya Civilization 630
The Postclassic Maya 631
• The Puuc Florescence 631
• Chichén Itzá 632
• Mayapan 632

Mesoamerica Discovered: What the Spaniards Found 633
The Maya of the Early 16th Century 633
The Aztecs and the Late Horizon: History and Myth 633
● KEY SITE Tenochtitlán: The Aztec Capital 634
The Aztec Empire in 1519 636
• Aztec Society 637
The Spanish Conquest 638

Summary and Conclusions 638

Further Reading and Suggested Websites 639

17 FROM VILLAGE TO EMPIRE IN SOUTH AMERICA 640
Michael E. Moseley and Michael J. Heckenberger, University of Florida

Main Environmental Regions 641
The Andes 641
• The High Sierra 641
• The Desert Coast 641
Amazonia 642
• Coasts 644
• Floodplains 644
• Uplands 644

Chronological Overview 645
The Andes and the Desert Coast 645
Amazonia and the Atlantic Coast 645

The Andean Preceramic, c. 3000–1800 BC 646
Early Mound Construction in Central and Northern Peru 646
Platforms and Sunken Courts along the Desert Coast 647
● KEY CONTROVERSY Maritime Foundations of Andean Civilization? 648
Mounds and their Builders at Caral and Paraiso 649
● KEY SITE Real Alto 650

Early Andean Civilization: The Initial Period and the Early Horizon 651
The Initial Period, c. 1800–400 BC 651
● KEY SITE Sechín Alto 652
Chavín and the Early Horizon, c. 400–200 BC 653
• Paracas 654
• Pukara 655

Andean Confederacies and States in the Early Intermediate Period, c. 200 BC–AD 650 655
Gallinazo, Moche, and the North Coast 655
● KEY SITE Sipán and the Presentation Theme 657
• The Temples of the Sun and the Moon 658
Nazca and the South Coast 659
• The "Nazca Lines" 660

The Rise and Fall of the Andean Empires 660
The Middle Horizon, c. AD 650–1000: Tiwanaku and Wari 660
The Late Intermediate Period, c. 1000–1470: Lambayeque and Chimor 662
• Lambayeque and Batan Grande 662
• Chimor and Chan Chan 663
The Late Horizon, 1476–1533: Cuzco and the Incas 665
• Origins and Expansion 665
• Cuzco and the Trappings of Empire 666
● KEY SITE The Sacred Valley of the Incas and Machu Picchu 667

Amazonia 668

The Amazonian Formative Period,
c. 1000 BC–AD 500 668
  The Linguistic Evidence 669
  The Archaeological Evidence 669
  ● KEY CONTROVERSY The Rank Revolution 670

Regionalism and "Classic" Amazonia,
c. AD 1–1500 670
  The Lower Amazon 671
  ● KEY CONTROVERSY Amazonian Mound Builders 672
  The Central Amazon 673
  The Upper Amazon 674
  The Orinoco and the Caribbean 674
  ● KEY CONTROVERSY Amazonian Urbanism? 675
  The Southern Amazon 675

Summary and Conclusions 677

Further Reading and Suggested Websites 677

18 COMPLEX SOCIETIES OF NORTH
     AMERICA 678
     *George R. Milner, The Pennsylvania State University and
     W. H. Wills, University of New Mexico*

The Eastern Woodlands 681
  *Adena and Hopewell: The Early and Middle Woodland
  Period, c. 800 BC–AD 400* 682
    • *Mounds and Earthworks* 682
    • *Exchange Systems and Cultural Ties* 683
    • *The Beginning of Food-producing Economies* 684
  *Settlement Patterns in the Late Woodland Period,
  c. AD 400–1000* 684
  ● KEY SITE Hopewell 685
    • *Warfare, Maize, and the Rise of Chiefdoms* 686
  *The Mississippian Period Mound Centers and Villages,
  AD 1000–15th/16th Century* 687
    • *Mounds and Burials* 687
    • *Settlement Patterns and Food-procurement Strategies* 688
  ● KEY SITE Craig Mound 688
    • *Increased Tensions among Northern Villages* 690
  ● KEY CONTROVERSY The Size and Influence of Cahokia
  690

The Southwest 692
  Preclassic and Classic Hohokam, c. AD 700–1450 692
  ● KEY DISCOVERY Hohokam Ball Courts 693
  Pueblo Villages on the Colorado Plateau 695
    • *Agricultural Foundations* 695
  ● KEY METHOD Tree-ring Dating 696
  Pueblo I Settlement Patterns, c. AD 750–900 696
  *Pueblo II: The Chaco Phenomenon,
  c. AD 900–1150* 698
    • *The Chaco Phenomenon* 698

  ● KEY CONTROVERSY Chaco's Population During the
  Bonito Phase 698
    • *Population and Agriculture* 699
  Pueblo III: Regional Population Shifts, c. AD 1150–1300
  700
  *Pueblo IV: Abandonment of the Colorado Plateau, 14th
  and 15th Centuries AD* 700
    • *Pottery Innovations* 702
  ● KEY SITE Pecos Pueblo 702
  Population Decline 703

The Plains 703
  Village Settlements 704
  ● KEY SITE Crow Creek: Scene of a Massacre 705
  Exchange Systems 706

The Pacific Coast 706
  Southern California 706
  The Pacific Northwest 707
    • *Village Life* 708
    • *Warfare and Population Decline* 708
  ● KEY SITE Ozette 709

The Arctic and Subarctic 710
  ● KEY SITE L'Anse aux Meadows 710
  The Dorset and Thule Cultures 711

The Collision of Two Worlds 712

Summary and Conclusions 713
  ● KEY CONTROVERSY Native American Population on the
  Eve of European Contact 714

Further Reading and Suggested Websites 715

19 THE HUMAN PAST: RETROSPECT AND
     PROSPECT 716
     Chris Scarre, University of Cambridge

Demographic Increase 717

Intensification and Degradation 718

Biological Exchange 719

Climate Change and Human Society 720

GLOSSARY 721

BIBLIOGRAPHY 726

SOURCES OF ILLUSTRATIONS 759

INDEX 762

CONTRIBUTORS

Chris Scarre is Deputy Director of the McDonald Institute for Archaeological Research, University of Cambridge, and editor of the *Cambridge Archaeological Journal*. He is a specialist in the prehistory of Europe and the Mediterranean with a related interest in the ancient Near East and the Classical world of Greece and Rome. He was editor and principal author of *Past Worlds: The Times Atlas of Archaeology* (1995); more recently he co-authored *Ancient Civilizations* (with Brian Fagan, 2nd ed., 2003). He has continued to direct and co-direct excavations at prehistoric sites in France and his current interests include the role of colour and landscape beliefs in the origins and structure of prehistoric monuments.

Susan E. Alcock is the John H. D'Arms Collegiate Professor of Classical Archaeology and Classics in the Department of Classical Studies at the University of Michigan, and Curator at the Kelsey Museum of Archaeology. Her research interests include the Hellenistic and Roman East, landscape archaeology, archaeological survey, the archaeology of imperialism, and the archaeology of the Caucasus, where she is co-directing a new project. Her books include *Graecia Capta: The Landscapes of Roman Greece* (1993) and *Archaeologies of the Greek Past: Landscape, Monuments, and Memories* (2002), and as co-editor, *Empires: Perspectives from Archaeology and History* (2001), *Archaeologies of Memory* (2003), and *Side-by-Side Survey: Comparative Regional Studies in the Mediterranean World* (2004).

Peter Bellwood is Professor of Archaeology at the Australian National University in Canberra. He has carried out field research in Southeast Asia (Brunei, Malaysia, Indonesia, Philippines, Vietnam) and many Polynesian islands. He has a special interest in archaeological and linguistic aspects of Austronesian prehistory in both Southeast Asia and Oceania, and in the prehistories of early farming populations in all parts of the world. He is the author of *Man's Conquest of the Pacific* (1978), *The Polynesians* (2nd ed., 1987), *Prehistory of the Indo-Malaysian Archipelago* (2nd ed., 1997) and *First Farmers* (2005).

David L. Browman is Professor of Anthropology and Chair of the Interdisciplinary Program in Archaeology at Washington University – St. Louis. His research interests mainly concern the New World, and include nomadic pastoralism, the development of economies based on domesticated species, the origins of prehistoric complex societies, Andean regional culture history, applied archaeology, historical archaeology, and, more recently, the intellectual history of archaeology; his multiple publications are on these topics.

John F. Cherry is Professor of Classical Archaeology and Greek in the Department of Classical Studies at the University of Michigan, Curator at the Kelsey Museum of Archaeology, and Director of the Interdepartmental Program in Classical Art and Archaeology. His research interests include Aegean and Mediterranean prehistory, regional survey, island archaeology, and archaeological theory. He has organized several archaeological surveys in Greece, has been involved in fieldwork in the UK, USA, and Italy, and he is now co-directing a project in southern Armenia. Of his co-authored or edited books, the most recent are *Pausanias: Travel and Memory in Roman Greece* (2001), *Side-by-Side Survey: Comparative Regional Studies in the Mediterranean World* (2004), and *Prehistorians Round the Pond* (2005). He has been co-editor of the *Journal of Mediterranean Archaeology* since 1990.

Robin Coningham is Professor of South Asian Archaeology and Head of the Department of Archaeological Sciences, University of Bradford. He has conducted fieldwork throughout South Asia, directing major excavations at the cities of Anuradhapura in Sri Lanka and the Bala Hisar of Charsadda in Pakistan, and has led seven UNESCO missions to the region. His publications include research on Anuradhapura (1999), the archaeology of Buddhism (2001) and the origins of Indian Ocean trade (2002), as well as two chapters in *The Archaeology of Early Historic South Asia* (R. Allchin, ed., 1995). His current research includes a survey of the hinterland of Anuradhapura and a programme of survey and excavation within Iran's Tehran Plain.

Graham Connah is an Emeritus Professor of Archaeology at the University of New England, Armidale, New South Wales, and is a Visiting Fellow in the School of Archaeology and Anthropology at the Australian National University, Canberra. He has excavated and conducted archaeological fieldwork in Britain, Nigeria, Egypt, Uganda, and Australia. His best known books are *The Archaeology of Benin* (1975); *Three Thousand Years in Africa* (1981); *African Civilizations* (2nd ed., 2001); *The Archaeology of Australia's History* (2nd ed., 1993); *Kibiro* (1996); and *Forgotten Africa* (2004). He was the founding editor of the journal *Australasian Historical Archaeology* (1983–88), and is a past President of the Australasian Society for Historical Archaeology (1993–97). His main interest remains the archaeology of tropical Africa, particularly the last 4000 years.

Susan Toby Evans is Professor of Anthropology at Pennsylvania State University and an archaeologist specializing in Aztec culture. She recently published *Ancient Mexico and Central America: Archaeology and Culture History* (2004). She has excavated at the Aztec site of Cihuatecpan, near Mexico City, and further research into Aztec palace life has led to numerous articles and to *Palaces of the Ancient New World* (2004), co-edited with Joanne Pillsbury. Other books include the Aztec period volumes of the Teotihuacan Valley Project Final Report (2001, co-edited with William T. Sanders), and *Archaeology of Ancient Mexico and Central America: An Encyclopedia* (2001, co-edited with David Webster).

Gayle J. Fritz is Professor of Anthropology at Washington University in St. Louis, where she directs research in the Paleoethnobotany Laboratory. Her research interests include plant domestication, the origins and spread of agriculture, subsistence and social change, and the archaeology of North America before and after European contact. Among her numerous publications are: "Paleoethnobotanical Methods and Applications," in *Handbook of Archaeological Methods* (H. Maschner, ed., 2005) and "Native Farming Systems and Ecosystems in the Mississippi River Valley," in *Imperfect Balance: Landscape Transformations in the Precolumbian Americas*, (D. L. Lentz, ed., 2000).

Michael J. Heckenberger is an Assistant Professor in Anthropology at the University of Florida. He has developed major research projects in the southern and central Amazon regions of Brazil, and has collaborated on archaeological research in northern South America, the Caribbean, and Eastern North America. He is the author of *The Ecology of Power: Culture, Place, and Personhood in the Southern Amazon, AD 1000–2000* (2005) and co-editor of *Os Povos do Alto Xingu: Historia e Cultura* (2001).

Charles Higham is James Cook Fellow at the University of Otago in New Zealand. He studied Archaeology at Cambridge University, and was appointed in 1968 to the Foundation Chair of Anthropology at Otago. He currently directs the Origins of Angkor research project in Thailand, having undertaken fieldwork in Southeast Asia since 1969. His many books include *Early Cultures of Mainland Southeast Asia* (2002), *The Civilization of Angkor* (2001), *Prehistoric Thailand* (1998), and the *Encyclopaedia of Ancient Asian Civilizations* (2004). A Fellow of the British Academy, he is also a visiting Scholar at St. Catherine's College and the McDonald Institute, Cambridge.

Peter Hiscock is a Reader in the School of Archaeology and Anthropology at the Australian National University. He is a leading researcher into prehistoric stone technology, with a record of developing models about prehistoric (Paleolithic) technology, both in Australia and elsewhere. He has worked extensively in Australia, although his current focus is the analysis of European Palaeolithic technologies.

Richard G. Klein lectures on human evolution at Stanford University in California and he has focused on the co-evolution of human anatomy and behavior. He specializes in the analysis of archaeological animal remains to illuminate how early people made a living. He has done fieldwork in Spain and especially in South Africa, where he has excavated ancient sites and analyzed the excavated materials since 1969. His numerous publications include *The Human Career* (2nd ed., 1999).

Roger Matthews is Reader in Archaeology of Western Asia at the Institute of Archaeology, University College London. He has directed field projects in Iraq, Syria, and Turkey. His research interests include long-term settlement studies, the rise of complex, literate, urban societies, empires and their regional impacts, and the development of the discipline of archaeology in Western Asia. Key publications include *The Early Prehistory of Mesopotamia* (2000), *The Archaeology of Mesopotamia: Theories and Approaches* (2003), *Ancient Perspectives on Egypt* (2003, ed., with C. Roemer), and *Excavations at Tell Brak, Vol. 4* (2003, ed.).

David J. Meltzer is the Henderson-Morrison Professor of Prehistory in the Department of Anthropology, Southern Methodist University, Dallas, Texas. He has research interests, and has published extensively in, the peopling of the Americas, Late Glacial environments and human adaptations, as well as the history of American archaeology. He has conducted archaeological fieldwork across North America, but especially on Paleoindian sites on the western Great Plains. He recently finished a long-term re-investigation of the Folsom Paleoindian type site, the subject of a forthcoming volume.

George R. Milner is Professor of Anthropology at the Pennsylvania State University. His research interests cover archaeology and human osteology, with an emphasis on prehistoric eastern North America. He has conducted field and museum-based work in several midwestern states, Denmark, Egypt, and Micronesia (Saipan, CNMI). Recent books include *The Cahokia Chiefdom: The Archaeology of a Mississippian Society* (1998) and *The Moundbuilders* (2004).

Michael E. Moseley is Interim Chair of the Anthropology Department, University of Florida. He directed the Chan Chan-Moche Valley project while teaching at Harvard. His research focus is now in the far south of Peru where he has been involved with field studies ranging from the Pleistocene arrival of the continent's first colonists through the region's conquest by indigenous empires and into the Spanish subjugation. His publications include *The Incas and their Ancestors* (rev. ed., 2001).

Paul Pettitt is Lecturer in Human Origins in the Department of Archaeology, University of Sheffield. His research focuses on the Middle and Upper Paleolithic of Europe and the Middle Stone Age of Africa. His specific interests are Neanderthal behavior and extinction, the origins of modern humans, Upper Paleolithic demography, burial, and cave art. In

2003 he and two colleagues discovered Britain's first Upper Paleolithic cave art. He has written numerous articles in specialist and academic journals.

Kathy Schick is Professor of Anthropology and Adjunct Professor of Biology at Indiana University, Bloomington. She is also Co-Director of the Center for Research into the Anthropological Foundations of Technology (CRAFT) and the Human Evolutionary Studies Program, Indiana University, and Co-Director of the Stone Age Institute, a non-profit research institution that studies the origins and evolution of human technology. She has conducted fieldwork in Kenya, Tanzania, Zambia, Ethiopia, Algeria, Spain, Jordan, and China. Her interests include paleoanthropology, geoarchaeology, and human evolutionary studies. Her books include *Making Silent Stones Speak: Human Evolution and the Dawn of Technology* (1993), and *The Oldowan: Case Studies into the Earliest Stone Age* (2004) (both with Nicholas Toth).

Nicholas Toth is Professor of Anthropology and Adjunct Professor of Biology at Indiana University, Bloomington. He is also Co-Director of the Center for Research into the Anthropological Foundations of Technology (CRAFT) and the Human Evolutionary Studies Program, Indiana University, and Co-Director of the Stone Age Institute, a non-profit research institution that studies the origins and evolution of human technology. He has conducted field work in Kenya, Tanzania, Zambia, Ethiopia, Algeria, Spain, Jordan, China, and New Guinea. His books (with Kathy Schick) include *Making Silent Stones Speak* (1993) and *The Oldowan: Case Studies into the Earliest Stone Age* (2004).

Trevor Watkins is Emeritus Professor of Near Eastern Prehistory at the University of Edinburgh. His research interests cover the beginnings of village-type communities in the Near East, and the economic transformation of early agriculture. He has directed fieldwork projects in Cyprus, Syria, Iraq and Turkey. His numerous publications include the excavation reports on Qermez Dere.

Patty Jo Watson is Edward Mallinckrodt Distinguished University Professor of Anthropology (Emerita) at Washington University, St. Louis; and Faculty Affiliate, Department of Anthropology, University of Montana, Missoula. She has carried out archaeological fieldwork in Iran, Iraq, and Turkey, as well as in USA. Her primary research interests include archaeological theory and method, early agricultural economies, ethnoarchaeology, and cave archaeology. Key publications include *Archaeological Ethnography in Western Iran* (1979), *Archaeology of the Mammoth Cave Area* (1974), and *Explanation in Archaeology* (1971), and *Archaeological Explanation* (1974; both with Steven A. LeBlanc and Charles L. Redman).

David Webster is Professor of Anthropology at the Pennsylvania State University. His main interests are the evolution of complex societies, human and political ecology, settlement and household archaeology, and ancient warfare. He has worked in Yugoslavia and Turkey, but his main research focus is Mesoamerica, and specifically Classic Maya civilization. Recent books include *Copan: The Rise and Fall of an Ancient Maya Kingdom* (with A. Freter and N. Gonlin, 2000), *Archaeology of Ancient Mexico and Central America: An Encyclopedia* (with Susan T. Evans, 2001) and *The Fall of the Ancient Maya* (2002).

W. H. Wills is Professor of Anthropology at the University of New Mexico. His research interests include the transition from foraging to agriculture, village formation, and the role of religion in economic change. He has conducted field research in several parts of the American Southwest and is currently directing archaeological investigations at Chaco Canyon, New Mexico.

PREFACE

Chris Scarre

Tuesday, Sept. 10 [1844]: Between nine and ten o'clock the members assembled on the Breach Downs to be present at the opening of some barrows [burial mounds].... Eight barrows were examined.... All contained the remains of skeleton much decayed; in some, traces of wood were noticed, and vestiges of knives. After the examination of these barrows, the whole party visited the mansion of the noble President, at Bourne, and having inspected his lordship's interesting collection of antiquities, and partaken of a substantial repast, attended the excavation of two barrows in his lordship's paddock.

The Archaeological Journal, volume 1, 1845

Archaeology has moved a long way from the early explorations of burial mounds, undertaken in a cursory manner as a diversionary entertainment for 19th-century gentlemen. Popular impressions of the subject still vary widely, however, from that of intrepid explorers trekking across deserts or hacking their way through jungles, to high-tech excavations in which crouching individuals carefully excavate minuscule flint flakes or delicately brush the soil from fragile bones day after day. The latter is more in line with current archaeological practice, and although it may be less flamboyant than romantic images of exploration, the discoveries that are being made are no less profound and significant. Indeed, within the last 50 years archaeology has grown dramatically to become our major source of information for the past 3 million years of the human story. It is only by appreciating that past that we can hope to understand the world we inhabit today.

The aim of the present volume is to provide an authoritative guide to those 3 million years, designed to be accessible both to beginning students in archaeology and anthropology and to any interested reader; the book assumes no prior knowledge of the field of prehistory. The timeliness of the endeavor is clear: at the dawn of the 21st century, new technologies and discoveries, as well as the increasing scale of archaeological research, are allowing us to see the patterns of the human past in fuller outline and in greater detail than ever before. What archaeologists have long sought to achieve – to construct a truly worldwide picture of the development of human societies, in all their diversity and across enormous spans of time – we are now able to do with new confidence.

The growing pace of archaeological research has been reflected in the development of university courses, and that, in turn, has triggered the production of several textbooks on the subject of world prehistory. Many of these seek to cover the entire field of the human past under the pen of a single author. These are valiant undertakings, increasingly so in an age when the rate of archaeological publication has reached levels that make it difficult even for regional specialists to keep up with new work in their own area. Gone are the days when a conscientious and well-informed individual could hope to gain mastery of an entire literature. Thus, the present volume has been conceived as a multi-authored text, with each chapter the work of an acknowledged expert in his or her field.

Our 24 authors are drawn from North America, Britain, Australia, and New Zealand, and together represent over 600 years of active archaeological scholarship. Specializations range from the first stone tools made by early hominins in Africa, to the complex societies of such disparate cultures as those of the Romans, Polynesians, and Aztecs. Together these scholars cover the vast panorama of the human past with a level of detailed understanding and expertise that is unrivaled in any other textbook of world prehistory. The present volume thus has an authority that is beyond the reach of any single-authored work: the texts are based on first-hand knowledge of the areas and issues under discussion, and represent an accessible, up-to-date, and uniquely reliable account of what we know today about the origins and development of human society.

Organization of the Book

The volume is divided into two main sections. Part I (chapters 2–4) focuses on human origins and developments up to the end of the last Ice Age – the period conventionally known as the Paleolithic. The second, longer, section (Part II, chapters 5–18) covers the postglacial period, the Holocene, from 11,500 years ago to recent times.

The book begins with an introduction (**Chapter 1**) that presents and explains a number of key concepts: what the disciplines of archaeology and prehistory comprise and how they originated; the ways in which archaeologists seek to learn about the human past (methods and techniques); and how they attempt to interpret archaeological remains in order to understand how societies have developed and changed (archaeological theory). The following three chapters cover the Paleolithic period, beginning in **Chapter 2** with hominin origins in Africa. **Chapter 3** describes the dispersal of early humans across much of the Old World and the development of new species of the human lineage, new lifestyles, and new technologies. **Chapter 4** covers the emergence and spread of fully modern humans, including their first colonization of the Americas and Australia.

Chapter 5 prefaces the second section of the book, setting out the main themes of the postglacial period around the world: climate change, the origins of farming, the inexorable rise in human population density, and the development of the social complexity that underpinned the emergence of cities and states. These themes are highlighted in the region-by-region chapters that follow.

The arrangement of material both within and between chapters is broadly chronological. **Chapters 6–14** take the reader on a world tour of Holocene developments, beginning in Southwest Asia and proceeding via East Asia, Australasia, and the Americas to Africa, Europe, and South Asia. The adjustment of human societies to postglacial environments, and the development of the new food-producing economies, provides a unifying theme across these chapters. The development of more complex societies is also covered – in Africa (**Chapter 10**), Southwest Asia (**Chapter 12**), the Mediterranean lands (**Chapter 13**), and South Asia (**Chapter 14**). More recent centuries are covered in **chapters 15–18**, which describe regional developments in East Asia and particularly in the New World.

This book provides a comprehensive introduction to world prehistory, and could form the basis of a complete undergraduate program. It could also be used more selectively, by taking a series of chapters to explore a particular theme or region. Thus chapters 9 and 16–18 provide an account of American prehistory from the Paleoindians to European colonization; alternatively, a comparative study of state societies might draw on chapters 12, 14, 16, and 17 for a selection of Old and New World examples (Mesopotamia, the Indus Valley, Mesoamerica, and Andean South America).

Within a multi-authored work of this kind there is necessarily less scope for a personal perspective, but the book is given coherence by its focus on key themes of adaptation, social change, and the development of social complexity. The final chapter brings these themes together in a brief retrospective that also looks to the lessons of the human past for the human future, in particular in terms of climate change and demographic growth. These form, arguably, the most important message that archaeology offers to the present world, though their implications are all too rarely taken seriously by planners and politicians. For the story of human evolution is not just about our past – it is intensely relevant to the most burning issues of contemporary humankind.

Special Features

The specialist scholarship of *The Human Past* is supported by a series of features that make the book accessible to the widest variety of readers:

Timelines Located at the beginning of each chapter, these give a simple, clear overview of the events covered in that chapter. Timelines also highlight the standard period divisions (with dates) for the area under discussion, and the chronological terminology commonly employed in each region ("Formative," "Neolithic," etc.).

Maps and Diagrams Each chapter is accompanied by a map showing the location of major sites and regional or cultural groupings. Additional maps and a wealth of plans, diagrams, and photographs illustrate specific themes or processes. Archaeology is an extremely visual subject, a fact that the high level of illustration in this volume serves to underscore.

Box Features Highlighted in each chapter, these fall into four main categories: "Key Sites," "Key Controversies," "Key Methods," and "Key Discoveries." "Key Sites" describe important individual sites or finds in greater detail than is possible within the flow of the main text. "Key Controversies," on the other hand, supplement the chapter text by focusing on important areas of debate such as the role of external trade in African state formation or who invented Mesoamerican writing. "Key Methods" describe some of the most important scientific techniques used today to date archaeological remains and to identify such major developments as animal domestication in South Asia and Africa. "Key Discoveries" include discussions of recent breakthroughs in long-standing archaeological enquiries such as the origins of Chinese metallurgy or the construction of the Egyptian pyramids, as well as descriptions of such world-famous discoveries as the Iceman of the Alps, and of experimental techniques used, for example, to understand early hominin toolmaking.

Summaries Provided at the end of each chapter, these give an overview of the chapter contents and a reiteration of the authors' conclusions. Links between chapters are indicated, making it easy to follow the developments of a particular region from their earliest appearance to later complexity.

Further Reading and Bibliography Each chapter closes with suggestions for further reading – carefully selected titles that will enable students to amplify and deepen their understanding of the key themes of that chapter. More detailed references are provided in a chapter-by-chapter bibliography at the end of the volume.

Suggested Websites A list of recommended websites is provided at the end of chapters where appropriate, chosen by the authors for particular usefulness, clarity, and scholarly reliability.

Glossary As far as possible, specialist terms are explained where they first appear in the book; in addition, a glossary is provided at the end of the volume for easy reference.

Website

A student web site has been designed to accompany *The Human Past*, which can be found at:

www.thamesandhudsonusa.com/web/humanpast

This offers students a range of materials specifically developed by Professor Tina Thurston of the University of Buffalo to reinforce what they have learned from reading *The Human Past* and to help them prepare for tests. The following are provided for every chapter in the book: learning objectives; chapter summaries; key terms; practice quizzes; flash cards to revise key terms; and useful internet links.

A Note on Dating

For the Paleolithic period (chapters 2–4) dates are given as "years ago" (years before the present). The other dates used in this volume have wherever possible been converted to calendar years (BC/AD). For an explanation of calibration and radiocarbon dating, see the box on p. 157.

Acknowledgments

I should like, first and foremost, to thank the individual contributors to this volume, who have provided an excellent series of texts and have patiently responded to a seemingly endless sequence of questions and comments. The success of the book is a testimony to this teamwork.

Editing this volume has been a learning process that has taken me into areas and issues of archaeology that I had not hitherto had occasion to visit, and I am grateful to all the contributors for their expert guidance.

Among the publisher's team, several people deserve thanks and recognition for their part in bringing this book to fruition. Colin Ridler has given it his unstinting support and encouragement at every stage; Diane Fortenberry transformed our occasionally chaotic drafts into elegant and coordinated prose; and Sarah Vernon-Hunt oversaw the project editorially during its final stages with great skill and efficiency. Sally Nicholls proved herself to be a tireless and imaginative picture researcher; while the book's designer, Rowena Alsey, has given it a handsome and distinctive visual presence. Thanks should also go to Shalom Schotten for an elegant cover design and to Celia Falconer for hard work on the production of the book.

We are grateful to other scholars for having read and commented on individual chapters:

Clive Gamble, University of Southampton; Kevin MacDonald, Institute of Archaeology, University College London; Ian Shaw, University of Liverpool; Andrew Sherratt, University of Oxford; and Lawrence Straus, University of New Mexico.

Terracotta figurines of women preparing maize for tortillas, from Nayarit, west Mexico, dating between c. 200 BC and AD 600.

SCALE VARIABLE   MILLIONS OF YEARS AGO

800,00

	7	6	5	4	3	2	1

CHAPTER 2
AFRICAN ORIGINS

Sahelanthropus tchadensis

• *Orrorin*

Ardipithecus ramidus

"Lucy"
First stone tools •   Oldowan

Homo rudolfensis to *Homo habilis*

• Bipedalism (walking on two legs)

Australopithecines

CHAPTER 3
HOMININ DISPERSALS IN THE OLD WORLD

Evolution of *Homo erectus* in eastern Asia? •

Homo ergaster

Oldest archaeological site/s in Europe

Possible use of fire in Africa •

CHAPTER 4
THE RISE OF MODERN HUMANS

20,000 BC	10,000 BC	9000 BC	8000 BC	7000 BC	6000 BC

CHAPTER 6
EARLY SOUTHWEST ASIA

Domesticated rye at Abu Hureyra •

Aceramic Neolithic   Ceramic Neolithic

Epipaleolithic hunter-gatherers

• Domesticated wheat and barley found widely in Hilly Flanks zone

Toward sedentary villages •

Pre-domestication   Domestication of sheep, goat, cattle and pig

Çatalhöyük

CHAPTER 7
EAST ASIAN AGRICULTURE

• Jomon pottery, Japan

Transition to rice and millet agriculture

Settled agricultural villages •

CHAPTER 8
AUSTRALIA AND THE AUSTRONESIANS

CHAPTER 9
THE HOLOCENE IN THE AMERICAS

• Clovis peoples

• Domesticated pepo and bottle gourd, Mesoamerica

Later Paleoindians

Dogs, eastern North America •

• Rock art, Pedra Pintada, Brazil   • Mummies, South America

CHAPTER 10
HOLOCENE AFRICA

Possible earliest • domesticated cattle, Sahara

Kharga Oasis: • wild cereals

CHAPTER 11
HOLOCENE EUROPE

Star Carr, Mesolithic hunter-gatherer camp, England

• First farmers, Crete

Bandkeramik farmers, central Europe

First farmers, Greece •

CHAPTER 12
LATER SOUTHWEST ASIA

(for this early time period see Chapter 6 above)

Irrigation •

CHAPTER 13
THE MEDITERRANEAN WORLD

(for this early time period see Chapters 6, 11, & 12 above)

CHAPTER 14
SOUTH ASIA

• First villages

• Domestication of zebu

CHAPTER 15
LATER EAST AND SOUTHEAST ASIA

(for this early time period see Chapter 7 above)

CHAPTER 16
MESOAMERICAN CIVILIZATION

(for this early time period see Chapter 9 above)

CHAPTER 17
SOUTH AMERICA

(for this early time period see Chapter 9 above)

CHAPTER 18
NORTH AMERICA

(for this early time period see Chapter 9 above)

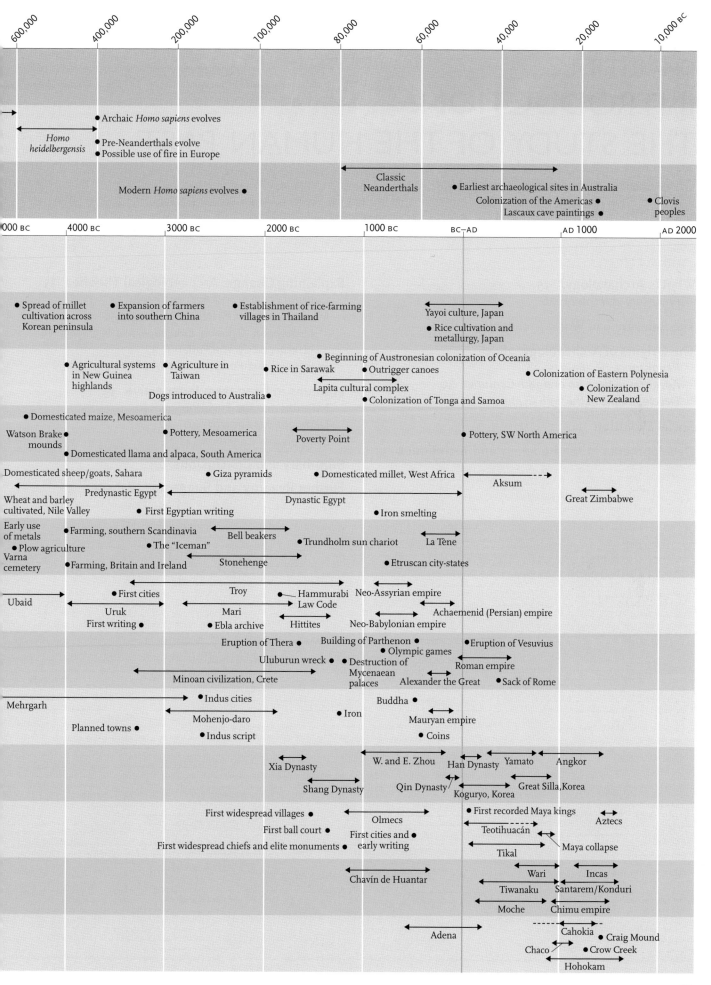

600,000　400,000　200,000　100,000　80,000　60,000　40,000　20,000　10,000 BC

→

• Archaic *Homo sapiens* evolves

Homo heidelbergensis

• Pre-Neanderthals evolve
• Possible use of fire in Europe

Classic Neanderthals

Modern *Homo sapiens* evolves •

• Earliest archaeological sites in Australia
Colonization of the Americas •
Lascaux cave paintings •

• Clovis peoples

5000 BC　4000 BC　3000 BC　2000 BC　1000 BC　BC–AD　AD 1000　AD 2000

• Spread of millet cultivation across Korean peninsula
• Expansion of farmers into southern China
• Establishment of rice-farming villages in Thailand

Yayoi culture, Japan

• Rice cultivation and metallurgy, Japan

• Agricultural systems in New Guinea highlands
• Agriculture in Taiwan
• Rice in Sarawak
• Outrigger canoes

• Beginning of Austronesian colonization of Oceania

• Colonization of Eastern Polynesia

Dogs introduced to Australia •

Lapita cultural complex

• Colonization of New Zealand

• Colonization of Tonga and Samoa

• Domesticated maize, Mesoamerica

Watson Brake mounds •

• Pottery, Mesoamerica

Poverty Point

• Pottery, SW North America

• Domesticated llama and alpaca, South America

Domesticated sheep/goats, Sahara
• Giza pyramids
• Domesticated millet, West Africa

Aksum

Predynastic Egypt

Dynastic Egypt

Great Zimbabwe

Wheat and barley cultivated, Nile Valley
• First Egyptian writing
• Iron smelting

Early use of metals
• Farming, southern Scandinavia

Bell beakers

• Plow agriculture
• The "Iceman"
• Trundholm sun chariot

La Tène

Varna cemetery
• Farming, Britain and Ireland

Stonehenge

• Etruscan city-states

Ubaid
• First cities

Troy
• Hammurabi Law Code

Neo-Assyrian empire

Uruk

Mari

Achaemenid (Persian) empire

First writing •
• Ebla archive

Hittites

Neo-Babylonian empire

Eruption of Thera •
Building of Parthenon •
• Eruption of Vesuvius

Uluburun wreck •
• Destruction of Mycenaean palaces
• Olympic games

Roman empire

Minoan civilization, Crete

Alexander the Great
• Sack of Rome

Mehrgarh
• Indus cities

Buddha •

Planned towns •

Mohenjo-daro
• Iron

Mauryan empire

• Indus script
• Coins

Xia Dynasty

W. and E. Zhou

Han Dynasty
Yamato
Angkor

Shang Dynasty

Qin Dynasty

Great Silla, Korea

Koguryo, Korea

First widespread villages •
• First recorded Maya kings

Aztecs

First ball court •

Olmecs

Teotihuacán

First widespread chiefs and elite monuments •
First cities and early writing

Tikal
Maya collapse

Chavín de Huantar

Wari
Incas

Tiwanaku
Santarem/Konduri

Moche
Chimu empire

Adena

Cahokia
• Craig Mound

Chaco
• Crow Creek

Hohokam

23

CHAPTER 1
INTRODUCTION:
THE STUDY OF THE HUMAN PAST

Chris Scarre, University of Cambridge

What is Archaeology? 25
  Prehistory vs. History 26

The Relevance of World Archaeology 27

The Origins of Archaeology 28
  Renaissance Beginnings 28
  Advances in the 17th and 18th Centuries 30
  Developments in the 19th Century 31

Social Evolution 32

Developments in Methodology and Techniques 33

Explaining Change: Archaeological Theories 35
  Cultural Ecology and Agency Theory 35
  Mechanisms and Patterns of Change 36
    • *Innovation, Diffusion, Emulation, and Migration* 36
    • *Linear and Cyclical Patterns* 37
  Processual and Postprocessual Archaeology 38

Humans in Long-term Perspective 39
  Humans and the Environment 40
  Demographic Growth 40
  Symbols and Cognition 41

Summary and Conclusions 43

Further Reading and Suggested Websites 43

Modern humans anatomically like us (*Homo sapiens*) have been living on the earth for around 150,000 years, an immense span of time when compared with the normal compass of human experience. Human ancestors go back even further, to the earliest so-called hominins of Africa 6 million years ago, or to the first of those who made stone tools, *c.* 2.5 million years ago. Archaeology, by contrast, is a young subject. Only 200 years ago, the Danish scholar Rasmus Nyerup (1759–1829) knew of numerous mounds and artifacts dating from ancient times, but had no way of knowing in what sequence they fell and how old they were:

Everything that has come down to us from heathendom is wrapped in a thick fog; it belongs to a space of time which we cannot measure. We know that it is older than Christendom but whether by a couple of years or a couple of centuries, or even by more than a millennium, we can do no more than guess. (Quoted in Daniel and Renfrew 1998)

The success of archaeology lies in the fact that over the past two centuries, and especially within the last 50 years, the prehistory of humankind has left the shadows of obscurity and moved decisively toward center-stage. The time-span of history, based on written records, remains short – a couple of thousand years or less for most regions. Although rich in detail, history lacks the long-term perspective that enables archaeology to study the origins of human behavior and how human societies developed over tens of thousands of years.

Archaeology deals alike with hunter-gatherers of the Ice Age and city-dwellers of ancient Mesoamerica, with the first farmers of Southwest Asia and early chiefdoms of Polynesia and Amazonia. Far from being ancillary to history, archaeology is our main source of knowledge of the human past, covering literate and non-literate peoples alike. It is the only field of enquiry that allows the broad canvas of the human past to be viewed as a whole. It illustrates the full diversity of human culture and society and shows how humans have changed and adapted, both to external factors such as climate and environment, and to new social circumstances and technologies. It reveals the degree to which humans have created themselves, in the form of culture and innovation, and at the same time studies how they coped with the demands of subsistence and reproduction, and how within the past few thousand years they have adjusted to the inexorable pressures of demographic increase. For while it is clear that few earlier societies have witnessed such a population explosion as we have seen over the past 30 years – a period during which the world's population has doubled in size – the steady growth in human numbers can be seen to be a significant measure of human success as a species. Population growth has brought social and environmental problems, however, and human societies through time have been forced to adapt, to find new ways of doing things, or perish. All of this is illustrated by the study of archaeology.

What is Archaeology?

Archaeology can be defined as the study of the human past from material remains. It is often considered (especially in North America) as one sub-field within anthropology. Anthropology – the study of humans – includes a number of other sub-fields, notably:

• *Cultural anthropology* (or social anthropology), the study of the diversity of living societies, often based on the work of ethnographers who live for a time within those societies and observe their behavior at first hand; traditionally, ethnographers have focused on non-Western societies, but increasingly today they are turning their attention to specific groups within Western societies, such as immigrant communities or inner-city groups;

• *Biological anthropology*, the study of human evolution and physiology, which may be divided into paleoanthropology (fossil and skeletal remains of early humans) and human ecology (human biological adaptation to environment and disease, including patterns of nutrition, fertility, and genetics, the latter also a source of information on human population history);

• *Linguistic anthropology*, the study of world languages, their development and interrelationships.

While archaeology remains at heart a humanity – the study of humans and human societies – it also draws on a range of other disciplines, including the sciences. Physics, chemistry, biology, botany, geography, and geology are employed for the discovery and analysis of excavated materials, to understand prehistoric lifeways, and to reconstruct key features of the environments in which past human societies lived. Archaeologists today make extensive use of computers, both to record material in the field, and for statistical and analytical techniques such as GIS (Geographic Information Systems) and computer modeling. Most archaeologists will also be familiar with human and animal anatomy, and with the technologies used to make the ancient artifacts that they study. The dependence on such a wide range of other disciplines is a key feature of the archaeological approach.

In terms of chronology, many consider that archaeology begins when early hominins first began to create material culture (stone tools) some 2.5 million years ago (Chapter 2). Material culture is often presented as one of the hallmarks of

1.1 *Religious imagery:* the Maya king of Yaxchilán, Shield Jaguar II, holds a flaming torch above the kneeling figure of his wife Lady K'ab'al Xoc who performs a bloodletting ritual, drawing a rope studded with thorns through her tongue. The first two glyphs in the text at the top of the panel give the date AD 709. (Lintel 24, Temple 23, Yaxchilán.)

underpin the ways in which humans understand the world, and these are frequently manifest in imagery or traces of ritual practice. Carvings and figurines may provide direct representations of mythical beings and religious ceremonies. Scenes in Egyptian temples and tombs, for example, show deities weighing the souls of the dead, while Maya artists depict rulers engaged in bloodletting rituals [**1.1**].

Burials, the ways in which people have disposed of their dead, indicate a growing concern with identity and the afterlife. The occasional burials of the Middle and Upper Paleolithic testify to the origins of human feelings of respect in the treatment of the dead. In more recent periods, the deceased may be inhumed (buried) or cremated, and equipped (sometimes lavishly) with objects and furnishings to assist life in the afterworld, or the journey thereto. The living, too, may be represented in statuary and art, throwing light on social practices and political power. Popular beliefs and household rituals are as much a part of archaeology's domain as the lavish stage-managed cults of state-sponsored temples and priesthoods.

Archaeology is famous for exceptional discoveries such as Tutankhamun's tomb [**1.2**] in Egypt (Chapter 10) or Qin Shi Huangdi's pottery army in China (Chapter 15). These catch the headlines but are only one small element of the story that archaeology tells us about the human past. What we can learn about the mundane details of daily life is often equally intriguing and arguably more significant. One of the greatest advantages of archaeology is that it deals with rich and poor, literate and illiterate, the ordinary and the exceptional, without fear or favor, dependent simply on the survival of evidence and the attentions of archaeologists themselves.

humanness; several other species use found objects such as twigs or stones to probe for food or to break open nuts, but none of them actually manufacture tools on a regular basis. The reliance on material culture, on tools, is hence distinctively human, and has given humans a substantial advantage in coping with a wide range of environments. Without key items of material culture such as clothing and shelter, humans would still be restricted in distribution to the tropical regions, where our closest primate relations, the gorillas and chimpanzees, live today. It is material culture that has allowed humans to populate the globe, and to develop large and complex settlements and societies. Thus, in a real sense, the rudimentary stone tools made in Africa 2.5 million years ago were a vital step in enabling the development of the human potential that we see around us today.

But archaeology is not just about technology. The material remains form part of the broader category of human culture that also includes non-material traces, such as oral literature, dance, song, belief, myth, and ritual practices. And the remains of material culture are also rich in evidence about the social, economic, symbolic, and religious life of past human societies: what we might call the human experience. Recent decades have seen a growth of interest in **cognitive archaeology** – the study of religious and symbolic behavior and of the development of the human mind. Powerful structures of belief and understanding

Prehistory vs. History

Archaeology has, in chronological terms, no upper limit. It doesn't end with Columbus's expedition to the Americas in 1492, or with the Industrial Revolution in England in the 18th and 19th centuries. It is not a method exclusively for the study of the early human past, but of the whole of the human past. It can as well be applied to contemporary societies as to those of the distant past, and to industrialized societies as much as to developing, non-Western ones. Indeed, one particularly flourishing sub-field of the subject is devoted to industrial archaeology – the archaeology of the Industrial Revolution, focusing not only on factories and machines, but also on the housing and living conditions of ordinary families of the time.

1.2 A spectacular discovery: *after many years searching for royal tombs in the Valley of the Kings in southern Egypt, archaeologist Howard Carter came upon the tomb of the boy-pharaoh Tutankhamun almost by accident in 1922. The wealth of material buried in the tomb made it one of the most spectacular discoveries of the 20th century.*

changing policies of the Soviet state in the 70 or so years since its construction (Buchli 2000).

If archaeology is essentially an approach to human societies based on the study of material culture, there is nonetheless an important distinction to be drawn between historic and prehistoric archaeology. History is the study of the human past from written records (or from recorded oral traditions). Since writing was first invented less than 5500 years ago in Southwest Asia, the whole of the human past before that time falls within the period of prehistory [**1.3**]. However, as writing was adopted at different times in different places, so the transition from prehistoric to historic (text-based) archaeology (Little 1992) occurs at diverse stages – in western Europe, for example, history proper begins with the Greeks and Romans in the south, and with the Middle Ages in the north. This transition is sometimes further complicated by a shadowy protohistoric period; here, archaeology continues to provide the primary source of information for those early societies where writing was known, but used only for limited purposes. The present volume includes such early literate societies and extends to the classical empires of Eurasia (Greeks and Romans, Achaemenid Persia, Han China) and to the first significant European contact in Australasia (18th century), the Americas (15th/16th century), and sub-Saharan Africa (15th century, in the most general of terms). Only within the past few centuries have written records revealed much about the daily life and circumstances of ordinary people, and for this aspect of human society archaeology remains an important complementary source of information.

The Relevance of World Archaeology

We live today in a global age, when every city and region of the world is bound together in an interlinked economic system, and where cultures and ideologies meet in diverse, multi-ethnic societies. We should be more aware than ever before of how varied past human experience has been. Yet there is still a profound ignorance about the more remote segments of the human story, those lying furthest back in time or in regions that

There have also been a number of projects on the archaeology of modern Western society, such as the Arizona garbage project, which studied the contents of domestic trash cans from Tucson, Arizona (Rathje and Murphy 1992). More recent still is the archaeological analysis of a 20th-century condominium in Moscow, the Narofkim Communal House, which sought to understand the building in terms of domestic life and the

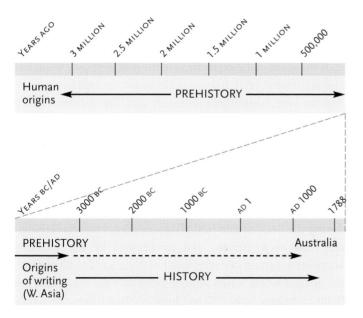

1.3 Prehistoric and historic archaeology: *writing was invented in Southwest Asia around 5500 years ago; prehistory, the period before written records, covers a vast timespan, for which material remains form our only evidence. Because writing was adopted at different times around the world, the transition from prehistory to history also varies.*

27

have hitherto been relatively little explored. This is all the more surprising given the level of general interest in ancient sites and remains, an interest that has been greatly increased by the rise of air travel and overseas vacations since the 1960s. Many Europeans and North Americans, for example, now combine a few weeks on a beach with a visit to Maya ruins or Mycenaean citadels.

As a discipline, archaeology has an advantage over history, in that it can tell us about both literate and non-literate societies, redressing the imbalance of a document-based history. Striking examples of the way in which this alters our outlook are Australia and southern Africa, both areas without any written historical record prior to the arrival of the Europeans, and both areas that archaeology now demonstrates to have had a rich prehistoric past.

The study of world prehistory also encourages us to view human development in long-term perspective. This can be seen most obviously in the early stages of human evolution, where the gradual expansion in human settlement and the ability to cope with varied and changing environments are major themes. The broad perspective of prehistory also encourages a similarly long-term view of human interaction with the environment, and allows us to pose key questions about the origins of agriculture, the development of cities, and various other phenomena that emerged, apparently independently, in different parts of the world. This perspective is all the more important since it was agriculture that led to the spread of sedentary societies and laid the foundation of the complex societies, urbanization, and states that have been a prominent feature of the recent past.

Thus, world prehistory is both enlightening and empowering. It is enlightening in that it offers a broad perspective, enabling local and regional developments to be better understood. It also allows events and circumstances in the recent past or at the present day to be set within the context of human developments stretching back over hundreds or thousands of years. The complex societies and conurbations of the 21st-century world can be seen as the heirs of cities and states that arose 4000 or 5000 years ago, themselves testimony to the way in which human social systems respond to large-scale demographic growth in certain predefined ways; in the last analysis, we are all descendants of the modern human hunter-gatherers who survived the Ice Ages and had colonized most of the habitable world by around 10,000 years ago.

World prehistory is empowering in that it documents the whole human past and is not restricted to dominant political players such as literate states and empires, with their rich iconography, military strength, and historical records. It tells us how the Bantu spread into southern Africa while the Roman Empire rose and fell, entirely oblivious, 2500 km (1500 miles)

to the north, in part in the same continent. It also documents the lives of ordinary people – how they farmed or herded, what they ate and made, how they buried their dead – subjects on which conventional historical sources have relatively little to say. It tells us about peasant farmers as well as the warrior elites, about slaves as well as their owners. It is also increasingly enabling us to rectify the serious imbalance that has generally emphasized male histories and roles and disregarded those of females; the recent growth of **gender archaeology** is throwing remarkable new light on women in prehistoric and early historic societies.

The Origins of Archaeology

World prehistory is, in essence, a subject of European and North American origin: a product of Western traditions of scholarship and enquiry. It has spread to other regions of the world largely through the work of Western archaeologists, sometimes within a colonial context. This has naturally brought it into contact, and sometimes into conflict, with the traditional understandings held by native peoples about their own pasts (Layton 1989). Recent decades have witnessed a growing and salutary sensitivity among archaeologists to the communities among whom they work, and this includes not only native Americans and Australians, but also local communities in urban Western settings. Archaeologists do not claim to "own" the past that they explore, and excavations today are generally undertaken only with the consent of local communities. Furthermore, the artifacts that are uncovered do not in any way belong to the archaeologists who excavate them, and in best practice are handed to a competent local authority for storage or eventual display.

Archaeologists must respect the beliefs and understanding of the people among whom they work and whose pasts they are recovering; moreover, the results are frequently of great interest to local communities, who are encouraged to collaborate with archaeologists in the exploration of the past. Empowerment has also occurred at a much larger scale, as archaeology has discredited the idea, widely held a century ago, that human culture arose first in western Europe; it has shown, instead, that we are all the descendants of hominins living and making stone tools in tropical Africa 2.5 million years ago.

Renaissance Beginnings

The origins of archaeology lie some 500 years ago in Europe, during the Renaissance [1.4] (Trigger 1989). Medieval scholarship had been directed and constrained by the authority accorded to certain key texts that had been handed down from the ancient world. Chief among these was the Bible, and the institutionalized power of the Christian church demanded con-

European intellectual horizons. A series of key developments came together to create the underpinnings of modern Western science, one of which was the invention of movable metal type and the printing press by Johannes Gutenberg in the mid-15th century. Books became cheaper and more readily available, and accompanied a gradual spread of literacy that took learning for the first time in centuries outside the confines of the religious specialists. Within the Christian church, a new spirit of enquiry led to the fragmentation of the previous orthodoxy and the rise of Protestantism, which challenged the traditional structures of

1.4 *(Left)* **Renaissance rediscovery of Classical antiquity:** *Maerten van Heemskerk (1498–1574) was a North European artist who in the 1530s spent several years in Italy, where he was inspired by the ruins of Roman buildings. These appear as the background of many of his paintings and engravings, as in this self-portrait in front of the Colosseum.*

1.5, 1.6 *(Below)* **Early ethnography:** *artist John White accompanied Sir Walter Ralegh on his voyage to establish the colony at Roanoke in Virginia in 1585. He recorded the local indigenous people along with local fauna and flora in a series of watercolors, and after returning to England 13 months later these watercolors, such as the North American chief (right) inspired his imaginary depictions of the pre-Roman inhabitants of Britain such as the Pictish warrior (left).*

formity and discouraged enquiry or experiment. For subjects lying outside the scope of the Bible, the Church relied on selected Classical authors, such as the 4th-century BC Greek philosopher Aristotle.

In the 16th century, the power of these traditional texts was weakened by the spread of learning and a general broadening of

1.7 The growth of antiquarian interest: *accurate surveys of European prehistoric monuments were first undertaken in the 17th century, as it came to be appreciated that careful observation and recording could yield much additional information about the character and purpose of these structures. Here students of Sir John Soane (1753–1837), the British architect and antiquarian, are measuring Stonehenge.*

authority. Reliance on ancient texts was gradually supplanted by new knowledge derived from direct observation and experimentation. At the same time, European economic expansion led to overseas voyages, which brought knowledge of distant and diverse societies. The Portuguese explored the coast of Africa, and Vasco da Gama rounded the Cape of Good Hope to discover the monsoon route to India in 1498. Six years earlier, Christopher Columbus had successfully crossed the central Atlantic and reached the Caribbean islands. Columbus's achievement was soon followed by European landfalls on the Central American mainland, which set in train the tragic effects of conquest and disease that devastated the indigenous societies of native America.

The voyages of discovery brought back to Europe new information and a new curiosity about human societies and technology that fed directly back into understanding of the European past. Thus, chipped stone tools from America were evidently human artifacts and not the "fulgurous exhalations conglobed in a cloud by the circumposed humor" that they had previously been supposed (although the old ideas lingered on; the quotation is from a text of the mid-17th century). Comparisons were drawn between the peoples met with in the newly encountered lands, and the prehistoric occupants of Europe; John White, for example, produced images of so-called "ancient Britons" with body painting based directly on his watercolors of the native North Americans [**1.5, 1.6**] he had seen in Virginia in 1585 (Moser 1998).

Advances in the 17th and 18th Centuries

It was Europeans who undertook these world voyages, and hence Europeans who were first faced with the perspective of global human diversity. Archaeology, however, was initially focused on the lands of northern and western Europe, and only later became a means of exploring the pasts of other peoples. In terms of field archaeology – the observation, recording, and excavation of archaeological sites – the Protestant nations of northern Europe led the way. The first serious investigations of British prehistoric monuments began in the 17th century, with John Aubrey's descriptions and plans of Stonehenge [**1.7**] and Avebury in southern England. The first hesitant steps towards archaeological excavation were made toward the end of the century, in northern France and Scandinavia, though much digging into ancient sites continued to have the aim of treasure hunting, with little or no attention to the contexts from which

objects came (Bahn 1996). Systematic excavation began only in the late 18th century, when the concept of **stratigraphy** began to be understood. Stratigraphy – the successive deposition of superimposed layers, either of natural or cultural material – laid the basis for chronological sequences, since lower deposits should have been laid down earlier than overlying layers. A pioneering example was the excavation of Native American burial mounds undertaken by Thomas Jefferson in 1784 (Willey and Sabloff 1993).

These early archaeological enquiries were innovative for their time, but were unable to overcome the most fundamental problem of prehistory: that of **chronology**. In much of western Europe, scholars could chart a historical sequence back to the Roman conquests of the 1st century BC or AD. Roman authors such as Caesar or Tacitus told of the native peoples who were conquered, and sometimes of those who lay just beyond the edges of the empire. Archaeologists in the 17th and 18th centuries were increasingly able to recognize that many of the remains they were studying were pre-Roman in date, but had no way of establishing their true age. The problem was compounded by biblical scholars, who set the age of the earth at around only 6000 years old.

Developments in the 19th Century

It was during the 19th century that the problem of chronology began to be resolved and the study of prehistoric archaeology was finally born (Daniel 1975; Trigger 1989). Early in the century, it came to be realized that archaeological materials could be sorted into sequences by means of their technology: stone tools had preceded metal ones, and among the latter, bronze had preceded iron. Thus the three-age system of Stone, Bronze, and Iron was established. It was widely used within Europe by the middle years of the 19th century, though it is important to observe that it was not applied to other continents – Africa, Australia, or the Americas – where different chronological terms were developed.

Closer study of the artifacts led to increasing subdivision of the European "three ages" on the basis both of technology and style; thus, the Stone Age was subdivided into an Old Stone Age (with tools exclusively of chipped or flaked stone) and a New Stone Age (with tools of polished stone). In the 1860s these two periods came to be known as the Paleolithic (Old Stone Age) and Neolithic (New Stone Age). The Bronze Age and Iron Age, too, were each subdivided into Early, Middle, and Late. These typological methods made it possible to sort objects into sequences that could be checked by excavation – did the different types follow each other in correct order in successive layers? – and thus provide a relative chronology. They did not, however, reveal any object's or layer's exact age, nor the length of the different phases or stages.

A crucial change in understanding of the human past came in the middle decades of the 19th century, with three interlinked developments (Daniel 1975; Grayson 1983). First was the demonstration in the 1830s that early human chipped stone tools could be found in the gravel terraces of European rivers, associated with remains of extinct species such as mammoth and woolly rhinoceros. This indicated both the great age of the human tools and gave a first insight into the dramatically different climate that early humans had experienced. Second was the

chance discovery of a pre-modern skeleton in a limestone cave in the Neander Valley in western Germany in 1856. This was the first fossil hominin – a Neanderthal [**1.8**] – to be generally recognized as such, and gave evidence of the development of modern humans from earlier archaic human forms.

The third key event was the publication of Charles Darwin's *On the Origin of Species* in 1859, followed by his *Descent of Man* in 1871 (Bowler 1990). In 1831, the young Charles Darwin (1809–1882) had embarked on a voyage of survey and exploration in the *Beagle*, which was mapping the coast of South America. His observations of the diversity and interrelationships of the species of plants and animals he encountered and recorded led him in the following decades to recognize the key role of natural selection in shaping the development of individual species over time (Chapter 2). Successful individuals within a species would be more likely to reproduce and pass on their characteristics to their offspring, and thus features that conferred an advantage – a longer beak, a different coloring – would spread through a population. Ultimately, a single species might be divided into sub-groups, each of which was increasingly specialized and successful within its particular environmental niche. This could lead eventually to the division of one species into two or more separate species, each of which would become increasingly different from the others as they respectively underwent further adaptations to their environment. Darwin's theory was revolutionary in suggesting that the diversity of life was not the result of divine creation, but of natural processes that could still be observed in the present day. Furthermore, what was true for animals could also be applied to humans.

Darwin's views brought him into fierce conflict with others [**1.9**], who continued to maintain that the account of divine creation contained within the Bible was correct. Gradually, however, his theory succeeded in winning general acceptance as the most persuasive explanation for the development of the diversity of life. It came to be appreciated that humans, along with other species, are not fixed in their form or behavior, but are constantly changing in response to the pressures and circumstances around them. The model of evolution through natural selection was given further support by advances in genetics, beginning with Austrian botanist Gregor Mendel's plant breeding experiments in the 1860s, which showed how particular characteristics are passed from parent to offspring. With the

1.8 The first fossil evidence for human ancestry: the skull cap and associated bones discovered in 1856 at the Feldhoffer Cave in the Neander Valley of western Germany were the first direct fossil evidence for human ancestry to be recognized as such, though it was dismissed by skeptics for many years. Further discoveries in the 1880s and early 1900s finally laid these objections to rest.

1.9 *The theory of evolution: Charles Darwin's theory of the origin of species through natural selection presented a powerful challenge to the Christian religious belief in a divine creation, but provided the context in which human evolution and the development of early societies could be understood. In the controversy that followed Darwin was lampooned in popular cartoons, but his theory eventually won the day.*

rapidly developing knowledge of DNA in the past 50 years, geneticists are now able to explain in detail how Darwinian natural selection operates at the level of the genetic code.

For some, however, these new understandings are unwelcome, and a number of people continue to believe in a creationist view: that the world, and all the species within it, were created in the form we see them today by divine action. Archaeology allows us to demonstrate that creationist views, though deeply held, are incompatible with the evidence of the past that is available to us. The fossil record of human evolution, with its numerous and increasingly well-dated remains of earlier hominin species, indicates clearly the steady morphological and behavioral change that preceded the development of the first modern humans some 150,000 years ago. Nor did natural selection stop at that point: to this day we are still continuously (if almost imperceptibly) changing in response to selective pressures.

Darwin's writings provided a new way of understanding humans and other species in the context of their total environment. This gave rise to the discipline of **evolutionary ecology**, which studies how species are adapted to their environments, in biological but also in behavioral terms. Human evolutionary ecology includes the study of culture as an adaptive mechanism (cultural ecology), a view that many archaeologists today regard as insightful, but too limited to provide a comprehensive explanation of human cultural behavior (see below).

Social Evolution

Darwin's thesis of human origins, coupled with the discovery of the Neanderthal fossils and the early stone tools, suggested that the human story went back much further than had previously been supposed, and could certainly not be accommodated within the 6000 years offered by the biblical time-frame. This was associated with a growing understanding of human prehistory that viewed it as a steady record of progress from primitive hunters to modern civilizations. Indeed, the concept of human progress has a very long history, and features in both Chinese and Roman writings of over 2000 years ago. It was during the 19th century, however, that the concept of universal stages of human progress was developed and applied to archaeological material. Among the most famous proponents were Lewis Henry Morgan (1818–1881) in North America and Sir Edward

Tylor (1832–1917) in Britain, both of whom argued that humans had passed through stages of savagery (as hunters and gatherers) and barbarism (as herders and cultivators) before progressing to civilization, which they equated with the invention of writing. Two separate ideas were embedded in this view of the human past: first, that each new stage was an improvement on the one that had preceded it; and second, that the pattern of progress was driven by a kind of social Darwinism, in which less efficient kinds of social organization were supplanted by more advanced social forms.

Archaeologists today would be very wary of interpreting changes in the human past as evidence of "progress," though the idea remained influential down to the middle of the 20th century. Terms such as "savagery," "barbarism," and "civilization" were still being used by eminent prehistorians such as V. Gordon Childe (1892–1957) in the 1940s (Trigger 1980). Though the concept of human progress was laid to one side in the 1960s, anthropologists continue to seek appropriate ways of classifying different kinds of human society, so that they may be better understood and compared. One widely influential scheme was that proposed by Elman Service (1962), in which he divided human societies into four major categories:

• *Bands*, characterized by small groups of 25–60 individuals who are related to each other through family and marriage ties – such societies consist typically of mobile hunter-gatherers;

• *Tribes*, generally settled farmers or pastoralist herders, numbering from a few hundred to a few thousand individuals whose identity is based on a concept of descent from a common ancestor; they are loosely organized without central control or strongly developed social hierarchy;

• *Chiefdoms*, which may number over 10,000 individuals, in which institutionalized differences of rank and status are embedded in a hierarchy of lineages ruled over by a chief; a key economic feature of chiefdom societies is redistribution, in which subordinate sectors of society pay tribute to the chief, who then redistributes it to his followers;

• *State societies* or *civilizations*, in which populations reach much greater levels of size and complexity, with a centralized and institutionalized control that overrides kinship ties, and in which differences of rank and wealth are fostered and protected.

This four-fold division of human societies has proved useful to prehistorians seeking to compare and comprehend archaeological materials. Thus, early farming societies have often been considered to have been tribal in character, whereas hunters and gatherers are imagined to have been organized into smaller-scale bands. Furthermore, it is clear that as human population densities have increased, there has been a general shift from bands to tribes to states (though the significance of chiefdoms remains more controversial). Although useful as a general scheme, however, this classification of human societies must be used with caution. It suggests that there are universal types of human social organization, whereas we know from both archaeology and ethnography that each society is different and indeed unique. In addition, it appears to propose a systematic pattern of social evolution, in which each stage succeeds the previous one in a standard and global pattern of human change, the only difference, region-to-region, being in the pace at which those changes have occurred; in other words, "progress" by another name. It also holds the danger that bands, tribes, or chiefdoms of the present day or recent past – the !Kung of the Kalahari Desert in southern Africa, the East African Masai, or 18th-century Hawaiians – may be considered fossil survivors of earlier social forms, rather than examples of the richness of human social diversity.

Developments in Methodology and Techniques

By the early decades of the 20th century, archaeological investigations had begun in virtually every corner of the habitable world. Long-established interests such as the Classical archaeology of Greece and Rome, the archaeology of ancient Egypt and ancient Mexico, or the prehistoric monuments of northwest Europe were now part of a much larger endeavor, which included Australia, North America, and sub-Saharan Africa. By the middle of the 20th century, the broad outlines of a world prehistory were beginning to become clear. Pottery and farming, cities and states could be studied and compared in a wide variety of regions. But the number of archaeologists was still small, and there remained a great obstacle to understanding the human past on a truly global perspective: the problem of chronology. Without adequate methods of dating it was impossible to establish whether Mexican cities predated those of China, or how long the various processes of social and technological change had taken. More difficult still was the dating of early hominin fossils such as the *Australopithecus* skulls that had been discovered in southern Africa (Chapter 2) or *Homo erectus* in Java (Chapter 3). What was needed was a method of absolute dating that would enable the whole of world prehistory to be viewed in its full chronological detail and extent.

The solution came in the late 1940s when, in a spin-off from research into nuclear physics, Chicago scientist Willard Libby (1908–1980) developed the first radiometric (absolute) dating technique: **radiocarbon dating** (also known as carbon-14 or C14 dating) [**1.10**] (see box, Chapter 4). The method was widely applicable to organic archaeological materials such as charcoal, bone, and shell, and a growing number of radiocarbon dates were published during the 1950s and 1960s. Many of these were surprisingly old – giving earlier dates than had been expected – but it soon became clear that a further correction (so-called "calibration") was needed, on account of changes in atmospheric radiocarbon over past millennia. Calibration revealed that many of the dates were in fact still older than they at first sight appeared. Despite certain problems and shortcomings with the method, notably the fact that the dates are not precise but carry an error margin, and the difficulty of ensuring that they relate securely to an archaeological layer or context,

1.10 *Scientific advances in archaeology: radiocarbon dating, invented in the late 1940s, is one of the key scientific methods used by archaeologists to establish the age of their sites and finds. Later advances, notably the introduction of the Accelerator Mass Spectrometer (AMS) technique, now allow samples weighing only 5–10 mg to provide dates as old as 40,000 BC.*

1.11 *Fieldwork: excavation remains a key component of archaeological research, with earth-moving machinery and modern computer technology assisting the work of the archaeologists. Here a burnt flint mound in the Cambridgeshire Fenland dating from the Early Bronze Age (late 3rd/early 2nd millennium BC) is being sectioned and recorded.*

radiocarbon dating has revolutionized the understanding of prehistoric and historical archaeology.

Radiocarbon dating is effective on materials up to 40,000 years old; beyond that date, the amount of radioactive carbon that survives is too small for accurate measurement. Thus it cannot be applied to the study of human origins or to the Lower and Middle Paleolithic. Other radiometric methods have, however, been devised to cover those periods, notably potassium-argon dating, used to date volcanic rocks and hence fix the age of many of the early hominin fossils from East Africa (see box, Chapter 2). It is on the basis of such methods, many of only recent development, that we can follow the chronology of human evolution from apelike ancestors to archaic and modern humans.

The account of the human past presented in this book is possible as a result of these new dating methods. But these are not the only major changes in archaeological methods over the past 50 years. The archaeologist now goes into the field armed with a battery of new techniques and approaches. Some of these will be practiced as fieldwork [1.11] proceeds: the planning and recording of layers and buildings (now generally using modern laser technology); the screening (sieving) of the excavated earth to ensure no finds are missed; the collection and labeling of samples for dating or analysis. Technology will also have been important before fieldwork commenced: aerial photography or side-scanning radar to locate sites; geomagnetic prospection or resistivity to identify specific below-ground features such as pits and hearths. When the field season closes, further work follows in laboratories, where the samples that have been collected are analyzed for remains of phytoliths (minute particles of silica from plant cells), pollen, or seeds; for traces of manufacture and

use-wear on stone and metal artifacts; for organic deposits surviving in the fabric of pottery vessels; for faunal and human remains (Renfrew and Bahn 2004). A recent addition to the range of techniques for the study of organic remains has been fossil DNA – preserved segments of the genetic code recovered from bones or seeds and used to reconstruct the relationships between past and present species. The technique has been especially helpful to our understanding of the origin and spread of domesticated plants and animals, and has also been applied to the issue of modern human origins (Chapter 4) (Jones 2001).

The traditional image of archaeology as excavation has also had to be revised. Many field campaigns today do not involve digging into sites, but rather collecting material lying on the ground surface. "Off-site" or "survey" archaeology enables broader patterns of human occupation to be established, sometimes including cities, villages, and individual farmsteads. Here again, new technology in the field and in the laboratory is revolutionizing the process, with GPS (Global Positioning Systems) to map sites and finds quickly and easily in the landscape, and GIS (Geographic Information Systems) to analyze their interrelationships.

These are important new technologies, but at its core, archaeology remains a humanity or social science. It does so because its subject is the human past. Our enquiry is focused on the development and diversity of humans, both as individuals and within societies, from earliest times. It is for this reason that there is much archaeological writing on interpretation and theory. The multiplicity of views and approaches may sometimes appear confusing, but it is symptomatic of the nature of the enterprise: of humans studying themselves.

Explaining Change: Archaeological Theories

Archaeology is the study of change: how human societies and their material culture have altered and evolved over the past 2.5 million years. When an archaeologist excavates a prehistoric settlement, he or she may in one sense be studying a specific moment in time – the burial of an individual, the abandonment of a dwelling – but this individual event is to be understood in the context of what came before and what succeeded it. The importance of change in the archaeological study of the human past becomes all the more evident when we reflect on long-term or large-scale processes, such as the adoption of agriculture and the development of cities. Change is a recurrent feature of human society, and the analysis and understanding of change lies at the heart of the archaeological endeavor.

Cultural Ecology and Agency Theory

Archaeologists have developed a number of approaches in seeking to study the mechanisms of change. One of the most important is the concept of **cultural ecology**: that one of the main causes of change in human culture and society has been the response of those societies to the challenges and opportunities of their environments. Cultural ecology became particularly influential in North American archaeology in the 1940s and 1950s through the work of Julian Steward (1902–1972) (1955) and Leslie White (1900–1975) (1959). Steward defined it as "the study of the adaptive processes by which the nature of society, and an unpredictable number of features of culture, are affected by the basic adjustment through which man utilizes a given environment." The social and political structures that characterize large-scale societies might thus be viewed as adjustments to the new needs created by the growing size of human communities. Steward's work on the role of irrigation in the rise of early state societies (Chapter 5) was a classic example of the cultural ecological approach. He concentrated on the way in which these societies had extracted their subsistence needs from their environment, and the impact that this had had on other aspects of culture. More recent proponents of this approach, such as Karl Butzer (1989), have described the core concerns of cultural ecology as "how people live, doing what, how well, for how long, and with what human and environmental constraints." Harvard archaeologist Gordon Willey (1913–2002) used a cultural ecological approach to interpret 1500 years of settlement patterns in the Virú Valley of Peru [**1.12**], against a background of changing environment.

1.12 Cultural ecology: *Gordon Willey examining the stratified sequence of deposits at Barton Ramie in Belize during the Belize Valley Project (1953–60). Willey pioneered the study of regional settlement patterns that went far beyond the confines of the traditional archaeological site.*

Nor has cultural ecology been exclusively the preserve of archaeology and the study of past societies. Anthropologist Roy Rappaport (1986) applied the approach to explain the New Guinea ceremonial feasts for which large numbers of pigs were slaughtered; they were timed to reduce the surplus when the herd became too large and used to create solidarity and alliance both within and between different communities.

Cultural ecology can be a powerful tool for interpreting social practices, settlement patterns, and cultural change. Opponents argue, however, that explanations such as these pay insufficient attention to the specific patterns of cultural behavior or to the role of individuals as agents of change. Societies are not monolithic entities, but consist of individuals, each with perceptions, aims, and desires. This perspective lies behind the recent development of **agency theory** in archaeology, which considers individuals in the past as knowledgeable actors: although constrained to a large extent by the traditions, norms, and beliefs of the society in which they live, they are nonetheless able, within certain limits, to effect change and achieve specific objectives (Dobres and Robb 2000). Whereas cultural ecologists such as Leslie White considered individuals in the past as unimportant – mere ciphers for changes operating at a much more fundamental level – agency theory highlights the impact of individuals. Agency theory is not, however, a reversion to 19th-century views of political history, which saw the past as a sequence of kings and dynasties, but rather an attempt to explain change in terms of individuals operating within societies.

1.13 ***Diffusion and emulation:*** *the gold stater of Philip II of Macedon (top) was one of the key models for several of the earliest coinages of temperate Europe, such as the Gallo-Belgic coinages of France (center and bottom), though the garlanded head (obverse) and 4-horse chariot (reverse) became increasingly stylized and abstract with growing distance from the Macedonian original.*

Mechanisms and Patterns of Change

Thus, cultural ecology and agency theory may be considered as contrasting but complementary approaches to understanding prehistory, operating at different scales: the former at the level of whole societies changing over the long term, in response to environmental change or demographic growth for example; the latter at the level of individual communities within a lifetime or across a few generations. Alongside these general frameworks of interpretation, archaeologists also study specific mechanisms of change.

Innovation, Diffusion, Emulation, and Migration One such mechanism is **innovation**, when a new artifact or technique – pottery-making, bronze-casting, or writing, for example – is developed. Such improvements often emerge from pre-existing technology developed for another purpose, and it is the transfer of that knowledge into a new domain that gives rise to innovation. A good recent example of such transmission is the adaptation of the traditional wine or olive press in 15th-century Germany to create the European printing press.

A second key mechanism is cultural contact. Societies are rarely isolated from each other, and usually engage in regular contact (whether hostile or friendly) with their neighbors. By this means, innovations and materials from one area can spread relatively rapidly into adjacent regions. This might take the form of actual imports, which subsequently trigger changes in the society that receives them. Thus the spread of Mediterranean coinages among the peoples of temperate Europe during the late 1st millennium BC led to the rise of native coinages based on the Mediterranean models [**1.13**]. This process is sometimes termed **diffusion**.

It is clear that diffusion has played a key role in change within human societies, but it has come to be regarded with suspicion by archaeologists, owing to its incautious use as an explanation in the earlier 20th century. Many innovations were explained through the impact of "higher" civilizations on "lower" ones around them, when a careful reading of the evidence would have shown there was no justification for such a link. Thus the megalithic tombs of western Europe were seen as local imitations of temples and tombs built by early state societies in Egypt and the east Mediterranean. The application of radiocarbon dating in the 1960s and 1970s exposed the fallacy of this explanation when it demonstrated that the megalithic

tombs were two millennia older than the models from which they were supposed to have been derived. So although diffusion is an important mechanism of change, assumptions based on it must be viewed with caution and with critical evaluation.

Another mechanism of cultural contact is, in essence, a form of **emulation**. Societies will frequently adopt features from their neighbors in a context of rivalry or competition. This is the basis for the concept of secondary state formation or peer-polity interaction, where new states form around the margins of existing states (Renfrew and Cherry 1982). The new states are, in many senses, indigenous in their social forms and beliefs: these are not imposed from outside. But the states may consciously adopt features such as writing or iconography (images of deities or other symbolic figures or objects) from their powerful and prestigious neighbors. Thus Minoan wall paintings copied the red/male, white/female color-coding of Egyptian art, and may well have adopted the practice of writing on clay tablets (and perhaps writing itself) from western Asia. In one sense this is another example of diffusion, but these specific cultural links support the theory that Minoan state formation itself owed much to the model of Egypt and the Levant. Thus significant social change in one region may have inspired social change, through emulation, in others.

The problem with cultural contact or diffusion as a mechanism of change is that it is sometimes difficult for the archaeologist to discount other possibilities. It is hard to demonstrate beyond question that changes in one area are the result of contacts with another, rather than simply the outcome of indigenous parallel processes. The same difficulty afflicts another important mechanism of change in human societies: **migration**. In the early 20th century, many instances of archaeological change – a new pottery type, new social and economic forms – were explained as the product of new people moving into an area and replacing or absorbing the indigenous inhabitants. Historical sources make clear that such migrations have been a feature of the recent past, though earlier documents or oral histories that tell of migrations may be more difficult to interpret. Archaeologists have experienced great difficulty in identifying migrations in the material record, and most of the changes in prehistory that have been attributed to migration are today explained by other mechanisms. It is clear that many accounts of migration and conquest are really references to elite dominance, where a relatively small group of warriors may take control of a region or society, and reshape its politics without radically altering its population or technology; a good example of this might be the Norman conquest of England in the 11th century AD.

In other cases, however, large numbers of people may have populated new areas, as in the Bantu expansion into southern Africa (Chapter 10), where the newcomers brought with them farming and iron tools. Faced with such examples, archaeolo-gists today must first decide whether the evidence of change is consistent with the hypothesis of migration, or is better explained in other ways. Furthermore, even where migration appears to be a justifiable interpretation, it is important to consider the scale of demographic movement (how many people were involved) and the impact on the indigenous inhabitants.

Linear and Cyclical Patterns Change in the human past can often appear unilinear and directional when viewed from the perspective of the present. Small-scale societies of hunter-gatherers with stone tools are succeeded by farming societies and states with metal technology and irrigation agriculture. We have already observed the shortcomings and dangers of such progressivist interpretations of the human past. Furthermore, many early societies understood change in very different terms, envisaging not a linear progression of time but a cyclical pattern of recurrent events, as is exhibited in the complex calendars of Mesoamerican societies (see box, Chapter 16) [**1.14**]. This notion corresponds to natural phenomena such as the pattern of the seasons or the movement of the sun, moon, and stars; these were used to track the progress of the year, but also revealed longer-term natural patterns, such as the 56-year lunar cycle. Cycles of birth, maturity, ageing, and death, visible in most living organisms, would also have served to inspire cyclical understandings of the passage of time.

1.14 Cyclical time: *the first page of the Codex Fejérváry-Mayer, with Xiutecuhtli (god of fire) in the center, surrounded by the 260 positions of the Maya Sacred Almanac; the 20 day-signs appear at intervals of 13 days (13 x 20 = 260). The Maya also used a second, solar calendar, based on a 365-day year.*

Processual and Postprocessual Archaeology

The study of archaeology today incorporates a diversity of theoretical approaches and perspectives, many of which grew out of debates that took place during the second half of the 20th century. Before 1950, many explanations of change in the archaeological record drew on hypotheses of diffusion and migration, as described in the previous section. In the 1950s, however, archaeologists became increasingly dissatisfied with such kinds of explanation, which did not enquire sufficiently closely into how it was that societies changed. It was clear from ethnographic and historical examples that internal processes were generally more significant than external forces; societies were not simply passive recipients of change introduced from outside. In order properly to understand prehistoric societies, therefore, new kinds of thinking were required.

It was against this background that **processual** archaeology (sometimes called the New Archaeology) arose in the 1960s. It takes its name from the focus that it placed on culture process: not simply recording what had happened in the past, but understanding how and why. The development of processual archaeology in the 1960s is associated particularly with the names of Lewis Binford (1972) in North America [**1.15**] and David Clarke (1937–1976) (1968) in Britain. Proponents of the new approach drew heavily on ethnographic parallels to interpret the features found in the archaeological record and to understand prehistoric societies as real, functioning entities. At the same time they wished to get away from earlier facile uses of ethnographic analogy, emphasizing that models taken from

ethnography must be tested independently against the archaeological evidence. Much use was made of computers, which were just then becoming widely available, and on explicit methods of reasoning, notably the "hypothetico-deductive" technique, in which archaeologists sought to generate hypotheses that they then tested against the archaeological material. The concept of testing was a key element of the new approach. Processual archaeology was also closely associated with the view of culture as adaptation, and with the major role played by the environment in generating change in human societies.

An important feature of the New Archaeology was the focus on formation processes – the processes that have affected the survival of materials from the past, and the formation of the archaeological record. American archaeologist Michael Schiffer (1987) has made the important distinction between C-transforms (cultural transformation processes) and N-transforms (natural transformation processes). The former relate to human activities – how sites were built and used, how artifacts were kept or discarded in garbage pits or deposited in graves – and the latter to natural processes such as decay, geological disturbance, and waterlogging. Some archaeologists have wished to extend the study of formation processes to create a body of Middle Range Theory, which would cover the whole of the interface between raw archaeological data and the general conclusions that may be drawn from them. Other archaeologists have sought similar information by living among traditional societies and observing how their activities would be represented in the archaeological record. A classic example of such **ethnoarchaeology** was Lewis Binford's work among the Nunamiut, a group of mobile hunter-gatherers in Alaska.

Closely related to these issues of matching archaeological traces with the activities that created them is the field of **experimental archaeology**, in which tasks or objects from the past are replicated and then compared with the archaeological remains. Experiments of this kind have thrown light on a wide range of archaeological issues, from flint-working and metallurgical production to building techniques and earthworks. They have been used, for example, to help understand how the massive stone blocks of Stonehenge could have been transported to the site and raised into position [**1.16**].

The clear methodology of processual archaeology, coupled with the extensive use of quantitative methods and ethnographic analogy, marked a major advance over previous, less rigorous approaches to understanding the human past. Many

1.15 Processual archaeology: *Lewis Binford became one of the most famous archaeologists of the 1960s and 1970s through his championship of the new "processual" archaeology. Focusing on processes of cultural change, this sought to escape from the limitations of traditional typological and culture-historical approaches.*

1.17 *A "time-capsule": the violent volcanic eruption of Vesuvius in AD 79 sealed the Roman city of Pompeii in southern Italy beneath a blanket of ash, burying streets, houses, people and artifacts. In 1860 Giuseppe Fiorelli discovered that by pouring plaster into the voids within the ash he could recreate the forms of the human and animal victims.*

archaeologists today would describe themselves as processualists. Since the 1980s, however, alternative approaches have developed, which challenge the assumptions of processual archaeology. This new school of thinking, which is customarily referred to as **postprocessualist**, rejects the idea that we can ever attain objective knowledge of the past, and questions the reliance of processual archaeology on specific rigid methodologies, such as the hypothetico-deductive approach. Other themes to have emerged within postprocessual archaeology include feminist archaeology (both the role of women in the past and as archaeologists today), the archaeology of ethnicity and identity (how groups use material culture to express their solidarity and distinctiveness), and the concept of multivocality, the idea that archaeologists should not be seeking a single official reading of the human past but accepting the validity of multiple alternative interpretations, including those of different members of an archaeological excavation field crew and especially those of living traditional societies whose past is being studied (Hodder 1998; Johnson 1999).

The fluidity of postprocessual archaeology has been seen as an attraction by some and a hazard by others. It has, however, led to a wider recognition of the important part played by symbolism, belief systems, and individuals in human societies. Most recent archaeological studies draw on elements of both the processual and postprocessual traditions.

Humans in Long-term Perspective

Archaeology deals both with long-term processes and short-term events. Famous sites such as Pompeii in southern Italy, overwhelmed by a volcanic eruption on 24 August, AD 79, provide a vivid illustration of the "instantaneous" character of some archaeological discoveries; sealed in time beneath layers of volcanic material are remains of individuals [**1.17**], their pets, and their belongings. Much earlier, the Australopithecine

1.16 *Experimental archaeology: the largest stones of Stonehenge in southern Britain were brought from a distance of 30 km (19 miles). An experiment in 1997 was set up to demonstrate how blocks of this size might have been transported. A replica block was mounted on a cradle and dragged along a greased timber rail. Considerable numbers of people pulling on ropes would still have been essential to provide the motive force.*

footprints at Laetoli in Tanzania, East Africa, likewise convey a graphic impression of a specific event, the crossing of a muddy ash fall by a small group of hominins one day 3.6 million years ago (Chapter 2, p. 60). Nor is this focus on individual past events confined to the spectacular. Most routine archaeological discoveries also reveal moments in time: a butchered animal carcass; a broken tool discarded; a dead body buried with grave offerings. These can provide snapshots into the lives of ordinary individuals and communities many millennia ago.

But alongside this capacity to reveal and study individual moments in time, archaeology is characterized above all by its enormous time-depth, stretching back over millions of years to the origins of the hominin lineage and the first stone tool-makers. This unique perspective allows us to understand the development of humans and human societies in a context of long-term change, and to consider recent periods of the human past in the light of the thousands or even hundreds of thousands of years that preceded them.

Such a long-term perspective conveys special insights, which recur in the chapters that follow as three key themes: the significance of environmental change; the impact of demographic growth; and the development of human cognitive and symbolic behavior.

Humans and the Environment

It has sometimes been observed that humans are an Ice Age species. The mild, stable, and relatively benign world climate of the past 11,600 years (the Holocene period) is far from typical of the conditions in which most members of our species have had to live. From at least 700,000 years ago, world climate has experienced a regular series of dramatic fluctuations between warm and cold conditions, the latter characterized by advancing ice sheets in the northern hemisphere and pronounced aridity in the tropics. These "ice ages" occur on a cycle of about one every 100,000 years, with short warm spells or "interglacials" of around 10,000 years duration between them. The harshness of the last Ice Age climate would have placed a severe brake on the development of human societies.

Another environmental factor may have played an equally significant role. Climatic information held in ice cores and submarine corals indicates that temperatures fluctuated rapidly during much of the last Ice Age, with short periods of warm and cold following each other in sometimes rapid succession: there were, for example, 10 such warm/cold oscillations within its final millennium. Dramatic changes appear to have taken place within a matter of years or decades – certainly within the timescale of a human lifespan. It is very likely that the capacity to adapt to rapidly changing conditions has been the key to human survival and success. For this, the development of technology and the control of fire would have been crucial, for these

enabled what was in origin a tropical species to spread northward into cooler environments, and to cope with the short-term environmental changes that they encountered.

The ride was probably a bumpy one: over the course of the past 3 million years, as we will see in Chapters 2, 3, and 4, all our close hominin relatives have become extinct, leaving modern humans the only surviving human species today. Thus the primary success of the hominin lineage, and of modern humans in particular, was the ability to survive and adapt in face of rapidly changing climate and environment, and to colonize the world in the process. What had been an exclusively African lineage 2 million years ago was present on every continent save Antarctica by the end of the last Ice Age.

Demographic Growth

It is very difficult to estimate the size of the human Paleolithic population, but we can be sure that it remained small. The constraints of the climate will have meant that any increase would have been followed by a shrinkage of numbers as harsher conditions returned. As humans became more skilled and technologically sophisticated, the overall size of the human population will have risen, but the pace of increase will have remained slow.

This pattern changed decisively as the last Ice Age drew to a close, and the mild, stable Holocene climate became established. Not only were food resources more abundant, but the erratic oscillations of Ice Age climate ceased, and human communities were able to develop more sophisticated ways of living in their local environments. The result was rapid population increase [1.18], and human demographic pressure has been one of the key causes of change throughout the Holocene period and up to the present day. This is not to claim that all societies everywhere were continually growing in numbers; some may have developed effective ways of stabilizing their numbers so as to live within their available resources. Other factors, such as war, famine, and disease, have also acted to keep population numbers low. Viewed at the global level, however, the key feature of the human story over the past 11,500 years has been the exponential increase in numbers of our species, leading today to the situation in which our planet supports some 6 billion people.

In order to feed the growing numbers of people, new lifestyles and technologies have had to be adopted. The most important of these is food production – farming – which has enabled communities to far outstrip the resources available from hunting and gathering. The development of farming was not a single act, but a steady intensification of production, from simple hoe agriculture to irrigation farming and use of animal fertilizers. Another key feature is the propensity of the growing human populations to cluster together in larger settlements

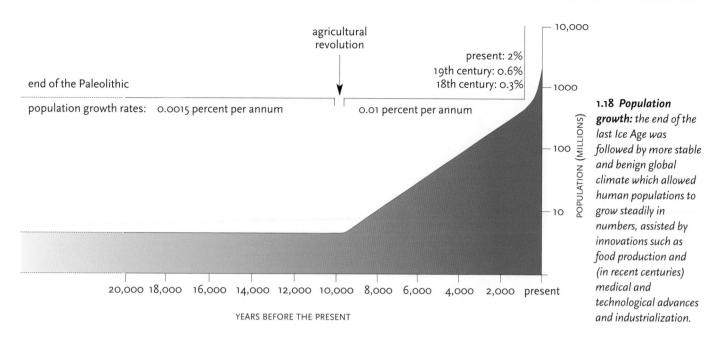

agricultural revolution

end of the Paleolithic

population growth rates: 0.0015 percent per annum   0.01 percent per annum

present: 2%
19th century: 0.6%
18th century: 0.3%

10,000
1000
100
10

POPULATION (MILLIONS)

20,000 18,000 16,000 14,000 12,000 10,000 8,000 6,000 4,000 2,000 present

YEARS BEFORE THE PRESENT

1.18 Population growth: *the end of the last Ice Age was followed by more stable and benign global climate which allowed human populations to grow steadily in numbers, assisted by innovations such as food production and (in recent centuries) medical and technological advances and industrialization.*

wherever possible. Towns such as Çatalhöyük [**1.19**] in Turkey (Chapter 6) may already have numbered several thousand people by 7000 BC, and the past few thousand years have been dominated in most regions of the world by the growth of cities, which typically number millions of inhabitants today. The fact that these same trends – toward food production, social complexity, and urbanism – are found as independent developments in different parts of the world suggests that they correspond to basic facets of human behavior that are common to all of us. Given certain sets of social and environmental circumstances, it seems, humans respond in similar ways.

Thus the long-term background of the ice ages must be set alongside the somewhat shorter-term pattern of the Holocene period, when human societies embarked on novel and often

parallel trajectories of development. It is from the latter period that the bulk of the archaeological evidence available to us today has survived, but both need to be considered in order to understand the full complexity of the human past.

Symbols and Cognition

What sets humans apart from all other species is not just their numbers, but their capacity for symbolic behavior, and its material expression in terms of structures and artifacts. The evidence for material expression begins with the first stone tools, and grows steadily more complex during the later stages of the Paleolithic period. As pebble tools are succeeded by deliberately crafted hand axes, and as these in turn give way to the flake and blade tools of the Middle and Upper Paleolithic, it is reasonable

1.19 The growth of urbanism: *Çatalhöyük in southern Turkey is the earliest large settlement to have been discovered by archaeologists, covering an area of 13 ha (32 acres). This agglomeration of close-packed rectangular houses, with decorated walls and benches, and burials beneath the floors, was founded in around 7200 BC and remained in occupation for a thousand years, forming a deeply layered settlement mound.*

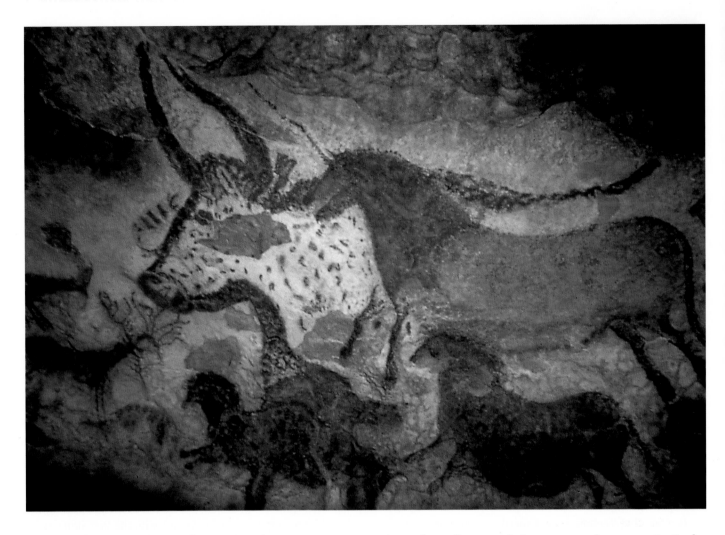

1.20 *Symbolic behavior:* *the cave of Lascaux in southwest France contains some of the most spectacular examples of early artistic representations by modern humans, including polychrome images of aurochs (wild cattle), horses, reindeer, and other animals. Many of these date to the Early Magdalenian period, around 17,000 years ago, though some may be more recent.*

to assume that we are witnessing the development of more intelligent and more capable hominins. It is with the appearance of symbolic behavior during the past 100,000 years, however, in the form of burials, personal ornaments, and "art" [1.20], that we begin to see evidence of fully modern humans that were not only anatomically like ourselves but were also for the first time behaving in ways similar to ourselves (Mithen 1996).

The increasing sophistication of symbolic behavior remains a major strand in the human story up to the present day. Humans use material symbols alongside language in a routine way to help them represent and conceptualize ideas and relationships, and to gain an understanding or interpretation of the social and physical world around them (Renfrew and Scarre 1998). Symbols may carry messages both explicit and uncon-scious, depending on their nature and context. Particular choices of clothing, for example, may indicate wealth and status, and also how individuals wish to be seen by their neighbors. Writing is a highly codified form of symbolic behavior, in which meanings are tightly specified and can be conveyed from writer to reader with little ambiguity. Elaborate ceremonies and rituals, involving special objects and settings, carry equally overt messages in a partly material form; the remains of buildings and artifacts survive for the archaeologist to explore. No less symbolic (and retrievable by the archaeologist) is the frequent practice of orienting a house in one of the cardinal directions or toward a particular feature of the landscape, such as a shrine or a sacred mountain, which is endowed by the inhabitants with special significance.

Symbolic behavior is thus a key focus of enquiry in our quest to understand the human past. Indeed, it is so thoroughly embedded in human behavior that it plays a part in structuring virtually all activities, from working in the fields to eating meals, making tools or visiting shopping malls. In the chapters that follow, we shall chart the rise of this symbolic complexity alongside issues of biological evolution, climate, and social change.

Summary and Conclusions

In this chapter we have discussed the nature of archaeology and how it provides new and fuller understandings of the human past. Archaeology arose first in Europe during the Renaissance, as part of a general movement toward obtaining secure knowledge of the world through direct observation, supplementing or displacing traditional beliefs derived from religious or Classical texts. In the 19th century, the discovery of fossil hominins, coupled with Darwin's theory of evolution by natural selection, led to models of human social evolution that "progressed" from the "savagery" of hunter-gatherers through the "barbarism" of early farmers and herders to the "civilization" of literate urban societies. World prehistory came of age only in the mid-20th century, when growing levels of fieldwork and reliable dating methods made it possible for the first time to review the whole of the human past in its proper chronological and geographical context.

The long-term perspective that archaeology provides makes it possible to identify key features of the human story. These include climatic and environmental changes, demographic increase, and the development of symbolic behavior. Modern humans are a product of the ice ages, but also of the novel strategies and trajectories that have been adopted during the past 11,500 years, including agriculture and urbanization. World prehistory sets all these developments in the context of a human story stretching back over 6 million years, to the appearance in Africa of the first recognizable hominin species.

Further Reading and Suggested Websites

Bahn, P. G. (ed.). 1996. *The Cambridge Illustrated History of Archaeology*. Cambridge: Cambridge University Press. Illustrated introduction to the history of world archaeology, from the first European antiquaries to the theoretical debates and new discoveries of recent decades.

Bell, M. & Walker, M. J. C. 1992. *Late Quaternary Environmental Change*. Harlow: Longman. The standard account of environmental change in the temperate zone during the late glacial and present interglacial period, with special emphasis on the impact of those changes on human societies, and the human contribution to environmental change.

Butzer, K. W. 1982. *Archaeology as Human Ecology: Method and Theory for a Contextual Approach*. Cambridge: Cambridge University Press. Reviews the dynamic interaction between human societies and their environments from the evidence provided by soils and sediments, faunal and botanical remains, and site locations.

Daniel, G. E. & Renfrew, C. 1988. *The Idea of Prehistory*. Edinburgh: Edinburgh University Press. A short and accessible introductory essay, charting the rise of prehistoric archaeology from the 18th century to the New Archaeology.

Lowe, J. J. & Walker, M. J. C. 1997. *Reconstructing Quaternary Environments*. (2nd ed.) London: Longman. Describes the various types of evidence used to reconstruct changes in climate and environment during the Quaternary period, from landforms and sediments to fossil assemblages and isotope ratios.

Renfrew, C. & Scarre, C. (eds.). 1998. *Cognition and Material Culture: The Archaeology of Early Symbolic Storage*. Cambridge: McDonald Institute for Archaeological Research. Collection of studies illustrating the use of material symbols by human communities from the Upper Paleolithic to 20th-century New York.

Roberts, N. 1998. *The Holocene: An Environmental History*. (2nd ed.) Oxford: Blackwell. An excellent short account of the climatic and environmental history of the past 11,500 years, with a focus on the interaction between environmental change and human society.

Schnapp, A. 1996. *The Discovery of the Past*. London: British Museum Press. Describes the rise of European antiquarian interest and the origins of archaeology, with extracts from key early textual sources, up to the early 19th century.

http://www.iath.virginia.edu/vcdh/jamestown/images/white_debry_html/introduction.html/ Website with John White's drawings of native North Americans.

http://www.culture.gouv.fr:80/culture/arcnat/lascaux/en/ Official French government website with images and information, including a "virtual visit," concerning the cave at Lascaux.

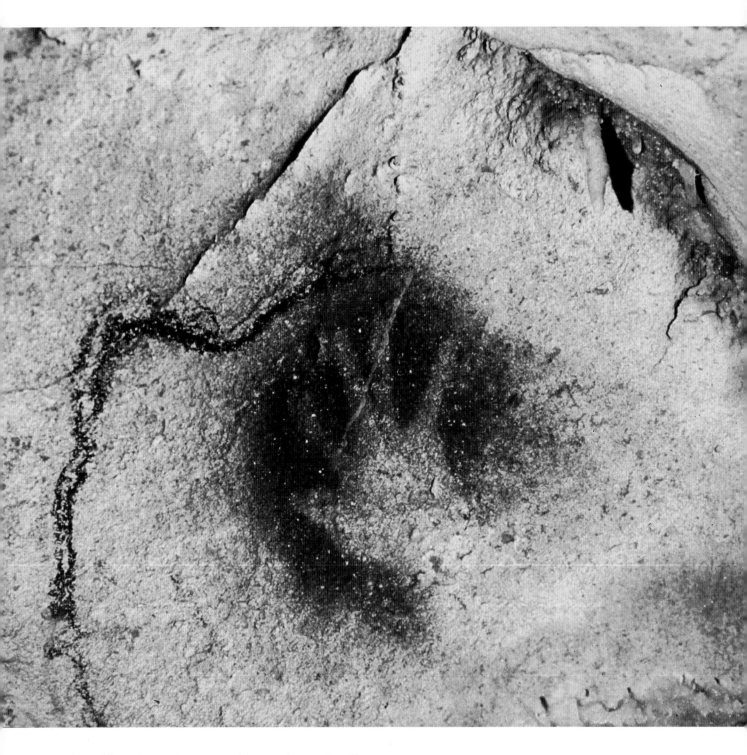

Hand stencil from Chauvet Cave, France; this was perhaps produced by spraying or spitting paint directly from the mouth or through a tube around a hand pressed against the cave wall.

44

PART I
THE EVOLUTION OF HUMANITY

6 million to 11,500 years ago

The human story begins for archaeologists some 2.5 million years ago, when early hominins in eastern Africa began to manufacture stone tools. This set them on a course of evolutionary change which progressively separated them from other branches of the primate family and gave rise to a pattern of behavior in which technology came to have an ever-increasing prominence.

Part I describes the development of hominins and early humans from their first appearance to the end of the last Ice Age some 11,500 years ago. Its three chapters present the evidence – in terms of fossils, tools, and environmental data – that enables us to trace the development of the earliest members of the human family tree and their descendants. The evolution of human anatomy and behavior must be set against the dramatic fluctuations in world climate which saw the successive advance and retreat of the ice sheets in northern latitudes from 700,000 years ago, coupled with major changes in sea-level, rainfall, and vegetation. It was against this stressful and ever-changing background that humans developed the adaptations that enabled them to expand from Africa into southern and eastern Asia, and then to Europe. Control of fire, the invention of clothing, and new skills in hunting and foraging lay behind this success.

By around half a million years ago, humans had reached most parts of the Old World, but they continued to evolve and new species emerged: Neanderthals and modern humans. The final chapter in Part I describes the origins and spread of modern humans (our own species) until, with the demise of the Neanderthals in Europe and *Homo erectus* in Asia, it became the only surviving hominin species. This survival owed much to the enhanced cognitive skills of modern humans, which are reflected in technology and creativity, and in the production of art. Whether modern humans were the first to possess the capacity for language, however, remains controversial. Their achievement culminated in the colonization of new lands, by sea across the Sunda Straits into Australia and by land across the Bering land bridge into North America. Successful in coping even with the extreme climatic conditions experienced at the height of the last Ice Age, modern humans were ably equipped to take advantage of the warmer conditions which set in as that Ice Age drew to a close. The ensuing social and cultural developments will be the subject of Part II of this volume.

CHAPTER 2
AFRICAN ORIGINS

Nicholas Toth and Kathy Schick, Indiana University

Evolution and Human Origins 47
Models of Evolutionary Change 48
The Human Evolutionary Record 49

The Primate Ancestors of Apes and Humans 49
What is a Primate? 49
Overview of Primate Evolution 50
• *Early Anthropoid Features* 51
• *Old World Monkeys and Apes* 51
Our Ape Ancestry: The Comparative Anatomical and Genetic Evidence 51
• *Anatomical Evidence* 52
● **KEY CONTROVERSY** Classifying the Primates 52
• *Genetic Evidence* 53

The Environmental Background 55
● **KEY METHOD** Reconstructing Paleoenvironments 56
Climate Change and Early Hominin Evolution 56

The Rise of the Earliest Hominins 57
The Australopithecines 57
● **KEY DISCOVERY** Discovering the "Ape Men" 59
● **KEY SITES** Hadar and Laetoli: "Lucy," the "First Family," and Fossil Footsteps 60
The Emergence of Homo 61

The First Stone Tools and the Oldowan 61
Technology 66
● **KEY SITE** Olduvai Gorge: The Grand Canyon of Prehistory 67
Who Made the Oldowan Tools? 68

● **KEY CONTROVERSY** Modern Apes as Oldowan Toolmakers? 69
The Nature of the Sites 70
● **KEY SITES** Regional Overview of Major Oldowan Sites 71
● **KEY METHOD** Dating Early Hominins and their Archaeology 74

Food Procurement and Diet 74
Hunters or Scavengers? 74
● **KEY DISCOVERY** What were Oldowan Tools Used For? 76
Food for Thought: Diet and Encephalization 77

The Behavior of Oldowan Hominins 78
Social Organization 78
Diet 78
Technology 78
Fire 79
Site Modification 79
Art, Ritual, and Language 79

Recent Trends in Approaches to the Oldowan 80
Experiments in Site Formation Processes 81
Isotopic Studies 82
Landscape Archaeology 82

Summary and Conclusions 82

Further Reading and Suggested Websites 83

Where does the human story begin? In this chapter we consider the evidence for the earliest members of the human lineage, who lived in Africa between 6 million and 2 million years ago. A proper understanding of these earliest hominins, as they are called, requires both a knowledge of their physical remains (fossil bones and skeletons) and the archaeological study of their behavior based on the evidence of stone tools, animal bones, and traces of early activity.

We begin with some general observations on the history of this quest, and the ideas and methods that have advanced it, and with the background to the emergence of the hominin lineage from within the order of Primates that includes our closest living relatives, the gorillas and chimpanzees. The crucial role played by environmental change in the development, spread, and extinction of different hominin species will also be described, before moving on to the first tool-using members of the hominin lineage in eastern and southern Africa around 2.5 million years ago.

The fragmentary nature of the surviving remains makes understanding the behavior of these first tool-users a daunting task, but a succession of new discoveries and analytical techniques now provides an unrivaled glimpse of the lifeways of early African hominins [see box: Dating Early Hominins and their Archaeology, pp. 74–75]. It was these initial African stages that paved the way for all later human developments, including the colonization of Eurasia and the ability to cope with a broadening range of diverse and often hostile environments.

In the century and a half since Charles Darwin and Alfred Wallace presented their arguments for the origin of new species through the process of evolution by natural selection (see below), prehistorians have conducted fieldwork throughout the world looking for paleontological (fossil-based) and archaeological (artifact-based) evidence of the emergence of the human lineage. For some time it had been believed that the human evolutionary pathway involved a unique combination of traits that evolved more or less contemporaneously, namely **bipedal locomotion** (walking on two feet), the **making of stone tools**, and significant **increase in brain size**.

The past few decades of research have undermined this scenario, however, producing evidence that these traits did not evolve together. Rather, their appearances were drawn out in a sequence over millions of years: bipedal walking preceded the first evidence for stone tools by millions of years, and brain expansion is evident only several hundreds of thousand of years after the beginnings of stone tools.

The fossil evidence indicates that bipedal hominins emerged in Africa from an ape ancestry by 6 million years ago. A number of different hominin species – possibly a dozen – are known to have existed between then and 1.5 million years ago; our own genus, *Homo* (a genus being a group of closely related species), emerged fairly recently, by at least 2 million years ago. Furthermore, the fossil record suggests that at many times during the span of this time more than one hominin species co-existed, indicating evolutionary complexity and possible niche separation during this phase of our evolution, with different lineages focusing on different foods and ecological habitats, rather than a single evolving hominin line. The earliest flaked stone tools are dated to between 2.6 and 2.5 million years ago and, by definition, herald the beginning of the archaeological record.

Evolution and Human Origins

It is now a well-established fact that plant and animal lineages change in form over long periods of time. This phenomenon, known as evolution by natural selection, was first recognized in the mid-19th century by Charles Darwin and Alfred Wallace (1823–1913). Darwin's book, *On the Origin of Species by Means of Natural Selection* (1859), was a watershed of intellectual thought – arguably the most important and influential book in the history of the life sciences. It presented a mechanism to explain how changes could occur in lineages over time (what Darwin called "descent with modification"), and how new species (distinct populations of plants or animals that can and do interbreed and produce fertile offspring) could emerge in the history of life.

All organisms produce more offspring than can be supported by the environment, and these offspring tend to show a range of physical and behavioral traits within a single species. Organisms with inherited traits that enable them to survive and reproduce at a greater rate than other members of their species tend to pass these favorable traits on to their offspring; over time, these traits should become more common in a population, since individuals without them will tend to die before reproductive age or reproduce at a lower rate. Darwin referred to this principle as "survival of the fittest." Those individuals having favorable (fit or adaptive) traits are "naturally selected" to survive and reproduce preferentially, thus providing the mechanism by which a species changes, shows descent with modification, or evolves over time. Evolutionary fitness is often specific to a certain environment or sets of environments; if the environment changes (in terms of temperature, precipitation, vegetation, etc.), new traits may be selected for and new evolutionary changes (or extinction) may occur in the species.

AFRICAN ORIGINS TIMELINE

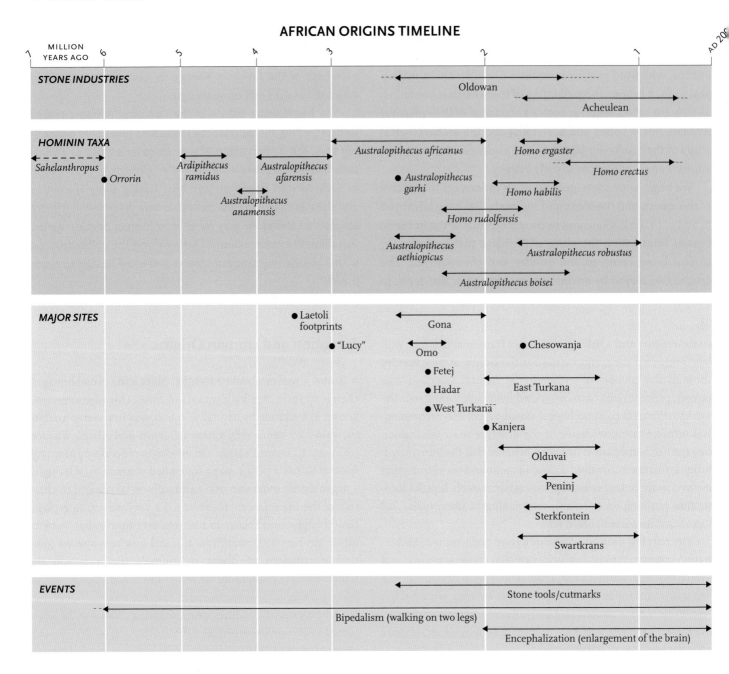

Darwin was not able to explain why such variation existed, or how novel traits ("sports," now called mutations) emerged in populations, but we now understand the genetic basis for inheritance that underlies the evolutionary changes observed in species. Evolution occurs at microscopic or genotypic levels, with changes in genes, chromosomes, or gene frequencies, as well as at macroscopic or phenotypic (visible) levels, with changes in such features as structure, size, or pigmentation.

Models of Evolutionary Change

Various models have emerged to describe the mode and tempo by which evolutionary changes have occurred in species. A model that had been employed by many researchers since Darwin's time is sometimes called **gradualism**, in which the gradual, rather slow and steady accumulation of small changes over a long period of time finally produces major changes in the descendants of a species. A more recent model for species change, at least for some species and at certain times, is called **punctuated equilibrium**, in which periods of more rapid, dramatic evolution over short periods of time are separated by longer periods of little change (or stasis). The latter model could apply to certain periods of dramatic environmental change, during which species underwent more significant natural selection processes, followed by periods of relative environmental stability, during which less profound evolutionary changes occurred.

Although tracing the evolutionary history of any single living species back in time may make it appear that it evolved in a single, unilinear trajectory, this is generally not the case. Natural selection can act on the variation within a single species to produce different evolutionary branches – closely related but distinct species, each of which pursues its own evolutionary direction. At times in the past, profound splitting of species may have even produced "bushes," or complexes of closely related, yet distinct, species. The fossil record suggests that the majority of these branches are ultimately selected against, or become extinct, leaving no descendants to evolve further.

At certain times in the past of various species, we can also see evidence of an **adaptive radiation** among a set of related species, in which members radiate and branch out to occupy and adapt to a range of niches in the environment. Thus, one or a few species can rapidly evolve into many related but diverse species, each occupying a slightly different ecological niche. This has happened within many lineages in the past, so that we talk of an adaptive radiation of reptiles during the Mesozoic, starting before 200 million years ago, a "mammalian radiation" after the end of the Age of Reptiles 65 million years ago, with a "primate radiation" soon afterwards.

The Human Evolutionary Record

The human evolutionary record shows evidence of a number of major splits in the past several million years, sometimes producing multiple lineages of contemporary, related species. Among the living primates, it appears that the human lineage diverged most recently from the African apes, with our last common ancestor living probably between 8 and 6 million years ago. Although the African apes are our closest living relatives today, at many times during the past few million years we had much closer relatives, now known only from their fossil remains. Sometime after our split with the other apes, the ancestral human lineage apparently developed bipedal locomotion (walking on two legs). This bipedal adaptation was not unique just to the lineage that ultimately led to us; there were a number of contemporary "cousin" species and lineages, including the various robust australopithecines. Descendants of only one of these, however, comprising the human species, survives today.

Behavioral patterns, either genetically programmed (i.e., "instinctive") or learned, may also be selected for. It seems certain that in the human lineage two important behavioral traits, the early development of tool use and the likely later development of symbolic communication (language), were highly adaptive and ultimately selected for in the course of human evolution. Any genetic basis to help support and promote these behaviors (larger and more complex brains, changes in hand morphology (form or structure), changes in vocal tracts, etc.) would have been selected for very strongly if they conferred higher survivorship and reproductive success. Technological traditions, represented by stone tools in the early prehistoric record, may thus have helped to set in train or support relatively rapid evolution of aspects of the brain and body involved in the development and maintenance of tool traditions. These tool traditions themselves, however, show very slow changes over time in the early archaeological record, perhaps until a sufficient development of proto-human culture and communication ability would support and promote more rapid diversification and innovation in technologies.

The Primate Ancestors of Apes and Humans

What is a Primate?

Within the mammals (the class Mammalia), humans are classified together with the apes, monkeys, and prosimians within one large order, Primates. There are currently more than 200 living species of primates, and together they share a number of traits and tendencies that reveal their common origin and shared ancestral roots. Primates consist of largely tropical and subtropical species, with 80 percent of species living in the rainforests of Africa, Central and South America, and Asia; some monkeys have also adapted to somewhat more temperate environments in Eurasia (Falk 2000). Humans are the major exception to this distribution pattern, as we have now spread and adapted to all the habitats of the earth.

The great majority of the primates are arboreal (living in trees), or spend a great deal of time in trees, searching for food, evading predators, or sleeping; even those that now spend little time there show an arboreal adaptation at some point in their ancestry, as evidenced by numerous physical characteristics including:

• hands and often feet that are manipulative, dexterous, and able to grasp, usually with opposable thumbs and great toes;
• a trend seen in most primate species is the replacement of claws (inherited from their mammalian ancestors) with nails, at least on most of their digits; some species show a combination of claws on some digits and nails on others, a lasting echo of this evolutionary transition.

Other important trends include:

• reduced emphasis on olfaction (the sense of smell) and increased reliance on eyesight, with stereoscopic and color vision a dominant mode of sensing;
• most primates also exhibit a locomotion that places great emphasis upon the use of the hind limbs (in contrast to that of many other mammals), and the common adoption of an erect trunk while foraging, climbing, and exploring their environment, although the front limbs can also play an important role in climbing, running, and guiding the body through trees and underbrush.

A very interesting development within primates overall is the tendency for the evolutionary development of larger brains in terms of a brain-to-body weight ratio and greater intelligence compared with other mammalian orders. This is on top of a pattern of significant increase in size of mammalian brains over those of animals in other vertebrate classes. This is a trend throughout the lineage, particularly prominent among the apes and carried to an extreme, of course, in modern humans.

These trends emerge gradually within the past 65 million years of primate evolution, with some groups exhibiting them more prominently than others. The two major subgroups (suborders) of primates are sometimes referred to as the "lower primates" and the "higher primates." The lower primates, the *Prosimii*, are observed to be somewhat closer in morphology and function to earlier primate species, and some of them even retain such "primitive" characteristics as an emphasis on an olfactory adaptation, retention of claws on some digits, and less highly developed grasping ability than is seen among the higher primates. Examples of lower primates today include lemurs, lorises, and tarsiers. The higher primates, the *Anthropoidea*, show morphological traits such as heightened enlargement of the brain and development of the visual senses, which emerged later in primate evolution and are considered more altered, or "derived," from earlier, basal primate characteristics [see box: Classifying the Primates, pp. 52–53].

Overview of Primate Evolution

There is now considerable accumulated fossil evidence for the evolution of life on the earth. In dealing with large-scale evolutionary changes it is necessary to refer to time-spans within the geological timescale, with long stretches of geological time divided into eras, eras into periods, and periods into epochs. Covering the past 600 million years or so are, first, the Paleozoic era, during which many forms of life such as fish, amphibians, and reptiles emerged; this was followed by the Mesozoic era around 225 million years ago, when reptiles dominated the land animals; and finally the Cenozoic or current era, starting about 65 million years ago, when mammals became the dominant land animals. Early primate evolution is observed in the fossil record during the early epochs of the Cenozoic period: the Paleocene and the Eocene.

The major evolution and adaptive dispersal of the primates occurred after the mass extinction event that happened 65 million years ago, generally believed to have been caused by a massive meteorite hitting the earth – this brought to an end the Age of Reptiles and at least three quarters of all species alive at that time, including the dinosaurs. During the ensuing Cenozoic era, mammals radiated into the environments vacated by the dinosaurs, evolved into multiple forms and lineages, and adapted to newly available ecological niches. One group to emerge in this mammalian dispersion, the early primates, adapted to arboreal environments and fed on the plants and insect prey

Table 1 *The Geological Time Scale and Major Evolutionary Events*				
Era	Period	Epoch	Million years ago	
	Quaternary	Holocene	0.01	
		Pleistocene	1.75	
	Tertiary	Pliocene	5	First hominins
		Miocene	22	
		Oligocene	35	First ape-like forms
		Eocene	55	
Cenozoic		Paleocene	65	First primates
	Cretaceous		135	
	Jurassic		190	First mammals
Mesozoic	Triassic		225	
	Permian		270	
	Carboniferous		345	
	Devonian		400	
	Silurian		425	
	Ordovician		500	
Paleozoic	Cambrian		600	First vertebrates
	Proterozoic		1000	
	Archeozoic		3000	
Precambrian	Azoic		4600	

available in this setting. Although the earliest members did not closely resemble any particular modern group of primate, dental and skeletal characteristics indicate their evolutionary connection to primates that emerged somewhat later. (For overviews of primate evolution, see Fleagle 1988; Conroy 1990.)

Between 60 and 35 million years ago, primarily during the Eocene epoch (which dates to about 55 million to 35 million years ago), primates emerged that show much more affinity than earlier types to some of the lower primates among modern groups, especially the lemurs and tarsiers. These primates, considered to be an early prosimian radiation, emerged and diversified in the spreading tropical environments of much of the world during a time of distinct global warming. They show many of the primate trends noted above, such as evolution of nails, some development of grasping hands and feet, and improvement of vision at the expense of olfaction.

As North America and Eurasia were still connected during much of this time, these early primates were widespread across the northern continental landmasses, as well as in Africa, where they may have originated. They are absent, however, in South America, since this continent had not yet joined with the North American continent. The rather restricted distribution of prosimians today reflects a distinct decline from this early phase of primate evolution, largely due to the shrinking of subtropical and tropical habitats as worldwide climate became cooler and drier, and to the simultaneous rise of the "higher primates," the anthropoids. The anthropoids came to occupy diurnal (daytime) niches at the expense of the prosimians, which became increasingly nocturnal except on the isolated island of Madagascar.

Although the origins of the anthropoids probably lie within the Eocene epoch, it was during the Oligocene (about 35 million to 22 million years ago) that distinct anthropoids begin to leave prominent traces in the fossil record. Meanwhile, prosimians began to decline in the drier, cooler, less forested environments of later Eocene and Oligocene times, and shifted their geographic distribution, disappearing in Europe and then North America but retaining a presence in southern Asia and Africa.

Early Anthropoid Features The early anthropoids show a number of dental and cranial (skull) features, such as a deeper jaw fused at the midline, which indicate their ties to present-day monkeys (New and Old World) and apes, rather than to the more primitive prosimians. Some of these early anthropoids evolved a distinct trait linking them with Old World monkeys and apes and distinguishing them from New World monkeys: the dental formula of 2.1.2.3 (that is, counting backwards from the front midline of each jaw, two incisors, one canine, two premolars, and three molars). It is only later in the Oligocene that distinct New World monkeys appear in deposits in South America, apparent newcomers on this continent from either Africa (across an expanse of Atlantic Ocean of over 160 km (100 miles) at that time) or, perhaps, from North America. The early Oligocene anthropoids, then, emerge as ancestral to all monkeys, apes, and humans. Although they cannot be linked definitively with any single lineage among the monkeys and apes, some of them, such as *Aegyptopithecus*, which was about the size of a small ape, could be on or close to the ancestral line leading to Old World monkeys and apes (including humans).

Old World Monkeys and Apes Starting about 20 million years ago, during the Miocene, we see fossil evidence in Africa for the emergence of distinct lineages of Old World monkeys and apes. Apes (or hominoids, members of the superfamily *Hominoidea*) were dominant for the first several million years of this anthropoid radiation, dispersing first within the forested environments of Africa, and then into Europe and Asia, and evolving into a multitude of species over this great geographic expanse. Among the many Miocene hominoids, *Proconsul* (an African ape from the earlier Miocene) is a good example of an early basal hominoid, with an apelike skull, enlarged brain, and reduced snout; the later, more evolved apes, *Kenyapithecus* (an African ape of the Middle Miocene) and *Dryopithecus* (a European ape), could be part of a lineage ancestral to the great apes (including humans); in recent years, *Sivapithecus* (an Asian ape) has emerged as a close relative or ancestor of the orangutan.

Ape species began to dwindle during the Miocene as the climate cooled and forests declined, while monkeys, which had been less prevalent, spread and diversified. By the end of the Miocene, about 5 million years ago, ape species were relatively few and more geographically restricted than in early Miocene times, a trend that has continued to the present. It is from this diminished, later Miocene ape stock that early human ancestors were to emerge, branching off from our last shared common ancestor with the other apes (probably the chimpanzees) apparently sometime between 8 and 6 million years ago. Most of the early fossil evidence for emergence of the human lineage and the beginnings of the archaeological record date from the Pliocene, starting around 5 million years ago, and the Pleistocene epoch, or Ice Age, *c.* 1.75 million to 11,600 years ago.

Our Ape Ancestry: The Comparative Anatomical and Genetic Evidence

In considering human origins, this fact that somewhere between 8 and 6 million years ago we shared a common ancestor with other apes is very important. Thus, it is more accurate to describe ourselves as apes and to speak of our divergence from *other* apes, than to characterize our evolutionary pathway as some radical departure from the ape lineage. We shared a common ancestry with other apes for many millions of years, and many aspects of our anatomy, genetic makeup, and behavior are rooted in that shared ancestry. The strong morphological similarities between humans and the great apes, particularly the African great apes (chimpanzees and gorillas), have long been recognized and taken as evidence that they are our closest living relatives. Now knowledge of the tremendous genetic similarity among the living apes corroborates this evidence from comparative anatomy, and further refines our understanding of the order and the timing of the evolutionary divergence of the diverse ape lineages.

Anatomical Evidence   Apes (including humans) are distinguished from their closest living relatives, the Old World monkeys, by a number of shared traits. Some of these are "derived" traits that evolved in our common lineage since our evolutionary divergence from the Old World monkeys. Among them are a broadened nose, a widened palate, the lack of a tail, and an enlarged brain. As a group, apes have, in fact, carried the primate evolutionary trend toward larger brain size and greater intelligence to an extreme. Other morphological features shared by humans and the great apes are a relatively mobile shoulder joint and many aspects of our trunk, which are likely components of an adaptation to hanging from and moving in trees. Human and ape hands, arms, legs, and feet also show many similarities, despite some major differences that have emerged since our common ancestor.

Prominent among these differences is **human bipedal locomotion**, involving numerous transformations in our spine, pelvis, legs, and feet. Later differences that emerged in the evolving human lineage include **smaller teeth**, particularly the reduction in the size of the anterior teeth (canines and incisors), but an increase in body size, and a very significant **expansion in brain size**. Another important human trait that emerged is a finely manipulative hand, with a long and opposable thumb. In addition, body proportions have changed substantially in the evolution of our lineage, with the development of longer legs relative to arms in humans, whereas apes retain relatively long arms and short legs.

KEY CONTROVERSY Classifying the Primates

Classification as currently practiced aims at reflecting evolutionary relationships, so that within any one grouping, members of a subgroup are more closely related evolutionarily to one another than to those of other "sister" subgroups. Thus, with the order Primates, the two major suborders, or subgroups, are *Prosimii* and *Anthroipoidea*, reflecting the fact that the prosimians (lemurs, lorises, and tarsiers) share traits and an evolutionary history that links them more closely to one another than to the other major subgroup, the anthropoids (monkeys, apes, and humans). The anthropoids likewise share a number of characteristics and an evolutionary record that unites them as a group. Further subdivisions are made according to the same principles. A group of animals at any one level of classification (suborder, infraorder, superfamily, family, and so on) can be further classified at each lower level, for instance the prosimians into their respective groupings for lemurs, lorises, etc., and further subgroups within each of these.

Since the 1980s, this classification system – particularly with regard to subdivisions within our superfamily, *Hominoidea* – has become quite dynamic, and the source of a great deal of controversy and debate. This is partially due to enhanced knowledge regarding the actual genetic closeness of ape species and the difficulty of reconciling this with morphological attributes, which may not always precisely mirror the genetic closeness of species or the amount of time since evolutionary divergence. As a result, a plethora of conflicting classification systems is available to the general public and to paleoanthropologists alike. Most differences among these involve ways in which the great genetic similarity between humans and our closest living relatives, particularly the chimpanzees and bonobos, are reflected, and how best to express this relationship and the overall evolutionary relationships among all the apes.

In traditional classifications, humans were isolated in their own family (usually *Hominidae*, or hominids), the great apes into a parallel family (*Pongidae*, or pongids), and the lesser apes (the gibbons and siamangs) into yet another. Many researchers felt that this classification system demanded a major overhaul in order to reflect adequately the great genetic closeness of humans to chimpanzees and bonobos, and the relative recentness of our evolutionary divergence (possibly between 6 and 8 million years ago). Thus, many new classifications have emerged. Most of these lower the hierarchical level of a distinctive human group (e.g. down to the level of subfamily or tribe, rather than the family level). In addition, many of them attempt to show ape affinities more realistically by linking humans with other apes at levels below the superfamily, for instance by putting humans and some apes into the same family, subfamily, or even tribe. The classification shown here is an attempt to reflect more accurately the evolutionary relationships among the different apes and to express these more fully. This schema diverges from ones common in past decades primarily below the level of superfamily, with family, subfamily, and tribe groupings devised to reflect current understanding of evolutionary relationships among apes and humans.

It is important to remember that different classification systems have a significant impact on the terminology used to describe

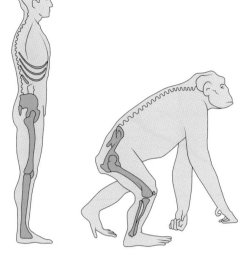

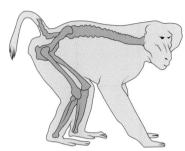

2.1 Anatomical evidence: the spines and lower limbs of bipedal humans (left), knuckle-walking chimpanzees (center), and quadrupedal baboons (right), show significant differences in posture for the different modes of locomotion.

Genetic Evidence The remarkable similarities between humans and apes that have been recognized since the time of Charles Darwin and the biologist T. H. Huxley (1825–1895) have now been corroborated by analysis and quantification of the degree of similarity among their proteins and even their DNA (deoxyribonucleic acid, a molecule that carries instructions from parents to offspring). From the late 1960s onward, scientists began looking at protein differences among primates and other

Order	Suborder	Infraorder	Superfamily	Family	Subfamily	Tribe	Common term
P R I M A T E S	Prosimii						Loris Lemur Tarsier
	Anthropoidea	Platyrrhini					New World monkey
		Catarrhini	Cercopithecoidea				Old World monkey
			Hominoidea	Hylobatidae			Gibbon
				Hominidae	Ponginae		Orang
					Homininae	Gorillini	Gorilla
						Panini	Chimp and Bonobo
						Hominini	Human

Table 2: Primate taxonomy

This table shows one interpretation of the classification of the Order Primates. Note that humans are at one and the same time anthropoids (at the suborder level), catarrhines (infraorder), hominoids (superfamily), homininae (subfamily), and hominini – or "hominins – (tribe).

the human lineage. In most traditional systems, the term "hominid" designates the human lineage since the split with the rest of the apes (equivalent to a human "family"). Among the modified systems of classification, the term "hominid" may refer to humans and the African apes, or, alternatively, to humans and all of the other apes. In the modified system presented here, the term "hominid" includes the African apes, the Asian great apes or orangutans, and humans within one great ape "family." It is only at the tribe level of classification, well below the family level, that the distinctly human group (*Hominini*, hence the term hominins) is distinguished from the African apes (the gorillas being a second tribe, the chimpanzees and bonobos a third). This classification thus reflects current realization that the distinctiveness of humans among the apes is not as great, and our common ancestry is much more recent, than was once thought.

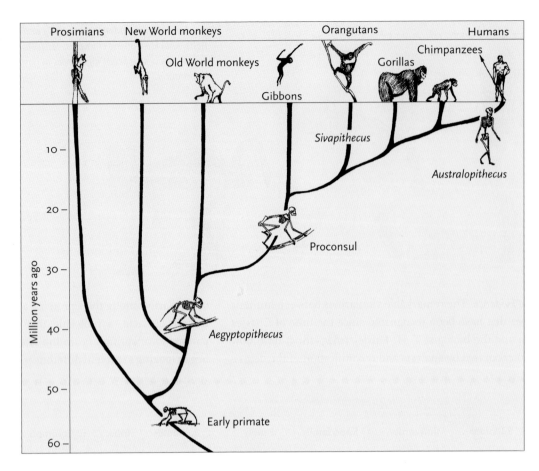

2.2 A simplified evolutionary branching diagram for the primates: *showing the order of branching or divergence for major groups within the primate order (arranged along the top, with a time scale in millions of years to the left). Some of the fossil forms are shown located at points along these branches. Note that the most recent branch in this diagram is between chimpanzees and humans, reflecting our very close evolutionary relationship with chimpanzees as observed in DNA comparisons.*

animals, albeit somewhat indirectly at first, through such techniques as antigen-antibody reactions (testing "immunological distance"). These gave quantifiable results indicating that humans possess a very strong protein similarity with African apes, somewhat lesser similarity with Asian apes, and successively less with Old World monkeys, New World monkeys, and prosimians.

Attempts were made to quantify the rate of genetic change responsible for the immunological distances observed, and thus to estimate times of divergence among species (calibrating immunological distance units with known times of divergence among major groups of animals). This produced a "molecular clock" model that gave an estimated time of divergence between humans and chimpanzees that was unexpectedly recent, only about 5 to 8 million years ago. This was surprising, as decades ago it was believed that this split had taken place much earlier, perhaps 15 to 20 million years ago, and fossils known at that time were mistakenly perceived to be already on a separate, distinctly human line (i.e., those attributed to *Ramapithecus*). Since the 1970s and 1980s, however, further fossil discoveries have largely vindicated the interpretations from the molecular evidence, and have corroborated the conclusion that our last common ancestor with the apes is indeed relatively recent, probably between 6 and 8 million years ago, as already noted.

Since the 1980s, other studies have looked in even closer detail at molecular biological similarities and differences among primates, with remarkably similar results to those obtained in earlier immunological studies. This research has entailed examination of amino acid sequences of specific proteins, the investigation of nucleotide sequences in DNA molecules, and DNA hybridization studies that detect overall similarities and differences between DNA molecules from different species. All these molecular tests indicate an extremely close genetic and protein similarity between humans and apes, in particular the chimpanzee. Most tests indicate that human DNA differs from that of the chimpanzee by only approximately 1.5 percent (see p. 147). On a microscopic scale also, there is remarkable chromosomal similarity between humans and chimpanzees in terms of their number (23 chromosomes in humans, 24 in great apes, with human chromosome number 2 the probable result of fusion of two chromosomes inherited from the human-chimpanzee ancestor), as well as their appearance and banding.

Taken together, the results of these diverse studies converge remarkably on basically the same branching sequence in hominoid evolution, with gibbons branching off first from the rest of the apes, followed by the orangutan and, much later, the gorilla. The chimpanzee-human divergence is now evident as the most recent of all. The genetic distance results conform remarkably well with the classification system suggested here [see box: Classifying the Primates], with humans differing genetically from the chimpanzee by 1.5 percent, the gorilla by about 2 percent, the orangutan by 3 percent, the gibbon by 4 percent, Old World monkeys by 6 percent, New World monkeys by 12 percent, and prosimians by over 20 percent. Thus, closer relatives – those that have branched off from our line more recently – are classified together with us at a lower level of classification than relatives that branched off much earlier from our ancestral line.

The Environmental Background

There is growing evidence that changes in the earth's climate had profound effects on the African landmass, altering temperature and rainfall and, subsequently, flora and fauna. Some of these major changes appear to relate to major changes in human evolution as well. While there is a danger of becoming overly deterministic when trying to correlate environmental changes with evolutionary ones, such correlations that can be documented in the prehistoric record are nonetheless intriguing and warrant further investigation [see box: Reconstructing Paleoenvironments, p. 56].

Global changes in climate greatly influenced the African continent and its environments during the time of the evolution of the African apes and the emergence and evolution of bipedal hominins. In addition, the mountain ranges of the African Rift created by tectonic uplift caused by movements of the earth's plates gave rise to a rain shadow in much of East Africa, gradually leading to drier, more open environments, particularly after the mid-Miocene, around 14 million years ago. This environmental trend continued, apparently also part of a global trend toward cooler and drier conditions, ultimately leading to pronounced cold glacial periods interspersed with numerous warmer interglacial periods.

This pattern of repeatedly oscillating climatic conditions, and the associated changes in plant and animal communities, was the environmental milieu in which our proto-human ancestors evolved and must have had a profound effect on the course of ape evolution and, ultimately, on the human lineage (deMenocal and Bloemendal 1995).

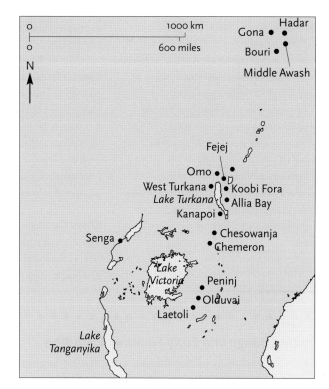

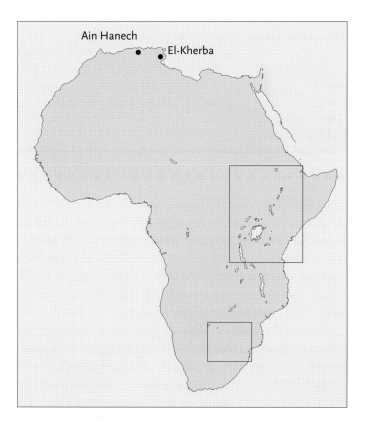

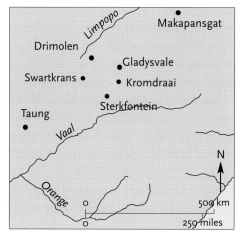

2.3 Map of Africa: *showing major archaeological and fossil site areas in the Eastern Rift Valley (in the inset above right), in South Africa (in the inset on the right), and North Africa.*

KEY METHOD Reconstructing Paleoenvironments

A wide range of types of prehistoric evidence can be employed in attempts to reconstruct paleoenvironments. These include:

Oxygen Isotope Chemistry of Deep-Sea Cores

During warmer periods, as the polar ice and glaciers melt, sea levels rise, producing oceanic waters with a higher percentage of the oxygen isotope ^{16}O. During colder periods, much of the oceanic water is locked up in the form of ice sheets and glaciers, effectively storing massive quantities of the lighter ^{16}O and creating oceans with higher percentages of the heavier isotope ^{18}O. These periods of cooler and warmer global conditions are reflected in changes in the ratio of the oxygen isotopes ^{16}O and ^{18}O found in the shells of microscopic *foraminifera*, or forams, a type of shelled protozoa.

Cores taken from the sea bed contain numerous layers that accumulated continuously over many millennia which can be dated using various methods. Examining the chemistry of forams found within particular layers of these deep-sea cores thus can provide information about glacial and interglacial stages going back tens of millions of years.

Terrestrial Dust in Deep-Sea Cores

Aeolian (wind-borne) dust, associated with wind erosion during arid times, found in deep-sea cores has been measured and shown to have existed in higher concentrations at certain times, notably at 2.8, 1.7, and 1 million years ago.

Carbon Isotopes in Soil Carbonates

The ratio of the carbon isotope ^{12}C to ^{13}C in soil carbonates can be an indication of the ratio of so-called C3 plants (primarily trees, shrubs, and montane (mountain-dwelling) grasses) to C4 plants (primarily heat-loving grasses), and thus provides an important clue to the presence of more closed or more open environments.

Carbon Isotopes in Bones and Teeth

As with soil carbonates, carbon isotopes in herbivorous animals can give an indication of the relative amount of C3 to C4 plant foods in their diets, and thus the probable presence of closed or open environments where they lived (this method is also be used to analyze diet, as discussed below).

Other Geological Evidence

The study of stratigraphy (superimposed layers of cultural or natural deposits) and geomorphology (land formations) can often indicate the environment in which the prehistoric earth deposition took place, such as river floodplain, river channel, colluvial slope (the soil of which has been washed to its base), delta, lake margin, lake, etc. Lavas and tephras (debris ejected by a volcano) can indicate volcanic activity and provide samples for radiometric dating. Certain minerals, notably evaporites and zeolites, may indicate arid, alkaline conditions.

Paleobotanical Evidence

Fossil pollen, seeds, wood, leaves, phytoliths (silica particles that survive from plant cells), and other plant structures can yield important evidence of the types of plant communities that were present in a given prehistoric habitat, and whether the paleoenvironment was more open or closed, or dominated by grassland, woodland, or forest.

Fossil Animal Remains

In most African settings, the majority of faunal remains tend to be mammalian, but they can also include birds, reptiles, amphibians, mollusks, and insects. Based on modern animal analogs, as well as isotopic evidence from tooth and bone, it is often possible to infer associated habitats (open vs. closed, wet vs. dry, warm vs. cold, etc.).

Climate Change and Early Hominin Evolution

Early in the evolution of the African apes, by the beginning of the Miocene (around 22 million years ago), the African continent was quite different from how it is at present. Lush tropical forests and woodlands covered much of the landmass in tropical and subtropical Africa, and the Sahara Desert had not yet developed. As already noted, as the drier, more open habitats started spreading in the mid-Miocene, the abundance of apes that had flourished and diversified in the wetter, more forested conditions dwindled dramatically. On the other hand, monkeys adapted well to the drier conditions; they underwent a major dispersal in these new habitats, and evolved into many species.

At least three major periods of climatic change can be correlated with early stages of hominin evolutionary change:

• *10–5 million years ago* During this time, the earth experienced another major cooling and drying phase, along with the spread of grasslands (and grazing animals) in many areas. Within this period of environmental change the first bipedal hominins emerged, evolving from some last common ancestor of the African apes and humans (presumably quadrupedal – walking on four legs – and predominantly arboreal).

The fossil record in Africa is fairly sparse for this time period, but it appears that by 6 million years ago small-brained, bipedal hominins were present in what are now Chad and Kenya (see Table 3). This was also a time of radiation of a number of other African faunal groups, including the bovids (ox or cow).

• *3–2 million years ago* At this time, during the Pliocene (which begins around 5 million years ago), another general trend toward cooling and drying (with many oscillations) saw the buildup of ice sheets in the Arctic and Antarctic and an overall increase in aridity in Africa. As well as chronicling the less dentally robust, "gracile" australopithecines (*A. afarensis, A. africanus*, and, later, *A. garhi*), this period also documents the emergence of the "robust" australopithecines (*Australopithecus* [or *Paranthropus*] *aethiopicus*), and subsequently *Australopithecus boisei* and *A. robustus*, and early members of the genus *Homo* (*Homo habilis* or its immediate precursor). (See below for a discussion of these species.) It is from this time that we find the earliest recognizable stone tools, and thus the beginning of the archaeological record.

• *Around 1.7 million years ago* During the Pleistocene (or Ice Age, beginning *c.* 1.75 million years ago) there was another major shift to drier, more open habitats, with the C4 grasses]see box Reconstructing Paleoenvironments, p. 56, and p. 82] spreading throughout much of East Africa. This was the approximate time of the appearance of *Homo erectus* (the earlier African forms of which are often, as here, assigned to *Homo ergaster*) and, soon after, the first Acheulean (hand axe and cleaver) industries, discussed in the next chapter. The earliest evidence of hominins outside Africa (for example at Dmanisi in the Republic of Georgia, Mojokerto on Java, and 'Ubeidiya in Israel; see Chapter 3), also occurred at around this time or shortly thereafter.

The Rise of the Earliest Hominins

A rich fossil record documenting the earliest hominins has now been discovered on the African continent, with perhaps a dozen hominin species identified as existing prior to 1.5 million years ago (see Table 3: Early Hominins). The fossil finds were initially concentrated in South Africa, but in more recent years significant discoveries have extended to eastern Africa and even further afield, in central Africa and the Sahara [2.3]. New discoveries have also expanded the known time

2.4 "Lucy": *this partial skeleton, discovered in the 1970s in Hadar, Ethiopia, represents a relatively small-bodied (approximately 1-m/3.3-ft tall) female* Australopithecus afarensis *from about 3.2 million years ago that shows adaptation to bipedal walking.*

depth of the hominin lineage, to perhaps as much as 6 million years. (For overviews of the human paleontological record, see Day 1986; Bilsborough 1992; Campbell and Loy 1996; Johanson and Edgar 1996; Klein 1999; Delson et al. 2000.)

Identification of early hominins that branched off since the last common ancestor of humans and African apes is usually based on one of two criteria: either (1) postcranial (referring to the skeleton below the skull) evidence of bipedality; or (2) derived dental characteristics that are shared with later hominins but not with apes. Prior to 4 million years ago, there is tantalizing evidence of this early stage of proto-human evolution in the discovery of pre-*Australopithecus* ("southern ape man") [see box: Discovering the "Ape Men"] fossils in East Africa and the Sahara.

The Australopithecines

The hominin fossil record becomes much better represented from around 4 million years ago, with the appearance of early australopithecines. A number of australopithecine species then appear over the ensuing 3 million years, with fossils attributed to the genus *Homo* appearing fairly late on the African scene, around 2 million years ago or slightly earlier.

These early hominins, including the earlier forms of *Australopithecus* – *A. anamensis* and *A. afarensis*, such as "Lucy" [**2.4**] – were characterized by being bipedal, with shorter legs and longer arms than modern humans [**2.5**]. They had ape-sized brains, with a cranial capacity of 375–500 cc (cubic centimeters) in the case of *A. afarensis* (the average for modern humans is about 1350 cc and around 450 cc for chimpanzees and gorillas), and skulls with prognathic (projecting) faces and large dentition (incisors and canines) [see box: Hadar and Laetoli, p. 60]. Sexual dimorphism (the difference in size between male and female of a species) was pronounced, with males approximately twice the body size of females (males of *A. afarensis* being perhaps 1.5 m (5 ft) tall and weighing around 45 kg (100 lb), while females were 1 m (3.3 ft) tall and weighed around 30 kg (65 lb)).

Some paleoanthropologists suggest that the proportionately long arms and apelike curved

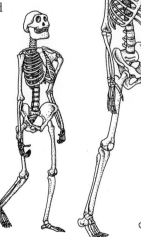

2.5 *(Right)* **Bipedal locomotion:** *comparison of the skeletons and stature of "Lucy" and a modern human, showing bipedal locomotion in each but a substantial difference in body size and limb proportions.*

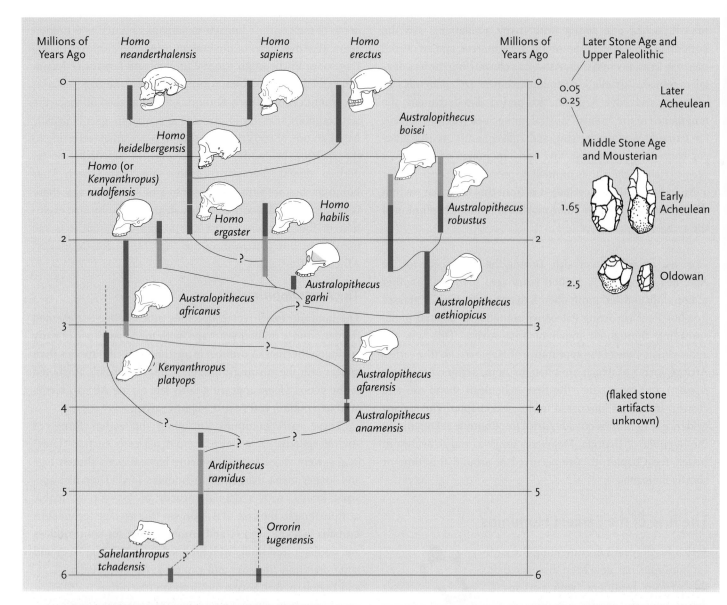

Millions of Years Ago — *Homo neanderthalensis* — *Homo sapiens* — *Homo erectus* — Millions of Years Ago — Later Stone Age and Upper Paleolithic

Homo heidelbergensis

Homo (or Kenyanthropus) rudolfensis

Homo ergaster

Homo habilis

Australopithecus boisei

Australopithecus robustus

Australopithecus garhi

Australopithecus aethiopicus

Australopithecus africanus

Kenyanthropus platyops

Australopithecus afarensis

Australopithecus anamensis

Ardipithecus ramidus

Orrorin tugenensis

Sahelanthropus tchadensis

0.05
0.25

Later Acheulean

Middle Stone Age and Mousterian

1.65 — Early Acheulean

2.5 — Oldowan

(flaked stone artifacts unknown)

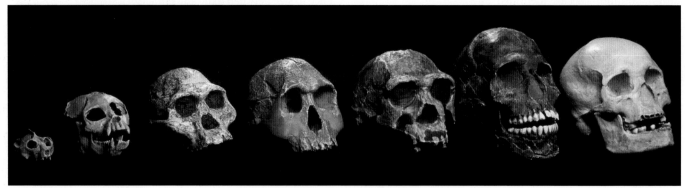

2.6 (Top) **Hominin phylogeny:** *chart showing one interpretation of hominin phylogeny within the past 6 million years. Major fossil species that have been identified are shown with possible evolutionary relationships noted (with more speculative links identified with a "?"). Major stages of the Stone Age are noted on the right.*

2.7 (Above) **Human ancestor skulls:** (left to right) Adapis (*a lemur-like animal that lived around 50 million years ago*); Proconsul (*a primate from 23–15 mya*); Australopithecus africanus (*3–2 mya*); Homo habilis (*1.9–1.6 mya*); Homo erectus (*before 1–0.5 mya*); *a modern human (*Homo sapiens*) from Qafzeh in Israel, which is around 92,000 years old; and a French Cro-Magnon human from around 22,000 years ago.*

phalanges (fingers) indicate that these creatures were still spending a significant amount of time in the trees. Other researchers contest this interpretation, however, seeing in the fossils a profound anatomical commitment to bipedality in such features as a broad and short pelvis, a femur (thigh bone) with a long neck, angled knee joint, and arched foot. There is no definitive evidence for the creation of artifacts during this early stage of human evolution; it is possible that the material culture of these early bipeds was of a type comparable to that associated with modern chimpanzees. Thus bipedality appears in the early hominid record before any expansion of the brain or evidence for tools.

Between 3 and 1.8 million years ago, during the Plio-Pleistocene (that is the period of the late Pliocene and early

---

KEY DISCOVERY Discovering the "Ape Men"

Charles Darwin correctly predicted that the earliest human ancestors would be found in Africa, since this was where the chimpanzee and gorilla lived, which appeared to be our nearest living relatives, based on comparative anatomy. Thus, it made biogeographical sense to look to the African continent for the fossil evidence for our emergence as a species. However, during the late 19th and early 20th centuries, many researchers decided that Asia or Europe was the cradle of humankind, and focused instead on research in these areas.

In the 1890s, the Dutch explorer Eugène Dubois (1858–1941) discovered the first remains of *Homo erectus* at Trinil, in Java (see p. 97). In the 1910s the notorious "discovery" in England of Piltdown Man (now known to be a forgery incorporating a doctored human braincase – the part of the skull enclosing the brain – and an orangutan jaw) was heralded as the "missing link" by many scientists.

The Discovery of *Australopithecus*

Enter Raymond Dart (1893–1988): an Australian anatomist, he became Professor of Anatomy at the University of Witwatersrand in South Africa, and encouraged people to bring him fossil specimens found in cave deposits during limestone mining operations in the region. In 1924 he was presented with a chunk of breccia (cemented cave sediment) from a quarry near Taung that appeared to have a small, apelike skull enclosed within. During the following year, Dart painstakingly cleaned the fossil, extricating it from the encasing limestone with his wife's knitting needles and other tools. What emerged was a juvenile skull that appeared to him to be a candidate for a human ancestor.

It was small-brained, but with teeth more human than ape and with a foramen magnum (the hole in the base of the skull through which the spinal cord connects with the brain) placed more forward and under the skull than among apes but similar to the human position and suggesting upright posture. Dart (1925) dubbed this discovery *Australopithecus* ("southern ape man") *africanus*, and suggested that this was the direct ancestor of the human lineage. This was the first of a number of fossil hominin species that represent a stage of human evolution characterized by upright walking, a small brain, and relatively large dentition, especially cheek teeth.

More Fossils, More Proto-Humans

Many in the scientific world, though, viewed this curious fossil as an ape, and met Dart's interpretation with great skepticism. In the next several decades, however, especially during the 1940s and 1950s, more fossils were found in the South African caves of Sterkfontein, Kromdraii, and Swartkrans, producing much more fossil evidence, including many adult individuals, to support Dart's claims that these African fossil forms were bipedal proto-humans.

As more fossils were retrieved from the South African cave deposits, it became clear that more than one form of proto-human was present: the earlier, smaller-toothed, smaller-

jawed form (*Australopithecus africanus*), and a later, larger-toothed, larger-jawed form that came to be called *Australopithecus* (or, alternatively, *Paranthropus*) *robustus*.

Today we know that the earliest hominins do come from Africa, as Dart had first realized, but we also know that they were present in many areas of the continent, with a great number of finds from many sites in South and East Africa, and fossil remains recovered more recently in northern Africa (Chad). Some of these are, in fact, predecessors of *Austalopithecus africanus*. There are possibly seven species of pre-*Homo* hominins presently known from various parts of Africa, and these numbers may eventually grow.

2.8 *Raymond Arthur Dart (aged 84) and the Taung specimen of* Australopithecus africanus, *discovered in South Africa in 1924. Dart was the first to recognize that the skull represented an early stage of human evolution. The specimen comprises part of a juvenile skull and mandible, with a cranial endocast.*

KEY SITES Hadar and Laetoli: "Lucy," the "First Family," and Fossil Footsteps

Between 4 and 3 million years ago, East Africa saw the emergence of an australopithecine that predated *Australopithecus africanus*. This species, named *Australopithecus afarensis* (after the Afar region of Ethiopia), is well represented from several sites, notably Hadar in the Ethiopian Rift Valley and Laetoli, about 50 km (30 miles) south of the main gorge at Olduvai in Tanzania.

Beginning in the 1970s, the Hadar project, originally led by Maurice Taieb, Donald Johanson, and Yves Coppens, has produced a rich assemblage of hominin fossil discoveries from many localities dating to this time period (Johanson and Edey 1981). These finds include a knee joint of a single individual at one locality; at another a partial skeleton of a 1-m (3.3-ft) tall female dubbed "Lucy" [see 2.4]; the spectacular find of the remains of at least 13 adult and juvenile individuals (the "First Family") at yet another locality; and, at one more, a nearly complete male skull.

The celebrated Lucy skeleton is approximately 60 percent complete, with body parts that include cranial fragments, a mandible with teeth, vertebrae, ribs, partial

2.9 *Donald Johanson and colleagues examine fossil remains of* Australopithecus afarensis *from Hadar, Ethiopia.*

scapula (shoulder blade), humeri, radii, and ulnae (arm bones), a pelvis, femur, tibia, and fibula (leg bones), and some foot and hand bones. This find, as well as that of the knee joint, were critical in pushing back the antiquity of bipedality.

The wealth of fossil specimens of *A. afarensis*, and the great diversity within the First Family collection of fossils, has also given anthropologists a much better appreciation of the range of variability and sexual dimorphism of this species.

Footsteps in Time

The Laetoli area, first explored in the 1930s, and investigated by a team led by Mary Leakey in the 1970s, has yielded a number of *A. afarensis* fossils, including the holotype (type specimen) mandible of the species. These date to between 3.7 and 3.5 million years ago.

2.10 *Excavation of the Laetoli footprints in northern Tanzania. These footprints, believed to be the product of three hominins (the larger tracks are the result of superimposition of the prints of two individuals) are dated to 3.5 million years ago.*

An amazing discovery was made here in the 1970s consisting of a layer of volcanic ash, or tuff, that preserved a set of animal footprints, including those of mammals, birds, and insects (Leakey and Harris 1987). The distinctive carbonatite chemistry of the tuff (highly alkaline; essentially a volcanic limestone) meant that, after a brief wetting with rain, it solidified into a concrete-like consistency that preserved the tracks of the animals that had walked across its surface.

The footprints chronicle the tracks of animals from insect to elephant size, including the famous set of footprints of three bipedal hominins that were all walking in the same direction. These hominin footprints have become an icon of paleoanthropological research, and remain one of the most remarkable and unexpected finds of recent decades. The Laetoli fauna, with grazing animals well represented, and the footprints showing linear and uninterrupted animal tracks, suggest fairly open grasslands, possibly with gallery forest along stream channels.

2.11 *Robust and gracile Australopithecines:* *the skulls of* Australopithecus robustus *(left) and* Australopithecus africanus *(right) from the South African Transvaal caves of Swartkrans and Sterkfontein, respectively.*

Pleistocene, around 3 million to 1 million years ago), two new trajectories in hominin evolution occurred alongside the continuation of the "gracile" forms of *Australopithecus* – *Australopithecus africanus* in South Africa and *A. garhi* in East Africa.

The first involved the appearance of the so-called "robust" australopithecines – *A. aethiopicus* and *A. boisei* in East Africa, and *A. robustus* in South Africa – sometimes referred to as *Paranthropus*. These exhibit a modest brain expansion – with a cranial capacity ranging from 400 to 550 cc – and the development of massive jaws and cheek teeth for grinding food. A saggital crest – a ridge of bone running across the top of the skull – for the attachment of powerful muscles for chewing, is found in adult males [**2.11**].

This trend is well established by at least 2.5 million years ago, when the first stone tools are found, establishing the earliest known archaeological record. The robust australopithecines were extinct by around 1 million years ago.

The Emergence of Homo

The second major development at this time is the emergence of early forms of the genus *Homo* between 2 and 1.8–1.7 million years ago, probably evolving from one of the non-robust australopithecines, perhaps *A. garhi* (see below). These early forms were *Homo rudolfensis*, *H. habilis*, and *H. ergaster* (the last, considered by some to be an early form of *Homo erectus*, is discussed more fully in the next chapter). Larger brains – the cranial capacity of *Homo habilis* ranges between 510 and 687 cc – and, usually, smaller jaws and teeth characterize these early *Homo* forms and define the species, although *H. rudolfensis* still retains large, australopithecine-like premolars and molars. The overall architecture of the skulls of some of these larger-brained forms seems to foreshadow many modern human cranial features. **Table 3** lists the species that are provisionally recognized in paleoanthropology and summarizes their major occurrences and features.

To recapitulate: the earliest bipedal hominins appear to emerge in the fossil record by 6 million years ago. During the Plio-Pleistocene, a major bifurcation in the hominin lineage led to the robust australopithecines as one evolutionary branch, or clade, and to the genus *Homo* as the other. In addition to bipedality, other hominin traits that emerged included longer legs, shorter arms, more dexterous hands with a longer thumb, reduced canines and incisors (and in early *Homo*, reduced molars and premolars), and brain expansion, again especially in early *Homo*. In the *Homo* lineage, body size tends to increase and sexual dimorphism appears to decrease through time.

The First Stone Tools and the Oldowan

The first recognizable objects modified by hominins – another significant step forward in the human story – are found approximately 2.5 million years ago in the form of flaked and battered **stone artifacts** from the Middle Awash Valley in Ethiopia. Most anthropologists assume that prior to this hominins may have produced and employed simple technologies that would leave little visibility in ancient deposits, either being made of perishable organic material, or being so little modified as to be unrecognizable as an artifact. The uses of material culture by wild chimpanzees in East and West Africa (e.g. trimmed grass stems and twigs to obtain termites and ants, stone and wood hammers and anvils to crack hard-shelled nuts, chewed leaf wads to dip for water or for cleaning) give some possible clues into such rudimentary technologies (Goodall 1986; McGrew 1992).

The earliest archaeological sites found have been assigned to the **Oldowan industry**, a term coined by Louis Leakey (1903–1972) and Mary Leakey (1913–1996), based on their work at **Olduvai Gorge** in Tanzania [see box: Olduvai Gorge, p. 67]. (For reviews of the Oldowan, see Leakey 1971; Toth 1985; Toth and Schick 1986; Isaac 1989; Harris and Capaldo 1993; Schick and Toth 1993, 2001; Klein 1999.) The Oldowan is characterized by simple core forms (the parent piece of rock from which flakes are detached), created from river-worn cobbles or angular blocks of stone; the sharp-edged, angular flakes and fragments detached from such cores (debitage); often battered hammerstones; and occasional retouched pieces (usually flakes, the edges of which were further modified by striking off tiny chips to reshape or sharpen the edge) [**2.12**, **2.13**].

Mary Leakey grouped cores and some battered stones into the category "heavy-duty tools," and most of the retouched forms into "light-duty tools." Her typology (Leakey 1971), which is usually used or adapted in some form by most researchers, is shown in **Table 4**.

At Olduvai Gorge, Mary Leakey distinguished between the chopper-dominated Oldowan industry and the Developed Oldowan industry, characterized by more retouched elements such as scrapers and awls, higher percentages of [–> p. 66]

Table 3 *Early Hominins*

Species	Time range (million years ago)	Key sites	Key fossils
Sahelanthropus tchadensis	7–6	Toros-Menalla, Chad	TM 266-01-060-1 (cranium), TM 266-02-154-1 (mandible fragment)
Orrorin tugenensis	Approximately 6	Lukeino Formation, Baringo Basin, Kenya	BAR 1215'00, BAR 1003'00, BAR 1002'00 (proximal femurs); BAR 1000a'00, BAR 1000b'00 (mandibular fragments); BAR 1004'00 (distal humerus)
Ardipithecus ramidus	5–4.4	Middle Awash (Western Margin and Aramis), Ethiopia; Gona, Ethiopia	Aramis, Middle Awash: ARA-VP-1-29 (mandible fragment); Aramis (partial skeleton); Western Margin, Middle Awash: ALA-VP-2/10 (partial mandible), ASK-VP-3/78 (distal humerus), ALA-VP-2/101 (humerus shaft and proximal ulna)
Australopithecus anamensis	4.2–3.9	Kanapoi and Allia Bay, Kenya	Kanapoi: KNM-KP 29281 (mandible), KNM-KP 29283 (maxilla), KNM-KP 29285 (tibia)
Australopithecus afarensis	4–3	Hadar, Ethiopia; Laetoli, Tanzania	Hadar: AL 444 (adult cranium), AL 288 ("Lucy" skeleton), AL 333 ("First Family"), AL 129-1A and -1B (knee joint)
Australopithecus garhi	2.5	Hata Member of the Bouri Formation, Middle Awash, Ethiopia; possibly isolated teeth from Members D and E from the Omo Valley, Ethiopia	Bouri, Middle Awash: BOU-VP-12/130 (cranial remains with dentition)
Australopithecus africanus	3–2	Taung, Sterkfontein, Makapansgat, and possibly Gladysvale in South Africa	Taung: Taung "child" (juvenile cranium and mandible); Sterkfontein: STS 5 (cranium), STW 505 (cranium), STS 71 (cranium and mandible), STS 36 (mandible), STS 52 (partial cranium and mandible), STS 14 (partial skeleton); Makapansgat: MLD 37/38 (cranium)

Cranial capacity	Morphology	Associated archaeology and other notes
Estimated to be 320–380 cc (one specimen)	Small, ape-sized cranium, large browridges, small canines, intermediate-thickness tooth enamel, anterior position of foramen magnum, low degree of facial prognathism; no postcrania to date	None
Unknown	Thick-enameled, relatively small teeth; postcrania consistent with bipedality	None
Unknown	Large canines, relatively thin tooth enamel; the partial skeleton has not yet been described	None
Unknown	Bipedal adaptation, thick enamel, large molars, great sexual dimorphism	None
375–500 cc	Bipedal adaptation, prognathic face, large browridges, sagittal cresting in males, ape-sized brain, primitive dentition, U-shaped dental arcade, large canines and incisors, thick-enameled and fairly large molars, curved phalanges, short and broad pelvis, relatively ape-like limb proportions (long arms relative to legs), females perhaps 1 m (3.3 ft) tall and around 30 kg (65 lb), males perhaps 1.5 m (5 ft) tall and around 45 kg (100 lb), high degree of sexual dimorphism	Some human paleontologists have suggested that other hominin species were contemporaneous with *A. afarensis*, including a fragment of mandible from Chad named *A. bahrelghazali*, and the highly fragmented and distorted cranium from Kenya dubbed *Kenyanthropus platyops*. Agreement on whether these specimens actually fall outside the range of *A. afarensis* will require larger samples from these localities.
c. 450 cc	Prognathic face, large anterior and cheek teeth, thick enamel, long arms and legs	Cut-marked bones at Bouri, Middle Awash, Ethiopia; no stone tools yet found *in situ* at Bouri, but these are found at Gona, Ethiopia (*c.* 80 km or 50 miles to the north) in roughly contemporary sediments
400–500 cc	Prognathic face, no sagittal cresting, parabolic dental arcade, relatively small canines but large incisors, relatively large premolars and molars, longer legs and shorter arms compared to modern humans, short and broad pelvis, females 1.2 m (3.8 ft) tall and 30 kg (65 lb), males 1.4 m (4.5 ft) tall and 40 kg (90 lb)	None in the South African breccia deposits, but *A. africanus* is contemporaneous with early Oldowan sites in East Africa

Table 3 *Early Hominins*

Species	Time range (million years ago)	Key sites	Key fossils
Australopithecus (Paranthropus) aethiopicus	2.8–2.2	West Turkana, Kenya (Lokalalei Member of the Nachukui Formation); Omo, Ethiopia (Shungura Formation Members C through G)	West Turkana: KNM-WT 17000 (cranium); Omo: Omo 18-1967-18 (partial mandible)
Australopithecus (Paranthropus) boisei	2.3–1.4	Olduvai Gorge and Peninj, Tanzania; East Turkana, West Turkana, and Chesowanja, Kenya; Omo and Konso Gardula, Ethiopia; Malema, Malawi	Olduvai: OH 5 (cranium); East Turkana: KNM-ER 406 (male cranium), KNM-ER 732 (female cranium); Peninj: mandible; Konso Gardula: partial cranium and mandible; Malema: RC 911
Australopithecus (Paranthropus) robustus	1.8 to perhaps 1	Swartkrans, Kromdraai, and Drimolen in South Africa; possibly also Sterkfontein Member 5	Kromdraai: TM 1517 (cranium and mandible); Swartkrans: SK 48, SK 46, and SK 79 (crania), SK 876, SK 23, SK 6, and SK 12 (mandibles)
Homo sp. indet. (possible early *Homo*, indeterminate species)	2.4–2.3	Baringo (Chemeron Formation), Kenya; Hadar, Ethiopia	Baringo: temporal fragment; Hadar: AL-666-1 (maxilla)
Homo habilis	1.9–1.6	Olduvai Gorge, Tanzania; East Turkana, Kenya; Sterkfontein, South Africa	Olduvai: OH 7 (partial cranium and mandible), OH 24 (cranium), OH 13 (partial cranium, maxilla, mandible), OH 8 (foot), OH 62 (partial skeleton); East Turkana: KNM-ER 1813 and KNM-ER 1805 (crania); Sterkfontein STW-53 (cranium)
Homo rudolfensis	2.3(?)–1.8	East Turkana, Kenya; Uraha (Chiwondo), Malawi	East Turkana: KNM-ER 1470, KNM-ER 1590, KNM-ER 3732 (crania), and KNM-ER 1802 (mandible); Uraha: UR 501 (mandible)

Cranial capacity	Morphology	Associated archaeology and other notes
410 cc (one specimen)	Small-brained, sagittal cresting in males, prognathic and broad face, large cheek teeth, very thick molar enamel	Contemporaneous with Oldowan sites in Shungura Members F and G of the Omo Valley (c. 2.3 million years ago) and early sites at Gona, Ethiopia
500–550 cc	Small incisors and canines, massive molars and premolars, molars with thick enamel, parabolic dental arcade, sagittal crest in males, broad and dished face, short and broad pelvis, sexually dimorphic with females approximately 1.2 m (4 ft) tall and 36 kg (80 lb), males 1.4 m (4.6 ft) tall and 45 to 80 kg (100 to 175 lb)	Contemporary with Oldowan and early Acheulean industries. Along with *Homo habilis*, in direct association with Oldowan artifacts at FLK Zinj site, Olduvai Gorge
50–550 cc	Wide, flat and dished face; sagittal crest in males; parabolic dental arcade; small incisors and canines; large molars and premolars; short, broad pelvis; female approximately 1 m (3.5 ft) tall and around 32 kg (70 lb), males 1.3 m (4.3 ft) tall and around 40 kg (90 lb)	Found within cave deposits in association with Oldowan stone artifacts at Swartkrans and Sterkfontein. At Swartkrans, these fossil hominins are also associated with polished bone fragments interpreted by some to be digging tools.
Unknown	Fragmentary remains suggest reduced premolars and molars relative to australopithecines	Oldowan artifacts from Hadar 666 locality
687 cc	Brain somewhat larger than australopithecines, moderately prognathic face and moderate browridge, no sagittal cresting, reduced dentition relative to australopithecines, proportionately long arms and short legs relative to modern humans, females perhaps 1 m (3.3 ft) tall and 30 kg (70 lb), males perhaps 1.2 m (4 ft) tall and 36 kg (80 lb)	Contemporary with Oldowan and Developed Oldowan industries at Olduvai Gorge, East Turkana, and Sterkfontein
750 cc	Brain significantly larger than australopithecines, large maxilla, large premolars and molars, flat face, browridge absent, no sagittal cresting, approximately 1.5 m (5 ft) tall, females 50 kg (110 lb), males 60 kg (130 lb)	At East Turkana, contemporary with Oldowan industries c. 1.8 million years ago

Table 4 *Major Types of Oldowan Artifacts*
1 *Heavy-duty tools (greater than 5 cm (2 in) maximum dimension)*
a Choppers: cores with a flaked edge around part of their circumference
b Discoids: cores with a flaked edge around most or all of their circumference
c Polyhedrons: heavily reduced cores with three or more edges
d Heavy-duty scrapers: thick cores with one flat surface and steep angles
e Spheroids and subspheroids: spherical stones, often flaked and heavily battered
f Proto-bifaces: artifacts intermediate between a chopper and a hand axe (also called a "biface," a flat cobble flaked over both surfaces to produce a sharp edge around the entire periphery; see Chapter 3)
2 *Light-duty tools (less than 5 cm (2 in) maximum dimension)*
a Scrapers: flakes that have been retouched along the side or end
b Awls: flakes that have been retouched into a pointed form
c Outils écaillés ("scaled tools"): thin cores or retouched pieces with flakes detached from opposite ends; some of these forms may be bipolar cores, flaked between a hammerstone and an anvil
d Laterally trimmed flakes: flakes with more casual, uneven retouch
e Burins: rare forms with a flake detached along the edge
3 *Utilized artifacts*
a Anvils: stones that show pitting in their center, suggesting use as anvils in the making of stone tools
b Hammerstones: cobbles or chunks of stone that show battering on particular surfaces, suggesting their use as hammers in the making of stone tools
c Utilized cobbles, nodules and blocks: pieces that show some chipping or blunting of edges
d Heavy-duty and light-duty flakes: flakes showing some chipping or blunting on edges
4 *Debitage:* unmodified whole flakes and fragments
5 *Manuports:* unmodified stones out of their geological context, which were presumably transported to sites by hominins

2.12 *(Right)* **Oldowan artifacts:** *a range of forms from East Turkana (Koobi Fora), Kenya.*

spheroids and subspheroids, and, at some sites, small numbers of poorly made bifaces, or hand axes. Most archaeologists now group the Oldowan and Developed Oldowan into the "Oldowan industrial complex" (Isaac 1976), but after *c.* 1.5 million years ago these sites are known to be contemporaneous with Acheulean hand axe and cleaver industries, so that some authorities regard them as a variant of the Early Acheulean. In this chapter, the term "Oldowan" refers to the Oldowan industrial complex unless otherwise noted.

Technology

Experimentation has shown that many of the artifacts that characterize the Oldowan industry can be explained by least-effort flaking strategies, reducing stone to produce flakes with sharp cutting edges and cores that could be used for chopping or hacking. Much of the variation seen in the Oldowan can probably be explained by differences in the nature of the raw materials available at different sites (the size, shape, and flaking quality of stones used for tools), as well as the amount of reduction (i.e., how heavily the cores had been flaked). Retouched flakes, however, suggest intentional modification to resharpen or shape the edges.

Some prehistorians have attempted to infer relatively sophisticated cognitive and technological abilities for Oldowan hominins, arguing for complex reduction strategies, platform preparation of cores (carefully shaping edges of cores for

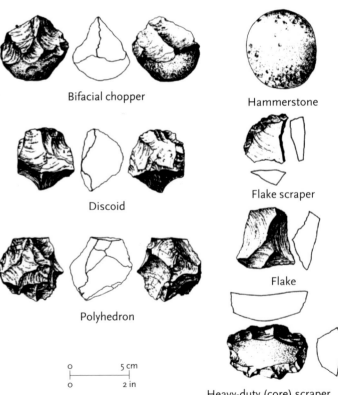

Bifacial chopper

Hammerstone

Discoid

Flake scraper

Polyhedron

Flake

Heavy-duty (core) scraper

KEY SITE Olduvai Gorge: The Grand Canyon of Prehistory

Olduvai Gorge, a 100-m (330-ft) deep, 50-km (31-mile) long gash in the Serengeti plain of northern Tanzania, is one of the most famous prehistoric sites in the world, and the closest we have to a time machine to take us back over the past 2 million years to document the biological and technological evolution of the human lineage in its environmental setting. One can literally walk through deep prehistory here, with layer upon layer of ancient sediments documenting an unparalleled sequence of ancient environments, animal communities, stone technologies, and prehistoric hominins during earlier (and later) periods of the Stone Age.

This impressive gorge was first described by the entomologist Wilhelm Kattwinkel, who was chasing butterflies across the Serengeti in 1911 when, in pursuit of an especially interesting specimen, he nearly fell into it. The German prehistorian Hans Reck led expeditions here beginning in 1913, and from their many years of fieldwork at Olduvai (the type site of the Oldowan industry), Louis and Mary Leakey gained an international reputation and a level of celebrity.

The Leakeys were able to establish a prehistoric sequence with chronological control that began about 1.85 million years ago in the lowest level, Bed I, with Oldowan sites and hominin fossils that included the type specimens of *Homo habilis* and *Australopithecus boisei* (originally called *Zinjanthropus*) (Leakey 1971; 1975).

Discoveries

The *Zinjanthropus* site (FLK Zinj) is one of the richest Oldowan sites ever excavated, containing well over 2000 stone artifacts and over 3500 fossil animal bone specimens, with over 1000 of the bones identifiable to taxon (unit of zoological classification, such as species, genus, or family) or body part; more than 90 percent of these belong to larger mammals. Bed II begins about 1.7 million years ago and contains Oldowan sites, some of which have relatively high proportions of retouched pieces and spheroids – what Mary Leakey called Developed Oldowan, with the

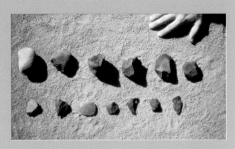

2.13 *Replicas of Oldowan artifacts: clockwise from upper left, hammerstone, unifacial chopper, bifacial chopper, polyhedron, heavy-duty scraper, discoid, 6 flakes, light-duty scraper.*

2.14 *Replicas of Acheulean artifacts: clockwise from upper left: ovate handaxe, pointed handaxe, cleaver, pick, three flakes, light-duty scraper, spheroid.*

2.15 *(Below) The FLK Zinj site at Olduvai Gorge, dated to approximately 1.8 million years ago.*

implication that this was a refinement of the Bed I Oldowan technologies.

By about 1.4 million years ago, the first early Acheulean industries appear in the sequence here, characterized by hand axes, picks, and cleavers. Bed II has also yielded fossils of *Homo ergaster/erectus* (Chapter 3). Beds III and IV, and the overlying Masek Beds, have yielded a number of Acheulean and Developed Oldowan sites, and the topmost beds, Ndutu and Naisiusu, contain Middle Stone Age and Later Stone Age sites.

Olduvai's Place in History

Olduvai Gorge holds a special place in the history of paleoanthropology because it established a long sequence of biological and cultural evolution in East Africa; it also set a number of standards for the varieties of evidence that could be gathered and the range of multidisciplinary investigations that could be fruitfully focused on such a rich paleoanthropological record.

A range of investigations have been focused on Olduvai Gorge's geology and paleoenvironmental setting, geochronological dating (using potassium-argon, fission track, paleomagnetism, tuff correlation, and biostratigraphic methods – see box: Dating Early Hominins and their Archaeology, pp. 74–75), its archaeological record of technological change, landscape archaeology, paleontological record, and its hominin fossils.

It is also a major tourist attraction for the Tanzanian government, in fact a UNESCO World Heritage Site, with a field museum and tours to many of the famous prehistoric sites in the Gorge. As such, it represents not only one of the foremost sites for primary research into human origins, but also an important destination for public archaeology and education in human prehistory.

further flake removal), and the removal of predetermined flake shapes in their manufacture of stone artifacts. These arguments, however, are not convincing. Clearly, Oldowan hominins were very good at striking off usable flakes from cores, but experimentation indicates that these technological patterns can emerge incidentally and simply through heavier reduction of cores without elaborate planning or sophisticated reduction strategies in the manufacturing process.

At some sites, notably Swartkrans and Sterkfontein in South Africa, polished and striated bone and horn core fragments associated with Oldowan artifacts have been interpreted as digging implements (Brain 1981). Clearly, much of the material culture of early hominins would have been made from organic, perishable materials such as wood, bark, and horn, or would have made use of unmodified materials that would leave little if any visible traces in the archaeological record to identify them as tools.

Who Made the Oldowan Tools?

The Oldowan industry is known from about 2.5 million years ago onwards; beginning around 1.5 million years ago, this simple stone technology begins to be augmented by larger tools, notably hand axes, cleavers, and picks. Between 2.5 and 1.5 million years, a number of hominin species (perhaps eight) are found in Africa, including the "robust" large, cheek-toothed australopithecines, as well as more "gracile" forms, and *Homo habilis*, *H. rudolfensis*, and *H. ergaster/erectus*. Which of these made these early stone tools?

Experiments with modern apes suggest that they have the cognitive and biomechanical capacity to flake stone and use stone tools [see box: Modern Apes as Oldowan Toolmakers?], and it is likely that early bipedal hominins had at least the same

ability. It is possible that all of these prehistoric species used technology to different degrees, some (or perhaps all) with flaked stone technologies [**Table 5**].

The fossil hominin record in this region for this crucial period between 2.5 and 2 million years ago is quite sparse, and the majority of crania, jaws, and isolated teeth that have been found have been assigned to the robust australopithecines, namely the earlier, possibly ancestral, species *Australopithecus* (*Paranthropus*) *aethiopicus*, and the later, possibly descendant, one, *Australopithecus* (*Paranthropus*) *boisei*. These two species share many features, most notably a relatively small brain, a pronounced sagittal crest (bony ridge) running along the top midline of the cranium, and massive jaws and large teeth for chewing (especially the molars and premolars). The smaller-toothed, more "gracile" species named *Australopithecus africanus* is known from three cave sites in South Africa dated to between 3 and 2.2 million years ago, but there are no stone artifacts associated with the hominin fossils in these deposits.

Since the late 1960s there had also been some evidence, notably in the form of isolated teeth from such localities as the Shungura Formation in the Omo Valley, Ethiopia, of a smaller-toothed form living contemporaneously with the robust australopithecines in the region. Unfortunately, no fairly complete cranium with a braincase, face, and dentition was known for this more gracile form. This all changed in the autumn of 1997, when the Middle Awash Research team, under the direction of Berhane Asfaw of Ethiopia and Tim White and J. Desmond Clark of the University of California at Berkeley, made a major new discovery in the Afar Rift of Ethiopia (Asfaw et al. 1999).

In the course of field survey in the 2.5 million-year-old Hata Beds, Berkeley graduate student Johannes Haile Selassie dis-

2.16, 2.17 *Oldowan toolmaking: examples of Oldowan artifacts and a diagram to show the method of manufacture of an Oldowan bifacial chopper using a hammerstone.*

KEY CONTROVERSY Modern Apes as Oldowan Toolmakers?

In the past half-century of detailed studies of ape behavior and adaptation in the wild, a range of toolmaking and tool-using behaviors has been documented, but there has not been a single observation of chimpanzees, bonobos, gorillas, or orangutans intentionally flaking stones to produce sharp cutting or chopping implements. Oldowan tools exhibit a level of technology not seen in modern apes in their natural setting. This may be due to a lack of any need for sharp-edged tools in their food-procurement and food-processing strategies within their respective adaptations.

Whether modern apes could produce Oldowan technology in an experimental setting given the proper incentive has been a subject of debate. Some anthropologists, such as Thomas Wynn and William McGrew, have suggested that there is little, if any, difference in the cognitive complexity of chimpanzees and Oldowan hominins (Wynn and McGrew 1989). Others, including the authors of this chapter, have suggested that there may be significant cognitive and biomechanical differences between Oldowan hominins and modern apes.

Experiments with Bonobos

Beginning in 1990, Nicholas Toth and Kathy Schick have had the opportunity to investigate this question in some detail in an experimental setting. They have been collaborating with cognitive psychologists at the Language Research Center in Atlanta, Georgia, notably Sue Savage-Rumbaugh and Duane Rumbaugh, who have been working with bonobos (or "pygmy chimpanzees"), teaching them to make and use stone tools.

Two subjects well known for their communication abilities – Kanzi, a large

2.18 *Kanzi, a tool-making bonobo ("pygmy chimpanzee" or* Pan paniscus*), has learned to flake and use stone tools in order to gain access to food in an experimental setting.*

male, and his half-sister, Panbanisha – have been the focus of this long-range study. Toth and Schick showed the apes by example how to flake stone and produce sharp flakes for cutting activities, such as cutting through a rope to open a box, or slitting a drumhead to obtain a desired food.

Kanzi and Panbanisha have been strongly goal-oriented in these experiments, and highly motivated to produce effective tools in order to gain access to food, just as early Oldowan toolmakers certainly had strong incentives to make tools for use in food procurement.

After a period of trial and error, these apes acquired the basic skills to fracture stone, and even showed some interesting innovations of their own: in one instance, Kanzi learned to throw a cobble against a hard floor or another stone and produce sharp flakes to use as cutting tools.

Nevertheless, despite the great strides they have shown, there remain, after more than a decade of experiments, interesting differences from Oldowan toolmakers (Toth et al. 1993; Schick et al. 1999). It is clear that bonobos can (on occasion) flake stone and produce cores and flakes that are reminiscent of the Oldowan, including unifacial and bifacial choppers and occasional flakes greater than 15 cm (6 in) in maximum dimension. Detailed analysis has demonstrated, however, that the early Oldowan tools at Gona in Ethiopia are more similar to flaked stone artifacts produced by modern humans than by bonobos, suggesting that early Oldowan toolmakers (perhaps *Australopithecus garhi*) were surprisingly skilled in their ability to reduce lava cobbles efficiently and produce sharp flakes and fragments.

This probably implies that these creatures had better biomechanical and cognitive skills than are present in modern African apes, as well as a well-developed tradition of stone toolmaking. It would not be surprising if future discoveries of even earlier archaeological sites someday push back the dates for flaked stone technologies several hundreds of thousands of years, perhaps close to 3 million years ago.

covered cranial fragments of a fossil hominin. Further surface survey and subsequent excavation yielded much more of the cranium and dentition of a new species, named *Australopithecus garhi* (the word "garhi" means "surprise" in the local dialect). This fossil showed surprisingly primitive characteristics, such as a small (*c.* 450 cc) braincase, a projecting (prognathic) lower face, and relatively large dentition, but with molars and pre-

molars not nearly as large as those of the robust australopithecines.

Many paleoanthropologists consider this species to be a probable maker of early Oldowan tools and a potential ancestor for the genus *Homo*. Fossils of large animal bones found near the hominin remains showed cut marks from stone tools, evidence of butchery. No stone tools were found near the hominin fossils, but the earliest tools known, in the form of flakes and cobbles, come from nearby Gona and date also to *c.* 2.5 million years ago. Although it is not possible to preclude the robust australopithecines as also being Oldowan toolmakers, and although there may still be other, as yet undiscovered, fossil species at 2.5 million years ago in East Africa, this discovery shows that there were at least two different forms existing in East Africa at the time of the earliest stone tools.

The genus *Homo* is characterized by larger absolute brain size and larger brain-to-body ratio than the australopithecines; it also exhibits a reduction in the size of jaws and cheek teeth. For many paleoanthropologists, these two changes would seem a logical consequence of hominins becoming more technological, slowly replacing their biology with tools, and expanding their diet breadth to include higher-quality foods procured and processed with the use of tools. Robust australopithecines get slightly larger-brained through time, but still maintain massive jaws and cheek teeth, becoming extinct by around 1 million years ago.

Some anthropologists, such as Randall Sussman (1994), have suggested that in the early Oldowan, stone tools could have been made primarily by the robust australopithecines. They are directly associated with early stone artifacts in East and South Africa (as is early *Homo*), and hand bones from the South African cave of Swartkrans exhibit features such as broad, rather than pointed, distal phalanges (the bones at the tips of the fingers) and a thumb with strong markings for the attachment of the flexor pollicis longus muscle more similar to modern humans than earlier australopithecines. Critics point out that these hand bones cannot be assigned with confidence to a hominin species, and question whether the anatomical features noted are in fact evidence of habitual tool use.

In any case, the Oldowan period established the critical biological and behavioral foundations for the later emergence of *Homo ergaster*, *H. erectus*, and the Acheulean industrial complex (Clark et al. 1966), which is characterized by large hand axes, picks, and cleavers. As discussed in the next chapter, the Acheulean developments emerged between 1.8 and 1.5 million years ago (though some believe the date may be pushed back to between 1.8 and 1.7 or 1.65 million years ago (Roche et al. 2003)), also believed to be the time that hominins moved out of Africa and into Eurasia

The Nature of the Sites

Archaeological sites during the Oldowan tend to be relatively small and low density, with stone artifacts and (preservation permitting) the fossil remains of animals. The majority of sites are found in sedimentary environments that include riverine floodplains and channels, lake margins, river deltas, and – in South Africa – karstic (limestone) cave infillings. Environments range from closed woodlands, often along stream courses, to more open or wooded grasslands. At some sites, substantial quantities of fossil bone are associated with Oldowan artifacts, yielding valuable evidence of the environmental context of these sites, as well as information about the possible procurement and processing of animal carcasses by ancient hominins. In general, raw materials for stone tool manufacture were transported short distances, usually less than a few kilometers.

There has been considerable debate as to how the prehistoric accumulations of flaked and battered stones and fossil bones formed. Some archaeologists, notably Mary Leakey and Glynn Isaac, suggested that these sites were "home bases," similar to modern hunter-gatherer camps (Leakey 1971; Isaac 1978). Isaac (1984) later used the more neutral term "central place foraging" to describe how these concentrations may have formed, with hominins radiating out on foraging rounds and returning to these sites for food processing and consumption. Lewis Binford (1981) suggested that these sites were simply carnivore leftovers that were scavenged by early hominins, primarily through marrow processing.

Richard Potts (1988) argued that the concentrations at Olduvai Gorge were "stone caches," where hominins created stores of stone raw material in areas where it did not occur naturally, and in proximity to areas in which they would be foraging. Robert Blumenschine (1987) postulated that these [–> p. 74]

Million years ago	Species	Association
	Table 5 *Hominin Species and their Association with the Oldowan*	
3.5–2.5	*Australopithecus afarensis*	
	Australopithecus africanus	
2.5–2.2	*Australopithecus africanus*	Oldowan
	Australopithecus aethiopicus*	
	Australopithecus garhi*	
	Early Homo sp. indet.*	
2.2–1.8	*Homo habilis**	Oldowan
	Homo rudolfensis*	
	Australopithecus boisei*	
	Australopithecus robustus*	
1.8–1.5	*Homo habilis**	Oldowan and
	Homo ergaster/erectus*	Acheulean
	Australopithecus boisei*	
	Australopithecus robustus*	

* Hominins directly associated with stone tools and/or cut-marked bones at a prehistoric site, or contemporaneous with nearby strata containing artifacts.

KEY SITES Regional Overview of Major Oldowan Sites

East Africa

• *Gona, Ethiopia* The world's earliest archaeological sites are known from the Gona study area of the Afar region of Ethiopia (Semaw et al. 1997; Semaw 2000). Gona is immediately adjacent to the Hadar study area, and has sedimentary deposits ranging from over 4.5 million years ago to less than 1 million years ago. Sites EG 10 and EG 12 have been dated by argon-argon and paleomagnetism to between 2.6 and 2.5 million years ago. These sites are channel floodplain deposits in fine-grained silts, and it is believed that the river conglomerates primarily composed of water-worn cobbles of lava that were the source of the raw material for stone tools were in the immediate vicinity of the archaeological sites.

The Gona artifacts consist for the most part of unifacial and bifacial choppers, as well as some more heavily reduced cores. The surprising skill in reducing stone casts doubt on the concept of a "pre-Oldowan" at Gona and other sites prior to 2 million years ago, as argued by Hélène Roche (1989). There is little fauna associated with these early sites, which may be more a function of preservation than reality, so that inferences about the function of the tools at Gona remain indeterminate.

• *Omo, Ethiopia* In the 1960s and 1970s, the Omo Valley of southern Ethiopia laid claim to the earliest archaeological occurrences known at that time. Omo Shungura Formation members E and F, dated to approximately 2.3 to 2.4 million years ago, yielded quartz artifacts from sites in fine-grained river floodplain deposits. The technology exhibited at the Omo sites consists primarily of quartz flakes and fragments, probably produced by bipolar technique (the production of flakes by resting the core on an anvil and splitting it with a hammer).

Fossil animal remains are rare or absent from these sites, but hominin fossils in these members indicate the presence of both *Australopithecus boisei* and some form of early *Homo* (Chavaillon 1970; Chavaillon 1976; Merrick 1976; Howell et al. 1987).

• *Fejej, Ethiopia* At Fejej in southern Ethiopia, artifacts made primarily in quartz and quartzite (but with some basalt also used) were recovered from river floodplain deposits dating to approximately 2.3 million years ago (Asfaw et al. 1991; Barsky et al. in press). An incisor attributed to early *Homo* was also recovered. At one site, FJ-1, almost 2000 artifacts have been excavated from two major layers, with a number of refitting pieces indicating that stone tool manufacture took place at the site and that it was buried under fairly gentle, low-energy circumstances.

• *Hadar, Ethiopia* At site AL-666 Oldowan artifacts made primarily in lava and a maxilla (upper jawbone) with dentition of a non-robust hominin were found on the surface, and excavations recovered more Oldowan artifacts *in situ* in river sediments that date to approximately 2.3 million years ago. The maxilla has been attributed to early *Homo*, with some anthropologists comparing it to *H. rudolfensis* (Kimbel et al. 1996).

• *West Turkana, Kenya* The oldest archaeological sites at West Turkana in northern Kenya are found in the Nachukui Formation, dating to approximately 2.3 million years ago, although younger sites between 2.3 and 1.3 million years old are also known here. Artifacts from the 2.34 million-year-old Lokalalei 1 site are made primarily in poorer quality lavas and consist of simple cores, debitage, and some retouched pieces. The Lokalalei 2C site, now thought to be perhaps 100,000 years younger than Lokalalei 1, consists of artifacts made in finer-grained lavas, and has cores that are more heavily reduced (Kibunjia et al. 1992; Kibunjia 1994; Roche and Kibunjia 1994; Roche et al. 1999).

• *East Turkana (Koobi Fora), Kenya* [2.19] A large number of Oldowan and Developed Oldowan ("Karari") sites are known from this study area, ranging in time from 1.9 to

2.19 *Excavation of the well-preserved Oldowan site, FxJj 50, dated to 1.5 million years ago, at Koobi Fora (East Turkana), Kenya.*

Regional Overview of Major Oldowan Sites (continued)

approximately 1.3 million years ago. These sites are found in river floodplain, river channel, and deltaic deposits. The predominant raw material at all these sites is lava, with smaller quantities of ignimbrite, quartz, and chert also used. Contemporaneous deposits have yielded the remains of *Homo habilis*, *H. rudolfensis*, and *H. ergaster* (Isaac and Isaac 1997).

• *Chesowanja, Kenya* In the Chemoigut Formation of Lake Baringo Basin in Kenya, two sites at the Chesowanja locality have yielded assemblages of Oldowan artifacts. Dated to *c.* 1.5 million years ago, these artifacts are made in lava and consist predominantly of flakes and debitage with very few core forms (Harris and Gowlett 1980; Gowlett et al. 1981).

• *Kanjera, Kenya* In southwestern Kenya, some Oldowan sites have been excavated at Kanjera that contain stone artifacts, mostly made in fine-grained lava, and fossil bone. Based on biostratigraphy and paleomagnetism [see box: Dating Early Hominins and their Archaeology, pp. 74–75] at Kanjera South, deposition of the artifact-bearing layers is believed to have begun around 2.2 million years ago.

Stable isotope analysis and the prevalence of grassland fauna (equids) are interpreted to suggest a relatively open, grassy habitat (Ditchfield et al. 1999; Plummer et al. 1999). At Kanjera North, Oldowan artifacts and fauna have been found at sites believed to date back to the Early Pleistocene.

• *Olduvai Gorge, Tanzania* This site complex in Tanzania [see box: Olduvai Gorge, p. 67] has yielded many Oldowan archaeological sites within lake margin, channel, and floodplain deposits in its lower levels, Beds I and II, dating between approximately 1.85 and 1.35 million years ago (Leakey 1971; 1975).

In the lowest level, Bed I, artifact assemblages consist of typical Oldowan cores and flakes made primarily from lava. By Bed II, starting about 1.7 million years ago, most

industries are assigned to the Developed Oldowan, quartz, quartzite, and chert becoming more common. There are high proportions of spheroids and subspheroids, and retouched forms such as light-duty scrapers and awls.

The early Acheulean industry appears here about 1.45 million years ago, but Developed Oldowan sites still predominate throughout the extent of Bed II until 1.35 million years ago.

• *ST Site Complex, Peninj, Tanzania* Eleven low-density Oldowan sites dating to between 1.6 and 1.4 million years ago have been identified at Peninj, Lake Natron, Tanzania. This concentration of sites, all within *c.* 250 m (820 ft) of one another, has yielded basalt-dominated artifact assemblages, with some nephelinite and quartz also used for tool making. The Oldowan materials are found on a paleosoil on top of a tuff (compacted lava particles or "ash") layer (T1) in a deltaic environment; they are roughly contemporaneous with early Acheulean industries found elsewhere at Peninj.

Core forms make up approximately 8 percent of the assemblages, and retouched flakes another 8 percent, with flakes and flaking debitage constituting the bulk of the artifacts found. Most of the core forms are not very heavily flaked, with types such as choppers and polyhedrons relatively scarce.

The sites also contain a large number of fossil animal bones, many of them showing cut marks and percussion fractures, supporting an interpretation of these sites as places where processing of fleshed carcasses was undertaken (Dominguez-Rodrigo et al. 2002; de al Torre et al. 2003).

• *Nyabusosi (Site NY 18), Uganda* This Western Rift Oldowan site, dated to 1.5 million years ago, contains an assemblage of approximately 600 artifacts. Located in a sandy horizon, above clays with ironstone, this assemblage is *c.* 80 percent quartz (Senut et al. 1987).

Central Africa

• *Senga 5A, Democratic Republic of the Congo (formerly Zaire)* Excavations at this site, located in lake margin deposits in the western Rift Valley, have yielded hundreds of artifacts, along with many fossil animal bones. The quartz artifact assemblage consists of cores and flaking debris (flakes and fragments). Dating of these materials has been somewhat problematic, however (Harris et al. 1987). Although the apparent level of the artifact horizon had been dated via faunal correlation to 2–2.3 million years ago, there has been some question concerning the context of the artifacts, in that they may have been incorporated within a recent slope wash deposit that includes materials of many different ages (de Heinzelin 1984).

• *Mwimbi, Chiwondo Beds, Malawi* Fossils of Plio-Pleistocene animals along with some quartz and quartzite artifacts have been excavated at Mwimbi in the Rift Valley of northern Malawi (Kaufulu and Stern 1987). The artifacts consist of typical Oldowan cores, retouched pieces, and flakes and fragments. Faunal correlations would indicate this site to be at least 1.6 million years old.

South Africa

• *Sterkfontein Member 5, South Africa* A large number of quartz and quartzite Oldowan artifacts have been excavated in member 5 of the breccia (cemented sediment) infill at the site of Sterkfontein (Kuman 1994; Field 1999). The artifacts consist of simple cores, debitage, and some retouched pieces. A hominin ulna (forearm) shaft and three *Australopithecus robustus* teeth have also been found within this member. This deposit is estimated to be between 1.5 and 2 million years old.

• *Swartkrans Members 1, 2, and 3, South Africa* At this site [2.20], members 1, 2, and 3 of the cave infilling contain artifacts made from quartz, quartzite, and chert. These consist of simple Oldowan core forms and debitage, as well as some retouched pieces. Member 1 is

estimated to be between 1.8 and 1.5 million years old, member 2 between 1.5 and 1 million years old, and member 3 less than 1 million years old.

Quantities of fossil bones have also been recovered from this site, including a number of hominins (*A. robustus* and *Homo* species) (Brain 1981; Clark 1991; Field 1999).

• *Kromdraai B, South Africa* A small, quartz-dominated assemblage of Developed Oldowan artifacts was excavated from cave deposits at Kromdraai B (Kuman et al. 1997; Field 1999). No hominins were associated with this assemblage, but *A. robustus* is known from the other cave deposit at this locality, Kromdraai A.

North Africa

• *Ain Hanech* [**2.21**] *and El-Kherba, Algeria* These sites are found in floodplain sandy silts overlying a thick cobble conglomerate. Biostratigraphic and paleomagnetic studies indicate that these sites are approximately 1.8 million years old (Sahnouni et al. 1996; Sahnouni and de Heinzelin 1998; Sahnouni

2.21 *The outcrops at Ain Hanech, Algeria, where Oldowan sites are dated to 1.8 million years ago. These are the oldest known sites in North Africa.*

2.20 *The Swartkrans cave deposits in the Transvaal region of South Africa have yielded Oldowan stone tools, fossil animal bones, and the remains of Australopithecus robustus and early Homo dating to between 1.8 and 1 million years ago.*

et al. 2002). The assemblages at these two nearby sites include numerous large limestone cores (choppers, polyhedrons, and faceted spheroids) and limestone debitage. There are also large numbers of artifacts made from small flint pebbles, producing small cores, debitage, and retouched pieces such as scrapers, denticulates (flakes or blades retouched to produce a ragged edge), and notches (denticulate tools with single indentation).

Earlier Pliocene deposits with well-preserved fauna are located approximately 13 m (43 ft) below these Oldowan horizons, but so far these have not yielded stone artifacts or fossil hominins.

• *The Casablanca Sequence, Morocco* In the 1950s, research in ancient beach deposits near Casablanca along the Atlantic coast of Morocco produced large numbers of Plio-Pleistocene fauna along with what were interpreted to be Oldowan stone artifacts (Biberson 1961). The latter, often referred to as a "Pebble Culture," were thought to represent a Stone Age occupation here that preceded levels with Acheulean tools in upper deposits in the sedimentary sequence.

Very recent research in these deposits has thrown serious doubt on evidence for a very early Stone Age presence here, however (Raynal et al. 2002). Stone objects found in deposits dating to the earlier part of the Early Pleistocene in the Casablanca sequence have been interpreted to be geofacts, stones shaped by high-energy wave action rather than by human manufacture.

The earliest known occupation of this region now appears to date to the late Early Pleistocene (*c.* 1 million years ago), as sediments of this age at Thomas Quarry 1 have been found to contain early Acheulean artifacts.

KEY METHOD Dating Early Hominins and their Archaeology

Both relative and absolute (radiometric) dating methods are employed in paleoanthropological research. A number of relative dating methods give a sense of chronological sequence or time equivalence among prehistoric finds. Although radiocarbon dating (discussed in Chapter 4) only extends back to about 40,000 years ago, some other absolute dating methods have been successfully applied to give a chronological age even to paleoanthropological evidence millions of years old. On most sites, multiple techniques, including some or all of the methods below, are used to corroborate and cross-check age assessments.

Stratigraphy and Superposition

This relative dating technique was recognized as early as the 18th century, but is still an important element of paleoanthropological research. Put simply, in a stratigraphic section (wherein a layer of sediment rests on top of the next), younger sediments overlie (are superimposed above) older sediments. The further down a stratigraphic sequence one goes, the further and further back in time.

In geological terminology, the smallest definable stratigraphical unit is referred to as a "bed"; beds are grouped together in terms of position and type of rock into "members,"

discrete stratigraphic and sedimentological layers; and related members are part of "formations."

Paleomagnetism

The earth's north and south poles are known to have switched back and forth in magnetic polarity over time. Metallic minerals in sediments and lavas align themselves according to this polarity ("normal," as today, or "reversed," where a compass needle would have pointed south rather than north). Sediments can be sampled and analyzed for their magnetic orientation and dip, determining whether the sediments are normal or reversed.

A master world paleomagnetic sequence has now been established for the entire period of human evolution, with good geochronological dates for the normal and reversed events. A paleomagnetic sequence is constructed for the stratigraphic layers of sediment or lavas at a particular prehistoric locality, and this site paleomagnetic sequence can then be compared with the master sequence for a possible fit.

Paleomagnetism in itself does not date a site, but these paleomagnetic events can often be tied to radiometric dates or other chronological markers, such as tuff correlations or biostratigraphy (see below). Paleomagnetism can also be used as a cross-

check for other dating techniques: for example, if a site is radiometrically dated to 2.4 million years ago, it should retain reversed polarity. Any site younger than 780,000 years old (the last major paleomagnetic reversal) should have normal polarity.

Tuff Correlations

When volcanoes erupt, their pyroclastic material may ascend high into the atmosphere as volcanic ash (tuff); this can then be deposited in thick layers across a broad geographical region as either air-fall tuffs or tuffs that have been spread and redeposited by water action in streams, lakes, or seas.

A volcanic eruption generally has a distinctive chemistry that can "fingerprint" the specific eruption of a particular volcano. Analysis of the proportion of different elements in volcanic ash can be used to match a tuff from one site or locality to that from another, over an area of hundreds of miles, and even to tuff deposits in deep-sea cores, indicating that the ash in these different areas was deposited at roughly the same time.

Dating a tuff at one site thus dates a correlated tuff found at another site. From this, regional sequences of paleontological and archaeological sites can be tied together and cross-checked using other dating techniques.

---

sites were areas where hominins brought scavenged body parts from carnivore kills and subsequently processed them. (The question of hunting or scavenging at this time is discussed in more detail below.)

It is likely that these Oldowan sites formed through more than one behavioral mode. As Kathy Schick (1987) has pointed out, the larger sites may well represent "favored places," where stones and bones were carried to an area that afforded some amenity, such as shade, protection, water, animal carcasses, or other resources.

In this model, stone may have been characteristically carried around by hominins for potential use, and sites developed where stone "imports" significantly exceeded their subsequent "export" when leaving the site, possibly because transport of foods took on a greater priority.

Food Procurement and Diet

Hunters or Scavengers?

Where bone preservation is good, Oldowan sites are often associated with fossil animal bones that are usually broken up and sometimes show distinctive grooves or scratches characteristic of cut marks from a sharp-edged stone tool, demonstrating a functional relationship between the bones and the stone tools. Since the beginning of the 1980s there has been an ongoing debate about the significance of these co-occurrences. Did early hominins intentionally bring parts of animal carcasses back to a central place to process and consume? If so, were these animal carcasses obtained through hunting, scavenging, or a combination of these two strategies? The African Early Stone Age (equivalent to the Lower Paleolithic in Eurasia) has proved to be

Biostratigraphy

Animals evolve through time. Some species become extinct, others are transformed from one recognizable form to another, while still others branch into two or more distinguishable forms. Biostratigraphy attempts to document these changes in the geological record, and to establish geochronological dates for the first and last appearance of species, and for faunal turnovers (times of significant extinctions and speciations in a range of animal forms).

In Africa, species of pigs, horses, and elephants evolved relatively quickly in the Plio-Pleistocene, around 3 million to 1 million years ago, and are especially good chronological indicators, since we know which particular species of horse, pig, or elephant were present at a given time.

Once a suite of animal species at a given prehistoric locality is confirmed as internally consistent (that is, the fauna are known to have coexisted at some time in the past), then that site can be placed within the time range of that set of prehistoric species.

Potassium-Argon and Argon-Argon Dating

The most important radiometric dating method used in paleoanthropology, potassium-argon dating, employs the principle of the radioactive decay of the isotope potassium-40 (^{40}K) into argon-40 (^{40}Ar); ^{40}K has a half-life – the time it takes half of it to decay – of 1.25 billion years. In principle, any rock just cooled from a molten state has the radioactive isotope ^{40}K, but no ^{40}Ar, as the latter radiogenic gas (produced by radioactive disintegration) is driven off during the heating of the volcanic magma. This heating thus sets the radiometric clock at zero; and as time progresses, more and more ^{40}Ar is produced and trapped in the rock as the ^{40}K decays.

Since the rate of radioactive decay is known, the amount of ^{40}Ar produced is a function, and thus a measure, of time. This method is especially useful in dating volcanic rocks, lavas, and ash falls (tuffs) with high potassium content. Fortunately, much of the volcanic rocks in the African Rift – where important sites such as Olduvai Gorge and Hadar lie – can be dated by this technique. Minerals such as potassium feldspars, biotite mica, and hornblende are particularly suitable for this dating method. The relatively young ages of the lavas and ashes (with respect to the very long half-life of ^{40}K) necessitate very precise measurement of the ^{40}Ar in the rock or ash.

Although the bulk of our knowledge about East African chronology was based on conventional potassium-argon dating in the 1960s through 1980s, a newer, variant method, argon-argon (^{39}A/^{40}Ar) dating, has generally replaced the traditional potassium-argon approach. This method is more accurate and requires smaller samples, sometimes a single crystal, and has allowed more refinement in establishing regional and global chronologies.

Fission-track Dating

Although not as widely used as argon-argon dating, fission-track dating is based on the spontaneous fission of uranium (^{238}U), which leaves microscopically identifiable tracks in volcanic minerals or glasses. ^{238}U has a half-life of 4.5 billion years, even greater than that of ^{40}K, and so is also well suited to the time range of paleoanthropological materials. The uranium-rich mineral zircon is especially useful for fission-track dating.

A mineral sample is polished and etched with acid to reveal fission tracks, and these tracks are counted for a given surface area. Then the sample is irradiated with neutrons, which causes another, more rare, uranium isotope, ^{235}U, to decay and produce additional tracks. The mineral is polished and etched again, and the tracks are again counted, giving a measure of the amount of ^{235}U in the sample. As this isotope is present in a known ratio to ^{238}U, this indicates the amount of ^{238}U as well. Then, the ratio of the spontaneously decayed ^{238}U (indicated by the original fission tracks) to the induced fission tracks gives an age estimate based upon the half-life rate of decay. This method is often used in combination with other methods, such as potassium-argon or tuff correlations, to confirm and corroborate age determinations.

---

a good testing ground to address these questions and try to develop theoretical and methodological approaches to answer them.

Prior to the 1980s, the conventional view was that these co-occurrences of Oldowan artifacts and animal bones were evidence of early hominin hunting and meat-eating. The "Man the Hunter" hypothesis emerged in the 1960s not only as an explanation for the animal bones found at early archaeological sites, but also as a model for the emergence of the human condition. In this model, bipedal locomotion, tool manufacture and use, and increased intelligence and social cooperation were all tied up in an adaptation involving efficient hunting of small and large mammals.

Then the hunting hypothesis began to be challenged by some archaeologists. Lewis Binford (1981) argued that Oldowan sites were the remains of carnivore kills and accumu-lations that were subsequently scavenged by hominins, who only had access to marrow and limb bones and relict scraps of meat on bones. This impoverished view of Oldowan adaptation gained support as time went on. Robert Blumenschine (1987) has also been a strong advocate of a scavenging mode, based upon his empirical studies of predation and scavenging in modern East African parks, and his analysis of Oldowan sites. He argues that the body part representation and cut-mark location and frequency are most consistent with hominins that were opportunistic scavengers exploiting the leftovers of carcasses killed and eaten by large carnivores.

Other researchers, however, notably Henry Bunn, Manuel Dominguez-Rodrigo, and Travis Pickering, have suggested that Oldowan sites were either the product of hominin hunters who could bring down game, or the product of hominin scavengers

2.22 Cut-mark analysis: *these cut-marks (magnified) on a 1-million-year-old fossil animal limb bone were made by a stone knife with an irregular edge.*

who were able to drive predators off kills and had access to complete or nearly complete carcasses (Bunn and Kroll 1986; Dominguez-Rodrigo 2002; Dominguez-Rodrigo and Pickering 2003). This Early Access model is also based upon empirical studies, body part representation, and cut-mark patterns [2.22]. In this interpretation, the bones at sites often represent the most nutritious parts of an animal carcass, notably upper limbs and crania, and the cut marks indicate removal of large, meaty muscle units. According to this model, then, early hominins were capable and efficient foragers with early or primary access to animal carcasses, rather than scavengers with late or secondary access to already ravaged kills.

KEY CONTROVERSY What Were Oldowan Tools Used For?

Determining the function of stone tools is a task that has challenged Paleolithic archaeologists for almost two centuries. Stone artifacts are in many ways a costly commodity, entailing time and energy to procure the stone material from a source on the landscape, to transport it to a site location, and to flake it into usable tools. Why bother? These tasks must have been done by early hominins for very good reasons, ones important enough in their adaptation to be conducted many, many times over an extensive prehistoric landscape and throughout long spans of prehistoric time.

Throughout much of the history of archaeology, the theoretical function of various stone artifacts was often left to the realm of imagination, which can sometimes hit the mark, but leaves little basis for critical assessment and evaluation. The ethnographic record and experimental archaeology, however, can provide valuable clues for relating artifact form to function.

Although these studies cannot conclusively show how specific prehistoric artifacts were used, they do help to identify the kinds of uses for which various stone tools may have been best suited. In addition to using such empirical studies to appreciate the more likely and efficient uses for various

artifact forms, archaeologists also try to identify the "smoking guns" of prehistory, such as cut-mark evidence on bone, or microscopic wear evidence on stone tools, which provide more direct evidence for the way in which prehistoric tools were used.

Experimental Studies

Experimental studies have been enormously valuable in identifying the potential tools among Oldowan artifacts and the possible uses for these tools. Experiments in manufacturing Oldowan-type artifacts (see 2.13, 2.14) have revealed that prior assumptions as to which Oldowan artifacts were "tools" and which were "waste" may be unfounded, and may in fact have led prehistorians somewhat astray in assessing Oldowan toolkits.

Experiments replicating Oldowan stone assemblages indicate that all varieties of core forms, long assumed to be deliberately shaped "tools," can result incidentally from flaking stone cobbles or chunks to produce sharp stone flakes. Likewise, experiments using Oldowan tool forms indicate that flakes are enormously useful tools, particularly for cutting, but that many core forms have much more limited utility. Thus, experiments in stone tool manufacture and use have revealed

that the so-called "core tools" at Oldowan sites may not have been target forms designed for use, but rather by-products resulting from the production of usable flakes, and that flakes may, in fact, have been important, primary tools and a major goal in the working of stone by early hominins.

Additional evidence for the importance of flakes is provided by cut marks on animal bones at Oldowan sites, usually in the form of fine, parallel striations (see 2.22). Experiments and microscopic analysis have shown that such cut marks are normally made by sharp, unmodified flakes (as opposed to unifacially or bifacially retouched edges). Such unmodified flakes were perhaps the most important tools in the Oldowan toolkit, and during animal butchery (skinning, disarticulating, and defleshing), these stone knives would have served as very useful tools to gain access to invaluable protein and fat [2.26].

Experimental studies of artifact manufacture also indicate that hammerstones and spheroids/subspheroids were used as percussors to detach flakes from cores and to retouch flakes. In addition, fractured limb bones at Oldowan sites indicate that stone hammers were also employed to break up bones in order to access

As new Oldowan sites are located, excavated, and analyzed, a clearer picture of early hominin adaptive behavior will emerge. The answers will probably be complex, showing a range of different patterns and indicating that the Oldowan is not some monolithic form of adaptation, but involves diverse behavior patterns in varying circumstances [see box: What were Oldowan Tools Used For?]

Food for Thought: Diet and Encephalization

The human brain is a voracious organ: although it makes up only 2 percent of our body weight, it demands 18 percent of our metabolic energy. No other primate has evolved such a high brain-to-body ratio as the human species, and this incredibly large brain has clearly given us the neurological foundation that is responsible for our complex technologies, food procurement strategies, symbolic and linguistic behavior, and culture. Since the time of Darwin, scientists have presented different explanations for brain enlargement (encephalization), suggesting such driving forces as tool use, hunting, gathering, food sharing, and increased socialization.

In 1995, anthropologists Leslie Aiello and Peter Wheeler published an article entitled "The Expensive Tissue Hypothesis." They noted that animals with diets that include large amounts of low-nutrient plant foods tend to have more complex digestive tracts and need to devote more metabolic energy to digesting and detoxifying these foods. Animals (such as carnivores and omnivores) with diets characterized by higher-quality foods (high in protein and calories, such as meat and fat) tend to have simpler, more streamlined digestive tracts and need substantially less energy for digestion, often allowing these species to evolve larger brains. Aiello and Wheeler argued that hominin groups that could process larger amounts of meat and fat (with

---

edible marrow [**2.25**]. Experiments have also shown that hammerstones could be used to crack open hard-shelled nuts [**2.24**], though there is no direct evidence of this.

Microscopic analysis

Microscopic wear studies of artifacts provide additional evidence as to the actual functions served by stone tools in the Lower Paleolithic. Analysis of microscopic polishes and other edge-wear patterns requires fresh, unweathered, and unabraded fine-grained artifacts, especially cherts and chalcedonies. Unfortunately, most Oldowan sites consist of lavas, ignimbrites, quartz, and quartzite, which are usually not suitable for such microscopic analysis, though a small number of artifacts are made in such favorable materials.

In a study of 54 fine-grained artifacts from Koobi Fora, Kenya, from between 1.9 and 1.4 million years ago, nine showed diagnostic wear polishes. These specimens were unmodified flakes and flake fragments, and showed polishes from animal butchery (four specimens), woodworking (three specimens), and cutting soft plant material (two specimens) (Keeley and Toth 1981). This range of activities, all conducted using flakes as tools, gives a small glimpse of the diverse uses to which stone tools were put by hominins even in the earlier phases of the Stone Age.

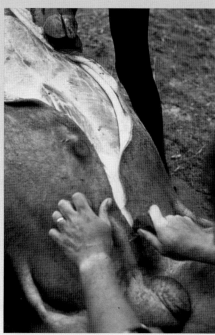

2.23, 2.24, 2.25, 2.26 *Experimental studies with replica Oldowan artifacts to perform various tasks have been extremely valuable in identifying the possible functions of these tools. (Top left) Chopping a sapling to make a spear or digging stick; (bottom left) nut-cracking with a stone hammer and anvil; (below) bone-breaking to extract marrow using a chopper and stone anvil; (right) skinning an animal with a sharp flake. All the animals used in these experiments died of natural causes.*

the assistance of technology) would need to consume fewer vegetable foods that require more metabolic energy to digest and detoxify. A more omnivorous diet would allow more metabolic energy to be devoted to a larger brain. Therefore, tool use, meat/marrow consumption, and brain expansion all evolved in tandem.

We have evidence in *Homo habilis*, which emerged between 2 and 1.8 million years ago, of a significant brain enlargement (510–687 cc) from the australopithecine condition; this occurred within a half million years of the first appearance of stone tools and cut-marked bones, if not sooner. While this is not proof that Aiello and Wheeler's hypothesis is correct, many anthropologists think that the close timing of the Oldowan and encephalization is more than coincidence.

The "expensive tissue" hypothesis is potentially testable by examining strontium-calcium ratios in fossil hominin bones and teeth to determine the degree of animal foods in the diet. The prediction would be that hominin species with larger brains would have more meat and marrow in their diet, and therefore lower strontium-to-calcium ratios. Robust australopithecines, for example, might be expected to have higher ratios than their contemporary early *Homo* counterparts (but see below, p. 82). And later forms of *Homo*, being larger-brained, should have lower ratios than early *Homo*. This chemical approach to hominin evolution is still in its infancy, with small sample sizes, but nonetheless it suggests that a significant inclusion of animal protein in hominin diet, accomplished through the use of tools, may have provided a critical impetus to the rapid evolutionary expansion of brain size in the hominin lineage.

The Behavior of Oldowan Hominins

We know that early hominin populations must have had distinctive patterns of social behavior, mating systems, vocal and non-vocal communication, dietary preferences and food procurement strategies, land use and ranging behaviors, and a wealth of other characteristics that did not involve stone tools and material culture. Many of these would leave little, if any, prehistoric visibility, but others can leave hard evidence behind.

Social Organization

Barring a Pompeii-like burial of toolmakers at an Oldowan site, our information about social organization of hominin groups is based on studies of modern primates and biological clues from hominin fossils. Prior to *Homo ergaster* (discussed in Chapter 3), it would appear that early hominins were highly sexually dimorphic, with males significantly larger than females. Primatologist Richard Wrangham (1987) has suggested that these forms lived in multi-male, multi-female groups. It is likely that males competed for access to females. A social group size of perhaps 30 individuals may have been typical, with seasonal fission/fusion patterns according to the availability of food and water resources.

Diet

Based on primate models, it is likely that plant foods formed the bulk of the early hominin diet, with animal foods an important but smaller portion of their food intake. The large molars and premolars of the robust australopithecines, and the microscopic striations and pitting that characterize their chewing surfaces, suggest that their diet included hard, gritty foods such as seeds or roots and tubers. The more gracile australopithecines and the early *Homo* forms may have had a more generalized diet. As mentioned, chemical studies of hominin bones (discussed in more detail below), may provide further evidence of dietary patterns, particularly the proportion of animal foods and the general types of plant foods consumed by different species.

Cut marks, hammerstone striae (fine lines or incisions), and fracture patterns on long bones show that Oldowan hominins processed large mammal carcasses (weighing several hundred pounds on the hoof) and thus incorporated some animal protein and fat in their diet. How much, how frequently, and by what means of procurement are, as we have seen, highly debated issues. In any case, the size of the animals these early hominins processed far exceeds the small body sizes of prey seen in the predatory behavior of chimpanzees and baboons. This suggests a new and unique adaptive pattern within the primate order, one achieved by hominins through the use of stone tools (and, presumably, other material culture), and one that would have pitted them in a competition for resources against predators and scavengers on the landscape.

Technology

We know that chimpanzees, as a species, possess a varied material culture, much of which is fairly casually made or used and would have no archaeological visibility after long-term burial. Given the variety of technologies observed among living chimpanzee populations, it would seem quite possible that early stone toolmaking hominins possessed a much greater range of tools made out of perishable or unmodified materials. Early hominins may have used a range of non-lithic materials such as animal skins, ostrich eggshells, or tortoise carapaces as containers; broken bones, horns, tusks, or wooden branches as digging tools; branches or long bones as clubs; and sharpened wooden shafts as spears. In addition, unmodified stones could have served as potentially deadly, hand-thrown missiles in offence or defense.

Fire

Controlled use of fire by early Oldowan hominins is a subject of some debate and controversy. There is evidence for thermal alteration of sediments and prehistoric materials at some Oldowan sites (Clark and Harris 1985). At Swartkrans in South Africa, burned bones are found in layers associated with stone tools and cut-marked bones (Brain and Sillen 1988). At other sites, such as the FxJj 20 site complex at **Koobi Fora** in Kenya, several patches of discolored, apparently baked sediment have been found, which have been interpreted as possible fire locations [**2.27**, **2.28**]. At these sites, some artifacts have also been found that show evident heating in a fire, producing discoloration, crazing, or heat-induced fractures (Bellomo 1994). In the absence of a discrete hearth structure, however, or spatially concentrated burned artifacts or bones, it is difficult to rule out completely the possibility that these features resulted from natural fires. (See also Chapter 3 for further consideration of fire use by early hominins.)

Site Modification

At present, there is no clear evidence for architectural features in the Oldowan. Mary Leakey (1971) suggested that a stone circle of lava cobbles at site DK in Bed I of Olduvai Gorge was the base of a hut structure, with stone artifacts and fossil bones within and outside the circular feature [**2.29**]. More recently, archaeologists have interpreted this feature as possibly a natural phenomenon, comprising natural exposure of chunks of the local bedrock. Of course, it is entirely possible that simple structures could have been produced out of perishable materials with no lasting impression, but without hard evidence, such

phenomena must remain in the realm of conjecture. Modern apes are known to build nests in the trees and on the ground, and it is likely that early hominins would have had similar nesting behaviors.

Art, Ritual, and Language

At present, there is little or no direct evidence for symbolic or ritualistic behavior among Oldowan primates. In fact, little evidence of features such as representative or abstract art, intentional burials with grave goods, or the collection of exotic stones or shells is seen until much more recent times, primarily only in the past 100,000 years. That having been said, some researchers, such as neuroscientist and evolutionary anthropologist Terrence Deacon, have argued that the encephalization and expansion of the prefrontal cortex of *Homo habilis* shortly

2.29 *Site modification: a partial plan of site DK, Bed 1, at Olduvai Gorge. The circular pattern of lava cobbles has been interpreted by some as the base of a hut structure, with a scatter of stone artifacts and bones. More recently, however, the feature has been seen as possibly a natural phenomenon.*

after 2 million years ago indicate the beginnings of a more symbolic communication system, and that "some nearly universal aspects of modern spoken language (e.g. constants of consonant articulation) may have occurred as early as 2 million years ago" (Deacon 1997: 358).

As Deacon wrote: "The introduction of stone tools and the ecological adaptation they indicate also mark the presence of a socio-ecological predicament that demands a symbolic solution. Stone tools and symbols must both, then, be the architects of the *Australopithecus-Homo* transition, and not its consequences. The large brains, stone tools, reduction in dentition, better opposability of thumbs and fingers, and more complete bipedality found in post-australopithecine hominids are the physical echoes of a threshold already crossed" (Deacon 1997: 348).

Recent Trends in Approaches to the Oldowan

Within the past few decades, specialists analyzing the Oldowan industrial complex have shifted their primary emphasis away from more traditional studies of artifact classification and typologies, and have instead stressed the making of inferences about hominin behavior patterns and overall adaptive strategies. Such approaches include the much more detailed zooarchaeological studies now standard at early African sites. Research focuses on faunal assemblage composition, including species representation, body part representation, age and sex indicators, fracture patterns, surface modifications such as cut marks and tooth marks, and bone-weathering stages. This information is used in an attempt to arrive at a synthetic understanding of these early prehistoric sites, including the influence of hominins, carnivores, or other agents for the collection and modification of the bones; the environmental indicators of the faunal assemblage; and the testing of such behavioral scenarios as primary vs. secondary access to carcasses.

Experimental archaeological approaches to understanding the nature of Lower Paleolithic occurrences can help identify techniques of manufacture (e.g. hard hammer percussion or bipolar technique) and determine what lithic patterns are the result of opportunistic flaking vs. more deliberate strategies. For example, experiments have shown that battered quartz and lava spheroids can be produced simply by their use as hammerstones over several hours (Schick and Toth 1994), whereas faceted limestone spheroids can be produced by heavy core reduction and exhaustion (Sahnouni et al. 1997). Many of the core forms (choppers, discoids, polyhedrons, heavy-duty scrapers) can be produced simply through opportunistic flaking, taking advantage of the shape characteristics of the core, without any special intent surrounding the final core morphology that is produced.

A recent emphasis in lithic analysis is the detailed reconstruction of patterns of stone reduction at archaeological sites (what French researchers now often call the "chaînes opératoires") through careful analysis of the materials, refitting studies, and experimentation. Ideally, one can reconstruct the "life history" of a stone artifact assemblage, from the acquisition of the unmodified raw material to final discard and incorporation of artifacts within the sedimentary and archaeological record. Such a history would commonly include considerations of raw material transport, artifact use, resharpening and rejuvenation, as well as site formation and taphonomic agents (i.e., those acting on an artifact between the time of its deposition and its discovery) that could have modified a prehistoric assemblage.

Experiments using Oldowan-type artifacts for activities deemed possible for early hominins (toolmaking, animal butchery, marrow processing, woodworking, nut cracking, etc.) not only can give us a much greater appreciation of the feasibility of using certain tools for certain functions, but can also help us to identify residual by-products in the prehistoric record. These can include cut marks and other striae on bones, fracture patterns on limb bones, use wear on artifact edges, and battering and pitting on stone hammers and anvils.

Pioneering studies by Sergei Semenov (1964) and Lawrence Keeley (1980) have established the means for inferring the function of stone artifacts based on microscopic polish and wear marks produced on a stone tool edge during its use. The potential of this approach, and its limitations, for the Oldowan, are explored in the box What Were Oldowan Tools Used For?

2.30, 2.31 *Site formation processes: the bones of a goat laid out after butchering the carcass with stone tools (below left) and after scavengers had been at work (below right), showing the processes potentially involved in the development of bone accumulations on the prehistoric landscape. The animal died of natural causes.*

Experiments in Site Formation Processes

Understanding the geological forces that can bury and alter Paleolithic sites can help determine which site contexts are primary (i.e., little disturbed in terms of their prehistoric spatial patterning), and which are more disturbed, or secondary, such that the composition of the artifact assemblage, its associations with materials such as fossil bones, and overall spatial pattern may be drastically changed from the time of the hominin activities that produced it. Experimental studies investigating the actual effects of sedimentary processes (on floodplains, in river channels, in deltas, along lake margins) on Oldowan-type assemblages have yielded valuable insights into site formation and deformation by the agencies of burial. Analysis of lithic assemblage composition (cores, flakes, and fragments), mean size and weight, vertical and horizontal patterns of materials, and dip and long axis orientation of artifacts can all yield important clues as to the degree of disturbance that a site experienced before final burial (Schick 1986; 1987).

Other important site formation studies in the past two decades have centered on the processes involved in the development of bone accumulations on the prehistoric landscape [2.30, 2.31] (e.g. Brain 1981; Blumenschine 1986). Of special interest has been the distribution and environmental location (open or closed habitat, near or far from river channels or lake margins) of kill or consumption sites of various carnivores, such as leopard, lions, hyenas, etc. Such studies have attempted to infer potential opportunities for tool-using hominins by such carnivore sites (i.e., how much meat, fat, marrow, or brains would be provided), and the mutual roles of the carnivores and hominins in carcass defleshing, dismemberment, and consumption.

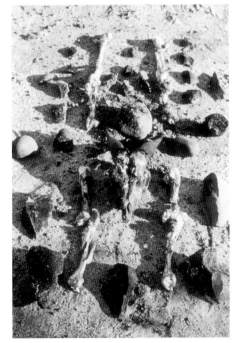

Isotopic Studies

During the past few decades, it has become established that fossil bones and teeth of prehistoric species can give important information regarding the animal's diet and paleoenvironment (Lee-Thorpe et al. 1994; Sillen et al. 1995). Studies of modern species have shown the relationship between diet and bone/tooth chemistry. For example, studies of stable carbon isotopes (^{13}C and ^{12}C) can give an indication of the relative amount of tropical grass (C4) versus shrub and tree foods (C3) in the diet of herbivores (reflected secondarily in the carnivores that eat them). Analysis of tooth enamel of *Australopithecus robustus* has indicated a diet rich in C3 foods from trees and shrubs, which could include roots, tubers, fruits, and nuts, but also some inclusion of C4-based foods, either grasses (stems and/or seeds) or, alternatively, animals that rely on C4 plants. Their diet and that of other hominins in South Africa appear very different from that of modern African apes, which is nearly entirely based upon C4 foods.

The ratio of strontium (Sr) to calcium (Ca) in bones and teeth can be an indication of how herbivorous, omnivorous, or carnivorous an animal is. Modern herbivores (with the exception of some browsers) tend to have high strontium-to-calcium ratios, while carnivores have much lower ratios. Studies of Sr/Ca ratios in *Australopithecus robustus* and *Homo* at Swartkrans have produced a somewhat unexpected pattern (albeit with small sample sizes), with the strontium levels of *A. robustus* lower than those of *Homo*, which could suggest that *A. robustus* was more carnivorous than *Homo*.

Andrew Sillen suggests, however, that the higher strontium levels in early *Homo* may be due to these individuals eating more geophytes, such as lily bulbs, which are available in the region today, or to their eating animals such as hyraxes, which themselves have quite high Sr/Ca ratios. Further research on bone and tooth chemistry should clarify the prehistoric picture, with the analysis of additional fossil specimens as well as an enhanced appreciation for the patterns and complexities seen in modern species.

Landscape Archaeology

Above and beyond conventional archaeological excavation, a relatively new approach to archaeology consists of studying the occurrences of stone artifacts, fossil bones, and other materials along erosional outcrops at a given stratigraphic horizon, ideally for a distance of several kilometers. This is done to get an appreciation of the nature and density of prehistoric materials in an ancient landscape and an understanding of the relationship of such features as nearby water (streams, lakes) to particular environmental niches and to stone raw material sources. These studies can also be conducted with small test excavations at intervals to see the relationships between densi-

ties of surface artifacts and fossil bone to *in situ* materials, and to make predictive tests of future patterns based on those currently perceived.

Such landscape archaeological studies have been conducted at Koobi Fora, Kenya (Isaaac and Harris 1980) and Olduvai Gorge, Tanzania (Peters and Blumenschine 1995; Blumenschine 1995; Blumenschine and Peters 1998).

Summary and Conclusions

The first bipedal hominins appear to have emerged in Africa from an ape ancestry in the late Miocene, between 8 and 6 million years ago. Between 5 and 2 million years ago, bipedal hominins (*Australopithecus/Paranthropus*) are characterized by having relatively small brains and large jaws and teeth, especially cheek teeth. The first archaeological sites, dated to around 2.5 million years ago, are found at Gona in Ethiopia, characterized by flaked stone technologies assigned to the Oldowan industry.

The hominins contemporaneous with these sites include *Australopithecus garhi* and *A. (Paranthropus) aethiopicus* in East Africa, and *A. africanus* in South Africa. Between 2 million and 1.8–1.7 million years ago, the first hominins that appear to show marked encephalization (brain expansion) are found. These forms are usually assigned to the genus *Homo*: *H. habilis*, *H. rudolfensis*, and *H. ergaster/erectus*. These forms are contemporaneous with the later "robust" australopithecines, *Australopithecus (Paranthropus) boisei* in East Africa and *A. (P.) robustus* in South Africa. It cannot be demonstrated with certainty which of these species made Oldowan tools. It is possible that all hominin species contemporaneous with the Oldowan made stone tools, but the fact that the genus *Homo* exhibits encephalization and tooth reduction over time, and continues after the extinction of the robust australopithecines, suggests that they were major players in flaked stone technology.

The Oldowan industry is characterized by simple core forms, battered stones, debitage, and retouched forms. There is a tendency for core forms to be more heavily reduced through time, and for higher percentages of retouched forms and spheroids to be present after *c.* 1.7 million years ago, at sites that Mary Leakey assigned to the Developed Oldowan. Both the Oldowan and Developed Oldowan industries are usually grouped into the Oldowan industrial complex.

Experimentation has shown that much of the variability in the Oldowan can be explained in terms of least-effort strategies to produce sharp flakes and chopping edges from cobbles and chunks of rock. Oldowan tools were probably used for a range of functions, including such activities as animal butchery, woodworking to make spears or digging sticks, and processing plant foods. Cut marks on bones, as well as functional experiments, show that Oldowan flakes were excellent knives for animal butchery. Such uses would have expanded the breadth of the hominin diet, incorporating larger quantities of high-quality foods. This change in diet would reduce gut size and allow encephalization over time.

The earliest archaeological sites tend to be situated in depositional environments such as river floodplains, river channels, deltas, and lake margins. Transport distances of raw materials were often less than 2 km (1.25 miles), and sometimes sites were situated in close proximity to a stream gravel source. At some sites, such as Olduvai Gorge, it appears that stone was occasionally transported distances of between 5 and 10 km (3–6 miles). Faunal remains are found associated with stone artifacts at some sites, notably FLK Zinj in Bed I of Olduvai Gorge. Bones of larger and smaller mammals are often present, usually heavily fragmented and sometimes exhibiting cut marks, suggesting that Oldowan hominins processed meat and marrow from animal carcasses. Zooarchaeologists argue whether this pattern represents hunting/primary access scavenging or more marginal scavenging, and a consensus has not yet been reached.

At around 1.8–1.7 million years ago, the larger-brained *Homo ergaster* emerged in Africa. Shortly thereafter, by around 1.5 million years ago, new technologies appeared, with larger flakes struck from boulder cores and subsequently flaked into hand axes, picks, and cleavers. These technologies are normally assigned to the Acheulean industrial complex, discussed in the next chapter. Oldowan and Acheulean technologies appear to coexist in Africa for hundreds of thousands of years; exactly what this variability means is not yet clear.

A wealth of evidence has now been uncovered regarding these early phases of human biological, technological, and cultural evolution. The hominin fossil record has now bushed and burgeoned into a multiplicity of different fossil forms, which evolved over a substantial amount of time and spread geographically over considerable distances and varying environments. Tighter chronological controls have allowed us to assign more precise dates to many sites and evolutionary events, to document the pattern of these emerging biological and cultural traits, and to try to explain them. Thus, what was once thought to be a monolithic package of bipedality, tools, and encephalization, is now observed to have evolved not all at once but rather in sequence. Africa was clearly the "cradle of humankind," witnessing the emergence of the earliest humans and the first archaeological record.

In Chapter 3 we describe the next stage in the human story, the expansion of hominins from Africa to Asia, and later to Europe. The ability to cope with new and challenging environments was put to the test as hominins moved beyond their tropical homeland to diverse and often less hospitable regions. The process of encephalization continued, and hominin behav-

ior became increasingly complex, with new tools and shelters, and later the control of fire. These new developments did not arise unpredictably, however, but have their origins in the biology and behavior of the earliest tool-using hominins just discussed.

Further Reading and Suggested Websites

Delson, E., Tattersall, I., Van Couvering, J. A., & Brooks, A. S. (eds.). 2000. *Encyclopedia of Human Evolution and Prehistory.* (2nd ed.) New York: Garland. This valuable paleoanthropological reference provides information on fossils, sites, artifacts, and dating techniques.

Isaac, G. L. 1989. *The Archaeology of Human Origins: Papers by Glynn Isaac* (B. Isaac ed.). Cambridge: Cambridge University Press. A good introduction to the sorts of evidence presented by early archaeological sites in Africa, and diverse approaches taken to understand them.

Johanson, D. and Edgar, B. 1996. *From Lucy to Language.* New York: Simon & Schuster. Superb photographs and accompanying text descriptions give an excellent and very visual introduction to many of our important fossil ancestors and relatives.

Klein, R. G. 1999. *The Human Career.* Chicago: University of Chicago Press. A comprehensive, detailed overview of the paleontological and archaeological evidence for human evolution, from early primates through modern humans.

Schick, K. D. and Toth, N. 1993. *Making Silent Stones Speak: Human Evolution and the Dawn of Technology.* New York: Simon and Schuster. This overview of the Stone Age stresses how experimental archaeological research sheds light on early Paleolithic patterns.

Schick, K. and Toth, N. 2001. "Palaeoanthropology at the millennium," in *Archaeology at the Millennium: A Sourcebook* (D. Feinman & G. Price eds.), 39–108. New York: Kluwer Academic/Plenum Publishers. A comprehensive synthesis of the Lower Paleolithic in the Old World.

Stringer, C. and Andrews, P. 2005. *The Complete World of Human Evolution.* London and New York: Thames & Hudson. A comprehensive and well-illustrated survey of the story of human evolution, with all the most up-to-date information.

Tattersall, I. 1995. *The Fossil Trail: How We Know What We Think We Know About Human Evolution.* Oxford: Oxford University Press. A well-illustrated introduction to the fossil evidence for human evolution.

http://www.stoneageinstitute.org A site showing a range of different approaches taken to understand the Stone Age by a research institute dedicated to Stone Age research.

http://www.mnh.si.edu/museum/VirtualTour/Tour/First/Human A virtual tour of the Smithsonian Institution's National Museum of Natural History, concentrating on human evolution.

http://www.leakeyfoundation.org/ The site of the Leakey Foundation, devoted to funding research on human evolution.

http://www.archaeologyinfo.com/ A good resource for information regarding both the archaeological and physical anthropological aspects of human evolution, with useful links.

CHAPTER 3
HOMININ DISPERSALS IN THE OLD WORLD

Richard Klein, Stanford University

Homo ergaster 85
  Anatomy 85
  • *The Turkana Boy* 86
  • *Human Evolution and the Inferences from the Turkana Boy* 88
  ● KEY DISCOVERY The Discovery of the Turkana Boy 89
  The Relationship of Homo ergaster *to Other Hominins* 92

The Acheulean 93
  The Acheulean Hand Axe Tradition 93
  ● KEY DISCOVERY The Acheulean Hand Axe Tradition 94
  Hand Axe Function 95
  Variation within the Acheulean Tradition 96

Homo erectus 97
  The Discovery and Dating of Homo erectus *in Java* 97
  ● KEY CONTROVERSY The Dating of Javan *Homo erectus* 98
  The Discovery and Dating of Homo erectus *in China* 99
  The Archaeology of Chinese Homo erectus 100

The Dispersion of *Homo ergaster* and the Fate of *Homo erectus* 101
  ● KEY CONTROVERSY Did *Homo ergaster* Disperse Partly by Boat? 102
  The Initial Expansion of Homo ergaster *from Africa* 102
  The Expansion of Homo ergaster *to Eurasia: The Dmanisi Discoveries* 102
  • *Dating the Dmanisi Fossils* 103
  • *Evidence that* Homo ergaster *Persisted to 1 Million Years Ago or Later* 104
  The Persistence of Homo erectus *in Java* 105

Homo heidelbergensis and the Earliest Occupation of Europe 106
  ● KEY METHOD Electron Spin Resonance Dating 107
  ● KEY SITE The Gran Dolina TD6 and the History of Cannibalism 108
  Unsuccessful European Colonizers: Homo antecessor *and the Ceprano Skull* 108
  Brain Expansion and Change within the Hand Axe Tradition 110
  The Evolution of the Neanderthals in Europe 110
  ● KEY METHOD Uranium-Series Dating 111

Evidence for Early Human Behavior apart from Stone Artifacts 112
  Raw Materials besides Stone 112
  ● KEY CONTROVERSY How did Human Fossils Reach the Sima de los Huesos? 113
  Site Modification 114
  Fire 116
  Art 117
  Diet and Food Procurement 118
  • *Plant Foods: Foraging* 118
  • *Animal Foods: Hunting and Scavenging* 119
  ● KEY METHOD Luminescence Dating 119

Summary and Conclusions 121
  ● KEY CONTROVERSY Acheulean Big-Game Hunters? 122

Further Reading and Suggested Websites 123

The course of human evolution can be described as a sequence of short, abrupt steps or punctuations, separated by long periods of stasis – the model referred to as punctuated equilibrium, explained in Chapter 2. That chapter described two crucial early steps in this development. The first, which remains poorly documented, occurred between 8 and 6 million years ago, when the australopithecine and chimpanzee lineages diverged. The australopithecines are the oldest well-known representatives of the human tribe, the Hominini (or hominins), and it is from one of them that all later humans evolved. The second step, which is much better documented, occurred approximately 2.5 million years ago, and produced the humans who created the Oldowan cultural complex, the oldest known stone tools.

This chapter focuses on a third key evolutionary step and its important consequences. This step occurred c. 1.8–1.7 million years ago, and resulted in a species that anticipated living people in every major respect of anatomy, behavior, and ecology, save mainly for its smaller brain. With this caveat in mind, its members can reasonably be labeled the first "true humans."

Their species is most commonly called *Homo erectus*, but for reasons that are provided below, its early African members are probably better called *Homo ergaster*. *H. ergaster* translates roughly as "working man," and the term was first applied to some fossils that were found east of Lake Turkana, Kenya, where the deposits also contain numerous flaked stone tools.

Homo ergaster is usually assumed to have evolved from *H. habilis,* or from one of its constituents, if there were two. (Variations within cranial volume and cheek tooth size have led some to see two species in *H. habilis* fossils: *H. habilis* (narrowly understood) and *H. rudolfensis*.) Early on, *H. ergaster* learned to strike much larger stone flakes than Oldowan people, and by 1.65 million years ago, it had created the hand axes and other more extensively flaked artifacts that archaeologists assign to the Acheulean culture or industrial tradition. Anatomical changes, more sophisticated technology, and other probable behavioral advances allowed *H. ergaster* to enlarge the human range to include drier, more seasonal African environments, where surface water and shade were relatively scarce. Even more momentous, at a time that may only shortly postdate its appearance, *Homo ergaster* became the first human species to expand to Eurasia. Its far-flung descendants then began to diversify into a variety of human types.

This chapter outlines the initial stages of the diversification process, from which at least three different human lineages emerged: *Homo erectus* in eastern Asia, *H. neanderthalensis* (the Neanderthals) in Europe, and *H. sapiens* (modern humans) in Africa. *Homo erectus* differentiated first, by 1 million years ago or before. *H. neanderthalensis* and *H. sapiens* appear to have shared a common ancestor as recently as 600,000–500,000 years ago, and they separated only after this ancestor, here labeled *Homo heidelbergensis*, spread from Africa to Europe. **Table 1** (pp. 90–91) summarizes the major occurrences and features of these species.

By modern standards, *Homo ergaster, H. erectus, H. heidelbergensis, H. neanderthalensis,* and even early *H. sapiens* were remarkably primitive in their behavior. The emergence of *H. heidelbergensis* 600,000–500,000 years ago may have coincided with the appearance of more sophisticated hand axes in Africa, and these, or the behavioral advance they imply, may

help explain how *H. heidelbergensis* was able to spread to Europe, where its descendants became the first permanent occupants. Still, archaeological evidence summarized in this chapter suggests that even as recently as 250,000 years ago, humans everywhere remained remarkably conservative in their behavior. They produced the same kinds of stone artifacts over long time intervals and vast regions, they rarely manufactured artifacts from bone or similar plastic materials, they produced little if any art, they hunted and gathered relatively inefficiently, and they left no firm evidence for structures. In these and other archaeologically detectable respects, they differed sharply from most historically observed hunter-gatherers.

The contrast with historic peoples persisted until much later, and only sites that postdate 50,000 years ago commonly provide archaeological residues that match the material culture of many historic hunter-gatherers. If we assume that the advanced, essentially modern behavioral repertoire developed in Africa about 50,000 years ago, it could explain how African *H. sapiens* subsequently managed to spread to Eurasia, where it swamped or replaced *H. neanderthalensis* and *H. erectus*. Most specialists accept the African origin of modern behavior, but they disagree on whether it appeared abruptly about 50,000 years ago or evolved more gradually before this time. The next chapter summarizes the debate and the archaeological evidence for different perspectives.

Homo ergaster

Anatomy

In the evolutionary scheme that is preferred here, *Homo ergaster* is a strictly African species that existed between 1.8–1.7 million and perhaps 600,000 years ago. Our understanding is based mostly on fossils from deposits on the eastern and western shores of Lake Turkana in northern Kenya, which date to 1.8–1.5

HOMININ DISPERSALS IN THE OLD WORLD TIMELINE

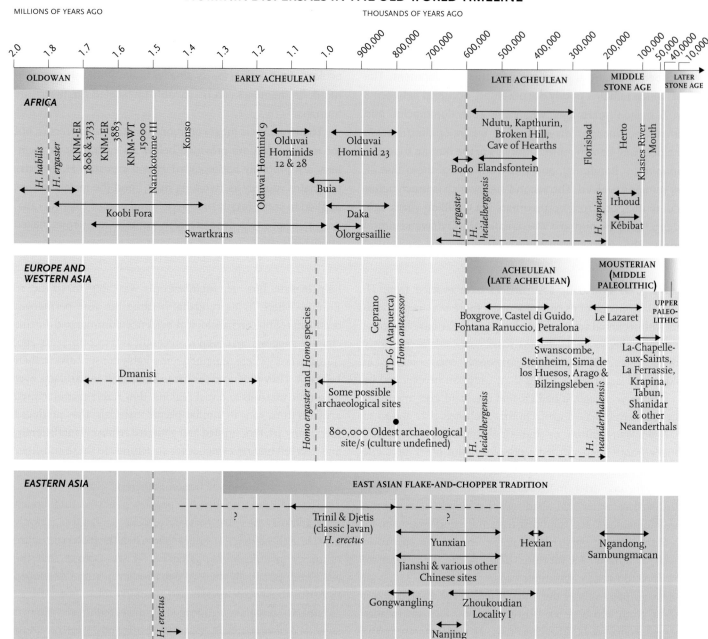

million years ago. The dating depends mainly on replicated potassium-argon determinations [see Dating Early Hominins box, pp. 74–75], and is remarkably secure. The principal specimens are two skulls, nine incomplete mandibles, a partial skeleton, and some isolated limb bones from Koobi Fora on the eastern side of the lake, and a skull and associated skeleton from Nariokotome III on the western side (Walker and Leakey 1993a). The individual fossils are commonly designated by serial numbers attached to an abbreviation for the Kenya National Museum (KNM) and to abbreviations for the two main regions: ER for East Turkana (formerly East Rudolf) and WT for West Turkana.

The Turkana Boy All the specimens from Lake Turkana have contributed to an understanding of *Homo ergaster*, but the West Turkana skull and associated skeleton are most important, because they allow unambiguous statements about body size and form (Ruff and Walker 1993). Skull robusticity and the shape of the sciatic notch (which permits passage of the sciatic nerve to the legs) on the pelvis indicate that the owner was male, while dental eruption (the appearance of teeth in pre-adults) and limb bone formation show that he was immature. His discoverers therefore dubbed him the "Turkana Boy," and specialists refer to him both this way and by his serial number, KNM WT 15000 [see box: Discovery of the Turkana Boy, p. 89].

Analysis of the surrounding sediments showed that he died and was then rapidly buried on the edge of a marsh about 1.56 million years ago (Brown and McDougall 1993). His skeleton is even more complete than that of the famous 3.3-million-year-old australopithecine, "Lucy," described in the previous chapter (p. 57), and it is still the most complete skeleton from any hominin who lived before 130,000 years ago [**3.4**]. Its significance matches that of Lucy, for if she left no doubt that her kind were bipedal apes, the Turkana Boy showed just as clearly that his kind were true humans.

Lucy was tiny – probably only about 1 m (3.3 ft) tall – and she had very long arms relative to her legs. She also had an apelike, cone-shaped trunk that narrowed upwards from her pelvis to her shoulders. From a distance, she probably looked very much

like a bipedal chimpanzee. The Turkana Boy was tall – about 1.62 m (5.3 ft) at the time of his death – and was destined to reach 1.82 m (6 ft) or more had he survived to adulthood. His arms were no longer, relative to his legs, than in living people, and he had a barrel-shaped chest over narrowed hips. From a distance, he would have looked very similar to the lanky herders who live around Lake Turkana today.

It was in his skull and face that the Turkana Boy differed most strikingly from living humans (Walker and Leakey 1993b) [**3.2**]. His brain was nearly full grown, but its volume was a mere 880 cc, only 130 cc greater than the maximum in *Homo habilis* (including all of its possible constituent species) and 450–500 cc below the average in people living today. The brain size increase from *H. habilis* all but melts away when the Turkana Boy's larger body size is considered. His braincase was long and low, and the skull walls were exceptionally thick. His forehead (frontal bone) was flat and receding, and it descended to merge

3.1 *Map: showing major sites and regions mentioned in the chapter.*

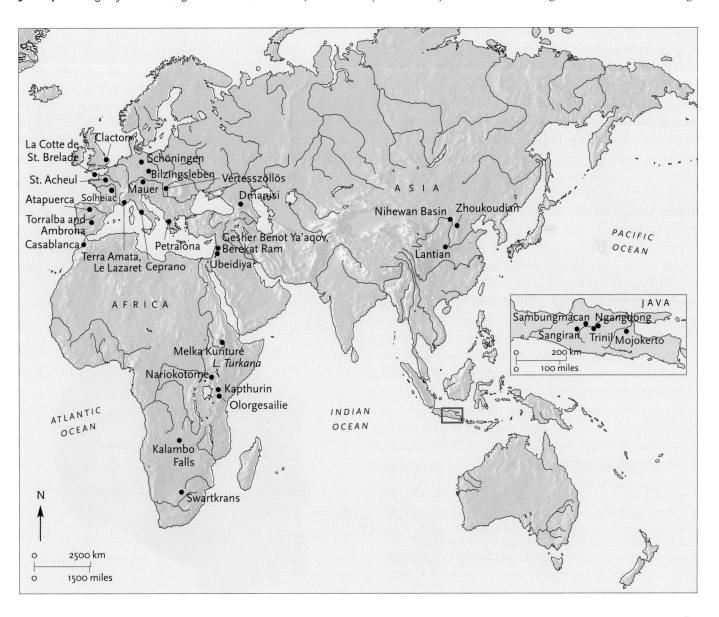

3.2 *Turkana Boy (***Homo ergaster***): a three-quarters facial view of the Turkana Boy's skull, showing the beetling brow, the large size of the face relative to the braincase, and the far forward projection of the face and jaws.*

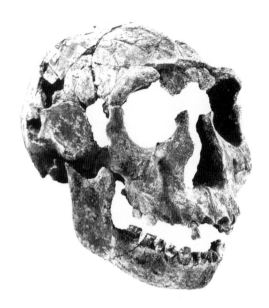

at an angle with the bony browridge over his eyes. His nose was typically human in its forward projection and downwardly oriented nostrils, and in this he differed from the australopithecines and *H. habilis*, who had apelike noses that were flush against the face. The nose aside, however, his face was striking for its great length from top to bottom, and his massive jaws were prognathic, projecting far to the front. These jaws contained chewing teeth that were significantly larger than our own, even if they were smaller than the average in *H. habilis* or the australopithecines. The bone below his lower front teeth slanted sharply backwards, meaning that he was completely chinless.

Human Evolution and the Inferences from the Turkana Boy It is impossible to exaggerate the significance of the Turkana Boy for what his skeleton reveals about the course of human evolution. The shortness of his arms relative to his legs signals the final abandonment of any apelike reliance on trees for feeding or refuge. A greater commitment to life on the ground meant an even greater emphasis on bipedalism, and this could explain the narrowing of the hips (pelvis) and the concomitant development of a barrel-like chest. The narrowed pelvis increased the efficiency of muscles that operate the legs in bipedal movement, and it would have forced the lower part of the rib cage to narrow correspondingly. To maintain chest volume and lung function, the upper part of the rib cage would have had to expand, and the modern barrel shape would follow. The narrowing of the pelvis also constricted the birth canal, and this may have forced a reduction in the proportion of brain growth that occurred before birth (Walker and Ruff 1993). Infant dependency could then have been prolonged, foreshadowing the uniquely long dependency period that marks living humans.

Pelvic narrowing must also have reduced the volume of the digestive tract, but this could have happened only if food quality improved simultaneously. Direct archaeological evidence for new foods is lacking or ambiguous, as noted in the previous chapter, but the choices are larger quantities of meat and marrow, greater numbers of nutritious tubers, bulbs, and other underground plant storage organs, or both. Cooking might also

be implied, since it would render both meat and tubers much more digestible (Wrangham et al. 1999). As discussed below, however, unequivocal evidence for fire is so far unknown before 250,000 years ago, long after *H. ergaster* had been replaced by more advanced species.

It was noted above that *H. ergaster* was the first human species to colonize hot, truly arid, highly seasonal environments in Africa, and this may partly explain why the Turkana Boy was built like a modern equatorial East African, with a slim body and long limbs. As the trunk thins, body volume decreases more rapidly than skin area, and greater skin area promotes heat dissipation. Long limbs provide the same benefit. In people like the Inuit (or Eskimo), who must conserve heat, we see the opposite: stocky bodies and short limbs that reduce heat loss. Adaptation to hot, dry conditions can also explain why *H. ergaster* was the first human species to have a forwardly projecting, external nose (Franciscus and Trinkaus 1988). In living humans, the external nose is usually cooler than the central

3.3 **Homo ergaster:** *facial and partial side view of skull KNM-ER 3733 from Koobi Fora, northern Kenya. The skull dates from roughly 1.8 million years ago, and it is one of the key specimens that signals the emergence of* Homo ergaster. *Note the forward projection of the nasal bones, which shows that* H. ergaster, *unlike its predecessors, had a typically human external nose.*

KEY DISCOVERY Discovery of the Turkana Boy

In late August 1984, Kamoya Kimeu was prospecting for fossils along the south bank of the ephemeral Nariokotome River, about 5 km (3 miles) west of Lake Turkana in northern Kenya. Kimeu had long assisted Richard and Meave Leakey in their quest for ancient human bones, and before his retirement in 1993, he had probably found more than anyone else.

On this occasion, his team had been in the field for two weeks, but their extensive fossil haul included no human specimens. They planned to move camp the next day, but while others rested or did chores, Kimeu continued the hunt.

Discovery

He picked a difficult, unpromising spot, a slight rise protected by an acacia tree within a sun-baked gully. The surface was littered with black lava pebbles, and any fossils that had eroded out were likely to have been trampled by local herds of goats and camels. Kimeu's chances seemed slim, but he had overcome such odds before, and he did so again now. He soon spotted a matchbook-sized piece of black bone, hardly distinguishable from the surrounding pebbles, and when he picked it up, he knew that it came from the forehead of an extinct kind of human.

Kimeu's assessment drew the Leakeys and their paleoanthropological colleague, Alan Walker, to the find spot, and over the next four years they led parties that meticulously excavated the deposits nearby. In the end,

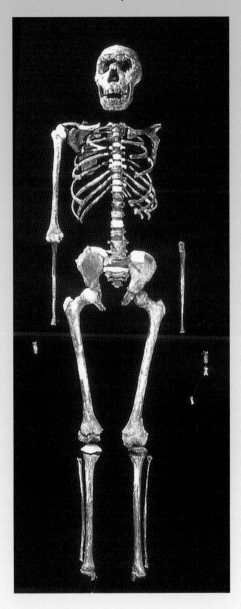

3.4 *The skull and skeleton of the "Turkana Boy." The skeleton has been dated to about 1.6 million years ago and it is the most complete skeleton of any fossil human before 130,000 years ago. It shows that* Homo ergaster, *the species the "boy" represents, had achieved fully human body size and proportions.*

they not only managed to piece together a complete skull, they also recovered most of the skeleton that went with it. The skeleton turned out to represent an adolescent male, whom his discoverers affectionately dubbed the "Turkana Boy."

Dating

Potassium-argon dating on tuffs (volcanic ash layers) that occur above and below the find spot bracket the Turkana Boy's skeleton between 1.33 and 1.64 million years ago. Assuming that the deposits between the tuffs accumulated at a constant rate, the ones that enclose the skeleton formed about 1.56 million years ago.

The excavators failed to recover only some small hand and foot bones, and the skeleton is more complete even than that of "Lucy," the famous australopithecine found in 1974 in deposits that are roughly 3.3 million years old (see Chapter 2). The value of skeletons like Lucy's or the Turkana Boy's cannot be too strongly emphasized, for they inform us of the evolution of human body form and proportions in a way that isolated bones and skull parts never can.

body, and it thus tends to condense moisture that would otherwise be exhaled and so lost during periods of heightened activity. Finally, given that *H. ergaster* was shaped for a hot, dry climate, we can speculate that it was also the first human species to possess a nearly hairless, naked skin. If it had an apelike covering of body hair, it could not have sweated efficiently, and sweating is the primary means by which humans prevent their bodies (and their brains) from overheating.

The other known fossils of *H. ergaster* confirm and extend the inferences from the Turkana Boy. The skulls combine large, forwardly projecting faces, large teeth, conspicuous browridges, receding foreheads, and thick skull walls with typically

human projecting nasal bones [**3.3**]. By modern standards, the braincases are small, with an average internal volume (endocranial capacity) of only about 900 cc. This was obviously large enough to invent new kinds of stone tools, discussed below, but it is also small enough to explain why the tools then changed little over the next million years or so. Judging by the state of eruption of the permanent teeth, the Turkana Boy was no more than 11 or 12 years old when he died (Smith 1993), and judging from the rapid rate at which his dental enamel formed, he might have been as young as 8 (Dean et al. 2001). Yet his stature compares more closely with that of a modern 15-year-old, and his brain with that of a modern 1-year-old. These facts [–> p. 92]

Table 1 *Later Hominins*

Species	Time range (years ago)	Key sites	Key fossils
Homo ergaster	1.8 to perhaps 600,000	East and West Turkana, Kenya; Buia, Eritrea; Bouri, Ethiopia; Swartkrans, South Africa; possibly Dmanisi, Republic of Georgia	East and West Turkana: KNM-ER 3733 (cranium), KNM-ER 3883 (cranium), KNM-WT 15000 (skull and skeleton), KNM-ER 730, 820, and 992 (mandibles); Swartkrans: SK 847 (cranium); Buia: cranium; Bouri: Daka cranium; Dmanisi: D2280, D2282, and D2700 (crania)
Homo erectus	From before 1 million to perhaps 50,000	Sangiran, Sambungmacan, Trinil, and Mojokerto, Indonesia; Zhoukoudian, Lantian, Hexian, Yunxian, and Nanjing, China	Crania, mandibles, and limb bones representing more than 70 individuals from Indonesian and Chinese sites
Homo heidelbergensis	600,000–400,000	Elandsfontein, South Africa; Kabwe (Broken Hill), Zambia; Lake Ndutu, Tanzania; Bodo, Ethiopia; Petralona, Greece; Arago, France	Crania
Homo neanderthalensis	400,000 to 40–30,000	Proto- or Ante- Neanderthals: Sima de los Huesos (Atapuerca), Spain; Swanscombe, England; Steinheim, Germany. Typical or Classic Neanderthals: La Chapelle-aux-Saints, Le Moustier, La Quina, La Ferrassie, Saint Césaire, and other sites in France; Neanderthal, Germany; Spy, Belgium; Krapina, Croatia; Amud, Tabun, and Kebara, Israel; Shanidar, Iraq	Crania, lower jaws, isolated teeth, and limb bones (including some nearly complete skeletons) from sites listed to the left and more than 200 others, mainly in Europe
Homo sapiens	400,000 years ago to present	Early or non-modern (transitional) *H. sapiens*: Jebel Irhoud, Morocco, and Florisbad, South Africa; early modern or near-modern *H. sapiens*: Klasies River Main, South Africa, Herto, Ethiopia, Dar-es-Soltan, Morocco, Skhūl and Qafzeh caves, Israel; modern *H. sapiens*: Cro-Magnon, France, Dolní Vestonice, Czech Republic, Kostenki and Sungir', Russia, and many other sites post-dating 40,000 years ago in Africa and Eurasia	Crania and limb bones

Cranial capacity	Morphology	Associated archaeology	Other
600–910 cc	Crania similar to those of *H. erectus* as described below, but somewhat more high-domed and more lightly built, with thinner cranial walls and a thinner, less projecting browridge; first human species in which body size and proportions clearly approximated those of living people	Contemporary with Oldowan and Developed Oldowan, and with the earliest Acheulean	
810–1250 cc, increasing through time	Long, low, thick-walled skulls with maximum breadth near the base, low, receding frontal bones, and a thick, shelf-like browridge over the eye sockets; short, wide, massive faces mounted in front of the braincase; prognathic jaws and no chins; body skeleton similar to that of living people, but remarkably robust	Flakes and core tools of the east Asian "chopper-chopping tool tradition"	
1225–1300 cc	Crania with large browridges, low receding frontal bones, broad bases, thick walls, and faces mounted in front of the braincase as in *H. erectus*; crania differ from those of *H. erectus* in a tendency towards larger overall size, greater rounding at the rear, outwards expansion of the sides, and broader frontal bones, with more arched (vs. more shelflike) browridges	Late Acheulean hand axes and associated flake tools	The African representatives of *H. heidelbergensis* are sometimes assigned to "early" *H. sapiens* and the European representatives to "early" *Homo neanderthalensis*
1125–1550 cc, increasing through time; the average in Classic Neanderthals approximated 1450 cc	Classic Neanderthals characterized by large heads, massive trunks, and relatively short, powerful limbs; crania exhibit unique specializations, including extraordinary forward projection of the face along the midline; tendency for the braincase to bulge outwards at the sides; depressed elliptical area of roughened bone on the back of the skull; array of bumps and crannies in the vicinity of the mastoid process (bone behind the ear), and a singular configuration of the semicircular canals of the inner ear; Proto-Neanderthals anticipated Classic ones in one or more of these novelties	Late Acheulean hand axes and associated tools with the Proto-Neanderthals; various kinds of Mousterian (or Middle Paleolithic) tools with the Classic ones	
900–2000 cc, averaging around 1350	Crania of modern or near-modern *H. sapiens* tend to be relatively short and high, with relatively small, non-projecting browridges and the face mounted below the forepart of the braincase; they totally lack Neanderthal cranial specializations; crania of early or non-modern *H. sapiens* also lack Neanderthal specializations, and they anticipate modern crania in basic form	Late Acheulean hand axes and associated tools with early or non-modern *H. sapiens*; Middle Stone Age or Mousterian tools with early modern or near-modern *H. sapiens*; Upper Paleolithic and Later Stone Age tools with fully modern *H. sapiens*	If biological change sparked the spread of *H. sapiens* from Africa, only people after 50,000 years ago should be referred to *H. sapiens*. Earlier people whose skulls anticipate those of *H. sapiens* would then have be assigned to another species (such as *H. helmei*, first proposed for the partial skull from Florisbad, South Africa)

suggest that by modern standards he was cognitively limited, and the same was probably true of everyone who lived between 1.8 million and 600,000–500,000 years ago, when brain volume seems to have increased rapidly to an average firmly within the modern range.

When isolated limb bones from other individuals are considered with the Turkana Boy's skeleton, it becomes clear that *Homo ergaster* was not only taller and heavier than earlier hominins, but also that the sexes did not exhibit any major dimorphism, differing no more in size than they do in living people. This stands in sharp contrast to the australopithecines and perhaps *Homo habilis*, in which males tended to be much larger than females (McHenry 1996). In ape species that exhibit a similar degree of sexual dimorphism, males compete intensely for sexually receptive females, and male-female relationships tend to be transitory and non-cooperative. The reduced size difference in *H. ergaster* may signal the onset of a more typically human pattern, in which male-male competition was more muted and male-female relationships were more lasting and mutually supportive.

The Relationship of Homo ergaster *to other* Hominins

Homo ergaster shared large browridges, a receding forehead, thick skull walls, massive prognathic jaws, and other distinctive features with the East Asian hominin *Homo erectus*, which was discovered earlier, in 1891 (see p. 97). When the first fossils of *H. ergaster* were unearthed in the early 1970s, their similarity to the East Asian remains led many specialists to assign them to *H. erectus* (Rightmire 1990). The antiquity of East Asian *H. erectus* is disputed for reasons discussed below, but the key specimens are probably all younger than 1.5 million years old, and the implication would therefore be that *H. erectus* originated in Africa before migrating to Asia.

The similarities between the East African and East Asian fossils are unquestionable, but some specialists have also pointed to subtle and potentially significant differences (Andrews 1984; Clarke 1994). On average, the African skulls tend to be somewhat higher-domed and thinner-walled than their East Asian counterparts, and they also have less massive faces and browridges. In these respects and others, they are more primitive or less specialized, and it is this that underlies their assignment to the distinct species *Homo ergaster*, though the separation of *H. ergaster* and *H. erectus* is not universally agreed.

3.5 *The Mauer Jaw:* *found in a quarry near Heidelberg, Germany, in 1907, it is the nomenclatural ("name") specimen for the species* Homo heidelbergensis *which spread from Africa to Europe about 500,000 years ago.*

The removal of the East African fossils from *H. erectus* to *H. ergaster* would be trivial if we accepted the once common notion that *H. erectus* was directly ancestral to *H. sapiens*, for *H. ergaster* would then be simply an early stage of *H. erectus*. Fossils that date from after 600,000 years ago, however, now indicate that *H. sapiens* evolved in Africa while *H. erectus* continued on largely unchanged in East Asia. Other fossils show that while *H. sapiens* was emerging in Africa, yet another species, *Homo neanderthalensis*, was evolving in Europe. Fossils and genes together suggest that *H. sapiens* and *H. neanderthalensis* last shared a common ancestor about 600,000–500,000 years ago (Hofreiter et al. 2001; Hublin 1996); as noted above, this ancestor has been designated *H. heidelbergensis*, named for a 500,000-year-old mandible (lower jaw) found in 1907 at Mauer, near Heidelberg, Germany. Thus, in form and geologic age, *H. ergaster* is well positioned to be the ancestor not only of *H. erectus* but also, along a different evolutionary branch, of *H. heidelbergensis* and thus of its descendants *H. sapiens* and *H. neanderthalensis*. Figure **3.6** illustrates the probable evolutionary relationships.

The ancestry of *Homo ergaster* is murky, but it may have evolved suddenly from *H. habilis* (or from one its constituent species, such as *H. rudolfensis*, if this split is eventually confirmed) in an adaptive response to a sharp increase in aridity and rainfall seasonality that occurred across eastern Africa about 1.7 million years ago. Alternatively, as the previous chapter pointed out, future research may reveal a bush of human species between 3 million and 2 million years ago, in which case *H. ergaster* could represent a branch totally separate from the variants of *H. habilis*. At Olduvai Gorge and perhaps other East African sites, *H. habilis* or one its variants may have persisted until 1.6 million years ago, but thereafter *H. ergaster* survived alone. Its history after 1 million years ago is debatable, because few relevant fossils are known, but on present evidence, it may have persisted in Africa largely unchanged until 600,000 years ago, when brain size increased rapidly and *H. heidelbergensis* emerged.

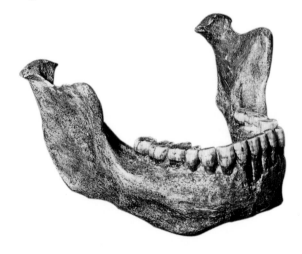

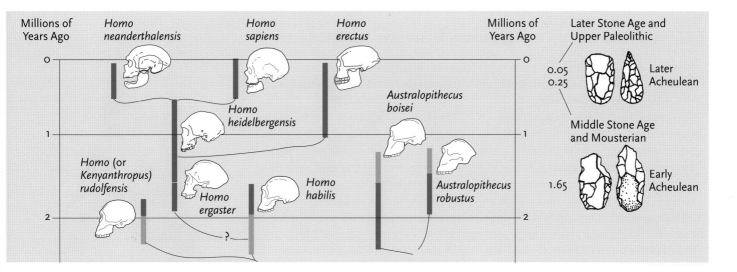

The Acheulean

A small brain surely means that *Homo ergaster* was less intelligent than people living today, and if brain size were all we had to go by, we might wonder if it differed cognitively from *H. habilis* or its variants. We also have artifacts, however, which show that it did. The tools imply a behavioral advance that helps us to understand how *H. ergaster* was able to colonize the more arid, seasonal environments to which it was physiologically adapted, and how it became the first human species to expand out of Africa.

The Acheulean Hand Axe Tradition

The previous chapter showed that the first toolmakers, the Oldowan people, had mastered the mechanics of stone flaking and were skilled at producing sharp-edged flakes that could slice through hide or strip flesh from bones. At the same time, they appear to have made little or no effort to shape the core forms from which they struck flakes, and to the extent that they used core forms, it was perhaps mainly as hammers to crack bones for marrow. For this purpose, core shape didn't matter very much. *H. ergaster*, however, initiated a tradition in which core forms were often deliberately, even meticulously shaped, and shape obviously mattered a lot.

The characteristic artifact of the new tradition was the **hand axe** or biface – a flat cobble or large flake that was more or less completely flaked over both surfaces (hence the term biface) to

3.6 *Human phylogeny:* *the family tree of the hominins after the emergence of the genus* Homo *about 2.5 million years ago. Flaked stone tools also appeared about 2.5 million years ago, and the right-hand column shows the large-scale categories to which archaeologists assign Paleolithic artifact assemblages.*

produce a sharp edge around the entire periphery [**3.7–3.10**]. Many hand axes resemble large teardrops, as they narrow from a broad base or butt at one end to a rounded point at the other. Ovals, triangles, and other forms are also common, and in some places, hand axe-makers produced pieces with a straight, sharp, guillotine-like edge opposite the butt [**3.11**]. Archaeologists often call such pieces cleavers to distinguish them from hand axes, on which one end tends to be more pointed. Together, hand axes, cleavers, and similar large bifacial tools define the Acheulean cultural tradition [see box: The Acheulean Hand Axe Tradition, p. 94], which spanned more than a million years and three continents.

Archaeologists commonly assign European and Southwest Asian Acheulean assemblages to the Lower Paleolithic, and those in Africa to the Earlier Stone Age (or ESA); the periods are more or less contemporaneous, the names merely reflecting commonly used terminology in the two

3.7, 3.8 *The Acheulean hand axe:* *a diagram to show the method of manufacture of an Acheulean hand axe and an example from Saint Acheul, France, the site that give the tradition its name. Hand axes were almost completely flaked over both surfaces, hence the term biface, to produce deliberately and meticulously shaped forms.*

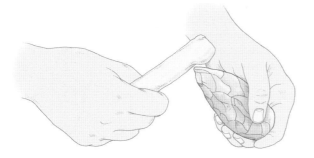

KEY DISCOVERY The Acheulean Hand Axe Tradition

John Frere (1740–1807), the great-great-grandfather of Mary Leakey, is sometimes credited as the first person to recognize the human origin and great antiquity of hand axes (Oakley 1964). In 1797, he sent a letter to the Society of Antiquaries in London, describing two carefully crafted hand axes he had recovered from ancient lake deposits at Hoxne in Suffolk, England. Bones of extinct animals occurred nearby, and Frere concluded that the hand axes had been "used by people who had not the use of metals" and belonged "to a very ancient period indeed, even beyond the present world."

Frere's archaeological colleagues largely ignored his opinion, and it was the French customs official Jacques Boucher de Perthes (1788–1868) who first forced the issue. Between about 1836 and 1846, de Perthes collected hand axes and bones of extinct mammals from ancient gravels of the Somme River near the town of Abbeville in northern France. He concluded that, "In spite of their imperfection, these rude stones prove the [ancient] existence of man as surely as a whole Louvre would have done."

His claims were initially spurned, but they gained credibility in 1854 when Dr Rigollot, a distinguished and previously vocal skeptic, began finding similar flint axes in gravels near Saint Acheul, a suburb of Amiens. In 1858, the eminent British geologist Joseph Prestwich visited Abbeville and Saint Acheul to check the claims for himself. He came away convinced, and the case was made. Archaeologists subsequently assigned ancient tool assemblages with hand axes to the Acheulean cultural or industrial tradition, named for the prolific locality at Saint Acheul.

Later, when similar artifacts were recognized in Africa, they were also assigned to the Acheulean, and we now know that the Acheulean was present in Africa long before it reached Europe, where it was almost certainly introduced by *Homo heidelbergensis*.

3.9 *Hand axe found by John Frere at Hoxne, Suffolk, England. He was probably the first to propose in print that prehistoric people produced such artifacts.*

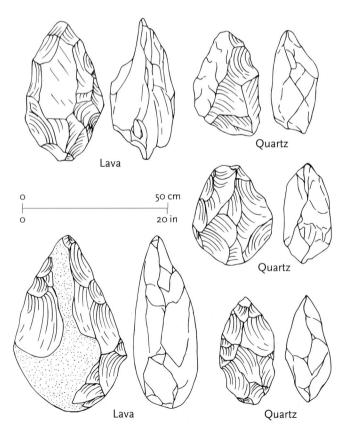

Lava

Quartz

Quartz

Lava

Quartz

0 ———— 50 cm
0 ———— 20 in

regions. The oldest known Acheulean tools are dated to 1.65 million years ago, and they come from the same West Turkana region of northern Kenya that provided the Turkana Boy, though not from the same site (Roche and Kibunjia 1994). Acheulean artifacts are also well documented at 1.5 to 1.4 million years ago at Konso in southern Ethiopia, on the Karari Escarpment east of Lake Turkana in northern Kenya, and at Peninj (Lake Natron) near Olduvai Gorge in northern Tanzania (Asfaw et al. 1992). In each case, potassium-argon dating has verified their antiquity just as securely as it demonstrates the

3.10, 3.11 *Acheulean tools: Early Acheulean hand axes from site TK in Upper Bed II, Olduvai Gorge (left), and a Late Acheulean cleaver from Elandsfontein, South Africa (right). Note that the Late Acheulean artifact is more extensively flaked and significantly thinner than the early Acheulean pieces.*

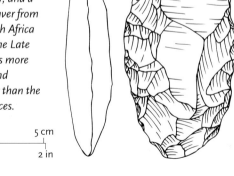

0 ———— 5 cm
0 ———— 2 in

presence of *H. ergaster* by 1.8 to 1.7 million years ago, and the close correspondence between the oldest *H. ergaster* and the oldest Acheulean is probably not coincidental.

Peninj has provided a mandible of the robust australopithecine *Australopithecus (Paranthropus) boisei*, but this shows only that the robust australopithecines persisted after *H. ergaster* emerged, not that robust australopithecines necessarily made Acheulean tools. Konso has provided an upper third molar and the left half of a mandible with four teeth from *H. ergaster*, and *H. ergaster* is the more likely toolmaker. This is not only because it had a larger brain than the robust australopithecines, but also because Acheulean tools continue on largely unchanged after 1 million years ago, by which time the robust australopithecines had become extinct.

The **Acheulean industry** surely developed from the Oldowan, and the oldest Acheulean assemblages often contain numerous Oldowan-style core forms and flakes (see Chapter 2, p. 70) alongside Acheulean hand axes. In a broad sense, the Oldowan core forms anticipate Acheulean bifaces, but no Oldowan or Acheulean assemblage contains tools that are truly intermediate between the two, and the biface concept seems to have appeared abruptly in a kind of punctuational event like the one that may have produced *H. ergaster*. The earliest makers of bifaces made one other noteworthy discovery that was often tied to biface manufacture: they learned how to strike large flakes, sometimes 30 cm (1 ft) or more in length, from large boulders,

and it was from these that they often made hand axes and cleavers. Ancient stone tool assemblages that contain large flakes can be assigned to the Acheulean even on those occasions when, perhaps by chance, the assemblages lack hand axes.

Hand Axe Function

The term "hand axe" implies that each piece was hand-held and used for chopping. Nonetheless, many hand axes are far too large and unwieldy for this, and their precise use remains conjectural. The puzzle is heightened at such sites as Melka Kunturé in Ethiopia, Olorgesailie in Kenya, Isimila in Tanzania, and Kalambo Falls in Zambia, where hand axes occur by the hundreds, often crowded close together and with no obvious signs of use. Such sites have prompted Marek Kohn and Steven Mithen (1999) to propose that the hand axe may have been the Acheulean equivalent of a male peacock's plumage – an impressive emblem for attracting mates. When a female saw a large, well-made biface in the hands of its maker, she might have concluded that he possessed just the determination, coordination, and strength needed to father successful offspring. Having obtained a mate, a male might simply discard the badge of his success, alongside others that had already served their purpose.

3.12 *Olorgesailie:* *a dense scatter of hand axes and other artifacts beneath the catwalk at the Olorgesailie Acheulean site, Kenya.*

3.13, 3.14 The Levallois technique: *this is a method of stone flaking by which a core was deliberately prepared (far right) so that a flake of predetermined size and shape could be removed with a single blow. The Levallois technique was practiced by people of various cultures and traditions, including the late Acheuleans.*

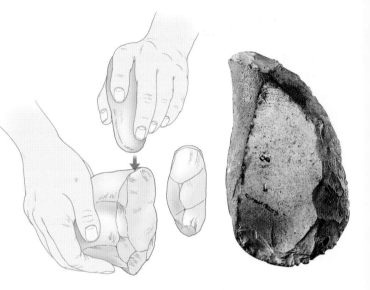

The mate selection hypothesis cannot be proven wrong, but sites with large concentrations of seemingly unused hand axes are less common than ones where hand axes are rarer and sometimes do show signs of use. Since the tools come in a wide variety of sizes and shapes, the probability is that they served multiple utilitarian functions. Some of the more carefully shaped, symmetric examples may have been hurled at game (prey) like a discus (Calvin 2002); other, more casually made, pieces may have served simply as portable sources of sharp-edged flakes (Jelinek 1977); and yet others could have been used to chop or scrape wood. Experiments have also shown that hand axes make effective butchering tools, particularly for dismembering the carcasses of elephants or other large animals (Jones 1980). The truth is that hand axes may have been used for every imaginable purpose, and the type probably had more in common with a Swiss Army knife than with a peacock's tail.

Variation within the Acheulean Tradition

Once in place, the Acheulean industry was remarkably conservative, and it is often said that it persisted largely unchanged from its inception at roughly 1.65 million years ago until its end about 250,000 years ago. Glynn Isaac (1977), who analyzed the Acheulean artifacts from a deeply stratified sequence at Olorgesailie, Kenya [**3.12**], remarked that the Acheulean displays a "variable sameness" and strikes "even enthusiasts as monotonous." By "variable sameness" he meant that changes in hand axe form seem to have been largely random from layer to layer or time to time, and there is no obvious directional trend. Often, where hand axes in one assemblage appear more refined than they do in another, the reason may be that the people had different raw materials at their disposal. Flint or chert, for example, is usually much easier to flake than volcanic rock, and where people could get large enough pieces of flint, their hand axes will tend to appear more finely made for this reason alone.

Still, despite the apparent sameness over long periods, early and late Acheulean artifact assemblages do differ in some important respects. Early Acheulean hand axes tend to be much thicker, less extensively trimmed, and less symmetrical. They were commonly shaped by fewer than ten flake removals, and the flake scars were usually deep (Mason 1962). Modern experiments indicate that such scars result from the use of hard (i.e., stone) hammers. Late Acheulean hand axes are often equally crude, but many are remarkably thin and extensively trimmed, and they are highly symmetric not just in plan form, but also when viewed edge-on. The final flake scars are shallow and flat, and replication efforts indicate that they were probably produced with soft (i.e., wooden or bone) hammers.

In addition, late Acheulean hand axes are often accompanied by more refined flake tools that foreshadow those of the Mousterian and Middle Stone Age (or MSA) people who came after the Acheuleans (discussed in Chapter 4). Mousterian and MSA assemblages differ from Acheulean ones primarily in the absence of large hand axes and other large bifacial tools. Like Mousterian people (who inhabited Europe and Asia between around 250,000 and 50,000–40,000 years ago) and Middle Stone Age people (who occupied Africa at around the same time), late Acheuleans knew how to prepare a core so that it would provide a flake of predetermined size and shape (Volman 1984). Archaeologists call such deliberate core preparation the **Levallois technique** [**3.13, 3.14**], named for a western suburb of Paris where prepared cores were found and recognized in the latter part of the 19th century. The term Levallois refers strictly to a method of stone flaking, not to a culture or tradition (Bordes 1968), and Levallois flaking was practiced by people of various cultures or traditions, including, especially, the late Acheuleans and their Mousterian and MSA successors. At any given time, people in some places employed the technique frequently, while people in others hardly used it at all. Most of the variation probably reflects differences in the availability of suitable stone raw material.

Most Acheulean assemblages are only weakly dated within the long Acheulean time-span, but future research may show that there were actually two periods of Acheulean stability, representing the early and late Acheulean respectively. They may have been separated by a short burst of relatively rapid artifactual change roughly 600,000 years ago, which resulted in the more refined hand axes of the late Acheulean and which coincided with the emergence of *Homo heidelbergensis*.

Homo erectus

Homo ergaster was the first human species to expand from Africa, but the timing of its dispersal is controversial. To understand why, we must back up a little and address the discovery and dating of its East Asian descendant, *Homo erectus*. The story begins with the Dutch physician and visionary Eugène Dubois (1858–1941) (Theunissen 1989).

The Discovery and Dating of *Homo erectus* in Java

Dubois was born in 1858, a year before Darwin published his landmark classic *On the Origin of Species*, in which he showed how natural selection could drive evolutionary change. Dubois developed a passion for human evolution, and he became the first professional paleoanthropologist when he decided to search full-time for human fossils. He focused on Indonesia, which was then a Dutch colony and which he and others reasoned was a logical place to start, since it still contained apes that might broadly resemble proto-humans. He arrived in Indonesia in December 1887, and in October 1891 found what he was looking for in river deposits near the village of **Trinil** on the Solo River in central Java. Here, together with bones of ancient animals, he discovered a low-domed, angular, thick-walled human skullcap with a large shelflike browridge [**3.15, 3.16**]. In August 1892, in what he thought were the same deposits, he encountered a nearly complete human femur (thigh bone) that was fully modern in every anatomical respect. The femur and the skullcap convinced him that he had discovered an erect, apelike transitional form between apes and humans, and in 1894 he decided to call it *Pithecanthropus erectus* ("erect ape man"). It was later transferred to *Homo erectus* by scientists who benefited from a much fuller fossil record and a more contemplative approach to the use of species names (Mayr 1950). The implication of the transfer was that *Homo erectus* did not differ from living people (*Homo sapiens*) as much as

Dubois believed. The change in naming is partly a matter of taste, however, and the important point is that *H. erectus* was far removed from its ape ancestors in both anatomy and time.

Dubois's claim for *Pithecanthropus* met broad resistance, anticipating the negative reaction that Raymond Dart received when he claimed that his newly discovered *Australopithecus africanus* was relevant to human ancestry [see Discovering the "Ape Men" box, Chapter 2, p. 59]. Dubois was discouraged, and after his return to the Netherlands in 1895 he gave up the search for human fossils. He was fully vindicated only from 1936 onwards, when G. H. R. von Koenigswald (1902–1982) (1975) described a second skull of *Pithecanthropus* from **Mojokerto** in eastern Java. The Mojokerto specimen represented a child who probably died before its second birthday, but it still exhibited incipient browridges, a flat, receding forehead, an angular (as opposed to rounded) occipital region (i.e., rear profile), and other features that recalled Dubois's Trinil find.

Then, between 1937 and 1941, von Koenigswald reported three additional partial adult skulls, some fragmentary mandibles, and isolated teeth from **Sangiran**, about 50 km (30 miles) up the Solo River from Trinil. Associated animal bones suggested that two of the Sangiran skulls were about the same age as the Trinil skull, and that the third was somewhat older. Between 1952 and 1978, the deposits at Sangiran produced three additional skulls, some skull fragments, and six partial mandibles, and there have been sporadic discoveries since.

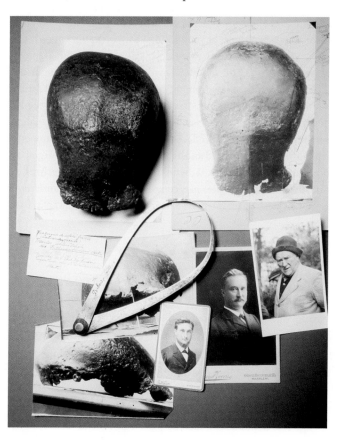

3.15, 3.16 *The discovery of* **Homo erectus:** *(above) a side view of the Trinil skullcap, showing the protruding browridge, sloping forehead (frontal bone), and angular rear region (occiput) that characterize* Homo erectus. *(Right) Its principal discoverer was Eugène Dubois, who is shown in the middle of the photo, along with a top view of the skullcap and other people important in its discovery and interpretation.*

KEY CONTROVERSY The Dating of Javan *Homo erectus*

In the Sangiran-Trinil area of central Java, *Homo erectus* fossils are commonly attributed to two successive stratigraphic units, each with its own distinctive set of animal species (Leinders et al. 1985; Theunissen et al. 1990). The older (lower) unit, which has provided relatively few *H. erectus* remains, comprises the Pucangan (or Putjangan) Beds with the Djetis (Jetis) fauna; the younger (upper) unit, which has provided most of the *H. erectus* fossils, comprises the Kabuh Beds with the Trinil fauna.

Dating Problems

Dates on volcanic tuffs from the Pucangan Beds range from 2 million to 570,000 years ago, while dates on tuffs and pumices from the Kabuh Beds vary between 1.6 million and 470,000 years ago (de Vos et al. 1994; Swisher et al. 1994; Larick et al. 2001).

The discrepancy is glaring, and it extends to paleomagnetic readings that contradict some of the dates. Finally, there are potassium-argon determinations that indicate that volcanic mudflows (lahars) below the Pucangan Beds formed only 1.7 million years ago (Sémah et al. 2000). If this age is correct, the Pucangan Beds must be younger than 1.7 million years old, and the *H. erectus* fossils must all be too, since the mudflows mark the first full emergence of Java from the sea.

Much of the dating inconsistency probably reflects stratigraphic reversals and other complications that were introduced when earth movements deformed and distorted the Pucangan and Kabuh Beds. With this in mind, the best age estimates may come from the southeastern quadrant of the Sangiran

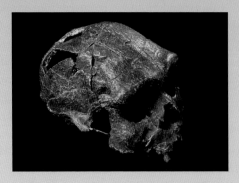

3.17 *Sangiran 17, the most complete skull of* Homo erectus *yet found. Note the long, low shape of the forehead, the powerfully built browridge, and the far forward protrusion of the upper jaw, all of which help to define* Homo erectus.

region, where deformation and distortion are minimal. In this quadrant, the Pucangan and Kabuh Beds are known as the Sangiran and Bapang Formations respectively, and they have provided nearly 80 *Homo erectus* fossils. The large majority are thought to come from the Bapang Formation, though none were found in the kind of carefully monitored fieldwork that produced most *H. ergaster* and other early human fossils in eastern Africa.

Still, it may be meaningful that a stratigraphically consistent suite of potassium-argon determinations places the fossil-bearing Bapang sediments between about 1.5 and 1 million years ago (Larick et al. 2001). The underlying Sangiran sediments must then be older than 1.5 million years, and this would support a widely publicized potassium-argon date of 1.66 million years on pumice overlying a central Sangiran layer that produced an *H. erectus* maxilla (upper jaw) and skullcap in 1978 (Swisher et al. 1994).

However, the researchers who produced the Bapang dates argue that the Sangiran Formation contains no pumice, and others have suggested that the dated pumice actually came from an underlying mudflow that was locally uplifted, so that it appeared to overlie the *H. erectus* find spot (Sémah et al. 2000).

Tektites

The Bapang dates may themselves be problematic, if it is true that a layer deep within the Bapang Formation contains tektites (Langbroek and Roebroeks 2000). These are small glassy objects that rained down widely over Southeast Asia following a large asteroid impact. They can be dated by the potassium-argon and fission track methods, and in every instance where dating has been done, the tektites turn out be about 800,000 years old (Hou et al. 2000). Their presence deep within the Bapang Formation would imply that the majority of *H. erectus* fossils could be no older than 800,000 years. Still, a 1.5–1.1 million year age estimate is broadly consistent with a 1.6–1.1 million year estimate for humans in China, and the evidence suggests that *H. ergaster* may have reached eastern Asia not long after it emerged in Africa.

Passage to Java could have occurred during an early Pleistocene glaciation, when a drop in sea level connected Java directly to the Southeast Asian mainland. The fossil mammals associated with *H. erectus* in Java demonstrate repeated connections under relatively dry, glacial conditions (Storm 2001). The times of connection probably promoted *H. erectus* populations, because forest cover shrank and more food became available at ground level.

Java is a land of volcanoes, and, in theory, it offers the same potential to date fossils as eastern Africa, since the fossil-bearing deposits often contain pumices (light porous rocks formed from solidified lava) or tuffs (layers of compacted lava particles or "ash") that can be dated by the potassium-argon method and by the less commonly applied, but equally reliable fission-track method, both described in the previous chapter [see Dating Early Hominins and their Archaeology box, pp. 74–75]. The deposits can also be placed in time at least roughly by paleomagnetism. As noted above also, the earth's magnetic field has pointed north for the last 790,000 years, which means that a layer that recorded a south orientation would have to be older than this. Potassium-argon and paleomagnetism have both been widely applied to Javan deposits that contain *H. erectus* fossils, but the results are controversial, partly because the regional stratigraphy is highly complex, and partly because the stratigraphic positions of the key fossils are so poorly known.

Based on different evaluations of the same dates, some specialists believe that *H. erectus* reached Java only after 1 million years ago, while others argue for a much earlier time, by 1.65 million years or before [see box: The Dating of Javan *Homo erectus*]. The difference has profound implications for human evolution. An arrival no more than 1 million years ago is fully consistent with the view offered here that *H. ergaster* was the first human species to leave Africa, and that it then gave rise to *H. erectus* in eastern Asia. In contrast, an arrival by 1.65 million years ago might mean that *H. ergaster* and *H. erectus* evolved separately from a shared ancestor that left Africa before *H. ergaster* appeared. It could even be used to support the possibility that an *H. erectus* population migrated from Asia to Africa and gave rise to *H. ergaster*.

The Discovery and Dating of Homo erectus in China

There is an equally important set of *Homo erectus* fossils from China, and they tell a similar story to the Indonesian ones. The discovery of *H. erectus* in China stems from the age-old Chinese custom of pulverizing fossils for medicinal use (Shapiro 1974). In 1899, a European doctor found a probable human tooth among fossils in a Beijing (then Peking) drugstore, and the search for its origin led paleontologists to a rich complex of fossil-bearing limestone caves and fissures on the slopes of Longghushan ("Dragon Bone Hill"), about 40 km (24 miles) southwest of Beijing, near the village of **Zhoukoudian**. In 1921, the Swedish geologist J. G. Andersson (1874–1960) began excavating in a collapsed cave at Zhoukoudian that was particularly intriguing, not only for its fossils, but also for quartz fragments that prehistoric people must have introduced. The site was called Locality 1 to distinguish it from other fossil-bearing caves nearby.

Andersson's excavations produced two human teeth that came to the attention of Davidson Black (1884–1933), a Canadian anatomist who was teaching at the Peking Union Medical School, and in 1927, excavation began again at Locality 1. Black died in 1933, and in 1935 he was succeeded by Franz Weidenreich (1873–1948), an eminent German anatomist. Excavations continued until 1937, and they eventually netted 5 more or less complete human braincases, 9 large braincase fragments, 6 facial fragments, 14 partial mandibles, 147 isolated teeth, and 11 limb bones [3.18, 3.19]. The specimens represented more than 40 individuals of both sexes and various ages.

Black had assigned the Locality 1 fossils to a new species, called *Sinanthropus pekinensis* ("Peking Chinese man"). In 1939,

3.18 Indonesian and Zhoukoudian Homo erectus: *Franz Weidenreich's restorations of* Homo erectus *skulls from Sangiran in Java and Zhoukoudian Locality 1. The features that unite the Sangiran and Zhoukoudian skulls in* H. erectus *include a thick, forwardly projecting, shelflike browridge; a large face with pronounced forward projection of the jaws; a long, low, flat braincase; a keel or gable along the top of the skull; and a highly angulated rear with a prominent occipital bar (torus).*

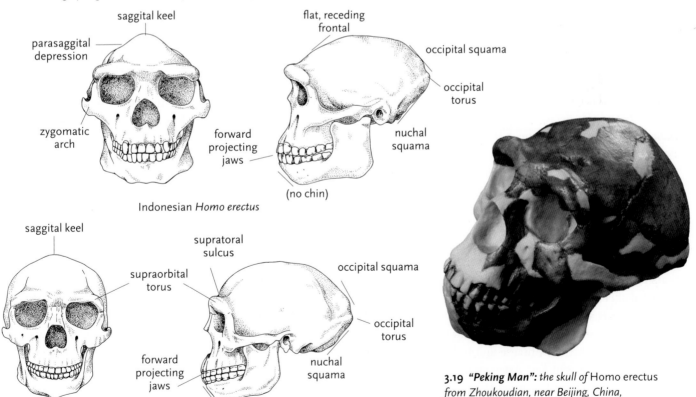

3.19 "Peking Man": *the skull of* Homo erectus *from Zhoukoudian, near Beijing, China, reconstructed from various parts; missing parts are represented by white plaster.*

3.20 *Zhoukoudian artifacts:* *sandstone and quartz artifacts associated with* Homo erectus *at Zhoukoudian Locality 1. The Zhoukoudian assemblage lacks hand axes and other typical Acheulean tools found at many sites in Africa, western Asia, and Europe, and probably represents a totally distinct, contemporaneous artifact tradition that was widespread in eastern Asia.*

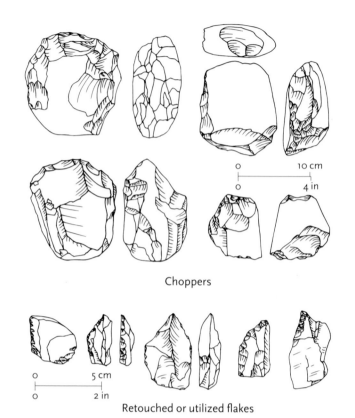

Choppers

Retouched or utilized flakes

Weidenreich and von Koenigswald compared the *Sinanthropus* fossils to those of Javan *Pithecanthropus*, and concluded that the skulls were very similar in their shelflike browridges, receding foreheads, low-domed braincases, thick, inwardly-sloping skull walls, and other features (von Koenigswald and Weidenreich 1939) [**3.18**]. For the sake of convenience, Weidenreich continued to call them *Sinanthropus pekinensis* and *Pithecanthropus erectus*, but he noted that they could be regarded as variants of a single primitive human species, *Homo erectus*. This anticipated a professional consensus that crystallized in the 1960s and continues to the present day.

The Locality 1 fossils were lost at the beginning of World War II, but Weidenreich had described them in detailed monographs and had prepared an excellent set of plaster replicas, now housed at the American Museum of Natural History in New York City. Excavations at Locality 1 produced a few additional fragmentary *H. erectus* fossils between 1949 and 1966, but following the original Locality 1 excavations, most diagnostic *H. erectus* fossils have come from other sites scattered across east-central China (Wu and Poirier 1995).

The Chinese *Homo erectus* fossils have been dated to between 800,000 and 400,000 years ago, mainly by paleomagnetism, associated mammal species (biostratigraphy), and climatic shifts recorded in the enclosing deposits. "Climate dating" depends on the assumption that local shifts can be accurately correlated with the dated sequence of global climate changes recorded in deep-sea deposits. The sum of the evidence suggests that the oldest Chinese *H. erectus* fossil is probably a skull from Gongwangling in Lantian County, Shaanxi Province, dated to 800,000–750,000 years ago or before. The youngest fossils come from Zhoukoudian Locality 1 and from Lontandong Cave in Hexian County, Anhui Province, where at least some specimens accumulated after 500,000 years ago.

Artifact occurrences discussed in the next section suggest that *H. erectus* may in fact have arrived in China by 1.6 million years ago, and dates from Chinese fossil sites indicate that it persisted after other kinds of people had emerged in the West. The Chinese *H. erectus* fossils differ from the Indonesian ones in some details, and the differences appear to grow with time. This may mean that the Chinese and Indonesian specimens represent two divergent East Asian evolutionary lineages, but the basic point remains the same: *Homo erectus* or its variants followed a separate evolutionary trajectory from like-aged populations in Africa and Europe.

The Archaeology of Chinese Homo erectus

China adds a dimension to the *Homo erectus* story that Java lacks, for unlike Java, China has provided numerous stone artifacts produced by local *H. erectus* populations. At most sites, the artifacts are attributed to *H. erectus* based only on similar geologic antiquity, but artifacts are directly associated with *H. erectus* fossils at the Lantian sites and especially at Zhoukoudian Locality 1 [**3.20**]. The oldest known artifacts come from the **Nihewan Basin**, about 150 km (90 miles) west of Beijing. The basin once housed a large lake, and the artifacts accumulated with fragmentary animal bones at sites on the lake margins. Paleomagnetic analysis, combined with the estimated rate at which the lake sediments accumulated, suggest that the oldest known artifact occurrence dates to about 1.6 million years ago (Zhu et al. 2004). The artifacts comprise crudely flaked stones, the human (versus natural) origin of which depends as much on their occurrence in fine-grained lake deposits as it does on their form; if they are genuinely artifactual and their age has been correctly assessed, they imply that human colonization of northeast Asia occurred at a remarkably early date.

It follows that we should expect to find equally early evidence for human presence on the eastward route from Africa, perhaps especially in the more temperate parts of Central Asia, and to the south, in southern China and Indonesia. Equally ancient discoveries in these regions are crucial for the acceptance of the remarkably old Nihewan dates and of their extraordinary implications for early human evolution.

In the 1940s, Hallam L. Movius (1907–1987) (1948) noted that neither Chinese artifact assemblages nor any others discovered east of northern India included hand axes. Instead, they tend to be characterized by less formal types of core tools and associated flakes. The larger pieces are sometimes as extensively flaked and shaped as Acheulean hand axes, and some that have been dated to 800,000 years ago in the Bose Basin of Guangxi Province in southern China recall contemporaneous African hand axes in the extent and quality of working (Hou et al. 2000); nevertheless, true hand axes remain unknown in East Asia. The contrast with Africa and western Eurasia does not depend on excavation, since in Europe and especially Africa, hand axes are often found on the surface, either because they have been eroded from their burial places or because they were never buried to begin with.

Movius drew a rough line through northern India separating the expansive Acheulean tradition of Africa, Europe, and western Asia from the non-Acheulean tradition in eastern and southeastern Asia [**3.21**]. Insofar as this line has stood the test of time, it sends the same message as the fossils, which is that from the time hominins first arrived in eastern Asia, they followed a different evolutionary track from their African and European contemporaries. If some of the Chinese and Javan dates that were discussed previously mean that people had colonized East and Southeast Asia by 1.3 million years ago, then hand axes might be absent because the colonists' ancestors left Africa before hand axes were invented. However, it is also possible that if these ancestors left after hand axes appeared, they may have passed through a kind of "technological bottleneck," perhaps a large region that lacked suitable raw material for hand axe manufacture, and by the time they emerged, they had lost the hand axe habit (Schick and Toth 1993). It was clearly not essential to their continued success, and thereafter, isolation by distance could have prevented its reintroduction. Such isolation probably explains why a strong artifactual contrast persisted between East and West even after 250,000 years ago, when humans in the West had given up hand axe manufacture.

The Dispersion of *Homo ergaster* and the Fate of *Homo erectus*

Artifacts and East Asian *Homo erectus* fossils indicate, therefore, that a human species had left Africa before 1 million years ago, and this species was almost certainly *Homo ergaster*. But aside from the question of who the hominins were, we may also ask why they left and what route(s) they took. Unlike many other questions in paleoanthropology, these are relatively easy to answer. Archaeology shows that about 1.5 million years ago, shortly after *H. ergaster* appeared in Africa, people more intensively occupied the drier peripheries of lake basins on the floor of the Great Rift Valley (Harris 1983), and they colonized the Ethiopian high plateau at 2300–2400 m (7600–7900 ft) above sea level for the first time (Clark and Kurashina 1979). By 1 million years ago, they had fully colonized the extreme northern and southern margins of Africa. The Sahara Desert might seem to provide an impenetrable barrier to movement northwards, but during the long Acheulean time interval, there were numerous periods when it was somewhat moister and more hospitable, and Acheulean people penetrated it readily (Wendorf and Schild 1980).

As to how and why people expanded through Africa and beyond, they almost certainly did so automatically, simply because their physiology and technology allowed them to colonize territories that no one had occupied before. A group on the periphery of the human range would periodically outgrow its resource base, and a splinter party would then establish itself in empty territory next door. Such a party probably rarely moved far, but given time, the splintering process would inevitably have brought humans to the northeastern corner of Africa. From there, members of a breakaway group would have colonized the southwestern corner of Asia without even knowing that they had left Africa. From southwestern Asia, the same process of population budding would inevitably lead other groups eastward toward China and Indonesia or northward and westward toward Europe [see box: Did *Homo ergaster* Disperse Partly by Boat?, p. 102].

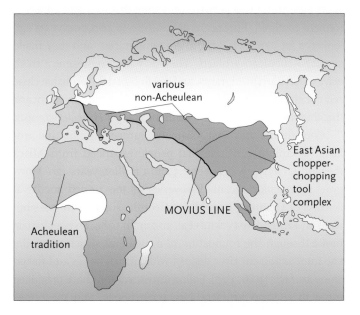

3.21 The Movius Line: *map showing the extent of the occupied world between roughly 1.7 million and 400,000 years ago. The stone artifacts from this time interval divide broadly between two distinct geographic traditions – the hand axe or Acheulean industrial tradition in Africa, western Asia, and Europe, and the chopper-chopping tool complexes in northern India. This division is commonly known as the "Movius Line" after the person who first identified it.*

KEY CONTROVERSY Did *Homo ergaster* Disperse Partly by Boat?

In theory, *Homo ergaster* could have dispersed to Eurasia not only by land through southwestern Asia, but also across the Strait of Gibraltar, across the Bab-el-Mandeb Strait at the southern end of the Red Sea, or even by island hopping across the central part of the Mediterranean Sea. Each of these routes would require seaworthy boats, however, even during those repeated intervals when the great continental ice sheets sucked water from the world ocean, and sea level dropped by 140 m (460 ft) or more. With one arguable exception, there is no evidence for such boats before 40,000 years ago, when modern humans must have used them to cross the sea from Southeast Asia to Australia.

The exception comes from the site of Mata Menge on the Indonesian island of Flores, east of Java. Flores would have been joined to

nearby islands during glacial intervals, when sea level fell and Java was joined to the Southeast Asian mainland, but the Flores cluster would always have been separated from Java by a 19-km (11-mile) wide deep-water strait.

Mata Menge has provided 20 basalt artifacts (flakes and fractured pebbles) associated with bones of *Stegodon trigonocephalus*, an extinct relative of the elephants that probably arrived in Java about the same time as *Homo erectus*. Fission-track dating (see Dating Early Hominins and their Archaeology box, pp. 74–75) suggests that the Mata Menge deposits formed 880,000–800,000 years ago, while paleomagnetism places them somewhat after 790,000 years ago (Morwood et al. 1998). At either time, *H. erectus* would be the presumed

maker of the basalt artifacts, and if the current strait were in place, people could have arrived only by boat. The presence of stegodon, however, suggests that the strait must have been much narrower, or even that it had been replaced by a transitory land bridge (Groves 1996).

Another reason for skepticism about the possibility that humans floated across to Flores is that proof of a human (as opposed to geologic) origin of the artifacts at Mata Menge depends not so much on their form as on their occurrence in fine-grained river deposits, where they are unlikely to have accumulated naturally. So long as Mata Menge remains unique, it will not be compelling, and additional sites will be necessary to demonstrate that *H. ergaster* or *H. erectus* could have dispersed by boat.

The Initial Expansion of Homo ergaster from Africa

Assuming that *Homo ergaster* lacked boats, its first stop on departing Africa would have been in what is presently Israel. It is not surprising, therefore, that Israel contains the oldest firmly documented Acheulean site outside of Africa. This occurs at 'Ubeidiya in the Jordan Rift Valley (Bar-Yosef and Belfer-Cohen 2001), where ancient lake and river deposits have provided nearly 8000 flaked stones. The tools include hand axes and other pieces that closely resemble early Acheulean artifacts from Olduvai Gorge and other African sites. They have been bracketed in the interval between 1.4 and 1 million years ago by associated mammal fossils, paleomagnetism, and potassium-argon dating of an overlying lava flow.

Most of the mammal species found at 'Ubeidiya are Eurasian, but some are African, and this reminds us of just how close Israel is to Africa. During the long time-span of human evolution, Israel was repeatedly invaded by African animal species, mainly during the warmer interglacial periods between the longer times of great ice sheet expansion. (The next chapter discusses the last such warm period, between about 125,000 and 90,000 years ago, when African immigrants included early modern or near-modern humans.) This raises the possibility that 'Ubeidiya marks a slight, transient ecological enlargement of Africa more than a true human dispersal to Eurasia. To demonstrate a genuine dispersal, we have to look further afield.

The Expansion of Homo ergaster to Eurasia: The Dmanisi Discoveries

Eastern Asia demonstrates that such a dispersal must have occurred by 1 million years ago and perhaps much earlier. Europe may have been occupied at the same time, but the oldest widely accepted evidence for human colonization there is only about 800,000 years old. The evidence comes from the Gran Dolina, a cave at Atapuerca, near Burgos, Spain, which is discussed below. Elsewhere in Europe, there is little or no indication that hominins were present before about 500,000 years ago, and it was perhaps only then that they gained a permanent foothold. Europeans at 500,000 to 400,000 years ago looked a lot like their African contemporaries, and they made similar Acheulean artifacts. They may thus represent a fresh wave of African immigrants, and it is to signal the probable close relationship between 500,000-year-old Europeans and Africans that they are commonly lumped in the species *H. heidelbergensis*.

Considering only East Asian and European fossils and artifacts, we might conclude that people expanded from Africa (beyond Israel) only between 1.3 and 1 million years ago. However, spectacular recent discoveries at the ruined medieval fortress of **Dmanisi**, Republic of Georgia, suggest the possibility of an earlier date (Vekua et al. 2002). In 1984, archaeologists broke through the foundation of a medieval structure on the site into an ancient river deposit with animal bones and flaked stone artifacts [3.26, 3.27]. Follow-up excavations have produced more than 1000 artifacts and 2000 bones, and the bones

3.22 The expansion of Homo: *a map showing the possible routes by which early Homo may have dispersed from Africa westwards to Europe and eastwards to China, with dates given in millions of years ago. The map also shows some of the principal sites that are thought to reflect this dispersal.*

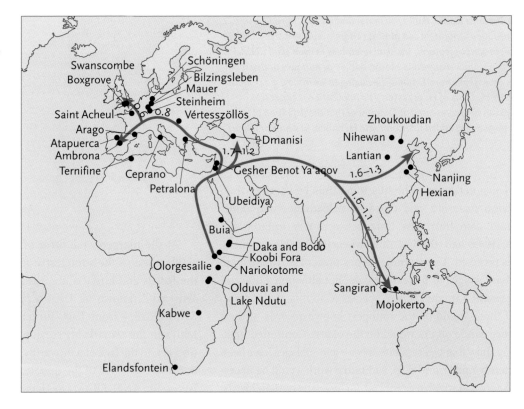

include four partial human skulls, two mandibles [3.23–3.25], and some elements from the skeleton below the skull. Human expansion from Africa is indisputable, since Dmanisi lies roughly 1500 km (940 miles) north of 'Ubeidiya, and its fossil fauna is overwhelmingly Eurasian.

Dating the Dmanisi Fossils The fossil-bearing deposits at Dmanisi overlie a basalt layer that has been dated to about 1.85 million years ago by potassium-argon. Research elsewhere has shown that the interval between 2.43 million and 790,000 years ago was characterized mainly by reversed magnetic polarity (when a compass needle would have pointed south). However, this long period was interrupted by shorter periods when the polarity was normal (like the present), and one such period occurred between 1.95 and 1.77 million years ago. The Dmanisi basalt would thus be expected to exhibit normal magnetization, and it does, as do the overlying river deposits. Since the surface of the basalt is fresh, the river deposits probably covered it shortly after it cooled, and they probably also formed before 1.77 million years ago. The human and animal fossils, however, occur in large hollows eroded within the normally magnetized river deposits, and the hollows are filled with deposits that exhibit

3.23, 3.24 The Dmanisi fossils: *(right) Skulls and lower jaws from the Dmanisi site, Republic of Georgia. The skulls and jaws closely resemble those of* Homo ergaster *in eastern Africa, and they suggest that H. ergaster had expanded from Africa as much as 1.7 million years ago. (Below) Lateral view of the Dmanisi skull pictured in the upper left of 3.23. Note the far forward projection of the upper jaw, the powerfully constructed browridge, and the long, low shape of the brain case.*

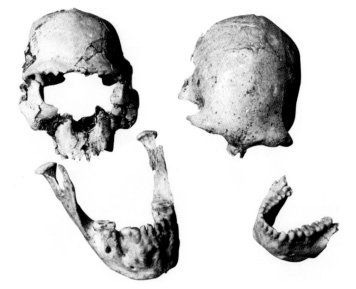

3.25 *The Dmanisi fossils:* *skull 2700 and mandible 2735 from Dmanisi, which were found separately, but almost certainly represent the same individual. In various features, the skull resembles Kenyan skull KNM-ER 1813, which is usually assigned to* Homo habilis *as narrowly understood. The three other skulls from Dmanisi (including those in 3.23, 3.24) more closely resemble those of H. ergaster. The implication is either two human species are represented at Dmanisi or that the definition of* H. ergaster *must be expanded to incorporate* H. habilis *in whole or in part.*

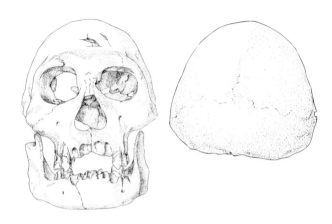

reversed magnetization. The fills must thus be younger than 1.77 million years old, and based on paleomagnetism alone, they could date from any time between 1.77 million and 790,000 years ago, the last time when the earth's magnetic field was reversed. The mammal bones present at Dmanisi are said to lend weight to the earlier date, but although Eurasian, they represent a unique mix of species (Gabunia et al. 2000); some of these would be the youngest known records of their occurrence, while others would be the oldest. Continued fieldwork may show that two separate species assemblages have been inadvertently mixed, and if so, additional work would be necessary to determine which assemblage includes the human fossils.

The Dmanisi artifacts include only flakes and flaked pebbles. There are no hand axes, and this could mean that the site formed before Africans invented hand axes roughly 1.7–1.6 million years ago. However, even long after this time, not all sites in Africa and Europe contain hand axes, for reasons that are obscure. The 800,000-year-old layers at the Gran Dolina, Spain, are an example, and there are others that postdate 500,000 years ago in the same parts of southern and western Europe that hand axe makers had widely settled. In short, the absence of hand axes at Dmanisi need not mean that the people were pre-Acheuleans, and the Dmanisi artifacts require more detailed description to determine whether they differed from Acheulean artifacts in fundamental flaking technology.

At the moment, the form of one of the Dmanisi human skulls presents the strongest argument that many, if not all, of the fossils and artifacts are actually 1.7–1.6 million years old. This skull, known as D2700 [**3.25**], closely resembles skull KNM-ER-1813 from East Turkana (Koobi Fora) in northern Kenya in the remarkably small volume of its braincase (about 600 cc), in the lack of a forwardly projecting, external nose, and in the overall form of the middle and upper face. Most specialists assign KNM-ER-1813 to *Homo habilis*, or, if *H. habilis* is split into *H. habilis* and *H. rudolfensis*, then to its smaller version, *H. habilis* as narrowly understood. The latest known occurrence of *H. habilis* is at Olduvai Gorge, in deposits that probably date from about 1.6 million years ago. The other two Dmanisi skulls that have been described (labeled D2280 and D2282), and one that has not, are much more similar to those of north Kenyan *Homo ergaster*, and on this basis they could also be 1.6 million years old or more. However, on current evidence, the basic skull form that marks *H. ergaster* persisted to 1 million years ago or later, and the relevant Dmanisi skulls could thus be much younger.

The apparent mix of human skull types at Dmanisi is puzzling, and whatever geologic age is preferred, the implication would still be either that two human species expanded from Africa early on, or that the definition of *H. ergaster* must be expanded to include fossils that would otherwise be assigned to *H. habilis*. Even if future research shows that the Dmanisi skulls date from two different time intervals, the form of D2700 would still argue that people left Africa by 1.6 million years ago. This forces speculation on how they could have expanded so far northward and then failed to move westward to Europe until after 1 million years ago.

Evidence that Homo ergaster *Persisted to 1 million Years Ago or Later* Excepting the Dmanisi specimens, there are only four

3.26, 3.27 *The site of Dmanisi:* *excavations underway (left) at the site of Dmanisi, a ruined medieval fortress in the Republic of Georgia (right), which has provided the oldest known human fossils and artifacts in Eurasia, dating to as much as 1.7 million years ago.*

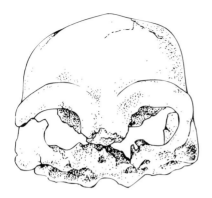

3.28 *The Daka skull:* *like skulls of broadly contemporaneous Far Eastern* Homo erectus, *the Daka skull has its maximum breadth near the base, a keel along the midline at the top, and a massive browridge. Its endocranial volume of 995 cc closely approximates the Far Eastern mean. It differs from classic Far Eastern* H. erectus *in the arching of the browridge over the orbits, the height of the vault relative to the breadth, the absence of a well-defined occipital bar, and the relative thinness of the vault bones. In the absence of a distinct occipital bar and vault bone thinness, it recalls earlier African* H. ergaster *and it is taken here to indicate the persistence of* H. ergaster *in Africa after* H. erectus *had emerged in the Far East.*

skulls between 1.5 million and 600,000 years ago that bear on the question of evolutionary change within *Homo ergaster*. These are a partial skull (Olduvai Hominid 9) from Olduvai Gorge that is thought to be 1.2–1.1 million years old (Leakey 1961), a fragmentary skull from Olorgesailie, Kenya, bracketed between 970,000 and 900,000 years ago by potassium-argon, paleomagnetism, and rates of sediment accumulation (Potts et al. 2004), a nearly complete skull from Buia, near the Red Sea coast of Eritrea in eastern Africa that is about 1 million years old (Abbate et al. 1998), and a skull [**3.28**] from the **Daka** Member of the Bouri Formation, Ethiopia, that has been fixed between 1 million and 790,000 years old by potassium-argon dating and paleomagnetism (Asfaw et al. 2002). The Olduvai skullcap is like those of East Asian *Homo erectus* in its massive browridge, thick walls, and angular rear profile, but in other, more detailed, characteristics it is like *H. ergaster* (Clarke 1990). The Olorge-

sailie, Buia and Daka skulls differ from the older *H. ergaster* skulls only in minor details, and they present a clearer case for long-term anatomical continuity.

The Persistence of Homo erectus *in Java*

By 600,000–500,000 years ago, hominins with larger, more modern-looking braincases had appeared in Africa, and based in part on the more or less simultaneous appearance of more sophisticated hand axes, it seems reasonable to hypothesize that they evolved abruptly from *Homo ergaster*. They closely resembled Europeans of 500,000–400,000 years ago, and, as noted above, it is this observation that has led specialists to group the Africans and Europeans together in *Homo heidelbergensis*. The expansion of *H. heidelbergensis* from Africa probably explains the introduction of Acheulean artifacts to Europe about 500,000 years ago.

It was suggested above that *Homo heidelbergensis* represents the last shared ancestor between the Neanderthals (*Homo*

neanderthalensis), who evolved in Europe after 500,000 years ago, and modern humans (*Homo sapiens*), who evolved in Africa over roughly the same interval, beginning somewhat later. The next chapter highlights the fossil and archaeological evidence for the expansion of modern humans from Africa after 50,000 years ago to replace the Neanderthals in Europe. But what then of *Homo erectus*, who was firmly entrenched in eastern Asia long before the Neanderthal and modern human lines diverged? The issue is difficult to address, because relevant East Asian fossils and artifacts are much sparser and more poorly dated than European ones. Still, the available fossil and archaeological observations indicate that *H. erectus* continued on its own divergent evolutionary trajectory after 500,000 years ago, when Neanderthals and modern humans had separated in the West. This suggests that *H. erectus* eventually suffered the same fate as the Neanderthals and died out.

The most telling late *H. erectus* fossils come from the site of **Ngandong** on the Solo River near Trinil, in central Java. Between 1931 and 1933, excavations in ancient river deposits by the Dutch Geological Survey in Java recovered more than 25,000 fossil bones, including 12 partial human skulls and two incomplete human tibiae (shin bones). Between 1976 and 1980, researchers from Gadjah Mada University in Yogyakarta expanded the excavations at Ngandong and unearthed 1200 additional bones, including two incomplete human skulls and some human pelvis fragments. Previously, in 1973, the same research team had recovered a similar skull and a human tibia from river deposits of comparable age near **Sambungmacan**, between Trinil and Sangiran. The Ngandong and Sambungmacan skulls are somewhat larger than those of classic

Indonesian *H. erectus*, but they exhibit the same basic characteristics, including a massive, shelflike browridge, a flat, receding forehead, thick skull walls, a tendency for the walls to slope inwards from a broad base, and substantial angularity at the rear. Based on these features, the Ngandong and Sambungmacan people are commonly assigned to an evolved variant of *H. erectus*.

Associated mammal species indicate that the Ngandong and Sambungmacan human fossils are less than 300,000 years old (Storm 2001), and electron spin resonance (ESR) dates [see box: Electron Spin Resonance Dating] on associated water buffalo teeth suggest an age between 53,000 and 27,000 years ago (Swisher et al. 1996). The reliability of the Ngandong and Sambungmacan ESR dates is questionable, but if they are valid, they provide strong circumstantial support for the survival of Southeast Asian *H. erectus* until it was replaced by modern human invaders after 60,000 years ago. However, even if the Ngandong and Sambungmacan skulls are actually closer to 300,000 years old, they still show that Southeast Asian populations were on a different evolutionary track from their European and African contemporaries.

Homo heidelbergensis and the Earliest Occupation of Europe

The previous sections argued that by 1 million years ago, humans had spread to the northern and southern coasts of Africa and had colonized eastern Asia as far east as China and Java. But what about Europe? The Dmanisi site puts people on the southern flank of the Caucasus Mountains in modern Geor-

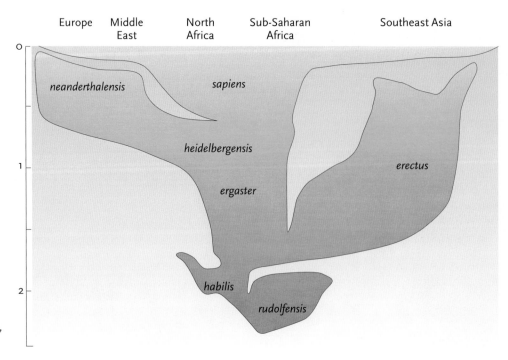

3.29 *The divergence of early* Homo: *a schematic representation of the pattern of human evolution after 2.5 million years ago, showing the geographic division into three distinct lineages:* Homo neanderthalensis, H. sapiens, *and* H. erectus.

KEY METHOD Electron Spin Resonance (ESR) Dating

The electron spin resonance (ESR) dating method depends on the observation that flaws in the crystalline structure of dental enamel accumulate electrons in direct proportion to radioactivity in the burial environment (Grün 1993). The principal sources of radioactivity are tiny but nearly ubiquitous amounts of naturally occurring uranium, thorium, and radioactive potassium. ESR is essentially a laboratory technique for measuring the number of trapped electrons of these elements. The yearly rate of irradiation, or "annual radiation dose," can be measured in the field, and if we assume that it has remained constant through time, the number of trapped electrons directly reflects the number of years since burial.

In practice, ESR faces many hurdles, of which the most serious is the possibility that teeth at any given site have experienced a complex history of uranium exchange with the burial environment. Exchange almost always involves uranium uptake from ground water, but it may also involve loss, and the precise pattern of uptake and loss will manifestly affect the annual radiation dose to which a tooth has been subjected. The possibility that this dose changed significantly through time often leaves ESR results open to question. Still, ESR dates are widely cited in paleoanthropology, in large part because ESR is commonly the only technique available for dating important archaeological or fossil sites that lack suitable materials for radiocarbon dating or that lie beyond the range of the radiocarbon method (i.e., before about 40,000 years ago). The deposits at Ngandong, Indonesia, with their late *Homo erectus* fossils, represent a prime example.

gia, at the "Gates of Europe," by 1 million years ago, and perhaps as much as 1.7 million years ago. Yet, despite searches that began in the 1830s (long aided by industrial activity), Europe has yet to produce a single site that is indisputably older than 800,000 years ago, and it has provided only one or two that are clearly older than 500,000 years. Enthusiasts have repeatedly proposed other sites that antedate 500,000 years or even 1 million years ago, but close scrutiny has shown that most such sites are dubiously dated, or that their artifacts could be geofacts, i.e., rocks that were naturally fractured by geologic processes (Roebroeks 2001; Roebroeks and van Kolfschoten 1994).

The contrast with Africa and southern Asia is stark, and it implies that Europe posed special obstacles to early human settlement, particularly during glacial intervals. The first permanent occupants of Europe were late Acheulean hand axe makers, who spread from Spain and Italy in the south to southern England in the north *c.* 500,000 years ago. Occasional human fossils such as those from **Petralona** [3.30] in Greece and Arago in France suggest that the hand axe makers resembled their African contemporaries, and the Europeans probably descended from an expanding African population that brought the late Acheulean tradition to Europe. It is this population and its immediate African and European descendants that is here called *Homo heidelbergensis*, named for a lower jaw found near Heidelberg, Germany, dated by associated animal species at near 500,000 years ago (p. 92).

Homo heidelbergensis shared many primitive features with *H. ergaster* and *H. erectus*, including a large, forwardly projecting face, a massive, chinless lower jaw with big teeth, large browridges, a low, flattened frontal bone (forehead), great breadth across the skull base, and thick skull walls. At the same time, it departed from both *H. ergaster* and *H. erectus* in its much enlarged brain, which averaged over 1200 cc (compared to about 900 cc for *H. ergaster* and 1000 cc for classic *H. erectus*), in its more arched (versus more shelflike) browridges, and in the shape of its braincase, which was broader across the front, more filled out at the sides, and less angular at the back. Like *H. erectus*, *H. heidelbergensis* probably evolved from *H. ergaster*, and in its anatomy and its geographic distribution it is a plausible common ancestor for the Neanderthals (*Homo neanderthalensis*), who appeared subsequently in Europe, and for modern humans (*Homo sapiens*) who evolved later in Africa.

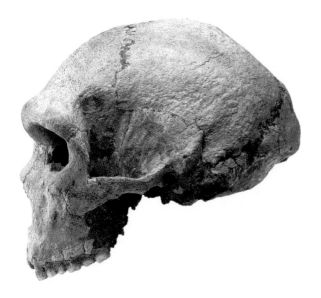

3.30 *The Petralona skull:* *it probably dates from between 500,000 and 250,000 years ago, and it anticipates Neanderthal skulls in the forward projection of the face along the midline. On the other hand, its braincase is more like that of* Homo erectus, *particularly in the angle of the occipital or rear region. The skull is here assigned to* Homo heidelbergensis *which was ancestral to the Neanderthals in Europe.*

KEY SITE The Gran Dolina TD6 and the History of Cannibalism

In layer TD6 at the site of Gran Dolina, at Atapuerca in Spain, the human remains, like the smaller animal species found at the site, are represented by a wide range of skeletal parts. Furthermore, 25 percent of the human bones show one or more forms of humanly caused damage in the same anatomical locations as appear on the animal bones (Fernández-Jalvo et al. 1999).

These include chop and cut marks where large muscles were severed or stripped away; roughened surfaces with parallel grooves or a fibrous texture that reflects "peeling," when a bone was partially broken by a blow and then bent across the break to separate the pieces; and percussion marks made when a bone was splintered for marrow extraction. There could be no more

compelling archaeological evidence for cannibalism.

The extent and positioning of damage marks suggest that the TD6 people butchered other people for food and not for ritualistic purposes, and it is tempting to draw a parallel to the situation on Easter Island when Europeans first arrived there in the 18th century AD (Chapter 8). The Easter Islanders had severely degraded their environment, and their once-thriving population had shrunk by 80 percent. In desperation, the survivors had adopted a wide range of bizarre behaviors, including dietary cannibalism.

In the short run, this helped some to carry on, but in the long term it could only have hastened the slide toward population oblivion. If cannibalism at TD6 reflects

similar nutritional stress, it could explain why *Homo antecessor*, the population that inhabited the Gran Dolina, was ultimately unsuccessful.

The Neanderthals also seem to have practiced cannibalism, but only on occasion, and if the custom led to extinction, it affected only local populations. As far as we know, the great apes do not turn to cannibalism when food is short, and the records from TD6, the Neanderthals, Easter Island, and late prehistoric sites in Europe and the American Southwest suggest that dietary cannibalism may be a specialized human tendency that *Homo antecessor*, *H. neanderthalensis*, and *H. sapiens* inherited from their last shared ancestor, *H. ergaster*.

Unsuccessful European Colonizers: Homo antecessor *and the Ceprano Skull*

Homo heidelbergensis was important as the first human species to gain a permanent foothold in Europe, but it was not the first to try. Cave deposits in the **Sierra de Atapuerca** near Burgos, northern Spain, reveal an earlier, if fleeting, attempt, and ancient lake deposits at Ceprano near Rome (see below) may record another. Despite its name, the Sierra de Atapuerca is not a mountain range, but a large limestone hill that is honeycombed with caves. Two of these – the Sima de los Huesos ("Pit of the Bones") and the Gran Dolina ("Large Depression") – are particularly remarkable. The Gran Dolina stands out because it has provided the most compelling evidence for human presence in Europe before 500,000 years ago. The Sima is famous for a mass of human fossils that document the local, European evolution of the Neanderthals from *Homo heidelbergensis*.

The **Gran Dolina** contains 18 m (60 ft) of sandy, rocky deposits first exposed in a now-abandoned railway trench at the turn of the 20th century. Excavations that began in 1976 and then accelerated after 1993 show that artifacts and fragmentary animal bones are concentrated in six discrete layers. The layer that interests us here is the second from the bottom, known as TD6, which has provided more than 90 fragmentary human fossils and 200 flaked stone artifacts [see box: The Gran Dolina TD6 and the History of Cannibalism]. An horizon that lies roughly 1 m (3.3 ft) higher records the shift in global magnetic polarity from the last long reversed interval to the present normal one (Parés and Pérez-González 1999). This means that

TD6 must be older than 790,000 years. Electron spin resonance dating brackets the TD6 fossils and artifacts between 857,000 and 780,000 years ago (Falguères et al. 1999), and bones of long-extinct rodent species support an equally great age (Cuenca-Bescós et al. 1999). With admitted uncertainties in mind, the excavators conservatively date TD6 to about 800,000 years ago.

The TD6 human fossils include 18 skull fragments, 4 partial jaws, 14 isolated teeth, 16 vertebrae, 16 ribs, 20 bones of the hands and feet, 2 wrist bones, 3 clavicles (collar bones), 2 radii (lower arm bones), a femur (thigh bone), 2 patellae (knee caps), and other fragments from a minimum of 6 individuals. The people were between 3 and 18 years of age when they died. The skull and jaw fragments are too incomplete for detailed diagnosis, but the jaws clearly represent humans whose faces were less massive and in some respects more modern looking than those of *Homo heidelbergensis*. The excavators have assigned them to a new species, *Homo antecessor*, from the Latin word for "pioneer" or "explorer." The relationship of *H. antecessor* to other human species is debatable, but it seems an unlikely ancestor for *H. heidelbergensis*, and it may have been an offshoot of *H. ergaster* that disappeared after a failed attempt to colonize southern Europe. Its doom may have been sealed by an inability to cope with one of the harsh glacial episodes that gripped Europe between 800,000 and 600,000 years ago.

The TD6 people made artifacts from pebbles and cobbles of flint, quartzite, sandstone, quartz, and limestone, all of which they found within a few kilometers of the cave (Carbonell et al.

1999). Their tools were mainly small flakes, some of which they modified by striking tiny flakes or chips from along one or more edges ("retouch"), in order to alter the shape of an edge, give it greater stability, or resharpen it after it had been dulled by use. In addition to flakes, TD6 has produced some hammerstones and a few cores from which the flakes were struck. Hand axes are totally absent, although they are commonplace in sites of similar age in Africa and Southwest Asia, and they occur in a higher Gran Dolina layer that formed after 500,000 years ago. Their absence may mean that, like *Homo erectus* in eastern Asia, the ancestors of the TD6 people lost the hand axe habit on their trek from Africa. Alternatively, it is just possible that a hand axe will turn up when the small artifact sample is increased through further excavation.

TD6 at Gran Dolina would be exciting if all it had provided were human remains and artifacts, but it has also produced

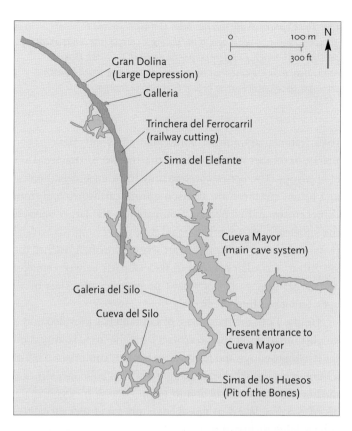

3.31, 3.32 Atapuerca: *plan showing the locations of different fossil and archaeological sites in the Sierra de Atapuerca, Spain (right). The two most famous sites are the Gran Dolina (below), where human fossils and artifacts, dated to about 800,000 years ago, are probably the oldest so far known in Europe, and the Sima de los Huesos (see page 111).*

3.33 *The Ceprano skull:* this has been tentatively dated to 900,000–800,000 years ago. If the dating is correct, the anatomical contrast with roughly contemporary fossils from the Gran Dolina, Atapuerca, may indicate that there were at least two failed human attempts to colonize Europe before 600,000 years ago.

1056 fragmentary animal bones that show cut marks, chop marks, or scrapes where flesh and marrow were extracted (Diez et al. 1999). The bones come mainly from pigs, deer, horses, and bison, but there are also some from carnivores and from rhinoceroses and elephants. Compared to the larger species, the smallest ones are represented by a wider range of skeletal parts, suggesting that smaller carcasses more often reached the site intact. A similar contrast in skeletal parts between smaller and larger species characterizes prehistoric campsites of all ages, and it was thus predictable.

Unlike TD6, the Italian site of **Ceprano** has provided only a single human fossil and no artifacts, but the fossil is important for its proposed age and for its form [**3.33**]. It comprises most of a human skullcap that was shattered when a bulldozer struck it during highway construction in 1994. Potassium-argon analysis of volcanic layers at possibly younger and older localities nearby suggest that the skullcap is 900,000–800,000 years old. It shares many features with skullcaps of *Homo erectus*, including a massive, shelflike browridge, extremely thick skull walls, a sharply angled occipital region (rear profile), and a small internal volume (estimated at 1057 cc). If the Ceprano skull had been found in Java, it might have been assigned to *H. erectus*, and if its dating is correct, the anatomical contrast with *H. antecessor* implies another early, failed attempt to colonize Europe.

Brain Expansion and Change within the Hand Axe Tradition

Beginning roughly 500,000 years ago, the makers of late Acheulean hand axes not only indicated their ability to hang on in Europe through thick and thin (or warm and cold), they also expanded into more northerly regions that *Homo antecessor* or other earlier Europeans apparently could not reach. The reason was probably that late Acheulean Europeans benefited from technological advances that occurred somewhat before 500,000 years ago in the African source land.

As demonstrated above, the Acheulean (hand axe) tradition began in Africa more than 1.6 million years ago, and it persisted in Africa, Europe, and the western Asian bridge between them until about 250,000 years ago. Most African Acheulean sites are imprecisely dated, but a previous section suggested that they may be divided between two stages: an earlier one before 600,000 years ago, when the hand axes tended to be relatively thick, weakly trimmed, and asymmetric, and a later one after 600,000 years ago, when they were commonly much thinner,

more extensively trimmed, and more symmetric, both in plan form and in edge view. Later Acheulean people also produced more refined flake tools that are indistinguishable from those of their successors. The greater technological sophistication of later Acheulean people may have been crucial to their successful colonization of Europe.

It has been argued that the early Acheulean ability to impose even crude, two-dimensional symmetry on a hand axe probably signals a cognitive advance over preceding Oldowan toolmakers (Wynn 1995). If so, then the wonderful three-dimensional symmetry of many late Acheulean hand axes may mark an equally important advance that now allowed their creators to rotate the final tool in their minds while it was still encased in the raw rock. The nature and timing of the shift from the early to the late Acheulean remain to be firmly established, but if the transition turns out to have occurred abruptly about 600,000 years ago, it could have coincided with a rapid expansion in brain size that may have occurred about the same time (Ruff et al. 1997). Careful analysis of fossil data suggests that between 1.8 million and 600,000 years ago, brain size remained remarkably stable at roughly 65 percent of the modern average; not long afterwards, it increased to about 90 percent of the modern value. If a spurt in brain size and associated changes in skull form sparked the appearance of *Homo heidelbergensis*, its emergence 600,000 years ago would signal a punctuational event like the one that may have introduced *H. ergaster* more than 1 million years earlier. The analogy would be especially apt if future research confirms a link between *H. heidelbergensis* and late Acheulean technology to parallel a postulated earlier one between *H. ergaster* and the origin of the Acheulean tradition.

The Evolution of the Neanderthals in Europe

The European fossil record after 500,000 years ago is critical to a full understanding of human evolution, for it shows that the Neanderthals were a European phenomenon, evolving in Europe over the same interval that modern humans were evolving in Africa. Occasional proto-Neanderthal fossils have long been known from sites between 400,000 and 200,000 years old (Hublin 1996), such as Swanscombe, England, and Steinheim, Germany. The certainty with which we can now reconstruct Neanderthal roots stems mainly from one site, however, which was mentioned above: the extraordinary **Sima de los Huesos** at Atapuerca, Spain, often abbreviated for simplicity as the Sima, or "Pit" (Arsuaga et al. 2003).

Unlike its sister site, the Gran Dolina, the Sima was never exposed by a railway trench or any other commercial activity, and its original entrance long ago collapsed. It is a tiny chamber with a floor area of about 17 sq. m (185 sq. ft), which can be reached today only via a 13-m (43-ft) vertical shaft located about half a kilometer (a third of a mile) from the entrance to the cave system. The chamber would probably be unknown to science if young men from nearby Burgos had not long been interested in exploring underground cave systems with torches and ropes. Graffiti show that they had entered the Sima system by the late 13th century AD, and in the mid-1970s an exploratory group told a paleontology student that the Sima abounded in bear bones. The bones were so striking and abundant that the Sima took its full name ("Pit of the Bones") from them [see box: How Did Human Fossils Reach the Sima de los Huesos?, p. 113].

Spanish investigators retrieved the first human fossil – a mandible, or lower jaw – in 1976, but the site was such a difficult place in which to work that they decided to direct their attention to other nearby caves. In 1982, however, they returned for another look and quickly found two human teeth. Beginning in 1984, they have returned every summer. Each season, the team excavates only about 1 sq. m (approximately 11 sq. ft) to a depth of just 20 cm (8 in), but the small volume of deposit typically yields 200–300 fragmentary human fossils, fragile and tightly packed. Most are postcranial, i.e., skeletal parts from below the head, but in 1992 the excavators recovered two skulls. In 1993, they found a third skull and a mandible that matched one of the previous ones. Uranium-series analysis [see box: Uranium Series Dating] shows that a fragment of cave flowstone (stalagmite or stalactite) that overlies the layer with human fossils formed at least 350,000 years ago, and the excavators believe that the fossil-bearing layer probably formed sometime between 500,000 and 400,000 years ago (Bischoff et al. 2003). This would place the Sima fossils early in the interval between *Homo heidelbergensis* and the emergence of the fully-fledged Neanderthals (see Chapter 4).

The Sima people were also intermediate between *H. heidelbergensis* and the Neanderthals in key anatomical respects. Neanderthal skulls were remarkably large, with an average internal skull volume of about 1520 cc. This compares to perhaps 1400 cc in living humans. Two of the Sima skulls are relatively small, with endocranial capacities of 1125 and 1220 cc, but the third has a capacity of 1390 cc, which is comfortably within the Neanderthal range. It is, in fact, the largest skull yet recovered from any site older than 150,000 years. Even more striking, the Sima skulls combine widely shared primitive skull characteristics with others that are distinctively Neanderthal. Thus, like virtually all humans except the Neanderthals, they had a primitive mastoid region with a large, distinct "mastoid process" (a downward-facing bony bump behind and below the ear), while unlike everyone but the Neanderthals, they had faces

KEY METHOD Uranium-Series Dating

The Uranium (or U)-series dating method depends on the observation that uranium occurs naturally in small quantities virtually everywhere, and that it is soluble in water, while the products of its radioactive decay, thorium and protactinium, are not (Schwarcz 1992). Thus, when uranium precipitates from groundwater, as, for example, in a newly formed cave flowstone (stalagmite or stalactite), the flowstone will initially contain no daughter products, but these will subsequently accumulate inside at a rate that is directly proportional to the rate at which uranium decays. The ratio between the daughter products and uranium can then be used to estimate the time when the uranium precipitated from groundwater, meaning, in the case of a flowstone, the time when it formed.

U-series dating is most reliable when it is applied to cave flowstones or to similar substances that subsequently remained closed to the addition or subtraction of uranium. In theory, it can be applied to fossil bone, since fresh bone contains little or no uranium, and the uranium in a fossil must then have been adsorbed from groundwater after burial. The timing and rate of adsorption, however, are generally unknowable, and adsorption can even alternate with loss (leaching). Thus, there is usually no way to set the clock to zero to determine when the bone was buried. U-series dates on bone from a single layer often scatter widely, and different dates have even been obtained on different parts of the same bone. Because suitable materials are relatively rare in ancient archaeological or fossil sites, the U-series technique cannot be applied as often as ESR dating [see box, p. 107]; but where reliable materials occur, the U-series method provides more secure dates, and it can provide ages beyond the reach of the radiocarbon method. One of its most important applications in paleoanthropology has been to show that human fossils accumulated at the Sima de los Huesos more than 350,000 years ago.

3.34 *(Right)* **Sima skull 5:** *facial view of skull 5 from the Sima de los Huesos, Atapuerca, Spain. The skull anticipates those of classic Neanderthal skulls in its double-arched browridge and pronounced forward projection of the midface.*

3.35 *(Below)* **The Pit of the Bones:** *the extraordinary assemblage of human bones from the Sima de los Huesos, Atapuerca, Spain. It includes more than 2000 specimens, meticulously recovered from a single deposit that probably accumulated sometime between 500,000 and 400,000 years ago. The sample is more than four times larger than the combined samples from all other sites of like age and includes multiple elements from nearly every part of the postcranial skeleton, together with three well-preserved skulls and fragments of more than six others.*

that projected far forwards along the midline (the line that bisects the face from top to bottom) and a conspicuous oval area of roughened or porous bone just above the upper limit for the neck muscles on the rear of the skull. In their retention of primitive skull features, the Sima people were not Neanderthals, but they were surely on or near the line that produced them.

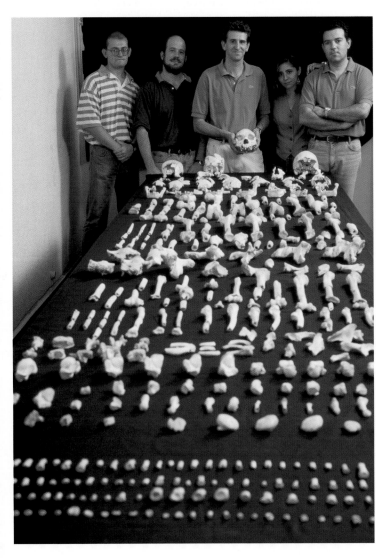

Evidence for Early Human Behavior apart from Stone Artifacts

The behavior of Acheulean people and their contemporaries must be inferred from fewer than 50 reasonably well-excavated archaeological sites. These are widely scattered in time and space, and the time dimension is poorly controlled, particularly outside Africa. Compounding these problems of small sample size and poor temporal control, the behavioral implications of excavated materials are often highly ambiguous, and non-trivial inferences are mostly tentative. With this caveat in mind, this section outlines what we can say about early human behavior apart from how people used stone.

Raw Materials besides Stone

Stone artifacts dominate the Paleolithic record because of their durability, but early humans surely used other raw materials, including bone and more perishable substances such as wood, reeds, and hide. Animal bones survive at many sites that Acheulean people or their contemporaries occupied in Africa, Europe, and Asia, and percussion marks or cut marks sometimes suggest that the people used individual bones as hammers, stone tool retouchers, anvils, or cutting boards (Villa and d'Errico 2001). A few, mainly European, sites have also produced bones that were percussion-flaked like stone. The most striking examples come from Fontana Ranuccio, Malagrotta, Castel di Guido, La Polledrara, and other open-air Acheulean sites in central Italy (Villa and Soressi 2000), and from the broadly contemporaneous non-Acheulean open-air site at Bilzingsleben, Germany (Mania 1998). At **Fontana Ranuccio, Malagrotta,** and **Castel di Guido,** the flaked bone artifacts include unequivocal elephant-bone bifaces. From **Bilzingsleben** come elephant-bone scraper-like and chopper-like tools [**3.36**]. Despite the variety of flaked bone artifacts, however,

KEY CONTROVERSY How Did Human Fossils Reach the Sima de los Huesos?

The fossils from the Sima de los Huesos ("Pit of the Bones"), at Atapuerca, Spain, have powerfully illuminated the broad pattern of later human evolution, but they have also raised a puzzle all their own: how did they get into the Sima (Arsuaga et al. 2003)? The layer in which they occur contains only fragmented human bones, and the bones are tightly packed. After nearly 20 years, the excavations have provided only a single stone artifact: a classic, beautifully crafted late Acheulean hand axe. Its form broadly confirms the 500,000–350,000-year age estimate for the human fossils, but the hand axe by itself obviously provides no reason to suppose that people inhabited the cave.

The excavated bone sample has grown to more than 2000 individual specimens, including three skulls, large fragments of six others, numerous smaller skull or facial fragments, 41 complete or partial mandibles, many isolated teeth, and hundreds of postcranial bones, i.e., bones from parts of the body other than the head.

How Many? How Old?

At least 32 people are represented by the bones in the Sima, and measurements on jaws and teeth indicate that they divide about equally into males and females. Tooth eruption and wear show that 17 of the 32 people were adolescents between 11 and 19 years of age, and 10 were young adults, of 20 to 25 years old; only 3 were younger than 10, and none were older than 35. Children may be rare because their relatively soft bones were more likely to disappear in the ground, and older adults may be absent because, perhaps like the Neanderthals, the Sima people rarely lived beyond 35 years.

Still, the age distribution is puzzling, for if it resulted from normal, everyday mortality events such as accidents and endemic disease, we would expect older, weaker people to be much more abundant relative to teenagers and young adults. The implication may be that the Sima people did not die from everyday events, but from a catastrophe that affected everyone equally.

Disease, Attack or Disposal of the Dead

One possibility is an epidemic disease, but we would still have to explain how the bodies ended up in the Sima. Another possibility that would cover both death and body disposal would be a devastating attack by a neighboring group. In this instance, however, the Sima bones should show wounds from spears or clubs, and there are none. Also, unlike the bones from the Gran Dolina, the Sima bones exhibit no stone tool marks, and cannibalism can be ruled out. The only damage is from the teeth of foxes or other small carnivores, which were probably attracted to the chamber by decomposing human remains.

Since the Sima sample includes virtually all parts of the skeleton, even the tiniest, the excavators believe that whole bodies reached the cave. Although the bones are mostly broken, the broken edges are sometimes smoothed, perhaps by sediment flow or by occasional animal trampling that would have disarticulated the bones and spread them across the cave floor. At the moment, a plausible explanation for the introduction of whole bodies is that other people dropped them down the shaft; we must then ask if the practice was ceremonial or simply hygienic. Ritual or ceremony can never be categorically rejected, but except perhaps for the single, well-made hand axe, the deposit contains no special artifacts, once-fleshy animal bones, or other items that we can interpret as ritual offerings or grave goods.

An understandable desire to dispose of bodies away from a nearby living site thus becomes a credible alternative. If the Sima people were simply practicing hygienic disposal, they may have anticipated the Neanderthals; these humans buried their dead, at least on occasion, but dug the smallest possible graves, into which they inserted bodies but no grave goods (see Chapter 4, p. 152). Much more conspicuous, elaborate graves with unequivocal ideological or religious implications show up only after 50,000 years ago.

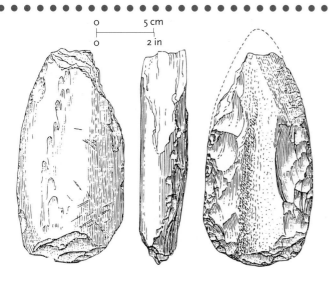

neither these sites nor any other of similar age have provided bones that were cut, carved, or polished to form points, awls, perforators, and so forth. As discussed in the next chapter, such artifacts become common only at the sites of fully modern humans after 50,000–40,000 years ago.

Artifacts in the most perishable raw materials are scarce by definition. Bamboo makes edges that rival or exceed those of

3.36 Flaked fragment of elephant bone from Bilzingsleben: *the site is 350,000–420,000 years old, and has provided more than 100 flaked bone artifacts as well as ones of stone and some human remains. The bone artifacts and similar ones from other sites (notably in Italy) show that early people sometimes flaked bone, but it was only after 50,000 years ago that they routinely carved or ground bone to produce formal artifacts.*

113

stone for sharpness and durability, and it is especially likely to have been used in eastern Asia, where it enjoys roughly the same distribution as the non-hand axe assemblages originally recognized by Hallam Movius (see above). An emphasis on bamboo could explain why East Asian stone artifact assemblages generally appear to contain a smaller range of artifact types than contemporaneous Acheulean assemblages from Africa, western Asia, and Europe (Pope 1993), but actual bamboo artifacts remain unknown.

Reed and skin artifacts are also lacking, and unquestionable wooden artifacts have been found at only four African, western Asian, and European Acheulean or Acheulean-age sites: **Kalambo Falls** (Zambia), **Gesher Benot Ya'aqov** (Israel), **Clacton-on-Sea** (England), and **Schöningen** (Germany). The sites are dated variously to between 790,000 and 300,000 years ago, and they are distinguished by unusually dense deposits that precluded air penetration and thus inhibited bacterial decay. In Africa, the artifact makers were probably early *Homo sapiens*; in western Asia, they could have been late *H. ergaster*; and in Europe, they were either *H. heidelbergensis* or early *H. neanderthalensis*. The pieces are mainly nondescript and of uncertain function.

At Schöningen, however, deposits that are about 400,000 years old have produced three complete, indisputable wooden spears (Thieme 1997) [**3.37, 3.38**]. Each was over 2 m (6.5 ft)

long, and the only issue is whether they were thrust or thrown. All three are heaviest and thickest near the pointed ends, like modern javelins, but they probably could not have been projected hard enough to penetrate an animal from a distance, and they are thus more likely to have been used as thrusting spears at close quarters. They provide the oldest, most compelling evidence for human hunting.

Site Modification

Early humans almost surely required shelters of some kind, particularly after they colonized Eurasia, but the surviving evidence is remarkably sparse and ambiguous. Cited examples include seemingly patterned arrangements of large, non-artifactual rocks at the possible pre-Acheulean site of **Soleihac**, France (Bonifay et al. 1976), and at four Acheulean sites: **Melka Kunturé** (Ethiopia), **Olorgesailie** (Kenya), **Latamne** (Syria), and **Terra Amata** (France). People at each site might have arranged the rocks to make the foundations of huts or windbreaks, but in each case the responsible agent could equally have been stream flow, soil creep, or some other natural process. The likelihood of a natural origin is particularly strong at Soleihac, where a 20-m (66-ft) long line of basalt rocks is associated with flaked stones, the artifactual origin of which is itself dubious (Roebroeks and van Kolfschoten 1994).

Many more sites contain clusters of artifacts, bones, and other debris that could mark hut bases or specialized activity areas. The evidence is more conjectural than compelling, but the most worthy examples perhaps include those from **Bilzingsleben** (Mania et al. 1994) and **Ariendorf 1** (Turner 1986) in Germany, and from **Le Lazaret Cave** (De Lumley 1975) in south-

3.37, 3.38 *The Schöningen spears:* one of the remarkable wooden spears, dated to about 400,000 years ago, in place at Schöningen (below), and a close-up of the pointed tip (below right). The Schöningen spears provide the oldest compelling evidence for active human hunting.

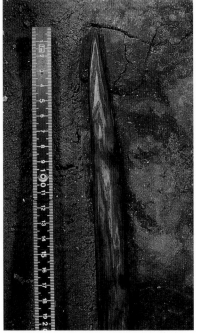

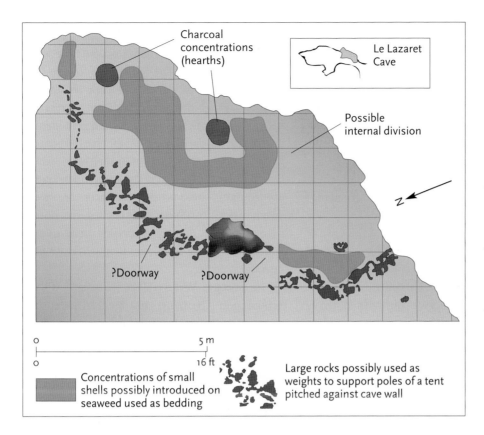

3.39 Site modification: *floor plan of an Acheulean layer at Le Lazaret Cave, southern France. Stone artifacts and fragmentary animal bones were heavily concentrated between the cave wall and a line of large rocks that may have supported the poles of a tent pitched against the wall. Artifacts and bones spilling out from between the rocks at two points might mark former doorways, while concentrations of small seashells could come from seaweed introduced as bedding. Two roughly circular concentrations of charcoal perhaps delineate former fireplaces (hearths).*

ern France. The sites vary in age from perhaps 400,000 years ago at Bilzingsleben, to a time within global oxygen isotope stage (OIS) 8 (301,000–242,000 years ago) at Ariendorf 1, and a time within OIS 6 (186,000–127,000 years ago) at Le Lazaret. (The isotope stages have been identified and dated in sediments on the deep-sea floor. They equate roughly with glacial and interglacial intervals recorded on land, and it is the assignment of terrestrial deposits to a particular glacial (or interglacial) interval that allows ancient archaeological sites to be dated by extrapolation from the deep-sea record; see also p. 127.)

At Ariendorf 1, several large quartz and quartzite blocks (measuring up to 60 x 30 x 30 cm, or 24 x 12 x 12 in) occur in a fine-grained, sandy-silty deposit, where they could only have been introduced by people. Conceivably, they mark the base of a structure, and they partly surround a scatter of artifacts and fragmentary bones. Refittable artifacts (which can be reconstructed to reveal the original core from which they were struck) and conjoinable bone fragments imply that many pieces were deposited at more or less the same time.

At Bilzingsleben, the ancient inhabitants camped alongside a stream flowing from a nearby spring to a small lake. They also settled on parts of the streambed that were periodically dry. The evidence for structures consists of one circular and two oval concentrations of artifacts and fragmentary animal bones (probable food debris) that occur with large stones and bones that could have been used to build walls. The concentrations are 2–3 m (6.5–9.75 ft) in diameter, and each is immediately adja-

cent to a spread of charcoal interpreted as a fireplace. Also nearby are clusters of artifactual "waste" that may represent workshops.

At Le Lazaret, the presence of a structure is suggested by an 11 x 3.5-m (36 x 11-ft) concentration of artifacts and fragmented animal bones bounded by a series of large rocks on one side and by the cave wall on the other [3.39]. The area also contains two hearths, as well as numerous small marine shells and carnivore teeth that could derive respectively from seaweed and skins that were introduced as bedding. The rocks could have supported poles over which skins were draped to pitch a tent against the wall of the cave. Contemporaneous concentrations of artifacts and other cultural debris surrounded or accompanied by natural rocks may represent structure bases in other French caves (especially La Baume Bonne and Orgnac (Villa 1976)), but the patterning is less compelling.

In sum, the evidence for housing before 130,000 years ago is remarkably sparse and equivocal, and the next chapter shows that it becomes abundant and unambiguous only after the advent of fully modern humans between 50,000 and 40,000 years ago. People before 50,000 years ago must have built shelters, particularly at open-air sites in mid-latitude Europe and Asia, but the structures were apparently too flimsy to leave unmistakable archaeological traces. The more substantial structures that appeared after 50,000–40,000 years ago help to explain how fully modern humans were able to colonize the most continental parts of Eurasia, where no people had lived before.

Fire

Homo ergaster (or *H. erectus*) may have had to master fire for warmth and cooking before it could colonize Eurasia, but direct archaeological support is tenuous. The oldest evidence may be patches of baked earth in deposits dated to 1.5–1.4 million years ago at Koobi Fora (p. 79) and Chesowanja in Kenya, but naturally ignited, smoldering vegetation might have produced the same effect (Clark and Harris 1985). Natural fires could also account for burning at most other early Paleolithic sites where dispersed ash, charcoal, burned bones, clusters of burned flint chips, or patches of burned earth have been found. The principal sites are Montagu Cave, Swartkrans Cave, and the Cave of Hearths (all in South Africa); Gesher Benot Ya'aqov (Israel); Olorgesailie (Kenya); Prezletice (Czech Republic); and Terra Amata (France). **Swartkrans Cave**, with burned animal bones, may provide the strongest case, because the burned bones appear only high in the sequence. They are absent in older layers where they might also be expected if natural burning were responsible. Swartkrans has produced a partial skull and other craniodental elements of *Homo ergaster*, dated by associated mammal species (biostratigraphy) to about 1.5 million years ago. If Swartkrans means that *H. ergaster* had mastered fire by 1.5 million years ago, fire use by its geographically scattered descendants might not require independent invention.

Swartkrans Cave aside, the oldest widely accepted evidence for fire comes from layers 10 and 4 at the classic *Homo erectus* site of **Zhoukoudian Locality 1** in China [3.40, 3.41]. The deposits at Locality 1 have been tentatively dated to between 500,000 and 240,000 years ago. The indications for fire consist mainly of numerous charred bones and dark lenses (very thin stratigraphic layers) interpreted as fossil hearths (Pei and Zhang 1985). Geochemical analysis has failed to identify wood ash or charcoal in the dark layers, but the charred bones have been confirmed, and the abundance of burned bones (about 12 percent of the total) recalls their abundance in much later (west Eurasian Mousterian) sites, where fireplaces are well documented (Weiner et al. 1998). As at later sites, the Zhoukoudian specimens are also directly associated with numerous artifacts, which adds to the likelihood that deliberate fire produced the burning.

In Europe, Vértesszöllös (Hungary), Bilzingsleben, and Schöningen (Germany), and Menez-Dregan (France) have all provided tentative evidence for fire in deposits dated between roughly 400,000 and 300,000 years ago (Roebroeks and van Kolfschoten 1994). If these sites are discounted, the oldest widely accepted European evidence for fire comes from the Penultimate Glaciation (OIS 6), between 186,000 and 127,000 years ago. It comprises occasional patches of ash and charcoal at **Pech de l'Azé** and perhaps other French caves (Villa 1976), and abundant carbonized bones, less abundant charcoal, and numerous burned flint artifacts at the cave of **La Cotte de St. Brelade**, Jersey (Callow, Walton, and Shell 1986) (see p. 120).

3.40 *The use of fire: an artist's reconstruction of* Homo erectus *people at Locality 1 Cave, Zhoukoudian, China.*

3.41 *Possible evidence of fire: dark lenses (very thin stratigraphical layers) found at Zhoukoudian Locality 1 in China, together with the presence of numerous charred bones, have been taken as poosible evidence of fossil hearths, though geochemical analysis has not identified the presence of wood ash or charcoal.*

Unequivocal fireplaces are obvious in many sites occupied by the European Neanderthals and their near-modern African contemporaries after 130,000 years ago (see Chapter 4), and it is reasonable to ask whether the paucity of older evidence indicates a more limited ability to make or control fire. The answer is, not necessarily, since the evidence after 130,000 years ago comes mainly from caves, whereas most well-known older sites are open-air occurrences near ancient water sources. Both individual charcoal fragments and thin concentrations that unambiguously mark hearths are much less likely to survive at open-air sites, and it is perhaps no accident that the oldest widely cited, if still equivocal, evidence for fire before 130,000 years ago comes from the Zhoukoudian Locality 1 cave. Unfortunately, caves of similar or greater antiquity are exceptionally rare, and reconstructing the early history of human fire use may thus always depend more on speculation than on hard evidence.

Art

It was noted above that beginning about 600,000 years ago, late Acheulean people often produced hand axes that appeal to the modern eye for their remarkable symmetry in both plan form and edge view. The makers shaped these hand axes extensively and meticulously, and there is the possibility that they were guided by an evolving aesthetic sensibility.

3.42 *Early art?: a proposed female figurine from the Acheulean site of Berekhat Ram, Golan Heights. The base object is a lava (tuff) pebble on which at least three grooves have been incised with a sharp-edged stone tool. If the object was intended to replicate a female figurine, it would be the oldest known example of representational art in the world.*

Alternatively, they might have been driven by the need to produce a piece that was finely balanced; the possibilities cannot be separated, since, as we have already seen, hand axe function remains largely conjectural.

Among other possible indications of art from Acheulean or Acheulean-age sites, three examples stand out. First, fragments of humanly introduced mineral pigment (ocher) have been found associated with Acheulean artifacts and animal bones at Kapthurin (site GnJh-15), Kenya (Tryon and McBrearty 2002), at Duinefontein 2, South Africa (Cruz-Uribe et al. 2003), and with like-aged non-Acheulean artifacts and bones at Twin Rivers, Zambia (Barham 2002). Second, an elephant tibia shaft fragment from Bilzingsleben, Germany (see p. 118), has incised on it a fanlike set of lines (Mania and Mania 1988). And third, above all, a 35-mm (1.4-in) long modified lava (tuff) pebble from Berekhat Ram [3.42] on the Syrian/Israeli border may represent a crude human figurine (Goren-Inbar and Peltz 1995).

At **Kapthurin** argon-argon dating on superimposed volcanic ash places the humanly collected ocher fragments before 285,000 years ago, while optically stimulated luminescence (OSL) on surrounding sands fixes the fragments from **Duinefontein 2** near 270,000 years ago [see box: Luminescence Dating, p. 119]. Uranium-series dating of flowstone suggests that pigment fragments at **Twin Rivers** began to accumulate by 270,000 years ago or before, although the associated stone artifacts belong to a Middle Stone Age variant (the

Lower Lupemban industry) that is commonly thought to succeed the Acheulean in the Twin Rivers region. The Twin Rivers fragments are particularly notable for their abundance and variety of colors, and for indications that some were modified by grinding or rubbing. At all three sites, the fragments anticipate those that occur commonly at succeeding Middle Stone Age and Mousterian sites dated between 250,000 and 50,000 years ago in Africa (Henshilwood et al. 2002) (see p. 143), western Asia (Hovers et al. 2003), and Europe (d'Errico 2003). Arguably, people before 50,000 years ago employed pigments as an ingredient in the mastic or glue used to fix stone tools to wooden handles or for some other utilitarian purpose, but in the absence of hard evidence, body painting or some other broadly artistic behavior cannot be ruled out.

Bilzingsleben is an ancient lakeside site cited above for its possible evidence of structures and worked bone. It is also well known for human skull fragments and for numerous animal bones and a flaked stone artifact assemblage that lacks hand axes. Electron spin resonance determinations and uranium series dates suggest that the bones and artifacts accumulated sometime between 420,000 and 350,000 years ago (Mania et al. 1994). Berekhat Ram is an ancient lakeside site that does not preserve bone but that has provided a rich artifact assemblage, including eight small hand axes and numerous well-made flake tools. Argon-argon dates on underlying and overlying basalts bracket the archaeological layer between 470,000 and 232,000 years ago. Based on the stratigraphic position of the artifact-bearing deposits, the excavators favor an age between about 280,000 and 250,000 years ago.

The incised marks on the **Bilzingsleben elephant tibia** fragment are noteworthy for their even spacing [**3.43, 3.44**], and for the extent to which they replicate each other in length and especially in cross-section. The strong similarity in form suggests that they were made in quick succession by a single stone tool. Their meaning is obviously debatable, but neither their placement nor their form suggests butchery marks.

The **Berekhat Ram pebble** is remarkable for three distinct grooves – a deep one that encircles the narrower, more rounded end, setting off the putative head and neck, and two shallow, curved incisions that run down the sides and that could delineate the arms [**3.42**]. The deep groove and, to a lesser extent, the shallower ones closely match marks produced by sharp-edged

flakes on the same material, and they are readily distinguishable from natural lines (d'Errico and Nowell 2000). The Berekhat Ram pebble was thus humanly modified, even if its final form only dimly anticipates the finely crafted, aesthetically attractive human figurines that appear in Europe and elsewhere after 40,000 years ago. Objects that exhibit the same degree of possible artistic intent also occur sporadically in sites occupied by the Neanderthals and their near-modern African contemporaries between roughly 130,000 and 50,000 years ago (d'Errico 2003). However, objects whose artistic meaning is unequivocal become commonplace only after 50,000 years ago, when they are associated with the origins and spread of fully modern humans from Africa (see Chapter 4).

Diet and Food Procurement

Plant Foods: Foraging As with control over fire, economic advances could help explain how *Homo ergaster* and its descendants managed to colonize new regions, though the evidence is very limited. Both logic and observations of historic hunter-gatherers suggest that, in general, early people everywhere depended more on plants than on animals. Tubers and other underground storage organs may have been especially important, since they were staples among historic low- and mid-latitude hunter-gatherers. It may not be coincidental that *H. ergaster* emerged at a time – 1.8–1.7 million years ago – when tubers had probably become more abundant, following a shift to a drier, more seasonally variable climate over much of Africa. As indicated above, key features of *H. ergaster* anatomy and behavior suggest that the species was well adapted for foraging in arid, highly seasonal environments. The evolution of *H. ergaster* has sometimes been tied to males' enhanced ability to hunt, but it may actually have depended more on females' enhanced ability to locate, excavate, and process tubers (O'Connell et al. 1999).

3.43, 3.44 Early art?: *an elephant tibia shaft fragment from Bilzingsleben, Germany, with a partial fan-like pattern of incised lines. The regular spacing of the incisions, their subequal lengths, and V-like cross-sections suggest that they were created at the same time with a single stone tool. The fragment is 350,000 to 400,000 years old, and it is only one of a handful of potential "art objects" from before 40,000 years ago.*

KEY METHOD Luminescence Dating

The luminescence dating method is a cousin of the electron spin resonance method described on p. 107, and it has the same advantage of being applicable at sites that lack suitable material for radiocarbon dating or that are beyond its range. The luminescence technique employs heat or light to release electrons that are trapped in crystal flaws within substances like flint or sand (Feathers 1996). As the electrons are released, the target object glows, and the intensity of the glow (luminescence) is directly proportional to the number of released electrons. The suitability of sand to luminescence dating is particularly fortunate, because sandy deposits are common worldwide and often enclose archaeological layers. The luminescence variant that is most often applied to sand involves exposure to intense light, and it is thus commonly known as optically stimulated luminescence, or OSL. Sunlight will also empty the crystal traps in sand grains, which means that the electrons released artificially must all have accumulated since the sand grains were last exposed at the surface, that is, just before they were buried. The rate at which electrons accumulated in the sand grains is directly proportional to natural, low-level, background radioactivity in the soil, and this can be measured in the field today to provide the annual radiation dose – in effect, the number of electrons that the sand grains must have accumulated each year since burial. Dividing this number into the total number released in the laboratory provides the number of years since the sand grains were buried.

In practice, luminescence dating often faces some daunting challenges, including the possibility that the annual radiation dose has fluctuated through time as groundwater circulation added or subtracted uranium or other radioactive elements. However, if potential problems can be overcome or placed aside, the luminescence method can often provide dates where no other method is directly applicable, such as at the Duinefontein 2 Acheulean site in South Africa.

Unfortunately, plant tissues that could illuminate the importance of tubers or other plants in early human diets survive at only a handful of Acheulean and Acheulean-age sites. **Table 2** lists the principal sites that have provided seeds or other remains of edible plants, but in each case there is the problem that the remains cannot be unequivocally linked to human activity. In the absence of indisputable plant food residues, plant consumption might be demonstrated by a chemical analysis of early human fossils, assuming that the diet of the living creature can be detected in bones whose chemical makeup has been altered in the ground. So far, the only fossil of primitive *Homo* that may provide a hint of diet is a partial skeleton of *H. ergaster* (KNM-ER 1808) from Koobi Fora, Kenya, dated to roughly 1.7–1.6 million years ago. The long bone shafts of this individual are covered by a layer of abnormal, coarse-woven bone up to 7 mm (0.25 in) thick (Walker et al. 1982). In a recent person, this could reflect yaws, an infectious disease related to syphilis, which induces such bone growth in its final stage. However, it could also follow from a toxic excess of vitamin A. If vitamin A poisoning was the cause, it could have been due to an overindulgence either of carnivore livers or on honeybee eggs, pupae, and larvae.

Animal Foods: Hunting and Scavenging Except perhaps at Koobi Fora, inferences about the subsistence of primitive *Homo* must be based almost entirely on the animal bones associated with artifacts at both Acheulean and contemporaneous non-Acheulean sites scattered throughout Africa and Europe. **Table 3** lists the principal sites. Until the 1970s, most archaeologists simply assumed that ancient people used the artifacts at such sites to kill and butcher the animals found there. It followed that the people were successful big-game hunters, since the animals often included elephants, rhinoceroses, buffalo, and other formidable prey.

Table 2 *The Main Early Paleolithic Sites with Plant Remains Possibly Eaten by Hominins*

- Kalambo Falls (Zambia)
- Gesher Benot Ya'aqov (Israel)
- Kärlich-Seeufer and Bilzingsleben (Germany)
- Vértesszöllös (Hungary)
- Zhoukoudian Locality 1 (China)

Table 3 *The Main Acheulean and Similarly Aged Sites with Closely Associated Animal Bones and Human Artifacts*

- Duinefontein 2, Elandsfontein, and Kathu Pan (South Africa)
- Olorgesailie (Kenya)
- Ternifine (Algeria)
- Revadim and Holon (Israel)
- Torralba, Ambrona, and Aridos (Spain)
- Cagny l'Épinette (France)
- La Polledrara, Isernia la Pineta, and Rebibbia (Italy)
- Bilzingsleben, Schöningen, Miesenheim 1, and Bad Cannstatt (Germany)
- Boxgrove and Hoxne (England)

3.45 *Evidence of early human hunting ability:* the cliffs at La Cotte de St. Brelade, Jersey, Channel Islands, over which Mousterian people may have driven elephants and rhinoceroses between 186,000 and 127,000 years ago.

In the 1970s, however, a growing number of archaeologists began to specialize in the analysis of animal bones, and after close scrutiny it was realized that a stratigraphic association between bones and artifacts need not imply a functional relationship (see Chapter 2). Most early archaeological sites were in the open air near ancient springs, streams, or lakes, which naturally attracted both people and animals. The animal bones at such sites could represent mainly human kills, or they could represent mostly carnivore kills or even natural deaths (from starvation, disease, etc.) that totally escaped human notice or that were subsequently scavenged by people (or carnivores). As has already been discussed in the previous chapter, sorting out the alternatives has proven remarkably difficult, and the most conservative conclusion today is that Acheulean people and their contemporaries definitely hunted big animals, though their success rate is not clear.

Assessing human ability to obtain animals, whether by hunting or scavenging, requires, at minimum, a site where people were the only, or at least the principal, bone accumulators. In this regard caves are generally more promising than open-air sites, because the main game animals available to early people do not, for the most part, enter caves voluntarily. In most instances, therefore, it is safe to assume that their bones were introduced by a predator or scavenger. If the cave fill contains numerous artifacts, hearths, and so on, and little or no evidence for carnivore activity (coprolites (fossil feces), chewed bones, etc.), then people are clearly implicated as the principal bone accumulators. Caves to which Neanderthals and their modern or near-modern African contemporaries surely brought most bones are well known after 130,000 years ago.

Unfortunately, caves themselves have a limited life span, and few survive from the era before 130,000 years ago. The famous Chinese *Homo erectus* site at Zhoukoudian Locality 1 is by far the most striking exception, and it was filled with bones from many species, ranging from small rodents and insectivores through rhinoceroses and elephants (Howell 1986). Two extinct species of deer were especially common, and it has sometimes been said that the Zhoukoudian people were proficient deerstalkers (Wu and Lin 1983). But this interpretation is complicated by the presence of numerous hyena bones and coprolites, and of bones plainly damaged by hyena teeth, indicating that these animals sometimes occupied the site. They may have introduced many of the animal bones, and their activities, combined with profile compaction and other post-depositional destructive pressures, could also explain why the

Zhoukoudian human fossils are highly fragmentary and why the crania lack faces and basal parts (Binford and Ho 1985). Cannibalism is unlikely, because the human bones lack obvious damage from stone tools. Pending the fresh excavation of a large bone sample, Zhoukoudian cannot unambiguously illuminate the predatory or scavenging prowess of *H. erectus*.

With one notable exception, the few European or African caves with deposits older than 130,000 years ago have been similarly uninformative. The main exception is the cave of **La Cotte de St. Brelade** on the island of Jersey in the English Channel (Scott 1989). Here, layers 6 and 3, which probably formed during the Penultimate Glaciation (OIS 6), between 186,000 and 127,000 years ago, have provided numerous Mousterian artifacts, together with bones of at least 20 mammoths and 5 woolly rhinoceroses. There are no securely associated human remains, but the people were probably early *Homo neanderthalensis*. Human butchering is strongly implied by the abundance of the associated artifacts (more than 1100 in level 3), by damage to the bones (especially to skulls, which may have been opened to obtain the brains), and by peculiar patterns of skeletal part representation: radii and ulnae (lower arm bones), tibiae (shin bones), wrist bones, ankle bones, foot bones, and vertebrae are all but absent in both layers. The missing parts are the least bulky ones, which people (and possibly other large predators) would have found easiest to remove. In addition, the compact, vertically restricted packing of bones within each layer suggests rapid accumulation, perhaps when people drove small groups of mammoths or rhinoceroses simultaneously over a headland just above the site [3.45]. Driving could explain why the mammoths and the rhinos were mainly subadults and prime-age adults. Unlike very young and old individuals, subadult and prime-adult animals would otherwise be difficult to obtain by either hunting or scavenging.

The evidence for butchering at La Cotte foreshadows abundant evidence for butchery by the Neanderthals and their African contemporaries after 130,000 years ago (Chase 1988; Stiner 1994; Milo 1998). Specialists agree that these people introduced large numbers of bones to many cave sites, where numerous cut or percussion marks indicate that the bones represent food debris (Chapter 4). The ages of animals at the time of death sometimes implies driving in Africa (Klein 1979) and in Europe (Levine 1983), but authorities disagree vigorously about whether hunting was more common than scavenging (Binford 1985; Chase 1988) [see box: Acheulean Big-Game Hunters?, pp. 122–23]. The issue may not be resolvable, but southern African observations indicate that whatever means people used to obtain large animals between 130,000 and 60,000 years ago, they did not succeed very often (Klein 1994). If it is fair to project backward, the more ancient people on which this chapter focuses were even less successful, and they probably rarely fed on the elephants, rhinoceroses, buffalo, or other large animals that dominate their sites.

Summary and Conclusions

The emergence of *Homo ergaster* 1.8–1.7 million years ago marked a watershed, for *H. ergaster* was the first hominin species whose anatomy and behavior fully justify the label human. Unlike the australopithecines and *Homo habilis*, in which body form and proportions retained apelike features, suggesting a continued reliance on trees for food or refuge, *H. ergaster* achieved essentially modern form, proportions, increased stature, and degree of sexual dimorphism. The evidence suggests that *H. ergaster* was the first hominin species to resemble historic hunter-gatherers not only in a fully terrestrial lifestyle, but also in a social organization that featured economic cooperation between males and females and perhaps between semipermanent male-female units.

H. ergaster was also larger-brained than earlier hominins, and this increased brain size was probably linked to the nearly simultaneous appearance of hand axes and other relatively sophisticated artifacts of the Acheulean industrial tradition.

The emergence of *H. ergaster* and the Acheulean recall the appearance of the genus *Homo* and of the first Oldowan stone tools roughly 800,000 years earlier. Both events reveal a close connection between biological and behavioral change in the early phases of human evolution. Arguably too, both occurred abruptly, in the punctuational (as opposed to the gradual) mode of evolution, and each may have been stimulated by a broadly simultaneous change in global climate.

The anatomical and behavioral advances that mark *Homo ergaster* help explain how it became the first hominin species to invade arid, highly seasonal environments in Africa, and how it became the first to colonize Eurasia. Its broad dispersal greatly enhanced the potential for natural selection, random genetic drift, or both, to promote genetic divergence among human populations. The eventual result was the emergence of at least three geographically distinct human lineages: *Homo erectus* in the Far East, *H. sapiens* in Africa, and *H. neanderthalensis* in Europe. *H. erectus* was probably the earliest to differentiate, and fossils and artifacts together imply that East Asian humans followed a singular evolutionary course beginning 1 million years ago or before. In contrast, fossils and artifacts indicate that *H. sapiens* and *H. neanderthalensis* shared a common ancestor as recently as 500,000 years ago, and their morphological differentiation is manifest only after 400,000 years ago. Arguably, eastern Asia was more distinctive because it was colonized (from Africa) only once, whereas Europe was colonized several times, and only the event at 500,000 years ago produced a permanent resident population.

The obstacles to earlier permanent European colonization remain obscure, but it is probably pertinent that the first permanent colonists arrived with the more sophisticated tools of the late Acheulean cultural tradition that probably appeared in Africa around 600,000 years ago, and that they may have been immediate descendants of the first Africans whose average brain size significantly exceeded that of *H. ergaster*. To begin with, the earliest permanent Europeans looked very much like their African contemporaries, and they are often lumped with them in the species *Homo heidelbergensis*. By 400,000 years ago, however, European skulls and faces had already begun to anticipate those of the classic Neanderthals.

By 250,000–200,000 years ago, craniofacial differences among *Homo erectus*, *H. neanderthalensis*, and *H. sapiens* were highly conspicuous, but all three lineages seem to have shared a tendency toward brain enlargement (encephalization). By 200,000 years ago, brain size, whether measured on its own or relative to body size, everywhere approximated the modern average, and only variation in braincase form might imply that the different lineages differed neurologically from each other or from later people, including present-day living ones. The shared natural selective forces that could have driven brain

KEY CONTROVERSY Acheulean Big-Game Hunters?

The Torralba and Ambrona Acheulean sites are located 2 km (1.2 miles) apart, about 150 km (93 miles) northeast of Madrid, Spain, on opposite sides of the Masegar River valley (Freeman 1994). Stratigraphic context and fauna (including especially teeth of the advanced, rootless vole, *Arvicola*, at Ambrona) indicate that the Acheulean artifacts accumulated roughly 500,000 years ago. This may have been only shortly after the initial Acheulean penetration of Europe, which could explain why the Torralba and Ambrona hand axes and other bifacial tools closely resemble contemporaneous African ones. The sediments and fauna also show that the sites were on the margins of a shallow, marsh-edged lake, which filled the Masegar Valley. Neither site has produced human remains, but if diagnostic remains were present, they would probably be assigned to *Homo heidelbergensis* or early *H. neanderthalensis*, as defined here. The large animal remains are heavily dominated by bones of elephants and horses.

At both sites, the stone tools and occasional tool-damaged bones imply some human role in the bone accumulations, but the tools are thinly scattered among the more numerous bones, and there are also carnivore coprolites (fossilized feces), bones damaged by carnivore teeth, and numerous bones abraded by flowing water. Among the bones of most species, axial elements (skulls, vertebrae, and pelvises) are relatively abundant compared to limb bones (Klein 1987). The limb bones are the meatiest parts, and the implication is that predators or scavengers often removed these from the site. However, either people or large animal carnivores would create the same pattern. Similarly, people, large carnivores, or especially natural mortality could account for an apparent overrepresentation of older adults among the elephants (other species are too poorly represented for the construction of age profiles).

The available data do not allow us to isolate the relative roles of humans, carnivores, and factors such as starvation, accidents, and stream action in creating the bone assemblages. In the current state of our knowledge, Torralba and Ambrona need not have differed significantly from the margins of historic African streams or waterholes, where the events that produce carcasses can be complex and need not involve people.

Certainly, as understood at present, the sites do not tell us how successful or effective *H. heidelbergensis* or early *H. neanderthalensis* was at obtaining meat.

Greater human involvement may be indicated at other broadly contemporaneous European sites, such as Aridos (Spain), Isernia La Pineta (Italy), and Bilzingsleben, Schöningen, and Bad Cannstatt (Germany), where stone artifacts, artifact-damaged bones, or both are more abundant; but even at these sites it is impossible to show that people significantly shaped the bone accumulations (Gaudzinski and Turner 1996). The human role is similarly ambiguous at contemporary or somewhat older African sites, including Ternifine (Algeria), Olorgesailie (Kenya), and Elandsfontein (South Africa), where the hunting or scavenging success of *H. ergaster* and early *H. sapiens* remains equally indeterminate. The uncertainty in each case stems partly from a heightened awareness of the natural factors that may have shaped bone accumulations near ancient lakes and streams, and partly from the incompleteness and ambiguity of the surviving evidence.

---

enlargement in each lineage are easy to imagine, but the pace of encephalization remains uncertain, partly because the relevant fossils are scarce, and partly because they are often very imprecisely dated. It is thus impossible to say whether enlargement occurred in sudden spurts or gradually, but a shared trend in three otherwise distinct lineages may argue that the increase was mostly gradual.

In addition, the archaeological record associated with each lineage nowhere reveals a striking behavioral advance that might reflect abrupt brain enlargement. Instead, even between 500,000 and 250,000 years ago, when average brain size was everywhere within the modern range, humans in both Africa and Eurasia remained extraordinarily primitive in their behavior. They produced a relatively small range of stone artifact types, their artifact assemblages varied remarkably little over long time spans and vast areas, they rarely, if ever, produced formal (standardized) artifacts from bone, ivory, antler, or similar plastic substances, they left little or no evidence for art, and they failed to build structures that would leave an unambiguous archaeological trace. In all these respects, the people differed little from their immediate successors between 250,000 and 50,000 years ago, and if there were differences, they were that the people between 250,000 and 50,000 years ago may have hunted more effectively than their predecessors, and may have been the first to gain full control over fire. Both contrasts, however, may reflect only the much smaller number of sites older than 250,000 years where evidence for hunting and especially for fire may be firmly detected.

Archaeologists agree that the pattern changed sharply after 50,000 years ago, when formal bone artifacts, art, housing remnants, and other items associated with historic hunter-gatherers appeared widely for the first time. It is thus only after 50,000 years ago that fully modern behavior became firmly established. Archaeologists disagree, however, whether completely modern behavior developed abruptly about 50,000 years ago or more gradually over the preceding 30,000–20,000 years. The next chapter outlines the evidence and the continuing debate.

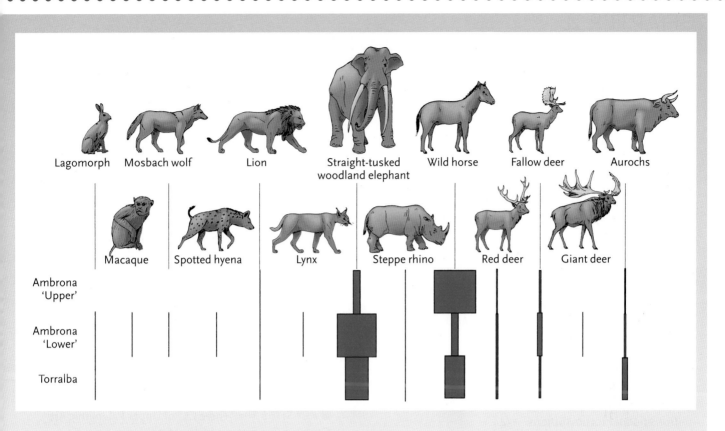

3.46 *The abundance of large mammals at the Torralba and Ambrona Acheulean sites, north-central Spain. The bars are proportional to the number of identifiable bones assigned to each species (NISP). Torralba is about the same age as Ambrona "Lower" and has been placed below Ambrona for display purposes only. Like other Acheulean sites, Torralba and Ambrona contain many bones of large mammals, including elephants, but as at other sites, the bones could represent natural deaths or carnivore kills, and so far it has not been possible to determine the hunting capability of Acheulean people.*

Further Reading and Suggested Websites

Deacon, H. J. & Deacon, J. 1999. *Human Beginnings in South Africa: Uncovering the Secrets of the Stone Age.* Cape Town: David Philip. A highly accessible introduction to the Stone Age prehistory of southern Africa and to how we reconstruct early human behavior and ecology.

Gamble, C. 1999. *The Palaeolithic Societies of Europe.* Cambridge: Cambridge University Press. A comprehensive, authoritative summary of European Palaeolithic prehistory with equal emphasis on archaeological observations and their synthesis.

Howell, F. C. 1965. *Early Man.* New York: Time-Life. A classic summary of human biological and behavioral evolution with a remarkably current perspective, despite its age.

Johanson, D. & Edgar, B. 1996. *From Lucy to Language.* New York: Simon & Schuster. A layman's guide to human evolution, with spectacular photographs of key fossils and artifacts.

Klein, R. G. 1999. *The Human Career: Human Biological and Cultural Origins.* (2nd ed.) Chicago: University of Chicago Press. A detailed overview that shows how human biological and behavioral evolution proceeded in tandem from the emergence of the human tribe 5–7 million years ago to the emergence of fully modern humans 50,000 years ago.

Tattersall, I. & Schwartz, J. H. 2000. *Extinct Humans.* Boulder, CO: Westview Press. A beautifully illustrated introduction to human evolution written for non-specialists, covering both ancient fossils and artifacts and the theoretical framework for understanding why they changed through time.

http://www.asu.edu/clas/iho/ The site of The Institute of Human Origins at Arizona State University, a multidisciplinary research institute dedicated to the recovery and analysis of the fossil evidence for human evolution.

http://www.indiana.edu/~origins/links/evolinks.html A site maintained by Professor Jeanne Sept of Indiana University, with up-to-date information on human evolution and links to many other key sites.

CHAPTER 4
THE RISE OF MODERN HUMANS

Paul Pettitt, University of Sheffield

The Climatic Background 125

Competing Hypotheses for the Origin of *Homo sapiens* 127
The Multi-regional Evolution Hypothesis 128
The Out of Africa Hypothesis 128
Other Hypotheses and Attempts at Consensus 128
● KEY CONTROVERSY Multi-regional Evolution and Modern Human Emergence in Asia and Australasia 130

The Anatomy of *Homo sapiens* 130

Evolution in Low Latitudes: Evidence for the Rise of Modern Humans in Africa 132
Earliest Homo sapiens 132
Transitional Homo sapiens 134
Anatomically Modern Humans 137

Genetic Keys to the Origins of Modern Humans 137
Mitochondrial DNA and the Theory of an Early African "Coalescence" 138
Other Theories and Potential Consensus 139
Mitochondrial DNA and the Evolution of Homo neanderthalensis 140

Archaeology and the Emergence of "Modern" Behavior in Middle Stone Age Africa 140
Artifactual Evidence 141
● KEY SITE Katanda and the Earliest Harpoons 142
Hunting and Dietary Evidence 142
Evidence of Site Modification and Art 143
● KEY SITE Klasies River Mouth: Middle Stone Age Hunters? 144
● KEY CONTROVERSY The Evolution of Language 146

Evolution in High Latitudes: The Neanderthals 146
The Anatomy of Homo neanderthalensis 146
Exploitation of Resources: Hunting, Gathering, and Scavenging 149
The Mousterian Lithic Industry 150
Neanderthal Behavior 151

Early Dispersals of *Homo sapiens* **into the Levantine Corridor** 152

The Colonization of East Asia and Australia 154
● KEY CONTROVERSY *Homo floresiensis*: A Small-bodied Hominin from Indonesia 155

The Colonization of Europe, and the Middle to Upper Paleolithic Transition 156
● KEY METHOD Radiocarbon Dating 157
The Aurignacian 157
Neanderthal "Transitional" Industries 158
Relations between Neanderthals and Incoming Homo sapiens? 159
● KEY SITES The "Three Cs" of Upper Paleolithic Art: Cosquer, Chauvet, and Côa 160

Developments in Modern Behavior: The European Upper Paleolithic 161
The Gravettian 161
Gravettian Behavior 162
The Magdalenian 163
● KEY CONTROVERSY The Meaning of "Venus" Figurines 164

Late Pleistocene Dispersals: Colonization of the Americas 166
Possible Source Populations 166
• *Archaeology and Human Remains* 166
• *Linguistic and Genetic Evidence* 166
● KEY CONTROVERSY Kennewick Man 168
The Archaeological Evidence for Pre-Clovis Sites 168
• *Interpreting the Evidence* 169
● KEY SITE Monte Verde, Chile 170
The Clovis Phenomenon 171

Summary and Conclusions 171
● KEY CONTROVERSY Big-Game Extinctions in North America 172

Further Reading and Suggested Websites 173

This chapter focuses on the origins and spread of *Homo sapiens* – anatomically modern humans – from *c.* 400,000 to 12,000 years ago. In the previous chapter we traced the dispersal of hominins across the Old World, from Africa to Asia and Europe, and saw the emergence of new species: *Homo ergaster*, *H. erectus*, and *H. heidelbergensis*. After 400,000 years ago, two more new species arose: *H. neanderthalensis*, the Neanderthals (through a pre-Neanderthal phase), in western Eurasia, and *H. sapiens*, modern humans, biologically similar to ourselves, in Africa.

In formal archaeological terms, this chapter covers the end of the Lower Paleolithic (*c.* 250,000 years ago) and spans the Middle and Upper Paleolithic (to *c.* 12,000 years ago). The transition from the Middle Paleolithic (known in Africa as the Middle Stone Age) to the Upper Paleolithic (Late Stone Age) at around 50,000 years ago coincides with the expansion of *Homo sapiens* and the demise of other hominin species. The success of modern humans is demonstrated not only by their replacement of *H. erectus* and the Neanderthals, but also by their spread to continents apparently unoccupied by earlier hominin species, including Australia and the Americas.

Although a century of research in the field and the laboratory has produced a large body of information about this period, the fossil database is still relatively poor. Furthermore, the archaeological record is strongly biased toward Europe, where both the history and the intensity of research have been far greater than elsewhere. There also remain serious gaps and limitations in absolute chronology – in our ability to date securely and precisely the finds and fossils that we wish to study. On the other hand, recent decades have seen a revolution in the understanding of modern human origins through the application of DNA research – the information embedded in all of our genes. This has played a particularly important part in the debate over the relationship between modern humans and Neanderthals.

The generally accepted view of human biological and behavioral evolution during the last half-million years of the Pleistocene, until around 12,000 years ago, can be summarized as follows:

● *Homo neanderthalensis* evolved slowly from at least 400,000 years ago in Europe and western Asia (**early pre-Neanderthals**), and **earliest** *Homo sapiens* somewhat later in Africa, both in the context of similar technological transitions, termed Lower to Middle Paleolithic in Europe and Early to Middle Stone Age in Africa. As explained in the previous chapter, the two species last shared a common ancestor, *H. heidelbergensis*, around 600,000–500,000 years ago.

The key story of the last 100,000 years of human history is the expansion of *H. sapiens* throughout the known world, replacing both *H. erectus* in eastern Asia and the Neanderthals in the West. The end result was a world dominated by a single hominin species – our own. The archaeology of this last 100,000 years reveals profound behavioral changes associated with modern humans, including the emergence of symbolism and art. How far these behaviors were shared with Neanderthals is the subject of considerable debate.

● Early *H. neanderthalensis* (**late pre-Neanderthals**) and early *H. sapiens* established distinct populations by at least 300,000 years ago. Alongside this is a possible early appearance and slow evolution of some "modern" behavior in Africa and, arguably, late in the Middle Paleolithic of Europe.

H. sapiens fossils dating to *c.* 250,000–125,000 years ago exhibit **transitional** traits, with elements of both primitive and modern human morphology.

● At least one dispersal of **anatomically modern** *H. sapiens* from Africa took place by 100,000 years ago, possibly followed by a major population bottleneck, i.e., a significant reduction in human numbers to perhaps as low as 10,000 individuals. These three groups of *H. sapiens* – earliest, transitional, and anatomically modern – are linked on the basis of recognizable human traits that clearly develop from the earliest appearance of the species in a single lineage.

Early Neanderthals developed by 150,000 years ago, and **Classic Neanderthals** in Eurasia by 70,000 years ago.

● The development of "modern" behavior in Africa at the transition to the Late Stone Age, and in Europe at the transition to the Upper Paleolithic, was accompanied by another dispersal of modern humans from Africa and western Asia, reaching Australia, southwest Siberia and Europe by *c.* 40,000 years ago.

● Population retraction at the Last Glacial Maximum, around 20,000 years ago, when the ice sheets were at their greatest extent, was followed by a major demographic expansion after *c.* 16,000 years ago, including the first colonization of the Americas around that time, and economic intensification leading to farming in some regions by 11,000 years ago.

The Climatic Background

Remarkably unstable climatic change forms the backdrop to the evolution of modern humans. "Saw-tooth curves" resulting from the study of fluctuations in the oxygen isotopes ^{18}O and

THE RISE OF MODERN HUMANS TIMELINE

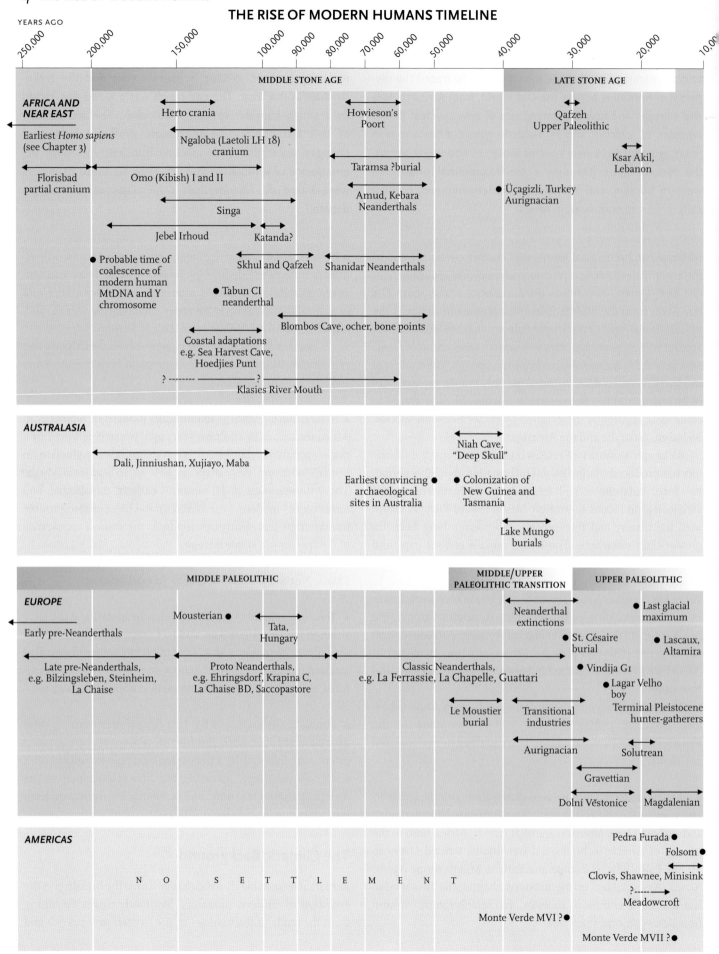

^{16}O in deep-sea cores from the Pacific Ocean or ice cores from Greenland (see Chapter 2) reveal at least four full interglacials (periods of warming), four severe glacials, and considerable climatic fluctuation within and between these over the last 400,000 years. Terrestrial evidence, such as geological and faunal indicators of broad environmental zones and relative ages, can be correlated to these oxygen isotope stages (labeled OIS12 to OIS1 from 475,000 years ago) [**4.1**].

In northern latitudes, the environmental effects of glacial/interglacial cycles and less dramatic stadial/interstadial fluctuations (respectively, relatively brief cold and warm stages within interglacial and glacial periods) were generally expressed in terms of the flourishing or dying back of grassland and areas of low shrub; as a result, there was an increase or decrease in the presence of herbivorous animals and in the extent of northern deciduous woodland. In Africa, however, the cycles expressed themselves more as arid or wetter periods, in which major geographical features such as the Sahara would expand and contract. In the periods when the region of North Africa now covered by the Sahara supported rich, well-watered, varied environments, human populations may have been widespread. Conversely, the contraction of such environments and the growth of desert may have forced small groups of anatomically modern humans out of Africa to the north or east. In eastern Asia, by contrast, climate appears to have remained relatively stable, perhaps explaining in part the lack of any major biological and behavioral evolution from *Homo erectus* and Lower Paleolithic variants of this species established there by at least 1 million years ago (Pope 1995) (see Chapter 3).

Competing Hypotheses for the Origin of *Homo sapiens*

As already explained, the key theme of this period is the origin and spread of modern humans, our own species. The question is, did we evolve in one specific region of the world and then spread to other continents, or did we develop from several earlier hominin species through parallel processes of evolution, e.g. from *Homo erectus* in East Asia and from *Homo neanderthalensis* in Europe?

In the 1940s, Franz Weidenreich (1947) suggested that modern humans had a multi-regional origin across the Old World. In such a view, which was rapidly developed by a number of scholars, *Homo sapiens* was seen to arise gradually from

Homo erectus populations sometime after they had established themselves in regions outside Africa; this process has come to be referred to as regional continuity. To Weidenreich, gene flow (the introduction of new genes into regional populations) would have ensured that these evolving regional populations remained essentially similar and resulted ultimately in one human species. This model of modern human origins has in recent years been developed by Alan Thorne, Milford Wolpoff, and others, and has become formalized as the multi-regional evolution hypothesis (Thorne and Wolpoff 1981; Wolpoff 1989).

Beginning in the late 1960s, however, a number of scholars, including Louis Leakey, W. W. Howells, and, later, Chris Stringer and Peter Andrews, suggested that modern human origins could be traced to a single geographic center, most often identified as Africa (Howells 1976; Stringer and Andrews 1988). Howells referred to this as the Noah's Ark hypothesis, and more recent terms have included the Garden of Eden, single origins, and Out of Africa hypotheses. Proponents of the two theories have never regarded them as entirely mutually exclusive, but they have tended to be portrayed as such, and the resulting polarization has hampered progress to a certain extent (Groves 1997). Other scholars have developed intermediary models, and the logic, predictions, and robustness of these models have been debated intensely since the late 1980s. Alongside such debates, modern genetics and, latterly, ancient DNA have played an

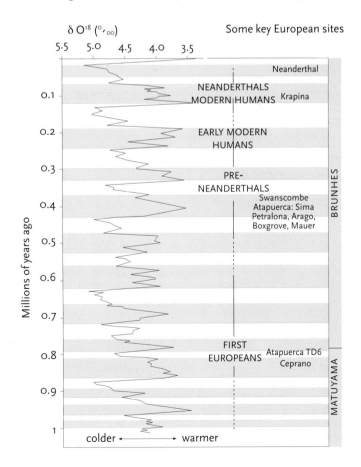

4.1 Oxygen isotope ratios: *diagram of fluctuating ratios of the oxygen isotopes ^{16}O and ^{18}O over the last 1 million years. Coloured and white bands correspond to oxygen isotope stages. Key sites and general evolutionary stages are noted to right, with far right bar showing Brunhes and Matuyama paleomagnetic phases.*

increasing role and have come to provide strong – but not unequivocal – support for the single African center.

The Multi-regional Evolution Hypothesis

This hypothesis, notably in its most recent incarnation, seeks to explain both modern human origins and modern human diversity. Modern "racial" differences are seen to have deep evolutionary roots (Wolpoff and Caspari 1997a), although gene flow is important in maintaining an overall reproductive and anatomical similarity. Central to the multi-regional argument are fossils from Asia and Australia, which have been interpreted as showing evidence for regional continuity in populations [see box: Multi-regional Evolution and Modern Human Emergence in Asia and Australasia, pp. 130–31].

The multi-regional evolution hypothesis predicts that modern human fossils should appear at broadly the same time throughout the Old World; that fossils transitional in form between earlier *Homo ergaster* or *H. heidelbergensis* and modern humans should be found in all or most inhabited regions; and that patterns of continuity should occur there also. Genetically, the hypothesis predicts that the coalescence of modern human genes should have a deep ancestry, and genetic variability should be broadly similar across occupied regions of the Old World, reflecting similar rates of change through random mutation and gene flow.

4.2 Human colonization of the world: *a map showing the spread of modern humans around the world, with very approximate dates, given as years ago.*

The Out of Africa Hypothesis

By contrast, this hypothesis is derived from the notion that some fossil specimens are more plausible candidates for modern human ancestry than others. For example, since the discovery in 1856 of the Neander Valley fossils near Dusseldorf, Germany, the Neanderthals were thought by many to be unlikely ancestors of modern humans, given their anatomical differences and chronological overlap with *Homo sapiens*. There was simply too little time for such a major evolution to have occurred. In its extreme form, the hypothesis assumes not only the dispersal of modern humans from a single center of origin, but also the absolute replacement of older, indigenous forms of *Homo* by this modern form, although the possibility of varying degrees of potential interbreeding have been acknowledged.

The single origins hypothesis predicts that the earliest fossils of modern humans will be found only in Africa, and that transitional fossils will also be found only in this region. It also suggests that modern-day human populations will not necessarily share links with earlier populations occupying the same region. One region, Africa, should show the greatest genetic diversity, reflecting a longer period of time for random mutation to have occurred than in regions to which humans dispersed.

Other Hypotheses and Attempts at Consensus

In 1982 Gunter Bräuer proposed an Afro-European *sapiens* hypothesis that envisaged a degree of evolution in both regions, with slow expansions out of Africa of emerging modern

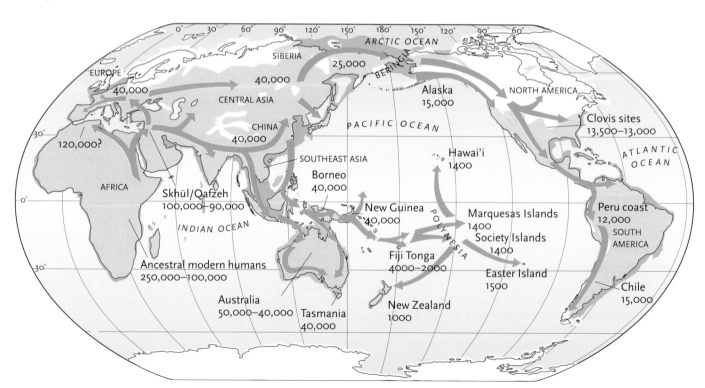

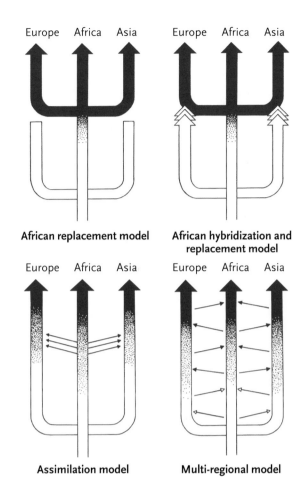

Europe Africa Asia

African replacement model

Europe Africa Asia

African hybridization and replacement model

Europe Africa Asia

Assimilation model

Europe Africa Asia

Multi-regional model

4.3 *Human evolution models:* *the main models for the origin and spread of anatomically modern humans originally comprised two – multi-regional and African replacement. Now, additional models accounting for more subtle and complex processes include assimilation and hybridization/replacement. White arrows indicate archaic humans, brown arrows anatomically modern. Small arrows indicate genetic admixture.*

humans, and varying degrees of genetic mixing. He later described this as a "hybridization and replacement model" (Bräuer 1989), which did not exclude a degree of regional continuity, and which saw modern human origins as complex, differing regionally in form, rate, and extent. In 1989 Fred Smith and colleagues proposed an assimilation hypothesis, in which an emergent *Homo sapiens* population from Africa would have affected evolutionary processes in other regions, ultimately assimilating regional early human groups into the modern human gene pool (Smith, Simek, and Harrill 1989). Furthermore, Marta Mirazón Lahr and Robert Foley (1994) suggested that multiple dispersals out of Africa were more probable than a single event, a notion that has been supported by recent genetic work (Templeton 2002).

To clarify the situation, Leslie Aiello (1993) distinguished clearly between four main hypotheses [4.3]: 1) an African replacement hypothesis, which argues that modern humans arose in Africa, dispersed from there, and replaced existing *Homo* species elsewhere, with little or no hybridization between the groups; 2) an African hybridization and replacement hypothesis similar to the former, but in which hybridization is variable but more significant; 3) an assimilation hypothesis, in which gene flow, admixture, and the effects of the already existing popula-

tion on an incoming African population are significant; and 4) a multi-regional evolution hypothesis, which denies the primacy of Africa in the origin of modern humans and instead emphasizes long-term population continuity and gene flow.

Since the 1980s, the multi-regional and single center hypotheses have been modified, and interpretational problems have arisen, particularly because the fossil and genetic databases may be seen to fit more than one hypothesis if they are poorly defined and flexible. To help overcome such problems, Chris Stringer (2001) has usefully distinguished between the four main hypotheses on the basis of their formal predictions. The **replacement** and **hybridization** hypotheses are similar in that they predict a relatively recent African origin for modern humans, and a high level of population replacement during their dispersal(s) out of Africa. The extent of gene flow between a dispersing *Homo sapiens* population and regional archaic *Homo* species defines the interaction between the two, from insignificant (replacement) to significant (hybridization). The replacement model in its extreme form would entail that the African population was a distinct species recognizable in the fossil record and incapable of producing viable offspring with populations outside Africa. Both of these hypotheses can be distinguished from the **multi-regional** hypothesis in that the latter assumes that the evolutionary origin of modern humans occurred in more than one region, and that the chronological period over which modern humans were emerging was considerably longer than is supposed in the replacement or hybridization hypotheses, i.e., that modern human populations were emerging outside Africa before *c.* 150,000 years ago. The **assimilation** hypothesis need not predict such a long chronology.

Although multi-regionalists continue to promote hypotheses of multi-center origins, it is fair to say that scholarly opinion is moving toward a consensus that modern humans evolved biologically in Africa. Even the complex Asian fossil record, which has been the mainstay of multi-regionalism, can no longer be held to refute the African origins hypothesis [see box: Multi-regional Evolution and Modern Human Emergence in Asia and Australasia, pp. 130–31]. Rather, research now centers on how many dispersal events occurred from an African or Southwest Asian center; how these are reflected in modern human genetics; whether a critical event such as the origins of sophisticated language was crucial to the process; and whether the emergence of modern behavior was gradual, perhaps paralleling the biological evolution of *Homo sapiens*, or whether it was a sudden, relatively late phenomenon. Only a vague picture of the subsequent spread of behaviorally modern humans across the Old and New Worlds is available to us, and the question as to when the earliest colonization of major continents such as Australia and the Americas occurred is still hotly contested. A major issue is whether dispersing members of our own species came into contact with indigenous archaic *Homo*

species such as the Neanderthals, and if they did, whether ideas, genes, or violence were exchanged.

The Anatomy of *Homo sapiens*

Reliable dating and informed interpretation of the fossil record are central to the testing of competing hypotheses of modern human origins. In particular, specific agreement as to exactly

---

KEY CONTROVERSY Multi-regional Evolution and Modern Human Emergence in Asia and Australasia

The status of the multi-regional evolution hypothesis, which holds that anatomically modern humans emerged in a number of geographical regions and maintained a morphological similarity by means of gene flow, has been severely eroded since the early 1990s. A number of genetic studies point to the primacy of Africa in the coalescence of the modern human gene pool, and the African fossil and archaeological record is the only one at present that bears reasonably convincing indications of the evolution of biological and behavioral modernity.

Nevertheless, the multi-regional hypothesis is thought by some to explain perceived long-term anatomical continuity in several regions of Asia. The complex fossil record of Asia has often been seen as representing a regional evolution from *Homo erectus* to *Homo sapiens*, resulting in the characteristic anatomical features of Southeast Asians and aboriginal Australians today, and some scholars believe that this is the last region in which an evolution toward modern humans independent of Africa may have occurred (Wolpoff 1989).

Chinese and Javan Fossils
Fossils from Java, China, and Australia play a central role in this debate. It is reasonably well established that *H. erectus* populations were present on Java (Sangiran, Trinil) and in China (Hexian, Yuanmou, Zhoukoudian) from at least 1 million years ago and down to 500,000 years ago (Chapter 3), and perhaps much later, for example at Ngandong. Four Chinese sites – Dali, Jinniushan, Xujiayo, and Maba – have yielded fossils bearing a variety

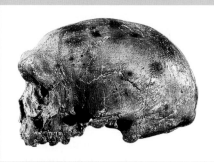

4.4 *The Dali cranium from China is approximately 200,000 years old and was originally classified as* Homo erectus. *It does possess traits of* Homo sapiens *and multi-regionalists see it as transitional between the two. The cranium is, however, highly distorted through post-depositional weight loading, and recent analyses have weakened this notion.*

of characteristics found in *H. erectus* and *H. sapiens*, in deposits dating to between 200,000 and 90,000 years ago (Brown 2001; Keates 2001).

The facial skeleton of the Dali cranium, for example, is modern looking in proportion and bears delicate cheekbones, and the Jinniushan partial skeleton has a large endocranial capacity (*c.* 1400 cc), a thin cranial vault, and a morphologically modern-looking face. To the proponents of the multi-regional hypothesis, these represent an intermediate stage between earlier *H. erectus* forms found at such sites as Lantian, Gongwangling and Yunxian, and later Holocene populations (after 10,000 years ago).

Unfortunately, the preservation of the Chinese fossil material is poor, and a number of facial skeletons, including those from Dali and Jinniushan, are severely distorted, particularly in diagnostic areas. Most

alarmingly, there are no hominin fossils securely dated to the period between *c.* 100,000 and 30,000 years ago, despite the intensity of archaeological research in China and in contrast to the adequate representation of populations before and after this time. This gap in the fossil record might explain the lack of any modern Chinese anatomical characteristics in fossils from before 100,000 years ago, undermining the model of regional continuity.

Whether or not they became regionally extinct long before the arrival of fully modern humans (see also box: *Homo floresiensis*: A Small-bodied Hominin from Indonesia, p. 155), Asian populations from before 100,000 years ago made little or no contribution to modern Asian peoples. Certainly the most tempting interpretation of the fossil and archaeological record is a replacement of existing populations by anatomically modern humans from elsewhere.

Australian Fossils
Similarly, hominin fossils from Australian sites such as Kow Swamp, Keilor, Wajak, and Willandra Lakes have been seen as an intermediate stage between Javan *Homo erectus* and modern aboriginal populations. These Australian fossils fail to show any features uniquely characteristic of *H. erectus*, and are clearly representative of *H. sapiens*. In particular, the remains from Kow Swamp in southeast Australia have fuelled arguments about a close link to *H. erectus*. Of a number of human remains, probably representing burials made in the Late Pleistocene and early Holocene, two crania (KS1 and KS5) possess a

---

how *Homo sapiens* may be defined anatomically is critical, as only through this may modern humans be recognized in the fossil record. Although opinions differ as to the specifics of what being "modern" actually means anatomically (see Wolpoff and Caspari 1997b for a useful critique), most authorities agree that there are global similarities in the **skull shape** of modern humans alive today, and where differences occur between regional populations this relates solely to size, which at this scale is not related to cognition or intelligence (e.g. Hennesy and Stringer 2002). This variable set of cranial traits provides a useful template with which to explore the fossil record, despite the retention of archaic traits on some of the early fossils generally classed as early modern humans, which push the frontiers of this definition [**Table 1**, p. 132].

Below the skull, limb bones are long relative to the trunk, and distal limb segments (tibiae and fibulae, radii and ulnae,

long shape, robust facial bones, a receding forehead, and low-set, rectangular-shaped eye sockets. The excavator of Kow Swamp, Alan Thorne, concluded that these represented a robust, archaic population of Australians that provided the link between *H. erectus* and modern Australians. Other discoveries, such as a cranial fragment and fragmentary postcranial material from the Willandra Lakes and a similarly robust cranium from Cohuna, were incorporated into this transitional group.

By contrast, more gracile remains from Lake Mungo stood in stark contrast to the population of "robusts," and Thorne (1971) thus envisaged two population events in Australia: an early event from the Indonesian *H. erectus* source, and a later spread of more gracile modern humans into Southeast Asia from mainland China, presumably including the gracile skull recovered in the Niah Cave, Sarawak, Borneo. Thorne saw aboriginal Australians as representing a hybrid of the two groups.

As with China, there are problems with the Australian material. Some of the fossils used by Thorne are not securely dated, and they may actually be much younger than suggested. In 1981 Peter Brown, on the basis of comparisons with a much larger sample of aboriginal cranial remains, demonstrated clearly that the peculiarly flattened foreheads of the Kow Swamp and Cohuna specimens were the result of artificial shaping. With

Brown's work, any sensible connection of the Australian "robusts" to Javan *H. erectus* was eliminated. Instead, Brown has suggested that a slow process of "gracilization" occurred in *H. sapiens* populations as people became smaller and less robust over the Pleistocene/Holocene transition.

Paul Storm (2001) has also noted that Asian *H. erectus* and *H. sapiens* occupied different ecological niches. There is no evidence that the former reached Sahul Land (the landmass formed by Australia, Tasmania, and New Guinea during low sea levels), but rather became regionally extinct with the spread of tropical rainforest, with which only *H. sapiens* could cope.

Conclusion

A general problem is that the physical features cited by multi-regionalists to support regional continuity in Asia are also found elsewhere, and cannot be held to be indicative of regional Asian traits or of a single regional evolutionary process (Stringer et al. 1984; Lahr 1996). In fact, a number of these features, such as the flatness of the frontal bone, the low position of maximum breadth between the sides of the skull, and a constriction of the skull behind the orbital area (the eye sockets), appear to have been general *Homo* characteristics, and this is true for both the Chinese (Brown 2001) and Australian (Storm 2001) material.

As a strong regional continuity in the Asian fossil record cannot be upheld, the anatomical basis of the multi-regional model is significantly weakened. Alongside the emerging evidence for African biological and behavioral change, and considerably mounting genetic arguments in favor of Africa, the issue must be nearing settlement. We are, it would appear, African in the main.

4.5 *The Niah Great Cave, Borneo, which was in use by humans from around 45,000 years ago. Excavations in the 1950s just to the right of this image yielded the "deep skull," the 40,000-year-old remains of a 14–15 year old, probably female,* Homo sapiens.

the bones between knee and ankle and between elbow and wrist) are long relative to the overall limb. Although variable, long bones (humeri and femora, the bones between shoulder and elbow and between hip and knee) are less robust than those of archaic *Homo* species. The selection for a tall, long-limbed, short-trunked body in *Homo sapiens* supports the notion of an African origin, as a biological adaptation to relatively mild tropical and subtropical climates.

Evolution in Low Latitudes: Evidence for the Rise of Modern Humans in Africa

The fossil record pertinent to the emergence of modern humans in Africa is still relatively poor, with the majority of a small fossil database belonging to the Middle Stone Age (after 100,000 years ago), and only a handful of relevant fossils covering the earlier period. This is possibly due to the fact that burial of the dead was apparently not practiced until well into the Later Stone Age in Africa (Rightmire 1989). A tentative pattern has emerged, however, in which the fossils fall into three chronological groups, as indicated above (p. 125) and shown in **Table 2**. The first, 1, consists of a sample dating to earlier than 250,000 years ago, in which *Homo sapiens* traits are clearly evident but in which a number of retentions from *Homo ergaster* are also evident; 2 is a transitional group with variable primitive and modern traits, dating to between 250,000 and 125,000 years

Table 1 *Characteristic Cranial Features of Anatomically Modern Humans*

- Cranial capacity usually in excess of 1350 cc (though admittedly this is variable)
- Relatively vertical frontal bone (forehead)
- High and parallel-walled cranial vault
- Rounded occipital region (the back of the head) lacking a prominent horizontal bulge (the occipital torus) and with a relatively flat angle of the cranial base (basicranial angle)
- Non-continuous brow ridge expressed more clearly in males
- Relatively flat, non-projecting face "tucked in" below the expanded frontal region of the braincase
- Distinct chin

ago; and 3 is a group comprising clear anatomically modern humans dating to less than 125,000 years ago. It should be emphasized, however, that a degree of morphological continuity is observable between these groups, and the division is therefore to some extent arbitrary.

Earliest Homo sapiens

The first group (1) is represented by material from sites that include Bodo in Ethiopia, Broken Hill (Kabwe) in Zambia, Elandsfontein (Saldanha) in South Africa, and Ndutu in Tanza-

Table 2 *Selected African Fossils, Grouped Chronologically (data from McBrearty and Brooks 2000)*

Group	Time range	Species	Key sites	Morphology
Group 1 Earliest	Early Stone Age (more than 250,000 years ago)	*Homo heidelbergensis, Homo leakeyi*	Ain Maarouf, Morocco; Bodo, Ethiopia; Broken Hill (Kabwe), Zambia; Cave of Hearths, South Africa; Elandsfontein (Saldanha), South Africa; Eyasi, Kenya; Melka Kunturé, Ethiopia; Ndutu, Tanzania; Olduvai OH9 (*Homo leakeyi*), OH23, OH28, OH34, Kenya; Omo (Kibish) 2(?), Ethiopia; Sidi Abderahman, Morocco; Tighenif, Morocco	Low braincase, broad and robust facial skeleton, thick bones, keeled forehead, large brow ridges
Group 2 Transitional	Middle Stone Age (late Middle/early Upper Pleistocene, *c.* 250,000– 125,000 years ago)	*Homo helmei, Homo sapiens*	Florisbad, South Africa; Hauah Fteah, Libya; Herto, Middle Awash, Ethiopia; Jebel Irhoud, Morocco; Mugharet el Aliyeh(?), Israel; Omo (Kibish) 1 and 2(?), Ethiopia; Porc Epic(?), Ethiopia; Singa(?), Sudan	Share characteristics with Group 1, but display in addition some modern characteristics, e.g. distinct chin, small brow ridges, rounded occipital
Group 3 Modern	Middle Stone Age (early Upper Pleistocene, *c.* 125,000–70,000 years ago)	*Homo sapiens*	Border Cave, South Africa; Dar-es-Soltan, Morocco; Die Kelders, Equus, and Sea Harvest caves, Hoedjies Punt, and Klasies River, South Africa; Mumba, Tanzania; Mumbwa(?), Zambia; Temara, Morocco; Taramsa, Egypt; Zouhra, Morocco	As Group 2, also considerable reduction in facial projection, brow ridge size, and tooth size

nia. These fossils have been classified variously as *Homo heidelbergensis*, *H. leakeyi*, *H. rhodesiensis*, and archaic *H. sapiens*. The cranium from **Bodo** was recovered in 1976, in deposits containing Acheulean tools that were dated by the argon-argon method to between 670,000 and 600,000 years ago. It possesses a number of features characteristic of *H. ergaster*, such as a low braincase, broad and robust facial skeleton, relatively thick bones, a "keeled" forehead (i.e., with a central bulge), and a massively constructed brow ridge. The Bodo cranium, however, bears more overall resemblance to crania dated to after 300,000 years ago, particularly in terms of endocranial capacity that has been estimated at close to 1300 cc. This is considerably greater than that of *H. ergaster*, and many scholars now include it in the same taxon (unit of zoological classification) as the African and European examples of *H. heidelbergensis* or early *H. sapiens* (Rightmire 1998, 2001; Conroy et al. 2000).

The Bodo cranium suggests that a gradual enlargement of the brain (encephalization) was occurring in African populations as early as 600,000 years ago. Unfortunately, no fossil material is known to date unequivocally between the age of Bodo and about 250,000 years ago, and it is only from that point that the fossil evidence becomes somewhat clearer, with demonstrably modern anatomical characteristics, particularly in the cranium, and clear associations with Middle Stone Age assemblages.

The remarkably complete cranium from **Broken Hill** (Kabwe) [**4.6**] has been dated biostratigraphically (i.e., based on the presence of fossils of known age in the stratigraphic layers; see Dating Early Hominins and their Archaeology box, pp. 74–75) to between *c.* 700,000 and 400,000 years ago, and was originally classified as *Homo rhodesiensis* ("Rhodesian Man"). Historically, it was seen by some as an African Neanderthal, although this can be ruled out today. It does, however, possess certain traits of *H. ergaster*, in combination with a number of advanced characteristics that link it with later specimens, such as the morphology of its nasal aperture, palate, and jaw region, and the proportions of the rear of the skull. Given its age and its apparent association with postcranial remains (the skeleton below the skull), most of the attributes of which are within the range of modern humans, it is best seen as another example of the varied emergence of modern human characteristics in Africa.

At **Elandsfontein** farm near Saldanha Bay in South Africa, a hominin calvarium (skull cap) [**4.7**] was discovered in 1953, associated with Acheulean stone tools. It shares some primitive characteristics with *Homo ergaster*, and compares closely to the Broken Hill cranium (Rightmire 2001). As it shares some traits with both modern humans and the Neanderthals, it could represent their last common ancestor, although according to Richard Klein, evidence of disease in the bone makes it difficult to evaluate this specimen with confidence. A similar hominin cranium was discovered in 1973 at **Lake Ndutu**, at the western end of the main gorge at Olduvai, Tanzania, also associated with an Acheulean industry. Philip Rightmire (2001) suggests that the age of the Ndutu material may be close to 400,000 years ago, on the basis of a tentative correlation with the Masek Beds geological formation in Olduvai Gorge. Although fragmentary, the endocranial capacity of the Ndutu cranium has been estimated at around 1100 cc, and enough of the brow ridge survives to reveal that it was fairly projecting, although not particularly thick; morphologically, it is similar to the fossils from Elandsfontein and Broken Hill. A cranium recovered from **Salé** in Morocco, which has been dated on geological and biostratigraphic grounds to *c.* 220,000 years ago (Hublin 2001), also possesses a number of derived, modern traits, despite having

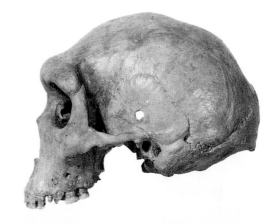

4.6, 4.7 *The Broken Hill and Elandsfontein crania:* *the Broken Hill (Kabwe) cranium of "Rhodesian Man" (above) and Elandsfontein (Saldanha) cranium (below) possess a mixture of traits characteristic of both late* Homo ergaster *and early* Homo sapiens.

several characteristics of *Homo ergaster*, including a cranial capacity of *c.* 930 cc, and best fits in this group of earliest *Homo sapiens*.

Transitional Homo sapiens

The second group (2), dating to between 250,000 and 125,000 years ago, contains notable fossils from **Florisbad** in South Africa [4.8, 4.9], **Omo** (Kibish) in Ethiopia [4.10, 4.11], and **Jebel Irhoud** in Morocco, and specimens have been variously classified as *Homo helmei* and *H. sapiens*. The partial cranium found in 1932 at Florisbad was originally classified as *H. helmei* by T. F. Dreyer to mark its distinctiveness, although subsequent workers recognized its affinities with other, apparently early, *H. sapiens* fossils, such as those from Ngaloba (Laetoli) in Tanzania, Singa in Sudan, Eliye Springs in Kenya, and Jebel Irhoud in Morocco. Damaged by hyena chewing, the fossil seems to have been part of a carnivore accumulation that became incorporated into vertical spring vents; tooth fragments have been dated by electron spin resonance [see ESR Dating box, p. 107] to between 300,000 and 100,000 years ago. A direct ESR determination of an associated hominin tooth dates the specimen to 300,000–200,000 years ago (Grün et al. 1996).

The base of the Kibish geological formation at Omo in Ethiopia has yielded a partial skeleton, including several craniodental fragments (Omo I) and, possibly, an almost intact cranial vault (Omo II). On geological grounds Omo I is dated to at least 100,000 years ago (Day 1986; Rightmire 1989). It is probable

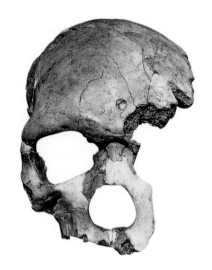

4.8, 4.9 *Florisbad skull and site:* *craniofacial fragment (left) excavated at the site of Florisbad, near Bloemfontein, South Africa (below). Between 150,000 and 120,000 years old and originally classified as* Homo helmei, *it bears a number of affinities with later* Homo sapiens *and is an exemplar of "transitional" forms.*

that Omo II is of broadly similar age, although some doubt as to its provenience exists, and Philip Rightmire (2001) has suggested that it may be older. Recent work by John Fleagle and colleagues, however, tentatively supports Karl Butzer's original interpretation that the two specimens originated from the same deposit, which can be placed between 200,000 and 100,000 years ago.

When compared to more recent *Homo sapiens*, Omo 1 and 2 are transitional in nature. Omo I has a number of distinctly modern characteristics, such as a chin, small brow ridges, and a rounded occipital region, but other features more closely resemble *H. ergaster*. Omo II, which is the more complete of the

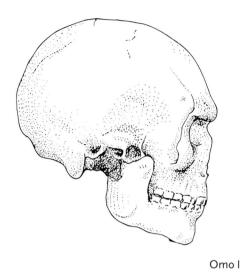
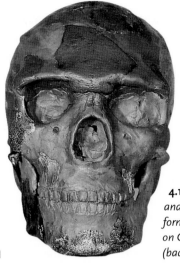

Omo I

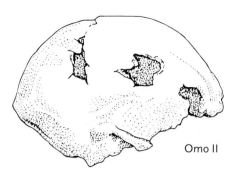

Omo II

4.10, 4.11 *Omo I and II: the reconstructed Omo I skull (left and center) and Omo II calvarium (right) from the Kibish formation in the Omo Basin, Ethiopia. Note modern characters on Omo I such as a pronounced chin, rounded occipital region (back of the skull), and reduced brow ridges.*

two specimens, has a long, low braincase with a strongly curved back of the cranial vault, which are archaic features linking this fossil to *H. ergaster*; but it also possesses a broad, flattened frontal bone and thin brow ridge, which link it to *H. sapiens*. The unclear proveniences of Omo I and II may suggest that they are of different age, and Omo II may better be seen as belonging to the first of our three groups. In this light, perhaps the unclear affinities between Omo II and modern humans are not surprising. This having been said, other scholars point to the incomplete nature of Omo I and suggest that a clear attribution of this fossil to *H. sapiens* may be premature. A cautious interpretation of the Omo material reveals the appearance of a number of modern cranial features at least by 130,000 years ago.

The recent discovery of two adult and one child's crania from **Herto**, in Ethiopia's Middle Awash region, has significantly increased support for an African emergence of modern humans (White et al. 2003). The crania were recovered from deposits beneath those dated by argon-argon to between about 160,000 and 154,000 years ago (Clark et al. 2003), which would appear to give them a minimum age. They display a variety of traits inherited from earlier African *H. ergaster* populations as well as clearly modern traits, and they lack any unique derived traits characteristic of the chronologically later Neanderthals. To emphasize the transitional nature of the Herto population, these have been classified as *Homo sapiens idaltu*, and it is suggested that they occupied an intermediary position in the regional evolution from *H. rhodesiensis* to anatomically modern *H. sapiens*. Archaeological associations

are both Acheulean and Middle Stone Age, as one would expect for fossils of such age.

Other, similarly aged fossils display this mosaic of archaic and modern features. The Upper Ngaloba beds at Laetoli, Tanzania, which have been estimated to date to somewhere between 150,000 and 90,000 years ago on the basis of geological correlation of tuff mineral contents, yielded a cranium – Laetoli Hominid [LH] 18 [**4.12**] – with clear *H. sapiens* affinities, such as a cranial capacity of *c.* 1350 cc and the occipital proportions of *H. sapiens*, although the cranium retained some archaic features more reminiscent of *H. ergaster*, such as a long, low cranial vault and a flattened, narrow forehead (Bräuer and Leakey 1986; Day 1986). Despite this, Philip Rightmire (1989) believes that this fossil presents even firmer evidence than those from Omo for a modern human presence in East Africa by *c.* 120,000 years ago. The cranium from Eliye Springs, possibly as old as 300,000 to 200,000 years ago, resembles LH18 in occipital shape.

In North Africa, five different specimens with a mixture of archaic and modern traits were recovered from the **Jebel Irhoud** (also spelled Djebel Ighoud) cave in Morocco. ESR dates on apparently associated faunal remains suggest an age for these

4.12 *LH18 hominid cranium: this skull from the Upper Ngaloba Beds at Laetoli, Tanzania, dates to between 150,000 and 90,000 years ago. The individual possessed a largely modern morphology while retaining some archaic features. Note the large endocranial volume and rounded occipital (rear).*

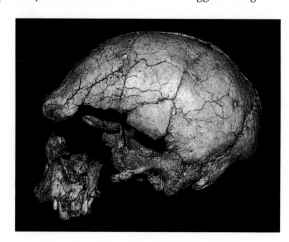

of between 190,000 and 90,000 years ago, and biostratigraphic data support this (Hublin 2001). The cranium and calvarium from this site (Irhoud 1 and 2 respectively) display a remarkable array of archaic and modern features, and were seen by some as evidence of African Neanderthals, but this view has now been discredited (Hublin 1993; 2001). Irhoud 1 is a large skull with an endocranial capacity somewhere between approximately 1300 cc and 1480 cc, and is modern in shape. It possesses a large, broad face similar to the Israeli Skhūl and Qafzeh specimens of group 3 (see below), and in many respects falls within the range of variation of early modern humans. In a number of ways, Irhoud 2 is even more advanced, and it is probable that the two come from the same population. A broken juvenile mandible (Irhoud 3) and a humerus mid-shaft

(Irhoud 4) are also within modern human size range. Importantly, none of the Irhoud fossils bear any traits that are unique to the Neanderthals. Given this fact and a number of overlapping characteristics with early modern humans, they can be excluded from a European, Neanderthal population. A braincase from the banks of the Blue Nile at Singa in Sudan may also reflect a population similar to the Jebel Irhoud remains, although a pathological condition that affected bone growth and resulted in relatively thick and broad skull sides confuses matters. It has been dated by a number of uranium series [see Uranium Series Dating box, p. 107] and electron spin resonance dates that fall into the range 145,000 to 95,000 years ago. Combining the U-series and ESR dates, the excavators prefer a date for the cranium of more than 130,000 years ago.

4.13 Fossil human types in Africa and Eurasia: the oxygen isotope stages (OIS) are listed to the left and major biological types are shown, with main artifact assemblage types.

Anatomically Modern Humans

In contrast to the previous two groups of fossils, those recovered from deposits dating to the period after 125,000 years ago clearly belong to modern *Homo sapiens* (group 3), and may be taken to indicate a succeeding group in which facial projection and brow and tooth size have decreased (Rightmire 1989). Teeth have been found at a number of sites, such as **Die Kelders Cave** and **Equus Cave** in South Africa, the latter of which yielded a fragmentary mandible with dimensions close to those of modern people (Grine and Klein 1985). While understandably limited in scope, the dimensions and morphology of such isolated teeth do not fall outside modern ranges. A jaw from the Cave of Hearths at **Makapansgat** in South Africa bears the hint of a chin (Stringer and Gamble 1993). **Border Cave**, again in South Africa, yielded a number of fossils that on the basis of ESR dates are certainly greater than 50,000 years ago; some of these are dated by luminescence to between 230,000 and 145,000 years ago – earlier than other group 3 examples (Grün and Beaumont 2001), although there is still some uncertainty over their stratigraphic provenience. All of these are anatomically modern, with crania falling well within the range of modern South African populations. Fragmentary human remains from Klasies River Mouth, dating to 110,000 years ago and thereafter (Deacon 1989), include a number of mandibles that fall within the modern range, as does the morphology and dimensions of tooth crowns (Rightmire and Deacon 2001).

Individuals may still have been robustly built at this time, as suggested by the remains from **Dar-es-Soltan**, Morocco, which are clearly modern but in a number of ways resemble the earlier Jebel Irhoud population, and are intermediate between these and remains from North African sites such as **Taforalt**, **Afalou**, and **Nazlet Khater**, dating to less than 50,000 years ago. The child from **Taramsa**, Egypt, which dates to between *c.* 80,000 and 50,000 years ago, is more similar to these Epipaleolithic (final Upper Paleolithic) samples than to the earlier specimens (Vermeersch et al. 1998). (For an explanation of the chronological terminology used for the end of the Pleistocene and the Upper Paleolithic, see A Note on Terminology, Chapter 5, p. 182.)

It is in group 3 that a number of fossils from the Israeli caves of the **Mugharet es-Skhūl** and **Jebel Qafzeh** can be placed. Between them, Skhūl and Qafzeh have yielded the remains of over 20 individuals, many of whom seem to have been buried in simple graves [**4.14**]. Consensus for the dates of these remains is 110,000–90,000 years ago, on the basis of ESR and luminescence dating (Bar-Yosef 1993). Although still possessing some archaic features, these individuals are essentially modern in a number of respects, and differ from Israeli Neanderthals that occupied the region up to 40,000 years later (Day 1986). The Skhūl V cranium, for example, possesses a modern-looking low basicranial angle and plane of the foramen magnum ("large hole," the opening at the base of the skull through which the spinal column and associated nerves and muscles join the head), and the Qafzeh 6 cranium, despite being robust (i.e., thick-walled), has a high and well-rounded vault; the Skhūl and Qafzeh mandibles have pronounced chins that are essentially modern, and postcranial remains from both sites are long and slender, in contrast to those of the Southwest Asian Neanderthals.

Genetic Keys to the Origins of Modern Humans

A number of genetics-based suggestions that the geographical origins of modern humans are to be found in Africa had been put forward by the early 1980s, notably based on nuclear DNA, but the first significant contribution was by Rebecca Cann and her colleagues (1987; see also Stoneking and Cann 1989), who demonstrated the particular strengths of the technique. Gradually, there arose a number of different measures of genetic variability – upon which evolutionary analyses are based – including blood groups, mitochondrial DNA, and the Y chromosome. Strong arguments in favor of the objective nature and complete database of genetics, as opposed to the theoretically biased and partial nature of paleontological evidence, were made early on (e.g. Wilson and Cann 1992). In retrospect, these were a little optimistic, and the central assumptions of the methods and problems that arose from them, as well as how sequences should be interpreted, were debated through the 1990s.

4.14 *Qafzeh burials:* *Qafzeh 9 (adult, interpreted as female) and Qafzeh 10 (infant) were apparently buried in the same grave, on the terrace of Jebel Qafzeh near Nazareth, Israel. Dating to between 110,000 and 90,000 years ago, the numerous burials at Qafzeh are in many respects anatomically modern.*

Mitochondrial DNA and the Theory of an Early African "Coalescence"

Cells contain two genomes (complete genetic components), by far the larger of which is nuclear DNA, which takes the form of the double helix of around 3 billion base pairs, nearly everything required to produce a human being. By contrast, mitochondrial DNA (mtDNA), which resides not in the cell's nucleus but in its walls, comes only in small, two-strand rings, unlike the long, double-helix fibers of nuclear DNA. The latter encodes (i.e., provides the molecular blueprint) for around 100,000 genes (sequences of base pairs) but mtDNA encodes for only 37. MtDNA is ideal for human evolutionary research, because it is not influenced by natural selection. In other words, it performs a specific function (in this case, in a system of energy production), rather than controlling the development and nature of a biological character. In addition, as it is only inherited through the female line – from mother to daughter – variability cannot be introduced by recombination with a father's mtDNA, which he will have inherited from his mother, but which he will not pass on to his offspring. Thus, only random mutation events should be responsible for variation in mtDNA sequences.

Empirical observations have suggested that random mtDNA mutations occur fairly rapidly, perhaps as many as 10 per 1000 reproductions. Thus they form a relatively reliable molecular clock that, assuming a rough mutation rate can be ascertained, will provide estimated dates for the period at which a particular phenotype (set of genes possessed by a particular group) appeared; this appearance is known as coalescence. Mutations accumulate in mtDNA some 10 times faster than in

nuclear DNA, making it particularly useful for reconstructing fairly recent human evolution. Variability in modern mtDNA can be analyzed statistically for similarities and distances between individuals, and a phylogeny, essentially a genetic family tree, drawn up. The variability of living human mtDNA is surprisingly low (some one-tenth that of chimpanzees), which suggests that modern human origins, that is, the coalescence of specifically modern genes, occurred very recently; or a population bottleneck event occurred, in which human population numbers and hence genetic variability reduced considerably; or both. A combination of the two is most likely.

From the outset, the genetic data were interpreted in favor of both African and multi-regional hypotheses (Thorne and Wolpoff 1992), as both theories assume an evolution of modern humans in Africa. In a genetic sense, then, the only difference between the two models would be that in the multi-regional hypothesis, such an evolution would also occur elsewhere. Thus the multi-regional model cannot be eliminated solely on the grounds that more variability can be observed in Africa. Instead, the timing of coalescence is crucial, as the multi-regional hypothesis predicts that this occurred at a time as early as 1.6 million years ago, reflecting the earliest populations to colonize the Old World. By contrast, the single origins hypothesis predicts a relatively recent coalescence, in the order of around 200,000 years ago.

In the burgeoning amount of work that has been undertaken in this area, no DNA suggestive of the much earlier coalescence has been found. While different genetic material will have different coalescence times – some of our DNA, for

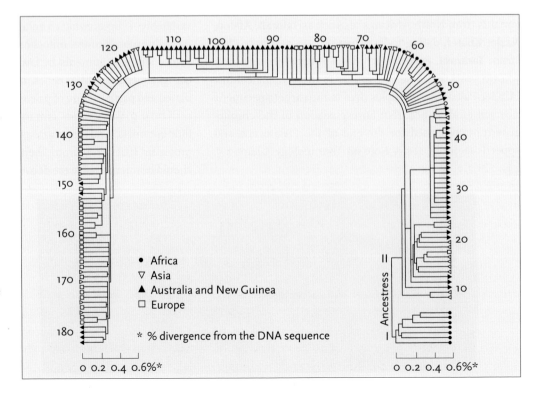

4.15 MtDNA genealogy:
diagram based on the work of Mark Stoneking and Rebecca Cann, relating 134 MtDNA types from 148 people in five geographical regions of the world. The tree displays branches showing ancestral relationships. Two primary branches clearly separate Africa (I) from the rest of the world (II). The amount of sequence divergence, the scale for which is at the bottom of the tree, shows that Africans have the longest period of genetic mutation. The tree is curved for convenience.

- ● Africa
- ▽ Asia
- ▲ Australia and New Guinea
- ☐ Europe

* % divergence from the DNA sequence

0 0.2 0.4 0.6%*

0 0.2 0.4 0.6%*

example, coalesced 35 million years ago – the clustering of coalescences around one major period will indicate the most likely date for the specific origins of *Homo sapiens*. Almost all coalescence data available to us today, especially mtDNA and Y chromosomes, cluster between around 270,000 and 200,000 years ago. Therefore, most studies point to recent coalescences that strongly suggest a single-center origin, and the greatest amount of genetic diversity is found in Africa; this strongly suggests that if coalescence occurred in one region only, it was probably south of the Sahara.

Rebecca Cann's discovery that mtDNA differences between regional populations in five areas – sub-Saharan Africa, North Africa/Near East/Europe, East Asia, aboriginal Australia, and New Guinea – were actually smaller than those within the regional populations is strongly indicative of mutation over a short period, and therefore of a recent coalescence that she and her colleagues estimated to have occurred around 290,000–140,000 years ago. Their analysis clustered individual sequences on the basis of similarity, difference, and degree of mutation [**4.15**]. This clearly reveals the primacy of a split between African and non-African groups, and Cann concluded that the simplest interpretation of this was that the common mitochondrial ancestor was African. Most of the genetic studies that have appeared since Cann's pioneering work support the Out of Africa hypothesis. Overall, many DNA sequences seem to have coalesced in Africa around 200,000 years ago (mtDNA), a little earlier (nuclear DNA), or a little later (Y chromosome).

Other Theories and Potential Consensus

These results, however, are not as straightforward as they might initially seem. Mutation rates have to be estimated, initially on the basis of calibrating mutation against the divergence seen between New Guinean and Australian populations, for which a maximum chronology can be ascertained from archaeological data. Such estimates suggest that divergence would be in the order of 2–4 percent per million years. Initial critiques centered on whether correct mutation rates had been applied. Why, for example, should the mutation rate between relatively small populations in New Guinea and Australia be at all representative of that in a larger African population? If mutation were slower in Africa, the date of coalescence would be older, perhaps even back around the time of the first Out of Africa dispersal, which might support the multi-regional hypothesis.

In addition, misconceptions quickly arose as to exactly what the genetic evidence was referring to. An example is the erroneous notion that all modern humans can be traced back to a single female, often known as "mitochondrial Eve." The rationale is straightforward. Alleles (variants of a gene) can be traced backwards from living individuals through their mitochondrial ancestors, ultimately to a single ancestral type, the coalescent. This, however, does not mean that "mitochondrial Eve" was the only female living, or that she was the only one who passed on mtDNA. An appropriate analogy involves surnames, and genealogy clearly shows how names can perpetuate or die out. Thus, modern mtDNA is representative only of a partial amount of the original genotype (a complete set of genes possessed by an individual).

Population sizes will also affect mutation: larger populations will reveal greater genetic diversity simply because more random mutation will prevail; on the other hand, a decline in population (a bottleneck) will reduce variability, often considerably. Many of these methodological problems were addressed early on, and a number of approaches to divergence rates, such as using chimpanzees as an outgroup, place this on a more secure footing. In the late 1990s, microsatellite DNA (short strands of DNA) were studied. These mutate so rapidly that mutation rates have actually been calculated in the laboratory, thus providing a far more secure basis for the estimation of coalescence. These studies suggest also that coalescence occurred recently, perhaps as late as around 150,000 years ago, which agrees with the previous studies (Relethford 2001).

The clarity of the genetic data has, however, been overestimated. Coalescence relates to specific genes, not directly to human populations; and as John Relethford (2001) has noted, much of the genetic data cannot be used specifically to eliminate other hypotheses. It is important to understand that while most genetic evidence as it stands is consistent with an African origin for *Homo sapiens*, it is often not inconsistent with a multi-regional one, or at least with the notion of a significant contribution to the modern human gene pool from Asia. This having been said, the relatively large degree of genetic variability observable in sub-Saharan African populations is indicative of a long pedigree of random mutation in the region, which certainly points to its primacy.

The emerging consensus is that the hybridization and replacement hypotheses put forward by Gunter Bräuer and others (see above) are most closely supported by the genetic data. Population genetics also support this notion. The greater genetic diversity of sub-Saharan African populations suggests that the long-term effective population size in the region was larger than elsewhere, and here one might expect greater rates of mutation, as well as gene flow out of Africa far more frequently than into it. Low levels of observed mtDNA diversity have been taken by some to reflect a population bottleneck, during which the number of female humans on Earth may have been as low as 1500. (If this is correct, then the multi-regional hypothesis is surely untenable, as it is inconceivable that such a small number of individuals could be spread across Africa, Europe, and Central and East Asia and still maintain considerable gene flow between populations.) The reason for this dramatically reduced population may have been the return to glacial conditions from around 70,000 years ago, although Stan Ambrose (1998) has suggested that the cause might have been the eruption of the Toba volcano in Indonesia around that time, which precipitated a volcanic winter. Henry Harpending and his colleagues (Harpending et al. 1998) have suggested that our population size may always have been small, and that it was fragmented into three distinct groups in Africa, which Harpending calls proto-African, proto-European, and proto-Asian. He argues that the bottleneck occurred following this fragmentation, and genetic variation was thus considerably reduced. Finally, a major population expansion occurred around 60,000 years ago, and at this time, he argues, the proto-African population was the first to expand, followed by the proto-European and proto-Asian groups, who dispersed into those regions.

Mitochondrial DNA and the Evolution of Homo neanderthalensis

The successful sequencing of mtDNA from Neanderthal fossils in 1997 has clarified their evolutionary position relative to modern humans. The general similarity of the resulting Neanderthal sequences, with regional differences one might expect from samples in Germany (Neanderthal 1), Croatia (Vindija Cave), and the Caucasus (Mezmaiskaya Cave), presents a strong case for genetic dissimilarity between Neanderthals and modern humans [see 4.21]. Whether this difference is enough to demonstrate that the two could not produce fertile offspring, however, is open to discussion (Ward and Stringer 1997; Relethford 2001).

The differences between a genetic sequence from the Neanderthal 1 fossil and a standard modern sequence is over three times the average difference between modern humans (Krings et al. 1997; 1999), and the overlap between the two is minimal. MtDNA sequences from a Neanderthal infant from Mezmaiskaya Cave in the Caucasus (Ovchinnikov et al. 2000) and Vindija Cave specimen 75 (Krings et al. 2000) were very similar to Neanderthal 1, which is a strong indicator of their accuracy. Despite inevitable caution about making inferences from such a small genetic database, the three sequences suggest very strongly that Neanderthals were dissimilar genetically to *Homo sapiens*.

The individuals from Germany, Croatia, and the Caucasus sequenced so far suggest that a long period of evolutionary divergence of perhaps half a million years separated Neanderthals from modern humans, and that Neanderthals did not contribute mtDNA to the contemporary human gene pool (Krings et al. 2000). The results also suggest that there was restricted mtDNA diversity among Neanderthals, which makes it highly unlikely that a divergent mtDNA lineage existed that

could have given rise to modern European mtDNA. The results clearly separate the two in genetic space.

MtDNA data from the Neanderthals is not completely without problems, however, and some scholars have urged caution in the interpretation of ancient DNA (Relethford 2001). Chemical damage occurring in Neanderthal bone from the time of death will break up DNA, and processes of decay may, for example, lead to the overestimation of differences between two sequences. But if specialists agree that the two populations are genetically different, the question still remains as to why they are. Do they differ because Neanderthals were a distinct species and therefore incapable of breeding with modern humans, or because they were merely a geographically isolated subspecies? The current consensus is that Neanderthals were a distinct species.

Archaeology and the Emergence of "Modern" Behavior in Middle Stone Age Africa

After 100,000 years ago, the archaeological record reveals evidence for a number of behavioral patterns that differ significantly from those of earlier times [**Table 3**]. These are usually seen as indicative of "modern" forms of behavior, and the broad coincidence of these traits with the biological emergence of anatomically modern *Homo sapiens* has suggested to many that

Table 3 *Archaeological Evidence for Modern Human Behavior after 100,000 Years Ago*

- Increased typological diversity and standardization of artifacts
- Greater frequencies of artifact/assemblage change over time
- Shaping of organic materials such as bone, antler, and ivory by carving into formal categories of implements such as needles, awls, and harpoons
- Jewelry of pierced shells and carved organics, often transported in the landscape
- Incontrovertible figurative and non-figurative art
- Clear organization of space, including dwelling structures and elaborate hearths
- Transport of lithic raw materials over longer distances, occurring more frequently
- Broad-spectrum economies incorporating small terrestrial animals, marine resources, vegetal resources, and often requiring trapping and processing technologies such as grindstones
- Storage
- Prey selectivity in large mammal hunting
- Occupation of more difficult environments
- Growth in population density

a new cognitive threshold had been crossed at this time by our own species. Traditionally, the emergence of modern behavior, as reflected in the Upper Paleolithic record of Europe and the Late Stone Age of Africa, has been seen as a relatively late phenomenon, and probably one that occurred outside Africa. The relatively intense amount of excavation and research in Europe, and the rich archaeological record that some European regions have yielded, have led to the notion that a European "human revolution" occurred when modern humans established themselves in these relatively northern regions and spread out from there, perhaps even back into Africa. Although the Upper Paleolithic in Europe seems to have appeared relatively suddenly around 40,000 years ago, a number of scholars have come to question both the suddenness of the transition, and whether all elements that are recognized as part of the late Upper Paleolithic/Late Stone Age appeared together at one time and in one place.

A growing number of Middle Stone Age sites in Africa have played an important role in this debate and in recent years attention has shifted away from Europe. It is very plausible that modern behavior has a much earlier pedigree in Africa than elsewhere in the world. Certainly, elements of modern behavior such as pierced shell, bone, eggshell, and stone jewelry appear earlier in Africa and Southwest Asia than in Europe, and red ocher, often in some abundance, is ubiquitous on Middle Stone Age sites dating to 100,000 years ago and younger. Although ocher can often have a prosaic function, such as for weatherproofing hides or repelling insects, the clear selection of ocher with saturated red hues, and use of this in the hand as crayons, judging from a number of small lumps from several Middle Stone Age sites that appear to have been artificially shaped by use, may suggest that it was primarily used to create two-dimensional symbols, or art. Similarly, the presence of cut marks apparently indicative of defleshing on three Ethiopian crania from Herto and one from Bodo (White 1986) suggest that complex mortuary ritual may have been practiced, at least on occasion, by 150,000 years ago (Clark et al. 2003). Whether existing archaeological data point to a slow evolution of behavioral modernity in Africa over a long period of time, or to a relatively sudden "revolutionary" emergence 50,000 years ago, as Richard Klein (1995) believes, it is only after this time that such modernity is demonstrated outside Africa.

Artifactual Evidence

In a provocative paper, Sally McBrearty and Allison Brooks (2000) argue that the notion of a sudden human revolution, in which modern behavior appeared as a package much later than the biological evolution of anatomically modern *Homo sapiens*, is fatally flawed. They argue that a number of elements of modern behavior can be found in Africa in deposits that often predate

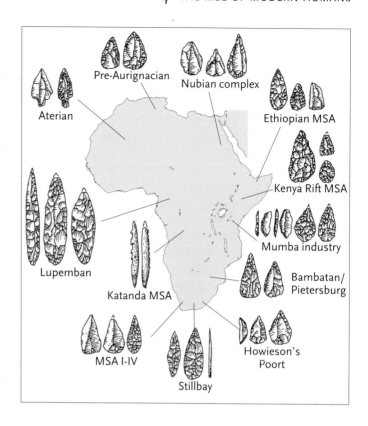

4.16 Middle Stone Age of Africa: *map of Africa showing regional variants of Middle Stone Age (MSA) assemblages. Essentially, these relate to variations in weapon points, such as tanged forms in the Aterian of the northwest, to leaf-shaped bifacial forms in the Stillbay of South Africa. Increasing regionalization of stone tools in the MSA may indicate developing social complexity.*

50,000 years ago. Possible bone points have been recovered from sites apparently dating to earlier than this period, such as in the **Aterian** of Morocco in the north. One was recovered from **Klasies River Mouth** in South Africa, although it was found out of context. Middle Stone Age points from **Blombos Cave**, South Africa, and potentially 150,000–90,000-year-old bone points from **Katanda**, the Democratic Republic of the Congo, may be a crucial piece of evidence here [see box: Katanda and the Earliest Harpoons, p. 142]. McBrearty and Brooks argue that geometric microliths (small standardized flakes), the hallmark of the Later Stone Age of Africa, appeared as early as 65,000 years ago at **Mumba** in Tanzania, and even earlier at such South African sites as **Howieson's Poort**, where they appear mixed with Middle and Late Stone Age lithics [**4.16**]. The Howieson's Poort assemblage, in which small pieces, their edge(s) blunted by steeply angled removals ("backing"), played an important role, and in which non-local lithics are particularly well represented, is securely dated to 70,000–60,000 years ago. It is possible that Howieson's Poort backed pieces functioned as arrowheads or as points for light javelins. Whatever the case, they appear to have formed part of a composite lithic system.

KEY SITE Katanda and the Earliest Harpoons

Three archaeological sites have been excavated at Katanda, in the Democratic Republic of the Congo (formerly Zaire), which yield potential evidence of "modern" behavior in the African Middle Stone Age (Yellen et al. 1995). These sites were located along the valley of a south-flowing proto-Semliki River, which at the time of occupation was fringed with stands of dense forest in an open grassland setting. All three sites, named Kt2, Kt9, and Kt16, have yielded abundant lithics, as well as faunal assemblages dominated by large catfish and terrestrial mammals; two have produced organic tools.

Bone Artifacts

Ten worked bone artifacts were recovered from Kt9, including seven points with uniserial (single-edged) barbs, and a long, tapering, pointed piece of unknown function, which the excavators describe as a dagger or knife. The points are well made and highly formalized, and microscopic examination has indicated that they were finished by a stone grinder; it is plausible that they were employed in river fishing. The excavators acknowledge that the form of the so-called dagger seems to indicate that its function was not to cut or pierce. It has an overall shape similar to the barbed points and is larger in dimension; it is therefore conceivable that it is a blank for the manufacture of these.

Dating

Dating of Kt9 is critical to the demonstration of an early emergence of some forms of modern behavior, namely river fishing and formal artifact production by carving and grinding. The fauna suggest that Kt9 is older than a neighboring site, Ishango, which has yielded bone uniserial and biserial (double-edged) points dating to around 25,000 years ago. In addition, the Kt9 Middle Stone Age horizons and overlying deposits have been dated by a combination of ESR, luminescence (both OSL and TL methods), uranium-series, and amino acid racemization. (The last is a dating method for fossil shell and bone based on the measured presence of particular amino acids; for the others, see specific boxes, Chapter 3). OSL and TL measurements suggest that the sands overlying the Middle Stone Age horizon date to between *c.* 98,000 and 66,000 years ago. ESR measurements on hippopotamus teeth from the Middle Stone Age horizon itself date to 130,000–45,000 years ago. Overall, the team concluded that the bone points at Katanda Kt9 must be at least *c.* 75,000 years old.

Questions of Site Formation

This is an impressive battery of dating for the site, and it probably indicates a reliable age for the archaeological horizon. The problem is whether the bone artifacts were recovered *in situ*, or whether they became incorporated into the horizon from younger deposits. All other examples of African barbed points come from deposits dating to at least 55,000 years younger.

As the excavators acknowledge, signs of abrasion and weathering on some of the lithics and animal bones indicate that the Middle Stone Age horizon was probably exposed to the open air for a significant period of time.

By contrast, the bone points are in relatively fresh condition, suggesting that mixing may have occurred. The nature of the geological deposits in which the finds were made – sands – indicate that the proto-Semliki River may have been responsible for the deposition of at least the artifacts other than the bone points as part of a gravel deposit, with the points being deposited later. The concentration lies on a slope and has been truncated by erosion. The archaeological layer, which the excavators interpret as an occupational "pavement," increases downslope, and size sorting is evident, with larger artifacts generally found lower down the slope. Clearly, some movement of artifacts over time has occurred.

Although the Katanda issue remains to be resolved beyond doubt, it does, nevertheless, provide strong indications of emerging modernity in the Middle Stone Age.

Hunting and Dietary Evidence

In addition to the evidence from Katanda, **broad-spectrum economies** as a feature of behavioral modernity are suggested by the recovery of fresh- and brackish-water fish remains at White Paintings Shelter in Botswana, and extensive Middle Stone Age shell middens at Klasies River and Herolds Bay caves and the Sea Harvest and Hoedjies Punt open sites in South Africa, in deposits of broadly Last Interglacial age, *c.* 130,000–115,000 years ago (Mitchell 2002). The recovery of fish remains, often of species that were too large to have been introduced into coastal sites by roosting seabirds, indicates the catching of various fish at a number of Middle Stone Age sites. At Blombos Cave, South Africa, these included large deep-water varieties, and at Klasies River and Die Kelders other marine mammals, such as Cape fur seals, indicate that the sea formed an important subsistence focus. The recovery of plant residues and even grinding stones on sites in savanna environments adds to the picture of a broad-spectrum economy.

On the land, large mammals comprise an important element of Middle Stone Age faunas, and have traditionally been the focus of the most intense debates about the cultural abilities of Middle Stone Age humans. Bones of medium-sized herbivores such as eland, other antelopes, and zebra, which are relatively easy to hunt, are common on Middle Stone Age sites, and probably reflect their numbers in proximity to habitation sites. Catastrophic mortality profiles for eland suggest that Middle Stone Age hunters on occasion took them in abundance. In comparison to Late Stone Age animals, however, dangerous species such as Cape buffalo and bushpig are rare on Middle Stone Age sites, which Richard Klein (1999) believes indicates that people of this time were not capable of hunting animals that were dangerous or difficult to catch. Furthermore, Middle Stone Age people seem to have targeted young or old and therefore vulnerable animals, perhaps even female Cape buffalo when they were giving birth.

Lewis Binford (1984) has taken an even more negative view of the competence of Middle Stone Age hunters as compared to Late Stone Age ones. He concluded from an analysis of the faunal remains from Klasies River Mouth that meat was procured by scavenging rather than hunting. His analysis ignored, however, many remains that were probably removed from the site by carnivores, and many scholars would now see the remains as reflecting hunted meat that, like the shellfish at the site, was shared. There are other indications from Klasies River that suggest that hunting was probably practiced [see box: Klasies River Mouth, p. 144].

It is most likely that a variety of meat-procurement strategies were employed in the Middle Stone Age, which included active and efficient hunting. The location and age structure of some faunal assemblages, for example, is strongly suggestive of ambush hunting at watering holes, while similar locations offered possibilities for the scavenging of larger animals such as hippopotamus (Mitchell 2002). McBrearty and Brooks argue that there are no grounds based on faunal evidence to suggest major intellectual differences between the Middle and Late Stone Age.

Evidence of Site Modification and Art

The organized use of space, including the construction of dwelling structures, is seen as a major hallmark of modern behavior, and unequivocal indicators of such organization beyond the focus of activities around hearths are extremely rare in European Middle Paleolithic (Neanderthal) contexts. A few examples of site modification exist in the African Middle Stone Age, such as arc-shaped "walls" of stone cobbles, possibly windbreaks or simple structures, but the evidence of organized use of space is as yet unconvincing.

Blombos Cave in South Africa [4.20], situated 35 m (115 ft) above sea level on the southern Cape shore of the Indian Ocean, has yielded important support for the notion of an early emergence of modern behavioral elements in Africa. Here, three Middle Stone Age phases were excavated, the entire sequence separated from the overlying Late Stone Age by sterile Aeolian (wind-blown) sediments (Henshilwood et al. 2002). In all three main phases, subsistence strategies were broad, including terrestrial and marine mammals, fish, shellfish, and reptiles. Wood ash scattered through all three phases indicates the regular lighting of hearths. Blade technology was practiced from the earliest phase, and lanceolate-shaped stone points [4.18] (called Stillbay points) appear in the middle phase and were abundant in the upper phase. In the middle phase, these points may have been supplemented by bone points [4.19] hafted as weapons, although it is unclear whether the few examples of these recovered from the site were shaped deliberately or by use, for example as digging sticks.

Over 8000 fragments of ocher have been recovered from the Middle Stone Age levels, two of which, from layers CC and CD in the upper Middle Stone Age phase, were associated with hearths and carry engravings. On one piece, both flat sides and one thin edge are worn by scraping and grinding, and one side bears a number of cross-hatched lines. The second piece also carries a row of cross-hatched lines, in addition to long lines across the top, center, and bottom of the cross-hatching [4.17]. These were clearly deliberate, and the similarity of the two objects suggests that these lines represent a deliberate design template. The association of these pieces of ocher with Stillbay points suggests an age in excess of c. 65,000 years ago, which is supported by thermoluminescence (TL) dates on burned samples from the upper Middle Stone Age phase and optically stimulated luminescence (OSL; see Luminescence Dating box, p. 119) dates on the overlying sterile sediments, which are in the order of 90,000–60,000 years old. The recovery from the c. 75,000-year-old level at Blombos of 41 tick shells apparently pierced for suspension, in addition to an ostrich eggshell bead of possibly similar age (Henshilwood et al. 2004), further strengthen the case for an early emergence of modern behavior at Blombos. Overall, the Blombos ocher fragments indicate the creation of intentional images by at least 65,000 years ago, possibly some of the earliest convincing examples of "art" objects in the world (though possible earlier examples are described in the previous chapter).

4.17 The creation of intentional images: *a red ocher "crayon" bearing engraved diagonal lines from Blombos Cave, South Africa. At least 65,000 years old, this and other examples found at the site represent some of the earliest convincing evidence of "art" objects in the world.*

KEY SITE Klasies River Mouth: Middle Stone Age Hunters?

The Klasies River main site, on the southern coast of South Africa, has been excavated since the 1960s. It preserves material in a number of different caves, all of which share a general stratigraphic sequence up to 16 m (52 ft) deep. The sequence reflects periods of occupation that began shortly after *c.* 125,000 years ago and occurred again around 110,000, before 90,000, and before 60,000 years ago (dated by ESR and luminescence). The gaps may reflect the absence of human populations in the region due to the difficulties of coping with arid periods.

Rich lithic and faunal assemblages have been recovered from Klasies, and they still form a major source of information about Middle Stone Age behavior (Singer and Wymer 1982; Rightmire and Deacon 2001). Artifactually, the sequence at Klasies comprises four sub-phases of the Middle Stone Age; a Howieson's Poort assemblage separates the Middle Stone Age II and III phases. The stone artifacts were rarely retouched, although a small number of fragments from bifacially flaked leaf-shaped points were found; there is evidence as well for the practice of backing (blunting one edge by means of steeply angled retouch) to facilitate the hafting of crescent and trapeze-shaped pieces in the Howieson's Poort assemblage.

The Howieson's Poort pieces from Klasies River and elsewhere clearly reflect a design "style" only found south of the Zambezi River, which has been imposed on hard stone materials with skilled knapping. The small size and backing of the Howieson's Poort lithics indicates that they were used as hafted elements in a composite toolkit, another aspect of behavioral modernity. Moreover, the material of which many of the Howieson's

Poort artifacts were made at Klasies River and elsewhere was obtained from non-local sources, and indicates either long-distance movement of people in the landscape or exchange.

The occupational lenses (very thin stratigraphic layers) at the Klasies River sites consist largely of shells, charcoal, and ash. Hearths are so common in the Middle Stone Age levels that the controlled use of fire must have been practiced routinely. The whole sequence is rich in faunal remains, from small terrestrial vertebrates, including reptiles, to large herbivores, and a variety of marine resources including fish and (rare) amphibians. There is no reliable indication of fishing at the main Klasies site, but shellfish accumulations are extremely deep in places, and would have been an important source of minerals. Conspicuous lenses of carbonized materials in the Howieson's Poort levels at the main Klasies site suggest that the gathering of plant food was important in this period.

Hunters or Scavengers?

There is considerable debate over the interpretation of the terrestrial mammal remains from occupation levels at Klasies River, arguments that are crucial to the debate as to whether Middle Stone Age populations were skilled hunters (Deacon 1989), or obtained most of their meat by scavenging (Binford 1984). Lewis Binford noted that the larger animals at the site, such as buffalo and eland, are mainly represented by the bones of the feet, whereas bones of the meatier parts of the limbs are rare; he took this to indicate that these resources were largely scavenged. By contrast, smaller animals such as steenbock and bushbuck were relatively well

represented by bones of the limbs, and may well have been procured by hunting. Binford's work has been criticized, for he included in his analysis bones that were probably deposited by nonhuman carnivores, and the bias in deposition by hyenas that may have selectively destroyed limb bones of the larger herbivores may explain their absence. Other difficulties with his analysis stem from the fact that carnivore gnaw marks are rare on the faunal assemblages, and patterns of humanly induced damage are highly suggestive of hunting.

Direct evidence also exists that hunting was employed to procure at least some of the animals: a weapon tip was found embedded in a vertebra of giant buffalo, for example. Different hunting strategies are suggested by herbivore species, however. Most buffalo represented are either very young or very old, suggesting that the occupants took advantage of natural deaths of vulnerable individuals or selectively preyed on them. By contrast, eland are represented mainly by prime-aged individuals, roughly in the same proportion as they are found in living herds. Such a mortality profile indicates the taking of the eland in large numbers with such catastrophic actions as driving, perhaps over a cliff edge. Such opportunities may have been rare, but they demonstrate considerable organizational skills in dealing with the hunting in number of these large herbivores.

Overall, the picture of Middle Stone Age subsistence at Klasies River, which is supported at other South African sites, is one of a broad-spectrum economy involving significant plant foods (some of which may have been processed), coastal resources, and a variety of terrestrial herbivores taken by various scavenging and hunting techniques.

It has to be said, though, that the data are still relatively poor for such a large continent, and in some respects examples similar to these ocher fragments can be found in the archaeological record left by the Neanderthals. This raises the question of exactly what "modern" behavior is, and whether it was restricted to *Homo sapiens* alone. Does a simple windbreak, or the use of pigments (for an archaeologically invisible function) denote modernity? If so, then it would have to be concluded that the Neanderthals were modern in at least some of their behavioral realms.

Overall, McBrearty and Brooks believe that a "fitful expansion" of modern behavior, occurring on an as-needed basis,

4.18, 4.19 *Artifacts from Blombos Cave: lanceolate bifacially worked Stillbay points (left above) and simple bone points (left below), which were possibly hafted as weapons, found in Middle Stone Age levels at Blombos Cave.*

4.20 *(Below)* ***Blombos Cave:*** *excavations in progress at Blombos Cave, South Africa. Caves on the Cape coast of South Africa contain deep sequences representing long time spans covering the period over which modern human behavior was emerging. Blombos continues to reveal increasing evidence of an early emergence of such behavior, including plausible evidence of symbolism.*

slowly unfurled over at least 100,000 years. By contrast, Klein (1995) believes that the qualitative differences between the archaeological record known prior to *c.* 50,000 years ago and that afterwards are indicative of a relatively sudden emergence of fully modern behavior at around this time.

Given the current paucity of evidence for a longer, gradual emergence of modernity, and the ambiguity of the available evidence, in addition to the possible agreement of Klein's transition with the emergence of language [see box: The Evolution of Language, p. 146] and the dating of the earliest emergence of modern behavior outside Africa, a straightforward reading of the data suggests that such a late and relatively sudden emergence is most likely.

KEY CONTROVERSY The Evolution of Language

In an almost unprecedented way in the biological world, *Homo sapiens* has become the only species of human on the planet, and has colonized an extreme variety of environments over much of its surface. How has this been possible? Archaeologists are drawn to the notion that one event or evolutionary mutation has marked us out as special. To many, this is the evolution of sophisticated language, which differs from simple speech in that it has syntax – organized ways of stringing words together to give variable meanings – as well as tenses to allow communication about things not necessarily in the present. Language facilitates considerable storage and communication of information, freeing the mind from the present and opening up a vast amount of adaptive potential.

Evidence from the Brain

The limited endocranial evidence that is available suggests that some language faculties developed gradually over the evolution of the genus *Homo*, even if theories of measurable "centers" of linguistic ability in the brain are now discredited. Strong lateral asymmetry of the brain is connected both to handedness and language. The former can be

traced back to the earliest stone tools, which display evidence of a clear dominance of right-handedness from the late Pliocene, *c.* 2.5 million years ago (Steele 2002). Although the two hemispheres of the brain interact in language production, the right hemisphere, which has grown larger in *Homo sapiens* at the expense of the left, actively interprets linguistic information in a very distinct way.

It is debatable as to whether any pre-modern hominins such as the Neanderthals possessed linguistic abilities approaching our own, although it is generally agreed that a certain linguistic ability arose slowly through the hominin lineage since the divergence from other hominoids (Lieberman 2002) (on the classification of humans, see Classifying the Primates box, pp. 52–53). Given the limitations of identifying all but the most general patterns of brain enlargement in human evolution, large brains cannot be taken simply to indicate increasing levels of verbal communication.

Debate currently exists as to whether our own capacity for complex language evolved slowly, perhaps in parallel with a gradual unfolding of modern behavior as discussed in the main text, or whether it was a sudden, and possibly quite recent, critical event. Linguists

have demonstrated that the first split between language families separated the !Kung of southern Africa and the Hadza of Tanzania, supporting the notion that the evolution of language as we know it occurred in Africa.

Genetic Evidence

Since the 1990s, a number of exciting projects suggest that a single mutation event did facilitate language. These suggest that biological modernity could derive originally from a mutation on the Y (male) chromosome (Crow 2002; Tyler-Smith 2002). Human Y chromosome lineages originated between 200,000 and 40,000 years ago, some time before which two substantial segments of DNA were duplicated onto the Y.

One of these – the FOXP2 gene – contains good candidate genes for the mutation that may have led to language as we know it, some time after 100,000 years ago and probably after 50,000 years ago; females would presumably have acquired language by means of imitation and participation. This mutation supports the belief of Paul Mellars (1989) and Richard Klein (1995) that behavioral modernity originated relatively suddenly in Africa around 50,000 years ago and spread rapidly from there.

Evolution in High Latitudes: the Neanderthals

The trajectory of anatomical change in the African *Homo sapiens* lineage differed markedly from hominin development in Europe. Among the former, most change occurred in the shape of the cranial vault, with relatively little change in the facial area. By contrast, in Europe the Neanderthals retained the primitive vault structure characteristic of *Homo heidelbergensis*, but it grew larger and had a characteristic shape as seen from the rear, with a large degree of modification of the facial area that occurred during foetal and early postnatal development. This development may reflect responses to pressures resulting from large biting forces that were employed habitually, or a degree of adaptation to cold conditions that maximized sinus tracts through which air could be warmed and moistened, but there is little conclusive indication that these explain the Neanderthal face. More simply, they could be the result of unique develop-

mental patterns that were not under natural selection (Franciscus 2003).

The Anatomy of Homo neanderthalensis

The Neanderthals retained the basic cranial and postcranial body of *Homo heidelbergensis* and adapted it to the cold, dry environments that they encountered in the northern tundra and to a lifestyle that was physically demanding (Trinkaus 1988; Stringer and Gamble 1993). Selection for a large brain – on average greater than that of *Homo sapiens* – also occurred. Genetic data indicate that many Neanderthal traits had coalesced by at least 250,000 years ago (i.e., the late pre-Neanderthals), and European fossils demonstrate that characteristic cranial features began to appear as early as 450,000 years ago on specimens classed as *H. heidelbergensis* at such sites as Swanscombe, England, and Mauer, Germany (Condemi 2000; Hublin 2000).

4.21 *Differences in DNA:* *histogram showing the distributions of pairwise sequence differences between modern humans, humans and Neanderthals, and humans and chimpanzees. The human-Neanderthal differences are much more numerous than was once thought and hence the Neanderthals are much more remote cousins of the human species, indicating that their classification as a distinct species is correct.*

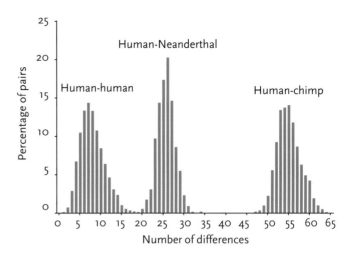

Although there is still some debate as to whether Neanderthals were related at the species level to *Homo sapiens* (thus classified as *H. sapiens neanderthalensis*), they are generally classed as *H. neanderthalensis*, the name proposed by William King in 1864. Some fossil evidence for the development of the species is listed in **Table 4** (p. 148). As Jean-Jacques Hublin (1998) has noted, the gradual evolution of the Neanderthals coincided with increased duration and amplitude of glacial/interglacial cycles, which would have had pronounced effects in northern latitudes. The sequencing of mtDNA from Neanderthal fossils reinforces the view that this evolutionary process occurred independently from that of *H. sapiens* in lower latitudes, and probably indicates that the classification of Neanderthals as a distinct species is correct [**4.21**].

Enough Neanderthal fossils are available from western Europe to Central Asia to permit a good understanding of their anatomy [**4.22**]; some of the major fossils are listed in **Table 5** (p. 148). Many of the traits that distinguish the Neanderthals from *H. sapiens* reflect their biological adaptation to severe northern latitudes [**4.23**]. The Neanderthal cranium contrasts with that of modern humans, as it retained the long, low vault of predecessors such as *H. heidelbergensis*, and possessed powerful biting musculature that modified the face by buttressing it to withstand such forces (Trinkaus 1987). Wear on Neanderthal front teeth suggests that these forces were not only generated through eating, but that the teeth were used as a vicelike tool. The nasal aperture was large, indicating well-developed sinuses that probably functioned to warm and moisten cold, dry tundra air to protect the brain and retain efficient respiration. Postcranially, Neanderthal bodies were large, limbs were robust (thick-walled), suggesting that physical stress was a habitual part of

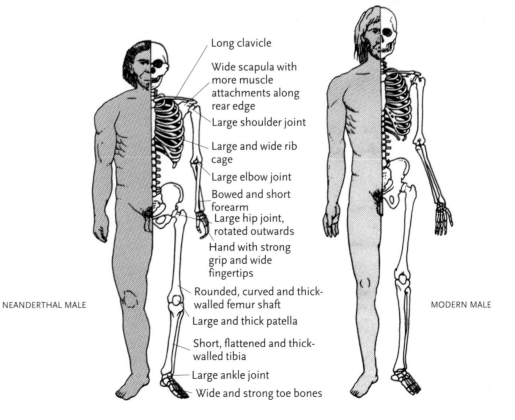

4.22 *Neanderthal anatomy:* *diagram comparing the anatomy of Neanderthals (Homo neanderthalensis) and modern humans (Homo sapiens). Note the shorter, stockier Neanderthal with relatively short limbs. Specific points of comparison are indicated.*

NEANDERTHAL MALE

Long clavicle

Wide scapula with more muscle attachments along rear edge

Large shoulder joint

Large and wide rib cage

Large elbow joint

Bowed and short forearm

Large hip joint, rotated outwards

Hand with strong grip and wide fingertips

Rounded, curved and thick-walled femur shaft

Large and thick patella

Short, flattened and thick-walled tibia

Large ankle joint

Wide and strong toe bones

MODERN MALE

Table 4 *Fossil Evidence for Neanderthal Evolution (after Condemi 2000)*

Species	Time range (years ago)	Key sites	Morphology
Early pre-Neanderthals	More than 300,000	Sima de los Huesos 4 and 5, Spain; Arago (Tautavel) 2, 13, 21, France; Petralona, Greece	Inflated maxillary (upper jaw) region, mental foramina (perforations in the mandible) below molars, lateral development of mandibular condyle (point of the mandible nearest the ear)
Late pre-Neanderthals	300,000–150,000	Bilzingsleben B4, and Steinheim and Mauer, Germany; Swanscombe, UK; La Chaise S, and Biache-Saint-Vaast 1 and 2, France	Lateral positioning of the zygomatic bone (cheekbone), low position of parietal (side of the skull) protuberances, double arched transverse occipital torus (mound of bone at rear of skull), large juxtamastoid eminence (large ridge of bone behind the base of the skull at the rear, the mastoid process)
Early Neanderthals	150,000–70,000	Ehringsdorf, Germany; Saccopastore, Italy; Krapina C, Croatia; La Chaise BD, France	Extended face, no canine fossa (bony depression above canine tooth)
Classic Neanderthals	70,000–30,000	Saint Césaire, La Ferrassie, and La Chapelle-aux-Saints, France; Guattari, Italy	Large nasal aperture, retromolar gap (behind third molar)

Table 5 *Some Important European Neanderthal Fossils*

Key sites	Years ago	Fossils
Engis, Belgium	?	Engis 2 child (cranial fragments and teeth)
Spy, Belgium	?	Spy 1 adult (bones of upper body); Spy 2 adult (partial skeleton); Spy 3 child (two teeth and right tibia)
Krapina, Croatia	c. 120,000	Fragmentary remains of over 13 individuals
Vindija, Croatia	40,000–28,000	Fragmentary remains of numerous individuals
Grotte du Renne, Arcy-sur-Cure, France	c. 34,000	Cranial fragment (temporal)
La Chapelle aux Saints, France	60,000–50,000	La Chapelle-sux-Saints 1 (partial skeleton)
La Ferrassie, France	>70,000	Ferrassie 1 adult (partial skeleton); Ferrassie 2 adult (partial skeleton); Ferrassie 3 child (partial upper skeleton); Ferrassie 4a foetus/neonate humerus and femur; Ferrassie 4b neonate (partial skeleton); Ferrassie 5 foetus (partial skeleton); Ferrassie 6 child (partial skeleton)
L'Hortus, France	120,000–70,000	Partial remains of at least 38 individuals (generally cranial & dental)
La Quina, France	>50,000	Quina H1-H27 fragmentary remains (generally cranial) of a number of individuals
Le Moustier, France	c. 40,000	Le Moustier 1 young adult (partial skeleton); Le Moustier 2 child (partial skeleton)
Marillac, France	c. 45,000	Marillac 1 adult (mandible); Marillac 2 (cranial fragments)
Regourdou, France	?	Regourdou 1 adult (partial skeleton)
Roc de Marsal, France	70,000–60,000	Roc de Marsal 1 child (partial skeleton)
Saint-Césaire, France	35,000–34,000	Saint-Césaire adult (partial skeleton)
Ehringsdorf (Weimar), Germany	>100,000	Ehringsdorf 1 adult (cranial fragments)
Feldhoffer Cave, Neanderthal, Germany	c. 40,000	Neanderthal 1 adult (partial skeleton); Neanderthal 2 adult (right humerus)

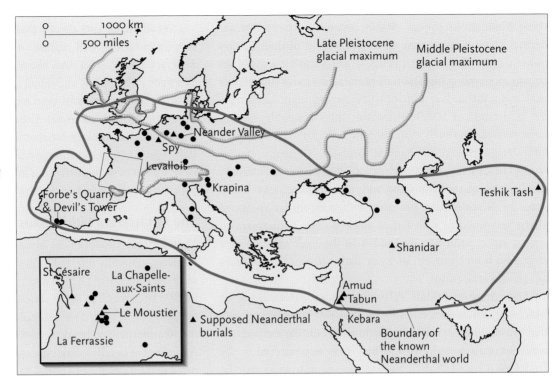

4.23 *The distribution of Neanderthal sites in Eurasia: at times, Neanderthals were as far northwest as Britain, as far south as the Levant, and as far east as Uzbekistan. This represents a sample of changing distributions over tens of thousands of years rather than a "carpet" spread at one time.*

their adaptation, and muscular insertions were pronounced, particularly on the upper body. Their limbs were short relative to their trunks, which is a biological response to the problem of retaining body heat in cold climates (Trinkaus 1981).

Exploitation of Resources: Hunting, Gathering, and Scavenging

Neanderthals seem to have lived relatively short lives, in which physical trauma was a common event. The ageing of Neanderthal remains suggests that most individuals died by their early 40s, although it is conceivable that some lived into their 50s. Large samples of early pre-Neanderthal and proto-Neanderthal remains, such as those from the Sima de los Huesos at Atapuerca in Spain and Krapina in Croatia, reveal mortality peaks in infancy (possibly connected to weaning) and in adolescence (possibly connected to childbirth and behavioral changes upon reaching adulthood, such as joining the hunt). Many Neanderthal postcranial remains show healed fractures, particularly to parts of the upper body, which closely parallel modern sports injuries found among rodeo riders (Berger and Trinkaus 1995) [**4.24**]. The dangerous activity of hunting large herbivores at close range presumably accounts for these.

Recent excavations, with improved recovery techniques, have revealed that plant resources played an important role in Neanderthal diet when available. The charred remains of legumes, including wild pea, and of grasses, acorns, and pistachio nuts recovered from Kebara Cave, Israel, hackberry from Dederiyeh Cave, Syria, and pine nuts from Gorham's Cave, Gibraltar (Akazawa et al. 1999; Albert et al. 2000; Gale and Carruthers 2000), indicate what is probably missing from many Middle Paleolithic sites where they have not been preserved by carbonization.

Animal resources, though, were critical for survival in the north, and a number of studies suggest that Neanderthals employed both scavenging and hunting strategies to obtain

4.24 *Comparison of injuries to modern rodeo riders and Neanderthals: diagram comparing the incidence of injuries found on Neanderthal skeletons with those recorded for modern rodeo riders. The close parallel between them is perhaps indicative of the results of the risks the Neanderthals faced in hunting large herbivores at close quarters.*

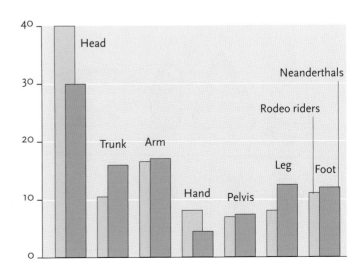

these (Gaudzinski 1999a). Stable isotope analyses of Neanderthal bones suggest that up to 90 percent of their dietary protein came from meat, which is not surprising given its importance among high-latitude populations today (Bocherens et al. 1999; Richards et al. 2000). Scavenging might account for the association of Middle Paleolithic lithic assemblages with large pachyderms such as mammoth at Pagnolo d'Asolo, Italy, and straight-tusked elephant at Gröbern, Germany (Mussi 1999; Gaudzinski 1999a). Numerous sites, however, attest to the hunting of medium-sized and, on occasion, large herbivores by Neanderthals, probably with hand-thrust spears of sharpened wood or with hafted stone points. A fragment of such a stone point was embedded in the neck vertebra of a steppe ass from Umm el Tlel, Syria, dating to over 50,000 years ago (Boëda et al. 1999).

The nature of Middle Paleolithic faunal assemblages, in which only rarely does one species dominate entirely, suggests that Neanderthals employed opportunistic hunting methods, in which animals were hunted as they were encountered in the landscape (Chase 1986). Some evidence points to more specific procurement strategies. Mammoth and woolly rhinoceros were apparently driven over a fissure at La Cotte de St. Brelade, on the island of Jersey, as early as 200,000 years ago (Callow and Cornford 1986) (see Chapter 3, p. 120). As Sabine Gaudzinski (1999a) notes, however, faunal assemblages overwhelmingly dominated by one species become prominent only after 150,000 years ago, and often involve the targeting of prime adult bison and aurochs (wild cow), such as at Mauran in France, Wallertheim in Germany, and Il'skaya in Russia. It is probable that Neanderthals employed a variety of hunting methods that varied in space and time. According to Mary Stiner (1994), they may have become more predatory after *c.* 55,000 years ago; she noted that around that time Neanderthals in coastal Italy replaced scavenging with a variety of hunting-based foraging strategies. As Steven Kuhn (1995) has noted, this change coincided with a reorganization of lithic technology, suggesting that the two were interlinked.

Neanderthals also ate any available small animals, such as tortoise, which is well represented at Shanidar Cave in Iraq, Kebara Cave in Israel, and elsewhere (Evins 1982; Speth and Tchernov 2002); turtle and rabbit at the Gruta do Caldeirão, Portugal (Zilhão 2000); and even scavenging birds at Il'skaya in Russia (Hoffecker et al. 1991). They exploited mollusks in coastal areas such as around the Mediterranean, for example in Latium, Italy (Stiner 1994), and at Vanguard Cave, Gibraltar [4.27], where large mollusks were carried 3–4 km (1.9–2.5 miles) and opened with the aid of heat from a hearth (Barton 2000).

The Mousterian Lithic Industry

Neanderthals produced an entirely Middle Paleolithic lithic industry, generally referred to as the Mousterian [4.25], named after the cave site of Le Moustier in France, one of the first sites to yield such material in the 1860s (Oakley 1964). There is considerable variability in the technological strategies employed by the Neanderthals to break up blocks of stone into usable units. A number of Levallois flaking techniques were common, allowing a certain degree of control to be exercised over the shape and size of resulting flakes and blades (see fig. 3.13), as were a number of simpler techniques such as the discoidal method, which produced as many flakes as possible in varying sizes and shapes. Flakes and blades were either used unmodified, or were modified by edge retouch into a small number of simple tool forms such as scrapers, denticulates (flakes or blades retouched to produce a ragged edge), notches (denticulate tools with single indentation), points, and bifaces (hand axes). Technological strategies and dominant tool forms vary over time.

The use of particular Levallois and non-Levallois techniques, in combination with the relative abundance of scrapers, as opposed to denticulates/notches, was documented by François Bordes (Bordes and de Sonneville-Bordes 1970), who suggested that five main Mousterian assemblage types could be recognized. The "Mousterian of Acheulean" tradition was the only assemblage to contain bifaces and, as the name implies, was assumed to originate in the European Lower Paleolithic Acheulean, discussed in Chapter 3. The Quina and Ferrassie Mousterian were dominated by scrapers, but were distinguished by the lack of Levallois technology in the former. Unlike these, the "denticulate Mousterian" was dominated by denticulates and notches. Finally, the "typical Mousterian" contained a general range of products without any in particular dominating.

Bordes believed that the differing assemblages reflected different Neanderthal groups, each learning different solutions to

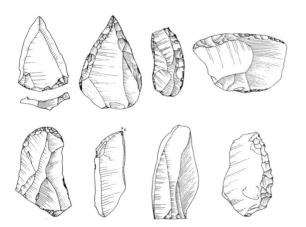

4.25 Mousterian tools: *typical Mousterian tool types, which probably served as weapon tips and pointed tools (above) and general purpose scrapers and knives (below). Wear traces and remains of sticky materials such as bitumen show that some of these were, on occasion, hafted.*

the same problems. This was challenged, however, by Lewis Binford, who suggested that the assemblages reflected different toolkits and, therefore, tasks (Binford and Binford 1966). The debate that ensued became known as the "Mousterian debate," and exists still as an object lesson in how archaeologists interpret the patterning they identify. Reflecting on the Bordes/Binford debate, Paul Mellars (1969) noted that there was some chronological patterning, with the Ferrassie Mousterian always preceding the Quina, and the Mousterian of Acheulean tradition always relatively late. This observation suggests that Bordes's hypothesis is incorrect, as the assemblage types (and therefore groups) seem not to have been contemporary; but by contrast, the lack of any convincing correlation between these different toolkits and differing environments or activities renders Binford's interpretation unconvincing also. The Mousterian problem has not been solved, but today there is a greater understanding of Neanderthal responses to materials in the environment. Their lithic technology seems to have been a very flexible one, with technological responses being made to the nature (size, form, quality) of available materials, and no correlation between specific tool forms and whether or not they were hafted, or the way in which they were hafted.

4.26 *(Right)* ***Excavations at Gorham's Cave, Gibraltar:*** *the wide coastal plain in front of Gorham's and Vanguard caves, Gibraltar, and a nearby estuary, offered a variety of animal and plant resources to Neanderthals who were operating in southern Spain down to around 31,000 years ago.*

4.27 *(Below)* ***Vanguard Cave, Gibraltar:*** *in the upper sediments of Vanguard Cave, the remains of marine shellfish were associated with hearths. The shellfish were probably carried to the site from the estuary, and opened naturally in the heat of the fire, as shown in this artist's reconstruction.*

Neanderthal Behavior

Neanderthals were also skilled workers of organic materials, such as **antler** and **bone**. While they seem not to have possessed the carving skills of modern humans from the Upper Paleolithic and Late Stone Age, the shaping of such materials into

points and other forms was probably common, as found, for example, at Salzgitter-Lebestedt in Germany and Buran-Kaya III, Crimea, in Ukraine (Gaudzinski 1999b; d'Errico and Laroulandie 2000). The recovery of pseudomorphs (casts of decayed organic items formed by brecciated sediments) of flat wooden items with rounded profiles, for example from the Abric Romaní rockshelter in Spain, and a preserved wooden spear from Lehringen in Germany, remind us that **woodworking** was probably a habitual Neanderthal activity, at least where tree cover was plentiful (Castro-Curel and Carbonell 1995).

Neanderthals commonly constructed simple **hearths** for warmth, light, and cooking (Meignen et al. 2001). Where wood was scarce, it seems that they transported coal up to 15 km (9.4 miles) from outcrops, as at Les Canalettes, France (Théry et al. 1996). Beyond the organization of activities around such hearths (Vacquero and Pastó 2001), and the paving of wet floors with stones, Neanderthal use of space seems to have been fairly simple, with certain areas reserved for disposal and messy tasks, and others for eating, resting, and maintenance (Kolen 1999). Some Neanderthal groups **buried certain of their dead**, at least on occasion, and most scholars agree that there are at least 20 clear examples of interment in shallow graves, although this has been the subject of some debate (Pettitt 2002). A number of sites, such as Shanidar Cave in Iraq and La Ferrassie rockshelter in France, were used for multiple burials interred over long periods of time, which suggests that particular sites may have been known as mortuary centers, although the majority of burials, from children to adults, are isolated.

Despite the abundance of used ocher fragments on a number of Middle Paleolithic sites, and the occasional collection of shells, there are no convincing examples of **art** from this period. A fossilized sea urchin from Tata, Hungary, dating to around 100,000 years ago, bears a crack across its surface, perpendicular to which another has been engraved, forming a cross within a circle; but the overwhelming lack of any other pieces of art suggests that it was not a common practice in Neanderthal society.

Early Dispersals of *Homo sapiens* into the Levantine Corridor

Available data for the colonization of the Old and New worlds by *Homo sapiens* are notoriously limited. Large expanses of land either have not been subject to excavation, or possess poor archaeological records that are open to debate and differing interpretations. With regard to the expansion of modern humans, Southwest Asia, Europe, Sahul Land (Australia and New Guinea), and the Americas form major areas of research. In at least Southwest Asia and Europe, the expanding modern human population replaced indigenous archaic *Homo*, with whom a degree of contemporaneity and possibly interaction may have occurred.

Throughout the Pleistocene, the Levant (modern Syria, Lebanon, Israel, and Palestine) formed a major corridor for human and faunal movements between Africa and Eurasia, as discussed in the previous chapter. Its fossil and archaeological record suggests an early establishment of modern humans in the region, possibly part of the initial dispersal out of Africa, although, given its environmental similarities with Africa, it is plausible that modern human origins occurred generally in the Africa/Southwest Asia region. ESR and luminescence dating of burials at the caves of **Skhūl** and **Qafzeh** indicate that robust modern humans were present in Israel by 110,000–90,000 years ago, as we have seen (Bar-Yosef 1993; Hublin 2000). The inclusion of fallow deer antlers with a burial at Qafzeh and a boar's jaw with another at Skhūl, and the presence of ocher at these sites, suggests that mortuary ritual was practiced at least on occasion. By contrast, Neanderthals were buried unaccompanied at **Kebara**, **Amud**, and possibly **Tabun** caves [4.28, 4.29] in Israel much later, between 60,000 and 50,000 years ago; following these, Neanderthals were buried elsewhere in deposits perhaps as late as 45,000 years ago at **Shanidar Cave** in Iraq and **Dederiyeh Cave** in Syria (Akazawa and Muhesen 2002).

The first unequivocal modern human burials accompanied by Upper Paleolithic artifacts occur at Qafzeh around 35,000 years ago, and at Ksar Akil, Lebanon, by around 29,000 years ago (Hublin 2000). However, modern humans may have been re-established in Southwest Asia somewhat earlier, by 45,000 years ago, on the evidence of the so-called Aurignacian stone and bone tools found at Ksar Akil, and bone jewelry at **Üçagizli Cave**, Turkey (Mellars 1993; Kuhn et al. 2001) [4.30], assuming the Aurignacian technocomplex (discussed below), characteristic of the Upper Paleolithic, was made only by modern humans. Furthermore, the burial of the C1 Neanderthal at Tabun, Israel, may be as old as 120,000 years ago, although there are doubts as to the stratigraphic position of this specimen. This confusing chronological picture may suggest that Neanderthals and modern humans were, on occasion, contemporary in this region. A simpler interpretation, however, is that several discrete occupations of the region reflect major biogeographic changes in the distribution of Neanderthals and modern humans, with the former occupying this region during the severe conditions between about 71,000 and 60,000 years ago, when the earlier modern human populations as represented by the Skhūl and Qafzeh remains had become locally extinct. Such a turnover would not be surprising, given the corridor-like nature of the region.

The picture is confused further by the archaeological evidence, which indicates that down to 50,000 years ago, both populations employed Middle Paleolithic toolkits. These have been described as Levalloiso-Mousterian and reflect the dominance of Levallois reduction techniques that were most often used to produce triangular points, many of which were hafted as weapons. A fragment of one such Levallois point was embedded in a neck vertebra of a wild ass from **Umm el Tlel**, Syria, as mentioned above (Boëda et al. 1999).

Although the lithic technology left behind by the two species was similar, there are indications that it was employed in very different ways, which reflect differences in how modern humans and Neanderthals exploited the landscape. Daniel Lieberman and John Shea (1994) have examined faunal and lithic assemblages from sites with hominin fossils in Israel. Incremental cementum deposition in animal teeth was used to determine the seasons in which mountain gazelle and other ungulates were hunted by Neanderthals at Kebara and Tabun and by modern humans at Qafzeh. At Kebara and Tabun, Neanderthals hunted these animals fairly evenly over both dry and wet seasons, whereas at Qafzeh they were killed by modern humans only during the dry season. In terms of the lithic assemblages from these sites, although a number of technical similarities exist, far more points (usually Levallois) occur at Kebara and Tabun, points that also had more impact fractures and use wear; raw materials tended to be procured only a short distance away from each site.

Lieberman and Shea interpret their data as indicative of differing seasonal exploitation and mobility strategies. They suggest that Levantine Neanderthals practiced a locally intensive "radiating" mobility strategy. Large, multi-purpose sites formed cores from which activities were organized, resulting in the formation of more specialized peripheral sites. In such a strategy, the Neanderthals were highly predatory within fairly small, circumscribed areas, producing relatively large numbers

4.28, 4.29 The Tabun caves: *these are situated on a wave-cut cliff at the foot of Mount Carmel (left). Major sedimentary units C and D (seen above) contained rich Middle Paleolithic assemblages with pronounced use of the Levallois technique. Neanderthal remains were found in Layer C.*

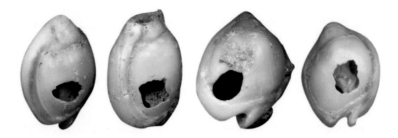

4.30 *Early Upper Paleolithic shell beads from Üçagizli:* *the beads, made from the shells of a Mediterranean species, come from layers probably dating to before 40,000 years ago.*

of weapon tips, and hunting throughout the year. By contrast, the Qafzeh modern humans seem to have practiced a strategy of residential circulating mobility, strongly organized around seasonal change. Movement would take them between several seasonal camps located in different environments, at which activities would differ according to season. This broader strategy, in which the hunting of gazelle and other ungulates was the focus of activity only during one season, put less demand on the production of weapon tips and presumably incorporated several other exploitation strategies, including gathering. If this is true, it may be that the circulating pattern of residential mobility of modern humans was more efficient in terms of energy expended than that of the Neanderthals, which may explain anatomical differences between the two regional populations. It is easy to see how such differing strategies and their associated nutritional demands and returns may have had evolutionary significance. The picture of Neanderthals as a

highly predatory species, which was suggested by stable isotope analyses, may have been significant in their being ultimately out-paced by modern humans.

The Colonization of East Asia and Australia

By 50,000 years ago, *Homo sapiens* was clearly established throughout much or all of Africa, and had already by this time occupied a range outside that continent, including Southwest Asia. By 40,000 years ago, modern humans had expanded their range considerably into new environments, dispersing at the same broad time period into Southeast Asia and Australia, northeastward into the Caucasus and southeast Siberia, and northward into Europe. As changes in the archaeological record largely indicate radical new behavior in a number of realms from this time, it is tempting to view these changes and human expansion as linked. In this sense, the resulting Late Stone

4.31 *Island Southeast Asia:* *at times of low sea levels in the Pleistocene, island Southeast Asia formed a large landmass from the Sunda shelf, while New Guinea, Australia, and Tasmania were linked as the Sahul landmass. The deep waters of Wallacea would still have provided a barrier between the two. The map shows major early modern human sites.*

KEY CONTROVERSY *Homo floresiensis*: A Small-bodied Hominin from Indonesia

A recent discovery on the Indonesian island of Flores of a new species of Upper Pleistocene hominin has raised issues of human speciation and the complexity of human evolution (Brown et al. 2004. Morwood et al. 2004). The Liang Bua cave, located in eastern Flores, has yielded an almost complete, partially articulated skeleton in sediments dating to before 38,000 years ago and perhaps down to as recent as 18,000 years ago. The LB1 skeleton includes a nearly complete cranium, mandible, and bones of the right leg, with partial preservation of the bones of the left leg, and axial elements such as the vertebral column, sacrum, scapulae, clavicles, and ribs. Arm bones may yet be excavated. Other remains of similar form have been found elsewhere in the cave.

On the basis of a unique combination of anatomical features the discoverers, Mike Morwood and Peter Brown of the University of New England in New South Wales, Australia, and their colleagues from the Indonesian Centre for Archaeology in Jakarta, have assigned the remains to a new hominin

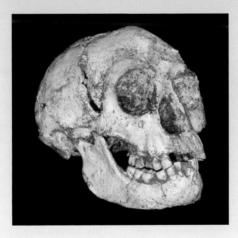

4.32 *The skull of* Homo floresiensis *found on Flores. From this and other associated remains, this female is estimated to have been around only 106 cm (42 in) tall.*

species, *Homo floresiensis*. The endocranial volume – 380 cc – is strikingly small for the genus *Homo*. The postcranial remains indicate that this was a committed biped and the general postcranial anatomy is within the range of variation in *Homo sapiens*.

The size of the LB1 femur (280 mm/11 in) is smaller than the smallest recorded for *Australopithecus afarensis* (Lucy). Estimated stature of the LB1 individual is around 106 cm (42 in) and is probably itself an overestimation. It therefore seems that adult stature was highly reduced in this species, although the combination of small stature and small brain size is not consistent with postnatal growth retardation such as the

various forms of dwarfism. Other mechanisms must therefore be responsible for the small body size of *Homo floresiensis,* and island dwarfing is the most likely. It seems that the isolation of ecological communities on the island of Flores brought about protracted endemic changes, both of *Stegodon* (an extinct relative of the elephants) and *Homo*. Such processes are well documented among mammals, and occur in response to local ecological conditions involving relatively impoverished resource availability and the limited supply of calories offered by tropical rainforests. Under such conditions selection should favour reduced energy requirements, leading to smaller body sizes.

The ancestor population from which *Homo floresiensis* evolved is as yet unclear. It is possible that it evolved from Indonesian *Homo erectus* populations, early populations of *Homo sapiens* in the region, or an as yet unrecognized ancestor population unknown to science. In either two former cases, a dramatic shrinking of the brain would be required, i.e. down to one third or less of average *Homo erectus* or *Homo sapiens* sizes. Given that this is unlikely to have happened, perhaps a more plausible ancestor population would be a small-brained species, perhaps similar to examples found at Dmanisi.

Age/Upper Paleolithic is as much a colonizing and dispersal phenomenon as it is a technological and social revolution. And recent discoveries on the island of Flores [see box: *Homo floresiensis*: A Small-bodied Hominin from Indonesia] have shown how complex the picture is.

Although archaeological data for the modern human colonization of southern Asia is very sparse, it seems that modern *Homo sapiens* was present at least in Sundaland (the continuous landmass formed by the Indonesian islands and Borneo during low sea levels) by c. 40,000 years ago, as indicated by recent re-evaluations of the anatomically modern human "Deep Skull" from the Niah Cave, Sarawak (Barker et al. 2002) (see p. 131). Sundaland, however, was always separated from Sahul Land (the continuous landmass formed by Australia and New Guinea in periods of low sea level) by the deep waters of the Wallacea Strait. This indicates that several island-hopping water cross-

ings would have been necessary to reach New Guinea and Australia, probably toward the northwest of the latter (see Chapter 8). Unlike the Americas (discussed below), the Pleistocene antiquity of the human colonization of Australia, New Guinea, and Tasmania is well established. The actual date of colonization, however, has long been debated. Existing radiocarbon dates, taken at face value, tail off around 40,000 years ago [see box: Radiocarbon Dating, p. 157], although this may reflect more the limitations of the technique rather than the earliest signs of human incursion, which many hold to have occurred much earlier. Furthermore, a number of distinct and differing colonization events may have occurred. Scholars who believe the fossil record of Australia represents two biologically different human populations have hypothesized that Sahul Land was colonized in two waves, an earlier originating in the *Homo erectus* population of Java, and a later originating in the gracile

4.33, 4.34 Burials at Lake Mungo: *at Lake Mungo in southeast Australia, burials were placed into sand dunes at least 40,000 years ago (right). The Mungo III skeleton (below) is that of an adult, probably male,* Homo sapiens, *and was apparently buried in the vicinity of a camp site that was represented by stone tools and hearths.*

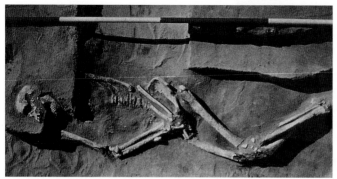

populations supposedly from China, although in Australia it is now clear that no taxonomic difference can be drawn between the human fossils from **Willandra Lakes**, **Kow Swamp**, and elsewhere [see box: Multi-regional Evolution and Modern Human Emergence in Asia and Australasia, pp, 130–31].

Well-dated archaeological sites on New Guinea and Tasmania, excavated in the 1990s, indicate that they were colonized by around 40,000 years ago, and a large number of sites exist in continental Australia that date to this period and thereafter. A small number, however, including the **Malakunanja** rockshelter in northern Australia, and burials at **Lake Mungo**, near the Darling River in southeast Australia [4.33, 4.44], have been held to suggest that colonization occurred before this watershed (Mulvaney and Kamminga 1999). Recent re-evaluations of the dating of these sites, however, have revised their age to around 40,000 years ago.

Perhaps it is no surprise, then, that the bulk of radiocarbon dates available for early human sites in Australia date to 40,000

years ago and younger. Although as already noted, some scholars see this as reflecting the limitations of the technique, others have convincingly shown that such a clustering of radiocarbon dates does not occur with naturally deposited animal bones, which throws serious doubts on this objection (Allen and Holdaway 1995). They conclude that while humans may have reached the continent before around 40,000 years ago, an occupational watershed may have occurred at this time, which renders humans far more visible in the archaeological record. This notion is not inconsistent with that of more than one dispersal event, and probably explains to some extent the broadly contemporary extinction of some fauna on the Australian mainland by 40,000 years ago, and on Tasmania a little later.

The Colonization of Europe, and the Middle to Upper Paleolithic Transition

The distinctive nature of the earliest truly Upper Paleolithic industry in Europe, the Aurignacian (from the Aurignac rockshelter in the French Pyrenees), indicates that *Homo sapiens* had reached at least the southern edges of Europe by around 45,000 years ago, and may have expanded to occupy other southern regions as far as Iberia by 40,000 years ago. This is indicated at sites such as Bacho Kiro and Temnata in Bulgaria, the Grotta de Fumane in northern Italy, and El Castillo in northern Spain. This early spread, possibly restricted to Mediterranean environments or even coastal areas, seems to have occurred during relatively mild climatic conditions (Mellars 1993). Although associations of the Aurignacian industry with modern human

KEY METHOD Radiocarbon Dating

Radiocarbon dating depends on the predictable decay to nitrogen of the unstable isotope carbon-14 (^{14}C). Experiments by Willard Libby in the late 1940s led to the discovery of the method, and measurements on samples of known age from the early 1950s confirmed the technique's usefulness. The resulting "radiocarbon revolution" brought about many surprises, not least of which was that the European later prehistoric period was twice as long as had previously been assumed, and that the origins of agriculture occurred much earlier than originally thought (see Part II).

Radiocarbon dating remains the most important absolute dating method for the period after 40,000 years ago, although it is not without considerable problems. These are central to the debate about Neanderthal and modern human contemporaneity and contact.

Basis of the Method

Carbon is present in all living things, entering plants through the process of photosynthesis, and then into animals which eat the plants and up through the food chain, from herbivores to carnivores. In theory, any organic sample can be dated, but bone, antler, and wood charcoal remain the most commonly sampled materials from Paleolithic sites.

Carbon occurs in three isotopes of similar chemical properties, each with a different atomic weight: ^{12}C, ^{13}C, and ^{14}C. Of these, ^{12}C and ^{13}C are stable, whereas ^{14}C is unstable, as it is radioactive. It takes about 5730 years for half the amount of ^{14}C in a sample to decay, a period known as its half-life. As the ratio of ^{14}C to the stable isotopes ^{12}C and ^{13}C is known, the original amount of ^{14}C in the sample at death can be estimated.

Modern methods of detecting existing amounts of ^{14}C in samples, such as accelerator mass spectrometers (AMS dating), are very accurate, and a precise estimate of the amount of ^{14}C that has decayed in a sample since that organism's death can be turned into a radiocarbon date using the half-life (see Aitken 1990 for a good summary of the history and principles of the technique).

The major assumption required by radiocarbon dating, however, is that the production of ^{14}C in the upper atmosphere has remained constant over time. Comparisons of samples dated by the radiocarbon method and by other, independent, methods such as dendrochronology [see Tree-ring Dating box, Chapter 18, p. 696] have demonstrated that this has not been so. On occasion the production has been much higher than today.

As the technique relies on the ratio of ^{14}C to the stable carbon isotopes, higher production of carbon will cause the radiocarbon clock to stand still, resulting in plateaux on the curves that compare dendrochronological dating and radiocarbon methods.

Calibration of Radiocarbon Dates

Such curves can be used to correct ("calibrate") radiocarbon dates, turning them into "real" dates. This can be done with a good degree of accuracy back to about 13,000 years ago, but beyond this, the lack of wood samples that can be tree-ring dated requires specialists to rely on other materials and methods. Most notable of these are calcium carbonate flowstones (stalagmites or stalactites) from caves, which can be dated by radiocarbon and uranium series methods, as noted in the previous chapter.

Such comparisons have demonstrated that considerable fluctuations in the production of ^{14}C have occurred over the period from around 40,000 to 10,000 years ago. A study by David Richards and Warren Beck (2001), using stalagmites from the Bahamas, demonstrated that radiocarbon dates of around 20,000 years ago were underestimating real dates by as much as 5000 years, and those at 40,000 years ago by almost 10,000 years. The reason for such anomalies is still poorly understood, but it is likely to involve fluctuations in the strength of the earth's geomagnetic field, as well as extraterrestrial sources of carbon such as supernovae.

---

fossils are rare (Churchill and Smith 2000), there is a general consensus that it was solely the product of *Homo sapiens* rather than of the indigenous Neanderthals.

The Aurignacian

The Aurignacian can be defined on the basis of definitive lithic tools such as carinated and nosed-end scrapers (the last with a protruding working end), retouched and often "strangulated" blades (ones in which the mid-region has been thinned to provide two concave edges, forming a "waist"), and a variety of small, retouched bladelets, in addition to various flat or oval-sectioned bone and antler points (Mellars 1994). Overall, Aurignacian lithic and organic tools appear fairly generalized and functionally flexible, probably an important requisite for a dispersing pioneer population (Davies 2001). From the outset, the Aurignacian reflects the employment of considerably more efficient and varied tools than those used by the Neanderthals.

By 35,000 years ago the Aurignacian was well established throughout much of Europe, and by around 31,000 years ago it is found on the northern European plain, for example in Belgium and Britain. From this time, evidence of the manufacture of **beads and other jewelry** from teeth and mammoth ivory, and the circulation of these and marine shells over several hundred kilometers, attest to the presence of established exchange networks. Although its abundance over flake technology is occasionally exaggerated, true prismatic blade technology (in which blades were struck off from the top of a core around its periphery, leaving a prismlike core) was widely employed, and a variety of bone and antler tools such as points, awls, needles, and more enigmatic pieces indicate the fashioning of elaborate clothing and use of sophisticated **weaponry. Tailored clothing** such as leggings and coats would have been far more effective in dealing with severe climates than the simpler furs and hides probably worn by the Neanderthals, and may have been a significant factor in the expansion of Upper Paleolithic populations into northern regions such as Siberia.

Art is present in the form of engraved ivory and bone, and painted and engraved cave walls. Examples of such Aurignacian art include figurines in mammoth ivory from Hohle Fels Cave in southwest Germany, animal carvings from the Vogelherd Cave in southern Germany, the lion-anthropomorph carvings on mammoth ivory such as that from nearby Geissenklösterle Cave, engravings of vulvae (especially common in France), and possibly some of the paintings of Chauvet Cave [see box: The "Three Cs" of Upper Paleolithic Art, pp. 160–61]. On the other hand, there are no convincing indications of burial of the dead or sophisticated dwelling structures, which suggests that although something of a behavioral revolution had taken place, this process was ongoing and far from complete at this time.

Neanderthal "Transitional" Industries

The Aurignacian overlaps in some regions with the late Neanderthals, who are represented either by late Middle Paleolithic industries or, it is generally agreed, "transitional" industries. The latest Neanderthal presence in some areas dates to around 30,000 years ago, and even as late as 28,000 years ago in Croa-

4.35–4.38 The Aurignacian: *these "split-based" bone points and carvings of a horse and mammoth on mammoth ivory from Vogelherd Cave, southern Germany (left), form some of the earliest traces of modern humans in Europe. Culturally, these derive from the early Aurignacian, of which split-based points are characteristic. More enigmatic is the "lion-anthropomorph" carving on a mammoth tusk, with a human body and a lion's head, from the neighboring site of Hohlenstein-Stadel (below).*

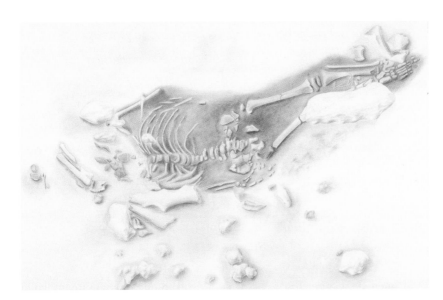

4.39 *(Left)* **Interbreeding?:** *the Lagar Velho child burial – a pierced shell pendant was found near left shoulder, a rabbit sacrum near the waist, and rabbit vertebrae over the lower legs. A fragment of pine wood charcoal may indicate a fire was lit prior to the child being placed in the grave. The red area is ocher.*

4.40 *(Below)* **Acculturation?:** *animal teeth pendants and waste from the manufacture of bone discs, from the Grotte du Renne, Arcy-sur-Cure, France. These are often used to suggest interaction between Neanderthals and modern humans c. 35,000 years ago.*

tia (Smith et al. 1999), where they remained highly dependent on meat (Richards et al. 2000). Many scholars now believe that a period of co-existence occurred between *Homo neanderthalensis* and *Homo sapiens*, at least in certain regions of Europe, and that interaction could have taken place. It is usually assumed that the Aurignacians possessed behavioral advantages over the indigenous Neanderthals – perhaps greatly improved hunting abilities, or broader spectrum economies that were more resilient to food fluctuations and crashes, or greater organizational abilities perhaps linked to language, symbolism, and art.

Arguments center on transitional industries thought to have been made by Neanderthals in the period after 40,000 years ago. These are so named because they are largely Middle Paleolithic in nature but possess some traits, notably true blade technology and some tool forms, which are characteristic of the Upper Paleolithic. Transitional industries are poorly understood and are usually restricted to fairly circumscribed regions of Europe. They may be characterized as variants on a theme: the production of fairly standardized points, which probably functioned in the main as weaponry, and which may suggest that late Neanderthals had improved their hunting prowess. **Table 6** (p. 160) notes these regional industries.

Relations between Neanderthals and Incoming Homo sapiens?

The mix of Middle and Upper Paleolithic elements in such transitional lithic assemblages has been seen by many to indicate a degree of acculturation of Neanderthals (i.e., influencing them culturally) by the incoming modern humans. An early Upper Paleolithic level of the Grotte du Renne at **Arcy-sur-Cure**, to the southeast of Paris, yielded a number of animal teeth that had been pierced and grooved for suspension, in addition to waste products from the manufacture of bone discs [**4.40**]. The Arcy evidence is often invoked in

such discussions of acculturation. In fact, this is difficult to demonstrate unequivocally, given the relative paucity of such assemblages and the imprecision of dating techniques available for this period.

An early modern human mandible from the Pestera cu Oase site in southwestern Romania may possess a mix of modern and Neanderthal characteristics dating to around 35,000–34,000 years ago (Trinkaus et al. 2003). More controversially, the burial of a boy of around four years old at **Lagar Velho**, Portugal [**4.39**], has been cited as evidence of local interbreeding between Neanderthals and modern humans. Evidence produced in support of this view includes traits such as hyperarctic body proportions (with short limbs relative to trunk, to minimize heat loss), which are Neanderthal-like, in the context of a fully modern body (Zilhão and Trinkaus 2002). There is, however, strong disagreement among scholars, some of whom point out that the growth of early modern humans in Europe is very poorly understood, and that hyperarctic body

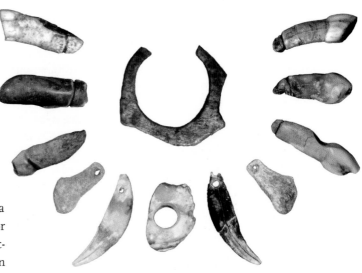

Lithic industry	Region	Characteristic production
Table 6 *Transitional Industries between 40,000 and 28,000 years ago*		
Blade technology is usually present, at least to some degree, in all transitional industries		
Châtelperronian	Southern France, northern Iberia	Small knives/points
Uluzzian	Central and southern Italy	Small crescents/points
Szeletian	Hungary, southern Poland, Czech Republic	Bifacial leaf points
Bohunician	Czech Republic	Levallois-technique endscrapers, leaf points, some burins
Bryndzenian	Moldavia	Leaf points
Lincombian/Ranisian/ Jerzmanowician	Northern European plain, from Britain to Poland	Blade/leaf points

proportions need hardly be indicative of a genetic relationship between the two populations. In addition, a number of Lagar Velho Boy's characteristics that one might expect to overlap morphologically with Neanderthals if he is the product of inter-breeding are fully modern, such as the inner ear canal and dentition, which make it less likely that this was the case.

It is difficult to demonstrate unambiguously a direct link between the arrival of modern humans in Europe and the broadly contemporary extinction of the Neanderthals. As Paul Mellars (1989; 1999) has noted, the chronological coincidence between the two phenomena in many regions of Europe probably suggests that they were related in some way. The pattern,

KEY SITES The "Three Cs" of Upper Paleolithic Art: Cosquer, Chauvet, and Côa

In the 1990s, three major discoveries changed our perceptions of Upper Paleolithic cave art. Jean Clottes (1998) has named these the "three Cs": the Cosquer and Chauvet caves in southeast France, and the open-air engravings in Portugal's Côa Valley.

Cosquer

The discovery of Cosquer Cave, which can only be entered underwater, extended the geographical range of French decorated caves (in this case to within 200 km (125 miles) of Italy), as well as the range of certain motifs, such as hand stencils and the depiction of sea creatures such as seals. As it is in part flooded by the Mediterranean, this cave reminds us that many sites have probably been lost due to the erosive processes of the sea.

Côa Valley

The petroglyphs pecked and engraved along at least 16 km (10 miles) of the deep Côa Valley and in neighboring Spanish open-air locations, such as at Domingo Garcia (Ripoll López and Municio González 1999), are

indications that Upper Paleolithic art was probably very widespread in the landscape, and the tendency for art to survive in caves is probably due to very lucky preservation.

Chauvet Cave

Chauvet Cave, discovered in 1994, is located by the Pont d'Arc, the impressive entrance to the gorges of the Ardèche in southeast France. It is a complex system containing large galleries, one of which was used by bears. In addition to a rich bear paleontology, and evidence for the arrangement of some of the bear remains by humans, abundant art appears on its walls, and numerous traces of human activity remain on its floors (Chauvet et al. 1996; Clottes 2003).

Chauvet was immediately hailed as a new Lascaux, due to the abundance of its engravings and its black (charcoal) and red (ocher) paintings, and to the number of sophisticated techniques and styles that were employed. Compositional groupings of grazing herbivores and predatory carnivores are probably scenes from life. The cave wall

was often prepared by scraping it clean prior to the creation of several panels, spatial perspective was created by a number of means, the natural relief of the cave's walls was used to enhance dynamism, and shading by spreading pigments around ("stump drawing") is common in the black animals.

A number of species are depicted at Chauvet that are rare in caves elsewhere, such as rhino and lion, and some animals, such as the long-eared owl, a panther, and a possible hyena, appear for the first time. Although differences exist between the red and black paintings as to the animals depicted and where the art is placed, stylistic similarities point to a degree of artistic unity in the art.

This having been said, radiocarbon dates, both directly on the black series art and on numerous charcoal fragments from hearths lit on the cave's floor, indicate that at least two periods of activity are reflected in the cave. A number of hearth charcoal fragments and two depictions (the "confronting rhinos," and a bison and an aurochs) have been dated to between 30,000 and 33,000 years ago.

however, varies across Europe. In some regions overlap seems to have been non-existent or relatively brief, but in others, such as Siberia, it may have lasted for up to 10,000 years, which suggests that more than one cause and process may account for the disappearance of the Neanderthals.

Developments in Modern Behavior: the European Upper Paleolithic

The Gravettian

The Aurignacian had come to an end in all areas of Europe by around 28,000 years ago. It was succeeded across most of the continent by more regionally distinct groups that shared general characteristics over a large area. This general techno-complex is referred to as the Gravettian; it lasted from at least 29,000 years ago down to 21,000 years ago in some regions, and much later in southern and eastern regions of Europe, where the late stage, down to *c.* 14,000 years ago, is usually referred to as the Epigravettian. This culture is named after the

site of La Gravette in the Dordogne, France, where it is found stratified above the Aurignacian and below the Solutrean (see below). Like the Aurignacian, its origins are unclear, although unlike that industry, which may have originated outside Europe and spread with modern human populations, the Gravettian is most likely to have originated within the indigenous later Aurignacian, possibly in central Europe.

The period from around 29,000 to 21,000 years ago, often referred to as the mid-Upper Paleolithic and brought to an end by the severe conditions of the Last Glacial Maximum, marks a number of behavioral innovations, such as **semi-sedentism**, **elaborate burial**, and **projectile technology**, which separate it from the early Upper Paleolithic Aurignacian.

The Gravettian represents innovations in subsistence, mortuary activity, organization in the landscape and on site, artistic endeavor, projectile technology, and other non-utilitarian aspects of behavior that together have led some to view it as a golden age (Roebroeks et al. 2000). Technologically, the Gravettian employed prismatic blade technology and a variety of points, often bearing steep backing (blunting) to facilitate hafting. A

Because of this, the Chauvet drawings have been seen as possibly the earliest evidence of painted art known, though some scholars have questioned these dates, on both stylistic (Züchner 1996) and dating (Pettitt and Bahn 2003) grounds. If these are the earliest known examples of art, the sophistication of techniques and style make them crucial to our understanding of how art emerged, at least in Europe.

4.41 *An Upper Paleolithic carnivore hunting scene? The left wall of the end chamber of Chauvet Cave in southeast France, contains a masterpiece of composition. A group of lions appear to be advancing towards a herd of bison. Note the shading ("stump drawing") and perspective.*

number of burins (flakes and blades with chisel-like edges) and end-scrapers attest to the working of skins and organic materials such as wood, bone, and antler. Of the latter, a profusion of highly designed weapon tips can be used to some extent to divide the period chronologically, resulting in a number of discrete phases. The small dimensions of some of these

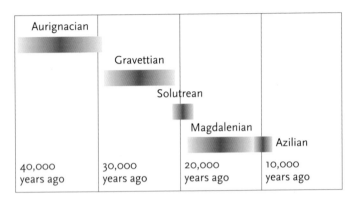

4.42 *Chronology of the European Upper Paleolithic: a simplified diagram showing the major periods.*

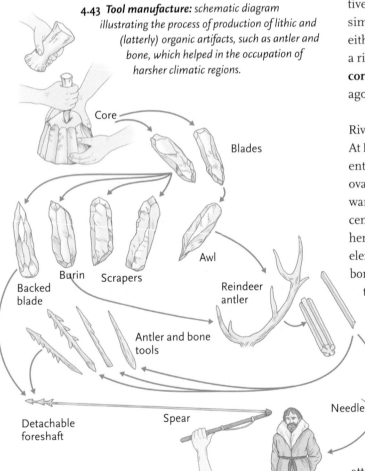

4.43 *Tool manufacture: schematic diagram illustrating the process of production of lithic and (latterly) organic artifacts, such as antler and bone, which helped in the occupation of harsher climatic regions.*

Core
Blades
Awl
Burin
Scrapers
Backed blade
Reindeer antler
Antler and bone tools
Detachable foreshaft
Spear
Needle
Tailored clothing

weapon tips suggest that the **bow and arrow** may have been invented at this time, although this is unproven, alongside the javelin thrown with the aid of a **spearthrower** (the "atlatl"). Some of the Gravettian phases appear to have developed locally as gradual changes in tool form, but some appear as abrupt transitions that most likely indicate population movements.

Gravettian Behavior

A number of regional centers of occupation may be recognized in the middle Upper Paleolithic, which to some extent seem to reflect large-scale population movements as responses to environmental changes. Southwest France has yielded a rich Gravettian record. In central Europe, particularly Moravia (in the Czech Republic) and Slovakia, early Gravettian settlements along rivers such as the Dyje seem to have been occupied for a number of months of the year, and a great amount of effort was invested in the construction and maintenance of **dwellings**. Here, site complexes such as Pavlov and Dolní Věstonice I and II in Moravia have yielded hundreds of bones of mammoth, bison, and reindeer, and complex patterning of artifacts suggestive of highly organized **campsites**. At both site complexes, simple firing of loess (silt) obtained from the banks of the Dyje, either deliberately as small animal figurines, perhaps as part of a ritual, or accidentally, has left us impressions of sophisticated **cordage**, **basketry**, and **textiles** dating to as early as 27,000 years ago (Adovasio et al. 1996).

Similarly, complex sites may be found on the terraces of the River Don in Russia, such as the numerous localities at **Kostenki**. At Kostenki I, a number of semi-subterranean dwellings, apparently roofed with mammoth ribs and furs, were organized in an oval, in the center of which a series of nine hearths provided warmth for a number of activities that were carried out in this central area. Pits cut into the permafrost and containing large herbivore bones indicate that storage of meat was an important element of Gravettian subsistence strategies. At all sites, the bones of fish and other small animals suggest that a broad spectrum of food resources was exploited; this is supported by stable isotope analysis of Gravettian remains from central and eastern Europe, which indicate that riverine resources contributed up to 50 percent of dietary protein (Richards et al. 2001). Clearly, a highly complex hunter-gatherer-fisher subsistence had emerged at least by 27,000 years ago.

Well over 40 **burials**, generally single but with some double and two triple examples, and the ubiquity of human remains amid settlement sites, attest to the development of Gravettian mortuary activity from France to Siberia. The high degree of ornamentation of most of these, and the inclusion of grave offerings with most burials, suggest considerable social complexity. Two infants buried

head to head around 24,000 years ago at **Sungir'**, Russia, for example, wore thousands of fox teeth and mammoth ivory pendants, and were highly colored with red ocher; their shallow grave contained numerous items of mammoth ivory and bone.

Mobiliary art (portable art produced during the Upper Paleolithic), particularly carving on mammoth ivory, is abundant across Europe, and may reflect the social importance of art and symbolic activity in the context of climatic deterioration toward the Last Glacial Maximum (Gamble 1991). The iconic "Venus" figurines [see box: The Meaning of "Venus" Figurines] are part of this Gravettian artistic flowering. Cave painting and engraving continues, with hand prints and stencils and human figurines alongside herbivores, as well as complex, multiphased panels such as the dappled horses and associated hand stencils of Pech Merle, France, which have been dated directly by radiocarbon to 25,000–24,000 years ago (Lorblanchet 1995).

The Magdalenian

As the climatic downturn reached its severest point during the Last Glacial Maximum at 21,000–18,000 years ago, northern Europe and circum-Alpine and other high-altitude areas were abandoned, leaving human populations in southern European refuges; here they underwent marked regionalization, probably due to their isolation from neighboring regions. Some areas witnessed a clear continuity from the Gravettian: in the Italian Epigravettian, backed points and ochered and ornamented burials continued down to the end of the Pleistocene. In other areas, new cultures emerged, such as the French and Iberian **Solutrean** (named after the site of Solutré, Saône-et-Loire), in which Upper Paleolithic flintworking reached its zenith. Flints were often heat-treated to improve their fracture mechanics, and pressure flaking was employed to create a variety of leaf-shaped weapon tips. These seem to have been produced to tight design specifications in terms of size and weight, probably reflecting the demands of hafting and aerodynamic efficiency of atlatl-propelled javelins [4.43]. Some of the weapon tips are so small and light it is conceivable that the **bow and arrow** was in use by this time, if not in the preceding Gravettian, although the

earliest direct evidence of arrows comes only from Stellmoor, Germany, at 10,500 years ago. (Earlier "arrowheads" are inferred from the size, weight, and design of stone tips, but are not unequivocally proven to be such.)

With the climatic amelioration from 18,000 years ago, depopulated regions of Europe were rapidly recolonized, and the late Upper Paleolithic Magdalenian technocomplex (from La Madeleine rockshelter in the Dordogne, France, the typesite for the industry) was soon established from its early roots in Iberia and southern France eastwards to Russia and across southern Europe. From around 17,000 years ago the improvement of the glacial environments of the northern European plain allowed this technocomplex to spread into this region, reaching Britain by 14,000 years ago, where it is known as the **Creswellian**. The long-distance circulation of lithic artifacts (quite commonly over several hundred kilometers and in some cases up to 700 km, or 435 miles) and the circulation of items of adornment such as marine shells, indicates that Magdalenian **social networks** were open and covered vast areas. Magdalenian environments were still cold, and reindeer, bison, and wild cattle (aurochs) were important resources, with red deer of more importance in the south, and ibex and chamois in montane regions. The recovery of fish bones from many Magdalenian sites indicates the continued importance of river fish. Of most use typologically are organic tools such as conical points, and **harpoons**, biserial (double-edged) and uniserial (single-edged) examples of which appear for the first time in the Late Magdalenian.

Some Magdalenian sites reached very large sizes and reflect large-scale occupation for several months of the year. The Madeleine rockshelter is more than 180 m (594 ft) long, and another shelter, Laugerie Haute in the Dordogne, is over 35 m (115 ft) from front to back. These seem to have been places where people congregated at certain seasons of the year, and they have often yielded large quantities of **mobiliary art** [4.44], as well as paintings and engravings on cave walls, such as at Altamira in Spain and Lascaux in France. In eastern Europe, where the term Molodovan is often used for this culture, **semi-permanent dwellings** of impressive size were constructed out of mammoth bones at sites such as Mezhirich [4.45], Mezin, Gontzy, and Yudinovo on the Russian Plain, rich sites among many that have yielded vast inventories of mobiliary art (Soffer 1985). In western Europe, the Middle and Late Magdalenian is the apogee of cave art, some 90 percent of which dates to this period.

Cave art is mainly known from Franco-Cantabria (southwest France and northern Spain), although examples are known

4.45 *Mammoth bone dwelling: with the rarity of trees on the Russian Plain, mammoth bone formed a useful fuel and architectural material. This is the Late Upper Paleolithic mammoth bone dwelling 4 at Mezhirich on the Russian Plain. Note the complex pattern of stacked mandibles to the right, with a vertebral column to the left of them.*

KEY CONTROVERSY The Meaning of "Venus" Figurines

Female carvings are known throughout the European Upper Paleolithic. Only a small number of depictions are known from the Aurignacian, such as the green serpentine Dancing Venus of the Galgenberg, Austria, and a mammoth ivory bas relief from Geissenklösterle Cave in southern Germany, both dating to around 33,000–31,000 years ago. In the Late Upper Paleolithic, stylized carvings of the female form are known from Magdalenian sites and contemporary cultures elsewhere. It was during the middle Upper Paleolithic (Gravettian), however, that the creation of female figurines flourished, one or two millennia either side of 25,000 years ago. Since their discovery in the late 19th century, the figurines have been the subject of much speculation, and some, such as the Black Venus of Dolní Věstonice in the Czech Republic, the Venus of Willendorf in Austria, and the "Dame à la Capuche" from the Grotte du Pape at Brassempouy, in southwest France, have become icons of the European Paleolithic.

Form and Function

Figurines were carved from mammoth ivory, soft stones such as steatite, and even limestone in the case of Willendorf. Scholars have often pointed to the emphasis on breasts and hips/buttocks, and the lack of attention to

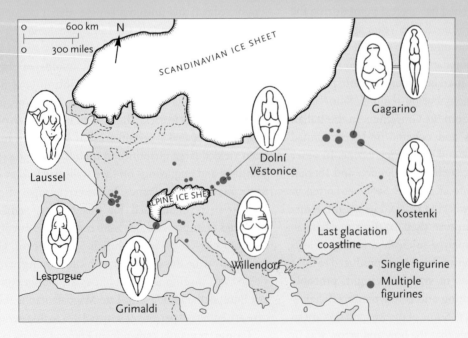

4.46 *(Left) Map showing the distribution of mid-Upper Paleolithic (Gravettian) Eurasian Venus figurines.*

4.47–4.49 *(Opposite) Three female carvings from the European earlier Upper Paleolithic. Left to right: bas relief on serpentine from the Galgenberg hill in Austria (Aurignacian); the fired loess "Black Venus" of Dolní Věstonice (Gravettian); and the limestone venus from Willendorf, Austria (Gravettian).*

from Italy, Germany, and Britain, suggesting that it was probably a widespread phenomenon in caves and also in open locations. Mobiliary art is remarkably abundant and diverse across Europe in this period, and included exquisitely carved animal heads and engraved and notated bones from the Pyrenees and southern France, stylized female carvings from Germany, engraved "batons" of bone and antler that may have functioned as spear shaft straighteners, line players for fishing or more spiritual functions, atlatl crooks for thowing javelins, and a host of other highly decorated pieces (e.g. Bahn 1984; Klein 1973). It is difficult to escape the conclusion that the Magdalenian world was highly decorative.

The last several thousand years of the Pleistocene, until around 11,500 years ago, saw pronounced climatic oscillations, from severe cold stadials such as the Older and Younger Dryas (17,000–15,000 and 13,000–11,500 years ago respectively),

between which occurred the Late Glacial Interstadial (15,000–13,000 years ago), in some regions divided into earlier (Bølling) and later (Allerød) phases. One effect of these oscillations was an increasing regionalization of European Upper Paleolithic societies, and adaptation to a variety of environments in regions where such climatic changes had the most effect – in the north of Europe. In southern France and Iberia, the **Azilian** industry (named after Le Mas d'Azil in the French Pyrenees) continued many traditions of the Magdalenian, with an economic concentration on red deer and the development of notational systems preserved on mobiliary art. In the north, by contrast, regional societies of Late Magdalenian character responded to open environments in relatively cold periods, in which reindeer were important, and, alternatively, to red deer and elk in the more forested landscapes of milder periods. It was, ultimately, just such a regionalized set of cultural

the extremities of the legs, arms, and heads, but interpretations of the function of the figurines often say more about the preoccupations of archaeologists than about mid-Upper Paleolithic society. Early in their discovery these figurines were seen as examples of cause-and-effect magic, i.e., with functions relating to fertility or childbirth.

André Leroi-Gourhan (1968) suggested that they respect a design grammar relating to structuralist principles that he also extended to cave art. Some have seen them as especially

linked to pregnancy, although Patricia Rice (1981) suggested, using ethnographic analogy, that they represented females at all stages of life, not just fertile and pregnant individuals, and speculated that they may have been a general symbol of womanhood.

Clive Gamble (1982) noted that their flowering coincided with a climatic downturn, and stressed their role in social negotiation. LeRoy McDermott (1996) suggested that some relate to self-expression among pregnant women, who were

communicating through the figurines their personal experience of their own bodies.

Since many were excavated in the infancy of archaeology, contextual information is often lacking. French figurines seem to have been tucked away in caves; in Moravia, some figurines (including the Black Venus) were found in domestic refuse, and at sites such as Kostenki and Avdeevo in Russia, female figurines were placed in pits, which may indicate that they were "goddesses" protecting stores, or were even buried accompanied by grave offerings (Gvozdover 1995).

The figurines are stylistically highly complex. They are often colored with ocher, which depicts items of clothing such as simple hats, or textile adornments such as belts and bands; there are several regional variants across Europe, from France to the Russian plain (Soffer et al. 2000). Some figurines may have been hidden or short-lived, others put on display.

It may be too simplistic to view them as possessing one function, and may be best to see them as having a variety of meanings, with regional variations, within a general theme. Whatever their function, they contrast markedly with actual mid-Upper Paleolithic burials, which are overwhelmingly male, and they may be at least a shadowy reflection of complex social dynamics from around 26,000 to 23,000 years ago.

adaptations that saw the production of increasingly microlithic toolkits (tiny bladelets set in composite weapons); these, which continued into the climatic amelioration of the Holocene, are formally classed as Mesolithic.

Late Pleistocene Dispersals: Colonization of the Americas

The question of when humans colonized the Americas is hotly debated, and the evidence – archaeological, linguistic, and genetic – often produces different possible dates, which we will examine here. Although occasional claims arise for pre-modern human presence in the Americas, no convincing evidence exists for any human colonization of the continent prior to the last 18,000 years, or possibly later, and most scholars agree that it was only the behavioral adaptations necessitated by living in the far north under glacial conditions that permitted modern humans to make this last, major terrestrial dispersal.

Possible Source Populations

Modern humans could have colonized the Americas in only a few ways [4.50]. In the glacial phases of the last 100,000 years, when sea levels were relatively low, the grassland of "Beringia" extended over what is now the Bering Strait and linked northeastern Siberia to Alaska. In its deglaciated areas, Beringia supported a "mammoth steppe" community of large herbivores, including mammoth, bison, and horse (Guthrie 1990). This extension of the Eurasian tundra would have been a rich food resource base for Upper Paleolithic hunter-gatherers, and it is very plausible that modern humans established in northern and eastern Siberia would occasionally move across Beringia into new land. This must have occurred before 10,500 years ago, when Beringia was submerged for the last time; any movement of populations southward may have involved an ice-free corridor between the Laurentide (eastern Canadian) and Cordilleran (Rocky Mountains) ice sheets that covered North America at this time, evidence for which has always been elusive. Alternatively, the same people may have made the trip by boat, either across the 55-km (18-mile) wide Bering Strait in a time of higher sea level, or by hugging the coasts of the Pacific Rim and exploiting a wide variety of coastal and inland resources en route.

A third, less plausible argument, based on perceived similarities between bifacially flaked leaf-shaped weapon points of western Europe and the USA, is that western European Solutreans made the first trans-Atlantic crossing. This is highly unlikely, given that the Solutrean predates the earliest convincingly dated leaf-shaped points in the USA by at least 5000 years, and given the difficulties of making such a crossing with the technology apparently known to these people.

Archaeological, linguistic, and genetic data point to eastern Eurasia as the major source population for the Americas, but scholars differ as to whether it was one or more population waves that brought humans to the continent, and whether linguistic and genetic data can be expected to reveal patterns similar to the archaeology. In addition, in situations of occasional, numerically small incursions into the continent, if and when a dispersal might be recorded and sampled archaeologically is a major question.

Archaeology and Human Remains   Although it is generally agreed that the source area for the colonization of the Americas is northeastern Siberia, the relatively poor archaeology of the region does little to provide direct evidence of American Paleoindian forebears. There is a possible archaeological link between the two continents later in time: finely worked spear points typologically similar to contemporary fluted and unfluted forms found in Alaska and further to the south have been found at Uptar, in northeastern Siberia, in a context dated to 8500–8000 years ago (King and Slobodin 1996). This may demonstrate a cultural link a few thousand years later than the most probable first dispersal, but does little else, and there are problems with context and the issue of whether or not the apparent fluting is deliberate. Archaeological traces of a probable source population come from the Upper Paleolithic Diuktai culture, which was established in the Aldan Basin of Siberia by 35,000 years ago. There are problems even here, however, since Diuktai stone tool assemblages bear little typological resemblance to American forms.

The few human remains available from this period do little to help, and the recent discovery of Kennewick Man has confused matters further [see box: Kennewick Man, p. 168]. Early historic skulls from Baja California may share similarities with Southeast Asian populations, suggesting to some that this region formed the source for the earliest human penetration of the continent, followed only later by larger-scale migrations from the north (González-José et al. 2003). Problems exist with this material, however, as this was an area of population isolation for long periods, and the link to Southeast Asia is somewhat tenuous.

Linguistic and Genetic Evidence   Linguistic and genetic evidence, while pointing overwhelmingly to a main Asian source population, does suggest that the process of colonization may not have been a simple one (Ward 1999). Some scholars see Native American languages falling into three main groups. Na Dene is spoken only in the northernmost parts of North America. The Eskimo-Aleut group is also found in the north, and the largest (i.e., most commonly spoken) group, Amerind, is found in the south of the USA through Central to South America.

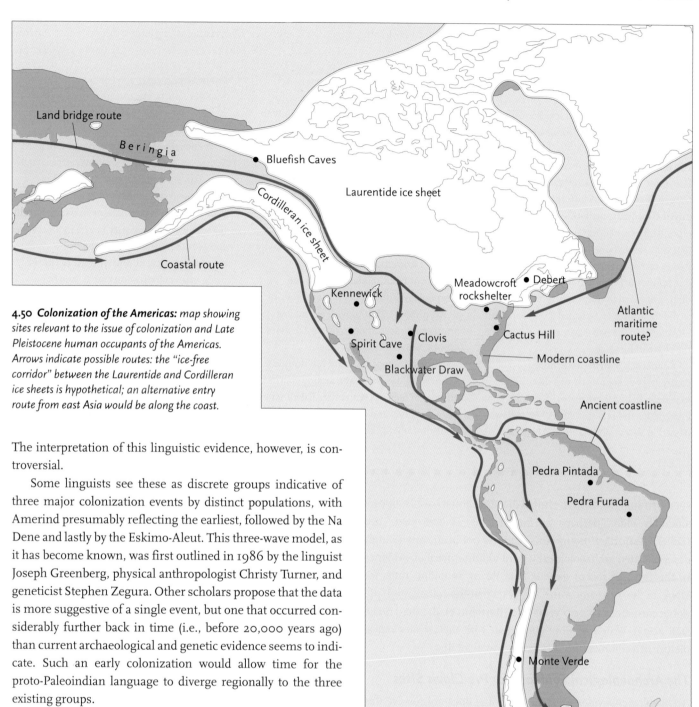

4.50 Colonization of the Americas: *map showing sites relevant to the issue of colonization and Late Pleistocene human occupants of the Americas. Arrows indicate possible routes: the "ice-free corridor" between the Laurentide and Cordilleran ice sheets is hypothetical; an alternative entry route from east Asia would be along the coast.*

The interpretation of this linguistic evidence, however, is controversial.

Some linguists see these as discrete groups indicative of three major colonization events by distinct populations, with Amerind presumably reflecting the earliest, followed by the Na Dene and lastly by the Eskimo-Aleut. This three-wave model, as it has become known, was first outlined in 1986 by the linguist Joseph Greenberg, physical anthropologist Christy Turner, and geneticist Stephen Zegura. Other scholars propose that the data is more suggestive of a single event, but one that occurred considerably further back in time (i.e., before 20,000 years ago) than current archaeological and genetic evidence seems to indicate. Such an early colonization would allow time for the proto-Paleoindian language to diverge regionally to the three existing groups.

Genetically, Amerindians fall into five main haplotypes or clades (groups with a common ancestor, i.e., a single evolutionary branch), which seem to cluster in southern Siberia. Some studies have, however, revealed that there is little correspondence between linguistic and genetic diversity, which raises the question as to how reliable linguistics can be as an indicator of dispersal.

Mitochondrial DNA from living Native Americans, such as the Nuu-Chah-Nulth of British Columbia, Mapuche of Chile, and Ngobe of Panama, is rooted in Siberia or Mongolia, where similar shovel-shaped incisors can also be found in local populations. A surprising degree of genetic similarity, however, can be found between Native Americans as geographically separate as the Alaskan Inuit and Brazilian Yanomamo, and probably indicates that one dispersal event played the most important role in the peopling of the continent.

Ryk Ward (1999) suggested that on genetic grounds, there is no reason to believe that humans have been in the Americas longer than about 800 generations – about 16,000 years. Others, however, believe that if humans were established in Tierra del Fuego by 13,000 years ago, as archaeological evidence

KEY CONTROVERSY Kennewick Man

Human remains predating the early Holocene are extremely rare in the Americas. In July 1996 a near-complete skeleton of an adult male was found eroding from early Holocene sediments in Kennewick, Washington state (Chatters 2000). He probably died at around the age of 40, was in fairly good health at the time of death, yet had suffered a number of physical traumas, including a fractured left elbow and a head infection. A radiocarbon date on a finger bone of 7880 ±160 years ago (when corrected for marine reservoir effects due to marine protein in Kennewick Man's diet) confirmed the antiquity of the remains, as did the willow leaf-shaped stone dart point embedded in the pelvis, which may have been the cause of his death.

Kennewick Man became the subject of controversy as soon as he was discovered, especially as he raised issues of identification, ownership, and repatriation. A federal law passed in 1990 – the National American Graves Protection and Repatriation Act (NAGPRA) – provides the legal basis for museums and the scholarly community to repatriate human remains to American first nations groups, and forms the context of the ongoing Kennewick debate.

In addition to Native Americans' call through NAGPRA for repatriation and reburial, and scholars' calls for detailed study first, controversy also revolves around his biological affinity. The skeleton is markedly different from modern indigenous Americans in craniodental traits, the morphology of the upper leg, and stature, and shows greater affinities with recent European immigrants, according to James Chatters (2000), who defined the remains as "caucasoid." These traits are not unique to Kennewick Man, however, and he shares a number of features with other Paleoindian male skeletons and early historic period skulls from Baja California that are older than around 8000 years ago (such as the 9400-year-old Spirit Cave mummy from western Nevada), which bear affinities with Southeast Asians and Pacific Islanders.

If such similarities are indicative of a Southeast Asian source for early Americans (and this is a highly debated point), this would suggest that there were a number of distinct physical populations in America, and that early settlement may have been more complex than initially thought. Such conclusions may fit well with the notion of three main colonization events (see main text), although scholars question the reliability of skeletally based affiliations here.

It is equally likely that Kennewick Man's affinities lie with Upper Paleolithic Asian populations, from which more recent Southeast Asians derive their own similarities; thus an origin in Siberia, as predicted in most colonization models for the Americas, cannot be ruled out.

seems to suggest, then the initial dispersal must have been considerably older, perhaps as far back as 20,000 years ago (Dillehay 2000), although this date has not been convincingly demonstrated archaeologically. And another piece of evidence in the form of recent genetic data, using mutation rates for DNA on the Y chromosome, suggests that the colonization did not occur before 18,000 years ago (Bortolini et al. 2003; Seielstad 2003), which is more consistent with the archaeological picture of a colonization somewhat later than this.

The Archaeological Evidence for Pre-Clovis Sites

Archaeological evidence in the Americas does not resolve this issue: at least 70 years of intensive research has done little to establish with confidence the date of the first arrival of humans in the Americas, dependent as it is on the recognition of humanly made artifacts and the dating of animal remains and charcoal associated with these by radiocarbon (Haynes 2002). The association of artifacts and extinct Pleistocene mammals was verified at Folsom, New Mexico, in the 1920s, when a spear point was found embedded in the bones of a bison species known to have become extinct before 10,000 years ago. Shortly after this, the association was pushed back to the centuries around 11,000 years ago, a date given the term "Clovis horizon" when the Clovis site in New Mexico was discovered in the 1930s. By the 1960s it was felt by many that the colonization of the Americas could not have occurred before 12,000 years ago, and the "Clovis barrier" was established. Since then, scholars have been divided into those who believe that the Clovis people were the first colonists of the continent, and those who believe that pre-Clovis populations were successful, perhaps for a considerable period of time before Clovis.

A number of sites now appear to break the Clovis barrier, indicating that at least small numbers of humans were operating in regions of the Americas as early as 15,500 years ago. A number of radiocarbon dates go back beyond 14,500 years ago at, for example, Meadowcroft rockshelter in Pennsylvania, Cactus Hill in Virginia, Taima-Taima in Venezuela, Guitarrero and Pikimachay in Peru, Monte Verde and Cueva del Medio in Chile, and Pedra Furada in Brazil; at Meadowcroft, Pedra Furada, and Monte Verde they are abundant and internally consistent for this timescale (Dillehay 2000; Haynes 2002). With most of these sites, however, the older radiocarbon determinations are either singular or very low in number, with the bulk clustering at Clovis or post-Clovis ages, or the samples dated are organic remains that may have accumulated at the sites naturally, and therefore have a questionable association with human activity.

The **Meadowcroft rockshelter** [4.51] is a rich site with a deep stratigraphy, and forms one of the most frequently cited examples of pre-Clovis occupation of the Americas (e.g. Adovasio et al. 1998). Numerous occupational lenses (very thin stratigraphic layers) contained abundant hearths and ash spreads, specialized activity areas, and pits that served for storage and refuse disposal. An abundance of radiocarbon measurements from these horizons indicate that occupation of the site occurred by at least 14,500 years ago, but scholars still argue whether apparent ages of up to 17,500 or even 22,000 years ago for levels underlying these lenses are reliable, or whether the few radiocarbon dates predating 14,500 years ago have been contaminated. The latter possibility seems unlikely (Goldberg and Arpin 1999), though an occupation around at least 17,000 years ago seems increasingly possible. Similarly, **Cactus Hill** contained bifaces (hand axes) and blades in a horizon below the Clovis, from which charcoal has been dated to 18,000 to 20,000 years ago; but the sediments are sand, through which small flecks of charcoal may be stratigraphically mobile, and in any case these need bear no relation to human activity at the site.

At **Pedra Furada** in Brazil, a series of hearths and possible stone tools are thought by the excavator to date back to 30,000–50,000 years ago, but no scientific support for these claims has yet been published. The "hearths" are, in fact, simple clusters of charcoal that may have accumulated naturally, as much material from the site seems to have, and many of the lithics seem to be of natural origin. At present, convincing use

of the site can only be pushed back to about 12,500 years ago, only from which time are unambiguous indicators of human activity present; before this time dated charcoal probably derived from natural causes (Meltzer et al. 1994).

Interpreting the Evidence It may be that the number of sites with archaeological remains clearly underlying Clovis horizons, the procurement of pre-Clovis dates at other sites (albeit not totally unequivocal), and a small number of dates associated with fairly convincing pre-Clovis occupation are, together, enough to demonstrate that colonization may have occurred as early as *c.* 17,000 years ago (Haynes 2002). The sophistication of foragers in Chile and Brazil, far from the presumed entry point in Beringia, suggests that the land was occupied and well known long before the earliest convincing archaeological traces appear, which adds support to Thomas Dillehay's notion that settlement may have occurred before 15,500 years ago [see box: Monte Verde, p. 170].

It seems reasonable to conclude, therefore, that occasional forays by small, highly mobile groups of foragers were made into the Americas at least 2000–3000 years before the Clovis peoples and their contemporaries, who by around 13,000 years ago had diversified into a number of environmental niches, from the northern tundra to the southern rainforests. Perhaps their explorations came to nothing and resulted in local extinction, or

4.51 Meadowcroft rockshelter: *the lowest levels at this rockshelter in Pennsylvania yielded stone tools and knapping waste that could date to as early as 19,000 years ago. The dating, however, is disputed, especially because Pleistocene fauna is absent. Whatever the actual date, some kind of pre-Clovis occupation of the site seems to have occurred.*

KEY SITE Monte Verde

Monte Verde in southern Chile is perhaps the most important pre-Clovis site in the Americas, as it clearly demonstrates that humans were established in the far south of the Americas much earlier than the Clovis people in the north. Excavations in the late 1970s revealed an open-air settlement on the banks of a small creek, in the vicinity of a bog and forest (Dillehay 2000; Adovasio and Pedler 1997). The site contains two broad archaeological layers: the controversial MV-I, with radiocarbon dates in the range of 33,000 years ago, and MV-II, with human occupation around 15,500–15,000 years ago. While scholars, including the excavator, realize that the MV-I occupation is dubious and remains to be demonstrated beyond doubt, there is general agreement in the validity of the MV-II occupation.

Archaeological remains at MV-II are exceptional. The expansion of the bog some time after the abandonment of the MV-II site covered it in peat, and led to the preservation of a large amount of organic material left by its Pleistocene inhabitants. This indicates the importance of plant food in the diet of early hunter-gatherers in the Americas, in addition to the meat of large herbivores such as mastodon. A wood and hide tent some 20 m (66 ft) in length provided shelter, and the relatively elaborate nature of its construction suggests that the occupants probably camped at the site for a long period. Another structure of wood and hide contained the remains of 18 different medicinal plants and is interpreted by the excavator, Tom Dillehay, as a special place of healing. Pollen remains show that while some of these plants grew locally (and are still used by local Mapuche people), many had been brought to the site from distances of up to 700 km (435 miles), indicative of an intimate knowledge of vast areas of land.

In addition to the medicinal plants carried over hundreds of kilometers, a wide variety of aquatic plants from lakes and the coast formed the bulk of the diet. Vegetables, including wild potato and other tubers, were also important. The meat of mastodon, an early form of llama, and many small animals

4.52 Foundations of a wood and hide tent in a wishbone shape at Monte Verde II, Chile. Mastodon hide, meat, and the remains of various medicinal plants were recovered from inside the tent.

was also eaten, although probably in far less abundance than the plant foods. The coast also provided salt, pebbles for flaking into tools, and bitumen to secure these to wooden hafts. It seems that the variety of resources available to the Monte Verdeans in this temperate forest and wetland environment was sufficient to allow them to exploit the region year-round in a broad-based economy of gathering, trapping, and hunting.

The number of radiocarbon dates from MV-II indicating that occupation occurred between 15,500 and 15,000 years ago are overwhelming, although Stuart Fiedel (2000)

has criticized inconsistencies in the excavations and possibly their results. Nevertheless, his assessment of the site does not necessarily undermine its credibility. Clearly, generalized foragers capable of considerable ingenuity in the use of the landscape, the construction of shelters, and the use of natural medicines were established near the tip of South America some 1500 to 2000 years before the advent of Clovis people to the north. This may not be the end of the story, as the lower, MV-I horizon is still being studied. Perhaps in the future, continued excavation will allow uncontroversial dating, or the recovery of clear human artifacts from this site. If this was to occur, and human occupation of this area tripled in age, the implications would be astounding.

4.53 Artifacts from Monte Verde II. Bifacial "knife" and unifacial tool (upper left), a "bola" (upper right) and other artifacts of ground stone. The scale is a 25 cent piece.

perhaps they were so few in number that it is impossible to find them archaeologically.

The Clovis Phenomenon

Archaeological visibility improves in quality and quantity with the Clovis phenomenon, which suggests at the very least that more humans were occupying the continent, or that behavioral strategies from this time were more likely to leave an archaeological record. The Clovis horizon is most clearly defined on the basis of characteristic small projectile points and knives that were artificially worked using pressure flaking and bear a basal flute to facilitate hafting [4.54]. Behaviorally, Clovis has been viewed by many as a fast-moving, west-to-east colonizing *blitzkrieg* of big-game hunters, explaining why its arrival around 13,500 years ago coincides with the extinction of several species of large mammal such as mammoth, mastodon, and giant sloth. Such a view also fitted with the three-wave model of colonization, in that it could be seen as the archaeological signature of the first (Amerind) migration. Research into Clovis behavior since the 1970s [see box: Big-Game Extinctions in North America, p. 172] has, however, overturned such simplistic notions. And the bones of smaller animals occurring on Clovis sites, such as muskrat, fox, beaver, turtle, hare/rabbit, and a variety of rodents, are now in many cases assumed to have accumulated naturally and not to have been directly related to diet.

Rather than concentrating largely on hunting, it seems that Clovis peoples were generalized foragers, and a more inclusive interpretation of faunal and other food remains at Clovis sites has been adopted today. Perhaps such a generalized subsistence is not surprising, as the late Pleistocene environments of eastern North America were a complex mix of open grassland, spruce parklands, and deciduous forests, which offered a variety of resources. The **Shawnee Minisink** site in Pennsylvania, dating to *c.* 12,900 years ago, yielded remains of grape, hackberry, plum, and blackberry. Grinding stones were recovered from **Blackwater Draw** locality 1 in New Mexico, and processing implements from **Debert**, Nova Scotia. Thus, while Clovis populations were certainly able on occasion to hunt mammoth and mastodon, even if their use of them appears to have been fairly wasteful (Haynes 2002), it seems that this occurred in the context of a fluid, technologically simple, generalist strategy.

At the same time as the Clovis peoples were active in North America, generalized foragers were exploiting the rich plant and small animal resources of the Amazon, as revealed by **Pedra Pintada** and other sites in Brazil (Kipnis 1998). Here, generalized lithic technologies, rather than the specific points of the Clovis system, were more suited to the extraction and working of vegetal material. Similarly, generalized strategies may have been used by populations in Mexico by at least 12,900 years ago, as stable isotope studies of human remains show sig-

4.54 A Clovis point socketed into the shaft of a spear: *a flute at the base of Clovis points facilitated hafting into a bone or antler sleeve.*

nificant amounts of plant protein in the diet (Gonzalez et al. 2003). By contrast, mammals were being hunted on the Argentinean Pampas, and while humans cannot be held totally responsible for a *blitzkrieg*, they certainly seem to have played a role, alongside environmental change, in the extinction of large animals, particularly mastodon and horse (Politis et al. 1995).

Summary and Conclusions

This chapter has described the evidence for human behavior and development during the last 400,000 years of the Pleistocene, up to the end of the last Ice Age some 11,500 years ago. The key theme of the period is the origins and spread of modern humans, and the extinction of all other hominin species. For the greater part of the Pleistocene, a number of different hominin species had co-existed: *Homo ergaster* and *H. erectus*, for example, around 1.5 million years ago, or *H. heidelbergensis* and *H. erectus* half a million years ago. The demise around 30,000 years ago of the last communities of *H. neanderthalensis* and *H. erectus*, however, left *Homo sapiens* – anatomically modern humans – the sole surviving hominin species on the planet.

This chapter has also discussed the new behaviors developed by modern humans, which may have given them an advantage in competing with other hominin species. Their brains were no larger than those of the Neanderthals, but they engaged in a much richer repertoire of cognitive and symbolic activity, which is manifest archaeologically in the evidence for cave art, personal adornment, and burial. Their success in coping with the vicissitudes of the Pleistocene climate is shown not only by their survival in relatively cold regions, such as central Europe, but also in their colonization of new territories, above all, Australia and the Americas.

Serious controversy about the origins of anatomically modern humans has polarized largely around two competing hypotheses through the 1980s, which saw modern humans arise either across a broad geographical front, with enough

KEY CONTROVERSY Big-Game Extinctions in North America

Some 35 genera of animals became extinct in North America toward the end of the Pleistocene, leaving the continent's fauna relatively impoverished by 12,500 years ago. The species that did not make it included mammoth, mastodon, a variety of large ground sloth, horses, deer, and a suite of carnivores dependent upon them.

Scenarios to explain these extinctions have shifted in recent years, from those that see humans as the main cause, to more ecologically based ones that invoke climatic change and see little human contribution (Barnosky et al. 2004).

The Human Overkill Hypothesis

The human hunting scenario, however, still captures the imagination. Paul Martin (1984) suggested that rapidly dispersing Clovis hunters were responsible for a *blitzkrieg*-style extinction of the megafauna, in particular mammoth and mastodon. This overkill hypothesis has attracted much attention, and relies on the apparent contemporaneity of the earliest secure human populations in North America and the last dated appearances of the animals in question.

Critics of the overkill hypothesis note that humans arrived in the Americas long before the Clovis phenomenon and the bulk of the

mammalian extinctions, and that recent analyses suggest that Clovis people were more generalized foragers than widely dispersing big-game hunters.

Dating resolution is poor, and at face value more than 20 of the 35 genera seem to have become extinct before the Clovis phenomenon. Certainly, there is no convincing evidence that all of the extinctions occurred over the very short period of time envisaged by Martin.

In addition, archaeological evidence for human hunting of most of the extinct species has not yet been discovered. Donald Grayson and David Meltzer (2002) noted that there is a surprising lack of Clovis kill sites. Their rigorous review of 76 Clovis sites with faunal remains demonstrated that only 14 of these actually provide unambiguous evidence of the hunting of mammoth and mastodon, and that there is in fact no archaeological evidence for the hunting of 33 of the 35 extinct genera.

By contrast, the species for which there is good evidence of Clovis predation – bison – survived the Clovis period. Grayson and Meltzer concluded that on the basis of existing evidence, Clovis populations could not have played a major role in North American big-game extinctions.

The Climate Hypothesis

The fluctuating climatic conditions toward the end of the Pleistocene had dramatic effects on the distribution and behavior of animal and human communities in Europe, and seem to have had similar effects in North America (Grayson 2001). It is possible that the extinctions related to ecological instability created by these fluctuations, although it is difficult to match the chronology of extinctions with specific climatic phases (Haynes 2002). A simple correlation of cold climate and faunal extinction has, therefore, not been demonstrated. A combination of climatically induced ecological changes, human (and carnivore) predation, and random fluctuation of species' size and ranges remains a plausible explanation for the extinction of several mammalian genera at least, but it remains to be tested and cannot explain why a number of the faunal groups became extinct.

Other plausible suggestions have been put forward, such as the spread of virulent disease among animal populations (MacPhee and Marx 1997). While elegant in theory, these remain to be tested against the available data. The bulk of opinion therefore rejects the overkill hypothesis, but there is no agreement as to alternative causes.

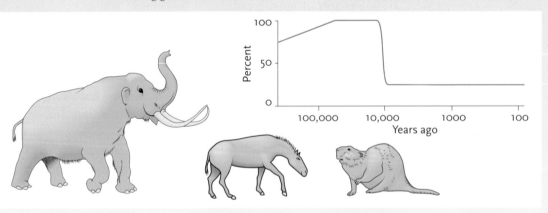

4.55 *A diagram to illustrate the sudden and dramatic decline in big-game animals in North America. There is still vigorous debate as to whether this extinction was a result of human hunting or other causes, including climate change or disease. Big-game animals which became extinct include the mastodon, horse, and giant beaver, as seen here.*

gene flow to keep the biological populations similar over vast distances (the multi-regional perspective), or in a single geographical area, from which they subsequently spread out in a series of colonizing events (the single center perspective). In the 1990s, the bulk of scholarly opinion, formed on the basis of

archaeology, anatomy, genetics, and other disciplines, converged largely on the view that modern humans evolved in a restricted geographical region in Africa, then spread out from there, occupying in an identifiable sequence regions of the Old World. By the end of the Pleistocene this included the Americas.

The last half million years of the Pleistocene saw two distinct evolutionary and behavioral trajectories that originated among *Homo heidelbergensis* populations in two broad geographic regions. In Eurasia, Middle Paleolithic populations evolved as a biological response to the often cold environments of northern latitudes, resulting in the Neanderthals, who had evolved into their recognizable form by 130,000 years ago and persisted until around 30,000 years ago. By contrast, in the southern latitudes of Africa (and perhaps including Southwest Asia), anatomically modern humans of the Middle Stone Age evolved as a response to very different selective pressures, possibly driven by social organization and language. To begin with, the behavioral repertoires of the two were similar. Many scholars agree that the Neanderthals, while exhibiting a variety of flexible approaches to stone tool technology and an intimate use of their landscape by scavenging and the hunting of large herbivores, only rarely buried their dead, apparently without obvious ceremony, and did not create art. By contrast, systematic blade technology, broad-spectrum hunting and gathering economies, elaborate burial, and art developed among modern human populations. There is ongoing debate as to whether the emergence of such modern behavior occurred rapidly, perhaps around 50,000 years ago, and was connected to the emergence of sophisticated language, or more gradually in Africa over a considerable period. Nevertheless, it is agreed that by 40,000 years ago, with the Upper Paleolithic or Late Stone Age, modern humans were clearly behaving very differently from their predecessors and from contemporary Neanderthals.

New behavioral innovations permitted for the first time the inhabitation of hostile areas such as Siberia, and the crossing of relatively short stretches of sea. These permitted the colonization of Australia and New Guinea by at least 40,000 years ago, and the Americas probably between 17,000 and 18,000 years ago, although there is considerable controversy in these areas. The long-held notion that human colonization of the Australia/New Guinea landmass (Sahul Land) and the Americas coincided with the local extinction of large herbivores is still problematic, although few archaeologists now see human overkill as the prime explanation for these events. In northern latitudes, the development of the Eurasian Upper Paleolithic reveals a number of modern behavioral patterns that developed over time, such as semi-sedentism, elaborate dwelling structures and settlement layouts, and multi-component weaponry, including altatl- (spearthrower-) driven javelins, and the bow and arrow. Collectively, these innovations indicate that the modern hunter-gatherer adaptation had evolved at least by 27,000 years ago, perhaps considerably earlier. It is likely that similar innovations in the material realm were also practiced at this time in Africa, although the current evidence is too poor to document this fully.

By the end of the Pleistocene, some 11,500 years ago, a single species of hominin, *Homo sapiens*, was established in every habitable continent of the world. The instability and frequent harshness of Pleistocene climate, with its succession of glacials and interglacials, stadials and interstadials, had played a major part in the evolution of these modern humans, but at the same time had severely limited the potential for demographic and cultural expansion. As the ice sheets melted at the end of the Pleistocene, however, temperatures rose, and plants and animals spread and multiplied. In this new world of much greater abundance, modern humans were able to use their social and cognitive skills to grow dramatically in numbers and to develop new kinds of lifeways. These developments are the subject of Part II of this book.

Further Reading and Suggested Websites

Dillehay, T. 2000. *The Settlement of the Americas*. New York: Basic Books. Surveys North and South American Paleoindian archaeology.

Gamble, C. 1999. *The Palaeolithic Societies of Europe*. Cambridge: Cambridge University Press. A scholarly summary and interpretation of the European record, with excellent coverage of Neanderthal and early modern human behavior down to 20,000 years ago.

Klein, R. 1999. *The Human Career*. Chicago: University of Chicago Press. Ambitious and comprehensive coverage of the biology and behavior of Neanderthals and modern humans; an ideal starting point for further reading.

Shreeve, J. 1995. *The Neanderthal Enigma*. London: Viking. An account of African and European Paleolithic archaeology, particularly strong on the Neanderthals and possible interaction with modern humans.

Stringer, C. & Gamble, C. 1993. *In Search of the Neanderthals*. London and New York: Thames & Hudson. Excellent general survey of African modern human origins and European Neanderthals, with a good balance between biology and behavior.

Stringer, C. & McKie, R. 1996. *African Exodus*. London: Pimlico. Surveys the origin of modern humans; also covers Neanderthals.

http://www.modernhumanorigins.com Informative site maintained by D. Kreger of Pennsylvania State University, with general coverage of human evolution and good sections on modern human origins; good links to other sites.

http://www.neanderthal.de Official website of the Neanderthal Museum, Germany, with general information pertaining to the Neanderthals and the Museum, and excellent related links.

http://www.cr.nps.gov/aad/kennewick/powell_rose.htm Web source for Kennewick Man.

Building M, at Monte Albán in the Valley of Oaxaca, Mexico. This site
was one of the first true cities in Mesoamerica, founded c. 500 BC.

PART II
AFTER THE ICE
11,500 years ago to the Early Civilizations

The end of the last Ice Age marks the onset of the warmer and less hostile climatic and environmental conditions of the Postglacial, that have continued (with minor fluctuations) up to the present day. Part II tells the story of the way that human societies across the globe took advantage of the new opportunities provided by this postglacial (or Holocene) world.

Diversity and change are two of the keynotes of these millennia. In several regions of the world there were important subsistence changes, as hunting and gathering gave way to more intensive methods of food production: what we today call agriculture. These in turn laid the basis for further social developments that culminated in populous and culturally complex cities and states in many regions: Egypt, the Maya, and Rome, to name but a few. One outcome of social complexity was the invention of writing, which from modest and limited beginnings has come to dominate the way in which we now understand and manage our world. Yet in many regions people experienced change at a different pace or in a different form: these include, for example, the highly successful long-term adjustments to desert environments of the native Australians, or the spectacular maritime achievements of the Pacific islands.

The chapters in Part II provide a survey of these developments, beginning with an overview of the major changes in environment, subsistence, and society that characterize this period. A series of chapters then take us on a tour of the Old World, beginning in Southwest Asia where the shift from hunting and gathering to farming is thought to have occurred earliest. Similar changes, however, are almost as old in parts of China, and in both these regions favorable river valley environments led progressively to more complex societies and ultimately to cities and states. In Africa and South Asia, the mosaic-like character of postglacial societies is the key theme, with foragers, farmers, pastoralists, and urban societies developing in different regions, and frequently in close proximity.

The same pattern is explored in the final series of chapters, devoted to the Americas. These begin with the transition from big-game hunting to farming, and then provide a region-by-region review of developments in Central, North, and South America up to the time of European contact. The diversity of human experience as expressed in the cultural remains is testimony to human ingenuity across this wide range of settings both social and physical.

A final chapter looks back across the human story to draw out the key themes and discuss what the archaeological perspective can tell us about the future of our species.

CHAPTER 5
THE WORLD TRANSFORMED: FROM FORAGERS AND FARMERS TO STATES AND EMPIRES

Chris Scarre, University of Cambridge

Climate Change and Faunal Extinction at the End of the Pleistocene 177

The Early Holocene Environment 179
  Coasts and Islands 179
  Forests and Deserts 181
  Hunter-Gatherer Adaptations to the Holocene 181

  A Note on Terminology 182

The Beginnings of Agriculture 183
  What is Agriculture? 183
  Domestication by Hunter-Gatherer Groups 183
  The Development of Domesticates 184
  The Geography of Domestication 184
  ● **KEY METHOD** DNA and Domestication 185
  Why Agriculture? 186

The Spread of Agriculture 187
  ● **KEY CONTROVERSY** Explaining Agriculture 188

The Consequences of Agriculture 190
  Settlement 190
  Social Complexity 191
  Material Culture 191
  Warfare 192
  Agricultural Intensification 192

Cities, States, and Empires 193
  The Development of States 194
    • *The Geography of State Formation* 195
    • *Archaeological Features of States* 195
  ● **KEY CONTROVERSY** Cities, States, and Civilizations Defined and Explained 196
  Toward History: The Adoption of Writing 196
  States and Empires 198

Summary and Conclusions 198

Further Reading and Suggested Website 199

In this chapter we survey the profound global transformation that followed the end of the Pleistocene, or last Ice Age, at around 9600 BC (11,600 years ago). This transformation had two components. The first was environmental change, notably the warming of the global climate, causing the ice to melt and a consequent rise in sea level, and the expansion of plant and animal species. The second was the human response to new opportunities provided by the warmer climate, and above all the development and spread of agriculture.

The domestication of plants and animals led to the establishment of new farming economies that could support much larger communities. The result was a growth in world population to much higher levels than were sustainable by hunting and gathering alone. Food production and demographic increase led, in turn, to other changes, notably in social complexity and technological development. Further change came when the first cities and states emerged in Mesopotamia and Egypt (4th millennium BC), South and East Asia (3rd and 2nd millennia BC), and Central and South America (1st millennium BC). Though cities and states, like agriculture, gradually spread to include greater and greater areas of the world, village farming continued to flourish in many areas, while hunting and gathering was still practiced down to recent times in regions where conditions are hostile to agriculture (such as dry deserts or Arctic wastes) or that were beyond the reach of expanding agricultural communities.

This mosaic of human societies and the changes it underwent are the subject of the remainder of this book, where they are described in detail on a region-by-region basis. In the present chapter these developments are viewed in a comparative perspective, on a global scale. We consider questions such as why agriculture arose in certain regions and not in others, and what it was that drove the development of the first cities and states.

The current postglacial period is only the latest in a series of interglacial periods, and is in many respects similar to interglacials of the previous 800,000 years – a return to glacial conditions may be expected at some point in the future. This latest interglacial – the so-called Holocene, or "recent" epoch in geological time – began around 11,500 years ago (c. 9600 BC). Temperatures rose to approximately their present level, vegetation recolonized northern latitudes, and sea levels approached or slightly exceeded their present height. Where this period differed from anything that had gone before, however, was in the human response to these climatic changes. Anatomically modern humans were now established on every continent of the globe save Antarctica, and once the climatic constraints of the last Ice Age were relaxed, human societies became increasingly prolific, and new forms of social and economic activity developed. Chief among these was agriculture, which arose independently in at least seven regions of the world during the earlier Holocene. The greater yields available through food production caused the steady abandonment of hunting and gathering, and the growth of large agricultural populations. Societies became more complex in their internal organization as they grew in size, and during the 4th and 3rd millennium BC, new kinds of settlement appeared in the form of the first cities, associated with the invention of writing and the development of the state.

It would be misleading, however, to regard the human story of the past 11,600 years simply as one of progress from scattered bands of hunters and gatherers to complex, densely peopled cities and states, as 19th-century writers saw it. Around 1880, for example, both American anthropologist Lewis Henry Morgan and his British counterpart Edward Tylor described the development of human society as moving from Paleolithic "savagery" to the "barbarism" of early farming societies, finally culminating in the "civilization" of Mesopotamia or Egypt (Daniel and Renfrew 1988). Such a simplistic "progressivist" view fails to account for the full diversity of human experience, or for the record left by hunter-gatherers and other less complex societies during these millennia. It should be borne in mind, for example, that while Maya temples or Egyptian pyramids may impress us by their size and sophistication, one of the greatest human achievements was the colonization of the far-flung Pacific islands by skilled seafaring horticulturalists using twin-hulled or outrigger canoes. Furthermore, the true significance of the archaeological record lies not in studying the spectacular, but in seeking to understand the full range of human behavior and experience in their material setting. In that respect, the greatest importance of the past 11,600 years lies in the rich body of material that has survived to throw light on such diverse human societies, far exceeding the rather slender remains left from the preceding Paleolithic.

Climate Change and Faunal Extinction at the End of the Pleistocene

At the height of the last Ice Age (or Last Glacial Maximum, c. 21,000–18,000 BC), the world presented a strange and largely hostile appearance. Land temperatures had fallen from present-day norms by up to 20°C (36°F), tropical sea temperatures by perhaps 2° to 5°C (4° to 9°F), and northern Europe and North America were blanketed by ice sheets over 4 km (2.5 miles) thick (Roberts 1998). With so much water locked up in the ice

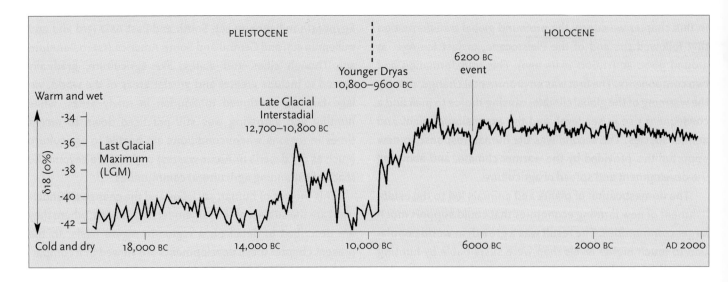

5.1 Temperature changes: *the fluctuating ratios of oxygen isotopes in ice cores such as this from Greenland provide a detailed history of temperature changes since the height of the last Ice Age. The diagram shows how the onset of warmer conditions from c. 14,000 BC was temporarily reversed by the cold conditions of the Younger Dryas. The warm stable climate that has characterized the Holocene became established relatively suddenly around 9600 BC.*

sheets, world climate was marked by aridity. Major deserts expanded far beyond their present limits, and the tropical rainforests of Africa and Amazonia were reduced to isolated pockets. Sea levels fell to 100 m (328 ft) below their present height, turning vast areas of what is now sea bed into dry land; this resulted in land bridges that linked Asia to Alaska and transformed much of island Southeast Asia into a vast, dry, low-lying peninsula called **Sundaland**, within which presently existing islands stood out as chains of hills or mountains.

Around 18,000 BC, the world began to warm, and the grip of the Ice Age climate began steadily to weaken. The process was slow and irregular, marked by both chronological and geographical disconformities. By around 13,000 BC, in the period known as the Bølling/Allerød interstadial, summer temperatures had reached almost their present levels, but in Europe deglaciation then went into dramatic reverse, and cold glacial conditions returned for a further millennium during the Younger Dryas phase (c. 10,800–9600 BC). Perversely, it was probably the melting of the northern ice sheets that was responsible for that reverse, by releasing large quantities of cold meltwater into the North Atlantic that weakened or stopped the warm "conveyor belt" North Atlantic current known as the Gulf Stream that brings water up from the tropics (Blanchon and Shaw 1995). Around 9600 BC, however, warm conditions re-established themselves fairly suddenly, with temperatures rising by 7°C (12.6°F) in only 50 years, ushering in the Holocene epoch [5.1].

At the end of the Ice Age, some of the large mammal species that had characterized the late Pleistocene world died out, notably the mammoth, the woolly rhino, and the giant elk. Carnivores that preyed on these species, such as saber-toothed cats, also became extinct at about this time. The causes for the extinction of these large mammal species, or megafauna, have been much discussed. As noted in the previous chapter [box: Big-Game Extinctions in North America, p. 172], some have laid the blame on human predation, suggesting that burgeoning groups of increasingly effective hunters and gatherers drove these species, with their slow reproductive rates, to extinction. Others have pointed to environmental change that dramatically altered the habitats of these large species and made them vulnerable to famine and disease. The fact that several species of small mammals, birds, and invertebrates also became extinct strengthens the case that climate change must have been at least partly responsible. In North America, however, hunters armed with spears tipped by pressure-flaked Clovis points appear at just the time that the mammoth were disappearing from the record, but the argument cannot be extended to the North American megafauna as a whole; only two of these species, mammoth and mastodon, are represented at kill sites (Grayson and Meltzer 2003). We must also recall that megafaunal species did survive in other parts of the world, such as tropical Africa; the difference there may be that climate change resulted in the expansion and contraction of existing habitats, rather than the complete disappearance of certain habitat types. A further twist has been given by the discovery of remains of dwarf mammoth on Wrangel Island, off the northern coast of Siberia; here the mammoths adapted to the changed conditions by reducing their body size, and by so doing were able to survive the demise of their larger ancestors by some 6000 years, becoming extinct only within the last 4000 years (Vartanyan et al. 1993). Thus environmental change must have been a key factor in megafaunal extinctions, though human predation must also have taken its toll.

The Early Holocene Environment

Coasts and Islands

The first 2000 years of the Holocene were a period of especially rapid change. Though summer temperatures had reached modern levels very early in this epoch, by around 9000 BC, the ice sheets took many centuries to melt, and sea levels at that stage were still over 50 m (165 ft) below those of the present. The melting of the ice sheets led to a rise in sea level (i.e., as a result of meltwater) that drowned low-lying areas, at a speed that must at times have been perceptible to human communities on a year-by-year basis [5.2]. In northern latitudes, the melting of the ice sheets had a reverse effect, as the removal of the weight of the ice caused land areas to rebound in a process known as isostatic uplift, which far outstripped the rise in sea level. In previously glaciated areas, early Holocene shorelines are now to be found well above sea level and far inland, whereas throughout most of the world, where there were no glaciers, the rising sea level drowned out coastal areas, and no early Holocene coastal sites are preserved. As a result, in most regions, save where isostatic uplift has preserved early shorelines, the history of human coastal exploitation can be traced back only to the middle/late Holocene, some 5000 years ago.

One notable effect of early Holocene sea-level rise was the creation of islands. Thus the Japanese islands were separated from the Asian mainland, Tasmania from Australia, and Britain from continental Europe. East Asia and North America became divided by the flooding of the Bering Strait around 8500 BC. In terms of geographical extent, however, the most dramatic of all late Pleistocene and early Holocene coastal losses occurred in Southeast Asia, where the Pleistocene landmass known as Sundaland, twice the size of India, lost over half of its land area to rising sea levels between 15,000 and 5000 BC, resulting in the creation of the Southeast Asian islands [5.3]. Most of the land loss occurred during the late Pleistocene, before 9600 BC, but Sumatra was finally separated from Malaysia with the formation of the Strait of Malacca as late as 6500 BC (Oppenheimer 1998). At about the same time, on the far side of the world, Britain became separated from the adjacent European mainland. The transformation of the North Sea basin from marshy lowland to open sea can be followed in detail, and artifacts dredged up from the North Sea floor testify to human occupation by Mesolithic hunter-gatherers across the whole region from eastern England to the Netherlands and Denmark. As sea levels rose, an area of low hills known as **Doggerland** became an island within the formative North Sea, until, ultimately, it too was submerged and became the rich fishing grounds known as the Dogger Bank (Coles 1998) [5.4].

By the time that changes in sea level began to slow appreciably, around 5000 BC, the shapes of continents and islands were

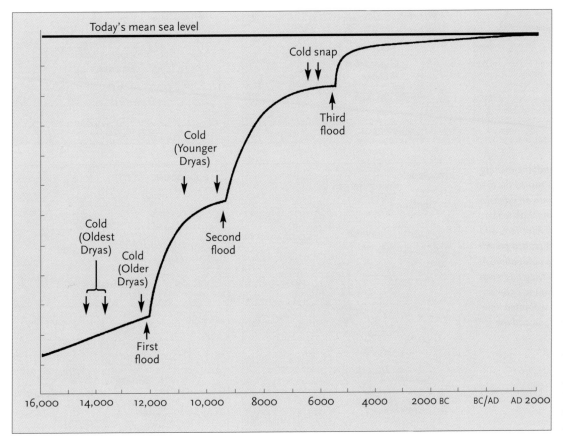

5.2 Sea-level changes: the melting of the ice sheets released massive quantities of water into the world's oceans, resulting in a substantial rise in sea level. Studies from Barbados have shown that this was not a steady progression but that there were three major phases of rapid sea-level rise, punctuated by standstills or regressions as temperatures warmed and cooled during the final millennia of the Pleistocene.

179

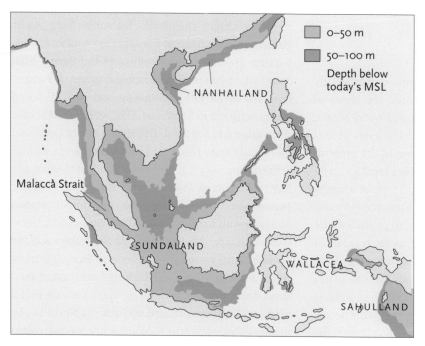

5.3 Sundaland: *at the height of the last Ice Age the islands of Borneo, Indonesia, and Sumatra were joined to the mainland of Southeast Asia to form a landmass known as Sundaland. Much of this landmass (an area equivalent to twice the size of India) was drowned as sea level rose with the melting of the ice sheets. The present-day geography of Island Southeast Asia came into being during the 7th millennium BC with the opening of the Malacca Strait.*

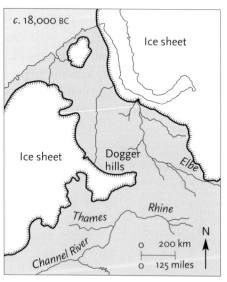

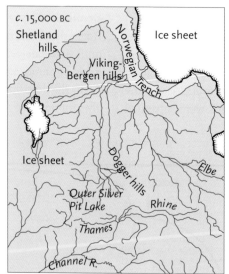

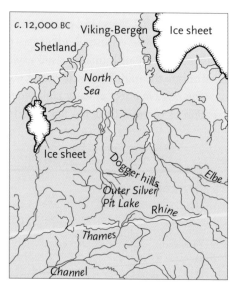

5.4 The drowning of Doggerland: *the melting of the north European ice sheets turned the area between Britain and Germany into an extensive marshy lowland, which was soon inhabited by groups of hunters and gatherers. Flint tools and other materials from the present seabed provide material evidence of this human occupation. As sea levels rose, however, the low-lying basin was progressively submerged until around 6500 BC when Britain became an island separated from mainland Europe by the North Sea and the Channel.*

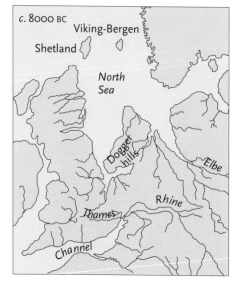

very much those of the present day. And although some former mainland communities now found themselves living on islands, this only rarely resulted in cultural isolation. The case of Tasmania, separated from mainland Australia by the stormy and impassable 250-km (155-mile) Bass Strait, is very much an exception. Still rarer are cases where such isolated communities died out, as on some of the smaller islands off the southern coast of Australia. The human response to changes in sea level and island formation was usually more innovative and positive, resulting in new strategies of marine exploitation and highly developed navigational skills. It was these that enabled Polynesian seafarers to discover and colonize the far-flung and often tiny islands of the Pacific during the 1st and early 2nd millennia AD, as discussed in Chapter 8.

Forests and Deserts

Vegetation zones expanded in response to increased temperature and rainfall. In Europe and North America, the boreal (northern) forest belt, with cold-climate trees such as birch and pine, was pushed northward as the ice sheets melted, and was replaced in the now more temperate latitudes by deciduous woodland, including oak, elm, and beech. The forests needed several centuries to establish themselves, spreading slowly outward from their glacial refugia as barren deglaciated landscapes developed soils capable of supporting them. The open tundra shrank in area, a change that may have played a part in the demise of North American and Eurasian megafauna referred to above. In their place came woodland species such as wild boar and red deer, offering new prey for human hunters in radically different and often thickly forested environments. The successive transformations of the northern forests left their imprint in the records found in pollen cores that have been extracted from lakes and bogs. The changing combinations of tree species revealed in these cores have led to the development of a sequence of "pollen zones," which divide the Holocene in these northern latitudes into vegetation units such as Boreal and Atlantic, though these are steadily falling into disuse (Roberts 1998).

Tropical areas were also affected by postglacial warming. During the earlier Holocene, the Inter-Tropical Convergence Zone, which carries rains through tropical Africa and via the monsoon systems across the Indian Ocean, moved north to pass over the Sahara. This became a region of lakes within an extensive savanna grassland, rather than the desert of the present day. By the 9th millennium BC, pottery-using fishers and hunters had settled the central and southern Sahara, and faunal evidence indicates the presence of domesticated cattle in the central Sahara by at least the 5th millennium BC. Only during the 3rd millennium BC did climate patterns change and the Sahara begin to take on the desert-like character it has today [5.5].

Hunter-Gatherer Adaptations to the Holocene

Human communities were among the many species favored by the warmer and moister Holocene climate and the vegetational and environmental changes it engendered. During the last Ice Age, human populations were most numerous in tropical and sub-tropical zones, and those living in more marginal areas would have been severely limited by the harsh glacial environment. The postglacial world, by contrast, offered enormous opportunities, especially to communities occupying or colonizing the temperate zones of North America, Europe, and Asia. The global distribution of human population expanded outward from warm central latitudes, and grew steadily in scale, as warmer climate increased the overall biomass of the planet and food sources became correspondingly more abundant. That is not to overlook the fact that there was considerable regional variation. Nor was the Holocene climate entirely stable, as the changes in the Saharan sequence illustrate. Areas of dense forest were not easily exploited, and human groups often chose to settle within breaks in the forest, beside lakes and rivers, where freshwater fish and waterfowl as well as game animals were available. Some of the best evidence for postglacial settlement comes from former wetland margins, such as the North Sea basin or the Florida swamps.

The technology and material culture of early postglacial groups was directly developed from that of their late Paleolithic forebears. **Microliths** – small standardized flakes – were used to make composite tools, with flint or chert cutting edges inserted into wooden or bone hafts. In Europe, microliths are a distinguishing feature of the Mesolithic [see A Note on Terminology, p. 182], the period between the end of the Paleolithic (the end of the last Ice Age) and the beginning of the Neolithic (characterized by the adoption of farming), though microliths had been used much earlier in Africa, where quartz and other fine-grained rocks formed the raw material.

Early Holocene communities gathered plant foods with stone reaping knives or dug up tubers with digging sticks, and hunted with spears and the bow. Like their Paleolithic predecessors, they exploited resources by moving around their landscapes, generally in small groups, occasionally coming together in larger seasonal gatherings at annual salmon runs or similar places of abundant resources. They were characterized by mobility, and though ethnographic parallels suggest that they probably maintained a complex network of kinship links, their societies were essentially small-scale in nature. The geographical and seasonal distribution of resources dictated the size and dispersion of these human communities, and set a limit to their numbers. For these were still gatherers, fishers, and hunters, not food producers, and they were dependent on the available natural resources.

Yet already during the final stages of the last Ice Age, certain groups of hunters and gatherers had begun to exploit their

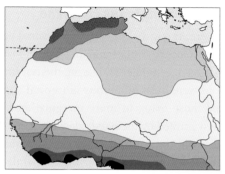

c. 16,000 BC: hyperarid

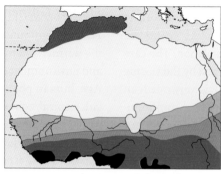

c. 10,000 BC: the eastern Saharan frontier moves north

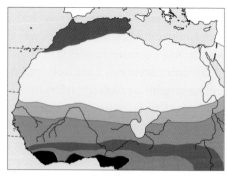

c. 8500 BC: western frontier moves north

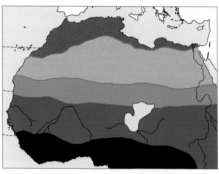

c. 6500 BC: greatest humidity

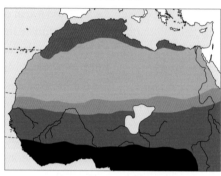

c. 4500 BC: less intense humidity

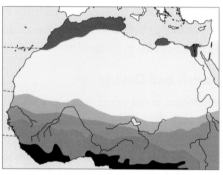

From 2000–1000 BC: present aridity

5.5 ***The Sahara:*** *during the early Holocene period North Africa experienced a wetter climate than today and much of what is now the Sahara desert became dry grassland. Rock art of the period depicts giraffe, elephant, and other animals now restricted to the sub-Saharan region; joined by herds of domestic cattle from the 5th millennium BC. Arid conditions returned during the 3rd and 2nd millennium BC.*

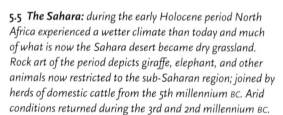

Extreme tropical desert

Temperate desert

Tropical semi-desert

Mixed semi-desert and subdesert steppe

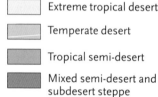

Grassland and dry savanna

Shrubby savanna

Mediterranean vegetation

Humid tropical forest

A Note on Terminology

The period up to the end of the Pleistocene (or Ice Age) is conventionally known to many archaeologists as the Paleolithic (Old Stone Age), but the nomenclature of the subsequent periods varies from region to region. In Europe and certain other areas, the Paleolithic is followed by the Mesolithic (Middle Stone Age). The distinction is one of chronology and environment rather than technology or material remains, though the Mesolithic is also distinguished from earlier and later periods by the use of small flint blades known as microliths, which were hafted in bone or wooden mounts to create composite tools such as knives, spears, and arrows.

The Mesolithic spans the time between the end of the last Ice Age (*c.* 9600 BC) and the adoption of agriculture, and is hence of variable length, depending on the date of the beginning of agriculture in the individual region.

In Southwest Asia, where cultivation began before the end of the Pleistocene, there is no Mesolithic; the final millennia of the Late Pleistocene are there labeled Epipaleolithic (Chapter 6). The term Mesolithic is not used in North America, the period instead being divided into Paleoindian, from first Late Pleistocene settlers to *c.* 7000 BC, and Archaic, from 7000 BC to the adoption of agriculture (Chapter 9). Nor is the term employed in Australasia or most of Africa.

The adoption of cultivation is normally equated with the beginning of the Neolithic or New Stone Age, though the precise associations of the term (based originally on the use of cutting tools made of ground rather than chipped stone) are not without their problems. Here, too, the terminology employed in Europe and exported by European archaeologists to other regions is

far from universally applied. Cultivation in the Americas begins during the Archaic, but in Mesoamerica the closest equivalent to the Neolithic would be the Formative or Preclassic (Chapter 16).

The different regional terminologies, where relevant, are explained in the chapters that follow. It must be emphasized that these are terms of convenience, which help us to discuss the archaeological evidence. Their origins lie in 19th-century classificatory schemes, and their limitations must constantly be borne in mind.

European Neolithic communities and North American Archaic communities, for example, were highly diverse, and must on no account be considered to form some kind of "natural" category, still less a universal stage in human progress.

environment in a new way, moving beyond simple collecting to the intentional management of selected plant species. Thus began the process of domestication and cultivation that has transformed the world. Spreading inexorably from its origins in a number of separate regions, the shift from food collection to food production dramatically increased the human carrying capacity of the planet. In the process, the environment was transformed, as modest clearings gave way to fields, and forests were felled to provide farmland for ever-increasing human numbers.

The Beginnings of Agriculture

What is Agriculture?

Agriculture is the establishment of an artificial ecosystem in which selected species of plants and animals are cultivated and reared. Its two basic premises are the intentional propagation of food (both plant and animal) by humans, and the isolation of the domesticated species from their wild relatives, leading to changes (intentional and unintentional) in their morphology such that domestic species may be distinguished. When describing early food production, a number of terms are used that have different, if overlapping, meanings, and it is important to clarify their interrelationship (Price and Gebauer 1995).

Domestication is a biological process that involves changes in the genotypes and physical characteristics of plants and animals as they become dependent on humans for reproductive success. Domestication may often be unintentional, resulting from continuing interaction between humans and wild species.

Cultivation is a cultural phenomenon that involves intentionally preparing fields, sowing, harvesting, and storing seeds or other plant parts. Cultivation required significant and deliberate changes in human technology, subsistence, and perspectives.

Herding, like cultivation, requires intentional changes in the relationship between humans and animals.

Agriculture is a commitment to this relationship between humans and plants and animals. It ultimately involves changes in the human use of the earth and in the structure and organization of human society, including the extensive clearance of forest, the cultivation of hard-shelled cereals or root crops that can be stored for long periods of time, and the invention and adoption of new technologies for farming and/or herding (plows, field systems, irrigation); this results in more villages, more people, and an increased pace along the path to more complex social and political organization.

Domestication by Hunter-Gatherer Groups

Although domestication – the human propagation of selected species – marks the key innovation toward agriculture, the radical transformation of societies came only with the adoption of cultivation practices, by which communities abandoned their primary reliance on wild species and invested time and energy in clearing forests and constructing storage facilities in which the annual harvest could be stored. This change is usually associated with sedentism, a residence pattern of permanent, year-round settlement, which replaced the mobility associated with most hunter-gatherer groups. The distinction may, however, be simplistic, as certain non-agricultural communities in favorable locations already had relatively permanent settlements. Our conception of hunter-gatherer lifestyles frequently draws heavily on the model of Australian or Kalahari Desert groups, or Arctic hunters, living in environments too hostile for agriculture. Hunter-gatherers in more favorable environments, such as the peoples of the Northwest Coast of North America, were living in villages of substantial timber houses at first European contact, and in at least some regions of the world (notably Southwest Asia; see Chapter 7) sedentary settlements preceded the shift to cultivation.

Nor was domestication an innovation that was restricted to farming societies. On the contrary, the first of all domestic animals – the dog – was domesticated by hunter-gatherers during the Paleolithic. Remains of domestic dog over 10,000 years old have been found at archaeological sites in northern Europe and southwest Asia, but analysis of DNA lineages suggests an initial domestication at least 14,000 and perhaps as much as 135,000 years ago. The domesticated form was distinguished from its wild ancestor, the wolf, by a shorter snout and modified teeth. The social structure of wolf packs facilitated their domestication, since a human could stand in place of the pack leader, and the striking allegiance of dogs to their owners is to be attributed to this ancestral lupine behavior (Vila et al. 1997; Pennisi 2002; Savolainen et al. 2002).

Dogs differ from most other domestic animals not only in the greater antiquity of their domestication but also in the reasons for it. Dogs can be (and in some societies certainly are) eaten, and there is archaeological evidence for the butchery of dog carcasses in prehistoric contexts. However, the primary utility of the dog in a hunter-gatherer context is not as a food source but as a hunting aid, and this is more probably the reason for its domestication. The special status of dogs as human companions is suggested by the burial of dogs within human cemeteries, as at the Mesolithic cemetery of Skateholm in southern Sweden (Larsson 1989). Burials of dogs and humans were also found at the pre-agricultural Koster site in Illinois, dating to c. 6500 BC (see The Archaic Dog box, Chapter 9, p. 326).

Hunter-gatherers often develop close relationships with key plant as well as animal species, which lead to practices verging on domestication. Australian Aborigines, for example, followed a practice of replanting parts of the yams that they dug up. In northern Australia the practice was to leave the main plant and its root, and to collect only the side tubers; in western Australia, people dug up the tubers, broke them into pieces, and returned some parts to the ground (Yen 1989). Even more elaborate practices are attested elsewhere: the Owens Valley Paiute of eastern California diverted streams so as to irrigate natural "fields" of water-meadow root crops (Smith 2001).

Two conclusions may be drawn from this. First, that hunter-gatherers were not simply passive bystanders in the history of plant and animal exploitation, but modified those species on which they relied, both intentionally and unintentionally; and second, that close relationships between humans and their food sources did not begin abruptly with the development of agriculture in the early postglacial period, but have a much longer history, stretching back tens of thousands of years into the Paleolithic.

The Development of Domesticates

Domestication involves the removal of species from the wild, and their propagation by humans within a sheltered or manipulated setting. As a result, domesticates are subjected to different selective pressures from their wild relatives, and so undergo morphological and genetic change from their wild ancestors through processes of natural selection [see box: DNA and Domestication]. Domesticated species are also subject to selection by humans, who may prefer smaller and more docile individuals in a herd, for example, or may breed new forms that have specially valued characteristics, such as woolly sheep.

Other consequences of human contact may be unintentional. In a now classic experiment, Jack Harlan (1967) harvested wild stands of cereals by hand in southeast Turkey, and showed that it was possible for a small family group to gather in only three weeks enough to sustain them for a year. It is important to consider the effect of such collection on the plant community, in particular on the way in which the plants reseed themselves. Those with brittle seed heads will shed their seeds as soon as they are touched; those with tougher seed heads will be preferentially gathered by the human collectors. Should the human collectors use the plants they have gathered as the basis of next year's crop, they will be sowing the tougher seed head variety, and thus altering the characteristics of the species overall. It may have been through this sort of process of unintentional selection that domesticated forms of wheat and barley first developed in Southwest Asia.

There were other common changes in domesticated species. A reduction in body size among animals occurred (either through intentional selection or as the unintentional result of breeding conditions); it should be noted, however, that size reduction is a widespread feature of postglacial mammals, and has affected humans as well as animals (Leach 2003). There is evidence also for an increase in size among cereals and tubers, through selective propagation. Studies in the dry valleys of Mexico have been effective in illustrating the dramatic size increase of maize cobs through intentional selection. In addition, incidental changes, such as twisted horns in goats, or the loss of natural coloring in cows or horses, may be due to the relaxation of natural selective pressures in the protected, humanly controlled environment; black and white Friesian cows, for example, would be conspicuous to predators and thus have reduced adaptive fitness in the wild.

The eventual result of these changes was the emergence of distinct domesticated species, many (though not all) of which could no longer survive in the wild without human intervention. Furthermore, the success of the new food-producing economy, based on effective combinations, or "packages," of domestic plants and animals (such as the triad of maize, beans, and squash in the Americas, discussed in Chapter 9), led to its relatively rapid expansion at the expense of hunting and gathering. As a result, species were carried by human action to areas far beyond the geographical range of their wild ancestors. Thus, cereals of Southwest Asian origin came to be cultivated in northern Europe, where there were no indigenous wild relatives. In these locations, there is no dispute or ambiguity about the domesticated status of the plants or animals concerned, and equally no possibility of any local domestication.

Aside from the domesticated species themselves, cultivation, herding, and agriculture leave a range of other archaeological traces. These include such **"technologies of cultivation"** as grindstones, sickles, storage facilities, or plows. Not all of these are reliable indicators, since grindstones may have been used for processing wild plant foods, and storage facilities likewise, but they are most commonly associated with sedentism and food production. More reliable indicators are **"technologies of the landscape,"** such as field systems, forest clearances, terracing, and irrigation. Finally, there is evidence in the social and demographic impact of cultivation, since large, concentrated settlements such as towns and cities would be beyond the capacities of hunting and gathering to support.

The Geography of Domestication

Only certain species of plants and animals are capable of successful domestication and of being combined into a full farming economy. Successful **animal domesticates** include a few large terrestrial herbivores, notably sheep, goat, cattle, pig, horse, camel, water buffalo, and llama, and a few smaller herbivore and bird species, including chicken, turkey, rabbit, and guinea pig. These represent only a tiny percentage of the total available species, and it has been argued that of the 148 available large terrestrial herbivorous mammals, only 14 have been successfully domesticated (Diamond 1997). Others do not breed readily in captivity or are very difficult to herd and manage.

KEY METHOD **DNA and Domestication**

The development of DNA analysis since the late 1980s has begun to provide new information about the ancestry, age, and place of origin of particular species of domesticated plants and animals (Jones 2001). In particular, it can determine on how many separate occasions (and in what regions) domestication of a given species appears to have occurred. Recent studies of cattle DNA provide a good example of this approach.

What is the origin of North African domestic cattle? Were they independently domesticated in North Africa during the middle Holocene, when the Sahara was greener than it is today, or were they taken to North Africa at an early date from an initial center of domestication in Southwest Asia? Domestic cattle exist today in two forms: humped or zebu cattle (*Bos indicus*), found mainly in South Asia, and taurine cattle (*Bos taurus*), found in Europe, Southwest Asia, and North Africa. These two forms are interfertile and hence are not separate species, but study of their genetic lineages has given new

insight into their history as domestic species (Troy et al. 2001). Mitochondrial DNA sequences indicate a split between zebu and taurine forms calculated to have occurred between 200,000 and 1 million years ago. Since domestication occurred only within the past 10,000 years, the two varieties of cattle must have been separately domesticated in South Asia and in Southwest Asia or North Africa.

The analysis of the DNA lineages further reveals that the common ancestor of European and North African taurine cattle probably lived around 26,000–20,000 years ago. This, again, is long before the earliest domestication of the species, and indicates that taurine cattle were independently domesticated in North Africa on the one hand and in Southwest Asia or Europe on the other (see The Domestication of Cattle in the Sahara box, Chapter 10, p. 362).

The genetic analysis is therefore most consistent with the model that cattle have been domesticated in three separate

locations: in South Asia (zebu), in North Africa (taurine), and in Southwest Asia or Europe (taurine). There is, however, a complication to this pattern. Humped cattle are also found in East Africa, as well as South Asia, and analysis of their DNA shows that they are related to taurine cattle through their mitochondrial DNA (the female line) but to South Asian zebu through their Y-chromosome DNA (the male line) (Hanotte et al. 2002). Hence, several thousand years ago, some zebu bulls must have been introduced into East Africa to mate with the indigenous taurine forms.

5.6, 5.7 *Studies of mitochondrial DNA illustrate the evolutionary history of wild and domestic cattle. The common ancestor* Bos primigenius *(below, from a 16th century painting) gave rise to domestic zebu in South Asia and to taurine forms in Europe, North Africa, and West Asia. The length of the individual branches of the tree diagram indicate the degree of genetic similarity between the different species and subspecies.*

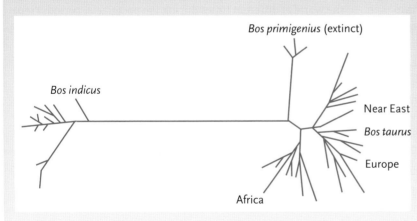

Bos primigenius (extinct)

Bos indicus

Near East

Bos taurus

Europe

Africa

Domesticated plant species are more numerous. They include several large-seeded grasses, namely wheat, barley, millets, sorghum, rice, and maize; tuberous root crops such as manioc, yam, and potato; and pulses such as beans, peas, and lentils. Especially important among these plants are the large-seeded grasses that formed the basis of some of the very earliest agricultural economies: wheat and barley in Southwest Asia (Chapter 6), millet and rice in East Asia (Chapter 7), maize in Mesoamerica (Chapter 9), and pearl millet in Africa (Chapter 10). Along with root crops such as yams and potatoes, these

constitute the staples that have proved an excellent source of carbohydrate, and are grown in many parts of the world today. Successful farming economies, however, needed to combine these carbohydrate-yielding staples with sources of protein from pulses or animal products. The combination of plant and animal species varied significantly from region to region, largely in response to the range of locally available domesticable species. It is significant, for example, that whereas all Old World agricultural economies relied on a combination of plants and animals, in much of the New World no suitable large herbivores were available for domestication. In Central and North America, early agriculture was based on the "Three Sisters" – maize, beans, and squash – which together provided the sources of carbohydrate and protein essential for a successful agricultural economy.

Research in recent decades has confirmed that agriculture arose independently during the Holocene in at least seven different regions of the world – Southwest Asia, East Asia, the New Guinea highlands, sub-Saharan Africa, Andean South America, central Mexico, and the eastern United States – at different times. These developments depended on different combinations of species, and some areas were only able to establish an agricultural economy by importing or adapting domestic species from neighboring regions. Yet agriculture was clearly not a chance discovery made in one specific region, which then spread rapidly and globally once its advantages were perceived. Instead, what we see is a parallel process of change among human societies in different regions, all of whom abandoned hunting and gathering in favor of food production. Why should this have occurred?

Why Agriculture?

Early writers assumed that agriculture brought such clear advantages that the obstacle to its development had simply been lack of knowledge: human societies did not have sufficient understanding of the plants and animals around them to undertake their domestication. Thus it was envisaged that once "invented," agriculture spread rapidly among prehistoric human communities, its progress stalling only where hostile environmental conditions intervened. This approach condemned hunter-gatherers to a marginal existence. As one anthropologist observed, "our text books compete to convey a sense of impending doom, leaving the student to wonder not only how hunters managed to make a living but whether, after all, this is a living. The specter of starvation stalks the stalker in these pages. His technical incompetence is said to enjoin continuous work just to survive, leaving him without respite from the food quest and without the 'leisure time to build culture'" (Sahlins 1968, 85).

The assumption that hunter-gatherers were constantly threatened by starvation was emphatically refuted by a number of ethnographic studies. In one famous example, Richard Lee (1968) showed that among the !Kung bushmen of southwest Africa, population levels were kept well within the capacity of the available food supply. For the most part, the !Kung had copious wild resources on which to rely, and enjoyed far more leisure time than peasant agriculturalists or, indeed, than working adults in westernized societies. Conversely, a few years before, in a study of cultivation systems, Ester Boserup (1965) had demonstrated the increasing amounts of labor that farmers needed to invest in order to increase the productivity of their

fields. More intensive agriculture can feed more people, but at a cost of much greater labor input per person, since if a plot of land is planted more frequently, with shorter and shorter fallow intervals between, it is necessary to devote an increasing amount of agricultural labor (weeding, fertilizing, irrigating) to each given amount of land.

These studies reversed the idea that early humans domesticated plants and animals to avoid drudgery and starvation. Indeed, they presented agriculture as an undesirable strategy that demanded greater labor input. Thus apologists for agriculture began to look at factors that might have forced postglacial communities to adopt it. The two most frequently cited have been **demographic increase** and **environmental change**, or a combination of the two. Climatic changes at the end of the Pleistocene have been given a major role in some accounts, especially in respect to Southwest Asia (Chapter 6); but however persuasive these individual interpretations, the global pattern and the chronological framework strongly suggest that agriculture may have been adopted for different reasons in different parts of the world. Agriculture may hence be best regarded not as a single monocausal phenomenon, but as a series of parallel adjustments and adaptations by human communities where particular conditions (social, demographic, and environmental) obtained [see box: Explaining Agriculture, p. 188].

Such conditions were clearly operative in various regions of the world at different times during the postglacial period. Pleistocene glacial climates were both too cold and too climatically unstable (with short-term climatic oscillations) for the development of agricultural economies, even in warmer regions such as central Africa. The last Pleistocene cold phase, the Younger Dryas, was marked by no fewer than 10 abrupt warm-cold cycles in only 1000 years, an erratic pattern of change that must have discouraged or precluded successful food-producing experiments. Holocene climates, by contrast, were sufficiently stable to allow the evolution of agriculture in vast areas that benefited from relatively warm, wet climates, or access to irrigation (Richerson et al. 2001). Furthermore, whatever the mechanism leading to the development of domesticates, it was a process that was very difficult to reverse, since more food led to population growth, which must very quickly have passed the threshold of what could be supported by hunting and gathering. There are exceptions (as in the American Southwest in the 12th and 13th centuries AD, for example; see Chapter 18), but in general, agricultural societies do not have the option of returning to hunting and gathering as a way of life. It is almost always a one-way transition.

Yet the concept that human societies were somehow forced by external circumstances (be it environmental change or population growth) to invent or adopt agriculture has been challenged on ethnographic grounds, and because it places too little emphasis on social factors. Canadian archaeologist Bryan Hayden (1995) has argued that **competition within societies** may have played a significant role in the development of agriculture. He points out that throughout the world, agriculture arose in societies of complex hunter-gatherers, such as the Natufian people of the Levant (Chapter 6). Excavation of Natufian sites has revealed that these societies possessed prestige items and practiced feasting and social competition. Ethnography shows that social status and power are frequently achieved through establishing relations of indebtedness or dependency, via principles of reciprocity. One of the most common ways in which ambitious individuals seek to gain power and status is by throwing feasts, which create indebtedness among those who attend but cannot reciprocate. Feasting is a conspicuous public display of wealth and status, and generates a powerful incentive for ambitious individuals to increase their food resources. Many of the first cultigens may have been chosen for their value as luxury foods, and some, such as the chili peppers that are among the earliest domesticates in highland Mesoamerica, can hardly have played a role in fending off starvation, for they are flavorings or additives (Hayden 1990; 2003). Cultivation may, therefore, have been adopted in part in order to provide the specially valued kinds of food and drink deployed in these competitive strategies.

Thus the reasons for the adoption of agriculture may have been diverse, and may have included both strategies of social competition and longer-term pressures toward food production imposed by demographic growth and instability in the less hostile postglacial world. Indeed, once the severe environmental constraints of the last Ice Age had been relaxed, the intensification of relationships between human communities and their plant and animal food sources might be regarded as both inevitable and unsurprising.

The Spread of Agriculture

As we have seen, archaeology has shown that agriculture was developed independently in a few, geographically dispersed centers of origin throughout the world [5.8]. Its development depended on the availability of wild species suitable for domestication, and on the successful combination of those domesticates to form sustainable farming systems.

Once established, these farming systems had huge potential, and within certain constraints of soils and climate were capable of expanding into neighboring regions. The general pattern during the Holocene is of the inexorable spread of farming and the progressive reduction of hunting and gathering, so much so that within the last few centuries the latter has largely been restricted to marginal areas where farming is impossible, such as arid deserts or the frozen Arctic. The expansion of farming was particularly rapid across Eurasia, where east–west similarities in climate and day length imposed few constraints on the successful transfer of cultivated plants to new areas. Farming spread much more slowly north and south through the Americas and sub-Saharan Africa, where tropical forests and greater climatic variations intervened (Diamond 1997).

The two major mechanisms of farming spread were the **adoption of farming by hunter-gatherers** from their neighbors, and the **displacement of hunter-gatherers by expanding farmers**. It is generally very difficult from archaeological evidence alone to distinguish between these alternatives. Farming clearly conveys a demographic advantage over hunting and gathering, since it is able to support many more people per unit area. It is not surprising, therefore, that where farmers and hunter-gatherers came into conflict over land, it was the former who usually prevailed. At the same time, it is probable that farming was often adopted from their neighbors by hunting and gathering communities, either under pressure of rising population, or through processes of social competition. In either case, the transition to the new way of life may appear relatively abrupt.

Several recent studies have looked to the distributions of **language families** and to patterns of **human genetics** to identify demographic spreads that might be the consequence of farming (Cavalli-Sforza 2000; Renfrew and Boyle 2000; Bellwood and Renfrew 2003). These argue that farming communities should have carried with them a distinct genetic imprint, which may still be recognizable in present-day populations. In a similar way, the geographical patterning of related groups of languages, or language families, around the world might reflect the expansion of the initially small farming communities that spoke the ancestral forms of those languages. These approaches have been applied with varying degrees of success in different regions of the world.

In the Pacific, speakers of **Austronesian languages** may have carried rice cultivation from southern China to Taiwan around 3000 BC, and thence to the northern Philippines around 2000 BC. There they adopted new domesticates, and with these they spread to the western Pacific islands *c.* 1500 BC, and finally to the far-flung Polynesian islands (including Hawai'i, New Zealand, and Rapa Nui, or Easter Island) between AD 700 and 1200 (Chapter 8). As already observed, the colonization of the Polynesian islands was one of the most impressive accomplishments of the postglacial period, and marks one of the final stages in the human colonization of the world. Easter Island is 2250 km (1400 miles) from its nearest neighbor, Pitcairn Island, and the total extent of Austronesian expansion from Taiwan to Easter Island measures 13,000 km (8080 miles).

In sub-Saharan Africa, the spread of the **Bantu languages** (spoken today by 200 million people over 9 million sq. km, roughly 3.5 million sq. miles) from their original homeland in

KEY CONTROVERSY Explaining Agriculture

The Oasis Theory

In 1936, Australian archaeologist V. Gordon Childe proposed one of the first coherent theories to explain the origins of agriculture. Like many later theories, this laid great emphasis on environmental change. Childe (1936) believed that at the end of the Pleistocene, a northward shift in the path of the Atlantic depressions (areas of low barometric pressure) from North Africa to Europe led to desiccation (extreme dryness) in countries that were always relatively dry. In the Sahara and Southwest Asia, grazing animals and their predators were forced to cluster around oases, where they came into contact with humans, and the result, Childe argued, was a symbiotic arrangement by which wild herbivores were allowed to graze stubble fields after the harvest, in turn becoming tame and accustomed to human contact. Selective culling by humans would subsequently have led to full domestication, by killing off intractable members in order to produce a docile herd, leading them to suitable pastures and water away from fields at the sowing season, and protecting them from wild predators.

The oasis theory suffers from two major shortcomings. First, it focuses very largely on animal domestication, and does not seek fully to explain the origins of plant cultivation, although stubble fields and fodder crops are an important part of Childe's model. In later writings, he argued that similar processes of environmental change and enforced proximity led to plant domestication and irrigation agriculture, but these arguments were less convincing. Second, the model was based on inadequate environmental information, which we now know to be incorrect, for in North Africa and Southwest Asia, rainfall increased rather than decreased at the end of the Pleistocene.

Childe referred to the adoption of agriculture as the Neolithic Revolution, one of those key changes in prehistory that could be likened in their impact to the Industrial Revolution of 18th-century Britain. In his account, the Neolithic Revolution was followed a few thousand years later by the Urban Revolution [see box: Cities, States, and Civilizations Defined and Explained, pp. 196–97]. While it is true that both agriculture and urbanism brought profound social and economic change, the term "revolution" implies a sudden and dramatic transition that does not accurately characterize the varied nature of these changes in different parts of the world. It also underemphasizes the important changes that continued to take place between these "revolutions."

The Hilly Flanks Hypothesis

Childe's hypothesis was very much an armchair theory. In the late 1940s, however, a group of American archaeologists, led by Robert Braidwood, set out a model of agricultural origins in Southwest Asia that they proceeded to test by fieldwork. Braidwood believed that farming would have begun not on the lowland alluvial plains, but in the hilly flanks of the Fertile Crescent, which were the natural habitat zone for a cluster of potential domesticates – barley, emmer and einkorn wheat, sheep, goats, pigs, and cattle – and which lay between the hot, dry floodplain and the cold, damp mountains.

From 1948 to 1955 he and his team excavated at sites in Iraqi Kurdistan, in the foothills of the Zagros Mountains (Chapter 6). Alongside the archaeologists were botanists and faunal specialists, and environmentalists who studied soils and river courses to track changes in climate and vegetation over the relevant period (Braidwood and Howe 1960). Braidwood's conclusion was that the invention of farming depended on the development of human knowledge and skill, coupled with a particular suite of locally available plant and animal species: "The food-producing revolution seems to have occurred as the culmination of the ever-increasing cultural differentiation and specialization of human communities. Around 8000 BC the inhabitants of the hills around the Fertile Crescent had come to know their habitat so well that they were beginning to domesticate the plants and animals that they had been collecting and hunting" (Braidwood 1960, 134).

This work preceded the studies of hunter-gatherers undertaken in the 1960s, and assumed that agriculture was fundamentally desirable and that the principal obstacles to its development lay in human knowledge and skill. "Why did incipient food production not come earlier? Our only answer at the moment is that culture was not yet ready to achieve it" (Braidwood and Willey 1962, 342).

Today the theory still has many adherents, and recent research at sites such as Çayönü in the Taurus foothills has confirmed the key role of the "hilly flanks" of the Fertile Crescent in the origins of agriculture in Southwest Asia (Chapter 6).

Demographic Theories

From the later 1960s, most theories of agricultural origins looked for factors that would have forced hunter-gatherers to

tropical West Africa may also be explained in terms of a spread of farming. The fact that speakers of one of the Bantu languages may be able to understand others suggests that this is the result of a relatively recent dispersal. In an initial stage, Bantu speakers spread into the lakeland region of East Africa, in the process adopting cattle herding and sorghum and millet cultivation. Then in the early centuries AD they spread rapidly southward, displacing hunter-gatherers and colonizing southern Africa up to the limits of agricultural viability (i.e., the edge of the Kalahari Desert). Earlier populations survived only in isolated pockets in tropical forest (e.g. the Okiek people of Tanzania) or in the arid Kalahari (Khoisan).

The **expansion of farming in Europe** has also been interpreted in terms of movements of populations and languages.

abandon their existing lifestyles and adopt the more labor-intensive agriculture. The American archaeologist Lewis Binford (1968) maintained that environmental change coupled with sedentism was the principal cause.

Environmental changes at the end of the Pleistocene, he argued, encouraged the exploitation of highly seasonal resources in resource-rich areas, and in several parts of the world (including Southwest Asia) these areas were sufficiently productive to allow the development of sedentary communities. These sedentary populations experienced population growth, as the abandonment of nomadism relaxed traditional constraints on reproductive rates; infant births became more closely spaced and offspring more numerous. Population pressure then led to expansion into more marginal zones outside these original resource-rich areas. It was in these more marginal, semi-arid zones, Binford argued, that incipient cultivation was developed in response to new population pressure from expanding groups.

Although discussed primarily in the context of Southwest Asian agriculture, Binford's theory had the merit of considering patterns at the global scale: why had agriculture arisen not only in Southwest Asia but also in other regions of the world at around the end of the last Ice Age? In terms of explanation, however, the theory may be held simply to shift the burden of the debate from "why agriculture?" to "why sedentism?"

Evolution and Intentionality

Alongside environmental or demographic theories were several that emphasized agriculture as the result of long-term relationships between humans and their food sources. Thus the idea arose that agriculture

should be viewed as one type of evolutionary adaptation between humans and other species. American archaeologist David Rindos (1984) argued that domestication was an unintentional outcome of relationships between humans and plants, and that the process followed three stages. First was incidental domestication: human dispersal and protection of wild plants in the general environment. Second came specialized domestication: the creation of locales in which plants and humans influenced each other fairly intensively. Finally there arose agricultural domestication: the culmination of the co-evolutionary process, producing plants adapted to a special set of humanly created conditions.

But Rindos also denied human intentionality in this process, seeing it as an outcome of natural evolutionary forces: "People could not intentionally domesticate a crop. However, they could, and surely did, favor those individual plants that were most pleasing or useful to them" (Rindos 1984, 86). This down-playing of human intentions would not today be accepted by many archaeologists, but the perspective that humans were adapting to plants and animals as much as plants and animals were adapting to humans gives an additional insight into the domestication process.

The Feasting Hypothesis

Reacting to those theories that envisage human communities as unwilling adopters of agriculture are those that consider the social context in which cultivation may have been developed, and the social factors that may have made it attractive. Thus British archaeologist Barbara Bender (1978) and Canadian archaeologist Brian Hayden (1995) have emphasized the key role that food and

feasting play in social competition. In many societies, those wishing to achieve rank and status do so by throwing feasts that create lasting dependencies between themselves and other members of the community who are unable to reciprocate on the same scale. Hunting and gathering would have provided only limited opportunities for this kind of social emulation, as the availability of wild resources was finite. The adoption of cultivation, however, made it possible for ambitious individuals to produce increasing amounts of food, which they could deploy in their strategies of social competition. Thus, despite the harder work that agriculture entails, it may in some circumstances have been eagerly embraced.

None of these theories provides an adequate explanation for the origins of agriculture in every region. Climatic factors may have played a key role, but these varied in importance from case to case. The co-evolution of human subsistence strategies and plant and animal domesticates highlighted by Rindos and others provides a key perspective in the understanding of longer-term change, but it does not explain why agriculture developed in specific times and places. The recognition that hunting and gathering are normally more cost-efficient than incipient agriculture strongly suggests that population pressure must have been one of the most significant factors. At the same time, the impact of human decisions and desires must not be overlooked, and social strategies will undoubtedly have played a part in individual cases at the local scale.

The pattern of radiocarbon dates reveals a gradual movement of domesticated plants and animals, earliest in the southeast and latest in the northwest and north. This has been linked by Colin Renfrew (2003) and others to the establishment of the Indo-European languages (see Chapter 11), and to certain genetic patterns among modern European populations. The evidence is not unambiguous, however, and the interpretation remains

controversial. In many regions of Europe, processes of indigenous adoption provide a more persuasive explanation for the transition to farming.

It is clearly very important to identify the nature of the agricultural transition in the various regions of the world, since the alternatives of demographic replacement vs. indigenous adoption open up radically different versions of human history. Was

5.8 *The origins and spread of agriculture:* *agriculture was developed independently in several regions of the world at different periods during the Holocene. From these "core areas," the productive new economy spread eventually to adjacent regions, allowing the development of more populous societies and leading ultimately to the demise of hunting and gathering in most areas of the world.*

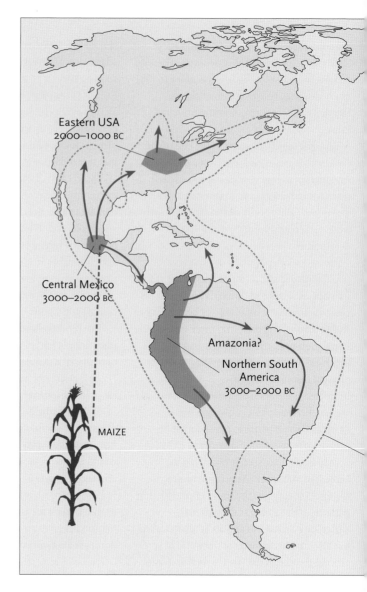

the initial colonization of the world by modern humans during the Paleolithic the primary basis of modern human populations? Or did the expansion of farming (and farmers) equally radically redraw the population map, resulting not only in much larger numbers of people worldwide, but also in the decline or eradication of many of the initial colonizing populations and their replacement by agriculturalists from other regions? Nor should we overlook the European and other colonizing enterprises of recent centuries. These have once again substantially altered the global patterning of human populations and are also associated in some regions (e.g. Australia) with an expansion of farming. The demographic impact of agriculture is fundamental to the human story.

The Consequences of Agriculture

The consequences of agriculture were more than simply demographic. Farming communities differed radically from hunter-gatherers also in terms of settlement, social complexity, material culture, and warfare, and their success led, almost inevitably, to agricultural intensification.

Settlement

Most farming communities are distinguished by being sedentary, their people living in permanent farmsteads or villages that are occupied year-round. Ethnographic and archaeological evidence shows that many hunter-gatherers, by contrast, were nomadic, moving camp regularly throughout the year as resources in different parts of their territory came into season. There are exceptions, however. In especially productive environments, hunter-gatherers too might become sedentary, as on the Northwest Coast of North America, referred to above; on the other hand in Africa, where spasmodic availability of water or low land fertility renders environments unproductive, there are many examples of seasonal and periodic mobility among agriculturalists, particularly herders. The essential difference is between societies that traveled between their food sources, and those that collected food and brought it back to a central place. The ability to store food is an important part of the latter strategy, and storage pits and ceramic containers are prominent features both of farming societies and among sedentary hunter-gatherers.

Farming settlements are larger and more substantially built than those of most hunter-gatherer communities. The greater productivity of agriculture allowed larger groups of people to

come together, and communities of several hundred could be supported by the produce of fields that lay within easy walking distance of a central settlement. The permanence of farming settlements encouraged greater investment in individual houses, which might be substantial structures built of timber, stone, mud-brick, pisé (rammed earth), or wattle-and-daub. These, in turn, revolutionized human experience of daily life (Wilson 1988). Households took on greater importance, their affairs hidden from the community at large. Nomadic hunter-gatherers live in conditions of great intimacy with one another, and are often very sensitive to the unspoken moods of others; they do not live isolated from the rest of the community in closed buildings (though they often have impermanent shelters for sleeping). Houses, by contrast, with their hidden spaces, allow the accumulation of household wealth. There is a constant tension between centrifugal tendencies (the well-being of the community or village) and centripetal tendencies (the success of the individual household). Sedentary settlements also

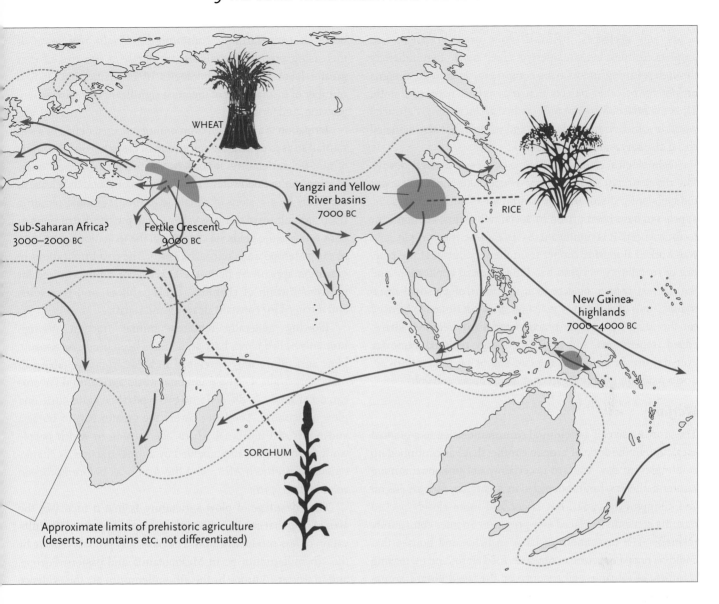

WHEAT

Yangzi and Yellow
River basins
7000 BC

RICE

Sub-Saharan Africa?
3000–2000 BC

Fertile Crescent
9000 BC

New Guinea
highlands
7000–4000 BC

SORGHUM

Approximate limits of prehistoric agriculture
(deserts, mountains etc. not differentiated)

provide fixed points within the landscape and become a focus of identity (the place where you live), ethnicity (the community to which you belong), and ancestry (where you and your forebears were born and buried).

Social Complexity

The development of larger communities led to corresponding changes in social complexity. Small-scale hunter-gatherer societies have flexible group membership, and disputes can be resolved simply by one or other party leaving to join another group. As group size increased with the adoption of agriculture, new types of social organization emerged. Kinship remained the key structuring principle, but questions of authority and differences in status and possessions became more contentious. In archaeological terms, the greater diversity of social roles may be shown by grave goods placed with the dead, or by differences in the number and quality of the objects associated with individual houses in a settlement. Prestige goods (already present in

the Upper Paleolithic) began to play an ever more prominent part in signaling social distinctions; these included items such as shell ornaments or carefully worked objects of exotic stone, traded from a distance. Social distinctions became increasingly institutionalized, as status that may at first have been based on individual achievement (e.g. personal prowess as a hunter or war leader) became transferred to particular lineages or families. In many parts of the world, these processes led ultimately to the emergence of systems of hereditary leadership.

Material Culture

Changes in material culture were an integral part of the transformation of human societies that followed the adoption of agriculture. Sedentism in itself allowed the accumulation of material goods, and the increasing adoption of containers made of pottery – heavy and fragile to transport – was a part of this trend. Yet many of the most conspicuous items of material culture were designed to be worn or carried on or around the body:

beads and necklaces, polished stone axes, bracelets, and amulets. Textiles, too, are attested, albeit most often indirectly through spinning and weaving equipment, or from the designs on pottery or other objects that may reflect patterned cloth. Thus material culture not only created an increasingly artificial world in which individuals lived and worked, but also signaled social diversity and social difference.

Technological change must also be viewed in social terms. The development of metallurgy, which, like agriculture, was independently discovered in a number of different regions, appears to have been driven by social rather than economic or technical need. It is significant that in Europe, for example, gold was worked alongside copper from the very outset of the practice of metallurgy, yet gold had little practical application, and the earliest copper objects took the form of personal ornaments. Tools of chipped or polished stone continued to be used for the majority of those practical tasks that required sharp-edged implements, and metal tools only replaced stone for everyday use in Europe in the late 2nd or 1st millennium BC, 4000 years after the first exploitation of copper and gold.

Warfare

The growing size of agricultural communities led to a gradual escalation in the scale of human conflict that has continued up to the present day. Warfare is certainly not unknown among hunter-gatherers, for it is depicted in Australian rock art (Taçon and Chippindale 1994); but larger and more closely packed farming settlements placed new pressures on inter-community relations. The investment of labor in fields and houses that could be raided or seized, along with food stores and increasing numbers of valuables, all encouraged the trend toward group-organized violence. Nevertheless, in much debate on the archaeological evidence for warfare [5.9], many supposedly defensive enclosures have been reinterpreted as livestock pens or ritual places. On the other hand, the discovery of mass graves containing skeletons that show marks of violent death, such as that from Talheim in Germany, dating to the late 6th millennium BC (see box, p. 411), provide graphic illustration of the reality of warfare among early farming communities.

Agricultural Intensification

The success of the new agricultural economies led to an increase in human population to levels far beyond those that had previously been sustainable by hunting and gathering. Nevertheless, early agricultural systems could afford to allow long fallow periods, when the land lay dormant and recovered some of its fertility, and cultivation was at first restricted to the more suitable soils and to areas where there was adequate natural rainfall. As populations continued to grow,

however, early farming communities sought new ways of increasing productivity, almost inevitably at the cost of ever greater labor input. "Technologies of intensification" took a number of forms, three of the most significant being irrigation, plowing, and terracing.

Irrigation is a means of overcoming seasonal deficiencies in rainfall so as to permit the cultivation of crops beyond the limits of rain-fed agriculture. It takes two primary forms: the storage of rainwater or floodwater in tanks and basins, and its release to the fields by a system of canals (e.g. the traditional receding flood agriculture of the Nile Valley in Egypt); the distribution of river water to the fields via canals (e.g. the irrigation agriculture of early Mesopotamia or coastal Peru). The cost implications of irrigation agriculture lie in the heavy labor input required for the construction of channels, banks, sluices, and reservoirs, and the need for constant cleaning and repair.

Plowing generally requires animal traction (though humanly pulled plows have sometimes been used). As a result, plow agriculture only developed in areas where suitable animals were available, and traditional world agricultural systems can accordingly be divided into two types: hoe agriculture and plow agriculture. The latter covers the greater part of Eurasia and north and northeast Africa; the former, in which people work the fields by hand, unaided by animal traction, is characteristic of southern Africa and the Americas before European colonization [5.10].

The advantage of plow agriculture is that it increases the area of land that can be cultivated, and makes practical the cultivation of less productive land. The plow was probably in use by the 5th millennium BC in Mesopotamia and eastern Europe, and in western Europe by the 4th millennium BC; the evidence takes the form of preserved plow marks, typically beneath burial mounds; preserved plows or ards (a simple plow) from wetland environments such as lakes and bogs; and pictorial representations in rock art. The major cost implication was the feeding and over-wintering of expensive plow animals.

5.9 Violence and warfare: skull of a 35–40-year-old Neolithic man from Porsmose near Næstved, Denmark. This individual had been struck by one arrowhead in the chest, and another in the face. Violence is far from unknown among hunter-gatherers but may have become more intense as farming societies grew in size and individuals and communities became subject to new social and economic pressures.

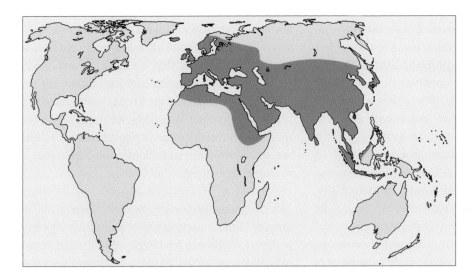

5.10 *Plow agriculture:* the development of the plow from the 5th millennium BC was restricted to areas of the Old World where domestic cattle provided a suitable source of traction. Elsewhere – in southern Africa beyond the tsetse fly belt, and in the Americas where there were no suitable traction animals – cultivation continued to rely on human muscle power and the hoe.

Terracing is designed to increase the area of cultivable land in rough or mountainous terrain by the construction of tiers of dry-stone walling to support fertile but often narrow and restricted fields; terraces also stabilize slopes and limit erosion. Agricultural terraces are sometimes combined with irrigation canals, and spectacular landscapes of terraced fields are found in Andean South America and the Philippines (Luzon); they are also a regular feature of Mediterranean regions, where the oldest date probably to at least the 5th century BC. The cost implications of such a system are obvious, though studies in Mesoamerica have shown that even quite elaborate terraces can be built and maintained by household labor.

Cities, States, and Empires

As we have seen, 19th-century anthropologists such as Lewis Henry Morgan and Edward Tylor envisaged the history of human society as falling into a number of stages, separated by significant transitions. One of these was the transition from hunting and gathering to agriculture, but another, no less important, was the rise of cities and states (what Tylor and Morgan called "civilization") [see box: Cities, States, and Civilization Defined and Explained, pp. 196–97]. Whereas the development of agriculture is perhaps the key story of the early postglacial period, the rise and fall of cities, states, and empires constitute a significant theme of the past five-and-a-half millennia. Such a perspective has the advantage of simplicity, of highlighting important changes in a global framework that is relatively easy to grasp. It is clear that agriculture allowed the growth of larger and denser populations that eventually, in certain regions, coalesced into still larger and more institutionalized social formations (states) and complex, concentrated settlements (cities).

This view, however, must be qualified in a number of important respects. We have seen how agricultural systems, with their reliance on different suites of domesticated species and differ-ent technologies of exploitation, are not a single standardized adaptation, but a series of individual adjustments to available resources and terrain. In the same way, cities and states are not a specific pattern-book response to rising population levels, despite attempts to demonstrate otherwise (e.g. Trigger 2003), but a cluster of diverse types of society, the differences between which were perhaps as significant as the similarities. Furthermore, too great an emphasis on the transition to states can easily obscure the fact that early states were very limited in geographical extent. It is true that some had impacts far beyond their borders, through trade or cultural borrowing, but it is nonetheless important to recall that during the 3rd millennium BC, when early states had emerged in several regions of the Old World, a majority of the human population worldwide still lived in non-state farming societies, including significant numbers of hunter-gatherers in several regions.

Finally, there is the danger of a progressivist view of human prehistory, which considers state societies (perhaps because they seem more familiar to us) as somehow "better" than early farming societies or hunter-gatherers. While state societies did produce elaborate monumental structures and artworks, and some of them left a literature that we can still read today, they must be considered but one among a mosaic of human social forms extending far back into the past.

The Development of States

States are centralized political institutions in which ruling elites exercise control over populations that may number between several thousand and several million individuals. Most early states, however, were toward the smaller end of this range, with populations in the thousands or tens of thousands. State institutions gather revenues from their subject population (either as agricultural produce, craft items, raw materials, or in labor dues), and in return offer protection and support in times of famine or warfare. State institutions usually reserve to themselves the

193

right to use force, either in external warfare or for internal control. Obligations (such as military service) owed by the subject population to the central institutions generally override kinship obligations, though kinship remains important. It is somewhat ironic, indeed, that whereas kinship plays a less prominent structuring role in state societies than in non-state societies, much of the internal history of states is focused on struggles for power and the succession among kin groups within the elite, in the form of ruling families. There has been some debate as to whether states should be considered beneficent institutions, operating for the good of all, or whether they are essentially exploitative, with governing elites gaining wealth and power at the expense of the majority; for most documented examples, the latter seems closer to reality. In terms of scale, however, it is only with the benefit of centralized state control that large populations can be integrated and supported; the collapse of states (as for instance the Classic Maya collapse, discussed in Chapter 16) is inevitably followed by population decline.

Canadian archaeologist Bruce Trigger (2003) has divided early states into two principal categories: those that develop around cities (city-states) and those that form within blocks of land (territorial states). In the latter, so the argument goes, cities appear through a secondary process, as administrative, economic, and political centers within the territorial state. Whether such a distinction is truly valid is unclear, and most early states were dominated by cities that were both centers of government and foci of population. Yet even in this regard, there is also considerable variation. Not all these early centers resembled the compact settlements that we associate today with the word "city"; those of 2nd-millennium BC China, for example, consisted of elite residential enclosures surrounded by a network of smaller settlements supplying the needs of the elite, a pattern that has been termed the "urban cluster" (McIntosh 1991). It was only during the 1st millennium BC that cities of more conventional form appeared in China.

The Geography of State Formation Early states developed in areas of high primary agricultural productivity, where sufficient food was available to feed large, concentrated populations; typically, they were located in fertile basins or river valleys. Thus the Egyptian state depended on the Nile, Mesopotamian city-states on the Tigris and Euphrates, and Harappan cities on the Indus and the Ghaggar-Hakra (the lost Saraswati; see Chapter 14). In China, the first cities developed in the valley of the Yangzi and the basin of the Yellow River (the Huang He), while in the Americas the great city-state of Teotihuacán developed in the

5.11 State formation: *state societies, like agriculture (see 5.8), developed independently in different parts of the world at different periods. Common features of these state societies are the reliance on high primary productivity from successful and often intensive agriculture, and the development of complex social organization that is frequently associated with the stylized or idealized portrayal of leaders and deities.*

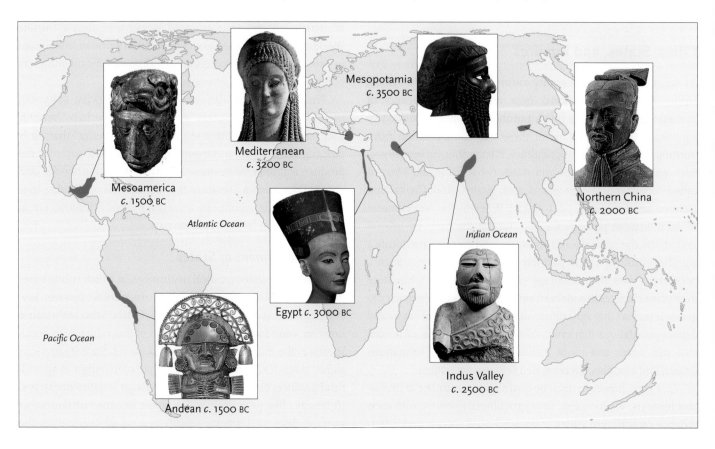

Mesoamerica
c. 1500 BC

Mediterranean
c. 3200 BC

Mesopotamia
c. 3500 BC

Northern China
c. 2000 BC

Atlantic Ocean

Egypt *c.* 3000 BC

Indian Ocean

Indus Valley
c. 2500 BC

Pacific Ocean

Andean *c.* 1500 BC

Mexican basin, and in coastal Peru, states formed within the river valleys running through the desert from the Andes to the Pacific. Most of these were in warm environments (some surrounded by desert), where high levels of solar energy permitted exceptional crop yields provided sufficient water could be brought to the fields. This was perhaps only to be expected, since several of the key staples (maize, wheat, and barley) had originated as desert-edge species of large-seeded grasses that flourished in hot climates. Thus hydraulic technology and irrigation were essential to support many early state societies, which might rely on receding flood agriculture (Egypt, Indus Valley, Angkor in Cambodia) or canal irrigation (Peru, Mesopotamia, highland Mexico).

The patterning of state development is in some respects similar to that of early agriculture, emerging in widely scattered regions of the world at different times, though in this case during the later Holocene. The first cities are generally believed to have developed in southern Mesopotamia around the middle of the 4th millennium BC. The origins of the Egyptian state may be placed at around the same period or very slightly later; exact chronologies are sometimes difficult to establish, since the earliest layers of many cities lie deeply buried beneath the remains left by later generations. In the Indus Valley, the aggradation (building up of the level) of the alluvial plain, and the high water table, have hindered attempts by archaeologists to study the origins of the Harappan cities, which are known to date from the first half of the 3rd millennium BC but could have had still earlier origins; deep soundings have discovered a modest walled settlement beneath the citadel of Kalibangan (Chapter 14). In China, cities appear during the 2nd millennium BC.

All these developments are generally regarded as having been independent of each other, in the same way that agriculture was an independent development in different regions. The possibility that trade contacts stimulated imitation cannot be excluded, however, since contacts between Egypt and Mesopotamia, and later between Mesopotamia and the Indus, have been documented by archaeological discoveries (e.g. of Mesopotamian cylinder seals in both regions).

Similar ambiguities are found in the New World, where states developed independently in the Andean zone and in highland Mexico during the 2nd millennium BC, but where contacts between these and neighboring regions may have stimulated social change and state formation. One powerful mechanism was the threat of war: smaller communities adjacent to burgeoning states sought safety by transforming themselves into states as well, in order to have greater resources of military manpower to resist their now threatening neighbors. The settlement of Tilcajete in Oaxaca, Mexico, for example, responded to the establishment of the city of Monte Albán in the 5th century BC by first doubling in size from 25 to 52.8 ha (62 to 130 acres), and later expanding to 71.5 ha (177 acres), though these measures did not prevent its eventual destruction and abandonment (Flannery and Marcus 2003).

Archaeological Features of States Though states clearly interacted with one another, and sometimes played a role in another's rise and fall, each was the product of its own specific circumstances. That is not to deny that they share many archaeological features, and it is these that allow us to label them as states. The key element is scale, and the level of resources and human labor that were available. Cities may cover hundreds of hectares with houses, temples, storerooms, and palaces, and are often enclosed within a defensive wall. Monumental scale is a consistent feature: public buildings are usually large and elaborate. Another feature of states is the propaganda of the ruling elite, seen in statues, palaces, and tombs, or in architectural settings where the rulers took their place in carefully stage-managed public performances.

Spectacular diversities of wealth and power are exemplified by luxury objects, which employ both elaborate craft skill and materials brought from far afield. Royal graves such as Pakal's at Palenque in Mexico (7th century AD) or Tutankhamun's in Egypt (late 14th century BC) are justly famous for their richness and the insight they provide into craftsmanship, ideology, and trade. Such discoveries do, however, risk diverting attention away from the lives of ordinary people in these early state societies. Archaeology has much to offer that is not available in the written records of those societies, which tend to focus on the central administration and the ruling elite.

The internal structure of early cities was often complex, with modest houses clustered along narrow streets, contrasting with the more spacious dwellings of the rich, which might sometimes be set in extensive gardens. In some cases, the power of the state was sufficiently strong to organize the foundation of new grid-plan cities in chosen locations, or to re-plan existing cities with a regular street grid. Examples of early grid-plan cities are known from China to the Indus Valley, the basin of Mexico and the Mediterranean. Yet early cities are characterized as much by their diversity as by their commonality. The palaces that are a feature of Maya or Mesopotamian urbanism are absent (or unrecognized) in the Harappan cities. Early Chinese and Maya cities appear to have been loose clusters of settlements around central elite residences and temples, rather than dense agglomerations bounded by a city wall. And while some cities may have had populations numbering in the tens or hundreds of thousands, others were small, more akin to villages in modern population terms, though they possessed political, economic, and social functions characteristic of the larger centers. Thus early cities were defined in qualitative as much as quantitative terms.

KEY CONTROVERSY Cities, States, and Civilizations Defined and Explained

One of the key problems in studying cities and states is the issue of definition: how can we understand the origins of these entities if we cannot reliably define them? The problem exists at two levels: the identification of states as functioning entities (i.e., the definition of currently existing states), and the identification of states in the past (from the archaeological evidence). Some have argued, for example, that state-level societies are characterized by a four-tier settlement hierarchy (cities, towns, villages, and hamlets), but while this may sometimes be the case, it is not clear why it should be either a necessary or a sufficient definition.

Gordon Childe (1950) listed 10 key characteristics of what he termed "civilizations," including features such as monumental architecture and full-time specialists, but not all states possess all of these (Andean states did not have writing, for example). Childe's list appears to be more an inventory of those features that recognized states are known to display, rather than a criterion for the identification of new states.

Scale and centralization are the twin pillars of any successful description of what we mean by states: states are large in both geographic extent and in population, and they are governed by centralized institutions that cut across traditional kinship ties. These qualities apply also to cities, which are in addition characterized by their unusual size and by their level of organization. While claims have been made that cities can exist outside of states, and there are certainly examples of states that are governed from administrative centers rather than true cities, the two frequently go together.

The other term that we have just mentioned, "civilization," is sometimes employed in discussing societies of this kind. The word is often used as a kind of shorthand to refer to urban state-level societies, and though it is sometimes applied more loosely, its main application is to regional traditions that may comprehend one or more separate states. Thus "Mesoamerican civilization" includes Olmec, Maya, Zapotec, Aztec, and others; "Mesopotamian civilization" includes everything from the first cities to the Assyrians and beyond; and the "Aegean civilizations" include Minoans and Mycenaeans, as well as societies of the Cycladic islands and the western coast of Turkey. In these cases, the various states grouped under the heading of a civilization usually share a number of cultural features, such as common scripts, specific artistic conventions, or similar rituals, such as the ball game in Mesoamerica.

Agricultural Surplus and Craft Specialization

In the 1930s Childe considered cities and states as the direct outcome of the transition to farming. Farming allowed surpluses to be generated, which made it possible for some individuals to be freed from the obligation to work on the land. The result was the emergence of a new category of full-time specialists, be they craftspeople or metalworkers, soldiers, priests, or bureaucrats. Where agricultural production was especially high, or where it could be made so by techniques such as irrigation, the numbers of full-time specialists could be correspondingly increased, leading to the

development of more and more complex societies with increasing divisions of wealth and expertise. These eventually coalesced in the formation of cities and states. Elements of this explanation, which combines agricultural productivity with demographic growth and social complexity, are retained in many of the more recent models of state formation.

Childe (1936) called the development of cities and states the Urban Revolution, by analogy with the Industrial Revolution of 18th-century Britain. It was the second major change in his account of human prehistory, following the Neolithic Revolution [see box: Explaining Agriculture, pp. 188–89] some millennia earlier. Few archaeologists today would consider the concept of a "revolution" helpful in the understanding of these changes, though the consequences of urbanism were ultimately both widespread and profound. Writers since Childe have sought to identify more precisely why urban societies developed in certain environmental or social settings.

The Hydraulic Hypothesis

Most early states developed in river valleys, where irrigation was essential for high crop yields. This observation led Karl Wittfogel (1957) to propose the theory (from his studies in China) that it was the control of irrigation systems that led to the rise of oriental despotism. The idea was straightforward: communities dependent on irrigation water for their survival could be forced to obey the demands of those (the emergent elites) who constructed and controlled those systems and who could regulate or cut off the water flow.

Anthropologist Julian Steward (1949) also believed that irrigation agriculture in arid

Toward History: The Adoption of Writing

A salient feature of early states that is of wide significance is the adoption of writing (Hooker 1990). This, again, is a technology that appears to have developed independently in a number of different locations [5.12]. The earliest known writing systems are those of Mesopotamia and Egypt (both of which originated during the 4th millennium BC), but writing was also a feature of the Harappan, Shang Chinese, and Aegean states from

the 3rd/2nd millennium BC, of both highland and lowland Mesoamerica from the 1st millennium BC, and of the Meroë and Aksum states in Africa from the late 1st millennium BC. The scripts differ widely in their mechanism and form, as we might expect given their independent development, though the possibility of stimulus-diffusion (the spread and borrowing of the idea of writing) cannot in all cases be excluded. The purposes for which writing was invented and used may also have been

environments provided the key to understanding the development of early state societies. Field surveys in Mesopotamia in the 1960s, however, showed that early irrigation systems were locally organized affairs, "which involved little alteration of the natural hydraulic regime and the construction of only relatively small-scale field and feeder canals that were wholly artificial" (Adams 1966, 68). Reconsideration of the Egyptian evidence likewise revealed that irrigation there was controlled at the local level and can have played no part in the rise of the state (Butzer 1976). Furthermore, in both the Nile and Indus valleys, communities probably made use of the annual river flood regime, holding back the water in basins and tanks as the floods receded, rather than a system of feeder canals. At the same time, while the hydraulic hypothesis has been abandoned as a general explanation of state formation, it is clear that any group establishing control over vital resources such as irrigation water would quickly rise to political dominance.

The Trade Imperative

The large agricultural communities that developed in the fertile lowland plains were rich in plant productivity but poor in several other essential materials. It is striking, for example, how Mesopotamian cities were built of mud-brick (and occasionally baked brick), but used very little stone. The clay on which scribes wrote and with which structures were built was available in abundance, but hard stone had to come from the surrounding uplands, at some considerable distance.

The Maya cities of Mesoamerica were similarly deficient in many vital resources such as obsidian, salt, and stone for grinding tools. Maya specialist William Rathje (1971) proposed that it was the need to procure such resources from a distance that led to the formation of cities. Those communities and elites that succeeded in establishing secure supplies gained considerable advantage over their neighbors, and grew in size and power as a result. Once again, however, the major flows of material produced by this model appear to have been a consequence of city formation, rather than its cause.

Warfare

Violence has been a feature of human society since the Paleolithic, as lesions on skeletons reveal. As communities grew in size, however, the scale of conflict increased. In 1970, Robert Carneiro argued that inter-community warfare might explain the formation of states in coastal Peru, where narrow cultivable valleys were separated by large expanses of desert. Conflict between communities, he proposed, may have led to one village or war-leader becoming dominant in each valley, thus forming a small state. Aggressive leaders may next have attacked other valleys, forming a larger, multi-valley state. The theory is hard to assess, though it is clear from historical and archaeological examples that non-state communities around the margins of an early state might have been obliged to form themselves into states (by a process sometimes known as "secondary state formation") in order to protect themselves from their more powerful, more populous, and more centralized neighbor.

Conclusion

Monocausal theories such as these were a common feature of archaeological explanations in the period up to the 1970s, but subsequent research has favored more complex, multi-causal explanations. Access to exotic trade goods may have enhanced the power and separation of elites, and may also have provided essential raw materials, but trade was a general feature of human societies and did not always lead to the formation of states. Irrigation systems were usually locally controlled, and while they enhanced village solidarity and led to increased population size (thus provoking social change), they did not inevitably lead to states and cities. Warfare certainly played a powerful role in forcing change upon societies, but it did not suddenly appear in Mesopotamia in the mid-4th millennium BC, or in Mesoamerica in the mid-1st millennium BC. Thus these explanations are elements of a pattern, in which they all may have played a significant part.

Coercion, insecurity, elite dominance, social differentiation, and new forms of wealth were most likely jointly in operation in the creation of these new kinds of societies. Furthermore, historical and ethnographic accounts emphasize the key role played by ambitious individuals in the establishment of several states, and such models may well be applicable to prehistory (Flannery 1999).

All of this supposes, of course, that states conform to a certain standard pattern that renders them capable of some universal explanation. The diversity of the states known through archaeology, ethnography, and history strongly suggests otherwise, however. Each state, each city, may bear the hallmark of a general set of processes (such as population increase, agricultural intensification, and heightened social competition), but each was the product of its own unique set of circumstances.

very varied. The greatest body of surviving early Chinese writings comprises short inscriptions on so-called oracle bones, recording the outcome of divination (Chapter 15). Egyptian and Maya texts are best known from monumental inscriptions on stelae, public buildings, and tombs, where they record the exploits of rulers. In Southwest Asia (Mesopotamia and adjacent regions), the bulk of surviving documents take the form of clay tablets, most of them records of administrative or eco-nomic transactions. It may be that the differences in the choice of writing materials and the consequent vagaries of survival have distorted the picture, and give a false impression of the purposes for which writing was used in these societies. One view is that Chinese script (like Mesopotamian) was invented for utilitarian economic or administrative transactions, but that these records, being on perishable materials, have not survived (Postgate et al. 1995). Others believe that Chinese writing arose directly from ritual practice and artistic conventions (Keightley 1996). The elaborate nature of some of the scripts, such as Egyptian or Maya hieroglyphic, lends support to the view that these were developed for display purposes – to be used, intricately carved and brightly colored, in public places – whereas others, such as Mesopotamian cuneiform, were perhaps designed more specifically for record-keeping.

The impact of writing on our knowledge of ancient societies is profound. Written testimony provides details of social and economic life, and of religious belief, which are unobtainable from archaeological remains alone. Early written records, however, concern only a tiny fraction of the activities of a very restricted number of early societies. Even within those societies, the proportion of people who could read and write was vanishingly small. In Mesopotamia, literacy was almost exclusively the preserve of professional scribes, and even kings were usually unable to read and write (Pollock 1999). More general levels of literacy are a feature only of modern times (with a few possible exceptions, such as Classical Greece). Most inhabitants of early cities will not have been able to read the inscriptions placed on public buildings and statues, a fact that only served to enhance the power of the mysterious signs.

We must also be cautious in defining what we mean by literacy. In Classical Athens, for example, where most (male) citizens may have had some basic ability to read and write, and could probably have deciphered the decrees posted in the marketplace, "the written texts of poetry and prose had a reading audience confined to the highly educated and wealthy elite, and their secretaries" (Thomas 1992, 11); for the rest, poetry and drama were disseminated orally. Thus the significance of writing in early societies must be carefully evaluated. It marks an important innovation, and a valuable source of information, but it was not essential for the successful functioning of early states. It was never adopted in Andean South America, for example, though the *quipu* system of knotted cords may have performed part of its role.

States and Empires

We have seen how early states arose mainly in lowland basins with fertile soil that could produce high agricultural yields with the benefit of irrigation. Cities and states subsequently developed in a much wider range of environmental settings, and warfare between them and their neighbors resulted in the formation of larger and larger political entities. The process was driven by a number of factors: the desire for security (by neutralizing or conquering potential enemies) or economic gain (by controlling greater and greater resources), or mere personal ambition on the part of rulers and elites. The process appears sometimes as a series of recurrent cycles, by which individual states became powerful and achieved regional dominance, only

to fracture and fragment as they failed to establish durable systems of integration and administration. Such cycles have been demonstrated for Mesopotamia, and for Central and South America (Marcus 1998).

At their most expansive, these accumulations of territory took the form of empires, such as the Roman Empire around the Mediterranean basin, or Peru under Inca rule. The distinction between state and empire is not an easy one to draw (Morrison 2001). Empires are territorially more extensive and organizationally more complex. They absorb other states and give them the status of provinces, with their own partially devolved governments and obligations to carry out taxation or provide other forms of tribute. They are typically multi-ethnic, multi-lingual, and sometimes multi-religious, though the same is true of many early states. What empires do represent, despite cycles of growth and collapse, is a general process of global development leading to the formation of larger and larger political units. The Spanish and British colonial empires are more recent steps along the same trajectory. The modern "global village," the dominance of the nation-state, and institutions such as the United Nations represent the most recent stage in a process of transformation that began with the first city-states of Mesopotamia some 5500 years ago.

Summary and Conclusions

This chapter has sought to provide an overview of the key developments in human societies during the past 11,500 years, focusing in particular on the transformation of the world in the earlier Holocene. As the ice sheets melted, temperatures and sea levels rose, and human communities took advantage of the new opportunities, growing rapidly in numbers where conditions were favorable. In several regions, population increase and the availability of suitable local plants and animals led to new patterns of exploitation, which resulted in the development of agriculture. The greater productivity made possible by food production ensured the further growth of farming communities and the extension of farming (and in many cases colonist farmers) to new areas. Farming came to dominate the world far beyond the confines of the original habitats of the domesticated plants and animals.

In favored regions, notably lowland river valleys, the potential for high agricultural yields was linked to the development of increasingly complex societies. These processes resulted in the formation of the first cities and states in the Old World, and later in the Americas. While local circumstances and individual historical trajectories were responsible for these changes in every area, the single most salient feature – both cause and consequence – was the growing size of human populations. The hunting and gathering lifestyle that had supported human soci-

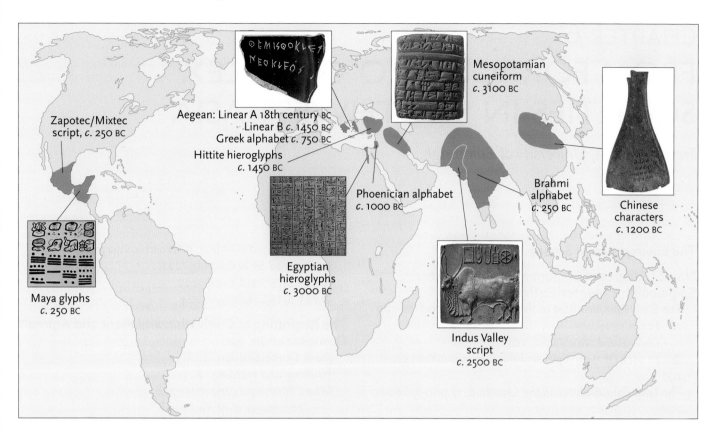

Zapotec/Mixtec script, *c.* 250 BC

Aegean: Linear A 18th century BC
Linear B *c.* 1450 BC
Greek alphabet *c.* 750 BC
Hittite hieroglyphs *c.* 1450 BC

Mesopotamian cuneiform *c.* 3100 BC

Phoenician alphabet *c.* 1000 BC

Brahmi alphabet *c.* 250 BC

Chinese characters *c.* 1200 BC

Egyptian hieroglyphs *c.* 3000 BC

Maya glyphs *c.* 250 BC

Indus Valley script *c.* 2500 BC

5.12 Writing: *the organizational requirements of early state societies led several of them to develop permanent recording systems in the form of writing. Most of these originated as pictographic systems but writing systems became increasingly stylized and abstract as the scripts came to be used more extensively and for an ever wider range of functions. Despite the spread of writing, literacy – the ability to read and write – has generally remained restricted to a small minority up to recent times.*

eties for tens of thousands of years had been pushed to the margins of the occupied world, and survived only in areas where agriculture was impossible. The rise of the modern nation-state and its sprawling conurbations are the outcome of processes that began with the intensification of human subsistence practices during the early Holocene.

Further Reading and Suggested Website

Alcock, S. E., D'Altroy, T. N., Morrison, K. D., & Sinopoli, C. M. (eds.). 2001. *Empires: Perspectives from Archaeology and History.* Cambridge: Cambridge University Press. A comparative survey of empires, Old World and New, from ancient times to the early modern period, drawing on both archaeological and historical material.

Feinman, G. M. & Marcus, J. (eds.). 1998. *Archaic States.* Santa Fe, NM: School of American Research. A compilation of papers on early states in different regions of the world (notably west and South Asia, Egypt, and Central and South America) with useful studies of their key features and patterns of development.

Jones, M. K. 2001. *The Molecule Hunt.* London and New York: Allen Lane. Accessible account of the contribution that is now being made by DNA studies to the understanding of the human past, with specific chapters on the domestication of plants and animals.

Mithen, S. 2003. *After the Ice: A Global Human History, 20,000–5000 BC.* London: Weidenfeld & Nicolson; Cambridge, Mass.: Harvard University Press (2004). A tour through the changing world of the last Ice Age and the early postglacial period, as seen through the eyes of a fictional time-traveler; rich in archaeological description and explanation of key times and places.

Roberts, N. 1998. *The Holocene: An Environmental History.* (2nd ed.) Oxford: Blackwell. An excellent short account of the climatic and environmental history of the past 11,500 years, focusing on the interaction between environmental change and human society.

Smith, B. D. 1995. *The Emergence of Agriculture.* New York: Scientific American Library. Well-illustrated and concise survey of the evidence for the development of farming, with coverage both of methodological issues and a review of farming origins in different regions of the world.

Trigger, B. G. 2003. *Understanding Early Civilizations.* Cambridge: Cambridge University Press. A comprehensive review of early state societies in terms of a series of common themes: socio-political organization, economy, and cognitive and symbolic aspects; a rich mine of information and insight by one of the leading scholars in this field.

http://instaar.colorado.edu/QGISL/bering_land_bridge/
Animation illustrating the flooding of the Bering Strait land bridge.

CHAPTER 6

FROM FORAGERS TO COMPLEX SOCIETIES IN SOUTHWEST ASIA

Trevor Watkins, University of Edinburgh

The Environmental Setting 201

New Strategies of Settlement and Subsistence: Epipaleolithic Hunter-Gatherers 204
The Early Epipaleolithic in the Levant, c. 18,000–12,000 BC 205
  • *Ohalo II and Neve David* 206
● **KEY SITE** Ohalo II: Epipaleolithic Lifeways in the Levant 207
The Late Epipaleolithic in the Levant, c. 12,000–9600 BC 208
  • *The Discovery of the Natufians* 208
  • *Evidence for Natufian Lifeways* 208
The Late Epipaleolithic Beyond the Levant 209
● **KEY SITE** Eynan 210
An Epipaleolithic Summary 212

Culture Change in the Aceramic Neolithic, c. 9600–6900 BC 212
New Stoneworking Technologies 213
Innovations in Art and Ideas 213
● **KEY SITE** Abu Hureyra: The Transition from Foraging to Farming 214
The First Large Settlements: Jericho and Çatalhöyük 216
  • *Jericho* 216
  • *Çatalhöyük* 217
Social Organization 217
Communal Buildings and Rituals 218

● **KEY SITE** Jerf el Ahmar: A Neolithic Village 218
Burials and Skull Caching 221
● **KEY SITE** 'Ain Ghazal 222
● **KEY SITE** Çatalhöyük 224

The Beginning of Cultivation and Plant and Animal Domestication 226
Plant Domestication 226
Hunting and Herding 227
Mixed Farming Economies 228
  • *The Evidence of Ali Kosh* 228
● **KEY DISCOVERY** The Colonization of Cyprus 229
Social Exchange and Networking 230

Transformation and the Ceramic Neolithic, c. 6900–6000 BC 231
The Levant 231
Syria and Turkey 231
Iraq and Iran 232

Summary and Conclusions 232

Further Reading and Suggested Websites 233

In the previous chapter we reviewed the profound transformation of climate and environment that accompanied the melting of the ice sheets, and the development of agriculture in different regions of the world during the milder Holocene period.

In this chapter we turn to the very first human societies to have adopted agriculture: those of Southwest Asia. Subsequent chapters will discuss the origins and spread of farming elsewhere in the world – in East Asia (Chapter 7), the Americas, Africa, and Europe (chapters 9–11).

The key period for studying the transition to agriculture in Southwest Asia starts around 18,000 BC, at the beginning of what is known as the Epipaleolithic period (the final Upper Paleolithic, *c.* 18,000–9600 BC), and ends at 6000 BC, by which time sedentary farming villages had been established throughout the region. The early origins of agriculture here have made Southwest Asia a special focus of interest to archaeologists seeking to understand the transition from mobile hunter-gatherer societies to sedentary farming villages. Since the 1950s, a series of archaeological expeditions have specifically sought evidence of agricultural origins in the region stretching from the Zagros Mountains of Iraq through the Taurus foothills of southern Turkey, down to the hill country and desert margins of the Levant. Coupled with environmental analysis, this work has focused on both the causes and the process of the transition to agriculture. Moreover, the story that has been revealed is not merely one of environment and subsistence. Remarkable carvings, sculptures, and wall paintings were produced by the communities of this region during the crucial period, from *c.* 13,000 to 6000 BC (the late Pleistocene and early Holocene), allowing us to see the period as one of cultural and perhaps cognitive innovation, accompanying the shift from hunting and gathering to food production.

We must begin near the end of the Last Glacial Maximum, when Epipaleolithic hunter-gatherer groups began to adopt new strategies of settlement and subsistence. They started to harvest and store plant foods, and began the shift from mobile foraging to life in permanent village communities. A number of these hunter-gatherer settlements, dated to the beginning of the Neolithic (around 9600 BC), have proved to be a good deal larger than our conventional idea of small-scale village communities. Clearly, life in societies with populations in the hundreds, and in some cases thousands, would have been very different from the old way of life in small, mobile groups of flexible membership, numbering 20 or so people at most, and these larger, more complex social groups turned out to be precocious in their development of complex symbolic worlds. It was these sedentary communities that went on in the early part of the Neolithic period to produce domesticated crops of cereals and pulses, and to herd the first domesticated flocks of sheep, goat, and cattle. So although the story may begin with foragers and end with farmers, there are important social, cultural, and cognitive developments that took place along the way.

The area covered in this chapter is sub-continental in scale, but its investigation has been very uneven. The best-explored area is undoubtedly the southern Levant – Israel, Palestine, and parts of Jordan. In other parts of Southwest Asia – Syria, Lebanon, Iraq, Iran, the Gulf States, and most of Turkey – much less research has been invested. Because we know very little about some parts of the region, however, we should not assume that they were unimportant. Archaeologists responding to requests to salvage sites ahead of the construction of major dams (on the Euphrates in Syria in the 1970s, on the Tigris in northern Iraq in the 1980s, and in southeast Turkey from the 1980s onward) have often found ancient remains of an unexpected scale, richness, and significance. Despite decades of research on the beginnings of farming in Southwest Asia, we are still on the steep part of a learning curve, where unexpected discoveries constantly require us to re-evaluate what we thought we understood.

The Environmental Setting

Southwest Asia is a region of great geographical variety and climatic diversity. The natural habitats of wild wheat and barley, and wild legumes such as lentils, peas, and beans, which were the ancestors of the first cultivated crops, overlap one another to a large extent, as do the original habitats of the wild sheep, goats, pigs, and cattle that were hunted along with other species. Moreover, they are not found everywhere in Southwest Asia. In the 1940s and 1950s, pioneering field research by Robert Braidwood and a multi-disciplinary team defined what Braidwood called the "nuclear zone," where the hunter-gatherers who exploited these plants and animals lived. It was not in the alluvial plains of the so-called Fertile Crescent, the arc stretching from the Nile Valley in Egypt, up the Levantine coastlands, across northern Iraq, and down to the deltaic alluvium at the head of the Persian Gulf, where the great civilizations of Mesopotamia had flourished. Rather, Braidwood identified what he called the "hilly flanks of the Fertile Crescent" as the place where foragers first began to harvest, store, and process wild foods (Braidwood 1960; Braidwood and Howe 1960) (see also Chapter 5, p. 188).

The wild ancestors of the plants that were first domesticated, specifically the cereals and pulses, prefer a hilly habitat (as do the first herded animals, sheep and goats). These plants

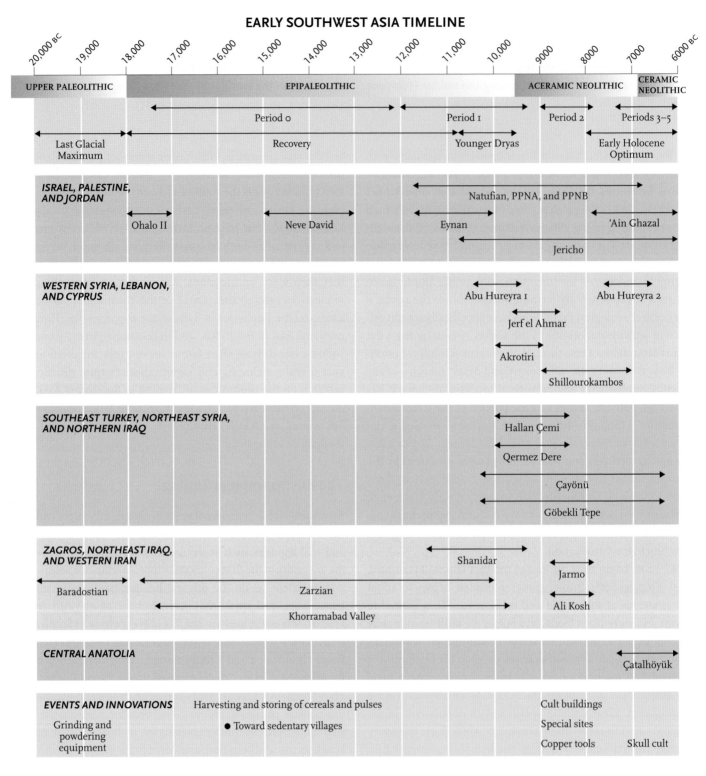

EARLY SOUTHWEST ASIA TIMELINE

cope well with hot, dry summers, and flourish where there is more than 250 mm (10 in) of mostly winter rainfall. Mobile hunter-gatherers could operate in the extensive semi-arid parts of Southwest Asia, but for farmers, the inter-annual variability around the 250-mm (10-in) annual rainfall contour was much less dangerous. Semi-sedentary and sedentary hunter-gatherers were more like farmers than mobile foragers; relying on harvests of wild cereals and legumes, they were subject to the

same risks as farmers, and since they lived in larger groups in permanent or seasonal villages, they lacked the mobility and flexibility of the classic hunter-gatherers. The "hilly flanks" environments were thus as suitable for them as for the plants and animals they ate.

During the harsher conditions of the Last Glacial Maximum (c. 21,000–18,000 BC), an open woodland zone of oak, *Pistacia* (a relative of the pistachio tree), and wild almond was restricted

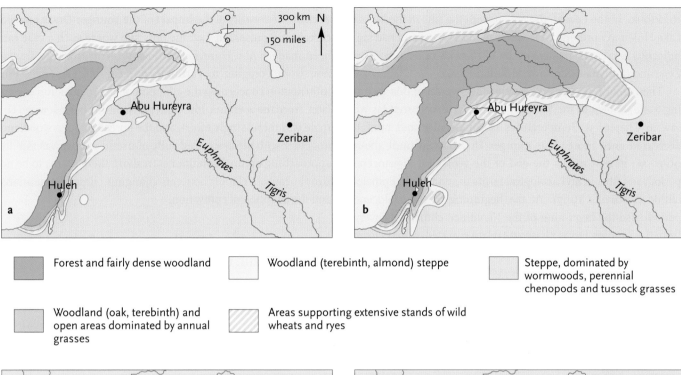

Forest and fairly dense woodland

Woodland (terebinth, almond) steppe

Steppe, dominated by wormwoods, perennial chenopods and tussock grasses

Woodland (oak, terebinth) and open areas dominated by annual grasses

Areas supporting extensive stands of wild wheats and ryes

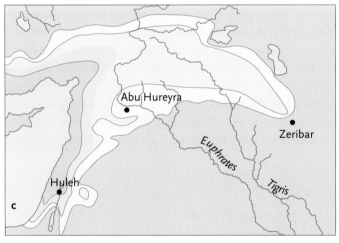

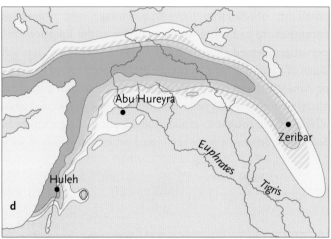

Areas dominated by trees, mostly probably growing as thin scatters

Partial die-back zone, with isolated pockets of trees with wild cereals and legumes

Total arboreal die-back zone, characterized by dead trees, with some terebinth and caper bushes in wadis

6.1 a–d The environmental setting: *a sequence of maps showing: (a) the extent of the forest and open woodland zones five millennia after the end of Last Glacial Maximum (c. 13,000 BC); (b) the further expansion of the open woodland (and with it the grasses, cereals, and pulses) by around 11,000 BC; (c) during the drier, cooler Younger Dryas phase there was significant "die-back," (c. 10,000 BC), and (d) the recovery in the early Holocene (c. 7500 BC).*

to a small zone around the Gulf of Antalya in southern Turkey, a strip behind the Mediterranean coast stretching from the Syrian-Turkish border south to the Jordan Valley, and possibly one or two other very small refugia in the northern part of the arc of the "hilly flanks" zone. Such open oak woodland is also the habitat within which are to be found many grass species – wild wheat, barley, and rye – and wild pulses. The tree species tend to dominate the pollen spectra recovered from lakebed cores, since they produce relatively large amounts of pollen; the grasses, cereals, and pulses are poorly represented. The best evidence we have for Southwest Asia shows that the warming trend that ended the Last Glacial Maximum began there somewhat earlier than the date recorded in the Greenland ice cores (see below), and that a climate similar to that of today existed by about 13,000 BC [6.1]. A major inland sea, the great Konya lake in the center of the Anatolian Plateau, had dried up by about

16,000 BC. In the Levant, the pollen from the silts in the bed of Lake Huleh in northern Israel show that oak woodland had significantly increased in density by *c.* 16,000–14,000 BC (van Zeist and Bottema 1982; 1991; Hillman 1996).

Then around 10,800 BC, a worldwide reversal of this warming trend, known as the Younger Dryas phase, occurred (as we saw in Chapter 5). Temperatures became cooler, and rainfall decreased once more. The Younger Dryas lasted until about 9600 BC; its end marks the end of the geological Pleistocene period, and thus in archaeological terms the end of the Epipaleolithic (Sanlaville 1997). At the beginning of the Holocene period (also the beginning of the Neolithic), climatic recovery from the Younger Dryas phase was relatively rapid, with warmer conditions re-establishing themselves within about 50 years.

It is important to note that the recovery from the Last Glacial Maximum proceeded differently in Southwest Asia from other areas, as recorded in the Greenland ice cores. It began earlier, and proceeded more or less smoothly. Even if the area within which hunter-gatherers could have turned to harvesting grasses, cereals, and pulses was fairly limited at 18,000 BC, the possibility of adopting harvesting, storage, and sedentism became more and more widely available as the Epipaleolithic period progressed. The Younger Dryas reversal, too, has left signs of a less dramatic impact than have been found in Arctic or Antarctic ice cores. Some scholars have assumed that the sharp changes seen in polar ice cores can be extrapolated globally, and have sought to explain the adoption of agriculture in Southwest Asia as a response forced on hunter-gatherer societies by the severity of the impact of the Younger Dryas on wild cereals and pulses. In fact, the only site where such a case can been made is Abu Hureyra [see box: Abu Hureyra: The Transition from Foraging to Farming, pp. 214–15]. Generally, our information concerning the adoption of crop cultivation comes later, from the aceramic (pre-pottery) Neolithic period, when climate was increasingly moist, and the spread of open woodland (together with the associated suite of useful plants) was rapidly approaching optimal conditions. In short, there seems to be no simple causal relation between changing climatic conditions and the adoption of cultivation.

New Strategies of Settlement and Subsistence: Epipaleolithic Hunter-Gatherers

In the Middle Paleolithic and the early stages of the Upper Paleolithic, Europe and Southwest Asia seem to have proceeded in parallel, with the significant difference that physical remains of *Homo sapiens* have been identified at two sites in Israel dating to between 110,000 and 90,000 years ago, long before the earliest attested appearance of the species in Europe (see Chapter 4). The cultural sequences of western Europe and Southwest Asia diverged, however, with the Last Glacial Maximum episode.

The Epipaleolithic cultural sequence in Southwest Asia was first defined in terms of a series of chipped stone industries. Dominating these assemblages were miniature blades – long, narrow, more or less parallel-sided flakes. Tools were fashioned by retouching these small blades (technically called "bladelets"

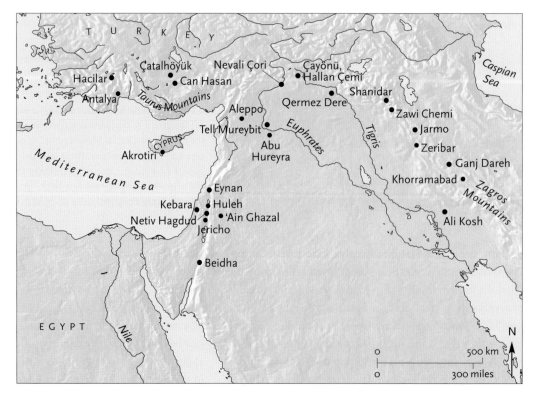

6.2 *Southwest Asia:* map showing major physical features and sites discussed in the text.

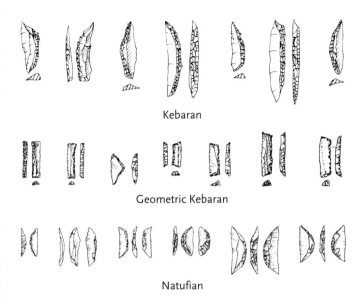

Kebaran

Geometric Kebaran

Natufian

6.3 Microliths: *formed with microscopic retouch on segments snapped from tiny bladelets, microliths are typical of successive stages in the Epipaleolithic in the Levant. Triangles and rhombus shapes are common in the middle Epipaleolithic, while crescentic pieces (called lunates) characterize the late Epipaleolithic.*

when they are less than 40 mm (1.5 in) long); microliths, mentioned in previous chapters, are a particularly striking category of tool formed from these bladelets. A microlith is created from a segment of a bladelet, its final shape finished with almost microscopic retouch. The end product may be geometric (triangles, rhombuses), or the basic shape may be retouched into a regular crescent, or given an asymmetrically curving back. Two or more microliths were combined to make new types of barbed arrowhead that were smaller and lighter in weight than earlier forms, and were probably devised for hunting small mammals and large birds.

These final Paleolithic assemblages with their microliths were generically labeled Epipaleolithic [**6.3**], a term that originally designated a sort of epilogue to the Paleolithic. Radiocarbon dating has shown, however, that the period was long-lived, lasting from the end of the Last Glacial Maximum (*c.* 18,000 BC) to the end of the Pleistocene and the Paleolithic periods (*c.* 9600 BC). The Upper Paleolithic exhibits more cultural diversity and cultural change in 20,000 years than the Middle Paleolithic shows in 200,000, but the Epipaleolithic in a span of under 10,000 years shows more cultural diversity and change than the Upper Paleolithic. *Homo sapiens* was using culture more and more as time passed.

The idea that microliths were designed for use as components in the making of sophisticated arrowheads supports the theory of a change in hunting strategy late in the Paleolithic period. Kent Flannery (1969) identified a "broad-spectrum revolution" as the critical factor in this change, supplanting Gordon Childe's old idea of a Neolithic, or "agricultural revolution" (Childe 1936). (For other general theories of the origins of agriculture at the end of the Pleistocene, see Explaining Agriculture box, Chapter 5, pp. 188–89.) In the Epipaleolithic, Flannery argued, hunter-gatherers developed a new hunting strategy that involved spending more effort on obtaining small

game, such as fox, hare, and birds such as partridge, as well as fish, shellfish, reptiles, and amphibians. They continued to hunt the larger herd animals, but their concentration on smaller species allowed them to remain longer in one place – a trend toward sedentism (living year-round in one place). Flannery believed that decreased hunter-gatherer mobility and the trend toward sedentism promoted an increase in birth frequency for females, and it was this population growth that drove the need to increase the food supply by introducing crop cultivation and animal herding.

This broad-spectrum hunting strategy, supported by microlithic tools and composite projectile points, was complemented by increasing reliance on harvests of large-seeded grasses, cereals, and pulses. As mentioned in Chapter 5, a classic field experiment in southeast Turkey showed that a family could harvest in three weeks enough wild wheat to feed them for a year (Harlan 1967). Seeds such as lentils, dried peas and beans, wheat, or barley can be stored, and stored food resources and sedentism clearly interrelate.

Thus, the Epipaleolithic hunter-gatherers in at least some parts of Southwest Asia diverged from their Upper Paleolithic contemporaries in Europe, not only in terms of their chipped-stone tool technology, but also in a trend toward reduced mobility, greater sedentism, a broad-spectrum hunting strategy, and stored harvests of cereals and pulses. Although plant foods leave much less evidence in the archaeological record than the animal bones that document hunting or herding strategies, there is a proxy indicator. Hard seeds need processing by either pounding (with a mortar and pestle) or grinding (with querns and grinders). These heavy implements begin to appear sporadically in the Upper Paleolithic, but increase steadily in frequency through time on Epipaleolithic sites (Wright 1994).

The Early Epipaleolithic in the Levant, *c.* 18,000–12,000 BC

The Early Epipaleolithic (*c.* 18,000–12,000 BC) is important for our understanding of the processes of increasing sedentism, larger resident communities, and food storage. Early 20th-century research was concentrated on cave sites and rockshelters in the Mediterranean woodland zone in Israel, and researchers since the 1960s have surveyed extensive areas of the Negev Desert in southern Israel, Sinai, the semi-arid regions of Jordan, and inland Syria. In all these regions, Epipaleolithic open sites have been found.

The effects of the Last Glacial Maximum, the amelioration of climatic conditions, and then the return to cooler temperatures and reduced rainfall in the Younger Dryas would, in theory, have been more critical in the marginal zones, the steppe or semi-desert regions, than in the Mediterranean woodland zone. Hunter-gatherer societies operating in semi-arid regions would thus have needed greater adaptive responses than were demanded of the groups occupying the Mediterranean woodland zone. It was surprising to learn, therefore, that the coolest, driest periods seem to have had little impact on hunter-gatherer occupation in those critical areas, though subsistence strategies continued to adapt and change.

There are sites of all stages of the Epipaleolithic period in the semi-arid zone (e.g. Garrard 1998; Henry 1995; Goring-Morris 1987), though the sparse remains comprise only stone tools and, at some sites, indications of the animal species exploited. Many of the sites are small and seem to document short-term, seasonal occupation by small groups. Among the stone tools, however, are heavy grinding and pounding implements, which indicate that stored harvests of dry grain and other seeds were being processed.

Don Henry (1995) has based his ideas of how hunter-gatherers might have used the landscape on the locations of sites in southern Jordan, which preserve no plant or animal remains. He reconstructs the settlement and subsistence strategy of Epipaleolithic groups as transhumant, that is, alternating seasonally between different locations. He identifies some low-altitude rockshelters as winter camps for large, aggregated groups; smaller, open sites in the piedmont and upland areas he believes were summer camps of smaller, dispersed groups operating in a more mobile mode. Nigel Goring-Morris (1987), working under similar constraints in the southern Negev and Sinai, hypothesizes the seasonal occupation of the different zones by reference to the likely climatic conditions, the availability of water, and the presumed distribution of plant foods. He suggests that base camps in the highlands would have been occupied in the late summer through to early winter, when groups would not have been "tethered" to the lowland permanent water sources. Nuts, fruits, and seeds would have been available during the summer at these high-altitude sites, and these nutritious harvests might have sustained the population through the autumn and into the winter, after which people operated at lower altitudes in smaller groups through the late winter and spring.

Ohalo II and Neve David The first excavated and best-known Epipaleolithic sites are in caves and rockshelters in the Mediterranean woodland zone, where people lived much as their Upper Paleolithic predecessors had done. However, two more recently discovered open-air sites in the Mediterranean woodland zone are noteworthy for their evidence of more advanced lifeways. **Ohalo II** is an Early Epipaleolithic occupation, firmly dated at around 18,000 BC, still within the Last Glacial Maximum [see box: Ohalo II: Epipaleolithic Lifeways in the Levant]. It is valuable for documenting a way of life that was practically sedentary and dependent on a range of stored plant foods at an unexpectedly early date. Apart from its chipped-stone industry and its radiocarbon dates, Ohalo II could easily be mistaken for a site of the end of the Epipaleolithic period, around 8000 years later.

The other site, **Neve David**, is at the foot of the western scarp of the Mount Carmel hills in northern Israel (Kaufman 1989). It dates to the later part of the Early Epipaleolithic period, and illustrates the tendency toward larger aggregations and longer occupations at base-camp sites. Neve David is only 1 km (0.6 mile) from the present coastline, but in final Pleistocene times the site looked out onto a coastal plain that was 10–12 km (6.5–7.5 miles) wide. The location of the site is one favored by many later Epipaleolithic and earliest Neolithic communities of sedentary hunter-gatherers: it sits on an ecotone, the boundary between contrasting ecological zones. On one side was the limestone massif of the Mount Carmel hills with their seasonally dry valleys, and on the other lay the Mediterranean coastal plain. The occupants chose a situation from which they had ready access to the complementary resources of different ecological zones.

The estimated extent of the occupation at Neve David is about 1000 sq. m (10,700 sq. ft), which is significantly larger than most sites of the period, which average around 400 sq. m (4300 sq. ft). More than 1 m (3.3 ft) of archaeological deposits were accumulated on this open site, which implies not only repeated use over a long period, but also that there were structures built of soil and clay that prevented its easy erosion by wind and weather between occupations. Base-camp occupation is also indicated by the density and variety of cultural and other debris, including a large quantity and variety of ground-stone implements, some in local limestone, the rest of black basalt brought from some distance.

One of the two burials encountered contained the tightly contracted body of a male of about 23–30 years of age (the other burial was poorly preserved). The grave pit was lined with stone slabs, and a stone mortar was placed upside-down over the skull. Part of a broken basalt bowl had been placed behind the neck, and there was a small piece of a flat grinding slab of basalt between the thighs. The grave's careful construction and the burial offerings of ground-stone implements presage the care and rituals that often accompany burials at later, Natufian sites, discussed below. At other Epipaleolithic sites of this age, there are also traces of the circular, semi-subterranean houses that characterize Natufian sites.

KEY SITE Ohalo II: Epipaleolithic Lifeways in the Levant

The site of Ohalo II in northern Israel, dated to 18,000 BC, provides a remarkable snapshot of Epipaleolithic lifeways in the Levant during the Last Glacial Maximum (Nadel and Hershkovitz 1991; Nadel and Werker 1999). This small settlement, with microlithic chipped-stone tools of so-called Kebaran type, was established on the marls of the retreating Lake Lisan (the inland sea that once filled the rift valley that now contains the Sea of Galilee, the Dead Sea, and the Jordan Valley). It was discovered in 1989, when the Sea of Galilee fell to an extraordinarily low level, and it is submerged under more than 2 m (6.6 ft) of water for much of the year.

Nature of the Site

The site comprises a tight cluster of several huts built of wood and brush, a number of external hearths and fire pits, an area where domestic waste was deposited, and a single grave at a little distance from the huts, which were slightly oval in plan, 3–4 m (10–13 ft) across. The huts had all been burned, the collapsed remains sealing the material that was on the floor when the hut was abandoned. One of the huts has been examined in detail, revealing that its wall had been formed of thick branches of oak, tamarisk, and willow set about 20 cm (8 in) into the ground. On the floor the excavators encountered a wealth of finds, including chipped stone, animal bone, and preserved seeds and plant fruits.

Among the houses there was a single burial. There are signs that this person suffered physical disabilities in the latter years of his life, to the extent that he would not have been a contributing member of his society.

Evidence for Diet

The waterlogging of the site has led to the exceptional preservation of some of the organic materials used at Ohalo II. Tens of thousands of seeds and fruits have been recovered, revealing that more than 100 plant species were in use. The people of Ohalo II gathered acorns, emmer wheat, and barley,

6.4 One hut at Ohalo II was examined in detail: the black ring is the charred remains of the wall of the hut, which was deliberately burnt at the end of its life, while the dark area inside the ring of the wall is the remains of the floor, which was covered with the debris of everyday life.

together with a range of legumes and many other plants. This diversity shows that they were collecting foods across the full range of altitude, from the valley bottom to more than 1000 m (3300 ft) above sea level, and across the full spectrum of ecological zones accessible from the site. Gazelle were hunted in numbers, and fish from the lake were also important. Other mammals that were exploited include fallow deer, fox, and hare, and plenty of birds. The plant remains indicate that people were present to harvest them through the spring, summer, and autumn, and the evidence of the cementum growth in the gazelle teeth, together with indications from the bird bones, suggests year-round occupation.

Overview

At Ohalo II, then, we have evidence for the exploitation of a broad spectrum of plants and animals, the extensive use of storable plant foods, and the year-round occupation of a settlement. It is the first site to confirm that the stone implements for grinding that are found on other Early Epipaleolithic sites were indeed used in the preparation of hard-seeded plant foods. Ohalo II is not typical of its period, for other Kebaran sites show evidence

6.5 A single burial has been found among the huts. The body was that of a man of 35–40 years of age at death and 1.73 m (5 ft 8 in) tall. He was buried lying almost flat, his head supported by three stones. His legs were folded tightly back at the knees so that the heels were in contact with the buttocks, and his forearms lay across his chest. Close to the head the excavators found a small implement made from a gazelle's limb bone that had been decorated with many close incisions.

of repeated, short occupations by mobile hunter-gatherer bands. But Ohalo II does demonstrate that some groups were already tending toward sedentism and the year-round exploitation of an ecologically diverse home territory.

6.6 Excavation in progress at Ohalo II at a time of summer low water. Since the site was drowned in the geomorphic movements that produced the Sea of Galilee there has been no erosion or disturbance, no subsequent occupation, and remarkable organic preservation.

The Late Epipaleolithic in the Levant, c. 12,000–9600 BC

We have seen that there is a long history in the Levant for the harvesting, storing, and processing of hard-seeded plant foods, increased hunting of smaller animal species, the habit of transhumance, and living in permanent and relatively large social groups in semi-sedentary or fully sedentary villages. In the Late Epipaleolithic period (*c.* 12,000–9600 BC) we can recognize a complex of material traits and cultural practices within specific geographical and chronological constraints that closely conform to the classic definition of a cultural group – **the Natufians**. The appearance of this culture has been described as a "threshold event" (Bar-Yosef and Valla 1991), and it has been claimed that the Natufian represents a "pre-agricultural revolution" (Henry 1989, 180). Such notions, however, need qualification in the light of the discovery of such earlier sites as Ohalo II and Neve David. Today, the step change seems much less stark than some authorities have claimed.

What impresses about the Natufian is the intensification. There were few cultural traits that were wholly new, but those that were first evident in the Early Epipaleolithic – sedentary or semi-sedentary settlements, large occupation sites, ground-stone implements for pounding and grinding, occasional deliberate human burials – were confirmed, expanded, and augmented during the Late Epipaleolithic. It is difficult to account for the numerical superiority of Natufian occupations over the Early Epipaleolithic ones except by accepting that there was probably an increasingly dense population. Natufian settlements are extremely varied, comprising small, ephemeral campsites and large, permanent villages occupied over many centuries. Communities ranged from small, traditional hunting and gathering groups in semi-arid locales to village societies of 200–300 people in particularly favorable locations. Here we shall concentrate on the "intensified" end of the spectrum.

The Discovery of the Natufians

The Natufian culture was first identified by Dorothy Garrod (1892–1968) (1932). In 1928 she excavated the cave site of Shuqbah in a dry valley called Wadi en-Natuf (from which the name "Natufian" derives), in the Mount Carmel hills of what is today northern Israel. The characteristic assemblage was clearly the latest in the sequence of Paleolithic industries from any of the caves that she went on to excavate, but the culture from which it came was unlike other Paleolithic cave occupations in four particular respects. First, among the chipped-stone tools there were numbers of small blades, blunted down one side and polished along the sharp edge from their use as elements in sickle blades (see below). Secondly, there were numerous and conspicuously large mortars and grinding stones. Thirdly, the occupation that Garrod excavated at **el Wad** had spread out well beyond the mouth of the Shuqbah

Cave, the inhabitants having built themselves living structures around the slope outside it; this was clearly a much larger community than any earlier Paleolithic group. Finally, more than 100 burials were found in a regular cemetery on the terrace and in the cave itself.

With the advent of extensive field survey in southern Israel and Jordan, more open-air settlement sites of Natufian date have been identified. Sites similar to el Wad have been found elsewhere in Israel, where the area of occupation debris and built structures extends well beyond the cave that was the focus of the settlement. When the French archaeologist Jean Perrot began salvage work in 1955 on the accidentally exposed site at **Eynan** ('Ain Mallaha) in the Huleh basin in northeast Israel [see box: Eynan, pp. 210–11], he found a Natufian-period, open village settlement, stratified and long-lived, consisting of houses with stone foundations. Salvage excavations in the Euphrates Valley in northern Syria in the early 1970s produced two more settlements dating back to the last millennium of the Epipaleolithic period – **Abu Hureyra** and **Tell Mureybit** (Cauvin 1977) – the material culture of which links them to the Natufian culture [see box: Abu Hureyra: The Transition from Foraging to Farming, pp.214–15]. Other Natufian sites discovered since Garrod's excavation have produced evidence of significant numbers of burials.

Evidence for Natufian Lifeways The Natufian chipped-stone industry is characterized by a low frequency of geometric microliths and a dominance of crescent-shaped microliths (called lunates). The **toolkit** was remarkably similar to earlier Epipaleolithic assemblages in the Levantine corridor, and there are no new tools for new functions. And with one exception – sickle blades – the changes that have been defined to differentiate the Natufian from its predecessors do not suggest a changing balance between different kinds of activities, but rather seem to be matters of cultural preference. Sickle blades, however, do provide evidence for a widespread change in cultural practice. Although bladelets are known already in the early Epipaleolithic, some of the bladelets and microliths from Natufian sites exhibit the characteristic gloss, or polish, that is produced by the silica in the stems of cereals, grasses, and reeds, signifying their use as harvesting implements.

A sharp increase in the numbers and variety of ground-stone implements on Natufian sites has been noted, reflecting an increased intensity in the harvesting, storing, and processing of dry seeds [**6.7, 6.8**]. In addition to the standard mortars and grinding slabs, we find bedrock mortars and deep "pipe" mortars formed in large boulders. Two features of the grinding and pounding equipment are striking. First, many are made from large lumps of vesicular black basalt, the geological sources of which are often tens of kilometers from the sites where they were used. And secondly, a number of the stone

6.7, 6.8 Natufian stone implements: *heavy ground-stone implements for grinding and pounding dry seeds (grasses, cereals, and legumes) increase in frequency in the late Epipaleolithic, and again at the beginning of the Neolithic. These large pestles and a black basalt mortar are from Hayonim, Israel.*

accompanied by the body of a dog (the earliest known occurrence of a domesticated animal). A very small number of bodies are lacking the skull, evidence of a ritual practice that became typical in the early Neolithic and is discussed in more detail below (p. 221).

Some Natufian sites (el Wad, Eynan, Hayonim) have produced dozens of burials in cemeteries, while other sites have no burials at all. On those sites with cemeteries, the several dozen burials by no means account for the population of the associated settlements, which were occupied over many centuries. Gary Wright (1978) attempted to show that the burials at el Wad consisted of groups of ordinary individuals clustered around the burials of people of higher social status. He argued that, since some of the higher-status burials were of children, the social group was stratified, and status was inherited rather than earned through achievement or seniority. Wright's methodology was criticized by Anna Belfer-Cohen (1995), however, whose study of the burials at Hayonim came to the opposite conclusion. While there is little or no evidence for the existence of social hierarchies, we still cannot account for the selection of a tiny minority of the population for ceremonial burial within or adjacent to certain settlements.

The Late Epipaleolithic Beyond the Levant

Beyond the Levantine corridor, we do not have anything that matches the concentration of excavation and research that has taken place in the southern Levant over more than 70 years. In the caves west of Antalya on the south coast of Turkey, excavations do show that there is a long stratigraphic sequence through the Epipaleolithic, and into the early Neolithic, but they are not yet fully explored or documented. In the piedmont and intermontane valleys of northeast Iraq and western Iran, cave sites have been investigated here and there, although no fieldwork has been possible since the 1960s. These soundings show that there was an Epipaleolithic presence, following upon Middle and Upper Paleolithic occupations, but that there was a break at the height of the Last Glacial Maximum, when the Zagros region was abandoned. The pollen evidence from a core taken from the bed of Lake Zeribar, in an intermontane valley of

vessels, both bowls and mortars, were decorated with carved geometric designs, or sometimes with designs in raised relief.

A common feature of Natufian sites is the frequency of items of **personal adornment**. In cemeteries such as that at el Wad, bodies were buried wearing caps, hair ornaments, capes, bracelets, and garters that were embroidered with dentalium shells, collected from Mediterranean beaches. There are shells of other species, mostly from the Mediterranean, but also from the Red Sea, as well as perforated animal teeth, stone beads, and pendants. On sites without burials, occasional finds of marine shells have been reported, presumably worn in life.

Most Natufian sites are tens of kilometers from the Mediterranean coast, and the Red Sea region is beyond the area of Natufian settlement. There were no sources of black basalt nearby, yet the Natufians possessed basalt basins, mortars, and grinding stones. These materials, along with the very rare occurrences on Natufian sites of obsidian (a volcanic glass that was chipped like flint) from central Turkey, indicate that long-distance exchange networks were in existence at this period. The basalt pounding and grinding tools played an important economic role, but the decoration carved on some of the mortars indicates that they also had social value. Obsidian was so rare that we must conclude that the social exchanges involved outweighed any functional or economic role. The extensive use of marine shells for personal ornament again stresses the social and cultural significance of the networks of exchange that linked together communities throughout the Levant and beyond.

While there are burials in small numbers here and there on Early Epipaleolithic sites, the occurrence of regular **cemeteries** differentiates the Natufian. Many of the burials are single inhumations in a grave pit, while others are multiple, the bodies apparently buried simultaneously in one pit. As already noted, some bodies were buried wearing clothes with shell ornaments, but scarcely any burials were accompanied by what might be considered to be grave goods; one female burial at Eynan was

the Zagros Mountains, shows that winter conditions were much colder than today, and woodland and other vegetation was much reduced. The Epipaleolithic culture in the Zagros region has been named the **Zarzian**, taking its name from a rockshelter called Zarzi, one of several sites in Iraqi Kurdistan that were briefly investigated by the intrepid Dorothy Garrod early in the 20th century.

It was Kent Flannery's experience of soundings in caves and rockshelters in the Khorammabad Valley of southwest Iran that fertilized his idea of a broad-spectrum revolution in the Epipal-

eolithic Zarzian (Flannery 1969). The work of Flannery and Frank Hole (Hole and Flannery 1967) demonstrated that the Zarzian culture had a long time span, as did the Epipaleolithic in the southern Levant, although there is little sign of this in terms of cultural change in the Zarzian chipped-stone industry. We have animal bone data that documents the extending of the broad-spectrum hunting strategy, but almost no information on the use of plant foods, and there is little evidence from the small-scale soundings for the use of heavy ground-stone implements for pounding and grinding. Thus we

KEY SITE Eynan

The Natufian marks a major change in the development of Epipaleolithic societies in the Levant, with larger and more permanent settlements, including some that were occupied year-round by communities of sedentary hunter-gatherers. Among the most important of these sites is Eynan (its Hebrew name), Mallaha (its Arabic name), or 'Ain Mallaha (after the nearby spring).

This large settlement lies in the far north of Israel, on sloping ground at the western side of a shallow basin that until recently contained Lake Huleh. In prehistoric times the location was ideal for sedentary hunter-gatherers, since a variety of rich resource zones were easily accessible. The lake provided fish, and there were other resources in its marshy margins, in the well-watered basin around, and in the hills rising behind the site. The inhabitants of Eynan hunted gazelle, fallow deer, wild boar, red and roe deer, hare, tortoise, reptiles, and amphibians, as well as the migrant waterfowl that visited the lake, and gathered terebinth (a bitter stoned fruit) and almonds, and probably wild cereals.

A Three-Phase Site

Eynan's long occupation documents the lifespan of the Natufian culture, from 12,000 to 9600 BC. François Valla (1991), who studied the chipped stone from Eynan and other Natufian sites, distinguishes three phases in the Natufian culture, all of which are represented at Eynan. The first two were characterized by substantial, stone-built

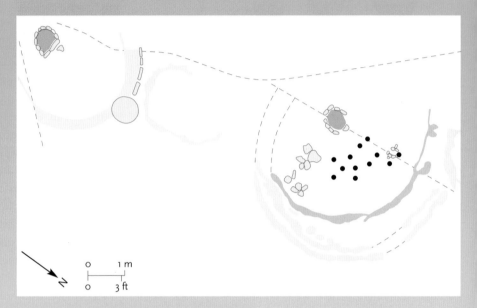

6.9 *Plan of the first period of occupation at Eynan. The cluster of dots to the right marks the positions of burials. Some time after the burials, structure 131 was built (see 6.10).*

structures, with smaller, less substantial ones in the third phase. In the two major phases, houses were constructed in circular holes some 0.5 m (1.6 ft) or more deep and several meters in diameter, with the sides of the cavity walled with dry-stone masonry. The larger houses had internal wooden posts to support the roof, which was probably of wood, brushwood, and thatch. Houses were entered

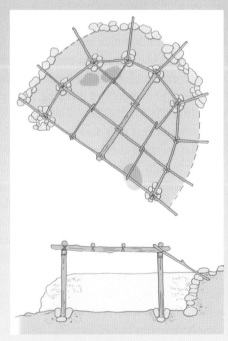

6.10 *Structure 131 was an open D-shaped structure with a complex timber roof. All sorts of materials were found on the floor, but as if deliberately deposited when the building was buried, rather than as a result of everyday use.*

do not know to what extent Zarzian communities had begun to collect storable wild harvests, or to engage in the trend toward sedentary village life.

Two sites excavated in the 1950s in the remote mountains of northeast Iraq, Shanidar Cave and the nearby open village site of Zawi Chemi, are tantalizing pointers to the presence of sedentary hunter-gatherer communities depending on stored harvests and a broad-spectrum hunting strategy in the last millennium of the Epipaleolithic (Solecki 1981; Solecki and Solecki 1983). The final Epipaleolithic stratum in **Shanidar Cave**, unlike earlier levels, produced ground-stone implements, small mammal bones, fish and shellfish, cobbled stone floors, and a number of burials. The small open village site of **Zawi Chemi** gave evidence of a sequence of circular, stone-built houses, burials within the settlement, and the use of personal ornament. More than 200 ground-stone implements were recorded, indicating the intensive processing of hard seeds such as grasses, cereals, or pulses. The animal bones from this Late Epipaleolithic settlement showed the intensive exploitation of wild sheep in a way that was different from earlier

---

through a doorway and down two or three steps. In the center of the floor was a hearth, sometimes defined by stone slabs, and the floors were cluttered with ground-stone implements for pounding and grinding grain and seeds.

The First Phase

In the first phase at Eynan the French excavation team encountered about 30 burials (Boyd 1995), many of which had been covered over by the structures of the same period. More bodies were interred after the buildings had been abandoned and filled in. Ornaments made of dentalium shell (a marine mollusk) accompanied some of the bodies, and one had a headdress embroidered with dentalium, as well as a necklace, bracelet, belt, and garter, all decorated with the same shells. A young dog accompanied another burial of an adult female.

The buildings that were erected over the early burials were larger than the normal, domestic structures; one of them, Structure 131, is unlike the houses in form, and seems to have been a special building. It was semicircular, its straight side formed by a line of posts. The roof was supported on a semicircle of posts set in stone-lined sockets, and it had two hearths, one close to the straight wall, the other consisting of two discrete areas at the rear of the building.

Around this double hearth was a concentration of flint blades, the little grooved stones that are believed to have served as arrow-shaft straighteners, and several heavy pestles (though no mortars or grinding stones). Also found were the polished and incised antler of a roe deer, two fragments of a piece of sculpted limestone, the vault of a human skull, half of a dog's jawbone, a heap of butchered gazelle bones, and a collection of small pebbles.

The Second Phase

In the second phase, the buildings seem to have been arranged in three ranges on terraces. They were generally smaller than the buildings of the first phase, but otherwise similar in construction and internal furnishings. Among the houses there were numerous cylindrical pits, some lined with stones, others with mud plaster. These would normally be understood as storage pits, but a

number of them were found to contain burials. Perhaps old storage pits were ultimately used as graves. Some bodies had been placed in the pits immediately after death; other pits contained multiple burials, all secondary (that is, the major bones of a skeleton were brought from elsewhere and reinterred here).

The Third Phase

The excavators once thought that the third phase of the site consisted only of seasonal occupations by a group that had returned to a mobile hunter-gatherer strategy. Further work has shown that the occupation continued, but that the community had shrunk in size, with smaller houses of less substantial construction; the site was eventually abandoned. This long-lived village, occupied for some 2000 years, bears witness to the size and success of Natufian settlements in the Levant before the adoption of agriculture.

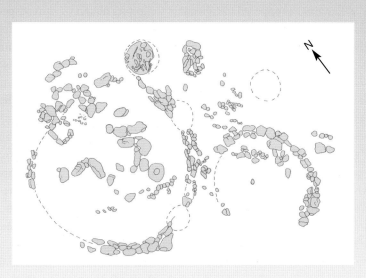

6.11 *Part of the second period village at Eynan. The circular houses were semi-subterranean. The larger house had a rectangular hearth at the centre of the floor. Many of the other stones are abandoned pestles, mortars and grinding stones.*

practice, with many more young animals eaten, though the claim that these were sheep on their way to domestication is not now generally accepted.

One further site deserves mention, because it too provides evidence that sedentary hunter-gatherers existed outside the Mediterranean corridor before the end of the Epipaleolithic period. **Hallan Çemi** is a small village site east of Diyarbakır in southeast Turkey, at the top of the arc of the "hilly flanks" zone. The settlement lasted from the last centuries of the Epipaleolithic period into the earliest Neolithic. The villagers built substantial circular stone structures, one of which was somewhat larger and more heavily constructed than the others; the skull and horns of a wild bull hung on its wall. Many ground-stone implements were found, especially large mortars and pounders. Careful sampling of the deposits by flotation and wet sieving has produced carbonized seeds of various legumes, plus almonds and terebinth (a bitter stoned fruit), but no cereals. Wild sheep dominate the animal bone sample, along with goat, deer, fox, hare, tortoise, birds, and fish. Michael Rosenberg and his team, who excavated at Hallan Çemi, have made a case (that probably needs further support) for early pig domestication (Rosenberg et al. 1998).

An Epipaleolithic Summary

In at least three different parts of Southwest Asia we can see that the Epipaleolithic period was substantially longer than was believed when the term was first coined, and that Epipaleolithic groups are defined by a good deal more than their characteristically small-scale chipped-stone industries. The more significant marker of Epipaleolithic societies is their shift toward a new strategy of settlement and subsistence. Based on his study of the anthropological literature concerning modern hunter-gatherers, Lewis Binford (1980; 1983; 1990) has described that strategy as foraging, as opposed to collecting. Collectors obtain the foodstuffs that they need for today, moving their base camp at relatively frequent intervals from one resource zone to another. Foragers move much less frequently, operating from one base-camp for several months, or even staying in the same place all year round. They operate in the environment using a logistically complex strategy, foraging for a variety of food resources from their base-camp or village.

The anthropologist James Woodburn (1982) described the same distinction among hunter-gatherer societies in terms of those who engage in immediate or delayed return strategies. Binford's collectors operate an immediate return strategy. His Epipaleolithic foragers, in contrast, operate a delayed return strategy that involves making an investment (building a fish-weir or a canoe, or making nets with which to trap birds) that will produce returns over a long period. Another form of investment against a delayed return is the intensive harvesting of a food resource (such as wheat, barley, or lentils) that can be processed and stored to supply food over a period of months. The French anthropologist Alain Testart (1982) showed that there are profound social implications to the practice of food storage, demonstrating a strong correlation between social inequalities within hunter-gatherer societies and the practice of food storage. It is reasonable to infer, therefore, that our Epipaleolithic hunter-gatherers in Southwest Asia, who were engaged in the harvesting of storable food resources, shared some of the characteristics of Binford's foragers, Woodburn's delayed return hunter-gatherers, and Testart's more complex hunter-gatherer societies.

By the late Epipaleolithic period, some societies (of whom the best known are the Natufians) had developed a settlement and subsistence strategy that enabled them to live in a variety of environments – not only in the best watered and most wooded parts of the Mediterranean woodland zone, but also in a variety of marginal and semi-arid sectors. Their growing concentration on storable plant foods was coupled with a tendency toward more permanent settlements. As well as having important social and socio-economic implications, life in sedentary or near-sedentary village communities represents a shift toward the creation of a "built environment," with substantial cognitive and cultural implications – a subject to which we will return at the end of the chapter.

Culture Change in the Aceramic Neolithic, *c.* 9600–6900 BC

The Epipaleolithic in Southwest Asia ends with the close of the geological Pleistocene, around 9600 BC, and the succeeding archaeological era, the Neolithic, coincides with the earliest part of the geological Holocene. There are changes of material culture, especially in ways of making chipped-stone tools, by which archaeologists can recognize the end of the Epipaleolithic and the beginning of the Neolithic, at least in the better-known parts of Southwest Asia.

This new era may itself be divided into an early, aceramic (pre-pottery) Neolithic (to 6900 BC) and a later, ceramic Neolithic (*c.* 6900–6000 BC). It is helpful to subdivide further the aceramic Neolithic into early (*c.* 9600–8800 BC) and later (8800–6900 BC) periods. As discussed below, these two subdivisions are frequently referred to in the archaeological literature as the Pre-Pottery Neolithic A and B periods (PPNA and PPNB), but these terms strictly apply only in the Levant. Even there, these somewhat crude labels are becoming increasingly unsatisfactory, as our understanding of the period becomes more subtle and complicated.

At first, the early Neolithic period was characterized by the term "village farming" (Braidwood and Howe 1960). We now know that farming was only beginning to play a role in the subsistence economy during the early Neolithic, and a number of the earliest aceramic Neolithic sites relied little, if at all, on cultivated crops. Only in the later aceramic Neolithic period can we identify communities that had come to depend on both domesticated plants and animals. In terms of subsistence economics, therefore, we can say that societies moved into cultivation at different rates, and adopted the practice of herding animals somewhat later, and again at different times. Further, the crops that people first chose to cultivate and the animals that they first herded differed from one area to another.

New Stoneworking Technologies

On the other hand, there are striking changes in material culture that mark the beginning of the aceramic Neolithic period. In most parts of Southwest Asia, the microliths that characterized the Epipaleolithic period rapidly dropped out of use at the transition to the Neolithic. A new and very striking pattern can be seen in the Levantine corridor, together with most of the top of the arc of the "hilly flanks" zone as far as northeast Iraq: societies began to make the same kinds of arrowheads. It is generally thought that many of the microliths of the Epipaleolithic were made to be used as components in compound arrowheads, and the one-piece arrowheads of the Neolithic [6.12] would seem to be a straightforward replacement of this tradition. However, there is no detectable change in the species that were hunted or the proportions of those species. Perhaps the new, intricately designed arrowheads should be understood in the context of human skeletons found with projectile points embedded in them, and settlements such as Jericho being surrounded with a massive wall and ditch (Watkins 1990; 1992a). It is at the beginning of the aceramic Neolithic, too, that heavy, sub-spherical, stone mace heads begin to appear. While the hunting of animals continued, a new factor arose within societies, and people began to produce weapons for display, for competition, and for inter-communal warfare.

The earliest type of Neolithic projectile point is known as a **Khiam point** (named after the site of el-Khiam in the Judean hills of Palestine). Its most obvious characteristic is a notch on either side near the base, and usually a slightly concave base. In almost all examples, the tip is retouched on both surfaces (the retouch on the underside being known as inverse retouch). The Khiam point is followed by other shapes, for example, points with two pairs of notches, leaf-shaped points, lozenge-shaped points, and tanged points. Extraordinarily, these new points come into favor or drop out of fashion at almost the same time throughout a very large area, and it is difficult to see any logic of technological improvement driving the changes. Some of the later types are long and were deliberately made thick and heavy; they may have been spear or javelin heads. The prominence of these many and varied types of projectile points within the chipped stone assemblages is very real – they may account for as much as 25 percent of all tools.

There are also less visible changes in stone tool traditions, both in the ways that cores were prepared and blades (long, parallel-sided flakes) were removed from the core. In the earlier part of the aceramic Neolithic, cores and blades remained small, even if the ways of preparing them changed. There are distinct regional traditions within Southwest Asia at this early period. In the later aceramic Neolithic, cores, blades, and thus retouched tools, became larger. Moreover, a peculiar way of preparing cores emerged and became very widespread, allowing the toolmaker to remove blades alternately from each end of a (bipolar) core. In its extreme form, cores were prepared that seem to have a "keel" when they are turned on their side (called naviform or bi-directional core technology). The extensive adoption of this new and complicated technology is evidence for the existence of long-distance exchange networks – material and cultural – throughout the region (see below, p. 230).

Innovations in Art and Ideas

The French prehistorian Jacques Cauvin (2001) noted further innovations in material culture at the beginning of the Neolithic period, which he defined as constituting a "symbolic revolution." To date, we have little in the way of figurative art from the Epipaleolithic, although there are a few Upper Paleolithic images of animals engraved on stone [–> p. 216]

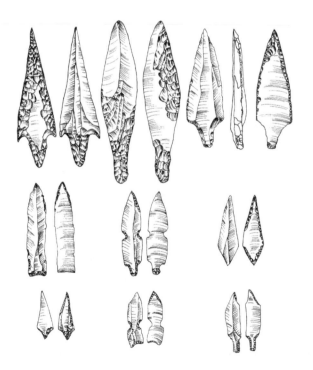

6.12 Projectile points of the early aceramic Neolithic: *these one-piece arrowheads replaced the microlithic technology of the Epipaleolithic.*

KEY SITE Abu Hureyra: The Transition from Foraging to Farming

A cherished aim of archaeologists studying the origins of agriculture in Southwest Asia has been to excavate a site where the transition from foraging to farming could be directly observed. Abu Hureyra, a prehistoric settlement on the edge of the Euphrates Valley in northern Syria, proved to be just such a site. It was discovered at the beginning of the 1970s during survey work ahead of the damming and subsequent flooding of that length of the valley. The Neolithic specialist Andrew Moore recognized the potential for obtaining information on the beginnings of cultivation and herding, and pulled together a young, multi-disciplinary team. Only two seasons of salvage excavation were possible before the site was drowned, but intensive wet sieving and flotation produced tons of floral and faunal data that has fueled a quarter of a century of investigation and research on the environment, the plant foods, and the exploitation of animals in this area (Moore et al. 2001).

The Epipaleolithic Settlement

The remains of a small Epipaleolithic settlement were found under the center of the later aceramic (pre-pottery) Neolithic village of Abu Hureyra. This earlier settlement consisted of round houses sunk into the ground, their thatched roofs supported on wooden poles. The villagers hunted gazelle, a few wild cattle and sheep, and a now-extinct species of zebra-sized ass (*Equus hemionus*). They gathered a great range of plants from a variety of different ecological zones, including wild cereals and grasses. The location of the settlement was well chosen to allow the exploitation of the complementary resources of the river, flood plain, seasonal watercourse valleys in the semi-arid zone, and the moist steppe.

The small village was established about 1000 years before the end of the Epipaleolithic period, *c.* 11,000 BC, just before the Younger Dryas cold phase. It was situated at a critically marginal location, and the effect of the cooler, drier climate has been documented in the plant foods collected. As cereals and trees such as plum and almond began to decline, people extended the range of small-seeded grasses and other plants that were gathered. These were harder to collect, required more processing, and were less nutritious. As conditions continued to deteriorate, the inhabitants turned to the intensive cultivation of rye, a cereal that could tolerate the harsh conditions. This intensive cultivation led to the emergence of a domesticated form of rye, the earliest instance of a domesticated species so far known.

The settlement was abandoned at the end of the Younger Dryas reversal, around 9600 BC, but was re-occupied toward the end of the early aceramic Neolithic or the beginning of the later aceramic Neolithic, *c.* 8800 BC.

The Aceramic Neolithic Settlement

The aceramic Neolithic settlement rapidly grew to become a large village, the remains of which were found wherever the archaeologists dug around the modern houses and cemetery. Since the houses of the prehistoric settlement were much more closely spaced than those of the modern village, we can infer that the population was substantial, probably numbering in the thousands, making Abu Hureyra one of the largest settlements of the aceramic Neolithic period. It was also long-lived, being abandoned early in the ceramic Neolithic period, when pottery was coming into use, and thus stretching over some 2000 years.

The mud-brick buildings of this settlement were rectangular in plan, and they seem to have consisted of storage rooms at ground-floor level, with the living accommodation on an upper floor. The ground-floor rooms were cells with no external doorways, and must have been reached from the upper floor by means of trap doors and ladders. These upper stories were more lightly built. As buildings became decrepit and were replaced time and again, several meters of stratified building remains and occupation debris gradually accumulated.

Changing Patterns in Diet

The first inhabitants of the aceramic Neolithic settlement brought with them domesticated wheat, barley, and pulses. They relied for much of their meat on the hunting of gazelle (and smaller amounts of wild ass and cattle), much as their Epipaleolithic predecessors had done (Legge and Rowley-Conwy 1987). There were also relatively small numbers of sheep

6.13 *Abu Hureyra: the Neolithic settlement covered a limestone promontory jutting into the floodplain of the Euphrates (in the foreground).*

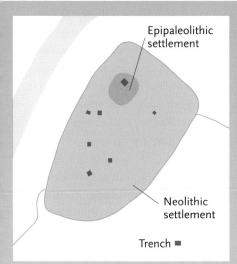

Epipaleolithic
settlement

Neolithic
settlement

Trench ■

6.14 *(Left) Site plan of Abu Hureyra: excavation (the trenches are the small rectangles) and surface indications showed that the aceramic Neolithic settlement became very extensive (the outer area). The Epipaleolithic settlement (the inner area) was found in one trench only, and probably extended over about 1 ha (2.2 acres).*

6.15 *Gazelle was the main source of meat for the Epipaleolithic inhabitants of Abu Hureyra. Gazelles are about the size of sheep or goat, and they moved seasonally around the steppe in large herds. They may have been driven between converging stone walls into stone-built killing enclosures. Many of these so-called "kite enclosures" survive throughout the steppe regions of Syria and Jordan.*

Human Remains

The skeletons from the burials of this phase have produced a new insight into the sexual differentiation of labor at the time. It is often assumed that the women worked mainly in the home, while the men worked the land and tended the flocks. Theya Molleson (1994) has found evidence on many mature females of wear on hip, knee, and ankle joints, leading to arthritis, and she relates this to hours of kneeling and rocking backwards and forwards as women ground seeds on saddle querns. The heavily worn molars of all the adults document the importance of ground cereals.

In the last phase of the aceramic Neolithic settlement, when pottery was coming into domestic use, wear of the molars was less pronounced, but dental caries began to make an appearance (Molleson and Jones 1991). This suggests that people were eating less

bones. The sheep were morphologically wild, but the age and sex profiles suggest that the population was being managed, representing a population in the early stages of domestication. Then, quite suddenly and sharply, the high percentage of gazelle bones drops to a very low figure, while the formerly small numbers of sheep suddenly become the dominant component among the animal bones. Sheep herding became a major element in the economy, and the hunting of gazelle in particular became an activity of minor economic significance.

baked food made from stone-ground flour, and more dishes such as gruel and porridge, which were boiled in a pot.

Overview

The range of information provided by the excavations at Abu Hureyra gives a unique insight into the changes affecting a community at the transition from foraging to farming. They reveal that the process was not a sudden, single shift from one lifestyle to the other, but a more gradual process extending over several centuries, during which domesticates made an ever-increasing contribution to subsistence. The remains of the site's inhabitants themselves also reveal the less desirable impacts of domestication on teeth and bones.

6.16 *At the bottom of Trench E, the excavators dug through more than 1 m (3 ft) of Epipaleolithic occupation to reveal the circular depressions where some of the earliest houses were dug down into the natural subsoil. The black holes are the cavities left where wooden roof supporting posts had decayed. In the upper part of the trench, there is part of a rectangular mud-brick house of the aceramic Neolithic period.*

(see Chapter 4) and some three-dimensional animal carvings from the Natufian. Cauvin pointed to a sudden explosion, in the earliest aceramic Neolithic, of small, three-dimensional figures, some modeled in clay, others carved in stone. The little human figures, when their sex is indicated, are clearly female. There are also many small animal figurines, among which bulls are often recognizable. Cauvin argued that these simple, schematic figurines represented, for the first time in human history, concrete representations of a female divinity and a divine male principle in the form of a bull. He believed that these figurines indicate a profound "psycho-cultural" change in human mentalities, with people for the first time being able to imagine a structured cosmos, differentiating between a "natural" human world and a supernatural world, and representing their most abstract notions in symbolic form. It is a provocative and controversial set of ideas.

The First Large Settlements: Jericho and Çatalhöyük

Robert Braidwood, who in 1948 identified the "hilly flanks of the Fertile Crescent" and worked first in the piedmont and the valleys of the Zagros Mountains in northeast Iraq, was a pioneer in the study of the early Neolithic here. He excavated the site of Jarmo, which became the model of a village society of the first farmers (Braidwood and Howe 1960), and coined the phrase "village farming" to describe the social and economic changes at the beginning of the Neolithic. We can now trace the

beginning of village societies to before the initiation of farming, but certain anomalies in the early Neolithic challenge the idea of the village society as the norm. While Braidwood was at work at Jarmo, Kathleen Kenyon (1957) was excavating Tell es-Sultan, ancient Jericho, in the Jordan Valley; in the early 1960s, James Mellaart (1967) started excavations at Çatalhöyük, on the Konya plain in south-central Turkey. Neither site conformed to the standard idea of early Neolithic farming villages.

Jericho Kenyon's central interest in excavating at Jericho was to investigate the Bronze Age city of biblical fame, but she knew from earlier excavations that there were deep deposits dating to the early Neolithic. Wherever she sank her trenches through the Bronze Age levels, Kenyon reached underlying Neolithic deposits that indicated an earlier settlement of about 2.5 ha (6 acres) in extent, as large as the Bronze Age city. There was no sign of pottery in these early strata, and she therefore named the two principal phases of Neolithic occupation Pre-Pottery Neolithic A and B (PPNA and PPNB, widely used, as already noted, to define cultural or chronological phases throughout the Levant). Radiocarbon dating was becoming available, and

6.17 The early aceramic Neolithic tower at Jericho: *the tower was built of solid stone set in mud mortar and was attached to the inside of the wall of the settlement, rather than the outside, as would be expected if it had a defensive role.*

Kenyon obtained sensational dates that indicated that Jericho had been occupied throughout a long aceramic Neolithic era, stretching between 9600 BC and almost 7000 BC (with an even earlier Natufian episode going back to around 12,000 BC). Even more surprises were in store, however.

Beneath the walls of Bronze Age Jericho, the excavators found that from early in the PPNA phase the settlement had a wall built of stones set in mud, with a rock-cut ditch around it. As the settlement mound had accumulated, the wall had been increased in height a number of times. In one trench, Kenyon found a great cylindrical drum of a tower, built of solid stone set in mud mortar in the PPNA phase [**6.17**]. Strangely, it was attached to the inner side of the wall, whereas defensive bastions usually project from the outside of the wall. Around the base of the tower was a series of very large mud-plastered "bins." The tower had a steep staircase through its core, down which several human corpses had been thrown at the end of its use. We should probably consider the tower, the wall, and the ditch as more symbolic and intended to impress than as actual defenses, for no settlement of remotely similar size has been found anywhere near that might constitute a threat to Jericho (Bar-Yosef 1986).

Çatalhöyük Çatalhöyük was a Neolithic settlement of extraordinary size – 13 ha, or 32 acres – more than five times larger than Jericho [see box: Çatalhöyük, pp. 224–25]. Even more striking than its size is its architecture, the imagery in paint and plaster modeling within the closely packed houses, and the many burials below the plaster floors. How were large and elaborate settlements such as Jericho and Çatalhöyük to be accommodated in the story of the emergence of village farming? Mellaart himself drew on Gordon Childe's list of the characteristics of the earliest cities (Childe 1936), and argued that Çatalhöyük was a precocious urban "supernova," which challenged the orthodox theory that urban civilizations emerged in Mesopotamia around 3000 BC. Certainly, communities that numbered in the thousands could not have operated in the same way as village societies that consisted of a small cluster of farming families. Moreover, the cultural phenomena exhibited at these sites imply elaborate belief systems and complex symbolic representations of a kind that show that social life extended well beyond the everyday demands of obtaining and processing food.

Social Organization

Since the late 1980s, a succession of discoveries has resulted in an array of sites that are clearly not simple villages. Especially in the later part of the aceramic Neolithic, we know of a number of very large communities on the scale of Çatalhöyük, for example Basta and 'Ain Ghazal in Jordan and Abu Hureyra 2 in Syria. Each of these settlements comprised many hundreds of houses, and must have had a population numbering several thousands.

In the Epipaleolithic period, the emergence of larger-scale sedentary communities implies a new type of society, different from the traditional small-scale hunter-gatherer band. In the aceramic Neolithic period, the scale of sedentary societies increases again. If Epipaleolithic sedentary hunter-gatherer communities were five to ten times larger than typical mobile hunter-gatherer bands, then aceramic Neolithic societies could be ten times larger again. Presumably the management of social relations would be complicated exponentially and the regulation of affairs would be critically important, since each community was totally dependent on the intensively exploited territory within one or two hours walk around the settlement.

Anthropological theory says that the larger the group, the more explicit is the exercise of authority and power, and the less egalitarian and more hierarchical the social organization. There are no signs in the aceramic Neolithic of social hierarchy or of individuals with higher status by virtue of their social role. Rather, we are probably looking at segmentary societies, in which a large community would be made up of a number of lineages (Renfrew and Bahn 2004). Lineages might have leaders whose authority and status were acknowledged on grounds of birth or seniority, and the group of lineage leaders might act as some kind of council of elders. The ways in which such segmentary societies may have operated is beginning to be investigated in the current research program at Çatalhöyük (Hodder 1996). In addition, the maintenance of a degree of egalitarianism and the restraint of any tendency for lineage chiefs to develop hierarchical power structures is now beginning to be discussed (e.g. Kuijt 2000a).

One feature of social organization within aceramic Neolithic communities may be seen to change with time. In the early aceramic Neolithic period, houses do not seem to have possessed individual storage facilities. There are indications that storage and tasks relating to food preparation for storage were managed at village level. At **Jerf el Ahmar**, Danielle Stordeur believes that the first large subterranean building was a communal storage facility, placed centrally among the households that it served [see box: Jerf el Ahmar: A Neolithic Village, pp. 218–19]. At **Qermez Dere** in northern Iraq (Watkins 1990; 1992b; 1995), the small village seems to have been zoned into two distinct areas. In one half were single-roomed, semi-subterranean houses with plastered walls and floors; there were no artifacts in them of the kind associated with food processing. Another zone within the settlement had no such houses, but around a rougher building of different design was found almost all the heavy stone equipment for pounding and grinding the hard-seeded food resources of the community. It seems there were separate places for doing distinct tasks, as well as clear ideas about what should and should not be done within the context of the house.

In the later aceramic Neolithic, house architecture is generally more complex, and there are signs that each household became a more self-sufficient unit, with its own storage and food-processing equipment (Byrd 2000). The implications of such a change are more than just economic. Early aceramic Neolithic village communities may have operated as self-organizing, organic social units. Larger settlements would seem to have been structured overall as cohesive village communities, and then internally as household units. The large communities, which would have numbered several thousand people, may then also have been organized further, at a third, intermediate level as lineages, or some other segmentary structure.

Communal Buildings and Rituals

In addition to Jerf el Ahmar and Qermez Dere, other settlements of both the early and the late aceramic Neolithic show signs of having been built to an overall architectural idea, their areas of domestic housing enclosing public areas with community buildings of special purpose. One site is **Çayönü Tepesi** in southeast Turkey (Özdoğan 1999; Özdoğan and Özdoğan 1990). The settlement was established some time in the early aceramic Neolithic and was abandoned at the end of the late aceramic Neolithic, *c.* 6900 BC. For much of its life, the houses were very substantial constructions, of which only their stone and mud foundations survive (Schirmer 1990). At ground level, the large rectangular houses had either a series of parallel walls that prob-

KEY SITE Jerf el Ahmar: A Neolithic Village

How were early Neolithic villages in Southwest Asia organized? Did they have standardized house plans and communal shrines or storage facilities? For an answer to these questions we must look to Jerf el Ahmar, a small Syrian village on the west bank of the Euphrates, occupied during the early aceramic Neolithic period (9600–8800 BC, filling the gap in the occupation of Abu Hureyra – see box, pp. 214–15).

6.18, 6.19 *This large subterranean structure (right) existed at the center of the earliest village at the site of Jerf el Ahmar and was originally roofed. At the end of its life, the roof was dismantled and the supporting posts were pulled out. In one of the empty post-sockets a severed human head was placed. A headless human corpse was spread-eagled in the center of the floor (above right) and the structure was burnt before being filled in; the bones of the corpse were scorched black by the intense fire.*

The site was discovered in the late 1980s and excavated through the 1990s ahead of the completion of a dam that has now drowned another substantial stretch of the Euphrates Valley (Stordeur et al. 1997; 2000; Stordeur 1999). Throughout its existence, the settlement's subsistence needs were supplied by wild animals and by cereals, pulses, and other seeds that were still morphologically wild.

An Aceramic Neolithic Settlement

Because Jerf el Ahmar was occupied only in the aceramic Neolithic, the excavator, Danielle Stordeur, has been able to explore the settlement in the horizontal dimension, seeing how the buildings related to one another. The early village, dating to the first centuries of the early aceramic Neolithic period, had houses of quite diverse plans. Some were simple, small, circular constructions built from lumps of soft limestone that had been cut to resemble the cigar-shaped mud-bricks used at the same period in Jericho. When the collapsed debris of one of these houses was removed, the skull and massive horns of a wild bull were found underneath. This spectacular trophy presumably had hung on the inside wall, as at one of the almost contemporary houses at Hallan Çemi in southeast Turkey and at Çatalhöyük. Other houses were larger and roughly rectilinear in outline, often internally subdivided into rooms. These tended to be at the center of the village, while the smaller, single- and multiple-roomed circular houses were built further away.

ably supported a raised living floor, or, at another stage in the settlement's history, a lattice of such walls that formed many small and doorless cells. These spaces below the living floors probably provided storage areas that could be accessed from above.

The settlement stood on a natural terrace above a small river, and the houses were built at right angles to the river. They form an arc that leaves a large, open, public space at the center of the settlement. The excavators found three buildings in the central "plaza," all different, and all quite unlike the domestic structures. They probably did not all exist at the same time, but their relationship to each other and to the stratified remains of the houses has proved very difficult to establish. It is reasonable to think of them as public buildings for the whole community.

One of the three, called the "skull building," was repeatedly modified and rebuilt. Under one end of the building were three square, stone-built cells full of human bones. One contained a heap of human skulls – hence the building's nickname – and analysis has shown that the pile of skulls had non-human blood poured over it. The disarticulated bones from the same cell are still being analyzed, and to date more than 400 different individuals have been identified. Another of the public buildings was almost square; it was built with a terrazzo floor (one made of small pieces of stone set into plaster) below ground level and had tall, stone monoliths set upright in the floor.

Also in southeast Turkey are two more recently discovered sites, Nevalı Çori and Göbekli Tepe. The small settlement of

An Enigmatic Communal Building

The open central area of the village contained a circular, subterranean structure, 8–9 m (26–30 ft) in diameter, much larger than any of the individual houses; the floor level of this building was fully 2 m (6.6 ft) below the ground level and was made on different levels, creating low "platforms" around the edge. Two thirds of the perimeter of the building was divided by mud-brick walls into two pairs of large cells (that is, walled spaces without doorways), with a smaller cell between the two pairs. The smaller, axial cell had a porthole-like creep hole in the middle of the wall facing the center of the building.

There was no trace of how this complicated structure was used, but its position and the large, doorless cells have led Stordeur to believe that it was a communal storage facility, shared by the whole village.

There is extraordinary information about the end of the life of this building. Before the complex was filled in and obliterated, it was completely emptied, and a headless human corpse was placed, face down, in

the very center. A human head was placed in a socket from which a substantial wooden post had been withdrawn. Finally, the building was burned and the cavity, amounting to some 100 cu. m (3500 cu. ft), was filled with soil.

All of this evidence, plus the fact that the greater part of the structure did not consist of storage cells, has suggested to the excavators that the building also functioned as a place for communal rituals. It is an interesting combination that brings together the shared food-store and the communal rites of the settlement.

In the succeeding phase, the village's center of gravity shifted to the south. There was another large, circular, subterranean

building, but its plan was distinctly different from the earlier one. Around the interior wall was a plastered platform, high enough to serve as a seat. A curb of long stones, their vertical faces carved with a geometric design, formed its edge. Set between the curbstones there had been six juniper posts supporting the roof. This building, too, was finally destroyed and filled in with dirt.

Overview

Jerf el Ahmar is evidence that villages of the early aceramic Neolithic period were structured to represent the organization of the village community, its component households, and the centrality of its communal life.

6.20 *A second communal structure of a quite different kind was built at Jerf el Ahmar when the village expanded. The roof was carried by wooden posts built into the wall, and there were six tree-trunk posts at the angles where the segments of a stone curb met. The stones of the kerb were decorated with pendant relief triangles. This building, too, was deliberately fired and obliterated.*

6.21 Nevalı Çori: the stone walls of the almost square central building at Nevalı Çori are revetments, for the plaster floor was well below ground level. Behind the revetment walls (to the top and to the right) are traces of similar walls for an earlier, larger version of the building. The surviving pillar is partnered by a gaping hole where another pillar once stood. At intervals in the stone bench around the building there were other stone pillars, but they were broken when the building was destroyed, leaving only stumps.

Nevalı Çori (Hauptmann 1993; 1999) is contemporary with Çayönü. It had massive rectangular houses, exactly like those at Çayönü, and they changed their floor plans in step with the Çayönü buildings. A small, almost square building at the center of the village was built with its hard plaster floor below ground level [6.21]. A pair of tall stone slabs, only one of which has survived, was set upright in the plaster floor. The surviving slab is a tall, narrow, T-shaped stone, but it was clearly intended as a stylized human form, for carved below its "shoulders" are the outlines of arms with elbows, hands, and fingers.

One of the German excavators of Nevalı Çori, Klaus Schmidt, went on to explore another site, **Göbekli Tepe**, on a hilltop near Urfa. Here the excavators have found only monumental, dry-stone walled structures that were dug 2 m (6.6 ft)

6.22, 6.23 T-shaped monoliths at Göbekli Tepe: this site consists of a series of special-purpose, subterranean buildings, all but the latest of them circular in plan. They contain free-standing pairs of T-shaped monoliths, similar to those from Nevalı Çori, and more monoliths set against, or partly within, the walls. The monoliths have low relief sculptures on their surfaces, no two stones the same.

6.25 Skull caching: *the clusters of plastered skulls found in the PPNB levels of Jericho were the first of their kind to be found. Since then, a number of other sites of similar date have also produced similar modeled and painted skulls.*

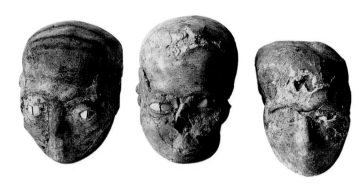

and more into the ground. There is no sign of everyday domestic occupation at or near Göbekli Tepe, and Schmidt (1998; 2000) suspects that the site may have served as a "central place" for the religious practices of a cluster of settlements in the region that are yet to be found. Each curvilinear structure contains one or two pairs of extraordinary tall, T-shaped monoliths [**6.22. 6.23**], and more monoliths are arranged around the perimeters of the structures [**6.24**] (as noted, the subterranean building at Nevalı Çori was similar in this regard). Bas-relief depictions of wild animals (lions, bulls), birds (cranes, storks, swans), snakes, and scorpions cover the surfaces of the mono-

liths. At the end of their lives, the enclosures were deliberately filled with domestic debris, stones, and dirt, and it is the cultural material in this fill that provides the dating. The latest of the structures is a small, rectangular building with two pairs of monolithic pillars – very similar in design and date to the central building at Nevalı Çori.

Burials and Skull Caching

Among the most surprising and striking discoveries in Pre-Pottery Neolithic Jericho in the 1950s were human skulls with facial features modeled in clay and eyes represented by cowrie shells [**6.25**]. Kathleen Kenyon's excavations found numerous burials among the houses, in many of which both cranium and

6.24 Göbekli Tepe: *the largest of the subterranean buildings at Göbekli Tepe is still being excavated. The tops of the central pair of 5-m (16-ft) tall, T-shaped monoliths are emerging. At regular intervals more relief-decorated monoliths are embedded around the dry-stone revetment wall. At the far side of the structure, a stone-flagged bench is beginning to emerge at the base of the revetment wall.*

jaw were missing. Since then, we have had repeated indications that rituals surrounding the burial of the dead within the settlement were important features of community life (Kuijt 2000b). At other sites in the south and central Levant, there are plentiful examples of burials that have been re-visited in order to remove the head; clutches of human skulls apparently were retained for a time and were then cached in small, shallow pits within the settlement. More examples of plastered skulls have also come to light. These are traditions whose roots can be traced back

through the late Epipaleolithic period, from which time archaeologists have found detached human skulls at several sites, including Eynan, as mentioned above. Skulls with facial features modeled in clay or lime plaster, sometimes finished with paint, generally belong to the later aceramic Neolithic.

At no site, however extensively excavated, are there sufficient burials to account for the population. It is clear that certain bodies were selected for burial among the houses or under their floors, and that a minority of those were selected for the detach-

KEY SITE 'Ain Ghazal

The site of 'Ain Ghazal on the outskirts of Amman in Jordan illustrates both the impressive size of some aceramic Neolithic settlements and their pattern of dramatic growth and collapse as environmental degradation set in. It has also yielded the earliest large-scale anthropomorphic statuary, and evidence for the cult of human skulls that characterizes Levantine settlements of this period.

The Settlement and Diet

'Ain Ghazal began life as a typical village of modest size, founded in the later aceramic Neolithic. It shared a number of characteristics with Jericho in its Pre-Pottery Neolithic B phase. The valley-side location required that the village site be terraced. The rectangular mud-brick houses conformed to a particular plan, each with an almost square main room and a smaller anteroom. There were substantial timber posts on either side of the doorway between the two rooms, which helped the mud-brick partition wall to

support the weight of the flat roof. The outside surfaces of the walls were plastered with mud, while the interior surfaces, floors as well as walls, were covered with a thick, white lime plaster, which was renewed every few years.

The people of 'Ain Ghazal grew the common range of cereals and legumes in

fields above the village, which was presumably sited on the valley slope for ease of access to water in the spring below (the Arabic name of the location means "the spring of the gazelle"). They also herded recently domesticated goat, and hunted wild animals.

6.26 *One of four buildings at 'Ain Ghazal, all of which date to a late stage in the history of the settlement, and which are distinctly different from the normal domestic architecture of the settlement. This small circular building has a frequently re-made plaster floor with a large circular hole at the centre. Under the floor, there were carefully constructed channels that may have been designed to carry away liquids poured into the central hole. Gary Rollefson believes that this is a small shrine intended for certain ritual practices.*

ment and further retention of the head. At 'Ain Ghazal in Jordan [see box: 'Ain Ghazal], where there are formal burials and evidence of detached skulls, Gary Rollefson has also found a number of human bodies that were thrown unceremoniously into refuse pits. At Çatalhöyük there may be as many as 68 burials under the floor of a single house, and no burials, or only one or two, in several of the neighboring houses.

It has been suggested that the burial of the dead within the settlement or within the house, and the recovery and treatment of skulls, represents some kind of ancestor cult (Kuijt 2000a, 2000b). If these rites were forms of ancestor reverence, only selected individuals in any generation were given this treatment, and the recovery of heads was even more selective. There are no indications in the form of grave goods that the bodies and skulls were selected on grounds of high status. They may have been leading members of important lineages, but, equally, their selection may have been on the grounds that their bodies or skulls were needed for periodic rituals.

Burials

Like many other communities of the period, the people of 'Ain Ghazal buried their dead beneath the floors of their houses or in the yards outside; also like other communities, they frequently re-opened graves in order to detach and retrieve the heads of the dead. At least one example of a retrieved skull was found to have the facial features modeled in plaster. Skulls were found by the excavators, Gary Rollefson and his team, in small caches of three or more, buried in shallow pits beneath house floors. In some of the areas outside houses they discovered a number of large pits that had been used for the disposal of domestic waste – ashes from the fire, butchery and cooking waste, and the like. Surprisingly, they also found human bodies that had been tossed unceremoniously into these refuse pits. Here was hard evidence that the bodies buried in contracted positions in grave pits, whose heads had frequently been removed, were only a small selection of the total population of the settlement. What cannot be learned, however, is why some were selected for ceremonial burial, while other bodies were simply discarded.

Anthropomorphic Statues

Rollefson (1990; 1998; 2000) found several buildings that do not conform to the norms of domestic architecture. Their different plans and special internal fittings suggest that these were shrines within which rituals were conducted, a theory supported by the dramatic discovery of two caches of half-size human figures, modeled in plaster on armatures of bundled twigs and small branches; these were found buried in pits,

apparently having functioned as ritual objects.

Population Growth and Its Effects

The settlement grew during the last centuries of the late aceramic Neolithic to four times its original size (i.e., to around 10–14 ha, or 25–35 acres), too rapid to have been the result of population growth within the community. Rollefson and his team hypothesize that other late aceramic Neolithic settlements further west were collapsing at this time, and refugee groups moved to join surviving settlements elsewhere. This additional population put further pressure on economies that were already close to ecological disaster. The cycle is illustrated at 'Ain Ghazal, where land was being tilled, exposing the soil to increased erosion, and trees were being cleared to

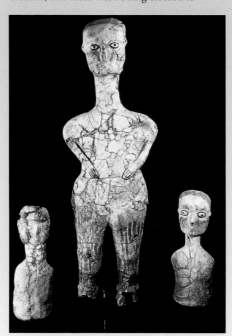

satisfy the demand for wood for domestic fires and for the preparation of lime for the vast quantities of lime plaster that were used. The intensive herding of goats only compounded the problem by preventing regeneration of the trees that helped to stabilize the soil. Population growth and subsistence activities generated a downward spiral of environmental degradation (Köhler-Rollefson 1992).

When life was no longer sustainable for such a large population, groups of people left 'Ain Ghazal to take up a new way of life, based on semi-nomadic herding and a modest amount of agriculture. Since the better-watered lands of the Mediterranean woodland zone had been despoiled, the hypothesis runs, people took to the extensive areas of moist steppe and semi-arid lands. Only a small community survived at 'Ain Ghazal itself, and they moved across the stream and built a small settlement close to the spring. There they could grow some crops in a few small plots in the valley bottom.

The story of 'Ain Ghazal appears to be one of the earliest examples of humanly induced ecological degradation followed by population collapse, a pattern that was to recur many times in different parts of the world.

6.27 *Three of the 32 plaster figures that were found buried in two caches. Of the 25 pieces in the first cache, 13 were full statues and 12 were busts. In the second cache, there were two full figures, three two-headed busts, and two fragmentary heads. The full figures are about half life-size. All were formed on armatures of reeds, and are made of the same lime plaster as was used on the walls and floors of the houses.*

KEY SITE Çatalhöyük

Çatalhöyük is one of the largest and most important Neolithic sites in Southwest Asia, and has drawn spectacular attention to the symbolic and cultural florescence that accompanied the rise of farming communities in the region. This extraordinary site was discovered in 1958 by British archaeologist James Mellaart (1967), who between 1961 and 1965 showed that Çatalhöyük was both very large (13 ha, or 32 acres) and very long-lived (there was 17 m, or about 56 ft, of stratified occupation debris). It was founded around 7300 BC, toward the end of the aceramic Neolithic period, and was occupied until at least 6200 BC (the last two occupation levels have not yet been radiocarbon dated). Mellaart's dramatic descriptions and vivid interpretation of the site have made Çatalhöyük famous worldwide.

In addition to believing that Çatalhöyük anticipated Mesopotamian civilization by more than two millennia, he thought that the site had been a cult center for the worship of a great mother goddess, prefiguring the ecstatic Anatolian cult of the goddess Cybele, famous in Roman times. In 1993, Ian Hodder (1996; 2004) resumed work at the site with an ambitious 25-year research plan and a determination to make Çatalhöyük accessible and comprehensible to the thousands who visit it. We are now seeing the first fruits of that program.

Location

The Konya Plain is the dry bed of a huge Pleistocene lake, lying in the middle of the Anatolian Plateau at an elevation of just over 1000 m (3300 ft). The area has the lowest rainfall in Turkey, only 200–250 mm (8–10 in) annually, too little for dry farming. The rivers that fed the former lake have formed alluvial fans around the margins of the plain, and Çatalhöyük was established far out on the largest of those fans. Braided streams provided the essential water, and the combination of alluvial soils, reed marshes, and seasonal swamps made the location potentially very productive.

6.28 *Detail from a painted plaster panel on the wall of a house. The overall scene shows many human figures around a massive wild bull. Here a man, painted in brick-red, runs or dances. He carries a bow and wears a strange, spotted costume around his waist.*

Archaeological survey has shown that there is a scatter of settlements earlier than Çatalhöyük, and a few more dating to the period after the Neolithic mound was abandoned, but no other site of the same date as Çatalhöyük on the alluvial fan. It seems that Çatalhöyük represents the coming together of a number of pre-existing communities at a new location beside the main stream running across the fan. The whole area was packed tight with housing, and the new super-community must have numbered several thousand people.

Architecture and Art

The architecture of the settlement is strikingly unusual. Houses were built like rectangular boxes pushed together, the four walls of one touching the walls of the four adjacent houses. There are almost no lanes or other approaches at ground level. Rather, the flat rooftops served as the means of access; each house had a trapdoor in the roof and a wooden ladder-like staircase against one wall, reaching down to the floor. Each house consisted of a rectangular main room, usually with a secondary, smaller room opening off it, used for storage. The floor of the main room had a series of low platforms of different heights around a square central area. The walls and floors were repeatedly plastered with a mud plaster made from the white marl of the Pleistocene lakebed. Floors were often painted red, and red, black, and white were also used to paint patterns, motifs, or whole scenes on the walls.

When houses needed to be replaced, the precious wooden roof support posts and main beams were withdrawn, and the mud roof was collapsed. The upper part of the walls was thrown down into the interior until the area was level; the new house could then be built with its walls sitting on the top of the stumps of the old. Because all the debris had to be disposed of within the walls of the old house, and because the walls (and mud roof) were thick, the buried wall stumps might be more than 2 m (6.6 ft) tall. Occasionally, when a house fell out of use, the roof would be removed so that neighboring households could use the considerable space for disposing of refuse.

Any of the accumulated coats of white mud wash on the interior walls of a house might have been decorated with red designs. Some of the surviving wall paintings consist of geometric patterns, while others are figurative. The scenes depicted include one with human figures engaged in a variety of activities, all centered around a colossal wild bull. Another painting shows schematically represented human figures lacking heads,

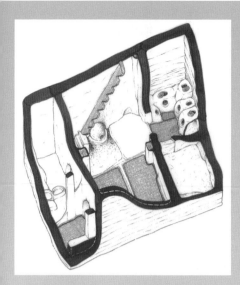

6.29 *A typical house interior. The main room was entered by a ladder from a trapdoor in the roof. A smaller room, accessed by a low doorway from the main room, was used for storage. Under the trapdoor and ladder, there was a clay oven and an open hearth for cooking. The floor of the main room was arranged in a series of plastered platforms at different levels.*

surrounded by vultures. In addition to paintings, a number of houses had three-dimensional sculptures attached to the walls. These might take the form of a bull's head, modeled in mud plaster around the actual cranium and horns of a bull. There are also sculpted goats' heads, and large, leopard-like cats. Finally, there are examples of human figures schematically represented in female form.

Burials

Mellaart found many burials below the plastered platforms of the houses, and the renewed excavations under Ian Hodder have shown that, while some houses have no burials, others may have as many as 68 bodies buried under the floor (including infants interred during the construction of the house).

Given the life of a mud-brick house of around 70 years, it is inconceivable that a family group living in a single-roomed house could have suffered on average one death per year. Some houses seem to have been special, and to have attracted many burials, perhaps functioning as the focal household in a lineage, or something similar.

Economy

The community relied on the farming of domesticated crops of cereals and legumes, and the herding of large flocks of sheep. The rich alluvium of the fan would seem to have been ideal for productive farming, but environmental research has shown that the locality around the settlement was prone to seasonal flooding. It now seems that the cultivated fields and the pastures must have been several kilometers away.

Exploitation of resources over a wide area is just one more of the peculiarities of Çatalhöyük. Its chipped stone tools were almost entirely made from obsidian, a volcanic glass, the geological origin of which was in the mountains of Cappadocia, about 125 km (78 miles) away. The timbers used in the houses were pines and slow-growing junipers brought from the mountains to the south and west. The people of Çatalhöyük also acquired venison from deer that would only have been found in the forested mountains.

With its extraordinary repertory of representational art, its size, and its complex reliance on distant resources, Çatalhöyük has a great deal still to reveal to the patient questioning of the large, international, and multidisciplinary research teams working on the site.

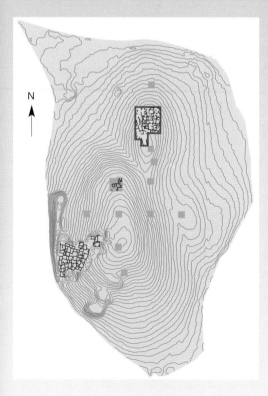

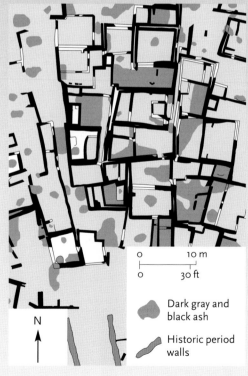

0   10 m
0   30 ft

Dark gray and black ash

Historic period walls

6.30, 6.31 *The east mound of Çatalhöyük (there is also a smaller, later, Chalcolithic period mound immediately to the west) is Neolithic from top to bottom (far left). A depth of more than 17 m (56 ft) of accumulated building debris extends over 13 ha (32 acres). Mellaart's excavations were in the southwest part of the mound. When the new research project explored another area near the north end of the site, they found similar architecture – the rectangular houses built against each other, with few lanes or alleys for ground-level access (left).*

The Beginning of Cultivation and Plant and Animal Domestication

Plant Domestication

Southwest Asia possessed the largest number of potential domesticates in the world – that is, plants that could be successfully and productively domesticated. In particular, there were chickpeas, several wild cereals, and several species of legume (peas, beans, and lentils). The main wild cereals were two species of wheat – generally known as einkorn and emmer – as well as barley. All of these would grow naturally in hilly country with rainfall of more than 250 mm (10 in) per year, which was how Robert Braidwood first identified "the hilly flanks of the Fertile Crescent" as a key area for research into the beginnings of farming. Fifty years of research and debate have produced theoretical distribution maps of the various species at the critical period, the end of the Epipaleolithic.

Domestication is defined by archaeobotanists as the altered status of a formerly wild species, when it has undergone genetic change sufficient to make it a new species that is effectively dependent on farmers for cultivation. To differentiate the domesticated from the wild species, the archaeobotanist looks for larger seeds, and, with the cereals, a change in the rachis, the tiny joining piece that connects the grain to the ear [**6.32**]. (The legumes are slow to change size, and the emergence of their domestication is therefore impossible to define.) With the cereals, the size differences in the grains are often not statistically distinct enough to distinguish domesticated from wild, and so carbonized rachis fragments can be the clinching factor. In wild cereals the rachis is brittle, and the grains are easily dropped as they ripen. But there is in nature a small minority of plants with a tough rachis, so that grains are retained on the plant. Complete rachises in a sample, with neat scars where

they separated from the ear and the grain, are evidence of a wild species. Broken rachis fragments indicate that grains with tough rachises have been harvested, suggesting the domesticated form.

The picture of plant domestication is likely to be something of a mosaic, since people in different parts of the region found it advantageous to intensify their cultivation of locally available species at different times. Present information indicates that cultivation of cereals was beginning at a non-intensive level (called "pre-domestication agriculture") in the early aceramic Neolithic period, or even at the very end of the Epipaleolithic period, from southeast Turkey through western Syria to Israel and the Jordan Valley (Garrard 1999). "Pre-domestication agriculture" means that methods of cultivation and harvesting were not sufficiently intensive as to induce genetic change in a domesticated species.

The British archaeobotanist Sue Colledge (1998) has recently tried multivariate analysis of the seed assemblages from several final Epipaleolithic and early aceramic Neolithic sites in Syria. She found that there were three assemblages at one long-lived site, starting with the harvesting of the wild cereals and grasses (plus the accidentally incorporated seeds of other plants), and finishing with the farming of domesticated species (together with the weeds of cultivation). She therefore suggests that the intermediate spectrum of cereals, grasses, and "weeds" represents pre-domestication agriculture.

The earliest evidence of the morphological changes that announce full domestication of a plant population comes from Abu Hureyra, where domestic rye appeared in the last few centuries of the Epipaleolithic period (Moore et al. 2001) [see Abu Hureyra box, pp. 214–15]. Abu Hureyra was abandoned soon after that, however, and rye was never a significant contributor to the harvests of later, Neolithic settlements.

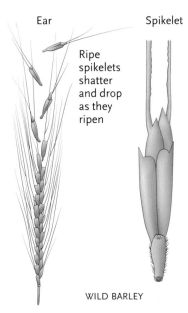

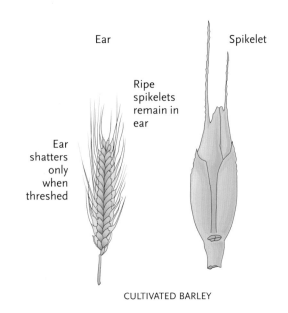

6.32 Wild and cultivated barley: the differences are slight, and the difficulty of identification is compounded by the fact that the archaeobotanist sees only fragments, never the complete ear, and the carbonized fragments have been distorted by being burnt. The cultivated grains are a little fatter, and the rachis (the piece that connects the grain to the ear) of the wild form is usually complete, while the tough rachis of the domesticated species is usually broken by threshing.

Ear   Spikelet

Ripe spikelets shatter and drop as they ripen

WILD BARLEY

Ear   Spikelet

Ripe spikelets remain in ear

Ear shatters only when threshed

CULTIVATED BARLEY

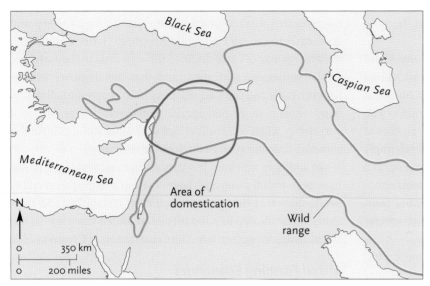

6.33, 6.34 *The domestication of sheep:* wild sheep were widely distributed in mountainous, hilly and piedmont landscapes in final Pleistocene times, as shown by the more extensive, gray outline. The area of southeast Turkey and north Syria within which sheep were probably first domesticated is enclosed by a tint outline. Wild sheep (below) and wild goat appear very similar, because the fleece that we associate with sheep has been bred into the domesticated species relatively recently.

Domesticated wheat and barley occur at several early aceramic Neolithic sites in the Jordan Valley and in southern Syria. At Jericho, just north of the Dead Sea, the evidence of domesticated barley, einkorn wheat, and emmer wheat was recovered in the form of fragments accidentally incorporated into mud bricks with chopped straw (Kenyon 1957; Hopf 1983). The Israeli archeobotanist Mordechai Kislev, who examined the carbonized barley from Netiv Hagdud, only a few kilometers to the north, found both morphologically domesticated (larger and fatter) grains and the smaller wild form (Bar-Yosef et al. 1991). The larger-grained type constituted 30 percent of the sample, whereas it should not exceed 10 percent in nature. He therefore argued that this percentage signified emergent domestication, though others are doubtful.

There is also evidence of domesticated as well as morphologically wild barley and wheat at another site, Iraq ed-Dubb, on the Jordanian side of the Jordan Valley (Colledge 1991). It may be that people cultivated some barley, but continued harvesting wild stands while they were available; or that their cultivation and harvesting methods only slowly brought about the genetic shift that we call domestication (Zohary and Hopf 2000).

Only at the end of the Epipaleolithic and into the early aceramic Neolithic period did some communities find it necessary to begin to practice cultivation; later, they moved on to more intensive modes of harvesting that produced the domesticated species. By the later aceramic Neolithic, the relatively intensive cultivation of domesticated species became the norm throughout most of Southwest Asia, as far east as southwest Iran, and as far west as central Turkey. It is notable that people intensified their cultivation at a time when Southwest Asia was actually recovering from the Younger Dryas reversal and moving toward a climatic optimum. This implies that their greater investment in labor was not a response to environmental change; it would

seem, rather, that they turned to more intensive farming methods as a result of population pressure or other social reasons.

It is thus clear that the adoption of intensive cultivation (with harvesting practices that induced the genetic changes that we call domestication) began around the end of the early aceramic Neolithic period. By the beginning of the later aceramic Neolithic, around 8800 BC, domesticated cereals are found very widely around the arc of the "hilly flanks" zone. Barley was the main cereal crop in the south of the Levant, but further north, einkorn wheat was the staple. Almost certainly, different species were the focus of attention in different parts of Southwest Asia. DNA studies are beginning to show that some of the so-called "founder crops" (einkorn wheat and chickpea in particular) most probably originated in their domesticated form in southeast Anatolia (modern Turkey).

Hunting and Herding

Similarly, the first intimations of animal domestication occur around the transition from the early to the later phases of the aceramic Neolithic. As well as plants, Southwest Asia possessed the world's largest number of potential animal domesticates. Epipaleolithic and early aceramic Neolithic hunter-gatherers were hunting species of deer (especially fallow deer in the Levant), species of gazelle, now-extinct zebra-sized equids resembling wild ass or onager (*Equus hemionus*), sheep, goat, cattle, pig, fox, hare, and many more small mammals. The most important hunted species differed from one part of the region to another, but the spectrum of hunted species remained remarkably constant between the Epipaleolithic and the early aceramic Neolithic.

The identification of animal domestication is cautious and complex. Many obvious morphological changes in an animal species – changes in the animal's size or shape of horn, for example – can be explained in terms of the wild animal as well as the domesticated one, as can details of sex or age profiles of remains within a species. More young animals killed can imply either deliberate herding or deliberate hunting strategies, and the presence of more older female animals could result either from the specific culling of young males from a herd or from the fact that male and female animals of a particular species tended to live apart.

The best evidence comes from long-lived settlement sites, and it suggests that animal domestication generally came later than plant cultivation. The first species to be domesticated (setting aside the dog, which was not used as a source of meat) were goat, sheep, cattle, and pig; while dates for sheep and goat domestication have tended to decrease in the light of sustained research and debate, the dates for cattle and pig domestication have moved in the opposite direction. We have more information about animal domestication than we do about plant domestication, simply because animal bone survives better than plant remains, and is more easily recovered in suitable quantities for research (Harris 1996). Bones from the domesticated herds usually dominate samples, where they are present, and the range of animals hunted is much reduced.

Wild sheep and goat were hunted throughout most of the "hilly flanks" zone and westwards through southern Anatolia; they prefer hilly and, in the case of goats, mountainous terrain. Bruce Smith (1995) has noted that the earliest dates for domesticated sheep and goat have come from sites in those areas where the animals were most significantly represented among the hunted animals of earlier sites. Thus, the earliest dates for goat domestication come from western Iran, in particular a small site called Ganj Dareh, where the age and sex ratios change in the early part of the late aceramic Neolithic, along with a statistically significant decrease in size. Within a short time, domesticated goat is found in the mountainous northeast of Iraq as well. The earliest occurrences of domesticated sheep (which, like goats, were hairy and horned – the woolly fleece is a relatively recent feature that has been bred into sheep) are found at sites in southeast Turkey and northern Syria, also early in the later aceramic Neolithic [6.33, 6.34].

Pigs are relatively easy to domesticate, and the area within Southwest Asia where pig provided significant amounts of meat stretches from Lebanon and southern Syria to southeast Turkey. Recent detailed work on the cattle bones from the long-lived settlement of Çayönü in southeast Turkey by the French archaeozoologist Daniel Helmer has shown that cattle were domesticated there at practically the same time as sheep and goat, early in the later aceramic Neolithic. Helmer found that the average size of cattle declined through time in the early part of the settlement's lifespan, and that the disparity in size between bulls and cows decreased as bulls became smaller. Perhaps smaller, more manageable bulls were preferred – not surprising, when one realizes that a wild bull stood taller at the shoulder than the average modern Western man.

In addition, new sites in Cyprus, where cattle and pig bones have been found alongside those of sheep and goat (and fallow deer), show that these species had been introduced and were either domesticated or substantially managed there late in the 8th millennium BC [see box: The Colonization of Cyprus].

Mixed Farming Economies

In sum, therefore, we can say that farming practices probably began sometime in the early aceramic Neolithic, and became generally more intensive around the end of that period, c. 8800 BC. By the later aceramic Neolithic most communities were relying on cultivated crops of pulses and cereals, together with domesticated sheep and goat, and in places domesticated cattle and pig. Alongside these observations, we can set another: there are many more later aceramic Neolithic settlements known to us than early aceramic Neolithic ones. Is this evidence of expanding population numbers? Can we link the adoption of intensive crop cultivation and animal herding with population growth? If so, did the production of more food encourage population expansion, or did population pressure force the adoption of more productive subsistence strategies? None of these questions is easy to answer on present evidence.

The Evidence of Ali Kosh One site at which we can observe some of the process of change in subsistence strategy is a small mound called Ali Kosh on the alluvial plain in southwest Iran (Hole and Flannery 1967; Flannery 1969). As we have seen, in the Epipaleolithic period, the hunting and gathering strategy of the people occupying the caves and rockshelters of the valleys of the Zagros Mountains changed, as people adopted what Flannery called a "broad-spectrum" hunting strategy combined with greater use of stored harvests of wild grasses, cereals, and pulses. The little village of mud-brick houses at Ali Kosh, out on the plain beyond the mountain valleys, represented the next stage but one in the sequence toward farming. To establish a permanent village community there, the settlers must have brought with them seed corn from domesticated crops. That step of first cultivation and the development of domesticated forms had already taken place.

Ali Kosh was established beside a seasonally marshy area from which food plants could be collected and where domesticated crops could be grown. The animal bones from the site

KEY DISCOVERY The Colonization of Cyprus

Recent discoveries on Cyprus have thrown new light not only on the early colonization of this island but also on the development of farming communities on the adjacent mainland – but they have also posed intriguing new questions. Up to the 1990s the island's Neolithic cultures had not been as extensively studied as later periods, since they seemed to lag behind the mainland by several millennia. This changed when archaeologists began to find new remains belonging to a much earlier occupation of the island.

First, an 11-year-old boy with an interest in archaeological exploration found the remarkable rockshelter of Aetokremnos at Akrotiri, on the southern coast of Cyprus. The American excavator Alan Simmons has concluded that this site was used around the end of the Epipaleolithic period by hunter-gatherers who left the butchered remains of hundreds of pygmy hippopotamus, a now-extinct species unique to Cyprus (Simmons 2001). These hunter-gatherers may have been seasonal visitors to the island, though it is also possible that Akrotiri was a hunting and butchering camp for a permanent community that had established itself elsewhere on the island.

The second surprise came from the site of Parekklishia-Shillourokambos, which has produced a sequence of dated occupation levels that extends back from the 7th millennium BC (the previously assumed date of colonization) to the mid-9th millennium BC (Guilaine and Briois 2001). Then, north of Paphos, Edgar Peltenburg and his team found a series of deep shafts below the Chalcolithic (4th–3rd millennium) settlement of Kissonerga-Mylouthkia (Peltenberg 2000).

The shafts contained no pottery, and radiocarbon dates on charcoal within them place them in the mid-9th to 8th millennium BC. Mylouthkia and Shillourokambos make it clear that Cyprus was occupied from at least the later aceramic Neolithic period.

Implications for Studying Domestication

The inhabitants of Shillourokambos enjoyed the meat of sheep and goat, cattle, pigs, and fallow deer; they also grew cereals and pulses. Botanists and zoologists are sure that none of these species would have been present on the island in the Pleistocene or early Holocene periods, implying that the first colonists must have introduced them to the island, and that they were already domesticated – it is beyond imagination to think of colonists sharing their boats with wild bulls and cows. The middle of the 9th millennium BC is not extraordinarily early for the possession of domesticated cereals and legumes, but the domesticated sheep, goat, cattle, and pig are remarkably early, and it is hard to find any mainland site with domesticated cattle at such a date. The best match for the suite of domesticated plants and animals at that time is from sites deep inland, in the Euphrates Valley of northern Syria and in southeast Turkey. The presence of fallow deer is a

6.36 *The large Mediterranean islands had quite a different fauna from the surrounding mainland, having been isolated for millions of years. Lacking predators, Cyprus had dwarfed varieties of both hippopotamus (above) and elephant. The arrival of human hunting parties around 10,500 BC soon brought an end to the island's native species.*

double puzzle. The species has never been domesticated, so their presence on Cyprus implies that the first settlers brought animals to the island in order to establish a breeding population to hunt. Yet there are no sites on the mainland coast whose inhabitants hunted fallow deer to a significant extent at this date.

The new evidence from Cyprus highlights the way in which colonist farmers brought domestic plants and animals to new areas from a very early period. It also indicates how much more is still to be learned about the early Neolithic, both of Cyprus and the adjacent mainland.

6.35 *The limestone headland of Aetokremnos at Akrotiri, Cyprus. In a collapsed rockshelter, animal bones were found with hearths, chipped stone tools and sea shells. Pygmy hippo bones account for 74 percent of the bones, accompanied by fish remains, bird bones, and a few dwarf elephants. There were four bones of fallow deer and a few of pig, neither of which were native to the island.*

show that the inhabitants also consumed mutton. Since wild sheep would not have been found living on the alluvial plains of southern Mesopotamia, it follows that the sheep were already controlled and managed and were brought there. The successive strata at Ali Kosh show the settlement becoming more and more solidly established, as the mud-brick buildings become larger, more complex, and more substantially built. The subsistence strategy changes in step, and reliance on cultivated crops grows steadily as the use of collected wild plants declines in importance.

The microcosm of Ali Kosh seems to represent a general but fragmentary pattern in the macrocosm of the aceramic Neolithic of Southwest Asia. Communities either developed their own domesticated plants or, when they needed to intensify the productivity of plant foods, obtained some already domesticated seed from neighbors. Paleobotanists tend to believe that each of the "founder" species was domesticated only once in one specific area of its natural range (Zohary 1996). Applying that principle, the spread of the cultivation of domesticated crops is to be accounted for by the spreading of domesticated seed and farming practice around the whole of the "hilly flanks" zone.

While one or two settlements of the earlier aceramic Neolithic period are large, there is a substantial number of such large communities in the later aceramic Neolithic. The ecotone situations where communities of hunter-gatherers numbering many hundreds or thousands of people could operate successfully were relatively few. However, once societies had shifted the balance to reliance on farmed crops, and once they also had flocks of domesticated sheep and goat, they could find many more locations where their substantial numbers could be sustained by mixed farming. The large-scale communities of the later aceramic Neolithic, such as Abu Hureyra in north Syria, Çatalhöyük in central Turkey, and 'Ain Ghazal in Jordan, all had populations of several thousand people and existed over many centuries. There are social implications that will be taken up in the next section, as well as an ecological dimension that we shall consider below.

Social Exchange and Networking

The communities we have been considering did not exist in isolation. Long-distance exchanges show that people were in touch with one another, and there is evidence that they shared cultural traits, adopting and incorporating new ones when they arose. The existence of exchange networks can be seen through the medium of obsidian and marine shells that occur on many sites that are hundreds of kilometers from the obsidian sources, and often distant from the sea.

The obsidian exchange networks and their geological sources in Neolithic Southwest Asia were first identified by Colin Renfrew, in collaboration with geologists Jim Dixon and E. Cann (Renfrew et al. 1968; see also Renfrew and Dixon 1976; Renfrew and Bahn 2004). They identified and characterized four key sources of obsidian, two in central and two in eastern Turkey, and correlated obsidian artifacts from early Neolithic sites with their geological sources. Further analysis by Renfrew showed that communities relatively close to a major source (Çatalhöyük, for example, is about 125 km (78 miles) west of the source of its obsidian) were found to have used obsidian for more than 80 percent of their chipped-stone needs.

Sites that were further away had rapidly declining usage, related to a significant extent to distance from the source. Renfrew proposed networks of "down-the-line" exchange. Each community kept and used a proportion of the obsidian that it received, but would exchange the rest with communities that were further away. Such exchanges carried obsidian from central Turkey as far as southern Jordan, and from sources in eastern Turkey to sites in southwest Iran. Such minute quantities as reached the furthest sites (about one piece of obsidian in every thousand pieces of chipped stone) were not of economic significance. Rather, they were elements in systems of social exchange, whereby the transfer of goods is embedded in, and a token of, the social relations between the partners who engage in the exchanges.

Another component in the network of exchanges is the complicated practice of preparing blades using the naviform core or bi-directional core methods already mentioned (p. 213). Instead of removing blades by pivoting the core a little after each removal, the flint knapper would prepare both ends of the core, and remove blades alternately from either end. Only a sophisticated user or an experienced worker would be able to recognize that the finished artifact had been made on such a flake derived from such a core. The very widespread adoption of this later aceramic Neolithic technology illustrates how communities, whatever their cultural preferences in terms of architecture or details of burial rite, nevertheless chose to participate in a commonwealth of tool types, in particular projectile points.

The shared cultural traits grew in number, especially in the later aceramic Neolithic, and their geographical extent grew wider and wider. This cluster of cultural phenomena was first identified and named by Kathleen Kenyon at Jericho; she called it the PPNB (Pre-Pottery Neolithic B) culture, as we have seen. Unfortunately, different archaeologists use different traits to define their idea of the culture, making it difficult to define and map an extensive PPNB culture. Jacques Cauvin (2001) saw the PPNB culture as a dominant, expansionist one, moving into southeast Turkey as local communities adopted it in preference to their indigenous culture, and being carried into other regions by an expanding population. Alternatively, the PPNB phenomenon has been interpreted as an interaction sphere (Bar-Yosef and Belfer-Cohen 1989), the result of cultural exchange between previously separate groups. This concept has been explored with great sophistication by Colin Renfrew (1986). Using his model of peer polity interaction (discussed in Chapter 1), we can watch the intensification and expansion of exchange networks in goods and symbolic cultural traits during the later aceramic Neolithic period. More and more communities chose to join this attractive and culturally dynamic sphere by adopting certain cultural practices, doubtless highly significant symbolically, and applying them in their own terms. In other words, there is no trend to an over-arching cultural uniformity, as Cauvin suggested; rather, each community embraced into its particular circumstances certain traits, be they technological, architectural, concerned with ritual, or involving the burial of the dead.

Transformation and the Ceramic Neolithic, c. 6900–6000 BC

Throughout Southwest Asia there is a marked discontinuity between the earlier, aceramic Neolithic and the later, ceramic Neolithic. The labels "aceramic" and "ceramic" imply that the significant difference between the two halves of the Neolithic is the addition of pottery to the techno-cultural repertory. In fact, in almost every part of Southwest Asia there were also significant changes in settlement type and location, architecture, the advent of dental caries (implying changes in diet and food preparation), and many other aspects of cultural life.

The Levant

Most work on this transformational period has been done in the southern Levant. Here there was a relatively short period of only a few centuries between the adoption of intensive mixed farming in the later aceramic Neolithic and what has been described as either a system collapse or a major transformation of farming societies and their economies. Jericho and more recently excavated late aceramic Neolithic settlements came to an end at different times in the later 8th millennium BC, and the evidence for the following centuries comprises merely a few small, short-lived sites with relatively ephemeral architectural remains. There is a huge contrast between these new sites and the size and solidity of the mud-brick and plaster settlements of the aceramic Neolithic.

Some archaeologists have argued that there was a climatic optimum in the earliest millennia of the Holocene period, which was brought to an end by a phase of reduced rainfall and serious aridification by the end of the 8th millennium BC; but the evidence for such a climatic change is slight. Others have proposed that the Pre-Pottery Neolithic B communities, with

their intensive cultivation and dependence on herds of goats, put too great a strain on their immediate environments. Gary Rollefson and his team, working at 'Ain Ghazal [see box, pp. 222–23], believe that they have reconstructed the history of this dramatic rise in population, followed by its rapid fall and the transformation of that community to a quite different way of life (Köhler-Rollefson 1992).

The story of 'Ain Ghazal's over-exploitation of its fragile environment may tell us what happened more widely in the southern Levant. If the landscape could not support intensive cultivation of crops and intensive pasturing of goats, then communities probably began to disperse into smaller groups, and to differentiate into small villages of farmers, or groups of nomadic pastoralists. There were probably also communities who found a solution somewhere between the two, maintaining a permanent village settlement in which some people lived and farmed year round, while others took away the village flocks to pasture in the semi-arid steppe for large parts of each year.

Syria and Turkey

In Syria and southeast Turkey, salvage archaeology in the Euphrates Valley has brought to light a number of Neolithic sites, almost all aceramic Neolithic in date. Abu Hureyra is a typical example, its aceramic Neolithic occupation continuing into the ceramic Neolithic, but only for a very short while. It was then abandoned, as other late aceramic Neolithic settlements had been – but there is no evidence of settlement sites of the ceramic Neolithic to replace them. This implies that populations moved elsewhere, as in the southern Levant, or shifted to a life of nomadic pastoralism in smaller communities. The best evidence for the appearance of nomadic pastoralism comes from the work of Andrew Garrard (Garrard et al. 1988) in northern Jordan. Garrard's team found hunter-gatherer sites in the semi-arid zone dating from the Epipaleolithic and early Neolithic periods. On sites dating to the very end of the aceramic Neolithic, significant amounts of domesticated goat bones replaced the bones of hunted gazelle, signifying the presence of nomadic pastoralists.

There is also a neat complementarity between the end of the large aceramic Neolithic settlements in the Euphrates drainage and the earliest evidence of settlement further west, toward the Mediterranean coast. In the 'Amuq basin west of Aleppo, in Syria, there was intensive occupation from the beginning of the ceramic Neolithic and on through the Chalcolithic period (Copper Age), and the Bronze and Iron ages. But none of the sites investigated have shown any evidence of occupation earlier than about 6900 BC.

In central Turkey we have only Çatalhöyük, which seems to bridge this period, to show us what was happening during this transformation. Nevertheless, Çatalhöyük too seems to have been abandoned some centuries later, no earlier than 6200 BC. We do not yet know why, but recent intensive survey work in the Konya plain around Çatalhöyük has shown that for the following period (the early Chalcolithic, starting around 6000 BC) there were several small sites scattered around the area. There was never another large settlement like Çatalhöyük.

Iraq and Iran

Across northern Mesopotamia, between the Syrian Euphrates and the Tigris in Iraq, a rash of small farming villages sprang up in the ceramic Neolithic period. The earlier, aceramic Neolithic sites were usually situated on the flanks of hill country or on terraces above the major river valleys – that is, in situations that would also have appealed to their predecessors, the sedentary hunter-gatherers. The new villages of the ceramic Neolithic period are scattered across the rolling plains, firmly in farming territory. This shifting of location is best documented in northern Iraq, where aceramic Neolithic sites occur in a range of limestone hills, the Jebel Sinjar, an outlying ripple of the Taurus Mountains further north. By contrast, survey work on the plains to the north and south of the Jebel Sinjar has produced a record of village sites that go back to the beginning of the ceramic Neolithic, but no earlier.

Clearly, there was a complete switch in the preferred location for settlements. The new villages produced distinctive and technologically sophisticated pottery, and their simple mud-brick architecture shows little resemblance to the buildings of the aceramic Neolithic period. On the other hand, chipped-stone tool technology, and in particular the taste for certain kinds of projectile point, show distinct continuity with earlier cultural traditions.

In the eastern part of the arc of the "hilly flanks" zone, the best-known region is in southwest Iran, where Frank Hole and Kent Flannery found no settlements of the aceramic Neolithic period in their study area in the Khorammabad Valley. Instead, they found that communities had moved out of the intermontane valleys onto the eastern edge of the alluvial plains of the major rivers that flow to the head of the Persian Gulf, a good example being Ali Kosh (Hole and Flannery 1967). With the passage of time, through the ceramic Neolithic and the following periods down to the Bronze Age, the number of village sites within their second study area on the alluvial plain of Khuzistan grew and grew. Ali Kosh itself was located close to an area of seasonal marshland, which allowed the growing of crops of cereals and pulses in the wet season. But there was a strict limit to such opportune locations in an area with annual rainfall insufficient to support dry farming. We must assume that, as the number of settlements began to grow, people were learning to manipulate groundwater resources and moving toward irrigation-based agriculture.

The social and cultural experiments of the aceramic Neolithic period were over – their societies were supplanted by very different cultures. Their rich architectural traditions and their imagery and symbolism disappear, and the following period belongs to a different world.

Summary and Conclusions

For more than 70 years, the focus of most researchers' interest in the period that we have surveyed has been in the origins of farming. From that point of view, we have seen that changes to the subsistence and settlement strategies of hunter-gatherers were the critically important precursor to the beginning of cultivation and the adoption of animal herding. To understand these changes, it has been necessary to go back to the end of the Last Glacial Maximum, *c.* 18,000 BC, when Epipaleolithic hunter-gatherers began to exploit their resources in new ways. In response to local pressures – at Abu Hureyra in response to the declining availability of plant food resources as a result of the Younger Dryas climatic reversal – communities began to cultivate certain crops, especially varieties of wheat, barley, lentils, peas, or beans. As cultivation and harvesting methods intensified, recognizably domesticated forms of wheat and barley began to appear late in the early aceramic Neolithic period, and the farming of cereals and pulses became widespread at the beginning of the later aceramic Neolithic. Soon afterwards people began to take control of flocks of goats and sheep and, in places, domesticated pig and cattle.

The adoption of a mixed farming economy by the sometimes large aceramic Neolithic communities seems to have led to severe environmental and population stress. Within Southwest Asia, some communities shifted to nomadic pastoralism, others to a combination of limited cultivation and seasonal nomadic pastoralism; still others founded new territories. They were realizing the potential portability of a mixed farming economy and, ultimately, its potential to be the fuel of major colonizing movements.

But the whole story is not told simply in terms of population and environmental pressures and changing subsistence and settlement strategies. Living in permanent village communities required new kinds of social organization that we can as yet only dimly perceive. The archaeological record reveals a remarkable burst of symbolic representation, in the form of architecture, statuary, sculpture, and painting. Human burials within settlements and the retention of detached skulls indicate important symbolic activities, and in a number of settlements we can recognize buildings that were created for the enactment of communal rituals. If living in permanent villages evoked new psychological and cognitive responses, then it was in the planning and architectural details of those villages that people began to materialize modes of symbolic representation (Wilson 1988; Renfrew 1998; Watkins in press), enabling them to create, for the first time, new ways of conceptualizing their world.

The chapters that follow describe the transition from hunting and gathering to farming in the other key regions of the world, beginning with East Asia (Chapter 7). These conversions to agriculture depended on a different range of plant and animal species in each of the regions where they occurred, and must hence be considered as independent of each other. Nevertheless, there are striking parallels among the early farming communities of these different regions, with pottery, sedentary village settlement, and increasing social inequality the ultimate result. In Southwest Asia, the early farming villages became larger and more complex after 6000 BC, and spread onto the lowland plains of southern Mesopotamia, leading to the rise of the first cities. This next stage in the Southwest Asian story is the subject of Chapter 12.

Further Reading and Suggested Websites

Bar-Yosef, O. & Meadow, R. H. 1995. *The Origins of Agriculture in the Near East, in Last Hunters, First Farmers: New Perspectives on the Prehistoric Transition to Agriculture* (T. D. Price & A. B. Gebauer, eds.), 39–94. Santa Fe, NM: School of American Research. An alternative view written from a Levantine perspective, by the doyen of Israeli prehistorians and a Harvard archaeozoologist.

Bar-Yosef, O. & Valla, F. R. (eds.). 1991. *The Natufian Culture in the Levant. International Monographs in Prehistory, Archaeological Series 1.* Ann Arbor: University of Michigan Press. A series of important papers on many different aspects of the most studied final Epipaleolithic culture, thought by many to be the pivotal culture for the period.

Cauvin, J. 2001. *The Birth of the Gods and the Beginnings of Agriculture.* Cambridge: Cambridge University Press. An original approach to the topic by the charismatic and innovative French prehistoric archaeologist Jacques Cauvin, translated from the French by T. Watkins.

Henry, D. O. 1989. *From Foraging to Agriculture: the Levant at the End of the Ice Age.* Philadelphia: University of Pennsylvania Press. Covers the Epipaleolithic hunter-gatherers of the Levant in authoritative but readable detail.

Kuijt, I. (ed.). 2000. *Life in Neolithic Farming Communities: Social Organization, Identity, and Differentiation.* New York: Kluwer Academic. A collection of contributions focusing on the social and cultural transformations that characterize the early Neolithic period.

Moore, A. M. T., Hillman, G. C., & Legge, A. J. 2001. *Village on the Euphrates.* Oxford and New York: Oxford University Press. Report on Abu Hureyra, the best-studied and thus the most important single site that we have for understanding the beginnings of plant domestication and the switch from hunting to herding.

http://www.france.diplomatie.fr/culture/culture_scientifique/archeologie French website (with English summaries) containing excellent pages on such sites as Eynan in Israel, Parekklishia-Shillourokambos on Cyprus, and Jerf el Ahmar in Syria.

http://catalhoyuk.com Website of the Çatalhöyük excavations, with information about the project and aspects of research being carried out.

http://www.asia.si.edu/jordan/html/jor_mm.htm Website mainly concerned with the conservation of the remarkable statues at 'Ain Ghazal, but with sections on the site and its discovery also.

CHAPTER 7
EAST ASIAN AGRICULTURE AND ITS IMPACT

Charles Higham, University of Otago

The Transition to Agriculture in East Asia 235
The Origins of Millet Cultivation: The Yellow River Valley 237
  • *Hunter-Gatherer Sites from before c. 7500 BC* 238
  • *Agricultural Sites from after c. 6000 BC* 238
● KEY SITE Cishan: The Transition to Agriculture in the Yellow River Valley 239
The Origins of Rice Cultivation: The Yangzi River Valley 240
  • *Gathering Wild Rice: Yuchan and Zhangnao* 241
  • *The Transition from Wild to Cultivated Rice: Diaotonghuan and Xianrendong* 241
The Development of Permanent Villages in the Yangzi Valley 242
● KEY CONTROVERSY The Origins of Rice Cultivation 243
● KEY SITE Bashidang: An Early Agricultural Village 244

The Growth of Agricultural Communities 245
Neolithic Cultures in the Yellow River Valley 245
  • *The Yangshao Culture* 245
  • *The Dawenkou Culture* 245
Neolithic Cultures in the Yangzi River Valley 246
  • *The Daxi Culture* 246
  • *Hemudu* 246
● KEY SITE Hemudu 247
  • *The Majiabang, Songze, and Chengbeixi Cultures* 247

The Expansion of Rice Farmers into Southeast Asia 248
  Initial Dispersal into Southern China 248
  From Southern China into Vietnam 249
  The Khorat Plateau, Thailand 250
    • *Early Rice Farmers in Thailand* 250
  Cambodia and the Mekong Delta 252
  The Bangkok Plain 252
    • *Khok Phanom Di and Ban Kao* 252
    • *Khok Charoen, Non Pai Wai, and Tha Kae* 254
  ● KEY SITE Khok Phanom Di: Sedentary Hunter-Fishers 254

The Expansion of Rice Farmers into Korea and Japan 256
  Korea 256
  Japan 258
    • *Jomon Antecedents* 258
    • *Yayoi Rice Farmers* 259
    ● KEY DISCOVERY Sedentism without Agriculture 260

The Linguistic Evidence 261

Summary and Conclusions 263

Further Reading and Suggested Websites 263

In the previous chapter we considered the origins of agriculture in Southwest Asia, from changes among late Pleistocene hunter-gatherers to the establishment of farming villages in the early Holocene. This chapter, too, is concerned with agricultural origins, but in a different region of the world: East Asia, including Japan, China, Vietnam, Korea, Thailand, and Cambodia.

Just as Southwest Asia gave the world the now-ubiquitous cultivated crops wheat and barley, so East Asia yielded the equally crucial crops rice and millet. Their cultivation allowed population numbers to grow, initially to support farming villages but later also towns, cities, and early states (discussed in Chapter 15).

Farming arose in East Asia between 8000 and 6000 BC in two separate areas, probably independently, with different suites of domesticated plants and animals: the loess (fine, wind-blown silt) plateau and central plain of the Huang He, or Yellow River, in the north (central China); and the central Yangzi River valley in the south (south China). Research into agricultural origins has been much less intensive in East Asia than in Southwest Asia, but a similar pattern emerges. As the late Pleistocene and early postglacial climate changed from cold and dry to warm and moist conditions, hunter-gatherer communities began to harvest and propagate millet in the northern part of this region, and rice in the south. This seminal cultural change, the adoption of agriculture, led to the establishment of permanently occupied villages and a transformation in the fundamentals of hunter-gatherer society. Houses were constructed, inhumation cemeteries increased, and populations surged. New crafts and skills developed: exotic stone jewelry, polished axes, wooden and bone spades, fine ceramics, woven fabric.

Alongside these changes, other hunter-gatherer groups continued their traditional lives. The interior tracts of East Asia were home to relatively small and at times mobile groups. The coasts, however, with their rich, self-replenishing supplies of marine food, sustained a myriad materially rich communities. From the Jomon groups of Japan south to the warm estuary of the Pearl River in southeast China, and from the Vietnamese coast to the Gulf of Thailand, marine fisher-gatherers made fine ceramic vessels, fashioned polished stone tools, and doubtless put to sea on trading voyages.

The Neolithic millennia from 6000 to 2000 BC exhibit a fascinating pattern of cultural interaction between hunter-gatherers on the one hand, and agricultural communities on the other. The latter proliferated in the core area of the Yangzi and Yellow River valleys, expanding along the coast and by river to all points of the compass. These agriculturalists took with them their material goods, their farming economy, their language, and, of course, their genes. This diaspora inevitably involved interaction with the indigenous hunter-gatherers; on some occasions the contrast between the two ways of life can be sharply defined, but in other areas the archaeological record of interaction becomes blurred. Perhaps there was exchange of goods and ideas, or intermarriage and a mixing of cultural tradi-tions. Hunter-gatherers may themselves have adopted rice farming, for example, if it suited their aspirations and interests.

Whatever the mechanics of interaction, tracing the resulting pattern of behavior on the basis of archaeological evidence is not straightforward, and interpretations are often controversial. Prehistorians can, however, currently participate in a fruitful dialogue with colleagues in the fields of historical linguistics and archaeogenetics. Expanding farming groups would have continued to speak their native tongues, and identifying cognate words and related languages over the vast regions of East and Southeast Asia is one way forward. Tracking genetic footprints on the basis of ancient DNA, a methodology still in its infancy, has profound potential. One approach involves sampling the genetic structure of the Y (male) chromosome and mitochondrial DNA (passed through the female line) of people living today, as a guide to their ancestry. Erika Hagelberg's samples from modern inhabitants of the Andaman Islands, in the Indian Ocean, show close affinities with Africans and New Guinea highlanders. She has suggested that this makes the islanders descendants of the first anatomically modern humans to expand into Asia from an African homeland (Hagelberg 2000). Such research can be combined, where possible, with analyses of DNA sequences that survive in ancient human remains, providing evidence for a direct genetic link between different groups. By this means, for example, it has been possible to track the origins of the Polynesians back to Asia (Chapter 8), and to begin the task of following the movement of different populations within the mainland of Asia itself (Li Jin et al. 2001).

The Transition to Agriculture in East Asia

The origins of agriculture in East Asia involve two major plant species: millet and rice. Millet was domesticated in central China, while rice was first cultivated in the Yangzi Valley to the south. The two regions, however, are virtually contiguous, and the establishment of settled farming communities took place over the same time span. The principal difference between the two areas lay in the environment, and in the indigenous plants available for collection by late Pleistocene hunter-gatherers. It is, therefore, vital to assess the origins of agriculture within the context of the pervasive changes in climate, flora, and fauna

EARLY EAST ASIA TIMELINE

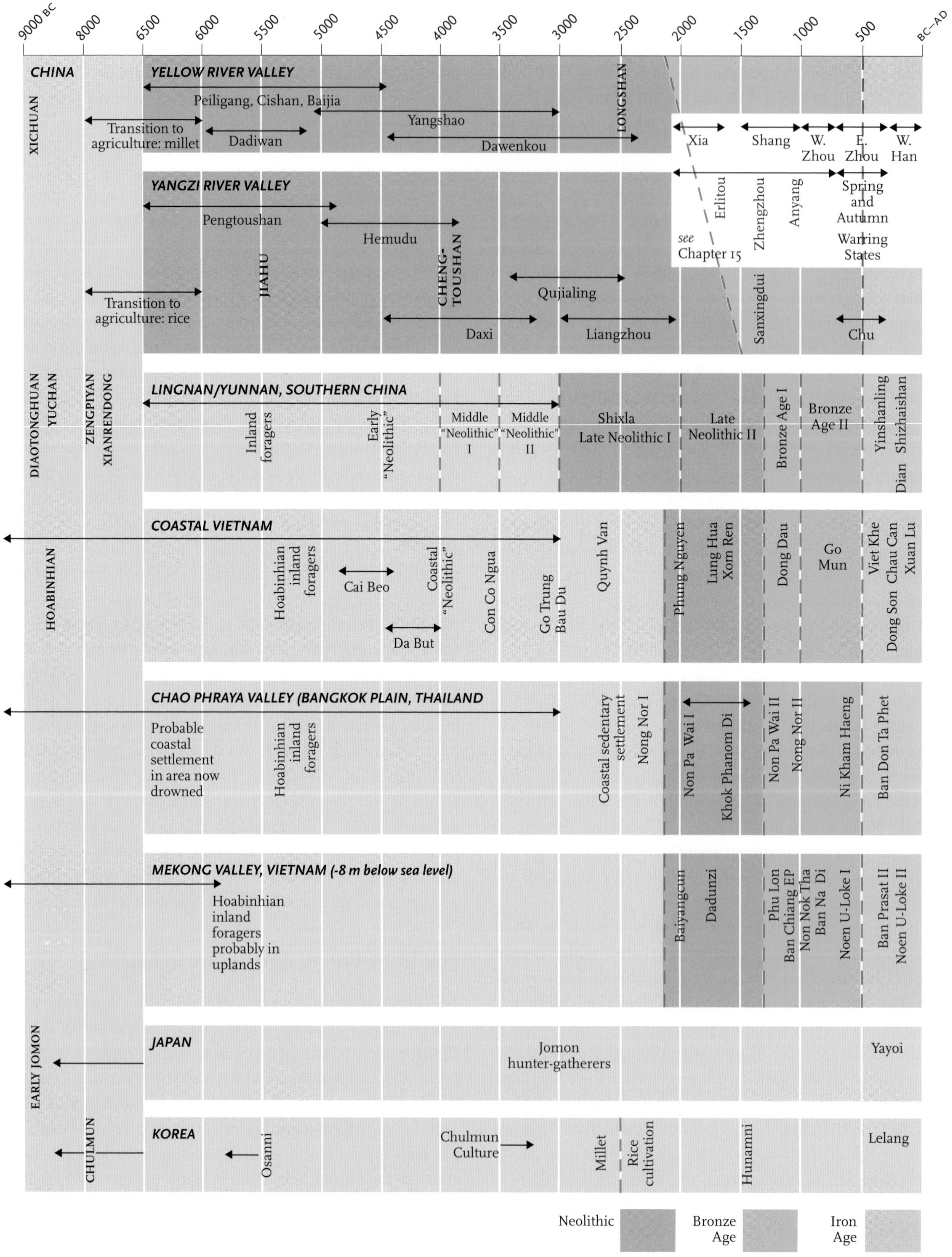

Timeline scale (BC): 9000 BC, 8000, 6500, 6000, 5500, 5000, 4500, 4000, 3500, 3000, 2500, 2000, 1500, 1000, 500, BC–AD

CHINA

XICHUAN

YELLOW RIVER VALLEY

Peiligang, Cishan, Baijia

Transition to agriculture: millet

Dadiwan

Yangshao

Dawenkou

LONGSHAN

Xia — Shang — W. Zhou — E. Zhou — W. Han

Erlitou — Zhengzhou — Anyang — Spring and Autumn — Warring States

see Chapter 15

YANGZI RIVER VALLEY

Pengtoushan

JIAHU

Hemudu

CHENG-TOUSHAN

Transition to agriculture: rice

Daxi

Qujialing

Liangzhou

Sanxingdui

Chu

DIAOTONGHUAN YUCHAN

ZENGPIYAN XIANRENDONG

LINGNAN/YUNNAN, SOUTHERN CHINA

Inland foragers

Early "Neolithic"

Middle "Neolithic" I

Middle "Neolithic" II

Shixla Late Neolithic I

Late Neolithic II

Bronze Age I

Bronze Age II

Yinshanling Dian Shizhaishan

COASTAL VIETNAM

HOABINHIAN

Hoabinhian inland foragers

Cai Beo

Coastal "Neolithic"

Da But

Con Co Ngua

Go Trung Bau Du

Quynh Van

Phung Nguyen

Lung Hua Xom Ren

Dong Dau

Go Mun

Viet Khe Dong Son Chau Can Xuan Lu

CHAO PHRAYA VALLEY (BANGKOK PLAIN, THAILAND

Probable coastal settlement in area now drowned

Hoabinhian inland foragers

Coastal sedentary settlement

Nong Nor I

Non Pa Wai I

Khok Phanom Di

Non Pa Wai II

Nong Nor II

Ni Kham Haeng

Ban Don Ta Phet

MEKONG VALLEY, VIETNAM (-8 m below sea level)

Hoabinhian inland foragers probably in uplands

Baiyangcun

Dadunzi

Phu Lon Ban Chiang EP Non Nok Tha Ban Na Di

Noen U-Loke I

Ban Prasat II Noen U-Loke II

EARLY JOMON

JAPAN

Jomon hunter-gatherers

Yayoi

CHULMUN

KOREA

Osanni

Chulmun Culture

Millet

Rice cultivation

Hunamni

Lelang

Legend: Neolithic — Bronze Age — Iron Age

that took place between about 14,000 and 6000 BC, the period spanning the end of the Pleistocene Ice Age and the first few millennia of the postglacial period.

The Origins of Millet Cultivation: The Yellow River Valley

In central China, the seminal changes took place in two distinct regions linked by the Yellow River. To the west lies the extensive loess plateau, while the North China Plain dominates the area east of the Taihang Mountains (Lu 1999). Archaeological research has highlighted the particular importance of the Wei River valley, the upper reaches of the Huai River and its tributaries, the Hebei plain, and the valley of the Fen River. Pollen analyses, particularly the long sequence from Fenzhuang, near Beijing in the North China Plain, have documented the extent of environmental change that occurred from about 14,000 BC. At that time sea levels were much lower than at present, and the climate so much colder and drier that vegetation was dominated by drought-resistant shrubs, herbaceous plants, and a few

coniferous trees. This steppe habitat also supported large herbivores, such as horses, deer, gazelle, rhinoceros, and sheep.

The climate became markedly warmer from about 11,000 BC, but this was short-lived, as the cold episode known as the Younger Dryas dominated from *c.* 10,800 to 9600 BC. Thereafter, the warm and wet conditions returned, with temperatures and rainfall rather higher than at present. This sequence is matched on the loess plateau west of the Yellow River. Deciduous trees now invaded the former steppe, and a new range of animals spread north, including deer, monkeys, and alligators. Archaeological evidence for the exploitation of fish and shellfish confirms these wet, warm conditions. It is vitally important to appreciate that during the period of dry and cold steppe conditions, i.e. for most of the period from around 14,000 to 9600 BC, seeds of grasses and herbaceous plants would have been available to hunter-gatherer groups. To identify the origins of plant domestication, we must consider the millennia preceding the establishment of agricultural communities, and the archaeological evidence for late Pleistocene hunters and gatherers.

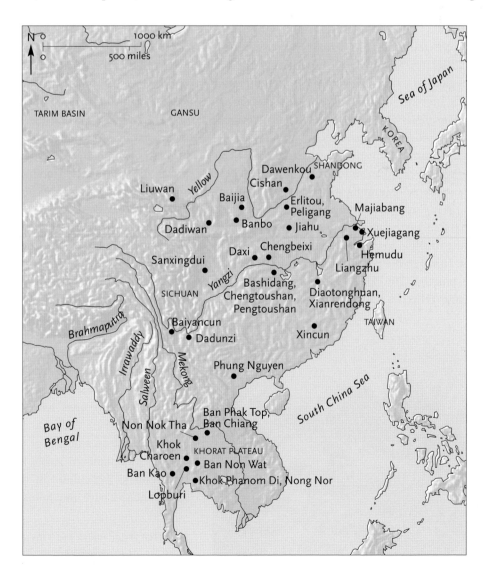

7.1 Map of China and surrounding countries: *showing the location of the main rivers and other geographical features, and the major sites mentioned in the text.*

Hunter-Gatherer Sites from before c. 7500 BC The Xiachuan basin lies in Shaanxi Province east of the Yellow River, before its confluence with the Wei. Settlements of hunter-gatherers have been found in caves and on open river terraces here, dated to the period of dry and cold steppe conditions toward the end of the last Ice Age (*c.* 36,000–16,000 BC). Excavations have recovered large quantities of stone artifacts, but little else. Nevertheless, the range of stone implements, and their likely uses, have illuminated a previously little-known period in East Asian prehistory. As might be expected, stone arrowheads flaked for attaching to a wooden shaft are commonly found, and were presumably used to hunt the sheep and wild cattle represented among the faunal remains. The open environment also encouraged wild grasses and herbaceous plants, including green foxtail millet [7.2].

This plant was the ancestor of the domesticated foxtail millet that was to dominate the subsistence of the farming communities of central China for millennia to come. Indeed, the stone assemblages of the Xiachuan sites, such as that of Shunwangpin, include a denticulate tool often bearing the gloss derived from its use as a harvesting implement (Lu 1999). The form also anticipates the sickles that became widespread in the first farming villages. It seems highly likely that late Pleistocene groups were beginning to harvest wild millet, an innovation supported by the presence of grinding stones with wear patterns very close to those observed on Australian Aboriginal implements used to process wild grass seeds.

Related sites are known to the northwest, in the valley of the Fen River. Sites such as Xueguan and Shizitan, located on loess river terraces, were bases for hunting steppic animals (predominantly gazelle), as well as for harvesting wild millet (Wang et al. 1983). Shizitan is thought to date to around 8000 BC. There was a similar hunting tradition to the north, in the Sanggan Valley west of Beijing, although the possible indicators of wild grass harvesting are missing. The pollen spectrum from one site here, Xibaimaying, reflects a cold and dry steppe climate with

little evidence for the presence of grass. The animals whose remains have been found at these sites, dominated by herd ungulates such as gazelle, wild cattle, horse, and deer, were presumably hunted with the stone arrowheads also found there.

As one moves east of the loess plateau and on to the North China Plain, further late Pleistocene sites provide evidence for hunting and gathering. Menjiaquan, located some 200 km (125 miles) east of Beijing, has yielded a stone industry containing microliths dating to about 11,000 BC. Nanzhuangtou was located near a marsh or lake, and the remains there, dating to 10,500–7500 BC, include a small sample of potsherds and a grinding stone, as well as possibly domestic dog and pig bones. These, if verified, would be the earliest known domestic animals in central China, while the pottery is also relatively early.

Agricultural Sites from after c. 6000 BC At present, no site transitional to the early agricultural villages has been identified; these should date to *c.* 8000–6000 BC. This is a vital area for future research, because it will provide insight into the origins of agricultural communities.

By 6000 BC there is abundant and widespread evidence for sedentary Neolithic villages. **Dadiwan**, located in the far western reaches of the Wei River valley in Gansu Province, dates to 5900–5300 BC and represents a cultural transformation. Instead of thin deposits dominated by stone tools and the bones of herd animals, we find the remains of a sedentary village incorporating semi-subterranean houses and storage pits; one of these pits contained the remains of cultivated broomcorn millet and rape seeds. Stone tools included spades and axes, and the inhabitants made cord-marked pottery and ceramic spindle whorls, used to spin fiber prior to weaving. The dead were interred in an inhumation cemetery. Technological parallels between the Xiachuan and Dadiwan assemblages in the production of small stone blades indicate cultural continuity between late hunters and early farmers in this region. Moreover, Dadiwan was not alone. Many more Neolithic village sites have been identified along the course of the Wei River, most prominently at **Baijia**, where similar house floors and storage pits have been found. Polished stone spades were used here to cultivate the soft loess soil, and shell sickles brought in the millet harvest. There was also an inhumation cemetery here too.

Similar village sites have been discovered in the North China Plain, where Cishan and Peiligang are prominent. **Cishan** is located on a terrace of the Nanming River, east of the Taihang Mountains in Hebei Province [see box: Cishan: The Transition to Agriculture in the Yellow River Valley]. Many sunken houses have been found cut into the soft soil here, asso-

7.2 Green foxtail millet: *this is the wild progenitor of the millet that fueled the rise to civilization in the Yellow River valley of China.*

ciated with hundreds of deep storage pits containing thick layers of carbonized millet grains; two pits had been used to store wild hackberry seeds, emphasizing the continuing role of collecting. Cultivation employed polished stone spades, and grain was processed on grinding stones. Bone shuttles and needles were probably used for making and repairing nets for fishing, and a variety of sand-tempered pottery vessels were used for cooking and storage.

Peiligang is located south of the Yellow River in Henan Province, and is one of many sites concentrated in the tributaries of the Huai River. Excavations between 1977 and 1979 uncovered 116 burials in the village cemetery, disposed in three clusters that might represent distinct clan groups within the community [7.5, 7.6]. Many polished spades and other agricultural implements were found [7.4, 7.7], as well as house floors and storage pits. Like those from Cishan, pottery vessels from this site were fired in the controlled conditions of a kiln [7.3].

Jiahu, one of the most southerly of the sites ascribed to the Peiligang culture, has produced the earliest evidence in central China for cultivated rice, found as impressions of husks in clay; radiocarbon dates suggest occupation by 6500 BC. As many as 30 house foundations and 300 burials have been uncovered at this important site, which has also yielded the

7.3, 7.4 Peiligang culture: *a pottery vessel (left) from Peiligang, height 14.5 cm (5.7 in); and a stone sickle from Egou, length 29.3 cm (11.5 in).*

KEY SITE Cishan: The Transition to Agriculture in the Yellow River Valley

The settlement of Cishan is of central importance to any consideration of the transition to agriculture in the Yellow River valley. The site covers about 8 ha (20 acres), an area compatible with a population measured in the low hundreds, and excavations here in 1976–78 uncovered two Neolithic layers, dated to between 6000 and 5700 BC.

The structural remains include small sunken "pit houses" and hundreds of pits, some up to 5 m (16 ft) deep, which had been dug into the soft loess substrate. These were apparently intended for the storage of grain for consumption during the winter months, for many contained the remains of domesticated foxtail millet, in one case lying 2 m (6.6 ft) thick. The remains of hackberry

seeds, walnuts, and hazelnuts indicate that gathering wild resources continued to be important.

The preservation of organic material has also illuminated other resources exploited by this early farming community. The bones of domestic pigs and dogs predominated, but aquatic resources included fish, shellfish, and turtles; evidence for woodland fauna comes from monkey and civet bones, as well as deer and wild pig; and many birds are represented, most wild but including domestic chickens.

This subsistence base stimulated related developments in the material culture of the community. Bone arrowheads and harpoons were used for hunting or fishing, and the presence of bone shuttles and needles suggests that nets were made. Some of the

pottery vessels bore the imprints of cordage, further evidence for the manufacture of nets and cloth.

Millet cultivation was facilitated by the production of stone spades, while harvesting and processing the grain was undertaken with stone pestles and mortars. Among the pottery vessels (fired at relatively high temperatures, some approaching 1000° C/1832° F) are low, flat-based platters and round bowls raised on three or four legs, as well as forms for cooking.

The excavations at Cishan have illuminated a vital stage in Chinese prehistory: the early agricultural village in which domestic stock and millet cultivation combined with hunting, gathering, and fishing to provide a stable subsistence base.

7.5, 7.6 Peiligang: cemeteries, such as this example from the early settlement of Peiligang, are a hallmark of early agricultural communities in China. The burials at this site occurred in three separate clusters, which may represent distinct clan groups within the community.

earliest known examples of turtle carapaces bearing incised symbols. These were to feature prominently in the much later written records of the Shang Dynasty, *c.* 1500–1045 BC (see Chapter 15).

The earliest Neolithic sites of the **Houli culture** of the lower Yellow River valley date from around 6300 BC, and the same pattern of sedentary village communities as has been outlined above has been traced at Houli itself and at the site of Xihe. Spades, grinding stones, and sickles recur, and pottery vessels were fired in closed kilns.

7.7 Early agricultural implements: this pestle and mortar for grinding millet come from Peiligang. These tools appear with the first farmers in the Yellow River valley of China.

The Origins of Rice Cultivation: The Yangzi River Valley

It is becoming increasingly apparent that the transition to economies that incorporated rice cultivation took place in the middle reaches of the Yangzi Valley, with a possible extension in the Huai River valley to the north. This low-lying, lake-filled region lies at the northern limits of wild rice, and it is highly likely that the availability of this grass changed with climatic fluctuations. (At its climatic extreme, wild rice will survive if rainfall exceeds 1000 mm (39 in) annually, and if temperatures are higher than 16° C (61° F) during ripening.) Any consideration of early rice cultivation must therefore incorporate the evidence for climatic conditions during the late Pleistocene and early Holocene (Lu 1999).

Evidence for the late Pleistocene climate in the Yangzi Valley comes from pollen cores, sediment sequences, and geomorphology (the study of changes in land forms). Conditions were much colder and drier than at present, as may be seen from the accumulation of the Xiashu loess, which has been dated to *c.* 18,000–11,000 BC; loess, a fine wind-blown dust, is typical of glacial conditions. Pollen cores taken from the Longquan Lake indicate a predominance of herbaceous plants with pine trees. For the lower Yangzi region, which would then have been far removed from the coast due to low sea levels, there is a similar pattern of cool, dry indicators.

Several brief periods of warmer climate occurred between 13,000 and 10,800 BC, but it was not until about 8000 BC that a long period of warming commenced. Sea levels rose rapidly, from about 18 m (60 ft) below present levels in 8000 BC until a marine transgression two millennia later began to inundate the lower Yangzi region and cause the expansion of lakes in the river's middle reaches. This rise was interrupted by a brief and possibly critical cold snap that began just after 7000 BC. This reconstructed climatic sequence indicates that rice was probably not available to the hunter-gatherers of the Yangzi Valley during the particularly cold spell that lasted until 13,000 BC. Thereafter, as noted above, this large area in the middle and lower reaches of the river hovered on the northern margins for wild rice.

Gathering Wild Rice: Yuchan and Zhangnao Several sites reveal the presence of late Pleistocene hunter-gatherers in the middle Yangzi Valley. The cave site of **Yuchan** in Hunan Province is probably the most significant. Although the radiocarbon dates are inconsistent, Lie Dan Lu's suggested range of 10,000–6000 BC is probably accurate (Lu 1999). Yuchan overlooks low-lying, swampy terrain, and excavations here have yielded many hearths associated with the remains of fish, birds, 40 species of seeds, and the phytoliths (minute remains of plant tissue) and husks of rice thought to be from a wild stand (Yuan and Zhang 1999). These last came from a context that included very poorly fired pottery sherds, and shell knives that

might have been used to harvest grasses. The stone industry is typical of the period, based on the flaking of pebble tools to shape choppers, scrapers, and knives; it has strong southern affinities. A similar flaked pebble industry has been recognized at the cave of **Zhangnao**, in association with the bones of giant panda, rhinoceros, and stegodon. The single radiocarbon date from this site falls in the mid-12th millennium BC.

The Transition from Wild to Cultivated Rice: Diaotonghuan and Xianrendong Although there are virtually no similar settlements of late Pleistocene hunter-gatherers in the lower Yangzi Valley, two caves contain long sequences vital to reconstructing the path to rice domestication and the establishment of agricultural village communities. These have enabled an attempt to integrate the cultural and climatic sequences.

At the cave of **Diaotonghuan** in Jiangxi Province, a deep accumulation of cultural layers has been divided into zones B to O, from top to bottom (Zhao 1998) [7.8]. The recovery of rice phytoliths that can be identified as coming from wild, domestic, or intermediate forms has provided important new information on the process of domestication. It has even been possible to distinguish between phytoliths from the leaf and those from the glume (the sterile bract that encloses the grain), which reveals whether people were bringing in the entire plant or selectively harvesting the grain. The deposits dating to about

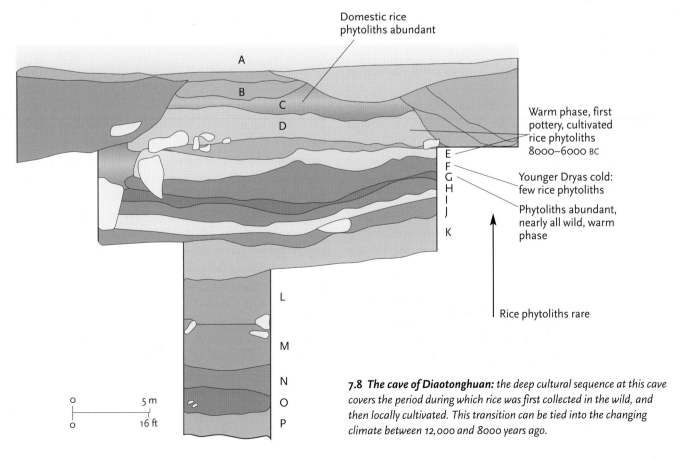

Domestic rice phytoliths abundant

Warm phase, first pottery, cultivated rice phytoliths 8000–6000 BC

Younger Dryas cold: few rice phytoliths

Phytoliths abundant, nearly all wild, warm phase

Rice phytoliths rare

7.8 The cave of Diaotonghuan: *the deep cultural sequence at this cave covers the period during which rice was first collected in the wild, and then locally cultivated. This transition can be tied into the changing climate between 12,000 and 8000 years ago.*

23,000–20,000 BC yielded few phytoliths, no layer producing more than 15. This number surged by a factor of ten in zone G, dated to the brief warm phase that began *c.* 11,200 BC. Of these, 29 samples were examined and determined to be either of the wild form or indeterminate. Two others might have been from a cultivated plant, but their rarity makes this unlikely. The hunters and gatherers of Diaotonghuan were probably collecting wild rice at this juncture.

There was a sharp fall in the frequency of rice phytoliths in zone F, which is thought to correspond to the cold of the Younger Dryas (*c.* 10,800–9600 BC), when wild rice would probably have retreated to its southern refugia. Rice remains were back in force during the accumulation of zones D and E, which correspond to the long period of warming between 8000 and 6000 BC. Perhaps significantly, it was in zone E that the first pottery sherds were recovered, since ceramic vessels often reflect a more sedentary lifestyle. The form of the phytoliths suggests that half are probably from a wild stand, the others closer to the cultivated form. Phytoliths remained abundant in zone C, and most of these fall into the domestic range of form and size.

Moreover, as more domestic phytoliths were found, so glumes were more frequently represented than leaves. This suggests grain harvesting, rather than the fortuitous arrival of rice remains in the cultural deposits. Thus at Diaotonguan we see a sequence in which the domestic form of rice grew steadily in quantity relative to the wild; it also reveals a harmony between the presence of rice and the changing climate [see box: The Origins of Rice Cultivation]. Spindle whorls were also found, indicating the preparation of yarn probably destined for weaving.

Xianrendong, a second major cave site, is located only a few hundred meters from Diaotonghuan and incorporates a similar cultural sequence. A preceramic phase of occupation at the base of the cultural layers probably dates to between 16,000 and 12,000 BC. As at Diaotonghuan, this was followed by layers dating to *c.* 11,000–6000 BC that provide evidence for the earliest use of pottery, in the form of cooking vessels. To this period is also dated a toolkit that included shells with polished cutting surfaces that may well have resulted from harvesting rice (Lu 1999).

These excavations disclose that the long warming period between approximately 8000 and 6000 BC saw the northward expansion of rice into the Yangzi Valley, linked with an increase in the frequency of rice remains at occupied sites – some, if not all, of it domestic. Pottery appears in cultural contexts in which the prevailing stone industry still includes forms common during the earlier phases of the late Pleistocene. This may indicate that hunter-gatherers were becoming more sedentary as they incorporated more rice into their diet.

The Development of Permanent Villages in the Yangzi Valley

As in central China, the sequel to this trend toward rice cultivation is a new form of settlement, in which houses, cemeteries, pits, and the remains of domestic activity accumulated in low mounds away from the limestone bluffs and on the plains surrounding the major lakes of the middle Yangzi, in Hunan, Hebei, and Jiangxi provinces. The survival of organic remains makes **Bashidang**, in Hunan Province, the most significant of these village sites [see box: Bashidang: An Early Agricultural Village, p. 244]. Excavations revealed a defensive ditch and an old riverbed that preserved many plant remains, including over 15,000 grains of rice claimed to have been of a cultivated variety (Pei 1998). Twenty other plants were represented, including the water caltrop and lotus, both edible plants which are easily propagated in the site's watery habitat. Other remains include wooden spades, which could have been used in agriculture, vestiges of houses raised on piles, pottery tempered with rice husks (i.e., with rice added to the clay to improve its firing qualities), and the bones of cattle, pigs, deer, and chicken. A cemetery containing at least 100 inhumation graves is compatible with a long-term, permanently occupied village (Higham and Lu 1998).

Excavations at **Pengtoushan**, located 20 km (12 miles) southwest of Bashidang, have revealed the remains of houses, a flourishing ceramic industry in which rice husks, straw, and grains were used to temper the clay, and an inhumation cemetery in which the dead were accompanied by siltstone ornaments and pottery vessels (Yan Wenming 1991). The radiocarbon determinations derived from rice remains used as a ceramic temper lie within the period 7000–6000 BC. The rice remains have not been conducive to identifying whether they came from wild or domestic plants, nor have any tools that could have been used for cultivation been found here. Nevertheless, the similarity of the pottery styles to those from Bashidang argues for contemporaneity, and for familiarity with rice farming. A second important discovery from Pengtoushan has been the realization that its stone industry, based on flaked pebbles, is closely related to the late Pleistocene hunter-gatherer sites of this region, thus providing evidence for cultural continuity during the period that witnessed the transition to agriculture.

By integrating the cultural and climatic data, which is not yet possible in central China for millet domestication, it is possible to propose a model for the transition to rice cultivation that recalls aspects of the one proposed for the Levant at the same period (Bar-Yosef and Meadow 1995). The Yangzi Valley lies at the northern limit of wild rice under warm conditions, but a fall in mean temperature makes it difficult, if not impossible, for this plant to survive here. Predominantly wild rice phytoliths from Diaotonghuan were abundant during a late Pleistocene warm phase, but fell away with the onset of the cold Younger

KEY CONTROVERSY **The Origins of Rice Cultivation**

There have been many twists and turns in the quest to trace the origins of rice cultivation. The plant is so adaptive, and there are so many varieties, that it is grown today in upland fields, in irrigated plains, on hill terraces, and along the margins of permanent lakes. It is basically a marsh plant, which relies as much on the nourishing qualities of water as on the fertility of the soil, and so harvests can be secured even on poor and sandy soils provided there is sufficient rainfall. Thus, rice has supported a greater number of people for a longer period of time than any other cultivated crop (Greenland 1997).

The wide distribution of viable rice cultivation today has made it hard for archaeologists to pinpoint the best place to seek its origins. In the 1960s, small rockshelters in the uplands of northern Thailand were canvassed as the focus for the earliest "Neolithic Revolution," i.e., for the development of agriculture.

One of these, Spirit Cave, is ingrained in the literature on the basis of its early evidence for plant domestication. The excavator of the cave, Chester Gorman (1972), found pottery sherds, polished stone axes, and small slate knives in the uppermost layers, which were then thought to date to the 6th millennium BC. The animal bones and plant remains both reveal a broad-spectrum pattern of forest hunting and gathering, as well as fishing in the local Khong stream.

The presence of resin on some of the potsherds has now allowed an AMS radiocarbon determination to be processed, and the result indicates a far later date than originally thought, falling between 1400 and 1200 BC. Spirit Cave, which has never yielded any rice remains, must thus take its place as a small and remote rockshelter occupied on occasion by transient hunters and gatherers.

During the 1970s, the site of Hemudu in the lower Yangzi Valley came to the fore as the earliest known site with cultivated rice, the oldest dates suggesting settlement by 5000 BC. However, the size of the settlement, linked with the sheer quantity of rice recovered and the well-developed agricultural tools, all pointed to earlier origins elsewhere [see box: Hemudu, p. 247].

In 1984, the large coastal settlement of Khok Phanom Di, located behind the Gulf of Thailand, was excavated to test an exploratory model suggesting that rice cultivation began as sea levels fell and freshwater conditions encouraged experimentation by hunter-gatherers. The structure of this model was based on the presence of rice remains at this site, in conjunction with radiocarbon dates as early as any then known for domesticated rice in Asia. However, the model was soon disproved, once it was found that the site was not as early as it had seemed [see box: Khok Phanom Di: Sedentary Hunter-Fishers, pp. 254–55].

7.9 *Wild rice is a marsh plant, as seen in this location in China. Cultivating it requires the replication of marshy conditions. The plant feeds on blue-green algae that must slowly circulate past the plant. Hence a dry spell and drying out of the rice fields can prove disastrous.*

Excavations at the caves of Diaotonghuan and Xianrendong in China have now traced a long sequence spanning the period from the late Pleistocene into the early Holocene (Lu 1999). It is clear that the presence of rice remains fluctuated with the climate: with increasing cold, numbers of rice phytoliths fell, whereas warmer conditions between 8000 and 6000 BC saw their return, with some grains now coming from a cultivated variety. Pottery vessels and a weaving industry were also developing at this time.

By 6000 BC the first fruits of this transition can be detected in the archaeological record, in the form of villages with permanent houses. New tools were developed specifically to cultivate the soil, but the strength of this new configuration, as seen at Bashidang [see box, Bashidang: An Early Agricultural Village, p. 244], was a subsistence strategy based on a wide range of plant foods, including lotuses and water caltrop. The adaptability and reliability of this strategy provided insurance against shortage, which sustained early farmers in the nuclear area and their descendants as they expanded into new lands.

7.10 *For at least 2000 years, peasant farmers in China have created marshy conditions for rice to flourish by building low banks to retain rainwater. Much bigger returns can be obtained by carefully transplanting rice seedlings at some distance apart, rather than broadcasting seeds into the fields.*

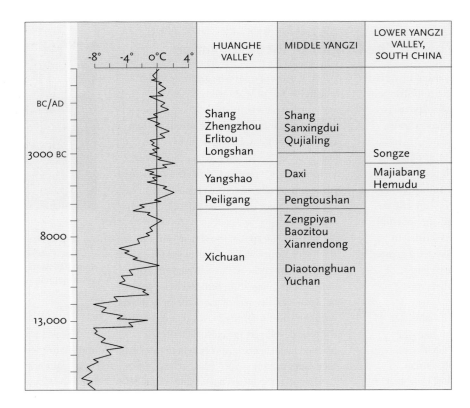

	HUANGHE VALLEY	MIDDLE YANGZI	LOWER YANGZI VALLEY, SOUTH CHINA
BC/AD	Shang Zhengzhou Erlitou Longshan	Shang Sanxingdui Qujialing	
3000 BC			Songze
	Yangshao	Daxi	Majiabang Hemudu
	Peiligang	Pengtoushan	
8000	Xichuan	Zengpiyan Baozitou Xianrendong	
		Diaotonghuan Yuchan	
13,000			

7.11 Temperature change and early Chinese sites: *a chart showing the relationship between early Chinese sites and the mean temperature.*

Dryas. In the long warming period that immediately followed, rice phytoliths, now probably of a cultivated variety, increased markedly, and did so in conjunction with the earliest evidence for ceramics, but so far only in cave sites. When the climate again cooled about 7000 BC, there was no retraction in the economic role of rice, but rather an expansion of the population into permanent open villages. Material culture in these settlements took on a new aspect as spades and sickles appeared, more pottery was made from clay tempered with rice chaff, cloth was woven, and the dead were interred in permanent cemeteries. It is suggested that, having become increasingly familiar with rice manipulation during the long warm phase, incipient or early rice agriculturalists withstood the next cold phase through a commitment to increasing the cultivation of a now domestic strain.

KEY SITE Bashidang: An Early Agricultural Village

The prehistoric site of Bashidang is located on the Liyang plain in northeast Hunan Province, between the Yangzi River and Lake Dongting. Excavated between 1993 and 1997, it produced two occupation periods, probably dating to c. 7000–6000 BC. In the upper of these levels, cultural remains covered at least 3 ha (7.5 acres) and were closely related to the culture of Pengtoushan, 20 km (12 miles) southwest of Bashidang. The layer below this horizon is of key significance, and comprises peat deposits containing postholes that might have been the foundations for houses raised above flood level.

This black peat deposit, which lay near an ancient channel, contained plant remains that included rice grains, some still within the husk. Initial analyses of this large sample have revealed a rice that was already domesticated but still retained a number of primitive features. It had a small grain, and had not yet differentiated between the two major domesticated varieties of rice, *indica* and *japonica*. This vital fact identifies the Pengtoushan culture, to which Bashidang belongs, as providing the earliest examples of the agriculturally based village in East Asia.

Further plant remains, such as water caltrop, enlarge our understanding of the subsistence base at that period. This plant can be easily propagated in wetlands, and the fruit stored for later consumption; the leaves can also be eaten. Remains of the lotus, an edible water plant that can be propagated by root division or by simply scattering the seeds, were also found. The context within which rice developed thus incorporated a range of other water plants as well, which would have contributed to the stability of the early farming village communities.

The fortunate discovery of a deep peat deposit in an area where acidic soils militate against the survival of plant remains has thus added another piece of evidence to help resolve what was once described as the $64,000 question of Asian prehistory: the origins of rice cultivation.

7.12, 7.13 Yangshao pottery vessels: *(left) the Neolithic Machang culture, part of the Yangshao complex, produced this extraordinary wine vessel standing 33.5 cm (13 in) high and found at Liuwan. It was embellished with the image of a bisexual human. It is highly likely that this figure was a shaman, who linked humans on earth with the mysterious world of gods. Perhaps the wine was drunk during rituals. (Right) The pottery vessels of the Yangshao culture in China are rightly famous for their spectacular decoration. This vessel from Banbo, 40 cm (16 in) across, bears the image of a shaman with two fish as earrings.*

The Growth of Agricultural Communities

Neolithic Cultures in the Yellow River Valley

Agricultural settlements based on millet cultivation proliferated in central China, and a pattern of increasing cultural complexity that culminated in the formation of early states can be identified. Two major cultures developed. On the loess plateau and the central plains of Qinghai, Gansu, and Shaanxi provinces, the sites are attributed to the Yangshao culture, whereas the sites of the Dawenkou culture are found further east, in Shandong Province.

The Yangshao Culture There are many regional aspects to the Yangshao culture, which is dated to approximately 5200–3000 BC. They have in common semi-subterranean houses, storage pits for the millet harvest, kiln-fired ceramic vessels bearing distinctive geometric painted designs and images, and extensive inhumation cemeteries. During the long existence of this culture there was a rising tide of social stratification, seen in particular in the grave goods placed with the dead. At Liuwan,

for example, over 1500 graves have been opened, the later examples displaying a wide range of variation in terms of offerings, from hardly any to over 90 ceramic vessels interred with individuals of evidently high status and wealth [7.12].

The best-known Yangshao site, that at **Banbo** in Xian, has been excavated over most of its extent. It was ringed by a defensive ditch, beyond which lay the village cemeteries; round houses were distributed within the defenses [7.14]. An important feature of the Yangshao culture is the accumulating evidence for shamanistic rituals [7.13] that formed the basis for later practices documented among the early states of this region. A painting on a floor at Dadiwan, for example, shows two shaman-like figures performing rites at a funeral.

The Dawenkou Culture The Dawenkou culture dominated the lower Yellow River valley, *c.* 4300–2400 BC. There is a consistent thread of evidence in favor of increasing population densities and social ranking among the people of this culture. Thus at the early Dawenkou site of Liulin, the five lobes of the village cemetery have been ascribed to members of different

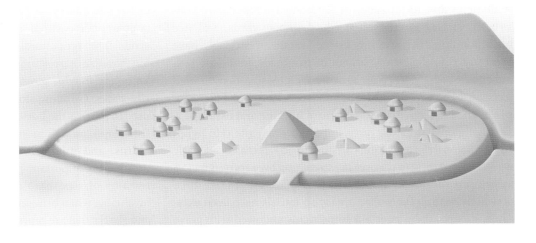

7.14 A Yangshao culture village: *the Neolithic village of Banbo near Xian has been extensively excavated. It was defended by a deep ditch all the way round, beyond which lay the cemeteries. Houses within were circular and widely spaced apart.*

descent groups. None stands out on account of mortuary wealth, but men and women were distinguished from each other, the former being interred with stone adzes and chisels, while females were accompanied by spindle whorls. The potter's wheel was invented during the middle phase of the Dawenkou culture (*c.* 3500–2900 BC), and at Dawenkou itself, mortuary offerings rose sharply in quantity and quality at this time. Jade ornaments, for example, increased, along with stone adzes and stone beads. By the late phase (*c.* 2900–2400 BC), there is compelling evidence for the emergence of specialists in the manufacture of jades and ceramic vessels, and a seamless development into the succeeding Longshan culture and early state formation (see Chapter 15, p. 555).

Neolithic Cultures in the Yangzi River Valley

In the heartland of early rice cultivation, centered on Lake Dongting in northeast Hunan Province, the site of **Fenshanbao** followed soon after the establishment of Pengtoushan and Bashidang. The three occupation layers here include much pottery bearing the impressions of rice, and some ceramic vessels accompany the dead in the village cemetery. Stone tools included the traditional flaked-pebble choppers and axes, but arrowheads had been polished. The pottery is sufficiently distinct from that of Pengtoushan, only 140 km (87 miles) to the west, to indicate that occupation probably took place between 6000 and 5500 BC. **Hujiawuchang**, 50 km (30 miles) south of Pengtoushan, is slightly later still, the radiocarbon dates falling between 5600 and 5100 BC. As with the other sites, excavations here revealed the remains of a sedentary agricultural village based on rice cultivation and hunting. Animal remains included hare, wild and probably domesticated pig, sambar deer, sheep, and water buffalo.

The Daxi Culture Thereafter, village sites in the middle Yangzi basin increased markedly in quantity and range. Dating to *c.* 4500–3300 BC, these are generally ascribed to the Daxi culture. Convenient spurs commanding wetlands were chosen for settlement, and rectangular, multi-roomed houses were constructed of clay, strengthened with bamboo, reeds, and rice husk bonding. The swampy terrain would presumably have been suited to the establishment of rice fields, and early (4th millennium BC) evidence for agricultural intensification through plowing has been identified. Domestic cattle and pigs were maintained, but not to the exclusion of hunting and fishing.

Chengtoushan is the most important Daxi site (He Jiejun 1995). Extensive excavations in the 1990s revealed an early walled town dating to *c.* 4000 BC, stretching over some 8 ha (20 acres); modifications to the walls took place on at least three occasions. Within the walled area, 700 burials have been excavated, most of them poor but some richly endowed with grave goods. One elite person, wearing two jade pendants, was buried with 50 pottery vessels and four individuals, who were interred in a crouched position in the corners of the tomb. Some houses incorporated a main room and a kitchen, others had corridors and several rooms. The 10-m (33-ft) wide moat contained the remains of wooden agricultural tools, bamboo and reed basketry, linen cloth, even paddles and rudders for boats that would have been in regular use in this flood-prone terrain. The importance of rice can be judged from the discovery of the earliest known rice fields near the eastern wall, complete with ridges to retain water, and irrigation ditches (He Jiejun 1999).

The site of **Daxi** itself is relatively late in the sequence, but has yielded two phases of burials. It is notable that the later ones contain jade jewelry and fine pottery vessels in place of the tools, such as spindle whorls and awls, found in earlier interments. At **Huachenggang**, Daxi occupation evolved locally into the Qujialing culture (*c.* 3100–2650 BC). Thus the central reaches of the Yangzi witnessed the development from the first agricultural villages to a walled center in little more than 2000 years.

Hemudu The expansion of agricultural communities downstream from the lakelands of the middle Yangzi Valley is best documented at Hemudu [see box: Hemudu]. This site is located on the southern side of the Hangzhou River estuary, on a low-lying plain close to the sea. There are four occupation layers, dating from 5000 BC at the base to 3000 BC at the top. Since the site was subject to marine transgressions, the resulting mantle of marine sediments has preserved organic material, providing a rare opportunity to examine a wide range of implements not normally preserved. These include wooden and bone tools and wooden house foundations, not to mention considerable quantities of rice grains, straw, and chaff that still retained their original color.

The foundations of three long houses with internal subdivisions for individual rooms, each made of fine wooden joinery, indicates permanent settlement, and since only about 5 percent of the site has so far been excavated, it probably possessed a population measured in the hundreds, possibly even thousands. The agricultural tools include well-used bone spades, but possible harvesting tools are very rare, though one bone knife has an edge gloss that could have resulted from cutting rice stalks. Grinding stones and stone pestles could have been used to process the harvest. The wide range of animal, bird, and fish bones, as well as such plant remains as water chestnuts, acorns, and jujubes, shows that hunting and fishing contributed an important part of the diet. Wooden oars and the remains of rope have survived, and boats would have been invaluable when bringing in the sea turtles, crocodiles, whales, and sharks that are represented by their remains at this site.

KEY SITE Hemudu

Until the discovery of the Pengtoushan culture in the Liyang plain, Hemudu was the oldest known site with clear evidence for the cultivation of rice (Lu 1999). When discovered in the 1970s, it was generally believed that plant domestication in China took place in the central plains. Excavations at Hemudu at once revealed the importance of the Yangzi Valley, and the role of rice.

Hemudu is located on a flat plain barely 1 m (3.3 ft) above sea level, in the lower valley of the Hangzhou River. Excavations have revealed four layers, beginning in about 5000 BC and ending two millennia later. A mantle of peat deposits over the cultural remains has led to the survival of organic material, including unparalleled samples of rice. Although only 5 percent of the site has been uncovered, it was clearly an impressive village, comprising stoutly constructed wooden houses that featured advanced joinery techniques. One house was 23 m (75 ft) long and 7 m (23 ft) deep, and featured a verandah. If such houses were distributed across the rest of the site, it would have had a population of many hundreds, possibly thousands.

The material items recovered document a wide range of activities. There are bone spades, fashioned from bovid shoulder

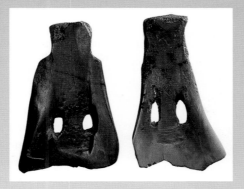

7.15 *By 5000 BC, rice was being cultivated at the important site of Hemudu. These shoulder blades of oxen found at the site were converted into spades; the holes were to lash the spade to a wooden handle.*

blades, which would have been used to cultivate the soft soil. Rice and other plant harvesting and processing was undertaken with knives, pestles, and mortars. Wooden oars stress the importance of water transport, and net sinkers and fishing spears, associated with the remains of sharks and whales, crocodiles and turtles, attest to the exploitation of marine resources.

There are bone shuttles, needles, and spindle whorls, which show an advanced weaving technology that incorporated looms. The whorls, used to produce yarns, were found throughout the site's occupation. There was also a very large number and variety of

animal bones, which illustrates intensive hunting as well as a varied environment within reach of the site. The remains of deer, water buffalo, tigers, and bears have been found, as well as small arboreal animals such as the macaque and civet, and domestic dogs and pigs were raised.

Almost a thousand ceramic vessels were found in the lowest stratum at the site, exhibiting a wide variety of shapes and styles. It is evident that some were used for cooking, for the remains of cooked rice were found still adhering to the inside of a rectangular vessel known as a *fu*.

Hemudu illustrates how rice farmers who probably expanded out of the middle Yangzi wetlands had, by 5000 BC, attained a high level of technological skill. Their economy, based on the cultivation of aquatic plants and widespread hunting, fishing, gathering, and raising of domestic animals, was adaptive to a process of rapid and relatively risk-free expansion. This site also lies at the threshold of the movement of groups across the Taiwan Strait to the island of Taiwan. The presence of oars and strong rope at the site, together with carpentry skills, are compatible with deep-water transport that may well have stood at the origin of the expansion of Austronesian-speaking people (Chapter 8)

Luojiajiao lies north of the Hangzhou estuary, and excavations there have shown that sites exhibiting Hemudu cultural characteristics had a relatively wide distribution in this region. The lowest layer at this site was contemporary with the initial occupation of Hemudu, and was found to contain the same evidence for wooden houses, agricultural tools, pottery, and rice agriculture.

The Majiabang, Songze, and Chengbeixi Cultures Further north still, on the margins of Lake Tai, sites in northern Zhejiang and southern Jiangsu provinces have been ascribed to the **Majiabang culture**. Again, initial occupation dates to around 5000 BC. Houses were constructed on raised ground that gave access to wet lowlands for rice cultivation, and to marshes or lakes for fishing and fowling. Cemeteries were established as the villages were occupied permanently, the dead being interred with grave goods that included pottery vessels, tools, and jewelry.

Majiabang and Hemudu sites are notable for their lengthy occupation periods, indicating the stability of rice as the basis for subsistence. Rice also has the great advantage of being storable for later consumption.

The Songze culture was a later stage of the Majiabang culture in the lower Yangzi region. The site of Songze, in Shanghai, was first occupied *c.* 4000 BC and has provided a pollen spectrum that indicates quite extensive forest clearance. The cemetery at this site reveals an increase in mortuary offerings over the numbers seen at Majiabang sites, and the dead were here laid out in rows or clusters. Women were often buried wearing jade ornaments, and with pieces of jade placed in the mouth. Some individuals were also endowed with markedly richer offerings than others. At Beiyinyanying in Nanjing, a cemetery site where 225 burials have been uncovered, some individuals wore fine jade and agate ornaments, while pottery vessels and stone axes lay beyond the head and

7.16 *Jade* cong: *a* cong *is a ritually significant artifact fashioned from jade, and particularly characteristic of the Liangzhu culture of the Lower Yangzi Valley. They have a circular interior and square exterior, and are often embellished with human masks. This example comes from Tomb No. 7, Yaoshan, Yuhang, Zhejiang Province.*

feet. The quality of the ceramic vessels and jades found at Xuejiagang was likewise far higher than those from Majiabang sites. The Songze settlements represent a long and important phase that culminated in the Liangzhu culture sites (discussed further in Chapter 15), in which the quantity of jades and the ritual component of aristocratic graves signaled early steps on the path to state formation.

Upstream from the Lake Dongting area, the major sites of the Three Gorges belong to the **Chengbeixi culture**. They are found on the lower river terrace, which would have been prone to regular flooding, and on surrounding hill slopes. Although the pottery from these sites resembles that from Pengtoushan, there is insufficient evidence to confirm whether the rice remains were from wild or domestic plants. Excavations upstream at the city site of Sanxingdui in Sichuan Province have revealed Neolithic settlement by 4000 BC, indicating that there had been a movement of early agriculturalists upstream toward this key geographic area, where the headwaters of the Mekong and Salween provide riverine access to the south.

The Expansion of Rice Farmers into Southeast Asia

Identifying the transition to rice cultivation in the middle Yangzi lakelands has opened to serious review the origins of the early agricultural villages of Southeast Asia [**7.17**]. The search for a similar transition there, however, has so far provided only negative results. All the early village sites reveal fully developed agriculture in association with a range of other pursuits. Fine pottery vessels were manufactured with broadly similar decorative patterns; weaving was undertaken; houses were built on piles; people were buried in permanent cemeteries; and domestic cattle, pigs, and dogs were raised. After his excavations at the central Thai site of Ban Kao in 1961 and 1962, Per Sørensen (1972) proposed that farming groups ultimately from China settled this and related settlements as part of a major expansionary

movement. His ideas were not adopted then, but recently they have been revived and given additional credence as new evidence has become available. Any review of this issue must be undertaken in conjunction with the pattern of rivers, and possible migration by sea. In both contexts, the recovery of wooden oars and strong rope from Hemudu (see above) provides sound technological evidence for maritime and riverine transportation.

Initial Dispersal into Southern China

The **Tanshishan culture** of Fujian Province lies south of the Hemudu complex of sites but exhibits a number of parallels in material culture. Its radiocarbon dates suggest a southern expansion of farmers by about 3500 BC. Further west, the Gan, Xiang, and Bei rivers provide links between lakes Poyang and Dongting and the sub-tropical and extensive territory of Lingnan, in the area of the Pearl River estuary in Guangdong Province, between Hong Kong and Macao. This area was occupied over many millennia by impressively large maritime hunter-gatherer groups, but the interior has yielded occupation only in small rockshelters.

Egress from the Yangzi Valley into this extensive region of warm lowlands by intrusive agriculturalists should have left an indelible archaeological signature. This been recognized by, among others, Au Ka-fat (1993), who has described close similarities in pottery – in terms of the temper, form, decoration, and color – between the Hunan Province sites around Lake Dongting and sites in Lingnan. The 3rd-millennium BC settlements of Shixia, Xincun, Chuangbanling, and Niling lie in the valley of the Bei River, which flows south to Hong Kong. In its earliest phase, Shixia had a cemetery in which grave goods included jade *cong* (tubes with square or circular cross-section), bracelets, pendants, and split rings typically found in the **Liangzhu culture** of the lower Yangzi Valley [**7.16**] (Chapter 15). It befell to the later 3rd-millennium BC **Nianyuzhuan culture**, which almost certainly resulted from an intrusive movement into Lingnan from the Yangzi basin, to encounter and interact with rich hunter-gatherer groups commanding the delta of the Pearl River.

Further west, the configuration of rivers that emanate from the eastern Himalayas resembles the spokes of a wheel, with Yunnan Province at the hub. The Yangzi takes an easterly course, while the Red (Yuan), Mekong, Salween, and Irrawaddy rivers flow generally south, and the Brahmaputra, west. Movement in or through the densely forested and folded landscape of this region was and remains most easily undertaken via these rivers. Yunnan and, to a lesser extent, the Sichuan basin, are nodal, and it is therefore important to stress the presence of rice farmers in the former province by the critical late 3rd millennium BC at **Baiyangcun**. This site has a deep stratigraphic sequence, involving over 4 m (13 ft) of accumulated cultural material. The initial settlement has been dated to 2400–2100 BC, and excavations over an area of 225 sq. m (2422 sq. ft) have revealed the remains of houses and inhumation burials. Many of the human remains were found headless, and grave goods were absent; the pottery from this phase was decorated with a distinctive series of patterns that incorporated parallel incised lines infilled with impressions. A second site at **Dadunzi** is rather later, the single radiocarbon date suggesting occupation in the mid-2nd millennium BC. When excavated, house plans were noted, often superimposed over earlier structures, and 27 burials were encountered. Adults were buried in extended positions with no preferred orientation, and infants were interred in mortuary jars. The style of pottery decoration matched that found earlier at Baiyangcun.

From Southern China into Vietnam

The Red River (called the Song Hong in Vietnam) flows directly from Yunnan Province to the broad lowlands of northern Vietnam that surround its confluence with the Black River (Song Da). The presence of maritime hunter-gatherers on the Vietnamese coast has been documented for many decades, and it was in the limestone uplands that flank the Red River floodplain that the **Hoabinhian** hunter-gatherer complex was discovered, named after the province where it was first recognized. These sites were occupied, it is now thought, between 16,000–14,000 and 5000 BC. More recently, however, a new settlement pattern has been identified at sites ascribed to the Neolithic Phung Nguyen culture. Two recently obtained radiocarbon determinations from the culturally similar sites of Phia Diem and Ma Dong lie respectively between 3355–2315 and 2925–2550 BC. Research at Co Loa has also revealed initial settlement during this phase, from about 2000 BC. Most settlements cover 1–3 ha (2.5–7.5 acres), and are found on slightly elevated terrain near small stream confluences. Phung Nguyen itself covers 3 ha (7.5 acres), of which 3960 sq. m (42,600 sq. ft) have been excavated.

7.17 Rice agriculture and languages: *the distribution of sites containing domestic rice remains in East and Southeast Asia suggests that the transition from hunting and gathering to farming took place in the Yangzi Valley. Agricultural communities then began an inexorable spread by the river valleys to the west and south. This probably saw the linked spread of Austro-Asiatic languages that are found today from eastern India to Vietnam, and from southern China to the Nicobar Islands.*

The material culture of the Phung Nguyen society represents a complete break in the cultural sequence of this region. Spindle whorls attest to a weaving industry, and bone harpoons suggest some form of hunting. Over 1000 stone adzes in a variety of forms have been found, as well as small stone chisels and whetstones. The inhabitants of Phung Nguyen also included highly skilled lapidaries who fashioned nephrite bangles and beads. There was a vigorous tradition of working clay, and changing decorative styles on pottery vessels have enabled the Vietnamese excavators to designate at least three phases to this culture. Significantly, the technique and motifs employed in decorating Phung Nguyen pottery [**7.18**] are seen also at Baiyangcun and Dadunzi in Yunnan Province. In addition, the form and decoration of the Phung Nguyen spindle whorls bear close parallels with those of the Tanshishan sites of Fujian Province in southeast China.

There are other parallels with Chinese sites. The site of **Trang Kenh** incorporates a workshop for the manufacture of nephrite bracelets and beads, involving working with chisels, drill points, saws, and grinding stones. Radiocarbon dates suggest that the workshop dates to about 1650–1500 BC, but the introduction of craft skills for working nephrite and jadeite ornaments represent a key link with the Chinese Neolithic. The value attached to stone jewelry and weaponry is also in evidence at **Lung Hoa**.

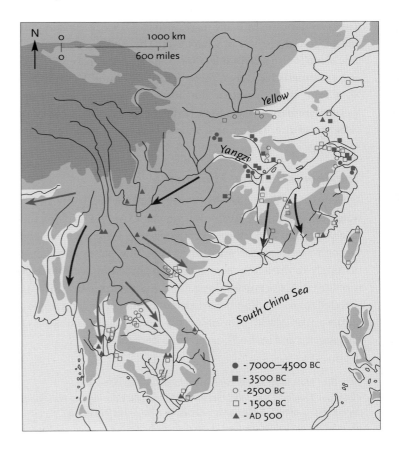

7.18 *Phung Nguyen pottery decoration: the pottery vessels at Phung Nguyen follow a widespread Neolithic preference for incised and impressed designs of considerable complexity. These examples probably date to between 2300 and 1500 BC. Their designs are widely paralleled among early farming sites in Southeast Asia and southern China.*

An increasing number of Neolithic contexts are now coming to light in this region, often deeply stratified beneath later Bronze and Iron Age deposits. Thus at **Ban Non Wat**, a large moated site in the Mun Valley of eastern Thailand, the Iron Age deposits were found to overlie first a Bronze Age cemetery, and then a Neolithic occupation horizon complete with evidence for rice cultivation, domestic animals, and burials associated with black ceramic vessels decorated with incised, burnished, and painted motifs. One male skeleton was found in a crouched position within a large, lidded vessel almost 1 m (3 ft) in diameter [**7.19**]. A charcoal sample from within the mortuary jar has been dated to about 2100 BC.

Early Rice Farmers in Thailand The establishment of rice-farming villages, which took place in Thailand according to present information from about 2300 BC, may be considered through this archaeological record, as well as from the study of cores taken from natural swamp or lake deposits. Most information from the core samples comes from a research program at Lake Kumphawapi, an extensive, shallow body of water in Udorn Thani Province, northeast Thailand (Penny et al. 1996; Kealhofer 1996; 1997). The study of the pollen evidence is handicapped by the difficulty of distinguishing between that of rice and other grasses, but increasingly wet conditions were noted from about 4500–3700 BC. In addition there were marked changes in the vegetation cover compatible with increasing rice cultivation over the last 2000 years, rather than

This late Phung Nguyen site is characterized by deep graves, some cut over 5 m (16 ft) into the ground and equipped, as in the Fubin culture of Lingnan (late 2nd millennium BC), with ledges. While it might be argued that the pottery, jade-working, and burial techniques could have had independent origins in Vietnam, definite links with China are seen in some imported jades. One *ge* (a halberd – an axe-like weapon) is particularly interesting, because it matches examples found in southern China and north into the early urban states at Sanxingdui and Erlitou, discussed in Chapter 15. The *yazhang* ceremonial jade blade is also a central feature of the latter two assemblages, and specimens have been recovered from Phung Nguyen and Xom Ren. It is clear that the intrusive Neolithic groups in Vietnam remained in contact with the increasingly complex societies of the Yangzi and Yellow rivers in China (Ha Van Tan 1993).

The Khorat Plateau, Thailand

The Mekong River provides a direct link between the headwaters of the Yangzi River and the extensive lowlands of the Khorat Plateau in northeast Thailand. After the river's passage through the dissected uplands of Laos, the plateau stretches invitingly to the south, access being provided by a network of tributaries. A site survey along these river courses in 1990–91 revealed many small settlement mounds that provided samples of the same black, pattern-incised pottery as was found at Baiyangcun and in the Phung Nguyen sites.

7.19 *Ban Non Wat: at the large moated site of Ban Non Wat in northeast Thailand, the initial settlement took place during the Neolithic period. Here, an adult man was interred in a huge pottery vessel. Charcoal found under the lid has been dated to 2100 BC.*

7.20 Southeast Asian Neolithic pottery: *pottery vessels from Neolithic sites in Southeast Asia display similar designs and decorative techniques. These mortuary vessels, dating between 2100 and 1400 BC, come from Ban Non Wat in northeast Thailand. The vessel to the left has a rim diameter of 42 cm (17 in).*

the period from 2100 BC, when the first Neolithic settlement is archaeologically documented. Cores from Lake Kumphawapi have also shed light on the activities of hunter-gatherers who occupied the area (e.g. White 1997).

The archaeological evidence for early rice farmers in this part of the Mekong Valley comes from several sites, although none has been extensively excavated. Two radiocarbon determinations from early Neolithic burial ceramics at the site of Ban Chiang, excavated in 1974, suggest that this site was first occupied by *c.* 2000 BC. One of the comforting aspects of this pair of dates is their conformity with the slightly earlier determinations from northern Vietnam and Yunnan Province in China. Twenty burials were uncovered at Ban Chiang, all but one coming from the second mortuary phase.

At least three more sites provide evidence for early rice cultivation. The site of **Non Nok Tha**, located about 140 km (90 miles) to the southwest, may have been occupied in the Neolithic period, according to the AMS (accelerator mass spectrometry) technique for radiocarbon dating (see box, p. 157). The earliest phase has furnished determinations of 2307–1858 and 1770–1310 BC. Either the initial settlement took place at about the same time as at Ban Chiang, or the site was first occupied in the middle centuries of the 2nd millennium BC.

In 1974, Richard Schauffler (1976) excavated a small trench at the Neolithic site of **Ban Phak Top**, located about 25 km (15.5 miles) southwest of Ban Chiang. He obtained a large radiocarbon sample dating to *c.* 2500 BC, interpreted as preceding the first occupation there. The lowest cultural level has a date of *c.* 2000 BC, and level 8 provided three dates of between 1500 and 1000 BC. Excavations at **Ban Lum Khao**, located further south in the upper Mun Valley, in 1995–96 encountered a Bronze Age cemetery, stratified over an initial occupation phase that yielded

the familiar black incised and impressed pottery style. The five well-provenanced determinations for this first occupation phase suggest initial settlement by about 1275 BC.

Detailed insight into subsistence and the environment on the plateau also comes from Ban Lum Khao, where several pits were found. The mammalian remains include bones from water buffalo so large as to fall well within the range for wild rather than domestic animals. One pit contained the bones from 11 Eld's deer, as well as an adult sambar deer and a muntjak; there were also bones of pig and domestic dog. A second pit contained the bones of three water buffalo and deer, as well as over 100 turtle carapace fragments. Riverine fish were remarkably abundant, most of them much larger than the current catch. Taken in conjunction with the large hunted water buffalo and deer, it seems probable that the first occupants of Ban Lum Khao, and probably the other late Neolithic sites from the upper Mun Valley, entered an uninhabited land.

There appears to be a consistent pattern to these radiocarbon determinations. On present evidence, the Neolithic period on the Khorat Plateau lasted for a millennium, from *c.* 2300 to 1300 BC. The first rice farmers introduced the inhumation burial rite, in which the dead were interred in a supine position with mortuary offerings that included pottery vessels [7.20], animal bones, and personal ornaments. At **Non Kao Noi**, for example, excavations in 1980 revealed a group of inhumation burials, one of which was accompanied by three incised pottery vessels, while another wore beads of an exotic green stone (Higham and Kijngam 1984). From evidence obtained from these sites we know that early settlers brought with them weaving techniques and domestic stock, and that they chose to live near gently flooded terrain suited to rice cultivation; they also intensively hunted, fished, and collected shellfish.

Cambodia and the Mekong Delta

Further down the Mekong Valley, the famous site of Samrong Sen in central Cambodia has produced pottery vessels virtually identical in their decorative motifs to those of the Khorat Plateau. Approaching the Mekong Delta and the nearby Dong Nai River valley, new sites are beginning to reveal a pattern of early agricultural settlement also similar to that of the plateau.

In 1963, the French archaeologist Louis Malleret (1959–63) could only describe the known prehistoric settlements in the most general terms. One site in particular, **Cu Lao Rua**, better known as the Isle de la Tortue, was the best documented, having been described as early as 1888 by Emile Cartaillhac. Excavations ensued in 1902 and 1937, and a local businessman assembled a collection of artifacts from the site, including shouldered and quadrangular adzes, much pottery, and stone bracelets, pendants, and polishers.

Now, however, archaeologist Pham Duc Manh (2000) has advanced a four-fold division of later prehistory in the Dong Nai Valley, of which the first phase belongs to the Neolithic period and dates within the period 2500–2000 BC. The sequence begins with the site of **Cau Sat**, which is characterized by shouldered adzes and stone arm rings with a rectangular or trapezoidal cross-section. The pottery from this site includes pedestalled bowls and tall jars with a flat base. The second phase incorporates sites described by Henri Fontaine (1972), of which **Ben Do** is best known. The excavator, Pham Van Kinh, has published the many large shouldered adzes from t his site; of these, the shouldered form is much more abundant than adzes with a quadrangular cross-section and no shoulder. Masanari Nishimura (2002) also finds evidence for four cultural phases in the Dong Nai Valley, with a sequence beginning c. 2000 BC.

There is further possible evidence for Neolithic settlement up the coast of southern and central Vietnam. Xom Con, for example, has yielded round-based and pedestalled pottery decorated with incised and infilled designs, in addition to polished stone adzes and barbed bone points. Inland, there are sites of similar age and parallel material culture, designated the Bien Ho culture.

The Bangkok Plain

The coast of the Gulf of Thailand and its interior broad floodplain of the Chao Phraya River, sometimes called the Bangkok Plain, present a varied tapestry of habitats and evidence for prehistoric adaptation. Excavations in the lower reaches of the Bang Pakong River valley have demonstrated a thick distribution of coastal settlements that were occupied by marine hunter-gatherers by at least the mid-3rd millennium BC. Nong Nor, one such site on the shore of an extensive bay, was occupied for a season in about 2400 BC; its inhabitants hunted marine mammals, brought in large sharks, and collected hundreds of thousands of shellfish. They also made pottery vessels and fashioned polished stone adzes, but they did not, as far as the evidence reveals, consume rice or have any knowledge of domestic animals, including the dog.

Khok Phanom Di and Ban Kao A few centuries later, c. 2000 BC, the same material culture and evidence for marine hunting and gathering is found at **Khok Phanom Di**, located only 14 km (8.75 miles) north of Nong Nor [see box: Khok Phanom Di: Sedentary Hunter-Fishers, pp. 254–55]. The first settlers chose to live at the mouth of a large estuary dominated by mangroves. Once again, there is no evidence for domestic dogs, but a small number of exotic potsherds were tempered with rice. Over the ensuing five centuries, environmental changes were closely tied in with changes in mortuary practices, material culture, and the economy. Thus, when sea levels fell and freshwater conditions prevailed, there is evidence for local rice cultivation. With a return to marine conditions, however, shell knives and granite hoes disappear. There is also some evidence for the arrival at the site of a new group of people, but not in sufficient numbers to replace the existing population.

The intrusive element at Khok Phanom Di, identified on the basis of slight changes in mortuary behavior, the arrival of the domestic dog, and preferences in material culture, must be considered in conjunction with the establishment of rice agriculture in newly founded settlements in the hinterland. Just north of Lopburi, the monotonous, flat floodplain of the Chao Phraya River is relieved by hilly outcrops that contain veins of copper ore. This area has attracted intensive research since the early 1980s, including a survey in which Karen Mudar (1995) identified a series of sites that, on the basis of surface finds, are probably Neolithic. Lisa Kealhofer (1997) has examined the Holocene vegetation history of this key area on the basis of two cores, one taken from an old river channel adjacent to the prehistoric site of Tha Kae (discussed below), and the second from an old floodplain meander 15 km (9 miles) to the north. Both reveal a sharp increase in carbon around 2500 BC, and evidence for agriculture is particularly evident at Tha Kae from about 2000 BC. These results indicate human modification of the environment virtually from the start of the sequences, including major changes consistent with agriculture in the period 2500–2000 BC. There is also, however, the possibility of some form of agricultural activity as early as c. 3700 BC.

Archaeological excavations in this area have so far failed to identify any occupation by rice farmers earlier than 2500–2000 BC. The Bang site near the village of **Ban Kao** was the first Neolithic site to be examined in detail in this area [7.23]. It lies in Kanchanaburi Province, near two tributaries that flow into the Khwae Noi River. It is not large, covering only 8000 sq. m

7.21 Stone adzes: these were ubiquitous in Neolithic Asian contexts, and would have facilitated forest clearance and the manufacture of houses and boats.

7.22 Ban Kao pottery: early Neolithic pottery vessels from Ban Kao in Central Thailand include distinctive tripod vessels that have been cited as evidence of links with southern China. The pot is 30 cm (12 in) in diameter.

(86,000 sq. ft), of which 400 sq. m (4300 sq. ft) were excavated in 1961–62 (Sørensen and Hatting 1967). A total of 42 inhumation graves were opened, divided into early and late Neolithic groups (radiocarbon-dated to c. 2300–1500 BC) on the basis of their depth below the surface and the form of the pottery vessels found as mortuary offerings.

There is some evidence for patterning in the burials: where it is possible to determine the sex of a skeleton, it seems that men and women were interred in pairs, women being found oriented with the head to the northwest, the men in the opposite direction. The burial of men, women, children, and infants in what were almost certainly family groups is widespread in prehistoric Southeast Asia. Only one infant interment was found at the Bang site, however, which means either that young and fragile bones did not survive, or that they were buried else-where. In the early phase bodies were buried with pottery vessels and stone adzes, while the later burials incorporated richer sets of grave goods, including more pottery vessels, adzes [7.21], shell disk beads, the bones of young pigs, freshwater bivalve shells, and stone beads.

The importance of this site goes well beyond the quantity of graves and the quality of complete mortuary assemblages. Stone bangles were manufactured there, and the bone fish-hooks and clay net weights reflect the role of fish in the diet. There are shell knives and stone sickles, probably used to harvest rice. Spindle whorls are evidence for a textile industry, and the whetstones were probably used to sharpen stone adzes. The Bang site also produced a wide range of pottery forms, the most distinctive being a bowl raised on tripod feet [7.22]. Similar forms have been found over a very wide area from

7.23 Ban Kao: the excavation of the Bang site at Ban Kao, Thailand, was the first major exposure of a Neolithic cemetery in Southeast Asia, and led the excavator, Per Sørensen, to suggest an inward movement of rice farmers from China.

Kanchanaburi south to peninsular Malaysia. Per Sørensen has noted their presence at Sai Yok, and at the site of Nong Chae Sao in Kanchanaburi Province, where two burials were found under what may well be the remains of a domestic building. Rasmi Shoocondej (1996) has described this pottery assemblage at Han Songchram and Rai Arnon, also in Kanchanaburi Province, while far to the south, parallels have been found at upper layers of the Lang Rongrien rockshelter, located in the Krabi River valley of Thailand, and at Jenderam Hilir on the western coastal plain of Malaysia. Leong Sau Heng (1991) has suggested that the latter site, dated from the later 3rd millennium BC, represents the intrusion of rice farmers.

Khok Charoen, Non Pai Wai, and Tha Kae Not long after the completion of the Ban Kao excavations, William Watson (1979) and Helmut Loofs-Wissowa (1967) began their investigations of **Khok Charoen**, a settlement located at the junction of two small streams, on an ecotone (a meeting of two environmental regions) between the Petchabun Range and the Pa Sak flood-plain. Trial soundings in 1966 revealed five inhumation burials accompanied by pottery vessels and polished stone adzes; major excavations began in 1967. Ultimately, almost 400 sq. m (4300 sq. ft) were excavated and 44 burials uncovered [**7.24**]. The burials follow a widespread pattern, being extended inhumations with an array of grave goods. The ceramic specialist Chu-mei Ho has concluded that there is a considerable differential in wealth between graves, the richest one being accompanied by 19 pottery vessels, stone beads, ten shell and nine stone bracelets, and many small shell disk beads. Other burials were less well endowed, though shell disk beads were found in the pelvic areas of some skeletons, and small, trapezoidal, polished stone adzes were common.

Pottery vessels found include examples with incised and impressed decoration recalling those from Tha Kae, Ban Chiang, and Non Pa Wai; others were cord-marked and red-slipped. Much of the shell used to make ornaments has a marine origin, *Trochus* being used for bracelets, ear ornaments, and possibly finger rings, and *Conus* for small rings that Ho believes could

KEY SITE Khok Phanom Di: Sedentary Hunter-Fishers

Khok Phanom Di is located about 23 km (14 miles) from the present shore of the Gulf of Thailand. It is unique in East and Southeast Asia for several reasons, including its special conditions for preservation. Partially digested food remains were found with one of the skeletons, and feces have documented the diet of humans and dogs. Wood survives in some of the postholes, and the excavation of a 10 x 10-m (33 x 33-ft) area in 1984–85, which involved the wet sieving of a sample of deposits, yielded an extraordinary range of biological data, including plant remains and microscopic shellfish, forams (*foraminifera*, skeletons of shelled protozoa), and ostracods (Higham and Thosarat 1994).

The site accumulated so rapidly between 2000 and 1500 BC that graves of members of descent groups were found superimposed over about 18 generations. The bone was very well preserved, allowing a detailed consideration of individual health and longevity. Many specialists have contributed to the analysis of the excavated material, permitting the history of a community to be tracked over a period of environmental change, which included growing interaction with intrusive groups of rice farmers into the hinterland of the site.

History of the Community

Despite such clarity of evidence, the interpretation of this site within the broad framework of Southeast Asian prehistory has not finally been resolved, although certain facts are well documented. The settlement was established around 2000 BC, when a group of marine hunter-gatherers settled near the mouth of a major estuary that was fringed with a dense belt of mangroves. There, they exploited the wealth of marine food, collecting shellfish from the mudflats, fishing, and hunting. They made their pottery vessels from the good-quality local clay, and imported stone adzes. By this date, rice farmers were already established upstream, and it is likely that these coastal hunters were in contact with them.

It is possible to trace the history of this community through seven mortuary phases. Men, women, children, and infants were interred in tight clusters during phases 2–4. Men had strong upper body musculature, most likely as a result of seafaring or taking their boats upriver, but anemia was widespread, probably caused by a condition known as thalassaemia, which had the advantage of conferring some immunity to malaria (Tayles 1999). Infant mortality was very high, with many babies dying at birth.

Freshwater indicators increased during mortuary phase 3. During this period also the presence of dogs is attested, and harvesting knives and stone hoes show that

7.25 *Pottery vessels were locally manufactured at Khok Phanom Di to a very high standard. The finest, special vessels were placed with the dead.*

7.24 Khok Charoen: *a general view of excavations at the site. By the end of the excavations 44 burials had been uncovered, showing considerable differences in wealth. Grave goods included pottery vessels, and stone and shell jewelry, as well as polished stone adzes.*

the inhabitants were cultivating some rice locally.

Perhaps some marriage partners came to Khok Phanom Di from agriculturally based villages in its orbit, for there were subtle changes in mortuary practices and in pottery decoration at this juncture. Marine conditions returned in mortuary phase 5, and rice cultivation ceased in favor of marine hunting and gathering. Five burials from this phase were fabulously wealthy in terms of grave goods, one woman being found with over 100,000 shell beads. By the following phase, people were being interred in elaborate mortuary buildings with clay walls.

Overview

Some specialists find it hard to acknowledge that Khok Phanom Di was the product of marine hunters and fishers. The ceramic vessels are of outstanding quality, and the community included individuals of very great wealth. This, they feel, is more consistent with the intrusive farming communities.

However, the biological and artifactual evidence indicate that rice farming was practiced only for a few generations, when conditions became favorable. The excavators,

Charles Higham and Rachanie Thosarat, believe that Khok Phanom Di documents the interaction between indigenous sedentary hunter-fishers and intrusive rice farmers, interaction that involved exchange and, on occasion, intermarriage.

7.26 *(Below left) The richest burial at Khok Phanom Di comes from Mortuary Phase 5. The woman wore over 100,000 shell beads, shell disks, a bangle, and ear ornaments. She was also interred with superb pottery vessels, and her tools for fashioning pots.*

7.27 *(Below) Burials at Khok Phanom Di were laid out in family groups, distributed in clusters. They were accompanied by fine ceramic vessels, bone and shell jewelry.*

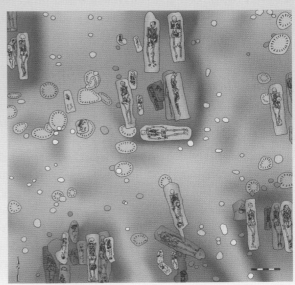

have been worn on the fingers. No radiocarbon dates are available. Some of the shell jewelry recalls the forms recovered at Khok Phanom Di, a situation similar to that of the site of Huai Yai, from which come H-shaped shell beads that were virtually identical with those unearthed first in Khok Phanom Di during mortuary phase 6.

Non Pa Wai, located in the Khao Wong Prachan Valley, is best known for its abundant evidence for the extraction and processing of copper ore. This began about 1500–1300 BC. The accumulation of slag and casting debris overlies a 75-cm (29-in) deep occupation layer rich in sherds, stone adzes, and marine shell jewelry (Pigott et al. 1997). The pottery was decorated with the incised and impressed designs common throughout the region, but there was also a new and localized style in which the pots were formed within baskets, which left an unmistakable surface texture; this pottery has been christened "elephant hide" ware. Sixteen Neolithic burials were also found, with grave goods including pottery vessels, stone adzes, and marine shell jewelry.

To judge from the shellfish and faunal remains recovered in this early context, the site originally lay within a low-lying and swampy habitat. In his study of the human remains, Anagnosti Agelarakis (1997) has noted that only one individual, a man, survived into his 30s, and there was relatively high mortality among those who were still in their teens. In general health was not good: eight out of ten skeletons displaying evidence of having suffered childhood stress. Dental wear, however, revealed a diet of well-prepared food compatible with an agricultural community.

Tha Kae is located a few kilometers south of Non Pa Wai, and the initial occupation at each is very similar. There are burials with red-slipped and black-incised and impressed pottery styles, along with shell beads, bivalve shells, bangles, and earrings. The motifs and forms of several pottery vessels recovered from earlier excavations at this site include incised and impressed decoration in the form of snakes and possibly stylized humans, the latter paralleled in late graves at Khok Phanom Di. The local manufacture of marine shell bangles also provides evidence for exchange contact with coastal groups (Ciarla 1992).

Fiorella Rispoli (1997) has undertaken a regional study of the decoration found on pottery vessels from these early Neolithic sites and has identified four main categories. The first is now familiar, the black-burnished ware with incised and impressed designs. The potters also applied a thick red slip to the rims and necks of some vessels, or red-painted designs. Elephant hide ware is another type, but has a very limited distribution. The recovery of such ceramics during site surveys suggests a dense distribution of sites in the eastern margins of the Bangkok Plain north of Lopburi, particularly where springs

7.28 Cow-shaped vessel: this unusually shaped vessel was found in a burial at the site of Non Mak La.

emerge from the surrounding foothills. At one of these, the site of Non Mak La, Neolithic burials were found, associated with impressive mortuary vessels and stone and shell jewelry. Excavations there in 1994 by Vincent Pigott and Andrew Weiss encountered an unusual pottery vessel in the form of a cow [7.28], and two burials in a cruciform pattern. Infants were often interred in ceramic vessels (Pigott et al. 1997).

The Gulf of Thailand and the Bangkok Plain thus present in microcosm a drama that must have unfolded in virtually every part of East and Southeast Asia where intrusive farmers met indigenous hunter-gatherers. The latter groups should not be identified as small and mobile groups of relative insignificance, for in Japan and the Pearl River estuary of southeast China, many communities were large and complex. The same situation is seen in the lower layers at Khok Phanom Di, where it has proved possible to pinpoint interactions through exchange and even the mixing of populations. Ultimately, however, it was always the agriculturalists who came to dominate the relationship.

The Expansion of Rice Farmers into Korea and Japan

Korea

Korean riverine and coastal settlements incorporating pit houses stretch from the Yalu and Tumen rivers in the north to the southern coast; they have been given the name **Chulmun** (comb ware) culture, after the pottery found there. Far too little is understood about the degree to which agriculture coexisted with the abundant evidence at these sites for maritime hunting and gathering, and only a few burials have been found. However, sites like Osanni, dating to between 6000 and 4500 BC, reveal the existence of round to oval dwellings centered upon hearths. Numerous stone fishhooks and weights, which probably represent net fishing, indicate a maritime orientation.

Tongsamdong, on Pusan Bay to the south, comprises a shell midden incorporating the remains of sharks, tuna, cod, sea lions, and whales; wild cattle and pig were also hunted. Sopohang, on the Tumen River near Russian Siberia, is a large mound in which oyster shells predominate, the superimposed house floors indicating a degree of permanence in settlement.

One house yielded 40 bone awls, perhaps evidence of some form of specialization (Nelson 1993). The recovery of the remains of millet, as at Chitamni, as well as slate hoes, suggests that agriculture was introduced into the region from northeastern China. This appears to have stimulated major population changes, for the number of Chulmun sites increased from the mid-4th millennium BC, and their area expanded in an easterly direction.

The cultivation of millet spread across the Korean peninsula from about 4500 BC. Rice cultivation was underway from the beginning of the 2nd millennium BC, and possibly by late 3rd millennium BC, and rapidly became a major domesticate. The question of why rice came so late to Korea, relative to millet, is easily resolved: Korean rice belongs to the *japonica* variety, which underwent a process of selective adaptation to the cold conditions of the peninsula compared with its sub-tropical homeland, a process that would have required many centuries. A pollen core from the Kimpo swamp has produced rice pollen dated to around 2000 BC, while at Kumgokdong, rice phytoliths have been identified in Mumun ("undecorated") pottery (Nelson 1999), the dominant pottery in Korea c. 500–300 BC.

Since rice is not native to Korea, it must have been introduced from China, but the conjunction of rice with distinctively local ceramics is a strong indication that it was incorporated into pre-existing agricultural communities, particularly when it is associated, as at Hunamni and Songungon, with millet and sorghum. Hunamni, dated to the mid-2nd millennium BC, produced spindle whorls and harvesting tools. Songungon is an important site because a conflagration there led to the survival of wooden tools, including a spade.

The fine red-ware pottery vessels, dated to the early 1st millennium BC, match those found in dolmen tombs [**7.29**] (most comprised of two large upright stones supporting a capstone) associated with rice-farming villages. The considerable size of these tombs (one capstone weighed over 160 tons) and the presence of fine ceramics and jade grave goods within them suggest strongly that the surplus provided by rice agriculture was associated with the rise of a social elite.

7.29 *Korean dolmen tombs:* *the dead were buried in dolmens of considerable size in Korea after the establishment of rice farming. This one is from Kangwha Island west of Seoul, and dates to about 1000 BC.*

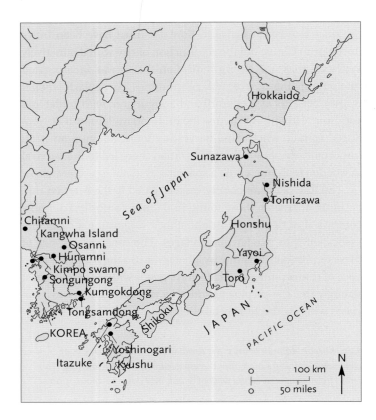

7.30 *Korea and Japan: map showing the major sites mentioned in the text.*

established by about 300–200 BC, along with local skills in casting bronze [7.32] and working iron. During the Middle Yayoi, there was a marked expansion of agricultural settlement from Kyushu, the southernmost of the main islands of Japan, then past the Inland Sea and into Honshu; sharp social divisions and large regional polities were forming during the Late Yayoi.

Jomon Antecedents Before the emergence of the Yayoi culture, however, Japan had been occupied by hunter-gatherer groups known collectively as the Jomon culture. Jomon means "cord-pattern," a characteristic of their pottery. This was one of the most complex and enduring hunter-gatherer traditions in the world, lasting from *c.* 10,500 to 300 BC (with an incipient phase beginning *c.* 14,000 BC) and responsible for a magnificent and early tradition of pottery manufacture. Pottery has long been associated with Jomon culture sites, and new discoveries are now revealing that it is even older than once thought. In central Honshu, pottery sherds have been found sealed by pumice deposited by Mount Asama; radiocarbon dates indicate an age in the vicinity of 14,000 BC.

Japan

Rice cultivation in Japan was only established widely during the period of the **Yayoi culture**, of which there are three major phases: Early (300–100 BC), Middle (100 BC–AD 100), and Late (until AD 300). This is a crucial period in East Asia, because it was during these six centuries that the foundations of Japanese civilization were laid. These rested on the firm base of rice cultivation [7.31], linked with bronze and iron metallurgy and increasing contact with China and Korea (Chapter 15). The critical issue of the origins of the Yayoi have not been completely resolved, even if the main points are evident: rice farming in prepared fields, following the developed Chinese method, was

7.31 *Yayoi agriculture: the Yayoi culture saw the arrival of rice farmers in Japan. These wooden agricultural tools survived at Kotoragawa, including a spade and a hoe. The spade is 114.5 cm (45 in) long.*

7.32 *Yayoi bronzeworking: bronze came to Japan along with rice agriculture. This period saw the rise of elites, and one of their major bronze items were decorated bells.*

7.33, 7.34: *Jomon pottery:* *some of the Jomon pottery of Japan reached levels of sophistication rarely encountered elsewhere in hunter-gatherer societies. The name Jomon means "cord-pattern," a characteristic of their pottery. The Middle Jomon vessel (left) is from Kamiina county, Nagano and is 61 cm (24 in) high, and the Late Jomon vessel (right) is from Horinouchi shell mound, Ichikawa, and is 42.5 cm (16.75 in) high.*

Many Jomon sites on the island of Honshu have yielded evidence for sea fishing, the haul including tuna and mackerel, dolphins, and turtles. The site of **Nishida** (Late Jomon, *c.* 1500–1000 BC), in northern Honshu, is not located on the coast, but its layout and size indicate long-term sedentary occupation [see box: Sedentism without Agriculture, p. 260]. The center of the site was set aside for burying the dead in rectangular graves, of which 192 were excavated. The cemetery was ringed by rectangular houses; beyond lay storage pits.

The occupants of such Jomon settlements made outstanding and complex pottery vessels, some for ceremonial use, others for food processing or cooking (Tsutsumi 1999) [7.33, 7.34]. The ingredients of preserved biscuits reveal how well the Jomon people lived: they included a flour made from ground walnuts and chestnuts, meat and blood, and birds' eggs. The Late Jomon people were familiar with rice, which has been found associated with their pottery (Yoshizaki 1997). They also began to cultivate some local wild plants, such as the beefsteak herb and barnyard grass (Crawford and Takamiya 1990; Barnes 1993).

As we have seen, by the beginning of the 2nd millennium BC the knowledge and practice of rice cultivation was spreading into Korea, and it was only a matter of time before it crossed into the Japanese islands. The basic issue is whether rice farming was introduced, along with bronze and iron metallurgy, into northern Kyushu by a wave of immigrant groups, or if it was brought more gradually into social contexts involving Jomon communities, which, in due course, integrated rice farming into their long-established economy.

Yayoi Rice Farmers At **Itazuke**, an important site in northern Kyushu, archaeologists have recovered Early Yayoi-style potsherds in association with Yusu ware. The latter has been assigned to the late Jomon culture, although there is a school of thought that assigns it to the Yayoi proper. Resolving this issue is relevant to the question of Yayoi origins, because the remains of irrigated rice fields at Itazuke have been found in association with Yusu pottery alone and date to about 500–300 BC.

The settlement, surrounded by a moat, occupied an area of about 100 x 80 m (330 x 260 ft), within which archaeologists have uncovered storage pits, and burials in jars and pits. Beyond, on an adjacent low terrace, embanked rice fields were fed by irrigation canals. Such a sophisticated system surely indicates contact with established rice-farming communities in Korea or even mainland China, probably involving the settlement of immigrant groups. This interpretation relies not only on the archaeological record of new subsistence activities and types of artifact. Although not abundant by any means, human remains indicate that the Yayoi were taller than their Jomon counterparts, and their heads were of a different shape. Estimates of the population of Japan during the late Jomon period and that typical at the end of the Yayoi, based on settlement sizes and numbers, also indicate that there must have been a considerable degree of immigration.

The establishment of intrusive rice-farming communities in Kyushu from about 300 BC was followed by a progressive expansion to the northeast into Honshu, the central and largest of the Japanese islands. The extreme climatic conditions of Hokkaido, further north, on the other hand, favored the

KEY DISCOVERY Sedentism without Agriculture

The tropical estuary is one of the three richest environments known in terms of natural bio-productivity. The food chain on the warmer coasts begins with the constant fall of mangrove leaves, which feed the many small marine organisms, and so to higher levels into which humans can tap for their food requirements. Fish, shellfish, crabs, and marine mammals are so abundant and regularly available in these regions that hunter-gatherers could, in theory, have settled permanently in one place. In the recent past, large and complex hunter-gatherer societies occupied the sounds of British Columbia and the warm shores of Florida.

During the height of the late Pleistocene in East and Southeast Asia, low sea levels left vast areas of the present continental shelves exposed. Prehistoric settlement along the old shorelines is a lost chapter in the prehistory of the region until about 3000–4000 BC, when the sea rose higher than its present level and thus formed shorelines that today lie inland. The absence of a wide continental shelf around Japan means that the long-term adaptation of hunters and gatherers to the rich coastal habitat can be traced there.

The hunter-gatherers of the long-lived Jomon culture, from its incipient phase (beginning *c.* 14,000 BC) until its final phase (ending *c.* 300 BC), attained remarkable levels of technical and social sophistication, and their sedentary way of life encouraged the development of skills normally associated with early farmers.

The Jomon people lived in relatively sedentary settlements, possibly related to seasonal hunting, gathering, and fishing activities. They made some of the earliest clay pottery known, used for cooking mollusks and preparing vegetable foods. Other examples of early pottery have come from this region, and from southern Kyushu.

On the Asian continent, equally early pottery manufacture has been found associated with hunter-gatherer sites from southern China to eastern Russia. At the Dayan Cave in Guangxi Province, for example, coarse pottery built up of slabs of clay dates to as early as 14,000 BC. This site illustrates an intriguing relationship between the incidence of pottery and gastropod shellfish, the flesh of which is easier to obtain once the shellfish is heated. Until the presence of coarse clay vessels, the shells were all crushed, but with the first potsherds, the shells were recovered undamaged.

Far less is known of rich and sedentary hunter-gatherer groups on the Asian mainland, due to the fact that the wide continental shelves they inhabited are now under water. However, at inland sites settled after the sea rose, we can explore the adaptive pattern that must surely have developed over many millennia.

At Nong Nor and Khok Phanom Di [see box, Khok Phanom Di: Sedentary Hunter-Fishers, pp. 254–55], both located behind the present Gulf of Thailand, marine hunters and gatherers enjoyed the opportunities afforded by the resources of the warm and shallow sea. Adept navigators, they brought in whales and dolphins, sharks, and many oceanic fish, and collected shellfish by the hundred thousand. The dead were interred with well-made pottery vessels and other grave goods, including polished stone adzes.

Ultimately, these sedentary hunter-gatherer groups were exposed to immigrant farmers (Barnes 1993). In Japan, the agricultural Yayoi culture rapidly replaced the Jomon groups in the late 1st millennium BC, save for those in the cold north of Hokkaido (the most northerly of the islands of Japan). In Thailand, two or three centuries of interaction took place between the two groups, possibly involving some transfer of marriage partners. Ultimately, however, it was the farming groups with their more adaptive and predictable subsistence base who came to dominate.

---

persistence of hunter-gatherers, whose descendants, in all probability, constitute the surviving Ainu people of today. The rapidity of this initial expansion – rice was being intensively farmed in northern Honshu only two or three centuries after its establishment in northern Kyushu – is a widespread feature of agricultural radiation that is also documented in Southeast Asia and Europe. In Japan, it is seen in the widespread distribution east and west of the Inland Sea of a pottery style known as Ongagawa ware.

This spread of rice cultivation appears to have moved north even by the end of the Early Yayoi period, as evidenced by the presence of rice fields at Sunazawa and slightly later fields at Tomizawa, located respectively in northern and northeastern Honshu. The growth in the numbers of settlements during the Middle Yayoi phase together with the expansion from low-lying coastal flats to elevated terrain overlooking river valleys both appear to have contributed to an increase in social friction: sites were ringed by defensive ditches, and stone arrowheads proliferated.

Tantalizing information on the Late Yayoi period comes from a Chinese historic text known as the *Wei zhi* ("History of the Kingdom of Wei"), which dates to the late 3rd century AD. It describes the Wa people of the Japanese islands as possessing a social hierarchy in which female shaman leaders were interred in large mounded graves. Some passages appear to have been confirmed by archaeology. At **Yoshinogari** on Kyushu, for example, excavations have revealed a settlement that covered 25 ha (62 acres) by Late Yayoi times, demarcated by a large defensive ditch supplemented with watchtowers [7.35]. The presence of a large mounded tomb covering an area of 40 x 26 m (130 x 85 ft), associated with ritual pottery deposits, suggests the presence of an elite rank within the local society.

Even the earliest Yayoi rice fields indicate a sophisticated method of cultivation. Chinese tomb models of the Han period (206 BC–AD 220) suggest that the construction of low banks around field plots to control the flow of water, linked with plowing and transplanting, underpinned the production of vital rice surpluses. This arrangement appeared fully fledged in Japan, and it is hard not to see it as a wholesale adoption of an established system. The Yayoi people occupied moated villages near their fields on a permanent basis, and maintained long-term cemeteries. Their tools of cultivation, as seen at the Toro site on Honshu, southwest of Tokyo, were solidly constructed in wood.

Nevertheless, it should be emphasized that there were other crops as well, some of which – wheat, barley, and two varieties of millet, for example – were better suited to dry land cultivation than to the marshy wetlands preferred by the rice plant. (The presence of wheat and barley are surprising so far east, and were probably introduced into East Asia along what came to be known as the Silk Road – see Chapter 15.) A range of fruits was consumed, and acorns and nuts collected; there is little evidence for the maintenance of domestic stock, but hunting and fishing were practiced.

The adoption of rice cultivation coincided with changes in technology. Pottery vessels had been a major aspect of Jomon material culture, but forms and decorative techniques changed with the Yayoi, and a set comprising cooking, serving, and storage vessels became the norm; these forms probably mirror the needs of rice farmers. The same can be said for stone tools, par-ticularly the arrival of pestles, mortars, and reaping knives. The form of these knives is widespread on the Chinese mainland, where they had been in use for millennia; wear on the blades proves their use in rice harvesting. The waterlogged conditions at such sites as Toro reveal the use as well of wooden hoes, spades, rakes, and forks. Weaving was also introduced into Japan, evidenced by many circular spindle whorls, and silk came to Kyushu from southern China.

The Linguistic Evidence

The years since the mid-1980s have seen a transformation in our understanding of the Neolithic in East and Southeast Asia. There is now a convincing sequence of cultural change leading from late Pleistocene hunter-gatherers directly into early rice farmers in the middle Yangzi lakeland. This is associated with environmental changes, which permit a reasonable, testable model for agricultural origins. While there are still many missing pieces, it is now possible to recognize the pattern of a complex jigsaw puzzle. It involves many archaeological sites distributed from eastern India to northern Japan, but its coherence is seen in the progressive expansion of rice farmers along riverine and maritime routes to occupy areas suited to their new subsistence economy.

This notion of expansionary movements needs to be tested, preferably by examining different forms of surviving evidence, of which there are two principal candidates: the spoken

7.35 Yoshinogari: *this settlement on Kyushu covered 25 ha (62 acres) by Late Yayoi times. It was demarcated by a large defensive ditch supplemented with watchtowers, seen reconstructed here.*

languages of Southeast Asia; and the genes of the prehistoric people. Although it is too early to say whether, for example, the early settlers of Non Pa Wai and Ban Kao in the Bangkok Plain shared similar genetic sequences with the prehistoric inhabitants of the Yangzi Valley, linguistic studies, supported by archaeological evidence, have been more forthcoming.

The study of historic linguistics in East and Southeast Asia confronts a remarkable complexity involving hundreds of languages and several major language families. According to Laurent Sagart (1993; 1994), there are five basic linguistic building blocks: Austroasiatic; Austronesian (discussed in detail in Chapter 8); Hmong Mien; Kadai with Tai; and Sino-Tibetan. In terms of the expansion of rice farmers from China southward, into Southeast Asia, it is notable that languages within the three major branches of the Austroasiatic family are distributed from eastern India to Vietnam, and south to the Nicobar Islands in the Indian Ocean (Diffloth 1994). There are strong grounds for suspecting that the inhabitants of much of Lingnan, in the Pearl River estuary in southeast China, also formerly spoke Austroasiatic languages (Norman and Mei 1976). The distribution of these languages is patchy, and in many parts of Southeast Asia we find Thai, Burmese, or Austronesian languages; these probably represent recent intrusions into what was once a more contiguous bloc.

Laurence Reid (1994) has identified structural parallels between the Austroasiatic languages of the Nicobar Islands, and Austronesian and other Austroasiatic languages, which suggest a common origin. If this linkage has any basis in fact, the search for a common homeland from which both language families emerged thus has a center of gravity on the Asian mainland. New archaeological evidence can now contribute to this issue, by specifying the place of origin of rice agriculture and by providing a logical platform for the expansion of human groups sharing a common ancestry. A burning issue lies in the relationship between the first settled rice farmers of Taiwan, home of the oldest Austronesian languages, and those on the Asian mainland. Judith Cameron has contributed important new information by identifying links in the morphology of spindle whorls between sites of the Dabenkeng (Tapenkeng) culture of Taiwan (c. 2500 BC; see Chapter 8, p. 283), and those of the Yangzi Valley. It would appear that spinning and weaving technology on Taiwan was introduced into the island. This is supported by the presence of similar items at the site of Fengpitou to the south of the island, and at Arku and Andarayan on Luzon in the Philippines.

It is thus possible to trace the progressive establishment of farming groups south from Taiwan and, ultimately, into the islands of Southeast Asia and the greater Pacific. As discussed in Chapter 8, these people probably spoke early Austronesian languages. Testing the archaeological construct of a similar expansion on the mainland can be undertaken by seeking the presence or absence of cognate words in the Austroasiatic Munda languages of India, east to the Vietnamese, Mon, and Khmer languages in Southeast Asia. The word for "dog," for example, is likely to be important. There is, in Southeast Asia, no native wolf from which to derive the domesticated dog. Yet the cranial characteristics of the prehistoric dog reveal beyond doubt a lupine ancestry. The nearest possible sources for the wolf are *Canis lupus chanco* in China, and *C. lupus pallipes* in India. Cognate words are present over the entire area of Austroasiatic language distribution, even into central India. The word for "child" is virtually identical between Kurku in central India and Bahnar on the eastern seaboard of Vietnam, a distance of almost 3000 km (1865 miles). "Fish" is another key word for any expansionary group of farmers in Southeast and South Asia, for excavations reveal the widespread exploitation of water resources. It, too, is clearly cognate across the area of Austroasiatic languages, linking small islands of speakers. The key words in the vocabulary, however, are those for "rice" in its various forms. Gordon Luce (1985) has considered the word for "husked rice" and "rice plant," and found them to be cognate across a wide range of Austroasiatic languages. He concluded that the only explanation for "this startling diffusion" is wet rice cultivation.

Munda is a branch of the Austroasiatic language family spoken in eastern India. In their review of the Proto-Munda vocabulary, Arlene Zide and Norman Zide (1976) have compared reconstructed words with those found in other Austroasiatic languages in Southeast Asia. They revealed that on the basis of the reconstructed Proto-Munda word list, the Munda were more advanced agriculturally than archaeologists had previously thought. They have concluded that proto-Munda speakers practiced subsistence agriculture at least 3500 years ago (1500 BC), at a conservative estimate, cultivating rice, millet, and at least three legumes. They also used husking pestles and mortars, the words for which go back to Proto-Austroasiatic.

This research is supported by Waruno Mahdi (1998), who has found that the Proto-Austroasiatic word for "rice" can be reconstructed in Munda, Mon-Khmer, Palaung-Wa, Viet-Muong, Old Mon, and Lamet. Ilia Pejros and Victor Shnirelman (1998) have also deployed linguistic evidence to suggest that neither the Austroasiatic nor Austronesian proto-languages reveal evidence for a tropical origin, but rather point to inland beginnings north of the tropical zone of eastern Eurasia. They identify the middle Yangzi Valley as a likely homeland, and feel that Proto-Austroasiatic began to divide in the 9th to 8th millennia BC. Within the Austroasiatic family, Munda and Mon-Khmer split from each other by the end of the 5th millennium BC. By the end of the 4th millennium BC, Mon-Khmer began to divide into Khmer, Bahnaric, and Viet-Muong.

The linguistic evidence summarized above is compatible with a homeland in the middle Yangzi Valley, from which at least the ancestors of the Austroasiatic and Austronesian languages originated and spread, the former largely by land, and the latter by sea. Linguists seem to agree that considerable time is necessary to account for the differences between the Munda and Mon-Khmer languages, and rather less for the divergence between the individual languages of the latter division.

Summary and Conclusions

We began this chapter with the indigenous hunter-gatherer societies of the Yellow River and Yangzi River valleys, and discussed the evidence for the development of agriculture in these two crucial areas: the cultivation of millet in the colder Yellow River valley, and the farming of rice in the warmer, wetter regions of the Yangzi River further south. This transition from foraging to farming, which must have taken place c. 8000–6000 BC (though actual transitional sites have not yet been located), was accompanied by the gradual establishment of permanent villages such as Bashidang and Banpbo, and the first archaeologically recognizable regional cultures. Larger agricultural communities eventually grew up in both areas, with attendant developments in material culture, social differentiation, trade, and political variance, leading at times to conflict.

From this crucible of agricultural development in central and southeast China, rice farming (and rice farmers) spread to Southeast Asia and beyond by the 2nd millennium BC, and possibly as early as the late 3rd millennium BC. The emerging pattern, rooted in firm archaeological evidence, reveals a pan-Southeast Asian settlement by farming communities, who would have initially encountered long-established hunter-gatherer groups, some of them sedentary, such as that at Khok Phanom Di. The southward spread of rice farmers may well have introduced Austroasiatic languages into this broad territory, based on the evidence of cognate words for "rice" and aspects of its cultivation.

The expansion of farming communities into Korea and Japan followed a rather different pattern. In the former, millet cultivation preceded rice by millennia, but once achieved (in the late 3rd or early 2nd millennium BC), rice cultivation was evidently adopted by local farming groups, for there is virtually no evidence for an intrusion of new people to match that in Southeast Asia. As in China and Southeast Asia, the adaptability and increased returns of rice, compared with millet, were soon manifested in the rise of social elites, seen in the provision of large tombs containing fine mortuary offerings. Rice cultivation became firmly established in Japan during the last centuries of the 1st millennium BC in the context of the early

Yayoi culture, spreading rapidly from Kyushu to Honshu before reaching an ecological barrier of cold to the south of Hokkaido. This was almost certainly associated, according to human anatomical evidence, with the intrusion of people from southern Korea.

This chapter has described the solid cultural foundations for East Asian society that were provided by its pioneering farmers, without which the civilizations of this region could not have developed as they did. The further development of East Asian agricultural societies and the rise of the first East and Southeast Asian states are traced in Chapter 15. In the next chapter, however, we turn southwards, to the postglacial societies of island Southeast Asia, Australasia, and the Pacific.

Further reading and Suggested Websites

Barnes, G. L. 1993. *The Rise of Civilization in East Asia*. London & New York: Thames & Hudson. Comprehensive coverage of the labyrinthine cultural sequences of China, Japan, and Korea, linking areas often treated independently.

Higham, C. F. W. 1996. *The Bronze Age of Southeast Asia*. Cambridge: Cambridge University Press. Describes the prehistory of Southeast Asia with particular emphasis on relations with China and India; dispels many myths concerning the early nature of agriculture and the Bronze Age in Southeast Asia, instead seeking a cohesive overall pattern to the region in its wider context.

Higham, C. F. W. 2002. *Early Cultures of Mainland Southeast Asia*. Bangkok: River Books. Highly illustrated description of Southeast Asian cultures from early hunters to the great states, with particular emphasis on Angkor in Cambodia.

Nelson, S. M. 1993. *The Archaeology of Korea*. Cambridge: Cambridge University Press. A synthesis of what is known about early Korea, from hunters and gatherers to the early states.

Nelson, S. M. (ed.). 1995. *The Archaeology of Northeast China*. London & New York: Routledge. Covers recent finds in the northeastern regions of China, opening many new and intriguing instances of cultural stimulus beyond the central plains.

Pearson, R. (ed.). 1992. *Ancient Japan*. New York: G. Braziller. Well-illustrated outline of Japanese prehistory, from the Jomon hunter-gatherers to the 1st millennium AD states centered on the Nara basin.

Portal, J. 2000. *Korea. Art and Archaeology*. London: British Museum Press. Well-illustrated introduction to the settlement of the Korean peninsula from early prehistory to the major states.

http://www.seaarchaeology.com Still in its infancy, the website of the Southeast Asian Archaeology group, based in Singapore.

http://www.ancienteastasia.org This website is a vital source for the latest information on East Asian archaeology.

http://sun.sino.uni-heidelberg.de/igcs/archaeology/ A source that gives the latest news and points to other websites of interest.

CHAPTER 8
AUSTRALIA AND THE AUSTRONESIANS

Peter Bellwood and Peter Hiscock, Australian National University

Australia 265
Early Foragers in a Changing Landscape 266
Technology in Uncertain Times 268
● KEY SITE Kenniff Cave 269
● KEY CONTROVERSY Explaining Technological Change in Australia 270
Changing Life in Tasmania 270
Changes in Aboriginal Perceptions of the Landscape 271
● KEY CONTROVERSY Why Did the Tasmanians Stop Eating Fish? 272
The Growth of Trade Networks 273
Population and Settlement Change 273
The Effects of Historic Foreign Contacts 274
● KEY SITE Barlambidj: Aboriginal Contact with Southeast Asia 275

The Islands of Southeast Asia and Oceania 275
Early Human Settlers in Island Southeast Asia 277
Early Agriculturalists in New Guinea 277
● KEY DISCOVERY Early Farming in the New Guinea Highlands 278

The Austronesian Dispersal 279
Who Are the Austronesians? 279
A Basic History of the Austronesian Languages 280
● KEY CONTROVERSY The Origins of the Austronesians 282
The Archaeology of Early Austronesian Dispersal 283
  • *Taiwan* 283
  • *Dispersals to Southeast Asia and Madagascar* 284

● KEY SITE Beinan 286
The Colonization of Oceania 287
Lapita Economy 288
● KEY CONTROVERSY The Origins of Lapita 289
The Settlement of Polynesia 290
  • *Eastern Polynesia* 290
● KEY SITE Talepakemalai 291
● KEY CONTROVERSY Expert Navigation or Sheer Good Luck? 292
  • *Why Migrate?* 294

The Austronesian World After Colonization 294
Polynesian Complex Societies: Easter Island and Elsewhere 294
● KEY CONTROVERSY Causes of Landscape Change 296
● KEY CONTROVERSY Easter Island and South America 297
Hawai'i and New Zealand: Varying Social Responses to Environmental Constraints 298
The Chiefdoms of Polynesia: Comparative Ethnographic Perspectives 299
  • *Theories of Social Evolution* 301

Seaborne Trade and the Transformation of Tribal Society in Southeast Asia 301

Summary and Conclusions 304

Further Reading and Suggested Websites 305

The previous chapter charted the origins of agriculture in East Asia and the expansion of farming communities during the millennia that followed. In this chapter we move south, to consider the development of human societies in Australia, island Southeast Asia (East Malaysia, Indonesia, and the Philippines) and Oceania (the islands of Polynesia, Melanesia, and Micronesia). In this diverse and geographically extensive region a number of significant archaeological developments occurred, including the hunter-gatherer prehistory of Australia, and an independent genesis of agriculture in the New Guinea highlands. To these can be added the prehistory of Austronesian agriculturalist dispersal since 3000 BC throughout island Southeast Asia, and the subsequent remarkable Austronesian maritime colonization of Oceania, a scatter of many archipelagos in the vast Pacific Ocean, some only permanently settled within the last 1000 years.

We begin this chapter with Australian prehistory, which represents an independent trajectory within the region. The initial colonization of the continent by modern humans around 40,000 years ago was described in Chapter 4, and this huge, relatively isolated continent continued to be a land of hunters and gatherers until the 19th century. A variety of foraging practices were used, usually involving the exploitation of plant food staples supplemented by hunting. Food procurement was sometimes sophisticated, involving not simply the harvesting of wild foods, but also managing plant and animal resources by burning vegetation, constructing dams and drainage channels, detoxifying poisonous plants, and storing and replanting seeds. Human populations were most dense near the coast, where resources were plentiful, but small, highly mobile bands also lived in the extremely arid regions of central and western Australia. Detailed records of these broad configurations of Aboriginal life come from historic observations. Archaeology records the drastic changes in Aboriginal foraging subsistence economy that occurred during prehistory.

We next look at the early Holocene in the islands of Indonesia and the Philippines, which provide the geographical and part of the cultural background to subsequent Austronesian dispersal. Hunter-gatherer cultures existed throughout the region prior to the spread of agriculture, and a few iron-using hunting populations still exist in remote areas of rainforest today, for instance in the Malay Peninsula and the northern Philippines. How the earlier Holocene hunter-gatherers related to the Austronesian-speaking populations, who spread through the region during the past 4000 years, is a matter of considerable debate.

Moving to New Guinea, we then examine the early Holocene development of agriculture in the island's highland zone – a very significant development for Melanesian populations, and one that appears to have occurred at around the same time as similar developments in the Levant and central China (Chapters 6 and 7). Over the long term, New Guinea and adjacent Melanesian islands contributed a number of important tree and tuber crops to the Pacific economy, and the early development of agriculture here allowed a culture of Papuan-speaking (i.e., non-Austronesian) agriculturalist populations to evolve with little external influence until European contact in the 19th and 20th centuries.

Finally, we consider the extraordinary migrations of the Austronesian-speaking peoples since 3000 BC, comprising the greatest dispersal of any identifiable ethnolinguistic population in world history prior to AD 1500. Before Christopher Columbus triggered the transformation of the tribal world, Austronesian founder populations had migrated through more than 210 degrees of longitude, from Madagascar (off the east coast of Africa) to Easter Island in the Pacific (perhaps even to South America), through an astounding 22,000 km (13,700 miles) of ocean and islands [**8.1**]. Today, over 350 million Austronesian speakers are distributed throughout island Southeast Asia, eastwards across the tropical Pacific, and westwards to Madagascar. Outside these regions, Austronesians also settled Taiwan, peninsular Malaysia, southern Vietnam and New Zealand. The ancestral migrations of these populations actually occurred over a period of more than 4000 years, but this does not diminish the overall achievement. The whole dispersal required considerable gestation time, allowing for the underpinning population growth and the necessary levels of socio-economic change and technological innovation that would eventually enable and encourage long-distance ocean crossings to new lands.

Australia

By around 8000 BC, Aboriginal hunter-gatherers had colonized most, if not all, of the environments of Australia and New Guinea. As already mentioned, humans had arrived in Australia by at least 40,000 years ago, during the last Ice Age, when exposure of the now-submerged continental shelf increased the continental landmass by nearly 50 percent, and when the climate was substantially cooler and drier than it is today. The end of the Pleistocene c. 9600 BC initiated climatic changes that reversed those earlier trends: the massive continental shelf of northern and southern Australia that had become home to many Aboriginal groups was submerged, creating geographical barriers that isolated other groups, and generating a sequence of landscape changes to which Aboriginal people had to adjust.

AUSTRALIA AND THE AUSTRONESIANS TIMELINE

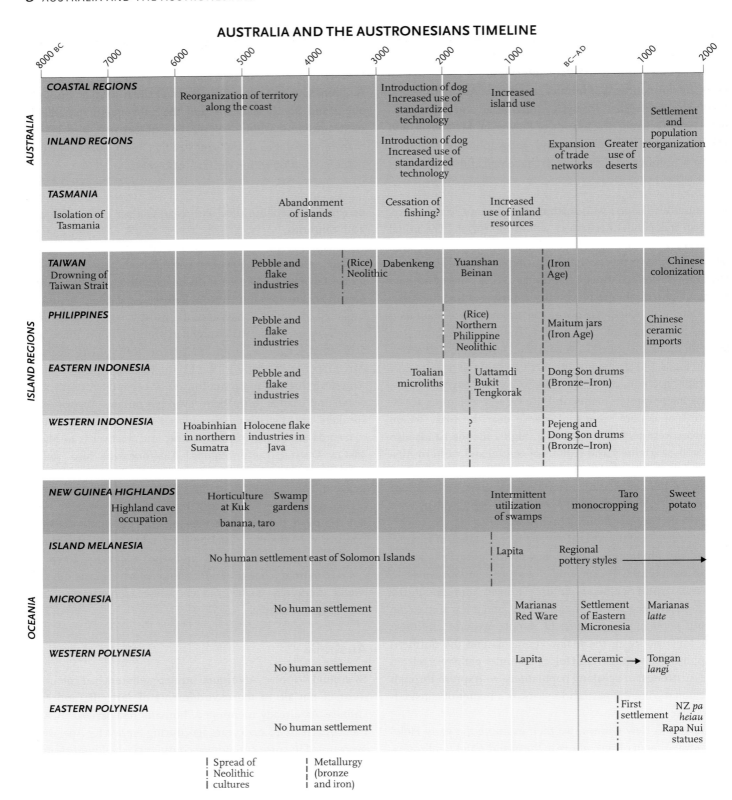

While the basic patterns of Aboriginal occupation had been long established, the continuous modification of the environment throughout the last 10,000 years triggered a series of economic and social alterations that are revealed in the archaeological evidence from Holocene sites across Australia.

Early Foragers in a Changing Landscape

Many of these modifications to cultural practice reflect responses to changes in the environment in which people were foraging. During the earlier part of the Holocene, sea levels rose and both temperatures and precipitation were higher than today, with summer rainfall being dominant. This changed between around 2000 BC and AD 1, when precipitation was reduced and summer rainfall uncertain. More frequent droughts and the re-initiation of dune building are visible in many regions during this phase. This was followed by a return to increased precipitation during the last 2000 years. A number of the alterations to subsistence strategies that have been recognized in the archaeological record correspond to the timing of these broad changes in climatic conditions.

Coastal landscapes underwent striking transformations at the end of the Pleistocene, as the large ice sheets of the northern hemisphere melted, causing the sea to rise until about 5000 BC. As noted above, in some regions this drowned the large continental shelf, forcing Aboriginal groups there inland, onto land already occupied by others. In Arnhem Land, in northern Australia, some panels of rock art that may be of this age seem to

8.1 *Map of Southeast Asia, Australasia, and the Pacific:* *showing the major areas and sites mentioned in the text.*

show battle scenes [8.2], perhaps a vivid rendering of the social dramas created by the inundation of coastal land (Taçon and Chippindale 1994).

Rising seas in other regions gradually created islands and archipelagos from what had once been a landscape of hills and valleys [8.3]. The most spectacular instance was the separation of Tasmania from mainland Australia by the creation of the enormous Bass Strait, completely isolating Tasmanian Aboriginals. These people responded by successfully adapting to their new island settings, but not all isolated foragers were able to survive the coastal inundation. Archaeological excavations on smaller islands off the coast of southern Australia, such as King Island and Kangaroo Island, reveal a more disturbing story.

These islands were more than 10 km (6 miles) from larger landmasses, and the water gaps were so treacherous that it was effectively impossible to voyage safely to and fro. Although there is clear evidence that people existed on these islands after rising seas isolated them, no one has lived there in the recent past, and the stranded Aboriginal people must have died out.

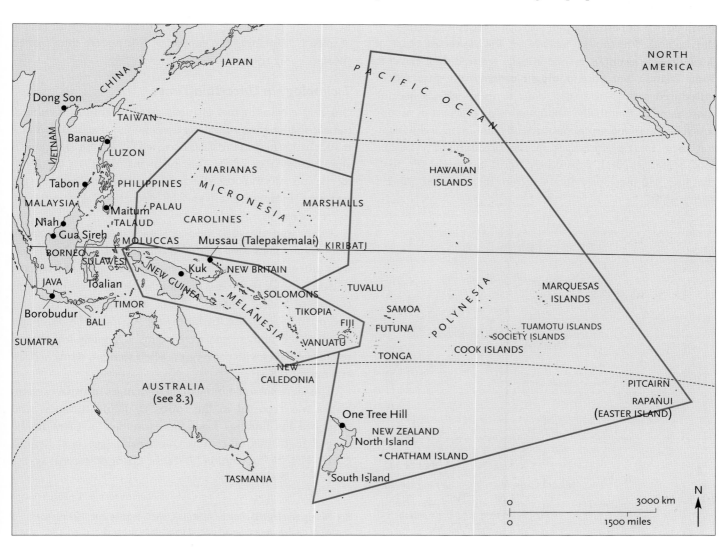

8.2 *Scenes of warfare:* *rock art from Arnhem Land (Australia) showing humans with spears is perhaps a reflection of increased social tensions caused by rising sea levels inundating coastal lands after the end of the Ice Age forcing some Aboriginal groups onto lands already occupied by others.*

The image of the last Aboriginal wandering alone across each island, awaiting death, is a chilling illustration of the effect of sea-level rise during this period.

A rise in sea level was not always fatal, however; elsewhere, the creation of an island landscape did not trap people, but provided new opportunities for social and economic change. In the tropical Whitsunday Islands on the northeast coast of Australia, for example, people initially reduced their travel to some islands, but once **outrigger canoes** were invented or introduced around 1000 BC, visits to these islands became more regular. Eventually, Aboriginal people began to occupy much of the island group permanently and intensively, adapting their foraging practices to the predominantly marine food resources and substituting local materials for tools that they had previously obtained from the mainland (Barker 1991; 1996).

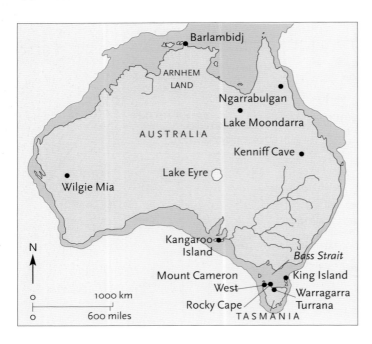

8.3 *Rising sea levels:* *map of Australia, showing the late Pleistocene coastline and archaeological sites discussed in the text.*

Coastal Aboriginal groups continued to adjust their new lifestyles to the constant changing of the coastal environments. For example, archaeological excavations in Moreton Bay, near Brisbane, show that people foraging on the coast made extensive use of mollusks; when sea-grass became widely established in the bay during the last millennium, Aboriginal people adapted by exploiting the enormous fish reserve thus created (Walters 1989; 1992).

Technology in Uncertain Times

Ongoing environmental changes acted to stimulate cultural transformations not only along the coast but also inland. A dramatic change in stone artifacts occurred during the Holocene in almost every area of the Australian mainland. In the Pleistocene and early Holocene the most common implements were scrapers – morphologically variable retouched flakes with curving retouched margins.

Then around 2500–1000 BC, standardized, finely made stone implements were produced and discarded in abundance, with different forms appearing in different parts of Australia (Hiscock 1994). In the east and south, the most common form comprised backed artifacts – flakes with steep retouch along one or more margins. In northwest Australia the dominant standardized implements were points – vaguely leaf-shaped retouched flakes with converging, often straight, retouched lateral margins [8.4].

The sequence and timing of these changes in artifact assemblages was reported in the 1960s by John Mulvaney, who described his findings from the excavation of caves in the rugged highlands of central Queensland [see box: Kenniff Cave]. His demonstration of these changes served as the

8.4 *Change in stone artifacts:* *a scraper from the early period of Australian prehistory (below) and a bifacial point (left) from the later period of Australian prehistory.*

change. A common pattern was the modification of foraging strategies when the climate switched from warm, moist, stable conditions prior to *c.* 2000 BC to cooler, drier, more variable conditions after that time.

The emphasis on small, standardized stone implements is best seen as the development of a means of moderating economic and social uncertainty. With these artifacts, hunters could conserve material while producing reliable tools, and when foragers were highly mobile and unable to predict the locations of resources, tools of this kind were highly advantageous (Hiscock 1994; 2002).

Some researchers have suggested that these tools might in fact have been introduced from Southeast Asia, and it is clear that Aboriginal people had contacts with visitors around 2000 BC, because dogs were introduced into mainland Australia at that time. However, the stone artifacts that became commonly made after that date had been in use thousands of years earlier than this, and contact with other groups is not a viable explanation for their emphasis (Hiscock 2002). The coincidence of changes in artifact assemblages and climate points to an indigenous economic response to changed conditions.

template for describing them across the Australian continent, and Mulvaney began the search for an explanation [see box: Explaining Technological Change in Australia, p. 270]. It is now recognized that these changes in toolkits occurred at different times in each region, and probably reflect local alterations to foraging caused by environmental and social

KEY SITE Kenniff Cave

Kenniff Cave produced the first evidence for the Aboriginal occupation of Australia during the Pleistocene. John Mulvaney's excavations in the spectacular cave, positioned in a sandstone cliff above Meteor Creek in Queensland, revealed a 3.4-m (11-ft) deep stratified deposit, consisting of horizontal bands of light and dark colored sands (Mulvaney and Joyce 1965). Mulvaney established that there were two distinct stratigraphic units, the lower one dating to the late Pleistocene; lying unevenly over this is a more recent unit covering the last 6000 years.

Although the impressive stratigraphic banding has led many archaeologists to see this deposit as a detailed and accurate record of human occupation, it is now clear that it has a complex history of formation. The absence of early Holocene sedimentation means that it cannot illustrate changes from the Pleistocene to the Holocene, making shifts in the artifact sequence seem more drastic than they are. Moreover, the site is not

unaltered: artifacts have moved vertically over short distances, making it impossible to assign very precise dates to events in the deposit (Richardson 1992).

As a result of these formational processes we have information from Kenniff Cave only of broad-scale events during the Holocene. It is likely that human occupation of the cave represents sporadic use of this dry landscape by mobile foragers after rainfall (Hiscock 2001). In the middle of the Holocene (*c.* 2000–1000 BC) a noticeable change occurred in the artifact assemblages, with small and precisely retouched stone artifacts being manufactured where none had existed previously. The reasons for this alteration in manufacturing activities have been the subject of extensive debate [see box: Explaining Technological Change in Australia, p. 270].

8.5 *Kenniff Cave, excavated by John Mulvaney in the 1960s, produced the first evidence for the Pleistocene Aboriginal occupation of Australia.*

KEY CONTROVERSY Explaining Technological Change in Australia

The explanation for changes in stone implements that occurred in Australia during the Holocene has been debated intensively for 40 years. John Mulvaney, the founder of modern Australian archaeology, offered one of the earliest coherent explanations. In the early 1960s, archaeologists believed that ground-edge axes, which were probably hafted, first appeared in Australia during the middle of the Holocene (Mulvaney and Joyce 1965).

Because he thought that the appearance of axes coincided with a new emphasis on smaller and more standardized implements, such as points and backed artifacts [see 8.4], Mulvaney suggested that the invention or introduction of hafting capabilities caused all of these technological shifts. He proposed that once foragers could manufacture composite tools with stone components, they invented or adopted suitable small and regular stone implements to use in those tools. Although plausible, this explanation was abandoned when edge-ground axes were found in archaeological deposits more than 20,000 years old.

In the 1970s and 1980s it was suggested that these kinds of standardized implements were the result of contact between Aboriginal peoples in Australia and various groups,

8.6 *A stone axe of the kind traded across thousands of kilometers of inland Australia.*

presumably Austronesian speakers, voyaging along the northern Australian shores during the mid-Holocene. Sandra Bowdler (1981) argued that alterations to Aboriginal social, territorial, and religious organization were stimulated by these outside contacts, and that small standardized stone implements were merely symbols employed as part of a new iconography to express these novel social perspectives.

Variation in regional patterns of assemblage change do not support this model, however; in some areas, the standardized implements were emphasized in the early Holocene (roughly 8000–4000 BC), in other regions the shift occurs during the mid-Holocene (c. 4000–1000 BC), and in some regions it does not take place until the late Holocene (after 1000 BC). This chronological variation is not consistent with the idea that change was stimulated by contact with foreign cultures at a single point in time.

In recent years there has been a return to the idea that we can explain the Holocene proliferation of small, standardized stone implements in terms of their economic function. Peter Hiscock (1994; 2002) has suggested that such implements represent technological strategies that reduce the cost of replacing tools and improve their readiness. These qualities would have provided a number of advantages to forager groups exploiting unfamiliar territories and resources. Since archaeological evidence now shows that implements such as backed artifacts and points were known in Australia for thousands of years before their proliferation, and that proliferation occurs at different times in different regions, at times of environmental and economic change, this explanation seems to be the strongest yet suggested.

Changing Life in Tasmania

The same environmental shifts, from warm, moist, stable conditions prior to 2000 BC to cooler, drier, more variable conditions after that time, were responsible for a number of changes in settlement, foraging, and social patterns in Tasmania. The most famous change was the complete cessation of fishing around 1800 BC [see box: Why Did the Tasmanians Stop Eating Fish?, p. 272]. This was one of many modifications to foraging practices that occurred as hunters expanded the range of resources and environments they exploited: diving to obtain sub-tidal mollusks and crustaceans, and spending more time hunting terrestrial game, such as the wallabies found in upland areas. At the same time, there was an increased emphasis on fat-rich animal resources such as seals and birds, and the minimization or removal from the diet of lean meat such as fish.

These changes in procurement strategies were linked to major reorganizations of foraging territory. In a number of non-coastal localities, open forests and grassland replaced closed forests c. 2000 BC. This probably reflects the changed climatic conditions prevailing at that time, although a number of archaeologists have suggested that Aboriginal burning practices may be implicated as well, perhaps exaggerating the effects of climate. Rockshelters in isolated inland valleys higher than 1000 m (3280 ft) above sea level were occupied more regularly after 2000 BC than before, indicating a greater emphasis on the exploitation of inland resources (Lourandos 1983). Occupation of many of the Bass Strait Islands also changed in the mid-Holocene. Many remote, isolated islands were abandoned c. 2000 BC, and, as noted above, on some islands the resident populations may have become extinct (Sim 1994). At about the same time, the use of some less remote islands intensified, another manifestation of the expansion of hunter-gatherers into a wide variety of environments (Bowdler 1988; Jones 1977; Vanderwal and Horton 1984).

These dramatic modifications to the distribution and nature of foraging activities involved alterations to territory size and residential locations, and must have triggered a reorganization of seasonal movements between landscapes within the territory of each group. Furthermore, given the scale of settlement and economic restructuring that occurred *c.* 2000–500 BC, it is likely that social and political organization was altered. This is consistent with the abandonment and relocation of artistic and ritual activities within the Tasmanian landscape. The impressive site at **Mount Cameron West** [8.7], for example, where sandstone walls were covered in deeply carved circles, was abandoned in the late Holocene (1st millennium BC or later).

8.7 *Social and political change:* *changes in territory size and residential locations between c. 2000 and 500 BC may have led to the abandonment of rock art sites in Tasmania, such as this one at Mount Cameron West.*

Changes in Aboriginal Perceptions of the Landscape

Somewhat similar environmentally stimulated changes to territory, group movements, and landscape use have been documented on the Australian mainland. In some instances these modifications of territory and land use may have been linked to changing conceptualizations of place and the production of stories about powerful creative beings such as the Rainbow Serpent. Archaeological evidence for these altered social perceptions comes in the form of abundant **rock art** found in many parts of Australia. Paintings and engravings dating to more than 20,000–30,000 years ago have been discovered, and long sequences of art document not only changes in lifestyle but also modifications in the way Aboriginal people thought of and depicted their world.

In western **Arnhem Land** the Rainbow Serpent imagery in rock art can be traced back to the major environmental changes

in the mid-Holocene (Taçon et al. 1996). Rising sea levels encroached on the region, converting it from a dry inland area to a diverse coastal region. Massive mangrove swamps appeared, and eventually extensive freshwater lagoons were established. Rock art sequences trace these environmental changes, as Aboriginal people depicted their changing life-styles: paintings of yams and terrestrial marsupials, for example, were suddenly replaced by paintings of riverine animals such as fish and turtles. While some of these images record animals with reasonable accuracy, other images served social purposes, and the transfiguration of images may reveal the incorporation of new social constructions of the landscape into the corpus of artworks.

It seems likely that the notion of the **Rainbow Serpent** may have been formulated at a time of marine encroachment, and was at first a depiction of a marine animal, the pipefish, before gradually being transformed into an imaginary, composite beast in more recent art [**8.8**]. This does not mean that recent Aboriginal religions were necessarily founded at that time, nor that they have remained unchanged since then. Yet because the iconography of creative beings becomes recognizable then, we may be seeing the reshaping of some older Holocene belief systems.

Modification of social life may be visible not only in rock art but also in landscape use. The reorganization of settlement and subsistence patterns was probably accompanied by a reconstruction of cultural frameworks for comprehending the environment. In some regions, such as Cape York in the northeast, alterations of religious practices were probably tied to changes in use of the land. An inland mountain at **Ngarrabulgan**, which in historic times was believed to be dangerous, was once regularly used for camping, hunting, and social events.

KEY CONTROVERSY Why Did the Tasmanians Stop Eating Fish?

After rising sea levels turned the Tasmanian peninsula into an island, foragers exploited numerous marine resources, such as seals and fish. Archaeological sites such as Rocky Cape South show that fish were an important element of the diet, contributing perhaps a quarter of the meat by weight. Then around 1800 BC, Tasmanian Aboriginals stopped eating fish, a change that has sparked a vigorous debate among archaeologists.

An "Economic Maladaptation"

Rhys Jones (1941–2001), the researcher who first established and precisely dated the cessation of fishing, argued that there was no satisfactory ecological reason to stop eating fish, and that it must therefore have been a cultural decision such as a dietary prohibition. Jones (1978) also suggested that the abandonment of fishing would have imposed dietary hardship, especially during winter. In view of this, he concluded that forsaking an obvious food source such as fish was disadvantageous to Tasmanian foragers and best viewed as an "economic maladaptation."

Other changes occurred at about the same time. For example, bone artifacts such as points and spatulas, made by splitting the long bones of wallabies, were common in archaeological deposits before 1800–1400 BC, but were not made more recently. Jones argued that these bone points were primarily used to make skin cloaks, and concluded that the disappearance of the points, and by implication the abandonment of cloak manufacture, represents the loss of a useful craft, again to the detriment of the Tasmanians.

Because he believed that cloak manufacture ceased at about the same time that fishing stopped, Jones (1977) thought these changes indicated a fundamental failure of the cultural system, as the Tasmanians lost many "useful arts" and were unable to invent replacements. This supposed inability to support and maintain a culture was also the mechanism Jones used to explain the apparent abandonment over the last millennium of engraving sites and stone arrangements, sites involved in ritual and social practices.

A Positive Response

Another proposal suggests that the changes to economic and social practices were a positive response to altered environmental circumstances. Harry Allen (1979), for example, explained that in the colder climate of the last few thousand years, hunters would increasingly need fat-rich foods. Switching from low-fat animals such as fish to fat-rich ones such as seal and sea birds would have been profitable for coastal Tasmanians, and that is precisely what occurred. The economic advantage of avoiding fish also explains the disappearance of bone points, because we now suspect that the bone points were not used to make clothes but were part of fishing technology (Bowdler and Lourandos 1982).

These changes in coastal foraging must be understood in the context of the overall economy, however. Around 1800 BC, drier and more variable climatic conditions meant that closed forests were replaced by open forests and grassland, allowing foragers to exploit inland areas more intensively. At coastal sites such as Rocky Cape, as well as high inland sites such as Warragarra and Turrana, we see archaeological evidence for this expansion inland, indicative of territorial enlargement and perhaps the development of larger trading networks (Lourandos 1983). This means that the cessation of fishing coincided with much greater resource procurement further inland. It is likely that the terrestrial foods more than made up for the loss of fish, resulting in a net gain of energy for Tasmanian Aboriginal society.

8.8 Rainbow Serpent imagery, western Arnhem Land: *the emergence of Rainbow Serpent imagery in rock art can be traced back to the major environmental changes in the mid-Holocene. The notion of this powerful creative being may well have been formulated at a time of marine encroachment, and was at first a depiction of a marine animal, the pipefish, before gradually being transformed into an imaginary, composite beast in more recent art.*

Archaeological excavations show that people abandoned the mountain only during the last 1000 years, and it was probably at that time that mythologies describing the area as dangerous were established (Fullagar and David 1997).

Rock art and landscape use may also reveal the emergence of well-defined group territories. Early art panels, often engraved and pecked, show generally uniform images across broad tracts of land; late panels, often elaborately painted with many colors, display regional distinctiveness. Such trends perhaps mark the emergence of regional political and social entities (David 1991; David and Cole 1990; Taçon 1993). Suggestions that Aboriginal groups were perhaps becoming more spatially tethered are reinforced by evidence for increasing numbers of **cemeteries** and large **base camps** in some regions during the last few thousand years.

The Growth of Trade Networks

The emergence of more highly defined and formalized group identity, bringing with it distinct territorial boundaries, may have been linked to the emergence of extensive trade networks. European explorers of the 18th and early 19th centuries observed organized exchange between neighboring Aboriginal groups. Sometimes this trade involved bartering at formal markets, and on other occasions it was practiced by reciprocal gift-giving before and after ceremonial events. In these ways objects might be distributed over large areas of Australia as each group received material from one neighbor and passed it on to another. In arid South Australia, for example, people received narcotic drugs from 400 km (250 miles) away in southern Queensland, stone axes from the Mount Isa region 1200 km (750 miles) to the north, grindstones from the Flinders Ranges some 300 km (190 miles) to the south, and pearl shell pendants from the northwest of the continent, more than 2000 km (1250 miles) away. While it is likely that these trading networks expanded and intensified during the historic period (see below), they were probably developing over at least the last 1000 to 2000 years. Archaeological evidence of this trade, such as long-distance transportation of goods and trade bundles, has been found at sites dating to the late prehistoric period, i.e., the last two millennia.

One consequence of the emergence of these ramified exchange systems was the need to supply large quantities of goods. In some places this market demand led to the restructuring of social and economic life. More effort was devoted to production of surpluses for trade, such as mining and manufacturing ocher or stone axes. Archaeological sites such as the deep ocher mine of **Wilgie Mia** in Western Australia, or the immense axe quarries at **Lake Moondarra** in north Queensland, illustrate the scale of activities required to supply the emerging trade networks (Hiscock and Mitchell 1993).

Population and Settlement Change

Reformulation of religious beliefs and the expansion of trade systems during the Holocene may reflect a cultural reaction to fundamental demographic and economic shifts. For example, during the last few thousand years archaeological materials increased in abundance in many regions of Australia: coastal and inland, islands and mainland. The rise in the number of archaeological sites occupied and in the artifacts recovered from those sites have been interpreted by many archaeologists as a reflection of a **population increase** during the later prehistoric period. While the magnitude of population change is difficult to measure, archaeological indicators suggest that the scale of change would be something like a tripling or quadrupling of population between 2000 BC and AD 1 (Hiscock 2003).

One consequence of population growth is the expansion of burial grounds. In the **Murray River valley** of southeastern Australia, the number of cemeteries and the density of burials within them increase substantially in the late Holocene (Pardoe 1988). The cause of population change in this period is poorly understood, but since the likely growth rates were only a minor departure from a long-term balance between births and deaths, we need not look for a dramatic process. Climatic change and an escalation of production driven by social competition have both been suggested as factors that might have been responsible.

During at least the late Holocene it is likely that people stayed longer at base camps in some regions. These foragers located themselves at places of abundant resources, such as lagoons or springs, sending parties away to gather resources that were not locally available. After a period, the local resources became depleted, and people walked to another resource-rich location. Archaeologists often find large scatters of artifacts and earth and shell mounds on or near the camping sites. In regions such as western Arnhem Land, hunter-gatherers moved during the dry season between swamps and lagoons, in response to pronounced seasonal changes in the location and timing of resources (Meehan et al. 1985). The residential shifts in such circumstances were relatively regular and predictable.

In other regions the concentration of people at particular localities was a response to deteriorating conditions, which may have been rare and difficult to predict. For example, around the margins of **Lake Eyre** in desert central Australia are large and dense concentrations of stone artifacts at natural mound springs. These are interpreted as places where people sought refuge during prolonged drought, basing themselves there until they had either exhausted the food at that location or until rain could be seen in the distance. The length of time spent at each location was only a few weeks or months, depending on the balance between resources at that location and elsewhere in the territory of the group. When the resources remaining in the vicinity of a camp fell to the level of resources generally available elsewhere in the landscape, people would usually have moved away.

Claims for **long-term sedentism**, in which occupation is permanently or semi-permanently based at one locality, have been overstated. Such claims rely on two kinds of ambiguous evidence. The first is the presence of structures such as earth mounds (e.g. at McArthur Creek in Victoria) and low stone walls (e.g. at Allambie in Victoria or High Cliffy Island on the northwest coast) that have sometimes been interpreted as house foundations. Some of these features were probably created by natural processes, however, and there are a variety of other explanations for such archaeological remains, including cooking mounds and ceremonial activities (Clarke 1994). Nevertheless, it does seem that some of these structures were foundations for small buildings, constructions that must have been advantageous in inclement weather. The existence of small-scale housing is an indication of repeated visitation by foragers to resource-rich areas, but people could have lived at these locations for perhaps only a few months each year.

Abundance of potential foodstuffs has also led to the idea of long-term sedentism. The most famous supposed proof of this claim is the "eel traps" of **Toolondo**. In this well-watered area of southeastern Australia, excavations have revealed artificial drainage channels up to 1 m (3 ft) deep, running between small swamps and creeks. Harry Lourandos (1980; 1987) has suggested that these ditches were used to breed and harvest eels. Nevertheless, although construction and maintenance of these ditches demanded a substantial investment of labor, it is unlikely that people would have been tethered to these devices year round. Since eels migrated seasonally to tropical waters, this food supply would only have been available for part of the year; and although recent evidence of possible meat storage in the form of eel smoking has been claimed, the scale and effectiveness of meat storage has not been established. It is improbable that smoked eel meat alone created a year-round food supply sufficient to allow permanent occupation of a single locality.

This conclusion applies not only to the eel harvesting in southern Australia, but also to the construction of other capture facilities, such as fish traps along the coast or in inland waterways. Targeting abundant food resources through construction of harvesting facilities and storage practices may have reduced the size of foraging territories and lowered the frequency of residential moves, but it probably did not create conditions suitable for permanent village life.

The Effects of Historic Foreign Contacts

One of the factors leading archaeologists to overstate the practice of sedentism during the late Holocene involves the observations by Europeans of large encampments of Aboriginal people near early colonial outposts. In many instances these historical records describe Aboriginal social and economic systems that had already been drastically changed by European contact. The historical lifestyles of Aboriginal people may, therefore, have only a superficial resemblance to pre-contact foraging societies.

KEY SITE Barlambidj: Aboriginal Contact with Southeast Asia

Copeland Island is a small speck of land located a short distance off the coast of western Arnhem Land in northern Australia. Located on a sandy flat on the southern edge of this island is an archaeological site named Barlambidj by local Aborigines. No water sources exist on the island, but the presence of rock platforms, sandy beaches, and nearby deep water and reefs means that abundant food is available.

Barlambidj has visible above-ground archaeological structures in the form of six stone lines and three depressions. The stone lines consist of sandstone cobbles and boulders arranged into a number of adjoining

bays about 1 m (3 ft) wide. Each bay served as a fireplace, with a large metal cauldron sitting on top. In addition to these structures there are shards of glass and earthenware pottery, mollusk shells, fish, and marine turtle bone spread across the sandy surface. Radiocarbon estimates and cultural material indicate that this surface material may date to less than 100–150 years ago, but excavations reveal an earlier shell midden below the stone lines. Dated to *c.* 1400–900 BC, this midden is similar to the more recent one, except that the fish come from a greater range of environments, and there is only a small amount of turtle bone.

Barlambidj provides a classic illustration of the effects on the Aboriginal economy of contact with Macassan fishermen from Southeast Asia. The contrast between the lower (pre-contact) midden and the surface (post-contact) midden reflects a number of economic changes initiated by introduced technology (Mitchell 1994). The major increase in turtle remains in the post-contact midden resulted from the adoption of dug-out canoes and metal harpoon heads, and the reduced diversity of fish taxa has been interpreted as evidence for the abandonment of this low-fat food as turtle became available.

The spread of smallpox and other rapidly transmitted diseases in the late 18th and early 19th centuries killed and injured many Aboriginal people (Butlin 1983). In some regions the majority of elderly, socially senior people may have perished, while in others a disproportionate fatality rate from disease among other sections of the community is suspected. By effectively creating power and knowledge vacuums, these contexts assisted social and political change. This process may have been exaggerated by the potential gains in political status that could be acquired by individuals or groups with privileged access to the valuable resources of non-Aboriginal people. By controlling negotiations with non-Aboriginal visitors and colonizers during the 18th and 19th centuries, some Aboriginal individuals and groups accrued new economic and political power. One way this was manifested was through the development of more extensive and intensive trading systems, probably stimulated by the desire for valuable introduced goods such as metal knives and axes (Mitchell 1994). The expansion of trading systems in response to the provision of foreign goods is likely to have stimulated the production of artifacts for trade, and ultimately to have led to a variety of economic changes.

One expression of economic change brought about by contact with non-Aboriginal groups involved the alteration to foraging and mobility patterns along the northern coastline of Australia. The introduction of new technologies, such as dugout canoes and metal fishhooks and harpoon heads, altered the food procurement conventions. Aboriginal foragers began intensively to hunt turtles and large marine mammals such as dugong [see box: Barlambidj: Aboriginal Contact with Southeast Asia]. Dugout canoes, manufactured for the first time

following the introduction of iron axes, enabled the meat of these large animals to be transported many kilometers back to base camps, effectively expanding the foraging radius of coastal Aboriginal groups. At the same time, steel axes probably made processing of some abundant plant foods economical for the first time. Large stands of pandanus (screw palm) on the tropical coast were probably first intensively exploited in the 18th century, when metal axes could be used to extract the nuts from the densely woven husk.

This combination of new and plentiful foods and more powerful capture and transport technologies enabled people to exist in larger groups and for longer periods in each location than they had in the prehistoric period, judging from increased site size and centralized site location on the northern coastline. Larger group size and less mobile settlement patterns must also have led to social and political change, exaggerating and shaping the influences that resulted from culture contact. The magnitude of these proto-historic and early historic modifications means that historical observations of Aboriginal society probably provide comparatively poor analogues for prehistoric Australian foragers, let alone ancient hunter-gatherers elsewhere.

The Islands of Southeast Asia and Oceania

Most of the islands of Indonesia and the Philippines were formed by the forces of earth movement (subduction) that operate along continental plate boundaries, creating chains of volcanoes and parallel formations of uplifted sedimentary rocks. Such volcanic arcs extend from Sumatra and Java into the

Moluccas (Spice Islands) and the Philippines; Borneo forms a relatively stable continental extension of Asia and lacks volcanoes. Other volcanic arcs occur in the western Pacific as far east as Tonga. Beyond Fiji and Tonga, i.e., in the ethnographic regions of Micronesia and Polynesia, the island chains have been formed mainly by "hot spot" activity emanating from zones of crustal weakness deep beneath the ocean surface (Nunn 1994).

The periodic lowered sea levels during the Pleistocene glaciations created a vast dry-land extension to the Asian continent that included the present islands of Sumatra, Java, Borneo, and Bali. This massive ancient landmass is termed Sundaland by biogeographers (see Chapter 4), and its modern islands have essentially Asian floras and placental mammal faunas. However, the islands of the Philippines and eastern Indonesia (Sulawesi, the Moluccas, and the Lesser Sundas) were never connected to either Asia or Greater Australia (Australia plus New Guinea and Tasmania) with land bridges, although the distances between them were sometimes much reduced. The eastern Indonesian islands belong to the biogeographical province of Wallacea, through which human migration toward Greater Australia has always involved sea crossings for animals, plants, and humans alike. Colonists in Wallacea found fewer animal resources, although a number of endemic placental mammal species existed in the Philippines and Sulawesi.

This brings up a major geographical distinction between the islands that were accessible to Pleistocene colonists, and those that were not. The islands of Wallacea and Near Oceania (the latter located from the Bird's Head peninsula of western New Guinea eastwards to the Solomons (i.e., western Melanesia)) were sufficiently close together that early populations of hunters and gatherers were able to reach many of them before 30,000 years ago [**8.9**]. The islands of Remote Oceania (Green 1991a), from the Santa Cruz Islands eastwards, including all of Micronesia and Polynesia, were only accessible to canoe-borne Austronesians after 1500 BC; those who traveled there entered terrain never before subjected to human presence.

To the east of New Guinea, with its marsupial mammal faunas, and moving into Oceania, native terrestrial resources diminished rapidly. The only mammals to extend their range east of the Solomons were bats. Snakes and large lizards did not extend beyond western Polynesia, so in most Polynesian islands (excluding New Zealand, which had flightless moas and lizards) there were virtually no terrestrial animals at all. Yet

8.9 *The migrations of early human populations into Island Southeast Asia and western Melanesia during the Pleistocene:* Homo erectus *populations possibly reached Flores, whereas early modern humans crossed wider sea gaps to reach Australia, the Philippines, and western Melanesia.*

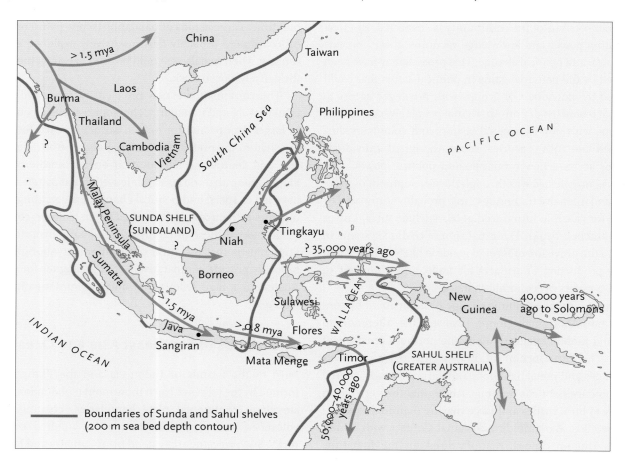

early humans in much of Remote Oceania were entering a veritable paradise of rich food, owing to the enormous and untapped resources of fish, shellfish, and birds, the latter doubtless naïve in the sudden presence of humans and all obliged to nest on land, whatever their flight capacities.

Early Human Settlers in Island Southeast Asia

Although not accepted by all paleoanthropologists (see Chapter 4), some scholars believe that the tropical world of the Southeast Asian islands was first settled, in the far west at least, by *Homo erectus* some time before 1 million years ago. This species was able to colonize Java, and might also have been able to migrate as far east as Flores Island in Indonesia by crossing narrow sea gaps. Whether or not its genes still survive among extant populations is a hotly debated issue in modern paleoanthropology. What is very clear is that anatomically modern human populations, who certainly do have living descendants, had spread through the region to as far east as the Solomons by at least 40,000 years ago.

These Pleistocene and early Holocene populations of Southeast Asia and western Melanesia established a cultural and genetic tapestry, now partly masked or replaced, to which later Austronesian colonists had to adapt during their migrations, at least to as far east as the Solomon Islands. The majority of these earlier populations were hunters and gatherers along coastlines and in forests, and possibly in parklands in some of the drier parts of Java and southeastern Indonesia. Flake and pebble tool industries favored chert or obsidian wherever such rocks were available; in cases where they were not, some populations, as in parts of the Moluccas, managed virtually without stone tools at all. Pebble tool industries (the so-called Hoabinhian industries, named after a province in northern Vietnam) dominated the Southeast Asian mainland, especially in the Malay peninsula. In the islands, pebble and flake industries are known from many cave sites, such as Niah Cave in Sarawak and Tabon Cave in the Philippines, associated with human skeletal material relating generally to recent Australian or Melanesian populations, at least during the Pleistocene. No suggestions of animal or plant domestication are present, and no one made pottery, but occasional pre-Neolithic occurrences of edge-ground axes in Vietnam and Malaysia perhaps hint at developments to come (for a general survey see Bellwood 1997).

The main variations in what was essentially a fairly unvarying cultural scene across Indonesia and the Philippines occur in the form of a number of industries of small, bladelike flakes that appeared initially in the mid-Holocene, after *c.* 4000 BC. The best known of these is the **Toalian** of southern Sulawesi, with its backed cutting tools and trapezoidal microliths. Similar industries appear in Australia at about the same time or earlier, and could relate there to adaptations to risk management and

stress alleviation [see box: Explaining Technological Change in Australia, p. 270]. However, the southern Sulawesi microliths belong to a much wetter climatic region and are very localized in occurrence, so the Australian explanation may not be appropriate here. Indeed, they are sufficiently restricted in distribution and sufficiently close in form to those of Australia to suggest sea-borne transference of technology from the latter region, although none have been found yet in intermediate islands such as Timor or the Lesser Sundas.

Early Agriculturalists in New Guinea

The islands of Southeast Asia and the Pacific witnessed a two-part development and dispersal of agricultural populations. The most significant one for later Austronesian dispersal commenced in China. But in the New Guinea highlands, agricultural systems based on the drainage of swamps for presumed taro cultivation and the shifting cultivation of surrounding slopes for yams, bananas, and sugarcane had developed indigenously by at least 4000 BC, at a time when highland temperatures were slightly warmer than now [see box: Early Farming in the New Guinea Highlands, p. 278]. The western Pacific region, including New Guinea, was homeland to a number of species of such useful plants exploited widely by pre-Austronesian populations (Lebot 1999; Swadling et al. 1991).

The New Guinea highland valleys are environmentally unique in this region – broad, fertile, mostly located 1500–1700 m (4900–5600 ft) above sea level and thereby malaria-free (Bayliss-Smith 1996). The cordillera, or mountain chain, that supports these valleys is also geomorphologically unique, being unparalleled in any of the volcanic islands of Southeast Asia or in Borneo. Thus, early Holocene populations in New Guinea were able to enter a highland world with a climate sufficiently equable for tropical crops to grow, but also close to their altitudinal limits. This perhaps encouraged climate-induced resource fluctuations (frost, drought) of a kind that are believed in some other parts of the world to have triggered early agriculture, as a means of maintaining short-term supplies of desirable foods (Bellwood 1996a).

The absence of cereals and domesticated animals in New Guinea meant that early farming populations were generally small and scattered. Pigs were not introduced until *c.* 1000 BC, in this case by Austronesians, and the American sweet potato, which is a major highland food source today, probably did not appear until after AD 1550 (although it might have arrived a little earlier, particularly if it could have been transmitted from prehistoric Polynesia, where it was present by about AD 1000: see Easter Island and South America box, p. 297).

The relatively low population and archaeological profile of the southern lowlands of New Guinea, in part a reflection of endemic malaria and in part due to extensive marine submergence

KEY DISCOVERY Early Farming in the New Guinea Highlands

The most significant site in New Guinea to reveal evidence for the indigenous transition to agriculture is Kuk, a former tea plantation near Mount Hagen in the western highlands of Papua New Guinea (the eastern half of the island of New Guinea). Research by Jack Golson (1977) since the 1960s, and more recently by Tim Denham and colleagues (2003), has revealed a series of drainage ditches cut into the swampy valley floor, presumably to control water flow for agricultural purposes, together with well-preserved wooden digging sticks.

The first evidence for human impact, in the form of a layer of redeposited soil believed to reflect forest clearing activities, dates to about 7000 BC. Mounding for cultivation commenced by about 5000 BC, and rectilinear gridlike ditching appeared by 2000 BC, associated with archaeobotanical evidence for taro (*Colocasia*) and banana cultivation (Bayliss-Smith and Golson 1992; Bayliss-Smith 1996; Denham et al. 2003). Finally, within the past few centuries, there appeared the close-set grid system of raised garden beds associated with current sweet potato cultivation practices.

Current botanical interpretations suggest that New Guinea might have witnessed an independent domestication of both taro and *Musa* spp. bananas during the early Holocene (Denham et al. 2003), together with some varieties of sugarcane and yams. The periodicity of ditch digging at Kuk, with major phases of swamp drainage being separated by long periods of abandonment, is thought to relate in part to the periodicity of severe drought and high levels of climatic variability (Haberle and Lusty 2000). During droughts, cultivators would tend to move into swamps, whereas during periods of higher rainfall they would be free to utilize more extensive methods of dry-land agriculture on surrounding slopes.

The deeper significance of Kuk and the New Guinea highlands transition to agriculture is that it can help to explain why New Guinea, apart from a few coastal pockets, never experienced any major Austronesian settlement. The New Guinea highlands are remote and difficult of access from the coastline, except via rare penetrative valleys such as the Markham, and today are entirely occupied by Papuan-speaking peoples who

show no signs of any significant prehistoric contact with Austronesians. Even pottery-making only reached the highlands in a very limited way, and this was the last region in the Pacific to be reached by European explorers, during the 1930s.

Given Austronesian success in the complete settlement of the island of Borneo by moving up the major rivers, one has to ask why nothing similar ever occurred in New Guinea. The answer, apart from sheer remoteness, is surely that the New Guinea continuous cordillera (a landform absent in Borneo) was conducive to an independent development of early agriculture, and that New Guinea highlanders were thereby sufficiently numerous and sedentary by 1000 BC to make any incursion by Austronesians very difficult. Settling new terrain (as opposed to simply governing it and extracting resources) became less successful as the indigenous population previously in place increased in number and economic complexity.

8.10 *(Left) Men holding two paddle-shaped spades from Kuk Agricultural Research Station, part of a larger collection found during drainage work at the station in the late 1960s/early 1970s (Kuk Phases 5 and 6).*

8.11 *(Right) The mounded paleosurface at Kuk, dating to 7000–6500 years ago.*

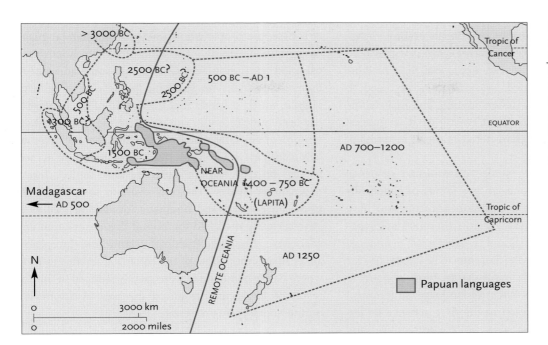

8.12 *Dates for Austronesian settlement: these are derived from correlations between the linguistic and archaeological records. New data recently emerging suggest a date of only 2000 BC for the northern Philippines and 1500 BC for western Micronesia.*

during the mid-Holocene (*c.* 4000–1000 BC), meant that no agricultural colonization of Australia, the last completely hunter-gatherer continent to survive until European contact, ever occurred.

The Austronesian Dispersal

The most dynamic series of events in Holocene prehistory in Southeast Asia and Oceania were the dispersal trajectories of the Austronesian-speaking peoples [**8.12**]. There are more than 1000 Austronesian languages, making it the second-largest language family in the world in number of languages, after the Niger-Congo family of Africa. With the exception of the various forms of Malay (the major *lingua franca* of Indonesia and Malaysia since the arrival of Islam about 600 years ago) and certain languages such as Javanese and Balinese, which were associated with pre-Islamic states, most Austronesian languages were spoken at European contact by relatively small populations of village agriculturalists. Some of the greatest linguistic diversity at this time, in terms of number of languages per unit of territory (a measure that has no relationship to genetic diversity, discussed below), existed in eastern Indonesia and Melanesia. On the other hand, in some Polynesian chiefdom societies, such as those of the Hawaiians, single languages with dialect variation were spoken by populations exceeding 100,000 people. Austronesian cultures in AD 1500 thus ranged from the Islamic and Hindu-Buddhist states of Malaysia and western Indonesia, through the colorful Philippine and Polynesian chiefdoms described in Spanish records and in 18th-century explorers' journals, to small and isolated clans of swidden (slash-and-burn) cultivators and tiny forager bands.

Economically, the variation was just as great. In western and northern regions of island Southeast Asia, many Austronesian populations depended on rice cultivation, whereas along the equator, and particularly in eastern Indonesia and Oceania, tubers and fruits provided most of the diet. Fish, pork, and chicken added protein in most regions, with cattle and water buffalo being husbanded in island Southeast Asia; dogs were relatively ubiquitous. Hunter-gatherers with access to Iron Age technology existed in the Philippines, interior Borneo, and Sumatra, and boat-dwelling fisher-foragers plied some of the sheltered seas of island Southeast Asia. By AD 1500, many people in Southeast Asia had already known both bronze and iron technology for about 1700 years (and had known bronze for far longer beyond the boundaries of the Austronesian world, in China, Thailand, and Vietnam; see Chapter 15), whereas all populations east of Indonesia were technologically Neolithic.

Who Are the Austronesians?

In general, the Austronesian dispersal has been an obvious and relatively recent one, particularly in Oceania; here Austronesians were the first human settlers, arriving everywhere beyond the Solomons within the past 3500 years (and much more recently in many places, perhaps only 800 years ago in the case of New Zealand). A careful look at the people who speak Austronesian languages, however, indicates that the primary dispersal was not one uniform and continuous migration, inbred and insulated from the rest of the world. Polynesians, Filipinos, Malays, Island Melanesians, and Negritos from the Philippine island of Luzon (Agta) certainly do not all share a single biological origin within the past 4000 years. This is as apparent now as it was to the naturalist Johann Reinhold

Forster, who accompanied James Cook on his second voyage through the Pacific in 1772–75. The early explorers witnessed a Pacific world that will never be seen again, and their insights should not be underestimated. Nevertheless, we need to progress beyond 18th-century understanding, and make some multidisciplinary observations about exactly what languages, artifacts, genes, and skeletal characteristics mean in terms of human history.

Absolutely central to the whole Austronesian dispersal process is the fact that Austronesian is a family of **genetically related languages** that share a common ancestor and have spread outwards from a homeland region. (Because languages are considered by many linguists and archaeologists to undergo descent from common ancestors, and thus to be candidates for cladistic (evolutionary) analysis, many use the term "genetic" to describe identifiable lineages such as language subgroups.) Thus, Austronesian history must in the first instance be linguistic history. But it must also be a comparative and multidisciplinary history if the past is to make sense. The archaeological record is crucial, since it tells us about the spread of material objects and economic indicators, such as artifact types, production systems, and domesticated crops and animals. Archaeology also provides absolute dates, something that the linguistic record is not well placed to do. Although some Austronesian languages, such as Malay, Javanese, and Balinese, were used with Indic scripts on stone and copperplate inscriptions from the 7th century AD onward, these are far too recent in time to inform us about Austronesian origins.

We must now ask a fundamental question: are the prehistoric records of dispersal derived from comparative linguistics and archaeology likely to tell the same story of the human past, or completely different ones? The answer will be "the same" if we can be sure that languages and native speakers spread together, as in recent situations of European colonization in Australasia and the Americas. But there must have been occasional (and by no means universal) situations in which people changed or shifted languages, so that the native speaker link down through the generations was broken. That such situations occurred in the Austronesian past is suggested by human biology. In some regions the biological data seem to correlate only partially with the linguistic and archaeological records and sometimes even contradict them, a situation perhaps to be expected whenever speakers of one language or members of one ethnic group are likely to mix with speakers or members of another.

All of this points to a prehistory that has been extremely complex. Many thousands of people, over a vast area of the earth's surface, have moved and interacted over several thousand years to form the ethnolinguistic patterns that we today term "Austronesian." So, who are the Austronesians? They are,

of course, the people who speak Austronesian languages – an easy group to identify, since within the main Austronesian distribution (excluding New Guinea and some adjacent regions) there are virtually no surviving pockets of other native languages, which suggests that the spread of the language family has been quite recent in world prehistoric terms, perhaps gathering steam in Taiwan at about the time that the pyramids were being built at Giza in Egypt (mid-3rd millennium BC; see Chapter 10, p. 376). Where Austronesians settled, few foreign populations have successfully overlain or replaced the Austronesian cultural and linguistic foundations, although they have certainly modified them, and this observation applies to successive Hindu and Buddhist, Islamic and European visitors alike. Apart from some of the colonized territories in Oceania where native populations were greatly reduced in numbers as a result of European-introduced diseases, Austronesia is still quintessentially Austronesian.

A Basic History of the Austronesian Languages

The Austronesian language family first "crystallized" in Taiwan, where nine of the ten primary subgroups of Austronesian still exist today (Blust 1995; Pawley 2003) [**8.13, 8.14**]. Taiwan thus has a strong claim to be recognized as the "Austronesian homeland" on the grounds of genetic diversity [see box: The Origins of the Austronesians, pp. 282–83]. The tenth subgroup of Austronesian, defined by the linguist Robert Blust as Malayo-Polynesian, is characterized by a number of widely shared innovations in pronoun forms, verbal prefixes, phonological (sound) mergers, and other linguistic features that occurred prior to its initial dispersal. Early Malayo-Polynesian languages were spread by human colonists from Taiwan to the Philippines and onward, eventually to reach all points of the Austronesian world from Madagascar to Easter Island.

The ultimate homeland of the Austronesian languages, according to many linguists, must have been the southern Chinese mainland, before ancestral groups actually migrated to Taiwan, although ancestry at this remote time is so faint that few worthwhile details can be added, apart from the very important observation that the languages most directly ancestral to Austronesian were probably spoken somewhere in coastal central or southern (see Chapter 7). The expansion of the Sinitic (Chinese) languages during the past 3000 years means that no unequivocal traces of such ancient languages remain today.

An examination of the linguistic reconstructions of lexical items and meanings that refer to the early Austronesian way of life in proto-languages results in the following inferences, in relative chronological order. First, the Proto-Austronesians who lived in Taiwan were agriculturalists who grew foxtail millet, sugarcane, and rice (having separate terms for field, husked,

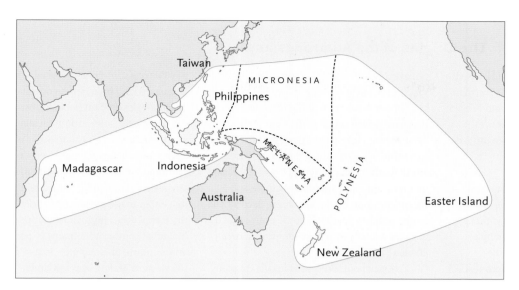

8.14 *Family tree for the major subgroups of the Austronesian language family:* Austronesian languages diversified in Taiwan (Formosa) for perhaps 1000 years or more before languages in the Malayo-Polynesian subgroup were carried further afield (after Blust).

and cooked rice). They doubtless grew some tubers and fruit crops, but linguistic reconstructions for these are not as strong as for the cereals. They made boats of some form (canoes and rafts – it is not certain if they had sails) and lived in timber houses; they kept pigs, dogs, chickens, and perhaps water buffalo; they had bows and arrows, some form of loom for weaving, and they used pottery, but they did not know how to cast copper or smelt iron. In archaeological terms, they appear to have been fairly classic Neolithic societies, with a material culture similar to that of many Austronesian communities in the Pacific Islands that survived to European contact without a knowledge of metallurgy.

Second, the break-up of the original Proto-Austronesian dialect chain into separate languages occurred within Taiwan as early Austronesian populations spread across the island. Possibly a millennium after this initial Austronesian colonization, the language ancestral to all the Malayo-Polynesian languages (Proto-Malayo-Polynesian) was carried from Taiwan by a seaborne migration to the northern Philippines. New crops added at this time, presumably in the tropical Philippines or Indonesia, included breadfruit, coconut, sago, and bananas. Yams and aroids (*Colocasia taro, Alocasia*) were certainly cultivated by this time and perhaps earlier. Unambiguous cognates now appear for the use of sails to power canoes – a very significant development for what was to come.

Third, after the move to the northern Philippines, a veritable tide of Malayo-Polynesian language dispersal seems to have been unleashed. The linguistic evidence for this is rather technical, but the early Malayo-Polynesian languages that spread from the Philippines through Indonesia and into the western Pacific were all very closely related in terms of their reconstructed vocabularies, sharing 80–90 percent of common, everyday words (Blust 1993; Pawley 1999). This situation points very strongly toward rapid dispersal, leading to a contin-

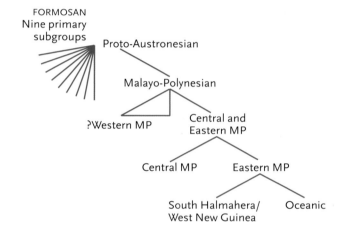

uous distribution of fairly homogeneous ancestral Malayo-Polynesian and Oceanic dialect chains. A boat-borne human diaspora flowed through the Philippines and northern Indonesia, eastwards to the Mariana Islands in Micronesia, through Island Melanesia (but not New Guinea initially) to Tonga and Samoa in western Polynesia, and southwards into Borneo, Sulawesi, and Java. The flow might have been slowed a little by the presence of non-Austronesian agricultural populations in parts of southern Vietnam and the Malay peninsula, and of course in New Guinea, since it is far easier for agricultural colonists to establish themselves where there are only small pockets of hunter-gatherers, rather than in an area already quite densely settled by other farmers.

Fourth, following the rapid language spread through island Southeast Asia and into the central Pacific, there seems to have been a pause. The languages of **Madagascar** and eastern Polynesia were definitely established much later, after AD 400. The former contains Sanskrit loan words that only spread to Indonesia from India after this time (Adelaar 1995). The Polynesian languages share so many unique linguistic features,

KEY CONTROVERSY **The Origins of the Austronesians**

Writing after traveling on the *Resolution* with Captain James Cook in 1772–75, the German scholar and explorer Johann Reinhold Forster asked his readers why the inhabitants of Tahiti in Polynesia should have been different in appearance from those of Vanuatu in Melanesia.

He suggested that "[the Tahitians are] nearly related in every respect to the Tagales in Luçon or Manilla [Philippines], so that we may now trace the line of migration by a continued line of isles … [through the Mariana or Ladrones Islands of Micronesia]." He went on to note: "I am therefore inclined to suppose, that all these dialects [Austronesian languages – Polynesian, Melanesian, Philippine, Malay] preserve several words of a more ancient language, which was more universal, and was gradually divided into many languages, now

remarkably different" (Thomas et al. 1996, 175, 187, 190).

Forster was here making two observations that have driven much of the enquiry into Austronesian origin questions over the past two centuries. First, the populations who speak Austronesian languages are very varied in appearance and are not of a single and recent common biological origin. Second, the languages they speak are sufficiently related to share a relatively recent common source [**Table 1**].

The viewpoint presented in this chapter differs little from that of Forster. Austronesian migrations commenced in the southern China-Taiwan-northern Philippines general region and progressed from there through movements of both people and languages. In some regions, such as western Melanesia or parts of the Philippines, indigenous

populations sometimes adopted Austronesian languages, and their genes continued to dominate descendant populations.

Such local "annexation" by language alone would have tended to occur in environments that for some reason were marginal for Austronesian settlement, or that already had large indigenous populations, due either to the presence of agriculture (in the New Guinea highlands, peninsular Malaysia, southern Vietnam) or perhaps arboriculture (dependence on tree crops, as in the western Melanesian lowlands).

In regions where incoming Austronesian settlers found few hazards or prior inhabitants, we can expect their Asian-derived genotypes to have dominated rapidly, as they did in most of island Southeast Asia, Polynesia, and Micronesia. Recent skeletal analyses (Pietrusewsky 1994) and genetic

none occurring in the Melanesian islands to the west, that a very long period of gestation is indicated (the build-up of innovations in languages, like the accumulation of mutations in genetics, requires time).

This gestation occurred in western Polynesia (Tonga and Samoa) and may have lasted for a millennium before any other Polynesian islands to the east were initially settled (Pawley 1996). This means that in Samoa or nearby, the dispersal of

Austronesians further toward the east was halted. Archaeologically, this could reflect the necessity of crossing much wider sea gaps, combined with a higher mid-Pacific sea level *c.* 1000 BC that would have caused most atolls to be partly submerged. The challenge of these sea gaps (1200 km (750 miles) if sailing from Samoa to the southern Cook Islands, 2000 km (1250 miles) to the Society Islands) seemingly induced major innovations in canoe technology.

Table 1 *Widely Shared Austronesian Words*

As recorded before 1778 by Johann Reinhold Forster. Original spellings are reproduced without original diacriticals; modern forms are in **bold**, together with modern Proto-Austronesian [**PAN**] and Proto-Malayo-Polynesian [**PMP**] reconstructions. For Forster's original table, see Thomas et al. 1996, 188–89. Modern forms and reconstructions courtesy Andrew Pawley and Meredith Osmond, Australian National University.

§ yams were grown in the northern North Island, but were not observed by Forster
* reconstructed form

English	Society Islands	Friendly Islands (**Tonga**)	New Zealand	Easter Island
Two	Rooa (**rua**)	Looa (**lua**)	Rooa (**rua**)	Rooa (**rua**)
Five	Reema (**rima**)	Neema (**nima**)	Reema (**rima**)	Reema (**rima**)
Coconut	Neea (**niu**)	Neeoo (**niu**)	none	none
Dead	matte (**mate**)	matte (**mate**)	matte (**mate**)	(not recorded) (**mate**)
Eye	Matta (**mata**)	Matta (**mata**)	Matta (**mata**)	Matta (**mata**)
Fish	Eiya (**i'a**)	Eeka (**ika**)	Eeka (**ika**)	Eeka (**ika**)
Ear	Tarreha (**tari'a**)	Taringa (**talinga**)	Tarenga (**taringa**)	Tarreean (**taringa**)
Yam	Oowhee (**ufi**)	Oofee ('**ufi**)	(none) (**uhi**) §	Oohee (**uhi**)
Eat	ai ('**ai**)	kai (**kai**)	kai (**kai**)	magho (**kai**)
Drink	Ainoo (**inu**)	ainoo (**inu**)	ainoo (**inu**)	hynoo (**unu**)

studies make this point strongly (e.g. Merriwether et al. 1999; Hagelberg 2001).

Recent Debates

There have been recent attempts to break down this fairly clear model (sometimes called the "express train" (Diamond 1989) or "out of Taiwan" model) into a more complex picture, involving a great deal of human dislocation between island Southeast Asia and Oceania. Matthew Hurles and his colleagues (2002) point out that it is difficult to trace the genes of Polynesians directly back to Taiwan.

This is perhaps not surprising, given the 4000 years since any likely common ancestry, for new genes mutate periodically, and then for various reasons (founder effects, selection, random genetic drift) can disappear or come to dominate in descendant populations, particularly in relatively isolated island groups.

Stephen Oppenheimer and Martin Richards (2001) take Hurles's argument much further, and claim that Polynesians are unrelated genetically to all the other Austronesians who live west of the Wallace Line (the eastern boundary of the Sunda Shelf), including those in Taiwan; their argument is founded on molecular clock calculations for Polynesian mitochondrial DNA based on assumed mutation rates (for an explanation of the use of mtDNA in human evolutionary research, see Chapter 4, p. 138). This viewpoint proposes a complete disassociation of language and mitochondrial DNA, a viewpoint not followed here, owing to the extreme levels of uncertainty associated with molecular clock forms of dating.

Linguistic and Archaeological Evidence

Leaving the genetics to one side, there is a very strong linguistic and archaeological correlation that emanates from recent research. Linguistically, a Taiwanese homeland for the Austronesian family is almost universally recognized by linguists; the idea of a Melanesian homeland (Dyen 1965) is no longer taken seriously. New discoveries in archaeology – especially in Taiwan, the Batanes Islands, northern Luzon, the Marianas, Sabah, and eastern Indonesia – make clear the overall directionality and chronology of the flow of Neolithic material culture related to the reconstructed early Austronesian lifestyle, even if many of the details are still obscure. The cultural and linguistic spread was from China and Taiwan southwards, albeit with very significant biological input from indigenous populations as far east as Melanesia.

These successive stages of Austronesian dispersal, it will be realized, are based essentially on linguistic reasoning. The absolute dating for them, together with many other details of the material cultures and economies involved in the population dispersal process, can only be provided securely by archaeology. As we shall see, the overall trajectories of the archaeological and linguistic records, in terms of major expansions and terminations, correspond with remarkable precision (Bellwood 1991).

Malay	Tagalas (Tagalog)	PAN	PMP
Dua (**dua**)	Dalava (**dalawa**)	*DuSa	*duha
Leema (**lima**)	Lima (**lima**)	*limaH	*lima
Neeor (**nyior**)	Niog (**niug**)		*niuR
Mattee (**mati**)	matayan (**patay**)	*maCey	*matay
Mata (**mata**)	Mata (**mata**)	*maCa	*mata
Eekan (**ikan**)	Yida (**isda**)	*Sikan	*hikan
Telinga (**telinga**)	Taynga (**tainga**)	*Calinga	*talinga
Ooby (**ubi**)	Obi (**ubi**)	*qubi(s)	*qubi
Macan (**makan**)	Cain (**kain**)	*ka'en	*kaen
Minnum (**minum**)	Ynom (**inum**)		*inum

The Archaeology of Early Austronesian Dispersal

In this section we examine the archaeological record for the appearance of Neolithic cultures that can, with reasonable assurance, be correlated with the material culture reconstructions for the various early proto-languages within the Formosan and Malayo-Polynesian subgroups of Austronesian [see **8.14**]. By 3000 BC, an agricultural way of life with pottery, stone adzes, rice, pigs, dogs, and possibly chickens had spread southwards through the coastal provinces of China to reach Taiwan. For the next 2000 years the archaeological record reveals a spread of related cultural complexes, with red-slipped and often stamped pottery, domestic animals, and similar kinds of stone and shell artifacts, right through the Philippines, eastern Indonesia, and the western Pacific, reaching western Polynesia (Tonga and Samoa) by about 900 BC. Later movements into the Caroline Islands of southern Micronesia occurred around AD 1, and into eastern Polynesia between AD 700 and 1250.

Taiwan The oldest Neolithic complex on Taiwan relevant to our discussion is that termed **Dabenkeng**, after a coastal site in the northern part of the island. Currently, Dabenkeng sites date between 3000 and 2000 BC and occur all around the coastal regions of Taiwan. Their incised and cord-marked pottery [**8.15**] is very homogeneous in terms of shape and decoration, this in itself being a clear indication that the Dabenkeng people belonged to a relatively unified cultural milieu and were perhaps immigrants into Taiwan from Fujian or Guangdong, where similar pottery occurs at the same general time (Chang 1995). The only archaeological assemblages in Taiwan older than the Dabenkeng are the flaked pebble tools left by the inhabitants of the Changbin caves and other sites in eastern Taiwan, but these assemblages show no signs of direct evolution into the Dabenkeng Neolithic.

Until recently, attempts to link the spread of the Dabenkeng culture through Taiwan with the early Austronesians were problematic, owing to the absence of any direct evidence for agriculture, even though Dabenkeng sites are large, numerous, and mostly close to good agricultural land. Several also occur in the Penghu (Pescadores) Islands in the Taiwan Strait, where there are sources of excellent basalt for adze-making (Tsang 1992; Rolett et al. 2000). But most Dabenkeng sites have been found on the ridges and hills that rise immediately inland from the modern coastal plain that runs down the western side of Taiwan. Such locations are excellent for archaeological visibility, since sherds are strewn everywhere, but very poor for preservation.

With recent discoveries at **Nanguanli**, in the southwestern coastal plain near Tainan, the difficulty in linking the Dabenkeng culture to the early Austronesians has been resolved. Rescue excavations here by Tsang Cheng-hwa during factory construction in 2000 exposed waterlogged deposits dating between 3000 and 2500 BC, 7 m (23 ft) below ground level and 1.5 m (5 ft) below modern sea level. They yielded Dabenkeng pottery with cord-marked, red-painted, and red-slipped decoration. Other Nanguanli artifacts include stone barkcloth beaters, perforated slate projectile points, shouldered stone adzes (some of Penghu basalt), baked clay spindle whorls, tanged shell reaping knives, and shell bracelets and earrings, most being items thought until recently to be absent or doubtful as Dabenkeng traits (Bellwood 1997; 2000). Nanguanli also has complete dog burials and carbonized rice and foxtail millet remains. Prior to the discovery of Nanguanli, the oldest remains of rice in Taiwan were those found in Suogang (Penghu Islands) and Zhishanyan (Taipei), dating to about 2000 BC.

By 3000 BC, therefore, Taiwan was well settled by Neolithic cultures with a material culture and economy that overlaps well with that reconstructed linguistically for early Austrone-sian communities. Many of the artifact types found in Nanguanli (red-slipped pottery, pedestals, knobbed lids, shell tools and ornaments, stone adzes) also occur in the younger archaeological sites that are found through the Philippines, Indonesia, and into Melanesia. However, the Taiwan assemblages most similar to those in the early Philippine and Indonesian Neolithic sites are not actually Dabenkeng, which seems to have remained firmly restricted to Taiwan itself, but later, post-Dabenkeng styles that contain *predominantly* red-slipped and often stamped pottery, without cord-marking. These developed out of the Dabenkeng, mainly after 2000 BC in northern and eastern Taiwan, and include the Yuanshan culture of the Taipei basin, and the Beinan culture of southeastern Taiwan [see box: Beinan, pp. 286–87], the latter being located in the probable source region for initial Neolithic movements into the Philippines.

Dispersals to Southeast Asia and Madagascar In island Southeast Asia, the archaeological traces of the Austronesian expansion of the 2nd and early 1st millennia BC are visible in a number of rockshelter and open sites with red-slipped pottery, shell artifacts, and polished stone adzes, found through the northern and central Philippines and Sabah (northern Borneo), the Talaud Islands, northern Sulawesi, and the northern Moluccas (Bellwood 1997) [8.16]. An open site called **Andarayan** in northern Luzon in the Philippines has yielded rice husks embedded in potsherds; these have been dated by AMS (accelerator mass spectrometer) radiocarbon to 1500 BC. Rice had already reached Sarawak before 2000 BC, where rice grains within a type of paddle-impressed pottery quite different from the Philippine and eastern Indonesian red-slipped ware, found in the cave of **Gua Sireh**, have been dated to c. 2300 BC (Ipoi and Bellwood 1991). It is possible that two cultural streams might have been involved in the movement from the northern Philippines: an eastern one with red-slipped pottery and a diminishing reliance on rice, and a western one, via Palawan and Borneo, with paddle-impressed pottery and continuing rice cultivation. But at the moment this is merely surmise; far more field archaeology is required in these regions.

As far as any hypothetical eastern stream is concerned, a large number of sites in the Batanes Islands between Taiwan and Luzon, in the Cagayan Valley of northern Luzon, in northern Borneo and eastern Indonesia, and in western Micronesia and Melanesia have now yielded closely related styles of red-slipped and incised and/or stamped pottery dating to the

8.15 Dabenkeng sherds: *Dabenkeng-style pottery is found right around the coastal regions of Tawian and in the Penghu Islands after about 3500 BC. These are from the site of Liohe in western Taiwan: (left) a cord marked body sherd; (right) an incised rim sherd.*

8.16 *(Left) Important Neolithic sites in island Southeast Asia:* those in italics have yielded Neolithic red-slipped pottery dating between 1500 and 500 BC, related to Lapita pottery in western Oceania.

8.17 *(Below) Dentate-stamped pottery from island Southeast Asia and Lapita sites in Melanesia: a) Xiantouling, Guangdong coast, China (pre-3000 BC?); b) Magapit, Cagayan Valley, Luzon (1000 BC); c) Yuanshan, Taipei, Taiwan (1000 BC); d) Nagsabaran, Cagayan Valley (1500 BC); e) Batungan Cave, Masbate, central Philippines (800 BC); f) Kamgot, Anir Islands, Bismarck Archipelago (Lapita – 1300 BC); g) Lapita (Site 13), New Caledonia (1000 BC); h) Achugao, Saipan, Mariana Islands (1500 BC). (All apart from (a) are red-slipped and have lime or white clay infill in the decoration.)*

ments that are very similar to those in contemporary Lapita assemblages in the western Pacific, described below.

Pollen studies from lakes in the highlands of Taiwan, Java, and Sumatra also indicate clearance for agriculture from *c.* 2000 BC onwards, although the exact dates for these activities are not very secure. Dates for Neolithic colonization in the large islands of Borneo, Sumatra, and Java remain uncertain, owing to the sparseness of the archaeological record, but settlements in the 2nd or 1st millennia BC seem very likely.

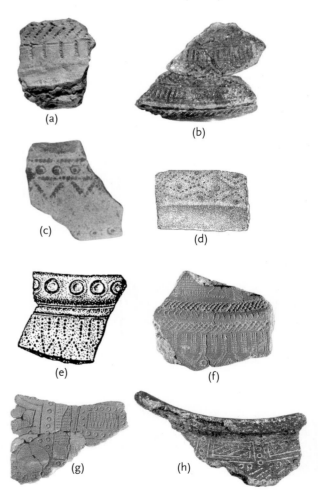

mid–late 2nd millennium BC. These sites are, according to radiocarbon dating, oldest in the north and west, and become gradually younger toward the south and east (Spriggs 2003). At the site of **Bukit Tengkorak** in Sabah, red-slipped pottery dated to *c.* 1300–500 BC onward was found with two rather surprising occurrences of a lithic nature: an industry of agate microblade drills used for drilling shell artifacts, and obsidian imported from sources in New Britain in Melanesia, located over 3500 km (2175 miles) to the east and probably representing one of the most distant transfers of a Neolithic commodity in world pre-history. Taiwan jade from a source near Hualien traveled almost 2000 km (1243 miles) and has been discovered at a similar date in sites in the Philippines.

Several sites in the Cagayan Valley in northern Luzon, especially Magapit and Nagsabaran, have yielded pottery with fine dentate-stamping dating from *c.* 1500 BC, closely paralleled in Lapita pottery from Melanesia and in contemporary pottery from the Mariana Islands of western Micronesia [**8.17**]. Such dentate-stamped pottery has not yet been found in eastern Indonesia, possibly because most excavations here have so far been in caves and rockshelters, where the use of fine pottery was not common. However, the other items of material culture from sites in this region include stone adzes and shell orna-

One of the problems in these large islands with their powerful erosion regimes is that the oldest coastal Neolithic sites, particularly on the northern coasts, are likely to be buried under huge depths of alluvium, and so difficult to find and excavate. The Malay peninsula, which still today has many interior regions populated by Austroasiatic-speaking (Aslian) populations, was probably only first settled in coastal areas by Austronesians less than 2500 years ago.

These Austronesians would have found Neolithic agriculturalists with strong cultural links to Neolithic populations in southern Thailand, for these ancestors of some of the ethnographic Austroasiatic-speaking peoples of the Malay peninsula were already in occupation from at least 2000 BC (on Austroasiatic languages, see Chapter 7).

In one of the most extraordinary feats of long-distance colonization in history, Austronesians sailed across the Indian Ocean west to **Madagascar** and the **Comoro Islands** (the latter now Bantu-speaking; see Chapter 10), probably in the mid-1st millennium AD – Madagascar was reached evidently by colonists from southern Borneo, perhaps with Malay- or Javanese-speaking leaders, according to recent linguistic analyses by Alexander Adelaar (1995). The archaeological record in Madagascar apparently commenced after about AD 500, although earlier hunter-gatherer settlement remains a possibility, despite the absence of preceramic lithic industries on the island (Dewar and Wright 1993; Vérin and Wright 1999). The Austronesian settlement was thus fully Iron Age, belonging to the period of trade across the Indian Ocean associated with Indic influence in Indonesia.

KEY SITE Beinan

The village site of Beinan, near Taidong in southeast Taiwan, with an extent of more than 40 ha (over 99 acres), is one of the most remarkable archaeological discoveries ever made on the island (Lien 1993). The excavations yielded remains of 50 dry-stone house foundations and over 1500 burials, dating mainly to between 1500 and 800 BC. The houses were constructed on rectangular stone pavements and laid out in rows, with adjacent rows of dry-stone walled storehouses. Some of the rows were separated by walls of boulders, suggesting possible lineage divisions of some kind within the village plan. The floors of the dwelling houses sealed slab-lined burial cists, an arrangement indicating an interest in ancestor veneration. The graves, many of them with multiple interments, revealed a high rate of infant and foetal death, for reasons at present unknown, but perhaps related to malaria.

8.18 *(Above) A slab grave of slate with jade grave goods (penannular earrings, tubular beads, perforated projectile points) excavated at Beinan.*

8.19 *(Left) General view of the Beinan excavations in 1987, showing stone pavements that served as house floors on the left, a line of stone-walled storehouses down the middle, and slab graves on the right.*

The Colonization of Oceania

In the western Pacific, Austronesian colonists between 1400 and 900 BC left an extremely clear-cut trail of pioneer Neolithic-sites belonging to the so-called **Lapita cultural complex** – named for its distinctive sand- or shell-tempered Lapita pottery – across about 6500 km (4050 miles) of ocean and islands from the Admiralty Islands north of New Guinea to as far east as Samoa, in western Polynesia (Kirch 1997; Spriggs 1997a; Clark et al. 2001) [see **8.22**]. This impressive migration correlates linguistically with the spread of Proto-Oceanic, the founder dialect chain in the Oceanic subgroup of Malayo-Polynesian, which today includes all the languages spoken in the Pacific Islands from coastal New Guinea eastwards [see **8.14**]. Although pre-Austronesian populations had reached the Solomons, all territories from New Caledonia and Vanuatu eastwards were subjected to initial human colonization by canoe-borne Austronesian groups. As noted, these settlers found a world well-stocked with marine and avian resources; like highland New Guinea, it was malaria-free beyond Vanuatu, and thus not subject to the very high infant death rates that probably afflicted contemporary populations in malarial regions of lowland New Guinea and Indonesia. Site sizes and numbers indicate that these populations grew rapidly during the early stages of colonization.

Lapita sites are generally well dated and well studied in terms of artifacts and economy, especially in comparison with contemporary sites in island Southeast Asia. Key features include pottery with sand or crushed-shell tempers (material added to clay to improve its firing qualities); forms included

Artifacts from the Site

The pottery from the Beinan graves is mainly a fine orange ware, sometimes red-slipped, with no other forms of decoration. The most common form appears to be a jar with two vertical strap handles (like Yuanshan pottery from the Taipei basin) and a ring foot. Beinan has also yielded clay spindle whorls, pig and dog figurines, stone barkcloth beaters, and stone reaping knives. The burials contained some remarkable items of Taiwan jade deposited as grave goods, including long tubular beads, bracelets, penannular earrings (in the form of an almost complete ring), some plain and some with circumferential projections (the so-called *lingling-o*, a very widespread form also found in the Philippines and Vietnam), anthropomorphic earrings, and perforated projectile points. Most adults had four of their upper teeth extracted (canine and first incisor on each side), and stained teeth attest to betel chewing.

An Associated Site

Current research in the Batanes Islands in the northern Philippines has revealed a possible extension of an early phase of the Beinan culture (or a southeastern Taiwan contemporary), dating to about 1200–800 BC at the site of Sunget on Batan Island. Similar pottery, slate projectile points, notched pebble net sinkers and stone adzes have been found there, and items of Taiwan jade have been found in the slightly younger site of Anaro on neighboring Itbayat Island. However, Sunget does not represent the initial movement of Neolithic populations from Taiwan, given that Neolithic sites further south in Luzon date back to almost 2000 BC, and a new finding of plain red-slipped pottery from Itbayat Island dates from 1600 BC.

Survival of the Austronesians on Taiwan

The Taiwan archaeological record is a remarkably rich one, continuing on through the Iron Age until mainland Chinese settlers arrived in large numbers in and after the 17th century. Prior to this time, Taiwan was entirely an Austronesian island, even though Austronesians of the island today (termed Formosans by linguists and anthropologists) only account for about 1 percent of Taiwan's total population of 22 million. Most groups today occupy the interior and the rugged east coast of the island.

8.20 *A reconstruction of the village at Beinan at about 1000 BC, showing an artist's impression of the buildings shown in foundation form in 8.19.*

8.21 *Artifacts from the Moluccas: stone adze and chisel (first and third from left, upper row), shell artifacts, and three bone points from the rockshelter of Uattamdi, Kayoa Island, northern Moluccas, c. 1300 BC. The chisel at top right is from Pitcairn Island, eastern Polynesia – an interesting parallel within the same Austronesian lithic tradition, even though perhaps 2500 years younger in time.*

globular cooking pots and open bowls, some with flat bases and others on high pedestals with cut-out decoration. Some vessel profiles are sharply carinated, and pots might have lug or strap handles and knobbed lids. Vessel surfaces are often red-slipped, and the decoration, generally in zones around the upper surfaces of some of the vessels, includes an intricate range of incised and dentate-stamped motifs of rectilinear, curvilinear, and even anthropomorphic forms, the latter perhaps indicating a concern with ancestors that was common to all Austronesian populations [see **8.23**].

Later Lapita pottery tends to have simpler designs, and dentate stamping faded in popularity after 750 BC in favor of plain ware in western Polynesia, although other styles of incised, appliqué, and carved paddle-impressed pottery continued until late prehistory in many of the Melanesian archipelagos. Recent work in the Philippines and Mariana Islands indicates the presence of pottery very similar to Lapita at around the same date (1500–1000 BC), so it is likely that the idea of dentate stamping, which replicates body tattooing and was probably carried out with a tool like a tattooing chisel made of bone, shell, or turtle shell (Ambrose 1997), originated much further north. Simple types of dentate stamping occur on coastal southern Chinese pottery that could be much earlier in date [see box: The Origins of Lapita].

Apart from pottery, other items of Lapita material culture include stone adzes (all untanged) with lenticular cross-sections, stone chisels, shell adzes, a range of shell ornaments (including beads and arm rings similar to those found in contemporary sites in the Moluccas [**8.21**]), and fishhooks for trolling and angling. The shell fishhooks suggest a technological adaptation confined mainly to Oceania, but bait (angling) hooks of shell are also found in a few western Neolithic sites, especially in Taiwan and Timor.

Lapita Economy

Economically, the Lapita culture was based on a mix of horticultural and maritime subsistence, mostly of a self-sufficient nature, despite the strong likelihood that some inter-island contact occurred after initial settlement took place (as evidenced by closely related sequences of pottery change in different archipelagos, for instance). The bulk of the pottery was made locally, and a theory that Lapita pottery was essentially a trade ware no longer has much support (Dickinson and Shutler 2000; Summerhayes 2001a). David Burley and William Dickinson (2001)

have, however, noted the presence in both Santa Cruz (southeastern Solomons) and Tonga of a few sherds with statistically indistinguishable petrological characteristics, all from an unknown Melanesian source.

Pigs, fowl, and dogs were all present in Lapita villages, although not all sites have yielded them, and it is clear that Lapita settlers, for a while at least, would have been distracted away from their domesticated food supplies by prolific wild resources in the areas they colonized, until these became reduced by extinction and local extirpation (Steadman 1999; Sand 2001; Burley et al. 2001). Plant remains from waterlogged sites in the Arawe and Mussau Islands include taro, coconut, candlenut, pandanus, and the canarium nut, most exploited as well by pre-Lapita populations in western Melanesia.

Village settlements, in some cases of stilt houses over shallow lagoons, occupied zones marked by sherds, earth ovens, hearths, postholes, and other features; they average about 1 ha (2.5 acres) in size in coastal and small offshore island locations, growing to a maximum of 7–8 ha (18–20 acres) in the Mussau Islands (Sheppard and Green 1991) [see box: Talepakemalai, p. 291]. A fairly healthy inter-island exchange of obsidian and other stones for tool manufacture was carried out in western Melanesia, from New Britain and Admiralty Islands sources to as far as the Santa Cruz Islands, and some of the obsidian was also carried in limited quantities much further afield, to Vanuatu, New Caledonia, Fiji, and even to Sabah in Borneo.

The **Mariana Islands** of western Micronesia were settled before 1500 BC by users of a thin-walled, red-slipped, and coral sand-tempered pottery very similar to Lapita. Linguistically, the Chamorro language of the Marianas can be traced to the northern Philippines, and the first settlers appear to have taken rice with them, the only occasion on which it was transported into Oceania (Blust 2000). The Mariana Islands were thus settled by a separate and possibly slightly earlier movement than that

KEY CONTROVERSY The Origins of Lapita

Archaeologists working in Melanesia have long debated the origins of the Lapita cultural complex (1400–750 BC), both there and in western Polynesia; many favor a direct connection with the spread of Austronesians from island Southeast Asia (Spriggs 1996; Bellwood 1997; Kirch 2000), while others prefer a local Melanesian origin, with only occasional interaction with peoples living to the west of New Guinea (Ambrose 1997; Swadling 1997). During the 1980s this debate became quite acrimonious, but today tensions have cooled, and the rapid accumulation of evidence from eastern Indonesia and the northern Philippines makes a completely isolationist Melanesian origin for Lapita increasingly untenable; nor does the Austronesian linguistic record suggest total isolation.

"Tattooed" Pottery

New finds of dentate-stamped pottery contemporary with and similar to that which defines Lapita have been made recently in northern Luzon, the Mariana Islands (Craib 1999), Taiwan, and along the coast of Guangdong Province in southern China. Such dentate stamping reflects the Austronesian cultural tradition of body tattooing, done in modern times in Polynesia with a small-toothed chisel of bone or shell. Lapita potters therefore "tattooed" their pots with complex designs that often appear to represent ancestors in human form (Green 1979).

The spread of dentate stamping is difficult to source to a particular homeland, although examples in China, the Philippines, and the Marianas seem to be slightly older than those in Melanesia. But like the obsidian from New Britain that traveled westwards to Borneo, ideas such as dentate stamping on pottery could have traveled back too.

One important clue to Lapita origins lies in the chronological context of the dentate-stamped pottery in different areas. In Taiwan it was preceded for at least a millennium by other styles of cord-marked or plain pottery, and the same may be true of the Cagayan Valley in northern Luzon and the Batanes Islands, where the oldest sites appear to have mostly plain pottery. In Melanesia, however, the oldest Lapita sites have not only the first pottery but also the most elaborate dentate decoration, which thereafter became simplified until it disappeared by about 750–500 BC. This suggests that an evolved form of dentate stamping was introduced widely through Melanesia by colonization *c.* 1400 BC, after initial development elsewhere. Unfortunately, the rockshelters excavated in Borneo and eastern Indonesia have not yet yielded dentate-stamped pottery of this precise kind (although there is plenty of related red-slipped and incised pottery), but this could reflect lack of research and a dominance of samples from relatively impoverished rockshelters rather than stilt villages.

Overview

One way out of the conundrum is to give credit where credit is due. Austronesians, with their potting traditions, agriculture, and the practice of tattooing, entered Melanesia

8.23 *A pottery sherd with a dentate-stamped schematic human face motif from Talepakemalai, Mussau Islands, Bismarck Archipelago,* c. 1400 BC.

from the west, probably via the Moluccas and western New Guinea if we rely on linguistic evidence, or perhaps from further north (the Philippines and Mariana Islands) if we rely on the archaeology as known at present. But the Lapita populations of island Melanesia developed the most complex ceramic art form ever to appear in the Pacific, and surely did it in part out of local initiative. They also adopted some arboricultural crops, obsidian-working, and doubtless many of their genes from the pre-Lapita indigenous populations of Near Oceania. As the founder populations of modern island Melanesians and Polynesians, and probably the southern Micronesians too, their prehistory involved both migration and interaction, not simply one or the other (Green 1991b).

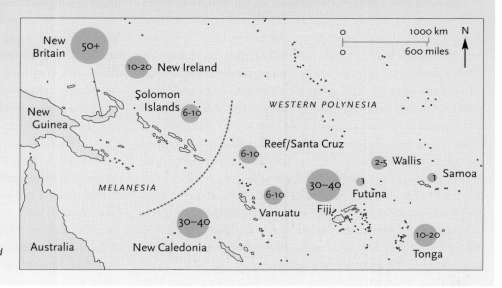

8.22 *Map of Lapita sites with dentate-stamped pottery in Melanesia and western Polynesia. The numbers in the circles refer to the numbers of recorded Lapita sites in each island group.*

indicated for Lapita, and the open-sea crossing to the Marianas from the Philippines, at least 2500 km (1550 miles), justifiably ranks as the first truly great voyage known to us in Austronesian cultural history. Strangely perhaps, we have no indication that the islands of southern Micronesia, especially the Carolines (mostly atolls), were settled before *c.* AD 1; like those of Polynesia, these colonizing populations soon abandoned the use of pottery (Rainbird 1994). The Palau (Belau) Islands to the west of the Carolines, on the other hand, have recently yielded signs of occupation perhaps dating back to 1500 BC or earlier (Welch 2002), so much is still being learned.

The Settlement of Polynesia

Lapita colonists reached **Tonga and Samoa** in western Polynesia by about 1000 BC. As in Melanesia, the decorated forms of Lapita pottery lasted for only a few centuries, with continuing simplification, eventually turning into a rather basic plain ware of increasing thickness before the eventual demise of pottery in Samoa and southern Micronesia *c.* AD 300. Oceanic cuisines, focused on fish, meat, and tubers, could manage perfectly well with earth ovens rather than pottery, although this does not explain why pottery-making continued until ethnographic times in some parts of New Guinea and Melanesia. Of course, pottery was difficult to make on coralline islands that lacked clay. But this cannot be the whole story, since Remote Oceania has many volcanic islands with good clay sources. Together with the losses of rice, millet, and loom weaving (and the associated clay spindle whorls for spinning fibers) prior to their entry into Oceania, it suggests that early Austronesian societies underwent "bottleneck" losses as small groups pushed ever further east, gradually losing contact with their more complex homeland cultures and leaving behind aspects of cultural knowledge.

Nevertheless, although Polynesians might well have lacked rice, pottery, and woven cloth, not to mention bovids, metals, and the wheel, they reversed inexorable cultural loss by inventing the double sailing canoe [see box: Expert Navigation or Sheer Good Luck?, pp. 292–93], a remarkable construction that allowed the discovery and colonization of islands located thousands of kilometers over the horizon, with a full suite of transported crops and animals. They also honed barkcloth and stone adze production to rarely equaled fine arts, and developed complex forms of terraced-field and canal-fed taro irrigation, as well as palisaded earthwork fortification, the latter reaching an apogee in New Zealand. Eastern Polynesians constructed massive stone platforms associated with competitive chiefly levels of society in the Hawaiian, Society, and Marquesas Islands. On Easter Island they adorned such platforms with those famous rows of top-knotted statues (see below).

The Austronesian migration process thus encouraged both losses and gains over the long term, as populations adapted to geographical variations in resources and opportunities. An example of such variations were those characterized as "the wet and the dry" by Patrick Kirch (1994) in his discussion of the agriculturally influenced rises and falls of Polynesian chiefdoms. In **Futuna and the Hawaiian Islands**, the most aggressive and expansive chiefdoms appear to have originated in risk-dominated situations in which agriculture depended purely on seasonal rainfall (the "dry"); these chiefdoms ultimately dominated those societies that held the most fertile alluvial soils (the "wet"), suitable for irrigated taro cultivation. The ultimate conquest of the Hawaiian Islands by the paramount chief Kamehameha ("the Great") in 1810, an achievement aided by the acquisition of firearms, is an excellent example of this: Kamehameha's homeland on the west coast of Hawai'i Island was one of the driest and most risk-prone regions weather-wise in the whole archipelago. As another example of adaptation, the Polynesians who settled New Zealand *c.* AD 1200 (see below) were the first Austronesians for over 4000 years to set foot in the temperate zone since the settlement of northern Taiwan *c.* 3000 BC. The response of the majority of the South Island Maoris, finding themselves living beyond the climatic range of their agriculture, was to return to a purely hunter-gatherer lifestyle that survived until European contact.

Eastern Polynesia The linguistic evidence described above suggests that the settlement of the islands in central and eastern Polynesia that lay beyond the Lapita zone – the Marquesas, Societies, Cooks, Australs, Tuamotus, Hawaiian Islands, Easter Island, New Zealand, and many others – occurred after a long period when population dispersal paused in western Polynesia. The archaeological record is now in perfect accord with this. Current interpretations of radiocarbon dates from archaeological sites suggest that none of the island groups just named were settled before AD 700, and some not until several centuries later. During this migration standstill, Proto-Polynesian society and culture developed in western Polynesia out of its Lapita (Proto-Oceanic) roots – the basic configuration ancestral to all the ethnographic societies of Polynesia, and one subsequently modified in each island group by differing processes involving chance, environmental variation, and interaction (Kirch and Green 2001).

Beyond Samoa, the first settlers became essentially aceramic in their technology, although a few appear to have taken the occasional pot with them, to judge from extremely rare undecorated potsherds found in the Marquesas and Cook Islands. Without Lapita, the crisp chronology derived from a refined but devolving art style tattooed onto pots is no longer available. Archaeologists are forced to fall back on radiocarbon dates with very little support from typological dating; this is problematic, since the young dates of Polynesian archaeology,

KEY SITE Talepakemalai

Talepakemalai, the largest Lapita site on record at 8 ha (20 acres), was excavated in 1985–88 by Patrick Kirch and his colleagues (2001) as part of the Lapita Homeland Project (Allen and Gosden 1991). The site is located on the coral islet of Eloaua, just off the southern coast of the larger island of Mussau, in the Bismarck Archipelago. The most significant part, area B, comprised the waterlogged remnants of posts from a stilt house that was originally constructed *c.* 1350 BC about 20 m (66 ft) offshore, over the shallow waters of a tropical coral lagoon.

Into the lagoon between the stilt house and the beach was dumped large quantities of broken but beautifully decorated Lapita pottery, together with prolific macrobotanical remains from an arboricultural economy that utilized pandanus, coconut, canarium, candlenut and many other seed and fruit species (Kirch 1989; see Matthews and Gosden 1997 for similar finds in the Arawe Islands). Some of these species were clearly selected for increasing size, a trend suspected to reflect careful human management.

Talepakemalai was the first excavated site to indicate the stilt-village nature of Lapita settlements; it also showed clear spatial differentiation in the distribution of the decorated pottery. The stilt-house dwellers used and discarded much of this, whereas contemporary groups living on the dry land nearby had almost none – a probable sign of either status differences or specialized activity. Stilt houses survive to this day in many regions of Southeast Asia and Melanesia, both over lagoons and far inland, in the latter case perhaps best known in the spectacular longhouses of the Iban and other peoples of Borneo. Other Lapita house plans are known from curving or rectangular posthole settings on dry land in New Caledonia and the Santa Cruz Islands (Sheppard and Green 1991). A rockshelter on the coast of the main Mussau Island was used by Lapita people for manufacturing shell artifacts, including trolling fishhooks of *Trochus* shell.

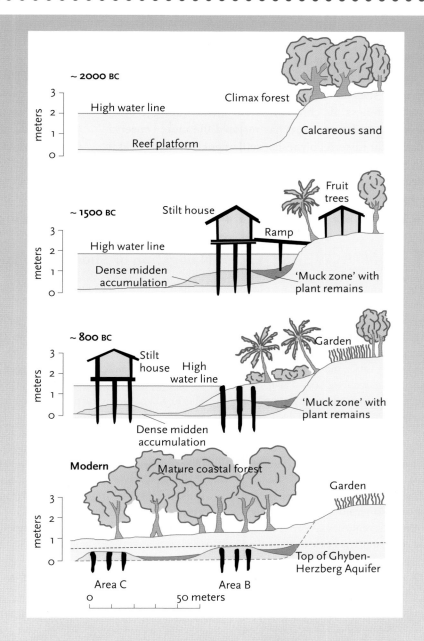

Talepakemalai has also yielded the oldest Lapita radiocarbon dates, interpreted to commence at 1500 BC by Kirch, although other Lapita scholars favor dates of about 1400 BC for the Bismarcks (Summerhayes 2001b); the pottery from the site is thus contemporary with the appearance of similar stamped pottery far to the north, in the Mariana Islands.

With the demise of the Lapita decorative style *c.* 750 BC, and its replacement elsewhere in Melanesia by other pottery styles (paddle-impressed in New Caledonia and Fiji, incised and appliqué in Vanuatu, the Solomons, and the Bismarcks), the region of the Mussau Lapita sites seems to have been left uninhabited until about AD 500.

8.24 *A diagrammatic representation of the probable stages of geomorphological evolution of the Talepakemalai Lapita site, 2000 BC to modern.*

for example, mean that standard deviations, or error ranges, often amounting to a century or more, produce radiocarbon dates that are frequently too broad to be useful. Archaeologists have an understandable tendency to use radiocarbon dates to make their sites as early as possible, but since the 1990s a greater awareness of "chronometric hygiene" (Spriggs 1989; Spriggs and Anderson 1993) has restored the more conservative dating for eastern Polynesian settlement that many held in the 1970s (Bellwood 1978). It is now believed that the bulk of central and eastern Polynesian colonization occurred in a short time span between about AD 700 and 1200 (Anderson 1995; Green 1998; Bellwood 2001). The main components of the oldest eastern Polynesian assemblages are shell fishhooks (both angling and trolling forms), bone harpoons, bone reels, and imitation whale-tooth pendants, along with stone adzes with triangular cross-sections, as well as the more widespread quadrangular and trapezoidal ones [8.25].

Why the rapid spread into eastern Polynesia should have occurred when it did, after such a long pause, is not clear. Possibilities could be that resource shortfall after some 1500 years of prior human settlement could have played a role in persuading populations to sail onwards from western Polynesia (although

KEY CONTROVERSY Expert Navigation or Sheer Good Luck?

The Polynesians who first saw Easter Island rise above the horizon around AD 700–900 had probably sailed 2000 km (1250 miles) for their reward, as had the first settlers of the Mariana Islands almost 2500 years before. At European contact, most Austronesians used sewn-plank sailing canoes with outriggers that were either single and kept to windward in Oceania, or double (one on each side of the canoe) in much of island Southeast Asia. (This leaves aside the large ships influenced by Indian and Chinese techniques of construction and rigging, which are known to have plied the Indian Ocean and island Southeast Asian waters since the early centuries AD.) The contact-period single outrigger canoes of the Caroline Islands, in particular, were very rapid tacking vessels with reversible ends and lateen (triangular) sails of pandanus matting, able to carry both crew and cargo on a platform amidships.

The precise antiquity of the outrigger canoe is not clear, but its wide distribution, plus linguistic reconstructions, suggest that it was known by at least Proto-Malayo-Polynesian times in the Philippines (c. 2000 BC), as, doubtless, was the use of sewn-plank (or lashed-lug) construction. This technique of shipbuilding is best known to the archaeological world in the royal barque of the 4th Dynasty Egyptian pharaoh Khufu, dismantled and entombed at the side of his Great Pyramid at Giza (c. 2500 BC) (see Chapter 10).

Double Canoes in Historical Times

The double canoe, however, appears to have been an invention of the Polynesians, possibly during the 1st millennium AD in western Polynesia, prior to their long journeys to the distant archipelagos of eastern Polynesia. By the 18th century, double canoes were also being used in warfare in the Society Islands, the warriors fighting on raised platforms. Johann Reinhold Forster recorded in 1778 (Thomas et al. 1996, 280–81): "The large war canoes cost the natives infinite labor, and afford the best specimens of their genius ... [On Huahine Island] I observed a double war canoe, which required 144 paddles, and eight or ten steersmen to move it forward; the stage for fighting was roomy, and could contain about 30 men. [The stage was] raised on six or eight pillars about four feet high ..." William Hodges fortunately painted for posterity a scene of war canoes assembled in Tahiti in 1774 for an attack on Moorea [8.27]. About 160 such canoes were assembled, according to Cook, with an estimated crew totaling 7760 men.

Naturally, the canoes of the period of European contact tell us little about the first voyaging craft of the Austronesians. Distributional facts imply that the pioneers

8.26 *An outriggered sailing ship carved on the Borobudur Buddhist stupa, central Java, c. AD 760–830. Ships like this plied the Indian Ocean trade routes during the later 1st millennium AD, and were probably involved in the settlement of Madagascar by Austronesians.*

8.25 *Eastern Polynesian adzes:* *stone adzes from New Zealand and Rarotonga, Cook Islands (second from right; casts of originals in Auckland Museum). All are of basalt, and some have tangs to assist hafting. Cross-sections vary from quadrangular through trapezoidal to triangular.*

we have no direct evidence that it did); that many western atolls were still below sea level until as recently as between 2000 and 1000 years ago (Kirch 2000); that more frequent El Niño events could have been associated with more frequent westerly winds; and that developments in canoe technology might have played a major role, particularly the invention of the double sailing canoe, perhaps somewhere in Tonga or Samoa (Anderson 2001).

understood the use of the sail and the outrigger, although the first voyages off the coast of Asia, including those during the Pleistocene to Australia, were probably tentative affairs with bamboo rafts and paddles. More contentious debate has centered on two questions of navigation.

Questions of Navigation

First, could Austronesians, especially those who settled Remote Oceania, have navigated regularly between distant islands, the locations of which were already known? The answer here is "yes," but only to a degree. From the period of European contact there are no records of regular voyaging over open-sea distances greater than a few hundred kilometers. Well-documented voyaging spheres at this time linked together Tonga, Samoa, and Fiji; the Societies and Tuamotus; and the Caroline Islands. European voyagers such as Cook and Andia y Varela (in the 1770s) recorded the islanders' use of stars, the sun, ocean swells, and other indicators of distance, speed, and direction, all described in greater ethnographic detail by David Lewis (1994).

The second question is more difficult to answer. Were early Austronesians, Polynesians in particular, able to navigate through unknown waters to find new land, and then return home to mount a full voyage of colonization? Captain Cook was not so sure, especially after he found survivors of an involuntary drift voyage from Tahiti on the island of Atiu in the southern Cook Islands in 1774. But drifting without sail on its own would not have allowed settlers to reach the

remotest parts of the Pacific, according to computer simulations using wind and current directions (Levison et al. 1973).

Polynesians had to use sails to reach many of their destinations, an observation recently underlined by experimental voyages such as those of the *Hokule'a*, first sailed from Maui to Tahiti in 1976 (Finney 1989). However, like the *Kon-Tiki* of Thor Heyerdahl [see box: Easter Island and South America, p. 297], these experiments belong in the known world of modern knowledge, not the unknown world of AD 800 – they tell us of possibilities, not certainties.

Cook's misgivings were emphasized two centuries later by Andrew Sharp (1963), who concluded that voyages of long-distance discovery could only have been one-way, without hope of a return home. There is actually nothing in the archaeological record that refutes this – the small quantities of pearl shell and basalt transported across Polynesia could just as well reflect one-way voyages by

8.27 *Double canoes with stages for hand-to-hand fighting preparing for war in Tahiti, 1774, painted by William Hodges on Cook's Second Voyage. The elite person on the stage at left is wearing a tall headdress of radiating tropic-bird feathers and a crescent-shaped gorget of coir, feathers, hair, and shark teeth on a cane foundation (Phelps 1975: 113).*

the first settlers as return ones. As noted by Geoffrey Irwin (1992) and Ben Finney (1989), both scholars with practical sailing experience, sensible would-be explorers would have waited for summer westerlies in the tropics or winter westerlies on the edge of the tropics to blow them eastwards. Sailing downwind on such westerlies would give them the chance to return home later (should they have felt the need to try) using the easterly trade winds that prevail during most of the year. Atholl Anderson (2001) also suggests that early Polynesian canoes had no fixed masts or standing rigging, and could only have been sailed downwind, not across or into it.

Once the process of eastern Polynesian settlement began, there is good reason to assume very rapid population growth in such healthy and disease-free environments, with so much wild food available to the first settlers. Demographic profiles from similar situations of first-farmer colonization, for instance from Pitcairn Island following settlement by the *Bounty* mutineers and their families in 1790, and from the colonial frontiers of the United States and Australia, leave no doubt about this. Just how fast early eastern Polynesian populations might have grown can be seen in **8.28**, taken from an analysis of the numbers of archaeological radiocarbon dates (as proxies for human population size) through Hawaiian prehistory. In this case, the curve indicates a human arrival a little before AD 1000 (older dates are probably not contemporary with human activity), followed by a very rapid population increase for the first 500 years or so. Population declined after this time, and in a case such as this the devastating effects of introduced diseases in the 18th and 19th centuries must be partly to blame. Unfortunately, radiocarbon dates are not accurate enough to separate this factor from any late prehistoric leveling-off of population, this also being very likely after such rapid early growth.

In terms of interaction between different islands, recent research has shown that early central and eastern Polynesian cultures were connected over thousands of kilometers by the long-distance transport of basalt, a volcanic rock used for adzes and other tools. Basalt from Samoa has been found widely in the Cook Islands, and that from the Marquesas in Moorea and Mangareva (Weisler 1998). That these connections involved regular two-way voyages seems doubtful [see box: Expert Navigation or Sheer Good Luck?, pp. 292–93], but in the early years of human settlement such return voyages would certainly have been assisted by the navigational aid provided by large flocks of homing birds with each sunset (Steadman 1997; 1999). As these flocks diminished with increasing human predation, this

aid would have been compromised; nevertheless, we know from European explorers' and ethnographic records, and from comparisons of late prehistoric artifact styles (especially stone adzes), that some inter-island contact was still occurring in the 18th century, and, indeed, until the 20th century, using traditional canoes and sailing methods in the Caroline Islands of Micronesia (Lewis 1994).

Why Migrate? Finally, why did all this island migration come about? Simply looking for new islands for agricultural land or other resources does not explain everything, given the huge sizes of many of the islands of Southeast Asia, even now underpopulated in some remote equatorial situations. Another suggestion assumes that like the youth of today, so the youth of millennia ago needed outlets for their energies, ways to gain self-esteem, success, and peer-recognition. The founding of new communities became a high-status activity and a major source for the embellishment of epics and mythology. In tribal agricultural societies with institutionalized forms of land ownership, where status and rights to land were to some degree determined by ancestry, gender, and birth order, there would always have been situations in which younger sons, able to found only lineages of junior rank at home, would have sought to establish a new senior line by the colonization of new territory. If such desires are institutionalized and given formal social approval (for instance, Maoris in New Zealand named many of their tribes after their founder figures), then a very powerful motivating force for active colonization will be unleashed (Bellwood 1996b). In the case of the Austronesians, this force appears to have become more significant as populations moved further and further east toward Polynesia.

The Austronesian World After Colonization

The achievements of Austronesian societies in the millennia since initial colonization derive from two cultural categories: those societies in the Pacific Islands that maintained Neolithic cultural traditions in relative isolation until European contact, and the societies west of New Guinea that became metal-using after about 300 BC. The latter also experienced the successive arrivals of Indian and Chinese influences, and those of Islam after AD 1250.

Polynesian Complex Societies: Easter Island and Elsewhere

The Austronesians of the more fertile Oceanic islands developed large and relatively complex societies, with chiefs, social ranks, and frequent warfare (see below). The most famous of these is that of **Easter Island** (Rapa Nui), first settled around AD 900, which also offers one of the best-known examples of social col-

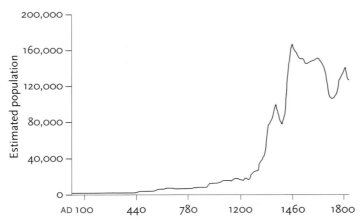

8.28 Population growth: *the demographic history of the Hawaiian Islands since AD 100, as modeled from archaeological data by Dye and Komori 1992. See text for explanation.*

lapse in Pacific prehistory [see box: Causes of Landscape Change, p. 296]. The massive stone statues (*moai*) of Easter Island, made of volcanic agglomerate, were carved in quarries in the steep inner and outer crater walls of the extinct volcano of Rano Raraku; they were transported by methods that are still uncertain, and erected in rows facing inland along the tops of raised stone platforms called *ahu* [**8.29, 8.30**]. The *ahu* were fronted by sloping paved ramps along one side of a large rectangular open space. Those statues that were finished and erected on *ahu* were provided with eyes of coral and obsidian, and many had separate "topknots" of a red volcanic rock quarried in the Punapau crater. These statues, perhaps representatives of deceased chiefs subsequently deified, were evidently carved *c.* AD 1100–1650 (Skjolsvold 1996). Some, too large ever to be moved, still stand partly buried in the quarry debris, mute testimony to a cultural system that seems to have over-reached its limits, in terms of both food supply and technology. By the time Europeans discovered the island in the 18th century it had been rendered almost treeless, the carving of statues had apparently

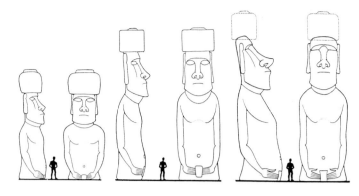

8.29, 8.30 *Easter Island statues:* *(above) Rapa Nui* moai *(statues) of different sizes and somatic forms. All are busts above the midriff, and all have hands meeting at the navel. The largest statue to be erected successfully on an* ahu *(stone platform) was 11.5 m (38 ft) high and weighed almost 100 tonnes. (Below) Statues re-erected with red tuff topknots on an* ahu. *Note the positions of the hands and the long fingers, also the distended and perforated earlobes that carried ornamental discs. Each statue has a stone plinth, aligned above the sloping cobbled ramp.*

KEY CONTROVERSY Causes of Landscape Change

That humans impacted quite heavily upon the environments of small Pacific islands is not in doubt – forest clearing for agriculture, soil erosion, bird extinction, and pressure on littoral resources must all have been a result of situations of rapidly increasing human population. Whether human impact affected the large islands of island Southeast Asia in such ways is not so clear at present, but we might expect that it did, particularly in a situation such as the apparent abandonment of the Penghu Islands, between Taiwan and the Chinese mainland, between 1500 BC and AD 1000 (Tsang 1992). The 4-m (13-ft) depth of sediment that has mantled the northern coastline of Bali since Indian contact began 2000 years ago (Ardika and Bellwood 1991) could well reflect human clearance for farming on the inland volcanic slopes. So, indeed, could the modern extents of the immense coastal plains that flank the northern coastlines of Sumatra and Java, burying some early Holocene preceramic shell middens in Sumatra under thick layers of sediment.

Evidence of Human Impact

Our best indicators of human impact come from the smaller Pacific islands. Bird extinction occurred on a dramatic scale – of flightless moas in New Zealand (Anderson 1989) and of hundreds of species, both flighted and flightless, in the tropical Pacific islands (Steadman 1997; 1999). Infilling of coastal flats and valley bottoms with alluvial soil released by forest clearance has been demonstrated for Tikopia in the Solomon Islands (Kirch and Yen 1983) and for many other islands in Melanesia and Polynesia, including New Zealand (Kirch and Hunt 1997). Nevertheless, much humanly caused landscape change in Oceania (e.g. infilled valleys and coastal plains) was probably beneficial for agricultural systems (Spriggs (1997b); human impact was not always deleterious.

Evidence for Other Factors

Moreover, there are growing claims that the emphasis on human impact may be somewhat overdone. Patrick Nunn (1994; 2000) has strongly suggested climatic variability, especially increased El Niño episodes between 1270 and 1475, as a major factor in Oceania leading to late prehistoric landscape change, warfare, reduction of voyaging frequency, and the abandonment of islands such as Pitcairn and Norfolk, once settled by Polynesians but uninhabited on European discovery.

A major arena for this debate is Easter Island, where the society was clearly in demographic and cultural decline at the time of European contact, resulting in the toppling of all the statues from their *ahu* platforms between 1770 and 1860. A number of archaeologists (Bellwood 1978; Flenley and Bahn 2002) have blamed prehistoric human impact for the demise, via overpopulation, warfare, and forest clearance. But now there are dissenting voices: Rosalind Hunter-Anderson (1998) points to adverse climatic change, and Paul Rainbird (2002) to the impact of diseases and other destabilizing factors introduced by Europeans. The reality may combine all these explanations in a causal sequence.

The Effects of Resource Instability

Whether human or natural, factors of environmental degradation and food resource instability must have acted from time to time to stimulate inter-island movement in Polynesia, particularly in the later periods of prehistory. For instance, David Porter's account of the Marquesas in 1813 records that there was frequent traffic at that time in double canoes sailing in search of new land (Porter 1823), apparently as a result of a famine that appears to have struck the islands around 1806–10.

Homelands characterized by great resource unreliability and risk are far more likely to spawn colonizing movements than those where food resources are secure. Both the Austronesian dispersal and the recent diaspora that took Chinese settlers into Southeast Asia and the Pacific Islands originated in part from one of the most drought-prone and stressed regions of coastal China – central and southern Fujian and northern Guangdong provinces.

---

ceased, and the inhabitants were described as living a fairly wretched existence. Subsequent tribal warfare rapidly led to the toppling of all the statues, a process probably underway by the time of the visit of La Pérouse in 1786, if not before.

While the statues of Easter Island stand as symbols of one of the greatest mysteries in Pacific prehistory [see box: Easter Island and South America], other island chiefdoms produced some very impressive stone monuments without undergoing social collapse. Polynesian shrine/temple platforms (usually known by the generic term *marae*), as constructed by the major chiefdoms of the densely populated and fertile islands of the Hawaiian Islands, the Societies, Cooks, Marquesas, and Tuamotus, were often major feats of construction, involving the use of very large stones and sometimes stepped pyramidal forms. Other very large constructions include the earthwork fortifications of the Fijians and the Maoris of New Zealand (see below), and the coral slab-terraced earthen burial mounds (*langi*) built for the Tongan nobility. The Micronesians of the Caroline Islands constructed remarkable enclosures, platforms, and tombs of prismatic basalt at **Nan Madol** on Pohnpei [**8.38**] and at **Leluh** on Kosrae. The people of the Mariana Islands carved massive stone pillar foundations (*latte*) for their raised-floor chiefly houses. Many island Melanesian and New Guinea coastal societies continued to excel in pottery-making, a craft otherwise abandoned everywhere in Polynesia and Micronesia soon after AD 1.

KEY CONTROVERSY Easter Island and South America

The issue of contact between Polynesia and South America was brought into prominence for a huge world audience by Thor Heyerdahl, (1914–2002) as a result of the *Kon-Tiki* balsa raft voyage from Callao, Peru, to Raroia in the Tuamotus in 1947. Heyerdahl's aim was to show that American peoples could have settled the Pacific Islands, and in 1952 he claimed that Polynesia had been settled by South Americans emanating from the civilization of Tiwanaku (Tiahuanaco) in Bolivia *c.* AD 800 (for Tiwanaku see Chapter 17). A second wave of Polynesian colonists, he claimed, arrived later, having sailed down from British Columbia between AD 1100 and 1300.

Heyerdahl led a major archaeological expedition to Easter Island in 1955–56 (Heyerdahl and Ferdon 1961). His conclusions (clearly not fully supported by all the professional archaeologists on his team) now were slightly different: he claimed that two separate waves of South American settlers had arrived on Easter Island, the later of which erected the stone statues, which were carved after 1100. Polynesians then arrived from the west after 1300 and eventually wiped out the South American population around 1680. Heyerdahl (1997) retained these views with little modification for the rest of his life.

Today, the inexorable progress of linguistic, archaeological, and biological research leaves open no possibility of any major South American or pre-Austronesian phase in Polynesian prehistory. The view that there was no contact whatsoever between Polynesia and the Americas is equally untenable, however.

Some form of contact between eastern Polynesia, especially Easter Island, and South America is clearly demonstrated by the existence in prehistoric Polynesia of the sweet potato (*kumara*, a word perhaps derived from Quechua *kumar*, the major tuber in Maori agriculture), the bottle gourd, and probably certain aspects of birdman iconography, as recorded in the famous Orongo rock carvings. These closely parallel the Chimu carved adobe figures of birdmen at Tucumé in northern Peru (Skjolsvold 1994). The finely cut stone facing of Ahu Vinapu 1 on Easter Island is also closely paralleled in the 15th-century Inca stonework of Sacsahuaman fortress near Cuzco (Bellwood 1987). Such massive and refined stonework is not found elsewhere in the Pacific in definite pre-European contexts, and Vinapu 1, furthermore, is not the only *ahu* with shaped stone on Easter Island.

Contact between Polynesia and Peru is best seen as ephemeral and involving Polynesian rather than South American craft, and it probably occurred on more than one occasion. Roger Green (1998) suggests that Polynesians might even have introduced the

8.31 *The seaward face of Ahu Vinapu 1, Easter Island, with its finely fitted stone masonry, including a shaped insert to fill corner imperfection, similar to stone masonry in Inca Peru.*

sailing raft to Ecuador, this being an artifact with a long Austronesian ancestry that still existed at European contact in Mangareva in eastern Polynesia. But had any major settlement from South America occurred, we might expect diagnostic Andean cultural traits such as pottery, maize, *quinoa*, and guinea pigs to occur in Polynesia, and these are all absent from the archaeological record. In addition, the most famous of Heyerdahl's claimed American traits in Easter Island culture, the huge stone *moai*, have parallels elsewhere in the Pacific and Indonesia, both in stone and in wood. Tiwanaku forerunners for these are not necessary.

8.32, 8.33 *Birdman figures carved in low relief on volcanic rocks at the Orongo crater summit, Easter Island (right), can be compared with a similar adobe birdman figure from the Chimu site of Tucumé, northern Peru (above).*

8.34 *Nan Madol: the basalt prism stonework in the enclosure wall of the tomb of Nan Douwas, Nan Madol, Pohnpei, Caroline Islands, is an example of the impressive stone monuments built by the Polynesians.*

Hawai'i and New Zealand: Varying Social Responses to Environmental Constraints

Comparisons of eastern Polynesian societies, all descended from a common cultural baseline over a period of about a millennium or less, indicate very clearly the relationships between these evolving socio-economic entities and the environments within which they existed. Two excellent comparative examples are the late 18th-century societies of the Hawaiian Islands and New Zealand, both first recorded in detail by Captain Cook and the scientists and artists on his three voyages between 1768 and 1780. **The Hawaiian Islands**, lush and tropical, comprised the major islands of Kauai'i, O'ahu, Lana'i, Moloka'i, Maui, and Hawai'i, plus several smaller islands (Kirch 1985). The first settlers, late in the 1st millennium AD, brought in a full range of domesticated plants and animals, including pigs, dogs, and chickens. Resulting population growth led to the formation of large social units, often termed "chiefdoms" by anthropologists, within which social rank was based on descent via primogeniture, mainly in the male line, from founder ancestors. By the 18th century, inter-group warfare and the varying fortunes of regional chiefs had led to the creation of a small number of stratified societies with separate commoner and chiefly land-managing strata, all becoming politically unified by force into a single kingdom early in the 19th century.

The archaeological record of the Hawaiian Islands reflects this development from small ranked founder groups to large stratified polities very clearly. By later prehistory, the Hawaiians were constructing massive religious structures (*heiau*) of uncut volcanic rock, normally consisting of terraced platforms and walled enclosures [**8.35**]. Hamlet-like clusters of house terraces, enclosures, and platforms indicate a settlement pattern that was spread in small nodes throughout all the cultivable areas of the islands, rather than being strongly nucleated.

Traces of ancient human activity are found in remarkable places: adze quarries in the basalts of Mauna Kea at 3780 m (12,400 ft) above sea level, and house and shrine foundations at 3000 m (9850 ft) around the summit of Haleakala on Maui. Field systems for the cultivation of taro, sweet potato, and gourd consist of parallel stone boundary lines running along or across contours, and extensive panels of rock-carving occur on flat lava surfaces [**8.36**].

New Zealand, by contrast, is temperate in climate and much larger in land area than the Hawaiian Islands (Wilson 1987). Social developments toward large chiefdoms progressed with population growth, as in the Hawaiian Islands, but without the tendency to such a marked degree of social stratification. The first Maoris, arriving *c.* AD 1200 (Anderson 1989; 1995), adopted a partial hunter-gatherer existence among the large populations of seals and flightless moa, but later were obliged, owing to dwindling wild resources, to focus more on cultivation of the only domesticated plant they were able to introduce that would grow in a climate with winter frosts – the American sweet potato. Even this would only flourish in the North Island and northern South Island, and had to be supplemented by the cultivation of the native fern for its starchy rhizomes. Tropical plants such as taro only survived at the frost-free northern limits of the North Island, and the dog was the only domesticated animal to be introduced successfully to New Zealand. As a result of this straddling of the limits of agriculture, the more southerly Maoris had little choice but to remain hunter-gatherers until the 19th century.

The result in New Zealand by the 18th century was a series of quite warlike northern chiefdoms, competitive in terms of rights to the use of cultivable land, but uninterested in the forms of competitive stone monument construction so prominent on the Hawaiian Islands and Easter Island. They turned instead to an intense preoccupation, after AD 1500, with the construction of fortified earthwork enclosures termed *pa*, of which

8.35 (Right) **Hawaiian religious structures:** *massive walls of unshaped volcanic rock enclose the rectangular courtyard of* Heiau Mo'okini, *northern Hawai'i Island.*

8.36 (Below) **Petroglyphs:** *these examples, comprising dots, circles, and lines, are carved in pillow lava at Pu'uloa, Hawai'i.*

over 5000 exist in the agriculturally rich coastal regions of the North Island and northern South Island. Some of these, particularly the terraced volcanic cones of the Auckland Isthmus [8.37], have dramatic visual impact even today. New Zealand is, in fact, one of the best examples in world prehistory of a short parallel trajectory from a common cultural ancestry, about 800 years ago, on the one hand to a warlike agricultural society of about 100,000 people in the north, and on the other hand to a thinly populated hunter-gatherer society in the south. Combined with the Hawaiian Islands and the other islands of eastern Polynesia, the ultimate differences in social and economic adaptation by societies of a common origin, over a period of less than 1000 years, are striking indeed. It is salutary to note that both Easter Island statue-carving and Maori fort construction had begun within 300 years of initial settlement, clear indications that population growth and cultural change could at times be very rapid.

The Chiefdoms of Polynesia: Comparative Ethnographic Perspectives

Invaluable eyewitness observations about many native societies made by 18th-century explorers were augmented by 19th-century oral histories and genealogies, but Polynesian societies were changing so rapidly following European contact that finer

8.37 A Maori pa: *this example was constructed by terracing the extinct volcanic cone of One Tree Hill in Auckland City, northern New Zealand. The terraces would probably have been palisaded, and used for housing or small plantations.*

details of late prehistoric social organization can often be in dispute; the early recorders themselves also acted as catalysts for change. Despite the uncertainties, a consensus view of how these societies were structured has guided much 20th-century comparative research on issues of Polynesian cultural evolution and ecological adaptation (Bellwood 1978; 1987; Kirch 1984; 2000; Kirch and Green 2001).

In terms of socio-political complexity, pre-contact Polynesian societies ranged from the internally stratified chiefdoms of large, close-set, and fertile archipelagos such as the Society, Samoan, Tongan and Hawaiian Islands, through the more gently ranked societies of temperate New Zealand and many of the smaller tropical volcanic islands and atolls, to the strife-torn warring polities of environmentally marginal islands such as Mangaia (southern Cooks), the Marquesas, and Easter Island. These differences in part reflect factors of island size and degree of isolation, and variations in soil fertility and rainfall reliability. They also track patterns of descent with modification from a Proto-Polynesian society that was already genealogically ranked by birth order to some degree (Bellwood 1996b; Kirch and Green 2001). This implies that, in the comparative evolution of Polynesian chiefdoms, shared ancestry was as

significant as adaptation to ecologically varied islands in determining the social kaleidoscope that forms the record of ethnography.

Polynesians defined rank in terms of closeness of descent from the founding ancestor of a tribal group, utilizing elder-younger distinctions and stressing patrilineality for inheritance of major status positions (rights to use food-producing land could often be inherited cognatically, i.e., passed down to a child of either sex). Chiefs functioned as ritually sanctioned stewards of land and food production, and as managers of community affairs and labor projects such as the construction of *marae*. By virtue of their genealogical rank, chiefs inherited supernaturally charged status, and their persons and statuses were protected by a range of behavioral taboos imposed on the chiefs themselves and on their subordinate populations.

Chiefs ruled using personal or family names in most of central and eastern Polynesian island groups, but high-ranking individuals in Samoa and Tonga were elected to specific transgenerational chiefly titles. Samoa developed the most complex system of titled office in Polynesia, with decision-making organized through a hierarchy of local and regional councils. The titled chiefs of Tongatapu headed the only pre-contact Polynesian polity to rule a whole archipelago through conquest and the imposition of tribute, this Tongan "empire" being extended by prestige exchange relations with eastern Fiji and Samoa. Other archipelagos, even the densely populated Hawaiian Islands, supported several late prehistoric chiefdoms, most maintained by strategic alliances until Europeans introduced firearms and unleashed the prospect of conquest-based total hegemony.

Theories of Social Evolution Polynesia has long served as a major anthropological "laboratory" for reconstructing courses of social evolution through ethnographic comparison. Marshall Sahlins (1958) ordered Polynesian societies in terms of intensity of social stratification, with Tonga, Tahiti, Samoa, and the Hawaiian Islands at the top, grading down through four divisions to the least stratified societies on small atolls, where Sahlins felt that the multiple social ties required to ensure survival militated against centralized control of resources. Sahlins's ranking reflected differing levels of food production and frequencies of feasting, thus relating social complexity fairly directly to variations in island ecology. Irving Goldman (1970) presented a similar ranking, based in this case on intensity of "status rivalry" and on the degree to which a "traditional" system of ascribed ranking based on kinship, without marked social strata (as in New Zealand, for instance), had been broken down either by warfare (Mangaia, Easter Island), or by super-stratification of an aristocracy above a dominated and sometimes exploited stratum of commoners (Tahiti, Tonga, Hawai'i).

Despite his focus on social rather than ecological causes, Goldman's overall rank order differed little from that of Sahlins. These rankings still receive strong support from archaeology, in that the largest stone monuments, whether for religious or burial functions, were associated with the largest and most centralized chiefdoms (hence the implications of the massive Easter Island *ahu* and *moai* for the perhaps centralized nature of that society prior to its decline).

In recent decades, a number of careful reconstructions of social evolution in single islands and archipelagos have been published. Patrick Kirch (1994) has emphasized, following a detailed study of the western Polynesian islands of Futuna and Alofi, that conquest and paramount chieftainship did not always emanate from the most fertile and densely populated regions, but often from relatively stressed environments with dry-land rather than irrigated agriculture; he has also applied this reasoning to the Hawaiian Islands (Kirch 1990). Not all such stimuli led to successful conquest, however. Nicholas Thomas (1990) describes how, by the time of European contact,

environmental poverty, drought, and overpopulation had reduced the chiefdoms of the Marquesas to warring polities dominated by inspirational priests. Easter Island underwent a related form of devolution during the 19th century, involving the toppling of the ancestor *moai* from their *ahu* platforms. In such circumstances, hereditary chiefs who could no longer ensure stability and fertility were replaced by non-aristocratic individuals perceived by the general population to be able to communicate with a higher world through trance, or to have been chosen by the gods in some way (as, for example, the 19th-century "Birdmen" in Easter Island).

Polynesian ethnography thus allows scholars to reconstruct how different societies might have evolved, in differing ecological and interactional circumstances, through the 1500 to 2000 years since Ancestral Polynesian Society achieved its post-Lapita existence in western Polynesia (Kirch and Green 2001). Differing island ecologies certainly did influence long-term social outcomes, as did the threads of common ancestry and interaction. Conquest was much easier and more attractive if islands were close together, and if there were major variations in food-producing capacities. The Hawaiian and Tongan Islands were far better placed in these respects, at least from the viewpoints of would-be conquerors, than the small and far-flung Cooks and Marquesas.

Was there a role for consensus, as well as competition, in the rise of paramount chiefs? In the first instance, at the Ancestral Polynesian level, it is quite possible that people rallied around individuals of high descent in order to achieve ritually sanctioned well-being and protection from competitors, particularly during the early phases of island settlement. With population growth and heavy human impact on fragile island ecosystems, however, human ingenuity turned ever more toward war, as the thousands of late prehistoric earthwork fortifications in New Zealand's North Island testify. The massive Tahitian war fleet painted by William Hodges on Cook's second voyage is one of the most evocative images of latent power on record from ancient Polynesia [see **8.27**]. One wonders what might have occurred had the Polynesian islands been left alone for another millennium. Would there have been merely local and cyclical repetition at the chiefdom level of complexity, or would Polynesia have witnessed a series of archipelago-wide conquest thalassocracies in Tongan style, or stratified "archaic states" in Hawaiian style (Kirch 2000)? We shall never know.

Seaborne Trade and the Transformation of Tribal Society in Southeast Asia

Around the western rim of the Pacific, in the islands of Southeast Asia, contact with the evolving civilizations of India, the Mediterranean, and China eventually had an enormous social and religious impact. The spread of **Hinduism and Buddhism** sprang in part from seaborne trading activities that occurred in the archaeological period known in Indonesia as the **Bronze-Iron Age**. In the period between about 500 BC and AD 500, much of the Old World experienced a rapid spread of iron, and both ironworking and bronzeworking (the latter occurring by as early 2000–1500 BC in Thailand and Vietnam, but not in the islands) spread through island Southeast Asia to as far east as the Moluccas during this time. This proliferation occurred, surely not by chance, at approximately the same time as the appearance of major empires in China (the Qin and Han; see Chapter 15), South Asia (the Mauryans and Kushans; see Chapter 14), and the Mediterranean and West Asia (the Hellenistic kingdoms and Rome; see Chapter 13). These empires exploited iron for tools and weapons and carried on trade in exotics, including tropical commodities such as Southeast Asia's spices and aromatics.

The repercussions from these major changes in technology and society were profound, expressed most clearly in the first appearance of urban settlements in Burma, Vietnam, Thailand, and Cambodia (Chapter 15). Urbanization did not spread at this time into the islands of Southeast Asia, however, and such

8.38 Borobudur: *the terraced Buddhist* stupa *of Borobudur, central Java, AD 760–830, from the air.*

changes never spread into the Pacific Islands east of New Guinea – these remained technologically Neolithic and quite remote from the turbulence of civilization until their discovery much later by Europeans. In island Southeast Asia after 200 BC there was, instead, a healthy expansion of long-distance trade with the civilizations of South Asia, and later China. South Indian pottery was carried to Java and Bali, and recent excavations at Sembiran in northern Bali have yielded Rouletted ware and other Indian pottery of the 1st and 2nd centuries AD, one sherd being inscribed with a graffito in Brahmi or Kharoshthi script (on the Kharoshthi script see Chapter 15, p. 584). Sembiran also produced part of a stone mold for casting a bronze kettledrum of the Pejeng type, manufactured at this time in Java and Bali, together with phytolith evidence for rice cultivation (Ardika and Bellwood 1991). The large bronze Dong Son kettledrums made in Vietnam were also distributed at this time through the Sunda Islands of Indonesia to the western tip of New Guinea, and there was a similar widespread dispersal of glass and carnelian beads ultimately of Indian inspiration (albeit often manufactured locally from local geological sources) [**8.40**].

Once seasonal monsoon sailing across or around the Bay of Bengal became a regular occurrence during the last few centuries BC, trade linked the coastlines of India and Indonesia into a vast network, through which spread the beliefs and philosophies of Hinduism, Buddhism, and, later, Islam. The massive

8.39 *Prambanan:* the Hindu temple complex of Candi Lorojonggrang, dating from the 9th–10th centuries AD, central Java.

Buddhist monument known as Borobudur (AD 760–830) [**8.38**], in central Java, is liberally decorated with scenes of large sailing ships at sea [see **8.26**], amongst the more than 1 km (0.6 mile) of reliefs devoted to scenes of Buddhist enlightenment. The terraced mountain shape of Borobudur, interestingly, is an Austronesian form, paralleled in terraced prehistoric stone constructions in Java, the Lesser Sundas, and in many Polynesian *marae*. Here is a true symbol of cultural interaction: Buddhist iconography from India imposed on a native architectural form. More purely Indian in its inspiration is the Hindu temple complex at Prambanan, constructed about a century after Borobudur [**8.39**].

During the 1st millennium AD, native Austronesian societies in Southeast Asia were transformed into complex societies unprecedented in the region, especially in such areas as the Malay peninsula, southern Vietnam, southern Sumatra, central Java, and Bali. Not all island Southeast Asian societies were drawn immediately into inexorable globalism, however. Local

8.40 *Evidence of long-distance trade:* carnelian and agate beads of probable Indian origin from the jar burial cave of Leang Buidane, Talaud Islands, Indonesia. Mid- to late 1st millennium AD.

cultures with local styles continued to evolve in much of the region, just as they did in the Pacific until European exploration. These local styles can be witnessed, archaeologically at least, in such remarkable 1st-millennium AD complexes as the bronze axes, drums, and ornaments of Java, Bali, and the Lesser Sundas; the stone-carvings of the Pasemah Plateau in southern Sumatra [**8.41**]; and the anthropomorphic burial jars of Maitum on Mindanao Island in the Philippines.

The use of large stones for tombs and memorials still characterizes many remoter regions of Indonesia today, especially in northern Sumatra and the Lesser Sundas. Creativity of a different kind can be seen in the remarkable rice terraces at Banaue in northern Luzon, the Philippines [**8.42**]. The centuries following AD 1200 witnessed the arrivals in Southeast

8.41 *Pasemah Plateau:* *a human head carved on a presumed pillar for a raised-floor dwelling, Tegurwangi, Pasemah Plateau, South Sumatra. Not dated, but associations are Iron Age, early 1st millennium AD.*

Asia of Islam, the Portuguese, and the Dutch, all long before the first phases of European contact in the Pacific Islands proper, which really only began in the 18th century (apart from occasional earlier Spanish contacts). The Southeast Asian islands have therefore undergone very different historical trajectories from the Pacific Islands during the past 2000 years, and this is perhaps why, when comparing Borobudur with the giant statues of Easter Island, one might wonder if they were really carved by two populations with a shared but very remote ethnolinguistic ancestry. Indeed, they were. Cultural history evolves in remarkable ways.

Summary and Conclusions

The prehistory of Australia and the Southeast Asian and Pacific islands involved diverse human activities, including the colonization of some of the remotest places on earth, the movement of people and the establishment of elaborate and socially important trade networks, the transition to agriculture and urban systems in some localities, and the persistence and refinement of mobile foraging systems elsewhere. These various trajectories reflect the history of economic and social opportunities and constraints encountered by each group. The archaeological evidence measures not only differences in the lifestyles of people

in each part of this region, but also the evolution of different cultural practices as people adjusted to new landscapes, climates, and neighbors. We can see that in all regions, modifications to economic and social life came about in response to combinations of internal adjustment and external contact, and that these modifications continued through the prehistoric and historic periods. However, the weighting of factors causing change, and the rate of cultural change, varied through time and space.

In Australia, periodic contacts with groups to the north led to a number of important introductions, including the dog, improved water craft, and, recently, metal tools. Symbolic and ideational systems may even have been modified in response to external contacts. However, it is clear that many possible intro-

8.42 *Hillside rice terraces at Banaue, northern Luzon, Philippines:* *the date of commencement of construction of these terraces, still in use today, is unknown, but rice remains are reported from other Philippine sites back to 1500 BC.*

ductions were not adopted, from projectile technology to domesticated plants and animals, and major changes to Aboriginal economy and society were indigenous responses to environmental, demographic, and cultural circumstances. Complex resource manipulation, technological strategies, and trade networks are all cultural practices that were modified throughout the Holocene as Aboriginal groups sought to reduce the impact of uncertain and changing environments and to enhance their lives. Change was ongoing, and some aspects of Aboriginal economy and social life were thoroughly transformed even as late as the last 500 years, as disease and cultural interactions altered technology and trade, procurement and politics.

In the islands that lie between Australia and Asia, Holocene prehistory commenced in a cultural matrix similar to that of Australia, then diverged through two seemingly independent processes. One was the generation of an agricultural lifestyle in the New Guinea highlands. The other was the externally catalyzed dispersal of Austronesian-speaking agriculturalists, a process that undoubtedly began in southern China in archaeological and linguistic terms, although genetically the input of aboriginal Southeast Asian and Melanesian populations also had a marked impact. Looking at the whole of Austronesian development, we can observe that a common baseline in terms of population dispersal can give rise to some remarkably different ultimate outcomes: compare the hunter-gatherer southern Maoris, Hawaiians, medieval Hindu Javanese, Philippine Agta hunters, and Melanesian coastal traders. It is the unravelling of these threads of common ancestry and subsequent differentiation that forms one of the most challenging tasks for modern prehistorians of this region.

As we have seen in this chapter, a strong case can sometimes be made for a close association between the spread of farming and the spread of farmers. The Austronesian example is one of several. Another will be covered in Chapter 10, in connection with the Bantu dispersal into southern Africa, and we shall see in Chapter 11 whether such explanations can be applied to still earlier agricultural expansions in Europe. In the next chapter, however, we consider the Americas, where no single model of agricultural origins and spread can be applied. Instead, a complex pattern of adaptations occurred, as communities of hunters and gatherers began to cultivate local plants or adopted domesticates from their neighbors. The result was a range of cultivation regimes, in many of which major staples such as maize only gradually assumed the dominant role.

Further Reading and Suggested Websites

Bellwood, P. 1987. *The Polynesians* (rev. ed.). London and New York: Thames & Hudson. A general text covering Polynesian prehistory and archaeology.

Bellwood, P. 1997. *Prehistory of the Indo-Malaysian Archipelago.* (2nd ed.) Honolulu: University of Hawaii Press. A review of prehistory in Taiwan, the Philippines, Indonesia, and Malaysia.

Bellwood, P., Fox, J. J., & Tryon, D. (eds.). 1995. *The Austronesians: Historical and Comparative Perspectives.* Canberra: Department of Anthropology, Research School of Pacific and Asian Studies, Australian National University. A series of edited papers on many aspects of Austronesian prehistory, linguistics, genetics, and anthropology.

Flood, J. 1995. *Archaeology of the Dreamtime.* (3rd ed.) Sydney: Angus & Robertson. An accessible introduction to Australian prehistory.

Glover, I. & Bellwood, P. (eds.). 2004. *Southeast Asia: From Prehistory to History.* London: Routledge Curzon. Contains summary chapters on all regions of Southeast Asia from the Neolithic to the Indic civilizations.

Irwin, G. 1992. *The Prehistoric Exploration and Colonization of the Pacific.* Cambridge: Cambridge University Press. An analysis of data pertaining to the actual colonization of the Pacific: navigation, environmental factors, chronology.

Kirch, P. 1997. *The Lapita Peoples.* Oxford: Blackwell. The sole book-length review of Lapita archaeology in the western Pacific.

Kirch, P. 2000. *On the Road of the Winds.* Berkeley: University of California Press. The most recently published text on Pacific Island prehistory and archaeology.

Lourandos, H. 1996. *Continent of Hunter-gatherers: New Perspectives in Australian Prehistory.* Cambridge: Cambridge University Press. An extended argument of the role of social mechanisms in ancient Australian life.

Morwood, M. J. 2002. *Visions from the Past: The Archaeology of Australian Aboriginal Art.* Sydney: Allen & Unwin. Australian rock art viewed from an archaeological perspective, with an emphasis on the methods of archaeological investigation.

Mulvaney, J. & Kamminga, J. 1999. *Prehistory of Australia.* Sydney: Allen & Unwin. A summary of conventional interpretations of Australian archaeology from the perspective of ethnohistory.

Spriggs, M. 1997. *The Island Melanesians.* Oxford: Blackwell. A review of the archaeological record in the Melanesian Islands from the Bismarcks to Vanuatu.

http://arts.anu.edu.au/arcworld/ippa/ippa.htm (mirrored at www.prehistory.org/ippa/) Website of the Indo-Pacific Prehistory Association, based at the Australian National University; many useful links.

http://arts.anu.edu.au/arcworld/arcworld.htm Archaeology website of the Australian National University, with news features, links, and details of archaeological activities of the university.

CHAPTER 9
ORIGINS OF FOOD-PRODUCING ECONOMIES IN THE AMERICAS

David L. Browman, Gayle J. Fritz, Patty Jo Watson, Washington University
The Late Paleoindian Period David J. Meltzer, Southern Methodist University

The Late Paleoindian Period 307
  The Plains 307
  West of the Rocky Mountains 311
  The Eastern Forests 311
  Central and South America 312
  Changes to Come 313

The Archaic Period, c. 9500 BC onward 313

The Mexican Archaic and the Origins of Mesoamerican Agriculture, c. 9500–2500 BC 313
  The Earliest Cultigens 314
  ● **KEY CONTROVERSY** The Domestication of Maize 316

Southwest North America 317
  The Archaic Period 317
  Agricultural Beginnings 317
    • *Models of Agricultural Adoption and Dispersal* 319
  Later Agricultural Developments and Systems 319

Eastern North America 321
  Early to Middle Archaic, c. 9500–4000 BC 322
  The Beginnings of Agriculture in the Middle and Late Archaic 323
  ● **KEY SITE** Koster: An Archaic Camp in Illinois 324
  ● **KEY DISCOVERY** The Archaic Dog 326
  Late Archaic Sites and Lifeways 326
    • *Bacon Bend and Iddins, Tennessee* 326
    • *The Carlston Annis Shell Mound in West Central Kentucky, and the Rockshelters of Arkansas and Eastern Kentucky* 326
    • *Horr's Island, Florida* 327
    • *The Earliest Pottery* 327
  Early Woodland Period, c. 1000–200 BC 328
  ● **KEY SITES** Watson Brake and Poverty Point, Louisiana 328
  Later Agricultural Developments 330
    • *Tobacco* 330

Western North America: Alternatives to Agriculture 330
  Great Plains Bison Hunting 331
  The Pacific Northwest Maritime Cultures 331
  The Great Basin Desert Archaic 332
  The Archaic Period in California 333

The South American Pacific Lowlands 334
  The North Pacific Coast 334
  The Peruvian Coast 334
  The Chilean Coast 336
  ● **KEY SITES** La Paloma and Chilca: Archaic Villages of the Peruvian Coast 337
  Southern Chile and Southern Argentina 338
  ● **KEY DISCOVERY** The Chinchorro Mummies 338

The Andean Highlands 338
  The Northern Andes 339
  The Central Andes 340
    • *Northern Peru* 340
    • *Central Peru* 341
    • *Southern Peru* 341
  The Southern Andes 342
  ● **KEY SITE** Asana: Base Camp and Herding Residence 343
  Andean Animal and Plant Domestication 343
  ● **KEY SITE** Caral: The Rise of Socio-political Complexity 345

The Amazonian Lowlands 346

The Atlantic Lowlands 347

Summary and Conclusions 348

Further Reading and Suggested Website 349

In this chapter, we discuss the spread of human populations into the Western Hemisphere (summarized in Chapter 4) and some highlights of cultural history in the Americas after the end of the Pleistocene. Our primary focus is upon the development of food-producing economies in North, Central, and South America. Developments in the Americas may thus be compared with those already discussed for other regions, such as Southwest Asia (Chapter 6) or East Asia (Chapter 7). Like those two regions, the Americas were the setting for the independent development of agriculture based on local plant and animal species. There were three, if not four, separate centers of agricultural origin: in Mesoamerica; Andean South America; and mid-continental North America; perhaps together with Amazonia. As in certain areas of Eurasia, agricultural economies in some regions of the Americas enabled intensification of food production, and the rise of those complex societies often known as civilizations, which are the subjects of chapters 16 through 18.

Much of the following discussion is based on new information and recently derived understandings, often dependent on AMS radiocarbon dating of the early domesticates themselves (on this method see box, Chapter 4, p. 157). Although many of the details and some of the generalizations presented will necessarily be revised as research continues, the processes that resulted in the establishment of agricultural, as well as highly stable non-agricultural, economies in the Americas will continue to be significant in charting global understanding of the human past.

As climate warmed during the early Holocene, the ice sheets disappeared from North America and were replaced by massive lakes fed by glacial meltwater; gradually these too shrank and disappeared, discharging their waters into the North Atlantic. This early postglacial period, when the first settlers were growing in numbers and learning to exploit a land rich in game, is known as the Late Paleoindian period, and begins with the abandonment of the widespread and distinctive Clovis point (see Chapter 4) around 11,000 BC.

The Late Paleoindian Period

The Clovis period marks the first and last time in North American prehistory that there was a broad, almost continent-wide similarity in artifact assemblages. That similarity may have been the result of several processes, not least the social mechanisms that would enable small groups of people, spread thinly across a vast landscape, to renew ties readily, and to exchange information and mates after long separations. Such mechanisms – flexible and fluid social relations, fewer languages, alliance networks – often leave no material traces, although they occasionally appear in the widespread distribution, use, and exchange of instantly recognizable and sometimes highly symbolic artifacts, such as the distinctive styles of Clovis projectile points.

Clovis points are broadly similar stylistically, technologically, and typologically across a vast area of North America, and may have served as one "currency" (a term not to be taken too literally) for an extensive social and mating network that maintained recognition and alliances, and helped check the attenuating effects of distance and time (Meltzer 2002). Gradually, however, the archaeological record changes. Although the timing varies in different areas, new **post-Clovis projectile point forms** begin appearing sometime after 11,000 BC in the central and western portions of the continent, and after 10,750 BC in eastern North America. By 10,650 BC, the once pan-North American Clovis form is replaced by a variety of regionally distinctive points.

Archaeologists do not place undue weight on formal change in projectile points, which may not relate to actual groups of people, their dispersals, or their adaptations. Nevertheless, if these new forms do mark cultural groups (however defined), and if different forms mark different groups in time and space, then the shift from a single broad and relatively homogeneous form to **multiple regional styles** between 11,500 and 10,650 BC can be interpreted in a number of ways: as evidence for the settling of colonizers in specific areas, for a relaxation in the pressure to maintain contact with distant kin (populations by then having increased in number), and for a reduction in the spatial scale and openness of the social systems. Moreover, these more regionally specific styles do seem to correspond with distinct adaptive strategies. They are more restricted geographically, are part of new and sometime prey- or region-specific foraging strategies (which occasionally involved newly invented technologies), and in places are made of stone obtained from nearby sources, indicating less extensive movement across an increasingly familiar landscape.

The Plains

The earliest replacement of Clovis occurred on the North American Plains, also the area where the Paleoindian complex was first defined in the 1920s. The Late Paleoindian period on the Plains (c. 11,000–7000 BC) is marked by a succession of archaeological complexes known by their **distinctive projectile points** (Folsom, Plainview, Goshen, Agate Basin, Hell Gap, Cody), all of which nevertheless share a common adaptive strategy: **bison hunting [9.1]**. This strategy appears to have "co-evolved" with

THE HOLOCENE IN THE AMERICAS TIMELINE

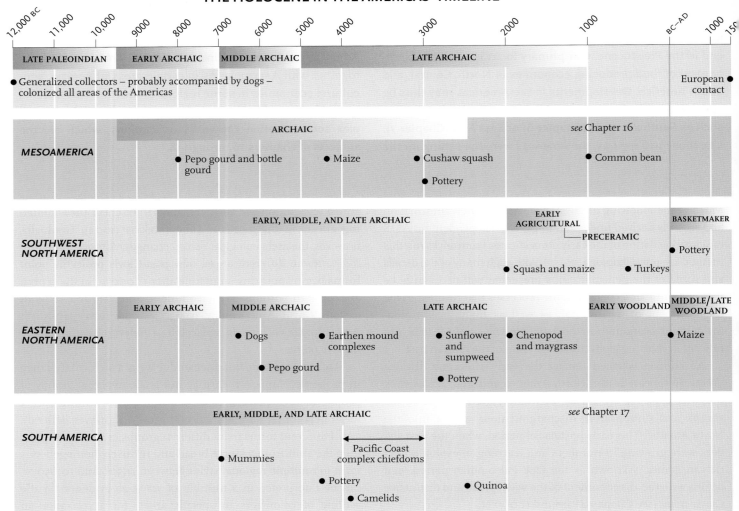

the bison on the Plains, numbers of which increased dramatically with the end of the Pleistocene and the demise of the large grazers (e.g. mammoth, horse, and camel) with which bison had previously to compete in this grassland niche – a niche that was itself changing, becoming increasingly dominated by warm-season grasses of the sort bison favored.

Bison are large, gregarious herd animals, and they group according to sex, age, season, and habitat. They have poor eyesight (though a keen sense of smell), and tend to stampede

9.1 Select North American Paleoindian projectile point forms found on the Plains: *the ticks along the edges mark the extent of grinding up from the base of the point; the Folsom point shown was heavily re-sharpened before being discarded. Points were likely ground along their lower edges for several reasons, not least that this is where the point was bound by sinew or plant fibers to a bone or wooden spearshaft, and the grinding served to dull the edges so they would not cut their bindings when under the stress of use as projectiles or cutting tools. These points are generally older to younger left to right.*

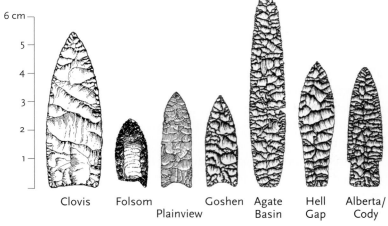

when frightened, making them relatively easily exploited by human hunters. This was accomplished in Late Paleoindian times by a variety of techniques, including **surrounds**, where animals were trapped in a topographically restricted space (e.g. a box canyon or high-walled sand dune) and killed, and **drives**, where animals were stampeded to their deaths over cliffs or into deep arroyos (rocky ravines or dry watercourses) (Frison 1991).

Late Paleoindian bison hunting began modestly enough: Folsom-age kills (11,000–10,050 BC) typically involved fewer than 30 animals. Within a matter of centuries, however, hundreds of animals were being slaughtered at single sites such as **Olsen-Chubbuck** [9.3] and Jones-Miller, both in eastern Colorado – testimony not just to the greater abundance of bison on the landscape, but also to the increasing efficiency of the hunters. Paleoindian hunters selectively targeted cow-calf herds, perhaps because these were not quite so dangerous and were more easily manipulated than bull herds. Given that hunting focused on herds rather than on individual animals, frequently more animals were killed than utilized. At Olsen-Chubbuck, Joe Ben Wheat (1972) found that 16 percent of the

190 animals killed were only partially butchered, and at least 10 percent of the animals at the bottom of the pile showed no butchering evidence at all.

Moreover, this was gourmet butchering: limited and select cuts of meat were removed, eaten, or prepared (by drying or freezing) for later consumption [9.4]. The processing of nearly entire carcasses for transport or storage, and the intensive processing of bones for marrow or bone grease for pemmican (a preparation of dried flesh and fat), characteristic of the historically known bison hunters of the Plains, was unknown in Paleoindian times (Todd 1991).

Consequently, the Paleoindian toolkit was relatively uncomplicated. Tools of stone and bone (the latter often fashioned on the spot) were geared to efficient butchering and easy transport of meat and carcass parts by groups who, over an annual cycle, might track hundreds of kilometers across the Plains

9.2 Map of North America and Mesoamerica: *showing the location of important sites discussed in the text.*

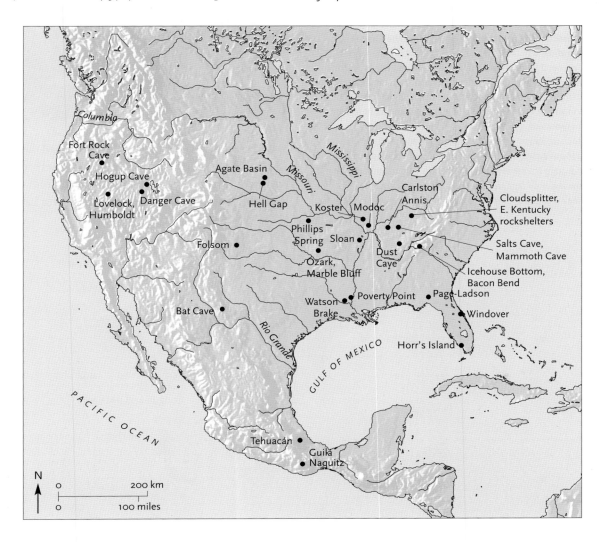

9.3 *The "river of bison bones" at Olsen-Chubbuck:* this was excavated in the lower portion of the long, narrow, V-shaped arroyo, into which some 190 bison had been stampeded and killed. The bison in the front of the stampede were the first to tumble into the arroyo and were then fallen upon by the remainder of the herd. Ultimately the arroyo was choked to the brim with bison heaped two to three animals deep. The hunters butchered most of the bison accessible at the top of the pile, but the carcasses at the base were left largely untouched, the hunters by then perhaps having acquired all the meat they could readily eat and transport.

landscape. These groups may even have traveled off the charts. As the ice sheets receded across Canada, and the land link between Alaska and the continental United States opened, grasslands filled the gap, and Late Paleoindian hunters may have followed the bison northward. The **Mesa complex** in Alaska (9500 BC) had an artifact assemblage remarkably similar to contemporary forms on the northern Plains (Bever 2001), though admittedly only limited evidence of bison predation.

The end of the Paleoindian period on the Plains is marked by a long, severe episode of aridity and drought, during which

9.4 *Generalized butchering pattern of the bison at the Olsen-Chubbuck Paleoindian site:* the diagram is based on archaeological evidence, supplemented by observations of bison butchering by historic Plains bison hunters: (1) the bison carcass was rolled onto its belly, and the hide was cut down the back and pulled to both sides to form a blanket of flesh on which the meat could be piled; (2) the front legs and hump meat were removed; (3) the rib meat was removed, sometimes with ribs still attached, exposing the inner organs which were then extracted and perhaps eaten on the spot; (4) the carcass was then severed just behind the rib cage to remove the pelvic girdle and attached meat; (5) the meat from the hind legs was then cut away, followed by (6) severing of the neck and skull, and removal of the tongue and neck meat.

bison populations were markedly diminished, and human foragers shifted their subsistence to a variety of other food resources (Meltzer 1999). That shift away from a bison-dominated diet was not altogether revolutionary, for Late Paleoindian

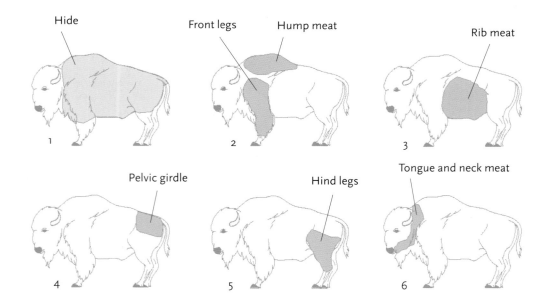

groups had always exploited other game species such as elk, deer, and rabbit, and perhaps also plants, though the evidence for the latter is meager (Stanford 1999).

West of the Rocky Mountains

Fluted point groups and their Late Paleoindian successors, marked by the so-called **Western Stemmed points**, were relatively rare across the west, their sites found in lowland settings across valley floors and near now-extinct lakes and marshes. Although we have only limited evidence of their diet, what does exist indicates that many resources were used, and that these varied by region. Plants were eaten, as well as a variety of small mammals and, where available, fish, frogs, and waterfowl (Beck and Jones 1997; Willig 1991).

The toolkits of these foragers were not unlike those of other Paleoindian groups: they were made to travel, consisting of generalized tools such as knives, scrapers, incising tools (burins and gravers), and projectile points, often obtained from distant sources. Mobility here, as on the Plains, was on the scale of hundreds of kilometers (e.g. Jones et al. 2003). Later, as the climate warmed still further and wetlands shrank (after *c.* 9000 BC), ground-stone tools appear with increasing frequency, presumably for use in plant and seed processing – resources that foragers turn to when more highly ranked foods disappear from the landscape. Because of the sometimes spectacular preservation of organic materials in the dry caves of the Great Basin, we also know that these groups possessed baskets, and used plant fibers to fabricate nets, line, and cordage for a variety of purposes. Surely such materials were used elsewhere in Late Paleoindian times, but the vagaries of preservation have eliminated much of that evidence from the archaeological record.

The Eastern Forests

The post-Clovis evolution of adaptations in eastern North America is tightly tied to the establishment of postglacial communities, a process that was completed early in the Southeast, where forests were essentially modern (comprised of chestnut, oak, hickory, sweet gum, and pine) by 9500 BC; Holocene vegetation came later to the Northeast and upper Midwest. In the latter regions, late glacial tundra gave way to newly arrived trees and forest, the composition of which changed over time – from spruce forest in late glacial times, to pine forests by 9500–8250 BC (depending on location), to mixed coniferous/deciduous forests, and finally to the deciduous oak- and hickory-dominated forests present today. Not all trees or forest communities are alike in terms of their food potential, and many adaptive strategies were used at different times in different areas in response to these changing habitats.

In the northern reaches of eastern North America, the archaeological record at the very end of the Pleistocene and into the early Holocene nearly goes blank. There are very few sites in this area in the centuries around 9500 BC, perhaps because earlier caribou-hunting groups followed the retreating tundra to the north, and/or because of the incursion into the area of a notoriously unproductive pine-dominated boreal woodland, which so limited the food options there was little incentive to stay. The few sites known are small and mark ephemeral occupations. Those human groups who did stay tended to locate themselves near lakes, which would have attracted game and provided fish. Indeed, some sites are on the floors of what were recently drained postglacial lakes, which would have provided open settings for grazing animals such as moose, deer, and elk (Ellis and Deller 1997).

Further south, in the lower Midwest and southeastern portion of North America, the most noticeable feature of the Late Paleoindian period is an explosion in the types of projectile points used in different areas (Lepper 1999). The distribution of these point styles is largely non-overlapping, perhaps signaling the advent of well-bounded territories. As noted, changes in point forms may not necessarily signal major changes in subsistence or settlement patterns, but within those territories there were subtle differences in adaptation, depending on local resources and environment; these are marked in places by newly invented artifacts such as the **Dalton adze** [9.5], which appears in the central Mississippi Valley at this time.

In general, and unlike the situation on the Plains, Late Paleoindian adaptations in the forests of eastern North America involved the exploitation of a wide variety of animal and plant resources, ranging from large to small mammals (deer to rodents), birds, fish, and many nut and fruit trees (Ellis et al. 1998). Joseph Caldwell (1965, 67), commenting on the evidence from one such Late Paleoindian site, observed that "Everything that walked, flew, or crawled went down the alimentary tract

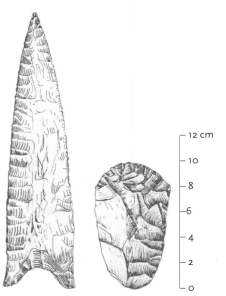

— 12 cm
— 10
— 8
— 6
— 4
— 2
— 0

9.5 New artifacts: *a Dalton projectile point (left) and a Dalton adze (right). The original specimens are from the Sloan site, Missouri. The adze appears to have been a wood-working tool.*

into the inhabitants of Modoc [rockshelter] at that time." The list of species indicates a broad-based utilization of closed-canopy climax forest resources (e.g. gray squirrel and nuts), as well as early successional species more commonly associated with edge areas (ecotones) and relatively open and more disturbed situations (e.g. cottontail rabbits, white-tailed deer, and pioneering seed-bearing plants). Unlike their Clovis predecessors, later Paleoindians in eastern North America were settling in, and not moving nearly so far and so regularly across the landscape. They frequented caves and rockshelters (Walthall 1998), their stone was routinely acquired from local sources, and we see for the first time what appear to be cemeteries, for example at Sloan, Missouri (Morse 1997).

Central and South America

The framework of the late Pleistocene prehistory of North America has often been applied wholesale to the archaeological records of Central and South America, to the dismay of archaeologists on both sides of the equator. This occurred most famously in the effort to send Clovis-like "big-game hunters" all the way to Tierra del Fuego, eliminating an entire hemisphere's Pleistocene fauna *en route*. There is virtually no secure archaeological evidence of big-game hunting across that range, however (Lavallée 2000; Roosevelt et al. 2002), and while Clovis (or Clovis-like) points are found in Mesoamerica, they occur in frequencies that diminish sharply to the south, disappearing around Panama (Ranere and Cooke 1991). Some South American points appear fluted or at least basally thinned (notably, the spottily distributed Fishtail points), and that feature is seen by some to link the continents technologically. Nevertheless, there is debate as to whether that similarity is historically meaningful, or merely a case of technological convergence (Lynch 1991; Politis 1991).

To be sure, the first groups in the southern hemisphere ultimately had ancestors who came through North America, but given the evidence from Monte Verde, this was well before Clovis times [see Monte Verde box, Chapter 4, p. 170]. There are structural similarities in the Late Paleoindian adaptations of the northern and southern hemispheres, but these reflect the evolutionary convergence of hunter-gatherer populations settling a new landscape, which in this instance involved adapting to environments that ranged from tropical Amazonian forests, to high Andean basins, to the semi-arid cold steppe of Patagonia. The Late Paleoindian archaeological record of Central and South America is unlike that of North America, save in the essential fact that it, too, reveals a variety of adaptive strategies and technologies, as one might expect of a relatively thin population dispersed unevenly across a vast continent.

Late Paleoindian sites in Central and South America are more common on the peripheries of the continents than in their centers: along the Pacific coasts and up into the adjoining Cordillera (the Andean mountain chain), but generally well below 4000 m (13,000 ft); on the coastal plain and eastern plateaus of the Atlantic side; and south to the tip of South America. Although it is tempting to suggest that this pattern indicates colonization from the outside inward, this may simply be the result of preservation and/or archaeological sampling. Large areas of this region, such as the Amazon basin, have not been thoroughly searched archaeologically. That said, there is evidence that some regions were not occupied by humans for some time. The highest regions of the Andes (above 4000 m, or 13,000 ft) were apparently not utilized in anything but an exploratory manner until at least early Holocene times and the postglacial re-establishment of modern plant and animal communities. Even then, and perhaps for many thousands of years afterward, these highlands may have been used largely seasonally by hunters of deer and camelids, the latter including the vicuña and guanaco.

In many regions, adaptations were tied to locally and regionally available resources. In the Peruvian coastal desert *c.* 10,850–7000 BC, for example, **Paiján** groups focused their subsistence on marine resources such as saltwater fish and shellfish, small mammals, reptiles, and invertebrates (Lavallée 2000). On the opposite side of the continent, at the Brazilian site of **Pedra Pintada** (a rare early human presence in the Amazon), the faunal remains included freshwater fish of varying sizes, small mammals, a variety of reptiles, and a wide range of plant foods (Roosevelt et al. 2002). And in the distant corner of the continent on the cold **Pampas**, Late Paleoindian hunters occasionally exploited large armadillos (at the site of **La Moderna**), but more often hunted camelids, birds, and rodents.

What is perhaps most striking about the Central and South American Late Paleoindian data is that in many areas foragers carried on a tradition first glimpsed at Monte Verde in Chile: notably, an unmistakable reliance on plants as food resources – and, for that matter, as medicine and construction materials (Dillehay and Rossen 2002). Such remains are not surprising at sites such as Pedra Pintada, but they were hardly restricted to such lowland settings, being found in Late Paleoindian times at sites such as **Guilá Naquitz** in the Oaxaca highlands (1926 m, or 6300 ft), and **Guitarrero Cave** (2580 m, or 8460 ft) and **Pachamachay** (4300 m, or 14,100 ft) in the high Andes; all of these yielded assemblages of edible plants (Dillehay 2000), at the latter two alongside the expected complement of deer and camelid remains. Although at first glance this might appear to contrast with the North American Paleoindian record, in fact it illustrates the same expansion of the diet we see in eastern and far western North America, and which likely occurred for many of the same reasons, as noted below.

Reflecting the broad range of resources being exploited, the **artifact assemblages** associated with these various complexes include a variety of hunting and animal processing implements, notably stone points, scrapers and knives, bone tools, and more specialized hunting implements, such as sling stones and bola stones (two or more stones strung together and thrown so as to entangle an animal), on the Pampas, and Paijan projectile points from the Pacific Coast, which probably served as harpoons. There were, as well, plant processing tools, such as pestles, mortars, and grinding stones.

Although some of these tool complexes are marked by distinctive bifacial projectile points, the explosion of regional point styles seen in the contemporary North American archaeological record does not occur here. Instead, the lithic technology is marked by an array of bifacial and unifacial industries, with the technological emphasis often on the latter (Dillehay 2000; Lavallée 2000). The stone tools in these assemblages were frequently made of stone of mediocre quality, such as quartzite, basalt, and andesite, suggesting that the purpose to which these tools were to be put did not demand the finest crypto-crystalline stone, as was arguably the case in Late Paleoindian North America (Goodyear 1989). Being able to make use of a wide range of stone had the incidental benefit of increasing the number of potential sources for raw material, thereby reducing the need to track great distances across the landscape to a favored rock outcrop. Not having to move far or often to procure vital resources helped to set the stage for early sedentary lifestyles.

Changes to Come

In North, Central, and South America, one can see a common set of trends, from the earliest securely known sites (Clovis in North America, Monte Verde in South America) until the end of the Pleistocene. There is throughout a continuing regional diversification in tool forms and technology over time, evidently reflecting reduced mobility, increasing heterogeneity, and a mosaic of cultures and adaptations. Underlying the process was probably an increase in the variety of food resources in the diet, which, along with the decrease in mobility, suggests that the Late Paleoindian world was slowly filling up. Hunter-gatherers use mobility as a means of coping with food shortages: once local resources were exhausted, they simply packed up and moved on, an option readily available when the landscape was still essentially devoid of other people, and territorial systems had not developed. When mobility is no longer feasible because someone else is already living at the destination, then one is forced to eat different kinds of foods and work one's way down the list of "preferred" food items, ending up with labor-intensive plant foods. From there, it is but a few evolutionary steps to the domestication of plants and intensive food production that ultimately followed in some portions of the Americas.

The Archaic Period, c. 9500 BC onward

The Paleoindian period, which saw the establishment of hunter-gatherer communities across virtually the whole of the Americas, was followed by the Archaic period, beginning at approximately 9500 BC and ending at different times in different regions. The Early Archaic coincides with environmental change following the retreat of glaciers during the terminal Pleistocene. By Middle Archaic times, the plant and animal communities known today were fairly well established.

The discussion that follows focuses on the dynamism between human groups and the flora and fauna that shaped them and were themselves continuously shaped and reshaped by human actions. In particular, we highlight the array of early food-producing economies that developed in the Americas, and the diversity of relations among hunting-fishing-gathering populations and agricultural or semi-agricultural ones.

Another theme is that of economic, social, and political relations or influences among the major geographic divisions of the Americas. Early ideas about prehistoric developments in the New World stressed the dominance of cultural achievements in Mesoamerica, with many other regions viewed as derivative or peripheral. For example, Mexico was once thought to be the source of all New World agriculture, and significant socio-political developments in adjoining regions were believed to have resulted from influence by high civilizations in Mesoamerica. Archaeological evidence accumulated since the mid-20th century, however, indicates a much more complicated situation, wherein each geographic region in North and South America has its own independent cultural trajectory. Hence, another point of emphasis in this chapter is the array of intricate, sophisticated, indigenous regional cultural histories that characterize the Americas.

The Mexican Archaic and the Origins of Mesoamerican Agriculture, c. 9500–2500 BC

The Archaic period in Mexico (c. 9500–2500 BC) was characterized primarily by **nomadic bands of foragers**, some of whom domesticated plants that became economic mainstays for Mesoamerican civilizations and, ultimately, for many cultures in North and South America. Across most of the region, current evidence indicates a long period of high mobility and low population density, in spite of the fact that increased numbers of plants were being domesticated. It was after this period, from around 1600 BC, that sedentary agricultural villages became common features on the landscape, and pottery-using people began constructing monuments.

Archaeological evidence for earlier sedentary communities or public architecture is sparse and controversial. There has so far been no unequivocal evidence in Mexico for 6000-year-old earthworks comparable to those at Watson Brake in Louisiana [see box, p. 328], or Archaic habitation sites with architecture, trash middens, burials, and domestic features as substantial as those on parts of the Pacific coast of South America or at Koster in the Illinois River valley.

The Earliest Cultigens

Most research on the Archaic period in Mexico has focused on plant domestication, dominated by the issues of how, when, and where **maize** was transformed from a wild plant (teosinte, *Zea mexicana*) to its domesticated state. It is now clear that the earliest cultigens were a **squash**, *Cucurbita pepo* ssp. *pepo*, and **bottle gourd**, *Lagenaria siceraria* [**Table 1**]. Desiccated specimens of the family *Cucurbitaceae* were found in the 1960s in early Holocene deposits at Guilá Naquitz (Flannery 1986), in the dry highlands of Oaxaca, and recently re-studied and dated by Bruce Smith (1997a; 2000). The earliest AMS-dated bottle gourd rind from Guilá Naquitz yielded a date range of 8030–7915 BC, and the earliest date for squash seed was also *c.* 8000 BC; nine additional dates range from shortly after 8000 BC to *c.* 6000 BC. Smith's careful examination showed that most of the *C. pepo* seeds are larger than those known for wild populations, putting to rest the suspicion that the earliest material might have come from wild plants.

Bottle gourd's nearest wild relatives live in Africa, and botanists and anthropologists assume that African gourds floated on ocean currents westward across the Atlantic Ocean to southeastern North America and Mesoamerica, where seeds from some such seafaring gourds sprouted to become established localized colonies that were eventually cultivated. The Guilá Naquitz specimens show that this process occurred very soon after the Pleistocene ended.

Like bottle gourds, wild specimens of *Cucurbita pepo* have hard rinds and thin, bitter flesh. The seeds are edible and nutritious, however, and the gourdlike fruits can be used as net floats, rattles, or containers. These plants require little care as crops, and squash and gourd apparently fitted easily into the subsistence strategies of Archaic foragers without conflicting with hunting trips or seasonal plant-collecting expeditions. If a band moved away from a territory where a patch of squashes and gourds was established, seeds could be planted at a new campsite, along an arroyo, or in another nearby alluvial zone. Gourds and squashes joined dogs as domesticated species tended by New World hunter-gatherers that did not necessitate a shift toward agricultural dependence.

In traditional interpretations of agricultural transitions in Mexico, proportions of domesticated plants consumed by Archaic people are said to have gradually increased, first enabling microbands (fewer than ten people) to coalesce sea-

sonally into larger macrobands, and eventually (by 3000–2000 BC) enabling semi-permanent base camps to be supported by a mix of wild and agricultural resources (MacNeish 1971; McClung de Tapia 1992). These formulations were based on now-outdated evidence for **maize** and bean domestication by 6000 BC. Although some archaeologists believe the process was well underway at that time, the earliest directly dated maize cobs (from Guilá Naquitz, at 4300 BC) are small and primitive, in the sense of retaining traits of teosinte, the wild ancestor [see box: The Domestication of Maize, p. 316]. The next oldest cobs (from the Tehuacán Valley of Puebla, dated to *c.* 3500 BC) are also small, and so different from modern maize that they were originally classified as wild (Mangelsdorf et al. 1967b). Unless and until older maize is validated by direct dating, there is no reason to infer that maize was domesticated before 4500 BC.

Common beans (*Phaseolus vulgaris*) have figured prominently in past discussions as dietary companions to early maize in Mexico, adding protein to the diet and fixing nitrogen in the soil of cultivated fields. Beans, however, may have been domesticated only once ceramic technology allowed them to be cooked long enough to render them edible. Beans from supposedly early levels of dry rockshelter sites in the Tehuacán Valley and Tamaulipas were found to be no earlier than 1000 BC when dated by the AMS radiocarbon method (Kaplan and Lynch 1998). On the other hand, an AMS date of 3080 BC shows that **cushaw squash** (*Cucurbita argyrosperma* ssp. *argyrosperma*) was cultivated during Late Archaic times, if not earlier (Smith 1997b), and the same may be true of other food plants, such as **grain amaranth** and **chili pepper**.

Increased reliance on agricultural produce might have been less gradual than previously envisioned, with most of the transition to food production occurring in the final 2000 years of the Archaic period (4500–2500 BC). With gourds and squashes being easily cultivated and transported, early Holocene hunter-gatherers would not necessarily have experienced seasonal conflicts that caused them to shift away from wild plant resources toward the two cultivated ones. The transformation of maize from teosinte shortly before or after 4500 BC may signal the earliest shift to effective food-producing systems in Mexico. In areas where wild resources were scarce or unpredictable, such as arid highland valleys in the state of Puebla, maize and other crops probably served as buffering agents that evened out imbalances. Where wild foods were abundant, as in some coastal estuaries, hunter-gatherers could have been more selective in adding domesticated plants to their diets.

On the Pacific coast of Oaxaca, late Archaic occupations dating between 3000 and 2000 BC have been studied using stable isotope ratios from human bone to track the introduction of maize or other C4 plants (primarily heat-loving grasses; see Chapter 2, p. 82). Two individuals who lived during the Archaic

Table 1 *Mesoamerican Crops*

Grains

Maize	*Zea mays* ssp. *mays*
Amaranth	*Amaranthus hypochondriacus* and *Amaranthus cruentus*
Huauzontli	*Chenopodium berlandieri* ssp. *nuttalliae*
Chia	*Salvia hispanica*

Legumes

Common bean	*Phaseolus vulgaris* (domesticated independently also in South America)
Sieva bean	*Phaseolus lunatus* (probably domesticated in both Mesoamerica and South America)
Scarlet runner bean	*Phaseolus coccineus*
Tepary bean	*Phaseolus acutifolius* var. *latifolius*

Vegetables/containers

Squash/Pumpkin	*Cucurbita pepo* ssp. *pepo* and *Cucurbita moschata*
Cushaw squash [9.8]	*Cucurbita argyrosperma* ssp. *argyrosperma*
Bottle gourd	*Lagenaria siceraria*
Calabash tree gourd	*Crescentia cujete*
Chayote	*Sechium edule*
Chili pepper	*Capsicum annuum* and *Capsicum frutescens*
Tomatillo	*Solanum ixocarpa*

Fruits, drinks, and flavorings

Papaya	*Carica papaya*
Soursop	*Annona muricata*
Sapota	*Pouteria mammosa*
Guava	*Psidium guajava*
Prickly pear [9.7]	*Opuntia* ssp. *(several species)*
Cocoa	*Theobroma cacao*
Vanilla	*Vanilla planifolia*
Annatto	*Bixa orellana*

Technical

Cotton [9.6]	*Gossypium hirsutum*
Agave	*Agave* ssp. (several species; uses include fiber, food, and drink)
Indigo	*Indigofera suffruticosa*

9.6 *Cotton:* Gossypium hirsutum

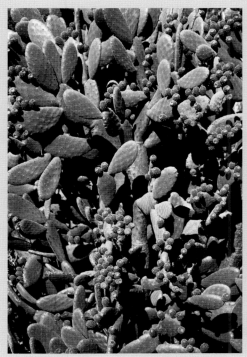

9.7 *Prickly pear:* Opuntia

9.8 *Cushaw squash:* Cucurbita argyrosperma

KEY CONTROVERSY The Domestication of Maize

The earliest solid evidence for domesticated maize (*Zea mays* ssp. *mays*) comes from the dry cave site of Guilá Naquitz in Oaxaca, Mexico. Two of the five small, desiccated cobs excavated in 1966 by Kent Flannery from an undated layer were recently submitted for AMS radiocarbon dating; they yielded calibrated dates of 4300 BC (Piperno and Flannery 2001). These cobs are quite small and display primitive traits that indicate an early stage of domestication, including a very low number of kernel rows: no more than four, as compared to later cobs with 8–16 rows or even more. The Guilá Naquitz cobs are not wild, however, as demonstrated by the rigid, non-shattering rachises (the tiny stalk that joins the kernel to the cob) of all specimens, and the presence on a few samples of cupules (cup-shaped wrapping) that bore two grains. Two of the cobs from Guilá Naquitz have two rows of cupules with a single grain per cupule, a trait of teosinte (Benz 2001). (For the use of rachises as evidence of domestication see Chapter 6, p. 226.)

The next oldest directly dated maize comes from the San Marcos and Coxcatlán rockshelter sites in the Tehuacán Valley of Puebla, Mexico. These maize remains were originally thought to be *c.* 8000 years old on the basis of stratigraphic position and associated charcoal, but AMS dates on 12 specimens range after calibration from 3500 to 1500 BC (Long et al. 1989). The oldest cobs (those predating 3000 BC) have between two and five rows of cupules, each of which would

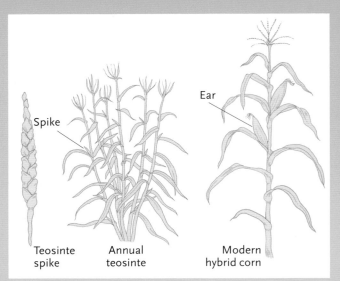

9.9 *Maize's wild ancestor, teosinte, differs from domesticated maize by having a narrow spike (left) bearing only two rows of grains – one grain per cupule – that shatter upon ripening. Ears of modern maize (right) have four or more rows of nonshattering cupules, and each cupule bears two grains.*

have borne two kernels, but have lost other anatomical traits of wild teosinte observed in the Guilá Naquitz specimens (Benz and Long 2000).

Molecular biologists are contributing greatly to an understanding of maize's domestication by studying the isozymes (variants of an individual enzyme) and DNA of modern maize and its close relatives. More debate has swirled around the ancestry of this domesticate than any other New World crop, but the current consensus among maize geneticists is that a wild annual teosinte (*Zea mays* ssp. *parviglumis*) growing only in southwest Mexico gave rise to maize (Doebley 2004; Matsuoka et al. 2002). The crucial genetic changes must be framed within the

context of human collecting and cultivating strategies, but the meager archaeological evidence for mid-Holocene harvesting of teosinte or planting of early maize makes it difficult to go beyond generalized scenarios. Most archaeologists envision people in central and southern Mexico from 5000 to 3500 BC as living in shifting, primarily foraging bands that aggregated seasonally into larger groups. Two sites – Zohapilco in the Basin of Mexico (Niederberger 1979) and San Andrés on the Gulf coast in Tabasco (Pope et al. 2001) – may demonstrate the possibility of more permanent and large-scale Archaic habitation where cultivation and domestication of food plants could have occurred, perhaps analogous to that uncovered in parts of eastern North America at the same time. Both sites, however, are surrounded by unanswered questions. Zohapilco is incompletely published, and compared with later Archaic sites in Mesoamerica, evidence for year-round or intensive occupation is insubstantial. *Zea* pollen from cores at San Andrés has been indirectly dated on the basis of associated organic remains to as early as 6000 BC, but directly dated remains are necessary to establish age, and cobs or kernels are needed to confirm domesticated status.

9.10 *These modern native maize varieties are grown along the Coatzacoalcos River, Mexico, and show great variety. They are better adapted to local climatic and soil conditions than those created by modern agronomists.*

period showed elevated consumption of C4 plants (possibly maize), indicating that their societies may have moved between the coastal estuaries (for fishing and shellfish collecting) and inland zones (for food production) (Blake et al. 1992). Future research will surely uncover unexpected developments leading up to the Formative period, but it is already clear that the transition to agriculture in Mexico is characterized by significant regional variability.

Southwest North America

The Archaic Period

After Pleistocene climatic conditions ended *c.* 9000 BC, inhabitants of the greater American Southwest, including those of northwestern Mexico, continued living as mobile hunter-gatherers for approximately 6000 years. The immediate post-Pleistocene period is poorly understood in the Southwest, and most archaeologists use 7000 BC as the starting point of the Southwestern Archaic tradition (Huckell 1996). Early and mid-Holocene rainfall and runoff patterns differed from modern ones in terms of seasonal monsoon cycles and stream flow patterns. Before 2500 BC, rivers cut narrow, relatively deep valleys rather than forming alluvial floodplains. After 2500 BC, climatic conditions seem to have been comparable to those documented historically; streams formed less entrenched valleys, with soil and moisture regimes suitable for cultivation and irrigation. The Archaic can be seen as persisting until the period between AD 1 and 400 if the appearance of ceramics is used as the defining criterion. Because the earliest Southwestern maize can be traced back to 2000 BC, using domesticated plants as the criterion would effectively end the Archaic much earlier, except in areas where farming was a late phenomenon.

Although regional stylistic and technical differences can be recognized among the stone tools, the subsistence and settlement patterns of **pre-agricultural Southwestern hunter-gatherers** shared many common elements. Animal remains and hunting tools (spear points and snares) demonstrate successful capture of larger mammals – deer, pronghorn antelope, mountain sheep, and occasionally bison – along with smaller game such as rabbits and various rodents (Cordell 1997). Grinding stones, choppers, and plant remains demonstrate the gathering of pinyon nuts, walnuts, agaves and yuccas, fruits of cacti and trees, and seeds of various grasses and other herbaceous species.

Before 2500 BC, there is no evidence in the Southwest for repeated or longer-term occupation at specific locales that approaches the substantial, Middle to Late Archaic middens in parts of the Eastern Woodlands (see below). Southwestern sites predating 2500 BC are small, artifact densities are low, and features other than hearths are infrequent. Although gradual

population increase throughout the Archaic has been invoked as a reason for the adoption of agriculture (Cordell 1997), it now appears that population densities remained relatively low, with material culture geared toward frequent moves.

Agricultural Beginnings

The northward spread of **maize**, **squash**, and other crops from central Mexico into the desert borderlands of northwest Mexico and the southwestern United States was underway shortly after 2000 BC. The timing of the initial transition to farming has been revised several times, as new evidence is uncovered and as cultigen fragments found during past excavations are AMS radiocarbon-dated. **Bat Cave**, in the Mogollon highlands of western New Mexico, long held the distinction of having yielded maize dating to *c.* 3000–2500 BC (Mangelsdorf et al. 1967a). After the site was re-excavated using modern stratigraphic controls, however, and both previously excavated and newly unearthed cobs were directly dated, the most secure estimates of maize's antiquity there centered around 1500 BC (Wills 1988; 1995). The 1990s brought a rapid succession of new material from sites in Arizona and New Mexico, and directly dated maize is now established at around 2000 BC. Sites with solid evidence of early maize agriculture (1000 BC or earlier) range from southern Arizona and south-central New Mexico to the Four Corners region of southeast Utah/northeast Arizona.

More significant than these chronological refinements is the apparent economic importance of maize for some Late Archaic people in the Southwest. Most archaeologists believed until quite recently that hunter-gatherers who planted crops were merely incorporating small numbers of cultigens into largely foraging patterns of subsistence, and persisting as low-level food producers until 2000 years ago or even later (Minnis 1992). Rather than occurring in small amounts in a limited number of samples, however, the maize from several sites predating 800 BC is as ubiquitous as from later sites, where serious farming is not in doubt. This indicates a less gradual transition than previously expected.

Rescue archaeology connected with construction for highways and canals in the Tucson basin of southern Arizona has recently resulted in excavation of several significant sites dating to the San Pedro phase (*c.* 1500–1100 BC) of what Bruce Huckell calls the Early Agricultural period. At the **Milagro**, **Las Capas**, **Valley Farms**, and **Wetlands** sites, settlements on river terraces consisted of shallow pit-structure dwellings and associated extramural storage and roasting pits. Projectile points, ceramic beads, marine shell beads and pendants, mica beads, fired clay figurines, stone pipes, stone vessels, and crude miniature ceramic vessels are characteristic finds at these sites and at other San Pedro-phase sites outside the Tucson basin. Maize was found in 85.7 percent of the features at Milagro and 87 percent of those at Valley Farms, making it more ubiquitous than maize from many Classic Hohokam sites of late prehistory. The explanation for this may be either that considerable amounts of maize were grown by these early Southwestern farmers, or that the earlier, smaller sites were more comprehensively covered with maize byproducts and that these can more readily be retrieved archaeologically, whereas later, larger, and more permanent settlements had more functionally segregated spaces, which would tend to result in smaller overall samples of cultigens (Wills 2001).

An astonishing discovery at **Las Capas [9.11]** is the presence of **irrigation canals** dating to as early as 1400 BC. The site was abandoned several hundred years later, when the habitation area was flooded and the canals filled with alluvium (Mabry 1999). Similar irrigation canals near **Zuni Pueblo** in northwestern New Mexico, on the Colorado Plateau, have been dated to *c.* 1000 BC, showing that early farmers outside the Basin and Range province of southern Arizona also practiced water con-

trol (Damp et al. 2002). Clearly, preceramic agricultural practices, at least in some places, were systematically implemented and important components of subsistence regimes, together with hunting and wild plant collecting.

Northern Chihuahua, Mexico, is another region where evidence for preceramic farming has recently been uncovered on terraced hills called *cerros de trincheras*. The largest of these is **Cerro Juanaqueña [9.12]**, a 140-m (455-ft) high basalt hill overlooking the Rio Casas Grandes valley. Nearly 500 artificially constructed, rock-lined earthen terraces (*trincheras*) cover large areas of the hill's flanks and summit. Archaeologists conducting surface survey on the terrace features during the early 1990s found many projectile points diagnostic of the San Pedro phase, as well as hundreds of basin-shaped grinding stones, but few artifacts diagnostic of the late pre-Columbian agriculturalists who lived in the Rio Casas Grandes valley (Hard and Roney 1998). Late Archaic inhabitants of this region were traditionally thought to have been too mobile and loosely organized to have been the builders and occupants of Cerro Juanaqueña, in spite of the fact that maize and squash were known to have spread into New Mexico by San Pedro times. Recent archaeobotanical studies, however, show that maize was present in 69 percent of the features analyzed at Cerro Juanaqueña, probably having been grown on the river terraces below the hill. Maize from 14

9.11 *Aerial view of the site of Las Capas:* one of several Late Archaic communities in the Tucson Basin of southern Arizona where high ubiquities of maize are forcing archaeologists to rethink models of early Southwestern agriculture. Irrigation canals predating 1000 BC were found at this site.

9.12 *Cerro Juanaqueña in northern Chihuahua, Mexico: this aerial view shows the hilltop terraces built by early agricultural people (c. 1300–1100 BC) for domestic structures. Crops were probably grown below, in the alluvial valley of the Rio Casas Grandes valley.*

samples has been AMS radiocarbon-dated to *c.* 1300–1100 BC, when most of the terraces were built (Hard and Roney 1998; 1999; Roney and Hard 2000).

Models of Agricultural Adoption and Dispersal The presence of what some archaeologists see as more sedentary and highly organized farming communities in the Southwest 1000 years earlier than previously expected has major implications, necessitating a re-evaluation of the conditions and mechanisms under which early agriculture spread across this region. (Some scholars interpret the increasing size of sites in this area as a palimpsest situation, derived from annual reoccupation of favored site locations by small family groups.) Popular explanations – based on the only evidence available until recently – portrayed Late Archaic people as nomadic hunter-gatherers who initially planted limited amounts of maize, squash, and possibly other crops to increase resource predictability in a region where climatic fluctuations, and therefore uneven levels of wild food productivity, are normal. These explanations might link the adoption of domesticated plants to growing population densities, or they could simply view early cultivators as taking advantage of attractive new foods without significantly modifying previous lifeways (Huckell 1996; Minnis 1992; Wills 1988; 1995).

Nevertheless, because there are now more substantial, village-like communities predating 1000 BC at lower as well as higher elevations, accompanied by domestic architecture, irrigation features, and storage pits yielding higher than expected frequencies of maize, some archaeologists no longer accept the view that the transition to agriculture was gradual, and that it had minimal initial economic impact. An alternative scenario has been receiving more attention in the past few years: the possibility that early Southwestern farmers actually moved up from the south. In other words, agriculture may have been introduced and implemented by Uto-Aztecan populations originating south of Sonora and Chihuahua, rather than having been adopted by indigenous hunter-gatherers recognizing a means to augment their long-term resource base (Diamond and Bellwood 2003; Hill 2001). Although this is not an entirely novel suggestion (e.g. Berry 1985), the "sociocultural intrusion" model in past years met nearly universal rejection (Wills 1990). It remains controversial, with a major obstacle to resolution being lack of research into Archaic-period cultures of western and north-central Mexico. Diffusion of cultigens versus migration of people may turn out to be a simplistic dichotomy when considering the whole greater Southwest. R.G. Matson (1999),

for example, proposes that **San Pedro Cochise** farmers from the south – whom he sees as having Mexican roots – colonized the western part of the Colorado Plateau, but that indigenous hunter-gatherers farther east later adopted crops and became farmers themselves.

Later Agricultural Developments and Systems

People began producing **pottery** and living in **agricultural villages** across most of the Southwest during the early centuries of the Christian era, developing distinct sub-regional stylistic and technological traditions, as described in Chapter 18. Agriculture appears to have been central to the economies of these societies, although their systems were probably still evolving in terms of water diversion, soil moisture retention, ground temperature control, and possibly also the species and varieties of crops being grown. We know by directly dated plant remains that **maize** spread across the region during the 2nd millennium BC, that a **squash** or **pumpkin** (*Cucurbita pepo* ssp. *pepo*) had either accompanied maize initially or joined it by *c.* 1400 BC, and that **common beans** were grown in New Mexico by 2000 years ago; **bottle gourds** have been found along with maize in preceramic contexts in dry caves, but none has been directly dated (Wills 1988; Tagg 1996).

A number of new crops may have entered the Southwest during the 1st millennium AD, contributing in significant ways to the diets and technologies of the developing agriculturalists. Two species of **squashes** – *Cucurbita moschata* (butternut) and *C. argyrosperma* ssp. *argyrosperma* (cushaw) – are among the Mexican crops apparently incorporated into established maize farming systems. The earliest **cotton** (*Gossypium hirsutum* var. *punctatum*) in the Southwest is also attributed to the middle or late 1st millennium AD (Cordell 1997; Ford 1981). Cotton seeds can be consumed, but the primary purpose of this crop was probably for woven textiles, which became crucial elements of costume, ceremonies, and trade. **Scarlet runner beans** (*Phaseolus coccineus*) are present in archaeological samples from Durango, Mexico, and were grown by historic Southwestern farmers. Two additional types of beans – **jack beans** (*Canavalia ensiformis*) and **sievas** or small **limas** (*Phaseolus lunatus*) – were grown historically in the Southwest and may have been present in pre-contact times as well (Cordell 1997; Ford 1981).

Of special interest is the **tepary** (*Phaseolus acutifolius* var. *latifolius*), a small bean whose wild ancestor is native to the Sonoran Desert, and which, therefore, may have been domesticated within the greater Southwest. Teparies were clearly an important food for ancient Hohokam farmers, and continue to be grown by the native O'odham (previously called Papago and Pima) who cultivate the desert of southern Arizona today (Bohrer 1970; Nabhan and Felger 1984). Teparies are known archaeobotanically in the late 1st millennium AD, but may have been present earlier.

Additional crops grown in late pre-contact Southwestern agricultural systems, especially in the Hohokam area, are **agave** (probably *Agave murpheyi* [**9.13**] and/or *Agave parryi*) and grain **amaranth** (*Amaranthus hypochondriacus* and *A. cruentus*), although their antiquity as cultigens is uncertain (Gasser and

Kwiatkowski 1991). Formerly overlooked as anything but wild resources, agaves are now recognized as having been planted in extensive rockpile fields on lower slopes of mountain ranges in the Sonoran Desert, above the zone where canal irrigation was possible but well below their modern range (Fish et al. 1985). As plants yielding food and fiber, they undoubtedly played a significant role in both the subsistence and exchange economies of farmers living in the challenging desert environment. Amaranth is infrequently identified as a domesticated species in the Southwest due to the difficulty of accurately categorizing charred specimens. Desiccated pale amaranth seeds and seed heads from Tonto National Monument, dating to AD 1400, are definitely cultigens, and charred specimens from Snaketown and other Hohokam sites probably represent domesticates as well (Bohrer 1962; Miksicek 1987). Two other native Southwestern plants known to have been domesticated are Sonoran panic grass and devil's claw, the latter used primarily for basketry fiber [**Table 2**].

A new, more productive variety of maize is sometimes seen as having played a pivotal role in intensified agricultural systems, accompanying the increase in size of pithouse villages, or the late 1st-millennium AD shift from pithouse to above-ground, room-block ("pueblo") architecture. Although Southwestern farmers may have adopted new varieties of maize from elsewhere or bred more productive varieties themselves, heightened agricultural productivity probably also stemmed from planting several species of squashes, beans, and in some places agave and grain amaranth, as well as in encouraging the weedy edible species that colonized gardens and fields. More sophisticated mechanisms of irrigation and temperature control were also implemented through time, as discussed in Chapter 18.

The **turkey** (*Melagris gallopavo*) was kept as a domestic animal in communities in the greater Southwest during pre-Columbian times. The current earliest evidence for domestic turkeys apparently comes from Tularosa and Jemez caves in New Mexico, where they are believed to be present by about 800 BC (Breitburg 1993); in Mexico, the earliest remains come from the Palo Blanco phases (200 BC–AD 700) in Tehuacán. For many years it was argued that the Southwestern turkey was domesticated only for its use as a ceremonial animal, that it was buried as a ritual animal, that its bones were used in ceremonial whistles, and that its feathers were used to make feather textiles, blankets, and ornaments, as well as prayer sticks, headdresses, and masks. There is now substantial evidence, however, that the turkey was also valued as a meat source.

9.13 Agave murpheyi: *one of the probable crops native to the Greater American Southwest.*

Table 2 *Crops Domesticated or Cultivated in the Southwest and Eastern North America*

Southwest North America

Grain

Sonoran panic grass	*Panicum sonorum*

Legume

Tepary bean	*Phaseolus acutifolius* var. *latifolius* (possibly domesticated in the Southwest and in Mexico)

Starchy food and fiber

Agave	*Agave murpheyi* and *Agave parryi* (cultivated and possibly domesticated in the Southwest)

Technical

Devil's claw	*Proboscidea parviflora* (used in basketry)

Eastern North America

Grains

Sunflower	*Helianthus annuus* var. *macrocarpus* (may have been domesticated in Mexico also)
Sumpweed	*Iva annua* var. *macrocarpa* (now extinct as a cultigen)
Chenopod	*Chenopodium berlandieri* ssp. *jonesianum* (now extinct as a cultigen)
Erect knotweed	*Polygonum erectum* (no longer cultivated)
Maygrass [9.14]	*Phalaris caroliniana* (no longer cultivated)
Little barley	*Hordeum pusillum* (no longer cultivated)

Vegetables/containers

Squash/pepo gourd [9.15]	*Cucurbita pepo* ssp. *ovifera*
Bottle gourd	*Lagenaria siceraria*

9.14 *(Left) Maygrass growing in northeastern Arkansas.*

9.15 *(Below) Free-growing eastern pepo gourd in Louisiana. Both were members of the pre-maize Eastern Agricultural Complex.*

Eastern North America

Major environmental processes in the earlier portion of the time-span from 9500 to 1000 BC center on postglacial alterations in landscapes – geomorphological, floral, and faunal (Schuldenrein 1996; Watts et al. 1996). Specifics vary greatly from place to place, but in the inland, more northerly latitudes east of the Mississippi River, lakes and hummocky, marshy terrain characterized regions that had been north of the maximum extent of the ice (the latitude of which was roughly that of St.

Louis, Missouri). Stream channels stabilized in the mid-Holocene (*c.* 7000–4000 BC), late Pleistocene floral and faunal zones shifted north, and in the Southeast, dominant vegetation patterns based on oak and herbaceous plants were replaced by pine and swamp- and lake-dominated regimes. Coastal plains and estuaries of the eastern seaboard began to assume their modern configurations, as water levels rose with the melting of the ice. The human groups who peopled the Americas brought with them toolkits that included not only stone, bone, wood, antler, and ivory artifacts, but also knowledge of a wide array of **vegetal fibers** that could be used to make clothing, cordage, baskets, nets, and other essential soft goods. **Weapons** included spears and spearthrowers (atlatls), but not bows and arrows, which do not appear until around AD 1–500, during Middle and Late Woodland times.

Beginning with the transition from the Late Paleoindian period, archaeological information for eastern North America comes from a few deeply stratified rockshelters and caves and several open sites. Late Paleoindian and Early Archaic lifeways were apparently broadly similar. Significant contrasts with Late Paleoindian/Early Archaic assemblages and the lifeways these are thought to reflect appear in the Middle Archaic, when, in general, floral and faunal distributions approximate those of the present. Hickory nuts became a staple forest food (Fritz et al. 2001), and the first cultivated plants – two kinds of gourd – appear in the archaeological record (Fritz 1990; 1999; Doran et al. 1990). Major earthworks were also created by these skilled gatherer-hunter populations in several different locales of the mid-South and Southeast (Russo 1996).

During the Late Archaic period in upland areas of the mid-South (Arkansas, Kentucky, Tennessee), archaeobotanical evidence from rockshelters and open sites documents the presence of several domesticated small-seeded plants, in addition to the two gourds found in Middle Archaic contexts. In some mid-continental riverine locales (e.g. the Ohio River and its tributaries, such as the Green River), Late Archaic sites are abundant and conspicuous because of the enormous quantities of **freshwater mussels** utilized by these river people, the remains of whose seasonal settlements form a site type called shell mounds or shell middens.

Early to Middle Archaic, c. 9500–4000 BC

This time period, *c.* 9500–4000 BC, is approximately equivalent to the early and mid-Holocene, the mid-Holocene warm interval, or "Hypsithermal," being warmer and drier than the early Holocene. By Middle Archaic times, regionally distinctive artifact assemblages are recognizable, especially diagnostic chipped-stone tools such as projectile points.

Knowledge of pre-Columbian peoples in the Southeast is enhanced greatly by research at wet sites in Florida (Milanich 1994; Purdy 1988), such as **Page-Ladson**. Located during systematic underwater survey of the Aucilla River, artifacts from this site date to 10,000–7500 BC, and include mastodon bones and dung containing, among other plant remains, *Cucurbita*

9.17 *(Opposite)* **Icehouse Bottom:** *excavation in progress at the Icehouse Bottom site on the Little Tennessee River in eastern Tennessee, an Early and Middle Archaic hunter-gather camp. The stratigraphic sequence documented here begins more than 9000 years ago in the Early Archaic period.*

pepo (squash or pumpkin) seeds (Newsom et al. 1993). These are evidence for a wild population of *Cucurbita pepo* plants more widespread in North America during the early Holocene than at present, and probably ancestral to the first cultivated plants in eastern North America.

Middle Archaic human remains have also been found at several Florida wet sites, including **Little Salt Spring**, a deep sinkhole in karstic terrain (a region of thick-bedded limestone, with numerous sinkhole caves and underground streams). The most famous of these is **Windover Pond** [9.16], a wooded marsh underlain by peat deposits that were used *c.* 6000–5000 BC for human burials. Because the peat has remained saturated to the present day, human tissues and many other ordinarily perishable materials are beautifully preserved. Each body was carefully shrouded in a textile wrap, then carried into the marsh and pinned securely to the peat by wooden stakes. A total of 168 bodies have been excavated, from 91 of which preserved brains were recovered. The Windover site seems to contain five or six episodes of mortuary activity within about 1000 years, and may represent a single, original local group with several descendant generations. DNA analyses as well as other biochemical and medical research are in progress (Doran 2002). The Windover peat yielded many well-preserved animal and plant remains as well, including at least one bottle gourd accompanying a burial (Doran et al. 1990), the earliest known bottle gourd north of Mexico; an array of fibers and textiles from clothing, bags, matting, and cordage; and many wooden artifacts (Andrews et al. 2002; Adovasio et al. 2002).

Other key sites for information on Middle Archaic life include **Modoc rockshelter** and **Koster** in Illinois [see box:

9.16 *Windover, Florida: excellent preservation conditions at this site allowed the recovery of at least seven different handwoven plant fiber textile varieties, which had been utilized for garments, bags, mattings, and coverings.*

Koster, pp. 324–25], and Eva and Icehouse Bottom in Tennessee. All of these sites are on or near permanent, mid-continental rivers. The site of **Eva**, on the Tennessee River in western Tennessee, was a long, oval mound of cultural deposit approximately 85 x 62 m in extent and 2 m deep (275 x 200 x 7 ft) (Lewis and Lewis 1961). Cultural deposits span most of the Middle Archaic, perhaps beginning in the late Early Archaic and ending in the Late/Terminal Archaic. The sequence is therefore chronologically comparable to that at Koster on the Illinois River, and the lower strata at Icehouse Bottom on the Little Tennessee River. The earliest inhabitants, probably descended from the Paleoindian populations whose characteristic projectile points have been found elsewhere along the Tennessee River, were seasonally sedentary hunter-gatherers, consuming deer, various forest plant foods (especially nuts), and freshwater mussels.

As at other Archaic sites in eastern North America, chipped- and ground-stone tools were found in abundance at Eva, including projectile points, scrapers, drills, flakes utilized as knives, pestles or pounders, atlatl weights, and two tubular pipes. There were also numerous bone and antler artifacts (including awls or perforators, needles, and fishhooks), and a few turtle-shell rattles. Eighteen dog burials and 198 human burials were excavated. Of the human burials, 57 (29 percent) were accompanied by grave goods. As at the Green River shell mounds in Kentucky (see below), the nature and distribution of grave goods indicate a basically egalitarian society, in which status was personally achieved.

Icehouse Bottom [9.17] was occupied *c.* 8500–6000 BC by Early and Middle Archaic hunter-gatherers camping seasonally near the Little Tennessee River (Chapman 1994). Their shelters were probably made of wood, brush, cane matting, or skins. Basketry and netting impressions were visible on many of the Icehouse Bottom hearths, enabling textile and fiber experts to say something about items relating to what would have been a very important and elaborate soft technology, not ordinarily preserved (Chapman and Adovasio 1977). Nuts, especially hickories, were a staple, and other plant remains indicate the use of fruits and berries, as well as seeds of weedy species.

Deer, rabbits, raccoons, opossums, squirrels, and other mammals were hunted (the larger ones with spears flung from spearthrowers), as were birds, especially turkeys and passenger pigeons. Turtles and tortoises would have been collected and presumably eaten before their shells were used for containers, rattles, net-mesh gauges, and other artifacts. Fish were taken by means of traps, hook-and-line, fish gorges, weirs, and nets, as well as being collected during their seasonal spawning aggregations in shallow water.

The Beginnings of Agriculture in the Middle and Late Archaic

Cultivation – defined here as intentional propagation of seeds (sometimes outside their natural ranges) without clear evidence of morphological or genetic change from the wild forms – may have begun with a native, gourdy **squash** as early as 6000 BC. AMS radiocarbon-dated *Cucurbita pepo* rind fragments from the Koster site in Illinois [see box: Koster] date to 6000 BC, and specimens from central Maine and northern Pennsylvania to 4500–3000 BC. Excavators and paleoethnobotanists who worked at these sites and analyzed the plant remains (Asch 1994; Asch Sidell 1999; Hart and Asch Sidell 1997) believe the most likely scenario for the presence and status of *Cucurbita* is that native gourds were obtained, probably by trade, from their natural range along the Gulf of Mexico and grown by mid-Holocene hunter-gatherers in the Midwest and Northeast.

An important early use, and the impetus for exchange and spread of this plant, was possibly for fishnet floats. The fruits could have been put to many other uses as well, including rattles, small containers, spoons and ladles, and of course food (seeds and flowers). Preferences for small, fist- or softball-sized, buoyant gourds to be used by net fishers would explain why seeds stayed small and rind remained thin. This changed later, when larger, heavier pepo gourds were bred for use as bowls.

At about 2500 BC, we do see larger-than-wild seeds from the **Phillips Spring** site in Missouri (King 1985). This represents a shift from casual cultivation of weedy little gourds with self-propagating tendencies to domestication of eastern squashes. Fruits could be used as containers if left to harden on the vine past the state of maturity, but some varieties became succulent, with non-bitter flesh and larger seeds requiring less processing to free them of bitter membranes. Modern summer squash varieties, including acorn, yellow crookneck, and scallop or pattypan, had their beginnings here, as did most of the small ornamental gourds that Americans north of Mexico buy at Halloween and Thanksgiving time. The Phillips Spring site also yielded bottle gourd seeds in 4500-year-old deposits, documenting the spread of a second container crop into the interior Eastern Woodlands (a vast expanse of deciduous forest east of the Great Plains stretching to the Atlantic coast and extending from the Canadian border to the Carolinas).

At least three native seed-bearing plants – sunflower, sumpweed, and chenopod – were modified during the Middle and Late Archaic to the point at which they could no longer reproduce without human aid. The first two underwent selection for much larger seeds, whereas seeds of the third were transformed through dramatic reduction in seed coat thickness. Other changes, such as monocephaly (having only a

KEY SITE Koster: An Archaic Camp in Illinois

Koster is a deeply stratified, open Archaic site at the base of a bluff on the eastern edge of the lower Illinois River floodplain, 41 km (25 miles) above the junction of the Illinois with the Mississippi (Brown and Vierra 1983).

Residential and Base Camps
The remains of a series of residential camps (as opposed to extractive or base camps) characterize the Early and early Middle Archaic strata at Koster. Extractive camps are places where a few people spent a short time performing some special task or set of tasks, whereas residential camps are locales where many people were present, engaged in a wider variety of activities.

Base camps appear in the later Middle Archaic levels at the site, where the whole population was living for extended periods and carrying out all the domestic activities necessary for long-term occupation. Remains of house platforms about 5 x 4.5 m (16 x 14 ft) in extent served as the foundations for rectangular structures with hearths. No walls

were preserved, but deep postholes indicated where they had once stood.

Numerous pits or basins for storage and food preparation (e.g. steaming of mussels and meat roasting) were also recorded.

Burials
A number of human burials were found in what the excavators think were specific burial plots within the last Middle Archaic horizon. Human burials were also present in Early Archaic levels, as well as the interments of five dogs; dated to 6500 BC, the latter are among the earliest dogs so far documented in eastern North America [see box: The Archaic Dog, p. 326].

Fishing and Fowling
The Koster archaeologists devoted an immense effort to the retrieval and analysis of plant and animal remains from the cultural deposits. It is clear that in addition to fishing the main river channel, the Middle Archaic people were obtaining large quantities of fish

from shallow lakes and swamps that seasonally occupied cut-off meanders and depressions in the floodplain between their village and the main river channel. These same wetland locales furnished seasonally abundant waterfowl (e.g. ducks and geese) that migrated twice annually along the Mississippi River flyway (an established route for migratory birds).

Hunting and Harvesting
Deer and other mammals, as well as several kinds of important plant foods, were collected from both floodplain and upland. In the uplands, hickory nuts were especially intensively harvested, and probably made into hickory oil and storable nutmeat products. Seeds from a number of herbaceous plants were also collected, and it is possible that the Middle Archaic people of Koster were tending vines that produced a gourdlike form of squash (*Cucurbita pepo* ssp. *ovifera*) with highly nutritious seeds, the shells of which could have served as net floats, rattles, and

single flower, as in the case of the sunflower), larger, more compact inflorescences (a clustering of blossoms along a stem), and the loss of natural shattering mechanisms (in the case of chenopod) accompanied changes in seed size and seed coat thickness.

Sunflower (*Helianthus annuus* var. *macrocarpus*) and sumpweed or marshelder (*Iva annua* var. *macrocarpa*) were domesticated in eastern North America *c.* 2500 BC, the same time that evidence appears for morphological change in pepo gourds. In addition to being eaten in various ways, the oil from the seeds of both may also have been used cosmetically on hair and skin, as sunflower oil was used historically. Domestication of sunflower and **sumpweed** is signaled by significant increase in size of the achene (seed surrounded by hard, dry fruit coat, or shell) (Heiser 1985; Yarnell 1978).

Native **chenopod**, or goosefoot (*Chenopodium berlandieri* ssp. *jonesianum*), was brought into the domestic sphere after 2000 BC, as shown by reduction in seed coat thickness. By 1300 BC, deposition along with cultigen-sized sunflower, sumpweed, and squash seeds is documented in storage contexts (Fritz 1997; Fritz and Smith 1988). Shortly thereafter, a buckwheat-

like seed plant, **erect knotweed** (*Polygonum erectum*), was also being stored, and may well have entered into a co-evolutionary relationship with people, eventually triggering an increase in average seed size and reduction in fruit coat thickness (Lopinot et al. 1991). An early-season grass called **maygrass** (*Phalaris caroliniana*) joins this eastern North American agricultural complex during the 1st millennium BC as a seed type occurring outside its modern natural range and found in storage contexts along with known domesticates.

The economic importance of these indigenous crops is difficult, if not impossible, to determine. Societies in different parts of the Eastern Woodlands clearly participated in pre-maize food production, or chose not to, in varying ways and to various extents. The mid-latitudinal zone south of the Great Lakes, north of the Gulf Coast plain, and west of the Appalachian Mountains was where the best-developed early agriculture took place. The Salts Cave paleofecal assemblage (see below) attests to heavy consumption of domesticated and cultivated seeds during the mid-1st millennium BC by Kentucky cavers and probably, by extension, the general Early Woodland population of that upland region (Yarnell 1969; 1974a; 1974b).

containers (Asch 1994; Fritz 1999). Two fragments of charred squash rind fragments have been AMS radiocarbon-dated to *c.* 6000 BC. These pepo gourds would have been an attractive resource, whether collected from wild populations (Decker-Walters et al. 1993; Smith et al. 2003), cultivated in small gardens next to houses, or simply encouraged when found growing spontaneously near the village.

Overview

Brown and Vierra (1983) emphasize that the evidence from Koster shows increasing commitment to seasonal sedentism, which is apparent well before the end of the Middle Archaic. They attribute this development to the rich resources of the mid-Holocene Illinois River floodplain that were not available in the early Holocene, when the river was adjusting to dramatic post-Pleistocene shifts in climate as the ice sheets melted and withdrew to the north.

9.18 *Excavation underway at the deeply stratified Koster site in west central Illinois. Archaeologists recovered a rich array of plant and animal remains enabling unusually detailed understanding of Archaic economic activities along the lower Illinois River over a span of several millennia.*

KEY DISCOVERY The Archaic Dog

Indigenous wild turkeys were domesticated prehistorically in what is now the Southwestern United States, and indigenous camelids, guinea pigs, and muscovy ducks were domesticated prehistorically in the Andes; but the only domesticated animal ubiquitously present in the Americas – the dog – is descended from Old World wolves, and accompanied those human groups who first peopled the Americas (Leonard et al. 2002).

The oldest archaeological remains of dogs currently known in the Americas date to the Early and Middle Archaic periods at Danger Cave in Utah (8000–7000 BC), Koster in Illinois (c. 6500 BC), and Dust Cave, Alabama (6000–5000 BC). The best-known early canine populations, however, are those of the Green River Archaic sites in Kentucky (c.

5000–1200 BC), where 178 were excavated in the 1930s from eight shell mounds and midden mounds. The Archaic dogs were sometimes buried with humans, but more often were placed in their own grave pits. One dog burial from the site of Indian Knoll is a pregnant female with three puppies *in utero* (Marquardt and Watson eds. 2005). Vertebral evidence on one of the Dust Cave dogs (from Middle Archaic deposits, c. 6000–5000 BC) suggests that this animal may have habitually pulled baggage loaded onto a wooden drag-frame (a travois) attached to its neck and shoulders, like the historically known Plains Indian dogs (Walker and Morey 2002). Pending further careful osteological analyses on other prehistoric canine skeleton remains, archaeologists tend to see Archaic dogs in eastern North America as companions, watch

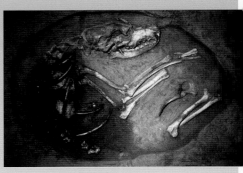

9.19 *Dog burial at an Archaic shell mound on the Green River in Kentucky. Ancestors of these Archaic dogs evolved in the Old World and accompanied early human migrants into North America. Dogs of the Late Archaic period in Kentucky and Tennessee were apparently valued companions in life; at death they were accorded their own individual graves in the same places where humans were buried.*

dogs, and perhaps aids in hunting. There is very little evidence that they were eaten.

Late Archaic Sites and Lifeways

As discussed in more detail above, several indigenous plants were first purposefully cultivated by Archaic peoples of eastern North America beginning at least as early as 2500 BC, during the Late Archaic period, and possibly as early as 6000 BC, in the Middle Archaic. The following is a sampling of the sites that provide evidence for early agriculture, as well as contemporary ones that do not.

Bacon Bend and Iddins, Tennessee Possible cultivated plants are reported from these two floodplain sites on the Little Tennessee River (Chapman 1994; Chapman and Shea 1981). Small fragments of charred squash rind as well as charred maygrass seeds found at the Bacon Bend site date to about 2400 BC. At the Iddins site, domestic sunflower and sumpweed were recovered from Late Archaic deposits, as were charred rinds of hard-walled gourdlike squash and bottle gourd.

In addition to macrobotanical evidence for increasing diversity and abundance of cultigens, palynological data (i.e., from pollen grains and spores) indicate forest clearance, presumably by people creating fields and gardens, at some places in Tennessee and Kentucky (Chapman et al. 1982; Delcourt et al. 1998).

The Carlston Annis Shell Mound in West Central Kentucky, and the Rockshelters of Arkansas and Eastern Kentucky Between 5000 and 1000 BC, hunter-gatherer populations living along the middle reaches of a tributary to the Ohio, the Green River of west-cen-

tral Kentucky, were gathering seasonally, spring to autumn, at shallow-water locales where mussels and other aquatic fauna were readily available, and where fish traps and weirs could be constructed and maintained. These semi-sedentary communities, known to archaeologists as the **Green River Archaic people**, were long-lived and had established far-ranging networks throughout mid-continental North America. They imported marine shell (whelk or conch) from the Gulf of Mexico and from waters off the southeast coast of North America, and copper and furs from sources in northern Michigan. These Late Archaic Green River societies seem to have been basically egalitarian, but, at least occasionally, some individuals engaged in raiding or warfare, and others were buried with relatively large quantities of the exotic items mentioned above (especially imported marine shell); many were laid away with no grave goods at all.

One Green River Archaic site, the **Carlston Annis** shell mound [9.20], has provided specific information about plant use (Crawford 1982; Marquardt and Watson 1983; Marquardt and Watson 2005). The Carlston Annis people made use of numerous riverine and forest foods, but at least while living at the shell mound, they were not using cultivated plants other than perhaps *Cucurbita pepo* ssp. *ovifera* (the small-fruited, gourdlike squash referred to above). There are hints of domesticated chenopod at rockshelter sites in the uplands away from the river, however, and the key sites elsewhere in the mid-South with evidence for early, domesticated, small-seeded plants are all rockshelters:

Cold Oak, **Cloudsplitter**, and **Newt Kash** in eastern Kentucky, and **Marble Bluff** in northwestern Arkansas (Fritz 1990; Gremillion 2002). The earliest farmers in these places lived seasonally in rockshelters, also using some of them as storage places for the harvests gleaned from fields on small streamside terraces, from the floors of coves and hollows, and from the lower slopes of hillsides above these (Fritz 1994; 1997).

Horr's Island, Florida In several regions of the Southeast, Middle and Late Archaic peoples created ritual earthworks [see box: Watson Brake and Poverty Point, Louisiana, pp. 328–29]. At one or two locales in Florida, they also built ritual mounds of sand and shell (Russo 1996). Horr's Island is one such locale, a sand dune on the Gulf of Mexico south of Fort Myers, Florida, which rises above the surrounding coastal mangrove forest. The site atop the dune includes a large accumulation of occupational debris partially surrounded by 7–9-m (23–30-ft) high artificially constructed shell ridges, which serve as substrates for several mounds varying in height from 1 to 6 m (3.3–20 ft). Present evidence indicates that the mounds were built *c.* 3000–2000 BC by relatively sedentary Middle and Late Archaic hunter-gatherers living in villages on the dune. The mounds do not seem to have been created primarily for mortuary purposes, but are thought to have been centers for ceremony and ritual, serving also as territorial markers.

The Earliest Pottery Dating to *c.* 2500 BC, the earliest fragments of **fired clay pots** in eastern North America, tempered with plant fibers such as Spanish moss and grass to prevent excessive shrinking and cracking during manufacture, are found on the coasts of Georgia and South Carolina and in the Stallings Island region of the Savannah River in the South Carolina piedmont (Sassaman 2002). Initially, pots were plain, but linear punctate (points or dots) designs were added by 2000 BC. Shallow, open bowls (the earliest forms) were probably used for cooking by the millennia-old indirect-heat method of dropping hot stones into a liquid, i.e., "stone boiling."

Foods processed this way might include hickory nut soup or "milk" (the dissolved, fatty nutmeats), steamed mussels, and marrow from large mammal bones. Coastal people seem to have switched early to direct heat (placing narrower ceramic bowls or jars over fire), possibly due to a scarcity of stone. By 1000 BC, people across the Eastern Woodlands were making and using pottery sturdy enough to withstand direct heat. It is

9.20 *Carlston Annis shell mound: situated on the Green River in Kentucky, the site is shown under excavation by federally funded work crews in 1940–41. Several such large, late Middle/Late Archaic shell mounds were investigated in the years just prior to World War II, and continue to yield detailed information about the seasonally sedentary fisher-hunter-gatherers who created them.*

significant that the earliest (Late Archaic) ceramic traditions of the Southeast are not correlated geographically with starchy seed crop production, but rather occur in regions where hunter-gatherers were becoming more efficient harvesters and processors of wild plants and animals.

Early Woodland Period, c. 1000–200 BC

By *c.* 1000 BC, the Eastern Agricultural Complex discussed above is evidenced in several regions of the Midwest and mid-South (Arkansas, Kentucky, and Tennessee) at rockshelters and open sites (Fritz 1990; Gremillion 2002). Beginning around 800 BC, Early Woodland cave explorers and miners left a marvelously detailed record of their diet in the dry passageways of **Salts Cave** [9.23] and **Mammoth Cave**, parts of the Mammoth Cave system in western Kentucky.

Thousands of human paleofecal deposits are perfectly preserved throughout the roughly 24–32 km (15–20 miles) of cave passages explored and mined between 800 and 300 BC (Crothers et al. 2002; Watson 1969; 1974; Yarnell 1969; 1974a; 1974b). These, together with stratified archaeobotanical remains from the entry chamber of Salts Cave, provide the most detailed documentation of an ancient agricultural complex known anywhere in the Americas.

The Early Woodland cavers were growing all the crops – chenopod, sunflower, sumpweed, maygrass, gourdlike squash, and bottle gourd – that we have seen first evidenced in Arkansas, eastern Kentucky, and Tennessee rockshelters and open sites, and they were also eating large quantities of hickory nuts, as well as a variety of other plant foods from the forest. It is possible that they and Early Woodland groups elsewhere in eastern North America were managing portions of the forest to promote abundant nut masts and robust stands of plants that provided medicine, fiber, and other desirable commodities, in addition to food.

KEY SITES Watson Brake and Poverty Point, Louisiana

The massive Poverty Point earthworks in northeast Louisiana (Gibson 2000) have puzzled archaeologists for years as monuments built on an unprecedented scale at a time (*c.* 1700–1200 BC) when most of eastern North America was occupied by non-mound-building foragers or their counterparts in initial stages of food production. Early suspicions that Poverty Point was constructed due to direct influence or even colonization by Mesoamerican maize farmers have been discounted. Long-distance trade was actively conducted by those who congregated at Poverty Point, but exotic artifacts and raw material such as galena, copper, chert, and steatite came from elsewhere in North America, rather than Mexico.

Watson Brake

A major recent development in North American archaeology is the recognition that construction of mounds and ridge-type embankments began more than 6000 years ago. Eight mound sites in the lower Mississippi River valley are now accepted as pre-dating Poverty Point, with Watson Brake (located 92 km (55 miles) southwest of Poverty Point) being one of the oldest, largest, and best studied (Saunders et al. 1997).

9.21 *(Left) Aerial view of Poverty Point, looking north, with remnants of the concentric ridges visible to the left and Bayou Macon to the right. Mound A is hidden in the trees near the left side of the photo.*

9.22 *(Right) Plan of the Poverty Point ridge-and-mound complex.*

9.23 Salts Cave: *a large passage in Salts Cave, Mammoth Cave National Park, Kentucky. Salts Cave and Mammoth Cave were extensively explored and mined for naturally occurring minerals (gypsum and medicinal sulphates) between 800 and 300 BC. The dry cave passages preserve a richly detailed record of the early agricultural complex created and maintained by these Early Woodland cavers and farmers.*

About 4000 BC, 11 mounds were built here around a circular, plaza-like area 280 m (900 ft) in diameter. An artificial ridge about 1 m (3.3 ft) high connects some of the mounds. The tallest is 7 m (22.8 ft) high and 165 m (536 ft) in diameter, and the others vary between 1 m (3.3 ft) and 4.5 m (14.6 ft) in height. Fish bones reflect use of nearby rivers and streams, and remains of deer, turkey, small mammals, turtles, mussels, and aquatic snails were also found, along with pecans, acorns, and wild seeds.

The Enigma of the Earthworks

We can only guess why the earthworks at Watson Brake and other Middle and early Late Archaic mounds in Louisiana – some large and elaborate, others consisting only of a few, relatively small mounds – were constructed. Mortuary functions seem unlikely, given the absence, so far, of burials. Evidence of trade is not extensive, but the prominence of micro-drills and stone beads foreshadows the elaborate Poverty Point lapidary industry to come. Whatever religious, economic, or social motivations brought people together to work and share food at Watson Brake, the mounds testify to the significance of this place on the cultural landscape.

Poverty Point

The Poverty Point phenomenon becomes far less enigmatic when seen in the perspective of this longer-term tradition of mound building in the lower Mississippi Valley. The scale, however, is more massive than before. There are six concentric semicircular ridges at Poverty Point, with a maximum diameter of 1.2 km (0.7 mile), following the west bank of Bayou Macon. As many as five aisles radiated through the ridges. The enormous Mound A is about 21.5 m (70 ft) tall, and four smaller mounds are located within or just outside the plaza-like area formed by the ridges. Competing views of social organization, population size, and duration of occupational episodes continue to be debated. Some see Poverty Point as a sizable town that was occupied year-round and possibly led by powerful chiefs, whereas others suggest that a small caretaker population was augmented periodically during trade fairs, where participants also negotiated social contracts of various kinds and took part in rituals (Gibson 2000; Jackson 1989).

Trade goods were brought to Poverty Point from up to 1100 km (660 miles) away. Exotic stone was worked into beautiful polished beads, pendants, plummets (weights), and other tools. Although archaeologists will probably disagree for some time about the level of socio-political complexity, subsistence at Poverty Point is clearly nonagricultural.

The Late Archaic hunter-gatherers in this resource-rich region continued the tradition of mound building begun by their predecessors at Watson Brake, and they passed it on to generations who followed them.

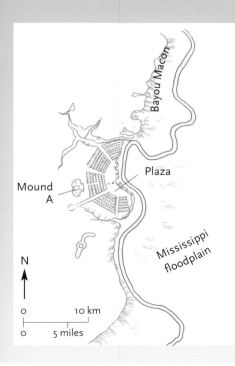

Bayou Macon

Plaza

Mound A

N

Mississippi floodplain

0 ——— 10 km
0 ——— 5 miles

Later Agricultural Developments

Middle Woodland (*c.* 200 BC–AD 400) peoples in Illinois, Ohio, Tennessee, Kentucky, and Arkansas left behind numerous crop seeds in middens, refuse pits, and storage rockshelters. At the same time, however, archaeobotanical remains in most of the Deep South, Great Lakes region, Northeast, and Atlantic seaboard reflect little interest in farming. Reasons for this stark regional variation may involve biogeographical factors such as higher productivity or predictability of native plants in the South, historical contingencies, and climatic conditions, the key one being a shorter growing season and consequent greater need for storable commodities in the Midwest (Gremillion 2002).

The spread and eventual intensified production of **maize** in eastern North America are topics of great interest, due to the later dominance of maize in some Native American diets and the significance this food has had on Euroamerican and global economies. Early eastern North American maize apparently came across the Great Plains from the Southwest (Doebley et al. 1986), and current evidence documents the presence of small amounts of maize at a handful of sites beginning about 2000 years ago (Riley et al. 1994; Crawford et al. 1997). The earliest securely dated maize in eastern North America dates to between AD 1 and 400 and comes from sites in Illinois, Ohio, and Tennessee whose occupants were already engaged in the production of native crops such as chenopod, sunflower, and maygrass. It appears that the new crop was added to the already flourishing Eastern Agricultural Complex without making much of an impact. Slightly higher frequencies of maize have come from sites in the Midwest, the Ozark highlands, and the Arkansas River valley, dating to approximately AD 400–800 (Hart 1999), but counts stay modest overall, and stable carbon isotope evidence from human bones indicates minor contribution of maize to the diet (Lynott et al. 1986). (For an explanation of this method of determining ancient dietary habits, see Chapter 2.) Maize spread into southern Ontario at this time, marking the earliest evidence recovered so far for transition to agriculture by previously non-food-producing people in this region.

The 9th and 10th centuries AD witnessed intensified output in Illinois, as revealed by the rapid rise of maize's contribution to all archaeobotanical indices at sites in the American Bottom area (the floodplain of the Mississippi River in Illinois opposite St. Louis, Missouri), where the Cahokia chiefdom would soon arise (Chapter 18). By AD 900, maize was an established part of the farming system, along with the pre-maize native crops that were seemingly also grown in greater quantities to feed the expanding population of Cahokia and surrounding mound centers (Lopinot 1994; 1997).

At about this time (AD 900–1100), hunter-gatherers to the south and east of the pre-maize farming zone described above adopted maize. This shift seems to be correlated, for the most part, with increasing socio-political complexity and the rise of Mississippian chiefdoms across the Southeast, as discussed in Chapter 18. Recent research reveals that unlike the situation in Mexico, **beans** did not accompany maize during its initial entry into eastern North America *c.* AD 100, where the earliest secure date on beans is AD 1200 (Hart et al. 2002). This is notable because it severs the nutritional link (in which beans augment the low available protein component of maize) assumed to characterize the earliest maize diet in this region. Maize, beans, and squash eventually became the Three Sisters, a Native American agricultural trinity, but their early trajectories in eastern North America were quite distinct.

Tobacco Discussion of early agriculture in eastern North America is incomplete without mentioning tobacco, an important crop that was ethnographically unique by virtue of its uses (ceremonial, spiritual, and medicinal) as well as its primary tenders (men). Tobacco seeds from Illinois dating to the very early 1st millennium AD demonstrate that a species of *Nicotiana* had reached the Midwest by that time, although most researchers infer from the earlier presence of pipes that it might have already been there for centuries (Asch 1994; Wagner 2000). All pre-Columbian eastern tobacco has long been assumed to be *N. rustica*, the species documented by Europeans when they reached the east coast of the continent; it would have spread up from a South American homeland. Archaeobotanists are now considering the possibility that a species native to California and Oregon – *N. bigellovii* – was the earliest tobacco in the Mississippi River valley. The ancient seeds that have been found share morphological characteristics with that species, and it was the type grown by Siouan speakers of the upper Missouri River region in historic times. The archaeological evidence also favors a spread from west to east, beginning at the confluence of the Missouri and Mississippi rivers. *Nicotiana rustica* might, then, have been introduced along the Atlantic seaboard or Gulf Coast during late pre-contact or very early proto-historic times. This is one of many currently unresolved issues in the general study of eastern North American agriculture.

Western North America: Alternatives to Agriculture

In the western portion of North America – **the Great Plains, the Great Basin, California**, and **the Northwest Coast** – sophisticated and effective means of gathering and collecting a wide array of plants were developed by human populations moving seasonally within well-established territories. They used dozens of different plants as food, medicine, elements for houses and other structures, and as sources of fibers for the manufacture of baskets, bags, cordage, nets, and snares. Some of these plant species were encouraged, propagated, and cultivated, but agricultural practices based on domesticated crops were not embraced. Early inhabitants of western North America also successfully hunted a variety of wild animals, from rabbits and other rodents to antelope, deer, and – at higher elevations – mountain goats and bighorn sheep. By Late Archaic times, they were skillfully managing the landscape itself, fire being especially important in this process.

California and the Pacific Northwest are especially interesting because of the sedentary, ranked societies that later evolved. These complex polities were supported by fishing, hunting, trading, and harvesting plants from ecosystems carefully managed by fire and other methods to increase productivity. In California, acorns, fruits, and seeds constituted the primary carbohydrate sources, whereas bulbs and tubers such as the camas lily balanced diets rich in salmon and other seafood for people living between Oregon and southeastern Alaska. The beginnings of classic, far western subsistence patterns are detectable archaeologically after 3500 BC, when sea levels stabilized and rainfall increased, following the mid-Holocene dry spell. Clear manifestations of hierarchical ranking, sedentism, and associated territorial competition and conflict, however, are phenomena that postdate 1300 BC in California. This chapter focuses on regions where food production developed, but it is important to recognize the persistence of non-agricultural societies along the Pacific coast, some of which had higher population densities and more stratified social systems than their counterparts who farmed the land.

Great Plains Bison Hunting

Sustained hunting of the American **bison** on the Great Plains began during the Late Paleoindian period (see above). The hunting pattern that emerged during this period and continued in subsequent Early Archaic times focused on the need for provisioning small bands of people throughout the winter season; thus, most large-scale kills seem to have occurred in the autumn. The climate at that period was colder and wetter than today, and the Great Plains had much harsher winters, necessitating a good winter food supply but also, serendipitously, providing the conditions for natural storage of the meat. The large number of animals ambushed in arroyos or driven off cliffs appear to have been quickly frozen and covered with snow, leaving a deep-freeze storage of bison that could be dug out and butchered throughout the winter as needed.

These sites are imposing, and tend to leave the impression that the populations survived by bison meat alone. At the spring-to-summer Early Archaic site of **Barton Gulch**, Montana, however, there is not a single bison bone. Here the people focused on gathering plants and taking small game. Plant remains come from 36 species; animal remains emphasize

smaller mammals such as rabbit, porcupine, and deer. The Early Archaic populations were exploiting all the resources available to them; bison were critical to their winter survival, but were not a year-round staple.

During the Middle Archaic, the environmental conditions varied, but were on average hotter and drier than in recent times. Grasses died back dramatically and were replaced by cactus, thorny bushes, and other unpalatable plants. Bison numbers dropped radically, and human populations depending on them for winter survival were forced to develop new options. Some may have moved to adjacent refuge regions, like the foothills of the Rocky Mountains, where groups developed new hunting strategies, such as the use of large nets to trap mountain goats and mountain sheep, and became successful at taking pronghorn antelope, deer, and elk to replace bison. Other groups remained on the Great Plains, expanded their diet, working their way down the food chain to incorporate more drought-tolerant species. In the far southern plains, at places like **Clovis** and **Mustang Springs**, the foragers dug water wells. Populations redistributed themselves on the landscape during this period, but while there was some local abandonment at certain times or places, it was not a Plains-wide phenomenon (Meltzer 1999).

The Late Archaic period on the Great Plains is marked by a shift back to more modern climate conditions; with increased moisture, bison populations once again grew rapidly, and people shifted back to communal bison hunting. This is the time of elaborate bison jumps, such as **Head-Smashed-In**, Alberta [**9.24**, **9.25**], where more than 125,000 buffalo remains, from innumerable hunts during the last several millennia, have so far been recorded. Bison jumps and ambushes in box canyons and dune traps, which had been practiced in the Early Archaic, were revived in the Late Archaic, but some groups added a new strategy: the bison pound, where animals could be trapped, and then killed as needed over an extended period, thus avoiding the spoilage problems associated with killing a large number all at once in warm weather. A new housing type is also developed at this time, the tipi or teepee, and the creation of large rock-ground constructions known as medicine wheels or sun circles began. These latter consisted of large stone outline constructions, of varying complexity, with astronomical, religious, locational, and other functions. In later times some may also have been the locations of the Lakota Indian sun dances.

The Pacific Northwest Maritime Cultures

The Early Archaic period on the Northwest Coast was a period of experimentation and development of an economy based heavily upon marine resources. Evidence from sites such as **Anangula** in Alaska, and **Namu** in British Columbia, indicates that line-fishing and sea-mammal hunting developed first, and

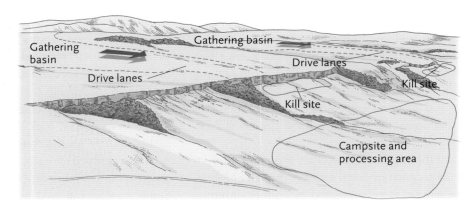

9.24, 9.25 *Head-Smashed-In bison jump site: at this communal, ambush-hunting bison jump, on the high plains of Alberta, large numbers of bison were driven over the cliffs, typically in the autumn for winter provisions. (Below) Some of the thousands of buffalo skulls recovered from the site.*

that concerted exploitation of shellfish, and fishing with nets and weirs, may not have evolved until the Middle Archaic period. Predictable access to maritime resources, which came about with essential sea-level stability around 6500 BC, appears to have been critical in the establishment of sustainable maritime exploitation techniques. The abundance of marine resources, brought about in part by the Japanese Current, and their year-around predictability, led to very early long-term demographic stability on the Northwest Coast. Elite social status markers such as labrets (lip or cheek plugs) and cranial deformation (cranial shaping or modeling), as well as fancy anthropomorphic and zoomorphic art objects, are present as early as 4000 BC. At about this time, cedar trees recolonized much of the coastal area. They were an essential resource for the canoes and longhouses that characterize the activities of the ethnic groups here, as well as for the woodworking and fishing industries.

Competition over control of resources led to nearly endemic **warfare** by 2500 BC in the northern half of the coastal area, apparently spreading to southern areas somewhat later. Archaeologists have recovered evidence of specialized regional economies by this date as well: fishermen in the Puget Sound area organized into highly cooperative gill-net sea fishing groups; peoples living on the Fraser, Skagit, Snohomish,

Columbia, and other large coastal rivers specialized in individual salmon fishing at weirs; and groups on the Olympic Peninsula focused on deep-sea hook-and-line fishing, and on whaling. Because of the seemingly incessant rains along the Northwest Coast, groups developed tribal styles of woven rain hats. Mudslides have preserved some examples (such as at the Hoko River and Ozette sites in Washington; see Ozette box, Chapter 18, p. 709), allowing researchers to marvel at the long-term stability of archaeological cultures. While the gear varies distinctly from one group to another, many styles remain relatively unchanged in specific locations over many centuries. The cultural roots of institutions such as slavery and the potlatch, which are so well known in more recent Northwest Coast culture studies, are clearly founded at this period.

The Great Basin Desert Archaic

West of the Rocky Mountains, the Great Basin (south-central Oregon, Nevada, Utah, and eastern California) was cooler and wetter during the early Holocene than later. There were mountain glaciers in the Sierra Nevada and Cascade ranges, and numerous pluvial (rain-filled) lakes in Great Basin valleys that later became arid deserts. There is considerable variation in the archaeological records for these far western locales, but for illustrative purposes we focus on two sites in the Great Basin: **Hogup Cave** and **Danger Cave**, both at the western edge of the Great Salt Desert, which lies west of Great Salt Lake.

The Desert Archaic begins about 7000 BC and is best known from rockshelters and caves such as Danger Cave, which overlooked shallow lakes and marshes. Hogup Cave is one of the few sites providing detailed environmental information, but both Hogup and Danger caves preserved abundant evidence of human activities spanning many millennia: approximately 8000 BC–AD 1400 for Danger Cave, and 7000 BC–AD 1400 for Hogup. Both caves overlooked salt flats containing salt marshes interspersed with small lakes, whence came the waterfowl and shorebirds whose remains are abundant in the archaeological deposits. The seeds of pickleweed, a plant native to the salt flats, were a staple food at both caves.

The aridity of such rockshelters has resulted in the astonishing preservation of ordinarily perishable organic material [9.27–9.29]. Artifacts made of wood, hide, feathers, vegetable fiber, reeds, bulrushes, and willow withies are abundant. In another Great Basin Archaic site, **Fort Rock Cave** in southern Oregon, several dozen sandals made of sagebrush bark fiber were found. A fragment of one of them was radiocarbon-dated in 1949 by Willard Libby, inventor of the radiocarbon dating technique: it was 9053 ± 350 years old. Large fragments of fiber cordage, baskets, open-twined cloth, nets, and wooden darts for atlatl-propelled spears enable detailed knowledge of a technology of raw material procurement and processing so successful that much of it was still in use in the western Great Basin until 150 to 200 years ago, as demonstrated by archaeological sequences in two other dry rockshelters – **Lovelock** and **Humboldt** – in west-central Nevada. Cultural deposits in these caves began *c.* 2500 BC. Tools and weapons common to both include twined and coiled baskets, nets, mats, cordage, skin and hide (including fragmentary moccasins), cloth, fire drills, and dart shafts.

The Archaic Period in California

Clovis points have been found in many parts of California, and direct dates on human bone from Santa Rosa Island show that the southern coast was occupied by 11,000 BC. Most of California's Paleoindian sites, however, are located near ancient interior lakebeds that dried up at the end of the Pleistocene, at the same time that mammoth and other megafauna disappear. Early Archaic hunters then broadened their subsistence base to include deer, pronghorn antelope, mountain sheep, hares, and rabbits. Bone awls and needles from 9000-year-old occupations are the first signs of the amazing **basketry tradition** that

native Californians developed into a fine art (Chartkoff and Chartkoff 1984). Coastal people in southern California began harvesting **shellfish** and hunting **marine mammals** during the Middle Archaic. At the same time, milling slabs (ground-stone tools for crushing seeds) appear in sites near the coast, documenting wider use of plant resources. Formal burials signify longer-term occupation of camps, although bands continued to migrate seasonally, taking advantage of California's diverse environmental zones.

By 4500 BC, in the Late Archaic, stone mortars and pestles were being used to process acorns and other nuts. Archaeologists infer that toxic tannins were being leached from acorns to render them edible, making California's oak savannas productive for harvesting and management. **Salmon fishing** also became a significant activity, and settlements expanded into coniferous zones that had not been much utilized in the past. The **Windmiller Tradition** was the earliest permanent occupation of the central California Delta region, and occupations appeared for the first time in the northern Sierra Nevadas, the southern Cascades, and the northwestern part of the state. Population growth is indicated by the geographical spread and more substantial nature of base camp occupations overall, but seasonal movements continued. The typical coastal round consisted of winter camps near the beach and summer camps in interior hills and valleys, while bands wintering at low elevations in base camps in central California moved to higher elevations for spring and summer.

9.26–9.29 *Artifacts of the Desert Archaic: mano and metate (top right), skein, and net from Danger Cave, Utah (below left and center), and a sandal from Fort Rock Cave, Oregon (below right). Dry rockshelters in the Great Basin of Utah, Nevada, and eastern Washington and Oregon preserve many such remarkable items of ancient technologies dating back to 9000–10,000 BC.*

Late Archaic cemeteries include burials with grave goods, mostly tools for hunting and plant processing, but also including marine shell ornaments that sometimes came from more than 160 km (100 miles) away. Steatite, obsidian, and other stone objects were also transported across the state, but in relatively modest amounts. Exchange patterns had commenced, but archaeologists find no clear evidence for status differentiation until later. Specialists who presided over religious ceremonies and healed the sick are manifested by the end of the Californian Archaic (2000 BC) by the presence of charmstones, quartz crystals, and other objects used by shamans into post-contact times. Over a period of 7000 years, the economic and ideological foundations for California's complex non-agriculturalists had been built.

The South American Pacific Lowlands

The Isthmus of Panama acted as a "bottleneck" through which peoples and ideas had to pass, moving either south or north. Early Archaic sites here are small campsites left by hunter-gatherers – transient sites much like those remaining from Paleoindian occupations. There is apparent evidence for early management of the landscape by burning after 9000 BC. At later sites such as Aguadulce, Cueva de los Vampiros, and Cueva Ladrones, plant collecting and gathering may have been augmented by cultivating squashes, bottle gourd, leren (grown for its tuberous roots), and arrowroot (Piperno et al. 2000; Ranere and Cooke 2003). Here and in Colombia, tubers and roots were being processed using edge-ground cobbles on grinding slab bases.

The North Pacific Coast

The northern Pacific coastal areas of Colombia and Ecuador experience a temperature and precipitation regime different from coastal areas to the south. Consequently, rather than the sand dunes characteristic of the southern coastlines, there are tropical forests inland from the northern coast. Early Archaic evidence is scarce. The Middle Archaic habitation site of **Las Vegas** on the Guayaquil peninsula of Ecuador had a mixed terrestrial and maritime economy (Stothert 1988; 1992). The inhabitants hunted deer and peccaries, fished, collected shellfish, and gathered cactus fruits and algarroba (mesquite) pods (Richardson 1999). The resource base was apparently rich enough to support a semi-sedentary village of 25–50 people from 8000 to 4700 BC, when the site was abandoned with the onset of a long dry period. A recent reanalysis suggests the presence of leren, cultivated squash, and gourds; an earlier reported claim for maize apparently has been dropped (Piperno and Stothert 2003). John Staller (2003) argues that the earliest maize did not appear in Ecuador until 2200–1900 BC, and then

only as a ceremonial plant, and that it did not become a significant food item for another millennium.

During the Late Archaic there was a rapid growth of more complex society along the Colombian and Ecuadorian coasts. Sedentary villages developed, pottery was introduced, and there may have been an agricultural component as well as a strong maritime focus (especially shellfish collecting and fishing). The earliest ceramics, ranging from 4500 to 3500 BC, come from sites such as San Jacinto I, Monsu, Puerto Chaco, and Puerto Hormigo in Colombia, and Real Alto and Loma Alta in Ecuador. These sites are all characterized by large villages of elliptical huts, 2–3 m (7–10 ft) in diameter, arranged in two parallel sections. The Ecuadorian sites, which have been more recently and more completely investigated, also reveal evidence of ritual or ceremonial mound construction associated with villages. At **Real Alto** in the Chanduy Valley (c. 3800–3000 BC, based on calibrated radiocarbon dates and ceramic evidence), the village consisted of large, oval houses with mud-plastered walls and thatched, gabled roofs, presumably containing extended families, around a long rectangular plaza divided into two segments by two larger, ceremonial buildings: one used for feasting and beer drinking, the other a charnel house for the bones of the dead (Bruhns 1994; Dillehay 1992) [see Real Alto box, Chapter 17]. In some cases, these Late Archaic villages were occupied or re-occupied over hundreds of years; upper levels may thus produce radiocarbon dates as recent as 2500–2000 BC. Plant remains from these upper levels were sometimes mixed prehistorically with lower levels, resulting in some anomalously early reports for cultigens.

The Peruvian Coast

On the north coast of Peru, the Early Archaic culture is usually identified as the Paijan complex, defined by a series of sites in and near the Pampa de los Fósiles. The economy included collecting shellfish, fishing, and hunting terrestrial fauna. The earliest evidence for shellfish collecting has been dated to 10,200 BC in Talara, and 9600 BC in the Pampa de los Fósiles (Lynch 1999; Richardson 1999), but most sites date between 9500 and 7000 BC. The long, thin, Paijan-style projectile point is now thought to be a stone harpoon point, indicating exploitation of marine animals as well. The maritime economy was apparently not standardized, however, as some sites have shellfish and maritime animal remains, whereas other contemporary sites have abundant fish, but no shellfish remains (Chauchat 1988).

Maritime economies expanded and flourished during the Middle and Late Archaic periods in Peru. At **Nanchoc**, in the Zaña Valley, a few archaeologists claim evidence for early agriculture during the Middle Archaic period – a precocious fishing-farming symbiosis. Nanchoc has a pair of small flat-top

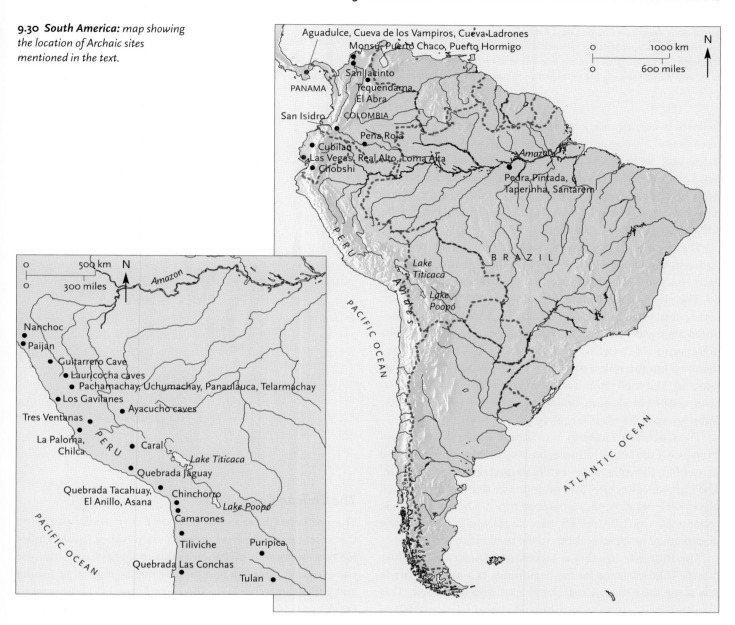

9.30 South America: *map showing the location of Archaic sites mentioned in the text.*

mounds, each *c.* 30–35 m (100–115 ft) long and 1.2–1.5 m (4–5 ft) high, defined in part by aligned stone facing. These are associated with a small ovoid hut, an area of lime processing (presumably for use in coca chewing), and nearby agricultural field furrows. Bottle gourd, squash, manioc, coca, peanuts, and a chenopod (assumed to be quinoa) were recovered in excavations. The mounds had a calibrated radiocarbon date of 5770 BC, leading the excavators to argue for an early farming economy, beginning in the 6th millennium BC (Rossen and Dillehay 2000; Rossen et al. 1996).

The problem here is similar to that at Tehuacán and Los Gavilanes: AMS radiocarbon dates on the actual plant specimens do not match dates for the rest of the deposits, suggesting a later disturbance of the site. For example, the direct AMS dates on the squash, peanut, and chenopod are no more than 200–300 years old. Thus we must separate the rather early mound construction at the site – not so unusual if we look at the Ecuadorian sites – from the agricultural plants, which clearly seem to be later intrusions.

The best evidence for development of maritime industries between 9000 and 7000 BC comes from the south coast of Peru, at locales such as the Ring Site, Quebrada Jaguay, and Quebrada Tacahuay. The **Ring Site** (also known as El Anillo) was 26 m (85 ft) in diameter and 2.5–8 m (8–25 ft) high. Although near the shore today, it would have been 5–7 km (3–5 miles) inland during the early Holocene. It is interpreted as a ring-shaped fishing village, where the inhabitants lived in houses around an interior circular plaza (Richardson 1999; Sandweiss et al. 1989). Shellfish made up the most abundant faunal remains; fish are the most numerous vertebrate animal,

335

9.31 South American Pacific Coast Archaic period fishing gear: *spear and throwing stick; composite harpoon with foreshaft; detachable foreshafts; composite fishing hooks and line; scaling and filleting stone tools; and a shell showing the manufacturing steps for a shell fishhook.*

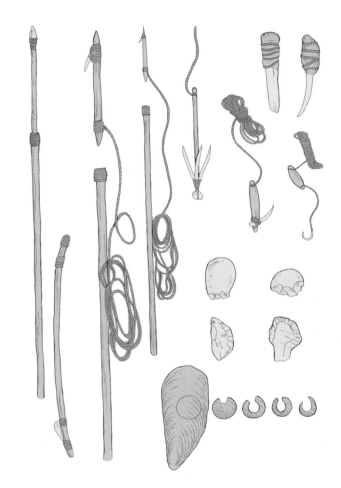

followed by cormorants, and then other birds. Although the site has a date of *c.* 9800 BC at its lowest levels, no tools were found in this unit, so there is no direct evidence of the earliest technology. The first good evidence for fishing (fishhooks) comes from 8500 BC. The main occupation levels date to 6500–4000 BC and have substantial evidence of hook-and-line fishing, but nets do not seem to have been employed.

The near-coast **Quebrada Jaguay** site, along the Rio Camana, would have been 8 km (5 miles) inland during the early Holocene. Human occupation may date as early as 11,300 BC. The site is a shell midden containing fish remains, with some possible fishnet and bottle gourd fragments perhaps associated after 9500 BC. Contact with the sierra, suggested by the presence of obsidian from the Alca source in Cotahuasi more than 100 km (62 miles) distant, may have occurred as early as 9500 BC. The shell mound also contained the remains of a circular semi-subterranean building *c.* 5 m (17 ft) in diameter (Moseley 2001; Sandweiss et al. 1998).

The **Quebrada Tacahuay** site dates to between 10,700 and 8500 BC. Of the faunal remains, birds were first and fish second in number; there are no land animals, and only a few shellfish. The number of anchovy present indicates that **net fishing** took place (Keefer et al. 1998; Richardson 1999). There was a single rectangular structure, rebuilt many times, and evidence of the placement of wrapped seabirds in the postholes as offerings.

The Ring Site, Quebrada Jaguay, and Quebrada Tacahuay provide solid evidence for the beginnings of a maritime tradition along the Peruvian coast by at least 9000–8000 BC. This maritime focus seems to have expanded after relative stabilization of sea levels *c.* 6000 BC, when net fishing became a dominant technique. Owing to the upwelling of nutrients from deep layers because of the Humboldt Current along the Pacific coast, fisheries in this zone are particularly productive.

The general model of maritime Peruvian Archaic cultures includes moderate reliance on fish during the Early Archaic, and increasing reliance on maritime resources, with use of specialized technology, during the Middle Archaic, when new technologies such as nets were integrated. By the Late Archaic, there was substantial specialization and intensification of maritime resource exploitation (Wise 1999). A perspective on the changing economies of the South Coast can be attained from looking at the Middle Archaic occupation of **La Paloma**, and the subsequent Late Archaic occupation of **Chilca**, only a short distance from La Paloma [see box: La Paloma and Chilca: Archaic Villages of the Peruvian Coast].

The Chilean Coast

The northern Chilean coast displays a very similar pattern to that of adjoining Peruvian areas. Lautaro Núñez (1998) argues for two modes of exploitation at this time: first, opportunistic use of coastal areas rich in resources, employing simple fishing and gathering technology; and second, use of more sophisticated hunting and fishing skills and tools, such as harpoons, fishhooks, rafts, and nets, to exploit resources beyond the intertidal zone. The early Holocene residents were semi-nomadic, relying upon both coastal and inland resources, as well as trading with highland residents to buffer food risk.

Typical of the Early Archaic northern Chilean coastal sites are **Tiliviche** (9000–8800 BC) and **Quebrada Las Conchas** (8800–8500 BC). Tiliviche was a semi-sedentary camp, where half the resources were marine and half terrestrial. At Quebrada Las Conchas, faunal remains include camelids and terrestrial animals, as well as the more abundant sea mammals, fish, and shellfish (Lynch 1999; Núñez 1998).

The northern Chilean Middle Archaic period is best known for the **Chinchorro** fishermen, who produced an elaborate mummy complex between 6000 and 1700 BC [see box: The Chinchorro Mummies, pp. 338–39]. Agustin Llagostera (1992) argues that the earlier Las Conchas and Tiliviche groups were no more than simple maritime gatherers, whereas the Chinchorro people were maritime specialists – the first true fishermen – with nets, fishhooks, and harpoons, who also collected shellfish, hunted sea lions, and butchered beached whales; bone chemistry analyses indicate that some 90 percent of the diet was marine-based (Moseley 2001). The Chinchorro lived in villages of small, circular cane-and-matting huts with stone foundations and plastered clay floors. Some of the adults from phases after 5500 BC exhibit auditory exostoses or aural osteomas, like those seen at La Paloma [see box], indicating repeated immersion of their heads below the sea surface (Arriaza 1995; Núñez 1998).

The Chinchorro mummies from the far southern coast of Peru and the north coast of Chile are the oldest intentionally prepared mummies in the world. Because the Chinchorro mummy tradition lasted for more than 4000 years, it should not be surprising that the material culture of this group changed, and that the reasons why the mummies were produced may also have changed. Subsistence altered over time: plant foods became more important after *c.* 5000 BC, when sites have more grinding stones; plants such as manioc and quinoa began to be used as offerings; and more inland animals were added to the diet, based on evidence from desiccated human

---

KEY SITES La Paloma and Chilca: Archaic Villages of the Peruvian Coast

La Paloma

The Middle Archaic Peruvian coastal site of La Paloma was continuously occupied from *c.* 6800 to 3700 BC. At its maximum size, the community was composed of 50 circular dome-shaped structures with an average of 11 sq. m (120 sq. ft) of floor space, placed in shallow, flat-bottomed pits *c.* 40 cm (16 in) deep. Cane was used as wall supports, and reeds and grass as thatch.

The economy was essentially maritime, with more than 90 percent of the recovered fauna from marine sources (Richardson 1992). There is also evidence of increasing use of plants, not only wild plants such as algarroba (mesquite) and cactus from the nearby lomas areas (a specialized fog vegetation ecotype), but also possibly domestic bottle gourds, guava, oca (a tuberous wood sorrel), squash, beans, and begonia by 6000–3700 BC. The distribution of artifacts – pigments, fishhooks, nets, cut-shell objects, exotic materials such as *Spondylus* shell from Ecuador, obsidian from the sierra, and monkeys from the rainforest – suggests a quasi-egalitarian society and exchange relationships with outside groups, perhaps to help manage subsistence risk (Benfer 2000).

The dead were partially preserved with salt and wrapped in reed mats; fires were built over the graves to help desiccate the corpses, resulting in partial mummification. Several of the males exhibit auditory exostoses (enlargement of bone in the ear) or aural

osteomas (tumors in the ear, composed of bone or bonelike tissue), a pathological condition resulting from extended immersion of the head below the water surface; archaeologists usually interpret this as evidence of deep-sea diving, documenting the importance of a new maritime pursuit.

Chilca

The fishing village of Chilca 1, located 72 km (45 miles) south of Lima, arose after the collapse of La Paloma, persisting from 3500 to 2500 BC. These fishermen invested more in plants, growing bottle gourd, lima beans, cotton, and perhaps even squash and tomatoes (Engel 1976; Moseley 2001). The richness of marine resources in central Peru, displayed at sites such as La Paloma and Chilca, gave rise to a hypothesis known as the Maritime Foundations of Civilization, discussed in Chapter 17, which has been employed to explain why complex society developed on the Peruvian coast prior to the adoption of maize agriculture.

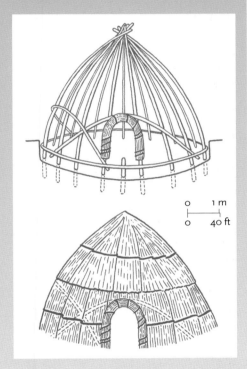

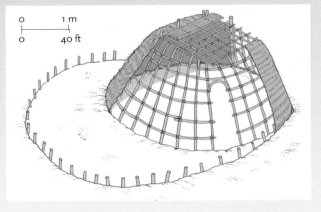

9.32, 9.33 *Chilca house (above) and La Paloma house (right) reconstructions, showing house styles along the Central and Southern Pacific coast. Where wood was not available, the framework was made of cane or large reed bundles, covered with matting of cane, or bundles of grass or reeds.*

feces. During the Late Archaic, additional domestic foodstuffs, such as sweet potato, potatoes, and squash, were added to the diet of people living in more nucleated, permanent settlements (Núñez 1998; Rivera 1995).

Southern Chile and Southern Argentina

In the far southern coastal areas, fisheries may be somewhat more recent. The earliest small, ephemeral fishing settlements appear *c.* 9000–8000 BC. The southern fur seal was the most important prey for the **Tierra del Fuego** groups, and second rank went to shellfish; fish, and land animals such as guanaco, huemel deer, and the ostrich-like rhea, were of less importance (Piana 2002).

Coastal peoples employed canoes in their maritime pursuits by at least as early as Middle Archaic times. These semi-nomadic peoples lived in circular huts covered with boughs and skins, and shifted camps frequently to exploit the rich littoral base. In the interior lowlands of Patagonia, the wild camelid guanaco was the main focus of the economy.

The Andean Highlands

Archaic populations in the sierra are best known from the high-altitude grasslands (called the páramo in the northern Andes, the wet puna and altiplano in the central Andes, and the dry and salt puna in the southern Andes), and from intermontane val-

---

KEY DISCOVERY The Chinchorro Mummies

The Chinchorro people of coastal Peru and Chile made the world's oldest intentionally prepared mummies, beginning at least two millennia before the better-known Egyptian tradition. More than 1500 Chinchorro burials have been found, though fewer than 250 of these were elaborate mummies (Lavalleé 2000; Moseley 2001).

Natural Mummies

There were four main varieties of mummy preparation (Arriaza 1995; Rivera 1995). The first type was that of slightly modified, naturally mummified bodies. Accidentally mummified bodies have been found as early as 7000 BC in this area, and deliberately prepared versions of these occur at the very beginning of the sequence, *c.* 6000 BC, and again at the end, after 1700 BC. The prepared naturally mummified bodies have faces painted with red ocher and black manganese, and may be wrapped in mats or animal skins; late examples are wrapped in elaborate woven woolen and cotton textiles. Otherwise little else was done beyond letting the hot, dry sands naturally desiccate the bodies.

"Black Mummies"

The most complex variety of artificial treatment occurred *c.* 5800–3800 BC; these are known as "Black Mummies" because of the black manganese used to draw facial features and other designs. The skin of the corpse was slit open and removed in segments. To arrest deterioration, the skin was treated with salt in early examples, and later with other procedures. The body was eviscerated, defleshed, and disassembled. The

interior of the cavity formed by the ribs was then thoroughly dried by means of fire, and the parts were then ready to be reconstructed. The main body cavity was filled with ash and clay. The back was stiffened with an elongated piece of wood attached along the vertebral column. The limbs were re-assembled using cane or wooden shafts for structural support, with the knee and elbow joints filed down to help make the limbs rigid. The limb bones were wrapped with mats of woven rushes;

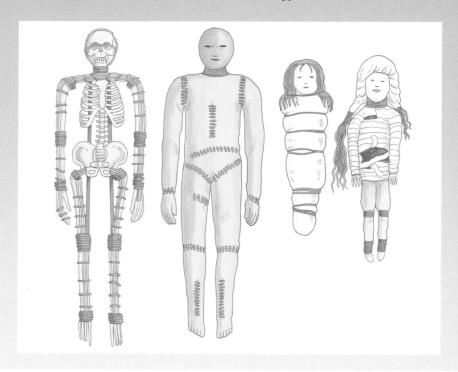

9.34 *On the left is a "black mummy-style" adult, showing internal preparation with joints bound with cords and body stiffened with wood sticks. This body was then stuffed and the skin sewn back on. On the right are two child mummies: one "red mummy style," one red-mummy bandage style variant.*

leys along the western slopes [9.36]. The early part of the period is marked by rapid change in environment, and hence in human lifeways. Early Archaic inhabitants were generalists: hunting and collecting, using spears, atlatls, nooses, snares, and traps to secure terrestrial animals, and more or less opportunistically collecting plants from local settings. Among the animals most frequently exploited were wild camelids, deer, various rodents, and birds. These Archaic populations were faced with patchiness of resources, low productivity and predictability, climatic instability, and high transport and mobility costs. Earlier solutions may have centered upon mobility or seasonal migration, whereas later populations reduced subsistence risk through exchange and storage.

The Northern Andes

Early Archaic highland sites in the northern Andes, in caves such as Tequendam and El Abra in the Sabaña de Bogotá, Cubilan near Quito, and Chobshi in southern Ecuador, seem to have been short-term residential base camps of semi-nomadic hunting groups. Thomas Lynch (1999) suggested that these Early Archaic people continued a substantial hunting focus, derived from his proposed "specialized big-game hunters" of the terminal Pleistocene. More recently excavated sites, however, where attention has been given to more detailed recovery procedures, indicate a strong collecting emphasis as well.

At **San Isidro** in Colombia, edge-ground cobbles (precursors to rocker mills, crushing and grinding devices of stone) have

9.35 *"Family" of six red-style mummies, both adults and children, from the El Morro 1 site near Arica in northern Chile.*

these were then tightly wrapped with cords for reinforcement.

The preserved skin was then sewn back onto the whole body. In order to restore some appearance of life, the body was coated with a layer of clay. The face was modeled and sculpted into a mask with eyes and mouth indicated by holes and incisions, often outlined in black. Both male and female sexual organs were frequently modeled in clay. The end result was a kind of sophisticated, rigid, vertical effigy.

"Red Mummies"

The "Red Mummy" period followed, *c.* 3800–2100 BC. The preparation of the corpse was not quite so elaborate, and mummies were prepared without disarticulation. The bodies were partially eviscerated, and the central cavity was dried over coals. Incisions were made so that sticks could be slid under the skin to add rigidity. Like the Black Mummies, the body was stuffed with ashes, soil, grass, shells, feathers, or other material. The Red Mummies also had an exterior coat of clay to permit sculpting and painting of facial and body details, although body modeling was less complex. Wigs of human hair were often fixed to the skull.

"Mud Coated Mummies"

The latest type of mummy was the "Mud Coated" variety, *c.* 2100–1700 BC. These corpses were smoke-dried, covered with a thick layer of mud, painted, and then usually wrapped in mats or textiles. Following 1700 BC, the Chinchorro returned to reliance upon natural desiccation in the hot sands.

The rigidity built into the mummies is thought to have helped in moving them from place to place, thus keeping them accessible to the living for an extended time, prior to final burial. The mummies exhibit various types of damage that were later repaired, such as refinishing of facial clay masks and repainting of body surfaces, suggesting an extended period of ritual use.

Early mummies are associated with mats, twined textiles, and basketry, but in later periods woven textiles of cotton and wool are common; highland-derived obsidian artifacts begin to appear at the same time as the textiles. The headgear of later mummies sometimes includes woven turbans, and "crowns" made from red, yellow, and blue tropical parrot feathers.

At the late Chinchorro site of Camarones 14, examples of South Andean hallucinogens were found with the mummies, including snuff (yaagi, *Banisteriopsis* sp.), snuff trays, inhaling tubes, spatulas, brushes, boxes, and other ritual containers (Rivera 1995). (For the possible relevance of the Chinchorro mummies to the rise of social complexity in this area, see Maritime Foundations of Andean Civilization box, Chapter 17, p. 648.)

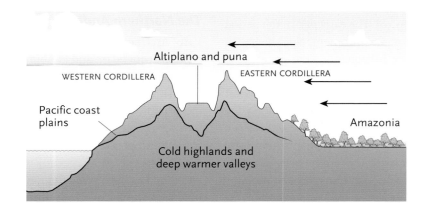

9.36 Diagram of a cross-section of the Central Andes from east to west: *rain storms originate from the Atlantic, lose most of their moisture as they cross Amazonia, with reduced rain falling in the altiplano or puna between the two cordilleras, and aridity on the Pacific coast.*

yielded starch grains and phytoliths from arrowroot, palms, and other edible forest taxa, dated to about 8000 BC and associated with digging implements or "hoes" (Mora and Gnecco 2003). In **Pena Roja** on the Rio Caquetá, a shift from hunting and gathering to plant utilization is proposed for *c.* 7000 BC, based on the occurrence of squash-family phytoliths. In later levels, bottle gourd, leren, eight species of palms, and several other wild plants were added to the subsistence base (Gnecco and Mora 1997; Mora and Gnecco 2003). These Archaic-period foragers apparently promoted the artificial concentration of useful plants prior to the advent of farming.

The Central Andes

Because more research has been conducted in Peru than in the rest of the Andean area, interpretations and models are heavily influenced by evidence from the punas and sierras there.

Northern Peru In the northern Peruvian sierra, early work at Lauricocha (Cardich 1958; 1966) and Guitarrero caves (Lynch 1980; 1999) suggested seasonal occupation, with groups heavily exploiting deer and camelid species in what was described as a pattern of seasonal transhumance. The **Lauricocha** assemblage is from a series of caves in two zones, 3880–4100 m (12,730–13,450 ft) above sea level. The caves were first occupied around 9000 BC, but in these early excavations, the accounts focus on the stone tools and on the human burials of *c.* 7000 BC, which were painted with red ocher and accompanied by hunting tools and turquoise and bone beads.

At 2580 m (8465 ft), **Guitarrero Cave** [9.37] is lower in elevation, and here it is the perishable materials that attracted the most interest. Remains include basketry, textiles, cordage, leather, fire-making tools of wood and other wooden tools [9.38], and possible domestic plants. The investigator originally thought there was evidence for domestic beans as early as 9000

9.37 Guitarrero Cave: *this cave, in the Cordillera Negra of the western Andes, near Yungay, was perhaps seasonally occupied. The photograph is of the mouth of the cave, 150 m (500 ft) above the Rio Santa, showing excavations in progress.*

9.38 *Guitarrero Cave:* *a sample of perishable artifacts recovered from the dry fill: a stick with cemented and bound end; the top of a gourd container in plan and cross-section; a bone awl; a fire-drill hearth; and a hide-wrapped scraper.*

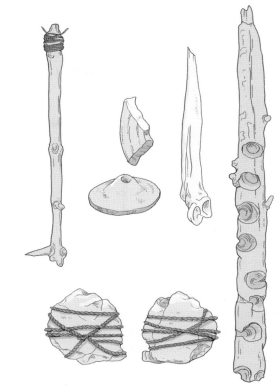

BC, as well as chili peppers, ullucu, and achira, but when the beans were finally dated using AMS radiocarbon techniques, they proved to be 5000 years younger.

In the northern Peruvian Andes, researchers posit a cultural anomaly that has also been proposed recently for the altiplano and the dry and salt puna of the south-central Andes (see below): a period of virtual depopulation during the Middle Archaic, roughly coinciding with the mid-Holocene warm period of *c.* 7000–4500 BC (Lynch 1999).

Central Peru In central Andean Peru, the Junin puna has been the focus of most explorations, particularly at sites such as Pachamachay, Uchumachay, Panaulauca, and Telarmachay, situated 4050–4425 m (12,250–14,500 ft) above sea level. Based on the exceptional quantities of camelid bones found at **Pachamachay** and nearby **Panaulauca**, John Rick (1980; Rick and Moore 2000) argued for limited-mobility hunting groups there around 7700–5000 BC, followed by year-round, sedentary, full-time vicuña hunters *c.* 5000–2000 BC, with a shift to camelid herding after 2000 BC. Rick thought that Pachamachay was a specialized permanent base camp for vicuña hunters, with other smaller rockshelters around the Junin puna employed as temporary hunting camps. His model is in sharp contrast to the one developed for Guitarrero Cave, where seasonal transhumance was proposed for Early and Middle Archaic highland groups. In new analyses of the Junin materials, others came to conclusions different from Rick's, suggesting, for example, that the zooarchaeological remains indicate seasonal utilization, rather than year-round occupation.

Work in nearby **Telarmachay** (Lavalleé 1987; 1990) also produced prodigious numbers of camelid bones, but detailed analyses indicate that this site was only occupied during the wet season, from November to March, despite the presence of permanent low stone walls delimiting and protecting the occupation area. Telarmachay adds to the corpus of information on early burial rituals in the sierra. Of particular note in the 6250–5900 BC levels are a child buried in a pit with five stone slabs set in an arc defining it, the body covered in red ocher, with a necklace of 99 discoidal white shell beads as well as shell pendants; and a woman buried with a hide-working kit, including 11 stone and six bone tools, incorporating needles, awls, knives, and scrapers (Lavalleé 1987; 2000). In conjunction with the Lauricocha evidence, we can identify a pattern of ritual treatment of the dead beginning in the Early Archaic, in which bodies were treated with red ocher, and individuals were buried with shell jewelry as well as tools and weapons.

Telarmachay provides the first good zooarchaeological evidence for a shift from the mixed hunting of deer and camelids to a focus almost exclusively on camelids by 5000 BC, the first existence of a domestic alpaca-like animal shortly after 5000 BC, and full-time pastoralism by 3800 BC. By 2000 BC, there is evidence of some quinoa and tuber agriculture in the Junin sites (Pearsall 1980). Only seasonal occupation of the north and central Peruvian puna sites is indicated during the Early and Middle Archaic, with permanent year-round occupations in the Late Archaic.

Southern Peru In the southern Peruvian zone, there are two well-known areas: the Ayacucho caves, at an average elevation of 2850 m (9350 ft), and the Asana site at 3435 m (11,270 ft). As with sites farther north in the highlands, the evidence from **Ayacucho** suggests seasonal occupation during the Early and Middle Archaic by large bands, which broke into smaller bands for dry-season seasonal camps (MacNeish et al. 1975; 1983). Ayacucho also provides evidence for the beginnings of guinea pig domestication during the Early Archaic, with llamas, alpacas, quinoa, squash, and bottle gourd added during the Middle Archaic, and several other plant species by the Late Archaic.

The evidence from the **Asana** site in the Osmore Valley [see box: Asana: Base Camp and Herding Residence, p. 343] has provided a different model for highland Archaic occupations, starting with transitory exploitation of sierra resources by coastal populations colonizing the sierra at the beginning of the

Early Archaic, to permanent establishment of a high sierra base camp utilized for the next several millennia, and finally a shift toward puna agro-pastoralism. The last included a new focus on plants such as Andean grains and tubers, and establishment of a pastoral herding camp and corral.

Mark Aldenderfer (2001; 2002) proposes two subsistence variations during the Early and Middle Peruvian Archaic: a high sierra pattern of camelid hunting, supplemented by some collecting, where the populations practiced a kind of seasonal transhumance; and puna and altiplano settlements, which were much more sedentary. Asana fits the first pattern; the site of **Quelcatani** in the Titicaca basin fits the second.

Populations in the Titicaca basin were closely constrained by the Archaic-period environment. During part of that time (6000–2300 BC), lake levels dropped more than 100 m (330 ft) and possibly as much as 200 m (660 ft) below current norms, leaving Lake Titicaca as a high saline, land-locked lake with no functioning outlet. Throughout the reduced rainfall period, the carrying capacity of the basin for herd animals, and for agriculture, would have been significantly reduced. **Quelcatani**, however, was situated in a small marshy zone, which would have served as a freshwater source. Hunters lived in small ovoid rock structures, employing the site as a short-term residential base camp until 2000 BC, when there was a shift over the next few centuries to herding llamas, raising guinea pigs, and the beginnings of potato, oca, ullucu, tarwi, and quinoa agriculture (Kuznar 2002).

Cave sites in this zone are well known for a variety of rock art, including images of deer, camelids, felines, humans hunting and herding, and various geometric patterns, rendered by successive generations of hunters and then herders. In the Titicaca basin, seasonal open-air village sites with oval semi-subterranean pithouses began *c.* 3200 BC; permanent sedentary villages were apparently not present until lake levels rose *c.* 2000–1500 BC.

The Southern Andes

The dry and salt punas of the southern Andes show evidence of Middle Archaic depopulation, as seen further north. In northern Chile, ancient lakes disappeared shortly after 7000 BC. As the area became progressively drier, populations either moved down slope (perhaps becoming part of the Chinchorro tradition on the coast), or adopted more sedentary patterns of resource use by settling close to the few perennial water bodies. Thus, in the Chilean sierra, archaeologists speak of the "silencio arqueológico" from 7000 to 2000 BC, when sites (such as Tulan 52 and Puripica 1) are known only in the very humid areas (Messerli et al. 2000; Núñez et al. 2002). Domestication of camelids began *c.* 3000 BC, and irrigated agriculture developed with the large-scale reoccupation of the sierra area when the lakes recharged, perhaps as early as 1500 BC.

Both Tulan 52 and Puripica 1 were sedentary villages of circular stone-slab houses. **Tulan 52** was a village of 20–25 agglomerated habitations, dated to 3000–2700 BC, situated on

9.39 Llamas and weavers: *the llama, domesticated by 4000–3000 BC, was first important for its meat and hides and later became the primary transport and cargo animal for Andean people. Its wool was also used in textiles.*

KEY SITE Asana: Base Camp and Herding Residence

The site of Asana lies in the Rio Osmore drainage in southern Peru at *c.* 3435 m (11,270 ft) above sea level. It displays a relatively continuous occupation record between *c.* 9500 and 2300 BC, providing evidence for the period from the first settlement of the high sierra through the beginnings of animal and plant domestication. The first use of this rockshelter was as a temporary hide-working camp for coastal groups *c.* 9500–8500 BC. From 8500 to 5000 BC, the site served as a base camp for a hunting band exploiting the high sierra and puna resources; the economy was based primarily on hunting deer, camelids, and various small mammals, and collecting wild fruits and tubers.

Use of the site changed *c.* 5000–3800 BC to a short-term occupation base camp, with the focus shifting again to a new, intensive exploitation of plant resources *c.* 3800–3000

BC. Asana's final use was as a pastoral camelid herding camp *c.* 3000–2300 BC (Aldenderfer 1993; 2000).

The site was located near prized swampy alpaca grazing areas. During the Early Archaic period, the residents constructed small circular residential structures covered with brush and hides, ranging from 3.5 to 6 sq. m (38–65 sq. ft) in floor area. There was also one larger ovoid structure with prepared white clay floors, possibly ceremonial, utilized *c.* 6000–5500 BC. In the near vicinity were short-term field camps (hunting blinds, butchery sites, plant-gathering loci) and resource extraction sites (e.g. stone quarries).

The shift to more intensive use of the campsite *c.* 3800 BC was accompanied by the building of a complex of ceremonial structures and a new emphasis on plant foods, including tubers and chenopod grains.

The ceremonial structures may have been employed for steam baths and rituals centering on earth worship. There is also possible evidence here for burnt offerings to the earth mother (later the Inca goddess Pachamama), and the beginning of the Aymara good luck (*alasita*) ceremonies (Aldenderfer 1991; Kuznar 2002).

By 3000 BC, the site's function changed dramatically and abruptly, no longer serving as a base camp for a group of hunter-gatherers, but as the herding residence (with corral) for a single extended family (Kuznar 1989; 2002). There is evidence of domestic chenopods (most likely quinoa) during this period. Other wild plant resources were exploited as well, such as algarroba (mesquite) pods, cactus fruits, wild seed plants, and wild tubers.

---

the edge of a large salt marsh in the San Pedro de Atacama area at 2925 m (9600 ft). The economy was based on wild camelid hunting, but there are also many grinding stones; numerous cactus seeds were also recovered (Núñez 1998; Núñez et al. 2002). Exchange items include Pacific seashells, copper ores, and various stone and shell beads. **Puripica 1** was a village of 30–40 dwellings, occupied around 2900–2600 BC. Based on the high incidence of neonate mortality, and evidence of the intense use of camelids, Lautaro Núñez (1992) believes that Puripica was a camelid herding settlement, thus suggesting a shift to camelid pastoralism here by 2900 BC. Later Archaic sites in this region also display evidence for the beginnings of agriculture, with quinoa, potato, beans, gourds, and chili peppers frequently cited.

Andean Animal and Plant Domestication

The Americas were impoverished in terms of varieties of domestic animals; for South America we are limited to llama [9.39], alpaca, guinea pig, and muscovy duck. The **llama** was initially important to prehistoric groups for its meat and hides, and llama dung later became a critical component of agriculture. By the time of the Incas and late prehistoric civilizations, llamas were the primary transport and cargo animals for Andean peoples. The **alpaca** was another special-function domestic camelid initially utilized mainly for meat and hides, like the llama, but later most valued for its wool. Textiles were

among the most important wealth items for Andean civilizations, and wool and cotton both became very important production fibers. Although there are conflicting evolutionary models for the derivation of llama and alpaca from the guanaco and vicuña (Browman 1989; Bonavia 1999; Stanley et al. 1994; Kessler et al. 1996; Kadwell et al. 2001), it appears that both animals had been domesticated by 4000–3000 BC.

Guinea pigs were raised primarily for food; in areas with little pasture, where alpaca and llama could not be herded in numbers, they were an important source of meat, as well as a particularly important animal for religious rituals. Guinea pig domestication has been dated from as early as *c.* 8000–6500 BC (MacNeish et al. 1981; 1983) to as late as 1000 BC (Lavalleé 1990). **Muscovy ducks**, a tree-nesting species native to lowland tropical regions of the Americas, were utilized for meat and eggs in coastal locations, but were never as important as alpaca, llama, and guinea pigs. The oldest archaeological remains come from Ayalan on the Santa Elena peninsula of Ecuador, where they were found with burial features ranging from 800 BC to AD 1150 (Hesse 1980); in Peru, clear ceramic images are known in the Moche area as early as AD 200.

One theory (Lathrap 1977) of the origins of South American agriculture suggests that it came with fishermen crossing the Atlantic from Africa to Brazil 16,000 years ago, carrying with them the domesticated **bottle gourd** and **cotton**, needed for fishing lines and nets, and for floats. According to this theory, the

Table 3 *South American Crops*

Grains

Quinoa	*Chenopodium quinoa*
Canihua	*Chenopodium pallidicaule*
Kiwicha or achita	*Amaranthus caudatus*

Legumes

Common bean	*Phaseolus vulgaris* (domesticated independently also in Mexico)
Lima bean	*Phaseolus lunatus*
Jack bean	*Canavalia ensiformis*
Tarwi	*Lupinus mutabilis*
Peanut	*Arachis hypogaea*

Vegetables

Squashes	*Cucurbita moschata*, *C. maxima*, and *C. ficifolia*
Bottle gourd	*Lagenaria siceraria*
Tomato	*Lycopersicum esculentum*

Roots

Potato	*Solanum tuberosum*, *Solanum stenotomum*, etc.
Oca	*Oxalis tuberosa*
Ullucu or papa lisa	*Ullucus tuberosus*
Isanu or mashua	*Tropaeolum tuberosum*

Achira	*Canna edulis*
Jicama	*Pachyrhizus tuberosus*
Arracacha	*Arracacia xanthorrhiza*
Manioc	*Manihot esculenta*
Sweet potato	*Ipomoea batatas*
Maca	*Lepidium meyenii*
Leren	*Calathea allouia*
Arrowroot	*Maranta arundinacea*

Fruits

Chirimoya	*Annona cherimola*
Avocado	*Persea americana*
Pacay	*Inga edulis*
Guava	*Psidium guajava*
Lucuma	*Pouteria lucuma*
Pepino	*Solanum muricatum*

Technical and ritual

Cotton	*Gossypium barbadense*
Aji and other chili pepper	*Capsicum baccatum*, *C. chinense*
Coca	*Erythroxylon coca*
Tobacco	*Nicotiana rustica*, *N. tabacum*

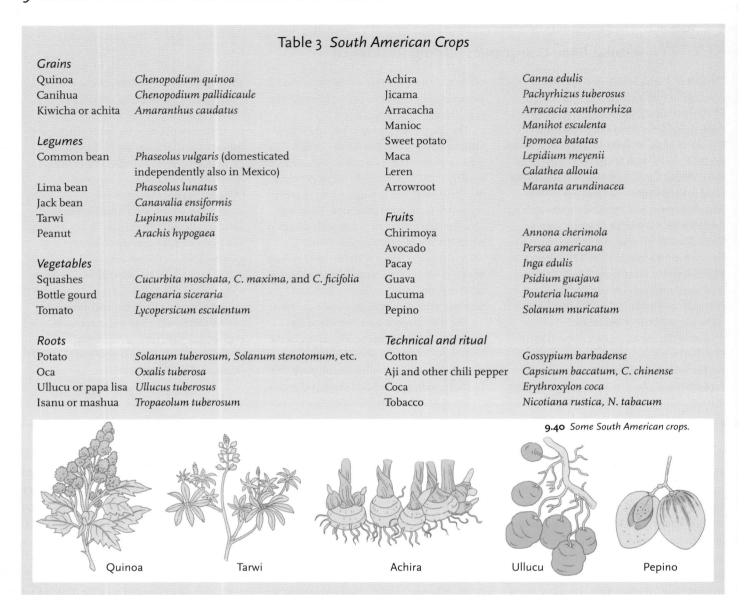

9.40 *Some South American crops.*

Quinoa   Tarwi   Achira   Ullucu   Pepino

cultivation of other Amazonian plants, such as bitter **manioc**, **sweet potato**, and **arrowroot**, developed by stimulus diffusion from gourd and cotton husbandry, and then spread from Amazonia into the Pacific lowlands and the Andean highlands (see also Piperno and Pearsall 1998). Although knowledge concerning the antiquity of specific domestic plants is insufficient to allow testing of these origin hypotheses, the best known of the lowland Pacific and Andean highland domestic plants are listed in **Table 3**.

Based on presumed radiocarbon associations, the first occurrence of potato, ullucu, bottle gourd, jicama, and perhaps manioc and sweet potato in the Tres Ventanas caves in the upper Chilca Valley of the central highlands of Peru were dated to 9000 BC, and three species of beans, cotton, and possibly tomato, from the site of Chilca 1 in the lower Chilca Valley, to 3000–2200 BC (Engel 1976). When examined by AMS radio-

carbon techniques, however, the **potato** dated to *c.* 5500 BC and the **ullucu** to *c.* 5100 BC, nearly 4000 years later than first estimated. These are still the oldest directly dated specimens we have, although their domestication status is not clear, as this is a zone where these two species occur wild.

The oldest **common beans** in the central Andes had for many years been believed to be those from Guitarrero Cave in central Peru. But as we noted above, although achira, beans, ullucu, and aji were reported to come from levels as early as 8000–6500 BC, when these samples were AMS dated, the earliest date for the beans was 3000 BC (Kaplan and Lynch 1998). Similar down-dating has occurred at other sites. Why have so many of the original reported dates turned out to be apparently too early? Sites tend to be either sandy coastal middens or dry rockshelters with loose, unconsolidated sediments. Small plant seeds and other botanical remains (especially phytoliths, starch

KEY SITE Caral: The Rise of Socio-political Complexity

The end of the Peruvian coastal Archaic is characterized by rapid development of cultural complexity. Perhaps most spectacular of the local florescences is the Supe religious tradition site of Caral, the largest and most complex of a score of communities that developed on the north-central Peruvian coast along the Rio Supe. Caral was located *c.* 20 km (12 miles) inland from the seacoast and was occupied *c.* 2600–2000 BC. It had an estimated population of 3000 people, scattered in eight planned neighborhoods around a large ceremonial core (Shady and Lopez 2000; Shady et al. 2001). To date, at least 32 mounds have been mapped, including six large pyramids – two with the circular subterranean temples so characteristic of the next historic coastal phase, described in Chapter 17.

Each major pyramid has a different layout, form, orientation, and configuration. The largest, Templo Mayor, is some 18 m (60 ft) high and 160 x 150 m (525 x 500 ft) at its base, with a well-developed entrance atrium fronted by a circular sunken forecourt. Warrens of ceremonial rooms crown the mounds, with access by aligned stairways that permitted large ritual processions. The pyramids are faced with cut stonework and adobe (dried mud), including adobe faces covered with multiple layers of colored plaster; the cores of the mounds are made up of piles of *shicra* (mesh) bags, each filled with *c.* 32 kg (70 lb) of field stone. Associated with each major pyramid are clusters of smaller platform mounds.

Irrigation agriculture appears to have been a major new economic industry supporting this complex. Not only were many food crops grown in irrigated fields, but there were also fields of industrial crops, such as cotton and gourds. These two plants were very important for the fishnets that secured anchovies and

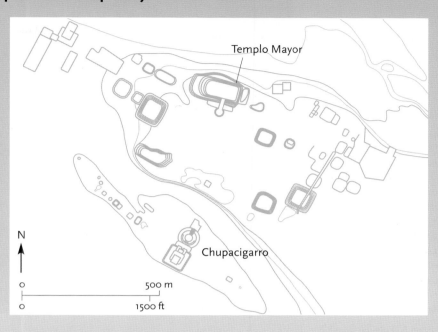

9.41 *Caral site plan, showing the layout of the largest of the platform mound pyramids at the site, demonstrating unexpectedly complex hierarchical political site structure for such an early date.*

other small fish; shellfish were also eaten. Preliminary evidence also supports the argument for production of large amounts of cotton for trade within an incipient textile industry. Maize was apparently not yet known

to the Supe peoples; it is not found at Caral, and is found at only one late transitional site, Aspero, perhaps no earlier than *c.* 1700–1500 BC. (For further discussion of Caral and its implications, see Chapter 17.)

9.42 *The mound of Chupacigarro, in one of the "suburbs" of Caral. The sunken circular temple associated with a platform mound complex with an elaborated atrium become typical of later north coast "Formative" or "Initial Period" temple complexes.*

9.43 *Rock art: rock paintings are common in Amazonian rockshelters, with a variety of styles occurring during the Archaic period. At the Serra da Lua site in the lower Amazon, designs are executed in vivid red and yellow pigments. Circles and geometric figures with complex shapes are common in the local style.*

grains, and pollen grains) can readily filter down to lower levels as the sediments are trampled and churned by humans and animals.

The evidence available indicates Middle to Late Archaic original domestication of most of the plants in **Table 3**. The shift in economic focus to managing domestic plants was characterized by very rapid development in socio-political complexity, particularly in the Pacific lowlands [see box: Caral: The Rise of Socio-political Complexity, p. 345].

The Amazonian Lowlands

The tropical rainforest of Amazonia is the focus of a continuing debate: was this environment a "lost paradise" for humans (Lathrap 1970; Roosevelt 2000), or a "counterfeit paradise" (Meggers 1995; 1996)? The rainforest argument is not limited to the New World: for both Africa and East Asia there are also ardent advocates on each side of the issue concerning suitability of tropical rainforests for humans with low-level technologies.

Betty Meggers, for example, believes that the environment was a very limiting factor. Initially she argued that human habitation was restricted to forested refuges, with colonization occurring only when drier periods opened up areas suitable for use (Meggers 1977; 1987). She has modified her position recently, but still holds that Holocene environmental change was a major limiting factor in Amazonia, resulting in low human densities and short-term occupations. According to this theory, the rainforest was unable to support dense sedentary populations until recently, owing to environmental uncertainty, subsistence stress, and risk avoidance behavior. Repeated cul-tural discontinuities and replacements seen in the archaeological record imply catastrophic climatic impact on human settlers.

Proponents of intensive tropical forest usage, such as Donald Lathrap and Anna Roosevelt, see this as unjustifiable ecological determinism, arguing that the carrying capacity of tropical rainforests with respect to humans employing low technology economies has been severely underestimated. (On this debate see also Chapter 17.) Unfortunately, scarcity of stone for tools, use of wood and other perishable materials, short-term duration of human settlements, continual oscillation of river channels with concomitant scouring and alluviation, and the dense vegetation of the tropical rainforest all make it difficult to find archaeological evidence for evaluating early human occupation in Amazonia.

For the Early Archaic period, the best-known site is **Pedra Pintada** in Brazil, occupied *c.* 8500 BC (Roosevelt 2002b; Roosevelt et al. 1996). Small, nomadic, forager-hunter groups, perhaps no larger than 5–10 people, exploited tropical forest nuts and fruits, small game, fish, and shellfish. Near the mouth of the Amazon, these nomadic groups were also successful in taking Atlantic manatee and dolphin. Their most visible signs are usually **rock art** [9.43], which includes such astronomical motifs as the sun, moon, and stars. Sticklike human figures and various animals, including rabbits, birds, fish, and the dolphin or manatee, are also rendered.

After the Early Archaic occupation of Pedra Pintada, the site was abandoned for *c.* 1700 years; its second occupation, at 6800–5700 BC, is associated with unexpectedly early **pottery**.

Roosevelt links this pottery to ceramics found in the lowest levels of the large shell middens at the site of **Taperinha**, near Santarem, dated to 5700–5000 BC, and argues for the origins of ceramics in Amazonia in the 6th millennium BC (Roosevelt et al. 1991). This is a very early date; elsewhere in South America, the oldest ceramics are found in northwestern Colombia, where they date no earlier than about 4500 BC. For this region of interior Amazonia, Roosevelt sees some impressive growths in density and complexity during the Middle and Late Archaic periods. There was continued reliance on fish and shellfish, supplemented by plant collecting, hunting, and, during the Late Archaic, by plant cultivation. Meggers and Miller (2003) suggest a more conservative date for these developments, placing the first occurrence of ceramics and agriculture at c. 3500 BC.

In the east-central Brazilian uplands, the environment was more open than in Amazonia during the Early and Middle Archaic periods. There is good evidence for considerable reliance on the hunting of small animals, as well as the collecting of palm nuts and other plant foods (Schmitz 1987; 1998). In addition to the atlatl and dart, found elsewhere in Amazonia as well, there are bolas, and polished and grooved axes. By the end of the Middle Archaic, sites are often associated with small habitation mounds, 5–6 m (16–20 ft) long, 2–3 m (6–10 ft) wide, and no more than 1 m (3 ft) high (Hurt 2002a).

Two distinct traditions can be identified after 4500 BC in the uplands: hunters who occupied open savannas, and fisher-gatherers of the various river tributaries (Lavalleé 2000). There was a significant increase in the number of plants and small vertebrates in the diet after 4500 BC, and a concomitant increase in

population. After 4000–3500 BC, ceramics are also found at habitation sites. Parklands began opening up with climatic shifts around 3500 BC (Meggers 1996; Meggers and Miller 2003). Perhaps associated with this was an expansion in the hunting of small animals and increased population growth, with villages of up to 100 inhabitants now common (Kipnis 1998; Hurt 2002b).

The Atlantic Lowlands

We have relatively little good evidence for Early Archaic utilization of the Atlantic coastal regions of eastern South America. Fishing and the collection of shellfish had begun by 9000–8000 BC, but few site reports are available (Schmitz 1998). The Middle and Late Archaic periods (6000–1500 BC) are characterized by maritime intensification, marked by development of *sambaquis* (shell mounds) [**9.44**].

The *sambaquis* appear only after c. 6800 BC, with the relative stabilization of sea levels, and most were abandoned by 1500 BC. These shell mounds were apparently both refuse and habitation mounds, with the best evidence for deliberate construction of habitation mounds post-dating 3500 BC. Buried between successively accumulated beds of shells are trampled, blackened hut floors of circular-to-elliptical houses, usually 5–6 m (16–20 ft) in diameter, in village clusters of up to 30–40 houses, usually with cemeteries on one side of the mound. While the *sambaqui* economies were primarily marine, with shellfish collecting, fishing with hooks and nets, and sea-mammal (seal and dolphins) hunting, there is some evidence for the hunting of

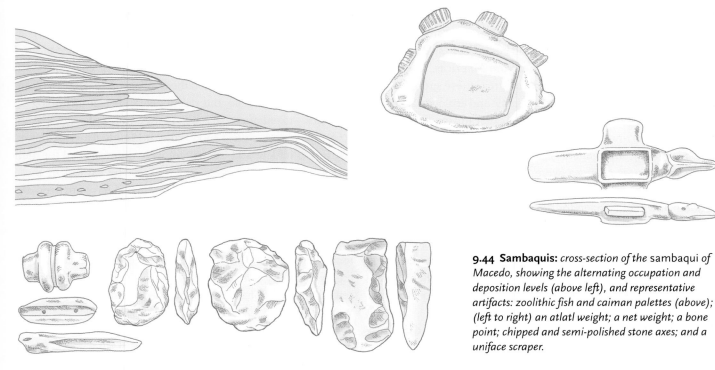

9.44 Sambaquis: *cross-section of the* sambaqui *of Macedo, showing the alternating occupation and deposition levels (above left), and representative artifacts: zoolithic fish and caiman palettes (above); (left to right) an atlatl weight; a net weight; a bone point; chipped and semi-polished stone axes; and a uniface scraper.*

inland rainforest animals (anteater, armadillo, capybara, deer, marmoset, peccary, and paca), as well as various other land animals and birds. There are also indications of plant use, such as nutting stones (stones with an indentation in the center to hold a nut, which was then hit with another stone, the pestle), thought to have been utilized in processing palm kernels. Among the best-known artifacts after *c.* 2500 BC are zoolithic sculptures (animal-form figures made of stone), thought to be totemic in nature (Gaspar 1998; Schmitz 1998).

Dolores Piperno and Deborah Pearsall (1998) argue from phytolith and starch grain evidence that domestication began in tropical forest environments by *c.* 8000 BC, and that by 6000 BC there was large-scale food production. They argue that food production began earlier in Panama, Ecuador, and Amazonia than it did in the central Mexican highlands or the central Andes, and that lowland tropical societies practiced food production for at least 5000 years before the emergence of sedentary village life. Their position in the "counterfeit" vs. "lost" paradise argument is to contend that tropical people were "pulled" into agriculture because the rainforest environment could not sustain large populations of hunter-gatherers. Because recovery techniques such as flotation have not often been applied systematically and intensively in Amazonian and Atlantic lowland sites, other researchers (Prous 1992; Roosevelt 2002a) take a more conservative stance, accepting the earliest good evidence for **maize** and **manioc** cultivation (the two plants usually associated with sedentary villages) at 1500 BC or later.

Summary and Conclusions

Late Paleoindian hunter-gatherer populations spanned the boundary between the Pleistocene and Holocene, thus witnessing the last vestiges of the Ice Age, and being the first to adapt to newly emergent environments across the Americas. Over several millennia, the timing varying by area, these groups and their descendants adapted to new climatic and ecological conditions, and along the way changed their diet (diversifying it in some areas, narrowing it in others), developed new tool forms and technology, and generally reduced their mobility on the landscape. These changes were more or less pronounced, depending on the structure of the habitats into which they were settling, and set the stage for the remarkable developments in domestication and intensive food production that followed. Indeed, as we have seen, that process may have begun even before this period, for domesticated dogs accompanied late Ice Age hunters who first peopled the Western Hemisphere. In a sense, then, there may never have been a time when Native Americans relied solely on wild animals and plants.

Shortly after spreading across North, Central, and South America, some groups began cultivating native gourdlike

Cucurbita squash plants. At about the same time (*c.* 8000 BC), early Holocene people began utilizing and planting bottle gourds, which evidently floated from Africa onto the shores of Mexico, Peru, and Florida. Five New World squash species were eventually domesticated, with uses ranging from food to containers, net floats, and other implements. In this regard, the earliest domesticated plants were similar to their counterparts in the animal kingdom, dogs – managed organisms that fitted conveniently into Archaic lifeways.

Domestication of maize in Mexico goes back more than 6000 years, but its economic impacts are difficult to recognize until approximately 2000 BC, when farming villages begin to appear across Mexico. Shortly thereafter, the presence of maize can be securely documented in the Southwest United States and in Andean Peru. Significant as maize is, more important crops preceded it in regions other than Mexico. The agricultural systems that developed independently in eastern North America after 2500 BC, for example, were based on sunflower, sumpweed, chenopod, maygrass, erect knotweed, and an indigenous squash that may have been cultivated as early as 6000 BC. In the greater American Southwest (including northwest Mexico), early farming was maize-based, but species of beans, squash, and several other crops, including cotton, became fundamental agricultural components; hunting and gathering of wild plants also remained important. Early arid-land farmers developed sophisticated systems of water control, expanded by later Hohokam and Ancestral Puebloan societies (Chapter 18).

Early and Middle Holocene coastal South American populations were very different from the nomadic Archaic bands of Mexico, living atop mounds of accumulated shellfish as early as 9000 BC. Deliberately constructed mounds that served as platforms for communal buildings date to as early as 6000 BC, and permanent villages appeared on the northern coast of South America by 5000 BC. People in these villages had begun to manage plants by 4500 BC and developed a special technology – ceramics – to enhance extraction of their nutrients.

Some of the earliest food crops in South America (leren, arrowroot, ullucu, and the potato) were domesticated for their starchy underground roots and tubers. The earliest of these date to *c.* 5000 BC, and although the remains have not been distinguished morphologically from wild plants, it seems likely that Andean people were selectively harvesting and possibly cultivating tubers at this time. The impressive suite of crops found at Caral near the Peruvian coast attests to irrigation farming by 2500 BC, and constitutes the earliest solid evidence for settled village life based on intensified agriculture in the New World.

Even if maize moved south from Mexico soon after its domestication there around 4300 BC, it did not become economically important in South America until 1500 BC. As in eastern North America, farmers in South America added maize to previously existing agricultural systems, and time was required for development of maize varieties that produced well under different regional environmental conditions. When and where fully integrated, maize had a major impact and became a critical cultural element ecologically, socio-politically, and ritually.

Indigenous North and South Americans developed many different ways of procuring and producing food and organizing their societies during the 6000–7000 years after the Ice Age ended and before state-level societies arose. Major crop plants and herd animals were domesticated, but commitment to agriculture was unevenly distributed across the continents, and it did not correspond to the degree of sedentism, use of ceramics, population density, or ceremonial complexity that is indicated by the construction of mounds and other large platforms and buildings. Where fish and wild plant foods were abundant, relatively sedentary societies – such as those on the Pacific coast of North America and in peninsular Florida – could flourish without agriculture or with low-level use of domesticated plants such as gourds. The high population density and political complexity of these people demonstrates that sophisticated non-agricultural systems were long-enduring, sustainable strategies in their own right.

Nevertheless, there would have been no Mississippian chiefdoms, and no Aztec or Inca empire without the eventual intensified production of maize, quinoa, beans, and many other crops (along with large-scale alpaca and llama husbandry in the Andean area). The New World agricultural systems that so impressed early European explorers had their roots in Archaic times. In their diversity, they provide a fascinating counterpoint to the rise of agriculture in other regions of the world, as well as providing the basis for a distinctive and creative range of more complex American societies that arose in the course of the following millennia. This story is taken up later in Chapters 16 (Mesoamerica), 17 (South America), and 18 (North America). Next, however, an account is presented of postglacial hunter-gatherers and the transition to agriculture in another continent: Africa.

Further Reading and Suggested Website

Anderson, D. and R. Mainfort (eds.). 2002. *The Early Woodland in the Southeast*. Tuscaloosa: University of Alabama Press. A thorough review of the current status of knowledge concerning Early Woodland cultures in the Southeast.

Bruhns, K. O. 1994. *Ancient South America*. Cambridge and New York: Cambridge University Press. A review of the archaeology of South America, with a particular emphasis on the Andean republics.

Cambridge History of the Native Peoples of the Americas. 1994–2000. Cambridge: Cambridge University Press. Three volumes on Mesoamerica, South America, and North America, respectively; edited and written by multiple experts, from prehistory to early contact periods.

Clutton-Brock, J. (ed.). 1988. *The Walking Larder: Patterns of Domestication, Pastoralism, and Predation*. London: Unwin Hyman. A worldwide review of animal domestication, including several papers on species in the New World.

Ford, R. I. (ed.). 1985. *Prehistoric Food Production in North America*. Ann Arbor: University of Michigan Museum of Anthropology, Anthropological Papers no. 75. Chapters summarize and interpret the evidence for early plant domestication primarily north of Mexico, but include a discussion of maize.

Fritz, G. J. 1994. Multiple pathways to farming in precontact eastern North America. *Journal of World Prehistory* 4, 387–435. Authoritative summary of early agriculture in the Eastern Woodlands of North America.

Lavalleé, D. 2000. *The First South Americans: The Peopling of a Continent from the Earliest Evidence to High Culture* (translated by P. Bahn). Salt Lake City: University of Utah Press. A review of the early settling of South America, with a particular focus on the periods prior to the beginnings of complex society.

Moseley, M. E. 2001. *The Incas and their Ancestors: The Archaeology of Peru*. (Rev. ed.) London & New York: Thames & Hudson. The standard textbook for defining and detailing the various Peruvian cultural events, culminating in the Inca.

Phillips, J. & Brown, J. (eds.). *Archaic Hunters and Gatherers in the American Midwest*. New York: Academic Press. A synthesis of Middle and Late Archaic archaeology in the mid-continental Unites States, emphasizing subsistence-settlement systems and sedentism.

Plog, S. 1997. *Ancient Peoples of the American Southwest*. London & New York: Thames & Hudson. Excellent introduction to the indigenous peoples of the Southwest, from Paleoindians to Spanish contact.

Sassaman, K. E. & Anderson, D. G. (eds.). 1996. *Archaeology of the Mid-Holocene Southeast*. Gainesville: University Press of Florida. Various experts provide good overviews of Archaic developments (including agriculture) for the mid-South and Southeastern United States.

Smith, B. 1998. *The Emergence of Agriculture*. New York: W. H. Freeman. A well-illustrated world survey of the earliest agricultural and pastoral economies, including those of the Americas.

http://infodome.sdsu.edu/research/guides/quipu This website features links to web resources on South American archaeology.

CHAPTER 10
HOLOCENE AFRICA

Graham Connah, Australian National University

The Environmental Setting 351

Intensification of Hunting, Gathering, and Fishing 354

  Southern and Central Africa 355
  • *Southern African Rock Art* 356
  Northern, Eastern, and Western Africa 356
  • *North Africa and the Sahara* 356
  ● KEY CONTROVERSY Symbolism in Southern African Rock Art 358
  • *East Africa* 359
  • *West Africa* 359
  ● KEY CONTROVERSY A Green Sahara? 360

The Beginnings of Farming 361
  The Sahara 361
  ● KEY CONTROVERSY The Domestication of Cattle in the Sahara 362
  The Nile Valley 363
  West Africa 363
  Northeast and East Africa 364

Ironworking Societies and the Adoption of Farming South of the Equator 365
  Movements of Bantu-speaking Peoples 366
  Ironworking Farmers 367
  ● KEY CONTROVERSY The Origins of African Ironworking 368
  Domesticated Plants and Animals 369
  Interaction Between Hunter-Gatherers and Farmers 369

Urbanization and the Growth of Social Complexity in Ancient Egypt 370
  The Predynastic Period 371
  The Early Dynastic Period 373
  The Old Kingdom 374

  ● KEY CONTROVERSY How "African" was Ancient Egypt? 375
  ● KEY DISCOVERY New Insights from the Pyramids 376
  The First and Second Intermediate Periods and the Middle Kingdom 376
  The New Kingdom and After 377

Urbanization and State Formation in the Rest of Africa 380
  Nubia and Ethiopia 380
  • *Kerma* 380
  • *Napata and Meroë* 381
  • *Aksum* 382
  North and West Africa 383
  ● KEY SITE Jenné-jeno: Origins of Urbanism in West Africa 383
  Eastern, Southern, and Central Africa 384
  • *The Zimbabwe Plateau* 385
  • *Remoter Parts of Central Africa* 385
  ● KEY SITE Great Zimbabwe 386

Africa and the Outside World 387
  The Mediterranean, Southwest Asia, and the Red Sea 387
  The Indian Ocean 388
  ● KEY CONTROVERSY Did External Trade Cause African State Formation? 389
  The Atlantic Coast 389
  ● KEY SITE Igbo-Ukwu 390

Summary and Conclusions 390

Further Reading and Suggested Websites 391

As we saw in Part I, Africa was the birthplace of humanity and probably the place from which *Homo sapiens* spread out to colonize the world. Chapter 4 described the evidence for the earliest modern humans in Africa up to the end of the Pleistocene. The present chapter takes up the story from the beginning of the Holocene, around 9600 BC. As in the Americas (Chapter 9), the African Holocene is characterized above all by a mosaic of diverse societies.

In some parts of the African continent, hunter-gatherers developed or adopted agriculture, while other groups retained their hunter-gatherer practices down to recent times. A few areas, such as Egypt, Zimbabwe, and West Africa, saw the development of states. The African Holocene was also witness to one of the most dramatic examples of farming spread, in the expansion of the Bantu (and Bantu languages) from west to southern Africa.

The early Holocene in Africa was characterized by substantial climatic changes that altered the extent and location of vegetation zones, sometimes resulting in deteriorating conditions to which people had to adapt, sometimes providing new environments that could be exploited. The result was often an increased range of subsistence strategies and a tendency for these to become both more intensive and more specialized. In the Sahara, for instance, with a moister climate than at present, **cattle** may have been domesticated by about 7000 BC (MacDonald 2000); in the lower Nile Valley, **barley and wheat** introduced from Southwest Asia were being cultivated by about 5000 BC (Rossignol-Strick 2002), and the domestication of indigenous **cereals** in West Africa began about 1500 BC (Neumann 1999). These and other changes led gradually to a variety of early farming economies, based on both indigenous and introduced animals and plants, some societies remaining mobile to a greater or lesser extent, others becoming increasingly sedentary. Although such developments began early in North Africa, they only reached the southern tip of the continent by the first few centuries AD.

Early farmers still relied on **stone-based technologies**, although the making of **pottery** was widely adopted; south of the equator, farming was, in most cases, first practiced by people who not only made pottery, but also smelted and used **iron**, for the production of which there is evidence from the 1st millennium BC onwards. Iron tools replaced those of copper and bronze in Egypt, where copper had been worked since the 4th millennium BC; in most of the rest of Africa, iron was the first metal to be used for tools.

Farming, whether based on cultivating plants or herding animals or a combination of both, probably resulted in population increase, and in resource-rich areas these aggregations of population led to socio-political changes involving growth in settlement size and the eventual formation of distinct urban communities, a process to which a knowledge of metallurgy must also have contributed. Such developments were already taking place on the lower Nile by the 4th millennium BC and later occurred on the middle Nile, in West and East Africa, and on the Ethiopian and Zimbabwe plateaus. In some instances, political and economic control was eventually extended by a powerful ruler over a number of cities and towns and the areas surrounding them, leading to the emergence of **African states**, of which pharaonic Egypt was the earliest.

Such states often depended for part of their power-base on the control and **exchange** of resources ranging from food to metals, ivory, aromatics, salt, and slaves, some of which commodities ultimately brought parts of Africa into increasing contact with the outside world. International traders took an interest in the continent as early as the 4th millennium BC, and this interest greatly expanded during the 1st millennium AD with the growth of commerce in the Red Sea and the Indian Ocean, as well as across the Sahara. External trade has grown enormously during the last 500 years, as European industrial development sought raw materials, new markets, and cheap labor. This led to the African diaspora brought about by the trans-Atlantic slave trade, to the impact of which should also be added the longer-lasting slave trade with the Arab world.

The Environmental Setting

To understand the later human past in Africa, it is essential to comprehend both the size of the continent and its environmental diversity through both space and time. Extending from about 37 degrees North to about 35 degrees South, it is larger than the United States, China, and Australia combined. Its landscape ranges from depressions below sea level to mountains over 5000 m (16,000 ft) high, and includes a number of major rivers and lakes. In places it has some of the world's highest temperatures, whereas in others they can fall below freezing point, and rainfall varies from over 4000 mm (156 in) a year at one extreme to virtually nothing at the other. The great variety of resulting environments is most clearly shown by the complexity of the continent's natural vegetation, spanning tropical rainforest, several types of savanna, sub-desert steppe, desert, Mediterranean, and montane [**10.1**].

Further complicating the situation are a marked climatic seasonality in many parts of Africa and both long- and short-term climatic fluctuations. For much of the continent the

HOLOCENE AFRICA TIMELINE

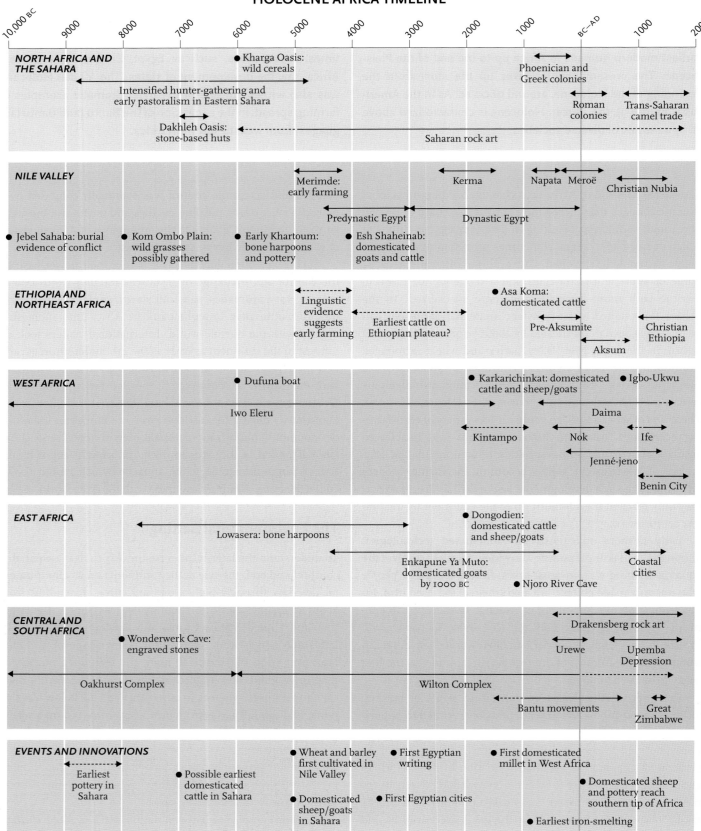

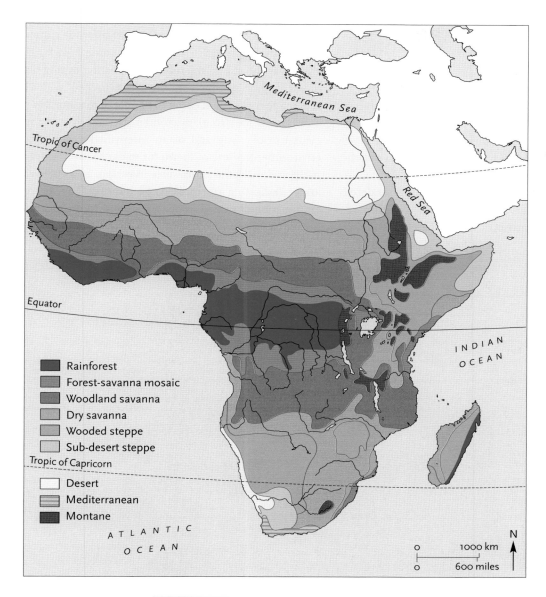

10.1 *Map showing African vegetation:* *the vegetation of Africa is characterized by a series of east–west zones each side of the Equator and a more complex pattern on the high country of East Africa. The vegetation ranges from rainforest through increasingly dry savanna and steppe to desert, with Mediterranean vegetation at the north and south extremes of the continent and montane vegetation in parts of East Africa.*

Rainforest
Forest-savanna mosaic
Woodland savanna
Dry savanna
Wooded steppe
Sub-desert steppe
Desert
Mediterranean
Montane

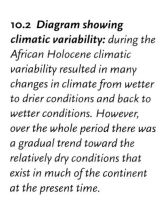

10.2 *Diagram showing climatic variability:* *during the African Holocene climatic variability resulted in many changes in climate from wetter to drier conditions and back to wetter conditions. However, over the whole period there was a gradual trend toward the relatively dry conditions that exist in much of the continent at the present time.*

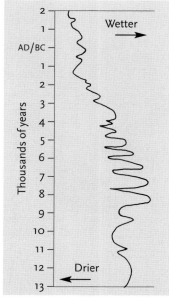

seasons consist of a hot, dry season and a cool, wet season, occupying opposing parts of the year north and south of the Equator, but this varies because of other factors, such as altitude. Moreover, climatic fluctuations over the last 14,000 years have included 30 major climatic events, varying from 700–1000 years in duration to 100–400 years, as well as smaller changes of 10–15 and 30–40 years [10.2].

The long-term oscillations of drier and wetter conditions have caused major shifts in vegetation zones, with deserts, savannas, and rainforests alternately expanding or contracting; short-term changes have resulted in droughts or periods of higher rainfall. This environmental kaleidoscope has presented the peoples of Africa with both constraints and opportunities, to which they have reacted with a variety of responses, including population movement, technological innovation, a variety of food-production strategies, socio-political changes, and ideological developments (Hassan 2002).

353

Intensification of Hunting, Gathering, and Fishing

The prehistory of Africa has most commonly been presented as a technological sequence, for the main stages of which it has been customary to use 19th-century epochal terminology of European origin, such as Early, Middle, and Late Stone Age, Neolithic, Early Iron Age, and Later Iron Age. Problems of definition and the increasing availability and complexity of data, for much of which there are now absolute dates, have rendered such subdivisions outdated, and, following more recent practice (Phillipson 1993a), they are not employed here.

A major characteristic of many later hunting, gathering, and fishing groups in Africa [10.3] (and of some early farming societies) was the use of **microliths**. Consisting of tiny blades and flakes of stone, of which one edge was "backed" with a blunting retouch to make them easier to handle or to mount in mastic in a composite tool [10.4], microliths are indicative of a more efficient use of stone and of an intensified exploitation of the environment. Some of them, for instance, were used as arrow barbs and mark the appearance in certain areas of the **bow and arrow**, indicating an emphasis on hunting. They represent the culmination of a development in stoneworking that had its origins long before the commencement of the Holocene period.

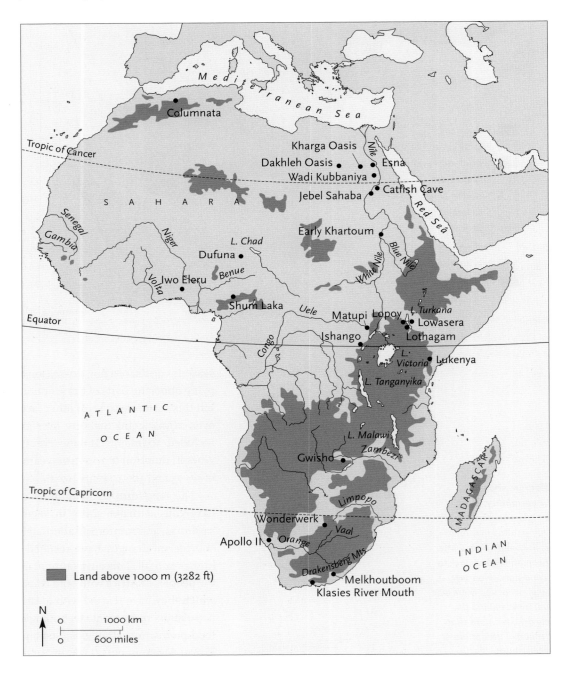

10.3 Intensified hunting, gathering, and fishing sites: these sites have been found in a wide range of environments and consist of both cave or rockshelter locations and open sites. In the south of the continent this economy survived until recent times, so that ethnographic observations can assist in the interpretation of the archaeological evidence.

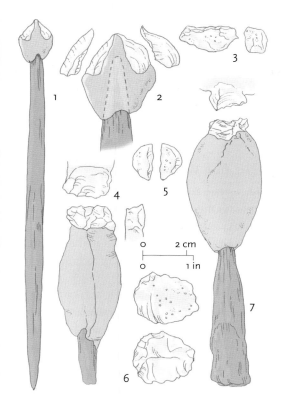

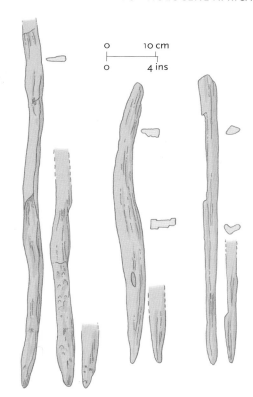

10.4 *(Left)* **Hafted microliths:** *(1 & 2) glass flakes mounted in wax on a wooden arrow-shaft by modern Bushmen; (3, 5, & 6) microliths with mastic adhering; (4) microlith mounted in mastic on a wooden handle; (7) microlith mounted in mastic on a rhinoceros horn handle.*

10.5 *(Right)* **Wooden digging sticks:** *these three examples were excavated from waterlogged deposits at Gwisho hot springs in Zambia. Wood was used for many purposes by hunter-gatherers but does not usually survive in African archaeological sites.*

Microliths dating to at least 30,000 years ago have been found at **Matupi Cave** in eastern Democratic Congo, and comparable elements exist in the Howieson's Poort industry from the cave complex at **Klasies River Mouth** in South Africa, where this industry has been dated to about 70,000–60,000 years ago, probably making its microliths the earliest yet known anywhere in the world [see Klasies River Mouth box, Chapter 4, p. 144]. Nevertheless, the tradition of core-tool manufacture that had been so characteristic of earlier periods, such as the Acheulean (Chapter 3), continued in some later hunter-gatherer societies (in the West African rainforest, for instance), producing axe and hoe forms that suggest the importance of woodworking and the digging up of plant food (Phillipson 1993a).

Southern and Central Africa

In much of southern Africa, later hunter-gatherers are best known archaeologically from the varied complex of stone industries known as the **Wilton**, dating from about 6000 BC onwards, in which microliths played an important part. Prior to that, the **Oakhurst Complex** (*c.* 10,000–6000 BC) was characterized by large scrapers, polished bone tools, and few or no microliths (Deacon and Deacon 1999). These and other Holocene industries appear to have been made by modern humans belonging to the Khoisan language family, who continued their foraging lifestyle in some parts of southern Africa until recent times. The substantial archaeological evidence for these people also includes organic remains from dry cave deposits in southernmost Africa, for example at **Melkhout-**

boom Cave (Deacon 1976), and from waterlogged sites such as **Gwisho** hot springs in southern Zambia (Fagan and Van Noten 1966; 1971). From such evidence it is apparent that wood was used for bows, arrows, digging-sticks, pegs, and wedges, bark was made into trays, leather was sewn into bags and clothing, and plants were an important source of food, as well as being used in other ways [**10.5**]. Plant remains, along with animal bones, also throw light on the seasonal movement of settlements. Groups in the southwestern Cape, for instance, moved regularly between the coast in winter and inland areas in summer.

Because of the late survival of some of South Africa's hunter-gatherers, it is possible to use ethnohistorical and ethnographic material culture and accounts to assist in the understanding of this archaeological evidence. The traditional arrows of the San Bushmen, for example, have suggested how microliths and bone or wooden points were mounted on arrow shafts, which were sometimes feathered and notched for the bowstring; the arrowheads were frequently poisoned (Clark 1975–77). Even more remarkably, arrows preserved in Predynastic and Dynastic Egyptian tombs have shown how some of these features persisted through both space and time (Clark et al. 1974).

Archaeology and ethnography also combine to provide information on other aspects of hunter-gatherer life in southern Africa (Phillipson 1993a; Dowson 1997; Mitchell 1997). It seems likely that seasonal movement included gatherings of people at resource-rich times of the year, when commodities could be exchanged and social relationships reinforced, and dispersal at other times, when resources were more limited. Bored stones that occur in some of the lithic assemblages appear to have served as digging-stick weights, to facilitate the exploitation of plant food. The dead were buried accompanied by tools, personal ornaments, and other items, sometimes including painted stones, perhaps indicating a belief in life after death. Personal adornment was common, and included beads and pendants of bone or ostrich eggshell or freshwater shell.

Southern African Rock Art Ocher and other coloring material were probably used for decorating the body and certainly for the rock paintings that, along with engravings, are abundant in southern Africa. Because they are usually situated in relatively exposed locations, in rockshelters or shallow caves or on rock outcrops, it is thought that many of the surviving paintings date only to the last few thousand years, although the engravings could be much older. However, at **Apollo 11 Cave** in southern Namibia, naturalistic paintings of animals have been found on loose stone slabs in contexts dated to as early as 26,000 years ago. Engraved stones have been excavated at **Wonderwerk Cave** in South Africa, from contexts dating to about 10,000 years ago.

The inclusion of subject matter of known date, such as domesticated animals or Europeans, shows that in some areas painting continued into recent times, although often maintaining traditional styles. This has allowed ethnographic observations from the 19th and 20th centuries to be used to interpret the art, particularly the rock paintings, the majority of which are naturalistic representations of animals and people. Frequent depictions of the eland, an animal that was important in San beliefs, and of people apparently in a state of trance, a practice known from the southern San, have been used to reconstruct aspects of prehistoric belief systems. Nevertheless, the extent to which such interpretations can be applied to the older rock art or to rock art in other parts of Africa remains controversial, as do some aspects of dating the art [see box: Symbolism in Southern African Rock Art, pp. 358–59].

The hunter-gatherer rock art of southern Africa extends as far north as Zimbabwe (Garlake 1995), Zambia, and Malawi (Summers 1959), and even to north-central Tanzania in East Africa (Phillipson 1993a). In contrast, it appears to be absent from much of central Africa, where climatic conditions and limited research combine to limit the archaeological record of later hunter-gatherers for the most part to stone artifact assemblages. Notable among these is the **Tshitolian industry** on the fringes of the equatorial forest, in northeast Angola and the Democratic Congo, in which there are microliths and small core axes, picks, and leaf-shaped points. There are indications that the proportion of this industry consisting of microliths is greater in the more densely forested river valleys than on the more open plateaus, suggesting contrasting subsistence strategies. It has been assumed that the makers of these artifacts were the ancestors of the scattered hunter-gatherers still to be found in the region, who are known to linguists as the BaTwa, and in the past were often referred to as "Pygmies" (Ehret 2002).

Northern, Eastern, and Western Africa

During the late Pleistocene and early Holocene, changes were taking place in hunter-gatherer societies in northern, eastern, and western Africa that were to provide the basis for later transitions to herding or cultivation or both. The earliest African farming is now thought to have formed part of a continuum of socio-economic adjustment over many thousands of years, rather than involving any rapid alteration in human adaptive strategies (although subsequently domesticated plants and animals from Southwest Asia did bring about rapid change in some areas).

North Africa and the Sahara Prior to the start of the Holocene, there were already indications of economic intensification and perhaps the beginnings of sedentism among some advanced hunter-gatherer communities in the Nile Valley, who were exploiting a relatively favorable but confined environment that contrasted with the generally uninhabitable Sahara of 20,000–11,000 years ago. For instance, as early as about 18,000–17,000 years ago, people at **Wadi Kubbaniya**, near Aswan in southern Egypt, with a stone technology mainly of backed bladelets, were relying on a range of plant and animal food that included fish and, particularly, tubers from a wild grass (*Cyperus rotundus*), which they processed on grindstones [10.6].

From about 15,000–11,000 years ago, during a period of high Nile levels, the occupants of Qadan sites further south fished, hunted wild cattle and other large animals, and gathered wild plant food, including grains. Evidence for the latter is provided by the numerous grindstones on Qadan sites and by the polished edges of many of their microliths, which were presumably used to cut grasses. The Qadan dead were buried in cemeteries, and that at **Jebel Sahaba** indicates the existence of violent conflict. Of 58 individuals buried in shallow pits usually covered with stone slabs, nearly half (men, women, and children) had died by violence, the evidence consisting of numerous stone flakes from arrows or spears both among and

10.6 Wadi Kubbaniya in southern Egypt: *one of the sites during excavation. Hunter-gatherers were living here about 18,000–17,000 years ago and exploiting a range of plant and animal food, that included fish and tubers from a wild grass that were processed on grindstones.*

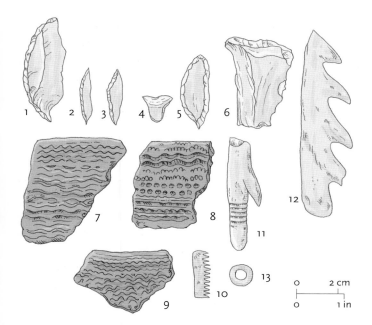

10.7 *Early Khartoum artifact assemblage:* *(1–5) microliths; (6) scraper; (7–9) wavy-line potsherds; (10) catfish spine probably used for decorating pottery; (11&12) fragments of bone harpoon heads; (13) stone bead. Stone grinders, rings and weights were also present.*

Other people in the Nile Valley were also making intensive use of available resources at this time. At some of the sites on the Kom Ombo plain, for example, wild grasses were possibly being gathered by about 8000 BC, and bone harpoons from **Catfish Cave** in southern Egypt suggest a particular interest in fishing by about 5000 BC, although they could also have been used in hunting and in human conflict. Far to the south, such harpoons appeared by about 6000 BC at **Early Khartoum** and other sites, where they were associated with a partly microlithic industry and with pottery that has a distinctive decoration of multiple-grooved wavy lines, which in later examples are elaborated with impressed dots [**10.7**]. Appearing as early as the 9th millennium BC in the central and southern Sahara (Phillipson 1993a), this pottery is a further indication of subsistence intensification, enabling the cooking of many otherwise unpalatable

embedded in their bones, which also showed cut marks. It seems probable that competition for food resources in the limited confines of the Nile Valley was causing severe competition between human groups (Robbins 1997).

but nutritious plant foods, particularly grains. Also at Early Khartoum were indications of mud-covered structures, suggesting the adoption of a more sedentary life than formerly.

In North Africa and the Sahara, the climate had become moister by about 9000 BC, although there were still periods of dry conditions [see box: A Green Sahara?, p. 360]. By around 6000 BC, people using varied, partly microlithic, industries known as Capsian hunted mammals and birds and collected land snails and plant foods at such places as **Columnata** in Algeria. At a roughly similar date, occupants of sites in the eastern Sahara, such as **Kharga Oasis**, appear to have been harvesting wild cereals and to have had affinities with people in the Nile Valley, while evidence of stone-based huts at **Dakhleh Oasis**, dating to about 7000–6500 BC, indicates at least a partly sedentary way of life (Phillipson 1993a). Elsewhere in the Sahara, mobility remained usual for people who, among other strategies, exploited the indigenous wild cattle (*Bos primigenius*). The oldest Saharan rock art, in the form of engravings of wild animals, might have been the work of such hunter-gatherers, although it has been argued that even the earliest examples also show domesticated cattle and sheep, and are therefore more likely to date from only 5000–4000 BC (Muzzolini 2000).

Another feature of the occupation of the central and southern Sahara was the number of sites on river and lake shores; although hunting and grain-gathering were also practiced, fishing and the collection of other aquatic food were important. Significantly, pottery and bone harpoons similar to those from Early Khartoum also occur at these sites, although the pottery might appear slightly earlier in the Saharan sites. Particularly indicative of the exploitation of aquatic resources at this time is the 8.5-m (28-ft) dugout canoe from **Dufuna**, in northeast Nigeria, beyond the southern edge of the desert. Found in alluvium at a depth of 5 m (16 ft) and dated to about 6000 BC, it is the oldest known boat in Africa (Breunig 1996).

KEY CONTROVERSY Symbolism in Southern African Rock Art

Wherever it occurs in the world, prehistoric rock art offers an intimate document of past peoples; but it is a document that has frequently frustrated archaeologists, because it can be read in different ways and is often difficult to date. Long-standing interpretations have included the idea that it was merely art for art's sake, or that it involved sympathetic magic, the artist depicting an animal in order to help him to hunt and kill it.

Research in southern Africa has now suggested that much rock art has deep symbolic meaning, and provides evidence of the thought processes of the society to which the artist belonged. Patricia Vinnicombe (1976) showed that the paintings of the Drakensberg Mountains, in southeastern South Africa, included more depictions of the antelope known as the eland than of all other animals, although the eland was not the major item of diet for the former Bushmen in the area.

From ethnohistorical and ethnographic sources, it was apparent that a strong ritual relationship had existed between the people and the eland, the animal serving as a link between the material and the spiritual worlds; the idealized and beautiful paintings providing ritual symbols that were a source of power. It remains unclear, however, how far back in time Vinnicombe's interpretations can be applied. Some of the Drakensberg art dates only from recent centuries, making the

10.8 *The eland, a type of antelope, was frequently depicted by Bushmen artists in South Africa. It is thought that there was a strong ritual relationship between people and the eland, the animal serving as a link with the spiritual world and therefore its representation providing a powerful ritual symbol.*

East Africa Evidence of an emphasis on aquatic resources has also been recovered from parts of East Africa, particularly from around Lake Turkana in Kenya, which about 8000 BC was 80 m (263 ft) higher than its present level (Phillipson 1993a). At **Lowasera**, bone harpoons were used from about 7000 BC, and pottery was subsequently present. The site of **Lothagam** yielded evidence of a similar adaptation, which appears to have continued for millennia around Lake Turkana as its fluctuating level gradually fell, being present at **Lopoy** until after about AD 1000. A comparable economy was also practiced at **Ishango**, on the shores of Lake Edward in the Democratic Congo, but its dating is uncertain; the site (which, significantly, lacked pottery) is at least 7000 years old but perhaps as much as 18,000–16,000 years old. Elsewhere in East Africa, as for example in the latest phase at **Lukenya Hill** in Kenya, hunter-gatherers continued to exploit the abundant terrestrial fauna, and increasingly used microlithic tools. These microliths also occur in the **Eburran**

industry of the southern part of the Kenyan Rift Valley, along with larger artifacts. The use of obsidian at some sites resulted in workmanship of a high quality; it was traded over substantial distances, providing further evidence of an intensified exploitation of the environment (Robbins 1997). As in southern Africa, some hunter-gatherer groups survived into recent times, although as relatively small, isolated groups. Ethnographic studies of the Hadza and Sandawe in Tanzania and the Okiek in Kenya are potentially useful in the interpretation of past hunter-gatherer societies.

West Africa Evidence for the intensification of hunting and gathering in West Africa has been found at a number of sites. One of the most important is **Iwo Eleru**, a rockshelter in the forest zone of southern Nigeria (Shaw and Daniels 1984). There a largely microlithic quartz industry was excavated, dating to *c.* 10,000–1500 BC, with an increasing use of a finer material,

---

use of the ethnohistorical sources quite reasonable, but it is less certain that they are relevant to older art, which may date back 2000 years or more and belong to a much more ancient tradition.

Research of David Lewis-Williams

A similar problem arises in connection with the research of David Lewis-Williams (1981; 1983; 1995; 2001; 2002; 2003), carried out in the same area. A central ritual for Bushman groups has been the trance dance, which is still practiced in the Kalahari. While women clap and sing songs about sources of supernatural power such as the eland or giraffe, some men are able to dance themselves into a trance or, as they believe, to enter the spirit world. Acting as shamans (individuals who can communicate with the spirits), they are said to be then able to cure the sick, resolve social conflict, and, in some cases, control game animals, including those that are thought to bring rain. Drawing on

19th-century ethnohistorical sources, Lewis-Williams was able to demonstrate that both the trance dance and the altered states of consciousness that it induced were depicted in the rock art of southern Africa, particularly in many of the paintings. Figures in a characteristic bent-forward position with blood pouring from the nose, and representations of fantastic creatures – part human, part animal – appear to relate directly to the trance dance and its experiences. The art, it seems, was not merely a record but a stored source of potency that made the shamans' contact with the spirit world possible.

Although some of this art is known to be relatively recent, painted stones from the southern Cape with similar depictions may be 2000 years old (Mitchell 2002), and the date

of much of the rest is unknown. Much of it seems to depict more mundane activities than trance dancing, and the question inevitably arises of the applicability of this symbolic approach to older rock art in southern Africa and to rock art in other parts of the continent. Rock art researchers in other parts of the world have similarly interpreted bodies of prehistoric art far removed in space and time, leading some to claim that visionary imagery is very widespread in such art, while others doubt this (Chippindale et al. 2000; see also Rock Art – Representation of Myth or Reality? box, Chapter 11, pp. 426–27). In the end, the subject of rock art interpretation raises fundamental questions about the extent to which archaeologists can use information from recent or near-recent peoples to interpret the remote past.

10.9 *Rock painting of a trance dance: a southern African depiction showing five men in a characteristic bent-forward position, who are supporting themselves on dancing sticks. To the left and right women are clapping the rhythm of a ritual song that intensifies the altered state of consciousness into which the men are entering.*

KEY CONTROVERSY A Green Sahara?

The Sahara Desert occupies approximately one third of the African continent and is thought to have existed for over 2 million years. However, it has not been a static phenomenon, but has been affected by numerous long-term and short-term climatic fluctuations. A change of particular significance for human settlement occurred about 11,000 years ago, when lower temperatures and higher rainfall rendered habitable parts of the desert that had apparently not been occupied during the previous dry period, producing what has been called a "green Sahara" (Davidson 1966).

There were lakes and marshes and even rivers in some places where there have been none for the last 4000 years or so, but continuing research has shown that the situation was far more complex than was once thought, with considerable variation in conditions across both space and time. Thus, rather than a bounteous environment characterized, for instance, by human groups who were able to benefit from distinctive aquatic adaptations, as has sometimes been claimed, it is more likely that Sahelian (grassland) and steppe conditions merely extended further north and Mediterranean conditions further south, complicated by the various Saharan highlands.

Furthermore, although generally moister conditions existed until the 3rd millennium BC, they were frequently interrupted by drier periods of varying lengths. To complicate matters still further, after the 3rd millennium BC the northern Sahara remained dry, but the southern Sahara continued to have moister conditions, although these were repeatedly broken by progressively longer drier phases, which by the 1st millennium AD resulted in true desert.

The impact on human settlement was equally complex. The moister conditions after about 11,000 years ago allowed hunter-gatherers to expand into regions where they then became vulnerable to subsequent short-term climatic fluctuations, necessitating a variety of adaptive strategies in order to survive: the collection of wild grass seeds, or snails, or fishing, or hunting wild cattle, for example. Climatic change did not determine what human groups did, but it did stimulate a range of human responses that in one way or another represented a more intensive exploitation by hunter-gatherers of their often marginal and unpredictable environments. In this way the foundations of the continuum of change were laid, that led eventually to food production.

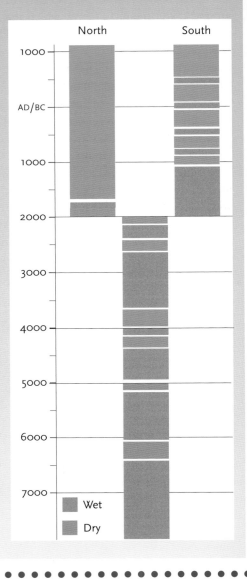

10.10 *Diagram showing Late Holocene paleoenvironments in the southwest Sahara.*

chalcedony, as time went on. The technological innovations of both **ground-stone axes** and **pottery** first appeared in the 4th millennium BC, and after about 2500 BC some of the microliths had sheen on their edges, as if used for cutting plant material. At about the same time there was a marked increase in the number of **grindstones**. Direct evidence of food production is lacking, but it seems likely that exploitation of the environment was being intensified, and this in an area where indigenous yams are thought to have been domesticated from *c.* 6000 BC, on the basis of linguistic evidence (Ehret 2002). Particularly important, because such evidence is so rare in this part of Africa, was a human skeleton from the lowest level of the site, which already displayed specifically West African features (Brothwell and Shaw 1971).

An even longer, although incomplete, stratified sequence was excavated at **Shum Laka**, a rockshelter in the montane Grassfields of southern Cameroon; this site also had a microlithic quartz industry (de Maret 1996). There is evidence here for discontinuous occupation from about 31,000 years ago until the 2nd millennium AD, with pottery appearing before 2000 BC, associated with partly polished, flaked, hoe-like stone artifacts.

The site also produced 18 human skeletons, of which the four earliest date to approximately 6000 BC; the presence of such burials suggests that the occupants were at least intermittently sedentary. As with Iwo Eleru, it seems probable that the people of Shum Laka were intensifying their subsistence strategies at about this time.

The Beginnings of Farming

The first African farming developed out of the intensification of hunter-gatherer strategies, and was based on both indigenous plants and animals and on some that were adopted from outside the continent. This development is best seen as a gradual change from food procurement to food production, in which increasing human control was extended over the sources of food.

It seems to have occurred in different places in a variety of ways, but the earliest evidence is almost all from north of the Equator [10.11]. A major trigger for the cultural adjustments involved was very likely the necessity to respond to complex environmental fluctuations.

The Sahara

The earliest African farming seems to have been an economy based on domesticated animals, for which evidence has been found in the eastern Sahara. The most important area is **Nabta Playa** in the far south of Egypt, a site complex where pits and traces of huts indicate some stability of settlement, though probably seasonal (Wendorf et al. 2001). By about 7000 BC, a stone-using people who made pottery but still hunted and harvested wild grasses and fruits (including wild sorghum), appear to have been keeping domesticated cattle at this place, although the evidence is disputed [see box: The Domestication of Cattle in the Sahara, pp. 362]. Indigenous wild cattle were present in the Sahara and were an important source of food for some hunter-gatherer groups. It is argued that the cattle whose bones were found at Nabta Playa must have been domesticated,

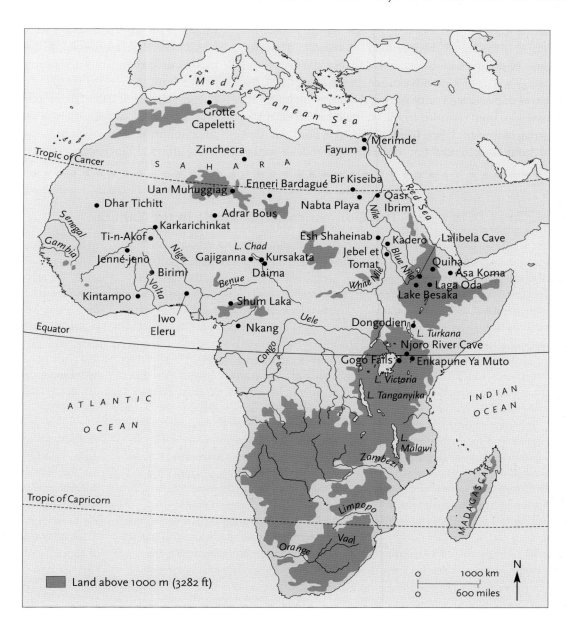

10.11 Early farming sites: these were occupied by people with a stone-based technology and were almost all situated north of the Equator. In many of these sites the evidence for the earliest animal domestication seems to be earlier than that for the earliest plant domestication and is thought to have involved both indigenous and introduced species.

361

10.12 *Saharan rock painting of a pastoralist camp:* this depiction from the Tassili area in the central desert shows huts and women on the right side of a rope to which is tethered a number of calves. Men and adult cattle are on the left of the rope. This layout conforms to ideas that were to persist for a long time amongst some cattle pastoralists in West Africa. (Painting by André Lhote.)

because the environment was so marginal that they could not have existed in the area without human intervention. However, the degree of domestication was probably very tentative at this early date. The site of **Enneri Bardagué**, in northern Chad, has evidence of domesticated cattle during the 6th millennium BC. They have also been recorded by the 5th millennium BC at **Uan Muhuggiag** in western Libya, **Grotte Capeletti** in northern Algeria, and **Adrar Bous** in northern Niger, and at later dates further

to the west and south (Hassan 2002). In contrast to the possibly earlier date for domesticated cattle, the remains of the earliest domesticated **sheep or goats** at Nabta Playa date to about 5000 BC, suggesting their probable introduction from western Asia. They were also present at Grotte Capeletti by a similar date, and were probably adopted rapidly in the Sahara because of their tolerance of the dry conditions in many areas.

Far to the southwest, at the large settlements of **Dhar Tichitt** in Mauritania, people were keeping both cattle and goats, as well as growing the indigenous cereal pearl millet by about the middle of the 2nd millennium BC. Nevertheless, it was pastoralism rather than cultivation that was important to Saharan groups, as is abundantly demonstrated by much of the rock art dating from this period [**10.12**]. Crop cultivation was a much later development (Dhar Tichitt providing the earliest unequivocal evidence), although by about the middle of the 1st millennium BC emmer wheat, barley, date, grape, and fig were being grown at **Zinchecra** in Libya (van der Veen 1999).

KEY CONTROVERSY The Domestication of Cattle in the Sahara

Although the subject is still the focus of considerable discussion, it now seems probable that the earliest cattle herding in Africa resulted from the domestication of indigenous animals in the area presently occupied by the Sahara Desert, rather than from their introduction from outside the continent, as formerly thought (Hassan 2000; MacDonald 2000). Wild cattle (*Bos primigenius*) were present in North Africa during the early Holocene, and appear to have been an important source of meat for some hunter-gatherers. Repeated spells of drought, resulting from climatic fluctuations during the 7th millennium BC, apparently led to attempts to keep cattle in areas where they could not have survived without human assistance, as at Nabta Playa, in the eastern Sahara.

Significant support for the African domestication of African cattle has come from mitochondrial DNA evidence (see box in Chapter 5, p. 185). This indicates that African and European cattle diverged from one another some 26,000–22,000 years ago, making it most unlikely that the long-horned humpless cattle of the Sahara originated from outside the continent. Nevertheless, the osteological evidence for their differentiation from wild cattle is inconclusive in the opinion of some authorities. However, the earliest stages of animal domestication inevitably are difficult to identify, simply because too little time will have elapsed for recognizable morphological changes to have taken place.

If what we are seeing at Nabta Playa and at Bir Kiseiba, also in the eastern Sahara, does represent the beginnings of cattle domestication in Africa, then its date of about 7000 BC would make it at least as early as the earliest cattle domestication outside the continent, in Anatolia, Syria, and Jordan.

Indeed, Christopher Ehret (2002) has gone so far as to claim that it is the first in the world. Others have been considerably more cautious but have generally accepted that domesticated cattle were present in the central Sahara by the 5th millennium BC. By then, cattle pastoralism was emerging there as a primary subsistence strategy, as indicated by the unfortunately poorly dated rock art. As conditions in the desert deteriorated from the 3rd millennium BC onwards, cattle herds were taken south into areas of West and East Africa that would have been unsuitable during earlier moister periods, because of the diseases transmitted by tsetse flies to both domesticated animals and humans. In short, whether or not cattle were domesticated in the Sahara, it was from there that the practice of cattle herding spread into much of the rest of Africa.

The Nile Valley

Farming began later in the Nile Valley than in the Sahara, but included cultivation as well as pastoralism. At **Merimde** on the western side of the Nile Delta, for instance, stone-using village dwellers were making pottery, cultivating barley, emmer wheat, and flax, and keeping cattle, sheep, goats, pigs, and dogs from about 5000 BC. The settlement covered an area of 18 ha (44.5 acres) and consisted of small mud dwellings set out along narrow lanes. The occupation debris at this site averages 2.5 m (8 ft) in depth, and the village appears to have existed for almost a millennium, although it was abandoned at one time. At about the same date, settlements in the **Fayum Depression**, west of the lower Nile, had a similar economy, although they were occupied more briefly. The most important evidence for their occupation consists of numerous storage pits for grain, which were often lined with matting; one pit contained a wooden sickle with a cutting edge of flaked stone inserts.

These developments along the lower Nile appear to have been relatively sudden, and to have been brought about partly by the introduction of plants and animals from Southwest Asia (Phillipson 1993a; Hendrickx and Vermeersch 2000). The people who occupied these settlements were possibly part of the Afroasiatic language family, which was then spread across north and northeast Africa, but to which Semitic languages also belong, thus illustrating the interaction between African and Asian influences that was to characterize the area (Ehret 2002). From this general base in and around the Nile Valley arose the Predynastic cultures, consisting of a succession of stone-using farming societies that gradually adopted the use of copper, and from which emerged the earliest dynasties of pharaonic Egypt by the end of the 4th millennium BC.

To the south, in Sudan, the site of **Esh Shaheinab** held evidence of domesticated goats and cattle at the end of the 5th millennium BC, although bone harpoons and shell fishhooks suggest that fishing was still important. Although the occupants of the site were now making axes and adzes by grinding both stone and bone, they still had a microlithic stone industry and pottery that resembled those of the older (hunter-gatherer) site of Early Khartoum. At a similar date, cattle, sheep, and goats were being herded at **Kadero**, also in Sudan; wild sorghum, finger millet, and panicum were exploited and may have been cultivated, hunting and fishing having become marginal activities.

To the north, along the middle Nile, the best-known early food producers were the 4th-millennium BC people that archae-

ologists call the **"A Group."** They cultivated wheat and barley and herded sheep, goats, and cattle, but were greatly influenced by contact with the later Predynastic occupants of the lower Nile, with whom they traded extensively. It is remarkable that although the southern part of the middle Nile formed the eastern end of the area in which **sorghum** is thought to have been domesticated, the earliest certain evidence for its cultivation dates only from the early 1st millennium AD, at the sites of **Jebel et Tomat** in Sudan, and **Qasr Ibrim** in southern Egypt. Considering the presence of domesticated sorghum up to 2500 years earlier in both Saudi Arabia and India, where it is not indigenous, it must have been domesticated in Africa, where it is, at an early date. The relevant evidence is still lacking, however, and there might be other explanations for this anomaly (Breunig and Neumann 2002).

West Africa

Less is known of the earliest farmers in the West African savanna, although cattle herders who also kept sheep or goats were present at Karkarichinkat in Mali by early in the 2nd millennium BC, at Gajiganna near Lake Chad by the end of the 2nd millennium BC, and at **Daima** [10.13], in the same part of northeast Nigeria, by early in the 1st millennium BC (Hassan 2000). As in the Sahara, there are indications that cultivation developed later than pastoralism, some of the earliest evidence

10.13 Continuity of farming settlement: *an archaeological excavation through deep occupation deposits at Daima, northeast Nigeria, near Lake Chad. A large mound had grown up as a result of some 2500 years of human occupation on the same spot, commencing early in the 1st millennium BC.*

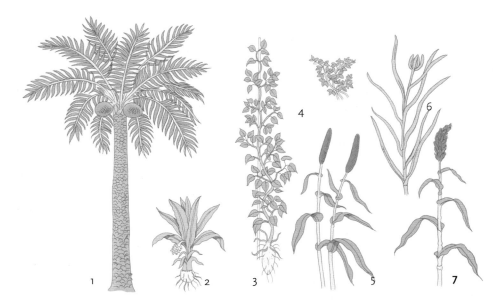

10.14 *Some major indigenously domesticated African crops: (1) oil palm; (2) the false banana, ensete; (3) two African species of yams; (4) cowpea; (5) pearl millet, also known as bulrush millet; (6) finger millet; (7) sorghum (various scales).*

being for domesticated pearl millet at **Birimi** in northern Ghana in the second half of the 2nd millennium BC, at **Ti-n-Akof** in Burkina Faso at the end of the 2nd millennium BC, and at **Kursakata** in northeast Nigeria by the mid-1st millennium BC (Neumann 1999; D'Andrea et al. 2001).

The important crops in the savanna zone, all indigenous to Africa, are likely to have been pearl millet, West African rice (different from East Asian rice – see Chapter 7), and sorghum. As mentioned in the context of the middle Nile, sorghum appears to have been domesticated late. The earliest date for domesticated sorghum in West Africa is only in the late 1st millennium BC, at the site of **Jenné-jeno** in Mali, which also had evidence of domesticated West African rice by a similar date (McIntosh 1995).

In the rainforest and its margins, yams and oil palms were probably important [**10.14**]. One of the **Kintampo** sites in Ghana produced **oil palm nuts** and (possibly cultivated) cowpeas from a context dated to the 2nd millennium BC, as well as indications that cattle and sheep or goats were kept by people who also hunted and gathered (Casey 2000). A useful sequence from the rainforest is in Nigeria at **Iwo Eleru**, where pottery and ground-stone axes, often but not exclusively associated with farming, first appeared in the 4th millennium BC. After about 2500 BC some of the microliths from this site had sheen on their edges, as if used for cutting plant material, and grindstones became more common (Shaw and Daniels 1984). Further to the east, at **Shum Laka** in Cameroon, pottery was in use before 2000 BC, along with partly polished flaked-stone artifacts that resemble hoes (de Maret 1996). Although these changes have already been cited as evidence for hunter-gatherer intensification at these sites, they could indicate tentative moves toward farming, and the uncertainty surrounding their interpretation serves to emphasize the continuum of change of which the development of food production was a part.

According to both botanical and linguistic evidence, this is the area in which both indigenous **yams** and **oil palms** were first domesticated (Ehret 2002); the later archaeological evidence from Iwo Eleru and Shum Laka might reflect that process. Particularly important is the recovery of banana phytoliths from the Cameroon site of **Nkang**, to the southeast of Shum Laka, from a context dated to the 1st millennium BC. Bananas are not indigenous to Africa and must have been introduced from Southeast Asia via the East African coast. That their cultivation had spread as far as the West African rainforest by such an early date is remarkable, and their adoption at that time would suggest that cultivation and management of local plants and trees was already well established. The site of Nkang also had evidence of domesticated sheep and goats by a similar date, and gathering, hunting, and fishing were still practiced (Mbida et al. 2000). Collectively, the Nkang evidence is a timely reminder of how much is still not known about early food production in the rainforest. Indeed, ground-stone artifacts and pottery of uncertain date occur as far south as the lower Congo, suggesting that early farming (most likely in the form of horticulture) may have been widespread in this region.

Northeast and East Africa

In Eritrea, Ethiopia, and Somalia, numerous rock paintings indicate the importance of herding cattle; unfortunately, their dating is unsatisfactory. Nevertheless, paintings showing long-horned humpless (taurine) cattle but lacking depictions of humped (zebu) cattle or camels are presumed to record early pastoral activities. Some indication of the time to which they might belong has been provided by the faunal evidence from **Asa Koma** in Djibouti, which showed the presence of domesticated cattle by about the middle of the 2nd millennium BC; in Ethiopia they appeared at a similar date at **Laga Oda** and at **Lake Besaka**, at the latter site along with sheep or goats (Marshall

2000). There is also evidence of domesticated barley, horse beans, chickpeas, cattle, and sheep or goats at **Lalibela Cave** in Ethiopia, in the second half of the 1st millennium BC (Phillipson 1993a). Furthermore, indications that domesticated cattle were on the Ethiopian Plateau by the 4th or 3rd millennium BC have been provided by the reanalysis of an old excavation at **Quiha** in northern Ethiopia, though only ceramic dating is available (Barnett 1999).

This is remarkably little archaeological evidence for an area that, particularly in the case of Ethiopia, has such ecological diversity and such a wide range of cultivated plants. Almost certainly the lack of such evidence is merely the result of limited research, because both botanical and linguistic evidence suggest a high antiquity for food production in Ethiopia. Introduced wheat and barley have been grown there long enough for a great number of varieties to develop, some of which are exclusive to the region. There are also a number of Ethiopian plants, such as the cereal teff, the oil plant noog, the so-called false banana, ensete, and the stimulants coffee and chat, which are indigenous to the region and were presumably domesticated there. It is surely significant that Ethiopia is the southernmost area in Africa to which the use of the ox-drawn plow penetrated, probably by the 1st millennium BC. As for the linguistic evidence, it suggests that the herding of domestic animals and the cultivation of cereals may have originated as early as the 5th millennium BC (Phillipson 1993b).

Another indication of a probable early date for farming in northeast Africa is provided by evidence to the south, in northern Kenya, where domesticated sheep or goats and cattle were present at the site of **Dongodien**, close to the eastern shore of Lake Turkana, by about 2000 BC. Fishing remained important at this site, hunting was still practiced, and pottery was in use (Marshall 2000). Still further to the south, in southern Kenya, the site of **Enkapune Ya Muto** has yielded evidence of domestic goats by about 1000 BC and perhaps earlier (Marean 1992). At other sites in central, southern, and western Kenya, and in northern Tanzania, there is also evidence for the herding of cattle and sheep and goats by the 1st millennium BC, by people who used pottery and stone bowls but either did not cultivate plants or did so in a very limited fashion. There appear to have been several of these pastoral groups, one of which, the Elmenteitan on the western side of the Kenyan Rift Valley, used obsidian for stone artifacts and had both pottery and stone bowls. One of the most remarkable of their sites is **Njoro River Cave**, where evidence from the late 2nd millennium BC indicated the unusual practice of **cremating** the dead. Other groups, who also used stone tools, pottery, and stone bowls, buried their dead under stone cairns or in crevices between rocks.

To the west, in Uganda and western Kenya, the makers of what is known as Kansyore pottery might also have been cattle pastoralists, although the 2nd-millennium BC evidence for this at the site of **Gogo Falls**, near the Kenyan side of Lake Victoria, has been treated with caution (Marshall 2000). Also in Uganda, the cultivation of bananas around the northern and western sides of Lake Victoria, where they were eventually to provide a unique subsistence base, could well have been established by the 1st millennium BC.

The southern limit to the adoption of pastoralism by stone-using hunter-gatherers seems for some time to have been northern Tanzania. For herding to spread into the southern part of the African continent, there had to be changes in the distribution of the tsetse fly and of trypanosomiasis (sleeping sickness in humans) to which so many domestic animals were vulnerable. It was probably only toward the end of the 1st millennium BC that climatic changes opened up fly-free corridors that allowed pastoralism to expand further to the south; by that time, many of the human groups involved had access to iron tools and weapons. Cultivation was also becoming well established by that time, and by clearing woodland was helping to reduce the extent of the tsetse-infested areas.

Ironworking Societies and the Adoption of Farming South of the Equator

Except in Egypt, the Sudanese Nile Valley, and parts of Mauritania and Niger, the earliest metallurgy in the African continent was based on iron, not copper. It remains unclear whether the knowledge of iron smelting and blacksmithing was diffused from Southwest Asia and the Mediterranean world, or resulted from indigenous development within Africa itself [see box: The Origins of African Ironworking. p. 368]. This is because ironworking seems to have been first practiced south of the Sahara at a date not appreciably different from that for its adoption north of the desert or along the Nile.

In west and west-central Africa, the earliest evidence belongs to the first half of the 1st millennium BC; the sites of **Do Dimi**, in Niger, and **Taruga**, in Nigeria, are particularly important, but early evidence has also been found in Cameroon, Gabon, and the Central African Republic. In East Africa it seems likely that iron was first smelted at a similar date, although several sites in Rwanda and Burundi have produced questionably early radiocarbon dates in the 2nd millennium BC. Certainly iron was being produced at **Kemondo Bay** in northwest Tanzania by the second half of the 1st millennium BC, and far to the north at **Meroë**, in Sudan, by about the middle of that millennium (having become commonly used in Egypt not much earlier). In sum, iron seems to have been widely known north of the Equator by the end of the 1st millennium BC [**10.15**], although in most of Africa south of the equator it was not adopted until the 1st millennium AD (Woodhouse 1998; Holl 2000).

One of the most remarkable of the early iron-using societies in West Africa was that of **Nok**, on the southern and western slopes of the Jos Plateau in Nigeria, to which the site of Taruga belonged. Numerous terracottas found in this area, mostly of humans and some life-size, display considerable technical and artistic ability and a unique style [**10.16**].

Heads and parts of limbs and torsos have been recovered, in some cases providing information about the society's material culture, dating from about the middle of the 1st millennium BC to the second quarter of the 1st millennium AD (Phillipson 1993a). The sculptural form of some of the terracottas suggests that the powerful tradition of West African woodcarving was already established, although direct evidence for it has not yet been recovered from archaeological contexts (Willett 1971).

Movements of Bantu-speaking Peoples

In Africa as a whole, iron appears to have been used at first for ceremonial, decorative, and high-value artifacts, and the speed and extent of its adoption varied greatly. Nevertheless, over the long term its possession had important economic and socio-political consequences. It provided tools and weapons of greater efficiency than those of stone, bone, or wood, and it must surely be significant that its adoption in the central and southern parts of the continent took place at much the same time as the later movements of Bantu-speaking people. Commencing at a time prior to the advent of iron technology, it is these people who are thought to have been instrumental in taking farming into most of Africa south of the equator.

On the basis of linguistic evidence (Vogel 1997), it has been postulated that this "Bantu expansion," as it has been called,

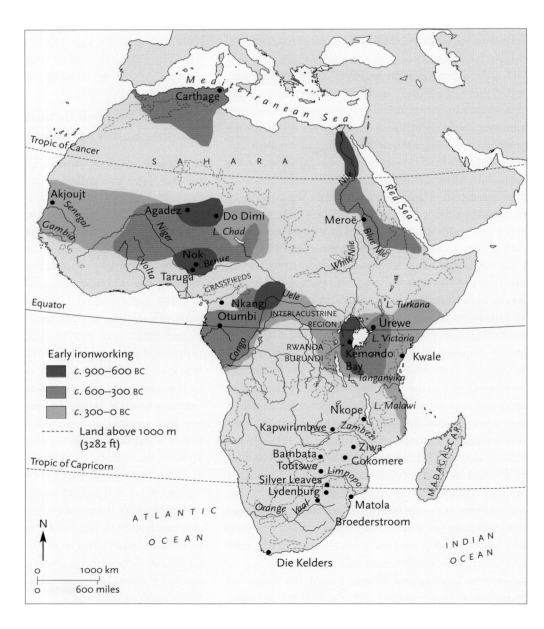

10.15 African sites with evidence for early metallurgy, and early farming sites south of the Equator: *in the southern parts of the continent iron was introduced by some of the earliest farmers in the region during the 1st millennium AD.*

Early ironworking
- ■ c. 900–600 BC
- ▨ c. 600–300 BC
- ▧ c. 300–0 BC
- ----- Land above 1000 m (3282 ft)

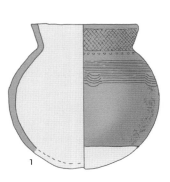

10.16 *(Left)* **Terracotta head from Nok, Nigeria:** *sculptures such as this were made by early iron-using farmers on the southern and western slopes of the Jos Plateau, from about the middle of the 1st millennium* BC *until the second quarter of the 1st millennium* AD. *Mostly of humans and some life-size, they formed parts of figures probably of ritual significance.*

10.17 *(Right)* **Chifumbaze pottery from central and southern Africa:** *note the similarity between pots from (1) western Kenya, (2) northern Zambia, (3) the Transvaal in South Africa. Pottery of this type was made by the earliest farmers and iron-users in the region.*

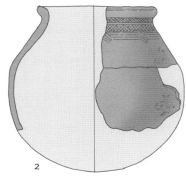

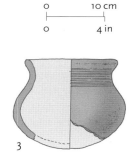

began in the Grassfields of Cameroon and gradually extended to the east through the savanna, until it reached the interlacustrine region of east-central Africa. From there it is thought to have moved southward and westward into the savanna south of the equatorial forest. Migrations might also have taken place along the Atlantic coast, along savanna corridors opened up through the forest during a dry phase, or along the many rivers of equatorial Africa. Probably a highly complex series of small movements was involved, beginning perhaps as early as the 2nd millennium BC and continuing until late in the 1st millennium AD. Although there is relatively little archaeological evidence that can be attributed with certainty to the movements of these Bantu-speaking peoples, it is apparent that they contributed significantly to the spread of both farming and ironworking south of the Equator (Sutton 1996).

Ironworking Farmers

The innovations of ironworking and farming spread remarkably quickly as far as the Transvaal and Natal in South Africa. The pottery from relevant archaeological sites throughout this enormous area shows sufficient similarity [**10.17**] for archaeologists to have bracketed it together under the title of the **Chifumbaze complex** (Phillipson 1993a). Nevertheless, different groups of people have been identified on the basis of variations in the pottery, of which the earliest is the **Urewe** group to the north and west of Lake Victoria, dating from the middle of the 1st millennium BC to the beginning of the 1st millennium AD. **Urewe pottery** has been found in Uganda, southwest Kenya, Rwanda, Burundi, adjacent parts of the Democratic Congo, and northwest Tanzania, in the last four countries associated with early evidence for iron smelting. The

Urewe people appear to have been village dwellers who smelted iron and probably kept domesticated cattle and cultivated finger millet and sorghum, though little is known about the details of their subsistence economy. Their agriculture and their ironworking might well have been the cause of a significant reduction in forest vegetation around Lake Victoria around the middle of the 1st millennium BC, indicated by pollen evidence from the lake sediments.

To the south of them, other groups belonging to the Chifumbaze complex appear to have been divided into at least an eastern and a western group. The eastern group expanded very quickly around the 2nd century AD from the coastal regions of southeastern Kenya, where it is represented by **Kwale ware**, to its southern limits in Natal, where the characteristic pottery is known as **Matola ware**, after a site in Mozambique. A distance of over 3000 km (1864 miles) appears to have been traversed in less than two centuries. The economy of the eastern group seems to have centered on cereal cultivation, probably finger millet and sorghum in particular, with domesticated animals being less important. Inland, other early iron-using farmers, represented by the **Nkope** and the **Gokomere/Ziwa traditions**, appear to have moved into Malawi, eastern Zambia, and much of Zimbabwe.

For people of the western group, who appear to have reached Zambia by the middle of the 1st millennium AD via the Democratic Congo and Angola, cattle seem to have played a greater role, as indicated by evidence from the site of **Kapwirimbwe** near Lusaka. The copper deposits of southeastern Democratic Congo and northwestern Zambia were exploited from the 1st millennium AD onward, and ironworking was important. For many southern African societies, for example at

KEY CONTROVERSY The Origins of African Ironworking

Attempts to explain how ironworking was adopted in Africa provide a good example of the common conflict between archaeologists promoting diffusion and those promoting independent invention. For a long time it was assumed that the associated technologies of iron smelting and forging must have originated in Southwest Asia, spreading into tropical Africa either via the Nile Valley or the North African coast. This was because most of the African continent lacked a period when metallurgy in copper or copper alloy was practiced, as in Europe and Asia, but instead changed directly (although hesitantly) from stone-based technologies to ones based on iron.

The Case for Diffusion

Smelting iron by the bloomery process, which was used in Africa and neighboring parts of the world, involves the achievement of a chemical reaction, not the melting of the metal from an ore. Iron melts at temperatures above 1540° C (2804° F), but the result is cast iron, which is unsuitable for blacksmithing. To produce metallic iron that can be shaped in a forge, it is necessary to reduce the iron oxide ore in a furnace environment that has a low level of carbon dioxide and a high level of carbon monoxide, a process that starts at 1150–1200° C (2102–2192° F). This entails maintaining a balance between oxidation and reduction: oxygen is needed to burn the charcoal fuel that is used to reach the necessary temperature, but too much oxygen will stop or reverse the reduction of the ore. The smelting of iron is more complex than that of some copper ores, and it has been

thought unlikely that iron smelting could have been developed independently in Africa without a prior knowledge of copper metallurgy and of the associated pyrotechnology of handling materials at high temperatures; ironworking must therefore have been introduced from outside the continent.

The Case Against

There are a number of factors that weaken the case for the diffusion of ironworking, however. First, copper-based metallurgy was known in some parts of the continent, most notably in the lower Nile Valley, from as early as the 4th millennium BC, but also at Akjoujt in Mauritania and Agadez in Niger from the early 1st millennium BC. Second, the earliest dates for African iron smelting are increasingly suggesting that it developed independently in several parts of the continent [see **10.15**]. Furnace remains excavated at Do Dimi in Niger, Taruga in Nigeria, and Otumbi in Gabon all date from the 1st millennium BC and seem to be at least as early as the earliest ironworking evidence at Meroë on the middle Nile in Sudan, a place long favored by diffusionists as a staging point in the hypothesized spread of ironworking into tropical Africa. Furthermore, a group of sites in Rwanda and

Burundi have produced dates for iron technology that extend back into the 2nd millennium BC, although these have been questioned. Nevertheless, the smelting of iron in Niger and Nigeria by the 1st millennium BC would suggest that the introduction of the relevant technology from Carthage in Tunisia, another source suggested by the diffusionists, is also unlikely, because that settlement only dated from about the same time. Relatively little is known of Carthaginian ironworking technology, and there is no real evidence that it diffused across the Sahara, as has sometimes been claimed.

Overview

Although the argument for a diffusion of ironworking into tropical Africa has been increasingly questioned, firm evidence for an indigenous origin or origins remains weak. Nevertheless, it seems likely that it will be found, ultimately, that iron technology in Africa was indigenous in origin and was developed in several different places. It has been suggested that, because the Mauritanian copper ores have a high iron content, it is possible that globules of iron might have formed accidentally during copper smelting. It has also been pointed out that similar accidental production of iron might have occurred during pottery firing, in which temperatures could approach those necessary for iron smelting, since in some areas crushed hematite (an iron ore) was used as a slip from the 4th millennium BC onwards. Moreover, the production along the Nile of pottery in which part of the body fired black and part fired red demonstrates that there must have been a knowledge of how to control reduction and oxidation (Woodhouse 1998). Thus the conditions for an indigenous development of iron smelting could have existed, though it has still to be demonstrated convincingly that it took place.

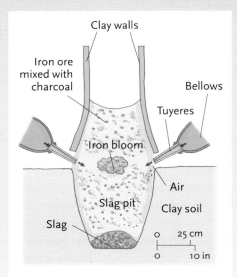

10.18 *Vertical cross-section through an iron furnace at Toumra in the Sudan: the design of African iron furnaces varied greatly but various forms of this shaft type of furnace seem to have been common. The iron bloom was formed at the centre of the furnace where the air blown in by the bellows had the greatest effect. This diagram is based on an ethnographic study of a furnace that was operated in recent times.*

Clay walls

Iron ore mixed with charcoal

Bellows

Tuyeres

Iron bloom

Air

Slag pit

Clay soil

Slag

0   25 cm

0   10 in

the **Toutswe** settlements of eastern Botswana, cattle were to become of major significance by the late 1st millennium AD. They made possible the exploitation of some of the drier environments of southern Africa, into which the earliest farmers in the region had not penetrated. In southeastern Africa they also provided a medium for the accumulation of wealth, whereas to the west, metal came to fill this role.

Valuable information about other early farming societies has come from sites in the Transvaal. At **Silver Leaves**, for instance, the pottery from which has a remarkable resemblance to Kwale ware far to the north, there is evidence for the cultivation of pearl millet by the 4th century AD, while a related site yielded cattle remains (Whitelaw 1997). At **Broederstroom**, west of Pretoria, the inhabitants of a large village of about the 7th century AD smelted iron, grew cereals, and herded sheep or goats and perhaps a few cattle. A mixed farming economy seems to have been well established in this part of southern Africa by about the middle of the 1st millennium AD, the consequent stability of settlement being reflected, perhaps, in the unique series of life-size terracotta human heads found at **Lydenburg**, in the eastern Transvaal. Presumably intended for some religious purpose, it is surely significant that one of the heads is surmounted by a representation of a domestic cow.

Domesticated Plants and Animals

The range of plant and animal resources exploited by southern Africa's early farmers was probably considerable, although insufficient is known about some of the plants and animals involved. In the savannas and higher areas of eastern and southern Africa, the important crops seem to have included pearl and finger millet, sorghum, and cowpeas (Phillipson 1993a) [10.14]. In the rainforest and its margins in central Africa, yams, oil palm and other useful trees were apparently of principal significance (Eggert 1997). A number of other indigenous root crops, pulses, and vegetables were probably grown in various environments.

In addition, a group of plants introduced from Southeast Asia must have had a greater impact in Africa than is often acknowledged. Most important of these were plantains and bananas (both of the genus *Musa*), Asian yam, Asian rice, sugarcane, coconut, and citrus fruits (Purseglove 1976). Linguistic evidence indicates that Madagascar was partly settled from Indonesia, and this has been suggested as the most likely route for some of these introductions. The settlement of Madagascar dates only from the mid-1st millennium AD (see Chapter 8, p. 284), and it is probable that settlers from the East African coast were also important. The chronology of Southeast Asian plant introductions is uncertain, but they could well have predated Madagascan settlement and have arrived on the East African coast itself. It has been suggested, for instance, that

plantains came to the northern part of that coast from India some 2000 years ago (Rossel 1996), and that they might have arrived in Africa more than 3000 years ago (De Langhe et al. 1996). The latter possibility is now supported by banana phytoliths dated to the 1st millennium BC that have been found at Nkang in Cameroon, far away on the other side of Africa. It seems likely that plantains and bananas played a greater role in early farming in Africa than was previously thought.

The story of domesticated animals south of the equator is equally complicated and also imperfectly understood (Blench 1993; Clutton-Brock 1993). Early cattle in the southern half of Africa are thought to have been humpless (taurine), but zebu cattle, both neck-humped and thoracic-humped, and usually assumed to have originated in India, were crossbred with them in eastern and southern Africa. This generated the "Sanga" types of cattle, and resulted in considerable regional diversity of breeds. Similarly, sheep consisted of a number of types, grouped into thin-tailed hair sheep, fat-tailed sheep, and fat-rumped sheep, the last probably the result of crossbreeding the first two. Although the bones of sheep and goats have not often been separately identified on archaeological sites, it seems that south of the Equator, goats were much less important than sheep. Of the two main types, dwarf goats were present in some rainforest areas, and savanna goats in the southern and eastern parts of the continent, either a short-eared brown variety or a lop-eared white one.

Other domesticated animals included donkeys as beasts of burden, dogs for hunting and other purposes, and chickens; these last, although common in Egypt by the late 1st millennium BC, seem not to have reached the rest of the continent until the second half of the 1st millennium AD. Like the Southeast Asian plants, chickens were introduced into Africa, having been domesticated long before in India and Southeast Asia. As with most domesticated animals in Africa south of the Equator, the archaeological evidence for these important birds is limited, and it is likely that they were present at an earlier date than has yet been recorded.

Interaction Between Hunter-Gatherers and Farmers

In spite of the rapid spread of iron-using farmers south of the Equator, groups of stone-using hunter-gatherers remained in both East and central Africa and particularly in Namibia and the Cape Province of South Africa. Yet even the Cape foragers were affected by the changes that had taken place across Africa. As early as the first few centuries AD, people in the southwestern Cape began to herd domesticated sheep and make their own distinctive pottery, as for example at the site of **Die Kelders**. It has been suggested that these practices might have been adopted as a result of influences from the **Bambata** group of southwestern Zimbabwe, via Botswana and Namibia. The earliest pottery in that area was associated at **Bambata Cave** with stone artifacts and the bones of domesticated sheep at a date around the 2nd century BC. However, the hunter-gatherers of the extreme south merely grafted herding and pottery-making onto their established economy, continuing to use stone artifacts and not adopting cultivation, the potential of which was limited in the dry area that they occupied.

Apparently at a later date, some of these groups added cattle herding to their subsistence strategies; in the southwestern Cape this involved a complex pattern of seasonal movement in order to exploit the available resources. It also needs to be emphasized that many early farming communities in Africa south of the Equator continued to hunt a variety of wild animals, which remained of economic importance as a source of food and other materials. Significantly, iron arrowheads and spear points occur in many sites (although possibly indicating conflict as well as hunting), and it has been claimed that sites containing the bones of wild fauna are more numerous than those with remains of domestic stock. Thus the adoption of farming in the southern half of the African continent is a far more complicated story than has sometimes been thought (Phillipson 1993a).

Urbanization and the Growth of Social Complexity in Ancient Egypt

Except in the case of highly mobile pastoralist groups, farming both facilitated and required a greater degree of sedentism than had often been the case with hunter-gatherers. This appears to have encouraged both a growth in overall population and an

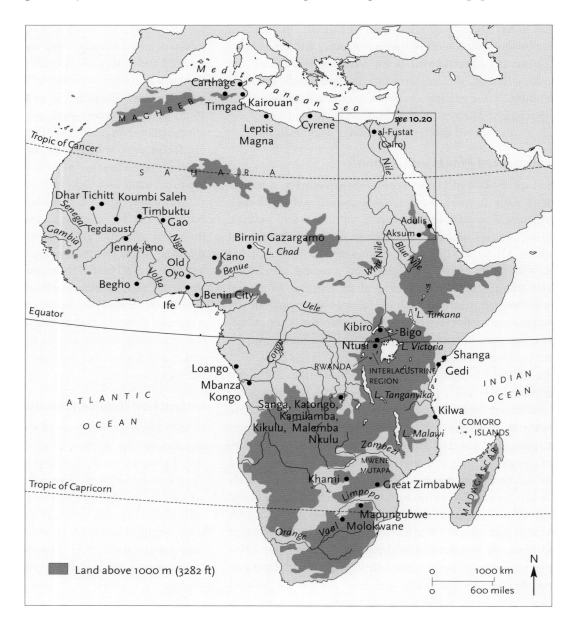

10.19 Sites and areas where urbanization and state formation occurred: these developments were widespread across the African continent, but the earliest were in the lower Nile Valley. The area within the rectangle is shown in greater detail in 10.20.

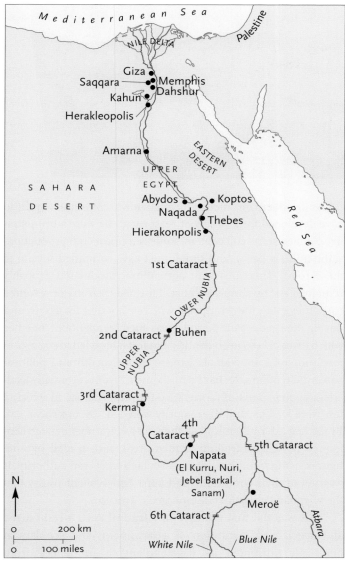

10.20 *Map of ancient Egypt and Nubia: sites mentioned in the text.*

covered had outstanding agricultural potential. Although water levels could vary greatly, sometimes being so high that settlements in the river valley were destroyed, and at other times so low that crops failed and famine resulted, it was this annual inundation that allowed Egypt to exist, and which dominated the lives and thoughts of its people. The floods supported a narrow strip of extraordinarily productive farmland, virtually surrounded by desert, resulting in a considerable aggregation of population and rapid socio-economic and political change. The main crops were emmer wheat and barley, plus lentils, chickpeas, vegetables, fruit, sesame, and flax. Livestock included cattle, sheep, goats, pigs, pigeons, ducks, geese, and bees.

The Predynastic Period

A series of cultural groupings, of which the principal ones are known to archaeologists as the **Badarian** and **Naqada I, II, and III**, developed an increasingly sophisticated material culture between about 4500 BC and 3000 BC (Hendrickx and Vermeersch 2000; Midant-Reynes 2000). With abundant agricultural resources, particularly in the form of cereals, came the growth of social stratification and trading contacts with Southwest Asia, whence the working of copper, gold, and silver was probably introduced. Although this Predynastic period is principally known from burial evidence, it is apparent that numerous villages were clustered along the Nile, and that by about 3500 BC there were large settlements at **Hierakonpolis**, **Koptos**, **Naqada**, and **Abydos**, all in Upper (southern) Egypt [10.20].

Ancient Egypt was at one time thought to have been a "civilization without cities," but it now appears that significant

increase in population density, particularly in resource-rich areas. A knowledge of metallurgy, usually concentrated on iron but sometimes on copper, improved the efficiency of such farming societies. The degree of nucleation of such settlement varied, depending on the environment, the subsistence economy, and the social organization of the people involved, but in some cases became strongly developed, so that villages gradually grew larger, and in time developed into towns or even cities.

The earliest example of this process in Africa occurred on the lower Nile in what is now Egypt, where archaeology and historical sources, together with exceptionally good preservation, provide a remarkably full picture (Baines and Malek 2000; Shaw 2000). Every year at a particular time, the Nile flooded the surrounding land, bringing both water and fertile silt from the African interior, which, unlike Egypt, was well provided with seasonal rain. When the floods receded, the areas that had been

Chronology of Ancient Egypt		
Predynastic and Dynasty 0	c. 4500–3000 BC	
Dynasties 1–3	c. 2950–2575 BC	Early Dynastic
Dynasties 4–8	c. 2575–2150 BC	Old Kingdom
Dynasties 9–11	c. 2125–1975 BC	First Intermediate Period
Dynasties 11–14	c. 1975–1640 BC	Middle Kingdom
Dynasties 14–17	c. 1630–1540 BC	Second Intermediate Period
Dynasties 18–20	c. 1540–1075 BC	New Kingdom
Dynasties 21–25	c. 1075–715 BC	Third Intermediate Period
Dynasties 25–30	c. 715–332 BC	Late Period
Macedonians/ Ptolemies	332–30 BC	Greek administration
Roman emperors	30 BC–AD 642	Roman/Byzantine administration

10.21 Reconstruction of a predynastic wall painting: *found in a tomb at Hierakonpolis dating to about 3500 BC, this shows boats, hunting, and warfare. The tomb possibly belonged to an early ruler.*

population centers already existed by the 4th millennium BC (Bard 2000); these seem to have been sprawling, low-density settlements, in contrast to later walled, brick-built towns of far higher population density, such as the early 2nd-millennium BC walled town of **Kahun**, built as a cult center for the nearby pyramid of a deceased ruler and laid out in a strict grid plan. However, much of the evidence for early urbanization in Egypt is probably buried deep beneath the Nile sediments or covered by modern occupation. Moreover, the ephemeral building materials sometimes used, a lingering tendency toward loose spatial organization, and royal residences that are known to have shifted their location periodically, add to the difficulties of archaeological investigation.

10.22 The Narmer Palette: *found at Hierakonpolis and dating to about 3000 BC, this ceremonial cosmetic palette of slate appears to record aspects of the early kingship that brought together Upper and Lower Egypt. It is carved on both sides, this side showing King Narmer smiting a captive foreigner.*

As time went on, ancient Egyptian towns and cities appear to have developed for a variety of reasons: some were administrative centers, some cult centers, some centers of craft production, some military bases, and some must have combined several of these roles. Their ties with agricultural production probably remained strong simply because it formed their major resource base. Inevitably, they competed with one another for assets, and during the Predynastic period it was such competition, together with a mystical sense of identity, that must have led to some centers and some individuals gaining more wealth and political power than others. As has been claimed, "from essentially leaderless aggregations of farmers, communities arose in which a few were leaders, and the majority were led" (Kemp 1989, 32). By the late 4th millennium BC there were a number of such centers of power, controlling limited areas and headed by elite figures using a combination of secular and sacred authority. It was out of their continuing and apparently violent rivalry that the Egyptian Dynastic state emerged *c.* 3100 BC.

This was the first example in Africa of such a centralized and specialized institution of government, and scholars at one time attributed its development to influences from Mesopotamia, with which Predynastic Egypt does seem to have had contacts, and where state formation was also in progress (see Chapter 12). However, the origins of the Egyptian state, headed by its sacred ruler, the pharaoh, lay firmly within the Nile Valley, expressly in the upper Nile Valley, centered on **Hierakonpolis** [**10.21**]. Significantly, it was there that the Narmer Palette was found, a ceremonial cosmetic palette of slate that appears to record aspects of the early kingship that brought together Upper and Lower Egypt [**10.22**].

Crucial to the emergence of the pharaonic state was the development of **writing**, which predated political unification and which, it has also been suggested, resulted from stimulus from Mesopotamia, where the earliest writing was thought to have developed. Recent discoveries at Abydos, however, have shown that there was an Egyptian system of writing even earlier than that of Mesopotamia (Davies and Friedman 1998). Furthermore, the two writing systems are so different that independent invention is more likely as an origin for Egyptian hieroglyphs. This distinctive type of monumental writing, with the cursive hieratic (for writing on papyrus, a type of paper made from an aquatic plant) that was developed from it and the later demotic script (the everyday script of Late and Greco-Roman periods), was to play a major role in the life of the Egyptian state. That state was essentially African in its origin [see box: How "African" was Ancient Egypt?, p. 375], but its position at the bridge between Africa and Asia gave it a unique character.

The Early Dynastic Period

From both historical and archaeological sources it is possible to trace the remarkable survival of the Egyptian state for some 3000 years, even though there were spells of virtual collapse, known as the First, Second, and Third Intermediate periods. Conventionally, this long stretch of time has been presented as a sequence of periods identified by ruling dynasties; the overall chronology adopted here is that of John Baines and Jaromir Málek (2000). The Early Dynastic period comprised the 1st, 2nd, and 3rd dynasties and lasted from about 2950 to 2575 BC. The beginning of this period seems to have been marked by an increase in the use of writing and by the founding of **Memphis** (near modern Cairo), from then on often the administrative and economic center of the state.

Most remarkable of the rulers during this period was Djoser, the first king of the 3rd Dynasty, who built the **Step Pyra-** mid at **Saqqara**, the oldest stone building of its size in the world [**10.23**]. Earlier, usually mud-brick, royal tombs at Abydos and tombs of high officials at Saqqara had been impressive structures, but the Step Pyramid was an important architectural innovation that inaugurated the practice of pyramid building, which was to be such a distinctive feature of the earlier phases of ancient Egypt (Lehner 1997).

It was a structure of six steps, unlike the smooth-sided pyramids of later times, containing 330,400 cu. m (over 11.6 million cu. ft) of clay and stone, measuring 140 x 118 m (459 x 387 ft) at ground level, with a height of 60 m (197 ft). The king's body was buried in a chamber beneath the pyramid, below ground level. The architect is thought to have been a man called Imhotep, and although there were numerous changes of plan during the construction of the Step Pyramid, it indicates great technical skill, as well as considerable economic power and administrative organization. It is apparent that by the end of the Early Dynastic period the Egyptian state was already sufficiently centralized and technically accomplished to provide the basis for what followed (Shaw 2000).

10.23 *The Step Pyramid at Saqqara: this was built for Djoser, the first king of the 3rd Dynasty, and is the oldest stone building of its size in the world. It inaugurated the practice of pyramid building, which was to be such a distinctive feature of the earlier phases of ancient Egypt.*

The Old Kingdom

The Old Kingdom, stretching from about 2575 to 2150 BC and comprising the 4th to the 8th dynasties, was characterized by economic prosperity and political stability, and was in many ways a continuation of the Early Dynastic period. The state was centrally organized around the pharaoh, who had both secular and sacred powers. He was regarded as a manifestation of Horus, the hawk god, and later as the son of Ra, the sun god. He also became associated with Osiris, the god of the dead and of the afterlife. As such, at least in theory, the ruler had immense power, and the Old Kingdom has often been described as a period of despotic rulers who sought to control disorder in whatever form it appeared and to see to it that the Egyptian concept of right order prevailed. It was the pharaoh's task to mediate between the gods and his people, and thus guarantee the regular change of seasons, the annual Nile floods, and safety from natural dangers and external enemies. During the Old Kingdom, the Egyptian people seem to have had a profound faith in the power of their ruler in such matters, a ruler who not only communed with the gods but also joined their company after his death.

It is in such a context that the massive expenditure of resources on public works that characterized this period is best understood. Usually these involved the construction of royal tombs or temples, and this is the period to which most of the pyramids of ancient Egypt belong. Most remarkable were the great pyramids built by the pharaohs of the 4th Dynasty, particularly the pyramids of Snofru at **Dahshur** and of Khufu and Khafre (known to the Greeks as Cheops and Chephren) at **Giza**. The pyramid of Khufu is the largest, with each side measuring 230 m (755 ft) and with a height of 146.5 m (481 ft); it has been estimated that it contains 2,300,000 blocks of stone, averaging about 2.5 tons each. Its sheer size still impresses, as it was clearly meant to do at the time of its construction some 4500 years ago. It was part of an extensive complex that included an enclosure wall, a mortuary temple, a long causeway to another temple situated in the adjacent Nile Valley, three small pyramids for queens, and a number of pits in which dismantled boats were buried.

The excavation of one of these pits enabled the reconstruction of one of the world's oldest boats, preserved by the dry atmosphere; it was 43.3 m (142 ft) long, with a displacement of 45 tons. Built of cedar that must have been obtained from Lebanon, the boat, like the rest of the pyramid complex, is evidence of the extraordinary resources that must have been devoted to the burial and subsequent worship of the deceased ruler.

It is surely significant that the truly gigantic stone pyramids were built during only three generations of rulers, later pyramids being much smaller in size. The successful completion of such major construction projects indicates the existence of a powerful centralized state, and their subsequent reduction in scale suggests a state whose control gradually weakened as it depleted its economic base.

The archaeological evidence for pyramid and temple building, together with information from inscriptions on stone and texts on papyrus, shed considerable light on the socio-political and economic organization of the Old Kingdom. The major pyramids are particularly rich sources of information [see box: New Insights from the Pyramids, p. 376]. It is apparent that a well-organized system of taxation existed, mainly in the form of agricultural products, other raw materials, and labor. To acquire these resources and to make use of them in major state projects required the involvement of a host of government officials, workmen, artisans, artists, surveyors, architects, scribes, managers, and others. A complex infrastructure existed, which was able to access materials even from outside the Nile Valley and from overseas.

This administrative machine was initially controlled by the ruler, who appointed members of his own family to its highest positions; the incumbents of these positions were also, in many cases, members of the priesthood. In a non-monetary economy, reward for their services consisted of the granting of royal estates and their produce, in theory until the official's term of office expired. However, the ruler's control over such appointments weakened as time went on, and their possession, along with the estates, tended to become hereditary. The increasing number of mortuary and other ritual centers needed support for the continuance of their associated ceremonies and for those who conducted them, support that was also often provided by the granting of estates or of their produce, theoretically in perpetuity. In a situation where productive land was limited but formed the basis of the economy, it was inevitable that the resources at the ruler's disposal were gradually reduced, and his power consequently weakened, as that of high officials and of the priesthood increased.

As with the Early Dynastic period, the Old Kingdom provided the foundation for much that followed, establishing many of the characteristic institutional, socio-economic, religious, and artistic traditions of ancient Egypt. During this period the Egyptian state extended its authority as far south as **Buhen**, far up the Nile at the Second Cataract (area of rapids), whence mining and trading expeditions were able to penetrate even further into the African interior. Nevertheless, the period ended with a weakening of state control, possibly brought on by a succession of low Nile levels and resulting famines, but more likely because wealth and power had become dispersed rather than being concentrated in the ruler and his court.

KEY CONTROVERSY How "African" was Ancient Egypt?

A mass of information on ancient Egypt has been accumulated since the days of Classical Greece, particularly in the course of the last two centuries. In contrast, little or nothing was known about human history in the rest of the African continent until fairly recently, so that Egypt tended to be studied in isolation, or in relation to neighboring parts of Southwest Asia and the Mediterranean. The idea of the state and the invention of writing were seen as the result of stimulus from Mesopotamia, and it was even suggested that the sudden appearance of the Egyptian state resulted from an invasion by a foreign "race" (Bard 2000).

Undoubtedly, the ancient Egyptians did have early trading contacts with peoples in Southwest Asia and some linguistic and ethnic interaction with them, but primarily they belonged to Egypt, and Egypt was not only part of Africa but could not have existed without it. If, as the Greek historian Herodotus remarked almost 2500 years ago, Egypt was the gift of the Nile, then the Nile was the gift of Africa. Both the water and the

fertile silt that were so essential for Egypt's existence were brought by this major African river from deep in the African interior. That same interior was the source of many raw materials lacking in Egypt, and at various times Egyptian trading interests extended far into Nubia, the land of the middle Nile, and along the Red Sea coast. Such interests at times even resulted in the establishment of Egyptian colonies far to the south, and in general imparted a veneer of acculturation that characterized such African societies as that of Meroë, near present-day Khartoum. So close were Egypt's ties with the African interior that for over a century during the early 1st millennium BC its pharaohs were black Nubians, the 25th Dynasty.

It is hardly surprising that as archaeological and historical research turned its attention to tropical Africa from the 1950s, some scholars (e.g. Bernal 1985; see also Chapter 13, p. 475) attempted to reclaim Egypt for Africa. All ancient Egyptians, they insisted, were black Africans, and as black Africans had led the world in scientific,

aesthetic, and abstract thought. Such a view is as much a myth as is the notion of an ancient Egypt divorced from its African context. The ancient Egyptians were very conscious of ethnic differences, and faithfully depicted the contrasting appearances of themselves, Asiatics, Libyans, and Nubians. Nevertheless, the population of the lower Nile Valley seems to have been an ethnic mixture that included a range of skin color and hair type, and the ancient Egyptians appear to have been fairly tolerant of such differences and more concerned about their own cultural identity (Shaw 2001).

Unique though that culture was, and increasingly oriented to Southwest Asia and the Mediterranean as time went on, it was nevertheless firmly rooted in African prehistory. Egypt's attainment of a literate, urbanized state is the earliest example of a development that to greatly varying extents was to take place repeatedly in the African continent. With its remarkable preservation of organic evidence and its documentary record, ancient Egypt provides a window through which we can observe this process in action. Furthermore, it reminds us of how much we still do not know about Africa's past, as we look at the technology of its bows and arrows (Clark et al. 1974) or at its experiments with animal domestication (Clark 1971). Indeed, the many Egyptian tomb models, mainly of the 2nd millennium BC, of people baking bread, brewing beer, counting cattle, plowing fields, sailing boats, and so on, are vivid reminders of how many aspects of past life in other parts of the African continent are imperfectly known to us. To understand Egypt we must know about Africa, but to know about Africa we must understand Egypt.

10.24 *Faience tiles from the ceremonial palace of Ramesses III at Thebes: these show four captive foreign chiefs and demonstrate the ancient Egyptian awareness of ethnic differences in both appearance and clothes. From left to right they are: a Nubian, a Syrian, a Bedouin, and a Hittite.*

KEY DISCOVERY New Insights from the Pyramids

Although primarily a place of royal burial and therefore a product of a powerful cosmology, with a major role in the state religion, the pyramids are also informative on many other aspects of Egyptian life. The earliest of them (particularly the giant examples at Giza) functioned as an economic engine that drove the pharaonic state. The sheer size of each monumental building project involved the collection and redistribution of resources on a massive scale, in order to support the necessary workforce and specialists associated with construction. The largest were all built within a century or so in the middle of the 3rd millennium BC, and it has been claimed that in addition to serving as "a major catalyst for ... the development of Egypt as one of the world's first true states," they also "represent an accelerated cultural development, comparable to our modern space programme or computer revolution" (Lehner 1997, 9 and 16).

Investigations of the pyramids' structures have shed considerable light on Egyptian astronomical and mathematical knowledge, and on ancient surveying, quarrying, transport systems, engineering, architecture, building methods, and stone masonry. It has become possible to understand something of the infrastructure, labor management, and site organization that would have been essential for the successful completion of such large and complex development projects. It has even been argued that the major pyramids have the capacity to refine the accepted chronology for the Old Kingdom.

Because they are oriented to true north with extraordinary precision, it seems likely that their alignment was based on observations of a selected pair of stars in the northern sky. This conclusion is supported by the progressive but slight deviations from true north of the pyramid alignments as time went on, reflecting, it is thought, the earth's extremely slow precession around its axis, of which the ancient Egyptians would not have been aware. Although there is some disagreement about which stars could have been used, and therefore about the chronological implications, calculations have indicated that the Pyramid of Khufu, for example, could date to 2480 ± 5 BC, a date somewhat later than that of 2554 BC currently accepted (Spence 2000; Rawlins et al. 2001).

10.25 *Aerial view of the Giza pyramids. Situated at the edge of the Nile Valley and built about 4500 years ago, their enormous size dwarfs the buildings of the encroaching city of Cairo. Although primarily intended for royal burials, they are informative on many other aspects of ancient Egyptian life.*

The First and Second Intermediate Periods and the Middle Kingdom

The First Intermediate Period followed the Old Kingdom, lasting from about 2125 to 1975 BC. For much of this time there were rival rulers centered on **Thebes** in the south (whose rulers comprised the early part of the 11th Dynasty) and **Herakleopolis** in the north (the 9th and 10th dynasties); it appears to have been a period of political instability, when unified rule gave way to competing principalities. The most important king of the more stable Theban Dynasty was **Mentuhotep** (variously given as I or II), who managed to reunite the Egyptian state.

This introduced the next period, known as the Middle Kingdom, which is dated to *c.* 1975–1640 BC and included the later part of the 11th Dynasty to the 14th Dynasty. Political uncertainty remained at times a problem, but the period seems to have been one of general stability, in which the state maintained control by means of less despotic pharaohs and a substantial bureaucracy. The capital was moved from Thebes back to **Memphis** by Amenemhet I, first king of the 12th Dynasty, with Thebes rising to prominence as a center for the worship of the god Amun. Pyramid building, which had almost ceased during the First Intermediate Period, was resumed, but on a relatively small scale, and the practice had virtually died out by the end of the Middle Kingdom. The period was, however, marked by other substantial building programs, including the construction of a series of powerful forts in the Second Cataract region by the 12th Dynasty kings Senwosret I and Senwosret III. There was an increase in both military campaigning and long-distance trade, in Nubia to the south and Palestine to the northeast, and large numbers of Asiatics settled in the eastern Nile Delta.

Some of these Asiatics, known as the **Hyksos**, took over the rule of northern Egypt as the 15th and 16th Dynasties around 1630 BC, while Theban kings continued to rule in the south as the 17th Dynasty from *c.* 1630 to 1540 BC – the Second Intermediate Period. Although this appears to have been a period of political and economic disintegration, it was also a reasonably stable one at times, during which foreign influences resulted in the introduction of several technical innovations, such as bronzeworking, new crops, the horse and chariot, composite bows, and even new musical instruments.

The New Kingdom and After

The first king of the 18th Dynasty, the pharaoh Ahmose, came to power in **Thebes** in *c.* 1540 BC, and by about 1520 BC had driven the Hyksos rulers from the north. His reign inaugurated the New Kingdom, which lasted until about 1075 BC and included the 18th, 19th, and 20th Dynasties. A series of powerful pharaohs, including Thutmose I, Amenhotep II, Sety I, and Ramesses II, not only held the state together, but at times extended its control both further up the Nile and further into Southwest Asia than ever before. Indeed, for a time Egypt became a great imperial power, one made wealthy by its access to Nubian gold resources. The period also saw the growth of an increasingly powerful army and priesthood. Many temples and other buildings were constructed, and numerous rock-cut tombs for royal and other privileged burials were created in the Valley of the Kings, on the west bank of the Nile at Thebes. Firmly held ideas about an existence after death resulted in

great care and expense being devoted to mummification and burial, for many lesser people as well as for rulers and important elites, in the New Kingdom and before [10.26]. The New Kingdom was also remarkable for the attempt by Amenhotep IV, otherwise known as **Akhenaten** [10.27], to replace traditional beliefs with a new religion based on the worship of the sun disk, or Aten (hence the heretic pharaoh's name change to Akhenaten, "beloved of Aten"). His successors, including his son Tutankhamun, speedily reverted to previous practices.

Of great value for the study of ancient Egyptian urbanism is Akhenaten's new capital city of **Amarna**, originally known as

10.26 Mummy of Ramesses II: *Ramesses II (c. 1279–1213 BC) was one of the most powerful pharaohs. Firmly held ideas about life after death caused great care to be taken with the preservation of the bodies of both rulers and others. As a result, mummies such as this one can provide valuable information on the health and diseases of ancient Egyptians.*

Akhetaten, built in the late 2nd millennium BC and abandoned at Akhenaten's death after only some 20 years of occupation. Extensive excavations at this site have provided a considerable insight into what seems to have been an ordered urban life [**10.28**], although prominent heaps of domestic refuse are a reminder of some of the problems that must have been generated by living in a city. The population has been variously estimated from 20,000 to over 50,000, and the spread of house sizes indicates a society grading from poor to rich without any major gaps, the great gulf being between the residents as a whole and the ruler and his family. A government office in the center of the city yielded a collection of clay tablets now known as the **Amarna Letters**. Written in cuneiform script, they throw an important light on the relationship of Egypt with its western Asiatic neighbors (Kemp 1989; see also Chapter 12).

By the end of the New Kingdom the areas of Egyptian control and influence had shrunk considerably, and Egypt once again disintegrated into a series of virtually separate states. (This occurred at the same time and probably for some of the same reasons as the decline of the Mycenaean Greeks and the states of Southwest Asia, a time of great instability in the eastern Mediterranean; see chapters 12 and 13.) There followed the Third Intermediate Period, lasting from *c.* 1075 to 715 BC, consisting of the 21st Dynasty to the early part of the 25th Dynasty. It ended with the reunification of Egypt, together with **Nubia**, by the Nubian ruler **Piye**, and there followed the so-called Late Period, from about 715 to 332 BC. This comprised the later 25th

Dynasty to the 30th Dynasty, during which Nubian, Egyptian, and Persian kings ruled at different times, and ended with the Second Persian period, brought to a close when Alexander the Great occupied Egypt. It was followed by the Greco-Roman period (332 BC–AD 642), during which Egypt was ruled by the

10.27 *(Above right)* **Fragment of a statue of Akhenaten:** *this sculpture comes from Akhenaten's destroyed temple at Karnak, near Thebes. The attempt by this 18th Dynasty pharaoh (c. 1353–1336 BC) to replace traditional beliefs with a new religion based on the worship of the sun disk failed. After his death, his successors speedily reverted to previous practices and tried to remove all traces of him and his ideas.*

10.28 **Reconstruction of part of the city of Amarna:** *this was the new capital city created by Akhenaten that was abandoned after his death. Because it was occupied for only about 20 years and not subsequently altered, excavations there have been able to provide a considerable insight into ancient Egyptian urban life at that time.*

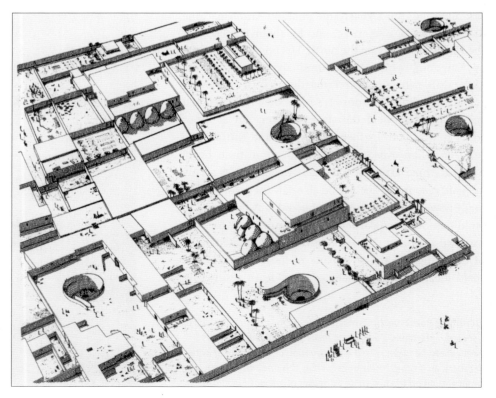

Macedonian and Ptolemaic dynasties and became a colony of the Roman Empire in 30 BC.

The foregoing politically based chronology originated in the work of a 3rd-century BC Egyptian priest called Manetho, and has tended to reinforce the impression of conservatism and continuity that has often been claimed to characterize the ancient Egyptian state. Indeed, all the trappings of statehood were present from the 3rd millennium BC onwards: a centralized government, a specialized bureaucracy, an official religion, substantial cities, monumental structures such as the pyramids and temples, and a unique form of writing. There was also a successful economic system that operated without coinage (which was only introduced at the end of the pharaonic period), and extensive trading interests. In addition, the early state possessed a varied and sophisticated technology, distinctive and original art forms, and an extensive knowledge of the natural world [**10.29, 10.30**]. The subsequent long survival of that state, in spite of periods of collapse, makes it seem as if there was little subsequent development. Nevertheless, a continual process of change and adjustment was active in many aspects of ancient Egyptian life, at both the national and regional level. An initially autocratic government evolved into one run by a complex bureaucracy that eventually controlled even the choice of ruler. The state became more militaristic in outlook, in time developing a powerful army that was able to dominate some of its neighbors. Even in its religion, there were gradual changes in ideas and practices, despite the powerful force of tradition.

10.30 *The Hypostyle Hall at Karnak, near Thebes:* built by the 19th Dynasty pharaoh Sety I (c. 1290–1279 BC), this part of the Great Temple of Amun-Re, with its huge columns and single-span lintels and clerestory, is one of the most impressive examples of ancient Egyptian architecture and building technology.

10.29 *Detail of one of the gold coffins of Tutankhamun:* the tomb of this short-lived 18th Dynasty pharaoh (c. 1332–1322 BC) was found in the Valley of the Kings, on the west side of the Nile near Thebes, in 1922. Its contents have shed considerable light on ancient Egyptian beliefs, rituals, technology, art, and other aspects of this remarkable society.

Urbanization and State Formation in the Rest of Africa

The process of urban development that has been observed in ancient Egypt also took place in many other parts of the continent [see **10.19**], although the form that it took varied greatly in space and time (Fletcher 1998). For instance, aggregations of population in resource-rich areas occasionally resulted in densely occupied centers that continued for long periods; sometimes such centers had populations that fluctuated seasonally or over a number of seasons, and sometimes the entire urban center shifted its site every few years. Such factors as the environment, subsistence economy, material culture, sociopolitical organization, religion, and trading contacts influenced the form, size, density, and degree of transience and mobility of settlements, at both the urban and the village level.

Outside of Egypt, the degree of government centralization and specialization involved in state formation also varied greatly. Some African "kingdoms," as they have often been called, were more like loose, amorphous federations. There are also the problems of distinguishing formally organized states from large "chiefdoms," and of recognizing that increasing social complexity did not automatically grow out of urbanization, nor were the static city or other forms of sedentism its only possible origins. Among the early pastoralists of the Sahara, for instance, it has been suggested that there emerged "mobile elites" who subsequently contributed to the appearance of the states of Kerma and ancient Ghana, discussed below (MacDonald 1998). The transient character of many African urban centers should also be remembered, for example those of Ethiopia for much of the 2nd millennium AD.

10.31 *Aerial view of part of the building traces excavated at Kerma, in Nubia:* this was a flourishing urban settlement by about the middle of the 2nd millennium BC. Situated just upstream of the Third Cataract on the Nile, there are indications that it was the center of black Africa's first identifiable state.

Nubia and Ethiopia

Kerma The people of Nubia on the middle Nile experienced a series of developments similar to those in Egypt, but slower and less comprehensive, probably because of a less productive environment (O'Connor 1993). Contact with Egypt during the Old and Middle Kingdom periods may well have stimulated growing social complexity, and by about the middle of the 2nd millennium BC there was a flourishing urban center on the Dongola Reach of the Nile, just upstream of the Third Cataract, in one of the most fertile parts of Nubia [see **10.20**]. This was the city of **Kerma**, founded in the middle of the 3rd millennium BC, which disappeared when Egypt's colonial interests in Nubia were at their most extensive during the New Kingdom (Kendall 1997). Excavations at Kerma have uncovered an extensive area with impressive building traces [**10.31**], mainly of rectangular houses of mud-brick or wood, and with an elaborate system of fortification consisting of a ditch and a mud wall with projecting rectangular towers. The economy appears to have been based on mixed agriculture, in which barley was an important crop grown on the Nile floodplain and in the annually flooded Kerma Basin; cattle, sheep, and goats played a major role, and hunting and fishing were still important. Trade in raw materials sought by the Egyptians seems also to have been a significant factor in the community's growth.

Kerma was probably the most important of a number of related settlements in its region, and there are indications that it was the center of black Africa's first identifiable state. Within the city, for instance, there was a very large circular building of wood and mud-brick, at least 10 m (33 ft) high and isolated from neighboring houses by a large rectangular enclosure – clearly an elite structure of some kind. There was also a monumental mud-brick temple, known as the Western Deffufa, its base measuring 27 x 52 m (89 x 171 ft) and its height probably far exceeding the 19 m (62 ft) that survived to modern times. Outside the city there was an extensive cemetery of several thousand graves, among which were two smaller monumental mud-brick structures and a substantial number of burial mounds. Some of the latter were unusually large and contained a principal burial accompanied by numerous other individuals, who appeared to have been sacrificed. In one of the mounds its excavator found 322 such sacrifices, and estimated that there had been as many as 400 before disturbance by tomb robbers. Collectively, the evidence from Kerma suggests the existence of a centralized political and spiritual authority (Connah 2001).

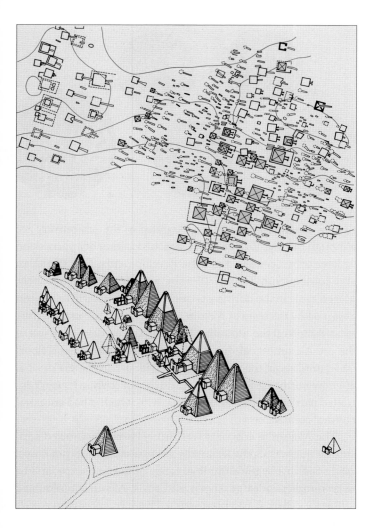

The cemeteries at the first three of these places have been interpreted as "royal" cemeteries and are characterized by tombs covered by small, steep-sided pyramids; mummification was practiced. Hieroglyphic inscriptions further reinforce the impression of Egyptian influence, and from Napata came the Nubian rulers who constituted Egypt's 25th Dynasty in the 8th and 7th centuries BC (Welsby 1996).

During the latter part of the 1st millennium BC and the early 1st millennium AD, the city of **Meroë** and the Meroitic state of which it formed the capital were of major significance in northeast Africa. Meroë was the most important of a number of large settlements; it covered an area of roughly 0.75 x 1 km (2462 x 3282 ft), and at its peak had a population that has been estimated at 20,000–25,000 people. Its principal buildings were of mud-brick, fired brick, and stone, and included a central walled complex interpreted as a royal precinct, as well as a number of temples dedicated to both Egyptian and Meroitic deities; most of its housing must have been of more ephemeral materials. Parts of the city area are still filled by large mounds of iron slag that indicate the former presence of industrial activities. Outside the settlement there are six cemeteries, containing between them a range of burials from common citizens to rulers and their families, the tombs of many of the latter being marked by small stone pyramids [10.32].

Meroitic society was supported by mixed farming. Sorghum, barley, wheat, millet, and other crops were grown, and pastoralism was particularly important. Its material culture

Napata and Meroë Kerma was followed by other urban and state developments further south, of which **Napata** was important during the first half of the 1st millennium BC. Located just downstream from the Fourth Cataract, it survived until the 4th century BC, when its capital was transferred to Meroë between the Fifth and Sixth Cataracts. The Napatan area contains major cemetery sites at **El Kurru** and **Nuri**, a cemetery and temple sites at **Jebel Barkal**, and a cemetery, temple, and town site at **Sanam**.

10.32 *(Above)* **The pyramids of Meroë, in Nubia:** *there are three cemeteries of small pyramids at Meroë – the West, the South and the North Cemetery. At the top is a plan of the West Cemetery and below is a reconstruction drawing of the North Cemetery. Nubian pyramids resemble non-royal New Kingdom pyramid tombs and were first built over 800 years after the last royal pyramid was built in Egypt.*

10.33 *(Right)* **Meroitic temple at Naqa, south of Meroë:** *this small stone building shows Roman influence in its capitals and rounded arches and Egyptian influence in its central lintel, a mixture of architectural styles characteristic of the Roman period in Egypt. The building is an example of how Meroitic society was able to adapt ideas from its north to its own purposes.*

10.34 Aksumite coins: *1) Both sides of a gold coin of about AD 300; 2) a gold coin of about AD 500; 3) a copper coin probably of the late 5th century AD; and 4) a copper coin of the early 7th century AD (2–4 obverse sides only). 1) shows the pre-Christian crescent-and-disk symbol but the three below have the Christian cross on them.*

was sophisticated [**10.33**] – some of the pottery, for example, was technically and artistically impressive. Numerous imports of luxury items such as fine glassware and metalwork indicate close trading relations with Ptolemaic and Roman Egypt, to which Meroitic traders seem to have been suppliers of commodities such as gold, semiprecious stones and other minerals, ivory, slaves, incense, ebony, wild animal skins, and other exotica from the African interior. The Meroitic state was partly literate, at first using Egyptian hieroglyphs for inscriptions but subsequently developing its own unique alphabet. Unfortunately, although such Meroitic writing can be read, the language of the writing cannot really be understood, in spite of intensive research (Welsby 1996).

Aksum The Meroitic state disintegrated in the 4th century AD, although the middle Nile Valley was the location of a succession of later urban centers and state developments, first Christian and subsequently Islamic (Welsby 2002). More immediately, Meroë's role in the northeast African region seems to have been assumed by the state of **Aksum** and the city of the same name, located high on the Ethiopian Plateau. Aksum developed out of the pre-Aksumite culture of the 1st millennium BC, and flourished until about the 7th century AD, with urban centers in what are now northeast Ethiopia and Eritrea. For a while it even controlled part of southwestern Arabia, with which it had ancestral cultural connections.

The Aksumite economy was firmly based on a mixed agriculture that was characterized by a remarkable variety of crops, made possible by the altitudinal range of the landscape, and by large numbers of cattle, sheep, and goats. Aksum's undoubted affluence seems also to have resulted from its successful participation in the trade of the Red Sea, to which it had access through its port of Adulis, supplying ivory, gold, and other African commodities and receiving in exchange a range of manufactured goods. Its political and economic success was reflected in its material culture, with monumental stone architecture for both tombs and elite dwellings. Its carved stelae (standing stones) that marked burials are justifiably famous [**10.35**], the largest, now fallen, being nearly 33 m (108 ft) in length and about 517 tonnes (509 tons) in weight. Aksum also minted its own coinage, in gold, silver, and bronze, the first state in tropical Africa to do so [**10.34**]. It developed its own form of writing; this can be read, and surviving inscriptions augment the other archaeological evidence. Aksum was one of the first states in the world to adopt Christianity as an official religion, and the Christian state of Ethiopia, which survived to modern times, was its direct successor (Phillipson 1998).

10.35 The largest of the stelae still standing at Aksum, Ethiopia: *these single pieces of stone marked the locations of burials, the largest of them probably royal burials. The example seen here, like some other large ones, was carved to represent a multi-storied building. It is 21 m (approximately 69 ft) in height and weighs about 150 tonnes.*

KEY SITE Jenné-jeno: Origins of Urbanism in West Africa

Since the late 1970s, excavations and other fieldwork at and around the site of Jenné-jeno, in Mali, have demonstrated that West African urban origins predated the development of trans-Saharan trade by the North African Arabs (McIntosh 1995). Jenné-jeno is situated in the Inland Niger Delta, an area subject to seasonal inundation that enabled abundant agricultural production and fishing, although surrounded by dry savanna and near the edge of the desert. Other raw materials, such as iron ore, could be obtained from a regional trading network that extended over a radius of at least 350 km (217 miles). Movements of commodities were particularly facilitated by canoe transport on the numerous branches of the Niger River.

Jenné-jeno originated around the 3rd century BC, had grown to at least 12 ha (30 acres) by the 1st century AD, and reached its maximum extent of 33 ha (82 acres) by about the 9th century AD, by which time it was surrounded by a mud-brick wall some 2 km (1.2 miles) long. If satellite sites within a 1-km (0.6-mile) radius of Jenné-jeno are included, then its maximum population could have been as high as 27,000. As it is only one of a large number of contemporary sites in the

Inland Niger Delta, it appears that the population of the area must have been substantial in the late 1st millennium AD. That was a time, it is thought, of greater rainfall than subsequently, when this and other sites were abandoned, in the case of Jenné-jeno being replaced in the early 2nd millennium AD by the nearby historical city of Jenné.

Although Jenné-jeno has shed important light on the indigenous development of West African urbanism, it has been less informative about the origins of West African states. The site has not produced evidence for a stratified social hierarchy or a centralized authority, leading to questions about the nature of its socio-political organization. Nevertheless, its role in long-distance trade, including that of gold from areas to its southwest, would suggest that at the very least the city was influential in its surrounding region. Within that region, a common material culture, a three-tier settlement hierarchy, and a greater diversity of artifacts on larger sites also indicate that this might have been so. Furthermore, by the late 1st millennium AD and the early part of the 2nd, evidence for an elite in the middle Niger area

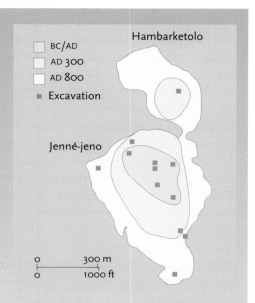

10.36 *Plan of the city of Jenné-jeno, Mali, showing its growth. This urban center played an important part in the trade of the Inland Niger Delta from the late 1st millennium BC till the late 1st millennium AD. It grew up before the development of the trans-Saharan caravan trade, from which West African urbanism was formerly thought to have originated.*

did exist, in the form of large burial mounds containing apparently high-status individuals accompanied by abundant grave goods and, in one case, human sacrifices.

North and West Africa

North African urbanization seems to have been stimulated by Greek and Phoenician colonial settlement during the 1st millennium BC, resulting in such centers as **Cyrene** and **Carthage**. In time these extended control over their surrounding regions, Carthage becoming a state powerful enough to challenge Roman ambitions during the Punic Wars of the 3rd and 2nd centuries BC (Chapter 13). These developments encouraged indigenous urban and state growth in North Africa, resulting, for example, in the emergence among the **Berber** people of the Numidian kingdoms of the Maghreb. In the archaeological record these kingdoms are best known from a number of impressive stone-built royal tombs showing influences from the Hellenistic world (Brett and Fentress 1997). By the early 1st millennium AD, Africa north of the Sahara was substantially under Roman control, and Roman cities such as **Timgad**, in Algeria, and **Leptis Magna**, in Libya, were established. Subsequently, during the second half of that millennium, the region became

part of the Islamic Arab world, and urban centers such as **Kairouan**, in Tunisia, and **al-Fustat** (the old city of Cairo), in Egypt, became important. Thus, North Africa had a long and continuing tradition of urbanization and state formation, as part of the literate world of the Mediterranean (Phillipson 1993a).

It was long thought that West African urbanization was inaugurated by Arab trading contacts across the Sahara from North Africa, commencing in the late 1st millennium AD, but archaeological evidence at **Jenné-jeno**, in Mali, has shown that urbanization originated about 1000 years earlier and had more to do with the resources of the Inland Niger Delta, just to the south of the desert [see box: Jenné-jeno: Origins of Urbanism in West Africa]. Indeed, the origins of West African urbanism are probably even older, for among the many dry-stone built settlement sites of the Dhar Tichitt-Walata area, in southeastern Mauritania, is the massive site of **Dakhlet el Atrous**, which covers 80 ha (198 acres) and dates from the late 2nd and early 1st millennia BC (MacDonald 1998).

By the late 1st millennium AD, both individual urban centers and state systems had appeared in parts of the West African savanna. Ancient Ghana, with its capital at **Koumbi Saleh**, was already in existence by the time of the earliest Arab written account of the area. Its immediate origins seem to date to about the middle of the 1st millennium AD, and are indicative of a growing social complexity in the West African savanna that is also suggested by the evidence from contemporary Jenné-jeno. There followed a succession of other states in various parts of the region during the 2nd millennium AD, including Mali, Songhai, Kanem, and Borno. Undoubtedly, the growth of trans-Saharan trade stimulated these developments, even though it did not initiate them. A number of important urban centers grew up on or near the desert margins as participants in this trade, including **Tegdaoust**, **Timbuktu**, **Gao**, **Kano**, and **Birnin Gazargamo** [see **10.19**]. Camel caravans from North Africa and parts of the desert itself brought salt, copper, manufactured products, dates, cowrie shells, and horses. Going north in exchange were slaves, gold, ivory, spices, pepper, alum, and fine leather. Moreover, the desert trade imported ideas as well as commodities to the West African savanna, and was instrumental in the introduction both of Islam and of limited literacy in Arabic.

Far to the south, in the rainforest and on its margins, other indigenous urbanization was in progress by the early 2nd millennium AD, for example at **Begho**, in Ghana, and **Ife** and **Benin City**, in Nigeria. By the 19th century the Yoruba, based in what is now southwest Nigeria, had become some of the most urbanized people in tropical Africa. Instances of state development include the Akan states in Ghana, the Yoruba state of Old Oyo, and the Edo state, centered on Benin City. Some of these developments expressed themselves in quite remarkable state-sponsored art, of which the copper alloy and terracotta examples from Ife [**10.37**] and the copper alloy ones from Benin City [**10.38**] have become world famous (Willett 1967; Dark 1973). Both of these cities were surrounded by protective earthworks, which in the case of Benin City were part of an extensive regional network. In contrast, in spite of a high population density, the Ibo people of eastern Nigeria had neither cities nor states until the colonial period, evolving their own form of social complexity in which authority was dispersed rather than concentrated. Their example suggests that explanations for urban and state development in Africa invoking population growth and increasing population density need to be re-examined (Connah 2001).

Eastern, Southern, and Central Africa

Towns and cities grew up along the Indian Ocean coast from Somalia to Mozambique (including the Comoro Islands and northern Madagascar) during the later 1st millennium AD. Archaeological excavations at **Shanga** and **Gedi** [**10.39**], in Kenya, and at **Kilwa**, in Tanzania, have shed particularly valuable light on this process (Kirkman 1964; Chittick 1974; Horton 1996). The origins of these urban developments were clearly indigenous, but their subsequent growth, during the first half of the 2nd millennium AD, owed much to their participation in the Indian Ocean trade and to their consequent interest in the products of the African interior.

The maritime trade brought fine ceramics and other manufactured goods from as far away as China, introduced the Islamic faith, and stimulated the construction of stone buildings that

10.37 (Left) **Brass head from Ife, southwestern Nigeria:** dating from the first half of the 2nd millennium AD, near-life-size heads such as this, of either brass or terracotta, appear to have been representations of rulers and members of their families. Holes above the forehead of this example were probably for the attachment of hair and the lines on the face represent scarification.

10.38 **One of the most famous of the brass heads from Benin City, southern Nigeria:** this is a near-life-size depiction of the mother of a king of Benin in the 16th century AD. She wears a beaded head-dress and a choker of beads around her neck. Distinctive scarifications are shown above the eyes.

10.39 *The entrance to the palace in the city of Gedi, Kenya: lime-mortared stone buildings were an indication of the economic success of the coastal trading communities that grew up along the East African coast, tapping the resources of the African interior and participating in the trade of the Indian Ocean.*

included mosques, elite houses, palaces, and tombs. The search for exportable commodities such as ivory, gold, rhinoceros horn, tortoiseshell, ambergris, copper, iron, rock crystal, frankincense, myrrh, mangrove poles, ebony, and slaves stimulated the growth of trading networks along the coast, among its islands, and deep into the hinterland. This brought the coastal traders into contact with gold producers on the Zimbabwe Plateau, adding substantially to the wealth of many in the coastal communities, whose settlements became important as entrepôts (centers for import and export). Subsequently, some of the larger cities appear to have become the centers of states, with members of the elite acquiring literacy along with their Islamic faith, and some rulers striking their own coins. The level of affluence attained by the more powerful of these individuals is apparent from the 14th-century palace and commercial center of Husuni Kubwa, just outside the city of **Kilwa**, with its audience court, open-sided pavilion, bathing pool, domed and vaulted roofs, and Arabic inscriptions. As time went on, coastal society developed its own common culture and language – Swahili – in which indigenous and exotic elements were combined (Kusimba 1999; Horton and Middleton 2000).

The Zimbabwe Plateau To the south and inland lies the Zimbabwe Plateau, bounded by the Zambezi River to its north and the Limpopo to its south. This region also experienced urban and state development during the first half of the 2nd millennium AD (Pikirayi 2001). Over 1000 m (3282 ft) above sea level and therefore not infested by tsetse fly, the plateau provided ideal conditions for cattle, which could also graze the adjacent lower savanna during the dry season, when it was relatively

tsetse-free. A suitable climate and areas of fertile soil allowed the successful cultivation of sorghum, finger millet, pearl millet, beans, and other vegetables. The plateau was also fortunate in its natural resources, which included gold, iron, copper, and tin, as well as numerous granite outcrops whose exfoliation provided ideal building material. The use of dry-stone masonry was widespread in much of Africa but reached its most sophisticated expression in the many "zimbabwe" walled enclosures of this region, most famously at **Great Zimbabwe**, one of Africa's most remarkable archaeological sites [see box: Great Zimbabwe, pp. 386–87].

Remoter Parts of Central Africa By the middle of the 2nd millennium AD there were indications that both urbanization and state formation were also in progress in some of the remoter parts of central Africa. Indeed, by the 19th century, when many parts of Africa were visited by outsiders for the first time, much of the African interior seems to have become a complex network of states whose fortunes, along with those of their cities, continually rose and fell. Relevant archaeological data is limited, historical records often too late, and oral traditions frequently difficult to interpret and of limited time depth. Nevertheless, the 16th-century kingdom of Kongo, with its capital of **Mbanza Kongo** in what is now northern Angola, was clearly of major importance, as were the somewhat later kingdoms of Bunyoro and Buganda, in the interlacustrine region of western Uganda (Robertshaw 1994).

The origins of these and other developments, such as the 17th-century city of **Loango** in Congo, and the later Ndorwa kingdom in Rwanda, were almost certainly due to indigenous factors, although external influences did play an increasing part as time went on. Control of production and trade in iron, salt, copper, and other commodities was probably the most common means by which elite power was acquired. The accumulation of wealth in the form of cattle in some areas, or tradable food resources such as dried fish or bananas in others, must also have been important. Archaeological excavations at **Ntusi** (Reid 1996), **Bigo**, **Kibiro** [10.19], and elsewhere have shed some light on the developments in what is now Uganda, but it is from southeastern Democratic Congo that some of the most inform-ative evidence has come. There, in the Upemba Depression, along lakes associated with the upper Lualaba River, it has been possible to trace the emergence of the Luba kingdom, of which little is otherwise known before about AD 1700 (de Maret 1997).

Excavation at the cemetery sites of **Sanga**, **Katongo**, **Kamil-amba**, **Kikulu**, and **Malemba Nkulu** [10.19] have allowed the construction of a cultural sequence from the 5th century AD to the beginning of the 19th century. The burials provide little

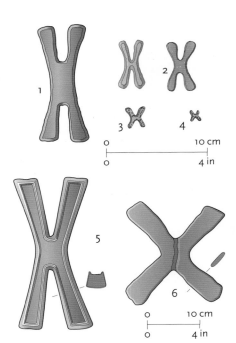

10.40 *Copper currency ingots from central Africa:* (1–4) are from Sanga in southeastern Democratic Congo and are examples of the four size categories in use during the 15th–18th centuries AD; (5) is from Ingombe Ilede, a southern Zambian site dated to the 15th century; (6) is from Democratic Congo and is probably the latest in date.

KEY SITE Great Zimbabwe

The site of Great Zimbabwe, from which the modern state of Zimbabwe takes its name, has been known to the outside world since the late 19th century, but it is only in relatively recent times that its dating, from the 13th to the 15th century AD, has been firmly established. It is even more recently that its character, as one of southern Africa's earliest cities, has begun to be understood. The impressive dry-stone structures are now realized to have been elite features in the centre of an extensive urban settlement, with a population that might have been as high as 18,000. Spatial analysis of this and comparable sites on the Zimbabwe Plateau also suggests that Great Zimbabwe was the capital of an early state in the region; it preceded similar states of a later date that are

historically documented, including that of the Mwene Mutapa, known to Portuguese traders in the 16th–17th centuries, and Torwa, with

its capital possibly at the 15th–17th-century site of Khami. In spite of earlier attempts to attribute the building of Great Zimbabwe to

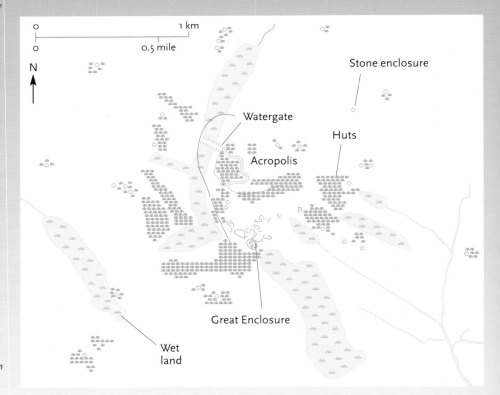

10.41 *Plan of Great Zimbabwe: the impressive stone structures were residential and ritual centers for the elite, in the middle of an extensive urban settlement consisting of huts of clay, wood, and thatch. The total population might have been as high as 18,000 and it is thought that Great Zimbabwe was the capital of an early state in the region.*

information about growing settlement size, but their numerous grave goods do indicate the gradual development of functional specialization, social stratification, and political organization. In particular, the 11th-century AD Classic Kisalian tradition was characterized by sophisticated pottery and metalwork, the latter making considerable use of copper, probably from the rich copper deposits to the southeast (Bisson 2000). Apparently important as an indicator of wealth, prestige, and status, after about the end of the 14th century it was also used as a currency, in the form of distinctive copper crosses known to archaeologists as "croisettes" [10.40].

Africa and the Outside World

From a European perspective, most of Africa remained unknown to the outside world until it was "opened up" by European exploration in the 19th century, with even the courses of Africa's major rivers, such as the Nile and the Niger, remaining a geographical mystery until then. From a broader perspective, however, this is less true, for there have been many instances of contact between Africa and the rest of the world for centuries, although they have varied greatly in intensity and duration. They consisted largely of trading interactions of one sort or another, but in some cases they involved actual immigration of people or the introduction of exotic plants and animals from outside the continent.

The Mediterranean, Southwest Asia, and the Red Sea

The areas adjacent to the African continent have had a long and complex relationship with it. Sheep and goats, domesticated animals of Southwest Asian origin, had spread through much of Africa by about 2000 years ago, and humped zebu cattle, usually thought to have come from Asia, and domesticated chicken, of South Asian origin, might also have arrived in Africa by this route by about that time. The domesticated

---

people from outside of Africa, it is now accepted that it was the work of the ancestors of the Shona, who still live in the area.

The Enclosures

The stone walls appear to have formed enclosures for the dwellings of the ruling family and their supporters, and other stone structures seem to have been intended for ritual purposes. The site consists of two areas of ruins, around which lay the rest of the city; one group of enclosures is clustered around the boulders at the top of a precipitous granite hill, and another lies on the far slope of an adjacent valley.

The principal structures were clearly intended to impress; they are monumental both in appearance and in the expenditure of resources implied by their creation. The main enclosure in the valley, for instance, has been called "by far the largest single prehistoric structure in sub-Saharan Africa" (Garlake 1973, 27). Its beautifully constructed granite wall is 244 m long, up to 5 m thick, and 10 m high (801 x 16 x 33 ft). Among the features within this enclosure is a unique conical tower of solid dry-stone masonry c. 5.5 m (18 ft) in diameter and over 9 m (30 ft) high.

Prosperity and Decline

How was such achievement possible? Almost certainly the successful mixed agriculture of the region was important, and elites with both secular and sacred power had probably gained control of large numbers of cattle and of areas with fertile soils. There appears to have been a flourishing internal trading network in iron, copper, salt, and other commodities, particularly gold and ivory, which brought Great Zimbabwe and its region into contact with the trading cities of the East African coast. Persian and Chinese ceramics and fragments of Southwest Asian glass have been found at Great Zimbabwe, along with other items, including glass beads, cowrie shells, and even a coin minted in Kilwa.

Significantly, the main period of stone building at Great Zimbabwe was at much the same time as the period of greatest prosperity in the coastal settlements, and both areas

eventually declined at about the same date, perhaps because of falling world gold prices. In Great Zimbabwe's case, however, environmental deterioration might have been an additional factor, the result of heavy demands made on the surrounding area by such a large population.

10.42 *The conical tower in the main valley enclosure at Great Zimbabwe: this solid dry-stone masonry structure is over 9 m (30 ft) high and might originally have been higher. Displaying a very high standard of skill, it is one of tropical Africa's most remarkable examples of precolonial building.*

cereals wheat and barley had been adopted from Southwest Asia by about 5000 BC, although they were only important in the northeastern parts of the continent. Given its location, it is hardly surprising that Egypt was for long a recipient of outside influences. Although the origins of the Dynastic period appear to have been substantially indigenous, as explained above, the lower Nile Valley was later to become a part first of the Greek world and then, in turn, of the Roman, the Byzantine, and the Arab worlds.

Along the north coast of Africa there was also substantial external influence, with Greek colonies on its eastern part and Phoenician colonies on its western parts by the early 1st millennium BC. The settlement of Phoenicians, who came from the Levantine coast at the eastern end of the Mediterranean (Chapter 12), was particularly significant, for these trading seafarers established the city of **Carthage** as well as a number of others, of which the furthest west was **Mogador** on the Atlantic coast (Aubet 2001). The Greek historian Herodotus, writing in the 5th century BC, even recorded a claim that Carthaginians had circumnavigated Africa, although he did not believe it, nor have most other people since. Subsequently, the whole of the North African coast became part of the Roman Empire, which at times sent exploratory expeditions deep into the Sahara Desert, though no archaeological evidence for Roman contact has ever been found to its south.

In contrast, the Nile provided an important trade route into the African interior, to Meroë and to the later kingdoms of the middle Nile, whose adoption of Christianity indicates the extent of external influence. Much the same happened around the Red Sea, where New Kingdom Egypt had earlier carried on maritime trade with the Land of Punt, thought by some to be in northeast Sudan or Eritrea. The Red Sea trade of the early 1st millennium AD contributed to **Aksum**'s affluence, in an area of Ethiopia in which groups of people from southwestern Arabia had settled by the middle of the 1st millennium BC, taking their form of writing and other aspects of their culture with them. The adoption of Christianity by Aksum, and its issuing of a coinage that included some Greek inscriptions, show how influential the Red Sea trading connection was. Indeed, when Aksumite participation in that trade dwindled with the rise of Islam and Arab power, so also did the state of Aksum, raising the question often met in the case of other African states, as to whether long-distance trade was a major causative factor in state formation [see box: Did External Trade Cause African State Formation?].

In North Africa, the Arab conquest of the second half of the 1st millennium AD and the expansion of Islam led not to a reduction in African trade but to a very considerable expansion. From late in that millennium there developed a substantial trans-Saharan trade, made possible by the extensive use of domesticated camels for transport. North African Arab traders found that the lands beyond the desert could supply commodities that were valued by Mediterranean and European societies, the most important of which was gold. The relationship that subsequently developed between North and West Africa had a deep and enduring impact on many of the inhabitants of the latter, resulting in the adoption of Islam and its way of life, including the acquisition of literacy. The trading connections also left clear evidence of their existence among the material available for archaeological study, such as the early 12th-century AD marble gravestones inscribed in Kufic (an early angular form of the Arabic alphabet), which were found at **Sané**, near Gao on the Niger in Mali, but which are thought to have been made in Spain. Some trade goods even penetrated to the far south, into the rainforest and its margins, such as the beads found at **Igbo-Ukwu** in southeast Nigeria [see box: Igbo-Ukwu, p. 390].

The Indian Ocean

For at least 2000 years the Indian Ocean has been a means of contact between the lands surrounding it, rather than a barrier. Much of the east coast of Africa has benefited from this situation, made possible by a seasonal reversal of winds and currents every six months. Moreover, many voyages could be made without ever losing sight of land. Ceramics excavated at **Ras Hafun**, near Cape Guardafui in the far north of Somalia, indicate trading contacts with the Red Sea, the Persian Gulf, and perhaps South Asia as early as the 1st century BC (Smith and Wright 1988). Indeed, on literary evidence, it has been argued that during the Roman period there was a "Cinnamon Route" right across the Indian Ocean, from Indonesia to East Africa (Miller 1969). Certainly the East African coast was known to the Roman world, as is indicated by works such as the *Periplus* ("account of a coasting voyage") *of the Erythraean Sea* and Claudius Ptolemy's *Geographia*. Furthermore, by the late 1st millennium AD, Arab seafaring was reaching as far as China in one direction and East Africa in the other (Hourani 1995). By the early 15th century, some Chinese ships had even reached the coast of East Africa, taking back a giraffe as a present for a Ming emperor (Wheatley 1975).

The impact of Indian Ocean contact on East Africa, indeed on Africa generally, was fundamental and diverse. A hoard of 3rd-century AD Indian coins found at **Debra Damo** in Ethiopia, two sherds of Roman pottery in a 5th-century AD context at **Unguja Ukuu** on the island of Zanzibar, 7th–9th-century AD imported Islamic ceramics at **Chibuene**, far to the south in Mozambique, glass beads apparently manufactured at al-Fustat in Egypt but found at the Limpopo Valley sites of **Bambandyanalo** and **Mapungubwe**, dating to the late 1st and early 2nd millennium AD – these and the imported materials in the

KEY CONTROVERSY Did External Trade Cause African State Formation?

In seeking to understand the factors that led to the emergence of states in various parts of Africa, the most popular explanation has been the growth of long-distance trade (Lonsdale 1981). The main argument for such an explanation is that such trade led to an increase in distributable wealth, placing power into the hands of those who controlled the trade, who consequently were able to control a growing number of people around them. Given that external trade was clearly important to the economies of many early African states, the idea is plausible enough. It has been criticized on a number of grounds, however.

The long-distance trade explanation originates from the former belief of many archaeologists that human societies only really change when subjected to some form of external stimulus. It is based on the assumption that diffusion rather than independent invention is the most likely cause of change. In the case of Africa, this idea seemed particularly justified by what was thought to be the changeless nature of past African societies, which were only likely to develop, according to this view, in response to outside influences. Such influences most commonly resulted from trading contacts with other, more complex, societies, either from some distant part of the continent itself or beyond the surrounding oceans.

Dynamic Societies

As archaeologists and historians have learned more about the African past, particularly over the last few decades, it has become increasingly apparent that African societies were often dynamic, not static, and were subject to a series of transformations that most commonly resulted from a combination of local factors. One argument has held that elite power was acquired by those who gained control of the most productive land or of important natural resources such as iron, copper, and salt. Another view has been that in such a generally under-populated continent, it was control of people rather than control of land that was the critical factor. It is also possible that different circumstances were relevant in different places at different times, the one common element being competition between groups of people and between individuals, from which some emerged victorious.

Moreover, as research has progressed, there have been increasing indications that both state formation and the process of urbanization, with which it often seems to have been associated, originated before the growth of long-distance trade (as at the site of Jenné-jeno, discussed above: see box p. 383). It appears that such trade facilitated the progress of these developments, rather than being an initial cause of them. It also seems that external trade, particularly from the world outside of Africa, was only possible because it was able to tap into already developed African trading networks.

Swahili cities and Great Zimbabwe are vivid reminders of this contact. There were more fundamental consequences, however, such as the immigration of people from Southeast Asia to Madagascar, the adoption of Islam and the arrival of at least some Arab settlers on parts of the East African coast, and the introduction of a number of domesticated plants of Southeast Asian origin, which were to become of great importance in many parts of Africa. Perhaps the most eloquent testimony of the wide impact of the Indian Ocean trade were the abandoned loads of a camel caravan, buried in a sand dune in the lonely Majâbat Al-Koubrâ, halfway across the Sahara Desert. Dating to the 12th century AD, a large portion of the loads consisted of cowrie shells of the species *Monetaria moneta*, over 9000 km (5600 miles) from their source in the Maldive Islands (Connah 2001).

The Atlantic Coast

For the Atlantic coast of the African continent circumstances were rather different, because adverse winds discouraged seaborne trade until improvements in European sailing technology during the 15th century AD. Contact expanded rapidly after that, and by the beginning of the 16th century European seafarers had rounded the southern tip of Africa and entered the Indian Ocean. Subsequently, the growing industrial economies of Western Europe had a profound effect on many coastal societies in Africa, with their increasingly aggressive search for both a widening variety of raw materials (such as palm oil) and new markets for their products. From about the 17th century onwards, those economies were also linked with the plantation production in the Americas of cotton, tobacco, and sugar, all of them demanding substantial labor. Thus there developed the trans-Atlantic slave trade, which had a devastating impact on many African societies, particularly in West Africa, just as a massive expansion of the long-established Arab slave trade had in parts of East Africa.

Nevertheless, European trade along the Atlantic coast also had positive aspects. It was the means, for instance, of the introduction of maize, cassava, tomatoes, peanuts, chili pepper, and potatoes, which were brought from the Americas from about the 16th century onwards. Less certainly of benefit, it also introduced various forms of Christianity, different ideas of economic and political organization, mass-produced alcohol, tobacco, guns, and gunpowder, and eventually even European immigrants. The impact of all this, prior to the European explorations of the 19th century, is difficult to assess. However, the image of Africa isolated from the world until recent times is certainly out of date. In the mid-1860s Samuel Baker, one of the first European visitors to central Africa, found tobacco already growing in what is now southern Sudan, just to the north of Uganda (Baker 1866), and archaeological evidence indicates that indigenous clay tobacco pipes were in use in many parts of Africa long before Europeans arrived. The conclusion is inescapable: that Africa has always been a part of the wider world.

Summary and Conclusions

During the Holocene, Africa experienced a series of important transformations in human societies. Already, prior to 10,000 years ago, some hunter-gatherers and fishers in northern and eastern Africa had begun to intensify their exploitation of particular animals and plants, as they were faced by an interplay of opportunities and constraints presented by climatic variability. For some human groups this intensification led eventually to the development of pastoralism, with varying degrees of mobility. Indigenous cattle were probably domesticated in a Sahara moister than at present, and sheep and goats already domesticated in Southwest Asia were also often adopted. For other groups, intensive gathering of wild grasses and other vegetable food led somewhat later to the cultivation of wheat and barley, which had been introduced from Southwest Asia, or of pearl millet and a number of other African plants. Such cultivation made possible a greater degree of sedentism, and although this

KEY SITE Igbo-Ukwu

The Nigerian town of Igbo-Ukwu is situated at the edge of the rainforest, to the east of the Niger River and a little north of its delta. Following accidental discoveries some years earlier, excavations in 1960 and 1964 uncovered three related sites: the burial of a clearly important individual, a repository of sophisticated regalia, and a ritual disposal pit (Shaw 1970). These sites produced, among other things, 685 copper and bronze objects, many of them highly ornamented lost-wax castings in a hitherto unknown art style, and some 165,000 stone and glass beads.

On the basis of radiocarbon dates, the complex was assigned to the end of the 1st millennium AD, a date that in the opinion of some scholars was too early, given the nature of the evidence. Nevertheless, the date has been generally accepted as correct, raising questions as to what the evidence means. Its excavator argued that the burial was that of a "priest king," and that the repository and pit were for associated regalia and rituals; but there was still the problem of how such apparent wealth had been accumulated.

The Mystery of Igbo-Ukwu's Wealth

At the time of the excavations, it was thought that there were no sources of copper in Nigeria, and that supplies of the metal for the recovered objects must therefore have been obtained from long-distance trade with the southern Sahara. This has since been shown

10.43 *Bronze roped pot from Igbo-Ukwu, southeastern Nigeria: this is the best known of the large number of copper and bronze objects, many of them highly ornamented lost-wax castings, that were found at this place. Dating to the end of the 1st millennium AD, it has been argued that they represent the regalia of a local "priest king" and the presence of many glass and stone beads suggests trading contacts with the outside world.*

not to be the case, and it is now known that the metal could have been obtained from within southeastern Nigeria, just as the tin for producing the alloy bronze could have come from the north of the country. However, this still leaves the problem of the glass and stone beads, many of the latter of carnelian; they, at least, must have resulted from long-distance trading connections, either across the Sahara or east-west through the Sahel. Gao, on the Niger River in southern Mali, has been suggested as an immediate source, from which transport down the Niger would have been possible (Insoll and Shaw 1997), but the Christian kingdoms of the middle Nile have also been proposed for this role. Current thinking has al-Fustat (the old city of Cairo), as a location for the manufacture of many of the glass beads, and the carnelian beads could also have originated in Egypt (Sutton 2001).

Some of the beads might, indeed, have come from even further away. Nevertheless, whatever the exact source or trade route, the question remains of just what the people at Igbo-Ukwu were giving in exchange for such luxury goods.

The usual answer has been to suggest that ivory and perhaps slaves were being exported from the area. Both would have been available there, but they could also have been obtained from sources much closer to the possible markets for these commodities. Instead, silver has been suggested (Sutton 1991), because it was a rare commodity of considerable international value at that time, particularly given the demand created by the currencies of both the Islamic and Christian worlds. There are, apparently, small quantities of silver to be found in the mineral deposits of southeastern Nigeria, but it is doubtful if the necessary technology existed to extract it, and there is no evidence that it was actually produced and traded. For the present, the Igbo-Ukwu mystery remains: wealth without a probable cause.

must have varied greatly, depending on the details of the subsistence economy, this probably led to an increase both in the overall population and in its density in resource-rich areas. As increasing attention was focused on selected plants and animals, so a range of different farming strategies gradually developed, often involving both pastoralism and cultivation. However, these changes were effectively limited to Africa north of the equator and to pottery-making people whose technologies were still based on stone.

The adoption of farming in central and southern Africa appears to have been the result of a complicated process of diffusion, as pottery-making Bantu-speaking farmers expanded eastward and southward across a huge area of the continent, from perhaps as early as the 2nd millennium BC. By the late 1st millennium BC they were acquiring a knowledge of ironworking, which had previously become established in parts of West, west-central, and East Africa, perhaps as a result of indigenous developments. By the early 2nd millennium AD farming in one form or another, along with iron technology, had spread over most of the continent south of the equator, except for some parts of eastern and southern Africa where stone-using hunter-gatherers persisted. Indeed, even in the furthest south, some of these people were already herding domesticated sheep.

In many parts of the continent as a whole, the adoption of metallurgy, particularly by sedentary people practicing mixed farming, probably encouraged a continued increase in both population and settlement size, leading in some more bountiful environments to the growth of cities. The need to maintain order within such larger human groups, and the emergence of elites who were able to control the means of production, sometimes led to the growth of states. Pharaonic Egypt is the outstanding example of these processes, although its metallurgy was based on copper and bronze, and only latterly on iron. Because of its abundant historical records and substantial archaeological evidence, ancient Egypt is also the best known of the African states. Nevertheless, such developments occurred in many places, although they varied greatly in scale and detail. They seem to have resulted in the main from complex adjustments in socio-economic and political relationships within areas of dense human settlement, rather than from any external influences, although such influences did contribute to their ongoing development, particularly when long-distance trade provided African rulers with both wealth and prestige. It was such trade with the outside world that eventually led to direct interference in African societies by Europeans.

This chapter has described the development of Holocene Africa up to the threshold of modern European contact. We must now step back in time and consider the development of Europe itself during the Holocene. The next chapter opens at the end of the last Ice Age and documents the expansion of hunter-gatherer communities in the Mesolithic period and the spread of farmers during the Neolithic. It then goes on to describe the later development of prehistoric societies in temperate Europe, up to the expansion of the Roman Empire in the 1st century BC.

Further Reading and Suggested Websites

Connah, G. (ed.). 1998. *Transformations in Africa: Essays on Africa's Later Past*. London & Washington: Leicester University Press. A series of studies of recent work on such major subjects as the development of farming, the origins of iron technology, the growth of urbanism, and the formation of states.

Connah, G. 2001. *African Civilizations: An Archaeological Perspective*. (2nd ed.) Cambridge: Cambridge University Press. A standard work on the archaeology of precolonial urbanism and state formation in tropical Africa.

Ehret, C. 2002. *The Civilizations of Africa: A History to 1800*. Oxford: James Currey. An historical study mainly based on linguistic evidence.

Hassan, F. A. (ed.). 2002. *Droughts, Food and Culture: Ecological Change and Food Security in Africa's Later Prehistory*. New York: Kluwer Academic/Plenum Publishers. A series of studies of human subsistence strategies examined in the context of environmental change.

Kemp, B. J. 1989. *Ancient Egypt: Anatomy of a Civilization*. London & New York: Routledge. An innovative examination of ancient Egyptian society and its development.

Mitchell, P. J. 2002. *The Archaeology of Southern Africa*. Cambridge: Cambridge University Press. A detailed text on the archaeological data from the southern part of Africa from the earliest to recent times.

Phillipson, D. W. 1993. *African Archaeology*. (2nd ed.) Cambridge: Cambridge University Press. The standard text on the precolonial archaeology of the African continent, covering all periods.

Shaw, I. *Oxford History of Ancient Egypt*. Oxford: Oxford University Press.

Shaw, T., Sinclair, P., Andah, B., & Okpoko, A. (eds.). 1993. *The Archaeology of Africa: Food, Metals and Towns*. London & New York: Routledge. A collection of conference papers that ranges widely over later African archaeology.

Vogel, J. O. (ed.). 1997. *Encyclopedia of Precolonial Africa: Archaeology, History, Languages, Cultures, and Environments*. Walnut Creek, CA: AltaMira Press. A multi-authored reference work that provides an introduction to a wide range of topics.

http://www.archaeolink.com/african_archaeology.htm A useful directory of websites relating to African archaeology, with many links.

http://safa.rice.edu/links.cfm Website of the Society of Africanist Archaeologists, based at Rice University.

http://www.sas.upenn.edu/African_Studies/About_African/ ww_anth.html Website of the African Studies Center at the University of Pennsylvania.

CHAPTER 11
HOLOCENE EUROPE

Chris Scarre, University of Cambridge

From Foraging to Farming 393
After the Ice: Europe Transformed 394
● KEY SITE Star Carr: A Mesolithic Campsite in Northeast England 396
Farming Comes to Europe 397
● KEY CONTROVERSY Replacement or Continuity? Population Genetics and the First European Farmers 398

Southeastern Europe 400
Neolithic Settlements 400
Figurines and Evidence for Social Complexity 401
The Introduction of Metals 402

The Mediterranean Zone 402
● KEY SITE The Varna Cemetery 403
Neolithic Settlements 404
The Emergence of Social Complexity 405

Central Europe 406
The Bandkeramik Culture 407
Later Regional Groups 408
● KEY CONTROVERSY The "Iceman" 408

Atlantic Europe 410
Mesolithic Settlements 410
● KEY SITE The Talheim Death Pit 411
● KEY SITE The Bandkeramik Settlements at Langweiler, Germany 412
Megalithic Monuments: The Neolithic Transition 413

Northern Europe 415
The Ertebølle-Ellerbek and Later Cultures 415
● KEY CONTROVERSY Stonehenge and Megalithic Astronomy 416
Neolithic Burial Practices 418

Toward Complexity: Europe from 2500 BC to the Roman Empire 419
Later Prehistoric Societies in Central and Western Europe 420
Beaker Pottery and Metalwork 420
Small-scale Settlement and Long-distance Contact 422
• *"Princely Centers"* 423

Later Prehistoric Societies in Eastern Europe 424
Urnfields 425
The Fortified Site of Biskupin 425

European Society at the Dawn of History 426
● KEY CONTROVERSY Rock Art – Representation of Myth or Reality? 426
European Societies Beyond the Mediterranean 427
The So-called "Celtic" Societies 428
• *Bog Bodies* 428
• *The Expansion of Roman Control* 429

Summary and Conclusions 429
● KEY CONTROVERSY Who Were the Celts? 430

Further Reading 431

In this chapter we follow the development of human societies in Europe from the end of the last Ice Age. The European continent lay beyond the initial center of agricultural origins in Southwest Asia (Chapter 6), but was profoundly affected by the spread of the new farming economy, which was adopted in southeast Europe around 6500 BC and reached the north and northwest 2500 years later. We begin c. 9600 BC, with the period when hunter-gatherer societies across the continent were taking advantage of the milder postglacial climate to increase their numbers and to colonize previously glaciated northern regions. These societies are conventionally known as Mesolithic (Middle Stone Age, between the Old Stone Age or Paleolithic hunter-gatherers of the Pleistocene and the New Stone Age farmers of the Neolithic). It is the transition from Mesolithic hunter-gatherers to Neolithic farmers that forms the central theme of the first part of this chapter. We then move on to the metal-using societies of the Bronze Age and Iron Age, and the development of a variety of increasingly complex societies across temperate Europe. The emergence of the first European states — in the Aegean during the 2nd millennium BC and in Italy during the 1st millennium BC — is the subject of a separate chapter (Chapter 13).

From Foraging to Farming

To understand the development of prehistoric Europe it is necessary first to take account of its diverse topography and climate, from the Arctic in the north to the Mediterranean in the south, and from the steppes and forests of the east to the warm ocean currents and rocky promontories of the Atlantic in the west [11.1]. The postglacial prehistory of Europe is correspondingly diverse, and can be divided into a series of regional narratives, with interplay between them. In the south, the Balkan, Alpine, and Pyrenean mountain chains separate the Mediterranean zone from temperate Europe to the north, but throughout most of the postglacial period the two geographical zones were linked by phenomena such as the spread of domesticates, the circulation of metals, or the impact of Mediterranean urbanism. Furthermore, topographical barriers were counterbalanced by the pathways provided by the major river valleys, notably the Danube, Dnieper, and Dniester flowing east and south into the Black Sea, the Rhône and Loire flowing respectively into the Mediterranean and the Atlantic, and the Rhine, Elbe, and Vistula debouching into the North Sea and the Baltic. Yet European diversity must not be underemphasized, and much of the broad-scale patterning of European prehistory must be understood against the background of a mosaic of soils and vegetation. Notable regional contrasts range from Mediterranean evergreen and deciduous forest in the south, now largely reduced to scrub, to the dense deciduous woodlands that colonized temperate Europe during the early postglacial period; this region was bordered by the steppe grasslands of Ukraine to the east and by coniferous forests and Arctic tundra to the north.

Large areas of Europe lay beyond the limits of human settlement during the last Ice Age, when a massive ice sheet covered the northern part of the continent, with smaller ice caps in the Alps and the Pyrenees. As temperatures began to rise, the ice sheets retreated, and modern climate and topography became established. Early postglacial hunter-gatherers – descendants of the first Upper Paleolithic settlers of some 40,000 years ago – are best represented along the coasts and rivers, and beside lakes and marshes. These Mesolithic communities were the first to inhabit the northern terrain made available by the melting of the ice sheets. This northerly colonization was followed by another expansion of quite a different nature, when, in the 7th millennium BC, the first farming communities appeared in southeast Europe, the region closest to the Southwest Asian area of agricultural origins, and most like it in terms of soils and climate. The spread of agriculture through central Europe and the Mediterranean, reaching the northern and western fringes around 4000 BC, appears to have been a hybrid process involving both the movement of farming communities into new territories and the adoption of domestic plants and animals by indigenous hunter-gatherers.

Diversity is a key feature of European societies during the millennia that followed. In some areas of the south and east, substantial villages formed mounds, or tells, but in most of Europe farming settlements remained small and scattered. In Atlantic Europe, burial mounds and standing stones are the most conspicuous remains of this period. The Balkan and Carpathian Mountains were exploited for copper and gold from the 5th millennium BC, and these and other materials became markers of social difference. During the 2nd millennium BC, the use of bronze became widespread across Europe, and social elites are more clearly identifiable in graves and other remains. Contrasts and contacts between the Mediterranean zone and temperate Europe remain a key theme during the 1st millennium BC, culminating in the expansion of the Roman Empire in the 2nd and 1st centuries BC. Much of Europe lay beyond Roman control, however, and in these regions, indigenous Nordic and Germanic societies continued to develop throughout the Roman period. Thus the European story in this chapter takes us from the hunter-gatherers of the early postglacial to sophisticated societies known to us not only from archaeology, but also through the writings of Greek and Roman authors. It is a complex and colorful story.

HOLOCENE EUROPE TIMELINE

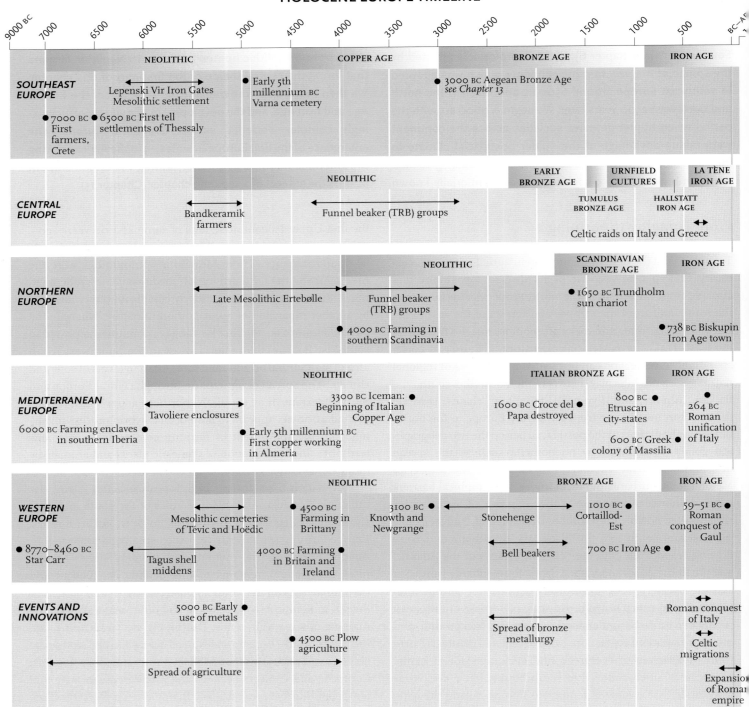

After the Ice: Europe Transformed

As we have seen in previous chapters, the earlier Holocene was a period of profound environmental change, as temperatures rose, and plants and animals recolonized areas that had been too cold and dry during the last Ice Age (Roberts 1998). The whole shape of the European continent changed, as rising sea levels flooded many lowland areas. The flooding of the North Sea that turned Britain into an island (Chapter 5) was one of the many consequences of sea-level rise. In areas that had been covered by the ice sheets, conversely, the surface of the land bounced back in response to the removal of the weight of the ice, such that early postglacial shorelines were raised up to 250

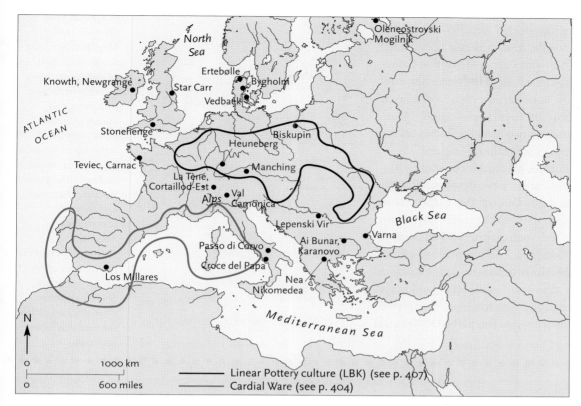

11.1 *Map of Europe:* 10,000 years ago much of Europe was thickly forested but rivers, coasts, and wetlands offered rich environments for hunter-gatherers. With the introduction of agriculture, plains and river valleys became centers of population and the growing demand for raw materials and pasture led to greater exploitation of mountainous upland regions.

11.2 *(Below)* **Franchthi Cave:** at the beginning of the Holocene, Franchthi Cave in Greece lay 2–3 km from the shoreline, but as sea level rose the sea moved closer. The changing character of the advancing shoreline is reflected in the kinds and numbers of shellfish collected by the inhabitants.

m (820 ft) above present sea level. Rainfall increased, and western Europe benefited from the newly re-established Gulf Stream, which brought warm tropical water to northern latitudes. As the forest spread, the open-country megafauna of the last glacial (mammoth, woolly rhinoceros, giant deer) died out, and reindeer and horse withdrew respectively to the northern and eastern margins. In their place came forest-adapted species – aurochs (wild cattle), red deer, wild pig. The warmer conditions and more abundant vegetation allowed human communities in postglacial Europe to place increasing reliance on plant foods as a source of nutrition, along with marine and riverine resources of fish and shellfish.

As already noted, many of the most significant postglacial hunting and foraging settlements were beside coasts, lakes, and wetlands, which offered a wide range of both marine or aquatic and terrestrial resources. At **Franchthi Cave** in southern Greece, occupation began in the Paleolithic and continued through the Neolithic period, and the frequency and species of shellfish in successive layers illustrate the changing character of the local shoreline, which came progressively closer to the site as rising sea level flooded the lowland plain (Shackleton and Van Andel 1980) [**11.2**].

Population levels rose across Europe as overall biomass increased and resources diversified, yet settlements remained small and seasonal for the most part, with few substantial structures. Cave and rockshelter occupations continued in many cases from the Paleolithic, but open sites are, for the most part,

characterized only by scatters of flints and food remains. In northern Europe the rise in sea level led to the waterlogging of Mesolithic coastal sites and the preservation of rich assemblages of organic remains. In the earlier Holocene, the whole of the area now occupied by the North Sea was a marshy lowland, home to communities of hunters, fishers, and foragers of the so-called **Maglemosian culture**. At the Continental end of this distribution, hut floors consisting of pine logs and bark sheets have been found at **Duvensee** and other sites. At the British end,

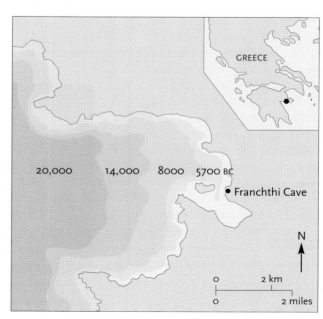

the lakeside site of **Star Carr** has yielded remains of a brushwood platform, a wooden paddle, and evidence of seasonal patterns of exploitation [see box: Star Carr: a Mesolithic Campsite in Northeast England]. From the floor of the North Sea itself have come artifacts such as the bone harpoon in a block of peat dragged up by a fishing boat in 1932 (Coles 1998). More recently in 2003, divers discovered two Mesolithic sites on the seabed off the coast of Tynemouth in northeast England.

In northern and eastern Europe, Mesolithic cemeteries suggest that communities in these areas were developing larger and more complex social groups. One of the earliest is at **Vasilievka III** in Ukraine, which dates to the 10th millennium BC. By the later Mesolithic period, such cemeteries had become more numerous and more complex. The 7th-millennium BC cemetery at **Oleneostrovski Mogilnik** in Karelia, in the Russian Federation, numbered more than 170 burials [**11.3**], and grave goods indicate social differentiation that has been interpreted in terms of clan moieties, or division into two parts (O'Shea and Zvelebil 1984).

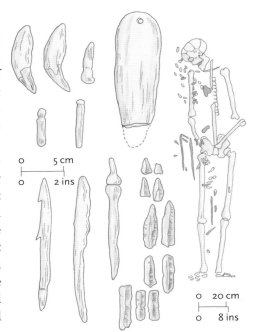

11.3 *Finds from Oleneostrovski Mogilnik:* this is the oldest and largest Mesolithic cemetery in northern Europe, with some 400 burials with rich grave assemblages including zoomorphic figures, maceheads, and axes. The graves illustrate the social and cultural complexity of Mesolithic communities and the iconography of the carved figures may refer to a northern cosmology which has survived into recent centuries.

KEY SITE Star Carr: A Mesolithic Campsite in Northeast England

Star Carr, on the shores of an extinct lake in northeast England, was one of many hunter-gatherer campsites of the early Mesolithic period; it owes its importance to the waterlogged conditions that preserved a wide range of organic materials (Clark 1954; 1972). The settlement centered on an accumulation of birch brushwood close to the edge of the former Lake Pickering.

The excavator, Grahame Clark, interpreted this as an intentionally laid platform, but there was no evidence that huts, tents, or other structures had ever stood on it. Some have suggested that it might not have been a humanly made structure at all, but a natural brushwood accumulation created by beavers and later taken over by the human occupants. Recent soundings, however, have revealed a wooden plank that was, without question, humanly worked.

Evidence for Human Settlement

The clearest evidence for human settlement and activity at Star Carr comes from its scatter of flint tools, remains of hunted animals, and worked pieces of wood, bone, and antler. Flint microliths would have been fitted into wooden shafts to form hunting arrows or knives for cutting reeds and other vegetation. Clark also discovered almost 200 barbed points, mainly of red deer antler, plus two of bone; elk antler was used for mattock heads, which were perforated for the fitting of a wooden haft. Surprisingly, however, few wooden implements were recovered, an interesting exception being a wooden paddle blade, probably used to propel a dugout canoe across the waters of the lake.

Craft Activities and Hunting Magic

The inhabitants of Star Carr no doubt carried out a number of craft activities in addition to the manufacture of tools and implements of flint, wood, and antler. One possibility is the working of hides (warm clothing would have been a vital concern), using flint scrapers to clean away the flesh and then birch pitch immersed in water (perhaps at the edge of the lake) to tan them. Alternatively, the tightly wound rolls of birch bark found at the site may have been a convenient way of storing resin for gluing microliths to their hafts.

11.4 *(Left)* This red deer frontlet (part of the skull of the deer with antlers still attached), from Star Carr, has been thinned internally to lighten it, and perforated so that it can be worn, perhaps in hunting rituals.

11.5 *(Opposite)* Waterlogged conditions at Star Carr (here under excavation in 1949—51) allowed the preservation of a wide range of organic materials including worked wood, bone and antler, and rolls of birch bark for pitch or resin.

At this period, or within a few centuries, cemeteries also appear at west European Mesolithic sites such as **Moita da Sebastião** and **Cabeço da Arruda** in Portugal, and at **Skateholm** and **Vedbaek** in Scandinavia. These may mark significant changes in social organization that prefigure the adoption of agriculture in those areas.

The European Mesolithic was not merely an interlude between the Paleolithic and Neolithic, however, nor just a prelude to what came later. The expansion of settlement, the adjustment to new and often changing environments, and the evidence for larger and more complex social groups illustrate the richness and diversity of these hunter-gatherer societies of the earlier postglacial period. Rock art and portable carvings and sculptures testify to the importance of the symbolic and spiritual dimension. The replacement of these ways of life by the spread of farming should, therefore, in no way be equated with the failure or inadequacy of Mesolithic communities, but rather with the demographic strength of the new food-producing economies.

Farming Comes to Europe

Farming came to Europe from Southwest Asia. This much is beyond question, since the domesticated plant and animal species involved have not only been dated earlier in Southwest Asia than in Europe, but their wild ancestors (notably sheep and goat, wheat, and barley) were in many cases restricted in their natural distribution to Southwest Asia, with at most a slight extension into areas of Greece (Chapter 6). While the Southwest Asian origin of the domesticates is relatively clear, the process by which farming spread to Europe remains controversial. Was it people who moved, or only the domesticated plants and animals?

Radiocarbon dates show that this spread began earliest in the southeast before moving westwards along the Mediterranean coasts to Italy and Iberia, and northwards through the Balkans to central, western, and northern Europe [**11.7, 11.8**]. In virtually every region, however, conflicting interpretations have been proposed, couched in terms of either incoming farmers or the uptake of domesticates by indigenous hunter-gatherers.

Not all the activities at Star Carr were purely utilitarian. Among the bone material were 21 frontlets of red deer skulls with the antlers still attached. Some were in fragmentary condition when found, but they consistently showed traces of intentional working. In the best-preserved specimens it could be seen that both skull and antlers had been scraped and thinned to reduce their weight, and the skulls had twin perforations, allowing them to be tied and worn as a kind of headdress. They may have been used in hunting magic. Red deer clearly formed a major element of the diet at the site, along with other species, such as roe deer, elk, pig, and aurochs. There were also bones of waterfowl, such as stork and crane. A surprising feature of the faunal record was the absence of fish remains, despite the proximity of the freshwater lake.

Recent Dating of the Site
The lake itself was the site's key attraction. Recent research (Mellars and Dark 1998) has thrown considerable new light on the local vegetation, through microscopic examination of sediment cores taken from the former lake bed. These have shown that reed swamp fringed by birch and poplar was dominant through much of the occupation, with open birch woodland on drier land.

Study of charcoal in these cores reveals a significant increase from previously negligible quantities at a point that corresponds stratigraphically with the worked plank referred to above. This suggests that human activity began around 8770 BC, and was associated with burning of the local vegetation. Large charcoal fragments were present through the following 7 cm (2.7 in) of sediment, representing a period of around 80 years, but were then scarce for a further 100 years until a second episode of burning, associated with some 120 years of human activity that ended *c.* 8460 BC. These new results provide a detailed chronology for the occupation of the site, showing that it was divided into two phases of seasonal use (perhaps annual, perhaps less frequent), separated by a period of abandonment.

KEY CONTROVERSY Replacement or Continuity? Population Genetics and the First European Farmers

The spread of farming across Europe has been the focus of considerable debate, with alternative views favoring an expansion of colonizing farmers on the one hand, or the adoption of domesticates by indigenous hunter-gatherers on the other. Albert Ammerman and Luca Cavalli-Sforza (1971) used radiocarbon dates, then newly available, to calculate the rate of spread of farming, and argued that the evidence was consistent with a demographic model in which farming populations grew rapidly in numbers (supported by the greater productivity of the new economy) and spread steadily into new areas, replacing or absorbing the indigenous hunter-gatherer communities. They proposed a rate of expansion averaging around 1 km (0.62 mile) per year, though they admitted that this average figure masked a high degree of regional diversity, with rates of spread varying from 0.7 km (0.43 mile) per year in the Balkans to 5.6 km (3.5 miles) per year in central Europe.

Recent reanalysis of the much larger body of radiocarbon dates now available has confirmed the general outline of Ammerman and Cavalli-Sforza's conclusions, with an average rate of spread of 1.3 km (0.8 mile) per year, although once again, regional variability is considerable (Gkiasta et al. 2003). Such models do not in themselves indicate the processes behind the spread of agriculture, and could just as plausibly be consistent with the progressive uptake of domesticates by indigenous populations upon the arrival of incoming farmers from the southeast. The degree of regional variability in the rate of spread, coupled with the distribution of archaeological traits such as pottery and house plans, strongly suggest a pattern of farming colonization in some areas (such as the central European Bandkeramik region) as opposed to indigenous uptake in others (e.g. Britain or Scandinavia), but here again the archaeological evidence is unable conclusively to resolve the controversy.

Mitochondrial DNA

A direct answer would be provided by the genetic profile of the various European populations before and after the introduction of agriculture, but attempts to extract DNA from prehistoric material have hitherto been hindered by poor preservation and problems of contamination. As an alternative, geneticists have analyzed the DNA of living European populations, and have sought to identify features that may indicate the relative contributions of different ancestral groups. These analyses can be divided into two categories relating to the part of the genetic code that is involved.

The first focuses on mitochondrial DNA (mtDNA), which is inherited through the female line. The rate at which random mutations accumulate in particular mitochondrial clades, or lineages, allows their relative age to be established and an estimate of their calendar age to be proposed. Thus we know that modern humans first entered Europe during the Upper Paleolithic, and that there was colonization (or recolonization) of many areas as the ice sheets retreated at the end of the last Ice Age. The study of mtDNA suggests that these Upper Paleolithic colonization events account for the vast majority of the modern European DNA; only 20 percent or so can be attributed to more recent population movements such as the spread of farming (Richards et al. 2000).

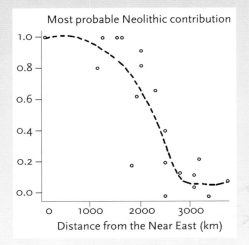

Most probable Neolithic contribution

The Y Chromosome

Hence on the evidence of mtDNA, the spread of farming must have been the result primarily of indigenous uptake, rather than the arrival of new populations. Analogous studies of the Y chromosome, however, have produced a very different conclusion, suggesting frequencies of "Neolithic" genes in excess of 85 percent in Greece and southeast Europe, falling to 15–30 percent in France, Germany, and Catalonia (northeast Spain) (Chikhi et al. 2002). The Y chromosome is restricted to males, and the difference between the results of the Y chromosome and mtDNA studies could be explained by an influx of male farmers marrying indigenous hunter-gatherer women. The Y chromosome pattern indicates a spatial trend from southeast to northwest, which mirrors the general direction of the spread of farming across Europe. It has also been compared with the distribution of Neolithic painted pottery and figurines, which are found in southeast Europe and Southwest Asia and could be taken to reflect the material culture of founder farming populations coming from Anatolia (modern Turkey) (King and Underhill 2002).

The assumptions behind these models remain largely untested, however, and in some cases are unpersuasive. The DNA studies are based on the genetics of modern European populations, and the chronology of the crucial genetic markers remains very approximate. Moreover, the archaeological evidence suggests strongly that the spread of farming was a mosaic-type process, varying significantly both from region to region and within individual regions.

11.6 *Studies of the variation among Y chromosomes in modern European populations have been used to model the contribution of incoming males to European genetic make-up. They suggest a Near Eastern contribution of 85 percent in parts of eastern Europe, declining to 15 percent in the west. Whether this relates to demographic movements or simply reflects long-standing interconnections between adjacent populations remains to be established.*

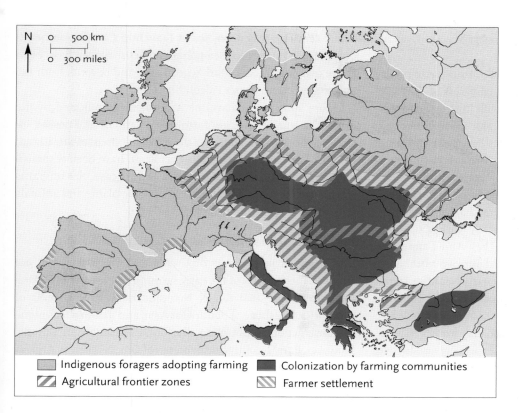

11.7 The spread of farming: colonist farmers may have carried farming across much of central Europe, while maritime pioneers may have established farming enclaves on the Mediterranean coasts of France and Spain, and the Atlantic coasts of Portugal. Elsewhere in Europe there is little to support the idea of an expansion of colonist farmers and it is more likely that the new plants and animals were adopted by existing hunter-gatherer communities, who made an indigenous transition from hunting and collecting to food production.

Indigenous foragers adopting farming · Colonization by farming communities
Agricultural frontier zones · Farmer settlement

11.8 The chronology of farming: the origins of farming in southeast Europe are indicated by the pattern of radiocarbon dates for the earliest farming settlements (areas shown in tint). The arrows show possible migration routes. Farming appears to have been carried by boat across the Aegean and to Crete soon after 7000 BC, and spread thence through the northern Balkans with particular emphasis of fertile plains such as Thessaly and river basins such as the Vardar and Moritsa valleys, reaching the Adriatic coasts and the Danube by the beginning of the 6th millennium BC.

Recent genetic studies have added to, rather than settled, this debate [see box: Replacement or Continuity? Population Genetics and the First European Farmers].

Alongside the question of how farming spread, we must also consider the nature of these early Neolithic communities, and above all their diversity. Archaeological evidence does not suggest that substantial farming settlements arose right across Europe at this time, and it appears that the new domesticates were integrated within a range of different cultural, social, and economic contexts. Thus, an early farming settlement from central Europe was very different from one in southern Scandinavia or the Balkans. To comprehend this diversity in the spread of farming across Europe, we shall look individually at five separate zones of the continent: the southeast; the central and western Mediterranean; central Europe; Atlantic Europe; and northern Europe.

Southeastern Europe

The first farming settlements in mainland Europe were established around 6500 BC on the fertile alluvial plains of Thessaly in east-central Greece. This was an area with little evidence for indigenous hunter-gatherer occupation; indeed, Mesolithic evidence is sparse in the whole of southeast Europe, suggesting that population levels were relatively low and communities small and scattered. The early farming communities soon formed settlement mounds, or tells (see below). They were established on the raised levees or in the channels of abandoned river courses, with access to light, easily worked silts that were watered every year by spring floods (Van Andel and Runnels 1995). Thessaly in this respect formed one of a number of lowland basins that became key centers of early Neolithic farming communities, others being Macedonia and Thrace from 5800 BC, the Sava and Morava valleys in the northern Balkans from 5700 BC, and Dalmatia (coastal Croatia) from 5700 BC. Early farmers may have targeted these especially productive areas; indeed, the spread of farming across southeast Europe may have been largely driven by the process of overspill, as population levels in each of the lowland basins reached a critical threshold, at which point groups split off to settle the nearest available pocket of prime arable land.

Thus the Neolithic may have been introduced to Greece by a migration of colonist farmers from Anatolia (modern Turkey) seeking new land. The absence of sites belonging to the earliest Neolithic period in Greece to the north of Thessaly suggests that such contacts would have been maritime in character, crossing the Aegean from island to island. Evidence for maritime traffic across the Aegean reaches back to at least the 11th millennium BC, when obsidian from volcanic sources on the island of Melos was deposited at **Franchthi Cave** in southeastern Greece. Patterns of sea-going contact may well have been active over the whole of the Aegean area and beyond, from the later stages of the Upper Paleolithic.

More substantial maritime movement is indicated by the establishment of an early farming settlement at **Knossos** on Crete c. 7000 BC, which marks the first settlement of this island; colonist farmers from Anatolia may again have been responsible (Broodbank and Strasser 1991). In this case, the migrants must have taken the full range of domestic plants and animals with them from their Anatolian homeland.

Neolithic Settlements

The Neolithic settlements of Greece and the Balkans do not share all the features of the early farming communities of Anatolia. It is true that Greek Neolithic houses were built of mud-brick like those of Southwest Asia, and that this technique of construction is not generally found elsewhere in Europe. However, Early Neolithic settlements of Greece, such as **Argissa** in Thessaly and **Nea Nikomedeia** in Macedonia [11.9], consisted of separate, small rectangular buildings, contrasting with the agglomerated architecture of south-central Anatolia and with the circular houses of contemporary northwest Anatolian sites such as Fikirtepe (Özdoğan 1997). Clay models portray houses with painted walls, steeply pitched roofs, and rectangular open-

11.9 Nea Nikomedeia: *excavations at this tell site in northern Greece revealed remains of three successive phases, each with six or eight rectangular timber-framed houses measuring between 6 x 8 m (20 x 26.25 ft) and 9 x 11 m (30 x 36 ft) in size. If similar houses were spread evenly across the unexcavated parts of the site the total community would have comprised at least 50 houses or some 250 people.*

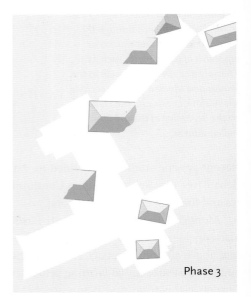

Phase 1   Phase 2   Phase 3

ings for doors and windows. On the other hand, there are close artifactual parallels with Anatolia in objects that required special care in their manufacture and may have related to status, such as carved and polished stone seals, ear studs, and stone vessels (Perlès 2001).

The use of clay (either mud-brick or daub) for building, coupled with the stability of settlement, led to the formation of **tells**. These are a feature of Neolithic communities not only in Greece, but in the whole of southeastern Europe, from Thessaly and Thrace to eastern Hungary. As houses decayed or were demolished, the mud-brick or clay daub accumulated to form the mound, a process that was repeated as new houses were built on the sites of those destroyed. The Neolithic tell of **Karanovo** in southern Bulgaria [11.10] grew to a height of 12 m (40 ft) and spread over 4 ha (10 acres) (Bailey 2000). Such mounds are not accidental creations but are the result of particular attitudes to place by communities that chose to remain at the same location over successive generations. The height and prominence of the tells themselves may ultimately have made them visual symbols of the importance (certainly of the longevity) of the community that lived there, and must have incorporated a memory of the generations that had occupied the site previously. This is in striking contrast to other regions of Europe, where prehistoric settlements were generally insubstantial and shifting in character. In areas such as eastern Hungary, tell settlements did not appear at the very beginning of the Neolithic, but developed around 1000 years later, their appearance marking a clear change in settlement practices (Chapman 1997).

Figurines and Evidence for Social Complexity

These early farming communities are also characterized by a rich material culture that includes painted pottery and modeled clay figurines. House models have already been mentioned; these indicate the likely appearance of domestic structures that survive only as mud-brick foundations or patterns of postholes. By the 6th millennium BC, more complex houses were being built, divided internally into several rooms. Clay models of furniture also survive, indicating something of the internal arrangements of domestic buildings.

The most populous category of clay models, however, is that of humans or animals. Many human figurines show female characteristics, though some are genderless and a few are explicitly male. Limited excavations at **Achilleion** in northern

Greece yielded fragments of 200 zoomorphic and anthropomorphic figurines, the earliest dating from the later 7th millennium BC, with human forms increasingly predominating over animals in succeeding phases (Bailey 2000). Many of the human figurines from Balkan sites of this period have no indication of gender, but where sex is shown it is predominantly female, with emphasis on hips, breasts, and belly. Traditional interpretations in terms of a "goddess" cult are increasingly being reassessed against the evidence that the figurines are not exclusively female, and their identification as deities or even ancestors is far from sure (Meskell 1995). These figurines may have played a diversity of roles in different contexts. Early figurines from Greece and the Balkans do tend to exaggerate sexual characteristics, and may have been associated with female fertility, but later figurines are more varied in form and function [11.11]. Some might represent supernatural beings, but many may have been tokens of living individuals or dead ancestors.

Some figurines were placed in graves, whereas others have been found, usually fragmentary, among settlement debris; but in both cases there is evidence that the fragmentation of figurines was often intentional: they were made and fired in such a way that they would easily break apart. This suggests that whatever the figurines stood for – whether living individuals, dead ancestors, or deities – the intentional dispersal of the fragments would have served to link together people or places, in a process that has been termed **enchainment** (Chapman 2000). Ethnographic studies suggest that for many societies, people are linked indissolubly to the objects that they have created or possessed, and that in giving away or depositing such objects (or fragments of them) they are giving or leaving a part of themselves. Thus the

11.10 Karanovo: *this 12-m (40-ft) high tell in southern Bulgaria is one of the most impressive and most deeply stratified mounds of the early farming sites of southeast Europe. Such tells are the product of continuous occupation stretching over several millennia coupled with specific social practices involving the demolition and rebuilding of mud-brick houses.*

11.11 *A figurine from Nea Nikomedeia, Greece, c. 6000 BC: baked clay figurines of human and animals are a feature shared between the early farming settlements of southeast Europe and those of Southwest Asia. They have in the past been invoked as evidence of a mother goddess cult, but may have represented living or recently dead individuals as much as divinities, and in many cases the sex is ambiguous.*

movement of objects materializes a chain of connections between individuals in a society, and between those individuals and the houses, pits, or graves in which objects may be placed or discarded.

Figurines are a symptom of the symbolic complexity of the early farming societies of southeast Europe, and are another feature that they share with Southwest Asia. During the 6th and 5th millennia BC this complexity began to assume new forms, as societies grew in size and organization. Tell settlements appeared in new areas, such as eastern Hungary and the lower Danube Valley; those of the latter region contained houses arranged in orderly fashion within a rectangular enclosure. Evidence of craft specialization appears at a number of settlements, and high-temperature kilns were developed for the production of thin-walled pottery that was either painted or graphite-decorated. Graphite decoration shared the light-reflecting qualities of copper and gold, which also came into use at this period (Bailey 2000). In some parts of the Balkans, burials were moved outside the settlement area in the early 5th millennium BC and began to be grouped into cemeteries, the grave goods placed with the dead indicating the increasingly varying social roles that were developing at this period. The most dramatic example is the cemetery of **Varna** on the shores of the Black Sea, where some 280 graves (including 56 "cenotaphs") were equipped with offerings of gold, copper, pottery, and stone [see box: The Varna Cemetery].

The Introduction of Metals

The introduction of metals does not mark a sharp break in the development of southeast European societies, although the term **Chalcolithic**, or **Copper Age**, is sometimes used to distinguish this period from the preceding Neolithic. But it does mark a stage in the increasing complexity of material culture, and an expansion of human settlement and activity across the landscape, perhaps associated with the introduction of the **plow**

(Sherratt 1981; Bailey 2000). Fertile lowland basins remained the principal population centers, supported by their rich primary agricultural productivity, but many of the special materials used in status displays came from the surrounding uplands, including metals and stone for axes. It is in these upland zones that the oldest recorded European **copper mines** are found, as at **Ai Bunar** in southern Bulgaria, where copper ore was mined in trenches up to 80 m long, 10 m wide, and 20 m deep (260 x 33 x 66 ft) from as early as 5100 BC (Chernykh 1978). A little later, mine galleries were being sunk for copper ore at **Rudna Glava** in Serbia. The distribution of the products (which can be traced by metal analysis) tied large areas of southeast Europe into complex networks of exchange, while the metal goods themselves stimulated the development of ever-increasing social differentiation in the farming settlements of the region.

The Mediterranean Zone

Within the Mediterranean basin, the domesticated crops of Southwest Asian origin were relatively easy to transplant and cultivate, since climates were broadly similar. Thus farming spread early from the Balkans to southern Italy, where on the Tavoliere plain, facing the Adriatic, domestic plants and animals were in use by 6000 BC.

The **Tavoliere** is similar in topography and agricultural potential to southeast European centers of early farming such as Thessaly in north-central Greece, and it is possible that domestic crops and livestock were brought by colonizing farmers from the Balkans. On the other hand, there are no tell settlements in southern Italy; the key Early Neolithic sites take the form of ditched enclosures containing numerous smaller C-shaped enclosures, as well as traces of houses and cobbled areas (Skeates 2002), the latter possibly hearths for feasting, or perhaps associated with other open-air activities. The site of **Passo di Corvo** [11.13] had three or more encircling ditches with over 100 house compounds within.

An integrationist model cannot be excluded: Neolithic features may have been conveyed across the Adriatic to the Italian peninsula in the course of routine maritime contact, and adopted by indigenous Mesolithic communities. There are some 500 Neolithic enclosures on the Tavoliere plain, and enclosures are also a feature of a second center of early farming sites in the **Stentinello** area of eastern Sicily. Both enclosure ditches and C-ditches were used for the burial of special deposits, including disarticulated human remains. Radiocarbon dating suggests that new enclosures continued to be dug on the Tavoliere for around 1000 years, down to 5000 BC. The earliest were associated with impressed ware pottery, later joined by fine painted ceramics.

KEY SITE **The Varna Cemetery**

The cemetery at Varna, on the Black Sea coast of Bulgaria, was discovered accidentally in 1972, and the abundance of metal and especially gold in some of the graves quickly attracted attention (Renfrew 1986). The cemetery itself is part of a wider 5th-millennium BC trend to community burial outside the confines of a settlement. Varna had some 280 graves, but larger cemeteries are known, such as Durankulak (some 50 km, or 30 miles, north of Varna), with over 800 burials. It is suggested that the development of cemetery burial served as a means of promoting greater social integration, taking burial outside the confines of individual households and placing it firmly in the public arena.

Analyzing the Graves

One quarter of the Varna graves were destroyed before excavation began, but details of the remaining 211 burials reveal striking differences in the amount and variety of material placed with the dead. Most of these graves (170) have up to ten items, but 23 graves have no grave goods that have survived, while 18 have large and spectacular assemblages of material. Grave 14, the occupant of which was a male aged 40–50 years old, had over 1000 objects, of which over 980 were of gold, including beads, rings, sheet ornaments, bracelets, and a penis sheath. There were also copper axes and other tools, as well as flintwork and pottery. Many of the richly furnished "graves" yielded no conclusive evidence of a body, and have been termed cenotaphs. No less than 60 percent of the gold from Varna was found in such cenotaphs, which may commemorate important individuals buried elsewhere.

The Gold Objects

The most abundant gold objects from Varna are beads, but more spectacular are the gold penis sheath, the hammered sheet pectorals, the gold appliqués (often zoomorphic in form) with perforated edges for sewing onto the clothing of the deceased, and the decorations added to axe, hammer, and scepter shafts. As archaeologist Douglass

Bailey has observed, most of these objects are ornaments, and would have been sewn onto clothes, attached to head or facial hair, pushed through holes in ears or lips, or worn around wrists and upper arms: "in almost all cases, gold was used to enhance the expressiveness of something else (a scepter, a face, a body)" (Bailey 2000, 219).

The association with the body is particularly significant: these were all objects to be displayed on or about the person, whether held in the hand or attached to clothing. Some, perhaps many, of them may have been produced specifically for burial, and their placement in the grave would have made the interment ceremony itself a setting for impressive visual displays of objects that most people would have very rarely seen.

The abundance of gold, along with copper and other prestige materials, suggests that Varna was the burial place of an important community. It also demonstrates how, by the 5th millennium BC, societies in southeast Europe were using elaborate material culture to signify differences between individuals. Gold is a particularly suitable material for status display, as it is rare, has a shiny

appearance, is relatively soft and thus easily worked and formed, and does not tarnish like most other metals. It has few practical uses, however, and its prominence and sought-after quality illustrates the social role of metal.

The Role of Copper

The earliest copper objects, likewise, were not tools or weapons but trinkets or beads, such as those found in the late 6th millennium BC settlement at Vinča in Serbia or at Cernica cemetery site in southern Romania. By early in the 5th millennium BC, copper was being cast into axes and copper ores mined in complex galleries at Ai Bunar in Romania and Rudna Glava in Serbia.

The copper objects in the Varna graves are copies of objects (axes, chisels, hammers) normally made in more mundane materials such as stone or antler. Whereas gold was used to decorate, copper was used to replicate. Both metals would have indicated control over distant sources of supply and knowledge of the technologies of transformation that copper, in particular, would have required. As the Varna graves show, however, their social role was significantly different.

11.12 *The richly furnished burials of the Varna cemetery testify to the growing complexity of communities in southeast Europe during the 5th millennium BC. The appearance of metals (copper and gold) was in response to the demand for new symbols of social display and differentiation, and the wealth of gold in some of the Varna graves illustrates the use of these materials to adorn the bodies of powerful individuals.*

As in Greece, Mesolithic settlement in Italy is concentrated in areas other than those where Neolithic farming settlements are principally found. It is likely that the first farmers and the last foragers co-existed for some time, and there may well have been contact between the two groups. In such circumstances, Mesolithic hunter-gatherers might have adopted pottery and domesticates from their farming neighbors. This is what we seem to find at sites such as the **Grotta dell'Uzzo** in western Sicily, where domesticates appear in an otherwise Mesolithic context (Whittle 1996).

Similar sequences have been documented in caves and rockshelters of southern France, such as the **Grotte Gazel** and the **Abri Jean-Cros**, where domestic animals appear in the course of the 6th millennium BC. Such sites were well located for hunting and the exploitation of wild resources, but were not ideal for farming, as they lacked suitable local agricultural land; it is not surprising that domesticates make a relatively late appearance at these sites. The most significant early farming settlements were probably situated in the alluvial plains, where traces of them are still relatively rare. A few open sites are known, however, including **Leucate** off the coast of Languedoc, and the lakeside settlement of **La Draga**, with wooden buildings occupied *c.* 5900–4900 BC (Barnett 2000). At La Draga, 75 percent of the fauna were domestic animals; this may be

contrasted with the Pyrenean rockshelter of **Dourgne**, where remains of domestic sheep were so rare that they may have been obtained by theft or exchange from nearby Neolithic groups (Binder 2000).

Neolithic Settlements

The earliest Neolithic sites of the central and western Mediterranean are characterized by "cardial" pottery [see 1.1], the decoration of which is executed by impressing the edge of a cardium shell into the wet clay before firing. Cardium shell decoration is often very elaborate, and underlines the role of the sea and maritime transport in the spread of the Neolithic. Cardial Ware [**11.14**] is unpainted, and hence provides a regional distinction with the red-painted or polychrome-painted wares of southeast Europe. Fishing communities along the Mediterranean coast may have played a significant part in the dissemination of domesticates and pottery technology, and smaller islands such as Malta and the Balearics were first settled during this period (Guerrero Ayuso 2002). Of the Mediterranean islands, only Sicily had continuous occupation from the Upper Paleolithic (Cherry 1990). Corsica and Sardinia were resettled by hunter-gatherers during postglacial times, but the smaller islands appear to have been permanently colonized for the first time by farmers or pastoralists in the 6th or 5th millennium BC. The continued importance of maritime contacts is demonstrated by the traffic in obsidian from sources on Sardinia, Lipari, and Palmarola to early farming sites on the Italian peninsula and in southern France.

The disparate nature of the Neolithic transition is especially clear in southern Iberia (modern Spain and Portugal), where enclaves of early farming settlement were established by 6000 BC. Cardial pottery at several deeply stratified cave sites, including **Chaves**, **Coveta del'Or**, **Cenres**, and **Cariguela de Piñar**, is dated to around 5900–5400 BC. The flint tools from these sites show marked discontinuity with the preceding Mesolithic tradition, and provide some support for the view that the Cardial settlements are intrusive and represent the arrival of small groups of farmers, though a few sherds at **La Cocina** (a cave site with a long Mesolithic sequence) may illustrate interaction with local hunter-gatherers (Zilhão 2000). If early farming did spread throughout the Mediterranean through the movement of small seaborne colonizing populations, the cultural repertory that they carried changed as they traveled west. It is most plausible to envisage short-distance movements from one enclave to the next, rather than long-distance displacements of people. Their boats must have carried both the plants and the animals

11.13 Passo di Corvo, southern Italy: *the multiple ditch circuits enclose an area of 28 ha (69 acres), within which are traces of some 90 house compounds. Traditionally interpreted as permanent villages, these may have been seasonally occupied by sheep and goat herders.*

11.14 *Cardial Ware:* so-called from the use of the edge of a cardium (cockle) shell to impress decoration into the surface of the vessel before firing, this is the characteristic pottery of the early farming communities of the west Mediterranean basin. It was first made about 5600 BC, but was preceded by a phase of non-cardium decorated "impressed ware" which marks the spread of pottery and domesticates into southern France and eastern Spain beginning around 6000 BC.

(sheep and goats) that they needed in order to establish themselves.

The Emergence of Social Complexity

Within a relatively short period, farming spread beyond these fertile coastal lowlands to the continental hinterland. Local communities of hunters and gatherers either adopted the new way of life or were absorbed by expanding farming groups. More complex societies began to develop. In the Toulouse area of southern France, a series of large enclosure sites dates to the late 5th millennium BC. These enclose rectangular, cobble-filled pits that appear to have been open hearths for communal feasting. The nature of social change is emphasized by the emergence of powerful individuals, represented by tomb A.185 at **St.-Michel-du-Touch**. Here a rectangular pit, probably lined with timber and covered by a tumulus of river cobbles, contained remains of two individuals. These two burials lacked the spectacular grave goods seen, for example, at Varna in Bulgaria,

but they are striking because the skeletons were reconstituted after being left to decay elsewhere (Beyneix 2003). The manipulation of bodies and skeletons is a regular practice of prehistoric societies, not only in Europe but throughout the world (see, for example, Chapter 6, p. 221), and indicates the complexity of burial practices and the beliefs associated with them.

In southeast Spain, the later 4th millennium BC witnessed the emergence of visible social complexity in the form of enclosed sites and communal tombs with rich assemblages of grave goods. The aridity of this region made water control essential, leading in part to the emergence of social complexity. The key site is **Los Millares** in Almería [**11.15**], where three circuits of dry-stone wall with bastions were once interpreted as a fortified settlement. Similar enclosures are found at **Zambujal** and **Vila Nova de São Pedro** in Portugal, and they are now generally interpreted as monumental settings for social and ritual practices (Whittle 1996). Close to the Los Millares enclosure is a cemetery of some 80 stone-built "tholos" tombs (circular tombs with a domed or conical roof). These contained multiple inhumations (1140 in total from 58 of the tombs, with up to 200 individuals per tomb) but were remarkable also for the nature of the grave offerings, which included copper objects and imported materials such as ivory and ostrich eggshell from North Africa, and variscite (a green-colored mineral) from Catalonia or northwest Iberia (Chapman 1990). There was also elaborately decorated pottery, and here again, as in the Balkans, we see how increasing distinctions of social status were associated with the elaboration of material culture and the collection of exotic materials. The invention of metallurgy is linked to these developments, and may have been an independent discovery:

11.15 *Los Millares, cross-section of a tomb:* this site in the arid region of southeast Spain consists of a promontory isolated by three concentric circuits of dry stone walling, and an adjacent cemetery of stone-built collective graves. Once considered a fortified settlement, Los Millares is more probably a high-status locale, marked by the impressive walls limiting access to the interior, and by the rich grave offerings in some of the chamber tombs.

the earliest evidence of **copperworking** has recently been dated to the early 5th millennium BC in Almería (Ruiz-Taboada and Monetro-Ruiz 1999).

Material and symbolic complexity are features of the central Mediterranean also in the 4th millennium BC. In southern France and northern Italy, communities carved stone statue-stelae with schematic faces, necklaces, belts, and daggers. Of approximately the same period are some of the Alpine rock carvings, notably those from **Mont Bégo**, where similar daggers are depicted. These upland sites may have been places visited by young men at the time of their initiation. Copper daggers of the kind depicted in the art are found in graves in the cemeteries of northern and central Italy, for instance those of the **Rinaldone** group in southern Tuscany, or at **Remedello** and similar sites in the foothills overlooking the Po Valley (Barfield and Chippindale 1997). Here, as in southeast Europe, or in Hungarian Copper Age cemeteries such as Tiszapolgar-Basatanya, the cemetery may have come to represent a communal focus for a series of communities living in the surrounding area. Small farming settlements are known from this period, some on the shores of the Alpine lakes, where the waterlogging of the remains has preserved details of the timber and other organic materials. The most vivid single insight into life in this part of Europe during the late 4th millennium BC is provided, however, not by wetland contexts, but by the freeze-dried body of the "**Iceman**," found in the high Alps in 1991 [see box: The "Iceman", pp. 408–09].

Central Europe

We have seen how farming spread westward from southeast Europe to Italy and Iberia. A second axis of farming spread took the new domesticates north into the Danube Valley and central Europe. By the end of the 7th millennium BC, farming settlements had begun to be established in Serbia and along the Danube Valley, at sites such as Divostin, Vinča, and Starčevo Grad. Further north, in eastern Hungary, small settlements such as **Endröd 119** (as its name suggests, just one of hundreds of known sites of this period) may have been occupied for only a short time, and it is clear that hunting and fishing remained important in many areas for several centuries after pottery and domesticates appeared. Only during the late 6th and early 5th millennia BC did some of these sites (such as Vinča) develop into substantial tells (Whittle 1996). The gradual accommodation of local Mesolithic communities to changing circumstances is visible at the hunter-fisher-gatherer settlement of Lepenski Vir (6200–5400 BC) [**11.16**], the latest in a series of significant Mesolithic sites in the Iron Gates region of the Danube (where the river cuts through the Carpathian Mountains on its way to the Black Sea). Distinctive trapezoidal houses at this site have stone-carved fish sculptures next to their central hearths [**11.17**]; pottery and radiocarbon dates indicate their contemporaneity with Early Neolithic farming groups in the Morava, middle Danube, and Tisza valleys (Boric 2002).

11.16, 11.17 *Lepinski Vir: fish played a major role in the economy and ideology of Lepenski Vir, a Late Mesolithic settlement (left) on the banks of the River Danube in Serbia. The distinctive sculptures hammered and pecked out of limestone boulders (below) combine fish and human features and were placed close to the hearths of the houses.*

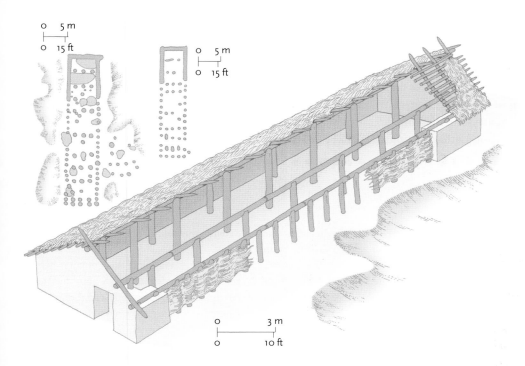

11.18 Bandkeramik longhouses: *of fairly standardized construction, these survive as patterns of postholes flanked by the long lateral pits from which the daub (adobe) for the wattle walls was extracted. Internal groups of massive timber posts supported the pitched roof (covered in thatch) which rested on and overhung the side walls. The northern end of these houses was often more massively built of split timber planks in a bedding trench; occasionally the whole of the outer wall was of timber plank construction. The extravagant use of such large timbers may be a response to the forested settings in which these houses were built.*

The Bandkeramik Culture

Around the middle of the 6th millennium BC, a distinctive cultural package developed in western Hungary, on the edge of this area of earliest Neolithic settlement. Called Linearbandkeramik (often abbreviated to Bandkeramik or LBK; sometimes anglicized as the Linear Pottery Culture or LPC), this subsequently spread across the whole of central Europe from Hungary and Austria to the Rhineland and the Paris basin in the west, and eastwards to Ukraine and Moldavia [see **11.1**]. Bandkeramik settlements are characterized by a number of distinctive features, notably the pottery with incised banded decoration that gives it its name, longhouses of fairly standardized construction, polished stone "shoe-last" adzes, single grave burials sometimes grouped in cemeteries, and particular types of site location and economy. From its earliest manifestation in Hungary and eastern Austria *c.* 5600 BC it spread relatively rapidly across Europe, reaching the Rhineland by 5300 BC, a distance of 650 km (400 miles) in 300 years, and the Paris basin a century or so later (Gronenborn 1999; Modderman 1988; Bogucki and Grygiel 1993).

Bandkeramik settlements took the form of massively built longhouses [**11.18**] grouped in twos or threes in forest clearings on gravel river terraces, which provided access to water and easily tilled soil. Successive generations of houses shifted over time, and Bandkeramik settlements typically display a palimpsest of postholes, but they never developed settlement mounds like the tells of southeastern Europe. Occupation of settlement sites was altogether less fixed and less intensive [see box: The Bandkeramik Settlements at Langweiler, pp. 412–13].

The rapid expansion of the Bandkeramik, and its relative cultural coherence, make it one of the strongest candidates for interpretation as a movement of colonizing farmers (Bogucki 2000; but see also Jochim 2000; Whittle 1996). The selection of light, easily worked loess (wind-blown silt) soils, and the clustering of Bandkeramik settlements in sub-regional groupings or "settlement cells," adds to the impression of dispersed communities moving steadily across central Europe, following the river valleys, planting small fields of cereals and legumes and pasturing cattle along the forest margins. From most of the Bandkeramik area there is little evidence of Mesolithic settlement, and here, as in other regions of Europe, the spatial segregation of late hunter-gatherer and early farmer activity foci is particularly striking (Gronenborn 1999).

As Bandkeramik settlement cells expanded, however, they would necessarily have come into contact with hunter-gatherer groups, and there is some evidence to suggest that the latter were ultimately absorbed by the growing agricultural populations. Analysis of strontium isotopes in human skeletons from the Bandkeramik cemeteries of **Flomborn**, **Schwetzingen**, and **Dillingen**, in Germany, and in the southern Rhineland indicates that a proportion of those buried had spent their adolescence in neighboring regions rather than on the fertile alluvial plains.

That the majority of these outsiders were female suggests that expanding farming groups were marrying women from local foraging communities, in a pattern of farmer-forager contact that has been recorded ethnographically (Bentley et al. 2002). The evidence for violence in Bandkeramik society, conversely, illustrates hostility between neighboring Bandkeramik groups rather than conflict with indigenous hunter-gatherers [see box: The Talheim Death Pit, p. 411].

Later Regional Groups

By 5000 BC the Bandkeramik had begun to be replaced by a series of regional groupings defined mainly on the basis of their pottery types: **Rössen** and **Michelsberg** in the west, **Lengyel** in the east. At first these retained the longhouse settlement mode but occupied a wider diversity of environmental settings, including the lowlands of the north European plain. Toward the end of the 5th millennium BC, a new type of pottery appears in northern and central Europe, characterized by beakers with a globular body and flaring out-turned rim and known accordingly as the **Trichterbecher** ("funnel-necked beaker") culture (TRB) (Midgley 1992; Price 2000). This culture is divided into a

KEY DISCOVERY The "Iceman"

On 19 September 1991, two German mountaineers discovered the oldest preserved human body ever recorded in modern times. The site of the discovery was the Italian South Tyrol, close to the main ridge of the Alps and only a little more than 90 m (300 ft) from the international frontier between Italy and Austria. This section of the Alps is known as the Ötztaler Alps, taking its name from the long, narrow Ötztal Valley, and the body is commonly known today by the nickname "Ötzi"; many, however, simply refer to the corpse as the "Iceman" (Fowler 2000; Spindler 1994).

The Finds

The body proved to be that of a man aged 25–45 years old. The excellent state of preservation meant that even the molecular structure of his tissues had survived, and the reason for this unusual degree of preservation lay in the sequence of events that led to and followed his death. It was thought at first that the man had died after being overcome by an early autumn blizzard. Then, in 2001, an X-ray of the body revealed that a flint arrowhead was lodged immediately below the left shoulder: he had been shot in the back (Gostner and Vigl 2002). Although the thin covering of autumn snow was not therefore the cause of his death, it was certainly the medium of his preservation, preventing attack from insect larvae as the corpse was gradually desiccated by autumn winds. In essence, what occurred was a natural freeze-drying. The condition of the corpse was already largely stabilized when the heavy winter snows covered it. Radiocarbon dating of tissues from the body, undertaken separately in four different laboratories for greater reliability, indicated that these events took place between 3300 and 3200 BC. The corpse lay buried for over 5000 years before melting of the ice, accelerated by wind-borne Saharan dust in July 1991, exposed it to view again.

The preservation of the Iceman is hence more remarkable than mysterious, but the circumstances of his death, and the significance of the objects that he was carrying, do pose many questions. Lying around the body in the ice hollow were a copper axe hafted in a yew handle, an unfinished bow, also of yew, a backpack of larch planks and animal hide, a flint knife and leather scabbard, a deerskin quiver with two flint-tipped arrows and 12 unfinished arrow shafts, and a calfskin pouch that hung from a belt. The remains of his clothing included fur leggings and cap, fur outer garment of poncho type, leather shoes stuffed with grass for warmth, and a grass cape that could have doubled as a groundsheet or blanket. This was a set of clothing well able to cope with the harsh Alpine climate, at least outside the winter months.

The same cannot be said of his equipment, for the unfinished nature of his bow and the majority of his arrows suggest that he was not well prepared for his journey. Furthermore, he was not in the peak of health. Analysis of one of his fingernails revealed that he suffered from serious illnesses (resulting in interruptions to fingernail growth) at least three times during the six months before he died. He also bore tattoos on his lower back, left leg, and right ankle and knee. These may have been

11.19 *The body discovered in the Similaun glacier in September 1991 had been preserved by a natural process of freeze-drying. Lengthy and detailed scientific analyses have since established that the man died over 5000 years ago, shortly after a violent struggle in which he was shot in the shoulder and sustained a probable knife wound to his right hand.*

series of regional groups and appears to represent an interaction zone – an interlinked series of communities among whom ideas, materials, and artifacts circulated widely. Most conspicuous among the materials involved in these exchanges is copper from the southeastern TRB area in Slovakia. This circulated through the TRB zone to reach northern Europe, where it appears in the form of axes and hoards of copper objects, such as that at **Bygholm** in Denmark, from around 4000 BC [**11.21**]. The early appearance of copper axes and ornaments in Denmark, far from the initial areas of metallurgy in southeast Europe, is all the more surprising in that Denmark has no metal deposits of its own (Ottaway 1973).

Coat of tanned domestic goat hide

Yew long bow, unfinished

Deerskin quiver

Grass cape

Dagger with flint blade

Leather loincloth

Fur leggings

Copper axe with yew haft

Leather shoes, stuffed with grass

Backpack of larch planks and hide

11.20 *The ice had preserved not only the body of the Iceman but also his clothing, which included leather shoes and loincloth, fur leggings and cloak, and an outer cape, open at the front, made from plaited grasses over 1 m (3.3 ft) in length. Capes of this kind, woven from straw or reeds, were still worn in parts of northern Italy in the 18th century.*

decorative but more probably had a therapeutic function, since the Iceman suffered from arthritis. Analysis of his colon contents has indicated that he also suffered from an intestinal infestation that could have given him chronic diarrhea. Most serious of all, however, was evidence that his right hand had been seriously injured, perhaps in a knife fight. A deep cut 4 cm (1.6 in) long across the palm of the hand would almost have immobilized two of his fingers.

The Interpretation

What precisely was the context of this violence, and of the bowshot wound that was the more immediate cause of death, we may never know. One theory is that the Iceman was a shepherd who frequented the mountains but died after becoming involved in a local feud. Analysis of moss from the body showed that it had come from the south side of the Alps, quite possibly from the Vinschgau, only 20 km (12.5 miles) due south of the place where he met his end. Isotope studies of the Iceman's bones, teeth, and stomach contents indicate that he spent his childhood in the Eisack Valley in the lowest Vinschgau, and as an adult migrated to slightly higher altitudes or a few kilometers upstream, or was perhaps engaged in seasonal transhumance (Müller et al. 2003). Pollen suggests that his death occurred in the early autumn, and he may have been shepherding his flock in upland pastures, and in none-too-good a state of health, when he was attacked or became involved in a fight. Further analysis showed that blood on his leather cape and knife, and on a broken arrow in his quiver, came from four separate individuals. The Iceman may have pulled the broken arrow from the body of one of his victims, and this, together with the wounds he had suffered, suggests that he survived for some time – perhaps as much as a day or two – after the encounter, before succumbing to the arrow wound in his back. It is becoming increasingly clear that violence was more frequent in prehistoric European societies than some earlier scholars have wished to suppose, as evidenced by the mass grave at Talheim in Bavaria, from a millennium before the Iceman [see box: The Talheim Death Pit, p. 411].

The nature of the Iceman's belongings have led some to argue that rather than being simply a shepherd or a village farmer, he was a shaman, or ritual specialist. The unfinished hunting equipment, the body tattoos, and a perforated bead of white marble with twisted leather tassels, have all been adduced in support. Shamans commune with the spirit world, often in remote locations, and this might explain his journey to the high mountains. Ethnographic examples indicate that bright or polished stones are often held to have special significance or power, though quartz, rather than marble, is the more usual material. The evidence that the Iceman was a shaman is not overwhelming, but it is a possibility that is difficult to discount.

The unique nature of the discovery, and the exceptional conditions of preservation, give us little with which to compare him. Were fuller evidence available, we might be less inclined to attribute to the Iceman some ritual or religious status, and more willing – notwithstanding curious features of his equipment – to regard him as a typical member of a high Alpine community of the late 4th millennium BC, distinguished more in the fate that befell him, and his body, than in his status in life.

11.21 *The Bygolm hoard: this hoard of copper objects was discovered in 1924 at Bygholm, Denmark. The objects date to around 4000 BC and comprise three armrings, four axes and a dagger blade. The armrings testify to the demand for personal ornaments that was a major stimulus to the adoption and spread of metallurgy, while the axes represent the transfer into metal of an artifact-type more commonly found in stone at this period in northern Europe.*

The 5th and 4th millennia BC witnessed other important changes in the Neolithic farming communities of central Europe. The introduction of the **plow**, probably in the 5th millennium BC, made it possible to bring new areas into cultivation, and the presence of **wheeled vehicles** is attested by finds of wooden wheels in wetland areas (for instance in Switzerland and Slovenia) and by ceramic models of wheeled vehicles from 4th-millennium BC graves at **Budakalasz** and **Szigetszentmarton** in Hungary. It has been argued that plowing, animal traction, milk, and wool were adopted together (some of them from Southwest Asia) at about this time, stimulating what has been called the "**secondary products revolution**" (Sherratt 1981). Milking is now known to have been practiced in northwest Europe by 4000 BC (Copley et al. 2003), and a more cautious view is that these innovations appeared gradually over a period of several centuries, being integrated in different ways in the increasingly diverse central European farming societies.

Atlantic Europe

In central and southeastern Europe, the principal areas of early Neolithic settlement appear to have been largely devoid of previous Mesolithic settlement, and a pattern may be envisaged in which farming groups exploited the fertile lowland plains and river valleys while hunter-gatherers preferred diverse upland and wetland environments. In western and northern Europe, however, evidence of Mesolithic occupation is significantly more conspicuous, and population levels and group sizes may have been correspondingly greater.

Mesolithic Settlements

Mesolithic settlement is best documented in favored coastal locations of Atlantic Europe, where marine as well as terrestrial resources could be exploited. Many of the key sites are marked by shell middens (concentrations of cultural debris, in this case shells), which indicate repeated occupations of the same place over periods of decades or centuries. Human remains (often scattered and disarticulated) are found at some of these sites, suggesting that feasting and mortuary rituals may both have been practiced. In northwest France and southern Portugal, Late Mesolithic shell middens are associated with cemeteries, and these would have formed significant focal points for seasonally mobile communities of hunter-gatherers. At three cemetery sites – **Moita da Sebastião** in Portugal and **Téviec** and **Hoëdic** in southern Brittany, in France – some of the burials were single interments and others double, while one grave (Téviec K) contained the remains of six individuals; evidence suggests that, as with the other multiple graves, these burials were the result not of simultaneous but of successive inhumations. At Téviec, several of the graves had a lining of stone slabs, creating a rudimentary cist, with a covering slab on which a fire had burned; this has been interpreted as evidence for funerary feasts [**11.22**]. Ritual hearths were also associated with the Hoëdic burials (Scarre 2002; Schulting 1996).

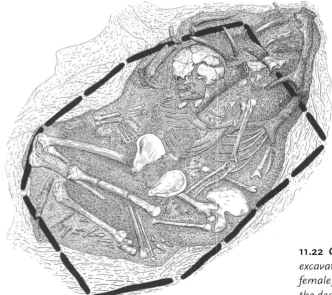

11.22 *Grave A at Téviec: the grave, in a Late Mesolithic cemetery in southern Brittany excavated 1928–34, contains the bodies of two individuals (an adult male and adult female), accompanied by red deer antler which may have marked the special status of the deceased. The grave is lined by a setting of stone slabs placed on edge.*

KEY DISCOVERY The Talheim Death Pit

Evidence for the relatively egalitarian nature of many early European farming settlements once led to the view that interpersonal or intercommunity violence was rare. This has been thrown into doubt by discoveries such as the mass grave at Talheim in Germany, where men, women, and children, perhaps victims of a hostile raid, had been dispatched by an axe-blow to the head and bundled into a pit.

Death at Talheim

Talheim is a Bandkeramik settlement site dating from the late 6th millennium BC. In a pit among the houses, archaeologists found the remains of 34 individuals: 16 children and adolescents and 18 adults, of whom at least 7 were females (Wahl and König 1987). Most of the bodies bore traces of violence. At least 18 had received blows from polished stone adzes, and analysis of the unhealed fractures allowed the individual weapons to be identified: 22 blows had been inflicted with the cutting edge of flat polished stone adzes, four by more massive adzes, and a further 14 bore the impact of blunt implements or the sides of adzes. Furthermore, three adults (at least two of them male) had received arrow wounds from behind. The absence of any evidence of resistance (in the form of injuries to the arms), and the position of the majority of head wounds on the rear of the skulls, suggests that these people were killed while attempting to flee.

The most probable interpretation is that these were inhabitants of the Talheim settlement who had been killed by raiders from a neighboring Bandkeramik settlement, though whether as part of a feud or simply to steal livestock or food stores cannot be determined. What the Talheim evidence does reveal is that the polished stone adzes of "shoe-last" form, a characteristic feature of Bandkeramik material culture, are not to be interpreted merely as carpentry tools; they had (or were capable of assuming) a much more aggressive role. This throws new light on the discovery of shoe-last adzes in the graves of older males at Bandkeramik cemeteries such as Nitra in Slovakia: they

11.23, 11.24 *Excavation of the Talheim death pit in southwest Germany with diagrams (below) showing the position of adult males (left) adult females (center) and children (right). The shape of the wounds in the skulls of many of these individuals indicates that their attackers were members of another Bandkeramik community, wielding characteristic Bandkeramik polished stone adzes, rather than (for example) neighboring hunter-gatherers.*

doubled as weapons of war, and were evidently male status symbols.

Evidence for Violence Elsewhere

Talheim is not the only Bandkeramik site to show evidence of violent death. At Schletz in Austria, skeletons had been thrown haphazardly into the ditch of a Bandkeramik enclosure, and of 67 that have so far been studied, all but one showed traces of violence – mainly, once again, blows to the head from shoe-last adzes (Vencl 1999). In this instance the enclosure itself may have been a defensive structure, and the discovery of further skeletons in the well within the settlement suggests that it was finally overrun and destroyed. Once again, it appears that we are

witnessing internecine warfare between Bandkeramik communities.

At the western edge of the Bandkeramik distribution, in Belgium, it has been argued that enclosures were built by colonizing Bandkeramik farmers to protect their settlements from hostile hunter-gatherers (Keeley and Cahen 1989). Not all (indeed, perhaps very few) Bandkeramik enclosures were defensive in nature, however, and the case for the Belgian enclosures has yet to be demonstrated. There is no conclusive evidence that violence was part of the relationship between Bandkeramik farmers and their hunter-gatherer neighbors.

KEY SITE The Bandkeramik Settlements at Langweiler, Germany

The Merzbach Valley on the Aldenhovener Plateau of western Germany is a key region for understanding the nature of the earliest farming societies in west-central Europe. Systematic excavations in advance of brown coal extraction have revealed evidence of 160 house plans from eight distinct settlement sites, plus three enclosures and a cemetery, belonging to the period 5300–4900 BC (Lüning 1982; Stehli 1989). Each settlement comprises one or more longhouses, massive timber structures up to 70 m (230 ft) in length. Successive longhouses were built to replace previous ones in the same location, each such sequence forming a settlement module termed a *Wohnplatz* or *Hofplatz*. Langweiler 8, the longest-lived of these settlements, spanned 14 successive house generations, representing an uninterrupted occupation of some 400 years. Langweiler 8 is also the largest of the Merzbach settlements, with 11 contemporary longhouses at its greatest extent. The Bandkeramik settlement of the Merzbach Valley as a whole grew from three houses in the first phase to a total of 16 or 17 in phases VII and XII, then fell away rapidly to only three houses in phase XIV and none in phase XV.

Settlement Types

The sites can be divided into three groupings on the basis of size: single farmsteads (Laurenzberg 8, Langweiler 16); clusters of 2–3 farmsteads (Langweiler 2, Langweiler 9, Laurenzberg 7); and 11 farmsteads (Langweiler 8). Each settlement had access to a portion of the valley floor, perhaps seasonal pasture for cattle, and to the drier gravel terraces for farming. Calculations suggest an average available area of some 10 ha (25 acres) per house. If 3–5 ha (10–12 acres) per farmstead were needed for cereals, each household would have had some 0.5 ha (1.2 acres) of valley floor and upwards of 5 ha (12 acres) of wooded hinterland for rough pasture or forest products (including timber for fuel and building). Since the parallel watercourses of this region are, on average, 3 km (1.9 miles) apart, we may envisage an area of uncleared woodland 1 km (0.6 miles) wide separating the more formally cultivated areas along each watercourse.

House Types

The houses of the Langweiler settlements fall into three types – long, medium, and small – and these are present in the proportions 83:12:5. Medium and small houses are found only in the middle and later phases of the Langweiler settlement cycle. Most houses are oriented northwest/southeast, perhaps in response to the prevailing wind direction in central and western Europe, but also indicating adherence to a long-established cultural norm. The tripartite plan of the houses has been interpreted in various ways; the central section is present even in the smallest category of houses, whereas only the larger ones have the plank-built northwest extension, which may have been designed for special ritual or household activities. House length appears to relate to household status, as it is the longest houses that have the highest percentage of decorated pottery.

Despite their massive construction (with oak posts measuring up to 0.5 m (1.6 ft) across), Bandkeramik houses do not appear to have had lengthy lives. Richard Bradley

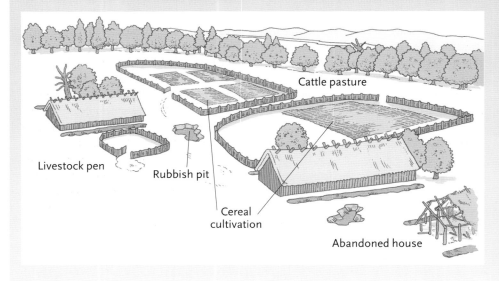

11.25 *Reconstruction of a Bandkeramik settlement. Small groups of longhouses would have been associated with fields and cattle pens in forest clearings. Settlements appear to have been divided up into individual residence plots, each of which would have one or two longhouses at any one time, together perhaps with the remains of other earlier houses that had been abandoned and left to decay.*

The groups represented by these cemeteries fall into the category of "complex" hunter-gatherers, with specialized foraging strategies, semi-sedentary settlements, and evidence of social competition. Their relationship with the earliest farming communities of their respective regions has long been a subject of debate. In Portugal, the shell middens of the Tagus and adjacent Sado estuaries may have continued in use until *c.* 4750 BC, almost a millennium after the establishment of the earliest Neolithic sites on the limestone Estremadura to the north. Thus in Portugal, and similarly in southern Spain, maritime colonist farmers may first have established themselves in enclaves some distance from the primary Mesolithic centers (Zilhão 2000). Over the centuries that followed, Mesolithic groups were absorbed into the successful and expanding farming societies, in a process sim-

(2001) has suggested that longhouses were closely associated with individuals, and may have been abandoned at the death of those individuals, taking on a funerary significance. This could explain why Bandkeramik houses were deserted long before they needed to be (in structural terms), and suggests that a Bandkeramik settlement might have consisted of longhouses in occupation interspersed with the remains of longhouses abandoned on the deaths of their owners, which would have collapsed to form low, long mounds of debris.

Farming Economy

The agricultural basis for these Bandkeramik settlements is reconstructed as small-scale cereal cultivation in fixed plots adjacent to the settlements. This replaces an earlier model that proposed shifting slash-and-burn agriculture as the typical Bandkeramik farming mode. Land may have been cleared for agriculture by burning off the vegetation, but the abundance of weed seeds suggests that fields were in use for periods long enough for persistent weed communities to become established. Bandkeramik faunal assemblages are dominated by domestic cattle, which replaced sheep and goat as the principal domesticated animal as farming spread to central Europe. For the Merzbach Valley, Petar Stehli (1989) paints a picture of limited cultivation around the settlements, with relatively little clearance of the forested hinterland.

"Settlement Cells"

The substantial nature of the houses, the evidence for long-term continuity and replacement of houses in the same locations, the arguments for fixed-plot farming, and the low incidence of hunted animals imply that

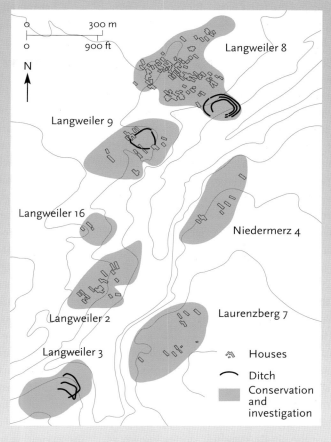

11.26 *Extensive excavations in the Merzbach Valley area of western Germany provide the clearest evidence of the landscape organization of Bandkeramik sites. Over a period of 400 years this "settlement cell" grew from a pioneer settlement at Langweiler to a pattern of hamlets and farmsteads covering the entire valley. At a late stage in this sequence, enclosures make their appearance, perhaps designed for communal gatherings or ritual activities.*

these were relatively stable communities, with a well-developed pattern for exploiting their local environment. The importance of cattle in the faunal record, however, has been used to argue alternative models of greater mobility, on the grounds that viable herds would require more extensive pastures and therefore demand higher levels of movement. The Merzbach Valley constitutes just a single Bandkeramik "settlement cell," which may well have depended on contact with similar clusters 20–50 km (12–30 miles) away for the exchange of breeding stock. There will also have been social exchanges, including, perhaps, marriage partners.

Ritual Activities

During the latest stages of the Merzbach Bandkeramik sequence, special enclosures were constructed that may have been the setting for social or ritual activities by whole communities. These were built in areas clear of houses, or on the edges of settlements, as if for special gatherings. The enclosure at Langweiler 9 is thought to have continued in use (for occasional feasts) after the adjacent settlement had been abandoned. Shortly afterwards, the Bandkeramik occupation of the Merzbach Valley came to an end.

ilar to that already described for other areas of Europe. An alternative view, however, holds that the inception of the Neolithic in Portugal owed little to incoming farmers but was the result of the adoption of pottery and domesticates by indigenous populations, even while Mesolithic communities in key areas such as the Tagus and Sado estuaries or southern Brittany continued to pursue their existing lifestyles for several centuries (Arias 1999).

Megalithic Monuments: The Neolithic Transition

Whatever the mechanism, the Neolithic transition in Portugal is dated to around 5500 BC, and pottery and domesticates were derived largely through contacts with the western Mediterranean. In northern and western France, the adoption and spread of Neolithic features drew on two separate sources: the early cardial pottery groups of the south, and the Bandkeramik farmers of the Rhineland and the Paris basin. By 4500 BC, farming had been adopted across the whole of the intervening region, and by 4000 BC it had spread to Britain and Ireland (Cooney 2000; Thomas 1999). The process was probably one of the adoption of pottery and domesticates by indigenous groups, but it may nonetheless have been marked by relatively sudden change in subsistence practices. In Britain, analysis of carbon and nitrogen isotopes in human bones has indicated that in coastal regions, marine foods such as fish and shellfish were largely abandoned at the end of the Mesolithic, and replaced by a concentration on terrestrial resources that would have included the new cultivated plants and domestic livestock (Schulting and Richards 2002). Lifestyles may still have been relatively mobile, however, with an emphasis, perhaps, on cattle herds as repositories of wealth and status.

The most visible impact of the Neolithic transition in Atlantic Europe is the construction of monuments, typically incorporating **megalithic** ("large stone") slabs together with mounds, cairns, or banks of earth or rubble. Many of these monuments take the form of stone settings, including circles and avenues in Britain and Brittany, or "cromlechs" (oval settings of standing stones) in Portugal. The most famous is the **Stonehenge** circle in southern Britain, oriented (at least in its final phase) on either midsummer sunrise or midwinter sunset [see box: Stonehenge and Megalithic Astronomy, pp. 416–17]. More numerous still are the single standing stones known as "menhirs," some of them carved with symbols of crooks, polished stone axes, and other motifs often difficult to identify.

Chambered tombs are the third major category of Neolithic monument: stone-built (or occasionally timber) chambers, usually, if not invariably, covered by a mound, and associated with the deposition of human remains. Many were places for collective burial, and may contain remains from hundreds of individuals. Associated mortuary practices frequently involved the removal, manipulation, and sorting of the skeletal elements. The tombs take a variety of forms: mounds or cairns may be circular or elongated, and may contain either a single chamber or a whole series; chambers were usually accessible by a door or portal, or by a more formal entrance passage in the classic "passage grave" form. Among the most elaborate passage graves are those of **Gavrinis** in Brittany and **Newgrange** [11.27] and **Knowth** in Ireland, where the megalithic orthostats (wall stones) are carved with spirals, circles, and lozenges in a style known as "megalithic art." Recent, highly controversial, interpretations have sought to relate these designs to images seen in drug-induced states, with the tunnel-like spirals indicating passageways through the stones (Dronfield 1995; 1996). A still larger repertory of motifs is found in the rock art of many regions of Atlantic Europe, some of which dates to this period.

While monuments of different types are fairly widespread in Atlantic Europe, a number of core areas developed, in which clusters of impressive monuments are found. One such is the **Carnac** area of southern Brittany, with remarkable stone rows incorporating ten or more parallel files extending for over a kilometer. Adjacent burial mounds of the late 5th millennium BC contain concentrations of polished stone axes, including sev-

11.27 Newgrange: the entrance to this passage grave in the Boyne Valley (Ireland) is blocked by an elaborately decorated curb stone, one of a series that fringe this impressive burial mound. The concentric patterns of running spirals and lozenge shapes are characteristic of "megalithic art," a body of non-representational motifs found especially in Ireland, northwest France, and Iberia, with examples also in adjacent regions. Visible in the background is the vertical tomb facade, built of quartz, granite and granodiorite blocks, which has been heavily reconstructed.

11.28, 11.29 *Jadeite axes: these examples (below) are from Cunzierton and Greenlawdean, Scotland, with (right) their distribution from a geological center of origin in the western Alps. The enormous distances traveled by these axes, together with their highly polished finish and sometimes exaggerated size, are evidence of the value and social prestige attached to them. In the Carnac region of southern Brittany axes of Alpine material were deposited in burial chambers beneath massive funerary mounds along with similar axes of other materials.*

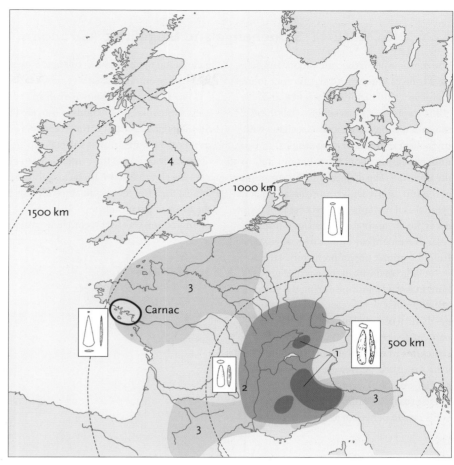

eral of jadeite [**11.28**], which had been obtained from sources in the Alpine foothills some 800 km (500 miles) distant (Cassen and Pétrequin 1999). Polished stone axes from known quarry sites were extensively traded among the Neolithic communities of Britain and France [**11.29**], and were prized as much for their origin and appearance as for their practical qualities. In flint-bearing areas, pits, shafts, and galleries were sunk, over 300 of them at **Grimes Graves** in eastern England. Here again, it was the appearance of the material that was at least as important as its technical properties, an observation confirmed by the wide-spread popularity and distribution of copper-colored Grand Pressigny flint from western France during the mid-3rd millennium BC, just as copper was being introduced and achieving wide circulation as a material of value.

Northern Europe

In northern Europe, as along parts of the Atlantic facade, the spread of farming came up against well-established and presumably relatively populous Mesolithic coastal communities. In the early postglacial period, the retreating ice sheets had reopened this area for human settlement, and hunter-gatherers had settled along lakes, marshes, and rivers in a broad band of territory from Karelia in the east to Britain in the west, at a time when the North Sea was yet to be formed. The wetland situation of these sites has led to remarkable circumstances of preservation in some cases, with wooden and other organic materials being preserved, for example at Star Carr in northern England [see box: Star Carr, pp. 396–97] or Stellmoor, near Hamburg (northern Germany).

The Ertebølle-Ellerbek and Later Cultures

By the middle of the 6th millennium BC, southern Scandinavia and the adjacent coasts of northern Germany were occupied by complex hunter-gatherers of the Late Mesolithic Ertebølle-Ellerbek. Their living sites include both large coastal settlements, perhaps permanently occupied, such as **Ertebølle** itself, and smaller, seasonally occupied camps. Coastal sites in northern Denmark are dominated by shell middens, though in eastern Denmark and Skåne there are large coastal sites without them. Special-purpose sites were devoted to the hunting of seals or swans. Ertebølle sites are characterized by pottery vessels of two distinct kinds: pointed-base pots of various sizes (with parallels across the north European plain eastwards and southwards to Siberia and Ukraine); and oval bowls or "lamps." The social complexity of Ertebølle communities is revealed by cemeteries

415

KEY DISCOVERY Stonehenge and Megalithic Astronomy

The movements of the sun, moon, and stars have been of interest and significance to most prehistoric and historical societies, and ethnographic accounts suggest that these movements may have been associated with mythological events or cosmological understandings about the origins or nature of the universe. The daily and annual movement of the sun, in particular, provides an obvious symbol and metaphor for processes of birth, decay, death, and rebirth, and an interest in solar movement can sometimes be postulated from the orientation of prehistoric structures.

A large majority of the passage graves built in western Europe during the 5th and 4th millennia BC face east, and the natural symbolism of the rising sun may have been particularly important and significant for structures in which the remains of the dead were deposited. At Newgrange in Ireland, a special "roofbox" was built above the entrance to the passage in order to allow the rising sun's rays to penetrate to the back of the

chamber at the midwinter solstice, even when the passage entrance itself was closed or sealed.

Probably the best known of all such megalithic solar orientations is provided by Stonehenge in south-central England. At dawn on the midsummer solstice, an observer standing at the center of Stonehenge sees the sun rise above (in fact, slightly to the left of) the Heel Stone and shine directly into the heart of the monument. This phenomenon was first recorded by antiquary

11.30 *The history of Stonehenge is complex and went through several phases before it reached the final form that we recognize today, as seen in this reconstruction, looking south.*

William Stukeley in the 1720s, and has in recent years drawn crowds to Stonehenge every year to experience and celebrate the event (Chippindale 2004).

The First and Second Phases

Excavations have shown that the history of Stonehenge is complex, however, and that the solar orientation probably only became significant in a relatively late stage of the monument's development (Ruggles 1999).

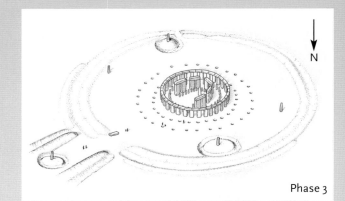

Phase 3

11.31, 11.32 *The astronomical alignment of Stonehenge has long been the subject of much controversy. In its initial form (right), the principal northeast entrance of Stonehenge was not aligned exactly on the midsummer sunrise and there was also a probable entrance to the south; arguments relating the northeastern entrance to the rising of the moon (far right) have not gained widespread acceptance.*

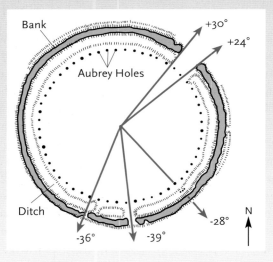

Bank
Aubrey Holes
Ditch
+30°
+24°
-28°
-36°
-39°
N

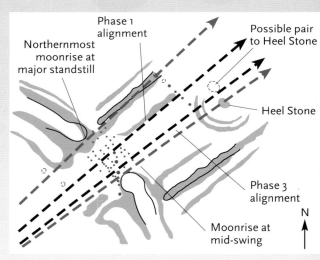

Phase 1 alignment
Northernmost moonrise at major standstill
Possible pair to Heel Stone
Heel Stone
Phase 3 alignment
Moonrise at mid-swing
N

---

such as those at **Skateholm** and **Vedbaek**, in which differential treatment of the dead, which may indicate social ranking, can be observed (Albrethsen and Brinch Petersen 1976; Larsson 1989; Tilley 1996).

Shortly before 4000 BC, the Ertebølle culture disappeared and was replaced by Early Neolithic groups forming a northern variant of the Trichterbecher culture (p. 408). The Late Mesolithic

communities had indeed been for several centuries living along-side farming neighbors to the south, and contact between the two is shown by occasional imports of polished stone axes by Ertebølle communities (Fisher 1982). There is strong evidence for continuity of population from Mesolithic to Neolithic in this region, but as in Britain, isotope studies indicate a significant change in diet even in coastal locations (although marine resources continued

Stonehenge began not as a circle of stones, but as a circular ditch with a low bank along its outer edge, measuring some 110 m (360 ft) in diameter. Within the ditch were 56 substantial timber posts set at approximately regular intervals in the so-called "Aubrey Holes," named after the 17th-century antiquary who first discovered them. Radiocarbon dates place the construction of this first, stoneless, Stonehenge at around 2950 BC (Cleal et al. 1995). There was a broad entrance gap to the northeast, and probably another to the south, but the northeastern entrance was too far to the north to frame the sunrise at any time of year. This orientation may instead be associated with the northernmost limit of the moonrise. The argument for this is based in part on the interpretation of the array of small postholes discovered in the 1920s in the entrance gap. These belong to the second stage of Stonehenge, at a time when timber settings were constructed also in the interior, though later disturbance has made it impossible to recover their complete plan. The postholes in the entrance line up in a series of rows that perhaps defined a number of restricted passageways into the interior of the monument; their relationship to the northernmost position of moonrise is imprecise and unclear.

The Third Phase

It is in the third phase, beginning around 2500 BC, that Stonehenge becomes a stone circle that inscribes a solar orientation on the midsummer sunrise and midwinter sunset. Some 82 "bluestones," followed by 84 much larger sarsen (gray) blocks were brought to the site and erected in a circle and horseshoe arrangement. At the same time, the entrance was realigned by the construction of the avenue against its outer face. The centerline of the new entrance was aligned exactly on the midsummer sunrise/midwinter sunset, and the stone uprights seem to have been arranged to give this axis still greater prominence. An unworked sarsen block, the Heel Stone, was erected within the terminals of the avenue, with another (now gone) immediately to its north. If these two stones stood together, they would frame the midsummer sunrise, and the rays would then pass through another gap between the now-recumbent Slaughter Stone and its lost neighbor E (marked only by its socket). The detailed chronology of these various elements is uncertain, however, and the precise effect must remain in doubt. Furthermore, whereas it is the midsummer sunrise that has caught the popular imagination, it may have been midwinter sunset (on the same axis but facing in the opposite direction) that was the focus of interest to the prehistoric builders of Stonehenge (Chippindale 2004, 236–37).

Despite this uncertainty, two observations remain clear: first, that the entrance of Stonehenge in its third phase was realigned on the midsummer/midwinter axis; and second, that the effect would only have been visible to a select few, given the restricted space at the center of the monument and the positioning of the stones that would have restricted the passage of the sun's rays. Thus the solar orientation of Stonehenge may have been associated with privileged access to sacred knowledge.

11.33 *At dawn on the midsummer solstice, the sun rises above the Heel Stone and shines directly along the main axis of Stonehenge, illuminating the central area. The same effect in reverse is produced at midwinter, when the setting sun in the southwest shines through the monument from the opposite direction. Recent studies suggest that it may have been the midwinter axis that was of primary significance to the builders.*

to play a role). Analysis of carbon isotopes in Mesolithic and coastal Neolithic skeletons from Denmark indicate a shift from high levels of marine diet in the Ertebølle skeletons – similar to that of modern Greenlanders – to a mixed terrestrial/marine diet in the Neolithic (Thorpe 1996; Richards et al. 2003).

That domestic plants and animals became a major element in subsistence is shown by pollen, by cereal grains and impressions, and by the faunal remains. The transition may not in all areas have been sudden or complete, and if we look beyond Scandinavia to Lithuania and the eastern Baltic, classic Neolithic markers such as pottery and ground-stone implements appear among communities still heavily dependent on hunting and fishing. Constraints on the development of early agriculture imposed by poor soils and harsh climate considerably delayed

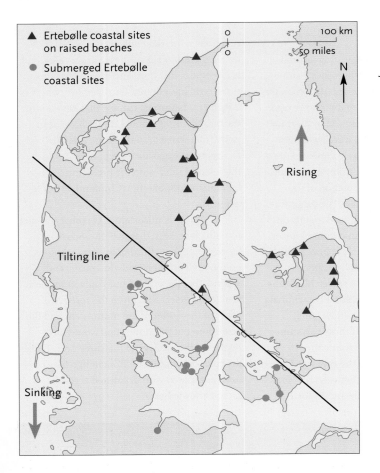

- ▲ Ertebølle coastal sites on raised beaches
- ● Submerged Ertebølle coastal sites

100 km
50 miles

N

Rising

Tilting line

Sinking

11.34 Changing shorelines: *much of the evidence concerning Mesolithic communities around the coasts of Europe has been submerged by sea-level rise. In northern Europe, however, the isostatic rebound of the land following the melting of the ice sheets raised Mesolithic shorelines and many Ertebølle coastal middens survive on raised beaches. The edge of the rebound is marked by a line through Jutland and the Danish islands.*

tradition. Such long mounds, however, vary significantly in their details, and in the kinds of burial feature with which they are associated. Some contain single burials in pits or cists; others cover multiple inhumations in timber mortuary houses that were burned or destroyed before the mound was built; still others cover megalithic chambers and passage graves.

Megalithic tombs were built in large numbers in southern Sweden, Jutland, and the Danish islands during the 4th millennium BC, and some of the greatest densities of tombs in the entire west European megalithic province are to be found in this region. Cemetery burial was also practiced, however, and may have been an Ertebølle legacy (Midgley 1992; Tilley 1996).

Another North European legacy of Mesolithic traditions was the deposition throughout the Neolithic period and beyond of pottery and other offerings in wetland or marshy locations, probably as offerings to gods or ancestors. These offerings include a number of human skeletons with marks or other signs of violence, such as the **Boldkilde** bodies (*c.* 3400 BC), the elder of the two with a rope round his neck (Bennike et al. 1986). These anticipate the well-preserved "bog bodies" of later prehistoric date (see below, p. 428).

Offerings were also made at dry-land locations such as megalithic tombs, and included highly decorated pottery vessels, which played an important part in ritual. Enclosures consisting of multiple circuits of ditches and banks with frequent interruptions or entrances were foci of ritual practice (Andersen 2002; Thorpe 2001). Within the ditches stood palisades, though these were intended more to define the internal space and to shield it from view than as any kind of defensive structure; some fence lines actually surround ditch segments. The deposition of special deposits such as burned pottery, stone axes, or animal bone was clearly one element of the purpose of such enclosures. Broadly similar enclosures are present in the British Neolithic, where they are known as **causewayed camps**, and analogous structures have been found in other parts of central and western Europe. The 30 enclosures known from southern Scandinavia [**11.35**] date to 3400–3150 BC and show characteristic evidence of frequent modification and recutting. It may be that the construction of these enclosures was itself the key aspect of ritual practice, though pottery, animal bones, and human remains from the interior indicate that feasting and mortuary rituals may also have been carried out there. One suggestion is that bodies of the dead may have been buried in the enclosure ditches and then exhumed after they had decom-

the adoption of farming in these areas, and demanded a different pattern of domestic plant and animal exploitation (Zvelebil and Dolukhanov 1991).

Neolithic Burial Practices

The Neolithic of south Scandinavia, however, benefited from the ameliorating effect of the Atlantic and North Sea maritime climate, and shared many features found in other areas of western Europe. Earthen long mounds covering timber mortuary houses, such as at **Barkaer** in Jutland, can be paralleled in Britain and northern France. The origin of such long mounds has been sought in the longhouses that were a characteristic feature of the Bandkeramik settlements of central Europe (see p. 407). Those communities buried their dead either in pits within the settlement area or in adjacent cemeteries, but did not raise mounds or other funerary monuments. It is around the northern and western margins of the Bandkeramik zone, by contrast, that long mounds make their appearance: in northern Germany, northern Poland, southern Scandinavia, northern France, and Britain. At **Balloy**, south of Paris, Bandkeramik longhouses are overlain by long mortuary enclosures that may have contained mounds. Thus the linear ideology of the longhouse appears to have been transformed and perpetuated during the 5th and early 4th millennia BC by the long mound

11.35 *Reconstruction of part of the Sarup enclosure:* within the palisade and short segments of perimeter ditch of this enclosure on the Danish island of Fyn were smaller fenced enclosures and almost 100 "offering pits" containing deposits of pottery, axes, and human and animal remains, many deliberately fragmented or burned. There were no traces of permanent buildings in the interior, suggesting that this was a ceremonial enclosure, perhaps used for feasting and mortuary rituals.

posed, the bones being placed in neighboring megalithic tombs. The fragmentation of bodies after death, and the circulation of bones as relics, appear to have been widespread practices in European prehistory.

Polished stone axes were a prominent feature of the north European Neolithic, and were once again connected with display and prestige, as well as with practical tasks. During the 3rd millennium BC, elaborate stone axes with shaft holes for hafting became common. Usually referred to as "battle axes," they are associated with a shift in burial practice to individual graves beneath circular mounds. This indicates a new concern with the expression of status, which was also associated with a new kind of drinking vessel, the **beaker** with cord-impressed decoration; the practice of individual burial with battle axe and corded ware beaker became widespread in northern Europe at this time, from the Moscow area to the northern Netherlands (Whittle 1996) [see **11.37**]. It anticipates the changes that were to take place in western Europe with the spread of bronze metallurgy a few centuries later.

Toward Complexity: Europe from 2500 BC to the Roman Empire

In the first part of this chapter we followed the spread of farming across Europe region by region, noting how colonization and indigenous adoption of the new domesticates were of varying importance in the different areas. Whatever the mechanism, farming did spread successfully across almost the whole continent within 2500 years. We have seen some of the social and demographic consequences of the change. Farming supports many more people per unit of land than does hunting and gathering, and with larger populations comes greater social

and material complexity. One result of these trends is the development of metallurgy, as a response to the increased social need for items of status and value. Demographic and social change did not stop at this point, however, but continued and sometimes accelerated in pace. The difficulty is to balance these long-term general trends against the extremely varied experience of the individual communities in different regions. Not everything happened everywhere in the same way or at the same speed.

By the middle of the 3rd millennium BC the continent of Europe, save for the Arctic fringes and the high mountains, was peopled by farming communities practicing plow agriculture and the raising of cattle, pig, sheep, and goat. In the southeast, many settlements had developed into mounds or tells that formed focal points in the landscape, and entire communities were represented in cemeteries of dozens or hundreds of graves. In the north and west, settlements were farmsteads or hamlets of a few timber or wattle-and-daub houses; the relative impermanence of these structures contrasted with a long tradition of burial mounds and other monuments. Over the following 2000 years, European societies underwent a series of changes, encompassing both technological and social developments.

The introduction of **bronzeworking** at the end of the 3rd millennium BC had little impact on everyday technology, but stimulated the development of new long-distance connections across Europe. Of the two constituent elements of bronze – copper and tin – the **copper** (which forms some 90 percent of the bronze alloy) came from a number of sources in mountainous regions, and copper mining on a relatively large scale is attested at 2nd-millennium BC mines such as those of the **Mitterberg** in the Austrian Alps, and at **Great Orme** in Wales (Harding 2000). Many smaller deposits were also worked at this period. Trace element and other compositional analyses have endeavored to determine the sources and distribution of copper from different areas, but with only limited success, owing to the practice of melting down damaged or obsolete copper objects and mixing the metal.

The second element of bronze, **tin** (10 percent of the alloy), is much less widely available, and the principal European sources exploited in prehistory were in northern Bohemia and the Atlantic zone: Brittany in France, Galicia in Spain, and Cornwall in Britain. The demand for tin from limited and distant sources set up a series of exchange networks across Europe, along which other prized materials, such as Baltic amber, also circulated. The result was a certain "international" character to the metalwork traditions of the European Bronze Age, where similar forms are found across wide areas.

In the early 1st millennium BC, Europe passed (in traditional terminology) from the Bronze Age to the **Iron Age**. The new metal had different and more abundant sources of supply, and although its impact may at first have been limited, its greater availability made it possible to use iron for a range of artifacts for which bronze had always been too costly. This included some 300 tons of iron nails used in the timber ramparts of **Manching** in Bavaria in the late 2nd century BC, and the development of iron or iron-tipped agricultural tools that made it possible to extend cultivation onto heavier soils (Manning 1995).

In the Mediterranean zone, the key development of the 1st millennium BC was the appearance of **city-states** – both the indigenous Etruscan cities of north-central Italy and the colonies founded by Greek and Phoenician (later Carthaginian) settlers along the Mediterranean shores of Spain, France, southern Italy and Sicily, and along the Black Sea coast (Chapter 13). These city-states brought with them a new scale of settlement architecture and social organization, and new commercial activity. Contact with the societies of temperate Europe and the steppes is shown by finds of Mediterranean products in those regions that may have been balanced by southward flows of raw materials to the Mediterranean and Black Sea cities. The peoples of the hinterland themselves emerge into history during the middle of the 1st millennium BC, notably the **Scythians** in the east and the **Celts** in the west, though the validity of the latter term has been challenged in recent research [see box: Who Were the Celts?, p. 430]. It was not Greeks, Etruscans, or Carthaginians who were ultimately to have the greatest impact on temperate Europe, however, but a central Italian city on the southern margins of the Etruscan

zone: Rome. Although in geographical extent the Roman empire even at its height encompassed less than half the land area of Europe, its influence extended much further than its immediate political control (Chapter 13).

Later Prehistoric Societies in Central and Western Europe

We begin, as so often in archaeology, with a new pottery type. Around the middle of the 3rd millennium BC a distinctive kind of pottery vessel, the bell beaker, came into widespread use in western Europe, from Spain to Scandinavia and inland as far as Bohemia. These vessels, which frequently accompanied their owners in death as grave offerings [**11.36**], represent the spread of a fashion or a drinking cult, and are associated with a range of other luxury items: copper daggers, gold ornaments, and fine stone perforated plaques interpreted as archers' wrist-guards. The origin of the beaker vessel itself may lie in western Iberia, but it was soon taken up and reproduced in numerous regional variants. Study of the contents, where these have been preserved, has suggested that the beakers may have held a honey-based (probably fermented) drink (Dickson 1978).

Beaker Pottery and Metalwork

Beaker pottery itself may not be very exciting, though individual vessels are well made and sometimes elegant. Its importance lies in its broader significance as an indicator of social and cultural changes taking place across wide areas of western Europe at this period. Of key significance is the evidence that these vessels provide for long-distance connections, especially along the

11.36 A Beaker assemblage: *a grave group from a burial found at Culduthel Mains, Inverness, Scotland, which contained a Beaker vessel, a scraper, eight arrowheads, an amber bead, a looped bone tube, and a wristguard.*

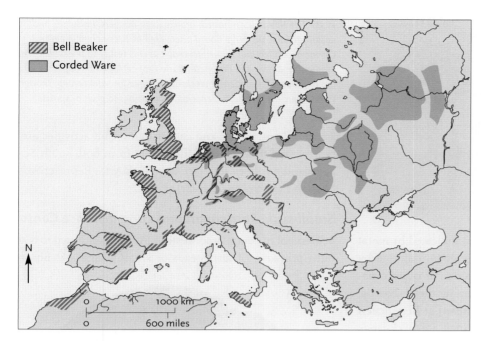

11.37 *(Left)* **Map showing the distribution of Corded Ware and Bell Beaker assemblages:** *these illustrate the growth of interregional contacts across northern and western Europe during the 3rd millennium BC. Both assemblages focus on a decorated drinking vessel, but include a characteristic range of other artifacts, found together especially in graves. Corded Ware vessels are frequently accompanied by polished stone battle axes, whereas Beakers are commonly associated with archery equipment and sometimes with copper daggers.*

11.38 *(Below)* **The "Amesbury archer":** *this burial excavated in 2002 is the most richly furnished Beaker grave yet to have been found in Britain. The grave pit (which may have been timber-lined, and covered by a small turf mound) contained the skeleton of a 35–45-year-old man.*

Atlantic seaways and the river routes such as the Rhine, leading into the European interior [**11.37**]. The new metallurgy of copper and bronze soon spread along the same routes. Metallurgy and beakers are directly associated at **Ross Island** in southwest Ireland, where from 2400 BC fire was used to extract copper ore from fissures in the limestone (O'Brien 2001). The earliest copper axes and daggers from southern Britain were made of Irish copper, while Beaker graves in the Rhineland contain metal from Alpine or central European sources.

The connection between Beaker pottery and metallurgy is also shown in grave finds. Beakers in graves are associated primarily with individual interments; where they occur in megalithic tombs, they were probably either offerings in their own right or accompanied the late introduction of an additional single body. The recently discovered "**Amesbury archer**" grave [**11.38**] in south-central England near Stonehenge (Fitzpatrick 2003) contained the skeleton of a man 35–45 years old, accompanied by archer's equipment (15 finely flaked barbed-and-tanged arrowheads of flint, and two polished stone wrist-guards), plus two decorated Beaker vessels, three copper knives, a pair of gold hair ornaments, and a black "cushion stone" for metalworking. Hence metallurgical knowledge and social status may have been directly connected. The Amesbury burial also demonstrated the interregional contacts characteristic of the Beaker phenomenon in another way, since oxygen isotope analysis of the man's teeth indicated that he had lived as a child in mainland Europe. Thus new skills and technologies may have been spread by the movement of individuals as much as by the transfer of knowledge. It also raises the question of how common long-distance travel may have been in prehistoric Europe; the notion that individuals lived and died within small-

scale local communities, never venturing a great distance outside their home territory, may be very far from the mark.

The single grave under a modest circular mound became a feature of northern and northwestern Europe during the early 2nd millennium BC. The Beaker vessel disappears from the

11.39 *The Bresinchen hoard: bronze axes, daggers, halberds, and neckrings from the large hoard discovered at Bresinchen in central Germany. Collections of artifacts such as this testify to the scale of metal production during the European Early Bronze Age. The objects may be the products of a particular workshop, buried for safekeeping, though some hoards were clearly deposited as offerings to gods or spirits.*

graves, but individual wealth and status are indicated by metal objects, now of bronze or gold. Male prestige is indicated by finely crafted bronze daggers, and by plaques or other ornaments of gold. Bronze objects also occur in metal hoards, especially in central Germany, where the hoard at **Bresinchen** contained 146 bronze axes, halberds, arm-rings, and neck-rings weighing 30 kg (66 lb) (Bradley 1990) [**11.39**]. A particularly flamboyant metalworking tradition developed in Denmark, rather unexpectedly given the lack of local copper ores. Danish Bronze Age societies did, however, have access to the highly prized Baltic amber that was used extensively in necklaces and ornaments and was traded as far afield as Italy and Mycenae in Greece. The bronze that was obtained in exchange was cast into axes and daggers and fashioned into special cult objects such as the "sun chariot" from **Trundholm** (*c.* 1650 BC) [**11.41**] and, some centuries later, the *lurs*, or horns, such as those found at **Brudevaelte**. A spectacular recent discovery from eastern Germany, the **Nebra sky-disk** [**11.40**], throws additional light on ritual practice during the Bronze Age, highlighting the special signif-

icance of sun, moon, and certain stars. Cult activities are also represented in rock art of the period from both south Scandinavia and northern Italy [see box: Rock Art – Representation of Myth or Reality?, pp. 426–27].

Small-scale Settlement and Long-distance Contact

Settlement in central and western Europe continued to take the form primarily of farmsteads or small villages. At **Elp** in the

11.40 *(Above)* **The Nebra sky-disk:** *this recent discovery from Germany provides evidence of the astronomical interest of central European societies during the 2nd millennium BC. The sun and moon, plus 32 stars and two (originally three) curving edge bands, are shown in thin pieces of gold sheet attached to the surface of the bronze. A cluster of seven stars in the center may represent the Pleiades.*

11.41 *(Left)* **The Trundholm sun chariot:** *this bronze wheeled-model of a horse pulling a large disk was discovered in a peat bog on the Danish island of Zealand in 1902. It has been dated to around 1650 BC and was probably buried as a ritual offering. One face of the disk is covered with gold leaf, representing the sun, while it has been suggested that the other face, left plain, represents the moon.*

11.42 Croce del Papa: *an eruption of Vesuvius in around 1550 BC buried and preserved this Early Bronze Age settlement, some 25 km (16 miles) from Naples in southern Italy. The inhabitants fled when the eruption began. An initial fall of pumice around the outside of the apsidal wood and wicker buildings was counterbalanced by the seepage of mud into their interiors, thus preserving them.*

Netherlands, a sequence of six large houses, four smaller houses, three barns, five sheds, and a number of other buildings was traced in the patterns of postholes (Waterbolk 1964). The building plans overlapped, and it is clear that a sequence of successive occupations is represented, usually with a major house, a minor house, and a set of ancillary buildings. These were originally thought to have followed each other closely in time, but new dating evidence suggests that the sequence spans no less than 800 years, suggesting that the farmstead may have been settled, abandoned, and resettled on the same spot several times (Bradley 2002).

In contrast to this is the snapshot of a small farming community provided by the site of **Croce del Papa** in southern Italy, overwhelmed and buried by a volcanic ash fall and mudslide around 1550 BC (Livadie 2002). The consolidated mud has preserved a cast of three houses up to a height of 5 m (16 ft); the light timber sides were continuous with a curving roof covered by thatch [**11.42**]. Within the huts were complete suites of pottery vessels and traces of wood and wickerwork containers. The inhabitants had fled as the ash began to fall, but they left behind footprints, goats, and a dog. The full extent of the settlement is unknown, but, as noted, most Bronze Age sites were small. A little larger are the lakeside settlements of the Alpine zone. **Cortaillod-Est** in Switzerland, for example, comprised some two dozen houses arranged in parallel rows within a palisade [**11.43**]. The houses were built and rebuilt in five successive phases over a 25-year period from around 1010 BC, then occupied with further minor repairs until 955 BC, before being abandoned after a life of only some 55 years (Arnold 1986). Thus even apparently substantial villages may have had only short lives.

During the 2nd and 1st millennia BC, agricultural settlements in western Europe became more fixed and substantial, a process that is also reflected in the development of field systems (Harding 2000). Celtic fields in southern Britain may date back to the middle of the 2nd millennium BC, and 1st-millennium BC complexes of small rectangular fields are known from Denmark and northern Germany, the Netherlands, Britain, and France.

11.43 Reconstruction of the Late Bronze Age settlement of Cortaillod-Est: *the rows of rectangular houses indicate a high degree of community planning and integration. Tree-ring study of preserved timber posts has allowed the history of the settlement to be traced in detail from its foundation in 1010–1001 BC, through its enlargement between 996 and 989 BC, to its eventual abandonment some 35 years later.*

"Princely Centers" By the end of the 8th century BC, most of Europe had adopted the working of iron, though bronze continued to play a major role for ornaments, alongside the rarer and more valuable gold. It is at this period (700–480 BC), labeled **Late Hallstatt** after the site in Austria where it was first defined,

11.44 *The Vix krater:* *this bronze krater or mixing bowl was probably manufactured at Tarentum, a Greek colony in southern Italy, in c. 530 BC. It was found in a richly furnished grave at Vix at the foot of Mont Lassois, one of the major princely centers of the Late Hallstatt period. Diplomatic gifts (such as this may have been) would have eased the flow of goods and raw materials to Mediterranean cities from areas north of the Alps.*

that the first indications of a political geography appear, with evidence for a series of "princely centers" across a broad band of central Europe from Burgundy to Bohemia. These were marked by hilltop enclosures such as the **Heuneburg** in Bavaria, with associated massive circular burial mounds at their feet containing richly furnished graves.

Contacts with the Mediterranean world are indicated by finds of Greek and Etruscan pottery and metal vessels, but whether these centers owed their origin to such contacts, or were the product of processes indigenous to central Europe, is open to debate (Collis 1984; Wells 1980). The Late Hallstatt grave at **Vix** in Burgundy, eastern France, yielded a massive bronze krater (mixing bowl with wide mouth and two handles) of Greek workmanship, dating to *c.* 530 BC, which is the largest metal vessel to have survived from the Classical world [**11.44**]. The Heuneburg hilltop enclosure [**11.45**] was embellished at around the same time (6th century BC) with a wall incorporating projecting rectangular towers, the whole in mud-brick on a stone base, a method of building more appropriate to the drier Mediterranean climate than to Europe north of the Alps. The graves also contain many indigenous objects and furnishings of gold, bronze, and other materials decorated in the so-called Hallstatt style.

A break in developments occurred early in the 5th century BC, when the Hallstatt princely centers were abandoned, and new sets of richly furnished graves occur further north in the Marne and Moselle regions (Collis 1984). These are associated with a new decorative style, named after the site of **La Tène**

beside Lake Neuchâtel in Switzerland. Elements of this art style came to be adopted and imitated across western and central Europe in the centuries that followed, and it has become closely associated with the identity of the peoples referred to by Classical authors as the "Celts" [see box: Who Were the Celts?, p. 430].

Later Prehistoric Societies in Eastern Europe

We have seen how in western Europe, the wide distribution of Beaker vessels hints at a "new internationalism" around the middle of the 3rd millennium BC. In eastern Europe, similar long-distance fashions and contacts are shown most strikingly by the distribution of bronzes. The extensive metal deposits of the Carpathian Mountains gave rise to a flourishing Bronze Age characterized by elaborately cast and decorated swords, axes, and metal vessels. These suggest that individuals were now able to set themselves apart by the possession and display of fancy metalwork, a trend that may ultimately have resulted in the rise of a warrior elite. The fact that many settlements became fortified is perhaps further evidence of the impact that the accumulation of portable wealth had on the societies of the time. Some of this wealth found its way into hoards of metal objects such as those from **Hajdusamson** in Hungary and **Apa** in Romania. These societies had connections eastwards onto the Russian steppes and northwards into Poland and Denmark; Hungarian imports may have stimulated the development of the south Scandinavian bronzeworking tradition described in the previous section. **Horse-drawn chariots** appear in eastern Europe at this period, and horses, first domesticated on the steppes during the 4th or

11.45 *Aerial view of the Heuneburg:* *a Late Hallstatt princely center in southern Germany; buildings excavated in one corner of the 3.2-ha (8-acre) enclosed area included workshops for bronze and other materials.*

3rd millennium BC but not yet used for riding, were another mark and repository of wealth and status (Harding 2000).

Urnfields

The trend toward the fortification of settlements continued in eastern Europe into the later part of the Bronze Age, after 1300 BC. There were also important changes in burial ritual, beginning in the east and then spreading through central and western Europe. Cremation became the norm, with the ashes of the deceased collected and buried in pottery urns. These burials usually have few grave goods, though they are sometimes accompanied by metalwork or sets of tableware. A key feature is the size of the so-called "Urnfields," or cemeteries, in which the cremation burials were often grouped: they may number several thousand, suggesting that for the first time the bulk of the population is finding representation in the archaeological record. Furthermore, most of these individuals received very similar treatment, with little indication of status differences. Wholly exceptional are the large mounded burials such as **Ockov** in Slovakia or **Seddin** in Germany, the latter with a stone vaulted tomb chamber and a rich display of pottery and metal objects (Kristiansen 1998). Most Urnfield burials are distinctly unpretentious, and this has led some to interpret the Urnfields as evidence for the spread of a common religious belief. The prominence of birds in the iconography of the period and in curious contexts (they are shown pulling boats or wagons, for example) may also be evidence of a specific belief system. Cremation becomes more common even in areas beyond the zone of classic Urnfields, and continues into the 1st millennium BC and the period conventionally described as the Early Iron Age.

Urnfield-period bronzeworkers were adept at the working of sheet metal; helmets and breastplates with elaborate chased and incised ornamentation were produced for the elite. These were probably for display rather than combat, as the thinness of the bronze sheet provided little real protection. The development of longer bronze slashing swords, with the weight concentrated toward the end of the blade, is more convincing evidence of actual conflict. In many areas this may also be evident in the systematic fortification of settlements by the building of ditches and ramparts or substantial timber stockades.

The Fortified Site of Biskupin

The Lausitz sites of northern Poland provide impressive examples of fortified settlements, above all the waterlogged and preserved timber township of Biskupin (Rajewski 1980;

Niewierowski et al. 1992) [**11.46**]. This was a 1.5-ha (3.7-acre) settlement on a low marshy island, rising only 1 m (3.3 ft) above the peat to the south and the waters of a lake on the other sides, an ideal location for security. The settlement was surrounded by a timber stockade 463 m (1519 ft) long and originally some 6m (20 ft) high. The rampart was built in box-type fashion, in two stages. The first stage, at ground level, consisted of oak log compartments 3–3.5 m (9.8–11.5 ft) square. Above these was a system of smaller boxes, each around 1 m (3.3 ft) square. Thus from front to back the rampart consisted of three lines of meter-square boxes, interlocked at the corners in log-cabin manner, plastered with clay to protect them from fire, then filled with sand and earth to create a solid structure. Along the top was a walkway for the defenders, protected by a timber screen or stockade along its outer edge, while a timber tower may have stood over the single gateway with double-leaf door.

Around the edge of the island a breakwater of 35,000 oak and pine stakes was placed, designed to prevent the lake waters from undermining the edge of the settlement. Within the stockade, the timber houses were tightly packed, laid out in terraced manner along parallel streets of split oak and pine logs originally surfaced with earth and sand. The regularity and order of the Biskupin settlement strongly suggests the operation of a

11.46 Biskupin: *dating to the late 8th century BC, the site owes its preservation to its waterlogged setting on a low promontory (originally an island) projecting into a lake. The main gateway and defensive tower have been reconstructed on the basis of discoveries made during excavations.*

powerful central authority. The scale of the project may be judged from the estimated 80,000 trees that were felled to construct it which could be tree-ring dated [see box: Tree-Ring Dating, Chapter 18, p. 696]. Most were cut in the winter of 738/737 BC, but felling continued down to 722 BC (Wasny 1993).

The degree of communal organization required by projects such as Biskupin or other hill- and marsh-forts of the early 1st millennium BC suggests that temperate European societies were becoming more centralized, though still relatively small in scale when compared with the developing polities of the Mediterranean zone. Toward the end the 1st millennium BC, however, complex societies developed in several parts of temperate Europe. Their emergence was a consequence both of indigenous change and of the growing impact of the expanding Mediterranean world.

European Society at the Dawn of History

In southern Europe, the archaeology of the 1st millennium BC is dominated by the development and expansion of city-based societies: Greeks and Etruscans in the Aegean and central Italy; Greek and Phoenician colonies in southern Italy and Sicily and around the shores of the western Mediterranean and the Black Sea (Chapter 13). Phoenician expansion may have been underway as early as the 9th century BC, with the major Phoenician foundation of **Carthage** in Tunisia traditionally placed toward the end of that century. Eighth-century BC Phoenician pottery has been found at sites along the Atlantic coast of Portugal, suggesting that Phoenician sailors were already exploring territories beyond the Strait of Gibraltar. Metals were one of the main objectives: in southern Spain, the silver of **Tartessos**

KEY CONTROVERSY Rock Art — Representation of Myth or Reality?

Representations carved onto rocks of northern Italy and southern Scandinavia provide images of the Bronze Age that some take as evidence of everyday life. The Alpine examples (notably those of the Valcamonica) include possible houses and field systems, but other scenes show combat, and those of south Scandinavia portray stylized ships and soles of feet ("footsoles"), which may be more symbolic than real.

Valcamonica Rock Art
The Valcamonica rock art, in a small valley between Lake Como and Lake Garda in northern Italy, occurs both on smoothed rock surfaces and detached boulders, many of which bear a confused mass of superimposed images. Overlapping between the different images sometimes allows a relative chronology to be established. On boulder 1 at Masso di Cemmo, for example, it is possible to divide the motifs into four distinct groups or phases (Anati 1972).

First, toward the top left of the stone, came a group of deer with curving antlers. Only one of these survives, but traces of the curved antlers of the others were left when the deer were recarved with straight antlers in the second phase. At the same time, a group of hornless quadrupeds (possibly elk) was added in the center and toward the right side

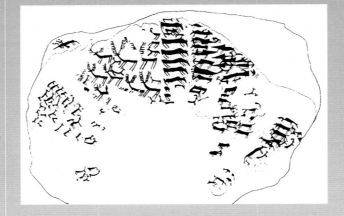

11.47 *Boulder 1 at Masso di Cemmo in the Valcamonica valley of northern Italy. Analysis of the individual motifs and the overlaps between them has enabled the sequence of carvings to be divided into four stages, beginning with the deer (top left), followed by the elk (right) and ending with the triangular daggers (top right) some of which have been intentionally carved over the elk.*

of the stone. In the third phase, a scatter of mountain goats, some with conspicuous curved horns, was carved across the whole of the surface. On the left-hand side the artists seem intentionally to have avoided the herd of deer, which must still have been evident, but elsewhere they carved between and across the earlier figures. The same is true of the fourth and final phase, in which a group of triangular-bladed daggers with narrow hilts overlay and obliterated parts of the earlier carvings. Quantities of coloring materials were discovered in excavations between and around the decorated boulders at Massi di Cemmo, and it is probable that the motifs were originally colored, which would have made them easier to distinguish.

Interpreting the Art
Emmanuel Anati (1984), who has spent a lifetime studying the Valcamonica art, has pointed to many features that suggest that the Valcamonica engravings had a religious or ritual significance. (For similar interpretations of rock art elsewhere in the world, see Symbolism in Southern African Rock Art box, Chapter 10, pp. 358–59.) A large number of carvings seem to show images from daily life, such as plowing, animals, warriors, or the famous "maps," but even these may have had ritual meaning. There are also numerous abstract symbols, and disembodied features such as carved footsoles. Anati interprets the latter as marks of worship or reverence, but this is highly

(Huelva), and further afield the tin resources of Galicia, Brittany, and southwest Britain (Cunliffe 2001). Greek colonies followed a little later, with the key cities of **Syracuse** in eastern Sicily founded in the late 8th century BC and **Massilia** (Marseille) in southern France *c.* 600 BC. Further east, the Greeks also founded a series of major colonies around the Black Sea coast, including **Olbia** at the mouth of the River Bug and **Panticapaeum** in the Crimea in the 6th century BC (Boardman 1999).

These were not all large urban centers, but they carried new concepts and techniques, and inevitably had an impact on the indigenous peoples living near them. Greek and Etruscan products came to be highly prized by some of these indigenous societies. The most striking examples are the Vix krater, already mentioned, made *c.* 530 BC in one of the Greek colonies of southern Italy and buried in a princely grave in eastern France, where it had perhaps been presented as a diplomatic gift, and the numerous finds of Greek painted pottery and jewelry in the richly furnished Scythian graves of the Ukrainian steppes. These goods include portable items in gold and other valuable materials that were probably manufactured by Greek craftspeople in the Black Sea colonies, but following Scythian models (Reeder 1999). The Scythian elite also adopted wine drinking from their Greek neighbors, and buried elaborate sets of gold and silver drinking vessels in their tombs.

European Societies Beyond the Mediterranean

It would be entirely wrong, however, to regard interactions between the Mediterranean colonies and the peoples of the continental hinterland in terms of the passive acceptance by the latter of the cultural and technological products of the former.

---

subjective. He is much more convincing when it comes to the scenes portraying sun disks accompanied by small human figures. A good example is rock 59 at Coren del Valento, where a rayed sun disk is surrounded by human figures with upraised arms. Anati interprets this scene, and others like it, as evidence of a prehistoric sun cult in the Valcamonica.

Elsewhere he sees representations of deities or idols, especially on the standing stones or "statue-menhirs" that were set up during the Chalcolithic period. A later scene at Zurla shows a large figure with stag antlers and upraised arms, and alongside it a similar, smaller figure, without antlers. The smaller figure may be a worshiper, and the larger one has been interpreted as the Celtic god Cernunnos. Austrian archaeologist Ludwig Pauli (1984) sees this scene as evidence that Celtic religious ideas from the Po plain gradually infiltrated the Valcamonica during the 1st millennium BC.

Rock Art of Southern Scandinavia
The rock art of southern Scandinavia has a different repertoire of motifs, yet is probably also ritual or mythological in nature. Among the carvings are many ship images, portrayed with numerous rowers (though at this period without oars). Some of the most famous of the carvings are scenes showing combat between shipboard warriors armed with axes or swords. These may be representations of actual warfare, though once again their real reference remains ambiguous. In Bohuslän, there is a dense distribution of Bronze Age burial cairns on the coast, with the largest cairns built on small islands off the coast.

Richard Bradley (2000) notes that ship carvings may be representations of the sea itself, and that they occur around inland hills capped by cairns: perhaps their role was to convert these hills to islands like those just off the coast, which were real islands girt by the sea. This is to be understood in an environment where postglacial sea level was falling owing to isostatic uplift, and former islands were indeed becoming hills. Furthermore, the footsoles depicted on these rock art panels are invariably moving vertically downslope, coming from the barrow cemeteries and cutting across the horizontally oriented ship carvings; perhaps these are the feet of the dead walking from the barrows down to the sea itself.

11.48 *Ships feature prominently in Scandinavian Bronze Age rock art, reflecting both their importance in daily life, for fishing and travel, along with their probable ritual or religious significance. This scene from Fossum in northern Bohuslän (Sweden) depicts armed men wielding axes on board a ship.*

The **Scythians** were a complex society who divided their territory into administrative districts under the overall control of a Scythian king. Nomadic in origin, they placed great value on horses, and buried large numbers of the animals (along with strangled retainers) in elite graves under large mounds known as "**kurgans.**" Livestock was the mainstay of the economy in the southern steppes, but to the north, in the forest-steppe zone, cultivation was practiced, and fortified settlements are known. The most impressive, at Bel'sk near Kharkov, was surrounded by ramparts 33 km (20 miles) in length (Rolle 1989). While there is evidence of cereal storage and permanent residence in the interior, how far these sites are to be regarded as proto-urban remains open to question.

Similar large settlements are found in western and south-central Europe during the last centuries BC, though here again the character of the occupation is sometimes difficult to assess. They include a class of sites labeled "**oppida,**" with timber-framed defensive circuits, such as **Manching** in Bavaria and **Mont Beuvray** in eastern France, enclosing 380 and 135 ha (938 and 334 acres) respectively. Within the defenses were houses and workshops, and although the density of settlement is unclear, and the range of functions may have varied from site to site, they have been described as the first arguably urban communities of non-Mediterranean Europe (Wells 1995).

By the late 2nd century BC, states may have begun to emerge in some parts of temperate Europe. In Austria, the kingdom of **Noricum** is referred to by Classical writers; it had a colony of Italian traders at its capital, the Magdalensberg (Alföldy 1974). In central and eastern France a number of peoples, including the Bituriges, Aedui, Sequani, and Arverni, have also been credited with the development of states at this period [**11.49**]. They

minted coins carrying the name both of their people and of individual rulers and elites (Cunliffe 1988). It is unclear whether these developments were an entirely indigenous process. These proto-states were distributed around the edges of the expanding Mediterranean urban zone, and extensive contact is shown by the spread of Mediterranean imports, including wine amphorae. Wine drinking became an important elite activity in these societies, though the contexts of feasting and consumption remained emphatically non-Roman. Coinage, too, was an idea taken from the Mediterranean world (modeled initially on the coinage of Philip of Macedon, father of Alexander the Great; see fig. **1.13**), but transformed by its temperate European imitators and certainly not the basis for a marketplace mode of purchase and exchange.

The So-called "Celtic" Societies

The societies of 1st-millennium BC western and central Europe are traditionally labeled "Celtic," from references by Classical writers. The term has been extended to encompass not only ethnic identity, but also languages and art, and its accuracy and utility have recently been challenged [see box: Who Were the Celts?, p. 430]. Greek and Roman writers do, nonetheless, constitute one of the key sources for our understanding of non-literate societies of the later 1st millennium BC, both in eastern and western Europe. The Greek historian Herodotus, for example, provides much information about the Scythians, and although these accounts must be regarded with caution as descriptions and interpretations of outsiders (and not always first-hand), they can, in many cases, be compared with and verified by study of the archaeological evidence. Thus the custom of decapitating enemies and displaying their skulls as trophies, which Greek writers attributed to the native peoples of southern France, is borne out at the site of **Entremont** in Provence by both stone sculptures of severed heads [**11.50**] and several skulls with nail holes for attachment to posts or buildings (Benoît 1975).

Bog Bodies The so-called "bog bodies" of northern Europe have also been compared with practices described by the Roman historian Tacitus (*Germania*, 12): "Traitors and deserters are hanged on trees; cowards, shirkers, and those guilty of unnatural vice are pressed down under a wicker hurdle into the bog."

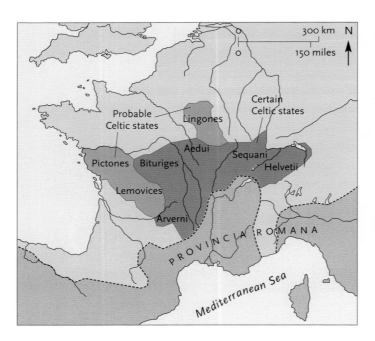

11.49 *State formation:* *beyond the edges of the Roman province established in southern France in 121 BC evidence suggests that a process of state formation may have been under way that was brutally interrupted by the conquests of Julius Caesar in 58–51 BC. Peoples such as the Bituriges, Arverni, Aedui, and Sequani had coinages, kings or magistrates, and fortified central places or oppida. Others, including the Pictones, Lingones and Lemovices, may have been developing similar patterns of government.*

11.50 *Carved limestone heads from Entremont in southern France:* *the eyes are closed in death and these are probably depictions of severed "trophy" heads, originally propped between the knees of a kneeling warrior statue. Nearby were found 20 humans skulls, three of them with nail holes for attachment to a pillar or building. Greek writers tell us that warriors of this region used to cut off the heads of enemies killed in battle and display them at the entrances to their houses.*

Roman provinces and the territories beyond, in the form of trade, cultural and technological borrowing, diplomatic exchange, and military action, until the Roman/non-Roman division dissolved in the late 4th and 5th centuries AD.

Summary and Conclusions

This chapter has described the development of societies in Europe from the end of the last Ice Age to the expansion of the Roman empire. A number of key themes have been identified. The first concerns the transformation of the European environment during the earlier postglacial period. This process had begun several millennia earlier as the ice sheets began to retreat, but reached its peak around 10,000 years ago, as sea levels rose steeply and human communities responded both to the new opportunities offered by the warmer climate and to the challenge presented by rapid environmental change. The successful outcome of these strategies is shown by the evidence of increasingly complex social organization in Late Mesolithic cemeteries in eastern, northern, and Atlantic Europe.

A second theme of this chapter has been the spread of farming, beginning earliest in the southeast and progressively supplanting hunting and gathering across the continent over a period of more than 2000 years. The origins of the domesticated

Studies of preserved bog bodies have shown that these are indeed not accidental deaths or casual murders, but the consequence of some structured and intentional act. **Lindow Man** from northwest England (1st century BC/AD) was knocked unconscious by two blows to the head, and then killed by having his throat slit and his neck broken by a garrote. **Grauballe Man** (1st century AD), along with other Danish bog bodies, had apparently had his throat cut, but also had a forehead wound and a broken leg, which were not accidental. The **Yde Girl** from the Netherlands (1st century BC/AD) was stabbed and strangled [**11.51**]. It is indeed remarkable how many of these bodies had been killed in a number of different ways (van der Sanden 1996). They may have been executions, but they could also have been sacrifices: the north European tradition of ritual offerings in lakes and bogs goes back to the Mesolithic period.

The Expansion of Roman Control From the 3rd century BC, the Mediterranean urban societies began to expand their territories beyond the coastal fringe and absorb large areas of the European hinterland. In Iberia, the Carthaginian settlements established in the southern half of the peninsula in the later 3rd century BC fell under Roman control by the end of that century, and 100 years later the Romans also controlled southern France. The conquests of Julius Caesar in the mid-1st century BC brought the Roman frontier up to the English Channel in the north and the River Rhine in the east. The invasion and conquest of Britain by the emperor Claudius in AD 43 marked the limit of Roman expansion in the northwest, and despite several attempts the Roman armies did not succeed in establishing effective control to the north or east of the Rhine. In eastern Europe, the River Danube formed the frontier of the empire. Over the centuries that followed, extensive interaction took place between the

11.51 *The Yde Girl: a naturally preserved "bog body" found in the Netherlands, the Yde Girl had been stabbed in the shoulder and strangled with a woollen band wound three times round her neck with a sliding knot that had been tightened beneath her left ear.*

KEY CONTROVERSY Who Were the Celts?

The word "Celts" derives from "Keltoi," the term used by ancient Greek writers to describe certain peoples of western and central Europe north of the Alps (Rankin 1987). Celtic peoples were also located in Iberia, where the Romans later encountered the so-called Celtiberians.

Herodotus, writing in Greece in the 5th century BC, placed the source of the River Danube in the territory of the Celts: "For the Danube, rising among the Celts, and the city of Pyrene, divides Europe in its course: but the Celts are beyond the Pillars of Hercules [Strait of Gibraltar], and border on the territories of the Cynesii, who lie at the western extremity of Europe." This may simply be a confused attempt to place the Celts in modern France; from the 6th century BC, Greeks would have come into close contact with the indigenous peoples in the area north of the Greek colony of Massilia (modern Marseille).

The Greek writer Poseidonius (2nd/1st century BC) traveled among these peoples, and described their social organization and customs such as the drinking of wine at feasts and the cult of trophy skulls. The Romans later referred to the Celtic peoples of France as "Galli," or Gauls. In the 4th and 3rd centuries BC, they and other peoples of northern Europe mounted a series of incursions into the Mediterranean, one group sacking Rome in 390 BC, another the Greek sanctuary of Delphi in 279 BC, whence a group of them, known as "Galatoi," crossed into Asia Minor (modern Turkey).

Identity of the Celts

Yet the identity of the Celts remains obscure and controversial (Megaw and Megaw 1996; Collis 2003). In the first place, the name is one assigned by Classical writers to certain of their "barbarian" neighbors. We know from other texts that these peoples themselves went by other ethnic names, such as Senones, Boii, and Scordisci. In later centuries the story becomes confused, however, and when the Romans invaded Gaul in the 1st century BC they made a clear distinction between the peoples of the new province of Gallia, whom they identified as Gauls or Celts, and those living east of the Rhine, whom they called Germans. In strictly ethnic terms, indeed, there may never have been a Celtic people as such: there is no evidence that they ever collectively called themselves "Celts."

La Tène Art and the Celts

"Celtic" is nonetheless still used by many archaeologists as shorthand for the peoples who occupied most of Europe north of the Alps in the 1st millennium BC. It is applied also to an art style (otherwise and more accurately known as La Tène) and by linguists to a group of interrelated languages. Yet there is nothing to connect the La Tène art style exclusively with a people or peoples known as the Celts. Paradoxically, the origins of La Tène art appear to lie in the Rhineland, an area that by Caesar's time was described not as an ethnic heartland, but as the boundary between the Celts to the west and the Germans to the east, though population movements between the 5th and 1st centuries BC may account for the apparent contradiction. La Tène art later spread to Iberia in the west, Bohemia in the east, and Britain and Ireland in the north, and while in some cases this extension is accompanied by other archaeological evidence indicating the movement of peoples (corresponding to the historically attested "Celtic" migrations), there is no reason to doubt that in other instances it was adopted by native elites as a fashion statement.

Britain and Ireland

The identity of the Celts becomes particularly problematic in Britain and Ireland. La Tène art is found throughout the two islands, but older models of Celtic invasion or immigration from the continent in either the 4th or the late 2nd century BC (or both) are now generally regarded with caution. Only in the early modern period did writers begin to describe the inhabitants of Ireland and parts of Britain as Celtic. The concept arose through the study of the Irish, Manx, Scots

11.52 *Detail of a La Tène sword scabbard from Lake Neuchâtel, with decoration of stags and foliage. La Tène art has sometimes been linked with the peoples known as "Celts" to Greek and Roman writers, but it is clear that this art style became widely fashionable in western Europe from the mid-5th century BC and is not the exclusive mark of one specific ethnic or linguistic group.*

Gaelic, Welsh, Cornish, and Breton languages around 1700. These were recognized to be interrelated, and the term "Celtic" was chosen to describe them. "Celtic" languages were also spoken by the pre-Roman inhabitants of Gaul, and in some regions of Spain. As one recent study has concluded, however, "the evidence seems quite clear that no one in Britain and Ireland called themselves a 'Celt' or 'Celtic' before 1700" (James 1999, 17). Thus the late prehistoric peoples of western and northern Europe shared many cultural and linguistic traits, but these are more reliably interpreted as the consequence of common origins or long-term interconnections, than as the result of a single "Celtic" people and its migrations.

plants and animals that were adopted lay in Southwest Asia, and farming strategies and some of the material accompaniments (such as tell settlements and painted pottery) have led to the proposal that colonist farmers from Anatolia introduced the new economy into southeast Europe. Such claims are difficult to evaluate, and although population movement appears to have played a significant role in southeast Europe and the Mediterranean, elsewhere – especially in northern and western Europe – the adoption of pottery and domesticates by indigenous Mesolithic communities is a more plausible scenario.

The key theme of the later prehistoric period is the development of social complexity. The adoption of copper and gold may not be significant in itself, but more a marker of other changes, notably the increasing differentiation of individuals and elites. The growing circulation of materials during the 2nd millennium BC created and reinforced connections between different regions, which are also reflected in the wide distribution of certain artifact types and in the spread toward the end of that millennium of Urnfield burial, indicating a new attitude to death and the individual in those regions where it is found.

Interregional connections continued to play a significant role in the 1st millennium BC, when urban societies developed in the Mediterranean zone. Connections along the Mediterranean and Black Sea coasts tied together the colonies founded by Greek and Phoenician communities, and it is tempting to view developments in temperate Europe, such as the rise of the Hallstatt princely centers, in the light of the demand for raw materials generated by these urban centers. Indigenous change, however, is as likely to have been a consequence of internal development as of contact with the Mediterranean.

During the 6th and 5th centuries BC, contacts between the urbanized Mediterranean and Europe north of the Alps appear to have been relatively peaceful. European raw materials were traded southwards, perhaps, in return for Mediterranean manufactures. Contact soon turned to conflict, however, and the Celtic and Germanic raids into Mediterranean territory during the 4th–2nd centuries BC reveal the capacity of temperate European warrior societies for concerted and effective action. The two sides in this exchange were ill-matched, however, and ultimately it was the Mediterranean, in the form of an expanding Roman empire, which triumphed, conquering western and parts of central Europe, though the north and east always lay beyond its control.

In the next chapter we travel east once again, to chart the development of complex societies in Southwest Asia. There, too, as in Europe, diversity in landscape led to a varying pace and direction of social and demographic change in different parts of the region, with farmers, pastoralists, and early states coexisting in sometimes uneasy proximity. The peoples of the hills and the peoples of the plains came into conflict on more than one occasion. Once again, the key changes in Southwest Asia were set in motion by the adoption of agriculture and the consequent rise of village farming; these were described in Chapter 6. The following chapter takes up the story from the time when farming settlement spread onto the Mesopotamian plain, and goes on to discuss the crucial process of urbanization; for it was in Mesopotamia that the world's earliest urban communities and the earliest writing systems came into being some five-and-a-half thousand years ago.

Further Reading

Bradley, R. 1998. *The Significance of Monuments.* London: Routledge. Good discussion of issues surrounding the construction of megalithic and other monuments in western Europe, and their relationship to the Mesolithic/Neolithic transition.

Collis, J. 1984. *The European Iron Age.* London: Routledge. Introductory survey, including both temperate European Hallstatt and La Tène cultures, and contemporary developments in the Mediterranean world.

Cunliffe, B. (ed.). 1994. *The Oxford Illustrated Prehistory of Europe.* Oxford: Oxford University Press. Authoritative and well-illustrated coverage of the whole of European prehistory, if slightly uneven.

Cunliffe, B. 2001. *Facing the Ocean: The Atlantic and its Peoples.* Oxford: Oxford University Press. Beautifully illustrated extended essay on the prehistory and early history of Atlantic Europe, from the end of the last Ice Age to the European discovery of the Americas; especially strong on maritime connections and the role of the sea as a unifying force.

Harding, A. F. 2000. *European Societies in the Bronze Age.* Cambridge: Cambridge University Press. Detailed account of the European Bronze Age (excluding the Aegean) organized on a thematic basis; rich source of information on settlement, economy, and society.

Hodder, I. 1990. *The Domestication of Europe.* Oxford: Blackwell. Reinterpretation of the European Neolithic as a process of ideological change, with domestication increasingly dividing farmers and their fields from hunting and the wild.

Kristiansen, K. 1998. *Europe before History.* Cambridge: Cambridge University Press. Lengthy account of the development of European societies 1100–150 BC, emphasizing central and northern Europe.

Price, T. D. (ed.). 2000. *Europe s First Farmers.* Cambridge: Cambridge University Press. Collection of essays on the transition to farming, focusing on issues of colonization vs. indigenous change.

Sherratt, A. 1997. *Economy and Society in Prehistoric Europe: Changing Perspectives.* Edinburgh: Edinburgh University Press. Studies of European prehistory written over a period of 20 years, including early farmers in southeast Europe, the "secondary products revolution," and megalithic monuments in the west.

Whittle, A. 1996. *Europe in the Neolithic: The Creation of New Worlds.* Cambridge: Cambridge University Press. Detailed account of the European Neolithic, emphasizing processes of indigenous and ideological change.

CHAPTER 12
THE RISE OF CIVILIZATION IN SOUTHWEST ASIA

Roger Matthews, University College London

Farmers of the Early Chalcolithic: The Halaf and Ubaid Periods, *c.* 6000–4200 BC 433
> *The Halaf Period,* c. 6000–5400 BC 433
>> • *Hunting and Warfare* 436
>> • *Religion and Society* 436
> *The Ubaid Period,* c. 5900–4200 BC 436
>> • *Eridu* 436
>> • *Ubaid Sites Beyond Lower Mesopotamia* 437

Urban Communities of the Late Chalcolithic: The Uruk Period, *c.* 4200–3000 BC 438
> *The Lower Mesopotamian Site of Uruk* 438
> *The Invention of Writing* 440
>> • *Cylinder Seals* 441
> *Uruk Expansion and Trade* 442

City-States, Kingdoms, and Empires of the Early Bronze Age, *c.* 3000–2000 BC 442
> *Sumerian City-States* 443
> *Upper Mesopotamian, Iranian, and Anatolian Cultures* 445
> *Kingdoms and Empires of the Later 3rd Millennium* BC 445
>> ● KEY SITE Tepe Yahya 446
>> ● KEY CONTROVERSY The End of the Early Bronze Age 448

Commerce and Conflict in the Middle Bronze Age 448
> *Lower Mesopotamia and the Persian Gulf* 449
> *Upper Mesopotamia and the Levant* 450
>> ● KEY SITE Troy 450
>> ● KEY SITE Ebla 452
> *Upper Mesopotamia and Anatolia* 453

Empires and States at War and Peace: The Late Bronze Age 453
> *Anatolia and the Hittites* 454
>> ● KEY SITE Hattusa, Capital of the Hittites 455
> *The Levant in the Late Bronze Age* 456
>> • *Ugarit* 456
> *Upper Mesopotamia and Syria: Hurrian Mittani* 458
>> ● KEY SITE The Uluburun Shipwreck 459
> *The Rise of Assyria* 460
> *Lower Mesopotamia: Kassite Babylonia* 461
> *Elam* 462
> *The End of the Late Bronze Age* 463

New and Resurgent Powers of the Iron Age 463
> *The Levant: Philistines, Phoenicians, Neo-Hittites* 463
>> • *The Philistines* 463
>> • *The Phoenicians* 464
>> • *The Neo-Hittites* 464
> *The Levant: Israel and Judah* 465
> *The Assyrian Empire* 465
>> ● KEY CONTROVERSY The Old Testament and Archaeology 466
> *Anatolian States* 467
> *Babylonia* 468
> *The Achaemenid Empire and the Conquest of Southwest Asia* 469

Summary and Conclusions 469
>> ● KEY CONTROVERSY Who Owns the Past? 470

Further Reading and Suggested Websites 471

Southwest Asia was of key significance in the development of human societies during the later Holocene period. As we saw in Chapter 6, the first steps in the development of settled communities supported by farming and animal husbandry were taken in this region shortly after the end of the last Ice Age. In the millennia that followed, these farming communities prospered, and in some parts of the region began to intensify their systems of agricultural production. Demographic and social changes made for large and increasingly complex societies, until, in the middle of the 4th millennium BC, Southwest Asia became the scene for the emergence of a new kind of society: the first city-states. Most of us today live in, or are socially and economically dominated by, urban conglomerations of some sort. The first steps toward urban life were taken in Southwest Asia in the context of a complex series of social processes often termed, as in this chapter, "the rise of civilization" [see Cities, States, and Civilizations Defined box, Chapter 5, p. 197].

In intimate association with early urbanism, the origins and development of various mechanisms of social control and expression can be clearly delineated, including early writing and bureaucracy, economic sophistication, social hierarchy, elite ideology, and the formation of states and empires. This chapter will trace the outlines of these complex social patterns through several millennia of the later prehistory and early history of Southwest Asia.

As explained in Chapter 6, the environment of Southwest Asia is highly varied in terms of topography, climate, and the distribution of natural resources. In geographical terms the region can be divided into four zones: the highlands; the foothills and upper plains; the alluvial plains; and the desert. The highland zone, principally in Turkey, Iran, Iraq, and Lebanon, includes the great ranges of the Zagros and Taurus Mountains [12.1]. In the foothills and upper plains, the first steps toward agriculture and the domestication of wild animals were taken. The alluvial plains, principally modern Iraq, were formed by the deposition of silt by the rivers Euphrates and Tigris and their tributaries. These rivers form the lifeblood of the region, enabling irrigation in an area where agriculture is not otherwise possible. It is in this flat, featureless landscape, surrounded by desert to the west and southwest, that the origins of urban life and writing are to be found, and it is on this region, known as Mesopotamia ("between the rivers"), that this chapter will principally focus.

The differential distribution of resources was a major factor in shaping the development and interaction of human communities throughout the prehistory and history of the region. In general, the alluvial plains are the most devoid of mineral resources, though rich in river water and soil, whereas the highland zone is rich in such materials as metal ores (copper, tin, and silver), utilitarian and semiprecious stone (obsidian, lapis lazuli, and carnelian), and timber. These commodities were all desired by the sophisticated societies of the plains, and to some extent the history of the region can be traced as a dialogue between the two zones, one rich in mineral resources, the other less so.

The terminology employed in this chapter is unavoidably rooted in the history of the discipline. The term Chalcolithic (literally "copper-stone") refers to the period 6000–3000 BC, when tools were still made principally of stone, although there was increasing use of copper implements through time. In the Bronze Age (3000–1200 BC), tools and weapons of bronze (usually an alloy of copper and tin) were most common. During the Iron Age (1200–334 BC), iron tools were more in use. These terms should be seen as convenient labels, and their use here is not intended to suggest that developments in metal technology were the sole driving force or key factor in the development of human societies through the entire period under consideration.

Farmers of the Early Chalcolithic: The Halaf and Ubaid Periods, *c.* 6000–4200 BC

By 6000 BC the human societies of Southwest Asia had developed into fully agricultural settled communities, living permanently in small villages and providing for themselves through animal husbandry, principally of sheep, goat, pigs, and cattle, as well as rain-fed crops such as barley, wheat, and legumes (Chapter 6). They still hunted animals such as wild cattle, onager (a species of wild equid), and gazelle. Population numbers were not high, as all the evidence indicates small-scale settlements widely dispersed across large swathes of the arable landscape. Around 6000 BC a major breakthrough came with the development of irrigation agriculture – the systematic use of constructed canals and channels to bring water from rivers to otherwise dry land, enabling fertile soils to be brought under cultivation. This single step opened up the broad plains of south Mesopotamia, today southern Iraq, for extensive settlement by human communities, and constituted a fundamental stage in the early development of complex societies, culminating in the rise of literate, urban civilization through subsequent centuries.

The Halaf Period, c. 6000–5400 BC

Archaeological sites with attributes typical of the Halaf period, named for the site of **Tell Halaf** in northern Syria, are found in a broad band of territory across the Fertile Crescent of Southwest Asia, ranging from western Iran across northern Iraq and Syria to southern Turkey and south into the Lebanon (Matthews

LATER SOUTHWEST ASIA TIMELINE

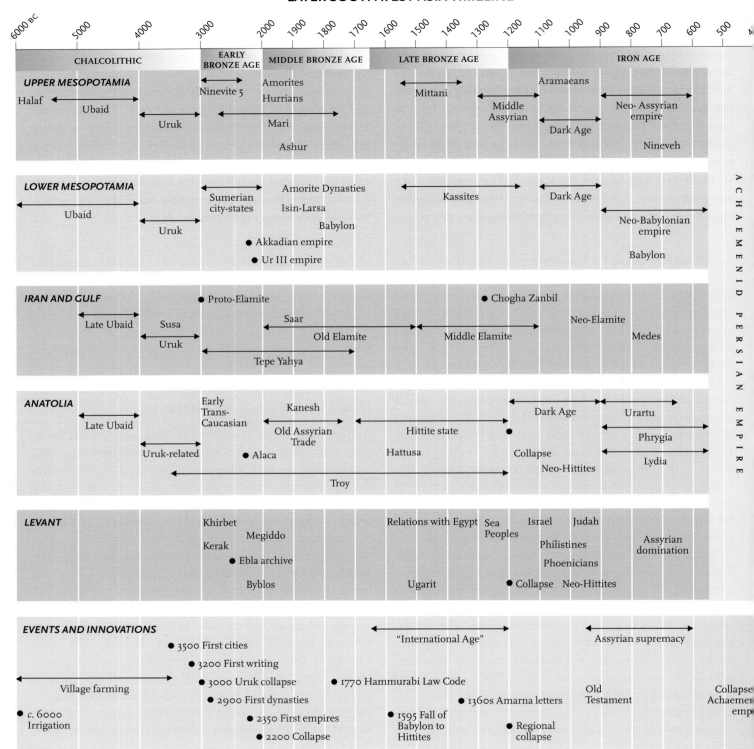

2000; Watson 1983) [**12.2**]. These sites are characterized by a distinctive package of material culture attributes, including circular buildings, high-quality painted pottery, female figurines, stone stamp seals, obsidian objects, and clay sling bullets. The distribution of Halaf sites is notable, situated as they are in rolling, hilly country with sufficient rainfall for dry farming. A great many Halaf sites were founded as new settlements, not overlying earlier human occupation, and this fact suggests a new peopling of sparsely inhabited areas, as farming techniques improved and populations increased.

Two major demographic stimulants may have been the introduction of **draft animals**, enabling tillage of deep, fertile soils, and, following the full domestication of cattle, a shift toward a **diet rich in dairy products**, which may have enabled women to produce greater numbers of children. A further factor may have been a pressure on human communities to increase their birth rates in the face of susceptibility to attack from predators such as the malaria-carrying mosquito, which flourished in the warmer climes of the post-Ice Age era (Groube 1996). Arguably, high incidences of malaria detected in assemblages of human remains suggest that life-or-death struggles

with devastating diseases may have been a recurring feature of Neolithic and Chalcolithic communities of Southwest Asia.

Halaf settlements were generally small, 0.5–3 ha (1.2–7.4 acres) in area, occupied by groups of perhaps 20–150 people. A few sites are much larger, covering areas of 12–20 ha (30–50 acres), but it is not yet clear whether these settlements were occupied in their entirety in a single period, or if they represent evidence for shifting partial settlement over long periods. There is some evidence for trade among and beyond communities. Analysis of the distinctive painted pottery found at all Halaf sites suggests that some sites, including **Arpachiyah** in Iraq and

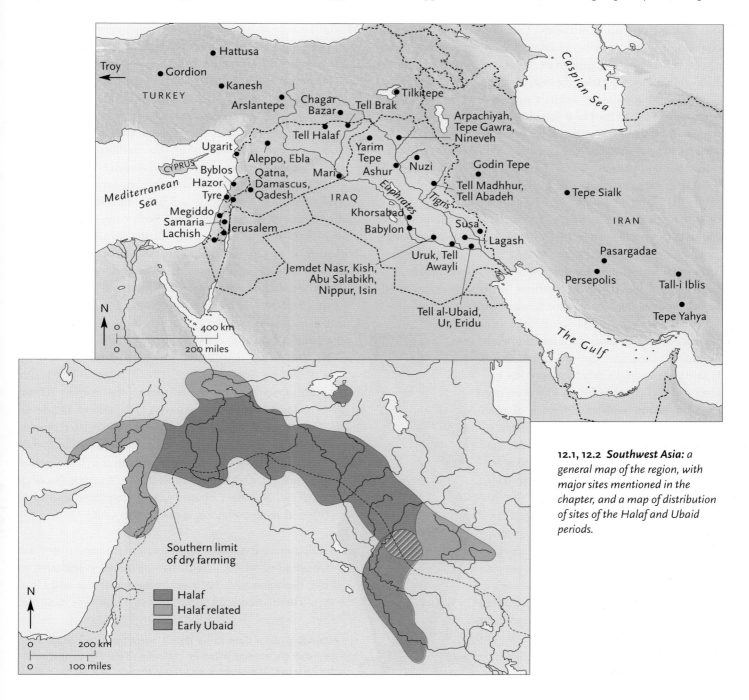

12.1, 12.2 Southwest Asia: *a general map of the region, with major sites mentioned in the chapter, and a map of distribution of sites of the Halaf and Ubaid periods.*

435

Chagar Bazar in Syria, functioned as pottery production centers (Frankel 1979). Obsidian, which occurs naturally in central and eastern Turkey, was also extensively traded, and was used to make tools and weapons, as well as items of jewelry. The site of **Tilkitepe**, located close to the shores of Lake Van in eastern Turkey, appears to have been a settlement specializing in the collection and preliminary working of obsidian prior to its shipment on to other Halaf sites.

Hunting and Warfare Although direct evidence for warfare is minimal, there is evidence for weaponry in the form of flat, pierced, stone wrist-guards for use by archers and huge quantities of hard clay sling missiles. On the existing evidence, however, it is not possible to determine to what extent these objects reflect hunting, or warfare, or a combination of both. It does seem that some Halaf sites were located as hunting camps along migration routes of animals such as onager and gazelle; but the mainstay of the Halaf economy was the suite of domesticated animals, especially sheep and goat, and crops, in particular emmer wheat, barley, lentils, and peas, that had provided the subsistence basis for human communities of Southwest Asia already for many centuries.

Religion and Society Our understanding of Halaf cult practices and religious beliefs is minimal. There are no clear ritual buildings, and human burials are treated in a variety of ways, including inhumation, multiple interments, skull burials, and cremations. Painted female figurines, often with exaggerated sexual features, may relate to the concern with fertility noted above [**12.3**]. There is little convincing evidence for social stratification within Halaf communities, although the so-called Burnt House at Arpachiyah may have been the residence of a village headman. The presence of stone **stamp seals**, and pieces of clay impressed by these seals (called "sealings"), is the earliest extensive evidence for the use of these objects in Mesopotamia; the practice was to have major significance in later Mesopotamian history, as we shall see. At Halaf sites, clay sealings were used to secure portable containers such as baskets and pots (Akkermans and Duistermaat 1997). This suggests a need by some people to exercise control over their possessions, perhaps while away on hunting or trading expeditions, and is a first hint of material possessiveness and social control that became fundamental elements of the later Chalcolithic period and beyond.

The Ubaid Period, c. 5900–4200 BC

Partially contemporary with these developments in Upper Mesopotamia, the first steps in human settlement of the Lower Mesopotamian plains were taking place. Modern alluvial deposits brought by the rivers Euphrates and Tigris have blanketed the earliest settlements under deep silt, making archaeological detection difficult, but some have nevertheless been located and excavated. Of profound significance at this time was the early development of **irrigation agriculture**, in particular the systematic exploitation of the waters of the Euphrates, as a means of enabling the cultivation of cereals. This single technological development, achieved in Lower Mesopotamia by about 5900 BC, allowed the settling and farming of the fertile plains of the area, and laid the basis for all subsequent cultural developments in this uniquely important region.

This period is called the Ubaid, after the site of **Tell al-Ubaid** in southern Iraq. Sites of Ubaid type occur throughout Lower Mesopotamia, where the earliest Ubaid-period sites are found, followed in later centuries by a spread into adjacent regions (Henrickson and Thuesen 1989). The earliest Ubaid phases remain obscure, but excavations at **Tell Awayli** (also spelled Tell el-Oueili) have reached beneath the modern alluvium to expose substantial mud-brick buildings, including a possible grain storage structure, associated with early pottery of so-called Ubaid 0 type. Other early Ubaid sites, such as **Hajji Muhammed**, lie 3 m (10 ft) below the modern plain surface, and give an indication of the wealth of archaeological evidence sealed, and partially protected, by the alluvium.

Painted pottery from the deeply stratified excavations at Eridu (see below) enabled a four-fold division of the Ubaid period into Ubaid 1–4, but later discovery of older material at Tell Awayli has necessitated use of the term Ubaid 0 for this first appearance of Ubaid material in Lower Mesopotamia. In broad terms, the earliest Ubaid material is contemporary with Halaf and earlier developments in Upper Mesopotamia, while later phases, from around 5400 BC, see a spread of Ubaid influence into Upper Mesopotamia, replacing the Halaf-period occupation, and beyond to southeast Anatolia (modern Turkey). Numbers of Late Ubaid sites have also been found along the shores of the Persian Gulf.

Eridu Eridu in southern Iraq is one of the most important Ubaid sites, where a sequence of temples dedicated to Enki, the water god, has been excavated (Safar and Lloyd 1981). These mud-brick structures are built one atop the

12.3 *Female figurine from Yarim Tepe II, north Iraq: a painted vessel in the shape of a woman; actual height 21 cm (8 in). The stopper or lid of the vessel would probably have been in the form of a woman's head.*

12.4 Successive temples of the Ubaid period at Eridu, south Iraq: *temples of increasing size and elaboration were built atop each other over a period of several centuries, culminating in the grand structure of level VII. This architectural sequence is good evidence for continuity of cult in a specific location.*

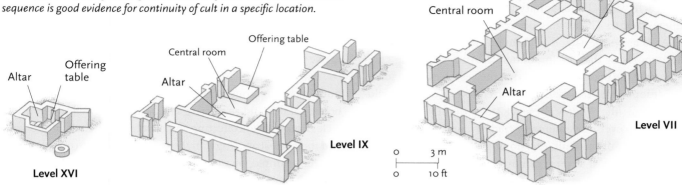

other in a chronological sequence spanning almost all of the Ubaid period [12.4]. From a small, single-roomed structure in the first phase, the temples were built on an increasingly grand scale, culminating, in the uppermost levels, in the classic Mesopotamian tripartite temple plan, with buttresses and recessed niches as well as altars and offering tables, the whole building set on a solid platform. Large amounts of ash and fish bones found in the upper temples indicate the offering of fish to the god. The sequence at Eridu is of particular importance as early evidence for the role of the temple within Mesopotamian society. Temples were highly significant elements in the origins of complex society in the region, their priests and administrators overseeing many aspects of daily life, including land and labor management, distribution of food, and, above all, the correct procedures for religious rites and rituals. Without such temples there would have been no early development of complex society on the Mesopotamian plains.

Excavation of an Ubaid cemetery at Eridu recovered some 200 graves of individuals buried in brick-lined pits, often with grave goods in the form of pots, jewelry, and food offerings. Figurines with lizard-like heads were found in these graves and elsewhere on Ubaid-period sites, and probably had some kind of religious significance [12.5, 12.6].

Ubaid Sites Beyond Lower Mesopotamia Beyond Lower Mesopotamia, Ubaid-period levels have been excavated at a range of sites. At **Tell Madhhur** in east-central Iraq, a domestic house which had been destroyed by fire was excavated, its walls surviving to a height of 2 m (6.6 ft) (Roaf 1989). The room-by-room inventory of objects, including pots, and tools of stone and clay, enables identification and localization of domestic activities within this spacious structure. Similarly grand houses of Ubaid-period communities have been excavated at **Tell Abadeh** and **Kheit Qasim** in the same region.

Further to the north, at **Tepe Gawra**, a complex of three temple structures was erected in the Late Ubaid period, *c.* 5200 BC. The presence of large quantities of clay sealings, used to seal containers or storerooms, found in a well in one of the Tepe Gawra temples may indicate a role for the temple in the collection and distribution of commodities in the name of the relevant divinity. The appearance of Ubaid-type pottery at sites in western Iran, including the site of **Susa**, where a rich cemetery has been excavated, demonstrates the interregional scale of activity and interaction during these centuries.

12.5, 12.6 Eridu figurines: *clay figurines with lizard-shaped heads and decoration in the form of painted spots and applied blobs of clay. These figurines are found in burials at Eridu and at other sites of the Ubaid period. Actual height: 10–15 cm (4–6 in).*

One of the most striking manifestations of the Ubaid phenomenon is the existence of some 50 sites in the Persian Gulf region, each with Ubaid pottery and other typical artifacts (Matthews 2001). These sites occur along the east littoral of Saudi Arabia, on the island of Bahrain, in Qatar, and on the western shores of the Oman peninsula. Analysis of the clays used to make the pottery suggests that the vessels were made in Lower Mesopotamia and then transported several hundred kilometers down the Gulf. These pottery distributions may represent low-level movements of traders and fishers up and down the coasts of the Gulf, exchanging items of material culture over a period of several centuries toward the end of the Ubaid period.

Painted Ubaid-style pottery fell out of use around 4200 BC, to be replaced by the largely unpainted ceramics of the Uruk period. Although much remains mysterious about the Ubaid period, especially as regards its earliest phases on the Lower Mesopotamian alluvium, it can nevertheless be appreciated that many aspects of later Mesopotamian civilization took their initial form during this period, including the institution of the temple as a community focus, the use of seals and sealings in economic and cult administration, the inter-community exchange of goods over long distances, and the sharing of material culture attributes, from pottery to architectural styles, over a region totaling several thousand square kilometers. It was on the foundation of these elements that the final steps toward civilization were taken in the following centuries.

Urban Communities of the Late Chalcolithic: The Uruk Period, 4200–3000 BC

During the 4th millennium BC, the alluvial plains of Lower Mesopotamia hosted large-scale human communities whose experiments in modes of living, warfare, craft production, administration, and social interplay gave rise to a phenomenon that we today characterize as "civilization." By 3200 BC, people in this region were living in communities that can be defined as urban, on the basis of size and complexity, as well as literate. The sophistication of these polities can be ascribed solely to autochthonous development, for there were no urban, literate communities prior to those of Lower Mesopotamia.

It is important to appreciate that the cultural achievements of what is called the Uruk period were firmly rooted in those of earlier ages. During the Ubaid period in particular, as we have seen, features such as long-distance trade and communications between Lower Mesopotamia and surrounding regions, the development of administrative technologies in association with religious authority, and, above all, the practice of irrigation agriculture had created a society that increasingly dominated and exploited its environment, locally and beyond. By careful irrigation and farming of the alluvial soils of the Lower Mesopotamian plains, communities were able to produce significant levels of surplus in staple commodities such as cereals, flour, fish, wool, and textiles. Civilization appears to have developed out of a concern by human societies to find ways in which to use this surplus staple wealth.

The role of the **temple** is once again critical, for these institutions acted as consumers of surplus wealth, accepting the bounty of the land as offerings to the gods, as well as serving as a clearing house, collecting the surplus on behalf of the gods and then redistributing it in the form of rations to temple-workers, for example, or as capital advanced to entrepreneurs who might then engage in commerce and long-distance trade (Postgate 2003). In this light, the stimuli to the rise of civilization in Southwest Asia were the fertility of the earth, the ability of the soil and the creatures that lived on it to generate staple surpluses and, crucially, the ingenuity of human beings in devising cultural mechanisms to dispose of those surpluses in ways that generated increasingly complex and self-reinforcing codes of conduct and practice.

Extensive survey work on the alluvial plains by Robert Adams (1981) has suggested that during the Early and Middle Uruk periods (4200–3500 BC), large settlements of up to 70 ha (173 acres) developed on the alluvium. A major shift in population distribution occurred in the Late Uruk period (3500–3000 BC), with the abandonment of many settlements on the northern plains around the important site of **Nippur**, and a complementary increase in settlement intensity in the southern alluvium around **Uruk**, with Uruk itself growing to some 100 ha (247 acres). By the Early Dynastic I period, around 2900 BC, Uruk had grown to the immense size of 400 ha (988 acres), the size of a modern small city or large town. It is possible that the north–south population shift at around 3500 BC was caused by a shift in the river courses of the Euphrates and/or Tigris, the rivers at that time joining together further north on the alluvium than they do today.

The Lower Mesopotamian Site of Uruk

Later 4th-millennium developments in Lower Mesopotamia are best appreciated by examining the great site of Uruk itself, from which the period takes its name (Nissen 2002) [**12.7**]. Uruk's modern name is Warka, and it appears in the Bible as the city of Erech. Early periods at the site have not been adequately explored, so that it is impossible to situate the Uruk-period developments in a detailed prehistoric trajectory; nevertheless, it is clear that Uruk must have been a major settlement in the 5th millennium BC and perhaps earlier. In the latter half of the 4th millennium BC we gain a clearer idea of the significance of the city. Uruk was the dominant settlement of the entire alluvium, and its temples would have been visible from

Before 2500 BC
2500–500 BC
After 500 BC
Mounded area

City wall

Palace of Sin-kashid

Ziggurat of Inanna

Bit-Resh

Kara-indash Temple

KULLABA

EANNA

White Temple

Uruk IV buildings

Ziggurat of Anu

Irigal

Mithreum

Temple of Gareus

City wall

N

0 — 500 m
0 — 1500 ft

designated structures and spaces for the execution of a broad range of social functions. Such structures and spaces include large-scale temples and associated administrative and residential buildings for priests and officials, open spaces for gatherings or worship, specialized craft production zones for pottery-making, stoneworking, and metalworking, and areas of housing. Although we find large agglomerations of people much earlier, for example at Çatalhöyük in the Neolithic period of Anatolia (Chapter 6), it is only in Late Chalcolithic Mesopotamia that we can detect a real multiplicity of function within those settlements, which enables us to identify them as true cities, as at Uruk.

Excavations at Uruk have concentrated largely on two major cult complexes, and have hitherto provided few insights into the everyday domestic life of the non-elite inhabitants of the town. The highly partial textual evidence, moreover, appears also to be associated with elite social elements of the city. The tenor and content of the available archaeological and textual evidence suggest that many aspects of daily life for all Uruk citizens were prescribed and controlled by elites, whose ideologies took shape in the form of massive religious buildings and associated technologies of control and command. The core of Uruk in the 4th millennium BC and beyond was dominated, in particular, by the cult complexes of the Eanna precinct [12.8], where Inanna, goddess of war and love, was worshiped, and the Anu temple area, dedicated to the sky god An.

Several massive structures have been excavated in the **Eanna precinct**, built principally of mud-brick with some limestone. Decorative use of baked-clay cones with colored heads typifies many of these buildings and other probable cult structures throughout Uruk-period Mesopotamia. The size and layout of a number of the Eanna precinct buildings suggest their use as temples, but some of the buildings may have served more as communal meeting houses or as residences of priests and

great distances across the level plains. Sustenance of the city would have involved the participation of large segments of the urban and rural population within a radius of at least 6 km (3.7 miles) of the city center.

It is fair to claim Uruk as the first genuine **city** in the world, by which we mean a large agglomeration of people, probably tens of thousands, living in a well-defined place that contained

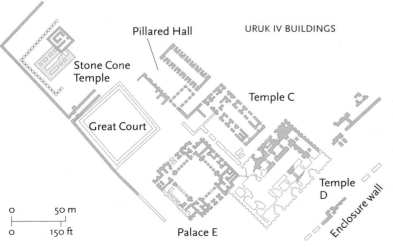

Pillared Hall

URUK IV BUILDINGS

Stone Cone Temple

Temple C

Great Court

Temple D

Palace E

Enclosure wall

0 — 50 m
0 — 150 ft

12.7 Uruk: *plan of the city of Uruk (modern Warka, biblical Erech); the site was occupied through many centuries and 4th-millennium levels have been investigated extensively only in the areas of the two main cultic precincts, Eanna and Kullaba.*

12.8 Plan of the Eanna cultic precinct at Uruk: *the area is dominated by a series of massive temples with large open courts, many of the wall faces decorated with stone or clay cones pushed into the mud-brick structures. The whole area had been severely truncated prior to later re-building and so these structures did not stand to a great height when excavated in modern times.*

officials. The temple was regarded as the residence of the god and was therefore often constructed in the form of a domestic house, albeit on a grand and elaborate scale. In the latest phase of Late Uruk building in the Eanna precinct, the largest structure, Temple D, measured 80 x 50 m (262 x 164 ft) – comparable in size to a small modern-day cathedral.

In the **Anu temple** area, to the west of Eanna, a series of successive temples, spanning several centuries, was built on terraces. The best preserved is the White Temple, smaller in scale than the Eanna precinct structures but in an imposing location, set on a platform 13 m (42.7 ft) high, a precursor of the ziggurats (high platforms surmounted by a small temple) that would in subsequent centuries feature so prominently on the Mesopotamian horizon. Within the White Temple, deliberate burial of a leopard and a lion cub may be traces of a foundation ritual. The painting of a leopard on the wall of a contemporary temple at the site of Tell Uqair, 200 km (124 miles) northwest of Uruk, may indicate a degree of uniformity in cult across Lower Mesopotamia at this time.

The Invention of Writing

Among the multitude of objects excavated over the decades at Uruk, some of the most significant are the more than 5000 clay tablets bearing evidence of early writing (Englund 1998) [12.9]. This writing takes the form of incised or impressed signs made by a stylus (a tapered instrument of wood or ivory) on carefully prepared soft clay tablets, in the script known as proto-cuneiform (cuneiform means "wedge-shaped") [12.10]. Some 850 signs are employed, but the lack of grammatical elements prevents secure identification of the language of these earliest written documents. It may be, however, that the lack of grammar was deliberate, allowing the texts to be read by individuals from a variety of linguistic backgrounds, almost certainly an advantage in the multi-ethnic context of Uruk at its interregional peak.

Uruk writing often employed pictographic signs, whose superficial meaning, at least, can be readily apprehended. Thus, corn or grain was represented by a drawing of an ear of grain. Additionally, most tablets have numerical signs, study of which

	Star	?Stream	Ear of barley	Bull's head	Bowl	Head and bowl	Lower leg
Pictographic sign *c.* 3100 BC							
Interpretation	Star	?Stream	Ear of barley	Bull's head	Bowl	Head and bowl	Lower leg
Cuneiform sign *c.* 2400 BC							
Cuneiform sign *c.* 700 BC, turned 90°							
Meaning	God, sky	Water, seed, sun	Barley	Ox	Food, bread	To eat	To walk, to stand

12.9 The development of the cuneiform script: *the general trend is for signs to become less pictorially representative through time as writing speed and familiarity with signs developed. The cuneiform script, like modern scripts such as Arabic or Latin, was used to write a host of often unrelated languages throughout its 3000-year history in Southwest Asia, including Sumerian, Akkadian (and its many dialects), Ugaritic, Hittite, Hurrian, Elamite, and Urartian.*

12.10 Proto-cuneiform: *clay tablet with proto-cuneiform ("wedge-shaped") script, dating to about 3000 BC. These texts are hard to interpret, as there are no obvious grammatical elements, but generally appear to relate to administration on the part of large public organizations, such as temples. In this case, the text accounts for the use of a very large quantity of barley grain over a period of 37 months.*

Quantity of the product:

c. 135,000 litres

Type of the product:

barley

Accounting period:

37 months

Name of the responsible official:

Kushim

Function of the document (?):

Final account? (inscribed over a partially erased sign)

Use of barley (?):

exchange

has demonstrated that different Uruk counting systems were used for specific functions. Thus, a sexagesimal system (units of 1, 10, 60, 600) was employed for counting discrete objects such as animals, humans, fish, implements, and so on; a bisexagesimal system (units of 1, 10, 60, 120, 1,200) for counting grain products and other items distributed within a rationing system; and a time system (using units of 1, 10, and 30) to form a calendar with months comprising three weeks, each of ten days (Nissen et al. 1993).

Where understood, the majority of the texts are of an economic and administrative nature, relating to such concerns as the disbursement of quotas of grain to laborers, the counting of flocks of animals, and the measurement and cultivation of fields belonging to officials. Other texts comprise lists of items such as professions, city or place names, and types of animals.

The very earliest texts date to the Late Uruk period (3500–3000 BC) and have so far been found only at Uruk itself, suggesting that the script may have originated there. The invention, whether or not at Uruk, of a new means of recording detailed information, albeit rooted in pre-writing systems of administrative control involving tokens, seals, and pieces of clay, constituted a quantum leap in administrative and organizational capability. From this time onward, cuneiform writing on clay tablets would delineate and police the internal boundaries of Mesopotamian society for some three millennia, until the disappearance of the cuneiform tradition around the time of Christ.

Cylinder Seals Intimately associated with early writing was the use of another weapon in the armory of administrative control, the cylinder seal (Collon 1987). Although early examples of cylinder seals have been found in Upper Mesopotamia and Iran, it is undoubtedly in the context of the rise of urban society in Lower Mesopotamia that these objects came to the fore. Cylinder seals were ideal for rolling over soft clay tablets, serving as both validation and identification of the participants involved in administrative activity. Additionally, cylinder seals were employed within a system of control over access to containers and storerooms by means of sealings affixed to pegs and coverings. This administrative use of seals was to be another characteristic feature of Mesopotamian society that endured for millennia.

The scenes depicted in cylinder seals tell us something about Uruk society (Boehmer 1999). Frequently depicted are bound captives brought before a skirted figure carrying a bow or spear, often identified as a priest-king. Other scenes show rows of offerings – animal, vegetable, and mineral – paraded before temples and high-status individuals [12.11]. Such a scene is also depicted in low relief on the famous **Warka Vase** [12.12], a stone vessel found at Uruk with figures bearing tribute into the presence of a ruler and the patron divinity of his city, the goddess Inanna. The atmosphere in all these scenes is of control, order, and hierarchy.

12.12 *The Warka Vase: this famous vase is carved with scenes around its exterior face of a cultic procession bearing offerings to a shrine, probably of the goddess Inanna. The vessel is made of alabaster and went missing from the Iraq Museum in Baghdad in April 2003, although it was later recovered. Height: 100 cm (39 in).*

12.11 *(Above)* **Cylinder seals:** *these were used as emblems and marks of authority in the context of early writing in Mesopotamia. The depiction of apparently cultic scenes on many of them, as here, reinforces the picture of temple involvement in these early stages of bureaucratic control. Seals were rolled over the soft clay of inscribed tablets and other clay objects in order to make an impression that would be seen and understood by officials working within the administrative system. Cylinder seal scene from Uruk, dating to c. 3200 BC.*

Uruk Expansion and Trade

The impact of these momentous social, political, and cultural developments in Lower Mesopotamia was felt in regions far from the city of Uruk itself; indeed, one of the characteristics of this period was the degree to which Uruk Mesopotamia interacted with its neighbors. Archaeological evidence from a host of contemporary sites paints a highly varied picture of the nature of relations between Lower Mesopotamia and adjacent regions (Rothman 2001; Postgate 2002). To the east, on the alluvial plains of southwest Iran, geographically at one with the Lower Mesopotamian alluvium, was the city of **Susa**, where a total adoption of Uruk-style artifacts and architecture was effected in the Late Uruk period. Following the collapse of the Uruk culture around 3100 BC, a local culture of complexity, called Proto-Elamite, carried the banner of early literacy for a century or so before dissolving. Further to the north, in the eastern Zagros Mountains, sites such as **Godin Tepe**, with its fortified residence of Mesopotamian colonists, were well situated to exercise control over routes of communication from the lowlands into the hills and high plateaus. The early development of sophisticated copper metallurgy on the Iranian Plateau, as demonstrated by material from sites such as **Tepe Sialk**, **Tepe Hissar**, and **Tal-i Iblis**, is likely to have been an important stimulant to highland-lowland interaction by the late 4th millennium BC at the latest.

A concern to oversee routes of communication is also marked by the location of the sites of **Habuba Kabira** and **Jebel Aruda** on the Euphrates River in northern Syria (Algaze 1993). Here there can be little doubt of the Lower Mesopotamian origin of the settlers, who brought with them a complete inventory of material culture resembling in almost every respect that of the city of Uruk itself, including religious architecture on a grand scale, distinctive pottery forms, and administrative technology in the form of cylinder seals and clay tablets with numerical signs. Missing from these sites, however, and from all other contemporary sites outside Uruk, are tablets with proto-cuneiform script, a lack that suggests that the collapse of the Uruk interregional system may have occurred at some time close to the invention of proto-cuneiform writing in Lower Mesopotamia.

Further northwards still, interactions between extrovert Uruk communities and local inhabitants took more complex forms, at least partly shaped by the nature of already existing societies in these hilly regions. Thus, at sites such as **Hacınebi Tepe** and **Arslantepe**, both on the upper Euphrates in Turkey, local polities maintained a strong sense of identity in the face of contact with Uruk-period Mesopotamia (Stein 1999). Indeed, there is every evidence that a considerable degree of political sophistication had been achieved prior to any such contact, as is especially clear at Arslantepe in the form of monumental buildings and intensive administrative activity (albeit without writing) in the earlier 4th millennium BC.

The engine for the expansion of the Uruk world in the later 4th millennium BC is seen by most scholars as the desire by powerful elite groups of Lower Mesopotamia to acquire the goods and commodities that were employed by them to validate their regime. Such resources included timber, semiprecious stones such as lapis lazuli and carnelian, and metals such as copper, gold, silver, and tin, as well as that most valuable and versatile of resources, human labor in the form of slaves. These resources were lacking in the Mesopotamian alluvium, and abundant in surrounding regions. Tapping into centuries-old prehistoric modes and routes of exchange and communication, it seems that the Uruk people of Lower Mesopotamia attempted to settle, domesticate, and exploit an entire landscape of several thousand square kilometers and all its resources, on an imperial scale, for the purposes of elite group enhancement at Uruk and other major centers of the south. Whether or not such an enterprise can have been feasible without a cloak of religious justification is debatable, but the occurrence at many sites across the region of typically Uruk temples, and the association with them of administrative technology, suggests that Uruk elites may have successfully married politics with religion in their expansionist endeavors.

The Uruk world system collapsed around 3100 BC, for reasons as yet unknown, although there are suggestions of climatic aridity at this time. Typically Uruk civilization was maintained at Uruk itself and at a range of other sites, including **Jemdet Nasr** (which gives its name to the period 3100–2900 BC), where the use of proto-cuneiform tablets and cylinder seals shows the determination of local elites to maintain their identities after the collapse. Seal impressions with names of Mesopotamian cities, including Ur, Larsa, Uruk, and Kesh, may demonstrate a need for cities to act in concert in as yet unclear ways (Matthews 1993). Outside the Lower Mesopotamian heartland, the peoples of the peripheries cast off the Uruk mantle and developed specifically local traditions of material culture. It may have seemed that the imperial experiment of the Uruk period had failed, but in their development of new technologies of exploitation and control, especially in the form of the written document, the people of Uruk-period Lower Mesopotamia had created a means of expression and accountability that would form an integral element of all later experiments in imperial activity in Southwest Asia and beyond.

City-states, Kingdoms, and Empires of the Early Bronze Age, *c.* 3000–2000 BC

Cultural and political developments of the later Chalcolithic period in Southwest Asia were consolidated and reinforced through the centuries of the Early Bronze Age. Urbanism, literacy, religious administration, and interregional trade continued to characterize societies of the 3rd millennium BC, following the collapse of the Uruk world system.

Increasingly abundant and rich textual evidence complements the wealth of archaeological material in defining and illuminating a host of distinctive human communities across the area. With varying degrees of access to sources of tin and copper – the ingredients of bronze – the societies of the region continued to develop their material and technological capabilities, engaging in both peaceful and hostile interactions through time. In this section we examine some of the more significant of these societies.

Sumerian City-States

In Lower Mesopotamia during the Early Dynastic period (2900–2350 BC), the alluvial landscape hosted a large number of independent city-states [12.13], each controlling a hinterland of productive agricultural and pastoral territory (Crawford 2004). This period is called Early Dynastic because, for the first time, written sources provide a list of kings and dynasties that held sway over cities or groups of cities in Mesopotamia.

Numerous cuneiform texts, especially from the later part of the Early Dynastic period, relate mainly to economic activity, but often also to religious, literary, and lexical matters. The language of these texts is Sumerian, unrelated to any known language, living or dead; but even among the earliest texts there is evidence for a Semitic element in the population of Lower Mesopotamia, indicating the mixed ethnic nature of Sumer at this time. By "Sumer," derived from an ancient term, we mean the area of modern south Iraq.

Sumerian city-states depended on irrigation farming, and the cutting and maintenance of canals feeding off the Euphrates and Tigris rivers was a major social responsibility for urban authorities (Postgate 1992). Conflicts between neighboring cities over land and water feature in the texts. The cities of the plain were built of mud-brick, with some use of wood and, rarely, stone. The people grew barley, wheat, pulses, fruits, and vegetables, and they herded cattle, sheep, goat, and pigs. Interactions between city-dwellers and pastoral nomads are hinted at in the sources and will certainly have played a significant role in the economy.

Many city-states grew wealthy on the produce of their lands, and exchanged surplus items, such as fine textiles, with their neighbors. Metals, semiprecious stones, and woods were the principal imports to Lower Mesopotamia, arriving from Iran, Anatolia, the Levant, and the Persian Gulf. These luxury items were often the preserve of social elites, epitomized by the palace and the temple. Rule of each city-state appears to have been by a "king" who combined secular and religious authority, ensuring his city's devotion to its principal deity. In addition to locale-specific deities, all Sumerian city-states recognized a pantheon of supreme divinities headed by Enlil, whose temple at Nippur was the holiest shrine of the land.

Despite their independent political status, Sumerian city-states show remarkable similarities in their material culture, with elements such as pottery, jewelry, statuary, seals, and even mud-brick shapes and sizes being uniform across the entire southern alluvium. These points of similarity argue for high levels of intimate and consistent interaction between city-states,

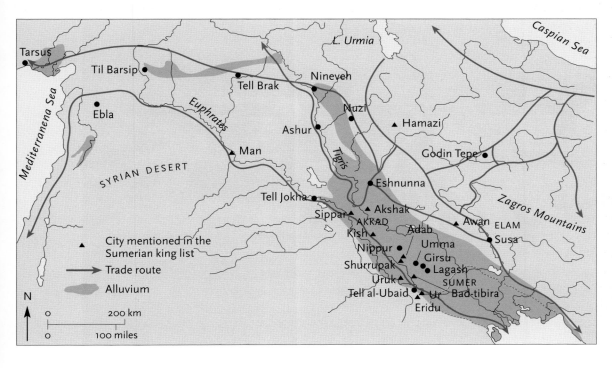

12.13 Map of Sumerian city-states: in the Early Dynastic period a large number of independent city-states were dotted over the alluvial landscape of Mesopotamia, each controlling its own hinterland of agricultural and pastoral territory.

443

their craft-workers, farmers, soldiers, architects, and builders, throughout the half millennium under consideration.

These city-states varied greatly in size, ranging from 12 ha (30 acres) or less, as at **Abu Salabikh** (perhaps ancient **Eresh**), to the enormous spread of **Al-Hiba** (ancient **Lagash**) at 400 ha (988 acres) [**12.14**]. But within each city a consistent repertory of services and facilities existed, including a city temple, a major residence for the ruler and his family, a city wall with gates, craft and production workshops, and domestic quarters for the populace. The dead were buried under the plaster floors of occupied houses [**12.15**], but special cemeteries are also known.

The famous royal cemetery of **Ur**, with its spectacular artifacts of gold, lapis lazuli, and silver [**12.16**], epitomizes the ability of city elites to accumulate wealth on the basis of agricultural production and interregional trade (Zettler and Horne 1998). In this cemetery, 16 tombs stand out as having lavish quantities of spectacular grave goods, as well as evidence of human sacrifice. These tombs may contain the bodies of either kings or high priests of Ur. To what extent divergences in wealth

12.15 *Abu Salabikh:* *burial of a human body under the floor of a domestic house at Abu Salabikh, south Iraq, Early Dynastic III period, c. 2500 BC. Burial of the dead under the floors of occupied houses has a long history in Southwest Asia, but burial in cemeteries is also attested.*

were predicated on the exploitation of lower-status social groups is hard to estimate, but at sites such as **Fara** (ancient **Shuruppak**) and Abu Salabikh, both dating to around 2500 BC, the evidence from archaeology and texts suggests that a significant element of city-states comprised a well-to-do middle class, occupying capacious houses, burying moderate wealth with their dead, and conducting economic and administrative business, sometimes on an ambitious scale, within their own homes (Postgate 1994).

12.14 *Ancient Lagash:* *excavations in progress at the site of Al-Hiba, ancient Lagash, in south Iraq. The site is a typical mound (tell in Arabic) of south Iraq, low in height and sprawling over an extremely large area. The buildings were constructed of mud-brick; walls of this material can be seen in the foreground, here dating to the Early Dynastic period (early 3rd millennium BC). Excavating such structures is a difficult and slow process.*

Upper Mesopotamian, Iranian, and Anatolian Cultures

Sumerian material culture such as pottery, cylinder seals, and statuary is found at some sites in Upper Mesopotamia during the earlier 3rd millennium BC, including **Mari** and **Chuera**; but otherwise this region hosted a locally based culture, known as Ninevite 5, after its first identification in Max Mallowan's excavations at **Nineveh**, in northern Iraq (Roaf 2000). Ninevite 5 settlements are mostly small, and appear to have lacked writing and monumental architecture. On the other hand, fine painted and incised pottery [12.17] stands in sharp contrast to the generally drab vessels of the Sumerian cities of the south.

During these centuries (3000–2500 BC), relations between Lower and Upper Mesopotamia were minimal, and the communities of the north reverted to a low level of social organization, compared to the preceding period of Uruk connections. Toward the end of this long spell, however, new cities erupted across the Upper Mesopotamian plains, including sites such as **Ebla**, **Tell Leilan**, **Tell Beydar**, and **Tell Brak** (ancient **Nagar**), in Syria. These cities never approached those of Sumer in size or grandeur, but they indicate a major increase in social development and regional administration, stimulated at least partly by renewed intercourse with the south.

In **Iran**, a similar situation prevailed through the period 3100–2500 BC. At the collapse of the Uruk phenomenon around 3100 BC, communities in Iran adopted radically new traits of material culture, including styles of pottery, cylinder seals, and even proto-cuneiform writing in the Proto-Elamite script (not, in fact, related to later Elamite texts). At **Susa**, all traces of Uruk connections ceased, to be replaced by objects of Proto-Elamite type. Some 1500 clay tablets in Proto-Elamite script, many with distinctive cylinder seal impressions, were found at Susa, and similar tablets have been found at a broad spread of sites across Iran following the cessation of contacts with Uruk Mesopotamia (Potts 1999). This dramatic switch in material culture introduces a new highland orientation of western Iran through these centuries. Interactions between Mesopotamia and Iran in the later 3rd millennium BC were shaped largely by the desire of Sumerian elites to obtain valuable commodities from the highland zone [see box: Tepe Yahya, p. 446].

In Anatolia, there is also clear evidence for a cultural break around 3000 BC, as illustrated at **Arslantepe**, where Uruk connections cease and are followed by evidence of material of so-called Early Transcaucasian type, including rich burials with metal objects (Frangipane 2001). Pottery of this type occurs from about 3000 BC throughout eastern Anatolia and down into the Levant, where it is known as Khirbet Kerak ware. It may be that a mass movement of peoples southwards from the Caucasus *c.* 3000 BC, perhaps caused by environmental change, brought about the collapse of the Uruk world system in Anatolia, Upper Mesopotamia, and beyond. Elsewhere in Anatolia, locally developing Early Bronze Age communities are spectacularly in evidence at the rich cemetery of **Alacahöyük** and at **Troy** [see box: Troy, pp. 450–51].

Kingdoms and Empires of the Later 3rd Millennium BC

The final three centuries of the 3rd millennium BC saw the rise of political entities interpreted as empires, by which we mean a large-scale political entity composed of both a core and areas subject to that core. Earliest of these was the **Akkadian empire**, initiated by Sargon (2334–2279 BC) (Liverani 1993) [see 12.22]. The dates of Sargon's reign can be tentatively reconstructed

12.16 *(Left)* **Sculpture from the Royal Cemetery of Ur:** *dating from the Early Dynastic III period, c. 2500 BC, this is the so-called "Ram in a Thicket" sculpture, actually more likely to be a goat. It is made of gold, silver, lapis lazuli, and shell over a shaped wooden core and formed part of an elaborate piece of furniture deposited in the tomb.*

12.17 *(Right)* **Ninevite 5 pottery, from Tell Brak, northeast Syria:** *variation in the decorative techniques and motifs of even small sherds of this pottery can be used to date associated structures and building levels at sites across Upper Mesopotamia; these fragments date to c. 2700 BC.*

KEY SITE Tepe Yahya

Throughout the 3rd millennium BC, relations between Sumer (Lower Mesopotamia) and what is now Iran were largely shaped by the desire of Sumerian city-states to acquire the mineral resources of the highland region. Lacking all but the most basic mineral resources, the cities of the plain used their agricultural and production surpluses to support a high level of foreign trade. These interactions encouraged the development of specialized production centers on the Iranian Plateau, of which Tepe Yahya is a striking example.

Tepe Yahya is located in southeast Iran, north of the Straits of Hormuz, and the site was occupied long before any contact with Mesopotamia. By around 3100–2800 BC there was a significant Proto-Elamite presence at the site, with 27 inscribed tablets dealing with local economic matters (Damerow and Englund 1989). These tablets employed systems of counting previously developed in

12.18 *Fragments of chlorite vessels from Tepe Yahya, in modern Iran. Motifs and styles can be traced across a large area of Southwest Asia in the later 3rd millennium BC. Ongoing excavations at the site of Jiroft, in the area of Tepe Yahya, are shedding new light on the early stages of this phenomenon.*

Lower Mesopotamia and known from the earliest written documents of Uruk, thus suggesting a continuing Mesopotamian influence on the highland region. The inscribed tablets were found in a well-built but otherwise unexceptional structure.

Debate continues as to whether the tablets relate to a purely local and domestic social context, as suggested by their contents, or if they are evidence for control of the area by a large-scale political entity centered at one of the major sites of the region, such as Susa or Malyan.

12.19 *Clay tablet with inscription in the Proto-Elamite script, c. 3000 BC. The language itself has not been deciphered but the number signs and systems employed in these texts show many similarities to contemporary number systems of Lower Mesopotamia.*

Abandonment and Re-birth

Whatever the context, the Proto-Elamite settlement at Tepe Yahya, as at other Iranian sites of the period, collapsed c. 2800 BC. Following a period of abandonment, the site gained major importance from 2400 to 1700 BC as a center for the production of carved vessels made of chlorite, a soft greenish stone mined locally (Lamberg-Karlovsky 1997). Thousands of fragments of these vessels have been found, decorated in low relief carving that includes figurative scenes with often mythical characters, as well as depictions of animals, snakes, birds, and temple facades, all in the so-called Intercultural Style. Vessels of this type, many no doubt manufactured at Tepe Yahya itself, have been found at sites in Mesopotamia, such as Ur, as well as in Bactria to the east and along the Persian Gulf.

from ancient sources, but it is important to bear in mind that there are several competing interpretations of the exact chronology of this period. Sargon's capital city of **Akkad** has not been located archaeologically but is believed to lie somewhere in northern Sumer, probably in the region of Babylon and Kish. Under Sargon's influence, an increased emphasis on Semitic aspects of language and society can be detected through the 150 years of the empire's existence, indicated by the preference for Akkadian soldiers as elite troops and the dominance of the Semitic Akkadian language in all forms of inscriptions.

The Akkadian empire began with Sargon's conquest of the cities of Sumer, and developed into an expansion into the world beyond, echoing the interregional connections of the Late Uruk period a millennium earlier. Thus, Akkadian influence is witnessed by archaeological and/or textual finds in Upper Mesopotamia, southeast Anatolia, and southwest Iran. The great city-state of Ebla was conquered by Sargon [see box: Ebla, p. 452], and in his inscriptions he boasts of reaching the Mediterranean coast beyond the Amanus Mountains (in southern Turkey). To the south, there is evidence for Akkadian connections with the lands of Dilmun, Magan, and Meluhha (Bahrain, Oman, and the Indus Valley, respectively). The engine for much of this activity must certainly have been the desire by Sargon and his successors to obtain goods and raw materials, such as timber, metals, and precious stones.

Art of the Akkadian empire displays a marked sense of naturalism and restrained composition that sets it apart from its Sumerian antecedents and successors. A particular masterpiece is the stela of Naram-Sin (2254–2218 BC), depicting that king in triumphant conquest over an enemy of the east [**12.20**].

The Akkadian empire collapsed *c.* 2200 BC in a flood of invading forces from the east, but there are indications also of a major, perhaps global, episode of climatic adversity, involving aridification and the abandonment of agricultural land, which may have undermined the economic basis of the Akkadian empire and of other contemporary states of Southwest Asia and beyond (Weiss 2000) [see box: The End of the Early Bronze Age, p. 448].

Following a period of regionalism, a grand return to imperial modes of power occurs with the empire of the **Third Dynasty of Ur**, or **Ur III**, which held sway from 2112 to 2004 BC (Klein 1995). Centered on the city of **Ur** in Lower Mesopotamia and covering much of the territory of the Akkadian empire, the Ur III empire oversaw a revival of the Sumerian language and culture, including a return to pre-Akkadian concepts and principles of art. At this time the city of Ur was completely rebuilt, with a massive ziggurat [12.21], magnificent temples, and large royal tombs. The Ur III kings ruled over large tracts of Mesopotamia and western Iran through a system of provincial governors, each in control of an extraordinarily rigorous bureaucratic administration that is bountifully recorded in thousands of clay tablets from this period. These texts, written in Sumerian, show a concern on the part of administrators and clerks to record every detail of the activities of empire, from labor devoted to canal-digging to animals provided as tax and tribute to the major shrines of Sumer located at **Nippur**. They provide a unique insight into the administrative mechanics of a Mesopotamian empire.

The Ur III empire disintegrated at the end of the 3rd millennium BC, again with significant impact from the armies of the east, the land of **Elam**. In this region, today southwest Iran, a dynamic dynasty of local origin had evolved at least partly in response to Mesopotamian stimulus. Centered on the site of **Susa**, where monumental building programs were pursued and inscriptions written in the Elamite language, the kings of Elam maintained their control over the city and its hinterland for some decades after the collapse of the Ur III empire (Potts 1999).

In the Levant to the west, a serious decline in urban settlement is also detectable in the last decades of the 3rd millennium BC, following the destruction of Ebla by the Akkadian dynasty. The collapse of the Egyptian Old Kingdom *c.* 2150 BC (Chapter 10), and of the Indus Valley civilization not long after (Chapter 14), adds to the picture of regional disintegration visible in the dramatic end to political entities across the entire area of Southwest Asia and beyond. The approximately simultaneous collapse of complex societies throughout the region argues strongly for, on the one hand, the existence of a factor or factors common to all, which may be climate change, and, on the other, for a high degree of at least economic integration between these early empires and polities, an integration abundantly clear in the movement of commodities and peoples between the states of the region.

12.20 *The stone stela of Naram-Sin, c. 2250 BC:* the carved scene shows Naram-Sin s victory over mountain tribes of the east. Naram-Sin is depicted with a horned helmet, a classic sign of divinity in ancient Mesopotamia, materializing his claim to be divine. The stela itself was later carried off as booty from Akkad to Susa in southwest Iran, where it was excavated in modern times. Height: 198 cm (78 in).

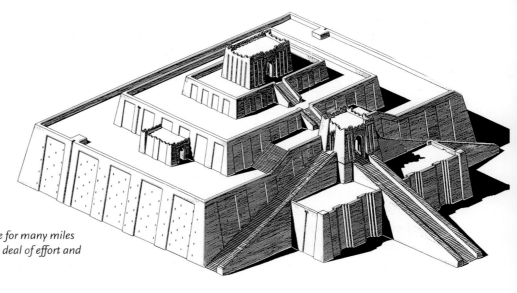

12.21 *(Right) Reconstruction of the ziggurat of Ur, c. 2100 BC:* ziggurats were staged towers, surmounted by shrines, with access by a series of staircases. In the flat and level landscape of Lower Mesopotamia these shrines would have been visible for many miles around. Kings of the Ur III dynasty invested a great deal of effort and labor in building ziggurats and temples.

KEY CONTROVERSY The End of the Early Bronze Age

A major episode of societal disruption occurred across Southwest Asia and beyond around 2200–1900 BC. The Akkadian empire of Mesopotamia collapsed, and there is widespread evidence for breaks in cultural trajectories and settlement patterns in most regions. There has been considerable debate about the possible role of climate change as a factor in these developments (Weiss 2000), but what is the nature of the archaeological evidence for collapse in the late 3rd millennium BC?

Mesopotamia

In Mesopotamia, the early empire of Akkad, which had exerted administrative and political control over Lower and Upper Mesopotamia for a period of at least several decades, came to an apparently sudden and dramatic end around 2200 BC, as suggested by evidence for the abandonment of landscapes and specific sites such as Tell Leilan and the Habur plains area of northeastern Syria.

In Lower Mesopotamia the Akkadian empire was succeeded by the Ur III state, accompanied by a mass immigration of population, perhaps those displaced from Upper Mesopotamia by the episode of collapse.

The Levant, Anatolia, and Egypt

In the Levant, the end of the Early Bronze Age is marked by a major phase of urban abandonment lasting for about 300 years from 2200 BC. Large fortified urban sites were replaced by modest settlements and

12.22 *Life-sized copper head, thought to be of the Akkadian king Sargon, found at Nineveh in north Iraq.*

temporary encampments, suggesting that significant elements of the population switched from settled agricultural ways of life to more mobile and flexible modes of subsistence, not so clearly detectable in the archaeological record.

Similar levels of social disruption and abandonment of hierarchical, urban settlement patterns feature in evidence from across Anatolia, again suggesting an increase in pastoral nomadism. In Egypt, the collapse of the Old Kingdom occurred at this time, followed by the First Intermediate Period, an episode of instability and flux spanning the years 2125–1975 BC (Chapter 10). In Greece and the Aegean world too, a serious decline in settled populations took place during this period (Chapter 13).

Climate Change as the Cause?

In sum, these centuries were characterized by imperial collapse, a switch from settled agriculture to pastoral nomadism, and an increase in population only in those regions where irrigation agriculture was practiced, such as Lower Mesopotamia. These factors have been taken as indicative of a severe and sudden climate change, most notable in a decrease in rainfall of some 20–30 percent. An episode of aridity on such a scale would have rendered marginal farming regions, common across Southwest Asia, totally unsuitable for large-scale human settlement, and would have seriously disrupted patterns of settlement and land use.

Evidence for climate change comes from a wide and ever-increasing range of sources. Cores through lake-bottom deposits provide information on pollen, rainfall, and fluctuations in water levels, while data from ancient tree rings can also be brought to bear. A reluctance to see human societal development as too tightly determined by environmental factors has led some scholars to doubt the validity or interpretation of the ancient climatic data, but as the evidence mounts up and increasingly coherent explanations are formulated, the scope for alternative explanations of this undeniably dramatic and widespread series of changes at the end of the 3rd millennium BC correspondingly diminishes.

Commerce and Conflict in the Middle Bronze Age

At the start of the 2nd millennium BC, new peoples appeared on the scene of Southwest Asia, perhaps taking advantage of, if not partly causing, the collapse of complex states of the late 3rd millennium BC. Their possible role in these collapses cannot be ascertained with accuracy, but when written records once more occur, the region hosts at least two new groups of people: the Amorites and the Hurrians.

Referred to in texts of the late 3rd millennium BC, the **Amorites** were a wave of Semitic intruders from the west and southwest desert fringes, like the Aramaeans and Arabs of later times. Doubtless they were attracted by the wealth of the settled states of the fertile plains of Syria and Mesopotamia. The Amorite legacy was to be considerable, for many of the Mesopotamian kings of the 2nd millennium BC, including Hammurabi of Babylon, explicitly traced their dynastic origins to the Amorite influx. The origins of the **Hurrians** are less clear, but they are often associated with the Early Transcaucasian movements of the early 3rd millennium BC. Their language, Hurrian, is believed to originate in the Caucasus region and is distantly related to that of the Iron Age kingdom of Urartu in eastern Turkey (see below). By 2000 BC, Hurrian communities had settled in large numbers across a broad swathe of Upper Mesopotamia, forming the basis for the state of Mittani (Wilhelm 1989).

From about 2000 to 1700 BC, groups of city-states competed for power across Southwest Asia. From contemporary documents, including royal correspondence, we know that several major kings each had a following of minor kings in train. A famous letter from Mari, dated to 1770 BC, reports, "There is no king who can be mighty alone. Ten or 15 kings follow Hammurabi, the man of Babylon; as many follow Rim-Sin, the man of Larsa, Ibal-pi-El, the man of Eshnunna, and Amut-pi-El, the man of Qatna, and 20 kings follow Yarim-Lim, the man of Yamhad."

Lower Mesopotamia and the Persian Gulf

The earliest dominant cities of the south, the former heartland of the Akkadian and Ur III empires, were the Amorite foundations of **Isin** and **Larsa**. The Isin kings saw themselves as successors to the Ur III empire. They purged the Elamites from Ur and established control of southern Mesopotamia, but power alternated between Isin and its main rival, Larsa. Both cities maintained vital trade connections with the Persian Gulf, already well established in the Akkadian period. This trade involved the import of copper, timber, and precious stones, and the export of wool, cloth, oil, barley, and silver. Excavations at sites in Bahrain, such as **Saar** (Crawford 1998), have investigated the settlements of local communities thriving on the profits of international trade at this time. Private entrepreneurs appear to have played the major role in organizing and executing this trade, although often with the participation of large urban institutions in the form of royal palaces and temples. With the increasing use of bronze for tools and weaponry, the import of copper from Oman (ancient Magan) was especially important. Evidence for these regional contacts includes the frequent and widespread occurrence of stamp seals of a particular style, known as Gulf seals, found throughout Mesopotamia, Iran, Anatolia, the Persian Gulf, and even the Indus Valley.

Within Lower Mesopotamia the increasing dominance of Amorite dynasties is notable, with Amorite kings established at many major cities, including **Babylon**, **Kish**, and **Uruk**. For a period of a century from 1865 BC the city of Larsa assumed dominance over Lower Mesopotamia, its kings carrying out massive programs of temple construction and restoration at many of the cities of the plains. The greatest Larsa king was Rim-Sin (1822–1763 BC), whose achievements in subduing the city-states of Lower Mesopotamia were exceeded only by those of his ultimate conqueror, Hammurabi of Babylon.

Hammurabi of Babylon (1792–1750 BC) was the most famous Mesopotamian king of the 2nd millennium BC (Vand De Mieroop 2005). Of Amorite origin, he created a state that almost transcended traditional city-state rivalries. Through the 1780s BC he increased his power-base by conquering the main cities of Lower Mesopotamia, including Uruk and Isin, before engaging in conflict with neighbors to the east and north – the Elamites, Guti, and Subartu. In 1763 BC he conquered Rim-Sin of Larsa, and in 1761 BC he captured the great city of **Mari**, finally destroying it in 1757 BC.

Hammurabi is famous today for his **Law Code**, one of the best-known documents from ancient Southwest Asia [**12.23**]. This text is inscribed on a stone stela, excavated at Susa in Elam, where it had been taken by eastern invaders at some point after Hammurabi's reign. The document commences by listing the gods and their cities that supported Hammurabi, including Mari, Tuttul, Ashur, Nineveh, Ur, Eridu, and Girsu. These widely scattered cities demonstrate the broad base of support that Hammurabi was able to establish in the earlier years of his rule. The Law Code is a social document as much as a legal one. Like all Mesopotamian kings, Hammurabi saw his rule as divinely sanctioned, a belief materialized in the stela in the image of the god Shamash handing the symbols of justice to Hammurabi. The king is shown as totally dominant in all aspects of the legal and social system addressed in the code, with the right to make decisions in any field of his society's affairs. Below the king were three social classes, the *awilum* or freemen, the *mushkenum*, of unclear dependent status, and the *wardum*, or slaves. In addition to his position at the apex of the Law Code, Hammurabi boasts of his public works, the construction and restoration of irrigation canals, temples, and fortifications.

12.23 *The Stela of Hammurabi: dating to c. 1770 BC, the scene at the top depicts Hammurabi receiving the symbols of justice from the deity Shamash, below which the Law Code is inscribed. Like the stela of Naram-Sin [**12.20**], this monument was found at Susa, where it had been taken by Elamite raiders of Mesopotamia in the late 2nd millennium BC. Height: 225 cm (89 in).*

An associated boom in private-sector commerce and industry accompanied the rise of palace power, evident in numerous cuneiform texts of the time. In archaeological terms, we know little of the Babylon of Hammurabi's time, for much of it lies beneath the remains of Iron Age Babylon. Houses of earlier 2nd millennium BC date have been extensively excavated at the city of **Ur**, however, and have provided a wealth of information on everyday life at this important city during the Isin-Larsa episode (Brusasco 1999–2000). A major program of research at the city of **Mashkan-shapir** has also shed light on urban structure in this period (Stone and Zimansky 2004).

The centuries following Hammurabi witness a steady decline in Lower Mesopotamia, with severe drops in land values attested in the few texts that come from the period (1700–1600 BC). With the Hittite sack of **Babylon** in 1595 BC, a dark age of some 150 years descends across Lower Mesopotamia, ended only with the arrival of the Kassites (see below).

Upper Mesopotamia and the Levant

Looking northwards and westwards from Babylonia, a main focus of attention is the city of **Mari**, in modern Syria, located on the Euphrates River at a key point where east–west and north–south trade routes meet (Margueron 1995). Trade in tin, in particular, seems to have underlain the prosperity of the city in this period.

The main architectural feature of the site is the great palace of **Zimri-Lim** (1775–1761 BC), famous in its day as one of the wonders of the region. It had been used as a royal residence for some time before Zimri-Lim's reign, over a period of about 250 years. The building was multi-storied, with over 260 rooms at ground level, and covered an area of about 2.5 ha (6.2 acres). As already noted, Mari was destroyed by Hammurabi in 1757 BC, and paradoxically his firing of the palace preserved much of its character, and its contents, for recovery by archaeologists, although the most valuable items had been removed before destruction.

KEY SITE Troy

Few archaeological sites have captured the public imagination as much as Troy, alleged location of the Trojan War as related in Homer's *Iliad*. Although written down in the 8th century BC, it is now believed that Homer's story had its origins in events of the Late Bronze Age, when the Mycenaean civilization of Greece and the Aegean was at its peak (Chapter 13). The mound of Hissarlık, in northwest Turkey close to the Dardanelles straits, has been identified with ancient Troy since the 1820s.

No textual evidence has ever proven this association beyond doubt, but in antiquity it was believed that the town of Ilion was the site of ancient Troy, and inscriptions have shown that Ilion was indeed located at Hissarlık. In looking at Troy we need to consider two major controversial issues. To what extent can we read Homer as a historical source? And how trustworthy are the results of the famous excavations at Hissarlık made by Heinrich Schliemann in the 1870s and 1880s?

12.24 *A reconstruction of Troy VI, in the Late Bronze Age, showing formidable fortifications and large structures within the citadel. A substantial lower town has been detected outside these walls.*

The walls of the palace still stand 4 m (13 ft) high in places, built of sun-dried mud-brick, with some use of baked brick and timber. Some rooms feature elaborate drainage systems, suggesting use as washing facilities. The main entrance was at the north, leading to a series of courtyards with surrounding rooms. The largest court covered a huge area (48 x 32.5 m, or 158 x 107 ft), and provided access to a room where wall paintings depicted mythological scenes. To the west of room 131 lay the official focus of the palace, with a throne room and attached facilities, constructed of monumentally thick walls. Elsewhere, other official rooms and spaces were decorated with wall paintings showing an investiture scene: Zimri-Lim receiving power from the goddess Ishtar in the presence of other deities [12.28]. A border around this scene suggests that textiles may have been hung on the walls. Other areas of the palace comprise shrines, administrative sections, and residences for the royal family and senior officials, as well as craft quarters, storerooms, and kitchens.

Within the palace, an archive of some 20,000 cuneiform texts has been recovered. Some 30 percent of these texts are letters, the remainder being economic, legal, and administrative documents. They are largely written in Akkadian, by this time the *lingua franca* of Southwest Asia, and they reveal a great deal about the role of Mari within the 18th-century BC world of politics, diplomacy, and conflict. It is clear that Mari participated keenly in the politics of the region. Zimri-Lim was married to a daughter of Yarim-Lim, king of **Yamhad**, a powerful kingdom centered on modern Aleppo. Zimri-Lim's predecessor, Yasmah-Adad, was married to a daughter of the king of **Qatna**, another powerful state of western Syria. There were also intimate connections with **Ebla**, and a range of interactions – political, economic, and cultural – with the major and minor states of Upper and Lower Mesopotamia and the Levant. The texts also tell of the important relations between the settled community at Mari and the pastoral nomads of the region – the Amorite tribes

Homer as History?

Schliemann was obsessed with proving the historicity of Homer's tales, and he set out to confirm his belief through excavation. His campaigns at many sites, including Mycenae and Tiryns in Greece, as well as Hissarlık, exposed the astonishing wealth of the Bronze Age societies of the eastern Mediterranean and provided a plausible context for Homer's story (Jansen 1995). No truly convincing historical evidence, however, has been found with which to verify or corroborate Homer's account of the ten-year siege of Troy.

Nevertheless, Schliemann and his successors did succeed in recovering and depicting a valid historical and cultural background, set in the Bronze Age, against which Homer's story could have been acted out. This background includes spectacular material wealth, represented by the gold treasures of Troy and the burials at Mycenae, for example, as well as evidence for fortification and conflict at many Bronze Age sites, including Hissarlık itself.

Excavating Troy

The excavations at Hissarlık by Schliemann and his successors established a sequence of nine successive cities (Troy I–IX) built one atop the other, spanning the years 3000 BC–AD 500. From small beginnings at the

12.25 *Gold sauceboat from Troy II. Many rich treasures were found within the buildings of level II at Troy, of the Early Bronze Age period, underlining the regional importance of the site at this early date.*

start of the Early Bronze Age, the city rapidly developed into an important regional power by c. 2500 BC. From Troy II came an immense wealth of treasure, found in 16 separate troves, comprising gold and silver jewelry, vessels, tools, and weapons.

The discovery of these treasures, dating to the later 3rd millennium BC, encouraged Schliemann to identify Troy II as the Homeric Troy, but it later became clear that these finds were 1000 years too early. In recent decades there has been considerable debate about the Troy II treasures (Traill 1995), with some evidence to suggest that Schliemann misleadingly augmented his finds with material he had collected from elsewhere. The fact that much of the treasure was illegally smuggled out of Turkey by Schliemann to Berlin (whence it was taken by

Soviet soldiers to Russia in 1945) has also clouded the issue. Despite these uncertainties, there is little doubt that Troy II was a wealthy and dominant regional center toward the end of the Early Bronze Age.

During the Middle and Late Bronze Ages, the city of Troy VI comprised a fortified citadel with major buildings inside; there was also an extensive lower town outside the citadel walls. The standard of defensive architecture was extremely high, and from within the citadel many examples of Mycenaean pottery have been recovered. Troy VI was totally destroyed c. 1250 BC, toward the end of the Late Bronze Age. All these factors suggest that Troy VI may indeed have been Homer's Troy.

KEY SITE Ebla

One of the most dramatic archaeological discoveries of recent times involves the lost city of Ebla, today the site of Tell Mardikh, near Aleppo in Syria (Matthiae 1980). In the 1960s and 1970s Italian archaeologists made the important discovery of a 3rd-millennium BC palace, Palace G, which had been burned down at some time between 2400 and 2350 BC, perhaps by Sargon of Akkad.

Within a suite of two rooms was found an archive of some 2100 clay tablets that had once been neatly stacked and filed on wooden shelves as a reference collection of working documents. With the burning of the shelves at the palace's destruction, the tablets had fallen onto the floor, but careful excavation and recording procedures enabled the reconstruction of precisely how the texts had been arranged on the original shelves.

Content of the Texts

The scribal practices revealed in this unique collection of texts show close links with Sumerian literate administration, and there is extensive use of the Sumerian language, as well as of a local Semitic language, called Eblaite by modern scholars. The texts deal principally with the economic organization of the city and its agricultural territory and produce. They concern the issue of rations to workers of various types, including court attendants, artisans, and manual laborers. Not surprisingly, given its location, the

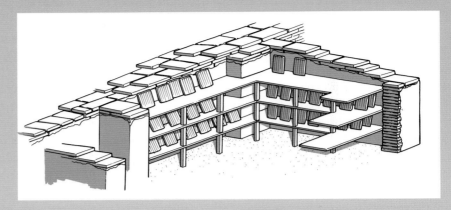

12.26 *Reconstruction of the mode of storage of clay tablets in the archive room of Palace G at Ebla. This was a working palace archive, where administrators could consult tablets for information relevant to a range of bureaucratic concerns; the tablets thus needed to be carefully classified and arranged, just as the books in a modern library, to facilitate consultation.*

archive indicates the important role played by the palace in the administration and economy of Ebla. Up to 20,000 people were involved in some capacity in palace activities, and the palace owned large tracts of land around Ebla, including entire villages. In the direct remit of the palace was control over animal husbandry, with herds of up to 67,000 sheep, and associated wool and textile processing and production. Textile workshops were organized at an intensive level, and employed large numbers of female personnel.

12.27 *Archive room of Palace G at Ebla, north Syria, c. 2400 BC. The clay tablets had originally been stored on wooden shelves; the texts give insights into the administration and economy of the city.*

Texts also reveal that Ebla participated in regional trade and commerce, particularly with the city of Mari and other towns of the Euphrates region, as well as engaging in political alliances and conflicts with neighboring states.

Ebla as a Regional Power

By 2400 BC Ebla covered an area of 56 ha (138 acres) and, with Mari on the Euphrates River, dominated the political scene of Upper Mesopotamia. The city's regional power base was the agricultural and grazing steppes of its large hinterland. Palace G and other buildings on the acropolis of Ebla, as well as the extent of the lower town, epitomize a local Upper Mesopotamian tradition of urban development and intensified rural settlement that accompanied, and certainly interacted with, the peak of Sumerian urban society on the Lower Mesopotamian plains at around 2600–2400 BC. Other sites in Upper Mesopotamia, such as Chuera, Beydar (also with cuneiform texts), and Leilan, further demonstrate the previously unsuspected sophistication of urban life in this region by the mid-3rd millennium BC (Dolce 1998).

Following its destruction, Ebla was rebuilt and continued as an important regional power in the early 2nd millennium BC, until another devastating destruction of about 1600 BC probably by the Hittite king Mursili I, destroyer also of Babylon.

12.28 Mari, the palace of Zimri-Lim: *wall-painting showing a scene of investiture. In the center the goddess Ishtar hands a rod and a ring toward the king; other elements include mythical animals, birds, and trees; c. 1775 BC.*

like those claimed as ancestors by the rulers themselves at Mari, Babylon, and elsewhere. These nomads might occasionally be conscripted into the army or employed for public projects such as irrigation works, as well as seasonally tending to animals belonging to city-dwellers.

For the Levant in the Middle Bronze Age, much of our information comes from the Mari archives, with frequent mention of the states of Yamhad and Qatna, as well as **Ugarit** and **Hazor**. The Middle Bronze Age in the Levant sees a reversal of the decline in urban settlement that took place at the end of the Early Bronze Age, with evidence for fortification of urban sites by 1800 BC (Ilan 1995). Many sites show evidence of large-scale temple-building, and the inhabitants of cities such as Ugarit, Megiddo, and Byblos thrived in the context of international trade and commerce conducted across Southwest Asia by the great cities and states of the time.

12.29 Statue, probably of a worshiper, from Mari: *the style and dress of the statue show strong Sumerian influence; the sculpture dates from c. 2500 BC.*

Upper Mesopotamia and Anatolia

During the Middle Bronze Age there is especially clear evidence for an episode of regional interaction in the form of the so-called Old Assyrian trade between the city of **Ashur** and the communities of Anatolia (Veenhof 1995). (The name "Assyrian" derives from Ashur.) Most of our knowledge about Old Assyrian trade with Anatolia comes from the site of **Kültepe**, ancient **Kanesh**, which lies north of the Taurus Mountains in the Cappadocia region of central Turkey, 1200 km (744 miles) northwest of Ashur. There are suggestions that there was already trade between this city and Upper, and perhaps also Lower, Mesopotamia, in the later 3rd millennium BC.

Kültepe has been excavated since the 1920s and is still being investigated. The main settlement, situated on top of a large mound, includes a massive palace belonging to the local Anatolian ruler of the city. Excavations have recovered some 15,000 clay tablets written in Old Assyrian in cuneiform script from a group of private houses located off the main settlement to one side. The texts from Kültepe show a flourishing trade organized by merchants from Ashur living long-term at Kanesh as part of a network of trade centers located throughout Anatolia. Each center was called a *karum*, from the Babylonian word for "quay," where trade was conducted. The network stretched across Anatolia, the northern Levant, and up to the shores of the Black Sea. Trade was by donkey caravan, each caravan taking 5–6 weeks to travel between Ashur and Kanesh. Donkeys carried finished textiles and tin from Ashur to Kanesh, and returned with silver and gold. The traded textiles were high-quality products – carpets and garments – produced in Assyria and Babylonia. The tin came from an unknown source, but was probably from Afghanistan via Ashur. The texts provide great detail on the conduct of this trade and the associated affairs of the traders.

In a violent end to the Old Assyrian trade, Kanesh was destroyed *c.* 1760 BC, probably due to conflict between local kingdoms. Other Old Assyrian trade sites were also destroyed at this time, as demonstrated by the burning of the two great Middle Bronze Age palaces of **Acemhöyük**, west of Kültepe.

Empires and States at War and Peace: The Late Bronze Age

During the Late Bronze Age a mélange of states, kingdoms, and empires existed throughout Southwest Asia, each based on the agricultural, technological, and commercial foundations established in earlier centuries [12.30]. In this section we examine the major states in turn, following a geographical sequence that commences in the north, in Anatolia, proceeds through the Levant, Mesopotamia, and Iran, before concluding with an overview of the collapse of Late Bronze Age societies *c.* 1200 BC.

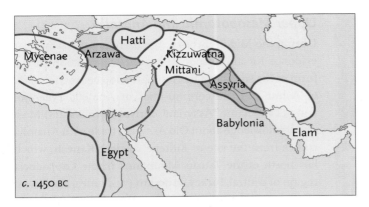

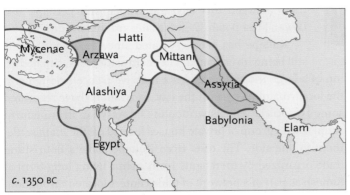

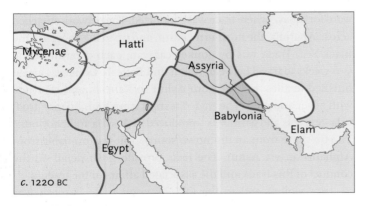

12.30 *Changing states in the Late Bronze Age:* *maps showing the fluctuating extents and interactions of the great powers of the Late Bronze Age – an "International Age." Hatti is the Hittite state.*

Our sources for the Hittites of the Late Bronze Age comprise both written documents and archaeological evidence (Bryce 1998). Research is ongoing at several major Hittite sites in Turkey, including Hattusa, so the picture is constantly developing. The fullest sources for Hittite history are the archives from Hattusa, mainly from the late period; most of these texts come from temples and the royal citadel. Further texts and archives have more recently been recovered from sites such as **Inandık**, **Maşat**, a frontier town in the east, **Ortaköy** (ancient Shapinuwa), a major site just east of Hattusa, and **Kuşaklı**, also to the east. Excavations at all these sites, and others, are steadily improving the breadth of our knowledge of the Hittite state (Yener 2002).

Hittite texts were written in seven different languages, including three Indo-European ones (Hittite, Luwian, and Palaic); other languages used by the Hittites, at least for writing, were Hattian, Hurrian, Akkadian, and Sumerian. This breadth of language use vividly underscores the cosmopolitan nature of the Hittite empire, and its role as a major international player through the Late Bronze Age. Texts were written on clay tablets using the cuneiform script, a Mesopotamian tradition, and in so-called Hittite hieroglyphs (not related to Egyptian hieroglyphs), which were reserved for high-status seals and rock-cut inscriptions.

The Hittites are the earliest Indo-European-speaking peoples securely attested anywhere. Hittite names occur in documents of the Middle Bronze Age, *c.* 1800 BC, from the site of Kültepe (Kanesh) in central Anatolia (see above). The proto-Hittites may have entered Anatolia in the Early Bronze Age, around 2300 BC, when there is material evidence for incursions of new peoples, but their origins are essentially obscure. According to their own account, the Hittites expanded from their original city of Kussara (modern location unknown) to control most of central Anatolia by about 1700 BC. By 1680 BC they had moved to a new capital, Hattusa.

The founder of this dynasty was called Labarna, whose name came to mean Great King, just as the personal name "Caesar" came to be used as a term of office by Roman emperors. Hattusili I (17th century BC) was the first Hittite king to campaign in northern Syria, including at **Yamhad (Aleppo)** and **Alalakh**; this expansion indicates the importance of access to the sea and control over trade routes for the Hittites, Hattusa itself being a long distance from the coast. Hattusili's successor, Mursili I raided far to the southeast, even sacking **Babylon** in 1595 BC, but after his death a period of strife inside the royal family led to a massive decrease in the size of the empire. This

Anatolia and the Hittites

Until the 19th century, the Hittites were a people lost to history, apart from occasional mentions in the Bible, where they were associated with the Levant, with no indication of their Anatolian roots. From the later 19th century onward, finds of carved stone blocks started to occur in Turkey, covered in a previously unknown hieroglyphic script. Excavations then began in 1906 at **Boğazköy**, *c.* 160 km (100 miles) east of Ankara in central Anatolia. Most of our knowledge of Hittite history comes from the thousands of clay tablets found at the site, which turned out to be ancient **Hattusa**, the capital city of the Hittites [see box: Hattusa, Captial of the Hittites]. It was once thought that specialization in the production and use of iron tools was a factor in the Hittites' success, but it is now clear that they were above all a Bronze Age society, with minimal use of iron.

KEY SITE Hattusa, Capital of the Hittites

Hattusa, by the modern village of Boğazköy in north-central Anatolia, was the capital city of the Hittite empire for almost its entire duration. Situated in a vulnerable location close to the northern mountains, where the enemy Kashka tribes lived, Hattusa persisted as a capital because it was regarded by the Hittites as the home of their gods, an attribute epitomized in the appellation "City of a Thousand Gods" (Bittel 1970; Seeher 1995).

Rise and Fall

During the Middle Bronze Age (2000–1650 BC), a trading post of Assyrian merchants operated at Hattusa, part of the network of trade and exchange in which Kültepe (Kanesh) played the dominant role within Anatolia. By 1650 BC Hattusa had become the main focus of the nascent Hittite state, which it was to remain until its final destruction around 1185 BC, at the end of the Late Bronze Age.

Excavations at Hattusa were begun by German archaeologists in 1906, and to this day continue to provide vital information on the city, both in terms of buildings and material culture, and also in the form of some 25,000 clay tablets in cuneiform script, an immense repository of information concerning cult, law, and royal correspondence.

Architecture of the City

The status of Hattusa as royal residence and imperial capital strongly affected the structure and architectural layout of the city. Situated across some 600 ha (1482 acres) of steppe, rock outcrops, and deep gorges, the city makes dramatic play of the contrast between nature and culture. In the Old Hittite period (1650–1400 BC), the focus of the city was the large citadel, where the king resided. Below lay the main temple and storage area, all enclosed by massive fortifications. In the Hittite empire period (1400–1185 BC), a dramatic expansion of the city occurred, reflecting the increased importance of the Hittites in the international arena.

An explosion of building took place at Hattusa in the empire period, which included

construction of the Great Temple in the Lower City, and a series of smaller temples and other structures in the Upper City, contained within a new defensive wall 3.3 km (2 miles) long. The royal citadel was expanded and rebuilt. At the same time, water reservoirs and massive silos for grain storage were constructed within the city, perhaps evidence of a concern to survive difficult times, whether induced by variable climate or by hostile action. So far, very few ordinary domestic quarters have been located or excavated at Hattusa, for much of the interior of the city is given over to temples and royal facilities.

The Rock Sanctuary of Yazılıkaya

The nearby rock sanctuary of Yazılıkaya was also completed in the 13th century BC. Here on vertical rock faces are carved images of Hittite deities in procession, culminating in a scene of the weather god, Teshub, and the sun goddess, Hebat. Hurrian influence on Hittite religion is evident in the fact that all of the major gods depicted here are Hurrian;

12.32 *Hattusa: a relief from the shrine at Yazılıkaya. Here the Hittite king Tudhaliya IV, late 13th century BC, is being led by the larger figure of the god Sharruma, perhaps as an escort for the king into the underworld after his death.*

12.31 *Hattusa: the King's Gate, 13th century BC. Although called the King's Gate, it is now believed that the relief figure depicts a deity, as indicated by his horned helmet, perhaps Sharruma, son of the weather-god Teshub.*

indeed, some Hittite kings had Hurrian names. Depictions of the Hittite king Tudhaliya IV suggest that the shrine may have been created as a memorial to him by his son Shuppiluliuma II in the 13th century BC. Slots in the wall of one of the rock chambers may have received the ashes of cremated kings, but no evidence survives, and no burials of Hittite royalty have ever been located.

Destruction

Hattusa was totally destroyed in the maelstrom of collapse that terminated the Late Bronze Age. Early Iron Age squatters made their homes in the burnt-out ruins, and in later centuries a major Phrygian Iron Age fortress was constructed on top of the Hittite citadel.

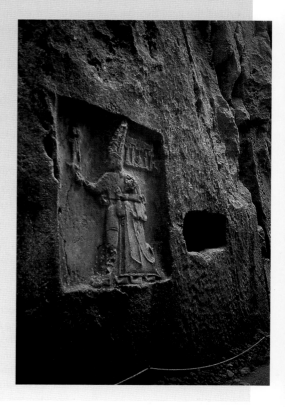

tendency to alternate between dramatic expansion and sudden contraction is a key characteristic of the Hittite state.

From 1420 BC a new line of kings came to the throne, headed by Tudhaliya I. These rulers had Hurrian connections and were keen on cultivating relations with Syria, where significant Hurrian populations were situated. The recent discovery that the site of Ortaköy is the heavily Hurrian-influenced city of Shapinuwa, however, demonstrates that Hurrian connections could be found quite close to home, in central Anatolia.

From 1345 BC Shuppiluliuma I conquered much of northern Syria, in particular the kingdom of the Mittani (see below). Kings of Aleppo, Carchemish, Ugarit, and other states all signed treaties with Shuppiluliuma I, a contemporary of the pharaoh Akhenaten in Egypt (see Chapter 10), with whom the Hittites dealt as equals at this time. There was considerable tension between these two great powers, largely due to rivalry over control of Syria and the Levant, and their prosperous trade routes. The culmination of this conflict came with the **battle of Qadesh** in the early 13th century BC when, contrary to Egyptian accounts of the campaign, it seems that the Hittites established control over much of the northern Levant and western Syria [**12.33**]. This conflict ended when the daughter of Hattusili III married the pharaoh Ramesses II in 1283 BC. During this period, the Hittite empire was at its most powerful, as is amply manifest in construction programs at Hattusa.

The Hittite empire collapsed around 1200–1185 BC, at the end of the Late Bronze Age, when all the Hittite sites of Anatolia show evidence of destruction and abandonment. The precise causes of the collapse are not clear, but it is certain that they formed part of a much broader picture of disruption and abandonment across much of Southwest Asia, as we shall see. Thereafter the Hittites disappeared from central Anatolia as a coherent cultural entity, but they survived in minor Iron Age kingdoms in southeast Turkey and northern Syria; these are the peoples referred to as Hittites in the Bible.

12.33 The battle of Qadesh: clay tablet bearing the Hittite version of a peace treaty with Egypt, agreed shortly after the battle of Qadesh, early 13th century BC. A copy of this text is today displayed at the headquarters of the United Nations in New York.

The Levant in the Late Bronze Age

The end of the Middle Bronze Age in the Levant is characterized by widespread destruction, of unknown cause, followed by reconstruction and reoccupation, but of a changed nature. The start of the Late Bronze Age coincides with major events in adjacent regions, including the expulsion from Egypt of the foreign Hyksos rulers and the fall of Babylon to the Hittites in 1595 BC (Bunimovitz 1995). The settlement distribution of the Levant in the Late Bronze Age is less hierarchical than that found in the Middle Bronze Age, suggesting a scattering of autonomous small cities rather than a series of major organized polities dominating the region. These cities contained well-appointed palaces and temples, and their elite were buried in tombs with rich grave goods, including pottery from Cyprus and the Mycenaean world to the west.

A major feature of this region in the Late Bronze Age, especially of **Canaan** (the southern Levant), was the relationship between the Canaanite states and their powerful neighbor to the south, Egypt. The domination of Egypt was pervasive enough to convert previously independent city-states into vassals, and the imperial demands of tax and tribute may have been so burdensome as to allow only the most resilient states to survive. In this light, the evidence for wealthy tombs, palaces, and temples at selected small city-states of Canaan indicates the ability of those states to thrive within a highly asymmetric relationship dominated by Egypt.

Much light is shed on the politics and diplomacy of the relationships between Egypt and the states of Canaan by the famous Amarna Letters of the 14th century BC [**12.34**], found at the pharaoh Akhenaten's capital city at modern Tell el-Amarna (Liverani 1990). These letters, in the form of clay tablets in cuneiform script, reveal that there were some 15–17 important city-states in Canaan, including known sites such as **Megiddo** [**12.35**], **Gezer**, **Lachish**, and **Hazor**. Each of these states controlled a territory of no more than 1000 square km (386 square miles), with a distance of some 35 km (22 miles) between nearest neighbors. Problems with labor supply appear to have exacerbated the settlement position in Canaan through the Late Bronze Age. Egyptian demands for labor in order to construct massive public works and to man the army had a serious effect on Canaan, driving urban and rural populations into the escape of pastoral nomadism and reducing the significance of urban settled communities.

Ugarit In the northern Levant, the site of Ugarit (modern Ras Shamra), situated on the Mediterranean coast of Syria at a point where routes of communication and trade converge, is of particular importance (van Soldt 1995). Overland routes up and down the Euphrates to the east readily reach the coast at Ugarit, whence sea routes to points west and south are open. Thus the

12.34 The Amarna Letters: *a text from the Amarna archive, a collection of tablets found at Tell el-Amarna in Egypt, mid-14th century* BC. *These texts, largely written in Akkadian, the* lingua franca *of the time, shed much light on interactions between Egypt and the city-states of the Levant, as well as on broader international relationships with states such as the Hittites, Mittani, Babylonia, and Assyria.*

history of Ugarit has to be viewed in the broad context of great power politics. The city thrived during the 14th century BC, when its eastern neighbor, the state of Mittani, was in decline, and while the Hittite empire was at its peak, particularly during the reign of Shuppiluliuma I.

For part of this time Ugarit fell under the direct control of the Hittite empire, and for all its existence Ugarit was intimately connected with political and economic features of that empire. Large quantities of grain, for example, were shipped through Ugarit to the ports of Anatolia and on to the Hittite heartland.

Excavations at Ugarit have uncovered a splendid palace, over 1 ha (2.5 acres) in area, which was famous even in antiquity [**12.36**]. Many clay tablets, written principally in Akkadian cuneiform, have been found there, as well as archives in other buildings. The city contained elite two-storied houses, and there was an acropolis with two temples, dedicated to the gods Baal and Dagan. A summer residence for Ugarit royalty was located some 5 km (3.1 miles) away at Ras Ibn Hani, where two palaces have been found, one belonging to a queen of Ugarit.

Ugarit specialized in trade, in particular in the export of olive oil, wine, and salt, as well as more specialized commodities such as bales of cloth, and purple linen and wool garments, the purple dye derived from the processing of locally available murex shells. Large amounts of gold and silver passed through the city, usually in the form of high-quality finished artifacts. Ivory carving and inlay are frequent finds, as is evidence for the use and export of locally available woods such as juniper, boxwood, and pine.

It was not only citizens of Ugarit who engaged in trade, but also foreigners who resided at the city, including people from Ura in Cilicia, and from Cyprus. It is probable that Minoan and

12.35 Aerial view of Megiddo: *this is one of a series of heavily fortified 2nd-millennium* BC *sites of the Levant, indicating the unsettled atmosphere of the period.*

Mycenaean merchants (see Chapter 13) also lived there, as revealed by their ceramics. Ugarit was thus a critical meeting place for peoples, commodities, and ideas from all over the eastern Mediterranean and beyond [see box: The Uluburun Shipwreck]. This cosmopolitan aspect of Ugarit shows itself clearly in the written texts found there. As noted above, they are written most commonly in Akkadian, the international language of the time, but also feature Hittite, Hurrian, and Egyptian hieroglyphic, as well as occasional Cypro-Minoan script. Most significantly, there is some use of a local cuneiform alphabetic script, the earliest known alphabetic script, employed for the indigenous West Semitic language of the region.

Ugarit was unavoidably involved in conflicts between the minor and major states of the region, and at one point called in help from the Hittites, who made Ugarit their protectorate. An Akkadian version of the late 14th-century BC treaty confirming this relationship was found at Ugarit, revealing that the city had to pay enormous tribute to the Hittites in return for protection from its neighbors. Texts from the late 13th century BC indicate a weakening of Hittite control over Ugarit and the region at this time. Ugarit was suffering badly from pirate raids and from the obligation to provide the Hittites with sorely needed ships and fighting men; one group of peoples mentioned in the text is the Shikala, who may have been one of the so-called Sea Peoples (see below). Ugarit was totally destroyed at the close of the Late Bronze Age, around 1185 BC.

Upper Mesopotamia and Syria: Hurrian Mittani

By the later 3rd and early 2nd millennia BC, a series of Hurrian states existed across Upper Mesopotamia, northwest Iran, and southeast Anatolia. Excavations at **Tell Mozan** (ancient **Urkesh**) in northern Syria, have been especially informative on one such kingdom (Buccellati and Kelly-Buccellati 1997). Hurrian names occur in texts from Mari of the 18th century BC, and the presence of Hurrian names of people and deities at Ortaköy in central Anatolia indicates the extent to which Hurrian influences had spread to the north.

For about 200 years up to 1340 BC, Upper Mesopotamia was dominated by the kingdom of **Mittani**, a state whose history, like that of Ugarit, is inseparable from that of the Hittites. Mittani's language was Hurrian, as was at least a part of its ethnic identity (Wilhelm 1995). Its capital city was **Washukanni**, the location of which has not been identified beyond doubt, though the heartland of the Mittani state was always the headwaters of the Khabur River, today northeast Syria.

Most of our information about Mittani comes from the 15th and 14th centuries BC, when we are able to correlate kings of Mittani with their contemporaries in Egypt and the Hittite empire. Mittani features as an important state in the 14th-century BC Amarna letters from Egypt, which include letters in both Hurrian and Akkadian languages from Tushratta, king of Mittani, to the pharaoh in Egypt. Hurrian was written in cuneiform script on clay tablets, but is unrelated to contemporary Semitic or Indo-European languages. Hittite-Hurrian bilingual texts found at Hattusa and Ugarit have helped scholars to decipher Hurrian to some extent, but much remains unclear.

The Mittani state and Hurrian material culture become clearest in the period 1500–1200 BC, especially as revealed in excavations at **Nuzi** in northeast Iraq, at **Alalakh** in the Hatay region of southeast Turkey, and at **Tell Brak** in northeast Syria. Texts from Nuzi date to 1500–1350 BC, when the city was part of the principality of Arrapha, itself part of the Mittani state. The special location of Nuzi, between the Hurrian and Babylonian worlds, is reflected in the use of Hurrian for personal names, in concert with Akkadian and Babylonian linguistic and religious

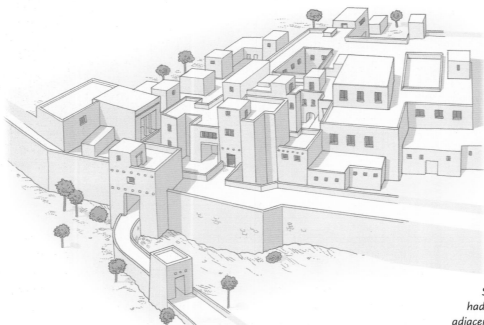

12.36 Reconstruction of the royal palace at Ugarit: *the site of Ugarit, modern Ras Shamra, on the Mediterranean coast of Syria, had a complex agglomerated plan of courts and adjacent buildings.*

KEY SITE The Uluburun Shipwreck

When it sank off the southwest coast of Turkey in the 14th century BC, the ship now called the Uluburun shipwreck was following a conventional course around the eastern Mediterranean, counter-clockwise from the Levant past southern Anatolia to the Aegean, and then south to the North African coast and Egypt.

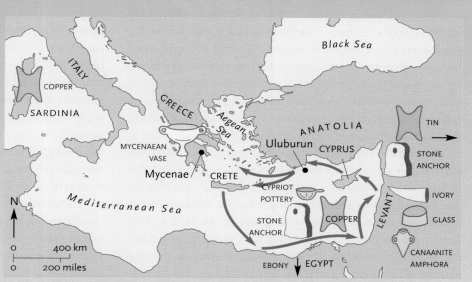

Ship's Cargo

The ship carried an immense wealth of cargo, the single biggest component being 350 ingots of copper from Cyprus, weighing 10 tons; there was also 1 ton of tin ingots. This massive amount of copper, when mixed with the tin in about the proportions represented in the wreck, would have produced enough bronze to make huge quantities of weapons, tools, and other objects. Other cargo items include 100 ingots of cobalt-blue and turquoise glass, a ton of terebinthine resin in amphoras (for use as a cosmetic or perfume component), ebony logs from Egypt, elephant tusks, hippopotamus teeth, ostrich and tortoise shells, and a host of fruits and spices.

Trading Contacts

Artifacts and cargo items from the ship, itself only 15 m (49 ft) long, vividly demonstrate the cosmopolitan flavor of Late Bronze Age trade and interaction. Pottery vessels on the ship originated from the Aegean, Cyprus, and the Levant. A gold scarab of Queen Nefertiti, wife of pharaoh Akhenaten of Egypt, appears to have been part of a jeweler's hoard of scrap items. Weapons range in type from Mycenaean to Levantine, while cylinder seals are in Kassite, Mycenaean, Syrian, and Egyptian styles. A hinged writing board, designed to hold wax upon which an inscription could be made with a stylus,

indicates that writing may have been an integral part of trade organization; unfortunately, none of the wax survived to tell us which language or languages were spoken, nor what was written. Nevertheless, the Uluburun shipwreck speaks volumes about trade and regional contacts of the Late Bronze Age eastern Mediterranean. While some of the cargo may have been destined for a single major end-user, it is likely that most was for sale or exchange at any point on the ship's journey; the vessel probably spent its life regularly putting into ports along its route in order to exchange items for locale-specific commodities at each stop.

12.37 *(Above) Map to show the location of the Uluburun shipwreck and the source of the traded items it carried, as well as the circulation of sea-borne trade in the east Mediterranean, partly dictated by the prevailing winds.*

12.38 *Underwater archaeologists working on cleaning and recording some of the copper oxhide-shaped ingots found in the Uluburun shipwreck, southwest Turkey.*

The discovery and total excavation of the Uluburun wreck has uniquely illuminated the intensity and richness of regional trade during the Late Bronze Age in the eastern Mediterranean (Bass 1995; Pulak 1998).

traditions. Alalakh also maintained a local identity within the Hurrian context. Archives from this site show that the city was subject to the Mittani kingdom but ruled by a local dynasty; one of its kings was Idrimi [**12.39**], whose statue of *c.* 1500 BC is adorned with a long inscription detailing the vagaries of contemporary regional politics. This text reveals that Mittani at that time controlled **Yamhad** (modern Aleppo) and **Emar**, as well as Alalakh. Excavations at Tell Brak have exposed a Mittani palace, and across Upper Mesopotamia distinctive styles of pottery and cylinder seals can be related to the Mittani presence (Stein 1997).

Ugarit came under the control of Mittani for a brief period, and at one point even the great city of **Ashur** on the Tigris fell within Mittani dominance. Thus, at its peak, under King Saush-tatar at around 1430 BC, the Mittani state dominated the region from Nuzi and Ashur in the east to Ugarit and Alalakh in the west, with sporadic control northwards into parts of Anatolia. Another key city of the period is **Qatna**, where a strong Hurrian element is clear in the 15th century BC, although the city seems not to have been under the direct control of Mittani. Ongoing excavations of a Middle and Late Bronze Age palace at Qatna are considerably enhancing the picture of elite life and death at this city (Morandi Bonacossi 2003).

The rulers of Egypt were not slow to appreciate the possible benefits of dealing with a power in Upper Mesopotamia that might be brought into play against their old rivals, the Hittites. The Amarna Letters delineate a long history of interaction, culminating in the marriage of a daughter of the Mittani king Tushratta to the pharaoh Amenhotep III. Egypt's main concern was to secure access to the rich territories and commercial interests of the Levant and Syria, while denying the same to the Hittites.

By 1340 BC Mittani was in severe decline, defeated by the Hittites and pressured by the rising might of Assyria from the south, a status clearly demonstrated in a text of that time, the Shattiwaza treaty. This treaty was imposed by the Hittite king Shuppiluliuma I after he had defeated Mittani in battle. The text, which survives as an Akkadian copy from Hattusa, relates the installation of Shattiwaza as a puppet ruler on the throne of Mittani, now subject to the Hittite ruler of Carchemish, himself a son of Shuppiluliuma I.

12.39 Statue of Idrimi, king of Alalakh: *the statue bears a long inscription relating the complex biography of Idrimi, king of Alalakh in northwest Syria, c. 1475 BC – a rare insight into the vicissitudes of royal life in ancient Southwest Asia.*

The Rise of Assyria

We have already mentioned the ascendant power of Assyria [**12.40**], and it is now time to look more closely at what was happening in the Tigris region of Upper Mesopotamia during the Late Bronze Age. We saw how the city of Ashur engaged in highly productive trade with the highland communities of Anatolia in the Middle Bronze Age, a trading network that collapsed around 1760 BC. From then until we reach the late 14th century BC, we have very little information about Ashur. For part of this period, as we have seen, Ashur belonged to the state of Mittani, but once Mittani collapsed c. 1340 BC, Ashur rose to increasing dominance, soon establishing relations with the other great powers of the day, including Babylon, the Hittites, and Egypt.

The sources for Assyria increase greatly during the 13th and 12th centuries BC, the so-called Middle Assyrian period (Saggs 1984). Most information comes from **Ashur** itself, where excavations have been conducted over the past century. The site lies on a limestone outcrop by a fork in the Tigris River, which protects the city on two sides. Excavated monuments include the city walls and moat, a quayside, ziggurats, temples, palaces, and some private houses. There are also increasing finds of material and texts of Middle Assyrian date from sites in Syria and Iraq outside the capital region, including **Kar-Tukulti-Ninurta**, **Sabi Abyad**, and **Tell Sheikh Hamad**. An initial aim of the Middle Assyrian kings was to consolidate their hold of the core territory around Ashur, including Nineveh, Nimrud, and Erbil. This core area constituted the rich agricultural heartland of the Assyrian state throughout its duration.

The Babylonians (see below) were naturally concerned by the rise of Assyria, as shown by a letter from the Babylonian king Burnaburiash II to the Egyptian pharaoh Akhenaten, stating that Assyrian envoys to Egypt should be expelled and claiming that they were vassals of Babylon. But by the time of the death of the Assyrian king Ashuruballit in c. 1330 BC, Assyria is treated as more or less an equal by the Hittites, Babylonia, and Egypt. Adad-nirari I (1307–1275 BC) succeeded in pushing back the Babylonian frontier to the Diyala River, as well as defeating the remnants of the Mittani state, thus extending Assyrian territory to the Euphrates at Carchemish. Assyria now became a neighbor of the Hittites, who were weak at this time and unable to react to Assyria's growing power. Shalmaneser I (1274–1245 BC) carried out administrative reforms in conquered territories, installing governors who lived in fortified residences, as excavated at Sabi Abyad and at Tell Sheikh Hamad, both in Syria. Local populations were expelled and Assyrian colonists brought in to farm the land. These dual policies of colonization and deportation were intended to result in an Assyrianization of the land.

Under Tukulti-Ninurta I (1244–1208 BC), Assyria fought in the mountains to the north and east, attempting to control com-

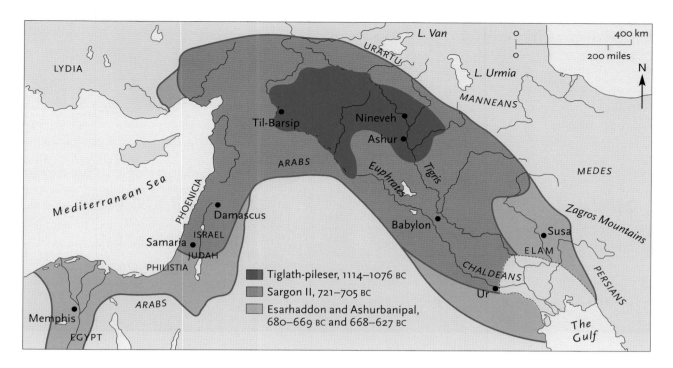

12.40 *The rise of Assyria:* map to show the phases of expansion of the Assyrian empire through the centuries of the Iron Age. At its peak in the 7th century BC, the Assyrian empire dominated Southwest Asia.

munication routes and ultimate access to resources such as copper, tin, horses, and lapis lazuli. Here, Assyria was competing with Babylonia and Elam for control of trade routes, and Tukulti-Ninurta fought a major campaign against Babylonia, bringing its king to Ashur in chains; puppet kings then ruled Babylonia for about 30 years. Following the assassination of Tukulti-Ninurta I by one of his sons, the rivalry of succession led to an unstable time for Assyria, during which Babylonia re-established its independence and Assyria fell into decline for a century.

With the accession of Tiglath-pileser I (1114–1076 BC), a marked revival of Assyrian fortunes took place, as told in the texts known as the Assyrian Annals. A serious problem at this time was the incursion of Aramaean raiders from the west, representing the next wave of pastoral nomads in succession to the Amorites almost a millennium earlier. By the time of Ashur-nasirpal I (1049–1031 BC), all of Upper Mesopotamia was lost to the Aramaeans, and Assyria was reduced to a small core territory around Ashur, Nineveh, and Erbil. For about a century from 1050 BC, the written sources in Assyria and Babylonia stop altogether.

Lower Mesopotamia: Kassite Babylonia

Babylon fell to the Hittites in 1595 BC, an event that brought to an end the Amorite dynasty there. In due course a new people rose in Babylonia, the Kassites, who are recorded in texts from the 18th century BC, usually as soldiers in the Babylonian army or as agricultural workers. It is not known where the Kassites came from, and their language is not related to any other known tongue (Sommerfeld 1995). Akkadian and Sumerian was used in their inscriptions, so there is little direct evidence for the Kassite language. The Kassite king called himself "king of Babylonia," that is, king of a country rather than a city-state, the first time that this concept of Babylonia appears. The Kassites' ceremonial capital was Babylon, home of their highest deity, Marduk.

Under Kassite rule (1530–1155 BC), Babylonia seems to have been unusually stable. For much of the period, however, the sources are sparse. Major Kassite archives come from Nippur and Ur, but in general this period has not received as detailed study as other periods of the Mesopotamian past. One of the fullest sources for the Kassites is, once more, the Egyptian Amarna Letters of the 14th century BC (Moran 1992). Earlier, after the army of the pharaoh Thutmose III had crossed the Euphrates River in 1447 BC, the Kassites sent emissaries to Egypt and established formal diplomatic contacts. By the 14th century BC there was a regular exchange of letters and emissaries between Egypt and Babylonia, and the pharaoh addressed the Babylonian king as "brother." According to the convention of the time, a daughter of Kurigalzu of Babylon was married to Amenhotep III (also married to a daughter of the Mittani king Tushratta, as noted above). Kurigalzu also distinguished himself by founding a new city, **Dur Kurigalzu**, just west of modern Baghdad. Excavations here have explored the large ziggurat [**12.41**] and exposed four grand palaces, one with painted walls and a mosaic of colored glass.

461

12.41 *The ziggurat of Dur Kurigalzu:* the lower stage has been *reconstructed in modern times; the upper courses of brick show the effects of centuries of erosion by wind, rain, and sun. It is located at 'Aqur Quf, near Baghdad, Iraq, and dates to the 14th century* BC.

Under the Kassites, major programs of building and rebuilding were undertaken at many towns across Babylonia, and there was a thriving trade and exchange with settlements established on the island of Bahrain in the Persian Gulf. Control over the trade in lapis lazuli, coming into Babylonia from the east, appears to have been especially important to the Kassites; they frequently presented lapis lazuli as a gift to the Egyptian pharaoh, receiving in return large amounts of gold.

By the late Kassite period, conflicts with Assyria and with Elam to the east were increasingly common and destructive. Like Assyria, Babylonia was badly affected by Aramaean raids, with all its major cities being sacked. As so often at a demise, the end of the Kassite period is shrouded in obscurity, and the period from 1100 to 900 BC in Babylonia is totally unclear.

Elam

Directly to the east of Lower Mesopotamia in the region of southwest Iran, the state of Elam experienced its height during the Late Bronze Age (Curtis 1989; Potts 1999). The Elamite language was used for inscriptions in the cuneiform script, but much of our information comes from Mesopotamian sources. Major Elamite sites of this period include **Haft Tepe**, only 10 km (6.2 miles) from the capital city of **Susa**. The principal structure at Haft Tepe is the tomb complex of King Tepti-ahar (1365–1330 BC), comprising a series of baked brick chambers containing many human skeletons, probably the remains of attendant individuals killed and buried upon the death of the king. Close to the tomb complex is a group of rooms with evidence of craft activity in clay, ivory, pottery, and mosaic, plus many cuneiform tablets. These remains are likely to represent the workshop quarters of a large temple associated with the royal tomb.

King Untash-Napirisha (1275–1240 BC) pursued an energetic program of temple-building throughout Elam, including 11 temples at Susa. Elamite expertise in metalworking, a long Iranian tradition, is best represented in the extraordinary cast bronze statue of Napir-Asu, wife of Untash-Napirisha, weighing an astonishing 1750 kg (3863 lb) [**12.42**]. Untash-Napirisha's major achievement was the foundation of a new city, named (for himself) Al Untash-Napirisha, today called **Chogha Zanbil**. No fewer than 6000 brick inscriptions declare his foundation of the city,

12.42 *Statue of Napir-Asu:* bronze statue *of the wife of king Untash-Napirisha, dating to c. 1250* BC, *found at Susa. It weighs 1750 kg (3863 lb) and is 129 cm (51 in) tall.*

major elements of which included a massive ziggurat, built of millions of bricks and thought to have been originally 50 m (163 ft) in height. Located around the ziggurat were numerous temples, at least four palaces, and a perimeter wall more than 4 km (2.5 miles) long. The city appears to have been abandoned at the death of Untash-Napirisha in 1240 BC.

A subsequent Elamite king, Shutruk-Nahhunte (1185–1155 BC), laid claim to the throne of Babylonia through his mother's line, as she was a Kassite queen. Shutruk-Nahhunte invaded Babylonia in 1158 BC and returned victorious to Susa, taking with him vast quantities of Babylonian booty, including such famous monuments as the stela of Naram-Sin (over 1000 years old by that time) and probably the law code stela of Hammurabi [see figs. **12.20** and **12.21**]. The final insult to Babylonian culture came with the Elamite capture of the statue of Marduk, patron deity of Babylon, and the plundering of the holiest shrine of Lower Mesopotamia, the temple of Enlil at Nippur. Revenge came later with the campaign into Elam of the Babylonian king Nebuchadnezzar I (1125–1104 BC), in which the statue of Marduk was retrieved from Susa and returned to Babylon. Following this total defeat, the Elamite state plunged into some 300 years of obscurity.

The End of the Late Bronze Age

A dramatic episode of destruction appears to have affected much of Southwest Asia to some degree in the period around 1200 BC, with collapse in the Levant, Anatolia, and, from the 11th century BC, across much of Upper and Lower Mesopotamia (Liverani 1987). The west saw the decline of Mycenaean societies in Greece and the Aegean, as well as destruction on Cyprus at around the same time. Similarly, Egyptian control of Canaan ceased at about 1150 BC. All these events were followed by a dark age lasting up to 300 years.

There is significant evidence for the mass movement of peoples at this time, including those known as Israelites, Aramaeans, Phrygians, and the "Sea Peoples" (Stager 1995). It may be that many of these peoples were displaced by poor harvests and economic decline. Overtaxing of rural communities by top-heavy empires may have been a factor in bringing collapse to the countryside. In time, however, the new arrivals were to build their own cities and states upon the ruins of the great Late Bronze Age societies of Southwest Asia.

New and Resurgent Powers of the Iron Age

In the centuries following the great collapse at the end of the Late Bronze Age, the lands of Southwest Asia hosted several major powers through the Iron Age. Some of these states, such as the **Neo-Hittites** and the **Assyrians**, took their inspiration from what had gone before, while others, such as **Urartu** and **Phrygia**, blossomed from influences and historical factors unique to the Iron Age. The use of iron for tools and weapons was still scarce until about 900 BC, when the technology of mixing iron and carbon to make steel was widely adopted. In this section we examine a selection of the most significant states of the 1st millennium BC, ranging from the Levant through Assyria and Anatolia to Babylonia.

The Levant: Philistines, Phoenicians, Neo-Hittites

We have already seen how the great states of the Late Bronze Age, including Egypt, the Hittites, and Mittani, as well as Mycenaean Greece (see chapters 10 and 13), competed for control and influence over the vital trading region of the Levant. In this atmosphere there was scope for quasi-independent states to flourish, such as **Ugarit**, **Lachish**, and **Hazor**. The Early Iron Age (c. 1200–700 BC) was a critical period for new peoples and powers, but by the later centuries of the Iron Age the region was dominated once more by external forces, especially the great empires of the east, Assyria and Babylonia.

The Philistines Among the so-called Sea Peoples active c. 1200 BC were the Philistines, who settled on the south coastal plain of the Levant (modern Israel and Palestine) in the Early Iron Age (Dothan 1995). It seems probable that the Philistines originated from the Aegean world, as Mycenaean-style pottery is found in the earliest Iron Age levels of sites such as **Ashdod** and **Tell Miqne** (Ekron) [**12.43**], but is locally made there. The distribution of Philistine pottery reflects the extent of their settlement, abundant along the coastal plain from **Tell Qasile** in the north to **Tell el-Far'ah South** in the south.

12.43 A group of Philistine pottery: *early types of this pottery show strong connections with Mycenaean pottery, suggesting a probable origin for the Philistines in the Aegean world.*

The Old Testament mentions the Pentapolis, or five cities, of the Philistines – **Gaza**, **Ashkelon**, **Ashdod**, **Gath**, and **Ekron**, all of which are archaeologically known. Excavations at Ashkelon (Stager 1993), Ashdod (Dothan 1967), and Ekron (Dothan and Gitin 1993) have revealed the massive extent of Philistine settlement overlying ruined Late Bronze Age towns. The scale of construction in the Early Iron Age suggests incursions of large groups of people familiar with urban structure and architecture on a grand scale. In addition to the Pentapolis, the Philistines founded many new settlements across the southern Levant, maintaining traces of their Aegean origins in such aspects of their material culture as figurines, pottery, and temple layout.

In economic terms, the Philistines made extensive use of cattle and pig, high consumption of the latter being in sharp contrast to their highland neighbors, the Israelites, whose Early Iron Age settlements show no use at all of pig. It may thus be that the Israelite cultural taboo against pork was an Early Iron Age ethnic or cultural distinction. An immense amount of trade was funneled through the Philistine cities, with the export of grain, wine, and oil. Egypt, in particular, was a major consumer of Philistine commodities.

The Phoenicians Turning north to the central Levant, the independent cities of the Phoenicians to some extent continued the commercial and cultural connections of the Late Bronze Age, with their major port cities at **Tyre** and **Sidon** in Lebanon (Harden 1980; Markoe 2000), perhaps indicating continuity of population in this region. Exports included the agricultural produce of the fertile plains, timber from the hills, and the product that gave the region its name, the purple dye made from the murex seashell (Phoenicia means "land of purple"). Trade in high-quality goods, such as carved ivory furniture fittings, glasswork, spices, and jewelry, keyed the Phoenicians into an imperial pattern of trade and connections that traversed all of Southwest Asia and beyond. Phoenician traders and artisans were heavily involved in Assyrian imperial projects to the east, as well as with the Early Israelite rulers, including David and Solomon.

A major achievement of the Phoenicians was the development of an alphabet before 1000 BC; unfortunately, few inscriptions are known from the region, as writing was executed mainly on perishable papyrus and parchment. The Phoenician alphabet was of supreme importance as the source of inspiration for subsequent alphabetic writing systems, including those of Hebrew, Aramaic, and Greek; it thus lies at the base of all modern alphabetic writing systems.

By the 8th and 7th centuries BC Phoenicia was impinged upon increasingly by the might of imperial Assyria, epitomized in the destruction of Tyre by the Assyrian king Esarhaddon in the 7th century BC, followed by the mass deportation of its people.

The Neo-Hittites Further north still, in the region of the northern Levant and southern Anatolia, a series of kingdoms dominated the political scene of the Early Iron Age from about 1200 to 700 BC. These states are known as the Neo-Hittites, as they appear to maintain several traditions of the Bronze Age Hittite state, including the use of monumental decorated architecture, the continued use of Late Bronze Age royal names, and the employment of Hittite hieroglyphic script for writing the Luwian language (Hawkins 1995) [**12.44**]. Neo-Hittite sites, such as **Carchemish**, **Zincirli**, and **Melid**, show consistent aspects of material culture, with spectacular carved wall reliefs in stone.

Neo-Hittite sites were located along vital routes of communication and show a continuing concern to control or influence trade routes. As with the entire Levant region, an increasingly urgent factor through the Iron Age is the dominance of Assyria (see below). In the late 8th century BC all the Neo-Hittite states were destroyed by the Assyrian king Tiglath-pileser III; several then came under the control of Assyrian provincial governors.

12.44 *Neo-Hittite relief sculpture:* *this pictorial relief from the site of Karatepe, near Adana, south Turkey, dates to the 9th–8th centuries BC. Also inscribed on these stone blocks is a rare bilingual inscription in Phoenician and hieroglyphic Luwian, composed by a ruler called Azatiwata.*

12.45 *Assyrian wall relief from the palace of Ashurnasirpal II at Nimrud: from the 9th to late 7th centuries BC, the Assyrian rulers decorated their palaces with carved stone slabs, depicting scenes such as battles, royal hunts, and cultic events. In all the scenes the aim was to glorify the achievements of the Assyrian kings, acting on behalf of the state god, Ashur. The message was reinforced by inscribed texts often written over the carved scenes. Their discovery at Nimrud, Khorsabad, and Nineveh by archaeologists in the mid-19th century confirmed and expanded on biblical accounts of the might of Assyria.*

The Levant: Israel and Judah

Part of the pattern of new states in the Early Iron Age is the rise of the kingdoms of Israel and Judah in the highland zones of the southern Levant, entities that can be characterized as nation-states, a stage beyond the existence of contemporary city-states sharing a common material culture. The origin of the settlers who founded the kingdoms of Israel and Judah is not certain, but archaeologists are increasingly suggesting that rather than a massive influx of new peoples from outside, the formation of these states is due to major oscillations in proportions of sedentary and pastoral-nomadic elements of society, with large-scale settling of previously mobile people in the 12th–11th centuries BC. In interaction, peaceful or not, with lowland neighbors, the settlements of the highland zone rapidly assumed the status of complex urban societies in the Early Iron Age (Holladay 1995).

At the end of the 11th century BC the communities of the highlands united to form a single state, the United Monarchy, a short-lived entity that soon broke down to a more familiar dual pattern of a kingdom of Judah, centered on **Jerusalem**, and an Israelite kingdom centered on **Shechem**, and later **Samaria**. Each had different political traditions reaching back into the Late Bronze Age. Histories of the kingdoms of Israel and Judah are recorded in the Old Testament, but it is notoriously difficult to match those histories with the archaeological evidence (Finkelstein and Silberman 2001) [see box: The Old Testament and Archaeology, p. 466]. As with other areas of the Levant, the impact of Assyria loomed larger as the centuries passed, culminating in the Assyrian termination of the kingdom of Israel in 722 BC and the mass deportation of the citizens of Samaria to Babylon.

The Assyrian Empire

At its peak in the 7th century BC, the Assyrian empire dominated Southwest Asia, reaching from the Persian Gulf in the southeast to the highlands of Anatolian Cilicia in the northwest, and from Egypt in the southwest to the Zagros Mountains in the northeast. The Assyrian state was rooted in political and cultural developments of previous centuries, with an identity that can be traced back to the Bronze Age, particularly an emphasis on the city of Ashur as the focal point of the state. We have seen

how Assyria suffered a period of decline and retreat in the aftermath of the Late Bronze Age regional collapse, but in the 10th and 9th centuries BC a series of strong kings campaigned successfully to re-establish Assyrian control over lost lands, culminating in 883 BC with the accession of Ashurnasirpal II, who built a new imperial capital at the site of **Kalhu**, modern Nimrud (Oates and Oates 2001). This action set a precedent for several subsequent kings, who chose new capital locations as arenas for massive programs of construction and display, involving palaces, temples, fortification walls, and associated irrigation works in the surrounding countryside. Thus, Sargon II (721–705 BC) selected the site of **Khorsabad** as his capital, whereas his son, Sennacherib (704–681 BC), moved the capital to **Nineveh**, where it remained until the collapse of the empire in 612 BC.

Each of these capital cities was a focus for imperial control and glory (Lumsden 2001). New palaces of great size and grandeur made manifest the might of the ruler, their walls lined with carved stone reliefs [**12.45**] depicting the king engaged in a restricted but highly explicit range of activities, including hunting lions, leading his army to battle, receiving defeated or honored guests, and participating in state cult practices (Curtis and Reade 1995; Reade 1998). In all these deeds the king was believed to be acting with the blessing of the state god, Ashur. Alongside this pervasive religious conviction, related factors in the success of the Assyrian state include the use of iron for weapons and, above all, the systematic training and equipping of a highly organized army.

During the mid-19th century AD, the capital cities of the Assyrian empire were excavated by archaeologists from Britain and France in particular, and many of the remains of Assyrian palaces now adorn institutions such as the British Museum in London and the Louvre in Paris (Larsen 1996). The major excavated palaces include those of Ashurnasirpal II at Nimrud,

KEY CONTROVERSY The Old Testament and Archaeology

The archaeology of Southwest Asia, as a modern discipline, has its origins in two main 19th-century intellectual strands. On the one hand there was a concern to situate the already well-known achievements of ancient Greece within a longer-term historical trajectory of cultural development; on the other, there was a desire to explore the historical background to the Bible, the Old Testament in particular.

Since the 19th century, study of the Bible and of its archaeology have proceeded hand-in-hand, with improved understanding of how the Bible was constructed as a historical text, and an increasingly subtle and complex appreciation of the material culture and physical conditions of the societies that existed in the periods and lands featured in it (Isserlin, 1998; Silberman 1998).

The Old Testament (often called the Hebrew Bible) is a highly complex document, written and assembled over several centuries in the 1st millennium BC. It contains a mass of varied material, including elements of history, myth, philosophy, poetry, law, and prophecy. How might this difficult document be approached and appreciated through the lens of archaeology?

Attempts to Prove the Bible's Historical Basis

Early explorations sought to provide historical verifications for places and peoples that featured in the Old Testament. Pioneering investigations by the American Edward Robinson in Ottoman Palestine in the mid-19th century attempted to identify and verify specific sites mentioned in the Bible, through detailed comparison of biblical names with modern Arabic place names. By these and other means, considerable numbers of modern sites and ruins were convincingly suggested as places that featured in the Bible.

This phase of biblical exploration appeared to lend support to those who contended that the Old Testament was constructed on the basis of historical reality, even if composed and written down at some temporal remove from that reality. Excavations at many sites in Israel and Jordan established a sequence of cultural development for the region, showing progress from early farming, through urban society, and on to complex statehood (Albright 1949).

Evidence from Egypt

As these researches proceeded in the Holy Land, contemporary explorations in the adjacent lands of Egypt, Syria, and Iraq began to shed light on the wider world of the Old Testament. The decipherment of Egyptian hieroglyphs from the 1820s onwards, as well as scores of excavations of archaeological sites in Egypt, brought the immensely rich world of the ancient pharaohs into the arena of biblical studies.

While providing an external check on the chronology of events recorded in the Old Testament, these developments in Egypt also yielded evidence for some very precise synchronisms between the Holy Land and Egypt, such as the victory stela of the pharaoh Merenptah, which, in 1207 BC, according to one chronology, recorded a victory over a people called Israel.

Evidence from Mesopotamia

At the same time, investigations in Mesopotamia provided dramatic evidence relating to the great empires of Assyria and Babylonia, with excavations of palaces and temples of the kings and gods at cities such as Nineveh, Nimrud, Khorsabad, and Babylon itself. For the first time in over two millennia, the physical remains of these states were revealed. They provided a wealth of material evidence within which to locate the world of the Old Testament, as well as numerous points of reference to specific events and individuals of the Bible. Thus, many of the kings of Israel and Judah are recorded in documents and depictions of the Assyrian royal court. The true importance of ancient Assyria in the history of the Holy Land in the Iron Age came to be appreciated.

Recent Trends

In more recent decades, biblical archaeology has shifted away from attempts to provide verification for events, places, or peoples featured in the Bible, and to a more generalized concern with exploring the past of the Holy Land in more anthropological terms (Finkelstein and Silberman 2001). This trend has brought biblical archaeology into the mainstream of intellectual developments within archaeology and anthropology, with exploration of issues such as diet, economy, administration, demography, and ideology.

At the same time, both archaeology and biblical textual studies continue to explore the specifics of the Bible as a historical document shaped and constructed within a complex and changing nexus of social, cultural, and religious factors.

Sargon II at Khorsabad, and Sennacherib and Ashurbanipal at Nineveh. The earliest use of extensive carved wall reliefs occurs in the palace of Ashurnasirpal II at Nimrud, and it is possible that this apparently sudden innovation owes its inspiration to Neo-Hittite stone-carving practices of the Early Iron Age.

From within Assyrian palaces, as well as other types of building, archaeologists have excavated thousands of clay tablets inscribed in cuneiform script, written in the Assyrian dialect of the Akkadian language. These texts, and those inscribed on the sculpted wall reliefs themselves, give an immense amount of information on the history, politics, and economic and legal structure of the Assyrian state (Postgate 1979). Additionally, extraordinary collections of tablets such as Ashurbanipal's library from Nineveh comprise a deliberately assembled treasure trove, containing literary, cultic, mythical, and other documents from many periods and places of the Mesopotamian past.

Anatolian States

Following the collapse of the Hittite empire *c.* 1200 BC, there is a long period of obscurity in Anatolia before Iron Age societies appear. We have already looked at the Neo-Hittite states of southeast Turkey and the northern Levant. Further to the east, centered around Lake Van, a major phenomenon was the state of **Urartu**, a contemporary and serious rival of its neighbor to the south, the Assyrian empire (Zimansky 1985; 1995). The state of Urartu features significantly in Assyrian texts of the 9th–7th centuries BC, and seems to be a "shadow empire" that came into existence as a direct result of Assyrian impact on the region. Indeed, Urartu assumed many aspects of Assyrian culture, although in distinctive ways, including its writing system (employing the cuneiform script, the Urartian language is distantly related to Hurrian but not to any other language) and its military equipment, tactics, and architecture, as well as some of its modes of artistic or ideological expression.

Urartian texts come mainly in the form of royal inscriptions detailing building programs and campaigns. Documents dealing with daily administration, subsistence, and economy are extremely rare – an aspect of the evidence that has naturally shaped how the Urartian state has been viewed by scholars. A major source for ancient Urartu is Assyrian records, which generally relate to war between the two states. We thus learn about Urartu from its bitterest enemy, again a significant element of bias in the historical record. The most important document is an account of the campaign of Sargon II in 714 BC in the upper Zagros region around Lake Urmia, in northwest Iran. This text provides great detail on the terrain, the sack of cities, and the huge amounts of booty taken from, in particular, the temple of Haldi at **Musasir**.

The geography of the region is critical: difficult for an army to march through but at the same time difficult to unify and orchestrate in defensive alliance. Agricultural land around the three great lakes – Van in eastern Turkey, Urmia in northwest Iran, and Sevan in Armenia – formed the economic basis of Urartu, and ambitious irrigation projects were a vehicle for regional cooperation in the state from an early stage. The rugged terrain meant that Urartu maintained a decentralized system of production and distribution, while exploiting locally available resources such as copper, silver, iron, and timber.

Urartian history is dominated by its long conflict with Assyria, leading to the construction of fortresses throughout its highland territory. These fortified sites, at locations such as **Tushpa**, **Toprakkale**, and **Ayanis** [12.46], formed the backbone of Urartian control, but associated with them, and archaeologically less well known, were outer towns and villages of agricultural laborers and their families. During the 7th century BC, more friendly relations between Assyria and Urartu allowed the appearance of an Urartian emissary at the court of Ashurbanipal in 643 BC. This occasion is the last Assyrian textual mention of Urartu, and the fall of Urartu was doubtless connected closely, like much of its history, with the vicissitudes of Assyria and its fall in the late 7th century BC.

In central Anatolia, the principal power of the period was the state of **Phrygia**, which by 800 BC had assumed control over the heartlands of the Hittite empire (Sams 1995). Early movements of Phrygian and other peoples from southeast Europe into Anatolia occurred *c.* 900 BC; these people brought with them European traditions such as the burial of elite dead under earthen mounds, or tumuli, often with spectacular grave goods.

The Phrygians are known to us from two highly disparate textual sources. From the west, the 5th-century BC Greek historian Herodotus tells us a great deal about them, and in particular about King Midas. The same king is known to us from an eastern source, in texts of the Assyrian empire. The major Assyrian concern was that the Phrygians would ally with Urartu and thus pose a significant threat to Assyria from the north and northwest.

12.46 Entrance to the shrine of Haldi: *temple of Haldi, the state god of Urartu, at Ayanis, east Turkey. Inlay materials have been removed, in ancient times, from the stone panels on the right, while to the left can be seen a long inscription in the Urartian language.*

The capital city of Phrygia was **Gordion**, in central Turkey, where excavations have uncovered palaces, temples, and fortifications (Voigt 1997). In the vicinity of the site are some 85 large burial mounds, the largest of which, at over 50 m (164 ft) in height, contained the burial of an adult male, laid upon a bench and buried in a tomb of juniper logs with a wealth of bronze vessels, decorated pottery, and exquisite wooden furniture. By the early 6th century BC Phrygia came increasingly under the influence of the rising power of **Lydia** from the west; in 547 BC Gordion was captured by Cyrus the Great, and Phrygia became part of the Achaemenid Persian empire (discussed below).

Babylonia

To the south of Assyria, the power of **Babylon** in Lower Mesopotamia became increasingly prominent through the 1st millennium BC (Beaulieu 1989). Assyrian attitudes to Babylonia were ambivalent. On the one hand, with its millennia of continuous cuneiform tradition, Babylonia was viewed as the cultural, religious, and literary fount from which the Assyrian court drew its inspiration. On the other hand, Babylon was itself a political and military rival for control over territory and trade

routes dominated by the Assyrians. Relations between the two states thus alternated between episodes of quiet respect and violent disagreement, leading to open warfare and conquest. Occasionally, Assyrian kings, such as Tiglath-pileser III (744–727 BC) and Shalmaneser V (726–722 BC), had themselves crowned as kings of Babylonia as well as of Assyria. Eventually, Sennacherib of Assyria captured and sacked Babylon in 689 BC, destroying its temples and palaces, a policy equaled in dramatic effect only by that of his son Esarhaddon (680–669 BC), who, ten years after their total destruction by his father, had all the temples of Babylon rebuilt in the belief that only by doing so could he maintain the favor of the gods.

Following the collapse of the Assyrian empire in 612 BC, in which the Babylonians and Medes were heavily involved, the Babylonian empire inherited the mantle of regional power in Southwest Asia, campaigning against Egypt and Judah in the west and Elam in the east. For about 75 years Babylon ruled supreme, an episode terminated by the Persian king Cyrus the Great in 539 BC. During this period the Babylonian king Nebuchadnezzar twice captured Jerusalem, exiling the Jews to Babylonia, an exile ended by Cyrus.

The city of Babylon was the focus of the Babylonian, or Chaldean, state of the 1st millennium BC (Oates 1979). Regarded as the home of Marduk, chief of the gods, Babylon had a long history of settlement prior to the Iron Age, most famously as the city of Hammurabi in the 18th century BC (see above). Under the Babylonian kings of the 7th and 6th centuries BC, Babylon was adorned with the magnificent palaces, temples, fortifications, and elite residences befitting the capital of a great empire (Van De Mieroop 2003). Contained within a double fortification wall, the Neo-Babylonian city was bisected by the Euphrates. At least three major palaces were situated within the inner wall, the so-called Northern, Southern, and Summer Palaces. These large structures were laid out on the traditional courtyard plan, with ranges of residences and other rooms surrounding open areas. A series of vaulted rooms in the northeast corner of the Southern Palace was originally believed to be the site of the famous Hanging Gardens, but is now thought to be a storage or administrative area.

Running parallel with the Euphrates' course, a major route through the city was the Processional Way, reaching from the massive Ishtar Gate in the north to the temple of Marduk in the south, which occupied an area of some 90 x 116 m (295 x 380 ft). Close by the temple stood the great ziggurat or staged tower, of which only the foundations survive. The Ishtar Gate itself was one of the most impressive of Babylon's monuments, heav-

12.47 The Ishtar Gate: *the gate was excavated, and then reconstructed in the Vorderasiatisches Museum, Berlin, as seen here, during German excavations at Babylon in the early 20th century.*

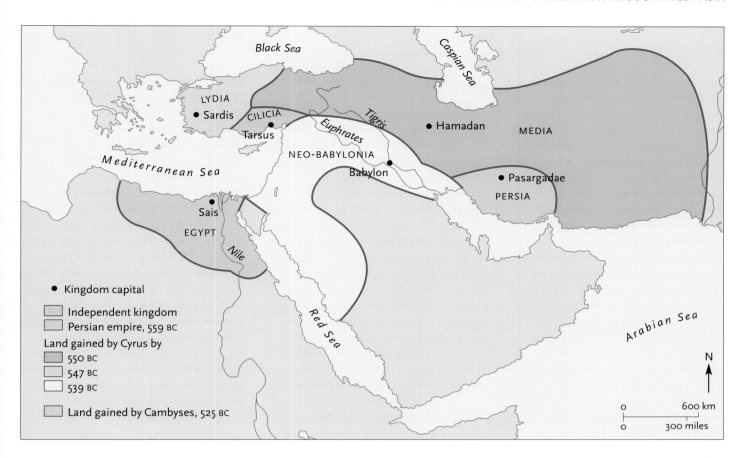

ily adorned with glazed bricks decorated with relief scenes of bulls and dragons (symbols of the deities Adad and Marduk) in yellow and white on a blue background; the gate can be seen today in the Vorderasiatisches Museum, Berlin [**12.47**].

The Achaemenid Empire and the Conquest of Southwest Asia

In 559 BC **Cyrus** became ruler of the Persians and embarked on a series of military campaigns that led to the creation of the greatest empire that had existed up to that time, the Achaemenid Persian empire (Briant 1995; Curtis 1989) [**12.48**]. The Persians were an Indo-European speaking people who had already settled in Iran for some time before the rise of the Achaemenid empire. As we have seen, Cyrus captured Gordion and Sardis in 547 BC, and Babylon in 539 BC. He founded a new city at **Pasargadae** in southern Iran, drafting in artisans and architects from parts of his newly established empire. Like the Assyrians before them, the Achaemenids incorporated Egypt into their empire. Darius I (died 486 BC) extended the empire toward Europe, and founded a new capital at **Susa** in southwest Iran. Defeats of Persian incursions in the 5th century BC by Greek armies formed the basis of Herodotus' famous histories.

With the invasion by Alexander the Great of Macedon in 334 BC, the Achaemenid empire collapsed at a dramatic stroke, and a new epoch of western influence on the east, and vice versa,

12.48 The Achaemenid empire: *map showing its growth and extent. This great empire was brought to an end by Alexander the Great.*

began. Fittingly, Alexander died in the great palace of the Babylonian kings at Babylon in 323 BC (Chapter 13). The world of ancient Southwest Asia lingered in cuneiform texts for a few centuries before fading from history, surviving as echoes of grandeur in the histories of the Greeks and the Old Testament (Dalley 1998), and transforming itself into the post-Hellenistic polities of the region.

Summary and Conclusions

With the collapse of the Achaemenid empire, a continuous line of cultural, linguistic, and religious development, stretching back for millennia appears to have come to an abrupt end. It is conventional to see this event as marking a significant cultural break with all that had gone before, with the subsequent history of the region viewed as a new phase that owed little to preceding centuries. Such a view is being increasingly questioned (Kohl 1989) [see box: Who Owns the Past?, p. 470]. At the most basic level, the vast majority of the population of Southwest Asia carried on their lives as they had for millennia, tilling their fields, husbanding their animals, raising their offspring, paying their taxes, and fighting the wars of their political masters. For them

KEY CONTROVERSY Who Owns the Past?

It is often claimed that the heritage of ancient Southwest Asia belongs to all humanity, not solely or even principally to those peoples who currently live in the region. The looting and destruction of Iraq's heritage in Baghdad in 2003 has been addressed by scholars in such terms, the loss being seen as having global significance. Many scholars have described a linear trajectory of cultural and social development from the past of Southwest Asia, through the biblical and Hellenistic worlds and on to our modern, Western-dominated one (Bottéro 1992). In this view, little or no credence is given to the role of the post-classical societies of Southwest Asia, including those of the Sasanian and Islamic eras, in nurturing and maintaining ancient traditions and transmitting them to societies that still reside in the region. A cultural fault line between the past and the present is discerned as falling somewhere around the time of Alexander the Great, when the thrust of cultural development shifts away from Southwest Asia and recommences its course in the context of ancient Greece.

Contrary to this attitude, other scholars situate the heritage of Southwest Asia within local traditions of cultural development, seeing fundamental continuity and indigenous maintenance of deeply rooted beliefs and practices up to modern times. They argue that the real break in Southwest Asia's past happened in our own times, with its hijacking into a trajectory of Western development, whereby scholars of the classical and biblical worlds sought origins for the intellectual and cultural development of those worlds (Larsen 1989; Bahrani 1998). In this view, since the start of historical and archaeological investigation of Southwest Asia by scholars from Europe and North America, the indigenous communities of the region have been excluded from genuine participation and exploration of the past of their own lands by the domination of a discourse conducted in non-native languages (English, French, German, Japanese, etc.), framed in academic practices and concepts developed outside the region (Al-Ansary 2000), and underpinned by a political and economic interaction that many characterize as imperialist exploitation of the modern lands in which these sites lie.

Archaeologists and historians of Southwest Asia are well placed to address and attempt to transcend the divisions outlined above. The following practices and procedures might contribute to such a development in future years. First, all scholars working at a senior level in Southwest Asia may be expected to have a proficiency in the language(s) of their host country. Second, Western academics should consider publishing their research in the language of the host country, as well as in their own tongue. Third, Western universities and museums should take steps to engage with their counterparts in the countries of Southwest Asia, for example by exchanging staff and students for courses and field projects, and by devising and executing truly collaborative research projects. Fourth, scholars working in Southwest Asia could be encouraged to consider and explore long-term historical perspectives that cross artificial divides between the ancient and the modern worlds (Kohl 1989).

Who owns the past? No one and everyone. It is up to all of us to respect the local and the global in the daily practices and attitudes that we bring to the exploration of the past of Southwest Asia, as with any region of the world.

---

it may have made little difference whether their ruler was a Sumerian king, an Akkadian emperor, an Assyrian governor, an Achaemenid satrap, or a Greek conqueror. As these people have left us little or nothing in the way of written records, and as archaeologists have not excavated many of their houses in adequate ways, we do not yet know how the shifting ideologies of elite power were accepted, molded, and rebuffed by everyday people of ancient Southwest Asia. But we can tell that the practices and procedures of their daily lives appear to have remained remarkably constant through the period covered in this chapter and on through pre-modern times (Snell 1997).

At the level of political and cultural development, however, there are some clear threads running through the subject matter of this chapter. Through the centuries of the Chalcolithic we see a steady trend toward increasing size and complexity of human communities. The Halaf societies of the earliest Chalcolithic phase, 6000–5400 BC, are characterized by small-scale settlements whose inhabitants were engaged in farming the land and hunting. The existence of a few larger Halaf sites, however, as well as evidence for trade in valued commodities such as obsidian and painted pottery, may indicate an initial move toward hierarchical society based on agricultural surplus. During the Ubaid period, 5900–4200 BC, partly overlapping with the Halaf, there is good evidence for increasing social differentiation, with the first clear temples, as at Tepe Gawra and Eridu, and some indications of long-distance trade, for example in the Persian Gulf region. A general lack of luxury goods on Ubaid sites, however, suggests that the social hierarchy of important Ubaid settlements such as Eridu may have been rooted in concerns of control over surpluses of domestic staple commodities rather than in the trading of high-status materials or artifacts.

This concern comes very much to the fore during the subsequent Late Chalcolithic period, c. 4200–3000 BC, when the first cities of the Mesopotamian plain, Uruk above all, clearly show an ability to master the gathering, redistribution, and exchange of massive quantities of domestic surplus in foodstuffs and secondary products, such as milk and wool. The act of achieving this mastery is itself the step that creates civilization and all its appurtenances, including a highly divided social hierarchy, an administrative system employing written records, a system of divine beliefs, rites, and rituals, and a hugely increased concern with trade in exotic, status-enhancing materials for use by elite groups of society.

After this step had been taken, at some time around 3500 BC, all the important cultural, social, and political developments of the Bronze Age and Iron Age in Southwest Asia can be seen as matters of scale. The basic framework of hierarchical, structured societies, dominated by institutions such as temples and palaces, with writing largely restricted to those institutions, stays the same throughout. States get bigger, of course, but it is arguable whether or not they get significantly more complex or intricate after 3000 BC. Even with the advent of empires, from the late 3rd millennium BC onward, the developments are still principally in scale rather than kind. Nevertheless, the mechanisms by which increasingly large and diverse empires manage themselves, particularly in the case of the Assyrian and Achaemenid empires, are intriguing subjects of study.

A consistent element in the past of Southwest Asia is that of trade and exchange. Marked by a highly irregular distribution of raw materials, particularly metals, timber, and stone, as well as of arable land and rainfall, the region hosted societies whose specific geographical location strongly affected their needs and opportunities for engaging in commerce and interaction with neighbors. Time and again we see the significance of trade and exchange as a formative factor in the rise, development, and collapse of cities and states.

At all levels of society, the story of civilization in Southwest Asia is one of consistency and continuity. Structures of power persisted as templates of social control, even while individual instances of kingdoms, city-states, and empires rose and fell with often spectacular alacrity. Even the specifics of elite ideologies show astonishing continuity across thousands of years, delineating the ruler as a divinely sanctioned source of all power – legal, religious, social, military. These aspects of ancient Southwest Asia can readily be tracked across the Achaemenid-Alexander fault line, and it is not too fanciful to discern them in modern examples, such as the recent regime of Saddam Hussein, latest in a long line of Mesopotamian rulers.

In the next chapter, we turn west from Mesopotamia to the Mediterranean basin. Here the rise of cities and states may have owed something to contacts with Southwest Asia, but the civilizations that developed there were distinctive and varied. State formation, as we have seen in Africa and Southwest Asia, and will be seen in South and East Asia, was, like agriculture, a globally distributed phenomenon, part of the human response to the challenges and opportunities offered by the Holocene world.

Further Reading and Suggested Websites

Curtis, J. 1989. *Ancient Persia*. London: British Museum Press. A highly readable and lavishly illustrated introduction to the archaeology and history of Iran.

Kuhrt, A. 1995. *The Ancient Near East, c. 3000–330 BC*. London: Routledge. Excellent historical introduction to ancient Southwest Asia, including Egypt.

Levy, T. E. (ed.). 1995. *The Archaeology of Society in the Holy Land*. London: Leicester University Press. Highly stimulating chronological treatment of the Holy Land, with an emphasis on long-term history and socio-economic archaeology.

Matthews, R. 2003. *The Archaeology of Mesopotamia: Theories and Approaches*. London: Routledge. A study of how archaeology is constructed and practiced within the arena of ancient Mesopotamia, using numerous specific case studies from Iraq, Syria, and Turkey.

Meyers, E. M. (ed.). 1997. *The Oxford Encyclopedia of Archaeology in the Near East*. Oxford and New York: Oxford University Press. Excellent reference work, offering succinct yet informative coverage of all aspects of the subject.

Pollock, S. 1999. *Ancient Mesopotamia*. Cambridge: Cambridge University Press. Thoughtful consideration of the archaeology of Mesopotamia, employing political economy and gender studies as its main approaches.

Postgate, J. N. 1992. *Early Mesopotamia. Society and Economy at the Dawn of History*. London: Routledge. Excellent study uniquely combining archaeological and textual approaches to the Mesopotamian past.

Potts, D. T. 1997. *Mesopotamian Civilization: The Material Foundations*. London: Athlone Press. Innovative study of the physical basis of an ancient civilization of Southwest Asia, using texts and archaeology in concert.

Roaf, M. 1990. *Cultural Atlas of Mesopotamia and the Ancient Near East*. Oxford: Facts on File. Wonderfully illustrated coverage of Mesopotamia and adjacent regions, full of insightful text, color images, and extremely useful maps; the best starting place for most issues.

Sasson, J. M. (ed.). 1995. *Civilizations of the Ancient Near East*. New York: Scribner. Superb collection of essays by leading academics on all aspects of ancient Southwest Asia, including history, culture, art, and archaeology.

Van De Mieroop, M. 2004. *A History of the Ancient Near East c. 3000–323 BC*. Oxford: Blackwell. Extremely useful and engaging survey of the history of all the major states and polities of the region, up to the start of the Hellenistic period.

http://www.mesopotamia.co.uk/ British Museum site; good introduction to ancient Mesopotamia, including Sumer, Babylon, and Assyria.

http://www.etana.org/abzu/ Excellent resource covering all aspects of ancient Southwest Asia.

http://www.ancientneareast.net/ Good resource for information on sites, museums, news, and activities.

http://www.hattusa.org Website relating to German excavations at the capital city of the Hittite empire.

CHAPTER 13
THE MEDITERRANEAN WORLD

Susan E. Alcock and John F. Cherry, University of Michigan

Defining the Mediterranean, Redefining its Study 473

The Bronze Age 476
- *Neolithic and Copper Age Settlement* 477
The Aegean Early Bronze Age 477
- ● **KEY CONTROVERSY** Early Cycladic Marble Figures 478
- *The Cyclades* 479
- *The Greek Mainland and Troy* 479
Minoan Crete: The Palace Period 480
- *Features and Functions of the Minoan Palace* 480
- *Life Outside the Palaces* 481
- *The End of the Minoan Palaces* 482
Mycenaean Greece 482
- *Mycenae* 482
- ● **KEY DISCOVERY** Linear B 484
- *Other Mycenaean Palaces* 485
- *Mycenaean Society and Overseas Influence* 485
- *The End of the Aegean Bronze Age* 486

Cultural Variety in the 1st Millennium BC 486
Greece and the Aegean 486
- *The Dark Age* 486
- *The Archaic Period* 486
- *The Classical Period* 487
Greek Colonization 488
- ● **KEY SITE** The Necropolis at Metapontum 489
The Phoenicians and Phoenician Expansion 490
The Etruscans and the Italian Peninsula 491
- ● **KEY CONTROVERSY** Who Were the Etruscans? 493
The Structure of the Archaic and Classical Greek Polis 494
- *The Hinterland: The Economic Foundation of the City* 494

- ● **KEY DISCOVERY** The Parthenon 494
- *Outside the City Walls: The Cemetery* 496
- *Life Within the City Walls* 496
- ● **KEY CONTROVERSY** The Silent Greek Countryside 498
- *The Commonality of Greek Culture* 499

Growing Powers, Growing Territories 500
Alexander and the East 500
- *The Conquests of Alexander* 500
- *The Hellenistic World* 501
- ● **KEY SITE** Alexandria-by-Egypt 502
Carthage and the Carthaginian Empire 503
The Rise of Rome 504
- ● **KEY SITE** The Tophet: Child Sacrifice at Carthage 505
- *Roman Expansion* 506

A Mediterranean Empire 507
Rome, Center of the World 508
The Provinces and Frontiers 509
- ● **KEY CONTROVERSY** Pompeii – All Problems Solved? 510
- *Reactions to Roman Annexation* 511
- ● **KEY SITE** The Mahdia Shipwreck 512
- *The Roman Army* 514
- *A Multiplicity of Gods* 515
The Later Empire 515

Summary and Conclusions 516

Further Reading and Suggested Websites 517

In Chapter 11, we followed the development of European cultures from the end of the Pleistocene through the Neolithic period, describing the spread of farming and the steady increase in social complexity that followed its inception; in Chapter 12 the development of urban state societies in Southwest Asia was described. Both these regions have borders on the Mediterranean Sea, and it is to Mediterranean societies that we now turn.

We take up the tale in the 3rd millennium BC, when first the Aegean and then (during the 1st millennium BC) the central and western Mediterranean began to pursue a development independent from that of the rest of Europe. The Minoan and Mycenaean civilizations of Crete and the Greek mainland rose and fell in the 2nd millennium BC, and the region subsequently witnessed the brilliance of Classical Greece, the expansion of the Etruscan state in Italy, and the spread of Hellenistic and Roman culture during the final centuries of the 1st millennium BC. These developments affected the entire shoreline of the Mediterranean, and thus spanned the continents of Asia, Africa, and Europe.

What's in a name? In the case of this chapter, a very great deal. In the Latin language of the Romans, "Mediterranean" means "in the middle of the land"; at 2.5 million sq. km (1.5 million sq. miles), it is the world's largest inland sea. This body of salt water, land-locked except for one natural outlet to the Atlantic Ocean, anchored an encircling Mediterranean world that depended upon and exploited its seaways and resources. Linked to one another by the sea, the peoples of the Mediterranean also interacted, often dramatically, with the neighboring regions discussed in previous chapters: notably with temperate Europe, Southwest Asia, and North Africa. Contact and exchange – of all kinds and with many consequences – are hallmarks of this Mediterranean world, which has consistently proven to be a fruitful crossroads of cultures.

The Mediterranean region is one of immense diversity. Fertile fields and pleasant climes still sought after today (consider the attractions of southern France) contrast with the arid and difficult environments in some of the eastern Mediterranean, such as parts of Greece or the Levantine coast. Even within individual modern countries, such as Italy or Turkey, topographic fragmentation is frequently the norm. While a Mediterranean climate (with wet winters and dry summers) reigns overall, the varied and broken landscape results in marked climatic irregularity, and thus agricultural uncertainty and risk. Diversity of landscape and unpredictability of life are constant motifs throughout Mediterranean prehistory and history (Horden and Purcell 2000; Braudel 1966). Yet these conditions fostered no single or simple response; on the contrary, over the centuries considered in this chapter (roughly the 3rd millennium BC into the 1st millennium AD), an astonishing array of social, political, and economic formations played out across the region. Whether palatial kingdom, city-state, or widespread empire, each shared the possibilities of movement, communication, and exchange opened up by the inland sea.

If one overriding trajectory can be identified over this long time-span, it is toward an increasing degree of regional integration. By the end of this chapter, we will have examined a Roman empire that not only embraced the entire Mediterranean (called by the Romans, proprietarily, *Mare Nostrum*, "Our Sea"), but also extended well beyond it. Yet the trend toward such extensive territorial units was no unwavering juggernaut, nor did it happen overnight. This chapter begins in the Early Bronze Age (around 3000 BC), and follows the development of relatively small-scale polities – a level of organization that would endure until late in the 1st millennium BC. Some of these societies have been much studied and celebrated, for example the Bronze Age palaces of Minoan Crete or the Classical cities of Athens or Sparta. Toward the end of the 1st millennium BC, expansionist states appear – those that resulted from the conquests of Alexander the Great and his successors in the eastern Mediterranean and Southwest Asia, the Carthaginian empire in North Africa and the western Mediterranean, and, building on and feeding off these entities, the over-arching *imperium* of Rome. Yet even within these large imperial territories, local distinctions survived, and local cultures persisted.

The Mediterranean, then, emerges as a superb laboratory in which to watch political evolution and cultural change in a region marked equally by uncertainty and opportunity. That statement summarizes the essential argument, and establishes the principal goal, of this chapter.

Defining the Mediterranean, Redefining its Study

Oddly enough, the Mediterranean does not always receive the attention it deserves in archaeological textbooks. Part of the problem may stem from the basic difficulty of defining the Mediterranean world: where do the region's boundaries lie in relation to other zones, especially temperate Europe to the north? This is an ongoing question, as contemporary geographers and political scientists debate the feasibility and utility of envisioning a modern Mediterranean world (Xenakis and Chryssochoou 2001) [**13.1**].

The shape of the Mediterranean sea in antiquity, at least following postglacial changes in sea levels and coastlines, seems relatively clear, although the effects of tectonic activity continue

THE MEDITERRANEAN WORLD TIMELINE

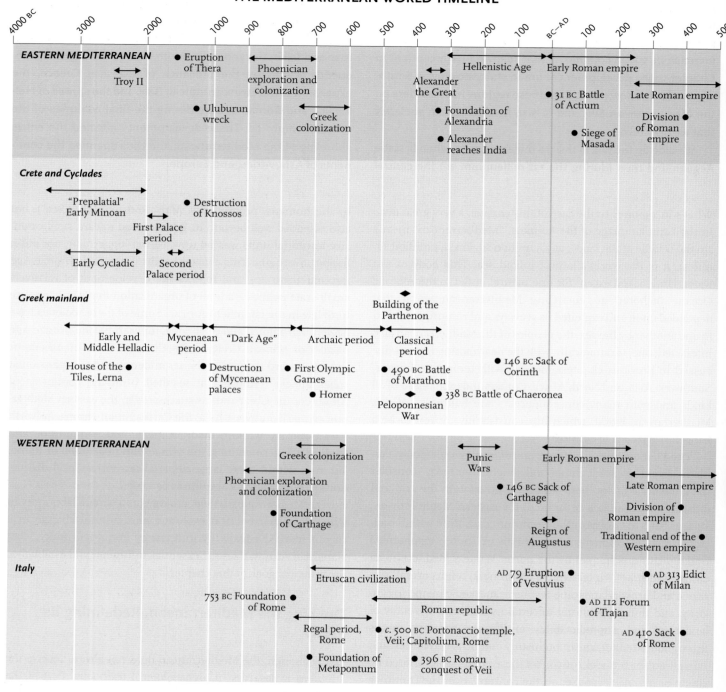

(the eastern end of the island of Crete, for example, is slowly sinking). Locating the cultural boundaries of the Mediterranean world is far more problematic, and various indices have been employed; one might be based on the rainfall and temperature patterns that allow olive cultivation, for the olive and olive oil are key elements (with grains and the grapevine) in the so-called "Mediterranean triad" of food staples [13.2]. A flexible interpretation of what comprises the Mediterranean is adopted in this chapter, a reading that embraces the littoral territories of

the inland sea in all directions. This vagueness of boundaries, and the resulting inevitable overlaps with other cultural regions, are very much part of the Mediterranean story.

Another reason for the relative neglect of the region as a whole, ironically, is the sheer fame of certain parts of its history – not least "the glory that was Greece and the grandeur that was Rome," in Edgar Allan Poe's famous phrase. To modern Western audiences, the Mediterranean world is best known as the home of those two cultures, the accepted foundations of Western civilization (Beard and Henderson 1995). The birthplace of democracy and Christianity, our model for state architecture and civic virtues – the influence of Greece and Rome is everywhere in the modern West. At its most pernicious, this rapt scholarly and popular attention to "core cultures" at the expense of all others reveals a deeply held bias that has come under increasing critical attack, most spectacularly in the often bitter debates stimulated by *Black Athena: The Afroasiatic Roots of Classical Civilization* (Bernal 1985; see also Lefkowitz and Rogers 1996). As its provocative title suggests (volume I is subtitled *The Fabrication of Greece 1785–1985*), Bernal's study accuses past scholarship of a profound Eurocentrism, even racism, in its exclusive reconstruction of the Classical past.

13.1 *The Mediterranean region:* map (above) of the Mediterranean world, and detail (below) of southern Italy, Greece, and western Turkey.

At very least, the "classic" status of Greece and Rome has obscured broader patterns of regional development. Unfortunately, it is not as easy as one might wish to rectify that situation and provide a wider context. The archaeology of the Mediterranean world, not surprisingly, long followed prevailing cultural biases, focusing by and large on the material culture of Greece and Rome (and even then, not on all periods in their lengthy histories). "Classical archaeology," for obvious reasons, is the title usually given to this discipline. The history of Classical archaeology is a long and fascinating story, and one quite distinct from that of archaeological schools elsewhere. Traditional training of Classical archaeologists laid heavy emphasis on the rich, much-admired Greek and Latin textual sources and on formal analysis of their remarkable artistic and architectural production. Fieldwork methodologies tended to the conservative, dominated by major excavations at large sites (Morris

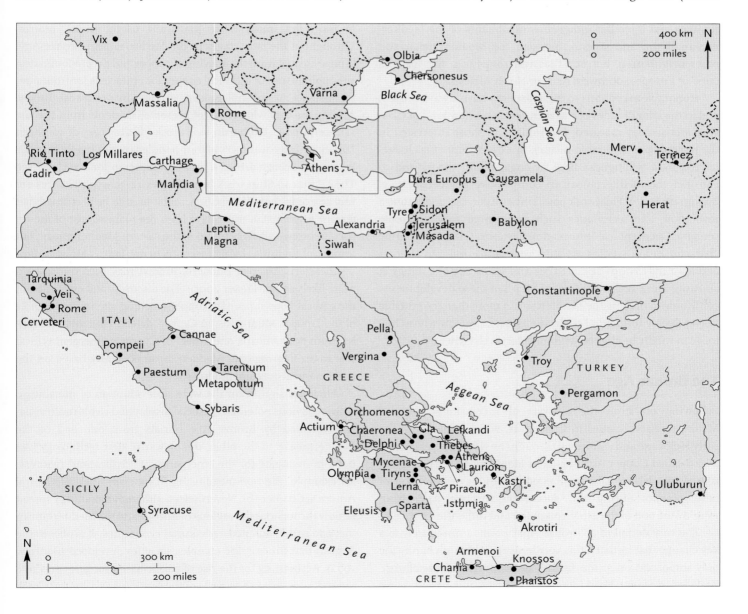

13.2 *Olive harvesting in action: as depicted on a late 6th-century Attic black figure vase by the Antimenes Painter.*

1994; Shanks 1995; Whitley 2001). Such attitudes and predilections led to unfortunate schisms in the understanding of the Mediterranean world: first, between the privileged Greeks and Romans and the other indigenous inhabitants of the Mediterranean basin; and second, between the Mediterranean and other neighboring, but non-Classical zones (e.g. the "barbarians" of Europe, Southwest Asia, or North Africa).

Honorable exceptions to these patterns have always existed, and in the later decades of the 20th century, a new kind of Classical archaeology matured. Led initially by those interested in the region's pre- and proto-history, this development is characterized by a willingness both to engage with theory and to consider the Mediterranean in comparative perspective (e.g. Snodgrass 1987). Fieldwork possibilities have also undergone a revolution, and techniques such as regional survey, remote sensing, Geographical Information Systems (GIS), or scientific characterization studies are now routinely employed (Barker and Mattingly 1999–2000; Sarris and Jones 2000; Gillings et al. 1999; Herz and Waelkens 1988). All of these developments contribute to making the Mediterranean more than the crucible of two deeply influential civilizations, and a region whose history can validly be aligned with trajectories elsewhere.

The Bronze Age

Following on from the analysis of increasingly complex Mediterranean societies in Chapter 11, which began with the early Holocene and continued through the Neolithic period and the so-called Copper Age (the latter identified by the escalating use of metals), we take up the story with an examination of developments during the succeeding Bronze Age, from roughly the end of the 4th through the 2nd millennium BC.

The very notion of a "Bronze Age" points immediately to a key change that initiated this very long era (although hardly the only important one): the further development of metallurgy. Knowledge of metalworking greatly predates this period, as we

have seen. As early as the 8th millennium BC at **Çayönü Tepe** in southern Turkey, native copper was being fashioned into various artifacts, while at 7th-millennium BC **Çatalhöyük**, crucibles and slag provide evidence for the melting and smelting of copper; objects of lead, a metal not native to Turkey, are also known from a similarly early period. The working of silver and gold dates from the 5th millennium BC, the earliest known use of the latter being at **Varna** in Bulgaria [see The Varna Cemetery box, Chapter 11, p. 403]. More complex metallurgical technologies evolved as time went on: recovering silver by cupellation (blowing air across a crucible of molten silver-bearing lead), for instance, is a 3rd-millennium BC development, for which there is evidence from sites in the Cycladic Islands.

The most important advance involved the alloying of copper to form the much more practically useful metal, bronze. Throughout the later stages of the Mediterranean Bronze Age, bronze created from the alloying of copper and tin predominates, although the use of arsenical copper for artifacts is far from rare, for instance at 3rd-millennium BC **Troy**, in northwest Turkey. Among the very wide range of preserved contents from the late 14th-century BC **Uluburun** shipwreck off the coast of southern Turkey are large numbers of four-handled copper ingots, smaller tin ingots, bronze artifacts, and bronze scrap for recycling [see The Uluburun Shipwreck box, Chapter 12, p. 459]. Tin ores are very scarce in their distribution, and it used to be presumed that distant Afghanistan must have been the main source of the tin used in bronze artifacts found in the eastern Mediterranean; but important tin mines located recently in the Taurus Mountains of southeastern Anatolia (modern Turkey) may turn out to be a more likely source (Yener 2000). The discovery and excavation of the earliest known primary copper-smelting site in the foothills of the Troödos Mountains on Cyprus, dated to the mid-2nd millennium BC, confirms one aspect of Cyprus's emergent critical role in an interregional Mediterranean economy based on the trade in metal ores and products.

However significant the wide-scale adoption of metallurgy, with its obvious potential for social display and wealth accumulation revealed by Bronze Age burials from one end of the Mediterranean to the other, this powerful new technology was not a prerequisite for the emergence of "civilization" (witness, for example, the non-metal-using Maya civilization of Central America, Chapter 16). Nevertheless, although metallurgy spread rapidly throughout the regions of Europe and the Mediterranean that had earlier adopted agricultural economies, it is only in the Aegean that Bronze Age complex societies developed (Renfrew 1972). Accounting for the rise of palace-based societies on Crete around 2000 BC, and in parts of the southern and central Greek mainland from the 16th century BC onward, thus poses an explanatory problem for the Mediterranean region: why did civilization not emerge more often? (Lewthwaite 1983).

Neolithic and Copper Age Settlement Although established at different periods in different regions and with diverse material culture assemblages, village farming communities became a common feature throughout the Mediterranean world several thousand years before the Copper and Bronze Ages (Chapter 11), each of them dependent on much the same package of domesticated plants and animals (of Southwest Asian origin; see Chapter 6). These communities were founded both on the mainland and on all of the largest islands (Cyprus, Crete, Sicily, Sardinia, and Corsica); the earliest known site on Crete, for instance, radiocarbon-dated to the 7th millennium BC, is a modest aceramic Neolithic farming hamlet, now deeply buried directly beneath the central court of the sprawling 2nd-millennium BC palace at **Knossos**. What processes led from hamlet to palace over the course of some 5000 years on Crete, and yet did not occur in other regions with comparable climates and natural environments, which were first settled at more or less the same time?

Throughout much of the central and western Mediterranean during the Copper and Bronze Ages, the size of individual sites and the scale of the human groups they housed remained in most cases as modest as in the preceding Neolithic, and was apparently little affected by the advent of metallurgy. Even in the case of the later 4th-millennium BC Copper Age Los Millares culture in southeast Spain (see Chapter 11, p. 405), where control of metal sources (and probably also water supplies in the very arid landscape) may have promoted the development of local elites, the type site itself is little more than

a village of some 5 ha (12 acres), enclosed by a stone wall with semicircular projecting bastions. And on copper-rich Sardinia, over 7000 distinctive stone-built fortresses known as *nuraghi* [**13.3**], constructed across the island between the early 2nd and late 1st millennium BC, suggest large-scale monument building and political power (Lilliu 1985; Webster 1996). Except for certain later examples, however, with multiple towers commanding fairly extensive agglomerated settlements, most are too cramped to have protected any sizable community; the same holds true for the *torri* on Corsica and the *talayots* of the Balearic Islands, both of comparable form and date. Throughout this entire region of the central and western Mediterranean, including peninsular Italy, the essential outlines of life and death in small-scale village farming communities remained largely unchanged until those villages felt the decisive impact of the various political powers of the 1st millennium BC – Greek, Etruscan, Carthaginian, Roman (Mathers and Stoddart 1994).

The Aegean Early Bronze Age

It is clear that the Aegean followed a different trajectory from some point in the 3rd millennium BC, but the explanations proposed to account for this by archaeologists over the past century have varied greatly. For Arthur Evans (1921–35), the first excavator of the palace at **Knossos** on Crete and creator of the label **"Minoan"** for the Cretan Bronze Age (from Minos, the legendary ruler of Knossos), Minoan Crete shared so many detailed points of resemblance with Predynastic and early Dynastic Egypt that it seemed self-apparent that the former must have emerged under the strong influence of the latter (for this reason, he termed the earliest form of writing in Crete "hieroglyphic"). The influential European prehistorian V. Gordon Childe (1926) adopted a more broadly diffusionist view, in

13.3 *Nuraghe Santa Sabina, near Silanus, Sardinia:* this single-tower nuraghe, dating to the early 2nd millennium BC, was probably a farmstead, occupied by an extended family engaged in agriculture and pastoralism in the surrounding territory.

KEY CONTROVERSY Early Cycladic Marble Figures

The sculpted white marble figures made in the Cycladic Islands of Greece during most of the Early Bronze Age (c. late 4th–3rd millennium BC) are among the most distinctive and instantly recognizable of archaeological objects. Some are less than 10 cm (4 in) tall, but almost life-sized examples have also been found. Nude females, especially those with arms folded across the belly, are commonest, but there exist many other types: male "hunter-warriors," flute players, seated harpists, two or three figures conjoined as a group, and purely schematic and other non-canonical examples. Traces of painted decoration survive on a few, but it is their brilliant whiteness, simple elegance, and severity of form that have made them so appealing to modern tastes (Renfrew 1991).

Although examples number in the thousands, almost every aspect of these figures remains enigmatic. What were they made for, and what did they mean to their makers or users? Did they serve domestic purposes (42 fragments were discovered in the excavated settlement of Agia Irini on Kea), or were they manufactured specifically for funerary use, since most of those with known contexts came from graves? Did they represent the dead person, or perhaps serve his/her needs beyond the grave? Were they divine representations, perhaps even of a "mother goddess"?

Their cultural context is that of small-scale village farming communities, and replication experiments have demonstrated that these figures could have been produced, laboriously, using abrasives and simple tools of obsidian and emery. Yet modern scholarship has, for the most part, written about them as art objects, employing terminology more appropriate to Renaissance

13.4 *Female folded-arm marble figure (height 75 cm/29.5 in) of the Cycladic Keros-Syros culture, c. 2600–2000 BC. Although often photographed or displayed in the upright position, the pointed toes make it impossible for these figures to stand unassisted.*

and later art: "master sculptors," "pupils," "workshops," "hands," etc. Established archaeological techniques for classification, based on context and date, have largely been supplanted by stylistic attributions to putative individual craftsmen, whose prehistoric anonymity requires the invention of modern names, such as the Goulandris Master (Getz-Preziosi 1987). Some scholars have even proposed that the artists employed complex schemes of proportion, involving precise geometric ratios, angles, or modules, although this has not yet been rigorously demonstrated.

Many of these uncertainties arise from the wholly unknown archaeological contexts of the majority of these sculptures. Once thought stiff and unexpressive, their appeal to modern artistic sensibilities has made them attractive and valuable to art collectors and dealers, leading to illicit excavation and looting on a massive scale, especially in the decades after World War II, and to the production of fakes and forgeries for which archaeology has, as yet, no reliable diagnostic tests.

A recent study (Gill and Chippindale 1993) has explored the devastating material and intellectual consequences of the fact that so few figures have a known find context or a well-documented history of ownership, and the fact that the corpus as a whole is corrupted – to an unknown degree – with modern fakes; indeed, their reliable archaeological study may no longer be possible. The question then arises as to whether archaeologists should study and publish these sorts of unprovenanced finds at all, since doing so may actually help to validate an illicit trade in looted material. This is a significant, and still largely unresolved, ethical dilemma that faces archaeologists worldwide, but one that these Cycladic figures raise in an unusually stark form.

which most of the significant technological, economic, and cultural changes throughout the Mediterranean and Europe were seen as the consequence of their spread from Southwest Asia (referred to by Classical archaeologists as the ancient Near East). In more recent decades, both the chronology and the impact of such influences have been questioned, with greater emphasis laid upon the search for causative factors internal to the Aegean itself (Renfrew 1972). Current scholarship, nonetheless, is also emphasizing the cultural links and economic and political structures that made Crete and the Aegean active players on the western periphery of a Near East-centered "world system" (Sherratt 1993; Sherratt and Sherratt 1998).

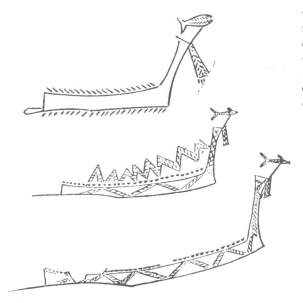

13.5, 13.6 *Depictions of Bronze Age boats of the Aegean:* (Left) *Paddled longboats, incised on clay "frying pan"-shaped vessels from the Cyclades, mid-3rd millennium BC. (Right) Deep-hulled ship with oars and sails, engraved on a Cretan seal, end of the 3rd millennium BC.*

Crete On Crete itself during the long centuries of the Early Minoan (or "Prepalatial") period, c. 3500–2000 BC, clear evidence of emerging social complexity is remarkably slight, from either domestic or mortuary contexts. Distinctive circular tholos tombs (also known as beehive tombs) were built and used throughout the entire period as communal places of burial (Branigan 1970); but although they often contained hundreds of corpses, the fact that these were deposited over many centuries indicates that the social groups who used them were – as their nearby settlement sites also suggest – quite limited. Prominent among the grave goods are riveted daggers of arsenical copper, and sealstones, both probably items of personal identity and display, which reflect both access to imported materials and enhanced craft skills. A handful of cemeteries, such as that at **Mochlos** in eastern Crete, provide plausible evidence of significant disparities of wealth between graves or family burial plots; on the other hand, such settlement sites as **Myrtos** and **Vasiliki**, also in eastern Crete, have proven to be far less convincing than was once claimed as precursors of the later palaces (Cherry 1983). Indeed, some of the very sites that later developed as palaces offer the best evidence for larger-than-average settlements (Whitelaw 1983), although size alone cannot tell us much about social or functional differentiation.

The Cyclades The picture is rather similar for the Cycladic Islands, although here another (modern) factor enters the equation. The central Cyclades are renowned for their pure white marble, used throughout the Early Bronze Age for making vases and anthropomorphic figurines in austere styles that resonate with modern sensibilities [see box: Early Cycladic Marble Figures]; the lamentable result has been the looting of Early Cycladic cemeteries, where most such sculptures are to be found (Gill and Chippindale 1993). Nearly all these cemeteries comprise at most a few dozen simple cist graves, although some exceptions are known: at **Chalandriani** on Syros, for instance, over 650 burials have been found associated with the nearby settlement at **Kastri**, which boasts fortifications and a maze of small buildings. Interestingly, it is from this site that many of the representations of paddled longboats [**13.5**] incised on a distinctive form of flat pottery vessel known as "frying pans" come, and it has been argued that such boats, possibly requiring cooperation from a number of small communities to build and operate, were used for trading and raiding throughout the islands; they may have fostered the prominence of certain sites, some of which became important centers in the earlier 2nd millennium BC (Broodbank 2000). Undoubtedly, maritime exchange played a significant role in Early Bronze Age societies throughout the Aegean [**13.6**].

The Greek Mainland and Troy Colin Renfrew (1972) characterized the mid-3rd millennium BC as a period with an "international spirit," based on the strong evidence of interregional contacts that began to transform hitherto independent cultures in different areas of the Aegean into a complex of related units. At some sites in the southern and central Greek mainland, for example, are found Cycladic marble figurines and pottery in forms that occur most commonly at **Troy** and other parts of the northeast Aegean; conversely, one of the most distinctive mainland pottery types, the "sauceboat" of the mid-3rd millennium BC, turns up on Cycladic and even Cretan sites.

The very ease with which mainland ceramics of this period can be recognized has led to the discovery of many hundreds of settlements, very few of which exceed small hamlet size. A significant architectural development at this time, however, is the rectangular, two-story "Corridor House" type (Shaw 1987), of which the House of the Tiles at **Lerna** [**13.7**] is one of the largest (at 25 x 12 m, or 82 x 39 ft) and best-known examples (Wiencke 2000). Provision for storage and finds of clay sealings (cly nodules into which carved sealstones were impressed) in the building suggest the mobilization or redistribution of commodities, but these Corridor Houses are far from monumental, and it is unwise to regard them as the functional predecessors of the later palaces. The same holds true of the series of rectilinear

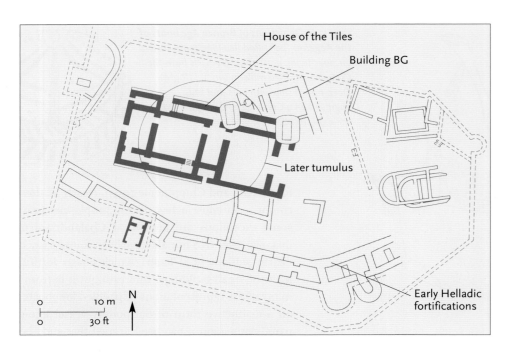

House of the Tiles

Building BG

Later tumulus

Early Helladic
fortifications

N

0   10 m

0   30 ft

13.7 *(Left)* **The House of the Tiles, Lerna:** *is a prototypical example of a distinctive architectural form, the "Corridor House." An earlier similar structure, Building BG, lies partially underneath it, and a circular tumulus was heaped up over it after its abandonment.*

13.8 *(Opposite below)* **The palace of Phaistos:** *view northwards over the paved central court of the Minoan palace at Phaistos, in south-central Crete. Ritual activities may have taken place here and in the Kamares Cave, in one of the distant peaks of Mount Ida, aligned with the court's north–south axis.*

buildings of this period known from an early phase (period II) of what later became the great site of Troy [see Troy box, Chapter 12, pp. 450–51]. In any case, this architectural tradition disappeared amid the upheavals that seem to have afflicted various parts of the Aegean toward the end of the Early Bronze Age [see The End of the Early Bronze Age box, Chapter 12, p. 448].

Troy II impresses in another way, however, as the source of the precocious metalwork in the various "treasures" unearthed by Heinrich Schliemann between 1872 and 1890; these disappeared from the Berlin Museums during World War II and resurfaced only in 1993 in museums in Moscow and St. Petersburg (Duchêne 1996; Antonova 1996).

Minoan Crete: The Palace Period

There are those who would say that the Minoan civilization is more the invention of its discoverer, Arthur Evans, than a past reality (MacGillivray 2000). Evans certainly interpreted his finds through the lens of later Greek myth (Minos, Theseus, Ariadne, and the Minotaur's labyrinth), and in the terms of his own Edwardian world (thus, separate quarters for kings and queens), and he boldly reconstructed much of the palace at Knossos in styles reminiscent of modern Art Nouveau and Art Deco. Nevertheless, he was also responsible for first identifying and publishing this prehistoric culture; as a result of his work, Minoan archaeology is today a very active field, and Crete has become a major tourist attraction – after the Athenian acropolis, Knossos is the most visited site in Greece.

Features and Functions of the Minoan Palace The palace at Knossos – Evans's "Palace of Minos," where excavations began in 1900 – may be the most famed, but it is not the only such com-

plex on the island. (The term "palace" must be used with caution, given its later associations; "regional center" may be preferable.) To the so-called **First Palace period** (*c.* 2000–1700 BC) can be dated the rise of the complexes at Knossos and Mallia in the north and Phaistos on the south coast of the island. These were remodeled, following destructive earthquakes, in the Second Palace period (*c.* 1700–1490 BC) and joined by others, such as Kato Zakros on the east coast; Petras, near Siteia on the northeast coast; Archanes, south of Knossos; Galatas in the Pediada plain in central Crete; perhaps Chania in northwest Crete; and a number of other sites with court-centered buildings (Rehak and Younger 1998).

While far from identical, the palaces share many features. They are monumental, but without defensive walls. Important elements include a large, open-air central court (the core of the palace), sometimes a secondary court to the west, residential quarters, and various spaces for entertainment and ritual performance, adorned with brightly frescoed walls and painted architectural elements. In other parts of the palaces were substantial magazines (some still crammed with gigantic *pithoi*, or storage jars), granaries, and even large subterranean pits, suggesting that the palaces served as points for the collection, storage, and perhaps redistribution of staple goods from surrounding areas. Various systems of seals and sealings, and several forms of script (dubbed hieroglyphic, Linear A, and Linear B) emerged as administrative technologies to account for and record the distribution of such commodities, held at the palace and/or produced in its hinterland. Unquestionably, Minoan palaces were multi-functional spaces.

Evans's assumption that elite persons ("kings") dwelled in and ruled from these palaces is generally accepted; but the iconography of power in Minoan Crete is, in fact, quite weakly developed, and virtually no clear examples of ruler portraiture are known (Davis 1995). Religious imagery, by contrast, is very apparent. Double axes, figurines of bare-breasted women grasping snakes, representations of bulls and of bull-leaping (a ritual act the feasibility of which is much debated), and "horns of consecration" (schematic bull horns) recur in a wide variety of contexts. Overtones of fertility and a strong female presence have led some to identify goddess worship on the island (but see critiques in Marinatos 1993; Goodison and Morris 1998).

The precise outlines and belief structures of Minoan ritual and religious cult remain difficult to discern, but they unquestionably played a major role in linking the island communities, and there is good evidence that palatial authorities sought to control religious power; this can be seen, for example, in the relationship of the palaces to sacred features in the landscape. The central court at **Phaistos** [13.8], for example, is aligned with the peaks of Mount Ida, high up on which lies the Kamares Cave, used for ritual purposes from early in the First Palace period; it gives its name to the beautiful Kamares Ware, a specifically palatial style of pottery first recognized there. **Knossos**, likewise, is visually linked with a major sanctuary atop Mount Iuktas; finds of cult apparatus and objects with Linear A inscriptions from this remote site again suggest strong links with palace culture. Peak sanctuaries such as these, as their name suggests, are shrines located in high places, at some remove

13.9 The "Peak Sanctuary" rhyton: *a chlorite rhyton (libation vase) from the Minoan palace at Kato Zakros, dating to the later 16th century* BC. *Once covered with gold leaf (some fragments of which still survive), the relief depicts a mountain sanctuary with "horns of consecration" and an altar, with birds and Cretan wild goats.*

from domestic settlement. They are known in most parts of Crete, many of them first established at the time of the rise of the palaces; a few (such as Iuktas) seem to have been embellished following their annexation to state control. A rhyton (a ceremonial vessel for pouring libations to deities) found at the palace of **Kato Zakros** [13.9] may provide a representation of one such peak sanctuary. Some of them (e.g. Atsipadhes, in west-central Crete) seem always to have served the needs of a more strictly local populace, to judge from the humble votives left there.

Life Outside the Palaces Although fieldwork in Minoan archaeology has always had a strongly palatial bias, certain other types of settlement in the countryside were recognized in the early years of the discipline. These include a number of substantial towns

(**Gournia**, first explored by the American Harriet Boyd Hawes in the early years of the 20th century, is the best example), and, in the Second Palace period, numerous "villa" complexes, such as **Tylissos** or **Vathypetro** in central Crete. Minoan villas are characterized by many of the features of palace culture – frescoes, use of script, storage facilities – and are assumed to be the residences of local elites, involved in the administration and exploitation of the Minoan countryside (Hägg 1997). Our understanding of settlement and other forms of activity below this level – villages, farmsteads, the life of the majority – is still under-explored, though regional surveys conducted in many parts of the island in recent years are beginning to address this imbalance.

The political organization of Minoan Crete – whether palaces and their territories were independent, or fell under the suzerainty of Knossos – remains uncertain, and may have varied over time (Cherry 1986). Whatever the political structures on the island itself, the developed sailing skills of the Minoans extended their influence well beyond Crete itself, and it is notable that the first Mediterranean representations of plank-built ships with sails are those depicted on Minoan sealstones from the time of the first palaces or a little before [see **13.6**]. Later Greeks spoke of the thalassocracy ("rule of the sea") of King Minos, although economic and cultural ties seem more assured than any formal political domination; Minoan imports and copies appear in the Cycladic Islands and on eastern islands such as Rhodes, for instance (Knapp 1993).

The End of the Minoan Palaces At the end of the Second Palace period, all but one of the palaces were destroyed, as were the satellite villas. Knossos survived, but a new administration was put in place, one employing certain new styles of material culture and, more strikingly, the **Linear B script** – a version of the Linear A writing that had been used in the palaces, but which expressed (somewhat awkwardly) the language of the Greek mainland [see box: Linear B, p. 484].

What precisely occurred is not known (Driessen and Farnoux 1997), and explanations range from an armed invasion to peaceful annexation. Some have argued that Crete had been weakened through the regional effects of a major volcanic eruption on the Cycladic island of Thera (Santorini) early in the Late Bronze Age, which blew the island apart and made a "Bronze Age Pompeii" of the vibrant and flourishing town at **Akrotiri** (Doumas 1983). This argument, however, is substantially undermined by a variety of scientific dating evidence that places the eruption much earlier than had previously been supposed, in the late 17th century BC (Manning 1999). Whatever the precise story, Minoan Crete passed into the political ambit of the new regional power in the Aegean, the Mycenaean society of mainland Greece.

Mycenaean Greece

Mycenae The eponymous site of this mainland civilization is Mycenae, in the northeast corner of the large peninsula of southern Greece known as the Peloponnese. This fortified citadel has been associated since Classical times and before with Agamemnon, king of the combined Greek forces that waged war on the Trojans, immortalized in Homer's *Iliad* (written in the Greek alphabet no earlier than the late 8th century BC). The Homeric legends prompted early archaeological work here, including excavations by Heinrich Schliemann in the 1870s, in between his two campaigns at Hissarlık, the site of Troy [see Troy box, Chapter 12, pp. 450–51]. At Mycenae Schliemann discovered one of two "grave circles" found at the site, containing rich burials of bodies interred with golden masks [**13.10**]; one of these inspired a telegram to the King of Greece, in which Schliemann claimed to have "gazed upon the face of Agamemnon." As with Minos on Crete, later Greek myth once again strongly influenced most interpretations of the Mycenaean world, but the direct relevance of Homer's poems to Mycenaean times has recently been thoroughly reconsidered (Morris 1992). In any case, we now know that the shaft graves found by Schliemann date to the formative era of Mycenaean society in the 16th century BC, long before the apogee of Mycenae's power and wealth in the 13th century BC.

The site [**13.11**] sits on a commanding hill, and, in contrast to Minoan centers, was strongly fortified with massive walls of Cyclopean masonry (named after the mythical one-eyed giants, the Cyclopes, their supposed builders). A defensible entrance led visitors beneath the towering walls and through the monumental **Lion Gate** [**13.12**] (topped with a sculpted facade of facing lions flanking a column), past the earlier grave circles, and up into the citadel proper.

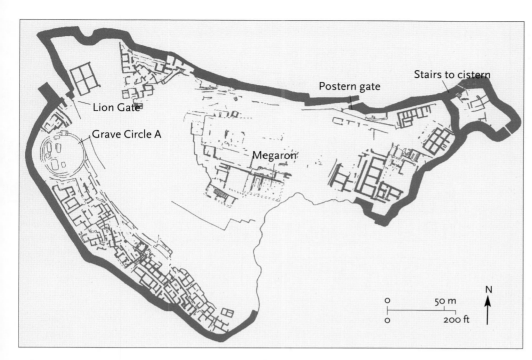

13.11 (Left) **Plan of the acropolis of Mycenae:** the pork-chop shaped citadel, fortified by massive Cyclopean walls, has been partially lost to erosion. Several excavation campaigns, chiefly by British and Greek archaeologists, have been conducted at the site since Schliemann's time.

13.10 (Opposite) **Gold mask:** the most famous of the golden masks, dating to the 16th century BC, discovered by Heinrich Schliemann in Grave Circle A at Mycenae in 1876. Schliemann, who relied heavily on myth in his interpretations, believed he was gazing upon "the face of Agamemnon."

13.12 (Below) **The Lion Gate, principal entrance to the citadel at Mycenae:** heraldic lions (their heads now missing) stand facing each other, with a column in between.

KEY DISCOVERY Linear B

In his very first excavation season at Knossos, on Crete, in 1900, Sir Arthur Evans discovered large numbers of inscribed clay tablets, the language of which was then unknown. Exploration soon afterwards at other major Minoan sites, such as Phaistos, Mallia, and Agia Triada, also yielded small quantities of tablets with inscriptions, but in a writing system related to, yet distinct from, that at Knossos. Both scripts seemed more highly developed than the arrangements of small pictures of objects sometimes found on engraved sealstones, clay bars, and other prehistoric objects.

As we now appreciate, these are the three main categories of Minoan script, which Evans termed, respectively, Linear B, Linear A, and hieroglyphic (from its generic resemblances to Egyptian writing). Hieroglyphic emerged *c.* 2000 BC, around the time of the first palaces, whereas Linear A was the principal script in use, mainly in administrative and ritual contexts, from the 18th century BC until the end of the Second Palace era, a little after 1500 BC. Linear B clearly developed from Linear A, and was in widespread use throughout much of the 14th and 13th centuries BC on the Greek mainland, at sites such as Pylos, Mycenae, Tiryns, Thebes, Eleusis, and Orchomenos, as well as at Knossos, Chania, and Armenoi on Crete.

Decipherment and Content

Evans's Knossian tablets remained unpublished until 1952, a dozen years after his death. Meanwhile, in the first week of excavations in 1939 at the Palace of Nestor at Pylos, in southwest Greece, Carl Blegen and his team encountered an archive room full of Linear B tablets baked by the fire that had destroyed the palace in the late 13th century BC. It was the publication of the first batch of these tablets in 1951 that finally provided the young British architect, Michael Ventris, with

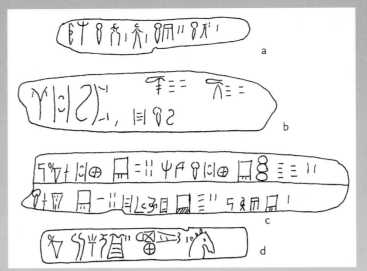

13.13 *Linear B tablets from Knossos showing ideograms representing: (a) a man, woman, two girls, and one boy; (b) 50 rams and 50 ewes; (c) different kinds of cloth; (d) a horse, chariot, and tunic. Examples of "leaf-shaped" tablets, they were created by forming a clay cylinder that was then squashed to provide a smooth writing surface.*

an adequate supply of material for a decipherment of Linear B as an early form of Greek. The story of this decipherment is a riveting one (Robinson 2002), and the eventual outcome was quite unexpected, since almost everyone had supposed Linear B to be a Cretan script used by Minoans who were not Greek-speakers (Chadwick 1958).

Mindful of the range of subject matter encountered in the immense archives of Near Eastern palaces (Chapter 12), there were those who had hoped that the Linear B documents would reveal Mycenaean legal and business records, letters, annals, royal inscriptions,

perhaps even an early version of Homeric poetry. Even prior to their decipherment, however, their brevity, layout, and easily recognizable ideograms made it obvious that these documents dealt mostly with the mundane administrative concerns of the palaces. Nevertheless, during the half-century since the decipherment, impressive amounts of information have been extracted from the several thousand tablets published (Chadwick 1976).

We now know a great deal about the detailed workings of palace-controlled industries concerned with textiles, flax, and perfumed oil, including the distribution of rations to different categories of female and male workers. There are sets of tablets dealing (enigmatically) with landholding; others provide powerful evidence that a number of Classical Greek deities (Athena, Poseidon, and Zeus, for instance) were worshiped already in Mycenaean times; and studies of place names have given some sense of the political geography of Mycenaean kingdoms on the mainland and in Crete. Most recently, new tablets and sealings from Thebes in Boeotia appear to reveal evidence of state-sponsored feasting. Considering how brief and fragmentary most Linear B texts are, and how routine and commonplace the subject matter of the majority of them is, it is remarkable how much valuable information has been extracted from them about Mycenaean society as a whole.

13.14 *Michael Ventris, the decipherer of Linear B, examining a tablet written in that script. Ventris, an architect and cryptographer, became a hero for his linguistic and archaeological "detective" work, but died tragically young in 1956.*

13.15 *Aerial view of the Mycenaean citadel at Tiryns in the Argive Plain:* this photograph was taken from a tethered balloon (the rope for which is visible at the top of the image). Tiryns is especially famed for its remarkable circuit of thick Cyclopean walls.

A key feature of the site (as of almost all Mycenaean centers) is the megaron: a three-roomed rectangular structure with columned porch leading to an antechamber, and then into a columned hall with central hearth. This is assumed to have been the seat of power of the Mycenaean ruler. Residential quarters, storage facilities, shrines, and workshops crowd the space within the massive walls of Mycenae, and some areas outside them as well; wall paintings and other fine craft products (many clearly reflecting Minoan influence) are common.

Other Mycenaean Palaces Mycenae is widely agreed to be the center of a kingdom, the precise boundaries of which remain undetermined; the impact of Mycenae's rise to power can be traced in the changing settlement patterns of neighboring valley systems (Cherry and Davis 2001). It was by no means the only such kingdom in Mycenaean Greece, however. Palatial complexes with broadly similar features are known at **Tiryns** (puzzlingly, only 15 km (9 miles) from Mycenae); at **Pylos** in the southwest Peloponnese; at the **Menelaion** near ancient Sparta, in the south-central Peloponnese; on the Athenian acropolis; at **Thebes**, in the Boeotian plain; and even as far north as Iolkos in central Greece. A number of other sites boast impressive defensive walls (those at **Gla** in central Greece run for some 3 km, or 2 miles), but seemingly lack a true palace.

Not all these sites are well preserved or accessible to the archaeologist. Thebes is little explored because the modern city sits on top of the ancient site, while later constructions on the Athenian acropolis have left scant traces of the Bronze Age palace there. But the astonishing Cyclopean fortifications of Tiryns were a wonder even in antiquity [**13.15**], and excavations at Pylos, begun in 1939 at the so-called Palace of Nestor (another Homeric hero), have revealed the best-preserved megaron of Mycenaean Greece, including even its painted

hearth. Each of these "palaces" (as on Crete, the term must be used with care) no doubt controlled a wide surrounding region, which both regional survey and the Linear B texts have helped us to understand [see box: Linear B]. The rich archive discovered at Pylos allows reconstructions of aspects not only of Pylian economy, society, and religious practice, but of political geography too, with its references to settlements throughout the "Hither" and "Further" provinces (Chadwick 1976).

Mycenaean Society and Overseas Influence The socio-political stratification of Mycenaean society is visible in its mortuary architecture (and in this respect is different from Minoan Crete). A range of tomb types, from plain rock-cut chamber tombs to highly elaborate, monumental tholos (or "bee-hive," from their shape) tombs has been identified. The so-called Treasury of Atreus (another of Mycenae's associations with later myth) is but the grandest of nine such tholoi that surround the citadel of Mycenae; examples are also known at a number of other major Myceanaean centers, such as **Orchomenos** in central Greece and at **Pylos**. The remarkable corbelled vaulting of the elaborately decorated Treasury of Atreus (wherein each higher level of stones slightly overhangs the previous one, eventually meeting at the top under a capstone), like the Cyclopean masonry of the citadels, demonstrates the remarkable skills of Mycenaean engineers. Road networks (especially around Mycenae), bridges, dams, port installations, and drainage projects such as the massive hydraulic works in the Kopais basin (where Gla is located), unrivaled before the modern era, all testify to what must have been state-directed development of the infrastructure of Mycenaean kingdoms.

Mycenaean influence overseas is today most readily traceable in the spread of its characteristic fine pottery (or local imitations of it), which is very widely found around the shores of the eastern Mediterranean in Egypt, the Levant, Cyprus, Crete, and many of the Aegean islands, as well as at sites in Italy, Sicily, and Sardinia. Trade seems to have been the principal mechanism involved, and the acquisition of metal resources necessary for bronzeworking may have been one of the motives for it. Shipwreck evidence such as the Uluburun wreck [see box: The Uluburn Shipwreck, Chapter 12, p. 459] suggests that Mycenaean trading activities constituted only one part of a complex network of exchange and multicultural interaction, involving participants from many regions and polities in the Late Bronze Age eastern Mediterranean. The extent to which certain areas of coastal Anatolia and the islands of the Dodecanese, heavily influenced by Mycenaean fashions in mortuary practice and material culture, reflect actual colonists, or simply political control from the Greek mainland, remains an open question. The Mycenaean annexation and administration of Minoan Crete during parts of the 14th and 13th centuries BC – a culture by which the Mycenaeans themselves had been much influenced – is somewhat less ambiguous.

The End of the Aegean Bronze Age During the 13th century BC, the citadels of Mycenae and Tiryns, and certain other Mycenaean sites, reveal signs of renewed or enhanced fortification, including the construction of defended underground cisterns as a provision for siege warfare [see **13.11**]. Despite such efforts, the Mycenaean palaces were destroyed or abandoned over the course of several decades toward the end of that century (c. 1200 BC). Invasions by a people from the north that the later Classical Greeks called "Dorians," or other interventions by foreigners (such as the so-called "Sea Peoples," see Chapter 12), no longer seem a likely cause. Troubles more local to the Mycenaean world – internecine warfare between kingdoms, internal unrest, crop failure – seem more plausible, although some scholars envisage complex scenarios whose details we can perhaps never know (Renfrew 1979). Occupation of a more modest sort continued at some sites (including both Mycenae and Tiryns), and overseas contacts never entirely dried up, but by around 1050 BC both the reality and the trappings of Mycenaean power – palace-sponsored luxury craft production, monumental burials, elaborately decorated architecture, great fortifications, and the use of writing – were over, and its monuments began to pass into memory and myth.

Cultural Variety in the 1st Millennium BC

The close of the 2nd millennium BC was a time of great instability in the eastern Mediterranean, and with the end of palatial civilization, a "Dark Age" cast its shadow over Greece and the Aegean. Out of these not entirely dark centuries emerged one of the principal developments of the 1st millennium BC – the

polity known as the Greek city-state. A cross-cultural phenomenon, the city-state appears in other Mediterranean contexts as well, and was widely distributed through the colonial activities of Greeks and Phoenicians (Nichols and Charlton 1997; Hansen 2000). Urbanization was thus a characteristic, if not universal, process in the 1st millennium BC. A multiplicity of local developments also marked the Mediterranean region, which emerges in this period as a mosaic-like distribution of different polities and cultures. Underlying this diversity, however, were population movements and networks of trade and exchange, which created strong currents of connection between these different zones.

Greece and the Aegean

The Dark Age Traces of the Greek Dark Age (c. 1000–750 BC), as its name suggests, are few and relatively impoverished; a sharp drop in population from the Late Bronze Age seems clear. As mentioned already, later Greeks, such as the 5th-century BC historian Herodotus, attributed this reversal to a so-called (and archaeologically invisible) Dorian invasion from the north. Few would accept that explanation today, preferring instead to consider internal factors, not least the collapse of the ruling state authority. The "darkness" of this Dark Age has also been increasingly re-evaluated. External contacts, especially with the east, appear to have revived quite quickly, as did some measure of internal social hierarchy. Both are demonstrated by the 10th-century BC "heröon" (a shrine or temple dedicated to a hero) at Toumba, Lefkandi, on the island of Euboea [**13.16**]. The interpretation of this large (40 m, or 131 ft, long) and complicated structure is controversial, but it contained, alongside human burials and horse sacrifices, exotic goods traceable to Phoenicia and Egypt (Popham et al. 1993; Whitley 2001).

The Archaic Period During the succeeding Archaic period (c. 750–480 BC) was born one of the more lastingly influential of all political formations, the Greek **polis**, or **city-state**. The polis was an autonomous unit that embraced both a central, urban settlement and its rural hinterland. Its people were bound together not only by political ties, but by economic and religious links as well; full members of this community (free-born males for the most part), wherever they lived, possessed the status of citizen. Not all parts of Greece followed this developmental path (league structures were another option), but Greek or Greek-influenced city-states would ultimately be established over a vast domain, stretching from the western Mediterranean to the eastern reaches of the Black Sea.

Charting and explaining the rise of the Greek polis has engendered major debate among Classical archaeologists. One influential argument revolved around the striking increase in population beginning in the 8th century BC, an observation

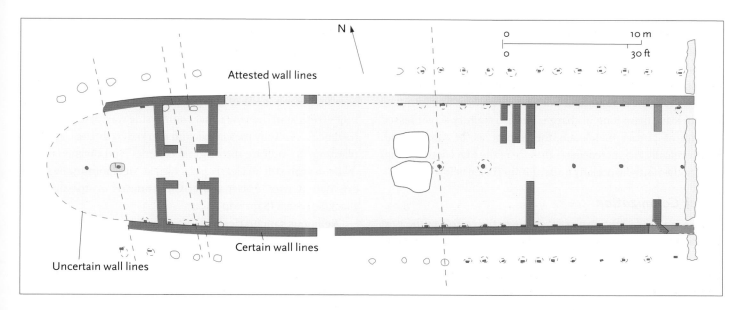

13.16 *Plan of the 10th-century BC 'Heröon' at Toumba, Lefkandi:*
which came first – the burials or the building – remains unclear.
Although frequently called a Heröon, the structure could have been a
house, a communal feasting hall, or some kind of early temple; perhaps
it served more than one of these functions.

based on the number of graves discovered (Snodgrass 1977; 1980). Reinterpretation of these data has suggested that the increase in grave numbers at this time reflects the formal burial of a complete population, not just an elite component of it, and thus perhaps the beginnings of the emergence of the citizen ideal (Morris 1987). The appearance of monumental temple architecture, and of bounded communal cult places (sanctuaries), is another element in the story. Relationships forged by cult would create ties within, and delineate boundaries between, developing civic territories (de Polignac 1995). Reconfiguration of domestic, urban, and mortuary space, as well as changes in military organization, also occur during this "age of experiment," to use Anthony Snodgrass's phrase, and seem both cause and symptom of this evolving political formation (Osborne 1996; Whitley 2001).

The Classical Period Once established, the political history of Archaic and Classical (480–338 BC) Greece becomes to a great extent the history of these cities and their mutual interactions. Each proudly strove for autonomy and independence, and warfare among them was endemic. Yet city-states were usually quite small in extent and population. The relatively small Cycladic island of Keos, for example, was home to four city-states simultaneously, the territory of one of which has been estimated at only 15 sq. km (6 sq. miles) in extent (Cherry et al. 1991). Individually, none of these could have sent many men to war, and, not surprisingly, political and military alliances often

resulted, usually led by one or another more powerful leader. Chief among these coalition leaders were **Athens** and **Thebes** in central Greece, and **Argos** and **Sparta** in the Peloponnese.

Even beyond such alliances (which tended to be volatile), Greeks acknowledged the bond of a shared language and shared gods; the poems of Homer (the *Iliad* and the *Odyssey*) were also treasured common property. Anyone outside that cultural circle was "barbarian," which originally meant incapable of speaking Greek properly (Cartledge 1993). Men thus perceived themselves as Hellenes (the later term "Greek" derives from the Latin name), as well as citizens of individual cities. This coalescing power was most clearly seen in the response to the **Persian invasion** of Greece under Darius I in 490 BC, and then again ten years later by his son, Xerxes. Greek states, against all the numerical odds, united to reject this barbarian threat. The success of this endeavor, particularly the victories at **Marathon** and **Salamis** in Attica (the territory of Athens) in 490 and 480 BC, respectively, dramatically boosted Greek, and particularly Athenian, self-confidence.

The 5th-century BC expansion of Athens into an imperial power, with tax-paying "allies" drawn from around the Aegean in a confederation called the Delian League (after its original base on Delos), grew from this new-found authority. What we call the Classical period was born around 480 BC from this post-Persian War enthusiasm, and memories of those great victories are showcased and explored everywhere in Classical art and architecture (Pollitt 1972).

If the Persian Wars formed one definitive event in 5th-century BC east Mediterranean history, the **Peloponnesian War** between Athens and Sparta was unquestionably another. This extended struggle (431–404 BC) was fought between rival and quite different powers; Athens prided itself on its imperial navy, whereas Sparta was thought unbeatable on land. The conflict

487

drew in much of the wider Greek world: a doomed campaign to colonial Syracuse on the island of Sicily decimated the Athenian forces, and even the despised Persian empire became involved. The Spartans won in the end, after a devastating siege of Athens, but the endless turbulence of political allegiances and enmities did not leave them long in charge. The 4th century BC witnessed the rise of Thebes in Boeotia, the resurgence of Athens, and, most critically, the increasing influence of the Macedonian kingdom to the north, especially under Philip II (see below).

Greek Colonization

Beginning in the 8th century BC and over the course of the next two centuries, some Greek city-states sent out parties of men to establish colonies in various parts of the Mediterranean world and beyond. Such initiatives targeted Sicily and southern Italy in sufficient quantity that the region became known as Magna Graecia ("Great Greece") [see box: The Necropolis at Metapontum]. Other zones of interest were the south of France, the North African coast, and the Black Sea region (Boardman 1999; Pugliese Carratelli 1996). These new communities went on to follow their own historical path, in some cases outstripping their home cities in splendor, wealth, and power. Good examples are Sicilian **Syracuse**, long a major military force in central Mediterranean affairs, or Italian **Sybaris** (whence our word "sybaritic").

No single motivation can explain all cases of this human exportation. Over-population at home and resulting land-hunger may account for some instances; ancient authors (albeit usually long after the fact) also cite internal civic tensions that led to the expulsion of unwanted or rebellious elements of the population. The location of many colonies suggests an interest in particular natural resources such as metal ores in the case of **Pithekoussai** and other western colonies, or fish in the Black Sea, or in fostering trade and exchange. Settling near the mouth of a river made sense for expanding contacts inland, as at **Massalia** (modern Marseille), near the River Rhône, or at **Olbia** on the north coast of the Black Sea (modern Crimea), near the Bug and Dnieper rivers. The observed long-distance movement of Greek artifacts (with pottery, as always, most visible) points to new systems of exchange and influence, both with other Mediterranean peoples, such as the Etruscans of central Italy, and with "barbarians" further away, such as the Celts to the west or the Scythians of the Eurasian steppes (Wells 1980; Tsetskhladze and De Angelis 1994; Osborne 1996).

Not surprisingly, given their far-flung geographical distribution and different mother cities, the composition of Greek colonies varied. Fundamental features of all, however, included some sort of urban center, with public buildings and residential quarters; a tomb or monument to the colony's founder was also common. As with Greek city-states, a rural hinterland was an essential component of the political unit. Given the community's fresh start, however, that countryside was, at least in some instances, carefully measured, and marked by ditches, roads, or plantings to indicate the original colonial land divisions. Such divisions can still be clearly perceived at **Metapontum** in southern Italy (Carter, 2005) and at **Chersonesus** on the northern Black Sea coast (Saprykin 1994).

Religious sanctuaries were also carefully located in the colonial landscape, within both the primary settlement and the countryside. One influential argument posits that their precise placement, often highly visible, served to signal and define the Greek presence, both to themselves and to indigenous observers. The appearance of monumental stone temples, constructed according to the mainland Greek architectural orders (either Doric or Ionic; see box: The Parthenon, pp. 494–95), was part of this development (de Polignac 1995). Our best-preserved Greek-style peripteral temples (i.e., structures with columns encircling an inner chamber containing a cult image, and usually adorned with external sculptural decoration) are actually located in these colonial settings, such as at Paestum in southern Italy [**13.17**], not in Greece itself.

13.17 *The temples of Hera I and II at Paestum (Greek Poseidonia) in southern Italy: the Greek city was founded around 600 BC; these two temples, testifying both to the popularity of Hera and the wealth of the community, date to roughly the mid-6th and mid-5th centuries BC.*

KEY SITE The Necropolis at Metapontum

Metapontum was one of the more famous Greek colonies in southern Italy, established by settlers from the northern Peloponnese in the later 7th century BC. The urban site controlled a rich and extensive rural hinterland (*chora*) that made it prosperous. Its territory has been studied in great detail: first by means of aerial photography and, over the past two decades, by intensive surface survey [see box: The Silent Greek Countryside, p. 498] within an area of about 40 sq. km (15 sq. miles). This work has revealed one of the largest and earliest Greek systems of land division, by which certain areas were divided into regular lots, served by roadways and irrigation ditches. Notwithstanding considerable disturbance from modern agriculture, as many as 1000 ancient farms have been identified dating to the peak period of rural settlement in the later 4th century BC, together with other types of special-purpose sites, such as small sanctuaries and cemeteries, some of which have been excavated (Carter, 2005).

Pantanello was one such cemetery, located at an ancient rural crossroads some 3.5 km (2 miles) from the city itself, and its remarkably pristine preservation allowed total excavation by a team from Texas between 1982 and 1986 (Carter, 1998). Astonishingly, despite centuries of tomb excavation in Italy, this is the first cemetery in Magna Graecia to have been excavated and published in its entirety. It produced 324 burials, primarily inhumations, most of them dating to between about 580 BC and sometime after 280 BC, almost certainly the graves of individuals who lived on farms in the vicinity.

Although not everyone was buried with grave goods, most had at least a few; over 1200 items were recovered, some of them artistically impressive. Interestingly, the physical anthropologists who aged and sexed the skeletons did so "blind," so that they were not tempted to make assumptions based on the grave goods, for instance that burials with mirrors must necessarily be those of females – although of the 18 mirrors, 14 were, in fact, found with females.

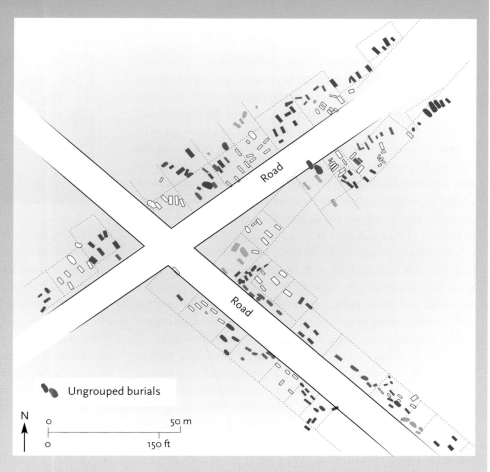

Ungrouped burials

N

0 — 50 m
0 — 150 ft

Good preservation, careful excavation and recording, and thorough specialist studies have resulted in the dating of most burials with some precision. This allows changing burial practices to be followed in detail, and enables one to say with confidence that female adult burials outnumbered males by a ratio of two to one. (Where, then, are the missing males?)

Perhaps the most unusual opportunity afforded by this necropolis arises from combining evidence about spatial layout with anthropological studies. The excavator, Joseph Carter, hypothesized that members of the same family would have been buried in a distinct grouping or plot, and the results of studies of blood groups and epigenetic (accumulated) traits showed that there were, indeed, biological linkages among nearby burials. Furthermore, the excellent

13.18 *Plan of the Pantanello necropolis, located at an ancient crossroad. It illustrates the presence of family plots (indicated by dotted lines) within the overall patterning of tombs, as well as the tendency of graves to line roadways.*

chronology and aging/sexing made it possible to reconstruct family trees, in some cases reaching over five generations, which can be mapped onto burial plots of standardized dimensions as hypothetical family groupings.

What gives this case study special value, apart from any interest in specific grave types or burial gifts, is the thorough and complete excavation of the cemetery, set against results from the region-wide survey; this meticulousness allows us to have confidence that we are dealing with a true cross-section of the rural, hybrid (Greek and local) population of this important colony.

13.19 *Bas-relief depicting a Phoenician trading-ship: the marine exploits of the Phoenicians have traditionally been the most celebrated aspect of their long and complex history.*

The vocabulary of colonization is, of course, highly colored by modern overtones of cultural superiority and ruthless economic exploitation. Great care must be exercised before making these same assumptions about the ancient Mediterranean. Despite the archaeologically obvious spread of Greek material culture, no evidence exists for an overt civilizing mission to the natives. The economic benefits of exchange, if favorable to the new settlements, appear to have flowed in both directions; apparent prestige gifts to indigenous rulers, such as the huge bronze krater found in a richly furnished Hallstatt grave at **Vix**, in eastern France (Chapter 11, p. 424), suggest that diplomatic relations were sought and achieved. Nevertheless, it remains true that our only textual sources, as well as the majority of archaeological evidence, come from the colonizer's side of the equation. For this reason, independent investigation into the lives of indigenous peoples, and their pre-colonial landscapes, has become an increasingly high priority for archaeologists.

What is already clear is that, far from becoming instant converts to all aspects of Hellenic culture, local populations interacted in various ways with the newcomers, sometimes adopting alien cultural practices, sometimes maintaining their own, sometimes creating new combinations of the two; the adoption in the west of wine-drinking, and what it signified culturally, is a good case in point. When we speak of the Greeks in the west, in the Black Sea, or wherever, what is actually under discussion is a complex of cultures which, despite participating in many widely shared Hellenic traditions, nevertheless followed unique and local paths of development (Lyons and Papadopoulos 2002).

The Phoenicians and Phoenician Expansion

This movement of peoples, goods, and ideas that began in Greece was paralleled in a wave of more or less contemporary activity by the Phoenicians, a Levantine people principally based along the coast of modern Lebanon (see also Chapter 12). Early in the 1st millennium BC they were organized in independent city-states (most notably **Tyre** and **Sidon**), which were eventually absorbed into the expanding Assyrian and Persian empires (Niemeyer 2000). Phoenician cities farmed the surrounding countryside, and they were centers of admired craft production, especially in ivory and glass. For all that, these people are most famous, and justly so, for their long-distance seafaring and trading interests (Moscati 1988; Aubet 1993) [**13.19**].

Scholars once tended to treat Greek developments in isolation from those of Phoenician cities, whose commercial orientation was much derided; this disdain for a more eastern, Semitic culture is an element in Bernal's *Black Athena* controversy, mentioned above. In fact, interaction between the two is manifest. It has long been acknowledged, for instance, that the Greek alphabet was borrowed from a Phoenician model in the 8th century BC, and subsequently passed west to Etruria and Rome (Osborne 1996; Powell 1992). Phoenician artifacts and architectural influence can also been seen in Greek sanctuaries such as that at the Cretan site of **Kommos**, which lay along sailing routes to the west (Shaw 1989; Hoffman 1997).

Phoenician exploration of the central and western Mediterranean began early in the 1st millennium BC, and by the 8th century BC they had established colonial foundations in Spain, North Africa, and Sicily. The juxtaposition of Phoenician and Greek colonies on Sicily, not to mention the proximity of these foreign colonies to native populations such as the Sikels and Elymians, resulted in centuries of intermittent tension and conflict. Phoenician colonial activity and site selection are agreed to have had fairly specific economic, exchange-oriented motivations. The locations chosen, coastal and blessed with good harbors, support this, as does a strong bias toward metal-bearing regions. Southern Spain and Portugal, for instance, produced great quantities of silver, as well as tin, copper, and gold; the Phoenician settlement of **Gadir** (modern **Cadiz**), founded on an offshore island near the Strait of Gibraltar, was deliberately placed to take advantage of that fact (Aubet 1993; van Dommelen 1998; Niemeyer 2000).

The most famous of these Phoenician establishments was **Carthage** on the north coast of modern Tunisia, set on a promontory reaching out toward Sicily and Italy. According to tradition, Carthage (from Qart-hadasht, or "New City") was founded by Tyre in 814/813 BC. It would later become the chief center of Punic culture (Punic being the west Phoenician dialect spoken there). Carthage developed into a major west Mediterranean power – a Carthaginian empire – through territorial expansion in North Africa, Spain, Sicily, and Sardinia, before finally being crushed, both militarily and symbolically, by the forces of Rome in the 2nd century BC (see below).

The Etruscans and the Italian Peninsula

By the middle of the 1st millennium BC, the peninsula of Italy appeared as a mélange of local cultures. These can be broken into three rough categories: the Greek colonies, chiefly to the south; the Etruscan cities of west-central Italy, north of Rome; and an assemblage of Italic peoples, such as the Samnites and the Umbrians of central Italy, among whom were the inhabitants of Rome in Latium (Cornell 2000).

Much of what we know of this last group from non-archaeological sources derives from later Roman authorities, whose often dismissive treatment of non-Roman groups must be read with some skepticism. The Samnites, for example, were often depicted as boorish unsophisticates, yet regional research has revealed a level of organization not unlike that of the contemporary community of Rome. The **Samnites** were major opponents of Rome's early expansion, having been finally defeated only after a series of wars in the 4th and 3rd centuries BC – an opposition that no doubt contributed to Rome's hostile characterization of them (Dench 1995). A major regional survey carried out during the 1970s and 1980s in Samnite territory (the Biferno Valley) provides a useful archaeological control for the partial historical accounts of these processes (Barker 1995).

On the other hand, the adjective once most frequently applied to the **Etruscans** (who flourished c. 700–400 BC) was "mysterious," thanks not least to debates over their origins and language [see box: Who Were the Etruscans?, p. 493]. More recently, early archaeological fascination with their very rich tombs, complete with bright and, to our eyes, incongruously cheerful paintings, has expanded into broader investigations of Etruscan regional landscapes, settlements, and non-funerary art and cult. These changing methodological approaches have rendered Etruscan society less alien, and more akin to Mediterranean developments elsewhere (Spivey and Stoddart 1990; Barker and Rasmussen 1998).

Etruscans resided in independent city-states, the 12 chief cities of which (including **Veii**, **Cerveteri**, and **Tarquinia**) united to form an Etruscan League (Torelli 2000). The organization of these cities remains relatively poorly known, but they were often well fortified and located in hilltop locations. At points in their history, the Etruscans followed an expansionist policy, moving south into the area of the Bay of Naples (and thus into tension with Greek colonies to the south of that) and north into the Po plain. The Latin community of Rome was also brought within their sphere of influence, probably from the 7th century BC. As for external relationships, finds (especially from sanctuaries and tombs) amply demonstrate that the Etruscans enjoyed extensive contact with Greeks and Phoenicians (and later Carthaginians) alike. Greek influence is clearly seen in the realm of Etruscan religious art and architecture, not least in the appearance of anthropomorphic deities and the concept of a

13.20 Reconstruction of an Etruscan temple, closely modeled on the Portonaccio temple at Veii: the figure of the "Apollo of Veii" would have been seen striding along the temple's roofline, behind the central chariot group.

13.21 *(Right)* **Banquet scene from the Tomb of the Leopards, Tarquinia, dating to c. 480–470 BC:** *below the snarling leopards, dining couples (male and female) recline at table; musicians and dancers are depicted on the adjoining walls. The entire tomb, including the ceiling, is brightly painted.*

13.22 *(Below)* **Aerial view of the Banditaccia necropolis, Caere (modern Cerveteri):** *in this photograph different types of Etruscan grave monuments can be clearly seen – both circular, heaped tumuli and tomb rows of rectangular construction.*

temple to house them. One of these temples, however, the Portonaccio temple at **Veii** (*c.* 500 BC), is not particularly Greek either in materials, proportion, or in its use of columns, which appear only to the front, on a high raised podium, rather than around all four sides of the inner building, on a low platform [**13.20**]. Statues marched along the Portonaccio temple's roofline in Etruscan fashion; one of these, the so-called Apollo of Veii, clearly responds to a Greek sculptural type, the young male *kouros* (discussed below), adapting its pose but eschewing Greek-style nudity.

Considerable evidence exists for a significant class hierarchy in Etruscan society, a structure most clearly seen in the realm of the dead. In their often very visible necropoleis ("cities of the dead"), elite tombs took several forms over time, developing from circular tumuli to rectangular constructions. Tumuli in the **Banditaccia** cemetery near **Cerveteri** could be over 40 m (130 ft) in diameter, with a rock-cut structure within, resembling the interior of a house [**13.22**]. Elite tombs might be ornately decorated, either with brightly painted scenes of feasting [**13.21**], athletic games, or deities and demons, or with relief sculptures of armor and weapons, domestic objects, or mythological scenes (Barker and Rasmussen 1998).

Etruscan tomb paintings, with their bright and vivid colors, are justly famous, none more so than those from the cemetery at **Tarquinia**. The frequent scenes of banqueting, probably depictions of funerary feasts, have received special notice and reveal the mixed reception of external fashions (Bonfante 1986; Spivey 1997). On the one hand, they point to the adoption of the eastern practice of reclining while eating; on the other, they show women dining with men – a distinct taboo in Greek culture and an indicator of the apparent social freedom of Etruscan women compared to their contemporaries elsewhere in the Mediterranean (Bonfante 1994).

Among the grave goods found in these tombs are thousands of imported Greek painted pots, especially the Black and Red Figure wares of Athens. An interesting debate has revolved around the extent to which these vases were themselves intentionally made for export, or whether they were merely ancillary elements to more significant economic exchange, as containers for valuable oils or perfumes, for instance (Osborne 1986; Spivey 1991). This debate is part of a wider argument about the value of Greek, and especially Athenian, pottery (Vickers and Gill 1994; Whitley 2001). Highly prized in the modern world,

its status in antiquity would have been somewhat less remarkable, since metal plate (gold and silver) was the most luxurious of tableware.

That does not erase the fact that these pots were perceived as desirable tomb goods in an Etruscan aristocratic context. Nor does it eliminate the sad fact that such precious finds have motivated tomb robbers throughout the ages; one enterprising 20th-century looter alone claimed to have ravaged some 4000 Etruscan tombs (Perticarari 1986). Despite concern and much publicity, the protection of Etruscan tombs and other antiquities, Italian and otherwise, still remains a heated issue in cultural heritage management (Graepler et al. 1993; Elia 2001).

KEY CONTROVERSY Who Were the Etruscans?

In the 1976 horror movie, *The Omen*, a terrifying scene involving the origin of the devil child Damien is set in an Etruscan necropolis. The selection of such a setting in many ways accords with long-held views of this culture. The Etruscans have been regarded as mysterious, cryptic, and death-obsessed, all thanks to a particular blend of scholarly preconceptions and prejudices.

Archaeological fascination with impressive tomb complexes had a part to play in these misconceptions, and even more fundamental was the perceived peculiarity of the Etruscan language. Unrelated to Latin or any other contemporary language spoken in Italy, Etruscan is not an Indo-European tongue (Bonfante 1990). A non-indigenous, exotic origin was once automatically assumed, specifically the one supplied by the 5th-century BC Greek historian Herodotus, who told of a westward migration from Lydia (southwest Turkey) to Italy. By contrast, later Roman-period authors claimed the Etruscans were autochthonous: a people who had always lived where they lived.

We have no idea what the Etruscans themselves believed. While some 10,000 Etruscan documents survive (and contrary to what is often asserted, these can be read), they are for the most part quite terse, only six being more than 50 words long. That silence has left the Etruscans vulnerable to many charges: as D. H. Lawrence (1960) remarked

ironically in *Etruscan Places* of 1932, "... the Etruscans were vicious. We know it, because their enemies and exterminators said so."

Modern Research

Most of the mystery behind Etruscan origins has now evaporated, thanks to a combination of new approaches and attitudes. First, the Herodotean story of a Lydian exodus has been re-evaluated as a piece of political and genealogical myth-making that fits its particular historical context. This kind of invention of tradition is now understood as having been extremely common in antiquity, thus requiring a flexibly critical reading of ancient sources. Detailed archaeological work has also demonstrated overwhelmingly that the roots of Etruscan society, the framework of its economic, social, and political system, lay in the later prehistoric communities of Etruria, in the Villanovan Iron Age (900–700 BC) (Barker and Rasmussen 1998).

External Contacts

This is not to suggest, however, that the Etruscans were impervious to external influence. Eastern contact, not least through Greek and Phoenician colonial activity, clearly had a major impact on the development of Etruscan culture. The occupants of "princely tombs" from the 7th century BC received luxury grave goods in Orientalizing (eastern Mediterranean) style, just as later elite burials

13.23 *Bronze mirror engraved with a scene of a (nude) man and (clothed) woman conversing. Dating to c. 300 BC, it is inscribed "mi thancvilus funial": "I [am the mirror] of Thancvil Fulni." Engraved mirrors were probably given to women at weddings or other significant occasions; they survive through being placed in the tombs of their owners.*

received Athenian vases; the Etruscans would adopt and modify an alphabet borrowed from the Greeks, just as the Greeks had borrowed it from the Phoenicians.

The unusual nature of the Etruscan language remains a mystery, but the Etruscans otherwise emerge as a complex product of the indigenous and the external – a very Mediterranean synthesis.

The Structure of the Archaic and Classical Greek Polis

It is impossible to describe the Greek polis as a uniform, universal entity, for each one varied according to its resource base, territorial concerns, patron deities and heroes, art and architecture, and civic histories and memories. Nor can we compensate by simply describing the best-known case, **Athens**, for that city is very far from the norm (Camp 2001). This section adopts a compromise, drawing heavily upon the Athenian case, while concentrating on those elements most widely shared among Greek cities.

The Hinterland: The Economic Foundation of the City As already noted, the polis comprised both urban center (*astu*) and rural hinterland (*chora*). Economic autonomy was no doubt a community goal, but given the exigencies of the Mediterranean climate, one that was surely almost never achieved. The Mediterranean triad of grains, olives, and grapevines, coupled with sheep and goat husbandry, continued to supply the chief elements of the Greek daily diet, and some cities possessed additional resources. Coastal settlements, for example, could turn to the sea, and fish, salt, and sponges were regularly exchanged goods (Osborne 1987). An Athenian word for fish

---

KEY DISCOVERY The Parthenon

The "discovery" of the Parthenon? Is that not somewhat paradoxical? After all, the temple to Athena Parthenos, patron goddess of Athens, located atop the high limestone plateau of the acropolis, has been visible ever since its construction (447–432 BC, with the cult statue dedicated in 438 BC). It is arguably the most instantly recognizable and well understood icon of Classical antiquity: a large peripteral temple in the Doric style, constructed of white marble from Mount Pentele.

Style and Decoration
The Doric order is an austere architectural style, with unadorned columns topped by a simple capital, and with a triglyth and metope pattern (a tripartite grooved element alternating with flat panels, sometimes

sculpted) decorating its external upper entablature, above the columns. The Ionic style, in contrast, was more ornamental, with volute-headed column capitals (like rams' horns) and a continuous (often sculpted) frieze on the external entablature.

The ornately decorated Parthenon employed a combination of these orders: it possessed the triglyphs and metopes of the

Doric style above the external columns, combined with an Ionic running frieze on the body of the inner temple, and it carried pedimental statues at the east and west ends. Certain key, widely popular, themes dominate these sculptures, notably conflicts reflecting struggles between "good" and its perceived opposite. The square panels of the metopes, for example, show battles between Greeks

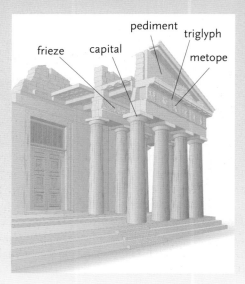

13.25 *(Left) Schematic cut-away of the Parthenon's architecture, showing the position of different components of its sculptural program, as well as their bright coloring.*

13.26 *(Right) The acropolis and the western façade of the Parthenon, as they appear today. The ruined pediment of this facade once depicted the contest between Athena and Poseidon, in their competition to become patron deity of Athens: Poseidon offered the people a salt spring, Athena an olive tree.*

(*opson*) was actually the general term for the more flavorful and interesting, non-grain-based portion of any Greek meal, and in democratic Athens, the eating of expensive fish came to have political overtones (Davidson 1997).

Mines and quarries could fall within the boundaries of city-states. Athens was especially rich, with silver mines located at **Laurion** in Attica, its hinterland. There slaves worked in conditions of great misery to mine and wash the ore (Jones 1982). This silver, coined into the famous "owls" of Athens [**13.24**], underwrote many endeavors and extravagances of the Classical period: the Athenian empire, the Parthenon [see box],

13.24 *An Athenian silver tetradrachm, or "owl":* the owl was a chief attribute of Athena, goddess of wisdom and the arts. Athena's head appeared on one side of these coins and the owl on the other, both signaling the city's devotion to their patron goddess.

and Centaurs, Gods and Giants, and Greeks and Amazons. Many of these conflicts were echoed on the colossal chryselephantine (gold and ivory) cult statue of Athena, created by the sculptor Pheidias, which dominated the temple's main room (Camp 2001).

Mysteries of the Parthenon

Yet for all this apparent understanding of and familiarity with the monument, many things about the Parthenon remain mysterious or problematic. For example, the Ionic frieze (a highly unusual feature on a Doric temple) could in practice only be viewed at a sharp angle from below, with columns interrupting the visual flow, and much of it in deep shadow. The frieze depicts a long and varied procession of men, women, sacrificial animals, riders, and a central scene of preparation for a sacrifice, watched over by the Olympian gods.

It is often thought that the scene represents the actual Panathenaic procession, part of the festival in honor of Athena, the participants in which would thus see themselves in the frieze. There seem to be some visual clues that link its iconography to Athens' finest hour against the Persians, the battle of Marathon in 490 BC. By contrast, it has also been suggested that the intended central sacrifice might be that of a child, a daughter of an early Athenian king, slain in order to save the city (a tragedy by Euripides relates this myth). A spectrum of possible meanings for this frieze is one element that makes interpretation of the Parthenon an endless process (Osborne 1998).

History of the Monument

The present sharply outlined, pure white look of the Parthenon also needs to be placed in context. Its sculptures would originally have been brightly painted, and over time the building underwent many additions and revisions. The temple has had a varied history, having been converted to a Christian church and a Turkish mosque, as well as – most devastatingly – an artillery store, which exploded in the late 17th century, resulting in the ruined state of building visible today.

Only in very recent times has the Parthenon stood largely isolated on the acropolis, the result of a reverential, but too thorough, clearing of numerous houses and other post-Classical structures in the service of tourism and Greek national pride. Considering the long-term history of the monument, it would seem that every age discovers – or, better, invents – its own Parthenon (Beard 2003).

13.27 *Photograph of Athens taken in the mid-19th century, before the development of the modern city. The Parthenon is visible on its high limestone plateau, along with an Ottoman-period tower. On the slopes below are other later monuments, such as the Roman-period Odeion of Herodes Atticus.*

korai, a clothed young woman) [**13.28**]. Both were used as votive dedications to a deity as well as grave markers (Stewart 1997); in the first of these roles, *korai* with remains of their original bright paint have been found on the Athenian acropolis (see below). The *kouros* form demonstrates how Greeks borrowed and adapted ideas and styles, for the sculptural concept of the standing youth originated in Egypt (albeit always clothed); the Archaic Greek *kouros* is shown nude and, over time, was depicted with an increasing naturalism very typical of the development of Greek art in general (Hurwit 1985). Grave markers of the succeeding Classical period are more modest; frequently they take the form of sculpted reliefs showing the deceased, in some cases bidding farewell to loved ones. The dead of Greek society, although kept outside the city, were far from invisible (Houby-Nielsen 1995; Morris 1992).

Life Within the City Walls Passing the necropolis and entering through a gate in the wall, travelers to the city would have many possible destinations. Each city had residential quarters (Nevett 1999), and most, if not all, had an acropolis ("high city"), to be turned to in times of danger and always important as a cult center. One especially likely destination, however, would be the city's marketplace, or agora [**13.29, 13.30**]. Agora means simply "open space" (as "forum" does in Latin), and dozens of activities and events that took place here – buying and selling, picking up prostitutes, running races – find mention in our ancient sources (Millett 1998). This variety is clear in the **Athenian agora**, which has been undergoing excavation since the 1930s by the American School of Classical Studies at Athens.

The administration of Athens was housed in public buildings lying to the west of the agora, including the council chamber (Bouleuterion) and the Tholos, where citizens being kept on call in case of civic danger were fed. Excavations here have recovered fragments of dining ware marked "public property" (Camp 1992). The agora also held several stoas, buildings with open colonnades to the front (sensible, given the Mediterranean climate), used for many purposes; the Stoic school of philosophy takes its name from conversations held in the Painted Stoa. Law courts, in the form of bounded enclosures, together with water-clocks and voting machines, attest to legal business. Buying and selling no doubt went on everywhere, and official sets of weights and measures indicate a high degree of civic control. The agora was also a central clearing house of information, with inscriptions recording honors to benefactors, dedications to the gods, and news for citizens. Finally, the gods

the Peloponnesian War. Stone quarries were more widely distributed in Greece than precious metals, but here too Attica was particularly well endowed: the marble quarries of Mount Pentele to the north of the city, for example, supplied the material to build the Parthenon and for its sculptures, as well as for numerous other famed statues and structures (Osborne 1987).

Outside the City Walls: The Cemetery For all the importance of the rural sphere, it was long ignored by scholars in favor of the urban center and its monuments [see box: The Silent Greek Countryside, p. 498]. Given the frequent warfare of the age, the urban center would have been walled. In the Athenian case, the so-called Long Walls ran to the port, **Piraeus**, allowing the city to be fed by its navy in times of siege. Approaching a city's walls, one would pass through cemeteries, which were kept firmly separate from the domain of the living. In Athens, the Kerameikos cemetery (literally, the "Potter's Quarter," named after evidence of ceramic production found nearby) lay outside the city, the road to which was lined with grave markers of various types. In Archaic times, wealthy individuals might erect a *kouros* (pl. *kouroi*, a statue of a nude standing youth) or *kore* (pl.

were everywhere in the agora. The Hephaisteion, a 5th-century BC Doric temple to Hephaistos and Athena, stood above it to the west; the Altar of the Twelve Gods (from which all distances in Athens were measured) lay within it; and statues of deities would have been ubiquitous. The major path across the agora, the Panathenaic Way, was the route followed by the ritual procession of the Panathenaia, a citywide festival held every four years in honor of Athena (Neils 1992).

Acropoleis were standard components in Greek civic organization; the Athenian example, a high limestone "table," is a particularly remarkable geological feature. In the Classical period, it was largely given over to the gods (Hurwit 1999). Although dozens of deities were honored on the acropolis, Athena, patroness of the city, was particularly venerated in many guises, from her warrior persona (Athena Promachos, Athena of the Vanguard), to her promise of victory (Athena Nike), to her

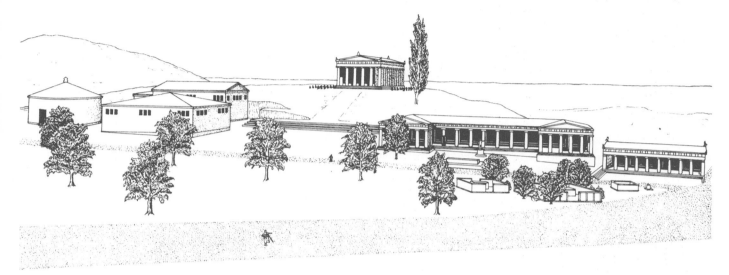

13.29 *(Above)* **Reconstruction of the west side of the agora, 5th century BC:** *public buildings here included the Tholos (the round structure to the far left), the Old and New Bouleuteria, the Stoa of Zeus Eleutherios and the Royal Stoa. The Hephaisteion, a 5th-century BC temple, stands on a hill above, overlooking the agora.*

13.30 *(Left)* **The Athenian agora:** *as it looks after seven decades of excavation by American teams. A modern-day reconstruction of the Hellenistic Stoa of Attalos stands to the left; the acropolis and Parthenon loom over the open space of the former marketplace.*

KEY CONTROVERSY The Silent Greek Countryside

Scholarly treatment of the Greek countryside has rightly been called a paradox (Osborne 1987). Agricultural activity carried out in the countryside provided the food on which all survival depended, and farming absorbed the energies of the vast majority of all pre-industrial populations. Yet ancient authors, overwhelmingly characterized by an urban and elite point of view, said very little of this productive sphere, and it is largely absent from Greek art. Later scholars, keen to study *objets d'art* or celebrated monuments, acquiesced in this neglect (Alcock 1998). Questions such as "how did people live in the countryside?" or "how did they work the land?" were neither asked nor answered.

That situation began to change in the later part of the 20th century. One key development was the introduction of regional field survey, an archaeological technique first pioneered in the New World. Survey investigations seek to establish patterns not on a site-by-site basis (as with excavation), but on a broader, more regional scale. Although methodologies vary, in essence this involves the intensive reconnaissance on foot of the earth's surface, by teams of fieldwalkers looking for traces of ancient cultural debris. Finds might include ceramics of all types, roof tiles, architectural remains, stone tools, agricultural processing equipment, religious votives, gravestones, and more. At first viewed askance by many Classical archaeologists, regional survey is today widely practiced in the Mediterranean world (Barker and Mattingly 1999–2000); and Greece, where scores of such projects have been undertaken in recent years, is now one of its most thoroughly explored countries (Cherry 2003).

When these surface finds are studied and mapped, their distribution in the landscape can be reconstructed on a period-by-period basis (in Greece, from the Paleolithic to the present), thus allowing a detailed look into the changing organization of life in the Greek countryside (van Andel and Runnels 1987).

Many scholars were stunned by the initial results for the Classical period, the 5th and 4th centuries BC, for far from being an empty zone surrounding the busy urban center, the countryside teemed with activity. While it remains clear that the majority of polis-dwellers lived permanently in the city, and "commuted" to their fields, other tiers of viable settlement have now been discovered: villages and very small sites, identified as farmsteads, rural cemeteries, and previously unknown rural sites such as shrines. Individual finds of "off-site" material also point to human presence and labor in the countryside, in some cases perhaps even revealing the mundane practice of manuring fields (Alcock et al. 1994).

As with all archaeological evidence, there are difficulties in the interpretation of regional data; there are, for example, issues of chronological precision, the definition of a site, and the comparability of different projects. Nevertheless, survey-based reconstructions of the ancient countryside can tell us much about patterns of landholding, the nature of rural settlement, and the intensity with which land was cultivated at different times – crucial factors in determining the economic and social framework of a given society. It has become very clear that these parameters varied in significant ways over time and space: the Mycenaean rural landscape does not match that of the Classical age, nor the Hellenistic that of the Roman. The Greek countryside was no static phenomenon; nor need it be a silent one.

13.31 *Archaeological survey in action in the northeastern Peloponnese, not far from Mycenae. The fieldwalkers are moving in parallel lines across the landscape, looking for artifacts such as potsherds, stone tools, roof tiles, or other traces of past human activity.*

virgin state (Athena Parthenos); to this last manifestation may belong the dedication of that most famous of all Greek temples, the Parthenon [see box: The Parthenon, pp. 494–95]. Below the acropolis of Athens lies the theater of Dionysos, a site sacred to the god of wine, ecstasy, and drama (Wycherley 1978; Green and Handley 1995). Starting from simple seating on a hillside, with a circular stage below, theater architecture grew more and more elaborate. Although Western drama is rooted in the Greek theater, the art form played a much broader and more significant role in ancient life than it does in our own.

13.32 An Athenian warrior's farewell departure for war: *marked by a symbolic handshake with an older man and by a woman offering a sacrificial libation to the gods. Red-figure vase, dating to the mid-5th century BC, by the Achilles Painter.*

The Commonality of Greek Culture Classical Athens was, of course, a democracy (rule of the people), and many aspects of its archaeology accord with the qualified "equality" of that regime (Morris 1992; Whitley 2001), apart from the infrastructure of chattel slavery that underpinned Athenian life. Burial and housing, for example, remained relatively modest for everyone, with wealth lavished instead on public structures and communal rituals; an ethos of civic dedication that included military service was also instilled. What constituted a good life and a good death in Athenian society was inculcated through images on red-figure pots [**13.32**], the numerous cults of Athena and of Victory, myths of Athenian greatness depicted on civic temples and enacted in the theater, and, not least, the very public, highly ritualized funerals provided for the war dead (Lissarrague 1989; Loraux 1986).

All Greek cities would have been bound together, through a complex mix of myth, ritual, imagery, and ideology, although their character would vary from case to case. For example, Athens' rival, Sparta, prided itself above all on military proficiency and personal austerity, relying on dependent labor (the serflike "helots") for food production and other practicalities (Cartledge 2003; Hodkinson 2000). Other poleis followed yet other socio-political paths, some democratic, some oligarchic (supporting the rule of the few). It is interesting how many of the elements observed in Athens appear in other cities as well, albeit usually on a less grandiose scale. Temples, dedicatory statues, fountains, bouleuteria, theaters, agoras: these were the standard urban furniture of the Classical polis.

For all the multiplicity of Greek cities and their endemic competitiveness, it is worth remembering their shared, overarching sense of kinship. Celebration and reinforcement of this inclusive Hellenic identity is highlighted in the phenomenon of panhellenic ("for all Greeks") sanctuaries. The four principal panhellenic sanctuaries were located on the Greek mainland at **Delphi**, **Olympia**, **Nemea**, and **Isthmia**; each held festivals and games on a four-year cycle, to which all Greek communities would send their best athletes and performers (Bruit Zaidman

and Schmitt Pantel 1992). Olympia, thanks to the 19th-century establishment of the modern Olympic Games, is without question the most famous of these sites. Events at ancient Olympia included competitions in chariot racing, wrestling, boxing, the pankration (a no-holds-barred fight), and running. A temporary sacred truce protected all who came to the games, even in times of war, and those who won at Olympia were honored forever by their proud home cities (Finley and Pleket 1976; Raschke 1988).

Olympia was sacred to Zeus Olympios. A large Doric temple (completed in 457 BC) held his colossal, chryselephantine (gold and ivory), seated cult image, which became one of the Seven Wonders of the Ancient World. The commission was given to Pheidias, sculptor of the Athena Parthenos of Athens; his workshop was discovered during the long-running German excavations at Olympia. The temple itself was decorated with sculpted metopes showing the 12 labors of Herakles [**13.33**], the quintessential Greek hero. One of the temple's pediments depicted the mythic battle between Lapiths and Centaurs, a very popular scene and one usually taken to indicate the distinction between human and animal, or Greek and barbarian, behavior (Ashmole 1972; Osborne 1998). Despite fierce inter-city competition, Olympia and the other panhellenic centers served to remind the Greeks of their desired unity – and superiority – in the face of the barbarian.

13.33 Metope from the Temple of Zeus at Olympia: *the panel represents the twelfth and final labor of Herakles. Here he holds up the world (with the assistance of Athena and a pillow), while Atlas (right) fetches for him the apples of the Hesperides.*

Growing Powers, Growing Territories

The Mediterranean world of the late 1st millennium BC would appear, in political and administrative terms, to be quite different from that described in the previous section. The eastern portion of the sea, from the Balkan peninsula to Egypt, formed part of the empire forged by Alexander the Great (356–323 BC), then inherited (and carved up) by his successors. To the west, the Punic power of Carthage had established control of a territory extending over much of the North African littoral and Spain. And in the central Italian peninsula, the small city-state of Rome had, through a series of military successes, expanded to annex an increasing number of its neighbors, capturing the major Etruscan city of Veii in 396 BC, for example, after a siege supposedly lasting ten years, much like that of Homeric Troy. These assertive powers, inextricably connected one to the other by the Mediterranean, ultimately came into collision. Only one would survive, to swallow up and build upon the others.

Alexander and the East

The proud city-states of Greece used to mock their northern neighbor, the kingdom of Macedon, the people of which were considered rustic and uncivilized, if not entirely barbaric. That perception was challenged by the rise of Philip II of Macedon (383–336 BC), a very able ruler who, it was said, persuaded his subjects to settle in cities and to stop wearing sheepskins. Philip engaged in the politics of southern Greece and participated in panhellenic games; his chariot at Olympia won on the very day his son Alexander was born. Aided by the rich gold mines of Mount Pangaion, Philip made Macedon a force to be reckoned with in the power politics of the 4th century BC.

At the battle of **Chaeronea** in 338 BC, Philip's forces – with the cavalry wing led by Alexander – defeated a coalition of Greek cities, including Athens and Thebes; many point to this as the end point of true Hellenic freedom. Philip was clearly turning toward expansion in the east when he was assassinated, in the theater of his capital at **Pella**, in 336 BC. The unbridled richness of Macedonian royal funerary practices is demonstrated by excavations in recent years at **Vergina**, the burial place of its rulers.

One tomb in particular has been associated with Philip himself [**13.34**]. In a style called "Macedonian," it consists of a building with a painted temple-like facade, in which human cremations and lavish grave goods were placed, the entire struc-

13.34 *Reconstruction of the possible tomb of Philip II at Vergina: a cut-away diagram of one of several lavishly appointed tombs excavated in the royal cemetery at Vergina in Macedonia. This vaulted, painted tomb has been claimed as the resting place of Philip II (d. 336 BC), father of Alexander the Great.*

ture then being covered with a massive earthen tumulus (Andronikos 1994). One of the cremations was incompletely burnt, allowing reconstruction of the deceased's face. Certain features – notably some distinctive war wounds – have convinced many (but not all) that this is indeed the burial place of Philip II (Prag and Neave 1997).

The Conquests of Alexander Alexander was only 20 when Philip was killed; he himself would die aged 33, in Babylon, at the heart of the Persian empire. The intervening years radically transformed the worlds of the eastern Mediterranean and the Near East, bringing them into ever closer contact within what came to be called the Hellenistic world. Alexander achieved this through military conquest. In a series of great tactical victories at the **Granikos River** and at **Issus**, in Turkey, and at **Gaugamela** in Iraq, the Macedonian forces defeated the much larger Persian army of Darius III [**13.35**], ultimately annexing domains that stretched from the Mediterranean to Afghanistan.

Along the way, Alexander also successfully besieged the Phoenician city of Tyre (332 BC) and marched into Egypt. His eastern campaigns led him as far east as the tip of northwestern India in 326/325 BC, when his troops mutinied and forced him to retreat. Alexander – whose motivations for conquest remain indistinct – is said to have wept and to have erected 12 massive altars as a thank-offering "at the end of the world" (Bosworth 1988).

Apart from his unquestioned military genius, Alexander emerges as a master of propaganda and a skilled manipulator of his personal image. He was very careful with his portraiture, allowing only three artists to create original depictions of him: one in paint, one in sculpture, and one in gems and coins (Stewart 1993). Over the course of his short career he increasingly

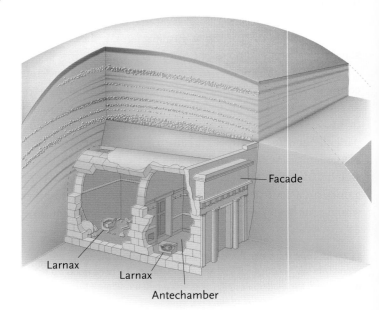

Facade

Larnax

Larnax

Antechamber

associated himself with the divine. When the Egyptian oracular shrine at the oasis of **Siwah**, in the desert west of the Nile, confirmed his descent from the god Zeus Ammon, Alexander adopted the rams' horns of that deity in some of his portraits [**13.36**], while in others he wore the lion skin of the hero Herakles. In his dress and behavior, he also distanced himself from his fellows, demanding, for example, the ritual prostration given to Persian monarchs. How far this was personal hubris, how far genuine belief in his divinity, and how far a desire to appeal to (and control) his new, non-Hellenic subjects is debated to this day.

Despite the speed of Alexander's conquests, an administrative and military infrastructure was implanted, and later built upon by his successors. City foundations were important instruments of this policy (Fraser 1996); usually named after Alexander, these new communities of Greek settlers were scattered from Egypt [see box: Alexandria-by-Egypt, p. 502] to Tajikistan. Few have been well explored, although a notable exception is **Ai Khanoum** (or Aï Khanum; possibly the ancient Alexandria in Oxiana) in modern Afghanistan (see Chapter 14, pp. 546–47). During the 1960s and 1970s French archaeologists there recovered what they first took to be a "purely Greek" city, complete with Greek-style temples, naturalistic sculptures, and philosophical maxims familiar from the sanctuary of Apollo at Delphi (e.g. "nothing in excess," and "know thyself") (Green 1990). The triumph of Greek culture in the east was thus assumed. More recent re-examination, however, paints a more nuanced picture of a hybrid community, exhibiting both local and Hellenic traits. Unfortunately, further work at Ai Khanoum will be difficult, if not impossible; it has been reported that the Taliban bulldozed parts of the site in the late 1990s.

13.35 *The "Alexander Mosaic," House of the Faun, Pompeii: this late 2nd-century* BC *mosaic, thought to be based on an earlier Greek painting, depicts a battlefield confrontation between Alexander the Great (the figure at the left) and Darius III, King of Persia (the figure in the chariot).*

The Hellenistic World After his death, Alexander's empire was quickly broken up by his generals and *de facto* heirs. Alexander's own son was born posthumously, and did not long survive. Following a period of conflict and political killings, three chief successor states emerged: the Antigonid kingdom based in Macedonia; the Seleucid empire, which at its height embraced much of Syria and the Near East; and the Ptolemaic kingdom of Egypt (Walbank 1992). The rulers of all these kingdoms claimed legitimacy through their connections to Alexander, now unequivocally worshiped as a god. Their portraits strongly resemble his in terms of his hairstyle, upward "melting" glance, and divine attributes, while still retaining their own, recognizable features (Pollitt 1986). Ptolemy I (died 282 BC), who seized

13.36 *Silver coin (tetradrachm) with a portrait of Alexander the Great wearing the horns of Zeus Ammon: the coin was issued by Lysimachos (d. 281 BC), one of the successors of Alexander.*

KEY SITE Alexandria-by-Egypt

Alexander the Great's rapid march of conquest as far as India destroyed existing political systems and disrupted local ways of life, but among its more constructive legacies was the foundation across a vast swathe of western and south-central Asia of new settlements ("Alexandrias"). As the 2nd-century AD Greek writer Plutarch put it, "Alexander established more than 70 cities among barbarian peoples, and planted all Asia with Greek magistrates, and thus overcame its uncivilized and brutish mode of life." The true total was certainly far less than this, and even in antiquity there was confusion about which places had been founded by Alexander, rather than by his successors. Nonetheless, some still-surviving cities in Afghanistan and Tajikistan – Herat, Merv, Termez, and Khodjend, for example – are certainly ancient Alexandrias (Fraser 1996).

By far the most influential, however, was Alexandria-by-Egypt, modern Alexandria, whose foundation in 331 BC is described in some detail by ancient sources. Its location provided Egypt with a new port unaffected by the Nile floods, and was chosen to bring Egypt closer to the Greek world. But Alexander also wanted to impress, by

constructing a veritable "megalopolis." The city was gigantic in scale, with walls over 15 km (9 miles) in circumference, a rectangular grid of broad streets, and an artificial mole 1 km (0.6 mile) long, linking the city to the islet of Pharos and thus creating two fine harbors. Alexander, dead only eight years after work began, saw none of this, although the city was to become his final resting place.

It fell to his successor Ptolemy I and a series of later Ptolemaic kings to embellish this increasingly cosmopolitan city with monuments worthy of Alexander's ambitions: a series of royal buildings, dozens of temples to deities such as Isis and Serapis, vast cemeteries, huge cisterns, canals, the 135-m (443-ft) tall lighthouse (the "Pharos"), which became one of the Seven Wonders of the Ancient World, and the vast library of Alexandria and its adjoining research institute, the Mouseion (whence our "museum") (Jacob and de Polignac 2000).

As Herman Melville wrote, however, "Alexandria seems to be paved with the crushed-up ruins of a thousand cities." This is a place with a long history, embracing Roman, late antique Christian, Arab, and Ottoman times, and it experienced massive, destructive rebuilding in the 19th and earlier

20th centuries (Empéreur 2002). For the archaeologist, little seemed to remain of the ancient city – the richest, most populous, and most powerful of the Hellenistic world. The Pharos collapsed, the Library was consumed in flames (though a new Bibliotheca Alexandrina opened in 2002), the temples have all gone, and the tomb of Alexander is still missing, despite 139 unsuccessful attempts over the past century to rediscover it.

Nevertheless, a surge of economic growth and associated construction in the late 20th century has led to much rescue archaeology both in the city (which has sunk 6–8 m (19–26 ft) since antiquity) and along its now-submerged edges. Geophysical explorations have traced the line of the mole, while excavations have revealed Hellenistic and Roman housing, cisterns, catacombs, and the vast western necropolis of the city, the earliest family vaults in which date back to the mid-3rd century BC.

Underwater mapping and excavation has attracted much media attention. Aside from locating a number of Greco-Roman shipwrecks, salvage activities begun in 1994 have revealed some 4500 submerged architectural elements (columns and blocks), over 30 sphinxes, and four obelisks of the pharaonic era. Most exciting of all is an immense granite statue, probably of Ptolemy II dressed as Pharaoh, and a dozen massive blocks weighing as much as 70 tons: this, it seems, is at last tangible evidence of the fabled lighthouse that once stood close to where these remnants now lie on the seabed (La Riche 1997).

13.37 *The raising in 1995 of the colossal granite statue of Ptolemy II from the harbor at Alexandria. This photograph illustrates both the heavy lifting-equipment necessary for this archaeological campaign, as well as the proximity of the ancient finds to the modern shoreline of the city.*

13.38 *The Battle of Gods and Giants:* *part of the frieze from the Great Altar of Zeus, Pergamon (c. 180 BC). Athena (who is being crowned by a winged Victory, or Nike, figure) grasps a Giant by the hair, while her snake also attacks him. His mother, Ge (Earth), stretches up in agony to intervene.*

Egypt as his own domain, went so far as to hijack the body of Alexander on its way back from Babylon to Macedonia for burial, interring it (mummified) in his own capital city. The location of Alexander's tomb has long been sought, but never found.

The large territorial states of the Hellenistic age (from the death of Alexander to the establishment of the Roman Empire: 323–31 BC) greatly facilitated an increase in trade links, intellectual exchange, and personal travel. The resulting synthesis led to profound developments in literature, philosophy, medicine, science, religion, and warfare; just two disparate examples would include the introduction of elephants into western warfare and the translation of the Old Testament into Greek (the Septuagint). In this more cosmopolitan world there developed a kind of cultural *koine*, or commonality, a shared communicative culture based on Greek language, styles, and practices (Pollitt 1986; Green 1990). Nevertheless, the depth of this *koine* should not be overestimated. Dozens of native languages (Aramaic, Phrygian, Egyptian, etc.) continued in use.

Aspects of Hellenistic art may have responded to the need to communicate to broad and culturally varied audiences, for example through colossal size (most famously, the Colossus of Rhodes), dramatic settings, and intense emotional expression. The Great Altar of Zeus at **Pergamon** [13.38], capital of a splinter Hellenistic kingdom in northwest Turkey, is a case in point. Created around 180 BC on a vast scale in a dominating location, the altar's frieze depicts the battle of gods and giants, as did the Parthenon's. This struggle between good and evil was now represented in very different style, however, with violence and

agony unmistakably highlighted (Pollitt 1986; Smith 1991). Moreover, the styles and customs of the conquered former barbarians might be adopted across the Hellenistic world. Most importantly, the rise of the ruler cult – recognizing the divine nature of living men – was profoundly non-Hellenic, yet became widely accepted as necessary for the governing of these multi-cultural, far-flung Hellenistic domains.

Carthage and the Carthaginian Empire

Carthage and its western empire was hardly a minor power, yet its story has been largely reduced to its final chapter, that of defeat by Rome. Perhaps even worse, it is the Roman version of Carthage that survives in the popular (and even scholarly) imagination. In Virgil's *Aeneid*, an epic poem of Rome's foundation by Aeneas, who was a refugee from Troy, Carthage is but a stop on the hero's way. There Aeneas loves and leaves the Carthaginian queen Dido, following his destiny to Italy and abandoning her to suicide [**13.39**]. Carthaginian peculiarity (not least in being ruled by a queen) and inferiority are here established, a tradition that runs through all the many subsequent literary, artistic, and operatic tellings of the story of Dido and Aeneas. It was also easy for Rome to characterize the Carthaginians as different, even barbarian, in respect to their religious practices. Being a Phoenician colony, Carthage had brought many aspects of Levantine practice to North Africa, and the gods of the city included Baal Hammon, Melkart, Astarte, and Tanit, deities honored in some cases by the ritual of child sacrifice [see box: The Tophet: Child Sacrifice at Carthage, p. 505].

13.39 *Fourth-century* AD *mosaic from the baths of a Roman villa at Low Ham, Somerset, England: various scenes from the* Aeneid *of Virgil are depicted; for example, Dido and Aeneas are shown embracing in the lower center.*

Nevertheless, it is clear that whatever Roman opinions were, the Carthaginian empire (at its height in the 3rd century BC) prospered. The agricultural hinterland supporting the capital city was fertile; one of the few Carthaginian texts to have survived (by being translated into Latin) was a treatise on scientific farming. Carthaginian exports included carpets, purple dyes, jewelry, timber, and hides; imports came from all over the Mediterranean world, and Egyptian and (especially) Greek influences in the city's artistic and architectural styles became increasingly prominent over time (Aubet 1993; Niemeyer 2000). The strongly maritime orientation of the culture is attested by the archaeological recovery of two Punic-period artificial harbors, one for commerce, one for warships.

The increasingly tense proximity of Carthaginian and Roman territory and interests was made clear when an implacable enemy of Carthage, Cato "the Censor," brought a fig into the Roman Senate: a fig still fresh, grown frighteningly close in Carthaginian soil. The **Punic Wars** raged in the 3rd and 2nd centuries BC, with victories going to both sides. During the Second Punic War (218–201 BC), the Carthaginian general Hannibal invaded Italy, bringing war elephants over the Alps, inflicting one of Rome's worst defeats at **Cannae** in 216 BC, and terrorizing the Italian population for some 16 years (Hoyos 2003). Ultimately, however, Rome prevailed, aided by the creation of a fleet to combat Carthaginian sea power. Carthage was sacked in 146 BC, the same year that the Romans also destroyed the important Greek city of **Corinth**. Romans could be generous in their treatment of enemies, but not in this case. The sack of Carthage is a good example of punitive Roman treatment of those to whom they wished to teach a lesson: its population was mercilessly slaughtered or enslaved, its buildings razed, the vast majority of its written records destroyed, and its territory

converted into the new province of Africa. It is not true, however, that the city's fields were sown with salt in order that they could never be cultivated again; both Carthage and Corinth, given their highly strategic positions, would later be re-founded as important Roman colonies.

The Rise of Rome

For all its later greatness, Rome began much like other communities in peninsular Italy (Smith 1996). The community occupied a promising setting: located on a river (the Tiber) running to a Mediterranean port (Ostia), and centered around seven hills, it was linked to the wider world yet protected from external threats, such as pirates. Its traditional foundation date is 753 BC, the work (according to a different origin story from that of Virgil) of Romulus, killer of his brother Remus (Wiseman 1995) [**13.40**]. Kings ruled early Rome, and Etruscan influence, if not outright control, was strongly felt. One of the most enduring symbols of authority in Rome, the bundle of rods known as the *fasces*, is, for example, of Etruscan derivation; the modern term "fascism," associated with the Italian dictator Benito Mussolini (himself a devoted supporter of Roman archaeology), derives from this symbol. The Roman regal period ended, we are told, with the expulsion of the Etruscan king Tarquinius Superbus, following his son's rape of a virtuous Roman

13.40 *Bronze statue of a she-wolf, a potent symbol of Rome: the wolf dates to c. 500* BC; *the suckling babies (Romulus and Remus, founders of the city of Rome) are much later restorations.*

KEY SITE The Tophet: Child Sacrifice at Carthage

Although some scholars have denied or downplayed the phenomenon, child sacrifice was practiced at Carthage as well as at other Phoenician colonies in the Mediterranean, for example on Sardinia and Sicily. Of the tophets where these sacrifices were carried out – sacred enclosures in which children were immolated and buried – the Carthaginian one, which lies south of the city at Salammbô, is the largest and best explored.

This example, discovered early in the 20th century, apparently saw uninterrupted use from the later 8th century to 146 BC, the year of Rome's sack of Carthage, and the scale of the practice there was significant. Thousands of cinerary urns containing cremated remains have been discovered, with over 20,000 dating to 400–200 BC alone; urns were sealed either by baetyls (sacred stones) or – from the 6th/5th century BC onward – by inscribed stelae.

Other distinct trends in this assemblage over time are apparent. Newborn babies, for example, tended to dominate at first (e.g. in the 7th century BC), whereas later burials (e.g. 4th century BC) seem to be of children between one and three years old. Investigators of the phenomenon argue that

earlier sacrifices seem principally drawn from the elite ranks, extending to lower social strata after the 4th century BC. Another clear shift lies in a willingness to undertake apparent substitutions, as some urns contained the burned bones of young animals. At first, during the late 8th through 6th centuries BC, one in three sacrifices were of animals; but this declined to one in ten in the 5th to 3rd centuries BC (Brown 1991).

What we know of the rite, from non-archaeological sources, comes from largely shocked and hostile Greek or Roman witnesses. It would appear from their accounts that the throats of the babies may have been slit before their bodies were burned.

The gods appeased by these acts, according to the stelae, were the divinities Baal and Tanit, who were native to the Phoenician homeland. Intriguingly, while the practice is indeed known there, child sacrifice was far more popular in the colonial west. How often the ritual took place is unclear, but it seems to have accompanied individual vows or times of emergency and crisis, such as periods of war or disease. Later Roman-period historians reported, for example, that in 310

BC, at the time of a Syracusan siege, Carthaginians repented a decline in sacrifice and the purchase of the children of the poor, and renewed the ancestral custom by sacrificing 500 children of noble birth.

Reasons for Child Sacrifice

Nothing would appear to explain the alien quality of Carthaginian society to ancient contemporaries, or to the modern audience, more than baby killing. Romans were hardly squeamish, but this is one religious rite they did not openly tolerate, although the practice continued secretly among the Carthaginians for centuries. Yet dispassionate examination of the ritual, taken in context, indicates that it was considered a pious act. Moreover, the performance of child sacrifice can be aligned with the internal constitution of Carthage, especially the ascendancy of its elite classes, and tophet distribution may well reflect Carthaginian intervention and political dominance in the western Mediterranean (Aubet 1993).

The particular rite may be repellent to us, but its role in creating social distinctions and forging political allegiances is, in fact, quite familiar from other Mediterranean cults.

13.41 *View across the Tophet, Carthage. The stelae seen here mark the location of thousands of cinerary urns, containing the remains of infants, small children and animals. Inscriptions on some stelae identify the burial as an offering to the gods; others bear the symbol of the goddess Tanit.*

matron, Lucretia. What followed was the establishment in 509 BC of a Roman republic (from *res publica*, Latin for "affair of the people"). This morality tale, testifying to Roman virtue and to the rejection of kings, became deeply entrenched in Rome's image of itself and its destiny.

Over the centuries of royal rule, Rome had acquired many of the urban features we have come to expect (Scarre 1995a). Temples and shrines dotted the city, and one of the most important, to the Capitoline Triad of Jupiter Optimus Maximus ("Best and Greatest"), Juno, and Minerva (the Latin equivalents of the Greek gods Zeus, Hera, and Athena), stood atop the Capitoline hill. This temple, the **Capitolium**, first built *c.* 500 BC and renewed and rebuilt over the centuries, possessed three chambers to accommodate the deities. Otherwise, it greatly resembled the Portonaccio temple at Veii, with its frontal columns and high podium; these imposing features went on to become highly characteristic of Roman temple architecture. Around 600 BC a low-lying area below the Capitoline and Palatine hills was drained; called the **Forum Romanum**, the space served the same multiple economic, religious, judicial, and political functions as the Athenian agora. The large-scale drainage that made the Forum habitable was facilitated by the early building stages of the **Cloaca Maxima** ("Great Drain") [13.42]; water control would prove a constant preoccupation of city officials, and the Cloaca Maxima ultimately developed into a remarkable, large-scale sewer system through which men could reputedly ride in boats.

Roman Expansion This community of Rome expanded through a series of wars and friendly annexations and alliances (Cornell 1995). Gradually, a mosaic of peoples – Italic tribes, Etruscan

city-states, Greek colonies – came under Roman control; the fall of the Greek colony of Tarentum (modern Taranto) in 272 BC is often taken as the final step in the peninsula's conquest. As a result of this process, what is normally considered Roman culture was actually one with diverse and complex roots. As for what drove this machine of expansion, one obvious factor is a system of Roman values and honors that rewarded military service and success with political and social authority. The extreme wealth that could be gained was equally appreciated, and this enrichment, of individuals and of the city as a whole, grew as Roman armies moved beyond peninsular Italy. The saga of Roman military activity is long and complicated, but over the course of the final centuries of the 1st millennium BC, the major powers (Carthaginians, Antigonids, Seleucids) all were defeated or much reduced; the last king of Pergamon simply willed his land to Rome, and it became the province of **Asia** in 133 BC. Julius Caesar first pushed the empire beyond the limits of the Mediterranean by conquering **Gaul** (modern France) in the mid-1st century BC. Victorious generals such as Caesar became astonishingly wealthy, as well as admired, men; they, in turn, adorned their beloved city with ever more spectacular and adventurous constructions, which only fed their popularity and influence. In the highly competitive elite culture of the Roman republic, this quickly led to factional disputes.

Thanks to almost constant interaction with eastern powers, Greek influence in the form of artistic booty, human hostages, and visiting artists and philosophers was powerfully felt, and widely emulated, in the Roman heartland. At the same time, other elements in Roman society perceived Greek culture as decadent and antithetic to fundamental Roman virtues. Choosing a path through this cultural minefield was no easy matter. For example, Pompey the Great (106–48 BC), a Roman general who consciously emulated Alexander in his behavior and portraiture, chose to build a permanent stone theater in Rome in 55 BC. The Greek stimulus is clear, although the actual construction of the concrete structure was very Roman. The theater made Pompey wildly popular with the masses (the plebeians) of Rome (Coleman 2000), but to the Roman aristocracy (the patricians) such gathering places were dangerous, and many grew to fear that Pompey meant to make himself a king. Struggles between the plebeians, in association with renegade patricians such as Pompey or Julius Caesar, and the senatorial aristocracy marked the last stages of the Roman republic, and led to bitter internal strife and civil war in the millennium's final century (Beard and Crawford 1985).

13.42 The Cloaca Maxima, the "Great Sewer" of Rome: *the sewer system served both for waste removal and storm-water management; thanks to its size and engineering skill, the Cloaca Maxima, seen here emptying into the River Tiber, was admired as one of the wonders of Rome.*

A turning point in the crises of the republic, and a new resolution with Greek culture, was reached with one of the most famous of Roman victories. The naval battle of **Actium** in 31 BC marked the end of the last of the great Hellenistic kingdoms, the Ptolemaic dynasty of Egypt. On one side was Octavian, heir of Julius Caesar; on the other a rival general, Mark Antony, and Cleopatra VII, the final Ptolemaic ruler (Walker and Higgs 2001). With this victory, the suicide of Antony and Cleopatra, and the acquisition of the fertile land of the Nile Valley, Octavian became sole ruler of the Mediterranean world. He is better known as Augustus, and as the first emperor (from *imperator*, which for the Romans simply meant "general") of Rome.

A Mediterranean Empire

At around the same time that he adopted his new title (27 BC), Augustus undertook a reorganization of the Roman empire, institutionalizing and systematizing its regional administrative units and consolidating its boundaries. He spent freely on his capital city of Rome, as he boasts in his "autobiography," the *Res Gestae* ("Things Done"), a text he ordered to be erected at several places in the empire, including his mausoleum in Rome. As the Latin biographer Suetonius said, "he boasted, not without reason, that he found [Rome a city] of brick, but left it [a city] of marble." His rule initiated several centuries of militarily enforced peace, which became known as the *pax Romana*. Dying in AD 14 at the age of 77, peacefully succeeded by his adopted son Tiberius, Augustus' signal success and longevity requires some explanation, considering the turbulence of the later republican age.

Part of Augustus' achievement stems from his masterful control of a wide-ranging propaganda campaign in literature, art, and architecture (Zanker 1988; Favro 1996). A new image of empire and imperial power was evolved during his reign, one that drew on Classical Greek models of control and authority, yet always possessed a particularly Roman stamp. One of his portrait types, the Prima Porta Augustus, represents this very well [**13.43**]. The balanced pose and proportions of the figure are based on the Doryphoros ("the spear-bearer"), a 5th-century BC Greek statue considered to embody the perfect man. Yet Augustus is here clad in the garb of an *imperator*, with his hand (unlike the Greek model) upraised in a gesture of power. His breastplate celebrates a victory over the Parthians, eastern barbarians now subdued by Rome. At his heroically bare feet, the dolphin and baby Eros symbolize Aphrodite (the Roman Venus), the

goddess of love born from the sea, a divine progenitor of Augustus' family line. With this careful modulation of style and subject, Augustus laid claim to divine ancestry without overdoing it, representing himself as a Roman general, not as a god or king (Walker and Burnett 1981; Elsner 1995). This selection of an already widely known "classicizing" style to proclaim Roman themes, which worked effectively both in Rome and the provinces, was copied by many of Augustus' successors during the early empire (roughly the 1st to the 3rd centuries AD).

Beginning with Augustus, a more or less unbroken chain of emperors ruled over the entire Mediterranean, as well as provinces in temperate Europe and the Near East. The size and shape of the empire changed constantly, at its greatest extent stretching from the Atlantic Ocean to modern Iraq, and from Scotland to the Sahara. The line of imperial succession, too, shifted over time, through assassination, adoption, and military acclamation (Scarre 1995b). Nero, for example, the last of the Julio-Claudian dynasty (the line of Augustus), committed suicide in AD 68 and was followed by a not particularly well-born,

13.43 *The "Prima Porta Augustus": this marble statue of Augustus (d. AD 14), is among the most famous and evocative of images from antiquity. Discovered in 1863, it was employed as a symbol by the newly reunified nation of Italy and, later, as a piece of Fascist propaganda by Benito Mussolini.*

but successful and popular general, Vespasian, who founded the short-lived Flavian dynasty. Likewise, Diocletian, a shrewd administrator who reorganized the empire in the later 3rd century AD, was an Illyrian soldier (probably from the region of modern Croatia) who rose through the ranks. In the provinces, living emperors were worshiped as gods with temples and sacrifices in their honor. In Rome itself, out of deference to the enduring and still respected senatorial aristocracy, this happened only at death, and then only if they were adjudged to have been good emperors (Price 1984).

Rome, Center of the World

For much of Roman imperial history, the city (*urbs*) of Rome remained the center of the empire, and of the known world. The capital city was fed and cosseted at the expense of the rest of the empire; paying no taxes, a proportion of its population received handouts of food, and all its residents were entertained courtesy of the emperors, not least by spectacles and games in the arena (Mattingly and Aldrete 2000; Garnsey 1988). "Bread and circuses" kept the people amused and content, and little expense was spared; emperors would stage entertainments that lasted for several days, with endless combinations of contests between animals and men. The need for wild animals, such as the African rhinoceros or the British bear, led to a veritable industry supplying the arena (Scarre 1995a). Gladiators, either slaves or criminals, were also called upon to fight, if by no means always to die. Amphitheaters were eventually built all over the empire to accommodate these activities. One of the best preserved, and certainly most prominent, is the Flavian Amphitheater, better known as the **Colosseum**, given as a gift to the people of Rome by the emperor Vespasian (Coleman 2000) and completed in AD 80.

Pleasing the people was especially desirable given the size of Rome's urban population, which in the early empire is thought to have approached 1 million (a city size not achieved again in the West until the 18th century). The city also grew increasingly complex in composition, both in terms of human diversity (with high levels of immigration, especially of slaves, from all over the empire and beyond its borders) and urban differentiation (for Rome possessed both elite residential areas and slums). Notwithstanding the construction of aqueducts to bring water to the city, and despite much urban legislation about matters such as fire fighting and waste disposal, Rome was not a healthy, or easy, place to live in for many of its residents (Scobie 1986).

As the city grew, further articulation was necessary to organize its multiple activities. Additional fora were constructed by emperors, both as personal showcases and as additional spaces for civic business. The **Forum of Trajan** (dedicated AD 112), for example, was a huge undertaking, paid for by the spoils of the Dacian wars north of the Danube [13.44]. The complex was made up by, among other elements, open spaces, basilicas (large columned halls used for judicial proceedings), libraries, imperial statuary, and a tall column sculpted with the story of Trajan's campaigns against the Dacian tribes (Packer 2001). **Trajan's Column**, with its spiral of highly detailed reliefs showing everything from the routine of building camp to the suicide of the Dacian leader, is an extraordinary depiction of Roman military life. It is also only one part of the overall message of this forum, which, in one representation after another, insists on the central significance of its creator, Trajan; indeed, the base of the Column ultimately became his tomb. This mix of entirely practical space and hard-hitting imperial symbolism was a peculiarly successful Roman blend, and it was witnessed in public spaces all over the empire [13.45].

13.44 Reconstruction of the Forum of Trajan (dedicated in AD 112): *in the middle of the court stands an equestrian statue of the emperor Trajan. Behind is the facade of the Basilica Ulpia (named after the emperor's family line), and – peeking up above – the top portion of the Column of Trajan (dedicated AD 113).*

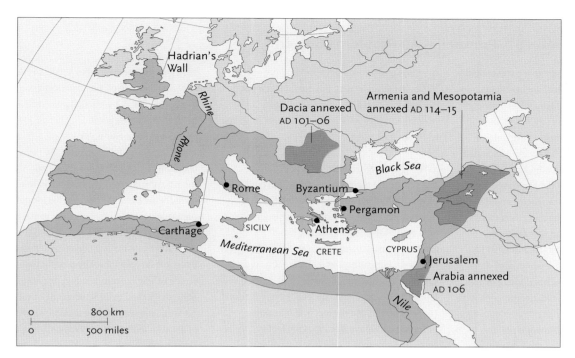

13.45 *Map of the spatial extent of the Roman empire: this shows the empire at its height in the early 1st millennium AD, reaching from the chilly wilds of Scotland to the barren environment of the Egyptian Eastern Desert.*

The city was first walled in Republican times and then again in the later 3rd century AD, when the empire began to experience troubles. These walls, as in Greek cities, defined the boundaries between the living and dead, and the radial roads (such as the Via Appia) that departed from Rome were lined with cemeteries, including monumental elite tombs. The burial of emperors such as Trajan within the heart of the city only served further to mark their unique status (Davies 2000; Walker 1985). In Roman Italy, and ultimately the empire at large, all roads truly did lead to Rome, and well-engineered, phenomenally straight roads became a hallmark of the imperial infrastructure [**13.46**]. Built in the first instance for military transport and rapid strategic communication, they also fostered economic exchange and the movement of peoples.

While Rome was unique in size and splendor, many of her urban features – fora, amphitheaters, temples, walls, roads – appear in other Italian cities and throughout the empire. Possessing such similar structures linked the cities of the empire; everyone would recognize the proper accouterments of a well-run community (Stambaugh 1988; Zanker 2000). It is true, however, that archaeologists of Rome have tended, not surprisingly, to become fixated on the public and the monumental, which are only part of the story of urban existence (Moatti 1993). A sense of day-to-day life under the Romans is better glimpsed elsewhere, above all in the buried city of Pompeii [see box: Pompeii – All Problems Solved?, p. 510].

13.46 *Aerial view of the Fosse Way: this Roman road linked the southwest of Britain to the rest of the province. Throughout the territory of the Roman empire, modern roads often tend, where possible, to follow the course of their Roman precursors.*

The Provinces and Frontiers

If Rome was the core of the empire, together with the imperial heartland of Italy, then the provinces could be called its periphery. Core-periphery models are often unsatisfactory, however, for they tend to privilege the needs and impact of the former over the reactions and responses of the latter. That said, imperial annexation had a profound effect on the societies brought within the ambit of Rome, and Rome certainly benefited from her provincial holdings. Taxes (in cash or in goods) were levied

KEY CONTROVERSY Pompeii – All Problems Solved?

A cynic might suppose that AD 79 must be the favorite year of the Classical archaeologist. In that year the eruption of Mount Vesuvius, near the Bay of Naples in Italy, led to the burial of several flourishing communities, most famously Pompeii. This city – its walls, forum, temples, amphitheater, houses, shops, tombs, and inhabitants – lay preserved by a layer of ash and volcanic pumice (*lapilli*) until exploration of the site began in earnest in the mid-18th century (Etienne 1992; Zanker 1998). Since that time, fascination with the buried city has never diminished, and archaeological activity has been more or less ongoing (albeit pursued in different ages with markedly different methods).

Pompeii is the most thorough urban excavation ever undertaken, and its range of finds, from wall paintings to latrines, provides predictable illustration for innumerable textbooks on Roman art and archaeology. The very nature of its destruction lends it a unique appeal: the existence of houses with walls, streets with sidewalks, and the evocative remains of the unfortunate

humans and animals trapped by the ash of Vesuvius explain why Pompeii (since 1997 declared a World Heritage site) is one of the most frequently visited archaeological places in the world.

The "Pompeii Premise"

This quite extraordinary and tantalizing degree of site preservation, extending right down to the discovery of food sitting ready to eat on the table, has tended to lead archaeological interpretation astray. Pompeii has been envisioned as a city frozen in time, preserved as a kind of perfect time capsule from the Roman past. Indeed, Lewis Binford (1981) dubbed the notion that human behavior can leave behind a perfectly transparent record, one easily read and understood by the archaeologist, "the Pompeii premise." Its dangers have been pointed out in a number of seemingly unrelated contexts, such as hunter-gatherer camps, shipwreck sites, or, most aptly, the "Bronze Age Pompeii" of Akrotiri on Thera in the Aegean Sea (Doumas 1983). What the

Pompeii premise ignores is the all-too-often confused nature of site creation and interpretation, as well as the significant impact of post-depositional taphonomic processes (Schiffer 1987).

At Pompeii, for example, the present site – far from being a fossil of its AD 79 incarnation, frozen in time – has been transformed in many ways. No longer a pleasant coastal resort, thanks to the eruption it today lies some 2 km (1.2 miles) inland. The contents of its houses, once believed to have been left largely intact by people fleeing the shock of the eruption, now appear to have been disturbed even in antiquity, and are very far from presenting the total house inventory of an archaeologist's dream (Allison 1992). Early exploration of the site (which usually meant the looting of precious artifacts and wall paintings) likewise drops a veil between modern interpretations and ancient realities.

Even more troubling, the unquestioning adoption of the Pompeii premise long prevented a range of interesting questions being asked about the site. By focusing solely on the moment of destruction in AD 79, for example, investigation of the site's previous centuries of existence as an Oscan community (a pre-Roman people who lived around the Bay of Naples and elsewhere) and later as a colony of Roman veterans was precluded.

Pompeii, the best known of all Roman cities, became Roman rather gradually, but that process, and its pre-Roman origins, has only recently begun to be seriously explored.

13.47 *The Via Abbondanza, Pompeii. This "Street of Plenty" (a modern name) was lined with a mixture of shops, bars, and houses. Graffiti, announcements, and electoral propaganda were painted on facades along what was clearly one of the town's busiest thoroughfares.*

across the empire. Cash taxes filled the imperial coffers, allowing imperial extravagance and display. Food distributions in Rome depended overwhelmingly upon provincial shipments, especially the flow of grain from Egypt. The army, ringing the empire on its frontiers, also had to be fed and clothed. In times of need, as after an earthquake or a famine, the center could

help the provinces, but the flow of financial support and supplies normally went very much the other way.

Natural resources, too, generally passed under imperial control. In the western provinces, in particular Spain and Portugal, these included silver, gold, and copper mines worked by slaves with the help of technological advances such as sophisticated

13.48 The Mons Claudianus quarry in the Egyptian Eastern Desert: *the abandoned columns in the foreground give a sense of the scale of this imperial operation. Despite the remoteness of the quarry, care was clearly taken to feed and nurture its workforce.*

pumping mechanisms (seen, for example, at the Rio Tinto complex of mines in southern Spain). The sheer amount of Roman mining activity has recently been measured by the pollution it created in Greenland ice cores (Greene 1986; Shotyk et al. 1998). In the eastern provinces, stone (often marble) quarries were more common. Apart from Rome's building boom, provincial elites also sought to adorn their public dedications and their private homes with these prized materials (Greene 1986). In some cases, the use of a particular stone was restricted to the emperors alone, most notoriously the "imperial purple" (granodiorite) from the **Mons Claudianus** quarry [**13.48**]. Lying in the eastern desert mountains of Egypt, exploitation of this remote resource demanded huge investments of labor and technical expertise; its very appearance in Roman monuments (for example, in the columns fronting the Pantheon of the emperor Hadrian) sent a clear message of an inexorable imperial will (Peacock and Maxfield 1997). Sea transport underlay much, if by no means all, of this endless movement of goods, skills, and power [see box: The Mahdia Shipwreck, pp. 512–13].

Reactions to Roman Annexation Despite many shared features in their treatment, the provinces reacted variably to Roman annexation. Factors guiding these responses, apart from location, topography, and natural resources, included the province's pre-existing social condition and political organization, as well as the nature of its take-over. The greatest impact was felt in the western provinces, chief among which were **Gallia**, **Hispania**, and **Britannia** – modern France, Spain, and Britain, respectively (King 1990; Keay 1988; Potter and Johns 1992). While indigenous pre-Roman societies in these regions were in some cases centered on large settlements and used coinage, by Roman standards they remained under-urbanized and loosely organized. Roman control encouraged civic development and more developed regional networks, articulated not least through the practice of the imperial cult. Communities in the western provinces also embraced many Roman cultural traits: baths, the games, education in Latin, styles of pottery. This process of Romanization (rather like the presumed Hellenization of Greek colonies) was once taken as automatic; now, the intricacies of cultural contact, and the use of Roman objects and actions to suit local needs and purposes, have become more apparent. Emulation and adoption may say less about a desire to appear Roman than they do about a desire by local groups or individuals to create internal hierarchies and differences; thus, far from replicating some central way of life, new

provincial cultures were created (Woolf 1998). It is equally true, however, that the local elites of the west were not reluctant to identify themselves with Rome and its authority. As one sign of this, the first non-Italian emperors came from the western provinces: Trajan and Hadrian from Spain in the very early 2nd century AD, and Septimius Severus from Leptis Magna in modern Libya, North Africa, at its very end.

Compared to those in the west, many of the eastern provinces were already heavily urbanized and possessed of a culture that Romans chose to emulate, rather than vice versa. The remark by the Latin poet Horace that "captive Greece took its savage victor captive, and brought the arts to rustic Latium" has, however, tended to be taken too literally. It had been thought that the Greek east experienced little change under Rome, but thanks to a growing archaeological interest in this period, the presence of Roman authority and expectations is now entirely visible, even in the Hellenic heartland of Greece itself (Alcock 1993). To consider just one index – the presence of the imperial cult – we may note that on the acropolis of Athens alone, a temple to Roma and Augustus was erected before the Parthenon's primary entrance, an honorary inscription to Nero was attached to its facade, and a statue of the emperor Hadrian stood within. Emperor imagery and shrines were equally ubiquitous in the Athenian agora. Far from being impervious to the shaping effects of Rome, Roman styles in such archaeologically visible domains as temple architecture, arena games, dining, and baths were widely adopted throughout the east. This does not mean that the Greeks sought to become Roman, however. In many ways – through the deployment of language, history, and rhetoric – they sought to maintain a cultural barrier between Greek and Roman, despite their peaceful inclusion within the empire (Swain 1996).

A remarkable fact about the Roman empire is the relative infrequency of serious internal revolt, although one clear

13.49 *Relief showing the triumphal display of spoils (including a menorah), from the interior of the Arch of Titus (c. AD 81): the scene on the arch's other side presents Titus in a chariot, crowned by Victory and led by the goddess Roma, on his triumphal parade through the city.*

exception came from the Jewish population of the eastern province of Judaea. By many historic standards, Rome was a society tolerant of other religions, so long as the imperial cult was properly honored with sacrifice, something not possible for Jews (or for the Christian sect in its turn). At least two major rebellions had to be suppressed in Judaea in the 1st and 2nd centuries AD. The first was commemorated on the **Arch of Titus** (*c.* AD 81) in central Rome, where the spoils from the destruction of the Temple in Jerusalem, including a giant menorah, were carried through the streets in triumph [**13.49**]. A landmark of this event is **Masada**, by the shores of the Dead Sea. A rebellious group, defying Rome during the First Jewish Revolt, had retreated to this high and isolated plateau, which fell only in AD 73 or 74 after a Roman siege. The massive siege ramp, and the camps built to house the Roman soldiers stationed in the desert to build it, can still be seen today [**13.50**]. The revolt ended, according to the historian Josephus, with a mass suicide of the

KEY SITE The Mahdia Shipwreck

Sponge fishermen first discovered the Mahdia shipwreck, off the coast of modern Tunisia, in the very early 20th century. Its astonishing cargo attracted several subsequent investigative campaigns, one involving famed underwater explorer Jacques-Yves Cousteau.

A Rich Cargo

The ship (40.6 x 13.8 m, or 133.2 x 45.3 ft) carried a rich and heterogeneous collection of material: some 60 marble columns, at least 30 marble column bases and capitals, numerous sculptures and decorative elements (such as candelabra) in bronze and marble, rotary and hand mills, transport amphorae, coarse (e.g. cooking) wares, lamps, anchors and more. The wreck has been dated to *c.* 80–70 BC on the basis of the pottery found aboard. It was traveling from east to west, probably from Piraeus (the port of Athens) to central Italy and Rome (Hellenkemper Salies 1994).

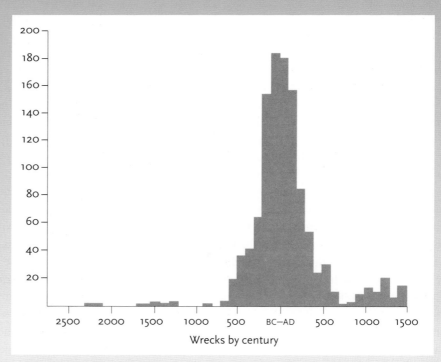

13.51 *Graph of the numbers, for each century from 2500 BC to AD 1500, of known Mediterranean shipwrecks. A peak during Roman times (in the last centuries BC/first centuries AD) is clearly demonstrated.*

13.50 *Aerial view of Masada, showing the siege ramp and the encircling Roman camps: the defensive possibilities of this isolated plateau had been noted before; King Herod the Great built a remarkable palace on it, with gardens and waterworks, despite the dry environment.*

The sculptures retrieved from the wreck initially received the most attention, both for their aesthetic merit and their ability to assist in dating other works of Hellenistic and Roman art.

It also became clear that certain statues and reliefs had been removed from their original contexts before being shipped out to the west. These discoveries led to an early and romantic reading of the wreck as a triumphant bearer of loot following the Roman sack of Athens in 86 BC. While this accords with both a willingness to take spoils and a mounting philhellenism on Rome's part, a more balanced assessment of the wreck complicates the story somewhat. It is clear, for example, that the ship's chief cargo (the first to be loaded and, at some 230 tons, the heaviest) were the marble columns and other architectural elements, all quarried from Mount Pentele in Attica, source of the Parthenon's marble.

Closer inspection of the other, humbler finds (mills, pottery, foodstuffs in amphorae) reveals that the ship also carried goods from all over the Mediterranean. If the removal of artistic masterworks was one motivation for the voyage, trade between various ports and the acquisition of freshly quarried prestige marbles were clearly others.

Trade and the Roman Economy

The Mahdia ship, rather like the Bronze Age Uluburun wreck [see The Uluburun Wreck box, Chapter 12, p. 459], is an exceptionally electrifying example of what can lie encapsulated at the bottom of the sea. On another level, however, analysis of the overall quantity and distribution of Roman shipwrecks, as well as their particular cargoes, can recreate complex and shifting networks of commerce, taxation, and the transport of tribute and booty (Parker 1992). Merely counting up the number of known wrecks, for example, strongly suggests an increase in sea traffic from 200 BC to AD 200.

On this basis, powerful arguments can be raised about the likelihood of overall expansion of the Roman economy (Hopkins 1980). Much debate surrounds the nature of the ancient economy as a whole, and the degree to which it was akin (or not) to its medieval or modern counterparts (Finley 1973; Scheidel and von Reden 2002). Such archaeological evidence as shipwreck data offers an opportunity to assess such behavior, and to quantify change over time, in an objective and comprehensive manner.

13.52 *One of the wonderfully well-preserved "dancing dwarves" from the Mahdia shipwreck of c. 80–70 BC.*

13.53 *Hadrian's Wall in northern England:* when complete, this ran for some 80 Roman miles (117 km, or 73 miles). The Wall was marked periodically along its course by forts and milecastles, allowing news and military orders to pass swiftly along the line.

13.54 *(Below)* **Statue of the god Mithras slaying the cosmic bull:** the fact that this sacred act was thought to take place in a cave is reflected in the frequently subterranean location of mithraea, shrines of Mithraism.

Jewish defenders. Archaeology of the site has proven controversial, in some interpretations supporting, in others disputing, this heroic account.

Whatever the truth of the matter, Masada has become a highly charged site of commemoration and pilgrimage, and a symbol for the modern nation of Israel (Yadin 1966; Ben-Yehuda 1995). This conscious modern appropriation of a Roman past is also evident in many other modern nation-states, such as Britain (Hingley 2000; 2001).

The Roman Army The Roman Tenth Legion assigned to break Masada was only one such unit, each of which consisted of some 5000 citizen infantrymen, carefully located around the empire. The legions, together with auxiliary units drawn from subject peoples, were placed chiefly along the frontiers or in provinces that promised trouble, as in Judaea (Cornell and Matthews 1982). One of the most efficient and successful fighting forces in world history, the Roman army battled when it had to, but was often more of a guarding, occupying force (Isaac 1990). The logistics and operation of this army can be studied via several archaeological techniques. In the east, much of what we know has been derived from aerial photographs, many taken before World War II (Kennedy and Riley 1990), in which a complicated landscape of camps, forts, and roads can be discerned. In the western empire, careful excavation has been undertaken at many military sites, particularly along **Hadrian's Wall** [13.53] in northern Britain. Such constructed barriers are relatively uncommon along the frontiers and seem, if anything, intended to control, rather than completely to prevent, movement across the border. Close connections between the military and civilian realms are also obvious from the rise of settlements that grew up in proximity to the army camps (Whittaker 1994). Whatever their functional purpose, military productions such as Hadrian's Wall also delivered a symbolic message, and a warning. Together with impressive imperial features such as aqueducts, which effortlessly spanned great distances, these monumental constructions reminded witnesses of the long arm of Rome. If the presence of the army was one coercive element behind imperial order, architectural and engineering feats played a parallel ideological role.

A Multiplicity of Gods Cult sites dedicated to many different gods were found along Hadrian's Wall, as well as in such other military contexts as Dura Europus, far away in the Syrian desert on the Euphrates River. The ready transplantation of troops accounts in part for this; Hadrian's Wall, for instance, welcomed soldiers from as close as northwestern Europe and as far afield as Syria. One deity worshiped both at the Wall and at Dura Europus was **Mithras**; this cult's strong sense of discipline and hierarchy proved popular with the Roman army. Originally from Persia, Mithraism represented a struggle between darkness and light, the triumph of the latter represented by the god's slaying of a massive cosmic bull [**13.54**]. Mithras, however, was but one of several eastern deities that traveled widely through the Mediterranean world and beyond, a transmission fostered by the open conditions of transport and trade. Other cults that spread in this fashion included the Egyptian gods Isis and Serapis, Artemis of Ephesus (a Greek city in southwest Turkey), and Christianity (Elsner 1997). Christians earned much Roman hostility for their rigid monotheism and refusal to participate in imperial cult practices; Nero and other emperors would employ them as scapegoats in times of trouble.

The Later Empire

Christian vulnerability to Roman attacks ended with Constantine (died AD 337), who "converted" to the new religion in AD 312 after seeing a sign in the heavens two years earlier, promising him victory in battle. The imperial attitude toward Christianity softened to the point of making it the new state religion, and with the **Edict of Milan** (AD 313), Constantine allowed its practice, thus adding an additional level of ecclesiastical administration and moral authority to the workings of empire. A colossal statue of the emperor [**13.55**], when compared to the Augustus of the Prima Porta [see **13.43**], demonstrates how imperial portraiture in the 4th century AD was both innovative and self-referential. Constantine's vast upturned eyes and the simple planes of his face are departures witnessed elsewhere in the art of the later empire; yet his short-cropped hair, clean-shaven face, and commanding gesture are reminiscent of the Prima Porta figure. That Constantine now points upward to the heavens, rather than gesturing to the world, has been taken as symbolic of a fundamental change in world view, although his personal devotion to Christianity has been much debated.

The fact that Constantine's conversion came at the battle of the **Milvian Bridge**, against his co-emperor Maxentius, signals one important change in the Roman imperial structure. Beginning in the 3rd century AD, the empire found itself, for myriad

13.55 Colossal head and body parts, including an upward pointing hand, of Constantine the Great (d. AD 337): originally placed in an apse of the Basilica of Constantine in the Roman Forum, and now in the Palazzo dei Conservatori, the head alone measures over 2.6 m (8 ft) in height.

reasons, increasingly less able to keep its domains in good order. One attempt to solve this problem involved dividing power among several emperors, initially a four-man team called the Tetrarchy [**13.56**], established by Diocletian in the later 3rd century AD; Diocletian's peaceful abdication in AD 305 testifies to the success of this strategy. To represent this structural change, there emerged an imperial iconography of *similitudo* (similarity) and *concordia* (harmony), along with the necessary creation of additional imperial capitals (thus diminishing Rome's central authority) located closer to the frontiers (for example, Trier in Germany), so as to allow a more rapid response to troubles. By the 5th century AD, mass movements of barbarian populations, attacking the edges of the empire from many directions, were a potent destabilizing force (Whittaker 1994). **The Huns** attacked both the eastern and western empire, invading Italy itself under their leader Attila (died AD 453); this had happened already some 40 years before, when Alaric the Visigoth sacked Rome in AD 410. In the course of his siege, certain elements of this once cosseted urban population were said to have been reduced to cannibalism.

The redistribution of imperial power, coupled with military reforms, did much to extend the life of an increasingly uncontrol-lable empire, but in the end it foundered. It did not precisely "decline and fall," as Edward Gibbon put it in his monumental 18th-century account. Instead, it divided along particular fault lines, being formally broken in two with the death of Theodosius I in AD 395 and then further fragmenting. The east remained more or less intact, with Constantine's foundation of the New Rome, **Constantinople** (modern Istanbul), as its capital. Later scholars would rename this eastern part of the Roman empire the Byzantine empire, although its own inhabitants long considered themselves "Rhomaioi" ("Romans"). This successor state only fell in AD 1453, to the Ottoman Sultan Mehmet II (Mehmet the Conqueror). Meanwhile, Carthage and much of North Africa were seized by Vandal rulers in the 5th century AD, while western Europe fragmented into several Germanic kingdoms.

Another key element in the transformation of the Roman world, of course, involved the 7th-century AD Islamic incursions into the Mediterranean region, ultimately monumentalized in the Moorish architecture of southern Spain. Yet from the imperial foundations left in Gallia (France) would rise the Carolingian kingdom of Charlemagne, who would be crowned "Emperor of All the Romans" in Rome in AD 800 (Moreland 2001). Given such a potent afterlife, it is no wonder that pinpointing the terminal date of the Roman empire is a subject for seemingly endless disagreement. What cannot be denied is the end of the political integration of the Mediterranean world, although exchange and contact continued, as always promoted by the existence of the inland sea (Goitein 1967–93).

Summary and Conclusions

At the outset, we referred to the Mediterranean as a superb laboratory in which to watch political evolution and cultural change in a region marked equally by uncertainty and opportunity. As one follows culture change and all manner of human activities taking place in and around this inland sea over many centuries – in this chapter, from c. 3000 BC to AD 500 – the trend toward ever-greater regional integration is very marked.

This can be traced from the multiple small-scale social units of the earlier Bronze Age, through the palace-based polities of the later Bronze Age Aegean and the city-states of the Classical and Phoenician worlds, with their offshoot colonies, to the more expansionist states of Alexander and his successors, or of Carthage, culminating in the virtually unchallenged Mediterranean-wide *imperium* of Rome – which swallowed up as

13.56 *Portrait statue of the four Tetrarchs embracing:* the dark reddish-purple stone (Egyptian porphyry) was used specifically for imperial representations. The great similarity of the figures is remarkable, although the older rulers are distinguished by beards from their smooth-faced younger partners. This sculpture is today located in St. Mark's Cathedral, Venice.

building blocks all such previous entities, as most empires tend to do.

Even under the sway of Roman rule, however, the Mediterranean was never characterized by a single, uniform culture, and certainly never by a single, common language. The geographically diverse regions that bordered this sea maintained and continually reworked their own local cultures and traditions. Such processes occurred, however, within a very active matrix of connection and contact. Apart from processes of outright conquest or annexation, the Mediterranean region was also bound together by links of colonization, trade and exchange, religious diffusion, and artistic influence – and these processes frequently worked independently of any political control. Connectivity, facilitated by the sea, was often driven in the first instance by need, given the variability of the Mediterranean climate and of natural resources. Cultural exchange, however, extended beyond issues of community survival. Imagery and concepts emerging from the Hellenic world, beginning in the Archaic and Classical periods, proved especially powerful as a shared "language" in the wider Mediterranean world, one that other Mediterranean peoples – Etruscans, Carthaginians, and Romans – would exploit in their own way.

The Mediterranean thus emerges as something of a paradox: a region of highly connected local societies; a crossroads of cultures in a fragmented and precarious natural environment; a region of uncertainty and opportunity. A disproportionate number of the world's most famous civilizations matured there, although such a statement is itself a reflection of past biases about just what constitutes a famous civilization. Trying to understand the genesis and operation of cultures such as Greece and Rome, the Etruscans and Phoenicians, is well worthwhile in its own right, and, moreover, is greatly enriched by considering them analytically and comparatively within the broader global patterns of the human past.

Chapters 10 through 13 have taken the story of Africa, Europe, Southwest Asia, and the Mediterranean world down to the later Holocene and the early historic period. We have charted the rise and diversity of urban state societies in each area, alongside less complex farming communities and (in parts of Africa) the survival of hunting and gathering. In the next two chapters the focus switches to the eastern half of Eurasia. In Chapter 14, we return to the beginning of the Holocene period in a new area, South Asia, and consider the mosaic of hunter-gatherer, agricultural, and urban state societies that developed there during the millennia that followed.

Further Reading and Suggested Websites

Broodbank, C. 2000. *An Island Archaeology of the Early Cyclades*. Cambridge: Cambridge University Press. A comprehensive study, with general reference to the Mediterranean and particular focus on the Early Bronze Age Cyclades.

Cartledge, P. (ed.). 1998. *The Cambridge Illustrated History of Ancient Greece*. Cambridge: Cambridge University Press. Beautifully illustrated chapters provide both a solid historical narrative and treatments of a wide range of provocative thematic topics.

Chapman, R. 2003. *Archaeology of Complexity*. Cambridge: Cambridge University Press. A general overview of how contemporary archaeology views social change, and the emergence of complexity, hierarchy, and inequality, illustrated by a detailed case-study of the later prehistoric societies of the western Mediterranean.

Coulston, J. & Dodge, H. (eds.). 2000. *Ancient Rome: The Archaeology of the Eternal City*. Oxford: Oxford University School of Archaeology, Institute of Archaeology. A collection of accessible essays, with up-to-date bibliography, on various aspects of the archaeology of urban Rome.

Garnsey, P. & Saller, R. 1987. *The Roman Empire: Economy, Society and Culture*. London: Duckworth. A clear and comprehensive review of Roman history, with a useful emphasis on social and economic developments.

Greene, K. 1986. *The Archaeology of the Roman Economy*. London: Batsford. A careful review of various facets of the Roman imperial economy, including transport, coinage, agriculture, and mining.

Horden, P. & Purcell, N. 2000. *The Corrupting Sea: A Study of Mediterranean History*. Oxford and Malden, MA: Blackwell. A sweeping examination of Mediterranean connections and regional fragmentation, ranging from later prehistory to early modern times.

Mathers, C. & Stoddart, S. (eds.). 1994. *Development and Decline in the Bronze Age Mediterranean*. Sheffield: Sheffield Academic Press. A Mediterranean-wide synthesis of Bronze Age archaeology; quite specialized.

Osborne, R. 1997. *Classical Landscape with Figures*. London: George Philip. Out of print, but worth tracking down, as one of the most accessible accounts of life outside the city in the Classical world, drawing on both archaeology and history.

Whitley, J. 2001. *The Archaeology of Ancient Greece*. Cambridge: Cambridge University Press. The most up-to-date and successful attempt to review the art and archaeology of Greece after the Bronze Age and through the Hellenistic period.

http://www.perseus.tufts.edu/ The Perseus Project is a large and evolving digital library of textual and visual materials on Archaic and Classical Greece, recently expanded to include the Roman and Renaissance worlds.

http://www.unc.edu/depts/cl_atlas/ Website of the Barrington Atlas (Princeton: Princeton University Press, 2000), with 99 full-color maps of the Greek and Roman world.

http://www.stoa.org/metis/ Website serving thousands of Quick Time photographs and plans of archaeological sites in the Aegean, with interactive links.

http://whc.unesco.org/heritage.htm/ A detailed list of the properties on the World Heritage List; Mediterranean sites are listed by country.

CHAPTER 14
SOUTH ASIA: FROM EARLY VILLAGES TO BUDDHISM

Robin Coningham, University of Bradford

Land and Language 519

The Foundations: *c. 26,000–6500* BC 522
 Western India 522
 The Ganges Plain 522
 Central India 522
 Sri Lanka 523
 Seasonality and Mobility 523

Early Neolithic Villages: The First Food Producers 524
 Western Pakistan 524
 ● KEY SITE Mehrgarh: An Early Farming Community 524
 Kashmir and the Swat Valley 526
 The Ganges Basin 527
 Peninsular India 527

An Era of Regionalization: Early Harappan Proto-Urban Forms 528
 ● KEY CONTROVERSY Foreign Contact and State Formation 1: The Indus Cities 529
 Kot Diji and Early Pointers Toward the Indus Civilization 530

An Era of Integration: The Indus Civilization, *c. 2600–1900* BC 532
 ● KEY CONTROVERSY The Decipherment of the Indus Script 532
 A Hierarchy of Settlement Forms 533
  • *Urban Settlements* 533
  • *Second Tier of Settlements* 533
 ● KEY SITES Mohenjo-daro and Harappa 534
  • *Third Tier of Settlements* 535
  • *Fourth Tier of Settlements* 535
 Character of the Indus Civilization 536
 Subsistence and Trade 536
 The Western Borderlands 536

An Era of Localization: The Eclipse of the Indus Civilization, *c. 1900* BC 536
 ● KEY CONTROVERSY The Social Organization of the Indus Civilization 537
 The Core Cities 537
 ● KEY CONTROVERSY The End of the Indus Cities 538
 Peripheral Areas 539
  • *Gandharan Grave Culture* 539
  • *The Ganges-Yamuna Doab* 539
  • *The Western Deccan* 540

The Re-Emergence of Regionalized Complexity, *c. 1200–500* BC 540
 Developments in the Northwest and East 540
 ● KEY CONTROVERSY Foreign Contact and State Formation 2: The Early Historic Cities 541
 ● KEY CONTROVERSY Dating the Historical Buddha 542
  • *Painted Gray Ware* 543
  • *"Great Territories"* 543
 Southern India and Sri Lanka 544
 ● KEY SITE Taxila 544

Reintegration: The Early Historic Empires, *c. 500* BC–AD *320* 546
 The Mauryan Empire 547
 Post-Mauryan Dynasties 548
 The Kushan, Satavahana, and Later Dynasties 549
 ● KEY CONTROVERSY Roman Contact and the Origins of Indian Ocean Trade 550

Summary and Conclusions 551

Further Reading and Suggested Website 551

In chapters 6 through 13 we followed the rise of farming and then the genesis of state societies in Africa, Europe, Southwest Asia, and the Mediterranean world. In this chapter we turn to South Asia – the modern nations of India, Bangladesh, Nepal, Bhutan, Pakistan, the Maldives, and Sri Lanka – and consider its development during the Holocene. Like Africa or Europe, it is a land of great contrasts in climate and geography, and the past 10,000 years have seen the creation within its boundaries of a correspondingly diverse mosaic of hunter-gatherers, village farmers, and early state societies. South Asia provides yet another example of the manner in which widespread changes such as agriculture and urbanism are manifest throughout postglacial Eurasia in settings of local cultural and social diversity.

Between 6500 BC and AD 500, South Asia witnessed a series of dramatic changes to the social and economic organization of its human inhabitants. These changes included the development and spread of early village-based communities in the 7th millennium BC, the emergence of the Indus Valley civilization in the 3rd millennium BC, the collapse of that civilization by 1900 BC, and the gradual re-establishment of cities and states during the 1st millennium BC.

Before 6500 BC, we have good evidence for communities of hunter-gatherers exploiting most regions of South Asia from the eastern edges of the Indus plain to the central hill country of Sri Lanka. These small communities appear to have been highly mobile, and have left indicators of increasing personal differentiation and territoriality. The dramatic discovery in the 1970s of Mehrgarh, 200 km (125 miles) west of the Indus in western Pakistan, completely changed the way archaeologists explain the relationship between these foraging communities and the later, Neolithic villages of South Asia. Mehrgarh has, at last, provided solid evidence that food-producing villages were established on the western flanks of the Indo-Iranian Plateau by 6500 BC, and that their inhabitants were actively intervening in the lifecycles of plants and animals, most obviously with the domestication of native cattle. This lengthened chronological backdrop now provides a solid foundation for the emergence of a network of South Asian villages and craft centers that steadily colonized the plateau and gradually moved down onto the Indus plain itself. By the 4th millennium BC these colonizers had built a number of regionalized proto-urban settlements, linked by the ceramic tradition known as Kot Diji. Although not on the same scale as its cultural successor, the mature Harappan, or Indus, civilization, the presence of a number of shared traits, such as rigid city planning, massive mud-brick walls, bull motifs, and carved sealstones, has led archaeologists to consider this development as a distinct formative phase.

The mature, or integrated, form of the Indus civilization emerged by 2600 BC, and its cities and their crafts have been well studied. Nevertheless, there is still no consensus among scholars as to the nature of the social organization binding this collection of cities, towns, and villages. Covering an area of over 500,000 sq. km (193,000 sq. miles), it was strong enough to facilitate the movement of raw materials down onto the alluvial plains of the Indus for manufacture and redistribution, but it left no evidence of palaces or royal burials. One of the greatest obstacles to our understanding of the Indus civilization is the failure of scholars successfully to decipher the Harappan script. Controversy also remains as to the factors responsible for the decline of the civilization in 1900 BC. While some scholars have identified invading Aryan speakers as the cause, others suggest catastrophic floods, earthquakes, and epidemics; still others point to a gradual exhaustion of the landscape.

Whatever the explanation, archaeologists have now successfully traced the steady development of a series of localized cultural groupings in the aftermath of the Indus civilization. Based in the northwest of the subcontinent and in the Ganges basin, these groupings spread throughout South Asia between 1200 and 500 BC and resulted in the re-emergence of urban forms at sites that collectively represent the so-called Early Historic civilization. A single integrated state, the Mauryan empire, emerged from these several political entities by 350 BC. Heavily involved in the state sponsorship of multiple religions (including Buddhism), and pluralistic in philosophy, it created under the emperor Asoka a centralized state incorporating most of modern South Asia, and had diplomatic relationships with its Hellenistic neighbors to the west as well as with Sri Lanka to the south. Its political and social organization was to provide a model for its successor states following its fragmentation in the 2nd century BC. The period covered by this chapter laid the social, economic, and cultural foundations for modern South Asia, a factor acknowledged in the Republic of India's choice of one of Asoka's lion-headed pillar capitals as its national crest.

The nomenclature adopted in this chapter blends more traditional terms, e.g. "mature Harappan," with those proposed by Jim Shaffer (1992), such as "era of integration," in order better to compare the development of South Asia's two great urban phenomena.

Land and Language

The nations that comprise South Asia, listed above, also have strong geographical, linguistic, historical, and archaeological links with parts of Afghanistan and Iran. Geographically, this region is recognizable as a single unit consisting of a roughly

SOUTH ASIA TIMELINE

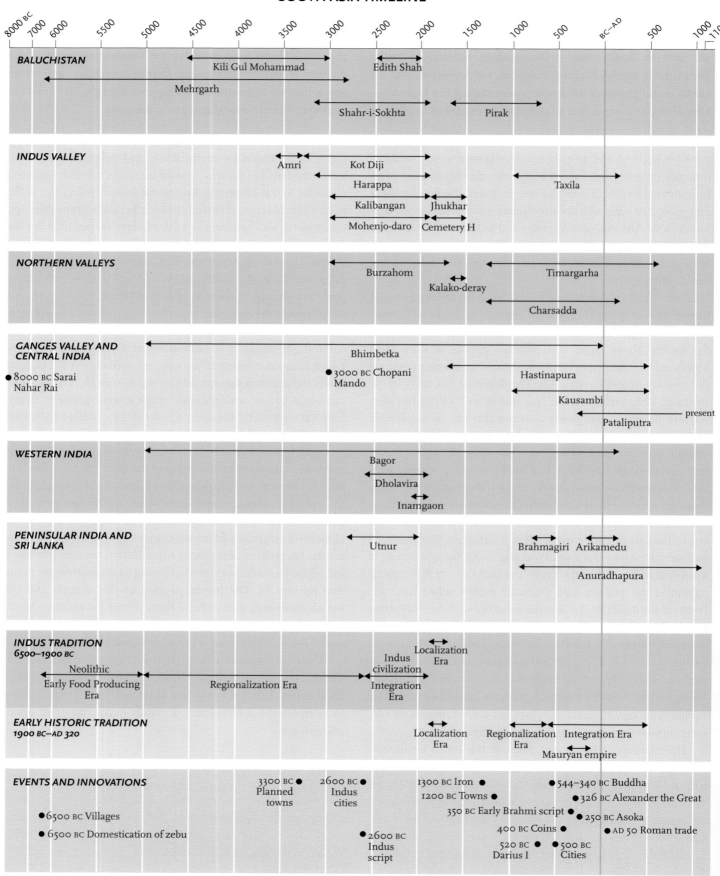

triangular landmass of 4 million sq. km (1.54 million sq. miles) [**14.1**]. It is defined on the east by the Bay of Bengal, on the west by the Arabian Sea, and on its northern edge by the mountain barrier comprising the Hindu Kush, Pamir, Karakoram, and Himalayan ranges (Robinson 1989). These montane and oceanic boundaries are not impervious, and indeed have for millennia facilitated contact with regions to the east, north, and south through seasonal passes and winds.

Although a single unit, South Asia possesses extremes of topography and environment, stretching from the glaciers of its northern barrier, with 95 peaks over 7500 m (24,600 ft), to the 1009 coral atolls of the Maldive Islands, none of which is more than 2 m (6.6 ft) above sea level (proving vulnerable to the tsunami or tidal wave of 2004). The most obvious features within the northern half of this landmass are the two great river basins, the Indus and the Ganges. Physically separated by the Thar Desert and the Aravalli range, and fed by the valleys and mountains to their north, their alluvium supports millions of inhabitants and some of the region's largest cities. The south-ern edge of the Ganges basin is defined by the east–west Vind-hyan escarpment and central India; further south lies the Deccan Plateau. This southern plateau is cut by a series of broad river valleys and is separated from its coasts by the Eastern and Western Ghats, rising to a maximum of 2524 m (8280 ft). South Asia's diversity is epitomized by the island of Sri Lanka at the southeastern tip of this land unit, where it is possible to travel from the arid northern peninsula to the lush central hill country in a single day.

This pattern of unity and diversity is also found within the region's languages, which largely belong to two families, the Indo-European and Dravidian; but such is the multiplicity of linguistic forms that India alone acknowledges 14 official lan-guages and 1652 native tongues (Robinson 1989). Most of today's 164 million speakers of Dravidian languages live in southern India, but the presence of a Brahui-speaking (i.e. Dra-vidian) pocket in western Pakistan has suggested to some scholars that there was a much wider distribution of these lan-guages in the past (Coningham 2002). This pattern, when

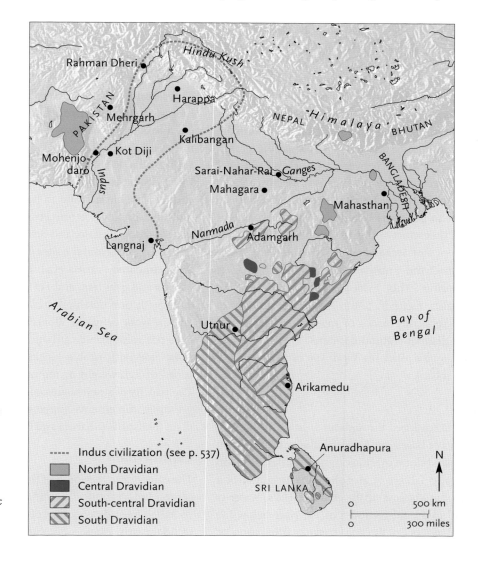

14.1 *South Asia:* this landmass of 4 million sq. km hosts one-fifth of the world's population, two of its great language families, seven of its major religious traditions, and has witnessed four distinct Neolithic developments and two major phases of urbanization.

----- Indus civilization (see p. 537)
North Dravidian
Central Dravidian
South-central Dravidian
South Dravidian

overlain by the distribution of Indo-European languages, has led many archaeologists and historians to suggest that Dravidian speakers were displaced by an invasion of Indo-European speakers (Parpola 1994). The pattern is repeated in microcosm in Sri Lanka, which has a core of Sinhalese, an Indo-European language, and a northern and eastern distribution of Tamil, a Dravidian language (De Silva 1981).

The Foundations: *c.* 26,000–6500 BC

The sequence of the peopling of South Asia is still uncertain, and research into this area is only now attracting the attention it deserves, despite the recognition of the region's first Paleolithic tools by Robert Bruce-Foote as long ago as 1863. Augmented by systematic research, the picture is improving, and the discovery by Helen Rendell, Robin Dennell, and their colleagues (Rendell et al. 1989) of a chopping tool in northwest Pakistan dating to 2 million years ago provides a much earlier date for initial occupation than the earliest hominin remains suggest. The remains of the earliest *Homo* species, "Narmada Man," date to only 250,000 years ago, and the earliest anatomically modern *Homo sapiens* examples, from Sri Lanka, date to 34,000 years ago (Kennedy 2002).

Despite these early uncertainties, most scholars would attribute the foundations of South Asia's complex societies to the period usually termed the Mesolithic. There are difficulties in applying European terminology to South Asia, including the use of the term Mesolithic (see Chapter 5, p. 182), as the sites to which it is applied range in date between 26,000 and 1800 BC. Nevertheless, this broad collection of sites is united by the use of microlithic blade industries with a developmental sequence from non-geometric to geometric forms – all that remains of the composite tools they must once have formed. The sites are united by the presence of archaeologically visible occupation levels and broad-spectrum subsistence strategies based on hunting and gathering. This evidence, although covering almost every ecological niche in South Asia, is grouped into four main regions, reflecting zones of intense archaeological activity rather than distinct cultural domains. These areas are western India, the Ganges plain, the Vindhyan escarpment and central India, and Sri Lanka.

Western India

The first grouping is scattered throughout western India, and includes the key sites of Bagor and Langnaj. **Bagor** is located on a 6-m (20-ft) high sand dune overlooking the Kothari River in Rajasthan (Misra 1973; Lukacs et al. 1983). At the center of a rocky plain in the rain shadow of the Aravalli Hills, water is retained year-round in an old meander of the river below the dune. The cultural sequence at the site stretches from 5000 BC

to AD 200 and is characterized by the presence of microlithic tools throughout; these are augmented by ceramics and copper objects from *c.* 2800 BC and iron objects from *c.* 600 BC. Occupation during Period I, dating to between 5000 and 2800 BC, consisted of schist paving and semicircular stone alignments, presumably windbreaks. No hearths were identified, but faunal remains indicated the hunting of cattle, deer, pig, turtle, and fish. A single inhumation with an east–west orientation belongs to this phase. Additional, wealthier burials were recovered from Period II (2800–600 BC), along with perforated ground-stone rings; the excavator has suggested that these represent weights for digging sticks. The evidence from Bagor is paralleled by that from **Langnaj** in Gujarat (Karve-Corvinus and Kennedy 1964; Sankalia 1965). Located on the summit of a dune overlooking a seasonal lake, it was occupied in the 3rd millennium BC. Although there was no evidence of structures, the site did produce midden deposits of faunal remains, charcoal, and 13 grave cuts complete with grave goods: microlithic blades, animal bones, and beads. Again, a broad-spectrum subsistence strategy was found, with wild deer, sheep or goat, cattle, horse, pig, fish, rhinoceros, and tortoise, alongside stone rings and querns, evidence for the grinding of grain.

The Ganges Plain

The second area to be considered comprises open-air settlements within the Ganges plain. Typically located at the edges of old meanders, or ox-bows, of the river and its tributaries, one of the best-preserved examples is the 9th-millennium BC site of **Sarai Nahar Rai** in the middle Ganges Valley (Sharma 1973). Lying on the bank of an ox-bow, it includes two structures, a cluster of 12 burials, and 12 hearths. Again, its faunal remains indicate a broad-spectrum economy, ranging from fish and tortoise to cattle, buffalo, and even elephant. Similar evidence has been recovered from the sites of **Mahadaha** (Sharma et al. 1980) and **Damdama** (Varma et al. 1985), the former with 301 stone querns and grinders, and 132 stone blades and bone tools, the latter with one notable burial that contained two arrowheads and an ivory pendant. Whereas most of the sites in this area have few recognizable structures, that of **Baghor** has postholes associated with rubble blocks, suggesting the presence of a series of lightweight or temporary windbreaks or sunshades. The paucity of stone blades and flakes and the large number of grinding implements suggest a reliance or concentration on plant foodstuffs (Sharma and Clarke 1983).

Central India

The evidence to the south of the Vindhyan escarpment and into central India is quite different, as most sites are associated with rockshelters and caves. One of the most important is the shelter of **Adamgarh**, where microlithic tools have been found (Joshi

1978). The broad-spectrum subsistence pattern of this site matches those of others, with finds of wild deer, hare, porcupine, monitor lizard, and shell, but the excavator has also suggested the presence of domesticated dog, cattle, buffalo, sheep or goat, and pig. Unfortunately, its radiocarbon measurement of 5500 BC was derived from an unreliable material for dating, questioning the antiquity of this remarkable site. The presence of bovid remains and microlithic blades in association with querns at the shelter of **Ghagharia**, overlooking the Son Valley, suggests that such sites were centers for the processing of animals as well as plants (Sharma and Clarke 1983).

The sites of this region are characterized by their large numbers of rock drawings and paintings. The complex of shelters at **Bhimbetka**, for example, has hundreds of paintings loosely associated with occupation floors that have yielded geometric microlithic tools and inhumations with grave goods of red ocher, bone points, worked antler, and even quern stones (Wakankar and Brooks 1976). Depicting humans hunting deer, cattle, buffalo, rhinoceros, monkey, and porcupine, as well as collecting honey and plants, the rock art has been analyzed more for its phasing than its possible function (Mathpal 1984). The site was occupied between the 6th millennium BC and the beginning of the Christian era, but sustained occupation ceased soon after the widespread distribution of iron tools at the beginning of the 1st millennium BC (Misra 2002).

Sri Lanka

Linked by a land bridge to the Indian mainland as late as the 6th millennium BC, the southernmost and fourth region, Sri Lanka, is remarkable due to the sheer amount of its evidence, collected almost entirely by the Deraniyagala father-and-son team (Deraniyagala 1992). As well as providing some of the earliest microlithic tools in South Asia (dating to c. 26,000 BC), the island has also revealed the earliest anatomically modern human remains, as well as demonstrating that such communities exploited almost every available ecological zone.

The fullest, and earliest, data have been recovered from rock-shelters in the island's central hill country. Although **Batadomba Lena** lacks clear evidence for structures, its midden deposits have yielded dates of 26,500 BC for geometric microlithic tools, bone points, shell beads, and human remains (Kennedy 2002). This evidence is augmented by plant and animal remains from the cave site of **Kitugala**, including pig, deer, squirrel, porcupine, and mollusks, along with banana and breadfruit; dates for this sequence range from 25,000 to 1400 BC.

At the northern end of the island, within the semi-arid lowlands of **Mantai**, evidence of a single incident of occupation dating to 1800 BC was recovered from a low sandbank beside a lagoon. This consisted of a number of geometric microliths scattered among the remains of a dugong (a herbivorous marine mammal) and various shellfish, within the inter-tidal shoreline. Further south, excavations at **Anuradhapura** in the island's dry zone have recovered scatters of microlithic tools covering an area of some 10 ha (25 acres) on a low gravel ridge above the active floodplain of the Malwattu River. Although the river is perennial, this scatter, dating to 3850 BC, may represent the exploitation of the site's natural ponds during the dry season.

Seasonality and Mobility

The breakthrough in understanding the functioning of all these South Asian communities did not occur until the 1970s, when G.R. Sharma (1973) identified a distinct difference between the lithic assemblages of the Ganges plains and those of the Vindhyan escarpments to the south. The latter had more and bigger tools, and their cores were larger and not worked for as long as those on the plains. Rather than interpreting these variations as representative of different cultural groups, Sharma suggested that they were evidence of **seasonal mobility**, or transhumance. He suggested that game moved from the plains to the hills in the temperate winter season and were followed by hunter-gatherers camping in caves and shelters. As the year became hotter and drier, there was a general exodus of animals down to the perennial ox-bow lakes in the plains, and people followed, augmenting their diet with plant and aquatic resources. This model of seasonality and mobility is also applicable to western India, where chalcedony found at Bagor has its source over 100 km (60 miles) to the southeast (Khanna 1992), as well as to Sri Lanka, with marine shell transported 80 km (50 miles) inland to the cave site of Kitugala (Deraniyagala 1992).

This pattern of serial mobility may have been accompanied by the development of **resource territoriality**, suggested by the presence of human remains within occupation middens, perhaps linking ancestors with resources; conflict may be indicated by the presence of a microlithic blade embedded in the ribs of one of the individuals buried at Sarai Nahar Rai. While the extended burials in the Ganges plain and flexed ones in Gujarat may represent the growth of regional diversity, the increasing presence of grave goods marks, perhaps, increasing individual differentiation. That this period witnessed increasing reliance on plant resources is indicated by the presence of querns and perforated and polished stone rings, perhaps used as weights for the ends of digging sticks, as well as by teeth worn by grit, indicating to some scholars a diet with as much as 60 percent plant content (Kennedy et al. 1992). Although the presence of microlithic blades and ground-stone tools at some sites may be termed Mesolithic, and at others aceramic Neolithic (Thomas 1997), there can be little doubt that these social and economic foundations were to lead some communities onto domesticated pathways, while others continued their hunter-gatherer lifeways until the end of the 19th century AD.

Early Neolithic Villages: The First Food Producers

In 1959 the British archaeologist Mortimer Wheeler suggested that the earliest evidence of Neolithic cultures in South Asia – polished stone axes – dated to 1000 BC and indicated the movement into central and eastern India of farmers from "Burma if not behind" (Wheeler 1959, 91). Since then, researchers have revised and vastly expanded this evidence, identifying four clusters of Neolithic communities that practiced pastoralism and agriculture, one of which dates to as early as the 7th millennium BC.

Each cluster is geographically and culturally distinct, suggesting a clear diversity of pathways in the approach to domestication, a feature supported by their very different dates. Two of the South Asian clusters, in the west and peninsular India, indicate a strong regional contribution toward the process of domestication; the remaining two, located in the Kashmir-Swat area and along the Ganges, are less convincingly of a South Asian origin.

As in other parts of the globe, these South Asian sites attributed to the Neolithic period are associated with ground-stone tools, domesticated plant and animal species, the introduction of ceramics, and the establishment of settlements. It should be noted, however, that these criteria are not always fully met in South Asia, and that continuity with the preceding period is strong. Some early Neolithic settlements do not appear to have been fully sedentary, wild as well as domesticated plants and animals were exploited, and polished stone tools were used alongside blades strongly linked to microlithic industries. Nevertheless, building on the strong foundations already laid, this period offers the first clear evidence for domestication, the agglomeration of large populations in villages, long-distance trade, and, perhaps, the storage of surplus.

Western Pakistan

South Asia's earliest known Neolithic communities were located in western Pakistan, at the eastern foot of the Indo-Iranian Plateau in Baluchistan. There, in the 7th millennium BC,

KEY SITE Mehrgarh: An Early Farming Community

Until the chance discovery of Mehrgarh, the earliest agricultural site known on the Indian subcontinent was Kili Gul Muhammad. Excavated in 1950, the latter provided evidence of a community of herders and farmers utilizing domesticated species, marked in its earliest phases by an absence of ceramics (Fairservis 1971). Dating to c. 4000 BC, the lack of an earlier phase here led scholars to assume that such sites had their origins to the west, and that their occupants moved east, exploiting the Indo-Iranian Plateau, before reaching the Indus Valley.

This model was completely revised in the early 1970s with the discovery of Mehrgarh by Jean-François Jarrige and his team. Noting an archaeological section that had been exposed by a flash flood at the mouth of the Bolan Pass, they discovered a site covering 2 sq. km (0.77 sq. mile), dating to 6500–2800 BC (Jarrige et al. 1995). While such a large area might indicate the presence of an urban settlement, the tell (an artificial mound formed by the accumulation of cultural debris) is actually formed by a series of interlocking areas of habitation, each chronologically distinct.

The First Settlement: Period IA
The earliest occupation at Mehrgarh, Period IA, dates to 6500–6000 BC. During this

14.2 *Pre-pottery Neolithic Mehrgarh, in western Pakistan, where evidence of the earliest farming community in South Asia was found. Dating from the 7th millennium BC, it consisted of clusters of mud-brick compartments measuring 1 sq. m. It is likely that they were used for storage rather than habitation, and may indicate that the settlement's inhabitants were largely mobile.*

small agricultural villages were established in the vicinity of the Bolan River and its pass, which links the uplands with the Indus plain (Jarrige et al. 1995). The earliest of these settlements is the site of **Mehrgarh**, mentioned above, which provides clear evidence of the development of a farming and pastoral community around 6500 BC; its people were reliant on wheat, barley, and domesticated cattle, augmented by wild plants [see box: Mehrgarh: An Early Farming Community]. A unique site discovered by chance, it is closely linked to a series of other small, but later, villages, such as **Kili Gul Mohammad** and **Rana Ghundai**, which spread across Baluchistan in the 5th millennium BC (Fairservis 1971). With mud-brick structures, these communities are characterized by their use of chert blades, bone points, and handmade (not wheelmade) ceramics, and all share a dependence on domesticated sheep or goat, cattle, wheat, and barley. There is also evidence that they were linked through trade networks that brought turquoise, marine shell, and steatite beads from communities to the north, south, and west.

The distribution pattern of these 5th-millennium BC villages further to the west and east is archaeologically unknown, as few scholars have surveyed on the Iranian side of the border, and the deep annual deposition of alluvium may mask related sites within the Indus plain. Before the discovery of Mehrgarh, most scholars had assumed that Neolithic communities from Southwest Asia gradually diffused eastwards, bringing with them the Neolithic package of settled villages, ceramics, wheat, barley, and sheep or goat.

The earlier dates for aceramic Neolithic levels at Jericho, and dates of between 8000 and 6500 BC for Neolithic deposits at Ali Kosh in southwest Iran (both discussed in Chapter 6), supported such a model of population movement from western to southern Asia with a postulated speed of 1 km (0.6 miles) per year (Renfrew 1987). However, the presence of Mehrgarh, with dates of at least 6500 BC, weakens this model, as it would require colonialists in Iran to have started this diffusionary process by at least 8600 BC in order to cover the intervening 2100 km (1300 miles).

---

period, the small settlement consisted of rectangular mud-brick structures internally subdivided into small compartments. As some of the later compartments measure little more than 1 sq. m (*c.* 11 sq. ft), they probably functioned not as habitations but rather as storage silos. This feature has led some scholars to postulate that occupation at the site was seasonally transhumant, a lifestyle still practiced in this part of Baluchistan today.

Many of the finds from this period were recovered from the settlement's burials and included exotic materials such as turquoise, marine shell, steatite beads, and even a single copper bead. In the absence of ceramics, baskets lined with bitumen were utilized as waterproof containers; this material was also used to fix short stone blades in sickles.

Rich plant remains, including barley and wheat, have been recovered from within bricks, where they were used as temper (material added to clay to improve its firing qualities). According to the site's archaeobotanist, Lorenzo Constantini (1984), although the wheat already appears to have undergone intensive domestication prior to arrival at the site, barley seems not to have

been completely domesticated. These cereals were augmented with dates and jujube fruit, and wild animal species such as gazelle, deer, and zebu cattle (*Bos indicus*).

Periods IB and II

This pattern changed significantly in Period IB (6000–5500 BC), a phase characterized by the appearance of ceramics, when the presence of many wild species declined and a subsistence strategy focused on cattle emerged. As this occurred at the same time that cattle declined in size, the archaeozoologist Richard Meadow (1984) has suggested that this is evidence of a localized domestication of zebu cattle. The size of cattle continues to decrease in Period II (5500–4800 BC), during the excavation of which a copper ingot was recovered; from this phase also comes a tantalizing report of

cotton, possibly providing the earliest evidence of its domestication in the world.

Overview

Mehrgarh is a key discovery because it provides the earliest undisputed evidence of the formation of farming and pastoral communities in South Asia. Its plant and animal remains provide clear evidence of ongoing domestication and, perhaps most importantly, a distinct Neolithic subsistence package based upon local zebu cattle. Finally, the longevity of the site and its relationship with the neighboring site of Naushahro (2800–2000 BC) provide a very clear continuity from the region's first farming communities to the emergence of its first cities (Jarrige 1984).

14.3 *The first Neolithic farmers: In addition to evidence for the local domestication of zebu cattle, Mehrgarh's inhabitants also cultivated barley and wheat. These crops were harvested with sickles made of geometric stone blades set into a wooden haft with locally available bitumen.*

More significantly, it is important to note that the development of farming in this region does not entirely imitate the Southwest Asian Neolithic package, as it relies heavily on the domestication of native cattle rather than sheep and goat. Indeed, posited western origins fail to account for this particularly South Asian character, nor do they explain why, if Mehrgarh's earliest occupation was the result of the diffusion of a developed Neolithic ensemble, it is both aceramic and probably seasonal. Collectively, these factors suggest that the earliest of South Asia's Neolithic complexes developed largely from local antecedents.

Kashmir and the Swat Valley

The second cluster of communities, the Northern or Kashmir-Swat Neolithic, emerged in the 4th millennium BC and is distributed across the southern valleys of the Karakoram and Himalayan ranges. The sites, of which there are more than 40, are characterized by the presence of ground-stone axes, rectangular stone sickles pierced for straps or handles, and bell-shaped pits. This cluster was first identified at **Burzahom** [14.4] in the Kashmir Valley during the 1930s, but the site was not subject to extensive excavations until 1971 (Singh 2002). It is located on an elevated plateau overlooking the valley's lakes, a position shared by the other related settlements in the region. Burzahom was occupied *c.* 3000 BC–AD 1700, the Neolithic occupation being restricted to Phases IA–C (Sharif and Thapar 1992).

Although the first phase (3000–2850 BC) appears to have been aceramic, with coarse, thick-walled, and over-reduced fired ceramics appearing in Phase IB (2850–2250 BC), the structures of both phases are similar. These are bell-shaped pits, the largest of which measured 4.6 m (15 ft) in diameter and 4 m (13

ft) in depth; some were plastered in clay, and a number included deposits of ceramics and faunal remains. Although the function of these pits is still controversial, a number of scholars have suggested that they represent underground dwellings, providing insulation from the cold winters of the foothills. Additional information has been obtained from the site of **Gufkral**, with data there suggesting a subsistence reliant on wild animals, domesticated sheep and goat, and wheat, barley, and lentils (Sharma 1982). Information from pollen sequences in the valley's lakes indicate frequent decline and growth of pine forests from 7000 BC, suggesting regular clearances (Singh 1964). No further pits were cut during phase IC of the valley's Neolithic occupation, which is typified by the erection of mud-brick and timber structures on the surface.

The evidence from Pakistan's **Swat Valley** is very similar, although somewhat later, with dates of between 1700 and 1400 BC; Neolithic sites there may extend as far south as Sarai Khola in Taxila (Halim 1972). The sites of **Kalako-deray** and **Loebanr III** are also characterized by the presence of large and small pits, the largest of which are bell-shaped and measure up to 4.7 m (15.4 ft) in diameter and 3.6 m (12 ft) deep (Stacul 1977; 1994). Some were stone paved, and others had evidence of burning. The pits contained terracotta figurines in human and animal forms, ceramic vessels, polished stone objects, rectangular stone sickles, hammer stones, grinding stones, bone objects, and jade beads. Paralleling the final Neolithic occupation in Kashmir and following the abandonment of the pits, rectangular mud-brick structures were erected on the surface.

The presence of jade beads, holed rectangular sickles, and underground dwelling pits has led some scholars to suggest contact with Neolithic communities in Central and East Asia (Stacul 1994). Indeed, Asko Parpola (1994) has further strengthened this link by noting that the languages of this zone are related to those of Central Asia. Others, however, have questioned the function of the pits as dwellings, and interpret their apparent domestic features as midden fills accumulated after their disuse (Coningham and Sutherland 1998). Such pits are probably better interpreted as providing sub-surface grain storage in the bitter winter months, while their transhumant communities moved south toward the plains before returning to the valleys in the spring for sowing. This hypothesis questions the Central Asian links of these communities as well as their characterized sedentary nature, but the specific origins of this Neolithic grouping are still unclear.

14.4 Burzahom's bell-shaped pits: *the Neolithic of the Kashmir and Swat valleys is typified by the presence of bell-shaped pits, and while some scholars have suggested that they represent dwellings, insulating the inhabitants from the region's cold winters, others have proposed that they were used as grain silos.*

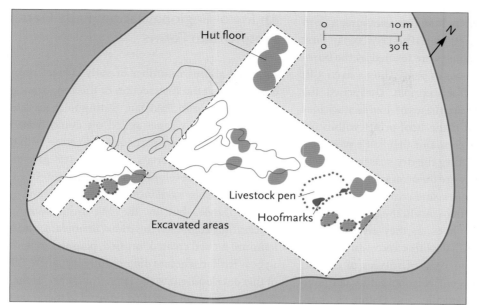

14.5 *Mahagara's Neolithic village:* excavations at Mahagara have revealed the plan of a small Neolithic village in the Ganges Valley. The huts (tint areas) appear to have formed eight discrete groupings, perhaps representing households, with a livestock stockade or pen, enclosing an area of 93.75 sq. m (1010 sq. ft), close to the center of the village.

The Ganges Basin

The third Neolithic complex is loosely centered on the Ganges basin, but the presence of polished stone axes in eastern India, including shouldered examples, suggests a much wider distribution. Some of the sites exhibiting this complex were established close to the seasonal settlements of the preceding period in the Ganges Valley and have their origins in them. This pattern is not entirely surprising, as many of the earlier sites, associated with microlithic tools and broad-spectrum subsistence, also relied heavily on the gathering of plant resources, as suggested by their utilization of stone querns for grinding cereals, as well as their possession of perforated and polished stone rings for possible use as digging-stick weights. The most substantive evidence of this complex was recovered from three sites closely clustered on the River Belan – Chopani Mando, Mahagara, and Koldihawa (Sharma et al. 1980).

The site of **Chopani Mando** is located on a former meander of the Belan and has a sequence stretching from the beginnings of the Holocene to the early or proto-Neolithic. Its final phase, dating to the 4th millennium BC, has revealed a settlement of 1.5 ha (3.7 acres), with 13 huts more substantially constructed than those in earlier phases. Although its Neolithic affiliations are indicated by the presence of cord-impressed, handmade ceramics, ground-stone tools, and numerous querns and other elements of food-processing equipment, the presence of wild rice and undomesticated cattle and sheep or goat suggest a settlement in transition.

It has been proposed by G.R. Sharma that **Mahagara**, located only 3 km (2 miles) from Chopani Mando, represents the next step in this development. Covering an area of 0.8 ha (2 acres), its Neolithic phase culminates in a settlement of at least 18 huts centered on a stockade or pen measuring 12.5 x 7.5 m (41 x 24.6 ft) [**14.5**]. George Erdosy (1987) has suggested that the huts were grouped into eight households, with a total population of 250 individuals, and that there was a degree of specialization among the inhabitants, suggested by the uneven distribution of querns and stone tools. Mahagara's final phase is associated with wild cattle, deer, and boar, and domesticated cattle, horse, and sheep or goat, together with cord-impressed ceramics, polished stone axes and stone blades.

Despite the apparent continuity in the Ganges from hunting and gathering to agriculture, there is controversy surrounding the identification, dating, and provenance of domesticated rice at the key Neolithic sites of Mahagara, **Koldihawa**, and **Chirand**. These factors, combined with the earlier development and spread of rice cultivation in East and Southeast Asia (Chapter 7), suggest to scholars of those areas that rice domestication was not introduced to South Asia until the middle of the 2nd millennium BC (Glover and Higham 1996). Many South Asian archaeologists, however, still favor the suggestion that rice domestication in South Asia was indigenous, the result of a steady development of food-producing communities from the foundations of the preceding period in this area (Singh 2002). Only further investigation will shed light on this debate.

Peninsular India

The final Neolithic complex to be examined is broadly limited to peninsular India, as there is not yet clear evidence of such communities across the Palk Straits on the island of Sri Lanka. The peninsula complex is dated to between the 4th and 2nd millennia BC and may be broadly divided between two categories of sites: **ash mounds** and larger **open-area settlements** (Korisettar et al. 2002). There are over 50 of the former, with concentrations in the Deccan; the largest example, **Kudatini**, measures 130 m (427 ft) in diameter and 10 m (33 ft) high (Paddayya 1973). First investigated in the 1870s, these sites were formed by the burning of successive phases of stockades or pens. The 3.5-m (11.5-ft) high mound at **Utnur** [14.6], for example, comprised the burned and vitrified remains of four phases of double stockades (Allchin 1963). The presence of cattle hoof-prints within the stockade suggested to the site's excavator that cattle were seasonally brought to these sites during the dry season and were augmented by wild cattle, which were then tamed.

Polished stone axes, stone blades, and coarse ceramics link these mound sites with larger settlements in the Deccan's granite hills. Less is known of these sites, as they are frequently covered by overlying deposits of Chalcolithic and even Iron Age date, but they appear to have consisted of villages of circular boulder-and-stake structures. Recent paleobotanical sampling at the sites of **Tekkalakota**, **Sangankallu**, and **Hallur** has indicated the presence of indigenous domesticated plants, including pulses, millets, and even tubers or rhizomes, again suggesting a strong regional development (Korisettar et al. 2002).

An Era of Regionalization: Early Harappan Proto-Urban Forms

As noted above, a number of early village communities were established at the intersection of the Indo-Iranian Plateau and the Indus plain in Pakistan. Dating to at least the 7th millennium BC, these villages relied on domesticated species and stored surpluses, and participated in trade with other communities for exotic materials. That they still preserved links with the preceding developments is apparent from their use of microlithic tools, a reliance on wild species, and even a transhumant lifestyle, but by the 4th millennium BC they had successfully colonized the Indus floodplain, and by the 3rd millennium BC had created fortified, planned settlements (Mughal 1990). Earlier scholars did not fully recognize the contribution of this development to the later emergence of the Harappan, or Indus, civilization, and thus referred to this stage as Pre-Harappan [see box: Foreign Contact and State Formation 1: The Indus Cities]. Subsequent discoveries, such as Mehrgarh, have provided new evidence, and archaeologists now acknowledge this period to be one of dynamic experimentation, which culminated in the emergence of a recognizable cultural complex *c.* 3200 BC (Shaffer and Thapar 1992). This complex stretched from Rehman Dheri on the west bank of the Indus to the dry bed of the Ghaggar in the east and from Balakot in the southwest to Surkotada in the southeast, with over 300 identified sites; it is frequently termed the **Early Harappan period**, or **Kot Diji phase**, although many scholars now utilize Shaffer's (1992) phrase, an **"era of regionalization."**

Following its Neolithic origins, the site of **Mehrgarh** continued to thrive, with a steady growth in settlement size. As the settlement expanded, it emerged as a regional center of ceramic production. Indeed, pottery manufacture is a distinctive characteristic of the Chalcolithic communities in Baluchistan and has been frequently divided and subdivided by archaeologists into numerous affiliations, such as Nal, Zhob, and Quetta (Fairservis 1971). These ceramic-producing communities populated the valleys of the Nal and Zhob watersheds, and have been broadly divided into the Kachi, Kili Gul Muhammad, Kechi Beg, and Faiz Muhammad phases (named after individual type sites), dating to *c.* 5000–2600 BC (Shaffer 1992; Shaffer and Thapar 1992). In addition to monochrome, bichrome, and even polychrome wheel-thrown ceramics, they also manufactured copper,

14.6 *The Neolithic ash mound of Utnur: when first encountered by archaeologists in the 1860s, the vitrified ash mounds of the Deccan were interpreted as slag heaps. Subsequent excavation has demonstrated that they date to the Neolithic period and that they mark the locations of pens for herding cattle, while scientific analysis has demonstrated that these mounds comprise many layers of vitrified cow dung.*

KEY CONTROVERSY Foreign Contact and State Formation 1: The Indus Cities

When Sir John Marshall, discoverer of the Indus civilization, retired to England in the 1930s, it was said of him that he left India 2000 years older than he found it. He also left considerable debate as to the origins of the Bronze Age civilization that he had discovered. Marshall himself was struck by the South Asian character of the great cities that he had excavated, even photographing their streets filled with modern local inhabitants for scale (Marshall 1931). This Asian character appealed to other archaeologists, but they were also aware that there were no known antecedents for the civilization, and so looked westwards. These early researchers, including Stuart Piggott (1950) and Sir Mortimer Wheeler (1953), could find little evidence of increasing complexity within the valleys of Baluchistan, so they turned their sights even further west, toward the great cities of Mesopotamia. Wheeler noted the similarities between these two great civilizations, with their "urban way of life," "civic consciousness," and cities planned on a grid, and, acknowledging the greater antiquity of Mesopotamia, suggested that the communities of the Indus basin had benefited from a diffused "idea of civilization."

Discoveries Since the 1970s

The basis of this debate altered dramatically in the 1970s with a major archaeological advance, the identification of a distinctive proto-urban phase. This was of vast significance, as it demonstrated clearly that the planned cities of the mature Indus phase were not suddenly imposed, but were built within an earlier context of experimental settlements such as Kot Dij, or Rehman Dheri, with its grid city plan. With dates of *c.* 3200 or 3300 BC, this development appears very similar to the contemporary foundation of Shahr-i-Sokhta on the Indo-Iranian Plateau to the west, further weakening the diffusionist theory.

The nature of this internal sequence is also illustrated by the findings at the Indus cities of Harappa and Kalibangan. At the latter, the proto-urban walled compound becomes the mature-phase citadel, while at Harappa the walled compound is later augmented by a number of adjoining walled enclosures. Also in the 1970s, the discovery of the site of Mehrgarh was of even greater significance, as it pushed the cultural traditions of the Indus civilization back to the 7th millennium BC and the pre-pottery Neolithic – fully overturning any diffusionist concepts.

Overview

Even though there is now a long developmental sequence for the Indus basin, it should be recognized that there remains a vast gulf between the 20-ha (49-acre) settlement of Rehman Dheri and the huge metropolis of Mohenjo-daro of 200 ha (494 acres); a similar gulf exists between the stamp seals and non-scriptural graffiti of the proto-urban phase and the Indus script and seals. It should be noted that the two periods occupied slightly different areas, and while Kot Diji-phase settlements thrived in parts of Pakistan's North West Frontier Province to the west of the Indus, this region was later largely uninhabited by settlements of the Indus civilization.

The mechanisms driving these transformations and changes are not well understood, and there is still debate as to whether coercion was involved, as suggested by horizons of burning at Kot Diji and Nausharo (Shaffer 1992). Moreover, other sites, such as Harappa, provide a sequence of uninterrupted continuity, confusing the situation. Only further excavations and a broader use of chronometric (absolute) dating will shed light on this, the most critical phase of the development of the Indus civilization.

14.7 *Kot Diji is one of a number of proto-urban towns established within the Indus watershed in the 4th millennium BC. These settlements have antecedents in the Neolithic communities of Baluchistan and indicate that the Indus civilization had a distinctly local formative stage and that explanations relying on concepts of diffusion from Mesopotamia are untenable.*

shell, and stone artifacts; they followed subsistence strategies dominated by domesticated cattle and sheep or goat, and buried their dead in formal cemeteries. They were in contact with other communities in the west, which were grouping together in large, permanent settlements on the Indo-Iranian Plateau and to its north. These western and northern sites, including **Shahr-i Sokhta** and **Mundigak**, were to become important entrepôts and manufacturing centers, facilitating the movement of materials across the plateau. Established in the 4th millennium BC, Shahr-i Sokhta was an important regional center that covered 12–15 ha (30–37 acres) by 2800 BC (Tosi 1983).

In contrast to the long sequence of settlement within the Baluchistan uplands, the earliest evidence for the colonization of the Indus plain has been recovered from the 4th-millennium BC site of **Balakot**, close to the Makkran coast, perhaps because earlier sites may be covered by alluvial deposits. The inhabitants of this settlement occupied structures with mud-brick platforms, made distinctive decorated wheel-thrown ceramics, and lived on domesticated cattle and sheep or goat, wild gazelle, shellfish, and cultivated barley (Dales 1979). Ceramics from the later occupation of this site are stylistically linked to those from a number of settlements of the lower Indus Valley. **Amri**, their type site, is dated to *c.* 3600–3300 BC; its people subsisted on domesticated cattle, with important contributions from fishing and hunting (Casal 1964). Paralleling the evidence from Mehrgarh and Kili Gul Mohammad (4300–3500 BC), Amri's earlier phases included rectangular mud-brick structures divided into small compartments.

Further north, another ceramic grouping, the **Hakra**, indicates the widespread exploitation of the plain from Bahawalpur in the east to Sarai Khola in the west, and even into the Swat Valley, within the Ghaligai Cave ceramic sequence (Shaffer 1992).

Overlapping the latter half of the Amri phase, vestiges of Hakra influence survived stylistically in northern parts until the middle of the 2nd millennium BC. It is notable that some of the well-known Indus cities were first established during this phase, most notably **Harappa**, and the survey by Rafique Mughal (1997) in the Cholistan Desert has identified a mixture of small, temporary settlements and a few larger, permanent settlements covering up to 26 ha (64 acres). United by a distinct wheel-thrown ceramic tradition, these Hakra settlements are associated with geometric microliths, terracotta figurines, and bone and metal artifacts.

Kot Diji and Early Pointers Toward the Indus Civilization

Out of this mosaic of regional centers and influences emerged the first clear indicator of cultural convergence within the Indus Valley – the ceramic style known as **Kot Diji**. With a distribution stretching from Kalibangan in the east to Rehman Dheri in the west, and south to Amri, it is a successor tradition to Hakra, and has origins in the central Indus Valley and the type site of Kot Diji (Mughal 1990). Dated to *c.* 3200–2600 BC, the Kot Diji style is usually identified by wheel-thrown globular jars of red ware with everted or flanged rims and with geometric decorations including fish-scale patterns and intersecting circles, as well as depictions of bulls' heads, fish, and pipal leaves (a type of Indian fig). One of the most striking features of its accompanying cultural assemblage is the presence of formally planned settlements of mud-brick buildings. Although fortifications have been identified at Kot Diji itself (Khan 1965), some of the fullest data come from the sites of Rehman Dheri, Kalibangan, and Harappa.

Rehman Dheri is located on the western bank of the Indus, at the southern tip of Pakistan's North West Frontier Province

14.8 Aerial photograph of Rehman Dheri: *located on the west bank of the Indus River, the 4th-millennium BC town of Rehman Dheri provides clear evidence of a pre-planned settlement. Differential erosion has picked out the settlement's system of roads as gullies, defining a rigid grid-iron plan lined with cardinally planned mud-brick structures and surrounded by a massive wall.*

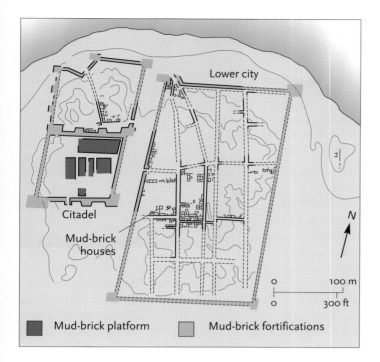

14.9 Continuity at Kalibangan: *nowhere is the continuity between the formative proto-urban stage and the integrated era of the Indus Valley clearer than at Kalibangan in Rajasthan. The Bronze Age city is well represented by a citadel mound to the west and a lower town compound to the east, but archaeologists have also identified an earlier settlement under the citadel mound, indicating that the proto-urban town followed exactly the same plan.*

of structures to the use of specific ceramic motifs [**14.10**]. The presence of a broad cultural convergence among the agricultural communities of the plains is further underlined by the presence of a series of shared motifs, such as the bull. Some scholars have suggested that this indicates the presence of a common ideology, enabling further convergence and the eventual formation of the Indus civilization. This is not, of course, to suggest that this development within the plains existed in isolation; the presence of Kot Diji ceramics at Burzahom in the Kashmir Valley, as well as within Sindh, Baluchistan, and southern Afghanistan, indicate the opposite (Shaffer 1978).

These contacts undoubtedly mark the paths of trade routes, which acted as channels for such raw materials as semiprecious stone to be exchanged for the products of the plains. The increasing economic role of settlements, and their specialization, is also suggested by the fact that of the 40 Early Harappan sites surveyed by Rafique Mughal in the Cholistan Desert, 35 percent exhibited multiple functions, such as craft and industrial specialization. The development of these routes of exchange and craft specialization is further evidenced by the presence of non-scriptural graffiti, indicating a demand for a recording medium (Coningham 2002). It is notable that, unlike the dynamic cultural convergence on the Indus plains to the east, the fragmented patterns of ceramic traditions in Baluchistan continued well into the 3rd millennium BC, and that this borderland was never integrated into the urban world of the Indus civilization. What had hosted the origins of the Indus complex was to become its periphery.

[**14.8**]. The site was first established around 3300 BC; its final, Kot Diji, phase has provided very clear evidence of a rectangular settlement with massive mud-brick walls enclosing an area of some 22 ha (54 acres) (Durrani 1988). Differential erosion at the site has helped to reveal on aerial photographs a rigid grid-iron street plan within its walls, even detailing individual structures. This element of formal planning is also found to the east of the Indus at the site of **Kalibangan**. There, under the Harappan citadel mound, B.B. Lal (1979) identified a 4.5-ha (11-acre) settlement enclosed by a 1.9-m (6-ft) thick wall. The parallelogram-shaped site includes mud-brick structures oriented to the cardinal directions and laid out in courtyard fashion [**14.9**]. Recent research at **Harappa** has successfully identified the presence of a wall surrounding an area of nearly 9 ha (22 acres) (Kenoyer 1998). Detailed settlement patterns have been revealed in the Cholistan Desert, where two larger settlements of between 20 and 30 ha (50 and 74 acres) dominated a hinterland of 38 smaller sites, suggesting increasing centralization (Mughal 1997).

Many of the features of the Early Harappan period are also found within the succeeding Indus civilization, suggesting degrees of artifactual and stylistic continuity. These range from the formal planning of settlements and the cardinal orientation

14.10 Cultural and ideological convergences: *anticipating the broad cultural integration of the Indus civilization, the proto-urban settlements of the Indus watershed began to display a number of common features – the "Kot Dijian" style. One of these features was the "horned deity," a key feature of later Indus ideology, suggesting that it had already been awarded iconic status.*

KEY CONTROVERSY **The Decipherment of the Indus Script**

Since the first publication in 1873 of a seal bearing the writing of the Indus civilization, the script's meaning, and even its language, has been a matter of controversy. From that date, the corpus of known inscriptions has expanded to over 2700, and find sites range from the Oxus to the Indus rivers and from South Asia along the Persian Gulf to the Euphrates (Parpola 1994). Composed of 170–220 simple signs and 170–200 composite signs, inscriptions are found on steatite, marble, ivory, silver, terracotta, shell, bone, and ceramic artifacts, including seals, axes, vessels, bangles, ladles, and sealings (the impression of a sealstone in clay). In addition to the signs, many inscriptions include a single standing animal, and a smaller number appear to depict a narrative scene. While some of animals, such as tiger, elephant, and rhinoceros, are recognizable as native to South Asia, others appear to be hybrid or mythical.

14.11 *The Indus script, as seen on this seal, has defied decipherment for well over 100 years and is likely to continue to do so until the discovery of a bilingual or trilingual inscription. The most we can advance now is that it probably represents a logo-syllabic script, with both word-signs and phonetic syllables.*

Challenges for Decipherment

Despite this large corpus, attempts to decipher the script are weakened by three factors. First, there are no bilingual inscriptions allowing a decipherment based on the comparison of a known and unknown script (such as the Rosetta Stone, which aided Jean-François Champollion in his decipherment of Egyptian hieroglyphs). Secondly, no single inscription is longer than 26 signs, defeating attempts to identify recurring sign patterns. Finally, there is no consensus as to the identification of the language, or languages, used in the inscriptions (Coningham 2002). This final factor is the focus of most controversy, with the debate ranging between a Dravidian or an Indo-European language. The argument relies on modern distributions of Indo-European languages in the north of the subcontinent and Dravidian ones in peninsular India, with the exception of Brahui, which is spoken in Baluchistan.

This distribution leads those favoring a Dravidian language for the script to argue that Indo-European speakers migrated after the end of the Indus civilization and pressed Dravidian speakers into the south, leaving a small pocket in Baluchistan (Parpola 1994). This intrusive model is contested by other scholars, who argue that there was a degree of Indo-European culture already present within the Indus civilization, and that its inhabitants spoke an Indo-European language (Srivastava 1984). To date, attempts at decipherment have been founded on an assumption that the language was either Dravidian or Indo-European, and so they have sought to demonstrate that the script conforms to pre-selected typological features or meanings. These approaches are weakened by such assumptions, and it is possible that the region's other major language families may have been represented, such as Austro-Asiatic or Sino-Tibetan or even a language since lost.

Overview

Despite this controversy, there is a degree of common ground between the 20 or so attempts to decipher the Indus script. First, it is agreed that the script was written from right to left. Second, most scholars would accept that numerical value signs for single units are indicated by a simple downward stroke, and units of ten by semicircles. (It should be noted, however, that the nature of the underlying numerical system is still debated.) Finally, it is generally acknowledged that the script was likely to have been logo-syllabic, possessing both word-signs and phonetic syllables. Beyond this, decipherment is unlikely unless a bilingual inscription or a series of longer inscriptions is discovered; until then, the Indus civilization will remain prehistoric.

An Era of Integration: The Indus Civilization, *c.* 2600–1900 BC

The **Indus, or Harappan, civilization** owes its names to the river basin where it was discovered, and to the type site – Harappa – where it was formally identified as a Bronze Age civilization. Since its discovery in the 1920s, many of its sites and cities have been identified outside the Indus River system, suggesting to some that its riverine title is too restrictive; these scholars argue that it should be renamed the Indus-Hakra or Sindhu-Sarasvati civilization (Chakrabarti 1999). Its mature, urban phase is dated to 2600–1900 BC, when it covered an area of 500,000 sq. km (193,000 sq. miles), extending from the Makran coast in the west to the Indo-Gangetic divide in the east, and from Gujarat in the south to parts of Afghanistan in the north.

The Indus civilization, termed an **"era of integration"** by Shaffer (1992), is typically identified at archaeological sites through the discovery of one or more of the following traits: cities; artifact standardization; four-tier settlement hierarchy; writing [see box: The Decipherment of the Indus Script]; long-distance trade; urban planning; craft and settlement specialization; and monumental public works. Frequently cited as uniform throughout this area, there are, however, elements of regional differentiation, referred to by some scholars as provinces and others as domains (Possehl 1993); these differentiations are frequently related to the immediately preceding pre-urban cultural sequences.

A Hierarchy of Settlement Forms

Urban Settlements At the peak of its settlement hierarchy, the Indus civilization possessed at least five sites that may be termed urban forms: Mohenjo-daro; Harappa; Dholavira; Rakhigarhi; and Ganweriwala. The first three covered areas of more than 100 ha (247 acres) each, closely followed by Rakhigarhi and Ganweriwala with 80 ha (198 acres). Analysis by Greg Possehl (1993) has suggested that Mohenjo-daro, Harappa, and Dholavira were all located as primary centers within the lower Indus, western Punjab, and western India respectively, while Rakhigarhi and Ganweriwala are situated close to the old course of the Ghaggar-Hakra River.

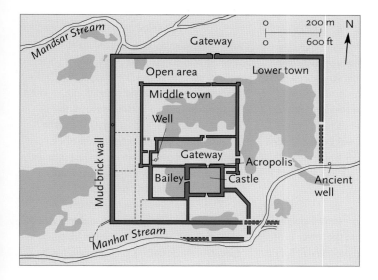

Harappa covers an area of over 150 ha (371 acres) and is located to the south of the old course of the Ravi [see box: Mohenjo-daro and Harappa, pp. 534–35]. Originally thought to share the same plan as Mohenjo-daro, recent excavations by Mark Kenoyer and Richard Meadow, building on the work of George Dales, have indicated the presence of at least four walled mounds clustering around a central depression, which may have held water (Meadow 1991). Each mound was entered through narrow gates and appears to have had little differentiation, each offering the same array of craft manufacture and finished artifacts. These mounds were linked by the excavators through the presence of molds from the same seals in different parts of the settlement (Meadow and Kenoyer 1997).

Dholavira is located in the Rann of Kutch and is one of the newest discoveries of the civilization (Bisht 1989) [**14.12, 14.13**]. Its most striking feature is its plan, which is quite different from any discovered previously. The urban element of the site is defined by a city wall measuring 771 x 617 m (2530 x 2024 ft), enclosing a complex of further walled rectangular and square compounds. The city was built of mud-brick and local sandstone, and the excavator has suggested the presence of large structures on the "acropolis"; the "lower" or outer town, with its evidence for craft activities, is subdivided by cardinal streets. Little is known of the plans of **Rakhigarhi** and **Ganweriwala**, as they were identified by surface survey and have not been significantly sampled through excavation (Mughal 1997).

Second Tier of Settlements The next tier of settlements includes some 32 sites that were significantly smaller than these urban centers, covering areas of less than 20 ha (49 acres). They vary considerably, but many appear to have been formally walled and internally planned. **Kalibangan**, for example, is located close to

14.12, 14.13 *Plan and artist's reconstruction of Dholavira: one of the most recently discovered Bronze Age cities, Dholavira possesses a unique plan and, unlike the better-known sites of Mohenjo-daro and Harappa, was largely built of locally available stone. Located in the Gulf of Kutch, its discovery demonstrates that western India was an integral part of Indus civilization.*

the former course of the Ghaggar-Hakra River in Rajasthan and had a plan very similar to that of Mohenjo-daro. Its rectangular citadel measured approximately 130 x 250 m (427 x 820 ft) and was located to the west of the walled lower town, which measured 235 x 375 m (771 x 1230 ft) (Lal 1993). The town was subdivided by cardinally oriented roads, and the citadel was divided into two by a large internal bastioned wall.

Lothal was somewhat different, with a rectangular plan measuring 300 x 225 m (984 x 738 ft). While the southwest, northwest, and northeast quadrants were filled with cardinally oriented mud-brick buildings and contained evidence for semiprecious stone manufacture, the remaining quadrant comprised an artificially constructed platform, topped by large structures (Rao 1973) [**14.14**].

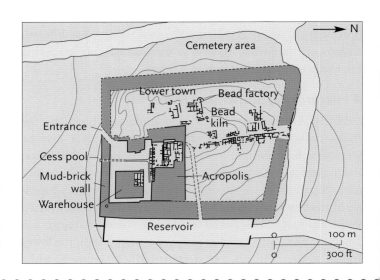

KEY SITES Mohenjo-daro and Harappa

The Indus civilization is best known for two cities, Mohenjo-daro and Harappa, simultaneously excavated in 1922 by Sir John Marshall (1931). That Marshall and his colleagues had discovered an unknown Bronze Age civilization was confirmed by the consistency between the artifacts discovered at the two sites, some 400 km (250 miles) apart, but was also attested at the time by the similarity of the two urban plans. Both had a pre-eminent "citadel" mound on the west and a lower residential "town" to the east.

Although the brick buildings on the summit of Harappa had been stripped for ballast for the Lahore-Multan railway,

excavation soon ascertained that the western mound at Mohenjo-daro was still crowned with a series of monumental structures. This cluster of civic and religious buildings contrasted with the regular residential streets of the lower town, laid out in a rigid grid pattern. The same pattern was later extended to smaller cities such as Kalibangan in northern Rajasthan.

Mohenjo-daro

Mohenjo-daro is the best-preserved city of the Indus civilization, located in the lower Indus Valley within the Pakistani province of Sindh. Recent surveys have suggested that its core

and suburbs may have covered an area as great as 200 ha (494 acres) (Kenoyer 1998); with 10 percent of the site excavated, it is the most studied city of the civilization. Crowned by a 3rd-century AD Buddhist stupa, the citadel mound rises 10 m (33 ft) above the surrounding floodplain on a mud-brick podium. Covering an area of 10 ha (25 acres), it was surrounded by a wall and contains a series of exceptional structures.

The first of these, the great bath, measures 12 x 7 m (39 x 23 ft) and is 2.4 m (8 ft) deep. Built of fired brick set in bitumen to provide waterproofing, it is surrounded by a colonnade and individual chambers, and would have held over 160 cu. m (5650 cu. ft) of water. It is immediately adjacent to the 6-m (20-ft) high granary, measuring 50 x 27 m (164 x 89 ft), of which nothing above its mud-brick foundation survives. The final monument is a pillared hall covering 30 x 30 m (99 x 99 ft) at the southern edge of the citadel, indicated by the presence of four rows of five brick pillars.

14.15 *The citadel of Mohenjo-daro: the key monuments include the most recent, a Buddhist stupa dating to the 1st or 2nd century AD, covering the Bronze Age buildings on the eastern side. To its west is the "great bath" and colonnade, abutting the mud-brick podiums of the "granary." There is a pillared hall to the south of the mound, close to a surviving portion of the mud-brick retaining wall.*

14.14 *(Opposite)* ***The "factory fort" of Lothal:*** *during the Bronze Age, a series of small walled settlements were built in western India, including Lothal. Here a mud-brick platform with storerooms occupied one quarter, with mud-brick structures filling the remainder of the settlement. The presence of a bead factory suggests that locally available semiprecious stone was collected and processed on site before being transported to the main cities.*

Third Tier of Settlements A third tier of settlements, small walled sites of 2–4 ha (5–10 acres), has been identified in western India. **Surkotada** in Gujarat, for example, consisted of a rectangular enclosure measuring approximately 65 x 130 m (213 x 427 ft), divided into two by a substantial internal wall (Allchin and Allchin 1982). Although the western division was higher than its eastern counterpart, both appeared to contain domestic structures. Even more diminutive is the walled site of **Kuntasi**, which hosted semiprecious stone bead production (Dhavalikar 1996).

Fourth Tier of Settlements At the bottom of the settlement pyramid are over 15,000 sites under 1 ha (2.5 acres), representing agricultural villages or economically specialized settlements, such as the shell-processing sites of **Nageshwar** in western India (Hegde et al. 1992) and **Balakot** in Sindh (Dales 1979). Moreover, survey in Gujarat has suggested that the urban characteristics of the Harappan civilization may mask a myriad other associated communities, such as those of hunter-gatherers and pastoralists, who were economically, rather than politically, drawn into the Indus sphere (Possehl 1979).

To the east of the citadel, the lower town lies on a 9-m (30-ft) high mound covering some 190 ha (469 acres). It was unfortified and was subdivided into six or seven blocks, with 10-m (33-ft) wide main streets; the blocks are further subdivided by smaller streets and lanes. Hundreds of individual houses are then grouped around their own courtyards within these smaller divisions and are entered from the smaller streets and lanes rather than directly from the main thoroughfares. The presence of bathrooms within most house compounds is very striking, as is the complex network of drains associated with them.

14.16, 14.17 *Plan and photograph of Harappa: recently it has become apparent that Harappa has a different urban plan from Mohenjo-daro. While the latter has a citadel mound in the west and lower town in the east, Harappa has at least four separate walled mounds centred on a central depression. Other differences are also apparent between the square podiums of Mohenjo-daro's "granaries" and the rectangular Harappan ones (below right).*

Harappa

As noted above, Harappa has been less studied, due to the lack of monuments on its citadel, but this has led archaeologists to concentrate on its sequence and development. Whereas Mohenjo-daro's earliest phases are not well understood because of the depth of alluvium and the high water table, Harappa's sequence has been expanded back to the Hakra phase and the beginning of the 3rd millennium BC (Meadow 1991). This work has also helped challenge many of the preconceptions associated with the civilization's cities.

For example, Harappa's urban plan was thought to be identical to that of Mohenjo-daro, but recent research has demonstrated that in addition to Harappa's "citadel" mound, each of the settlement's other mounds was also fortified. The granaries of the two cities are also different, and even the concept of twin capitals is challenged by the discovery of Ganweriwala and Dholavira; the latter has an urban plan unlike any encountered previously.

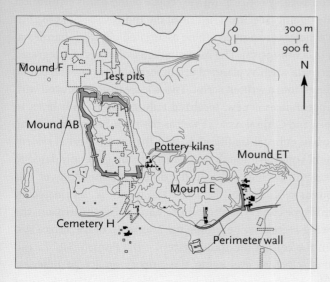

Character of the Indus Civilization

Portrayals of the Indus civilization as inherently peaceful are common (McIntosh 2001) and may be traced back to John Marshall, excavator of Mohenjo-daro and Harappa in the 1920s. He was himself trained by Arthur Evans, excavator of Knossos on Crete (see Chapter 13) and creator of the concept of a peace-loving Minoan civilization, a notion since largely abandoned. Based on perceived defects and shortcomings in weapons and defensive architecture, such assumptions also focus on the absence of elite martial grave goods and the absence of representations of war or warriors. There is little evidence of elite differentiation anywhere within Indus settlements, however [see box: The Social Organization of the Indus Civilization], suggesting that conspicuous martial displays should not be expected; moreover, representations of war may have been made on materials unlikely to survive in the archaeological record (Kenoyer 1998).

Finally, the presence of massive mud-brick walls in both the Early and mature Harappan stages suggests a substantial investment in conspicuous defenses, although they may also have had symbolic, ritual, or even utilitarian functions (e.g. against floods). It is likely that the Indus civilization experienced as much violence as its neighbors to the west, although it did not necessarily celebrate or ritualize warfare in the same way.

Subsistence and Trade

It is notable that the majority of the Indus settlements were located within the floodplains of the Indus and Ghaggar-Hakra rivers, at elevations below 1200 m (3940 ft). This location, like those of the cities of Mesopotamia and Egypt, allowed the establishment of large agglomerations of population close to stretches of fertile land that was annually refreshed by inundation. Recent archaeozoological and archaeobotanical research has allowed the identification of the key staples of the Indus civilization (Weber 1991). They included seasonal crops of wheat and barley, pulses, and millets, with limited evidence for fibers/oilseed, melons, cucumbers, squashes, and rice. For meat, milk, hides, and wool, the civilization relied heavily on cattle and water buffalo, with goat and sheep, augmented by hunted species (Fuller and Madella 2002; Meadow and Patel 2002).

While the location of a city within the floodplains had the advantage of silt, good for cultivating crops, it had the disadvantage of the poor availability of raw material resources. Urban economies nevertheless provided the core surplus necessary for the civilization to function as a unit through exchange [see box: The Social Organization of the Indus Civilization]. Indeed, Mark Kenoyer (1998) has proposed a series of trade, or rather resource, routes linking the urbanized centers and hinterlands with source materials such as lapis lazuli, carnelian, and steatite, as well as shell for objects and inlay, chert for blades, and tin, copper, and gold. The Harappan chert factories of the Rohri Hills and the lapis seams of the Afghan province of Badakshan all attest to this system of redistribution.

Furthermore, the presence of copper tools and drilled beads within settlements of hunter-gatherers, such as at **Bagor**, suggest the exchange of nodules of semiprecious stone for finished goods. Indeed, so strong is this model that analogies have been drawn between the small processing sites of western India and the first 17th-century European East India Company "factories" in Surat (Dhavalikar 1995). These Indus civilization materials, once processed to a highly standardized format, were redistributed within the settlements of the civilization, and the surplus was traded across the Persian Gulf as well as through plateau entrepôts such as **Shahr-i Sokhta**, as far west as the cities of Elam and Mesopotamia.

The Western Borderlands

As already noted, the Baluchistan borderlands were never absorbed into either the Early Harappan culture or the Harappan civilization, but their southern area was internally integrated, as suggested by the broad distribution of Kulli-phase ceramics (2500–2000 BC) (Shaffer 1992). In contact with the Harappan cities to the east, these communities built major public complexes of boulders and mud-brick at **Las Bela** and **Nindowari**. One of their largest constructions, at Edith Shahr in Las Bela, was 10 m (33 ft) high with at least three terraces or steps; it was crowned by a fired mud-brick structure (Fairservis 1971). These complexes may be the final attempts of the communities of the borderlands to compete with, or mimic, the cultural explosion to the east.

An Era of Localization: The Eclipse of the Indus Civilization, *c.* 1900 BC

The controversy concerning the eclipse of the Indus civilization is still ongoing [see box: The End of the Indus Cities, p. 538], but most scholars are agreed on the associated physical manifestations (Allchin 1995a). The most marked is the loss of integrated urban traits, such as planned urban forms, monumental public buildings, and a written script. These losses are associated with the appearance of new, localized cultural traits with links to western and Central Asia, as well as the reconfirmation of local, pre-urban cultural traditions within the greater Indus system (Possehl 1979). Although these changes are generally dated to *c.* 1900 BC, the regional patterns differ, and the study of this period, as with that of the Early Harappan, is dominated by ceramic types and type site culture names. For this reason, the following section will examine the aftermath of the urban system in the core of the Indus system – the Punjab, Sindh, and Gujarat – before evaluating the impact on its peripheries, notably Afghanistan, Baluchistan, the North West Frontier Province, the Gangetic plains, and the western Deccan.

KEY CONTROVERSY The Social Organization of the Indus Civilization

Since its formal identification in the 1920s as the last Bronze Age Old World civilization to be discovered, scholars have been struck by the uniformity of the Indus civilization. Common features include the standard urban plan of citadel mound and lower town, a uniform script, a common weight series, and even standardized artifact forms and decorative motifs. Although less homogeneous than first thought [see box: Mohenjo-daro and Harappa], its uniformity is all the more striking because the majority of the civilization's urban forms were located in the Indus floodplain, an area devoid of raw materials, necessitating an enormous network of procurement, manufacture, and distribution. As these features of consistency and standardization stretched across an area of 500,000 sq. km (193,000 sq. miles) and over a period of some 600 years, most scholars since the time of Stuart Piggott (1950) have assumed that they were enforced by the presence of a rigid state-level organization.

Absence of a Visible Elite

Such a system is usually identified by the presence of a number of archaeological characteristics, including elite residences, the gathering of great wealth, depictions of the elite, full-time craft specialists, and vast investment in pre-eminent burials with rich grave goods, as exemplified by the pyramids of ancient Egypt or the royal burials at Ur (chapters 10 and 12).

None of these archaeological characteristics, so well known in contemporary riverine civilizations, have been found within the Indus civilization, however. Indeed, an analysis of space at Mohenjo-daro has failed to distinguish a single elite residence within the city (Sarcina 1979), and separate studies of grave goods have failed to discover any evidence of elite communities (Miller 1985; Rissman 1988). The absence of prestige objects, hoards, and seals on the citadel mounds further undermines the concept of a visible elite.

Models of the Indus Civilization

Despite this apparent paradox – the presence of uniformity and the absence of an elite – scholars have applied a variety of models to the civilization, ranging from empires and theocracies to city-states, chiefdoms, and even a caste system.

Some earlier scholars, such as Sir Mortimer Wheeler (1953) and Stuart Piggott, chose largely to overlook the absence of differentiation, and sought evidence of a priest-king elite resident on the citadels; a number of more recent scholars have offered alternative models of organization. B.B. Lal (1993) based his model upon the presence of a caste system. Walter Fairservis (1986), rather creatively, suggested that the Indus civilization was never a state-level society, but rather a chiefdom, and that the elite was not located in cities but moved with the symbols of wealth – cattle – on the grassy peripheries. Others have suggested a blend of traders and priests.

Paul Rissman and Danny Miller, however, have successfully focused attention away from standard values and models. Miller has argued that the artifactual uniformity of the Harappan civilization implies the scorning of material wealth and indicates that its inhabitants sought equality (1985).

Rissman further advanced this concept by observing that little wealth differentiation was visible in public burials, but that hoarded wealth was present, suggesting that a conscious masking or hiding of wealth was carried out by the civilization's elites.

14.18 *Binary weight system from Mohenjo-daro: during the long period of Bronze Age integration within the Indus watershed, metal and ceramic objects and even bricks became strikingly standardized in form. A further degree of standardization can be found among the polished stone cubes, which are thought to represent weights as they follow a binary system from 1, 2, 4, and 8, up to 12,800.*

The Core Cities

In one of the core centers of the Indus urban system, the great cities of the Punjab, such as Harappa and Ganweriwala, were lost, together with their distinctive urban traits. In their place came fewer and smaller communities with little evidence of the highly specialized settlements of the preceding period. Frequently dubbed **Cemetery H** or the **Late Harappan**, evidence for this post-urban phase comes from the excavations at **Harappa** (Shaffer 1992). At this site the Cemetery H sequence suggests that the Harappan tradition of extended burials was replaced by the placing of disarticulated remains within burial vessels that had a very characteristic black paint on red slip decoration (Kenoyer 1998).

The shapes and the style of designs – such as the dog and peacock – indicate both continuity and change. Settlements in Cholistan were similarly affected, and the survey by Rafique Mughal (1997) has registered a drop in number of almost 50 percent as sites became fewer and smaller. This pattern of change is also found to the east, following the disappearance of urbanized traits.

KEY CONTROVERSY The End of the Indus Cities

Around 1900 BC, most of the characteristics of the Indus civilization were lost, including its urban forms, centralized storage facilities, script, artifact standardization, long-distance trade, and even its system of weights. Longstanding cultural uniformity was replaced with a variety of different cultural traditions, such as the Cemetery H culture in the Punjab or the Jhukar culture in Sindh.

The Invasion Hypothesis

The rapidity of this change was first explained as the result of the movement of peoples from outside the civilization, who destroyed cities and favored their own alien cultural packages. This model was most firmly advocated by Sir Mortimer Wheeler (1947), who famously accused the Hindu god Indra and his followers, the Aryans, of the destruction of the civilization. The evidence on which he based his accusation included the presence of massacred victims at Mohenjo-daro, exotic adze axes and ornaments, burnt settlements in Baluchistan, abandoned cities throughout the Indus basin, and new ceramic and artifact forms with Central and western Asian affinities.

This archaeological evidence was augmented by the modern distribution of Indo-Aryan or Indo-European speakers in the northern half of the subcontinent, with the exception of a pocket of Dravidian speakers in Baluchistan – perhaps isolated survivors of the massacres (Parpola 1994). The case was completed with reference to the *Rigveda*, a collection of ancient Hindu hymns commemorating the destruction of the cities of the Dasas or "slaves" by the gods of the Aryans or the "pure."

Other Monocausal Explanations

The invasion hypothesis was abandoned during Wheeler's lifetime because it became increasingly apparent that elements of "Aryan culture" were already present within the civilization, such as the fire temples at Kalibangan or the *lingam* and *yoni* stones (the first a phallus-shaped rock symbolizing the god Shiva, the second a representation of the female vagina, symbol of the goddess Sakti). The "massacre" was reinterpreted as a formal burial (Dales 1964) and the period described by the *Rigveda* given a much younger date than 1900 BC. It was also recognized that many of the post-urban regional cultures actually reflected a resurgence of pre-urban traditions.

In place of humanly caused catastrophes, a series of models were advanced that favored natural disasters. Some scholars advocated models in which tectonic activity caused a damming of the Indus, flooding its southern cities (Sahni 1956; Dales 1965; Raikes 1967), while others suggested a shift in the course of the Indus away from the cities (Lambrick 1967), and others the drying up of the Ghaggar-Hakra river system (Lahiri 2000; Ratnagar 2000).

A Combination of Factors

What these monocausal explanations failed to address was how a change in one region of the Indus experiment could cause the collapse of the civilization as a whole. This is a weakness also of arguments based on the drying up of trade with the cities of Southwest Asia, deforestation and salination, the appearance of new crops more suited to the Ganges basin, and even epidemics of malaria. Such catastrophes do not account for the proven element of continuity and growth within the Punjab and western India (Coningham 1995a).

Instead of advocating one disaster over another, there is growing consensus among South Asian archaeologists that a combination of some or all of these factors may have destabilized the networks of trade and redistribution that bound the Indus communities so closely, resulting in loss of authority by the established elites, and the emergence of new regional elites with fresh symbols of currency and power. The exotic Central and western Asian materials, so visible within the post-urban period, may represent such symbols. Until the Indus script is deciphered and its social organization understood better, however, the end of the civilization is likely to be as enigmatic as its origin.

14.19 *The Mohenjo-daro massacre? This scene was used for many years to illustrate that the end of the Indus civilization was brought about by an invasion of Indo-Aryan speakers at the end of the 2nd millennium BC. More recently, it has been reinterpreted as a peaceful mass burial, complete with grave goods, and the evidence for an invasion found lacking, leading many to stress continuity between Bronze Age and Iron Age rather than contrast.*

14.20 *The Gandharan Grave culture: this title is given to assemblages of ceramic vessels and terracotta and metal objects recovered from the valleys of Dir, Swat, and Chitral. First appearing between 1700 and 1600 BC, some scholars have attributed it to a migration of Indo-Aryans; however, the sequence at the rock shelter at Ghaligai suggests a high degree of continuity with earlier periods.*

A similar decline is registered in the lower Indus province of Sindh. The cities of **Mohenjo-daro** and **Chanhu-daro** were largely abandoned, with evidence at the latter of what has been termed "squatter" occupation (Mackay 1943). This post-urban phase, known as the Jhukar, presents evidence of stamp seals as well as exotic items such as copper pins and shaft-hole axes with western or Central Asian affinities. Sindh's loss of urban forms and literacy is also paralleled in Gujarat, but it is important to note that smaller settlements actually increase in number here, with 120 such settlements, as opposed to only 18 dating to the Harappan period (Possehl 1980). A number of cultural styles and traditions, which had characterized this region prior to urbanization, also re-emerged (Possehl 1993).

Peripheral Areas

While one might expect the peripheries of the Indus system to be similarly affected by the loss of Harappan urbanized traits and general settlement dispersals, the evidence from the site of **Mundigak** in Afghanistan presents a great contrast to the core cities. There, on the remains of an enormous palace structure, a further monumental brick structure was erected, indicating a continued success in the mobilization of surplus lost to its east (Casal 1961). By now, Mundigak's cultural links had shifted away markedly from the south, west, and east, moving north to the Central Asian sphere. A number of settlements in Baluchistan, to the south of Mundigak, were abandoned around 1900 BC (some, such as Rana Ghundai, were apparently burned), while at the same time the number of exotic items with Central and western Asian affinities increased at Mundigak. Such exotics include the gold bull pendants, gold chalice with lion frieze, and stone "scepters" of the Quetta hoard (Jarrige and Hassan 1989), as well as the copper shaft-hole axes from the Sibri cemetery (Santoni 1984).

This general pattern was significantly distorted by the excavation of the site of **Pirak**, however (Jarrige and Santoni 1979). This 9-ha (22-acre) site is of great significance because it appears to have been occupied between 1700–1600 and 700 BC. It demonstrates clear settlement continuity, as well as evidence of the survival of trade and exchange networks bringing ivory from the Ganges plains, shell from the Arabian Gulf, lapis from Afghanistan, and carnelian from western India. Furthermore, there is evidence from the site to suggest the survival of craft specialization, indicated by the concentrated working of bone, stone, and copper. These activities were later augmented by iron, but with little social or economic change to the site.

Gandharan Grave Culture To the north of both the Early Harappan and Harappan urban experiments, the northern valleys of the North West Frontier Province remained loosely linked to the plains, as demonstrated by the long cave sequence of **Ghaligai** (Stacul 1987). However, by 1700–1600 BC, a new and distinctive assemblage of materials, known as the Gandharan Grave culture, spread across the valleys of Chitral, Dir, Swat, and the upper Indus [**14.20**]. As shown by excavations in Dir, at the sites of Balambat and Timargarha, and in Swat at **Aligrama**, **Bir-kot-ghundai**, **Kalako-deray**, and **Loebanr I**, it is a homogeneous culture, represented by similar grave and burial patterns, pottery assemblages, and other artifacts (Dani 1967; 1992; Stacul 1987; 1989). Its more distinctive features include stone-lined burial pits, some of which are surrounded by stone circles, and the presence of horse burials, horse ornamentation, copper shaft-hole axes, vessels of "Burnished Red ware," and gray ware pedestal cups with western Asian affinities. This core of Gandharan sites has been extended north and west to Chitral (Stacul 1969; Ali et al. 2002), and it may be assumed to extend into Afghanistan, but little fieldwork has been carried out there. More notably, its presence to the south is now well supported by sites in the Vale of Peshawar (Khan 1973; Ali et al. 1998), and some assign to it the cemetery of **Sarai Khola** in Taxila (Dani 1986), Peshawar and Taxila both being areas of later Iron Age development. It is also very tempting to add to this complex the stone-lined burials in the southern Himalayas of Uttar Pradesh (Agrawal et al. 1995), further stressing the presence of a cultural sphere linking the Neolithic cultures of the northern valleys of Pakistan with those to the east.

The Ganges-Yamuna Doab As noted above, archaeologists have also been successful in identifying the presence of a small number of settlements with links to the Harappan period as far east as the Ganges-Yamuna doab (the tongue of land between the two rivers) (Dikshit 1982). During the post-urban period, this region became the focus of a distinct cultural continuum, which eventually culminated in the emergence of a number of Early Historic states and cities over 1000 years later (see below). The first indication of this development may be found in the distribution of Ocher Colored pottery, which is found tightly clustered in the Ganges-Yamuna doab. This ceramic complex has frequently been noted for its distinctive links to the red ware of the Harappan tradition (Allchin and Allchin 1982; Erdosy 1995a). It is restricted to small settlements, is frequently associated with copper hoards, and has been dated to c. 1700–1200 BC. Notably, it has been recovered from the base sequences of a number of sites that later emerged as the centers of city-states in the Early Historic period, such as **Hastinapura** and **Atranjikhera**.

The Western Deccan To the south and west of this development are the complex communities of the western Deccan, also noted for their copper and bronze objects, which flourished c. 2100–700 BC. The presence of a chiefdom centered on the settlement of **Diamabad** has been suggested, with a three-tier settlement hierarchy and sub-regional centers such as Prakash and Inamgaon [14.21] sited above smaller agricultural sites (Dhavalikar et al. 1988). Detailed research at **Inamgaon** has provided very clear evidence that by 1000 BC, 13 percent of the settlement's buildings were utilized for specialized production, including the manufacture of ceramics, and metal-, bone-, and stoneworking. This regional post-urban complex was even linked to a port site, **Malvan** (Allchin and Joshi 1995), and finds of marine shell, gold, ivory, carnelian, and copper suggest firm connections with existing networks. Thus, while much of the former core of the Indus urban system witnessed a decline, communities to its north, south, and east were intensifying, resulting in a notable shift in urban distribution during South Asia's second phase of urbanization, that of the Iron Age.

The Re-Emergence of Regionalized Complexity, c. 1200–500 BC

The period between the end of the Harappan or Indus civilization and the emergence of the Early Historic or Gangetic civilization was once frequently referred to as a "dark age" [see box: Foreign Contact and State Formation 2: The Early Historic Cities]. More recently, a growing number of scholars have cited the broad evidence for continuity within the archaeological sequence, and new radiocarbon dates have reinforced their position (Shaffer 1993; Coningham 1995a; Weber 1999).

This period, between 1200 and 500 BC, saw the establishment of fortified settlements, the emergence of states, the use of seals, the creation of planned urban forms, the re-introduction of graffiti that utilized script, and the mass production of ceramics and other artifacts. Another important feature is the first appearance of iron tools, although the emergence of iron within South Asia's sequence did not bring about immediate change. It was a period of increasing complexity, and it witnessed the emergence of a number of heterodox religious teachers, such as the Buddha [see box: Dating the Historical Buddha, p. 542]. A period of dynamic change, it was brought to a close with the integration of the western parts of the subcontinent into the Achaemenid, or Persian, empire in the late 6th century BC through the conquests of Darius I; at this time the subcontinent witnessed a new expression of unity, indicated by the wide distribution of Northern Black Polished ware.

Developments in the Northwest and East

Those western areas, extending as far east as the Indus and north into Afghanistan, became Achaemenid satrapies or provinces. Each satrapy was centered on an administrative center; these were few in number – Taxila, Begram, and Kandahar among them – although a substantial Achaemenid presence is not always supported by the archaeological evidence.

14.21 *Plan of the village of Inamgaon:* *at the same time as the breaking up of the Indus watershed integration, agricultural communities in the western Deccan were flourishing. One such community, the 5-ha (12-acre) village of Inamgaon, comprised rectangular structures all oriented to the cardinal points, demonstrating a degree of pre-planning at 1600 BC.*

KEY CONTROVERSY Foreign Contact and State Formation 2: The Early Historic Cities

Sir Mortimer Wheeler (1959) referred to the period following the collapse of the Indus civilization as a "dark age," a period of social and economic instability, with refugees fleeing the destructive power of the Aryan barbarians; he was perhaps inspired by his experience of the chaotic Partition of British India in 1948. He suggested that this confused period was ended by the annexation of Gandhara (Afghanistan and northern Pakistan) by Darius I in the 6th century BC, and the foundation of the first urban administrative centers in the northwest region.

Historical evidence for the Achaemenid claim to Gandhara is found in Darius' inscription at Behistun in Iran, as well as in depictions of its subject people offering tribute on the elaborate staircase at the dynastic complex of Persepolis. Additional evidence includes the presence of *sigloi* (Persian bent bar coins) at Taxila, a Persian-style pillared hall at Pataliputra, and the fact that many of the Mauryan emperor Asoka's inscriptions in the northwest, dating to the 3rd century BC, are in Aramaic, the official language of the Persian empire.

Support for the Diffusionist Model

This diffusionist model for the origins of South Asia's second urbanization was strongly supported by excavations at the Bala Hisar or "high fort" of Charsadda in 1958 [see 14.24]. Wheeler (1962) cut a trench some 22 m (72 ft) deep from the summit of the tell down to natural soil. Working before the general use of radiocarbon dating, he regarded the presence of iron objects in the

14.22 *The great processional staircase at Persepolis, in Iran, the spring capital of the Achaemenid Persian empire, depicts the subject peoples of the empire bearing tribute to Darius I, "the Great." Dating to the 6th century BC, subjects from Gandhara are identified by their gifts of humped zebu bulls from South Asia.*

lowest levels as indicators of contact with the Achaemenid empire to the west, since he believed that both ironworking technology and urban forms had diffused to the Indus region at the same time. The output of his excavation, a comprehensive typological sequence, became one of the most widely used references in the northwest of the subcontinent, and is still frequently used to date other sites on the basis of relative chronology.

New Evidence for Indigenous Development

A new trench beside Wheeler's deep cutting was excavated in 1996 in order to recover a chronometrically dated sequence (i.e., based

on absolute dates) (Ali et al. 1998). The new dates suggest that the site was first occupied toward the middle of the 2nd millennium BC, some 800 years earlier than previously thought. Most importantly, the lower levels show little evidence of contact with the Achaemenid world, but demonstrate very close affinities with the Gandharan Grave culture of Pakistan's northern valleys and the Taxila Valley, thus suggesting an internal dynamic. This evidence of continuity and development from immediate post-urban and post-Indus communities in the northwest is mirrored by the development of Chalcolithic and later Iron Age communities within the Ganges basin to the east, reinforcing the concept that this was a period of dynamic development and not a "dark age." Moreover, it demonstrates that South Asia's second, Early Historic urbanization was founded on a long internal developmental sequence prior to its dramatic collision with the expansionist worlds of the Achaemenids and Macedonians to the west.

The sequence in **Kandahar** provides the most material evidence for this imperial expansion, with the erection of a 30-m (99-ft) high citadel measuring some 200 sq. m (2150 sq. ft) and a casement curtain wall enclosing a roughly rectangular area of some 0.5 km (0.3 mile) square (Helms 1982). Supported by the presence of fragmentary Elamite tablets (the language of the Elam state, which was absorbed into the Achaemenid empire; see Chapter 12), this Achaemenid horizon sits firmly on what appears to be a substantial, earlier settlement. Most significantly, this pre-Achaemenid settlement was already forti-

fied by a massive 15-m (49-ft) thick clay rampart (McNicoll and Ball 1996), providing evidence of a complex urban core already established by the first quarter of the 1st millennium BC on a critical route from the Indus plains to western and Central Asia.

A parallel development has been identified at the twin capitals of the satrapy of Gandhara in northern Pakistan, **Taxila** and **Charsadda** (or Pushkalavati), although the evidence of Achaemenid occupation is far less secure. Survey of the western edge of the Hathial ridge in the Taxila Valley has identified

KEY CONTROVERSY Dating the Historical Buddha

The re-emergence of complexity in the northern half of South Asia in the middle of the 1st millennium BC took place during a dynamic period marked by increasing trade and commerce, the creation of planned settlements, and a growing militarization and expansion of newly emergent city-states. The introduction of taxes, centralized administration, and portable wealth (i.e., coinage), combined with the pacification of the countryside, assisted the growth of a powerful merchant class.

Frequently grouped into guilds and trade organizations, they did not sponsor the traditional sources of religious authority (the Brahmans, or priests, who were frequently portrayed as being at the apex of society – high above merchants and traders – on account of their ritual purity, but able to perform crucial intercessionary sacrifices for lower castes.) Instead, the new mercantile elite appears to have been strongly attracted to the radical teachings of the traveling renouncers of the Ganges plains, individuals who challenged the authority and practices of the Brahmans by abandoning ritual, wealth, and family. One of the most successful and influential of these was Siddhartha Gautama, known as the Buddha, or "Enlightened One."

Textual Evidence

Despite the wealth of information concerning his teachings and philosophies, the Buddha's life is still surrounded by controversy. The date of his birth and death and even the location of his childhood home, Kapilavastu,

are still hotly debated (Coningham 2001). This controversy does not deny the historical presence of the Buddha, but rather highlights most Buddhist scholars' dependence on texts, along with the poor understanding and development of "Buddhist" archaeology. For example, possible dates for the Buddha's passing at the age of 80 vary, with most scholars advocating either a long, uncorrected "southern Buddhist" chronology of 544/543 BC, or a long, corrected "southern Buddhist" chronology of 480 BC, and a short one of 340, 368, 383, 384, 386, or 390 BC (Bechert 1995). This variation is partly due to the fact that many of these calculations are reliant on regnal years, or the span of time between the passing of the Buddha and the accession of the Mauryan emperor Asoka, and different sources provide very different dates for these.

The Contribution of Archaeology

Archaeology has, unfortunately, played little part in this debate, as the majority of the great sites of Buddhist pilgrimage – Lumbini, Bodhgaya, Sarnarth, Kusinagara – were largely cleared and conserved in the 19th century using very rudimentary recording systems. This position has led many scholars to ignore the assistance that archaeology can play in narrowing this date range. For example, many of the cities associated with the life of the Buddha – Rajghir, Sravasti, Kausambi – have been dated to between the 5th and 4th centuries BC, and the great pilgrimage sites have little evidence of the development of ritual monuments before the 3rd century BC. This evidence favors the younger date ranges for the life of the Buddha, but only more scientific analysis at these sites will provide reliable answers.

Whatever the date, it is clear that the splendid cities, palaces, and monasteries described in the Buddhist scriptures belong to a period long after the passing of the Buddha, when monks were trying to illustrate his life with reference to the worldly experiences surrounding them.

14.23 *Lumbini, birthplace of the Buddha. Despite over a century of archaeological research at sites associated with the historical Buddha, we are no closer to ascertaining the actual date of his birth. There is no confusion as to the location of his birthplace, Lumbini, as it is clearly designated in an inscription on a pillar erected by the Mauryan emperor Asoka in the 3rd century BC.*

an area of some 13 ha (32 acres) associated with a spread of **Burnished Red ware** (Allchin 1982) [see box: Taxila, pp. 544–45]. Subsequent excavation has suggested that this ware belongs to the ceramic traditions of the Gandharan Grave culture, and it is also found in the basal layers of the sequence at the **Bala Hisar** or "high fort" of **Charsadda** [14.24].

Covering an area similar to that of the Hathial ridge, this settlement was first occupied c. 1300 BC. Artifacts from the Bala Hisar indicate strong links with the communities in the valleys to the north, and include Burnished Red wares, rippled rim forms, a female figurine, and even what appears to be a frag-

ment of a ground-stone sickle, well known from the Neolithic sites of the Swat Valley. This degree of similarity is further accentuated by the presence of a small anthropomorphic ceramic figure at Charsadda, identical to one recovered from Timargarha in the Dir Valley (Dani 1967). It would appear that the earlier developments within the valleys were restricted by terrain and seasonal differences, but that once established, settlements in the Vale of Peshawar and the Taxila Valley expanded rapidly, based on an agricultural subsistence augmented by the seasonal movement of livestock by transhumant communities.

Painted Gray Ware To the east, the number of small settlements in the Ganges-Yamuna doab region expanded significantly, and their allegiance to the Ocher Colored pottery tradition was replaced by the new **Painted Gray ware** (Erdosy 1995a). Painted Gray ware vessels were constructed of clay filtered through water to reduce coarse particles, covered with a thin gray slip and decorated with black lines. Dated to between the beginning of the 1st millennium BC and the 6th or 7th century BC, this ware is associated with the use of iron within the Ganges Valley. It remains an important chronological indicator, and was only superseded in the 6th century BC, when Northern Black Polished ware, a direct descendant, spread throughout the subcontinent (Erdosy 1995b). Painted Gray ware indicates increasing craft specialization and object standardization, as well as an emergent unifying tradition drawing together the disparate regions of South Asia.

Few of the settlements associated with Painted Gray ware have been excavated and published, but the site of **Hastinapura** provides clear details of the settlement's development (Lal 1955). Established as a small settlement using Ocher Colored

14.24 *The Bala Hisar of Charsadda: refuting Mortimer Wheeler's findings of the 1950s, recent excavations have revealed a sequence of occupation stretching back to 1300 BC. The material in the lowest levels is closely associated with the tradition known as the Gandharan Grave culture, suggesting that the Achaemenid Persian empire seized a region that had already advanced toward urbanization.*

pottery, it expanded to cover an area of 6.5 ha (16 acres) between 1100 and 800 BC. This expansion was not limited to the key centers, but was paralleled by the colonization of the Ganges basin, with a massive 38 percent population rise from the previous, largely Chalcolithic settlement (Lal 1984). This rise was accompanied by the successful concentration and mobilization of significant numbers of people, as indicated by the creation of Kausambi's ramparts, which contained almost 1 million cu. m (35.3 million cu. ft) of soil.

A number of these centers emerged in the 6th century BC in the Ganges basin and central India, emulating one another by constructing large earthworks; each was centered on what became known as a *janapada* or "territory." Further physical signs of this nascent political identity can be seen in the emergence of coinage in the 5th century BC, also a sign of a growing economy as well as a mechanism for the easy storage and movement of surplus and wealth.

"Great Territories" By 500 BC the emergent *janapadas* had coalesced into 16 *mahajanapadas*, or "great territories," each associated with a capital and ruler, supplemented by ministers and courts, supported by taxes and campaigns, and vying with one another for supremacy. One of the best expressions of this change within one of the emergent kingdoms is **Vatsa** (Erdosy 1987). By the middle of the 1st millennium BC this kingdom was centered on the fortified capital of **Kausambi**, covering an area of some 50 ha (124 acres), with a further tier of settlements,

such as **Kara**, offering provincial authority. Below that was a third and finally a fourth tier of settlements, the last below 2 ha (5 acres). The lowest categories of settlements practiced agriculture and herding, and the third category was responsible for manufacturing iron, ceramics, and stone tools as well as low-level administrative tasks. The second tier of towns was responsible for the manufacture of similar materials, but also processed luxury items, while the uppermost tier was responsible for political control.

Southern India and Sri Lanka

In contrast with the developments in the northwest and east, southern India and much of the Deccan Plateau pursued an alternative pattern of complexity, with massive investment in funerary complexes. A number of the Neolithic settlements, such as **Brahmagiri**, **Maski**, and **Hallur**, were continuously occupied from the 3rd millennium BC into the Early Historic period. Their subsistence strategies appear to have remained largely unchanged, despite the appearance of copper objects within the sequence, and iron artifacts from 1100 BC (Korisettar et al. 2002). This continuity is also found within mortuary practices, with the earliest burial to utilize stone identified at **Watgal** and dated to 2700–2300 BC.

From these early beginnings, experimentation with the use of stone increased; stone circles surrounding pit burials gave way by 800 BC to the creation of complexes of central stone cists, complete with portholes (McIntosh 1985) [**14.28**]. Covering tens of hectares in many cases, these very visible monuments make the absence of settlement sites more notable. Recent intensive surface survey now suggests that

KEY SITE Taxila

The scattered ruins of three cities – the Bhir Mound, Sirkap, and Sirsukh – in a valley north of the Margala Pass in northern Pakistan were first surveyed and planned by Sir Alexander Cunningham in 1864. Using topographical descriptions of the region recorded by Roman historians of Alexander the Great and later Chinese Buddhist pilgrims, Cunningham suggested that these ruins represented the ancient site of Taxila, a city taken by Alexander and later occupied by the Mauryans and Indo-Greeks.

The cities were not subject to detailed investigation until Sir John Marshall, Director-General of Archaeology in India, began excavating in 1913 with the aim of finding evidence of Greek influence; his program was completed 21 years later. Marshall (1951) opened enormous trenches at the three sites and was rewarded with an exceptional urban sequence that reflected different geopolitical and cultural influences. His work has provided the foundations for subsequent studies of the development of the urban form in Asia.

The Bhir Mound: The Earliest Settlement

Although Marshall discovered no structural evidence of the Achaemenid Persians, finds of Persian bent bar coins (*sigloi*) and seals suggested to him that Taxila had been part of the Persian satrapy of Gandhara. The earliest remains uncovered were found on the Bhir Mound, a 6-m (20-ft) high mound covering some 1100 x 670 m (3609 x 2200 ft). Dated to between 425 BC and AD 50, it had never been fortified and consisted of houses and shops lining meandering streets and lanes. These irregular streets, combined with the encroachment of thoroughfares and the lack of street drainage, suggested to Marshall the absence of civic authority. This haphazard plan of an organic Asian settlement was strongly contrasted with the extreme gridlike regularity of its successor, Sirkap.

Sirkap

Located less than 300 m (985 ft) from the Bhir Mound, Sirkap formed a rectangle measuring 1300 x 850 m (4265 x 2789 ft),

14.25 *The Bhir Mound, Taxila: succeeding the "Burnished Red ware" settlement on the Hathial ridge, the Bhir Mound represents the valley's first urban settlement. Its irregular street plan combined with the lack of a central drainage system, have suggested the presence of an organic, rather than a pre-planned, settlement.*

14.28 *Megalithic cist burial at Brahmagiri:* *while urban forms began emerging to the north and south, the Iron Age communities of the Deccan invested in funerary monuments of stone. Brahmagiri has well over 300 cists and its position, close to an Asokan edict, suggests that its concentration of skills, authority, and surplus marked it for the location of a later administrative center as Mauryan hegemony expanded (see p. 547).*

most megalithic burial sites are associated with settlements, but that the latter are far less visible than the former (Rajan 1994).

The south Indian sequence is in stark contrast to that of **Sri Lanka**, where older diffusionist models have been revised by the new chronological data from the city of **Anuradhapura**, in the north-central plains [**14.29**]. The island's capital until the 11th century AD, excavations indicate that the settlement was

with a rocky "acropolis" at its southern end. Occupied between 175 BC and AD 100, Marshall believed that it had been founded by a dynasty of Indo-Greeks, descendants of Alexander's troops, who had moved from their kingdoms in Afghanistan and Central Asia. In his enormous trench (measuring 595 x 234 m or 1952 x 768 ft), Marshall revealed straight streets lined with shops, temples, and monasteries, and smaller roads and lanes leading to houses built around courtyards. The chance recovery of a reused slab with an Asokan inscription strengthened Taxila's identification as a Mauryan capital.

Although Marshall's identification of a palace is not entirely convincing, he did uncover a gigantic apsidal temple measuring over 43 m (141 ft) long within a courtyard of almost 3500 sq. m (37,675 sq. ft). In addition to the presence of trade items from the Hellenistic world, sculptures suggest the practice of many different beliefs, ranging from Buddhism to cults of the Indian deity Hariti, the Greek god Hermes, and even the Egyptian god-child Harpocrates.

Sirsukh

Sirkap was, in turn, replaced by a new foundation, Sirsukh, occupied *c.* AD 100–200. An irregular rectangle measuring 1375 x 1000 m (4511 x 3280 ft), its plan and rounded bastions with arrow slits indicate strong links

with Central Asia. Indeed, most scholars assume that it was founded by members of the Kushan dynasty, who wished to demonstrate their hegemony with a new capital.

This important sequence has been extended back into prehistory with the discovery in the 1980s of an earlier site at the western edge of the Hathial ridge. This stone-built settlement covered an area of some 13 ha (32 acres) and was associated with scatters of "Burnished Red ware," also found within the Gandharan Grave culture (Allchin 1982). Dating to 1000–400 BC, it firmly places the origins of urban development in the Taxila Valley within South Asia.

14.27 *Sirsukh, Taxila: the final urban form within the valleys, Sirsukh was constructed between the 1st and 2nd century AD. Its rectangular plan and stirrup bastions suggest a Central Asian influence and even, perhaps, a Kushan foundation.*

14.26 *Sirkap, Taxila: the contrast between Sirkap and the Bhir Mound could not be greater, as the former has a rigid grid-iron plan with very visible divisions between acropolis and lower town. It was occupied between the 2nd century BC and 1st century AD and was probably founded by a Hellenistic dynasty from Afghanistan or Central Asia.*

14.29 *The citadel of Anuradhapura: recent excavations at trench ASW2 at Anuradhapura have revealed a sequence running from 900 BC to AD 1100. Mapping the growth of the settlement from a small Iron Age village into one of South Asia's great medieval capitals, it demonstrates the importance of internal dynamics and long-distance trade to South Asia's second urbanization.*

Reintegration: The Early Historic Empires, *c.* 500 BC–AD 320

The regionalized development of centers of complexity within Afghanistan, Gandhara (northern Pakistan), the Ganges basin, central India, and Sri Lanka was interrupted in the northwest, as we have seen, by the annexation of the region by the Achaemenid Persian empire in 520 BC and the siting of administrative centers at **Kandahar**, **Charsadda**, and **Taxila**. The bas-reliefs of Persepolis, the royal capital in Iran, depict tribute from the eastern provinces [see **14.22**], but the actual impact of Persian rule is less clear, although the presence of inscriptions in the Kharoshthi script (which originated in Gandhara; see also Chapter 15, p. 584) in the northwest from the middle of the 3rd century BC indicates a continuum.

In parallel, archaeological evidence relating to the later invasion and partial Hellenistic colonization of the Indus region by Alexander the Great [**14.30**] in 326/325 BC is extremely poor, perhaps limited to the site of **Birkot** in Swat. Indeed, despite a century of study, we are still unable firmly to identify the cities sacked or founded by Alexander in this region. To some extent, this places the Alexandrian incident in perspective – his actual presence was not of outstanding significance, unlike the southern spread of Hellenistic art, architecture, and script some 200 years later.

The closest example of a classic Greek presence is the Hellenistic city site of **Ai Khanoum** (also spelled Aï Khanum) in northern Afghanistan (see Chapter 13, p. 501) [**14.31, 14.32**], complete with quotations from the oracle at Delphi (Bernard 1994); but, again, the immediate impact of such communities is not clear. Despite these interpolations, it is now apparent (largely as a result of the partial adoption of the regalia and

first established around 900 BC (Coningham 1999; Deraniyagala 1992). A simple community of circular structures, reliant on a mixture of cultivation, pastoralism, and hunting, it had reached an area of some 26 ha (64 acres) by 450 BC. Its manufacturing debris suggests the working of iron, copper, bone, ivory, and semiprecious stone, while the presence of horse bones, a non-endemic species, indicates maritime links. Most striking is the identification of four sherds scratched with inscriptions of early Brahmi, indicating the re-appearance of a written script by 400 BC. That the inscriptions are all in the genitive or dative case (indicating "of" and "to" or "for") suggests that they are part of the paraphernalia necessary for managing trade and exchange (Coningham et al. 1996).

14.30 *Silver decadrachm of Alexander the Great: this coin was minted at Babylon after Alexander's pacification of the eastern extremes of the Achaemenid empire. Although the obverse depicts a horseman in Greek dress attacking two figures wearing conical hats seated on an elephant, it does not necessarily depict Alexander's famous duel with Porus, King of Taxila, but may be a symbolic representation of the relationship between Alexander and India.*

14.31, 14.32 *The Hellenistic colony of Ai Khanoum:* despite a long search, archaeologists are yet to uncover one of the many Alexandrias that Alexander founded in the east. Although Ai Khanoum, in northern Afghanistan, is the only undisputed Hellenistic colony in the region, complete with acropolis, gymnasium, and theater, it contains no reference to Alexander and there is no record of the city in Alexander's histories.

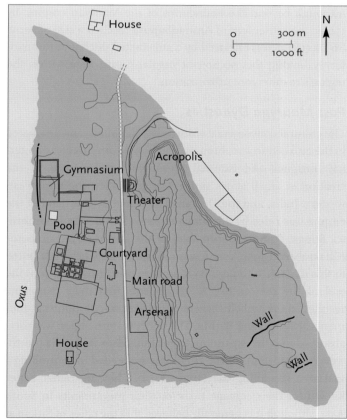

mechanisms of kingship), that competition, emulation, amalgamation, and religious patronage resulted in the convergence of the 16 *mahajanapadas* of central India into a single integrated unit, the Mauryan empire, by 350 BC.

The Mauryan Empire

The Mauryan dynasty ruled for more than 150 years (*c.* 325–185 BC), but many archaeologists argue that the region's history only starts with the third emperor, **Asoka** (reigned 272–235 BC), since we have testimony of his rule in the form of edicts displayed on boulders, erected on stone pillars, or written on stone slabs (Thapar 1961). These edicts, in combination with early texts such as the *Arthasastra*, a study of political science reputedly written by a Mauryan chief minister, have allowed a reconstruction of aspects of the empire, and many archaeologists assume that their distribution, from Bangladesh to Afghanistan and Karnataka, in south-central India mark the limits of Mauryan power [**14.33**]. The inscriptions allow a tentative reconstruction of the administration of this vast empire. Authority was centered on the capital at **Pataliputra**, modern Patna on the Ganges, and enforced through a series of governors based in the provincial capitals of **Taxila**, **Ujjain**, **Sisupalgarh**, and **Maski**, with ministers in lesser centers.

Asoka's edicts also demonstrate that his empire represents one of the first attempts to create a pluralistic unity from the diverse populations of South Asia. This factor is well illustrated by the transcription of Asoka's edicts into different languages (Greek, Aramaic, and Prakrits) and scripts (Greek, Kharoshthi, and Brahmi), presumably relating to constituent populations and traditions within the empire (Allchin and Norman 1985). The edicts also encapsulate philosophical elements of the Early Historic world: forsake violence and greed, show reverence for animals, establish works of public benefit, rectify bureaucracy and other administrative evils. It is also recorded that Asoka's

547

14.33 *The extent of the Mauryan empire, 3rd century* BC: *most scholars have mapped the extent of the Mauryan empire from the distribution of the emperor Asoka's rock and pillar edicts, which stretch from Bangladesh to Afghanistan, and from Nepal to Brahmagiri. The presence of edicts written in Greek, Aramaic, and Prakrits, attest to the presence of many different populations and traditions within the empire.*

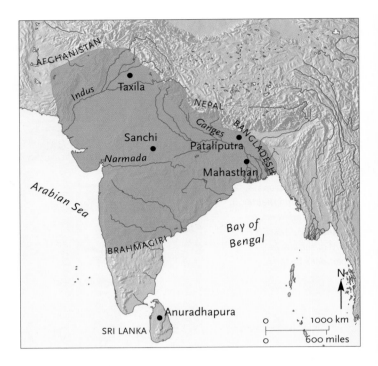

patronage resulted in the dispersal of Buddhist missionaries to the north and south of the subcontinent, resulting in the conversion of Sri Lanka (Coningham 1995b).

Archaeological evidence from this period is very full, and includes many of the great urban establishments of South Asia. Excavations at the 1350-ha (3336-acre) city of **Pataliputra** have uncovered a large stone-pillared hall, Persepolis-style stone pillar capitals and sculptures, and massive timber ramparts. Pataliputra is now covered by modern housing, and there is little evidence of its hinterland, but it once stood at the summit of a six-tier settlement hierarchy (Allchin 1995b). **Mahasthan** in Bangladesh represents one of the most complete examples of an Early Historic city with ramparts, capped by later additions, rising 8 m (26 ft) above a 100-m (328-ft) wide moat and enclosing 130 ha (321 acres) [**14.34**]. Once a Mauryan provincial capital, Mahasthan has over 40 mounds marking the ruins of major brick-built monuments in its immediate surroundings. These represent religious institutions surrounding the city, whereas the hundreds of tanks and ponds record the location of simple agrarian settlements – the economic base of the city. This pattern is repeated in microcosm in the sub-provincial center of **Bhita**, complete with a grid layout of streets of merchants and traders operating out of their courtyard-centered houses (Marshall 1912).

The pacification of much of South Asia by the Mauryans allowed greater freedom of movement, the enhancement of networks for trade and commerce, and the emergence of artifact standardization. This standardization, presumably assisted by increasing craft specialization, is found within imperial products – for example, all the pillars inscribed with Asokan edicts were quarried from a single site on the Ganges, Chunar near Varanasi – but also within more utilitarian objects, such as

14.34 *Silver punch-marked coin:* South Asia's earliest coins appeared in the 5th century BC together with the emergence of the 16 mahajanapadas or "great territories." They represent the demands of a growing economy as well as a revolution in the storage and mobility of surplus and wealth. They were punched with a variety of symbols: this one appears to have been authorized by the Mauryan court.

ceramics, coins [**14.34**], and terracotta figurines (Allchin 1995c). Although beyond the boundaries of the Mauryan empire, by 350 BC the settlement of **Anuradhapura** reached a size of some 66 ha (163 acres) enclosed by a substantial ditch and rampart, firmly linking this section of insular South Asia within the region's re-emergent urbanization.

Post-Mauryan Dynasties

The cultural convergence enforced by the Mauryans dissipated in the 2nd century BC, brought about by a combination of internal intrigues and external pressures, and resulted in the creation of small states in the Ganges Valley, the northwest, western India, and the Deccan. The Gangetic heartland of the empire was ruled by the **Sunga dynasty**, founded by Pushyamitra Sunga, commander-in-chief of the last Mauryan emperor (Chakrabarti 1995). Very few monuments have been attributed to this dynasty, although its members ruled this area until the end of the 1st century BC. It appears that their patronage resulted in the embellishment of the Mauryan Buddhist monuments at **Sanchi** and **Barhut**. The northwestern region was soon absorbed into the expanding Greek kingdoms in **Bactria** (northwest Afghanistan). These kingdoms succeeded in controlling a vast area straddling the Hindu Kush. They are rather better known for their coinage than for their monuments in South Asia, although it is generally believed that the cities of Sirkap at Taxila and Shaikhan Dheri at Charsadda were founded at this time (Marshall 1951; Wheeler 1962).

The last Indo-Greek king, Strato III, still ruled an area of the western Punjab in the 1st century AD, but territorial control had already been weakened in the 1st century BC by the appearance of a people known as the **Sakas**, reputedly of Central Asian origin. The Sakas, who adopted Hellenistic-style coinage and titles, appear to have controlled a loose confederacy encompassing much of the northwestern and central areas (Puri 1994). Nevertheless, their influence was steadily reduced to that of a small provincial dynasty in western India, called the **Western Satraps**, by the first centuries of the 1st millennium AD. Although the northwest region was never formally absorbed into the expanding Parthian empire of this area, it was incorporated into the Indo-Parthian kingdom of Gondophares (reigned AD 20–40). Artifactual and architectural remains of the cities of Sirkap at Taxila and Shaikhan Dheri at Charsadda illustrate, however, the survival of Hellenistic influence on both Saka and Indo-Parthian dynasties (Marshall 1951; Dani 1966).

The Kushan, Satavahana, and Later Dynasties

It was not until the first half of the 1st millennium AD that union was reintroduced into the region as the result of the rise of two dynasties, the Kushans in the north, and the Satavahanas in the south. The **Kushans**, or Yuezhi, were a nomadic Central Asian tribe that had established a small kingdom in Bactria in the 2nd century BC (Puri 1994). By the 2nd century AD, under the emperor Kanishka, they had transformed this provincial center into an empire stretching from Central Asia to the Indian Ocean. During their rule, which ended in the 3rd century AD, they had a vast impact on urban planning and religious patronage (Rosenfield 1967) and established a series of dynastic foundations, such as the cities of **Sirsukh** in Pakistan and **Dalverzin-tepe** in Uzbekistan, while still developing other established urban sites such as **Begram** in Afghanistan.

With the creation of major dynastic cult centers such as the fire temple at **Surkh Kotal** in Afghanistan, along with the building of new complexes and the restoration of still more, this period represents a renaissance of Buddhism in South Asia. It also saw the spread of the Kushans' own brand of Buddhism into Central and Eastern Asia along the Silk Route (Chapter 15). These trading routes, linking the Han Chinese and Roman worlds, provided an important means for the exchange of ideas, values, and goods, exemplified by objects found at the city of **Begram** in Afghanistan, such as a hoard of South Asian ivories, Chinese lacquerwork, and Roman metalwork and glass, including a vase depicting the lighthouse of Alexandria in Egypt (Hackin 1939). Although remnants of the Kushan dynasty still ruled parts of Kashmir and the Punjab as late as the 5th century AD, the provinces of Bactria and the upper Indus were annexed by the expanding **Sasanian empire** of Iran under its founder, Ardashir I (reigned AD 224–240).

To the south, the **Satavahana** dynasty emerged in peninsular India, filling the vacuum left by the Mauryans; under Satakarni I (reigned 27–17 BC) it expanded to cover much of the Deccan Plateau, until its decline in the 3rd century AD (Kulke and Rothermunde 1986). The extent of Satavahana power appears to have depended on individual rulers, who, despite being a Hindu dynasty, represented an important source of patronage for the construction of monumental Buddhist art and architecture, perhaps stressing the legitimacy of their succession to Mauryan rule (Seneviratne 1981). Satavahana rulers were active in establishing dynastic and provincial capitals, including the dynastic center of **Pratisthana (Paithan)** and the cities of Sannati, Dhayakataka, Satanikota, Ter, and Bhokardan. They were all engaged in maritime Silk Route trade (Chapter 15), as revealed by finds of Roman bronzes, coins, ceramics and glass (Wheeler 1946; Casal 1949) [see box: Roman Contact and the Origins of Indian Ocean Trade, p. 550].

14.35 *The Early Historic fortifications at Mahasthan:* the rampart and moats at Mahasthan in Bangladesh represent one of the best-preserved fortifications of Early Historic South Asia. Surrounding one of the Mauryan dynasty's provincial capitals, its rampart rises 8 m (26 ft) above a ditch with a span of over 100 m (328 ft). Its construction represents a great communal investment, and the strength of the centralized authority of the Mauryan empire.

KEY CONTROVERSY Roman Contact and the Origins of Indian Ocean Trade

Scholars have frequently suggested that South Asia can be geographically separated into two major cultural spheres, north and south, with the River Narmada marking the dividing line (Wheeler 1959). This division may be rather more complex in reality, but its application appears to hold true for identifying differentiated development in the emergence of South Asia's Early Historic cities and empires. With their lack of distinct cities, the inhabitants of the south are rather better known for their investment in complex megalithic tombs and urn-burial cemeteries, often covering hundreds of hectares (McIntosh 1985; Rajan 1994).

This largely agrarian and pastoral landscape, frequently identified as egalitarian and mobile, was transformed into a series of literate, dynamic kingdoms linked with trading partners throughout the Indian Ocean region by the 1st centuries AD. The catalyst for this transformation remains controversial, some scholars identifying an external source – the Greco-Roman world – and others autochthonous origins.

Roman Traders

The external contacts hypothesis was put forward by Sir Mortimer Wheeler (1976), and was based on his findings at Arikamedu. Excavating in 1945, he identified the transformation of a small fishing village on the southeast coast into a brick-built complex of warehouses and vats, complete with Italian Arretine wares and amphorae, which he termed an "Indo-Roman trading station" or a "Roman market" (Wheeler 1946).

Using models derived from 17th- and 18th-century European trading companies, he suggested that the first Indian Ocean routes were operated by merchants who discovered the cyclical pattern of the monsoon winds. Once harnessed, this information allowed them to sail to the subcontinent and trade for six months before returning when the winds changed. Wheeler (1954) suggested that such traders also exploited the interior, converting "unenterprising" fishing villages into permanent trading centers. Certainly, the failure to identify evidence of trade networks within the pre-Arretine levels at Arikamedu appeared to fit his model very well: urbanization and international trade had been kick-started by the appearance of Roman traders in the Indian Ocean.

Indigenous Origins

Such was the persuasive nature of Wheeler's model that until recently it has been scarcely challenged, and then only on account of inescapable evidence from excavations at two key archaeological sites, Arikamedu and Anuradhapura. The former has in fact demonstrated that there is evidence of regional trade networks in the pre-Arretine levels at Arikamedu in the form of Rouletted ware, a locally manufactured flat dish with wheel decorations (Begley 1996). The evidence from Anuradhapura is much fuller and refutes Wheeler's theory entirely by indicating that powerful trade networks were already in place by the 4th century BC, linking this inland site with maritime communities (Coningham 1999).

These networks are revealed by the presence of carnelian beads from Gujarat, lapis lazuli from Afghanistan, as well as marine turtle and early Brahmi script. These materials are only later augmented with Hellenistic glass and metalwork and Roman coins, indicating that such "western" objects arrived in the Indian Ocean region through routes already hundreds of years old (Coningham 2002). The full extent of these later routes can be best illustrated by the distribution of locally manufactured Rouletted ware, the find sites for which stretch from Egypt in the west to Vietnam and Bali in the east – routes that spread Buddhist and Hindu thought and cosmographies into Southeast Asia (Chapter 15).

14.36 *Excavations at Arikamedu in 1945. Sir Mortimer Wheeler argued that his wartime excavations at Arikamedu indicated that Indian Ocean trade had been established by Roman traders in the 1st century AD. Subsequent excavations at Arikamedu, in southern India, and Anuradhapura, in Sri Lanka, have disproved this hypothesis by revealing evidence of trade dating back to at least the 4th century BC.*

To the south, the Sri Lankan state continued to thrive, with **Anuradhapura** established as capital of the entire island in the 4th century BC, and a monastic hinterland covering some 15 sq. km (6 sq. miles) in place by the 3rd century AD (Coningham 1999; Bandaranayake 1974). Finally, the establishment of the **Gupta empire** of northern India by Chandragupta I (reigned AD 320–335) represented the end of the fragmented remains of the Early Historic period, and ushered in a new era. With the installation of a new imperial system consisting of a core run by royal officials and governors, and a periphery of individual states run by client kings, this new era marked the abandonment of the centralized socio-economic and religious integration of the Mauryan model of kingship.

Summary and Conclusions

This chapter has presented the foundations of modern South Asia from the formation of the first agglomerations of population and the domestication of plant and animal species to the end of the Early Historic world in the 4th century AD. The archaeology of this enormous region is still by no means fully understood or agreed upon by scholars, and some of the major debates concern such fundamental issues as the nature of the Indus script, the civilization's social organization, and even the causes of its demise. The enormity of South Asia's archaeological resource is apparent from, for example, the tremendous impact of the chance discovery of the site of Mehrgarh in the 1970s, following a flash flood of the Bolan River.

This chapter has also concentrated on the developmental sequence and morphology of two great phases of urbanization, the Indus, or Harappan, and the Gangetic, or Early Historic; both share pervasive developmental sequences within the region, the shared nature of which is further stressed by the use of Shaffer's (1995) reference to eras of regionalization, integration, and localization. The Harappan sequence is becoming increasingly better understood as a result of pioneering research at Mehrgarh and the proto-urban settlements of the Early Harappan period. The exact processes that transformed settlements such as Rehman Dheri and Kalibangan into ones of the enormous proportions of Harappa, Mohenjo-daro, and Dholavira are still uncertain, but the phasing and morphology of that change are now clearer.

Similarly, the abandonment of the concept of a post-Harappan "dark age" has greatly simplified our understanding of the emergence of the second, Iron Age, urbanization of South Asia. Rather than relying on a series of invasions – Aryan, Achaemenid, and Greek – archaeologists are concentrating on the regional sequence from the Chalcolithic to the Iron Age and have successfully identified the presence of proto-urban settlements pre-dating evidence of foreign contact. Again, we may not be certain of the exact nature of the dynamics involved, but the characteristics of the resultant changes are now well understood on an intra- and extra-settlement basis. Only further research within the region will enable us to fully comprehend these transformations, but the increasing use of radiocarbon dating and high-quality excavation and survey techniques bode well for the future of this sub-discipline.

In the next chapter we move eastwards, and take up the parallel story of the rise of state societies in East and Southeast Asia, from the point at which we left off in Chapter 7. That chapter discussed the rise of farming societies in this region, and in Chapter 8 an account was given of the further dispersal of farming through island Southeast Asia. In the next chapter we describe the earliest state societies of mainland East and Southeast Asia, beginning in the 3rd millennium BC, down to and including the Indianized states of Angkor and its neighbors in the 2nd millennium AD.

Further Reading and Suggested Website

Agrawal, D. P. 1982. *The Archaeology of India*. London: Curzon Press. Data-heavy text concentrating on India.

Allchin, B. & Allchin, F. R. 1982. *The Rise of Civilisation in India and Pakistan*. Cambridge: Cambridge University Press. The best available student textbook, despite its early date; heavy on data but with little theoretical context.

Allchin, F. R. (ed.). 1995. *Early Historic South Asia: The Emergence of Cities and States*. Cambridge: Cambridge University Press. One of the best available textbooks on Early Historic archaeology, with chapters reflecting the specialist interests of each contributor.

Dani, A. H. & Masson, V. M. (eds.). 1992. *History of Civilisations of Central Asia, Volume I: The Dawn of Civilisation: Earliest Times to 700 BC*. Paris: UNESCO.

Harmatta, J. (ed.). 1994. *History of Civilisations of Central Asia, Volume II: The Development of Sedentary and Nomadic Civilisations: 700 BC to AD 250*. Paris: UNESCO.

Harmatta, J. (ed.). 1996. *History of Civilisations of Central Asia, Volume III: The Crossroads of Civilisations: AD 250–750*. Paris: UNESCO. This and the previous two volumes contain collections of edited chapters with good detail.

Kenoyer, J. M. 1998. *Ancient Cities of the Indus Valley Civilisation*. Karachi: Oxford University Press. Good introductory textbook with excellent detail on the Indus Valley.

Settar, S. & Korisettar, R. (eds.). 2002. *Indian Archaeology in Retrospect, I: Prehistory: Archaeology of South Asia; II: Archaeology of the Harappan Civilisation*. New Delhi: Indian Council of Historical Research. Both volumes offer up-to-date collections of edited chapters with good detail; main coverage is India, but still a very valuable resource for the rest of South Asia.

http://www.harappa.com/indus2/harpframe.html The website of the Harappa Archaeological Research Project.

CHAPTER 15
COMPLEX SOCIETIES OF EAST AND SOUTHEAST ASIA

Charles Higham, University of Otago

China 553
   The Rise of Complex Societies 553
    • *The Liangzhu Culture* 553
    • *The Hongshan Culture* 554
   The Longshan Culture 555
   The Lower Xiajiadian Culture 556
   The Xia Dynasty, c. 1700–1500 BC 557
   The Shang Dynasty, c. 1500–1045 BC 558
   ● **KEY DISCOVERY** The Origins of Chinese Writing 558
   ● **KEY SITE** Zhengzhou: A Shang Capital 561
   ● **KEY DISCOVERY** Southern Rivals to Shang Culture 562
   The Changjiang Culture 562
   The Western Zhou Dynasty, 1045–771 BC 563
   ● **KEY SITE** Sanxingdui 564
    • *Western Zhou Bronzeworking* 565
   The Eastern Zhou Dynasty, 770–221 BC 566
   ● **KEY DISCOVERY** Confucianism 567
   The Qin Dynasty, 221–207 BC 568
   The Han Dynasty, 206 BC–AD 220 569
    • *Administration* 569
    • *Agriculture* 570
   ● **KEY SITE** Tonglushan: A Copper-Mining Site 571
    • *Religious Beliefs* 571
   ● **KEY SITE** Mawangdui 572

Korea 574
   Koguryo 574
   Kaya 574
   Paekche 575
   Silla 575
   Great Silla, AD 668–918 577

Japan 578
   Early Yamato 578
   The Growth of Yamato Power 578
   Decline and Civil War 580
   The Asuka Enlightenment 580
   ● **KEY DISCOVERY** The Origins of Chinese Metallurgy 582
   The Transition from Yamato to Nara 582

The Central Asian Silk Road 583
   Khotan 583
   Shanshan 584

The Southeast Asian Maritime Silk Road 585
   ● **KEY CONTROVERSY** The Origins of Southeast Asian Indianized States 585
   Funan, the Mekong Delta 586
   Angkor, Cambodia 586
   ● **KEY SITE** Angkor: Capital City of the Khmer 587
   The Arakan Coast, Burma 590
   The Pyu of Burma 590
   The Dvaravati of Thailand 590
   The Cham of Vietnam 591

Summary and Conclusions 593

Further Reading 593

The preceding chapters have reviewed the Holocene prehistory of the Old World continent by continent, and have highlighted the theme of growing cultural complexity as human populations increased almost everywhere. In this final Old World chapter we complete the story by describing the development of state societies in East and Southeast Asia.

The development and spread of farming villages in East and mainland Southeast Asia was described in Chapter 7. As these early agricultural communities grew in size and complexity, they initiated a process that culminated in the rise of many states, large and small. The earliest developed indigenously during the late 3rd and early 2nd millennia BC in China, in the valleys of the Yellow and Yangzi rivers, though from

their inception they received stimuli along the steppes from the west. These polities co-existed, usually belligerently, until 221 BC, when the Qin Dynasty was established under Qin Shi Huangdi, the first emperor of China. The expansive nature of the Qin and Han empires, whose rulers encouraged trade links with India and Rome, stimulated the genesis of myriad states on their borders and along burgeoning trade routes. To the northeast, one can discern the origins of the early civilizations of Korea and Japan. To the northwest and south, the emerging states that clustered along the Central Asian Silk Road and the coasts of Southeast Asia exchanged exotic goods and ideas with Mauryan and Gupta India, and ultimately Rome and the west, as Chinese silks and ceramics were traded through remote desert or maritime cities.

China

The Rise of Complex Societies

The establishment of agricultural communities in the valleys of the Yellow and Yangzi rivers between the 8th and 7th millennia BC was followed by a surge in population and the foundation of new settlements. Millet in the former region and rice in the latter were the bases for the development of increasingly complex societies. By the 4th and 3rd millennia BC we can identify the establishment of large defended centers associated with cemeteries that included the graves of elite members of society. These developed into the earliest states of East Asia.

Most research in China has concentrated on the central plains of the Yellow River, and it was here that Sima Qian (c. 145–86 BC), author of the *Shi Ji* ("Records of the Grand Historian"), the first history of China, placed the shadowy Xia and Shang dynasties (Nienhauser 1994). Archaeological research in the Yangzi Valley has now provided new insights into early Chinese civilization there. As described in Chapter 7 (p. 246), excavations at the Daxi culture site of **Chengtoushan** have revealed a walled and moated center dating to as early as *c.* 4000 BC. Some of the dead were interred with unusual wealth, one individual being accompanied by 50 ceramic vessels, two jade pendants, and four people. When compared with the majority of graves, this suggests social stratification within the community, as does the presence of specialist potters, and evidence that the elite lived in fine houses provided with corridors and several living rooms.

The Liangzhu Culture Further downstream, the Liangzhu culture (c. 3300–2250 BC) was contemporary with the middle and later phases of Chengtoushan. Sites distributed chiefly in Jiangsu and Zhejiang provinces reveal a rich and sophisticated

society, with an economy based on irrigated rice agriculture and the raising of domestic stock. Craft specialists wove silk, made lacquerware, fired splendid ceramic vessels, created baskets, and, above all, fashioned outstanding jades (Huang Xuanpei et al. 1992) **[15.1]**. Settlements were located next to rivers, and wooden boats and oars, even a jetty at the site of Longnan, reveal the importance of water transport.

A strong ritual element is seen in the elite graves and ceremonial sites. **Sidun**, for example, incorporated a circular mortuary platform within its moated precinct. Here, a young man was accompanied in death by 24 jade rings and 33 *cong* cylinders, the latter bearing ritually significant carved images of ancestral animal masks and birds. Elsewhere, a mound at the site of **Fanshan** incorporated 11 elite tombs, and 12 burials were found in a raised precinct at **Yaoshan**, the dead having been buried in double wooden coffins, accompanied by many precious offerings. Jade items, which were locally manufactured in the Liangzhu area, were vital components of elite mortuary rituals.

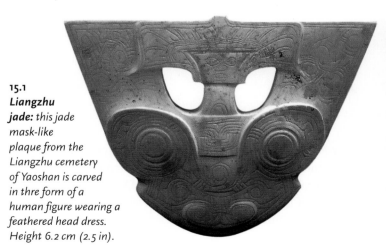

15.1
Liangzhu jade: this jade mask-like plaque from the Liangzhu cemetery of Yaoshan is carved in thre form of a human figure wearing a feathered head dress. Height 6.2 cm (2.5 in).

COMPLEX SOCIETIES OF EAST AND SOUTHEAST ASIA TIMELINE

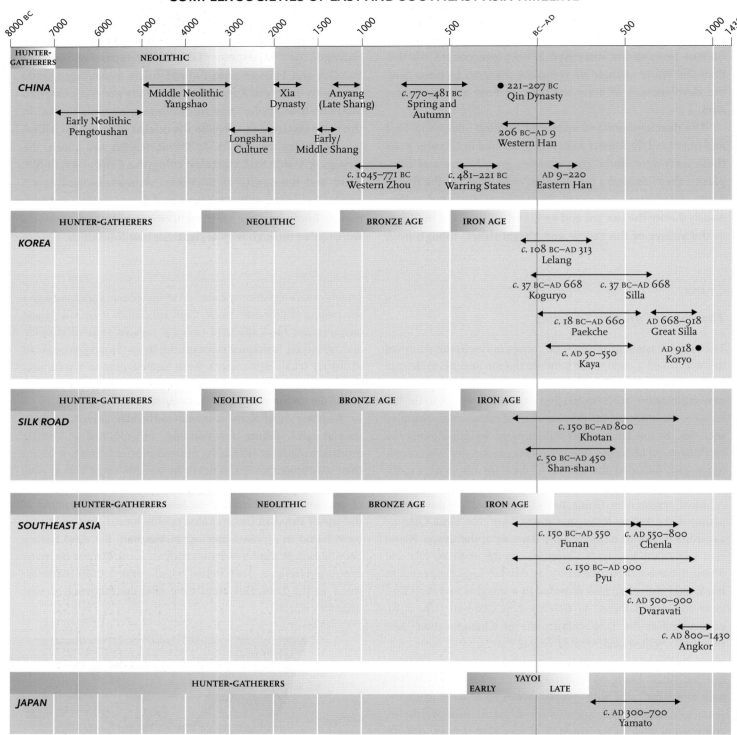

The Hongshan Culture There are several groups of sites in central and northern China that reveal trends toward social complexity similar to those in the Yangzi Valley. The Hongshan culture of Liaoning Province and adjacent Inner Mongolia, for example, features ritual sites associated with rich burials dating to *c.* 4700–2900 BC (Nelson 1995). **Niuheliang** is notable for its

spirit temple surrounded by an extensive area of mounded tombs [15.3]. The temple itself covers 22 x 9 m (72 x 30 ft), and was constructed of wooden-framed walls on stone foundations; the inner walls were plastered and painted. Several clay female figures were found within, as well as representations of dragons and birds. Burial mounds clustering around the sacred structure included stone mounds raised over stone-lined graves. The presence of some particularly rich burials, as measured by their jade grave goods, indicates an early development of social ranking. Furthermore, some of the jade figures, such as the coiled dragons, animal masks, and turtles, are matched by later developments in Shang and Zhou art. This suggests that a lengthy development of similar rituals was emergent long before the establishment of early states. Like the Liangzhu and Yangshao cultures (the latter discussed in Chapter 7), social complexity had early beginnings in several regions of China.

The Longshan Culture

The *Shi Ji* refers to a remote period of the Five Emperors, naming kings and cities, battles and rival kingdoms. The *Han Shu* ("History of the Former Han"), written by Ban Biao (AD 3–54) and completed by his son Ban Gu, mentions early walled cities that may well relate to the late Neolithic Longshan culture, distributed from the central plains to Shandong Province (Dematte 1999; Underhill 1994). Longshan sites reveal an increasing social complexity, and cemeteries such as those at **Chengzi** and **Taosi** [15.2] included a few elite graves as well as many for the less exalted. Up to 200 offerings were found in wealthy graves at Taosi, including jade rings and axes, and two wooden drums, each with a striking surface of crocodile skin. (Historic texts refer to drums as being associated with royalty.) A middle group of about 80 graves included jade axes, *cong* tubes, and rings, as well as pigs' mandibles, but the vast majority of poor graves had few offerings. Taosi also yielded a bronze bell, and a few bronzes have been found at other Longshan sites, but metal is in general very rare at this period.

15.2 *Longshan pottery:* *the pottery vessels from the Longshan cemetery of Taosi are of outstanding quality. Height 19.2 cm (7.5 in).*

Excavations at **Chengziyai** in Liaoning Province have uncovered inscribed oracle bones dating to between 2500 and 1900 BC. These anticipate the Shang practice of making divinations using animal bones by interpreting cracks generated through the application of heat. Symbols on pottery that anticipate the Chinese script have also been found at **Dinggong** and **Jingyanggang**. Many Longshan sites incorporated stamped-earth walls (those at Jingyanggang enclosing 38 ha, or 94 acres), and sacrificed adults and children have been recovered from house and wall foundations in Shandong Province, again antecedents of later Shang human sacrifices.

15.3 *The spirit temple of Niuheliang:* *this aerial view shows the shape of the temple, built of wooden-framed walls on stone foundations.*

15.4 China and Southeast Asia: *map showing major sites and places mentioned in the text.*

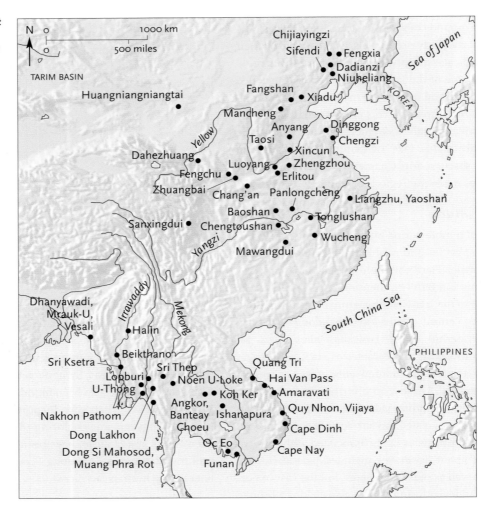

These defensive walls, rich burial assemblages, the adoption of metallurgy, an increase in artifacts associated with armed conflict, and evidence for craft specialization in jade carving and ceramics all reveal a quickening of social complexity in the Longshan culture. Both defended settlements and craft expertise were rooted in a long preceding Neolithic period, in which stamped-earth enclosures and growing settlement sizes were already appearing by the end of the 4th millennium BC. During the Longshan culture period, well-placed communities grew further in size and constructed large walls and platforms for elite buildings. A growing density of sites and population increase accompanied the trend toward sharp social distinctions, at a time of increasing warfare. During the late 3rd millennium BC, Longshan centers sustained a hierarchical social structure on the brink of state formation, but they were not alone in northern China.

The Lower Xiajiadian Culture

The Lower Xiajiadian culture of Inner Mongolia and Liaoning and Hebei provinces was contemporary with the Longshan culture (Guo Da-shun 1995). Based on excavations at **Fengxia** in

Liaoning, three developmental phases can be identified, and the 2000 known sites fall into three groups based on size and the presence of defenses. The largest walled site covered more than 10 ha (25 acres), while smaller defended sites and those without defensive walls clustered round a large central place, such as at **Chijiayingzi**. Many stone walls included bastions, and the houses were at least partially underground, constructed of stone or stamped earth, with plastered walls and floors. At **Sifendi** in Inner Mongolia, houses were circular, with a diameter rarely exceeding 4 m (13 ft). They were accessed by a set of steps, and a hearth dominated the single room within. The economy was based on millet cultivation, and many storage pits were probably dug to hold millet for winter consumption. Agricultural implements included stone hoes and sickles, as well as spades fashioned from animal shoulder blades. Bones of domestic pigs, dogs, cattle, goat, and sheep indicate the raising of livestock, while deer were hunted. Pigs were placed in graves as ritual offerings.

Some 800 burials have been excavated at Dadianzi, where the mortuary ritual involved single inhumation burials. The elite were interred in large, richly endowed graves up to 8.9 m

15.5 Erlitou: *the Xia Dynasty center of Erlitou incorporated the earliest palace structures in China, as well as elite graves and fine bronze vessels and weapons.*

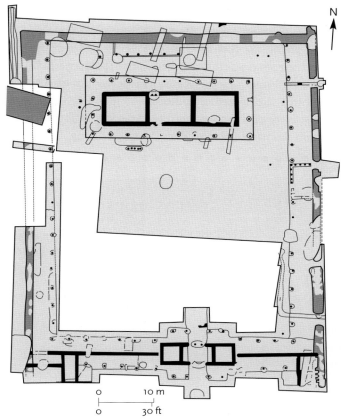

(29 ft) deep. A wooden coffin lay at the base, while fine painted ceramic vessels [**15.6**] and the limbs of domestic pigs were placed in side niches. Polished stone battle-axes, lacquerware, rare jades and bronze ornaments, and the skeletons of dogs and pigs were also found. The craft specialization exhibited in these graves and on other Xiajiadian sites provides evidence of increasing social distinctions in a region relatively remote from the central plains. Parallels for the bronzes lie to the west, with the Andronovo culture of the steppes, and in the case of decorative finials, in Bactria (northwest Afghanistan), suggesting that the steppes provided a conduit for the introduction of bronze-working into China [see box: The Origins of Chinese Metallurgy, p. 582]. Long-distance trade would have brought jade and marine shells to the Xiajiadian communities. The drilling and heating of animal scapulae for divination purposes was widespread, a hint that the Lower Xiajiadian culture was at least in part ancestral to the Shang civilization.

The Xia Dynasty, c. 1700–1500 BC

The Xia Dynasty has long been regarded as the first dynasty of China, documentation in the main coming from Sima Qian's *Shi Ji*, and more recently from archaeology. This dynasty, which involved many kings over a period of at least two centuries, presents an exciting challenge to archaeologists, with the discovery of the city of Erlitou, located south of the Yellow River in Henan Province, representing a major breakthrough (Fitzgerald-Huber 1995).

Erlitou covers over 300 ha (741 acres) and has four occupation phases falling in the first half of the 2nd millennium BC [**15.5**]. The first two phases relate to the Longshan culture, but the third and fourth reveal marked changes, as seen in the elite burials, ritual bronze vessels, and the presence of two palaces.

Aristocrats were interred in painted wooden coffins, accompanied by bronzes cast using the piece-mold technique (in which the vessel was cast in sections, which were then joined with mortises and tenons). There are also bronze dagger-axes (a weapon combining the functions of both) and a battle-axe, and ceremonial *yazhang* blades [**15.7**], knives, and ritually important *cong* cylinders made of jade. Several symbols on pottery vessels represent early written characters, and a sheep's shoulder blade had been used for divination. The excavations at Erlitou, one site of many of the same period now identified in the Yellow River valley, give substance to Sima Qian's historic description, written 1500 years after the event.

15.6 *(Far left)* **Pottery vessel from Dadianzi:** *the many burials uncovered at Dadianzi, of the Lower Xiajiadian culture, incorporated spectacular mortuary vessels as offerings for the dead, such as this Hu vessel. Height 40.5 cm (15.75 in).*

15.7 *(Left)* **Yazhang:** *such blades of jade were ritually important in early Chinese states. This example from the Xia site of Erlitou was found on an elite individual's chest. Height 54 cm (21.25 in).*

The Shang Dynasty, c. 1500–1045 BC

Sima Qian also set out the king list of the second dynasty of the central plains, the Shang. Until the closing years of the 19th century, the *Shi Ji* was the principal source for this period. Then in the late 1890s, the recognition of an archaic text inscribed on some turtle shells used in traditional Chinese medicine led to the discovery of the source of the carapaces at the village of Xiaotun. Archaeological evidence for the Shang Dynasty (*c.* 1500–1045 BC) suddenly appeared, for this was the site of **Anyang**, the last Shang capital, situated on the southern bend of the Huan River in Henan Province.

Further fieldwork has identified more sites, as well as over 100,000 oracle bones used by Shang kings for divining the future (Keightley 1978). Oracle bones were created when heat was applied to pits dug in the underside of the bone, thus generating cracks [15.9]. Both the questions posed and the

KEY DISCOVERY The Origins of Chinese Writing

Chinese writing has very early roots. The earliest evidence for a written script comes from Jiahu, a Neolithic site in the Huai River valley in Henan Province, dated to *c.* 6500 BC. It has yielded turtle carapaces that were pitted and inscribed with symbols. The Longshan site of Chengziyai in Shandong Province has produced fragments of inscribed bones used to divine the future, dating to 2500–1900 BC, and symbols on pottery vessels from Dinggong are thought to be an early form of writing. Symbols of a similar nature have also been found on pottery sherds from the Liangzhu culture of the lower Yangzi Valley.

Shang Dynasty Pictograms

By the time of the Shang Dynasty these had developed into a fully-fledged system of writing that used pictograms to represent objects and ideas. Since this early script is ancestral to modern Chinese written forms it can be translated, enabling scholars not only to produce a king list and to date specific events, but also to probe issues that concerned the court.

One of the foremost of these was the making of sacrifices to appease the ancestors, frequently by killing an animal in the ancestral temple. Another concern involved military campaigns. An inscribed oracle bone might read, positively, "This season, the king should attack the Shu, because he will gain assistance on this occasion." The opposing negative would read, "This season, the king should not attack the enemy, because if he does, he might not receive assistance." The cracks formed by the application of heat to the bone would determine whether to attack or not. Other texts reveal the king's concern with a consort's pregnancy, whether or not to go hunting, and how to cure the royal toothache. Much concern was also devoted to the success of the millet harvest.

Over 100,000 oracle bones have been recovered, mainly from Anyang, but these

Table 1 *The Evolution of Chinese Writing*

	Oracle bone inscriptions *c.* 1400–1200 BC	Bronze inscriptions *c.* 1500–700 BC	Small seal script standardized after 221 BC	Chancery script *c.* 200 BC–AD 200	Standard script *c.* AD 200 onward	Standard printed style *c.* AD 1400 onward	Cursive script *c.* AD 200 onward
Pictograph							
Differentiated pictograph							
Pictographic compound							
Phonetic compound							

subsequent interpretation of the cracks as answers were afterwards recorded in writing on the surface, allowing archaeologists an insight into royal policy [see box: The Origins of Chinese Writing]. There was much concern with war, hunting, rainfall and the success of agriculture, and the health of members of the royal family. Desired outcomes were influenced by the sacrifice of humans or animals to the divine royal ancestors. Archaeologists have also explored the earlier Shang city at

Zhengzhou, in Henan Province (Bagley 1999). City walls enclosed 335 ha (828 acres), while the extramural area covered 25 sq. km (9.7 sq. miles) and included bronze, bone, and ceramic workshops, cemeteries, and the homes of specialist craftspeople [see box: Zhengzhou: A Shang Capital, p. 561]. A moated palace lay within the city walls, near richly endowed graves containing bronze ritual vessels and jade and bronze ornaments.

were not the only Shang use of texts. Vermilion-colored writing has been detected on some oracle bones prior to their being traced with incisions, and one image took the form of vertical strokes joined by wavy lines. These represent bamboo slips, joined sequentially with threads to form a scroll that could be opened to read, and then folded to be stored away. Common in later periods, none has survived from the Shang Dynasty, but they clearly existed.

The Zhou Dynasty

With the establishment of the Zhou Dynasty in 1045 BC, oracle bones continued to be used, but they are very rare. In their place, we find that texts were cast into bronze ritual vessels,

Draft or "grass" script 200 BC onward	Simplified script standardized AD 1956	English translation
马 (grass)	马	Horse
上 (grass)	上	Up, to ascend
莫 (grass)	莫	Sunset; negation
柳 (grass)	柳	Willow

providing vital evidence for the history of this period. Thus, the Song *gui*, an inscribed bronze vessel in the form of a low-footed bowl, was cast to commemorate a court appointment under King Xuan (reigned 827–782 BC). It describes in detail the ceremonial investiture of a court official named Song to supervise warehouses, for which he was awarded a black embroidered jacket and other choice gifts from the sovereign. Bamboo records were clearly widely used, for the text then describes how Song "suspended the strips from his jacket in order to withdraw." It would seem that a copy of the document appointing him, written with ink and brush on the bamboo slips, was presented to him during the audience.

A bronze *jia* (a tripod vessel) from the rich hoard of bronze found at Zhuangbai in Shaanxi Province, dating to about 975 BC, mentions the court scribe Zhe and his title *Zuoce*, meaning "Maker of Strips."

Bamboo Slips

Texts on bamboo slips have been recovered from tombs dating from the period of the Warring States (481–221 BC); most derive from southern China, where conditions for the use and survival of bamboo are more favorable than in the north. The tomb of Shao Tuo at Baoshan has yielded a series of such texts, found together with his brush for writing and knife for erasing errors. The texts were largely concerned with legal issues, although there was also an inventory of the

15.8 Annals written on bamboo slips, from Yunmeng County, Qin Dynasty. A total of 53 slips were found, written in ink, mostly recording accounts of wars by the Qin to unify the country.

tomb contents, and divinations. The last set of texts even included continuing references to Shao Tuo's declining health.

Another set of early texts comes from the tomb of Xi, an archivist who lived during the reign of the first emperor of Qin, Qin Shi Huangdi. He was buried in tomb 11 at Shuihudi, and was accompanied by about 1200 bamboo slips bearing historic texts that Xi might well have written himself. One document records events that took place, rather like a diary, including references to the life of Xi. Often, bamboo tomb texts have provided copies of histories thought to have been lost forever.

Records on Silk

Written records have also survived on silk, particularly in the south. One set was discovered at Mawangdui, in a tomb dated to 168 BC. It comprised a series of documents that included the Daoist text *Daode jing* by Laozi, with four appendices. The latter have proved controversial, some scholars identifying them as the records of the mythical Yellow Emperor (*Huangdi sijing*), lost to historians for over 2000 years.

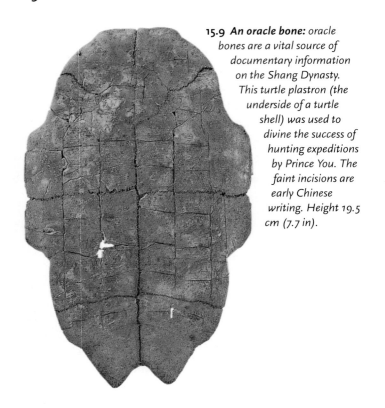

15.9 An oracle bone: oracle bones are a vital source of documentary information on the Shang Dynasty. This turtle plastron (the underside of a turtle shell) was used to divine the success of hunting expeditions by Prince You. The faint incisions are early Chinese writing. Height 19.5 cm (7.7 in).

palace precinct has been found in the center of the walled area, covering over 10 ha (25 acres) and incorporating at least 25 individual buildings. Outside the eastern wall, a 10-m (33-ft) wide and 1.5-km (0.9-mile) long road has been identified, still retaining the rut marks left by wheeled vehicles. Further excavations at this remarkable site have the potential to illuminate a crucial period of Shang history.

The Shang capital at **Anyang** covered at least 25 sq. km (9.7 sq. miles), but no surrounding walls have been found [**15.10**]. The center contains the foundations for the palace precinct, as well as ancestral temples and repositories for the oracle bone records. Some pits discovered here contained complete chariots, as well as the skeletons of their horses and charioteers. It is now possible to compare dated chariots from China with those excavated in sites further west, leading to overwhelming evidence of an exotic source for Shang chariots. The site of Lchashen in Armenia, for example, has yielded the remains of two chariots that anticipate Shang examples dating from the reign of Wu Ding, who died in 1189 BC (Lubotsky 1998; Puett 1998).

The royal necropolis at Anyang includes 12 subterranean tombs up to 13 m (43 ft) deep, each containing a wooden chamber approached by four descending ramps oriented to the cardinal points. Several huge bronze vessels and fine jades, overlooked by robbers, hint at their former wealth. Two bronze cauldrons were found in the central pit of one tomb, 2 m (6.6 ft)

Zhengzhou was in due course superseded as the Shang royal capital, though it continued to be a major center in its own right during the Warring States period (481–221 BC), and the Han (206 BC–AD 220) and, later, the Ming (AD 1368–1644) dynasties. There was a chronological gap, however, between the abandonment of Zhengzhou as a capital and the foundation of Anyang – a gap that was closed in 1999 with the discovery of the city of **Huanbei**, just northeast of Anyang itself. Preliminary excavations have dated this vital site to within the period 1400–1200 BC, making it the likely Shang capital of **Xi'ang**. A

15.10 The late Shang capital of Anyang: this complex site incorporated an area for royal graves (Xibeigang) and another for the palace center (Xiaotun), where the oracle bone records were stored. There were also workshops for bronze casting, areas for the elite and commoners to live, and lineage cemeteries. (Various scales.)

Royal cemetery at Xibeigang

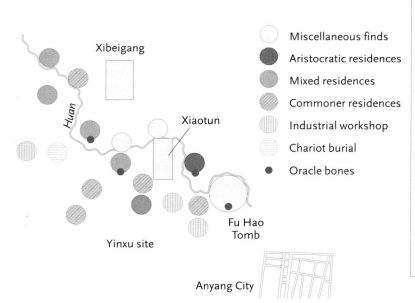

Xibeigang

Huan

Xiaotun

Yinxu site

Fu Hao Tomb

Anyang City

◯ Miscellaneous finds
● Aristocratic residences
◐ Mixed residences
▨ Commoner residences
▦ Industrial workshop
▭ Chariot burial
● Oracle bones

Temple

Hall

Great Hall

Palace-temple complex at Xiaotun

KEY SITE Zhengzhou: A Shang Capital

The site of Zhengzhou has seen virtually continuous occupation since the middle Shang Dynasty. In the absence of Shang texts from this site, other than a small assemblage of oracle bones, its original name is not known. The word *zhen* on the oracular texts implies ritual divination, making it highly likely that Zhengzhou was a royal center. It might well have been the city of Bo, the first Shang capital, or Ao, founded by the sixth king, Zhong Ding.

It was strategically placed at the junction of two rivers, commanding the link between the loess uplands to the west and the Yellow River plains to the east. Today, the stamped-earth Shang walls reach a width of 36 m (118 ft) at the base and still stand in parts to a height of nearly 10 m (33 ft); they probably date to c. 1650 BC.

Excavations within the walls have uncovered the stamped-earth foundations of a probable palace precinct, represented by large postholes to receive columns. This same area included pits filled with dog skeletons and human skulls. Dogs were often sacrificed to the ancestors, whereas human beings were slaughtered when major new buildings were constructed. Opulent graves with fine mortuary offerings in this part of the ancient city also indicate the presence of an elite, probably royal, presence.

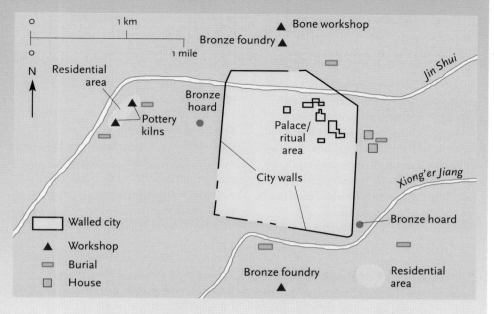

15.11 *A plan of the Shang city of Zhengzhou. The city was surrounded by walls which are 36 m (118 ft) wide at the base and still reach a height of nearly 10 m (33 ft) in places. Inside the walls is a probable palace precinct, while outside are various specialist manufacturing areas.*

The extramural area of Zhengzhou incorporated a series of specialist manufacturing areas. One workshop was found in which large ceremonial bronze vessels and weapons were cast; the skill of the bronze-casters, who surely worked under royal control and patronage, can be judged from one recovered vessel known as a *ding*, which weighed 86.4 kg (190 lb). Another area was used for shaping and firing ceramics, the homes of the specialists being located nearby. There were workshops for boneworkers, whose output included hairpins and arrowheads. Four extramural cemeteries for the non-elite Shang populace have been investigated; mortuary offerings include ceramics, bronzes, and jade ornaments.

---

above the top of the wooden burial chamber. The cauldrons overlay 360 spearheads and 141 helmets, as well as jade figurines of turtles, frogs, and monsters. Hundreds of nearby graves contained the skeletons of beheaded young men, while others contained only the skulls; children had been buried alive. These grisly finds confirm the sacrifice of human victims described in the oracle bone texts.

The location of queens' graves is not known, but the discovery in 1976 of the tomb of Fu Hao, a consort of Wu Ding, revealed the wealth of a lesser member of the royal house (Zheng Zhenxiang 1996). A wooden chamber at the base of her mortuary pit contained nested, lacquered wooden coffins, and 16 men, women, and children accompanied her in death. Mortuary offerings included 468 bronzes incorporating ritual wine and food vessels, some inscribed with her name [15.12]. There were also about 7000 cowrie shells, 755 items of jade,

15.12 *Bronze wine vessel in the form of an owl: from the tomb of Fu Hao at Anyang. Fu Hao was a consort of King Wu Ding and a lesser member of the royal house, but the offerings in her tomb included 468 bronzes as well as numerous shell, jade, and bone ornaments. Height 46.3 cm (36.75 in).*

KEY DISCOVERY Southern Rivals to Shang Culture

When he compiled the *Shi Ji*, his history of China, in the 2nd century BC, the Han historian Sima Qian devoted many pages to the Shang Dynasty. He provided the names of kings, cities, and events, placing this state in the central plains of the Yellow River valley. During the course of the 20th century, archaeologists have verified the historic reality of this dynasty and explored its cities. At Zhengzhou, they have traced the outline and extent of an early capital city, while the last capital at Anyang has yielded royal tombs, chariot pits, temple foundations, and extensive cemeteries. A hitherto lost Shang city was found in 1999, just northeast of Anyang at Huanbei.

Archaeologists have also uncovered a treasure trove of texts in the form of oracular pronouncements incised on animal bones. Whether or not to go to war with other states is one of the recurrent themes in these oracle bone texts, and they make it clear that the Shang people did not exist in isolation. Many of these other states lay on the periphery of the Shang domain and were probably minor players on the political scene. Recent research in the south, however, where rice rather than millet was cultivated, has provided a new view of early Chinese civilization.

The Changjiang Culture

Rice was brought under cultivation in the middle Yangzi lakeland by the 8th millennium BC (Chapter 7), and urban sites such as Chengtoushan existed even earlier than similar sites in the central plains. It is, therefore, not entirely surprising that a southern state, named Changjiang by Chinese scholars, is now being identified. The existence of this society, apparently unknown to Sima Qian and other early Chinese historians, is requiring a new interpretation of early polities in East Asia.

Sanxingdui is the dominant site in this new view of early China [see box: Sanxingdui, pp. 564–65]. Located in the heart of the rich Chengdu plain in Sichuan Province, this walled city was contemporary with Anyang. The discovery of two pits here, filled with bronze, gold, jade, and ivory artifacts, has astonished scholars. The bronzes are quite distinct from Shang objects, tending toward the massive: masks, human faces, and statues of trees and human figures are unmatched. The energy expended, first in their production and then in their destruction and burial, could only have come from a powerful state.

Further down the Yangzi Valley, other settlements reveal the widespread nature of this southern society. Panlongcheng in Hubei Province (Bagley 1977) and Wucheng in Jiangxi, for example, were substantial and wealthy urban centers contemporary with Zhengzhou, while the tomb at Xin'gan is hardly less wealthy, in terms of grave goods, than the burial complex of Fu Hao, consort to the Shang king Wu Ding (see p. 561).

---

many hundreds of bone ornaments, and three ivory cups with turquoise inlay.

Temples formed a major portion of the royal precinct of Anyang. Rituals were dedicated first to the supreme god Di, whose command over natural forces ensured his influence over agriculture. One oracle text divined that "Di, in the fourth moon, will order rain." He also encouraged war on enemy states, though after the reign of Wu Ding, the ancestors increasingly assumed this role – they were dominated by former kings in direct line of descent, and mothers of kings.

The Shang landscape was dotted with villages with their associated millet fields. Cultivation was a central concern of the Shang kings, who owned extensive estates, as was domestic stock; the bone workshops of Anyang processed the remains of cattle, sheep, pigs, dogs, and horses.

Supplies of copper and tin were strategically important, and jade (the nearest known source for which was nearly 400 km (249 miles) from Anyang) was converted into elite ornaments and ritual objects. Cowrie shells were a currency unit, and some of these had to come from tropical seas thousands of kilometers to the south; turtle shells for use in divinations were also imported from the south.

The Changjiang Culture

The cultures of the central plains have long dominated our interpretation of early Chinese states. The discovery of **Sanxingdui**, however, a walled city in Sichuan Province that has been assigned to the newly named Changjiang culture, has emphasized the equal importance of the Yangzi Valley [see box: Southern Rivals to Shang Culture]. Known for many years as a source of early jades, Sanxingdui rose to prominence with the discovery of two remarkable ritual pits dating to the 12th or 13th century BC [see box: Sanxingdui, pp. 564–65]. Further research is necessary to illuminate the nature of this city more clearly and the early state of which it must have been a part. However, we now know that the rice-growing region of China, centered in the Yangzi Valley during the 2nd millennium BC, produced a civilization rivaling in splendor that documented at the Shang capital of Anyang.

Further down the Yangzi Valley, there is evidence for the Changjiang culture at the necropolis of **Xin'gan** and the associated city of **Wucheng** in Jiangxi Province (Bagley 1990; 1993). The large royal tomb at the former site dates to the late Shang period and contained hundreds of ceramic vessels, 150 jades, and 475 bronzes [15.13]. Of the bronzes, about half were weapons; there were also 50 vessels and 4 bells. We find a distinctive southern bronze tradition in the casting of tigers onto the handles of bronze vessels and the *nao* form of bell, which had an elliptical cross-section and was supported mouth-upwards on a tubular handle. Like Sanxingdui, the discovery of the Xin'gan tomb has revealed a powerful early polity in the Yangzi Valley, which would have provided the necessary base for the future rise to power of the state of Chu, which came to dominate this region.

The Western Zhou Dynasty, 1045– 771 BC

The end of the Shang Dynasty came in 1045 BC, when the powerful and ambitious king of the state of Zhou, based in the Wei Valley, sent his chariots and the Tiger Warrior infantry north to defeat the Shang at the **Battle of Muye**. With the establishment of the Zhou Dynasty, we enter a period well-documented both in terms of texts and in the archaeological record.

Traditional historical texts, particularly the *Shi Ji*, are important sources of information on the Zhou, and we also have the *Bamboo Annals*, a narrative history of China up to 298 BC (Shaughnessy 1986). A steadily increasing number of inscriptions on ritual bronze vessels document this period, and archaeologists have investigated Zhou settlement and cemetery sites, adding much to our available information (Shaughnessy 1991). During the Western Zhou (1045–771 BC), the capital was located at **Zongzhou** (Hsu and Linduff 1988). When it was sacked, the court moved east to **Luoyang**, initiating the Eastern Zhou Dynasty (770–221 BC; see below).

Thirteen Western Zhou emperors ruled until 771 BC, making it one of the longest-lived Chinese dynasties. This dominance may be partially explained by the innovative Zhou approach to war, and an arsenal that included new forms of armor, halberds, and cast bronze swords. Early Western Zhou emperors adopted an expansive policy, in which peripheral states were conquered and ruled by members of the royal clan. A text on the Mai *zun*, a ritual bronze vessel, describes how Xinghou Zhi was authorized to command a border area. The king presented him with horse harness and fine clothing, soldiers, and 200 families to found a new settlement. This policy was initially sound, but proved to be a double-edged weapon as blood relations thinned and provincial rulers grew more powerful.

Jin, with its capital at **Tianma Qucun** in Shaanxi Province, was one of these new states (Rawson 1999). Excavations of 600 burials have revealed varying degrees of wealth, with some tombs incorporating remarkable jade facial images. There were, as well, fine bronzes and pits for chariots and horses. Rich burials have also been excavated in the cemetery of **Xincun** in Henan Province, which belonged to the state of **Wei**. The deep tomb chambers were associated with pits containing horses and chariots. Further east, small states were established in Shandong Province, and to the north, the state of **Yan** was founded; there is documentary evidence that the founding prince of this state enjoyed very high status in the Zhou royal line. The cemetery of **Fangshan**, near Beijing, contained extremely rich burials and was probably associated with another of these provincial states. Bronze vessels were of the highest quality, and there were also multiple chariot burials and horse interments.

One of the key points to emerge from recent archaeological research involves the early Zhou adoption of ritual and mortuary practices from the Shang. We find, for example, the casting of typically Shang forms of bronze ritual vessels, used in banquets to feast the ancestors. Many such vessels contain inscriptions

15.13 *(Left)* **Bronze vessel from a royal tomb:** the Xin'gan tomb in Jiangxi Province dates to 1400–1200 BC and contained many fine bronzes, including this fangding, a vessel for cooking meat. It weighs 49 kg (108 lb). Height 97 cm (38 in).

15.14 *(Below)* **Inscribed bronze vessel:** the history of the Western Zhou dynasty has been greatly enriched through the recovery of texts cast into bronze vessels. The Shi Qiang pan from Zhuangbai is part of a hoard of bronzes, and its inscription records the succession of the first seven Western Zhou rulers. It dates to the end of the 10th century BC. Height 16.2 cm (6.4 in).

willing their use for generations lasting 10,000 years. During later times of danger, such vessels were accumulated and placed in underground hoards, such as the exceptionally rich one unearthed at **Zhuangbai** [15.14]. As we have seen, the interment of chariots, horses, and charioteers in pits associated with the nobility was also a Shang practice, while the form of the chariots themselves is a clear link between the two dynasties. Nevertheless, the Zhou expressed their own preferences in their bronzes (see below), and there were marked regional styles.

While cemetery excavations have yielded a rich harvest of information, cities and other settlements provide a more rounded picture of the Western Zhou state. The foundations of a palace, for example, have been uncovered at **Fengchu** in the Plain of the Zhou, Shaanxi Province (Wu Hung 1995); it is notable for the discovery of oracle bones, suggesting that it was occupied by a high-ranking member of the royal family. Raised on a stamped-earth foundation, it incorporated wooden pillars forming two enclosed courts. A hall dominated the center

KEY SITE Sanxingdui

Sanxingdui, located north of Chengdu in Sichuan Province in southern China, was a walled city of about 450 ha (1112 acres), with extramural occupation and industrial areas covering at least 15 sq. km (6 sq. miles). It incorporated specialist workshops for the manufacture of bronzes, lacquerware, ceramics, and jade (Jay Xu 2001). Excavations of the walls, which had a maximum width of 47 m (154 ft), reveal that they were constructed *c.* 1400–1400 BC, contemporary with the Shang culture of the Chinese central plains. Until the discovery of two unique ritual pits here in 1986, the Shang state dominated any review of early Chinese civilization, but these pits have required a fundamental revision of this supremacy.

The first pit contained layers of burnt animal bones together with 13 elephant tusks,

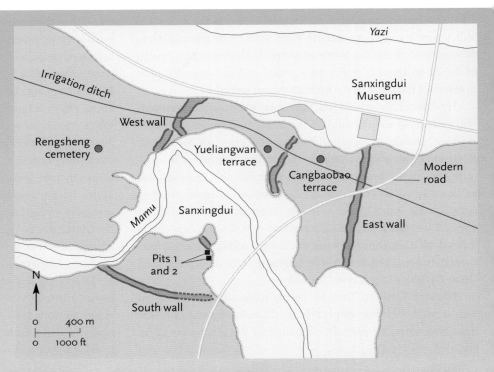

15.17 *The plan of the ancient city of Sanxingdui shows the remains of the massive walls that enclosed an area of 450 ha (1112 acres). Beyond these lay the cemeteries, occupation, and manufacturing centers covering at least 15 sq. km (9.65 sq. miles).*

15.15, 15.16 *Two ritual pits at Sanxingdui contained items of unprecedented grandeur for this period in China – huge bronze masks, splendid jades, and ivory– and were probably ritually associated with the royal Shu dynasty.*

then ceremonial jade *yazhang* blades and *ge* daggers. Lower layers included 178 items of bronze, four gold artifacts, 129 jades, and other objects of stone and pottery, together with many cowrie shells. The second pit contained further items of bronze, jade, gold, and stone, including bronze castings of trees, and diamond-shaped fittings. The next layer comprised a gigantic bronze statue of a man,

between the two courtyards, which were flanked by covered passageways providing access to subsidiary rooms; the structure was drained by a complex system of ceramic pipes. The building formed part of a much larger complex that included a further palace. The most important result of the excavations at this second palace has been the uncovering of the foundations of a great hall, measuring 22 x 14 m (72 x 46 ft) – possibly where royal ceremonies took place. The structure incorporated substantial postholes 1 m (3.3 ft) wide to accommodate the supporting columns; one particularly large one in the center, almost 2 m (6.6 ft) across, would have held a column to take the main weight of the roof. This site also included specialist bone, ceramic, and bronze workshops.

Western Zhou Bronzeworking The location of bronze foundries in a major settlement with a palace precinct recalls the layout of earlier Shang cities such as Anyang. The Zhou bronze industry was related to that of the Shang both in terms of the types of

44 bronze heads, bronze masks, a bronze tree complete with birds perched on the branches, and bronze vessels containing jades and cowrie shells. This layer was capped by 60 elephant tusks. The final count totalled 735 bronze items, 61 of gold, 486 jades, turquoise ornaments, tigers' teeth, ivory, and cowrie shells.

Remarkable Bronzes

The bronzes are of a size and form unparalleled in China. The complete statue of a man stands 2.61 m (8.6 ft) high and weighs 180 kg (397 lb). He wears a crown, and a tunic richly embellished with images of dragons, animal heads, and crowns. His hands are held in a position suggestive of holding something curved and heavy, such as an elephant's tusk. A second unique bronze comprises a tree, complete with leaves, fruit, and buds, and with birds perched on its branches; it stood nearly 4 m (13 ft) high. A series of huge human heads with masklike features, some of gold, stand apart from any other bronzes of this period in China; one bronze mask with eyes protruding on stalks was 1.4 m (4.6 ft) wide.

These pits may have been connected with the burials of the kings of Shu, a state mentioned in the Shang oracle archives, but as yet no royal tombs have been uncovered (Bagley 2001; Gao Dalun 2001; Sage 1992). The burning of the contents, despite their value, rarity, and beauty, suggests a sacrificial or ritual purpose.

The quality of the offerings indicates great wealth, and some of the smaller objects provide clues to the use of items deposited in the pits. The function of the 57 *yazhang* jade

15.18 *(Above left) This statue of a man from Sanxingdui probably once held a curved object, such as an elephant tusk. It stands 2.61 m (8.6 ft) high, and weighs 180 kg (397 lb).*

15.19 *(Above right) The tree from Sanxingdui is probably the most remarkable of all the bronzes contained in the two sacrificial pits. It stands 3.96 m (13 ft) high.*

blades, for example, is represented by a small bronze figure who holds one of these blades, shown in a kneeling posture indicating a form of worship or sacrifice. The massive bronze human heads were probably the components of one or more ritual structures similar to those depicted on a model altar, while the numerous jades would also have had a ritual role.

The rulers of Sanxingdui supported a distinct bronze-casting tradition dedicated to the gigantic. There are few, if any, parallels in the ancient world for the size of the freestanding statue of a man, the trees, or the masks with animal features and eyes on stalks. The trees reveal innovative skill, and even the jades show a taste for the spectacular and novel.

vessels and weapons cast and the techniques of manufacture. It is also likely that the early Zhou rulers brought Shang specialists to their own workshops.

Excavations at **Luoyang** in Henan Province have uncovered a bronzeworking area that covered 700 x 300 m (2297 x 984 ft). Apart from the dwellings of the workers, it has also produced many fragments of clay molds and furnaces used to heat molten bronze. Production, which lasted from early in the dynasty until the second half of the 10th century BC, was intensive. The casting technique employed clay piece-molds, which could be decorated or incised with texts prior to being fired. As many as ten separate pieces were necessary in the case of complex vessels; these were then fitted together using mortise and tenon joints. There is evidence in other foundry areas for specialized production, wherein vessels were cast by one group, and chariot fittings or weapons by another. Such bronze workshops were established both in the royal domain and in the vassal states, enabling the latter to cast their own important ritual vessels, as well as weaponry that would in due course lead to competition and civil friction.

Indeed, it is in part through the analysis of the bronzes that social change, described by Jessica Rawson (1989) as a "ritual revolution," can be traced. This widespread change dates to the first half of the 9th century BC and is best documented in the mortuary record, the manner in which chariots were interred, the increasing importance of jade grave goods, and, most significantly, in ritual bronzes and the forms of the vessels being cast. Where formerly there had been a range of vessels to serve food or wine, now sets of virtually identical forms were cast, much heavier than their predecessors and with longer and similar, or even identical, inscriptions. Wine containers and serving cups are no longer found, and a series of new vessel forms was introduced. Well-tried vessel types, formerly rendered in clay, were now cast in bronze, and individual rank could be indicated by the number of virtually identical vessels that an individual possessed. Bells were adapted from southern prototypes. It seems that the sets of bronzes, which could be added to in number if resources permitted, were a means of exhibiting the status and achievements of particular lineages. Such a move encouraged the mass production of practically identical pieces, and the commercialization of a bronze industry hitherto dedicated to the provision of specific items for court ritual purposes.

The Western Zhou Dynasty was a vital and formative period in Chinese history: literature, music, and poetry flourished, bronzes reflect changing cultural preferences, and growing trade encouraged new administrative structures. Nevertheless, by the 8th century BC the Zhou court faced mounting external pressures. In 771 BC, the rulers of the eastern states moved King Yi Jiu to Luoyang. As King Ping, he reigned for 50 years until 721 BC, but now as first ruler of the dynasty known as the Eastern Zhou.

The Eastern Zhou Dynasty, 770–221 BC

The Eastern Zhou Dynasty is divided into the periods of the **Spring and Autumn Annals** (770–481 BC), and the **Warring States** (481–221 BC), both named after contemporary historical documents that recount the period in question (Li Xuequin 1985). The kings at Luoyang were too weak to control the power of the regional lords, and in place of a central authority, large and potent regional states had become established, known as the Five Hegemonies. Some of these, the Hua Xia states, controlled the old heartland of the central plains, and the center of gravity during the Spring and Autumn period was firmly placed there and east to Shandong Province. From the perspective of this center, other states were viewed as barbarous. The states themselves were also subject to factionalism and splintering, depending on the strength of the ruler of the day. Friction and rivalry came to a head during the aptly named Warring States period, when the states of Qi, Chu, Yan, Han, Zhao, Wei, and Qin, being the most powerful, were collectively known as the Ten Thousand Chariot states.

In addition to the known historical texts, archaeological research is now providing many more important documents from Eastern Zhou graves. Perhaps the most informative comes from the **tomb of Xi**, an archivist and lawyer whose grave contained many texts written on sets of bamboo slips. These describe battles and historic events, legal regulations, details of the unification of measurements, and accounts of legal decisions governing the establishment of Qin rule in the recently defeated state of Chu. Texts on silk and on official seals are also important sources of historical information, and as already noted, bronzes and pottery vessels were occasionally inscribed. A hoard of bronze weaponry from the Han city of **Zheng Han** contained items inscribed and dated with the name of the official in charge, indicating the importance of mass production of weaponry at the end of the Warring States period.

Although the dynasty continued, the Eastern Zhou court was virtually shorn of power after its move to Luoyang, and relied on the support of the major states (von Falkenhausen 1999). As feudal ties broke, it became accepted practice for states to expand through naked power shorn of morality or the bonds of kinship. It was in this milieu that the philosopher Confucius arose to rail against such perceived immorality from his eastern base, the state of Lu [see box: Confucianism]. At the same time, southern states beyond the pale of the Eastern Zhou empire rose in power, particularly the Chu of the middle Yangzi basin, the Wu and the Yue of the lower Yangzi, and the Shu of Sichuan. Adapting to this situation led to the development of the *Ba* system, in which the dominance of the ruler of one major state was accepted by the others. The *Ba* state was on occasion Zheng, Qi, or Jin, and toward the end of the period, Yue.

KEY DISCOVERY Confucianism

Confucius was China's most influential political philosopher and teacher. Named Kong Qiu, his students called him Kongzi, "Master Kong." As he grew in stature and reputation, he became known as Kong Fuzi, or "Our Master Kong," a title that was written in English as Confucius. He was born in 551 BC in the state of Lu, located in modern Shandong Province, into a high-status but impoverished family, and he was only three when his father died.

He showed an interest in scholarship from an early age. His first employment was in minor government positions, but his

15.20 *Fragment of a tablet inscribed with the "Xiping Stone Classics," the earliest Confucian writings inscribed on stone, dating from the Eastern Han dynasty. Seven Confucian classics were engraved on 46 stone tablets, which were later destroyed and survive only as fragments.*

passion for and skill in the Six Arts – calligraphy, history, poetry, archery, ritual, and music – soon equipped him as a teacher and sage. His approach to teaching, to instill knowledge and concern for public service, can be seen as a major turning point in Chinese education. He rose through increasingly important public positions in Lu, ultimately becoming the Minister of Justice, but disillusioned by the administration, he left Lu in self-imposed exile. During this time he visited the leaders of other states to outline his moral code, returning 12 years later to continue his teaching, editing of ancient texts, and writing on political philosophy. He died in 479 BC.

Teaching and Writings

Confucius's ideals are recorded in the *Analects*, meaning "a selection." In Chinese, they are known as the *Lunyu* ("Conversations"). These 20 chapters of recollections of conversations with their master were written by Confucius's followers after his death. Confucius lived at a time of weakening central Zhou authority and constant friction between rival rulers, but

instead of militarism and force, he advocated the concept of *ru*, meaning virtue or civility, which would lead to a person becoming *junzi*, that is, deserving of moral power through noble behavior.

In his scholarly role, Confucius is credited with editing and commenting on a number of significant historical documents. He is said, for example, to have added commentaries on the *Yi Jing* ("Book of Changes"), a notable text that explains the interpretation of divinations. He edited the *Shu Jing* ("Book of History"), which includes statements made by early kings, and possibly the *Li Ji* ("Record of Rites") and *Shi Jing* ("Book of Odes"), with commentaries.

Perhaps his most notable contribution to Chinese literature, however, was the *Chunqiu* ("Spring and Autumn Annals"), which recorded the history of the state of Lu, his own birthplace, between 722 and 481 BC. By compiling and safeguarding these texts, Confucius assured for himself an enduring place in the history of Chinese thought.

His influence was also felt well beyond his native China. With the Asuka Enlightenment in Japan (see p. 580), for example, the Yamato prince Shotoku issued injunctions incorporating Confucian ideals on proper behavior. In AD 603, a system of court ranks was established in the Yamato capital, and each of the 12 grades was accorded a name recalling Confucian virtues, beginning with the rank of Greater Virtue and ending with the rank of Lesser Knowledge.

There was also a new or secondary trend toward a feudal system, the result of the difficulties posed when a smaller state was subjugated. The answer to the problem of who was to be placed in control of the new territory was resolved by appointing men chosen for their loyalty. While this was a useful expedient, it held the seeds of future trouble because it led to the formation of regional elites, who might rise up against the center. Thus Jin was carved up into the new polities of Han, Wei, and Zhao. Moreover, contested succession led to a widespread policy of murdering descendants of previous kings. This set the stage for a political philosophy that, despite the efforts of Confucius and his disciples, followed the path of absolutism and self-interest.

Technological and Social Changes The Warring States period witnessed major advances in military strategy, and wars of increasing intensity led to the annihilation of states and their ruling houses. These events were fueled by the spread of a new metallurgical technology, involving the casting of molten iron into molds; this technical achievement required the control of very high temperatures, not matched in the West for centuries to come. Furthermore, rapid advances in agriculture meant that permanent armies could be raised. Successful states were led by kings with powerful ministers and well-organized social and economic systems, tending increasingly toward totalitarianism. Ultimately, no power could resist the state of Qin, which, under its ruler Qin Shi Huangdi, brought the Eastern Zhou dynasty to an end in 221 BC.

This competitive milieu encouraged art, architecture, industry, and warfare. New cities sprang up, and their internal layout changed. The state of **Zhang**, for example, had three capitals between 425 and 386 BC. The city became an anchor for the social elite in times of political stress, and civic plans thus required strong defenses. Moreover, increases in trade and the rise of the mercantile classes led to wholesale changes in the nature of the city. Formerly a royal administrative center, it became a metropolis of many classes and occupations, with the royal palace as the centerpiece. In place of the enclosed privacy of courts linked at ground level, palace designs stressed height and grandeur. At **Linzi** in Shandong Province, the foundations for the palace still stand 14 m (46 feet) high. At **Xiadu**, capital of Yan, in Hebei Province, the palace stood on top of a high mound that dominated the rest of the city.

Bronze and iron workshops kept specialists within reach of the ruler and his ministers, and bronze-casting during the Eastern Zhou period underwent a series of significant changes. The rise of powerful ministerial families and layers of bureaucrats spread the demand for fine pieces, leading to a hierarchical provision of bronzes in tombs. Meanwhile, war demanded weapons of unparalleled tensile strength, while ostentatious display led to the development of new decorative techniques. Exceptional bronzes were cast, represented at their peak by the *pan* and *zun* ritual serving vessels and the magnificent set of 65 bells, inscribed with the names of their tones in gold, from Leigudun tomb 1, the tomb of the Marquis of Zeng (433 BC) [see box: Tonglushan: A Copper Mining Site, p. 571]. Decoration on bronzes included patterned inlays of gold or silver, which are found on vessels as well as ornaments such as belt buckles, and luxury items such as the mirrors that proliferated in this period.

15.21 Gold vessel from the tomb of Marquis of Zeng: *this golden bowl and spoon were almost certainly used by the Marquis of Zeng at his dining table. They date to the mid-5th century BC. Height 11 cm (4.3 in).*

The Qin Dynasty, 221–207 BC

In 221 BC the head of the state of Qin, who had conquered the by-now impotent Zhou Dynasty, took the name Qin Shi Huangdi ("august emperor of Qin") and became the First Emperor of China. (The name "China" derives from Qin, pronounced "chin.") His reign saw sweeping reforms (Lewis 1999). He created 36 commanderies (provinces), each subdivided into counties. These commanderies were placed under a centrally appointed governor, who was a military commander and an inspector who ensured compliance with the Emperor's wishes. Qin Shi Huangdi ordered the adoption of a uniform system of writing known as the small seal script (*xiaozhuan*), a vital step in consolidating his grip on power. Uniformity was also applied to weights and measures, the gauge of wheeled vehicles, and the currency. The legal system was applied equally across the empire, based on the basic tenet of mutual responsibility.

Based on a principle of strong encouragement for agriculture at the expense of trade, the state maintained huge resources of labor. These were deployed on new roads that radiated out from the capital, and on the creation of a canal system. Some 300,000 men were set to work on the Great Wall, which ran along the borders of northern China to keep out the marauding Xiongnu, powerful steppe horsemen. More than 600,000 were engaged on the **Emperor's tomb** at **Lintong**, near modern Xi'an [**15.22**]. Whole communities were uprooted and sent into thinly populated regions, or dispatched to strengthen defenses and increase agricultural production.

Qin Shi Huangdi died in 210 BC at the age of 49, during a tour of inspection; his body was interred in his massive mortuary complex at Lintong. Texts describe the interior of his tomb, which has never been excavated, as being filled with the Emperor's personal belongings. The roof reflected the heavens in pearls, while the ground displayed the extent of the empire, with rivers of flowing mercury. The subterranean chambers that surrounded the central pyramid of the tomb were filled with the famous life-sized terracotta replicas of the Emperor's armies, including infantry, chariots, cavalry, and a command center [**15.23**]. Each soldier, mass-produced but then individually modeled, was painted and armed. Chambers also contained a replica of the imperial zoological garden, and a half-sized copy in bronze of the royal chariot, resplendent with four horses and the charioteer.

Following a court intrigue, Qin Shi Huangdi's legitimate successor was ordered to commit suicide on the basis of a forged directive, and the throne passed to Er Shi Huangdi ("second august emperor"), who was then aged 21. His reign was brief. Rebellions broke out in 209 BC, and the Second Emperor committed suicide two years later, bringing the Qin Dynasty to an early end.

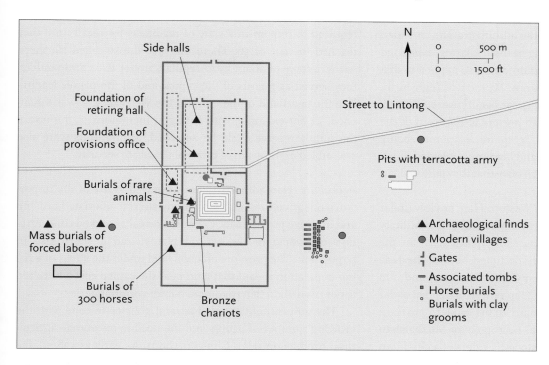

Side halls

Foundation of
retiring hall

Foundation of
provisions office

Burials of rare
animals

Mass burials of
forced laborers

Burials of
300 horses

Bronze
chariots

N

500 m

1500 ft

Street to Lintong

Pits with terracotta army

▲ Archaeological finds
● Modern villages
⌐ Gates
— Associated tombs
▪ Horse burials
° Burials with clay
  grooms

15.22 (Left) **The tomb of China's first emperor:** the tomb complex of Qin Shi Huangdi is one of the largest the world has seen. The Emperor took with him to the afterlife all his possessions and followers. The former were buried in pits or placed inside his mausoleum. The latter, represented in bronze or terracotta, were interred in huge underground chambers.

15.23 (Below) **Terracotta army:** the warriors of Qin Shi Huangdi emerge from pits near his tomb. Each terracotta model is about life size. Their armor, weapons, and disposition reveal the nature of warfare during the period of the Warring States.

The Han Dynasty, 206 BC–AD 220

The Han Dynasty was seminal in the development of Chinese civilization, initiating changes that are still part of the fabric of China (Twitchet and Loewe 1986). Like the Zhou Dynasty, the Han is divided into two halves, with an interregnum between AD 9 and 23. The earlier period is known as the Western Han Dynasty, and the later the Eastern Han. These names reflect the location of the capital, for after a long sojourn at Chang'an, the Eastern Han moved the capital in that direction, to Luoyang. The period of the interregnum saw the former regent Wang Mang take power, establishing the short-lived Xin, or "New," Dynasty.

Administration The inheritance of an empire with an administration based on legalist principles posed unique challenges. Although some dependent states were permitted, ruled by centrally appointed kings, the commandery system was maintained. The need for able administrators led to the foundation of a central training institution, where before entering government service students were taught by scholars versed in Confucian ethics. Toward the end of the Western Han Dynasty, there were 120,285 officials in the administration (Bielenstein 1954; Wang Zhongshu 1982). Government was headed by the Chancellor, the Imperial Counselor, and the Commander of the Armed Forces. Below them were nine ministries, one of which oversaw finance and the management of the economy. From 120 BC, when it was resolved to nationalize key industries, this ministry supervised the production and marketing of iron, salt, and alcohol products. The Commandant of Waters and Parks was an office created in 115 BC; among other duties the holder of this post controlled the royal mint.

The marked hierarchy within the administration, in which bureaucrats were ranked according to their salaries, expressed as annual payment in bushels of grain, was also applied to that powerful institution, the royal harem. Women of high birth, unimpeachable personal life, and great beauty were selected, attended by eunuchs who were also present at the court of the Empress. With so many child or infant emperors being enthroned, the Dowager Empress and her family wielded much power, attracting in many cases such envy that they suffered virtual extinction.

The territorial expansion of the Western Han, notably under Emperor Wudi (140–87 BC), required a strong army. Military force was deployed to take new territory, particularly in the northwest, where huge tracts were occupied beyond the Jade Gate (a fortified outpost in far west Gansu Province) and into the Tarim basin. To the south, the Han empire extended as far as the rich Red River basin in Vietnam; in the modern province of Yunnan, excavations at the royal necropolis of **Shizhaishan** have revealed the tombs of the aristocratic rulers of a chiefdom that succumbed to the imperial reach of the Han. To the east, colonization also spread into the Korean peninsula (see below). Thereafter, it was necessary to provide for frontier defense, particularly along the extended **Great Wall** [15.24], where the Xiongnu horsemen were a constant threat. There was also a problem of security within the empire itself, for provincial discontent and uprisings, such as those of the Red Eyebrows and the Yellow Turbans, were always possible.

Conscription was compulsory except for top aristocrats and those who could afford to buy exemption. At the age of 23, a young man underwent a year of military training within his home commandery before being posted for another year to active service. Survivors could then return home, but were required to remain in a state of readiness for recall until they reached the age of 56. There was also the so-called Northern Army, a force of about 3500 regulars under five commanders; they served as guards of the capital and of the passes leading into the heartland of the empire, the Wei Valley. If war threatened, as, for example, with Xiongnu incursions in the north, the militia reserve could be deployed. Militia units were also assembled in the event of internal threats to security.

Agriculture Han administrators were well aware of the importance of agriculture, and took many steps to alleviate hardship and improve productivity. Censuses reveal a marked concentration of people in the central plains, and a sharp rise in population. The pressure on good land under the stress of a rising population meant that land near the capital cost a hundred times more than that in remote border commanderies.

The government adopted several policies to cope with the growing number of people and the need to encourage agricultural production (Hsu Cho-yun 1980). As early as 178 BC, the adviser Zhao Zuo urged the settlement of farmers in the northern border regions as a bulwark against incursions. Land was provided, housing constructed, and there were tax remissions and medical facilities. In 119 BC, this policy was intensified following a serious flooding of the Yellow River, when over 700,000 people were moved north. There was also a steady drift to the south, and into the area where rice replaced millet as the staple.

Irrigation was one of many techniques applied to increase production. Provincial administrators often took the initiative in devising and implementing irrigation schemes. Both the construction of canals and dikes, and agriculture itself, were facilitated by the increasing abundance of iron, which was turned into plows, sickles, scythes, spades, and hoes. In 85 BC,

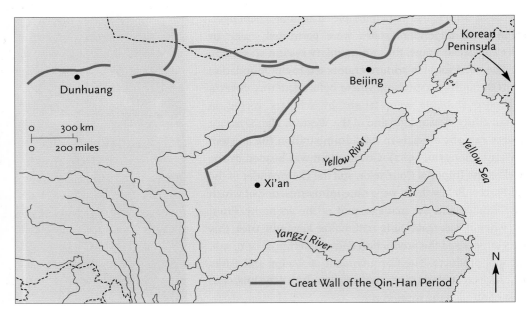

15.24 *The Great Wall of China: the construction of defensive walls was a common practice during the period of Warring States in China. With the unification of the country by the Qin emperor, hundreds of thousands of workmen were deployed in the north to begin the construction of a massive wall to defend China against the Xiongnu, warrior horsemen from Mongolia. The wall has been extended, embellished, and repaired for over 2000 years, up to the present.*

Dunhuang

Korean Peninsula

Beijing

300 km
200 miles

Yellow River

Xi'an

Yellow Sea

Yangzi River

N

—— Great Wall of the Qin-Han Period

KEY SITE Tonglushan: A Copper Mining Site

Tonglushan, which means "great smelting place," is the best preserved of all copper mining sites in China (Zhou Baoquan et al. 1988). It is located about 140 km (87 miles) south of Wuhan in Hubei Province, and thus would have been, for most of its existence, within the territory of the state of Chu. It was discovered in 1965, and intensive research began in 1974, including excavations of the mining pits and surface smelting features.

Mining began here during the late 2nd millennium BC and continued for at least 1000 years, the complex so intensively exploited that it covered at least 140 ha (346 acres) and yielded over half a million tons of ore.

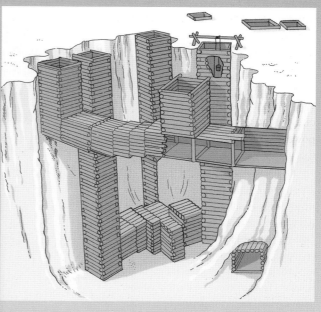

15.25 *A schematic cross-section drawing of the Tonglushan copper mine, the best preserved in China. It was in use for at least 1000 years from the late 2nd millennium BC on, and is estimated to have yielded over half a million tons of ore. Some shafts were 60 m (197 ft) deep.*

Demand for Copper

Knowledge of bronze – an alloy of copper and tin – came to China from the west via the ancient Silk Road [see box: The Origins of Chinese Metallurgy, p. 582]. As well as copper, China is rich in sources of tin, and by the late 3rd millennium BC bronze was being cast in northwestern China into small artifacts such as knives and awls. With the Xia Dynasty, the first large bronze vessels were being cast at Erlitou, and there was a huge increase in the quantity and size of ritual bronzes and weaponry during the course of the Shang and Changjiang states of the 2nd millennium BC [see box: Sanxingdui, pp. 564–65]. This placed continuous and growing demands on copper sources.

Mining and Smelting

At Tonglushan, the mine shafts probed up to 60 m (197 ft) into the ground, so deep that they pierced the water table; wooden troughs channeled water to special sumps, where wooden buckets and windlasses raised it to the surface. Before iron became available, the ore was secured with bronze pickaxes and mattocks, but iron hammers and spades made for more efficient extraction.

The narrow mine pits and shafts, only 50 cm (19.6 in) wide, were now given enlarged entrance galleries and shafts, and lined with wood. Where air has since been excluded from the lower workings, wooden supports, buckets, and windlasses have survived to the present day. The cuprite and malachite ores, when brought to the surface, were hand-sorted and crushed with anvils to aid smelting. Iron was employed as a flux (i.e., used to promote the fusion of the ore), and ingots comprised 93 percent copper and 5 percent iron. Enclosed furnaces for the actual smelting had a main firing chamber and a second chamber for tapping the metal.

Copper from Tonglushan was cast into some of the finest bronzes known. Pride of place must be accorded the unrivaled *zun* and *pan* vessels from the tomb of the Marquis of Zeng at Leigudun. These were made first by the traditional piece-mold system, but then incorporated a modification developed in the 6th century BC known as the pattern-block technique, a form of mold-making that enabled the mass production of decoration.

Decorative embellishments, most in the form of dragons and mythical serpents, were cast by the lost-wax method, in which the original model is formed in wax, then coated with clay; the object is then fired, melting the wax, and the resulting clay mold is filled with metal. The figures thus created were then fixed to the vessel with solder.

---

the official Zhao Guo introduced the seed drill. In this the plow-share itself was pierced by holes through which the drill was inserted, so that plowing and seeding were undertaken simultaneously. The Han dynasties witnessed other vital innovations in productivity, such as waterpowered bellows used in the production of iron, and the application of waterpower to milling grain.

A manual on field techniques in agriculture, compiled in the reign of Emperor Zhengdi (33–7 BC), reveals the rapid advance of farming methods under the Western Han. It covers the cultivation of a wide range of plants, including wheat, mil-let, soybeans, hemp, and mulberry trees. One innovation, the pit field system, showed how 15,000 plants could be grown in a plowed field measuring only 42 x 11 m (138 x 36 ft).

Religious Beliefs Religious beliefs under the Han Dynasty comprised a mixture of old forms of worship and new, exotic ones. There was also a distinction between court ceremonials and those of the countryside. The former began with the worship of Di, the supreme god. The concept of Di had been enlarged during the Qin Dynasty to four aspects, and under Emperor Guang

KEY SITE Mawangdui

Mawangdui is located in a suburb of Changsha in Hunan Province, southern China. Three intact tombs investigated there contained the remains of Li Cang, the Marquis of Dai; his wife Xin Zhui; and their son. The Marquis, who had been Chancellor to the king of the Western Han state of Chu, died in 168 BC.

Each grave was marked by a tumulus with a diameter of about 60 m (197 ft), below which lay a rectangular pit sunk up to 17 m (56 ft) into the ground. The cypress-wood chambers were encased in thick layers of charcoal and clay to protect the contents from air and damp, thereby preserving the organic remains from decay. The tomb chambers were divided into compartments, which contained the nested coffins and mortuary offerings.

Lady Dai

In Tomb 1, the latest and best preserved of the three, the body of Xin Zhui ("Lady Dai") had been placed within the innermost of four coffins, each elaborately decorated in lacquer and painted scenes showing clouds, monsters dancing and playing zithers, and auspicious animals. The innermost coffin was covered in fine silks decorated with embroidery and feathers, over which lay a silk tomb banner.

Xin Zhui's body was perfectly preserved, down to the presence of red blood in her veins and the remains of the melons that comprised her last meal. She was 1.54 m (5 ft) tall, and overweight. The ingredients that were present in her tomb for treating heart problems – magnolia bark, peppercorns, and cinnamon – had not prevented her fatal heart attack.

15.26 *The tomb banner from Mawangdui tomb 1. Placed over her inner coffin, this banner would have been carried in Lady Dai's funerary procession. It was an illustrated guide for her soul to reach heaven.*

All requirements for eternal life accompanied her. A tiny theatre in a compartment beyond her coffins contained her couch, walking stick, and slippers. Some 162 wooden figures exhibit the courtly life of a Han aristocratic family: models of musicians perform on zithers and panpipes, accompanied by eight dancers. An actual zither was found in a brocade bag and had 25 strings still in place, while a set of pipes was also found in its original bag.

A complete wardrobe of fine silks filled bamboo cases. One silk gown with sleeves almost 2 m (6.6 ft) long weighed just 49 g (1.73 oz). Xin Zhui's personal cosmetics were included, together with a hairpiece and mittens. Food and chopsticks awaited her use, laid out on lacquer platters, and the texts on the 312 bamboo slips, which neatly catalogued all these offerings, included menus for her favorite dishes, including a venison and taro stew. Her fare also included lotus root, chicken, peaches, melons, dried ginger, and pickled vegetables.

Paintings on Silk

The passage of Xin Zhiu's soul to paradise is illustrated by the silk tomb banner that had in all probability been carried in her funerary procession and then placed over the coffin. It portrayed the lady in life, supported by her walking stick, and provided a guide for her spirit to ascend to heaven. The painted scenes show her being laid out after death, surrounded by mortuary vessels and attendants, with the underworld below her. Above, she is seen standing in an elegant robe accompanied by divine messengers, while the passage to paradise is seen higher up, guarded by two leopards. Once through this portal we see heaven itself, with the sun, moon, and celestial beings.

The burial in Tomb 3 of Xin Zhiu's son followed the same pattern: fine coffins, a tomb banner, and personal belongings. His silk paintings showed a long procession and images of fitness exercises. There is a military map, and classical histories such as the *Yi Jing* ("Book of Changes"), and one of the bamboo documents from his library provided the world's first known sex manual.

Wudi (reigned AD 25–75) to five, each determined by a different color. Emperor Wudi further expanded the official deities to include new gods and goddesses, including those known as the Earth Queen and the Grand Unity. Imperial rituals involved animal sacrifices and burnt offerings. Mount Dai, a peak of great holiness in Zhejiang Province, was scaled by emperors Qin Shi Huangdi, Wudi, and Guang Wudi. In 31 BC, there was a change in favor of the deity Dian, Heaven, and new forms of

worship were put in place to link the ruling dynasty with this god's heavenly mandate.

The religious beliefs of the Han, in particular in the quest for immortality, are closely linked with the development of mortuary rituals (Loewe 1982). The major Han emperors, as well as the nobility, invested much labor in their tombs, and in ensuring that all their needs in the afterlife would be catered for. They thus bequeathed to history remarkable assemblages of their

15.27 *Han tomb model:* *such models were often placed in Han dynasty graves, and these are a vital source of information on everyday life. Here we see a rural farming scene, including people working in the rice fields, ducks, and a crab.*

possessions, from clothing to libraries, furniture, and retainers represented as clay or wooden models. Such treatment of the deceased was based on the notion that on death, the body resolved into the soul (*hun*), which with proper assistance could enter paradise, and the body (*bo*), which remained behind on earth. The *hun* required directions for its passage to paradise, and had to pass through several strictly guarded gates before it could join the gods. The *bo* had to be accompanied below with the goods necessary to continue the lifestyle to which the dead person had been accustomed, and this was best achieved if the body could be preserved from corruption (see below).

The mortuary complex of Emperor Jingdi (156–141 BC), near **Xi'an** in Shaanxi Province, lies under a steeply sided mound of earth, surrounded by a walled enclosure that formerly contained four entrance gateways oriented to the cardinal points. Between the wall and the mound were many pits, of which 86 have so far been identified and 11 opened by archaeologists; the contents represent departments of state. One pit contains the models of about 400 dogs, 200 sheep, and many pigs laid out in neat rows. Two others contain official seals, one from the kitchen. There are also 40,000 clay models of individuals,

including foot soldiers and cavalry, court women, and eunuchs, all of whom once had wooden movable arms and fine silk clothing. The adjacent tomb of the Empress has at least 31 pits of its own, and there is also a mound covering the tomb of a favorite concubine.

No imperial Han tomb chamber has been opened under scientific conditions, and many, if not all, were looted in antiquity. However, the wealth of goods placed in the tombs of high-status private individuals can be seen in a handful of intact burials, and may give some idea of what has been lost from royal tombs. Three such elite graves at **Mawangdui** contained the remains of Li Cang, the Marquis of Dai, and his wife and son (Wu Hung 1992) [see box: Mawangdui].

Only emperors and very high-status aristocrats could be buried in the jade suits that were believed to preserve the body uncorrupted, thus continuing the life of the *bo*. The status of the deceased determined whether the wafers of jade were stitched together with gold, silver, or bronze thread. The tomb at **Mancheng** of Prince Liu Sheng, the older brother of Emperor Wudi, was opened in 1968. It had been cut into the living rock to a depth of 52 m (170 ft), and incorporated a lateral chamber 37 m (121 ft) wide. A second tomb, which housed his wife, was found 100 m (328 ft) away. The entrance to Liu Sheng's tomb opened onto a long lateral corridor that housed his chariots and horses; half of this was filled with rows of ceramic containers for food and wine. The central hall was filled with his bronze vessels, lacquer bowls and containers, and fine ceramics. To the back of the complex lay the burial chamber itself, together with superbly crafted artifacts of gold, silver, and jade. Both the prince and his wife had been interred in jade suits [15.28]. Liu Sheng's was made of 2690 wafers, stitched together with gold thread; his wife's suit incorporated 2156 pieces of jade. Each suit would have taken one craftsman ten years to complete.

15.28 *The jade suit of Prince Liu Sheng:* *jade suits such as this one were supposed to give immortality. They were incredibly expensive, and reserved for members of the royal family. It dates to 113 BC and was made of 2690 finely shaped wafers of jade, held together with gold thread that weighed over a kilogram. It was found in Liu Sheng's tomb at Mancheng.*

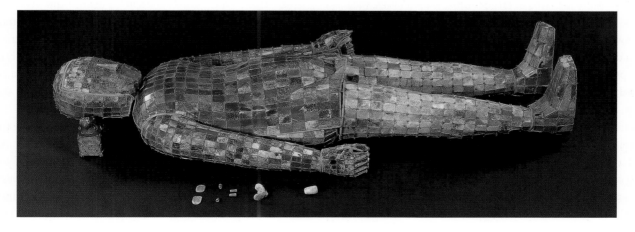

The fact that the Han Dynasty brought relative peace and prosperity to China for four centuries, after an equally long period of internecine strife, is a testament to the adroit manner in which the administration knitted together the fabric of the empire. Its rulers maintained a central mint and the means to collect broadly based taxation. They invested in agriculture and transport, and organized the production of iron for a wide range of purposes. Their system of selection for the civil service has stood the test of time in many other states, and through aristocratic patronage, the arts and literature flourished. The Han Dynasty also saw China expand to frontiers still recognizable in the political map of East Asia.

Korea

In 108 BC, Han armies occupied the northern part of Korea and founded four provinces. The longest lived, Lelang, near modern Pyongyang, remained under Chinese domination for approximately four centuries, during which the local elites were accorded Chinese titles and administrative functions. The Chinese presence provoked resentment, however, and the rise of indigenous states. The period of ascendancy of three of these states – Koguryo, Paekche, and Silla – became known as the Three Kingdoms period (57 BC–AD 668) and lasted until Silla unified the peninsula in alliance with the Tang Dynasty of China, thus opening the period Great Silla (AD 668–918).

Koguryo

According to tradition, Koguryo was founded in 37 BC, and it survived until its defeat at the hands of its southern rival, Silla, in AD 668. It was recognized as an independent and powerful polity after AD 313, when its forces successfully defeated the Lelang commandery (Hyung Il Pai 2000; Portal 2000). It was for long the dominant force in the politics and economy of northern Korea. Although good agricultural land was scarce and the climate harsh, trade and agriculture flourished, and the Koguryo kings have bequeathed a rich archaeological legacy that includes the remains of large tombs, walled cities, palaces, temples, and defensive walls.

Following the defeat of Lelang, the Koguryo leaders established a university in AD 372 to train their rising administrators, with a preference for Confucian ethics. Imports from China included paper, as well as silk clothing and weapons; in return, Koguryo exported furs, gold, and silver. Weaponry was important in the expansion of Koguryo to the south, as is recorded in an inscription from Ipsongni in Chinese characters dated to the mid-5th century AD, which recorded a military victory.

The early Koguryo capital at **Jian**, in the Yalu River valley, is impressively surrounded by stone walls and a moat. A reservoir lay within the walled precinct, together with a royal palace. In AD 427 the capital was moved south to **Pyongyang** on the Taedong River, where walled defenses, a palace, and the foundations of Buddhist temples survive. Another walled city, **Fushun**, incorporated gateways within which archaeologists have recovered plowshares, coins, and chariot fittings.

Elite Koguryo tombs comprised mounds raised over stone chambers. Although all have been looted, wall frescoes [15.29] have survived. The tombs at Jian include many vigorous scenes. Tomb 1, known as the Tomb of the Dancers, includes images of festive activities. The dead man and his consort are depicted in tomb 12, together with paintings of hunting scenes in which mounted noblemen hunt deer, tigers, and bears with bow and arrow. Mountains are figuratively depicted, and some paintings were enhanced by the inclusion of gold inlay and jeweled ornaments. At **Chinpari**, 15 tombs have been counted, the fourth being embellished with stars in gold foil on its ceiling. **Anak** tomb 3, in the lower reaches of the Taedong River, is particularly interesting, for the mound covered stone chambers in the form of a palace. The inscription records that this was the burial of Dong Shou, who was interred in AD 357. He was depicted in a carriage attended by a procession of 250 servants (Barnes 2001).

Kaya

Kaya was a confederation of city-states located in the southern tip of Korea, an area dominated by the Naktong River. This region is noted for the quality of its iron ore. From the early centuries of the 1st millennium AD until it was absorbed by the kingdom of Silla between 532 and 562, Kaya was heavily engaged in the smelting and export of iron utensils, armor, and ingots. Although a few fortresses are known in this region, most information on Kaya comes from its burials, which comprise pit graves dug into hillsides, as well as mounds raised over stone-lined tomb chambers.

Kaya's small size, and its vulnerability in respect to its two powerful neighbors, Silla and Paekche, underlay its need for self-defense. At **Paekchonni**, iron armaments have been recovered from the graves. Near Pusan, the cemetery of **Pokchondong** has furnished iron armor, helmets, and horse masks (the Kaya military were renowned for the strength of their cavalry). The presence of iron armor is particularly intriguing: most such finds in Korea concentrate in this area, and the style is closely identified with armor from 5th-century AD Japanese burials (Nelson 1993).

A royal grave of the 3rd century AD at **Taesongdong** included rows of pottery vessels beyond the head and feet, while a Scythian bronze vessel originally from the steppes of southern Russia reveals widespread trade contacts. There was much commerce also with the growing states of Japan. Tomb 38 at this site included no fewer than 16 suits of armor, Han-style

15.29 Koguryo fresco: *wall painting from tomb 3, Anak. In this scene a nobleman is served by his wife.*

mirrors from China, quivers, swords, and shields. Bronze ornaments of Japanese origin were also recovered.

The most remarkable graves come from the royal cemetery of **Chisandong** near Koryong. Two were opened in 1979, to reveal not only the large central mortuary chambers for the royal dead, but also smaller stone-lined tombs for sacrificed victims immolated with their deceased ruler. These people ranged from girls barely over seven years old, to men and women in their 50s. This mortuary tradition stresses the authoritarian nature of a state constantly under threat up to its final subjugation in the 6th century AD.

Paekche

The state of Paekche, located in southwestern Korea, was traditionally founded in 18 BC, and its economy was basically agrarian. The court was literate in Chinese by the 4th century AD, and adopted Buddhism in AD 384. Paekche was arguably the most cultured of the early Korean kingdoms, and exercised considerable influence over Japan (see below), sending the first Buddha images there in AD 552. Wars with Koguryo and Silla resulted in at least two moves of the capital, and Paekche was finally confronted by an alliance between the Chinese Tang Dynasty and Silla in AD 660.

Military defeat was accompanied by widespread destruction and looting, such that few structures survive intact. Nevertheless, archaeological research has uncovered many sites. At **Mongchon**, the walls and moat enclosed an area of nearly 23 ha (57 acres), within which lay a palace and a reservoir. Imported Chinese ceramics attest to occupation during the late 3rd and early 4th centuries AD, but the city was eventually taken by Koguryo forces. Another fort at **Isong Sansong** was defended by an extensive stone wall; it also contained a palace structure. A large urban site has been identified at **Pungnamni**, covering an area of at least 1500 x 300 m (4921 x 984 ft), with walls at least 5 m (16.4 ft) high.

Paekche mounded tombs had a re-entry passage, which facilitated looters. Tomb 3 at **Sokchondong** still contained two gold earrings, part of a gold crown, and Chinese pottery of the 4th century AD. Wooden coffins were found at the **Karakdong** cemetery, whereas to the south at **Naju**, mounds covered jar burials in which two vessels were placed mouth to mouth; one contained part of a gilded bronze crown. At **Kongju**, the tomb of King Muryong, who died in AD 523, has been found intact. The land was purchased from the earth god, the price being recorded on an inscription that still bore the coins used in payment. Within, the two royal corpses had been buried with a wealth of superb grave goods, including gold crowns that would have been joined to silk caps.

Silla

The most powerful of the early Korean kingdoms, Silla was located in the southeastern part of the peninsula; with Chinese help it overcame Kaya, Koguryo, and Paekche during the 6th and 7th centuries AD. Mythical and much later historic records ascribe the origins of Silla to a confederation of clans that in 37 BC resolved on alliance against external dangers. Gradually this group developed into a powerful state that came into regular conflict along its borders with Koguryo to the north and

Paekche to the west. The king originally held the title *Kosogan* ("big man"), but by the 4th century AD, a crucial period in the development of Korean states, he had become the *Maripkan*, or hereditary king. The rules of succession incorporated queens, and three are known to have reigned. The early prowess of the Silla state may well have been based on the rich iron ore deposits of Hwangsong-dong, which lie near the capital of **Kyongju**. Iron was among the most likely of Silla exports to Japan.

The ranks of the Silla state were determined by ancestry, the highest being *songgol* ("holy bone"), for those with a right to rule. The *chingol* ("true bone") came next, before three further ranks and then the commoners. This last group was largely engaged in rice agriculture, or worked in one of the 14 state departments specializing in the production of fine silk, leather goods, metal weapons and implements, woolen garments, tables, and wooden containers. Much of this output was traded, particularly with China. Unlike Koguryo and Paekche, Silla preferred to retain its own shamanistic religious practices against the spread of Buddhism, which failed to take hold until the early 5th century AD.

The Silla capital and associated burial mounds at **Panwolsong**, in the Kyongju basin, have attracted much archaeological research. The earliest phases of state formation might well be represented at **Choyangdong**. Dating to the 1st–2nd centuries AD, the pit graves from this site have furnished Han-style bronze mirrors and exotic glass beads. The burials from **Kujongdong** also include pits containing wooden coffins, along with grave goods such as iron spears and bronze swords.

The six principal phases of Silla mortuary remains date to AD 300–550. They are dominated by the royal graves at **Kyongju**, where 155 mounds survive. A unique type of tomb was created here, consisting of a wooden chamber covered by a stone mound. One of these, the tomb of the Heavenly Horse [**15.30**], was 6.5 m long and 4.2 m wide (21 x 14 ft). A lacquered wooden coffin was placed within the chamber, positioned so that the head pointed to the east. A wooden container for mortuary offerings lay adjacent to the coffin. This chamber was then covered by a massive tumulus comprising thousands of heavy river boulders, rising to a height of 7.5 m (25 ft), with a diameter of 23.5 m (77 ft); there was no re-entry passage. In turn, the stone mound was covered in earth to a height of nearly 13 m (43 ft).

The contents of such royal graves reveal a rich and opulent society. Foremost are the golden crowns, which took the form of tree- or antler-like projections [**15.31**]. Jade and gold ornaments were attached to the trees, some in the form of leaves; other gold attachments fell as tassels from the ring of the crown. The royal dead also wore elaborate gold belts, that from the Tomb of the Golden Crown attaining a length of 2 m (6.6 ft). They, too, were embellished with dangling gold ornaments, including a model of a fish and a basket. The Tomb of the Washing Vessel, so-called after the bronze vessel found within, yielded a lacquered wooden mask embellished with blue eyes and a golden background. Gold finger- and toe-rings, bracelets, and heavily ornamented earrings are also regularly encountered. The kings and queens wore bronze shoes with gold attachments on the soles, an impractical form of footwear possibly worn only on ceremonial occasions, when the monarchs may have been carried aloft. Male burials included much armor – iron swords, arrowheads, and helmets – as well as accoutrements for horse riding, such as saddles, harness, and stirrups.

The Silla landscape was dominated by fortresses, several strategically placed around the capital. Panwolsong is the most significant, because it housed the royal palace. A stone-walled fort also protected the port of Pusan. Buddhist temples were

15.30 (Right) **The Tomb of the Heavenly Horse:** *the painting on birch bark that gives the tomb, at Kyongju, Korea, its name. It belongs to the Silla kingdom of the 5th–6th centuries AD. Height 53 cm (21 in).*

15.31 (Opposite above) **Silla gold crown:** *the Silla kingdom was renowned for its goldwork. This crown comes from the Gold Crown tomb at Kyongju. 5th–6th centuries BC. Height 27.5 cm (11 in).*

15.32 (Opposite below) **The Sokkuram Buddha:** *carved in granite, this sculpture dates to the 8th century AD. Height 3.3 m (11 ft).*

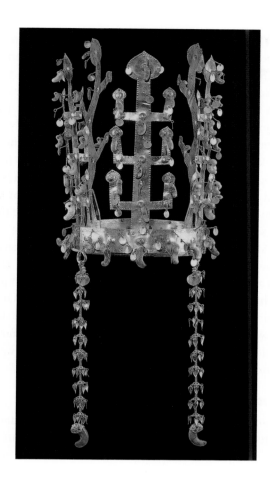

The Buddha is seen here within a cave, flanked by two *bodhisattvas*, followers of the Buddha who chose not to attain *nirvana*, but rather to stay on earth to help others. Silla craftspeople were also adept at casting bronze figures, as seen in the late 7th-century AD guardians from the **Kamun-sa temple**, each standing about 22 cm (8.7 in) in height. Gold was also used as a medium for portraying the Buddha. Two fine examples come from the **Hwangbok-sa** temple at Kyongju.

A specific Silla style of architecture and associated sculpture developed by the 8th century AD, the most prominent example being the **Sokkuram cave temple** at Mount Toham, near Kyongju. This famous site comprises three chambers constructed of granite blocks; the circular shrine room, with a diameter of 8 m (26 ft), contains the finest Silla Buddha sculpture, standing 3.3 m (10.8 ft) high [**15.32**]. The Buddha sits serenely on a throne, and was accompanied by images of *bodhisattvas* and disciples. One unusual aspect of later Silla sculpture was the casting of images of the Buddha in iron, which was then gilded. Some Silla specialists continued this tradition after the rise of the Koryo state in 918, and the transfer of the center of power in Korea to Kaesong, north of Seoul.

constructed, one of which, built in Kyongju by Queen Sondok in AD 645, survives to this day. Investigations there have revealed the presence of Chinese porcelain of the Tang Dynasty (AD 618–906), confirming trade with China.

Great Silla, AD 668–918

With the unification of Korea in AD 668, we enter the period known as Great (or Unified) Silla, which endured until Silla was conquered by the state of Koryo in AD 918. Great Silla was at its height in the 8th century AD, and was in regular contact with the Tang court in China. Indeed, it is said that the capital of Kumsong, modern Kyongju, was modeled on the Chinese city of Chang'an, and might have attained a population of over a million. Excavations at Kyongju have provided a rare glimpse of palace life, particularly the restoration of the Anapchi Lake, with its ornamental pavilions and bank depicting the outline of Korea, Japan, and Taiwan. The mud at the lake bottom has provided a rich array of artifacts relating to palace life, including wooden tablets bearing administrative records.

Buddhism flourished under Great Silla, and many temples with statues of the Buddha were spread across the landscape. Granite was widely employed in sculpture, which has permitted the survival of complete works of art. A fine example comes from **Mount P'algong**, 60 km (37 miles) northwest of Kyongju.

Japan

Early Yamato

The Japanese kingdom of Yamato, centered in western Honshu, developed from the Late Yayoi culture (discussed in Chapter 7) in the 3rd century AD (Barnes 1988). It was ruled by *okimi*, or great kings, whose burial mounds were known as *kofun*. The kingdom was undergoing rapid development by about AD 300 (dated on the basis of imported Chinese mirrors from burial mounds), and lasted for about four centuries. Our knowledge of Yamato comes from three main sources. The first are two early historic accounts compiled by royal order in the early 8th century AD, known as the *Nihongi* and *Kojiki* (Aston 1995). There are also some inscriptions, for example on swords recovered from elite tombs; finally, there is the evidence of archaeology (Pearson 1986).

Kofun burial mounds concentrate around the shores of the Inland Sea, between Honshu, Kyushu, and Shikoku islands, and match in many respects contemporary tombs in Korea. Particular stress in Japan has been given to the huge mounded tombs found in the Nara basin, southeast of Osaka, as representing the earliest phase of Yamato. This reflects the political domination of this region in the early 8th century, during the compilation of the *Kojiki* and *Nihongi* historic texts. The rulers at that time sought local origins for their royal ancestry, and the names of the early Yamato kings are thus recorded; attempts

have been made to match them with particular burial mounds. In general, this early phase of Yamato was characterized by large tumuli, in which dead leaders were interred in wooden coffins sunk into the tops of the mounds. They were associated in death with such exotic prestige goods as jasper and tuff jewelry, bronze mirrors, and iron weaponry, including body armor.

According to the histories, the earliest dynasty, named after the first king, Sujin, comprised five kings, who reigned from AD 219 to 346. Sujin, described as "he who ruled first," was closely involved in the worship of the *kami* (deity or spirit) of Mount Miwa, in the southeastern flank of the Nara plain, and thereby sought sacred powers of legitimacy. It is here, at the foot of Mount Miwa, that six colossal *kofun* mounds have been examined; they vary in length from 207 to 310 m (679 to 1017 ft). Sujin is also described as a military leader who sent out princes to fight his enemies, and took captives, implying that there were rival polities around the Inland Sea and into Kyushu. That the period was one of competition and militarism is documented archaeologically in the widespread placement of iron weapons and armor in elite tombs.

The Growth of Yamato Power

The second dynasty of Yamato is named after its founder, Ojin, whose reign dates traditionally fall between AD 346 and 395. It was during his rule that Korean tutors brought literacy to Japan. The political center initially moved north in the Nara basin to **Saki**, where a group of very large *kofun* is located. However, by AD 400 the power base had moved west, out of the Nara basin and onto the Osaka plains near the shore of the Inland Sea. Six subsequent rulers are named in the early historic accounts, ending with Yuryaku (reigned AD 457–479). If these dates are accurate, Ojin would have been the ruler to whom the Shichishito sword was presented by the ruler of the Korean kingdom of Paekche in AD 369. This gold-inlaid ceremonial weapon, which is still kept in the Isonokami shrine in Tenri, south of Nara, reflects the strong relations that existed between Paekche and Yamato, a relationship that brought much valued iron to Japan.

While it is clear that the Yamato kings of the 5th century AD commanded considerable military power and engaged in political relations with contemporary Korean states, little is known of their administration. They must have controlled labor in order to construct their massive tombs and excavate irrigation works. Chronicles refer to a number of court positions, such as guards, and sword- and quiver-bearers, while the close relations with Korea brought immigrant scribes. There were also specialist craft-workers. The rulers, again according to the early historic accounts of the period, were less concerned with rituals than

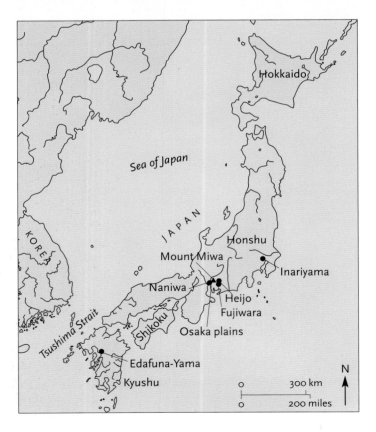

15.33 Japan: *map showing major sites mentioned in the text.*

15.34, 15.35 *(Left, below left)* **Nintoku's tomb:** *the tomb of Emperor Nintoku at Mozu, Japan. This is the largest keyhole-shaped kofun known, with a total length of nearly 500 m (1640 ft).*

15.36 *(Below right)* **Terracotta** **haniwa:** *figures from Japanese mounded tombs portray the dress and activities of the kofun period elite. This example shows a seated female, possibly a shaman, from Oizumi-machi, Ora county; c. 6th century AD. Height 94 cm (37 in).*

earlier kings, and spent more of their time organizing such secular activities as the provision of irrigation works and the suppression of regional dissent.

The move of the political center onto the Osaka plains involved the erection of probably the largest earth-mounded tombs ever constructed. The **Furuichi** group contains the so-called Ojin tomb, which attained a length of 420 m (1378 ft), while the **Mozu** group incorporated the tomb associated with the Emperor Nintoku, which is 486 m (1595 ft) long [**15.34, 15.35**]. These massive tombs also incorporated coffins formed by joining together large stone slabs. The grave offerings in the elite tombs of this period that have been examined included huge caches of iron weaponry and armor, as well as tools; one interment located near the Ojin tomb contained 77 iron swords. From AD 450, gold and silver ornaments of Korean inspiration were also found. Elite tombs were now surrounded by moats and ringed by clay *haniwa*, representations of houses, people, and animals [**15.36**]. Tomb chambers were lined with massive stones, and coated with clay to counter damp; charcoal and pebble-based drains were used for the same purpose.

The change from tomb offerings such as bronze mirrors, which stressed ritual, to increasing quantities of weaponry and armor has been cited as evidence for an actual invasion by foreigners who introduced cavalry warfare. This much-debated theory has not been sustained by archaeological evidence. The alternative, and more likely, hypothesis is that the second Yamato dynasty developed from the first with a change in its

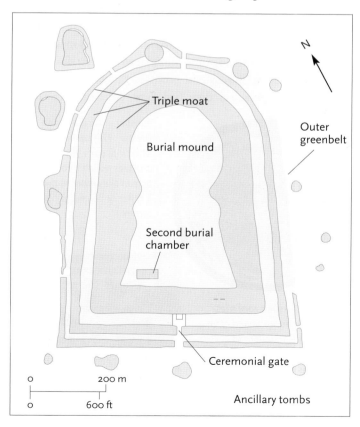

Triple moat

Burial mound

Outer greenbelt

N

Second burial chamber

Ceremonial gate

Ancillary tombs

0   200 m

0   600 ft

political center, perhaps to take advantage of the power of local clans, in a context of increasing political contact with Korean counterparts. This trend involved territorial gains by the Yamato rulers against former rivals to the west, intent no doubt on securing access to the Tsushima Strait and therefore to Korea (Totman 2000).

Inscribed swords also provide evidence for the extension of Yamato control during the 5th century. That from **Inariyama** in Sakitima Prefecture is dated to AD 471, during the reign of King Yuryaku (reigned AD 457–479). It had been owned by a member of the sword-bearer guards of the royal palace; its owner thus appears to have been an official of a court then located over 300 km (186 miles) to the west (Kiyotari 1987). A second inscribed sword dating to the same reign, from the mound of **Edafuna-yama** on the far west coast of Kyushu, included the word for king, *okimi*, and thus confirms central control over a region 550 km (342 miles) to the west.

Decline and Civil War

In AD 507, Keitai ascended the throne. This has been described in some quarters as a dynastic break, but he had the same royal credentials as his predecessors, and there was no serious change in tradition. The court center and the royal tombs were now relocated back to the **Mount Miwa** area of the Nara plain. Fifteen kings and three queens were to rule until the end of Yamato, following the death of Empress Genmei (reigned AD 707–715). The first signs of decline in power came within Keitai's reign. Yamato drew upon Korean iron for its weapons industry, particularly from areas under its own control in the confederation of Kaya. These regions were uncomfortably located between the might of Silla to the east and Paekche to the west, and during the course of Keitai's reign, Silla encroached into Kaya, taking territory traditionally loyal to Yamato. An expedition to halt this move collapsed in AD 527 due to an insurrection in Kyushu, where a local leader refused to cooperate. This required a diversion of forces to cope with a rebellion that was symptomatic of rising independence in the provinces.

In AD 585, the rivalries between powerful senior clans reached the royal court itself, and civil war broke out over the successor to Emperor Bidatsu, who died that year. The problem of the succession was exacerbated by the lack of primogeniture, whereby the oldest son naturally followed the previous king; there was, therefore, a proliferation of possible claimants. Two protégés of Soga no Imako, leader of a particularly powerful clan, were successively placed on the throne. Yomei lasted only two years before his death, and Sushun five years before his assassination was arranged by Soga; he was succeeded in 592 by the Empress Suiko. With her nephew Prince Shotoku as her nominated successor and prince regent, the Empress reigned until 628, a remarkably long span for that period.

The Asuka Enlightenment

The political situation in Japan was now strongly influenced by events in China. After centuries of fragmentation, China was reunited in AD 589 under the Sui Dynasty. Yamato and the three Korean states sent tribute missions to the Sui court in 600, and returned impressed by the imperial power. Not only had the Sui emperor Wendi (AD 581–604) ordered the building of a new capital and palace, but he also initiated the construction of the Grand Canal, lacing together the empire with a waterborne transport and communication system. Moreover, through the Confucian ethic of obedience he received the obligatory homage of his subjects; the registration of individuals and an efficient system of revenue collection in China added to the impression of a powerful state. The members of the official mission returned to Japan armed with these new ideas, bringing with them currents of change that contributed to what has been called the Asuka Enlightenment, named after the new court capital, **Asuka** [15.39], located in the Nara basin (Brown 1993).

This enlightenment involved not only the rapid entrenchment of writing based on the Chinese script, and the construction of palace capitals on the Sui model – it also brought Buddhism (which by the time it reached Japan, initially in the mid-6th century AD, had been transformed from its Indian roots by contact with Daoism, Confucianism, and geomancy). The struggle over the succession which had led in 592 to the enthronement of Empress Suiko had also divided the protagonists on the basis of their preferred religion, with Soga no Imako and Prince Shotoku favoring the new Buddhism. Buddhist monks were imbued with the charisma of divination and miracle-working, and both Soga and Shotoku vowed that if successful in the succession, they would promote Buddhism to the full. True to their promise, they had new temples constructed,

number of Asuka-period sites. (Below) This square tile is from Myoon-ji, early 7th century, and was nailed through the hole in the center to the end of a rafter or beam; 38 cm (15 in) square.

15.37, 15.38 *Asuka roof tiles:* (above) tile from the end of an eave, from Asuka-dera at Asuka, c. 596; diam. 15.1 cm (6 in). The Asuka-dera seems to have been the first timple to have had roof tiles, but examples are then found at a

employing immigrant craftsmen. Soga sponsored the construction of the **Asuka-dera temple** at Asuka [**15.37**], while Shotoku was responsible for the **Shitenno-ji temple** in **Osaka**. Both broke new ground in the size and splendor of religious structures. Buddhism spread rapidly under royal patronage, particularly at the hands of Prince Shotoku, and it is recorded that nobles vied with each other to construct temples. Temple offerings of horse-riding equipment and gold and silver ornaments recall the mortuary offerings found in the *kofun*, and, indeed, continued the same tradition. A census taken in AD 623, less than a century after the first arrival of Buddhism, recorded that there were 46 Buddhist temples in Japan, staffed by 816 monks and 569 nuns.

Korean immigrants were prominent players in the Asuka Enlightenment: their priests were numbered among the 816 monks of the AD 623 census; Korean equine equipment occurs among the widespread evidence for armored cavalry of the period; and Korean influence can be seen in the architecture of the grand new temples and in the burial goods found in elite tombs. At the same time, the Enlightenment saw the establishment of imperially appointed ranks based on merit and ability. The Twelve Ranks were identified on the basis of the color of the feathers worn in a purple silk hat embellished with gold and silver. The role of Confucian ethics can be seen in the titles, beginning at the top rank with Greater Virtue and descending through such titles as Greater Propriety and Greater Justice to the lowest of all, Lesser Knowledge. These ranks replaced the former system of hereditary access to positions of influence. The Seventeen Injunctions, said to have been formulated by Prince Shotoku in 604, confirm a Confucian approach to life,

integrated with complete deference to the emperor's wishes. The Injunctions range from the requirement that officials must always obey the emperor, to an order not to disturb farmers at critical times of the agricultural cycle.

Interest in Chinese administration, art, and culture was magnified through diplomatic missions sent by the Empress Suiko to the Sui court, a situation that became even more accentuated following the fall of the Sui and the establishment of the Tang Dynasty in AD 618. In 622, however, Prince Shotoku died, followed by Empress Suiko six years later, leading to a period of factional politics in the court. The obvious choice as Suiko's successor was Shotoku's son, Prince Yamashiro, but this was opposed by the strong Soga clan, and first the ineffectual Emperor Jomei acceded, followed by his wife as Empress Kogyokui (reigned 642–645). Serious bloodletting followed. Yamashiro and his family were eliminated at the hands of Iruka, a leading member of the Soga clan. In 645, Iruka himself was murdered in the royal audience hall, setting the stage for the appointment of Emperor Kotoku (reigned 645–654). One of his first actions was to move the capital from Asuka to **Naniwa** on the coast, followed on New Year's Day, AD 646, by a series of major reforms that provided greater powers for the emperor and improvements to the tax system. These, known as the Taika Reforms, exhibit recurrent features in the development of early states. There was a census, and the tax on agricultural production was set at 3 percent of the yield. Cloth to be given in tax was set against the area of land owned. Other goods required as tax included horses (one horse per 100 households), labor on government projects, weaponry, and armor.

15.39 *The palace at Asuka: a section of the remains of the Asuka Itabuki palace, Asuka village, probably mid-7th century.*

KEY DISCOVERY The Origins of Chinese Metallurgy

Although bronzes dating from about 1800 BC include weaponry, much energy was dedicated by the Chinese to casting richly decorated vessels used in rituals to feast the ancestors. The bronze-casting tradition established in China during the Xia and Shang dynasties produced vessels of such remarkable size and form, by such singular techniques, that it is hard not to see it as unique and indigenous. The origins of metallurgy in China, however, have come under close scrutiny. The key issue lies in finding early evidence for bronze-casting to the west of China, from an area that could have transmitted the necessary expertise.

From West to East

Such evidence is now being identified. The Afanasievo culture of the Irtysh, Ob, and Yenesei valleys in southern Siberia probably represents an eastward movement of a pastoral nomadic people belonging to the Yamnaya culture, who occupied the steppes of Central Asia north of modern Turkmenistan. Yamnaya sites, which date to about 3500 BC, have provided evidence for both copper-based metallurgy and the presence of domestic horses and wheeled carts (Anthony 1998). The potential of rapid horse transport across the steppes may well have been a key element in the intrusion of new technologies from west to east.

Afanasievo cemeteries include copper beads as grave goods, as well as the remains of horses, sheep, and cattle. The metal industry becomes much more sophisticated in the succeeding Okunevo culture sites, for by now copper was being alloyed and cast into knives, awls, fishhooks, and bangles.

Bronzeworking in the Tarim Basin

The spread of bronze technology into the Tarim basin in northwest China followed. The Gumugou cemetery of the Konqi River valley, west of Lop Nur lake, is a key site for appreciating the chronology and cultural affiliations of the Tarim basin Bronze Age. During the early period, dated to 2000–1500 BC, grave goods included copper, bone, and jade ornaments, together with wheat grains. Gumugou burial rituals hint at an origin in the Afanasievo culture, including the provision of animal remains and the enclosing of the graves by a fence. Similar copper-based knives, awls, bracelets, and earrings are also found.

There is convincing evidence as well, in the form of the remains of domestic goats, sheep, cattle, and wheat, that the Gumugou economy incorporated agriculture and stock raising, in association with hunting and gathering. The preferred location for settlements was along the oases, where rivers flowed from the surrounding mountains into the arid Tarim basin.

The Western Chinese Bronze Industry

These sites provide an answer to the intriguing issue of why the earliest bronzes in China are found in the far west of the country. The Neolithic Majiayao and Machang cultures in Gansu, Qinghai, and Xinjiang provinces include cast and forged copper knives and other tools dated between 2740 and 1900 BC.

This western Chinese bronze industry continued with the Qijia culture, which comprises a series of agricultural villages dated to 2300–1800 BC.

At Qinweijia in Ningxia Autonomous Region, for example, storage pits have been found to contain a few objects in bronze and copper. In Gansu Province, millet was found adhering to a copper knife at Dahezhuang. Huangniangniangtai has provided 32 copper-based items, including knives, awls, chisels, and a possible hairpin. The Siba culture of the same region dates to 1900–1600 BC, and grave goods from the site of Huoshaogou include gold and bronze earrings, bronze knives, daggers, spearheads, and socketed axes.

Bronze in Eastern China

The first rare bronze artifacts east of Gansu occur in a series of settlements ascribed to the Longshan culture. Part of a bronze bell was recovered from one of over 1000 graves excavated at Taosi, while Meishan has yielded two fragments of crucible, enough to confirm that a knowledge of bronze-casting was now entering the Yellow River valley.

Once established, the bronze industry of the Xia and Shang dynasties took on their singular and essentially Chinese pattern. Vessels were cast in piece molds to satisfy court ritual requirements, leading to individual castings weighing over 800 kg (1764 lb). This was to continue, with many further innovations and refinements, for another 1500 years of dynastic history.

The Transition from Yamato to Nara

The defeat in AD 663 of Paekche, Yamato's ally in Korea, and then in 668 of Koguryo by the combined forces of Tang China and Silla, had a profound effect upon Yamato. Predatory enemies, in the form of the might of the Tang empire and a unified Korea, were now on Japan's doorstep. Defensive forts were constructed from Kyushu east into the heartland of Yamato. The capital at Asuka was abandoned in favor of the more easily defended position at **Otsu**. The strength of the ruling dynasty under emperors Tenji (reigned 668–671) and Tenmu (673–686) increased at the expense of the powerful clans. The investment in charismatic authority of the emperor was manifested in the construction of magnificent palace-capitals along Tang lines, such as **Fujiwara** and **Heijo**. The 14-year reign of Emperor Tenmu saw the construction of the Kiyomihara Palace at Asuka, a portent of the royal capitals to come, and increased central control over the armed forces.

All of this was associated with a series of edicts that laid down the legal basis of imperial rule. Historic records charting the godly origins of the royal dynasty were designed as a legitimizing force, and Buddhism was encouraged as the state religion. The *sutras* (Buddhist texts) favoring royal rule were widely read. Tenmu was succeeded by his widow, the Empress Jito, who resolved to construct a great new capital at **Fujiwara** on the Nara plain, a city she was able to occupy by 694. It was designed along continental Chinese lines on a grid layout, with the royal palace at its heart. In 702, the Taiho Code was issued, a set of laws that institutionalized the aristocratically based Fujiwara regime. Succession was not restricted to the male line, and the empress was succeeded by her sister Genmei. One of the new ruler's first decisions was to abandon Fujiwara after less than a decade, and move the capital to **Heijo-kyo**, located 20 km (12 miles) to the north. This move established the Nara state, although the transition from Yamato was seamless and involved the same dynasty.

The Yamato state, over a period of four centuries, saw the development of an increasingly powerful civilization that grew in tandem with the three states of Korea, and finally with Tang China. It received much influence in terms of ideas and goods from the continent, but throughout displayed a specific Japanese ideology. Thus, while accepting Buddhism, the local *kami* spirits retained their importance, as they do to this day. The rulers developed increasingly efficient forms of rice cultivation, the basic prop of the court centers, and had sufficient disposable wealth to deploy a fleet and armed forces across the Tsushima Strait in support of their ally, Paekche.

Royal and elite tombs were constructed and filled with opulent grave goods. Heavily armed cavalry, another Korean import, was maintained. Large cities, palaces, and temples were built, again on continental models. Writing was adopted from the Chinese script, and records of tax payments written on wood have survived. Japanese civilization can look back at Yamato as its seminal period of development, leading directly into the Nara state.

The Central Asian Silk Road

The Silk Road that linked China with India and Rome had its roots deep in antiquity. It comprises the routes followed by Indo-European-speaking people who brought wheat and barley and Western styles of dress to the Tarim basin oases, along with the Tocharian language, an ancient Indo-European tongue spoken by immigrants who may have come from east of the Caspian Sea in the 2nd millennium BC. It was also the conduit for the spread of bronzeworking [see box: The Origins of Chinese Metallurgy] and the horse-drawn chariot into China.

With the expansion of Han domination to the west, along the Gansu corridor and beyond the Jade Gate (so called because of the jade merchants who passed this way), trade flourished as never before. Merchants plied the maze of routes that skirted the Taklamakan Desert, journeying across the steppes to Ferghana and the Syr Darya Valley in Central Asia and on toward the Caspian Sea; from there, the traveler could move on to the Mediterranean lands. Many states – some ephemeral, others extensive and powerful – developed through the control of trade along these routes, the potential of irrigated agriculture, and the exploitation of natural resources, such as jade and lapis lazuli.

Khotan

Khotan was one such state, located in the southwestern corner of the Tarim basin, south of the Taklamakan Desert. Here, the rivers that flow north from the Kunlun Range form delta oases before their waters dissipate in the desert sand. Khotan was known to the Chinese as Yutian, and was renowned as a source of jade (Bailey 1970; Stein 1907). The ancient capital is located at the modern site of **Yotkan**. Formerly walled, it has been virtually destroyed by looting for gold, jade, and other precious artifacts. In 1913 the Hungarian explorer Aurel Stein found many artifacts from Yotkan for sale, mostly terracotta figurines

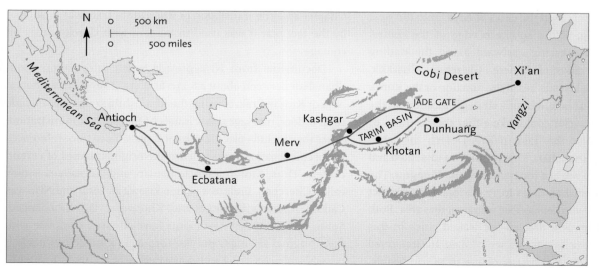

15.40 The Silk Road: *this was a series of routes linking east and west traversed by merchant caravans. It brought great wealth to the merchants involved, although also much danger and hardship. It saw not only the carriage of goods, but also the transmission of ideas, not least the spread of Buddhism from its home in India to China.*

of men and women, or of animals such as camels, horses, and monkeys. He also collected some stone seals, agate and glass beads, and fragments of stucco ornamentation.

The Khotanese spoke a dialect of the Middle Iranian Saka language, closely related to the southern Saka languages of Mathura, Sistan, and Gandhara. Many cognate words provide clues to the social order of the society, including expressions for "supervisor," "rich," "greatness," "ruler," "lord," and official titles. Written in the Indian Brahmi script, this language was the vehicle for Buddhist texts written in the region, some of which were sought after and taken to China, for Khotan was an important stepping-stone between East and West. The Tibetan document known as the *Li Yul* annals provides some indications of Khotanese history. It describes 56 kings, with Buddhism being introduced 404 years after the Buddha attained *nirvana*, i.e. around 104 BC, during the reign of King Vijaya Sambhava. The 14th king, Vijaya Jaya, married the Chinese princess who brought silk worms to Khotan to found the local silk industry.

A brief period during the 1st and 2nd centuries AD is also illuminated by the corpus of local bronze coin issues. These bear Kharoshthi (see below) and Chinese inscriptions, the former naming a series of kings with the family name of Gurga and the titles *Maharaja* ("Great King") and *Yidaraja* ("King of Khotan"). Some also carry the symbol of a Bactrian camel. Evidence for an extensive exchange system that incorporated Khotan is also provided by the presence of Chinese and Kushan coins. The Kushan empire (Chapter 14) incorporated Samarkand, Bokhara, and Ferghana in Central Asia, bordering on the state of Khotan, as well as Gandhara (northern Pakistan and Afghanistan) further west.

Shanshan

Shanshan was founded in the 1st century BC in the southern and eastern margins of the Tarim basin (Rhie 1999). At its greatest extent, it encompassed the cities of **Niya** far to the west (now modern Minfeng, at the southern edge of the central Tarim basin), and, progressing eastward along the trading route, the areas and cities of **Endere**, **Cherchen**, **Charklik**, **Miran**, and **Loulan**. The last site lies at the junction of the Kuruk Darya River and Lop Nur lake, a highly strategic location on the Silk Road where the traveler could take either the northern or southern routes around the Taklamakan Desert; the latter involved the transit of Shanshan. This region was unsettled and continuously subject to warlike incursions by the Xiongnu. The origin of the name Shanshan dates to 77 BC, following conflict with the Han Chinese, who kept a close watch on this area. Both the *Shi Ji* and the *Han Shu* discuss the walled cities in this region. The latter describes the state of Loulan (renamed Shanshan) as comprising 1570 households with 14,100 people,

located 1600 *li* (c. 400 km, or 250 miles) from the Jade Gate, the official western border of the Han empire. It was said to be a region of sandy and salty soil and few agricultural fields, lying on the Han communication route westward.

During periods of strong central power in China, Shanshan was a client state, but when the central government was weak, as during the late 2nd and early 3rd centuries AD, Shanshan would have been independent. In AD 222, its ruler sent tribute to the Chinese court, and during the reign of the Western Jin emperor Wudi (AD 265–289), a period of relative stability in China, the western routes were cleared of threats from nomadic horsemen and other enemies. Surviving documents on wooden slips, cloth, and paper provide insight into late 3rd-century AD Shanshan; most date to the Western Jin dynasty, with a concentration in the years AD 266–270. These documents, issued by local officials, describe the presence of Chinese military commanders, and those who supervised agriculture. The son of the Shanshan king was sent as a hostage to the Western Jin court in AD 283.

While most of the Shanshan documents were written in Chinese, those from further west, at Niya and Endere, are inscribed in the Kharoshthi script. Kharoshthi documents on silk have also been found at Miran. Kharoshthi is a script with a wide but patchy distribution, which was employed between the mid-3rd century BC and the 6th century AD. It originated in Gandhara, and was employed from the 3rd century AD in Sogdiana and Bactria under the Kushan empire, in the Krorän kingdom of the Tarim basin, and even as far east as Luoyang in China. There, a Kharoshthi text was found on a wall surrounding a well, describing the activities of a group of Buddhists who lived in Luoyang during the reign of the Han emperor Lingdi (AD 168–189). Coins of northern and western India also bear Kharoshthi legends. The script almost certainly derives from an Aramaic script at a time when Gandhara was under Achaemenid (Persian) dominance in the 5th century BC (see Chapter 12). The translation of Kharoshthi texts was facilitated by the fact that it was used in tandem with Greek names on coinage.

Documents from Niya provide much information about Shanshan between about AD 230 and 335. They were written at Niya or Krorän Prakrit, using the Kharoshthi script, and include royal orders, messages, and issues of Buddhist administration. Since they include place names, it is possible to trace references to specific locations and to learn the original names of certain centers. Thus, Krorän refers to Loulan, and Calmadana is now called Cherchen. Endere was then known as Saca, and Niya was Cadota. Khotan's former name, Khotamna, is little changed. Some of the wooden documents have survived complete with their original sealings, and the corpus as a whole has made it possible to reconstruct with some degree of accuracy the names

KEY CONTROVERSY The Origins of Southeast Asian Indianized States

The origins of the indigenous states of Southeast Asia can only be understood and explained by examining the late prehistoric societies as they were developing on the eve of the transition to civilization. In the absence of such information, any model of origins is bound to be speculative, and over-reliant on later historic data. This is particularly true of the civilization of Angkor, which, though officially founded in AD 802 by Jayavarman II, had its roots deep in the prehistoric period.

The Indian Origins Model

Until research focused on illuminating this question of prehistoric transition to state-based civilization, historians of Southeast Asia dedicated their research to unraveling the dynastic sequence, based on historic inscriptions, and studying and restoring the ruinous brick and stone temples. The principal texts of the inscriptions were usually written in Sanskrit, the language of Hinduism, in a script derived from India. The temples were built following Indian designs, for the worship of Hindu gods or the Buddha. Kings of Angkor had Indian names. The early Vietnamese port city of Oc Eo contained many Indian imports, as did other major sites of the state of Funan in the Mekong Delta,

occupied c. AD 200–550. Until the initiation of major archaeological research in the 1970s, all these factors encouraged the leading scholars of the day to see the origins of such states as the result of contact with a superior Indian civilization (Cœdès 1968; Sedov 1978). In this model, the indigenous inhabitants played a supine role from a base of cultural simplicity.

Indigenous Origins

Recent re-evaluations of historic inscriptions have stressed the fact that supplementary texts were written in old Khmer, and mentioned local deities. This has led Michael Vickery (1998) to describe the Indian influence as merely a veneer over a solid local culture. Moreover, excavations of late prehistoric sites that were occupied up to the transition to statehood have revealed that rather than being comprised of simple farmers, communities were large, vibrant, and culturally complex. Thus, at Noen U-Loke in the Mun Valley of northeast Thailand, the dead were interred in clay-lined graves filled with burnt rice. Some individuals were lavishly equipped with mortuary offerings: gold and silver ornaments, bronze belts, finger- and toe-rings, bangles, glass, carnelian

and agate beads, eggshell-thin ceramic vessels, and iron knives, sickles, hoes, and spades. Iron Age settlements were encircled by wide moats, wherein the water was diverted and managed by banks. These date back to the late 1st millennium BC, indicating that water control was not introduced from India. The manufacture of salt was undertaken on an industrial scale, and war increased, as seen in the proliferation of iron arrowheads and spears.

A New Model

This new evidence requires the formulation of a new model to account for state origins. In the case of Angkor, it revolves round the increasing cultural complexity of the indigenous people, who participated in an expanding maritime trade network and selectively adopted exotic cultural practices, such as building in brick and writing, to their own advantage. In other parts of Southeast Asia, evidence for similar trends is emerging on the basis of new archaeological research, and it appears that increasingly complex Iron Age societies were also developing in coastal Vietnam, central Thailand, Java, and Burma.

---

of the seven kings of Shanshan and their approximate reign dates. Their royal titles began as *Maharaja*, but this was to change to *Maharaya*. The fourth king, Amgvaka, who probably reigned from AD 255–258 to 293–296, had his documents sealed with the title "The Chinese High Commissioner for Shanshan," which indicates a degree of Chinese influence in administration.

The kingdom of Shanshan was a major center for Buddhism, and during his journey west in AD 399, the Chinese monk Fa Xi'an noted that the then ruler was a Buddhist, and that the state included several thousand monks. Beginning in AD 442, Shanshan was attacked by Chinese armies; it succumbed to the northern Wei in 445. This was not the final foreign domination of Shanshan. In due course, the Hephthalite Huns controlled this region, followed in the 6th century by the Turks. The Tang Chinese returned in the mid-7th century, permitting the local rulers a considerable degree

of autonomy until 751, when the Tang dynasty was defeated by the Arabs.

The Southeast Asian Maritime Silk Road

The end of the Eastern Han dynasty in AD 220 resulted in the division of China into three major states, called the Three Kingdoms (AD 220–280). The Wu emperor of southern China, cut off from the Silk Road, sent emissaries south to seek out an alternative, maritime route to trading partners in the West. This was already developing, as Indian and Southeast Asian venturers had been traveling the sea-lanes for centuries. The imperial Chinese agents, to their surprise, encountered in Southeast Asia kings and their palaces, cities, intensive rice cultivation, systems of taxation, and writing. Even by the turn of the millennium, two centuries before, many small states had been testing their strength to secure their share of maritime trade.

Funan, the Mekong Delta

One of the best-known states controlled the strategic Mekong Delta (Higham 2001). Called Funan by the Chinese, it incorporated large walled cities linked by canals stretching for tens of kilometers across the flat deltaic landscape. Archaeological research at **Oc Eo** in Vietnam and **Angkor Borei** in Cambodia, two walled and moated urban centers linked by a canal system, have revealed the adoption of Sanskrit names for kings, use of the Brahmi script, worship of Hindu gods, and adherence to the teachings of the Buddha, wooden statues of whom have been dredged from the mud [see box: The Origins of Southeast Asian Indianized States, p. 585]. Brick temples have been uncovered, containing pits for cremated human remains. Grave offerings found in these pits include gold plaques embellished with sacred Buddhist inscriptions and images of Hindu deities.

This polity flourished until the mid-6th century AD, as trade with China and India brought many new goods and ideas to Funan. Changing patterns of Chinese maritime trade then skirted Funan, however, and political power moved inland to new and thrusting principalities known collectively as **Chenla**, again according to Chinese accounts. Several growing kingdoms emerged, living in a state of regular competition and war. The best known was centered at **Ishanapura**, just east of the Great Lake (Tonle Sap) in Cambodia, where a dynasty of kings is recorded in inscriptions (Vickery 1998). These rulers progressively adopted the characteristics of fully-fledged states, with a central court, splendid temples, water-control measures, and a bureaucracy of office holders. The leader of one such state was unmatched in charisma and military prowess, and founded the state of Angkor toward the end of the 8th century AD. His name was Jayavarman II.

Angkor, Cambodia

Angkor is the modern name given to a complex of cities, temples, and reservoirs [15.41] located between the Great Lake (Tonle Sap) and the Kulen hills in northwest Cambodia [see box: Angkor: Capital City of the Khmer]. Between about AD 800 and 1435, it was the center of a kingdom that controlled most of lowland Cambodia and adjacent parts of Thailand and Laos. The name Angkor is derived from the Sanskrit *Nagara* ("Holy City"). Its location next to the Great Lake provided limitless supplies of fish, and access to the Mekong River and the sea. Small rivers issuing from the Kulen hills to the north also supplied the city with constant fresh water. It was first encountered by Europeans in the 16th century, when Portuguese missionaries visited and described a gigantic, abandoned stone city, encroached by the jungle (Groslier 1958). The Angkorian inscriptions were written in Sanskrit and archaic Khmer, leaving no doubt that the people responsible for this state were the ancestors of the present population of Cambodia.

The earliest historic occupation probably took place just west of the main complex of buildings at Angkor. At Banteay Choeu, a large, rectangular enclosure now partially covered by the Western Baray (reservoir) can be seen from the air, and temples lie within or just beyond the precinct, including Ak Yum, Prei Khmeng, and Phnom Rung. A second rectangular enclosure can be seen to the north. Banteay Choeu has been

15.41 Angkor: *the site reached its greatest extent during the reign of King Jayavarman VII (AD 1181–1219). His rectangular walled city of Angkor Thom housed a large urban population, and was dominated by his temple-mausoleum, known as the Bayon. The city was flanked by several huge reservoirs. An earlier center, known as Hariharalaya, lies to the southeast.*

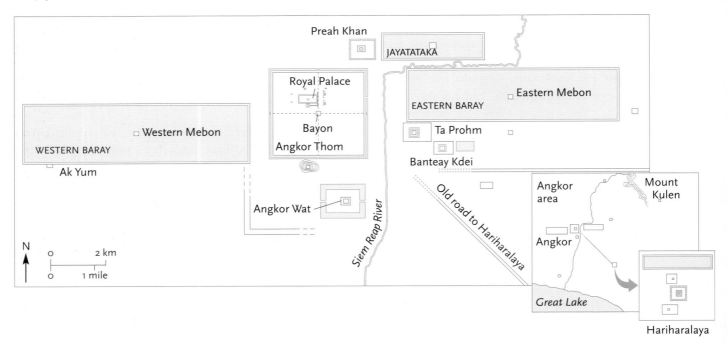

KEY SITE Angkor: Capital City of the Khmer

Angkor consists of successive city foundations and temples constructed by the kings of three dynasties over a period of about 600 years. Unraveling a long and complex sequence has shown that the area was first occupied during the prehistoric Iron Age (*c.* 400 BC–AD 150 in this region). During the 7th and 8th centuries AD, it was the center of a small state, for inscriptions have mentioned a ruling queen in this area. In the late 8th century, Jayavarman II founded his kingdom in the area now covered by Angkor. In AD 802 this king was consecrated *Chakravartin*, or supreme ruler on earth.

Jayavarman II (reigned 802–835) founded a dynasty that endured for two centuries, and his successors built their own temples and reservoirs. While temples were built in brick and stone, and have therefore survived, residential buildings were constructed in wood, and only excavations can reveal their location and form. We know that Indravarman had a large new center built at Hariharalaya, dominated by a series of brick shrines to the ancestors and a huge reservoir named after him. His inscriptions also describe a royal palace. His son Yashovarman (reigned 889–910) left this capital to build a new one, along with a fabulous temple, on top of the Bakheng hill about 20 km (12.5 miles) to the northwest.

Such temple mausolea were constructed in the form of Mt Meru, home of the Hindu gods, to worship the ancestors and to receive the cremated remains of individual kings. They dominate the Angkorian landscape: there is Ta Keo of Jayavarman V (reigned 968–1001) and the Baphuon of Udayadityavarman II (reigned 1050–1060), but the largest and most admired is Angkor Wat, built by Suryavarman II.

Angkor Wat

This magnificent structure was built in sandstone, much of which bears bas-reliefs showing the king, his court, and iconographic scenes drawn from the Hindu religion. Much of the surface was apparently once covered in gold. Many kings also built rectangular reservoirs, the purpose of which is controversial. Some argue that they were essentially symbolic, representing the oceans that surrounded the Hindu home of the gods and serving a ritual function. Others feel that they also served an irrigation function by supplying rice fields located between the city and the Great Lake to the south.

Angkor Thom

One of Suryavarman's successors, Jayavarman VII, was responsible for most of the layout of the Angkor as the visitor sees it today. His huge walled and moated city, known as Angkor Thom, was dominated by the central temple mausoleum known as the Bayon. He also constructed a large new reservoir and many temples dedicated to royal ancestors.

In 1296, a Chinese diplomat, Zhou Daguan, stayed at Angkor Thom for ten months and wrote an account in which he described the city at its height. There was a large population, who lived within the city walls. The royal palace was itself enclosed by its own set of walls, and the king's progresses were spectacular. Archaeology is now confirming Zhou's description. Under the direction of Jacques Gaucher (2004), excavations that began in 2000 have revealed numerous canals, houses, ponds, and roads within the city, and have yielded evidence not only for a large staff of palace retainers, but also for artisans, slaves, and a strong leavening of Chinese merchants.

15.42 *Angkor Wat is one of the largest religious monuments known. It was the temple mausoleum of King Suryavarman II of Angkor (reigned AD 1113–1150).*

interpreted as a possible early foundation of Jayavarman II, though its rectangular outline could also represent the dykes of a later reservoir (Pottier 2000). It was this king who, in AD 802, had himself consecrated *chakravartin*, the supreme king on earth, and founded the Angkorian kingdom.

Another complex, known as **Hariharalaya**, lies to the southeast of Angkor. Its temples lie south of the Indratataka, a reservoir of unprecedented size to that time (3800 x 800 m, or 12,500 x 2600 ft). From much later inscriptions it is known that Jayavarman II lived here during his declining years, until his death in about AD 835. Most of the Roluos Group of buildings, however, was constructed during the reign of Indravarman (877–889). The royal center of this king incorporated two major temples, known as **Preah Ko [15.43]** and the **Bakong**. With the death of Indravarman in 889, his son Yashovarman abandoned Hariharalaya in favor of a new capital, centered on a low sandstone hill known as the **Bakheng**. Yashovarman also inspired the massive Eastern Baray, the dykes of which are 7.5 x 1.8 km (4.6 x 1.1 miles) in extent. He also had Hindu monasteries constructed south of his new reservoir, and temples built on hills surrounding the capital.

15.43 The temple of Preah Ko at Hariharalaya: *this was a monument dedicated to the ancestors of King Indravarman I (AD 877–889). It was formerly covered in brightly painted stucco. The name means "sacred ox," after the sandstone oxen that guard its entrance.*

After a brief interlude when Jayavarman IV established his capital at **Koh Ker**, to the northeast of Angkor, Rajendravarman II (reigned 944–968) returned to the old center and had two major state temples constructed; one is now known as **Pre Rup**, the other as the **Eastern Mebon**, built on an island in the center of the **Eastern Baray**. The former honored the king and his ancestors within the context of the god Shiva. Its five major towers rise on two tiers of laterite (a clay formed by weathering of rocks in the tropics). The largest and centrally placed brick sanctuary housed Rajendrabhadresvara, the royal *linga*, or stone phallus, which was an object of veneration. The architect Kavindrarimathana designed the Eastern Mebon. The central tower held a *linga* named Rajendresvara, and the four subsidiary temples on the uppermost platform housed images of the king's forebears. Rajendravarman II was succeeded by his ten-year-old son Jayavarman V. Jayavarman continued to reign at Angkor, and his state temple, then known as **Hemasringagiri** or the Mountain with the Golden Summits, was built to represent Mount Meru, the home of the Hindu gods.

The reign of Jayavarman V was followed by a period of civil war that left the state in serious disarray. The victorious king, Suryavarman I (reigned 1002–1050), established his court at Angkor, with its focal point at the temple of the **Phimeanakas**. This comprises a single shrine, surrounded by narrow roofed galleries on top of three tiers of laterite, each of descending size.

15.44 The Bayon, Angkor: the huge heads that dominate the Bayon temple-mausoleum at Angkor are thought to represent the king, Jayavarman VII, as a bodhisattva. He was a follower of Buddhism, and his ashes would have been placed below the central tower after cremation rituals.

The royal palace would have been built of perishable materials, and will only be traced through the excavation of its foundations. These buildings were located within a high laterite wall with five entrance pavilions ascribed to this reign, enclosing a precinct 600 x 250 m (2000 x 900 ft) in extent. Suryavarman also began the construction of the **Western Baray**, the largest reservoir at Angkor. The **Western Mebon** temple to Vishnu in the center of the reservoir was built in the style of Suryavarman's successor, Udayadityavarman. Such island temples provide some evidence for the purpose of the reservoirs: one inscription describes how pilgrims would cross the sacred water to wash away their sins.

It was under the succeeding dynasty of Mahidharapura, from about 1080, that Angkor attained its present layout. **Angkor Wat**, the largest religious monument known, was constructed by Suryavarman II (reigned 1113–1150). This temple incorporates one of the finest and longest bas-relief sculptures in the world, and the scenes do much to illuminate the religious and court life of Angkor during the 12th century. One scene shows the king in council, another reveals the Angkorian army on the march [**15.45**], while a third shows graphic scenes of heaven and hell. High-status princesses are seen being borne on palanquins. The main temple incorporates five towers, representing the peaks of Mount Meru.

The second king of the Mahidharapura dynasty, the Buddhist Jayavarman VII (reigned 1181–1219) was responsible for the construction of Angkor Thom, the rectangular walled city that today dominates Angkor. It centers on the Bayon, a temple embellished with gigantic stone heads thought to represent the king as the Buddha [**15.44**]. Jayavarman VII also ordered the construction of the northern reservoir and the central island temple of Neak Pean, formerly known as Rajasri. According to contemporary inscriptions, visitors to this temple would wash away their sins in the water that gushed from four fountains in the form of a human and animal heads. Foundation inscriptions also describe how Jayavarman VII founded and endowed two vast temple complexes, **Ta Prohm** to his mother and **Preah Khan** to his father. Each temple also incorporated shrines dedicated to ancestors of the aristocracy.

Following the death of Jayavarman VII, building activity slowed. By the 14th and 15th centuries, the Angkor state was under stress from the encroaching Thais; it was abandoned in the mid-15th century (Cœdès 1966; Higham 2001). Although much of the site was then overgrown by the jungle, Angkor Wat

15.45 Relief from Angkor Wat: this section of the huge bas-relief decorating Angkor Wat shows the Angkorian army on the march.

was never completely abandoned. It, and the other temples, retain their sanctity to this day.

The Arakan Coast, Burma

As noted, increasingly complex societies were developing elsewhere in Southeast Asia as well, helped by maritime trade and cultural contacts with India and each other. The Arakan coast of western Burma (Myanmar) occupies a key geographic position in the Asian maritime exchange route that developed during the early centuries AD (Gutman 2001). It faces India across the Bay of Bengal, and was thus a natural stepping stone when, for example, the Mauryan emperor Ashoka sent Buddhist missions from India to Southeast Asia. Tradition has it that the Buddha manifested himself in Arakan, when an image of him, known as the *Mahamuni* ("Great Sage"), was cast in his likeness. Although the history of Arakan has hardly been tested archaeologically, it is known that two major cities spanned the 5th to the 8th centuries AD (Gutman 2001).

The earlier of these, **Dhanyawadi**, lies on the Tarechaung River, by which boats can reach the Kaladan River and thence the Bay of Bengal. The city's encircling brick wall encloses 442 ha (1092 acres), within which lay a second walled precinct containing the palace. The early history of the site is recorded on the inscription in the Shitthaung Pagoda of King Anandacandra of the city of Mrauk-U, dated to AD 729. It lists the kings who preceded him, noting that it was King Dvan Candra who first defeated 101 rivals before founding the city in the mid-4th century AD, and ruling from 370 to 425. His city, so the inscription records, "laughed with heavenly beauty."

Vesali superseded Dhanyawadi as the capital during the early 6th century AD, lying beside the Rann Chuang River, which provided access to the Bay of Bengal. The outer moat and brick walls enclose an oval area covering approximately 540 ha (1334 acres), and a second walled precinct in the northern half of the city housed the palace complex. Excavations in the 1980s revealed a number of Buddhist foundations, for Buddhism dominated at Vesali.

The Shitthaung inscription describes how the king founded monasteries and donated slaves, fields, and buffaloes for their maintenance. He also sent gifts to the monastic communities of Sri Lanka. The commerce centered at Vesali is reflected in the locally minted coins that have been recovered there. One side has the image of a bull, symbol of the ruling family, and the other has the *srivatsa* motif, symbolizing prosperity. Some Vesali coins have been recovered from sites in Bangladesh. Trade also brought to Vesali an intaglio ornament (i.e., with the design hollowed out) that originated in the Mediterranean, and gems bearing brief inscriptions in south Indian characters. In this respect, the site falls into a wide range of other port cities in Southeast Asia.

The Pyu of Burma

The Pyu or Tircul people of Burma were first mentioned in a mid-4th century AD Chinese text, in a list of tribes on the frontier of southwestern China (Stargardt 1990). The author, Chang Chu, described them as the Piao. Other early Chinese records that survived in later editions describe the Piao as civilized: "where prince and minister, father and son, elder and younger, have each their order of precedence." Archaeology has revealed that the Pyu state developed in the dry zone of central Burma between about 200 BC and AD 900.

The state is best known on the basis of three large walled cities: **Beikthano**, **Sri Ksetra**, and **Halin**. All were located in tributary valleys of the Irrawaddy River, where it was possible to harness the local rivers or streams for irrigation. There is compelling evidence at Beikthano for a pre-Buddhist mortuary tradition involving large brick and timber halls containing the cremated remains of high-status individuals. By the 4th or 5th century AD, however, Buddhism had taken root, and many large public buildings were constructed for this faith, including *stupas* (domed buildings often containing Buddhist relics) and monasteries. Meanwhile, the cremated dead were interred in mortuary jars set in brick structures outside the city walls.

The Pyu spoke a Sino-Tibetan language, employed Indian scripts in their inscriptions, and took part in a widespread trading network that incorporated India. They were proficient bronze-casters, one set of figurines from Sri Ksetra showing dancers and musicians richly dressed and ornamented. Skilled artisans also made silver Buddha images of great beauty. The culture was ultimately succeeded in the 9th century AD by the state of **Pagan** [15.45]; there is a major destruction layer at Halin, which may relate to this change of regime. Nevertheless, many Pyu arts, crafts, and ideas were incorporated into the Pagan state. It is recorded that King Anawratha of Pagan removed votive tablets and offerings from Sri Ksetra and placed them in his Shwesandaw temple at Pagan (Donovan et al. 1998).

The Dvaravati of Thailand

The civilization of Dvaravati flourished in the valley of the Chao Phraya River of central Thailand from about AD 400 to 900 (Brown 1996; Skilling 2003). It then came increasingly under the influence and, at times, control of Angkor. The people spoke Mon, a language closely related to Khmer. The few inscriptions include references to the Sanskrit name Dvaravati, meaning "having gates," perhaps referring to the gates giving access through the city walls. The names of Dvaravati rulers occasionally survive: a mid-7th century AD inscription from U-Thong reads "Sri Harshavarman, grandson of Ishanavarman, having expanded his sphere of glory, obtained the lion throne through regular succession." The king had given meritorious gifts to a *linga*, and described his exalted ancestry and military achieve-

15.46 Pagan: *one of the greatest centers of Buddhist temples in Southeast Asia. In the foreground is the Anada Temple.*

ments. A further text, also dated to the 7th century, records that "In the year ... a king who is nephew of the great King, who is the son of Pruthiveenadravarman, and who is as great as Bhavavarman, who has renowned moral principles, who is powerful and the terror of his enemies, erects this inscription on ascending the throne."

The archaeology of Dvaravati is dominated by a series of large, moated city sites of irregular oval or sub-rectangular plan. The favored location was near a stream to feed the moats. Excavations have frequently revealed the foundations of religious buildings constructed in laterite and brick, covered in decorated stucco with Buddhist figures or symbols. The buildings include *stupas* and *caityas* (barrel-vaulted shrines), to house relics or images of the Buddha. **Ku Bua** is a notable site, for it has furnished stucco images of Semitic traders, emphasizing the importance of international trade to the rise of this state. The major sites in the western group, such as **U-Thong** and **Nakhon Pathom**, are strategically located on the flood plains of the Maeklong and Chao Phraya rivers. The central region is dominated by the sites of Lopburi, Ban Khu Muang, and Sri Thep, while the eastern area incorporates Muang Phra Rot, Dong Si Mahosod, and Dong Lakhon.

The Cham of Vietnam

The Cham people occupied the coastal plains of Vietnam from Saigon (Ho Chi Minh City) to the Hai Van Pass. They spoke an Austronesian language most akin to the languages of Borneo, and their ancestors probably settled this coastal strip during the 1st millennium BC. Cham territory is divided into a series of restricted coastal enclaves, backed by the Truong Son cordillera. Centers were located where major rivers cross these coastal plains.

The most southerly region of Champa lies from the eastern margins of the Mekong Delta to Cape Dinh (south of modern Phan Rang), an inhospitable stretch of coastline with thin, sandy soils. Between Cape Dinh and Cape Nay (south of Tuy Hoa) are three well-watered valleys separated by low passes, and an area known to the Chams as Panduranga. North of Cape Dinh, the coastal strip broadens into a plain about 70 x 70 km (43 x 43 miles) in extent. There are many sites here in a region known to the Chams as Vijaya.

The region of **Amaravati** lies between the Hai Van Pass and Quy Nhon, and was the dominant area of Cham political centrality. It has a reasonable area of land available for agriculture, and several well-sheltered harbors. The last area lies north of the Hai Van Pass, with most archaeological sites being concentrated in the vicinity of **Quang Tri**. The relative importance and political reach of these polities, named in inscriptions, almost certainly changed markedly over time (Glover and Yamagata 1998; Guillon 2001).

It is most unlikely that Champa was ever a unified state. Louis Finot described the regions of Champa known from the inscriptions as "provinces," based on an inscription from Po Nagar, set up by King Jaya Harivarmadeva in 1160 (Southworth 2000). Jia Dan (AD 730–805), a Chinese traveler and eyewitness, confirmed that Champa was a group of kingdoms, rather than one unified state.

Chinese records contain many references to the Chams, who appear as a constant irritant to the maintenance of peace on China's southern frontier (Maspero 1928). There were episodes of warfare and raiding that were either repulsed by punitive expeditions or resolved through diplomacy. These episodes ceased during periods of central strength in China, which saw the restoration of tribute missions to the Chinese court. The Chinese histories recorded such missions (the first of which occurred between AD 220 and 230) as coming from the state of **Linyi** (effectively Champa, but known as Huanwang after 757). It is from such Chinese histories, too, that we are informed of the civil centers of Linyi, while the names of their overlords up to the early 6th century AD are known almost exclusively from Chinese sources. Toward the end of the 3rd century AD, a Chinese text recorded that the Linyi (the Chams) comprised numerous tribes that cooperated in resisting Chinese expansion. Border unrest was recorded in the *Hou Han Shu* ("History of the Later Han") in AD 137 and again in 192; at this point, the texts refer to the first dynasty of Linyi.

Fan-Wen was a prominent early Cham ruler, and was succeeded by his descendants Fan-Fo (from AD 349) and Fan-Hua (399–413). One of Fan-Hua's inscriptions contains a text written in Cham, confirming that the Linyi were Cham speakers by the end of the 4th century AD. During his reign, Sanskrit names were adopted, and the inscriptions refer to a King Bhadravarman. The establishment in his temple of a *linga* called

15.47, 15.48 Champa art and architecture: *(above) a statue of a seated Deva; height 91 cm (36 in); (right) the kalan (tower) of the temple at Po Klaung Garai; 11th–15th centuries.*

Bhadresvara confirms the development of the state cult of the named *linga*, which also provided a unifying force in the early states of Cambodia.

Summary and Conclusions

Civilization in China developed in the central plains of the Yellow River and along the course of the Yangzi River during the 2nd millennium BC. In the former area, the Xia and Shang dynasties dominated, while to the south, major centers were located in Sichuan and downstream in the area of lakes Dongting and Poyang. Later Chinese histories, now supplemented by archaeological research, have provided a compelling insight into the origins of these early states. Moreover, contemporary written records, in the form of divinatory incisions on turtle carapaces, give access to the thoughts and actions of individual kings.

The royal tombs of Shang, and major new archaeological discoveries such as the Shang city of Huanbei, reveal a powerful royal dynasty, responsible for the maintenance of craft specialists, a bureaucracy, and far-flung trade relationships. Warfare was endemic, and the western chariot was deployed in battle. In 1045 BC the Shang Dynasty was defeated at the Battle of Muye by the Zhou. The Zhou Dynasty ruled for longer than any other in Chinese history, although during the second half of its life, from 770 to 221 BC, it was overshadowed by the growing power of other states. The leader of one such state, known as Qin, defeated all its rivals, and in 221 BC established the first unified Chinese state under its emperor, Qin Shi Huangdi. The death of this emperor brought a period of civil strife that resulted in the establishment of the Han Dynasty in 206 BC. This engendered a period of imperial expansion that had a profound impact on those now increasingly brought within the Chinese sphere of influence.

To the northwest, Han interest in international trade led to the rise of many small states along the so-called Silk Road. To the east, Han colonialism in Korea was followed by the rise of indigenous states, while the rise of civilization in Japan took place in the context of Chinese trade and influence. Further south, the development of a maritime link with India and Rome played a part in the development of many Southeast Asian states. The Chams of central Vietnam, for example, profited from the passage of trade vessels along their long coastline. The Funan and Chenla states of Cambodia sent regular tribute missions to China. In central Thailand, the state of Dvaravati controlled this strategic link in a chain that stretched further west still, to central Burma and the Arakan coast. In due course, we can trace a progression from these early states to the modern nations of Southeast Asia.

In the next chapter we move back to the Americas, and resume the story that was begun in Chapter 9. There we traced the development of human societies during the early and mid-Holocene, down to 2500 BC, and in particular the transition from hunting and gathering to cultivation in key regions. There are strong parallels with some of the developments that we have described in the Old World – the rise of cities, monumental architecture, and intensive cultivation techniques, to name but three. But as in the Old World, each of the major regions to be discussed in the following chapters – Mesoamerica, South America, and North America – had its own distinctive trajectory and its own cultural and social character.

Further Reading

Bagley, R. (ed.). 2001. *Ancient Sichuan*. Seattle & Princeton: Seattle Art Museum. A magnificently illustrated volume by several experts that charts the prehistory and early history of Sichuan Province in southwest China, concentrating on the site of Sanxingdui.

Barnes, G. 2001. *State Formation in Korea*. London: Curzon Press. An up-to-date survey of the formation of the Korean states during the 1st millennium AD.

Brown, D. M. 1993. *The Cambridge History of Japan*. Cambridge: Cambridge University Press. Guide to the development of the early states of Japan, in which the coverage of the 1st millennium AD, in particular, relies on contemporary texts and recent major archaeological finds.

Higham, C. F. W. 2001. *The Civilization of Angkor*. London: Weidenfeld and Nicolson. A description of the civilization of Angkor from its prehistoric origins, describing the complexity of the local Iron Age cultures that led to the early states of Funan and Chenla, and then covering the three major dynasties of Angkor itself by means of contemporary inscriptions and the evidence of archaeology and surviving buildings.

Li Xueqin. 1985. *Eastern Zhou and Qin Civilizations*. New Haven: Yale University Press. The most complete available text describing the Spring and Autumn and Warring States periods.

Loewe, M. & Shaughnessy, E.L. (eds.). 1999. *The Cambridge History of Ancient China*. Cambridge: Cambridge University Press. An encyclopaedic consideration of Chinese history from the early prehistoric period to the end of the Warring States period and formation of the Qin empire, written by acknowledged authorities.

Rawson, J. (ed.). 1992. *The British Museum Book of Chinese Art*. London: British Museum Press. An informative and lively review of Chinese art, edited by the leading authority on the Western Zhou period.

Rawson, J. (ed.). 1996. *Mysteries of Ancient China*. London: British Museum Press. A richly illustrated compendium of major archaeological discoveries in China, providing glimpses of the extraordinary wealth of the early states and empires.

CHAPTER 16
MESOAMERICAN CIVILIZATION

David Webster and Susan Toby Evans, The Pennsylvania State University

The Landscape and its Peoples 595

The Spread of Agriculture and the Rise of Complex Societies in Preclassic Mesoamerica 598
● KEY DISCOVERY The Mesoamerican Ball Game 599
The First Agricultural Communities 600
● KEY SITE Paso de la Amada and the Emergence of Social Complexity 601

The Olmecs, *c.* 1200–400 BC
(Early to Middle Preclassic) 602
San Lorenzo and La Venta 602
The Olmecs as a "Mother Culture"? 604
West Mexican Polities, c. 1500 BC–AD 400 604
● KEY CONTROVERSY Were the Olmecs Mesoamerica's "Mother Culture"? 605

Late Preclassic Mesoamerica 606
Calendars and Writing 606
● KEY DISCOVERY The Mesoamerican Calendar 606
● KEY CONTROVERSY Who Invented Mesoamerican Writing? 608
● KEY CONTROVERSY Metallurgy in Mesoamerica 610
Kings, Courts, and Cities 610
  • *Monte Albán* 612
  • *Teotihuacán* 613
● KEY SITE Teotihuacán 614

The Classic Period: Teotihuacán and its Neighbors 616
Teotihuacán's Wider Influence: The Middle Horizon 616
● KEY CONTROVERSY The Teotihuacán Writing System 617
● KEY SITE Classic Monte Albán 618
Cholula, Cantona, and the Teuchitlan Cultural Tradition – Independent Polities? 620
The Demise of Teotihuacán 620

Epiclassic Mesoamerica, AD 600–900 621

The Classic Maya 623
Kingdoms and Capitals 624
Maya Society 625
  • *Royalty* 625
  • *Lords and Officials* 625
  • *Commoners* 626
  • *Warfare* 627
● KEY SITE Tikal 626

Postclassic Mesoamerica 627
● KEY CONTROVERSY Mesoamerican Urbanism 628
The Rise of the Toltecs 628
● KEY CONTROVERSY The Collapse of Maya Civilization 630
The Postclassic Maya 631
  • *The Puuc Florescence* 631
  • *Chichén Itzá* 632
  • *Mayapan* 632

Mesoamerica Discovered: What the Spaniards Found 633
The Maya of the Early 16th Century 633
The Aztecs and the Late Horizon: History and Myth 633
● KEY SITE Classic Tenochtitlán: The Aztec Capital 634
The Aztec Empire in 1519 636
  • *Aztec Society* 637
The Spanish Conquest 638

Summary and Conclusions 638

Further Reading and Suggested Websites 639

This chapter is the first of three describing the peoples and cultures of the Americas during the period from 2500 BC down to European contact and colonization in the 16th and 17th centuries. The earlier background, from the adoption of agriculture to the development of settled village farming, was set out in Chapter 9. Here, we follow the rise of complex societies and early states in Mesoamerica from the Olmec through the Maya, Toltec, and Aztec, up to the arrival of the Spanish adventurer Hernan Cortés in 1519.

When the Spaniards made their first landings in Mexico early in the 16th century, they encountered a world much more sophisticated than the one they had met with up to this time in the Caribbean. Kings and lords ruled over dense populations of farmers who supported them with taxes and tribute. Well-tended agricultural landscapes, often ingeniously irrigated and terraced, produced lush yields of maize, beans, and many other crops (Whitmore and Turner 1992; 2001). Lavish stone palaces, temples, and ball courts dominated impressive towns or political centers, the grandest of which were populous urban places comparable to the major cities of, for instance, Europe and North Africa. Professional merchants brought feathers, gold, jade, chocolate, and other costly goods to great urban markets. Scribes recorded the tribute of empire in brightly painted books, along with the genealogies of kings, the histories of peoples, and accounts of world creation. Priests scrutinized elaborate calendars for propitious times to celebrate a bewildering variety of rituals. Presiding over all were the powerful gods of war, rain, maize, and the sun, whose visages, along with those of kings, graced countless carved and painted monuments.

Particularly distinctive in this new world was a set of specific ideological beliefs, ritual practices, aesthetic conventions, and intellectual achievements (Miller and Taube 1993). Local societies broadly shared writing, shamanism, the use of 260- and 365-day calendars, a reverence for jade and other green stones, human sacrifice (especially through heart excision), traditions of multiple world creations, the belief that the earth was divided into four cardinal directions associated with particular colors, complex concepts of the human soul, carved stone stelae and altars, and a ball game that was played for both recreational and ceremonial purposes. Also shared were certain conventions of cosmetic or bodily presentation, most notably the use of ear flares, cranial shaping, and modification of the teeth by filing and inlays.

While some of these occurred elsewhere in the New World, taken together they form part of a distinctly Mesoamerican "package" of cultural features. Writing especially impressed the Spaniards as an essential hallmark of civilization (Boone 2000), and the Classic Maya are famous for their use of the mathematical concepts of "zero" and "place," which formed the basis for their highly accurate Long Count calendar (Sharer 1994) [see box: The Mesoamerican Calendar, pp. 606–7].

Despite their common features, however, Mesoamericans were never ethnically unified. The estimated 260 separate languages spoken in the 16th century illustrate the striking diversity that characterizes the region even today, when over 80 are still in use. Nor was any power ever able to unite all of Mesoamerica politically, not even the expanding Aztec empire with which the Spaniards collided in 1519. Nevertheless, there were long periods, conventionally called horizons, when vigorous regional cultures exerted unusually strong cultural, ideological, economic, or political influence over very wide areas. Such influences emanated at various times from several dynamic and precocious core regions, such as the Mexican Gulf Coast and the Basin of Mexico.

The distribution of many elements of Mesoamerican civilization (e.g. human sacrifice, the 260-day ritual calendar, the ball game) may reasonably be attributed to diffusion from restricted areas of origin. But "... the really significant development in the evolution of any civilization is the increase of societal size and internal heterogeneity, that is, the emergence of class and occupational divisions; and this is a process, not an invention to be diffused from place to place" (Sanders 1972, 152). This fundamental civilizing process took place in a remarkably varied landscape over several thousand years, and was heavily influenced by local environmental and ecological conditions.

The Landscape and its Peoples

When the Spanish arrived in Mesoamerica there were many thriving regional cultures and populations, stretching from what is today central Mexico to the northwest to El Salvador to the southeast [16.1, 16.2]. The imperial Aztecs and other Nahua-speaking peoples dominated the Basin of Mexico and adjacent highlands. To the west loomed the expanding empire of the Tarascans. Farther south, Mixtec and Zapotec peoples occupied Oaxaca and its neighboring valleys, while a solid block of Mixe-Zoque speakers extended from the Gulf Coast to the Pacific. Maya speakers were concentrated in the northern part of the Yucatán Peninsula and in the highlands of southern Mexico and Guatemala.

A distinctive feature of the mature Mesoamerican cultural tradition is that by 1519 it included virtually no hunter-gatherer societies, although farmers typically augmented their diets by

MESOAMERICAN CIVILIZATION TIMELINE

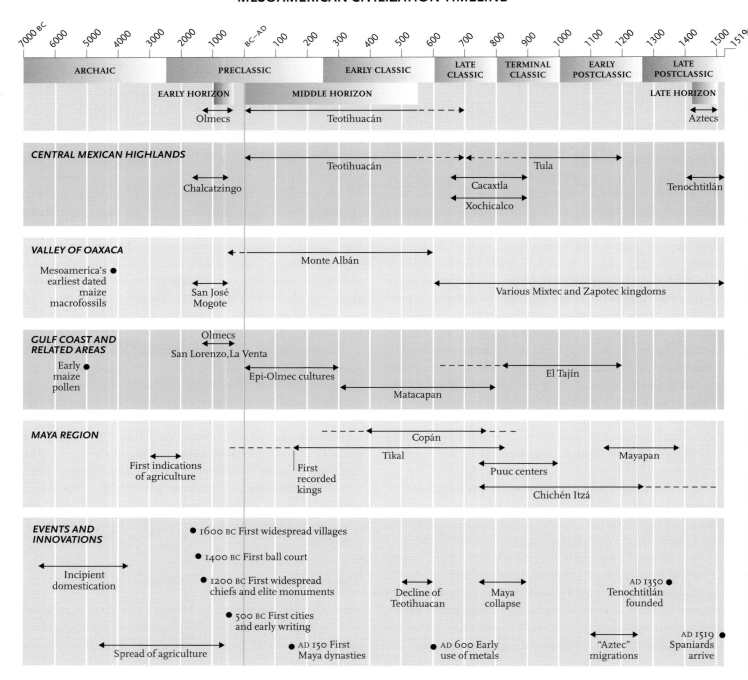

hunting, fishing, or foraging. Equally distinctive is that an impressive array of domesticated plants was poorly supplemented by domestic animals; particularly lacking were large herd animals. Introduction of Old World livestock after the Spanish conquest stimulated rapid and dramatic ecosystem transformations (many of them deleterious), and drastically affected social and economic behavior. Old World livestock allowed humans to exploit zones marginal or unsuitable for agriculture, thus enlarging their effective niches. Varying degrees of pastoralism not only affected diet (animal fat in par-

ticular was highly desirable), but also created patterns of group mobility and territoriality, divisions of labor, capital accumulation, and exchange that were very different from anything seen in pre-hispanic Mesoamerica.

Neither at the north nor the south was Mesoamerica delimited by sharp natural topographic or climatic boundaries. Its limits shift somewhat over time, depending on climatic change, population movements, and cultural interactions, but wherever they are positioned, Mesoamericans were certainly not isolated. To the north, native peoples in the Hohokam region of the southwestern United States constructed ball courts and possessed copper bells, macaws, and other things native to Mesoamerica (Chapter 18). Turquoise was imported into Tenochtitlán, the Aztec capital, from sources in northern Mexico and the southwestern United States. Gold from distant Colombia and Panama found its way into burials and offerings in Yucatán, and the first Mesoamericans sighted by Europeans were probably Maya traders who plied the waters of the Gulf of Honduras in large dugout canoes. Despite all these external contacts, however, the coherent package of cultural traits outlined above served to make Mesoamerica as distinctive as ancient Egypt, China, Mesopotamia, or the other precocious civilized regions of the Old World. It was, moreover, the only part of the ancient New World that developed true writing systems, thereby uniquely contributing to our understanding of the Mesoamerican past.

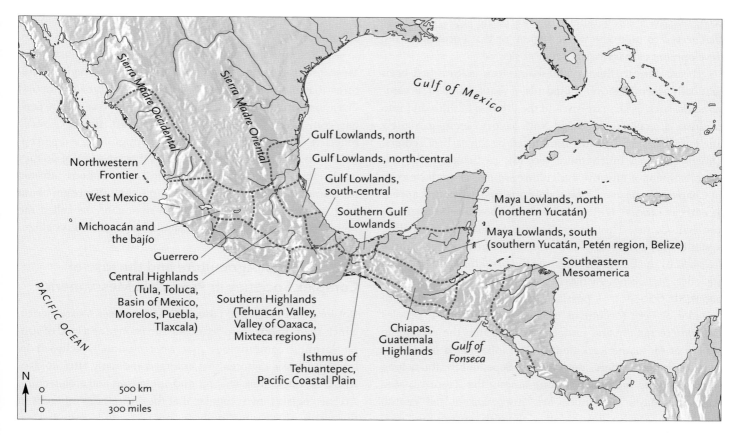

16.1 (Above) **Major physiographic and natural regions of Mesoamerica:** with the northern and southern boundaries of Mesoamerica, and major cultural regions within them.

16.2 (Right) **Major sites and cultural regions of Mesoamerica.**

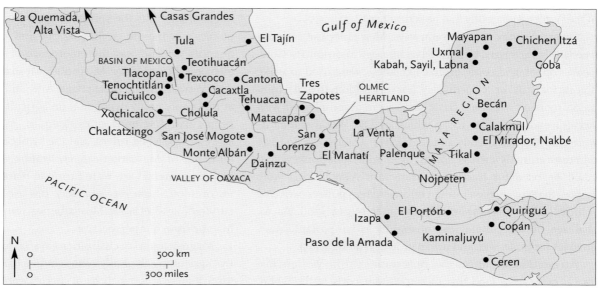

When Hernan Cortés visited the Spanish court and was asked to describe the lands he had conquered, he purportedly crumpled up a sheet of parchment and threw it on a table, saying, "That is Mexico!" This bit of drama graphically illustrates the rugged mountain systems that dominate much of Mesoamerica. Topographic compartmentalization stimulated much local cultural and ethnic diversity, and people had to adapt to environments ranging from high, cool mountain valleys to lowland tropical forests. There were, moreover, no great navigable rivers comparable to the Nile or the Tigris/Euphrates that served to unite the whole region, or that encouraged the development of massive irrigation works.

The mature tradition of Mesoamerican culture had been gradually assembled over thousands of years. Some of its components, such as shamanism and the division of the world into cardinal directions associated with colors, seem extremely ancient, and were arguably introduced by the earliest settlers. Others emerged much more recently, particularly after the establishment of effective agriculture, which, as we have seen in Chapter 9, was itself a long, slow process. Ball courts appear as early as 1400 BC (Hill et al. 1998) [see box: The Mesoamerican Ball Game]. The earliest certain Mesoamerican writing systems only emerged c. 600–300 BC (Marcus 1992), shortly followed by the first great cities and the first kings and stratified societies. Metallurgy, such as it was, appeared even later – after about AD 600–800 – possibly stimulated by contacts with Ecuador or Peru (Lechtman 1984). Nor were ancient peoples everywhere rapidly and uniformly drawn into the expanding sphere of Mesoamerican identity. The inhabitants of western Mexico, among others, developed independently for a long time. Ancestor veneration, strong among the Zapotecs, Mixtecs, and Maya, was much less important in the central highlands of Mexico. Even as late as the 16th century, the Tarascans, who conquered their own impressive empire to the west of the Aztecs, apparently had no writing at all.

Diverse as they were in some ways, Mesoamerican societies were all characterized by marked technological simplicity. Gold, silver, copper, and some bronze-like alloys were used to make objects for ritual or social display, but very seldom to make utilitarian tools or weapons. Basic tasks were accomplished with stone, wood, and fiber tools, which by Old World standards were comparatively crude and ineffective. There were no large domestic animals such as horses, oxen, mules, or donkeys that could be used for traction or transport. Also lacking were devices that augmented human effort, such as pulleys, wheeled vehicles, sails, or complicated machines of any kind. As we shall see, these technological constraints had important consequences for trade, war, and urban growth (Hassig 1985).

An evolutionary lesson that runs counter to the Western historical experience (and that of some other parts of the world, such as China) is that dynamic social and cultural change can be largely unrelated to technological innovation. A Mesoamerican magically transported from the time of Christ to the eve of European contact would find few tools, materials, or construction methods (metallurgy apart) that were very different from those of his own time, although the sheer scale of buildings or irrigation systems might dwarf anything he knew. What would disorient and impress our visitor would be the enormous populations, the huge settlements, the complex and powerful institutions and offices, and the landscape transformations all about him.

As a framework for our discussion of this distinctive Mesoamerican cultural tradition and the many regional cultures that manifested it, we will use several broad temporal divisions, with the caveat that these mainly represent time periods convenient to archaeologists. They are not necessarily reflective of thresholds or episodes meaningful or even perceptible to ancient Mesoamerican peoples themselves, nor do they imply that important changes in one region affected Mesoamerica as a whole, or at the same time. We begin about 2500 BC, when something that can reasonably be called the Mesoamerican tradition of civilization first began to crystallize.

The Spread of Agriculture and the Rise of Complex Societies in Preclassic Mesoamerica

Not long ago Preclassic (also called Formative) Mesoamerica, which spans nearly 3000 years, was envisioned as a land of simple farming communities that were eventually eclipsed by brilliant Classic cultures that emerged suddenly after AD 250, with their huge cities, writing, and opulent art and architecture. Archaeologists now recognize that the abruptness inherent in this picture was wrong, for it does not take into account the two major evolutionary trends that dominated the long Preclassic interval. First was the spread of agriculture, with all its social, political, economic, technological, and demographic consequences. Second was the emergence of social, political, and ideological complexity. At 2500 BC, Mesoamerican populations were very small, and most people were still hunter-gatherers, or at most only partly dependent on agriculture. By AD 250 these people had developed cities, temples, palaces, and dynasties of well-established rulers, and the symbolic/ideological accouterments of Mesoamerican civilization, including calendars and monumental art, were firmly in place. Writing was as yet uncommon, however, and very few early inscriptions have survived, so Preclassic Mesoamerica remains essentially prehistoric from our perspective.

All great agrarian civilizations are based on systems of effective agriculture, typically centered on a handful of staple crops. More than 100 domestic plant species were eventually grown in

Mesoamerica, but only a few contributed heavily to the diet, and by far the most important of these was **maize**. Maize was not just the basic food, but also a plant of extraordinary ideological and spiritual significance, much as rice is in parts of eastern Asia. Mesoamerican cosmology sometimes envisioned the surface of the world as a maize field, and it was widely believed that the gods created humans partly from maize. Rituals of sacrifice and renewal mimicked the lifecycle of the maize plant, and maize deities ranked high in the pantheon of Mesoamerican gods. Even some forms of human sacrifice, such as ritual beheading, are thought to be metaphors for harvesting ears of maize. Cultivating maize was an annual act of consecration for humble farmers, and a family that could not grow its own maize was not quite respectable – an attitude that survives in many parts of Mesoamerica today.

Maize seems originally to have been domesticated from its wild ancestor teosinte during the Archaic period, sometime before 4300 BC, with its primary center of dispersal in the upper Balsas River valley of southwestern Mexico (Matsuoka et al. 2002) [see The Domestication of Maize box, p. 316]. Maize fragments from Guilá Naquitz, a dry highland cave in the Valley of Oaxaca, date to 4300 BC, and indirect evidence suggests that the plant may have been grown in lowland zones such as the Mexican Gulf Coast by 5000 BC (Piperno and Flannery 2001; Pope et al. 2001). Clearly, maize was a crop that could be fairly rapidly adapted to many environmental circumstances. What is surprising, then, given its later importance, is how long it took for maize (along with other cultigens) to trigger the kinds of changes that we commonly associate with the adoption of agriculture, such as sedentism and the use of pottery – both

KEY DISCOVERY The Mesoamerican Ball Game

The Mesoamerican ball game could be played on any flat surface, but generally required a formal facility consisting of a long rectangular court flanked by structures with vertical or sloping sides. Scoring was accomplished in several ways, but basically involved striking a rubber ball (without using the hands or feet) through an "end zone" or, more rarely, through a stone ring set high up on the sidewall of the court. The court itself was conceived as a liminal place connecting the surface of the earth and the underworld; some versions of the game had great cosmological significance, and appear to have been associated with human sacrifice. Some ball games also functioned as events in which powerful chiefs or kings hosted emissaries from other polities, and so had great political significance. Other games seem to have been purely recreational, especially during Postclassic times (AD 1000–1519), and observers wagered vast amounts of personal wealth on their outcomes.

16.3 *The ball game, seen here on a Maya vase of c. AD 600–800, had great symbolic significance, and the losers of the contest on the court sometimes also lost their lives.*

16.4 *The site of Copán has one of the largest ball courts in the Classic Maya Lowlands, built in the characteristic I-shape with sloping sides.*

16.5 *The Valley of Oaxaca: San José Mogote was a large "dispersed village," but other early agricultural communities in the Oaxaca Valley were smaller and seem to have been politically autonomous.*

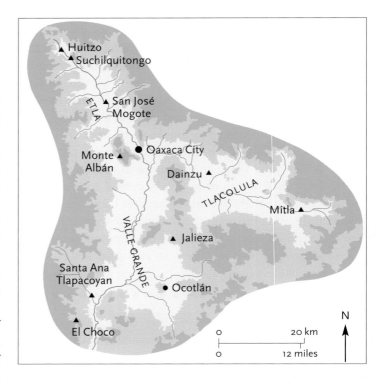

hallmarks of the Early Preclassic. One probable reason for this slow impact is that, unlike the various wild wheats of Southwest Asia, teosinte is a very unlikely candidate for domestication (Iltis 2000). Wild teosinte produces abundant seeds, but these are small, difficult to process into usable form, and not very palatable. Many generations of human selection were required to produce large-kernelled maize cobs, and early maize was, for a long time, not an effective staple, but rather a useful adjunct to a traditional diet largely consisting of wild resources, as described in Chapter 9.

Use of pottery was once thought to be a good marker for the onset of the agricultural way of life, and one reason for setting the beginning of the Preclassic at 2500 BC is that the first pottery appears at about this time at sites on the Pacific coast of Mexico. A century or so later it was present in the Tehuacán Valley, and thereafter it became increasingly widespread. Much of this early pottery is rather crude, and some of its basic shapes seem to mimic earlier vessels made from gourds or carved from stone. Over the next few hundred years, ceramic assemblages increasingly included vessels carved or painted with complex designs. A somewhat later, but very important, Preclassic innovation was the production of distinctive stone tools called prismatic blades. First appearing *c.* 1500 BC, these were usually struck or pressed from carefully prepared obsidian cores. Such blades (or cores) were widely traded and remained the most common Mesoamerican cutting implements right up to the 16th century.

The First Agricultural Communities

The first widespread and reasonably permanent agricultural communities date to around 1600 BC, almost a millennium after the first pottery. Early agricultural settlements typically consisted of small clusters of simple houses with earthen floors, walls of wattle and daub, and roofs of thatch. Often, as at **San Jos Mogote** in the Valley of Oaxaca [**16.5**], the spaces between houses [**16.6**] were used for gardens, the produce from which supplemented deer, rabbits, quail, and other wild resources (Marcus and Flannery 1996). Slightly larger structures probably had specialized communal purposes. A big "dispersed village" such as San José Mogote might have had about 200 inhabitants in 1400–1300 BC. Other communities in Oaxaca at the time were smaller, and all seem to have been politically autonomous. Imported macaw feathers and shells of

oysters and turtles hint at differences in wealth, but there were as yet no unusually large residences or elaborate burials. Burned remains of an apparent timber palisade at San José Mogote suggest that raiding and warfare were present even as the first villages were established (Flannery and Marcus 2003).

Similar communities, such as **Chalcatzingo** (Grove 1984), were established in the central Mexican highlands at about the same time, part of a colonizing process that introduced agriculture into the high, cold valleys of the Basin of Mexico (although various plants might have been cultivated there as early as 3000 BC). Not until about 1000 BC is there substantial evidence for farming communities in the tropical Maya lowlands, although signs of forest disturbance consistent with cultivation appear at least 2000 years earlier (Pohl et al. 1996). Elsewhere in the low-

16.6 *San José Mogote: a reconstruction of a civic building at the site, which probably served communal purposes.*

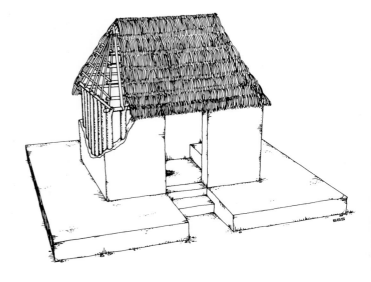

land tropics, agricultural communities were well established by about 1600 BC; some show signs of unusual size and precocity, and the first glimmerings of increased social complexity [see box: Paso de la Amada].

The ethno-linguistic affiliations of these various early Pre-classic peoples remain unclear and controversial, in part because there were many population movements. In some cases archaeological evidence suggests considerable continuity – early farmers in the Valley of Oaxaca almost certainly spoke ancestral forms of modern Zapotec. The first villagers in some parts of the Maya lowlands, however, might have spoken a non-Maya language, perhaps of Mixe-Zoque affiliation, before being pushed to the west by intrusive Maya speakers (Ball and Taschek 2003).

KEY SITE Paso de la Amada and the Emergence of Social Complexity

Paso de la Amada (c. 1550–850 BC) is located on the Pacific coastal plain near the modern border between Mexico and Guatemala (Blake 1991). This region was covered by heavy tropical forest, and the inhabitants of Paso de la Amada occupied a sandy ridge near old river channels and lakes – an excellent set of microenvironments for gardening, gathering, hunting, and the exploitation of riverine and marine resources.

Foundations of more than 50 residences have been mapped, and the community eventually covered at least 50–75 ha (124–185 acres). Two parallel mounds delineate a level area about 80 m (262 ft) long and 7 m (23 ft) wide – the earliest ball court (and one of the largest) so far discovered in Mesoamerica.

Controversy centers on Mound 6, an unusually large earthen structure c. 20 m (66 ft) long, which was rebuilt six times between about 1350 and 1250 BC. The excavator interprets it as a chiefly residence, given its architectural features and the abundant associated domestic refuse. Other archaeologists believe that it was some sort of public building, perhaps a young men's house. Both views might be correct, for the houses of prominent leaders often had important communal functions later on. This is an important issue, because although we know that social ranking and stratification evolved during the Preclassic, tracing their earliest archaeological manifestations is challenging. Another impressive building, Mound 4, has been interpreted as a residence or temple.

Paso de la Amada seems to have been the largest of a number of villages in the region during the Early Preclassic, and might well have functioned as a kind of chiefly capital or central place for people living in nearby communities. Ornate serving bowls and dishes suggest frequent feasting, and non-local materials such as obsidian and jade were imported from sources hundreds of kilometers away. On the other hand, the numerous burials recovered were all given simple mortuary treatment, suggesting few social or political distinctions and little concentration of wealth. Although maize might have been eaten early on, it was not a dominant part of the diet, judging from studies of stable isotopes in human bone samples.

This was obviously an impressive and long-lived community, the architecture of which hints at emergent elites or political leaders, or at least considerable expenditure of organized community labor. So why is this social differentiation not reflected in burial rituals, as it is later in Mesoamerica? Another question is whether Paso de la Amada thrived on a subsistence economy that featured marine/estuarine resources rather than agriculture.

Whatever the answers, the presence of the ball court helps to reveal the origins of one of the most distinctive features of the Mesoamerican cultural tradition. Even more important, Paso de la Amada somewhat predates the Olmec culture, which left one of the most flamboyant archaeological records of any ancient Mesoamerican people, and which was long envisioned as the most precocious Early to Middle Preclassic society.

16.7 *Earthen floor of Mound 6 at Paso de la Amada. This has been interpreted either as a chiefly residence or a public building, or possibly both.*

The Olmecs, *c.* 1200–400 BC (Early to Middle Preclassic)

During the mid-19th century, archaeologists and collectors began to recognize distinctively decorated objects of pottery, jade, and other materials that did not fit the canons of better-known Maya, Zapotec, or Aztec art (Benson and de la Fuente 1996; Clark and Pye 2000; Diehl 2004). Such objects were small and portable and turned up in many parts of Mesoamerica, but in 1862 the huge monolithic sculpture of a stone head in this mysterious style was found at Tres Zapotes on the Mexican Gulf Coast, clearly in or near its original location. Eventually the term "Olmec" (derived from the Aztec name for the people who lived in this region in the 16th century) became attached to this art style. Surveys and excavations beginning in the 1920s confirmed that the style was associated with large Gulf Coast sites such as La Venta and San Lorenzo, and so the label was also applied to the ancient inhabitants of this presumed "homeland." Just who the Olmecs were, what language they spoke, and their relationships with other Mesoamerican cultures have stirred intense debate ever since.

Most immediately controversial was Olmec chronology, an issue difficult to sort out before World War II, in the absence of sophisticated dating methods. Archaeologists devoted to the idea that the Classic Maya were the great "Mother Culture" of Mesoamerican civilization refused to believe that the Olmecs predated the Maya, while an opposing camp asserted that the Olmecs were much older. The advent of radiocarbon dating in the 1950s resolved this issue, and we now know that Olmec culture thrived roughly between 1200 and 400 BC. Olmec influences were especially pronounced and widespread during the Middle Preclassic (1000–400 BC), creating what is sometimes called Mesoamerica's **Early Horizon** – a time when art and symbols, and presumably the ideologies behind them, were widely shared.

San Lorenzo and La Venta

Non-chronological issues could not be resolved so easily. Archaeologists agree that there were impressive Olmec polities in the Gulf Coast lowlands, where meandering rivers flowed through dense tropical forests. The earliest of these was dominated by **San Lorenzo**, *c.* 1200–900 BC (Cyphers 1996), where the Olmecs leveled the top of a natural plateau standing about 50 m (165 ft) higher than the surrounding countryside. On the summit they erected an impressive building called the Red Palace, probably an elite residence, and created an elaborate system of what appear to be ceremonial ponds and drains. Water seems to have been of great ritual significance; spectacular offerings, including carved wooden effigies and large rubber balls, were placed in the nearby spring-fed pond of **El Manatí**. Whether many people lived on top of the San Lorenzo plateau is unclear, because the Olmec levels are covered by accumulated debris from much later occupations. About 500 ha (1235 acres) of artificial terraces with associated house foundations have been mapped on the adjacent slopes, however. Some of these are Early Preclassic residences, although it is uncertain how much of this habitation zone dates to Olmec times. Surveys have located long, causeway-like features around San Lorenzo that linked settlements, supported houses, and possibly channeled water in this frequently flooded environment.

Archaeologists have recovered scores of large basalt monuments at San Lorenzo, including ten of the trademark **colossal stone heads** [16.8]. All were probably originally set up in public places on the plateau top. They were carved from stone quarried 60 km (37 miles) from San Lorenzo; this material was sufficiently valuable that old, unwanted monuments were cut apart and recycled into smaller sculptures or other objects in work-

16.8 Colossal head: *this example is from San Lorenzo, but each such image wears a distinctive cap similar to those sometimes later worn by ball-players.*

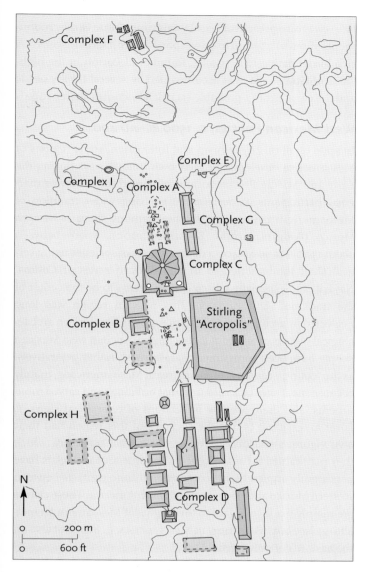

monuments, including colossal heads, stelae (upright stone slabs), and huge rectangular thrones [**16.10**], were set up in La Venta's public spaces. Frequent renovations to these spaces included the deliberate burial of huge numbers of slabs, mainly of the imported green mineral serpentine, some arranged to depict abstract effigies of animals or gods. Some La Venta notables were interred in richly carved sarcophagi, and two infants were placed in an elaborate tomb made of natural basalt columns, accompanied by a rich array of mortuary offerings. This last tomb provides some of the earliest evidence for inherited rank and social position in the Mesoamerican archaeological record. La Venta was once envisioned as a vacant ceremonial center, but abundant domestic refuse and the remains of houses indicate a permanent population that probably included rulers and their families as well as commoners (about whom we know almost nothing).

Around San Lorenzo and La Venta is a constellation of smaller sites, some the remains of tiny hamlets or rural households, others well-established villages. Houses were made of perishable materials, much like modern dwellings in the region. A few of the bigger settlements have their own large earthen structures and carved monuments. Clearly, San Lorenzo and La Venta were political capitals where powerful leaders resided, supported by sizable outlying populations numbering in the thousands. Several other such capitals, as yet inadequately tested by archaeologists, might have coexisted

shops near the Red Palace. Olmec artisans also polished exotic iron minerals brought from the Mexican highlands into mirrors, which were used in shamanistic displays and as objects of wealth and status. Other imports included obsidian and, no doubt, many other, perishable materials, such as feathers of the quetzal bird. Olmec carvings of blue-green jade are particularly distinctive, the raw material having come from the upper reaches of the Motagua River in Guatemala.

San Lorenzo's decline *c.* 1000–900 BC coincided with the rise of **La Venta**, another large, sprawling center about 88 km (55 miles) to the northeast [**16.9**] (Gonzales Lauck 1996). Its most impressive feature is an earthen pyramid over 33 m (108 ft) high, around which cluster many lower earth structures and associated courtyards. The most famous of all Olmec carved

16.10 *Olmec throne from La Venta:* the carvings show gorgeously dressed adults holding naked, baby-like figures with fanged, snarling mouths.

with them in the Olmec heartland. Although earlier signs of Preclassic social and political complexity are glimpsed at Paso de la Amada and elsewhere, the Gulf Coast Olmecs do appear unusually precocious for their time.

The Olmec as a "Mother Culture"?

Archaeologists are divided about what all this means. Some believe that heartland Olmec polities had all the institutional and symbolic trappings of true civilizations, such as those found later in Mesoamerica, and that centers such as La Venta were complex urban places. Flamboyant art and architecture notwithstanding, others assert that Olmec social and political organization were on the simpler, chiefdom level, and that places like La Venta mainly served as elite residences and ritual centers (the view taken here).

Fueling this controversy is intense disagreement about the nature and implications of "Olmec" art and symbolism. Some of the classic manifestations of the style, such as the colossal stone heads, are confined to the Gulf Coast. These heads are generally interpreted as portraits of individual chiefs or kings, and plausibly represent the beginnings of a long Mesoamerican tradition of monumental ruler depiction. Gorgeously dressed figures are frequently shown on stelae or thrones (particularly at La Venta), and this pronounced hierarchical theme in Olmec monuments points to considerable political centralization and social ranking. Although no Olmec ball courts are known, some figures display elements of the ballplayer's costume (Whittington 2001).

Much "Olmec" art is not restricted to the Olmec heartland, however, but is scattered throughout Mesoamerica. Some archaeologists think this distribution reveals the Gulf Coast Olmecs as the most dynamic of all Early and Middle Preclassic cultures – indeed, as the "Mother Culture" of later Mesoamerican civilization. Others argue that the heartland Olmecs were just one of many Mesoamerican societies that independently evolved complex institutions and cultural patterns, despite undoubted trade and other interactions [see box: Were the Olmecs Mesoamerica's "Mother Culture"?]. Contributing to the confusion is the fact that many "Olmec" objects come from looted sites, so their original contexts are lost, and not a few have turned out to be fakes.

Whatever one's opinions concerning the "Mother Culture" hypothesis, or whether even the most complex Early to Middle Preclassic cultures warrant the label "civilization," many basic elements of the Mesoamerican cultural tradition, including effective agriculture, marked political ranking and centralization, large centers with monumental architecture and sculpture, and the ball game, were firmly in place by the end of the Middle Preclassic, *c.* 400 BC. Another more sinister aspect of Mesoamerican life that later became very prominent – war-

fare – was also present at least by this time. Some Olmec monuments show what seem to be weapons and militaristic scenes. A rich burial dating to *c.* 500 BC, found at **El Portón** in the highlands of Guatemala, was accompanied by several trophy heads and the corpses of 12 probable sacrificial victims (Sharer 1994).

West Mexican Polities, c. 1500 BC–AD 400

In spite of all this dynamism and interaction, some regions of Mesoamerica developed in their own unique ways during the Early and Middle Preclassic, and remained for centuries marginal participants at best in the evolving wider tradition of Mesoamerican culture. Conspicuous among them is western Mexico (Weigand 2001a; Beekman 2000), where between about 1500 BC and AD 400 a distinctive set of societies using vertical **shaft tombs** emerged in the Mexican states of **Colima**, **Nayarit**, and especially **Jalisco** (which seems to be the center of the tradition). Unfortunately, this western region was long neglected by archaeologists, and many of its best-known archaeological objects come from looted tombs. Ancient west Mexican people have been sometimes characterized, rather pejoratively, as the "country cousins" of mainstream Mesoamericans, mainly because most sites lack monumental buildings and carved monuments, and there are few indications of calendrical signs. A fairer assessment is that the societies of this region had their own vigorous and distinctive developmental trajectory, which they maintained for many centuries. Some archaeologists have persistently argued that there were maritime contacts between western Mexico and northwestern South America. These claims are mainly made in regard to the origins of Mesoamerican metallurgy [see box: Metallurgy in Mesoamerica, p. 610], but also on the basis of ceramic forms.

Such possible influences aside, it is clear that various polities in Preclassic western Mexico were hierarchically organized, and that their chiefs and other elites were buried in deep shaft tombs. Some tombs included only single interments, but others were ossuaries that seem to have served large groups for generations. Weapons, tools, ornaments, and elaborate pottery accompanied the dead. Most impressive of all the mortuary goods (and the principal reason for the looting) are large, hollow figurines of dogs, warriors, rulers, and religious practitioners. Among the most informative of these sculptures are complex models of houses, rituals, ball games, musical performances, and people being carried in litters. All this complexity seems to reflect a politically fragmented landscape and much elite rivalry. By the beginning of the Late Preclassic period there was a shift from this preoccupation with mortuary ceremonies focused on tombs, to the construction of unusual surface-level architectural complexes with concentric circular layouts. These distinctive Teuchitlan cultural tradition communities appear more politically centralized, and they endured until AD 600–900.

KEY CONTROVERSY   Were the Olmecs Mesoamerica's "Mother Culture"?

Objects and motifs now labeled "Olmec" were widely distributed across Mesoamerica, particularly during Middle Preclassic times, *c.* 1000–400 BC. This period coincides with the flourishing of La Venta and is sometimes called the Early Horizon, when broadly shared aesthetic/symbolic patterns can be discerned throughout much of Mesoamerica for the first time.

Sculptures found as far away as Chalchuapa in El Salvador closely resemble monuments from La Venta, and cave paintings at Oxtotitlan in western Mexico show human/animal figures sitting on La Venta-style thrones. Some smaller portable objects in the Olmec style appear to have been exported from the Gulf Coast, and locally made ones are decorated with Olmec designs.

Two routes of communication seem particularly important. One led up into the highland valleys of Puebla and Morelos, and then farther away to the Basin of Mexico and western Mexico. Another ran through the Isthmus of Tehuantepec, from there to the Pacific piedmont of Mexico and Guatemala, and eventually all the way to El Salvador.

The Case For ...

All this evidence for widespread influence, plus the precocity of San Lorenzo and La Venta in terms of public architecture, large stone monuments, and sophisticated art and iconography, convinces some scholars (e.g. Diehl 1996) that the Gulf Coast Olmecs were great innovators who not only invented many of the basic elements and institutions of Mesoamerican civilization, but also transmitted them widely to less developed societies through trade, diplomatic exchanges, religious proselytizing, war, and other forms of direct or indirect contact. In short, the Olmecs were Mesoamerica's "Mother Culture."

... and Against

The alternative and more prevalent view (e.g. Grove 2000) is that the Olmecs were only one of many regional societies in Mesoamerica

16.11 *This sculpture from Teopantecuanitlán, in west Mexico, has characteristic Olmec elements, including the snarling, downturned mouth.*

that were rapidly evolving new and more complex social and political institutions during the Early and Middle Preclassic, along with their attendant aesthetic, intellectual, and ideological traditions. Interregional contacts certainly played a part, but the most fundamental evolutionary processes were local ones.

Many of the shared traits, for example those related to shamanism, might have been inherited from a commonly held set of very ancient beliefs. The Early Horizon was, in fact, created not by the overwhelming dominance of the Gulf Coast Olmecs, but instead by this larger sphere of interaction and shared origins, to which many regional societies eventually contributed as equals.

Among the objections to the "Mother Culture" interpretation is that some sites, such as Paso de la Amada, show evidence of considerable social complexity, along with specific features such as ball courts, centuries before comparable evidence appears in the Olmec heartland. Moreover, many so-called "Olmec" icons or stylistic elements seem to originate elsewhere in Mesoamerica, so their distribution does not imply a primary role for the Gulf Coast people. In addition, some parts of Mesoamerica that show signs of early sophistication, such as the Maya lowlands and the highlands of Guatemala, yield few or no indications of direct Olmec influence.

Nor were the Olmecs necessarily the first great builders. Early monumental architecture is found elsewhere, such as in the planned arrangement of large earthen structures at Chiapa de Corzo in Mexico's Grijalva Valley, built *c.* 700 BC, plausibly as early as La Venta's great pyramid. Temples, elite residences, and elaborate burials accompanied by what appear to be sacrificial victims all appeared in the Salama Valley in highland Guatemala *c.* 800–400 BC, and many more examples of such precocity could be listed.

Overview

Proponents of either argument can point to specific sites to bolster their claims. Supporting the "Mother Culture" perspective, for example, is Teopantecuanitlán. At this site in the highlands of western Mexico are Olmec-style zoomorphic monuments, along with an impressive arrangement of sunken ritual courts and terraces, all built *c.* 1000–800 BC. On the other hand, nothing comparable has been found in the Basin of Mexico at the same period, although it had long had its own thriving agricultural communities.

Chalcatzingo in Morelos was established as a farming village by 1500 BC, and within a few hundred years was a dominant center of the region. Distinctly Olmec carvings appear within the community itself and on nearby natural rock faces *c.* 700–500 BC. Yet the ceramic traditions of Chalcatzingo are firmly rooted in those of the central highlands of Mexico, and its inhabitants were not in any sense Gulf Coast Olmecs, although people from there must have visited the site. Finds at Chalcatzingo illustrate why it is so difficult to resolve the "Mother Culture" issue to everyone's satisfaction – one can use them to support either perspective.

KEY DISCOVERY The Mesoamerican Calendar

The most widely shared of all Mesoamerican calendars tracked cycles of 260 days and 365 days. While the latter period closely approximates to the solar year, the former (referred to as the Sacred Almanac) does not correspond directly to any particular astronomical cycle. It is close to the human gestation period, but it might simply result from the permutation of the number 20 (Mesoamericans counted in increments of 20, rather than 10) and the 13 levels thought to comprise the heavens.

Calendrical notations were made using the vigesimal (base-20) system of counting, in which dots and bars signify, respectively, the numbers one and five. These signs could be combined to represent larger numbers, and the lowland Maya also had a symbol for zero and the concept of place, allowing them to express and accurately manipulate very large numbers.

Although there were many local variations of the two calendars, they generally worked as follows:

260-day calendar Each day was designated by a number from 1 to 13, and one of 20 names. The same designation thus repeated itself every 260 days (13 x 20).

365-day calendar Solar cycle days were designated by one of 20 day names and 18 month names, for a total of 360 days (20 x 18). To this was added a period of five days to bring the total close to the solar year.

Calendar Round Any given day had a "compound name" of four signs that resulted from the combination of designations from the 260- and 365-day calendars. If the calendars were conceptually meshed, this same day came around again only every 52 years, a long cycle called the Calendar Round. The reappearance of the conjoined days that signaled the beginning of the two subsidiary cycles was of great cosmological and ritual import.

The Long Count A third calendar, the Long Count (also called the Initial Series), tracked such a very long cycle that for all practical purposes it functioned as a linear count of time. Each day thus had a unique date, not one that repeated itself cyclically as in the other calendars. Although invented elsewhere, by Classic times (AD 250–800) it was used only by the lowland Maya, who perfected it.

Like the Gregorian calendar in the West, the Long Count began on a specific day: on or about 11 August 3114 BC. To express a particular Long Count date the Maya began with the most basic unit, the day (called a *kin*), and then combined days into longer periods called *uinals* (20 days), *tuns* (360 days), *k'atuns* (7200 days), and *baktuns* (144,000 days). There are even larger units, but these are the most fundamental ones.

Notice that the progression of units here is always by a factor of 20 except for the *tun*, which is not 400 as expected (20 x 20), but rather 360 (20 x 18), an accommodation Maya mathematicians probably introduced to better fit this unit to the length of the solar year. (Even so, Long Count reckonings accumulated an error of more than five days each year.) The "completions" of some of these periods, particularly *k'atuns*, had great significance.

Full Long Count dates recorded on ancient Maya monuments consist of a sequence of numbers that expresses these units in order. For example, a date given as a sequence that runs 9 *baktuns*, 15 *k'atuns*, 6 *tuns*, 14 *uinals*, and 6 *kins* indicates the collective number of days that has elapsed since the count began over 5000 years ago. This date corresponds to 1 May AD 738 in the modern calendar. According to the conventional notation used by Mayanists, such a date would be written 9.15.6.14.6, and the Maya would often have appended the corresponding Calendar Round date as well.

Because Long Count dates can be correlated with our current calendar, they provide archaeologists with a very precise chronological control.

Ancient Mesoamerican peoples employed all these calendars in very complex ways, using them to track the cycles of the sun, the moon, Venus, and other celestial bodies. Specific days governed the fate of individuals, and in some cultures a person's name was derived from his birthday. Important events were dated in historical or genealogical records.

Late Preclassic Mesoamerica, 400 BC–AD 250

Despite the decline of the Gulf Coast Olmecs, the Late Preclassic period (400 BC–AD 250) saw the first great flowering in this region of what, by any standards, was a major world civilization. Fueling this florescence was rapid regional demographic growth. Lowland Maya populations burgeoned after about 400 BC, as witnessed by the many sites that yield their characteristic red-slipped Chicanel pottery, and population in the Basin of Mexico more than doubled between 300 BC and AD 100. Stimulated by such demographic changes, large polities with impressive centers became much more common. Some were the regal-ritual capitals of kings, but at least two of them – Monte Albán in Oaxaca and Teotihuacán in the Basin of Mexico – developed into the earliest true cities in Mesoamerica. Before turning to these political and urban transformations, however, we examine the evolution of Mesoamerican calendars, writing, and art, all of which emerged rapidly during the several centuries immediately following the demise of the Olmecs (a time sometimes called the Epi-Olmec period).

Calendars and Writing

Various Olmec objects are embellished with signs that seem to prefigure mathematical, calendrical, or written symbols; calen-

Cycles recorded by calendars had great divinatory significance, and certain calendrical events were particularly important. For example, the cusp of a 52-year Calendar Round repetition was thought by the Aztecs to herald a moment of great danger for the world, and was attended by elaborate ceremonies and sacrifices.

16.12 *The Maya version of the intermeshed 260-day ritual calendar (left) and the 365-day solar calendar (right), which together constitute the 52-year Calendar Round.*

drical glyphs appear slightly later. Working back from their knowledge of Classic Maya calendars, archaeologists long ago documented the Late Preclassic origins of the Long Count [see box: The Mesoamerican Calendar]. A monument discovered in 1939 at Tres Zapotes, deep in the Olmec heartland, yielded a Long Count date corresponding to 31 BC, recorded using the characteristic bar-and-dot signs common on later Classic monuments (Diehl 2000) [**16.13**].

Both the 260-day ritual and the 365-day solar calendars are probably much older. What might be an early calendrical notation in the 260-day cycle (apparently used as a personal name) is found on a carved stone slab [**16.14**] at San José Mogote (Mar-cus and Flannery 1996), possibly dating to just before the abandonment of that site *c.* 600–500 BC (some archaeologists think it is much later). Stelae at Monte Albán also have bar and dot numerals that might date as early 500–400 BC. Although the origins of the solar calendar remain more uncertain, it too was probably used in Epi-Olmec times.

Writing seems to have originated more than once in Mesoamerica. We know that its origins and spread were associated with several major groups of languages ancestral to those still spoken today – Nahua, Maya, Mixe-Zoque, Mixtec, and Zapotec. In the early 16th century, all but Zapotec and Mixe-Zoque speakers still retained writing, although Maya literacy

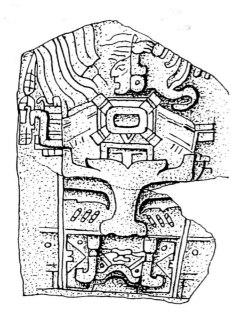

16.13, 16.14 *Early calendrical inscriptions:* *fragments of this Epi-Olmec monument from Tres Zapotes (left) have one of the oldest Long Count dates – corresponding to 31 BC. (Right) Monument 3 from San José Mogote shows a mutilated victim with the calendrical sign for "One Earthquake" between his legs – a very early Zapotec inscription.*

KEY CONTROVERSY Who Invented Mesoamerican Writing?

Most epigraphists define writing as systems of signs that record speech in visual form, although some prefer a broader definition that would include images or pictures less directly related to spoken language (Boone 2000). One reason for this disagreement is that although some scripts, and all Mesoamerican ones, consist of pictographic elements combined with signs that signify words or sounds, the exact mix differs from one script to another. Aztec (Nahuatl) writing emphasized the pictographic principle, and used many elements that had to be "decoded" into spoken words. Classic Maya writing, by contrast, was primarily logo-syllabic (i.e., glyphs directly represented words or sounds) and probably could have recorded any verbal utterance. Although writing has long been inappropriately bound up with our concepts of "civilization," immense empires such as that of the Inca flourished without writing in the strict sense, and even very small and comparatively simple communities have maintained scripts, for example the Rongorongo inscriptions of Easter Islanders.

Nahuatl and Mixtec scripts used in the 16th century can still be read, and Maya writing has been largely deciphered. Ancient Zapotec inscriptions are still unreadable, however (apart from some calendrical labels and ruler names), as are some other early scripts, the linguistic affiliations of which remain uncertain. Fortunately, the close relationship of all ancient inscriptions to art, along with knowledge of their contexts, allows some reasonable interpretations. A case in point is Monument 3 at San José Mogote, in the Oaxaca Valley, which shows a slain captive with glyphs that might refer to his day-name in the 260-day ritual calendar [see **16.14**]. Monument 3 could have been carved around 600 BC, and is thought by some to be a very early expression of Zapotec writing (Marcus 1992). Other epigraphists think that it is several centuries younger, contemporary with the hundreds of so-called "Danzante" carvings found at nearby Monte Albán. Each of these latter figures seems to show a slain and mutilated war captive accompanied by what might be his name glyph, or perhaps titles or toponyms (place-names). In any case, inscriptions are clearly very ancient in Oaxaca and plausibly record an ancient form of the Zapotec language.

The La Mojarra Stela
Many archaeologists suspect that Mixe-Zoque speakers developed writing at least as early as the Zapotecs did, building directly on earlier Olmec foundations. The Olmecs are thought to have transmitted their influence from the Gulf Coast across the Isthmus of Tehuantepec, and thence along the Pacific coastal strip where many early sculptures are known.

A puzzling monument from this "Isthmian" tradition is the La Mojarra stela, retrieved from a river in Vera Cruz on the Gulf Coast. It depicts a ruler accompanied by a long inscription, including two Long Count dates equivalent to AD 143 and 156 (Diehl 2000). One provisional decipherment assigns the script to an early Mixe-Zoque language, but many epigraphists find this interpretation controversial. Still, if the La Mojarra stela is not a fake (as some archaeologists suspect), it is unquestionably early, and has a style of presentation and a set of themes similar to those found on later Maya stelae.

The Maya and Beyond
Although the lowland Maya eventually perfected Mesoamerica's most sophisticated script (Coe 1992; Houston et al. 2001), they did not invent writing, and for the present it is probably best not to try to assign the origins of

quickly succumbed to Spanish suppression. A problem in tracing the beginnings of these scripts is that all Mesoamerican writing systems made use of pictorial signs or glyphs. Only some of these, however, are true pictographs, while others might represent whole words or even syllables. Thus it is difficult to disentangle early true glyphs from other kinds of iconographic depictions that might precede or accompany them, or to know exactly what linguistic element an individual glyph conveys. Adding to this difficulty is the characteristic close association between art, calendrical notations, and writing. The earliest writing seems to have been used to convey very limited kinds of information, and probably was not as closely linked to speech as it was later (e.g., in Classic Maya inscriptions).

All Mesoamerican scripts were recorded in three basic media. Glyphs were carved or painted on stone stelae, altars, thrones, tombs, building facades, and other architectural elements. They also embellished a host of small, portable objects such as ceramic vessels, jewelry, bones, and shells (and, undoubtedly, less durable items of cloth and wood). The longest inscriptions were painted in accordion-fold books called codices, made of bark paper or animal parchment pages sized with washes of lime plaster and enclosed in wooden covers. All the surviving Mesoamerican books that are still legible were made shortly before the arrival of the Spaniards, so archaeologists must rely on the other kinds of inscriptions to trace the origins of writing. This is a much-debated issue, in part because of a widespread, if wrong-headed, idea that the possession of a sophisticated writing system is a *sine qua non* of true civilization [see box: Who Invented Mesoamerican Writing?].

Although many historians, linguists, and anthropologists see an almost inevitable association between writing and the evolution of complex societies, patterns of the adoption, spread, and obsolescence of writing systems are actually quite variable. The early and precocious "Isthmian" scripts of southeastern

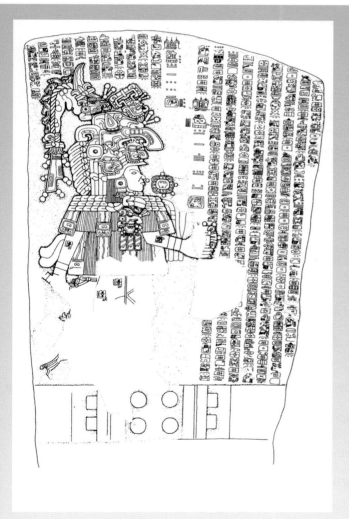

16.15 *The Epi-Olmec La Mojarra Stela from the Mexican Gulf Coast has one of the longest early inscriptions. It includes two Long Count dates equivalent to AD 143 and 156.*

Mesoamerican writing to any particular people, region, or time. Glyphs that resemble later Classic Maya inscriptions are found on El Portón Monument 1, erected around 400 BC in the Guatemalan highlands. Nearby, at Kaminaljuyú in the Valley of Guatemala, there are stelae with elaborate, undeciphered Late Preclassic texts (possibly independent of the Isthmian scripts) that plausibly record some Mayan language. The first proto-inscriptions in the Maya lowlands might result from contacts with these highland sources.

Writing did not take hold everywhere quickly, or at all – as was until recently believed to be the case at the great city of Teothihuacán [see The Teotihuacán Writing System box, p. 617]. Scores of impressively carved stelae at Izapa show extremely complex iconography *c*. 300–50 BC, but none has a date or inscription. The brief florescence of Late Preclassic writing at El Portón and Kaminaljuyú quickly faded away, with no subsequent inscriptions known in highland Guatemala. Still, however fragmentary and poorly understood the Preclassic corpus of inscriptions might be, some basic themes of later Mesoamerican writing are clearly present: rulership, war, and sacrifice, concern with gods and ancestors, and designations of titles, places, or dynasties.

KEY CONTROVERSY Metallurgy in Mesoamerica

Why did metallurgy develop so late in Mesoamerica, and why was metal use so markedly confined to nonutilitarian objects? These questions have long intrigued Mesoamerican archaeologists (Hosler 1988; 1994). Suitable mineral ores are admittedly scarce to the south and east of the Isthmus of Tehuantepec, but they are abundant in western Mexico, and New World people elsewhere showed considerable early sophistication in extracting and shaping metal for many purposes.

For centuries, chiefs in Panama, Costa Rica, and Colombia used precious metals, particularly gold, to make objects for display, trade, and grave offerings. To the south, in Ecuador and Peru, a spectacular tradition of metallurgy emerged before the time of Christ. Extraordinary objects of gold, silver, and copper were buried in elite tombs, such as those recently unearthed at Sipán on the northern Peruvian coast (see Sipán and the Presentation Theme box, p. 657).

In stark contrast, the first intimations of metal use in Mesoamerica date back only to *c.* AD 600, with metal items – particularly small bells used as jewelry – becoming common over the next few centuries. The beginnings of this metalworking tradition are found in western Mexico, where the most accessible mineral sources are located.

Casting by the lost-wax method (in which a wax effigy is replaced by molten metal in a clay mold) might have been introduced by overland contact with Colombia. Metal artifacts are rarely found in the intervening Maya parts of Mesoamerica, however, although Maya artisans did make objects from sheet gold imported from Central America.

Long-Distance Contacts?

Archaeologists have also long suspected that some sort of contact by sea with Ecuador or Peru introduced knowledge of metalworking. There are some striking similarities between aspects of the culture of the Central Andes and Mesoamerica, although no artifact from the former area has ever been found in the latter. For example, the highly distinctive "hairless" dog, a favorite food of Postclassic Mesoamerican peoples, was found in only two parts of the Precolumbian New World: west and central Mexico and Ecuador. In addition, Tarascan ethnic dress shared strong similarities with that worn in Ecuador (Anawalt 1997). In any case, west Mexican peoples were the most accomplished Mesoamerican metal users, and metal objects of many kinds figured particularly in the political economy and ritual life of the Tarascans, the western neighbors (and enemies) of the Aztecs.

Postclassic Metal Use

Metals were used in many ways during Postclassic times. At Chichén Itzá, in northern Yucatán, the Maya threw gold into the Sacred Cenote as an offering to the gods, and Postclassic lords in the Valley of Oaxaca were buried with elaborate gold jewelry. More prosaically, thin axe-shaped copper objects served as a kind of currency in highland Mexico.

Tribute in gold dust was paid to the Aztec empire, where gold and silver were valued as the "excrement" of the Sun and Moon gods. Aztec expansion was partly geared to control mineral sources, one reason for friction with the Tarascans. High-status artisans

16.16 *Elaborate status objects such as this golden pectoral were sometimes placed in Postclassic tombs. This one is from Tomb 7 at Monte Albán.*

transformed metal into ear ornaments, lip plugs, and other objects that signaled the social rank and office of their owners; other objects made of precious metal were probably used in ritual contexts.

Despite the sophistication of contemporary metalworking, few 16th-century people made much effective use of metal tools or weapons, although needles, awls, tweezers, and small cutting tools of copper or bronze (a copper-tin alloy) show up in excavations. Metal objects were instead appreciated for their colors and for the sounds that they made (associated with thunder, rain, and snakes), and for their rarity. Mesoamericans remained for all intents and purposes Stone Age people in utilitarian technological terms.

Mesoamerica flourished for a time in the Late Preclassic and then disappeared, as did another contemporary, but probably unrelated, short-lived script found on monuments at Kaminaljuyú, in highland Guatemala. Other scripts, such as Classic Maya and Zapotec, seem tied to specific communities and ethnic/linguistic groups, whose cultural and political decline they did not effectively survive. Late scripts such as that used by the Aztecs were more pictorial and less clearly tied to particular spoken languages. Although regarded by some as therefore more "primitive," such scripts could be used by diverse linguistic/ethnic groups for precisely this reason, and so had a certain vigor.

Kings, Courts, and Cities

Writing, calendars, and monumental art are symptomatic of two more fundamental and closely related transformations in Late Preclassic Mesoamerican society: the rise of kingship, and the emergence of the first great urban centers and territorial states. There were powerful leaders or rulers in earlier times, but only during the Late Preclassic does a constellation of traits emerge that later came to characterize the institution of kingship. By far the best evidence of early kingship anywhere in Mesoamerica comes from the Maya lowlands, where large carved monuments exhibit royal portraits and dated inscriptions – our first certain glimpses of "historical" individuals. The **Hauberg Stela** [16.17], dedicated in AD 197, is the earliest generally legible one (although unfortunately looted, so its place of origin is unknown). It depicts a king nicknamed by scholars Bone Rabbit dressed as a rain god impersonator, and its general themes include autosacrifice, agricultural fertility, world renewal, and human sacrifice, all closely associated with later Maya rule and warfare (Newsome 2001). Such monuments became increasingly common after about AD 250, one reason why the Classic period threshold is placed at this time.

While Late Preclassic texts are rare and often ambiguous, the Classic Maya frequently inscribed retrospective texts on their monuments, recounting the names, titles, and deeds of much earlier kings. Such accounts, along with supporting archaeological evidence, enable epigraphists to trace the historical founders of several royal lines, most conspicuously Tikal's, back to about AD 100. Judging from the archaeological record, these well-documented founders were not the first Maya kings, though they appear to have been singled out because of their subsequent dynastic significance.

What might be royal burials occur in earlier contexts at Tikal and elsewhere. Even more suggestive of kingship are two huge centers that emerged in the Mirador basin of northern Guatemala in Late Preclassic times (Matheny 1986). **Nakbé** was settled *c.* 1000 BC by simple farmers. An astonishing burst of construction *c.* 400–200 BC produced buildings as high as 30–45 m (98–148 ft), and Nakbé's sculptors created some of the first lowland Maya carvings, showing gorgeously attired human figures who might represent kings. Eclipsing Nakbé between about 200 BC and AD 150 was the even grander nearby center of **El Mirador**, where a vigorous tradition of stela-like monuments, accompanied by what appear to be glyphs, was present by around 200 BC. Nakbé and El Mirador are both good candidates for the seats of very ancient Maya kings, as are smaller, roughly contemporary centers such as **Lamanai** and particularly **Cerros**, in Belize, where elaborate temples have facade sculpture and inscriptions that prefigure later royal iconography, including the royal *ajaw* title. More extensive excavation should eventually reveal the first elite residences, including royal palaces. The

scale and complexity of construction of temples, ball courts, causeways, and other buildings at these sites suggests marked centralization of authority and an impressive capacity to organize communal labor.

Classic Maya rulership was closely associated with war, and unambiguous signs of large-scale conflict extend much farther back in time. A possible defensive wall has been mapped at El Mirador, and one of Mesoamerica's most impressive fortifications, the huge system of earthworks at **Becán**, was constructed at the end of the Late Preclassic. In addition, there is good osteological evidence for the ritual sacrifice of war captives that later features so prominently in Classic Maya art, and trophy heads seem to be portrayed on some early monuments. War is probably implied by the three severed bodies shown on the Hauberg Stela, and possibly by mass Late Preclassic Maya sacrifices found at **Cuello**, in northern Belize (Hammond 1999).

Some archaeologists believe that the roots of lowland Maya kingship and royal display lie in the artistic traditions of the

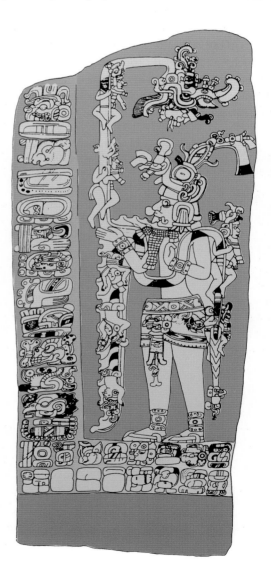

16.17 *The Hauberg Stela:* this carved stone slab has an early inscription (AD 197) and its themes, including sacrifice, agricultural fertility, and world renewal, prefigure those of later Classic Maya monuments.

Epi-Olmec cultures, particularly in the Guatemalan highlands at Kaminaljuyú, where Late Preclassic rulers were buried in extravagant tombs with scores of vessels and other costly offerings, as well as sacrificial victims.

Monte Albán Impressive as all these Maya developments are, even more striking transformations took place in the Valley of Oaxaca and the Basin of Mexico, where the first great cities emerged in Late Preclassic times. Although neither art nor texts reveal much about kingship in these regions, vigorous royal dynasties were no doubt integral to this process of urbanization.

San José Mogote, for centuries the largest center in the Valley of Oaxaca, was abandoned by all but a few farmers around 500 BC. By that time there were several nearby independent polities, and there is evidence that enemies burned some of San José Mogote's buildings; there is also evidence for newly built defensive systems in the southern arm of the valley at around the same time. Apparently, competition stimulated the sudden founding in *c.* 500 BC of the Zapotec city of **Monte Albán** on a previously uninhabited mesa (a high, flat-topped hill) in the central part of the valley; the settlement was a defensible center from which a powerful confederation of communities embarked on the unification of the entire region (Blanton et al. 1993; Marcus and Flannery 1996). Shortly afterwards, the Danzante warrior frieze – so-called because the figures were once

thought to represent dancers, but which are now thought to depict slain enemy captives – was erected, again suggestive of warfare [**16.18**].

Monte Albán's subsequent growth was dramatic. By 200 BC its hillsides were packed with more than 17,000 people, while the summit was crowned with a complex set of acropolis buildings, including elite residences, and carved stelae with dates. The whole conglomeration covered an area of about 6 sq. km (2.3 sq. miles), and scores of smaller settlements clustered around the new capital. Outside this ring of settlements were more distant ones, many fortified, attesting to still unstable conditions. Sophisticated irrigation systems underpinned much of the food supply.

Between 200 BC and AD 100 the top of the Monte Albán mesa was leveled off, and a new, grand design of buildings was laid out. Although much of this early architecture is today buried under later phases of construction, we know that the new arrangement included a ball court, about 20 temples where offerings were made to sky gods and other deities, huge palace-like residences built of adobe (unbaked clay) bricks, and

16.18 *Monte Albán: the Danzante figures from Building L; these figures, remnants of a much larger frieze, were once thought to be dancers but are now interpreted as dead or sacrificed enemies of Monte Albán, along with glyphs that might name them or their polities.*

elite chamber tombs. At this time the entire population of the Valley of Oaxaca totaled some 41,000 people, living in 518 settlements that exhibited several levels of size and complexity, a pattern often associated with early territorial states. Impressive outlying communities (including a resurgent San José Mogote) were probably administrative centers under Monte Albán's control. Some, such as **Dainzu**, possessed their own ball courts, which were potent political symbols. Unification of the whole Valley of Oaxaca entailed considerable human cost however; there was a decline of about 20 percent of its population compared to the previous period.

The Monte Albán urban state might have controlled far more distant areas at this time as well. Over 40 so-called "conquest slabs" associated with Building J in the great plaza of the city are carved with what seem to be place glyphs or political toponyms. Some archaeologists think that these represent distant polities conquered or otherwise subject to Monte Albán, although the glyphs might refer to places within the Valley of Oaxaca itself. In any case, a centralized and expansive Zapotec state was clearly present by the end of the Preclassic.

Teotihuacán The ancient Basin of Mexico environment had two main attractions for early agriculturalists: an extensive lake system with an abundance of aquatic resources, and fertile volcanic soils (Sanders et al. 1979). Nevertheless, farmers colonized the region fairly late – about 1600 BC – partly because they had to adapt their tropical crops to the high (over 2240 m, or 7349 ft), cold environment. About 10,000 people lived there in small communities when the Olmecs began carving monuments at San Lorenzo on the Gulf Coast, around 1200 BC; by the time the Early "Olmec" Horizon ended *c.* 400 BC, the population of the Basin of Mexico had increased to around 80,000. There were five or six large polities with emergent capitals dominated by pyramid mounds, chief among which was **Cuicuilco**, with its distinctive circular pyramid, located in the comparatively humid southwestern part of the Basin.

Hardly any farmers lived in the much drier Teotihuacán Valley to the northeast. Then, during a period of rapid population growth between 300 and 100 BC, this formerly marginal northern zone was heavily colonized, and **Teotihuacán** suddenly emerged as a huge urban center with 20,000 to 40,000 people. A century later it had burgeoned to 60,000 people in an area covering 15–20 sq. km (6–8 sq. miles). This remarkable growth was partly accomplished by attracting or otherwise concentrating 80–90 percent of the entire population of the Basin within the city's limits, and by eliminating all the other polities.

Eruptions blanketed 80 sq. km (31 sq. miles) of the southern Basin in volcanic deposits about this time, destroying Cuicuilco's landscape, and repeated eruptions between 250 and 350 BC affected much larger areas in the Puebla-Tlaxcala region to the east. (Two of Mesoamerica's major deposits of obsidian, a volcanic glass, are in or near the Teotihuacán Valley, including the source of the widely traded, greenish-gold Pachuca obsidian.) Quite possibly, many people displaced by these catastrophes migrated to Teotihuacán.

As at Monte Albán, Teotihuacán's rapid rise and its reordering of regional settlement seem to be associated with a check to the previous pattern of demographic growth in the Basin of Mexico. Whether warfare was part of this process of urbanization, as in the Valley of Oaxaca, is unknown. Whatever the cause, Teotihuacán was incomparably the largest city in the New World. Equally remarkable was the immense construction program that started at the beginning of the 1st millennium AD and created the ceremonial core of the city over the next 350 years, including the imposing pyramids of the Sun and the Moon [see box: Teotihuacán, pp. 614–15]. Most unusual, and in striking contrast to the situation in Oaxaca, is the paucity of settlements outside the city proper, particularly in the formerly heavily occupied and well-watered southern parts of the Basin of Mexico. Most of the people who lived at Teotihuacán must have been part-time farmers who lived in the city, but who cultivated fields a considerable distance away. The city depended heavily on a huge irrigation system watered by copious local springs and seasonal streams, all within about a day's walk.

We do not know the ethno-linguistic identity of the Teotihuacános, because we have no written texts comparable to those available for the Maya [see box: The Teotihuacán Writing System, p. 617]. Indeed, until the 1940s, archaeologists thought that Teotihuacán was no older than the 14th century, or immediately pre-Aztec. The Aztecs (who lived a millennium later) revered the older city as a sacred place where the world had been created, and it was they who gave it its name, which in Nahuatl means something like "place where the gods live." They also christened the Street of the Dead and the pyramids of the Sun and the Moon.

A widespread Mesoamerican belief features a great mythical metropolis, inhabited by prosperous and accomplished people and ruled by benevolent priests and kings, representing an ideal human condition to be recreated in the present world. The Aztecs called this idyllic, enchanted city Tollan, which literally means "place of the rushes," signifying a populous place. For a long time scholars thought that Teotihuacán was the Tollan of the Aztecs, but we now know that the Aztec Tollan was actually Tula, a site to the north of the Basin of Mexico. Belief in Tollan long predates Tula and the Aztecs, however, so there was not just one such utopia. Quite possibly the first Tollan in the Mesoamerican imagination was someplace like La Venta, but the dominance of Teotihuacán during the Early Classic period probably made it a Tollan in its own right.

KEY SITE Teotihuacán

Teotihuacán reached its peak of power and influence between the 4th and 6th centuries AD, when its estimated 125,000 inhabitants made it one of the largest urban places anywhere in the world (Berrin and Pasztory 1993). Unlike many other ancient cities, its remains have not been buried or heavily destroyed by subsequent activity, and so are very accessible to archaeologists. What visitors see today are mainly the ruins of Teotihuacán as it existed sometime in the 7th and 8th centuries AD, but there was a long sequence of earlier development.

The Ceremonial Core

Late Preclassic occupation seems to have been concentrated in the northwest sector of the site, but Classic Teotihuacán eventually sprawled over about 22 sq. km (8.5 sq. miles). Its ceremonial backbone is the Street of the Dead, the northern parts of which were laid out around the beginning of the 1st millennium AD, along with the first stage of the Pyramid of the Moon which stands at the northern terminus.

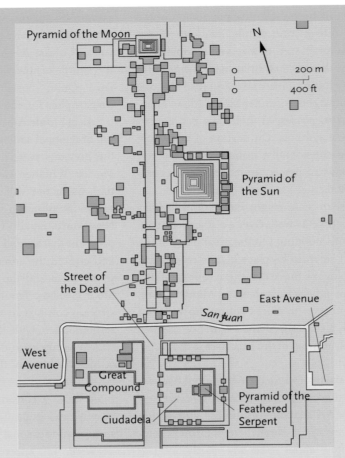

16.19, 16.20 *Plan (left) and view (below) of the ceremonial core of Teotihuacán. The view is from the Pyramid of the Moon looking south down the Street of the Dead, with the Pyramid of the Sun on the left. Unlike most archaeological sites, Teotihuacán was not buried or destroyed in subsequent ages.*

Roughly a century later, construction started on the immense Pyramid of the Sun, a west-facing building erected over an artificial sacred cave. Completed in two main stages over the next 50 years, it was as large at the base as the Great Pyramid of Khufu in Egypt (Chapter 10), and even without its summit temple it still stands 63 m (207 ft) high.

The Street of the Dead was later extended farther to the south, and along its western side was erected an immense enclosure, 440 m (1444 ft) on a side, later called the Ciudadela ("Citadel") by the Spaniards. Within it sits the Pyramid of the Feathered Serpent, famous for its many associated sacrificial victims. On the other side of the street is the even larger complex called the Great Compound, which was probably the principal marketplace.

Completion of these southern projects around AD 250, along with the final enlargements of the Pyramid of the Moon *c.* AD 350, completed this immense ceremonial zone. Today these grand streets and buildings strike visitors as rather plain, because, with the exception of the Pyramid of the Feathered Serpent, architectural sculpture was not emphasized at Teotihuacán. Instead, the plaster surfaces of the buildings were brightly painted with polychrome murals, only fragments of which remain. Surprisingly, no ball court has been found on the site, although we know the game was played there – from depictions in paintings – probably in some suitable but informal open space.

The Residential Layout

At about the same time the Ciudadela was finished, there was a vast and apparently coordinated reorganization of Teotihuacán's residences, resulting in a grid-like arrangement of rectangular house compounds aligned along narrow streets or alleys. This shift in the residential layout of the city is so profound that many archaeologists think it reflects a period of internal political and social upheaval. At the very least, it must have been centrally planned and organized. Within the new grid were erected many solidly built stone apartment complexes surrounded by walls.

Recent work by Mexican archaeologists in "vacant" parts of the city have revealed more modest, apparently unwalled, house groups that were simply oriented to conform to the grid alignment. If this almost invisible universe of residences proves to be widespread at Teotihuacán, then we will have to revise population estimates upward.

Apartment Compounds

Some 2000 "apartment" compounds have been mapped. Inside most of them were complexes of residential rooms and courtyards that housed the city's inhabitants. Only a few of these compounds have been systematically excavated, revealing kitchens,

storerooms, patios, shrines, dense deposits of domestic refuse, and numerous sub-floor burials. A few have elaborate courtyard shrines that cover the rich burials of adult males, who possibly represent revered ancestors. Each compound housed up to 100 people, and even the smaller ones had facilities for four to six families. Some have spacious and comfortable layouts, while others are cramped and barracks-like. Most were solidly built of plastered masonry, roofed with wooden beams, and had well-engineered drains.

A few compounds are so elaborate and beautifully decorated that they deserve to be called palaces; at the other extreme are shoddy adobe residences. All this variation among the internal features of the compounds is difficult to explain simply on the basis of differences in rank and organization among families, and many compounds might have had quite specialized functions that we do not yet understand. Clearly, however, many Teotihuacános lived in social groups larger than the nuclear family, and just as clearly there was great variation in status and wealth among the inhabitants.

16.21 *(Above) The Temple of the Feathered Serpent is one of the few buildings at Teotihuacán with impressive facade sculpture.*

16.22 *(Left) This example of Teotihuacán mural art shows a gorgeously attired female deity, with water dripping from her hands.*

The Classic Period: Teotihuacán and its Neighbors

During its initial rise to power, Teotihuacán directly controlled the Basin of Mexico; some archaeologists believe it also governed a much larger region of about 25,000 sq. km (9653 sq. miles) in the neighboring highlands to the east and south. Such a core polity might have had roughly 500,000–750,000 Early Classic inhabitants. But the city's influence reached far beyond central Mexico, especially between the 4th and 6th centuries AD. Many archaeologists call this interval the **Middle Horizon** because evidence of Teotihuacán's contacts is so pervasive throughout Mesoamerica.

The Middle Horizon appears to coincide with Teotihuacán's mature urban phase (Berrin and Pasztory 1993). Not only did the city have a population of at least 125,000, but a surprising number of the apartment compounds show evidence of some sort of specialized economic activity. Most conspicuous is the manufacture of obsidian implements, some intended for export, others used locally as tools. Other workshops made ceramic vessels, grinding stones, shell objects, jewelry, and pottery, and no doubt numerous items of wood, fiber, and feathers that have left few archaeological traces. Presumably many of these specialized products were exchanged in urban marketplaces, particularly at the Great Compound, the city's principal market.

Even in earlier, Late Preclassic times, Teotihuacán was a cosmopolitan place. Sherds of Chicanel pottery from the Maya lowlands dating to the 1st century AD have been found in deposits near the Pyramid of the Sun, and later evidence suggests that people from western Mexico, the Gulf Coast, and the Valley of Oaxaca not only visited the city, but actually lived there in special residential enclaves. Some of these residents were artisans, others probably merchants. The so-called Merchants' Barrio in the eastern zone of the city has the highest concentration of foreign pottery known anywhere at Teotihuacán, along with a set of distinctive round buildings that some archaeologists identify as residences, but which are probably storehouses. Cotton, cinnabar (a mineral used as a pigment), textiles, and feathers all might have been brought there from tropical regions to the east and southeast. Most resident foreigners were probably of rather low status, but one epigraphist suggests that the Tetitla compound, the murals from which show many exotic influences, was a kind of international clearinghouse for nobles, ambassadors, or other high-ranking visitors (Taube 2000).

We know very little about the social and political structure of Classic Teotihuacán, largely because of the lack of comprehensible inscriptions. Nor are the murals much help, because Teotihuacán art does not emphasize royalty, as Classic Maya art does – instead they mainly depict deities, fantastic animals, and abstract and repetitive designs. Moreover, virtually all the murals postdate the vast reorganization of the city's residential plan *c.* AD 250, and so do not reveal much about organization during the early period of rapid urban growth and monument construction.

For a long time there was a puzzling lack of elaborate tombs at Teotihuacán, though several spectacular ones were discovered in the 1990s. Buried beneath the Pyramid of the Feathered Serpent are the looted remains of at least one major tomb, along with some 40 sacrificial victims. The pyramid seems to have been built to cover this central set of interments. Scores of other sacrificed victims, mostly men of military age accompanied by weapons and war regalia, along with some women, were placed in shallow trenches beneath and around the pyramid as it was completed. Studies of bone isotope signatures reveal that most of these people were natives of distant places, or at least had lived elsewhere for long periods. They were probably not captives, and if they represent a cross-section of Teotihuacán's armed forces then recruitment must have been very broad. The Feathered Serpent tomb was very publicly looted some time after AD 250. Most of its sculpture was stripped away, and its front facade was buried beneath a later pyramid, signaling internal troubles and perhaps a new regime that emphasized more collective and impersonal leadership.

Since 2000, several other rich burials have been excavated from the later construction stages of the Pyramid of the Moon. All these impressive mortuary episodes date to AD 150–350 and may indicate the presence of powerful rulers and a well-established institution of early kingship, although most of the interred individuals appear to be sacrifices.

Whoever made the political decisions at Teotihuacán would have required administrative facilities, probably combined, in good Mesoamerican fashion, with palatial residences. Some archaeologists believe these functions were concentrated in sets of buildings within the Ciudadela, just to the east of the Pyramid of the Feathered Serpent. This might have been the original royal compound, but William Sanders (1972) thinks it later shifted to the huge Street of the Dead Complex, a walled section of the city's core just to the northwest of the Ciudadela.

Teotihuacán's Wider Influence: The Middle Horizon

On 15 January AD 378, a dramatic event occurred at the Classic Maya center of **Tikal**, in northern Guatemala, some 1000 km (621 miles) distant from Teotihuacán. A lord named Siyaj K'ak' arrived there, his approach recorded eight days earlier at the site of El Peru. On the same day, the incumbent Tikal king seems to have died, or at any rate is heard from no longer (Stuart 2000). Siyaj K'ak' had strong connections to Teotihuacán and might even have come from that great northern metropolis. His name

KEY CONTROVERSY The Teotihuacán Writing System

Until very recently many scholars believed that Teotihuacán had no tradition of writing, despite the fact that it was incomparably the most dynamic and culturally dominant center in all of Classic Mesoamerica, where writing was widely used. Teotihuacáno nobles, soldiers, and traders certainly knew about the existence of writing in Oaxaca, the Maya lowlands, and elsewhere, so how could one account for its apparent absence at the city itself? One possibility is that Teotihuacános wrote, but on some completely perishable medium. Still, one would expect at least fragments to survive.

Recent Discoveries

Numerals and glyph-like signs appear in Teotihuacán murals, but these do not occur as long inscriptions and could not be deciphered. Recently, however, Mexican archaeologists found 42 obvious glyphic signs painted in red on the floor of a patio nicknamed the Plaza de los Glifos in the walled La Ventilla compound (Taube 2000). These glyphs were arranged singly, though occasionally they occur together, in a grid of red lines reminiscent of the layout of 16th-century codices, particularly that of Aztec tribute lists.

One epigraphist recognized that there were two styles of writing, or "fonts" at Teotihuacán – one condensed and simple, as at the Plaza de los Glifos, and a second consisting of very large and elaborate emblematic glyphs. Many of the mural arrangements can potentially be read as texts, and armed with this new perspective, epigraphists are beginning to identify toponym signs, as well as short labels that seem to give the names or titles of associated human figures.

Overview

It appears increasingly likely that Teotihuacán had a well-developed writing system, and that its emblematic expression or "font" was particularly suited to large mural presentation. While similar in some ways to Mixtec and Classic Maya inscriptions, the Teotihuacán system had many distinctive elements, some

16.23, 16.24 *Glyphs (left) found painted on the floor of the Plaza de los Glifos (below), in the La Ventilla compound at Teotihuacán. Usually found singly, they were also occasionally arranged in groups, within a grid of red lines.*

of which prefigure later Aztec writing. Such a resemblance is particularly significant because the origins of Aztec writing remain obscure, as does the ethno-linguistic identity of Teotihuacán's inhabitants and those of the larger Basin of Mexico.

Quite possibly, Aztec writing had its roots at Classic Teotihuacán, where people might have spoken an ancient form of the Nahua language. On the other hand, if some non-Nahua language was widely spoken in Classic times, what happened to this population? Was it displaced by northern Nahua-speaking migrants during Postclassic times, or do these late migrations represent just a final phase of movements of Nahua people into the region?

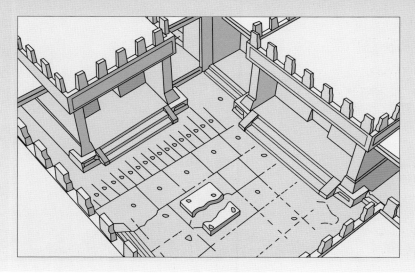

KEY SITE Classic Monte Albán

Monte Albán takes its name from a Spaniard who once owned the land on which the site sits. Its original Zapotec name is unknown, but may have been something like "hill of the tiger." The city attained its peak early, during the Late Preclassic (Blanton et al. 1993); its urban population subsequently declined slightly, and other communities in the Valley of Oaxaca asserted more autonomy. Actual conflict is suggested by the construction of the first of a series of impressive defensive walls protecting vulnerable points around the lower slopes of the hills.

Monte Albán's rulers still exerted control over distant areas to the north, however, and the city as we know it today assumed its basic form in Classic times, between AD 300 and 700. Some 2000 terraces were constructed on the slopes of the hill to accommodate the city's growing population. Nearly 3000 separate residences have been mapped on these terraces, most of them quite simple, consisting of several adobe structures arranged around a courtyard. Some 57 others are unusually elaborate, and might be elite houses. Interestingly, far less evidence for basic commodity production has been found

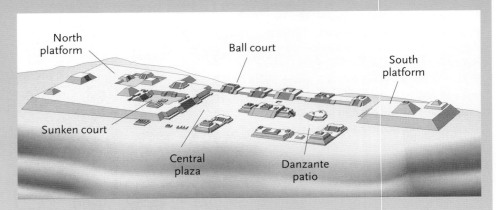

in Monte Albán's residences than at contemporary Teotihuacán, although ceramic kilns are associated with some houses.

The Main Plaza

Monte Albán's rulers and highest elites occupied the Main Plaza on the summit of the hill, which remained rather isolated from the rest of the community and difficult of access. We cannot read their inscriptions (some names and dates excepted), but monuments in the Main Plaza, as well as in elaborate tombs, show rulers, their accessions to power, their military victories, and royal

16.25, 16.26 Reconstruction of the summit of the Monte Alban mesa during Classic times, from the southwest (above), and a view of the impressive site today.

ancestors or relatives. Some also depict personages dressed in Teotihuacán style, interpreted as diplomats or ambassadors. Architecture around the Main Plaza assumed an extremely monumental and integrated form. This huge space, some 300 m (984 ft) long, was delineated on its northern and southern ends by two enormous platforms, and along its east and west sides by lines of smaller temples and a compact ball court. The North Platform was a gigantic palace complex, where Monte Albán's royal family lived amid the administrative and ritual facilities essential to their rule; elaborate tombs with carved and painted chambers lay beneath the floors.

Decline

By AD 700 Monte Albán's population had probably reached 25,000 people. About that time a severe decline is signaled by cessation of large-scale construction and much reduced ritual activity in the Main Plaza. Like Teotihuacán, the city was not permanently deserted, and thousands of people continued to live on the residential terraces. Nevertheless, it never regained its former dominance of the Valley of Oaxaca. In Postclassic times, many small Zapotec and Mixtec kingdoms coexisted uneasily in and around the Valley of Oaxaca, until the Aztecs established their own hegemony there in the 15th century.

16.27 *Teotihuacán influence:* *plan of Tomb II in Structure E-III-3 at Kaminaljuyú, in which the tomb's main occupant was laid on a wooden litter and surrounded by sacrificial victims and grave goods including Teotihuacán offerings.*

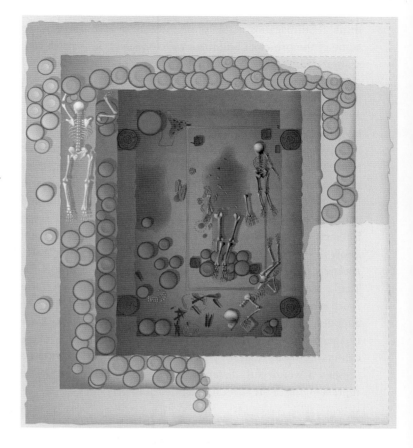

is also recorded on monuments at other centers, suggesting that his prestige and influence were widespread.

The following year, the son of one of Siyaj K'ak's entourage was enthroned as Tikal's king. Half a century later, something very similar happened far away on the southeastern frontier of the Maya lowlands, where **Copán**'s dynastic founder, Yax Kuk Mo, also arrived as an outsider with some sort of relationship to Teotihuacán. Long before these political intrusions, around AD 250–300, Teotihuacán materials, including Pachuca obsidian, were interred with a burial at **Altun Ha** in northern Belize. Teotihuacán might even have been implicated in the troubles that resulted in the construction of the Becán fortifications at the end of the Preclassic period, mentioned above. Nor was Teotihuacán's influence in the Maya lowlands only political and military. Central Mexican iconography became important to royal presentation, and Maya architects incorporated Teotihuacán forms into their buildings. Both artistic and architectural signs of Teotihuacán presence have recently been discovered at several sites in Yucatán, for example **Acanceh** and **Chunchucmil**.

Elsewhere, evidence for Teotihuacán presence is even more compelling. Great lords were buried with Teotihuacán offerings at **Kaminaljuyú**, in highland Guatemala, around AD 400–550 [**16.27**], and at the end of this period a huge "acropolis" was built there using Teotihuacán-style architectural elements [**16.28**]. Perhaps not coincidentally, Kaminaljuyú is very close to the El Chayal obsidian source that supplied much of the Maya lowlands. Teotihuacán-style pottery and architecture also appeared *c.* AD 350–400 at **Matacapan**, in the Tuxtla Mountains of the Gulf Coast, a community apparently founded as a Teotihuacán enclave (Santley 1994). For the next century or so, Matacapan

burgeoned as a regional power and ceramic production site, all the while maintaining close ties to the Basin of Mexico.

Nor did **Monte Albán** remain aloof from all this interaction [see box: Classic Monte Albán]. Pachuca obsidian and imported Teotihuacán vessels, as well as locally made imitations, show up there between AD 200 and 600. Some tomb paintings have derivative Teotihuacán motifs, and carved monuments depict visiting Teotihuacán notables. Recently it has even been suggested that Teotihuacán actually attacked or conquered Monte Albán. Only west Mexico's Teuchitlan tradition polities seem to have largely escaped Teotihuacán's influence, for reasons that are poorly understood.

Although Teotihuacán's power mainly extended south and east, it reached to the north as well. Around AD 400–450, at the hitherto modest center of **Alta Vista**, far away in northwest Mexico, construction projects at the site core incorporated typical Teotihuacán architectural elements, along with a new innovation: skull racks hung with the remains of sacrificial victims. As at a number of other sites, artifacts at Alta Vista display both Teotihuacán and more local features, and some archaeologists

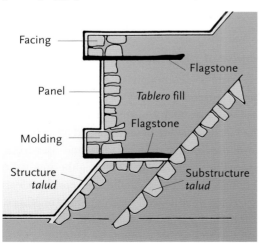

16.28 *Teotihuacán architectural elements:* *large Teotihuacán buildings feature combinations of rectangular (tablero) and sloping (talud) elements. Murals are often painted on the inset panels. These architectural elements often appear at sites far from Teotihuacán.*

think Teotihuacános actually migrated there. Around AD 850 some of the principal buildings were burned and demolished; scattered human remains also attest to some sort of violence.

Many more such examples could be given, but what does it all mean? Few archaeologists believe that Teotihuacán had an empire achieved through conquest like the Aztecs' centuries later. Quasi-military intrusions as at Tikal, and possibly at Kaminaljuyú or Becán, might instead reflect the opportunistic activities of noble Teotihuacán factions detached from their homeland by political events – a process very evident in later Mesoamerican ethnohistoric accounts. Undoubtedly, trade and commerce were fundamental to much of this Middle Horizon interaction, but in the absence of historical records we do not know if it involved professional merchants like the later Aztec *pochteca*. Outright colonization of strategic locales such as the Tuxtla Mountains seems very likely, and we cannot discount more intangible kinds of cultural influence, as reflected in the adoption of Teotihuacán dress, weapons, political and military imagery, and ritual. Teotihuacán might have been a pilgrimage center for many Classic people, and for others it no doubt seemed a wonderful, distant metropolis, probably coming to represent one of the several imagined Tollans.

Cholula, Cantona, and the Teuchitlan Cultural Tradition – Independent Polities?

Teotihuacán's influence was by no means present everywhere, however, nor did it lack competitors. As yet unclear are its relations with **Cholula**, a contemporary Classic city located in the fertile agricultural landscape of neighboring Puebla. Cholula's remains are blanketed by modern urban sprawl, so it is not well known archaeologically. With an estimated 30,000–40,000 people, it was much smaller than its giant neighbor, but its main pyramid grew by accretion to become the largest structure in the New World. Although its architecture shared some similarities with that of Teotihuacán, in other ways Cholula retained its own cultural identity and survived as a major highland center until the Spaniards arrived.

Even more intriguing is **Cantona**, a unique Classic center 190 km (118 miles) due east of Teotihuacán, which archaeologists are just beginning to investigate (Cook 1998). The sprawling 14 sq. km (5.4 sq. mile) city is located in a badlands zone with little agricultural potential, a locale so inhospitable that the Spaniards called it the Gran Despoblado ("Great Wilderness"). There are, however, nearby fertile valleys and several major obsidian sources. Cantona boasts many workshops and an astounding 25 ball courts, some of which are parts of larger complexes that include extensive plazas and possible elite residences. Low walls enclose stone platforms that probably supported light, perishable superstructures, an unusual form of construction given the elevation of well over 2000 m (6562

ft). Established at least by AD 100, one estimate (almost certainly too high) puts its peak population at 90,000 in the centuries from about AD 600 to 900, when Teotihuacán was in decline.

Cantona seems to share remarkably few architectural features with Teotihuacán, and has its own distinctive ceramic tradition. Unlike other centers of comparable size, it lacks monumental sculpture or other surviving symbolic statements of ritual or political power (ball courts aside). Well situated to dominate trade between the central Mexican highlands and the Gulf Coast, Cantona probably exchanged obsidian and other commodities. Its local microenvironment is ideal for growing agave, an extremely important plant that produced fiber and the mildly alcoholic drink *pulque*, both mainstays of the highland economy from early times. One possibility is that Cantona was a highly specialized outpost established by El Tajín (see below) or some other Classic polity, and that a large population lived there only seasonally, when intense production activities were carried out.

Further afield, western Mexico continued to develop in its own distinctive fashion, as exemplified by remains of the **Teuchitlan cultural tradition** (Weigand 2001b). Between AD 400 and 700, clusters of elaborate shaft tombs were associated with local polities dominated by hierarchies of impressive centers. Each sub-region was distinguished by its own somewhat different ceramic, figurine, and tomb styles. At the cores of the biggest Teuchitlan sites were monumental circular buildings and sets of ball courts, one of which is 130 m (426 ft) long. One huge habitation zone has thousands of residential compounds interspersed with obsidian, ceramic, shell, and stone workshops, all scattered over an area of 2.5 sq. km (1 sq. mile). Teuchitlan people built complex systems of drained fields and canals to utilize the many swamps and lakes of the region, and these prefigure the famous *chinampas* (artificial fields constructed in a shallow lakebed) that later supported the dense Aztec populations of the Basin of Mexico. Also distinctive of western Mexico was the emergence *c.* AD 600 of a metallurgical tradition that developed during the following centuries [see Metallurgy in Mesoamerica box, p. 610].

The Demise of Teotihuacán

For many years it was thought that Teotihuacán collapsed as a major power around AD 700–750 (Millon 1988). Violence was implicated, because archaeologists detected extensive burning and deliberate destruction of temples and other buildings along the Street of the Dead, in the Ciudadela, and elsewhere. Just who was responsible is unknown. No neighboring polities seem strong enough to be likely candidates, nor are clear signs of invading foreign enemies reflected in pottery or other artifacts.

An alternative possibility is some internal, factional conflict that destroyed the major symbols and facilities of traditional rule. This latter explanation gains plausibility because we know that on at least two earlier occasions Teotihuacán experienced internal crises: *c.* AD 250, when the city's residential layout was dramatically reorganized; and slightly later, when the Pyramid of the Feathered Serpent was so openly looted and its tombs despoiled (Sugiyama 1998). Whatever ultimately happened not only caused political and social upheaval, but also the disappearance of a religious and ideological order that had long integrated much of Mesoamerica.

The traditional timing of Teotihuacán's demise was convenient because it offered one possible trigger for the slightly later collapse of Classic Maya society (discussed below). More recently, however, the Teotihuacán catastrophe has been pushed back in time. Teotihuacán's strongest external influences seem to peak early, *c.* AD 250–500, and there is evidence from archaeomagnetic dates (based on correlating the magnetic direction of iron particles in baked clay structures such as kilns and hearths to known variations in the earth's magnetic direction) that the destruction and burning of the city might have taken place as early as AD 500–550. Quite possibly, Teotihuacán was a spent force by the early to mid-6th century AD, although its reputation haunted the Mesoamerican imagination long thereafter.

Archaeologists disagree about whether or not the city was abandoned for a short time, but Teotihuacán never perma-nently lost its urban population. Some 30,000–40,000 people continued to live in urban enclaves around the old ceremonial core, and many well-established communities elsewhere in the Basin of Mexico continued to thrive. As late as the 16th century, Teotihuacán remained the center of a city-state with its own resident king and about 10,000 inhabitants.

Epiclassic Mesoamerica, AD 600–900

Monte Albán was too weak to fill the political vacuum created by Teotihuacán's collapse. Instead, a series of local centers and polities rose to become regional powers during what is called the Epiclassic period, a chronological label mainly applied to that part of Mesoamerica west of the Isthmus of Tehuantepec and dated there to AD 600–900. Cantona, as already noted, seems to have prospered, possibly in tandem with **El Tajín** [**16.29**], a major center in Vera Cruz on the Gulf Coast lowlands that might have been its trading partner. Closer to the old Teotihuacán heartland, two other upstart centers also flourished for a time. Near Cholula is **Cacaxtla**, a hillside site with a huge, palace-like complex of buildings protected by a dry moat (McVicker 1985). Built over many stages, Cacaxtla, along with a nearby ceremonial complex called Xochitecatl, dominated the fertile Puebla-Tlaxcala Valley and its important trade routes during much of the period between AD 650 and 900. Its resident

16.29 Regional powers in the Epiclassic: *the Pyramid of the Niches dominates the sprawling center of El Tajín, the capital of a major Gulf Coast polity.*

population was small, perhaps 10,000 people, but its buildings are famous for their polychrome murals depicting military confrontations between groups with central highland (including some Teotihuacán-related) costumes and regalia, and others with distinctly Maya characteristics. Cholula was probably defeated by warriors from Cacaxtla, but still survived as a considerable urban center in its own right.

About 25 km (15.5 miles) southwest of modern Cuernavaca lies **Xochicalco**, the best known of all Epiclassic sites and roughly contemporary with Cacaxtla (Hirth 2000). Large architectural complexes crown five separate hills, one of which is much more impressive than the others. This hilltop location seems to have been chosen mainly with an eye to defense, because the surrounding landscape has poor agricultural potential. The core of the community was heavily protected by earthworks, ramparts, and terraces. Much of the population of 10,000 to 15,000 people lived in residential neighborhoods on terraces on the hillsides. Excavations have revealed evidence of complex economic activities, including long-range trade, craft production, and internal market exchange. Carvings on the Pyramid of the Plumed Serpent show warriors and what appear to be toponyms representing outlying towns that paid tribute to Xochicalco [**16.30, 16.31**]. Several stelae are incised with name glyphs of kings –

among the earliest known for central Mexico. Sometime around AD 900 the site was suddenly and violently destroyed by unknown enemies, and never subsequently reoccupied.

Far away in northern Mexico, just inside the geographical limits of Mesoamerica proper, lies **La Quemada**, another hilltop center of Epiclassic date. While the main community is small, it is quite complex, with artificial terraces, numerous residential patio complexes, temple and palace-like structures, and ball courts, all protected by a defensive wall. Archaeologists have unearthed unusual concentrations of cut, broken, and burned human bones, along with clear evidence that human skeletons were displayed in some buildings, perhaps as war trophies.

Clearly, the centuries after Teotihuacán's fall from power were violent ones in the Mexican highlands, though none of Teotihuacán's squabbling successor states was strong enough to reestablish the order and prosperity of the old Classic system. The greatest eventual beneficiary of the decline of Teotihuacán

16.30, 16.31 *Epiclassic Xochicalco: carvings on the Pyramid of the Plumed Serpent (below) depicted warriors and toponyms of towns; the open mouth in the glyph (right) might relate to tribute.*

was **Tula**, founded after AD 700 some 80 km (50 miles) to the northwest; from this beginning emerged the huge Postclassic city destined to become the legendary Tollan of the later Aztecs.

The Classic Maya

By far the best known of all Mesoamerican cultures is that of the lowland Maya, both because it has attracted an inordinate amount of archaeological attention, and because we have long been able to understand its complex calendars and its texts (Sharer 1994; Grube 2001; Coe 2005).

The early sophistication evident at Nakbé, El Mirador, Tikal, and other Maya sites matured over a region in the Yucatán Peninsula of roughly 250,000 sq. km (96,530 sq. miles), or about the same size as Great Britain or the state of Colorado. Most of this landscape has comparatively little relief and is hotter and more humid than the Mesoamerican highlands. There are marked wet and dry seasons, natural vegetation is distinctly tropical, and large rivers or streams are rare. After a widespread Late Preclassic crisis, the distinctive markers of the Classic Maya tradition spread very widely – in particular altars and stelae carved with royal and ritual statements – enabling epigraphists and archaeologists to chart a network of interacting kingdoms (Martin and Grube 2000). These phenomena most strongly affected the southern lowlands; societies in northern Yucatán developed in somewhat different ways.

Early Classic (AD 250–600) inscriptions and art are less abundant and informative than those of the Late Classic, but many of the latter are retrospective, helping us to understand the political dynamics of earlier times and the evolving institution of kingship. We have already seen that during the Early Classic, Teotihuacán had a direct hand in the fortunes of some dynasties, particularly Tikal's. By the early 6th century AD, Tikal was a Maya superpower in its own right, and head of a coalition embroiled in protracted struggles with another great alliance led by the rulers of Calakmul. All this mayhem ushered in a period of Early Classic population decline and political crisis sometimes called the "Hiatus." Some previously vigorous centers, such as Piedras Negras and Tikal, did not raise royal monuments for much of the 6th and 7th centuries AD. Other polities, including Caracol and Copán, continued to prosper, however, so this crisis was by no means universal. Nevertheless, it did stimulate considerable reorganization of Maya society and culture. Maya monuments after AD 600 presented kings in more highly personalized ways, attributed new titles to them and to subsidiary lords, and increasingly emphasized warfare.

All this conflict served as a prelude to the great flowering of **Late Classic** Maya society between AD 700 and 800, a period for which we have unprecedented information. The Maya are the only Classic-period Mesoamericans who have left a corpus of intelligible inscriptions that can be assembled into something like an indigenous historical record. About 15,000 texts have been recovered, some carved or painted on monuments or buildings, but most recorded on smaller objects such as pottery vessels [**16.32**] that were used in palaces or elite residences, or placed in tombs; no Classic books have survived intact. All the texts seem to have been written in an archaic, courtly Maya language that functioned somewhat like Latin in medieval Europe (Houston et al. 2000). In combination with associated architecture and art, these texts convey rich information about the elite of Maya society, including names and titles of rulers and lords, gods and ancestors, emblems of dynasties and polities, and toponyms, as well as specific events such as births, deaths, accessions, wars, rituals, and alliances. Linked to many texts are calendrical notations in traditional Mesoamerican cyclical calendars, and, most importantly, the Long Count, in which each day, for all practical purposes, is unique [see The Mesoamerican Calendar box, pp. 606–07]. Such chronological precision allows us to place sequences of real events in their proper order.

Unfortunately, Maya inscriptions are not found at all sites, and they become common only after about AD 600. Nor do they tell us much about the size of polities, the details of social and political organization, or economic institutions or behavior. Particularly lacking is any information about the lives of common people. Nevertheless, in conjunction with archaeological evidence, the texts allow us to reconstruct many aspects of Classic Maya life.

16.32 *Maya writing:* this large Late Classic plate shows Hunahpu, the father of the Hero Twins, as a scribe, with a brush in his right hand with which he is writing in a screenfold book.

The mature Late Classic phase of Maya culture began just about the time that Teotihuacán declined, *c.* AD 600, and Teotihuacán's misfortunes did not disrupt the general course of Maya culture history, as some archaeologists long believed. While the early influence of the great highland city on the lowlands may have been dramatic and direct, it was probably inconsequential after the beginning of the 7th century. It may be no coincidence that some murals at Cacaxtla show central Mexican warriors being defeated by others who look more like Maya. But this is itself puzzling, because it is one of the few examples of Maya intrusions or cultural influence far beyond their own ethnolinguistic borders; we do not know how to interpret the events depicted, except, possibly, as the overthrow of native Pueblans by Olmeca-Xicalanca migrants.

Kingdoms and Capitals

The southern Maya lowlands were never politically unified, and during Late Classic times at least 45–50 separate kingdoms are indicated by their associated emblem glyphs. These distinctive signs always occur in combination with the names and titles of kings, and serve to identify a dynasty or its polity. Beneath the veneer of similar art, writing, and architecture, these kingdoms varied greatly. Some, like Tikal, were very ancient, while others were newcomers. Some had large populations and territories, while others were much smaller. Polities, or more properly their dynasties, were identified with different sets of patron gods. Several Maya languages and dialects were spoken, and pottery and tools in use differed from one region to another. Political and social arrangements no doubt varied among kingdoms as well, as suggested by the use of different royal titles. Nevertheless, an underlying "Mayaness" clearly united all these kingdoms, reinforced by trade, military alliances, intermarriage among elite families, common rituals and religious beliefs, and the periodic movement of peoples. This last is particularly important. Centers, polities, and whole regions experienced political and demographic instability and marked cycles of prosperity and decline throughout Maya history. The abandonment of Nakbé and El Mirador, for example, probably contributed to the rise of such sites as **Tikal** [see box: Tikal, pp. 626–27].

Each major Late Classic kingdom focused on a central precinct dominated by large masonry pyramid-temples, the palatial residences of kings and lords, spacious public plazas with altars and stelae, and ball courts. Often these huge complexes grew by accretion, and in the process incorporated the elaborate tombs of rulers and other elites. The most famous such tomb is that of K'inich Janaab' Pakal [**16.33**], the great 7th-century king of **Palenque** (Martin and Grube 2000). Despite their impressive appearance, however, some Maya centers were extremely short-lived. All the large buildings at Pakal's capital, for example, were erected in less than a century [**16.34**].

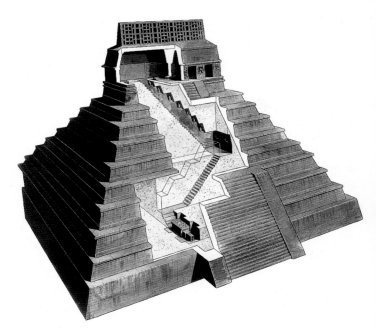

16.33, 16.34 Palenque: *reconstruction of the Temple of the Inscriptions (above), where the great king Pakal was buried, which is visible in the left center of the view of the central part of Palenque in the photo opposite.*

Radiating out from these zones of monumental architecture were the households of lesser people. It is often difficult to determine where the edges of these communities lie, because settlement typically thins out gradually with distance, merging with the outlying rural households of the farmers who formed 80–99 percent of the population. This kind of settlement distribution is much less urban-looking and more dispersed than that visible at Teotihuacán, Monte Albán, and other highland cities. Nor is there evidence for the multiplicity of functions or economic complexity found at Teotihuacán. Maya centers are best envisioned as enormous courtly and ritual places from which royal rule emanated, although there are some exceptions [see box: Mesoamerican Urbanism, p. 628].

Most Late Classic kingdoms probably had territories small enough to walk across in a day or two, although some were larger. The kings of Copán, on the southeastern margin of the southern lowlands, might have had 20,000–25,000 subjects in the 8th century AD. Tikal's region would have been more populous, with perhaps 120,000 people. Complicating such estimates is the fact that some kings occasionally dominated or "possessed" lesser ones through alliance, conquest, or some other kind of system of loose suzerainty or patronage. Some archaeologists believe that larger polities consisting of hundreds of thousands of people were patched together in these ways by superpowers such as Tikal or Calakmul (Martin and Grube 1995), but if so, they must have been very fragile.

Maya Society

Royalty Maya social and political organization was strongly hierarchical, and central to all was the institution of kingship, symbolized in the ancient *ajaw* title borne by rulers and their immediate relatives. Maya kings were sacrosanct, hedged about with ritual and sacred duties. Their most important obligations were to ensure balance and stability in the cosmos, and particularly agricultural fertility. Kings impersonated gods at royal ceremonies and were custodians of mysterious "god bundles." Some of them, such as Palenque's Pakal, were resurrected as gods themselves. Deceased royal ancestors exerted powerful influences over the living world. Day-to-day activities were focused on royal courts, which were places of elegance, indulgence, and conspicuous display (Inomata and Houston 2001; Miller and Martin 2004).

From very early times, some kings seem to have been more exalted than others, who were social or political inferiors and perhaps in some sense subordinates. Copán's dynasty, for example, seems to have overseen the founding of Quiriguá's, so the Quiriguá line might have constituted a cadet lineage. Conflict could overturn such relationships, however, as when Copán's ruler was killed at Quiriguá in AD 738, and the smaller polity asserted its independence. Similarly, the kings of Yax-

chilán were overlords of the rulers of Bonampak, where celebrated wall murals completed on the eve of the Maya collapse record such relationships.

Succession to kingship focused on suitable males in royal patrilineages, but in the absence of an acceptable male heir, women could serve as regents or occasionally queens in their own right, and pass on the title. Kings were expected to be powerful warriors, and their monuments often boast of the capture and sacrifice of enemies. Males of royal lineages who did not ascend the throne had other responsibilities; signatures show that some of them were artisans who made stelae and other precious objects, and they probably were the repositories of the highest levels of literacy and calendrical lore. Some of the most talented sculptors and painters were apparently "loaned" to lesser communities within multi-center kingdoms.

Lords and Officials Ranked below royalty were other great lords and officials. Some of the most exalted had titles such as *sajal* or *aj k'uhuun*, respectively meaning a kind of subordinate ruler, and a close associate and "provisioner" of the king. Inscriptions suggest that such titles were both bestowed by kings and inherited in family lines. Women sometimes bore them as well as men, and some titled officials were royal relatives. Texts often characterize titled individuals as "owned" or "possessed" by kings. Living in their own palatial residences, they attended on the courts of their royal masters, and served various governmental and ritual functions. Rulers and elites were leaders in ritual, war, tax collection, diplomacy, and construction projects, but whether Maya kingdoms had a bureaucracy in the modern sense is unknown.

Commoners Supporting all this complexity were commoners, mostly farmers, who made up the vast bulk of the population, paid taxes in kind or labor, probably served in war, and who are known mainly from the remains of their modest households (Sheets 1990). Where population densities were low, they practiced various forms of swidden (slash-and-burn) agriculture, augmented in other regions by more intensive systems of cultivation utilizing terraces and drained fields.

Because of the technological limitations that affected all Mesoamerican societies (the lack of metal tools, traction animals, and wheeled vehicles), each farming household could cultivate only limited amounts of land, and so produced only small surpluses with which to support kings and nobles. Cheap, heavy products such as maize could not be efficiently moved in bulk over great distances, and so agrarian economies were quite local.

KEY SITE Tikal

Tikal is one of the largest Classic centers in the Maya lowlands, and many conceptions of the ancient Maya derive from research done there since the late 1950s (Harrison 1999). The architectural history of the site can be divided into two main periods: Late Preclassic/Early Classic; and Late Classic. During Late Preclassic and Early Classic times, Tikal's kings were buried in the imposing North Acropolis; a series of temples with astronomical orientations was built in the nearby Lost World complex, whose 30-m (98-ft) pyramid was, until the 8th century AD, the tallest building at Tikal. In the 4th century AD the great king Jaguar Paw I built a palace that became the nucleus of the residence that housed his successors.

Early Classic Earthworks

Despite the "foreign" disruption in AD 378, when a lord named Siyaj K'ak' arrived, possibly from Teotihuacán, Tikal continued to prosper, and Teotihuacán architectural elements were incorporated into some buildings. Another Early Classic project was a 9.5-km (6-mile) long earthwork built to delineate Tikal's northern boundary; part of another to the southeast has also been found. Surveys in 2003 revealed a previously undetected western earthwork, so that the system as presently known is almost 26 km (16 miles) long. Altogether the earthworks delineate a region of several hundred square kilometers that formed the core of the polity.

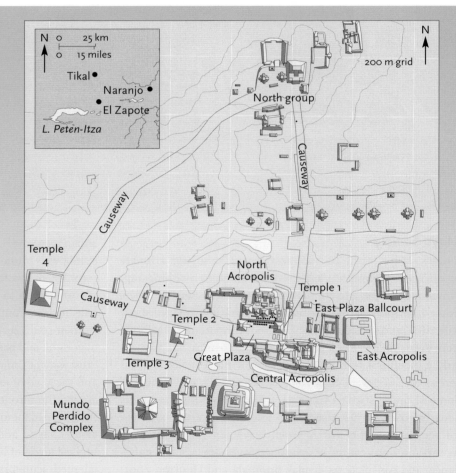

Although it has long been assumed that the earthworks were fortifications, many sections make little defensive sense. In any case, they represent a set of boundary features that show us what parts of the landscape the inhabitants of Tikal thought should be delimited by a formal boundary. If some parts of the earthworks were fortifications, they did not

16.35 *Plan of the center of Tikal in the 9th century* AD. *Imposing groups of buildings were joined to the Great Plaza by wide causeways.*

prevent Tikal's military defeat by Calakmul and its allies, however, and between AD 562 and 692 construction waned and no dated monuments were raised.

Warfare Warfare is now known to have been virtually constant among the Classic Maya, who not long ago were envisioned as a uniquely peaceful civilization (Webster 2000). Wars were fought to capture sacrificial victims, avenge past defeats, acquire titles and status, neutralize enemies, exact tribute, and almost certainly to annex territory. No particular polity or coalition, however, ever became powerful enough to unite for long any appreciable part of the Maya lowlands. By the late 8th century AD there were more kingdoms than ever before, and populations reached unprecedented densities over very large areas. Many of the most spectacular building projects were initiated at this time, but all this apparent vitality and prosperity masked underlying stresses that soon brought down one kingdom after another [see box: The Collapse of Maya Civilization, pp. 630–31].

Postclassic Mesoamerica

Until the 1950s, when scientific techniques such as radiocarbon dating became available, our conceptions of the chronology of Mesoamerican cultures were strongly anchored in Maya Long Count dates. These seemed to indicate a crisis between AD 800 and 1000, so it made sense to begin the Postclassic period for all of Mesoamerica at about this time. Postclassic societies in

The Late Classic Site

The heavily reconstructed Tikal visible today, sprawling over an area of about 4 sq. km (1.5 sq. miles), represents the mature site as it looked *c.* AD 800, vastly enlarged by resurgent kings after Calakmul was defeated in its turn by Tikal in AD 695. Around the Great Plaza is the most imposing set of buildings. On the west is the North Acropolis, burial place of Tikal's kings, and across from it the huge Central Acropolis, with its hundreds of rooms and courtyards that housed living kings, their families, and their retainers. Temples I and II are on the north and south, and altars and stelae are displayed in the plaza itself. Artificial reservoirs were constructed to provide water, and drainage was carefully arranged to fill them. Other imposing sets of buildings are attached to the Great Plaza by wide causeways. On the hilly terrain around Tikal are thousands of smaller clusters of buildings, most of which represent residential compounds built on high ground with good drainage. Population density drops off markedly with distance from the major palaces and temples, but still some 60,000 people probably lived within the protected hinterland.

Tikal began to decline after about AD 800, and its last royal monument is dated to AD 869. Most of its population disappeared around AD 830–950, although the larger region was never completely abandoned.

16.36 *The pyramids of Tikal rise steeply out of the surrounding forest. Temple I is is about 52 m (170 ft) high, and topped by a roofcomb.*

KEY CONTROVERSY Mesoamerican Urbanism

All great ancient civilizations had imposing central places, and archaeologists have traditionally spent inordinate amounts of time excavating them. Does it make sense to call all such places on the ancient Mesoamerican landscape "cities," in some Western sense of the word? Much controversy swirls about this issue for several reasons (Sanders and Webster 1988; Smith 1989), most important being the obvious variability these centers exhibit. Olmec La Venta was a very different kind of community from Teotihuacán or the Aztec capital Tenochtitlán, and central places such as El Mirador or Monte Albán are in many ways microcosms of their larger societies; thus, understanding what each was like is vital. In addition, many people think that any civilization worthy of the name must be urban in character, just as it must have writing. According to this point of view, saying that some ancient cultures lacked true cities somehow devalues them.

If monumental temples and palaces, ball courts, and great plazas with sophisticated public art make cities, then ancient Mesoamerica abounded in them. If, on the other hand, we include less directly observable features, such as large, dense populations and a wide array of urban functions, particularly economic ones, then identifying urbanism becomes more problematic. Classic Teotihuacán, with its huge population, density of settlement, and all the obvious economic specialization evident among its apartment compounds, certainly was an impressive urban center by anyone's definition. Monte Albán, Xochicalco, Tula, and Tenochtitlán also clearly qualify, as do several other less well-documented cities, such as Texcoco, Cantona, and Cholula. On the other hand, Olmec and most Classic Maya centers such as Tikal or Copán appear to have had much smaller and less dense populations, and far simpler economic institutions. Major 16th-century capitals in the Maya highlands of Guatemala are essentially fortified elite strongholds.

Cities and Regal-Ritual Centers

Many archaeologists believe that despite their obvious variation, all these places were true cities, and assert that we should not impose our own urban models on a distinctive, non-Western urban tradition. Others think that calling all of them cities obscures important aspects of variation in the ways in which they developed and in the functions they served. According to this view, centers such as La Venta, Tikal, or Copán were essentially regal-ritual capitals of great lords and royal dynasties, which lacked both the scale and complexity of Teotihuacán or Tenochtitlán. Instead, they were the gigantic households of rulers or lesser lords, centered on palaces and courts, and having the temples, tombs, ball courts, art, and other facilities essential to

rulership. Falling between these extremes are such sites as the small Maya center of Cancuen, which has a huge palace and workshop facilities, but no large temples. Postclassic Mayapan had a very dense population concentrated inside a wall, and the Early Classic site of Chinchukmil in northwest Yucatán has a similar but larger layout, though not much in the way of impressive palace or temple architecture; some archaeologists think it was a major mercantile emporium (Dahlin 2000).

Conclusion

The position taken here is that true cities developed in Mesoamerica only where distinctive urban ecologies allowed large, dense populations to be supplied with food and other necessities, overriding the strong energetic constraints imposed by simple technology and transport. For example, Teotihuacán depended heavily on its local irrigation system, and Tenochtitlán benefited from the enormous productivity of *chinampa* (drained field) agriculture and effective canoe transport on the surrounding lake.

In both cases, the resulting dense urban populations generated new economic institutions, such as huge markets, as well as the demographic base to expand their political and economic influence, which in turn allowed for the acquisition of taxes and tribute over very wide regions.

---

general were widely believed to be less sophisticated, more war-like, and more "decadent" than their splendid Classic forebears. Such perceptions now seem quaint and wrongheaded. There was no sudden, uniform process of florescence and decline that simultaneously affected all of Mesoamerica (Smith and Berdan 2003). Both Classic Teotihuacán and Monte Albán lost their power and influence centuries before the Maya collapse, and many Postclassic societies such as the Aztecs were extraordinary civilizations by any standard. Fortunately, we know a great deal about Postclassic Mesoamerica, because these late times bring us within the range of reliable oral histories, surviving indigenous books, and, ultimately, the complex interface between natives and Europeans that produced detailed descriptions of all aspects of life in the early 16th century.

The Rise of the Toltecs

Foremost among the Early Postclassic kingdoms celebrated in Mesoamerican myth and history is **Tula**, the great urban successor to Teotihuacán (Mastache et al. 2002). For the Aztecs Tula was Tollan, the legendary city, and they called its inhabitants Toltecs. The Aztecs imagined the Toltecs to be rich and accomplished at every conceivable craft, and their name came to be synonymous with "skilled artisan." Toltecs are said to have lived harmonious lives under their ruler Ce Acatl Topiltzin Quetzalcoatl, whose splendid palaces were adorned with shell, turquoise, silver, and gold. They worshiped a principal god also called Quetzalcoatl, who required only the sacrifice of butterflies. Toltec fields produced crops effortlessly and unfailingly, and even the cotton grew in brilliant colors. Toltec wise men

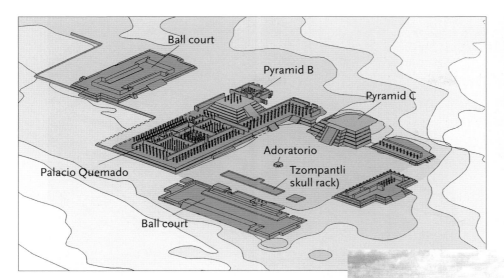

Ball court
Pyramid B
Pyramid C
Palacio Quemado
Adoratorio
Tzompantli
skull rack)
Ball court

16.37, 16.38 The sacred precinct of Tula: *reconstruction drawing (left) of the pyramids and large colonnaded buildings at the core of Tula. Pyramids B and C dominate the central quadrangle. (Below) Pyramid B, with pillars in the form of warrior figures, overlooks the Palacio Quemado ("Burned Palace"), a vast colonnaded set of buildings.*

invented the arts of medicine and the counts of the days and years. Tula finally fell, so the myths said, when Quetzalcoatl and his followers were tricked by evil enemies linked to the malevolent god Tezcatlipoca, and fled to distant lands in the direction of the rising sun.

The real Tula emerged on the fringe of the Basin of Mexico some 80 km (50 miles) northwest of Teotihuacán. This region of about 1000 sq. km (386 sq. miles) receives comparatively little rainfall but has several large rivers, making it attractive for irrigation agriculture. In Classic times the area was heavily colonized by people with strong connections to Teotihuacán, many of whom probably produced lime for making plaster. Around AD 700 a little community grew up around a modest group of civic structures at a place called Tula Chico. Ceramics and other artifacts found there show strong connections with areas to the north and west, consistent with stories that Tula was founded by intrusive Tolteca-Chichimeca peoples migrating from those directions. Following a slight shift in the location of the ceremonial core of the community, Tula matured into a huge city between AD 900 and 1200, with a population as large as 60,000 people concentrated in an area of about 16 sq. km (6 sq. miles). Many of its inhabitants may have been new migrants from southern parts of the Basin and Tula's culture represents a fusion of central Mexican and northern influences; other influences (especially religious) and perhaps populations came from the Huasteca on the northern Gulf Coast. Clearly, the city was a very cosmopolitan place, although most of its people were probably Nahuatl speakers (the language of the Aztecs).

Tula sprawled over a landscape of low hills, valleys, and swamps at the confluence of two major rivers. It derived much of its support from numerous outlying rural communities, especially to the east, where 30–40 percent of the population resided. Houses in the city itself took several forms, a common one being a set of rectangular, adobe structures, each with mul-

tiple rooms, built around a central courtyard. Such compounds probably housed several nuclear families. A high proportion of city dwellers must have farmed nearby irrigated land or perhaps cultivated agave, a plant perfectly suited to the dry environment. As at Teotihuacán, there are many remains of workshops that manufactured special products such as obsidian tools, mold-made pottery, and stone vessels.

At the highest point in the center of the city is a huge sacred precinct composed of large pyramids, ball courts, and spacious colonnaded halls [**16.37, 16.38**]. Building facades are decorated with panels showing jaguars and deities, and supporting pillars are carved in the form of warrior figures. Above the heads of some of these warriors are undeciphered glyphs resembling later Aztec writing, which probably represent names. Both the general arrangement and specific architectural elements of Tula's monumental buildings show similarities with Teotihuacán.

During Tula's hegemony, strong links were forged with other parts of Mesoamerica, including regions beyond its borders. Objects were imported from great distances, such as marine shell from the Pacific and Gulf of Mexico, and pottery from as far away as Central America. What appear to be Toltec

16.39 *The House of the Governors at Uxmal: the facade, with its distinctive mosaic sculpture, is the most famous Puuc-style building.*

KEY CONTROVERSY The Collapse of Maya Civilization

Contrary to popular belief, the so-called Classic Maya collapse was not a sudden catastrophe, nor did it affect all ancient Maya people (Webster 2002). The whole northern half of the Yucatán Peninsula was comparatively unscathed, and remained impressively civilized until the Spanish conquest. In the old southern heartland, however, kingdom after kingdom eventually failed over an area of about 150,000 sq. km (58,000 sq. miles), roughly the size of the state of Florida; eventually most of the population of this region, estimated at about 5 million people, also disappeared.

Chronology of the Collapse
The traditional barometer of this collapse is reduction in the rate at which dated royal monuments were set up; the decline began about AD 760 in the western kingdoms and accelerated during the next century. A few sites still dedicated monuments with Long Count dates as late as AD 909 or slightly later, but the early 10th century saw the effective end of a tradition established almost a millennium before. Fewer and fewer royal construction projects were completed, and

some were left unfinished. No more kings were buried in elaborate tombs.

Clearly, the collapse was not a sudden event, but a process of decline that occurred over about 150 years. The worst effects of this decline, as well as many subsequent cultural readjustments, are notably apparent between AD 800 and 1000, a period sometimes called the Terminal Classic. Particularly evident are rejection of the old polychrome pottery tradition, with its many court scenes, and the monumental art and inscriptions so closely associated with kings and elites.

The Fall of Kings
What all such evidence mainly signals is failure of the Maya royal institution. It was long believed that lords and commoners disappeared at about the same time as kings, making the collapse much more mysterious and dramatic. Some polities did indeed experience this kind of abrupt and total collapse, but elsewhere the process was much slower. At Copán, some noble residences were still occupied as much as 200 years after the royal dynasty fell, and the commoner population dwindled away over about four

centuries. A few polities, such as Lamanai in Belize, never collapsed at all, and the Classic kingdom of Coba survived to play a major role in later Postclassic conflicts. Still, by the time the Spaniards first penetrated the old heartland region in 1524 they found it almost deserted, apart from the vigorous Itzá kingdom near the ruins of Tikal. However long it took, something dramatic did eventually destroy Maya civilization in the southern lowlands. The collapse is best viewed from the perspective of particular kingdoms, although in some sense it was a communicable failure as well.

Possible Causes
Such a protracted and variable process of decline does not lend itself to simple explanations. Many "prime mover" causes have nevertheless been singled out, including peasant revolts, soil exhaustion, epidemic diseases, earthquakes, ideological fatigue, and, most recently, drought. No explanation goes very far by itself to justify the complex patterns of the collapse, and some (e.g., earthquakes) are simply unconvincing. Many archaeologists agree that a complex set

trading colonies have been identified as far south as El Salvador (Fowler 1989). Equally important were exchanges with outlying peoples far to the north, beyond the Mesoamerican frontier, for example Casas Grandes in northern Mexico.

While not a power on a par with Teotihuacán, Tula certainly dominated sizable territories. Later traditions mention several centers tributary to Tula, all located near the northern fringe of Mesoamerica, and some archaeologists think that all of the Basin of Mexico fell under its hegemony. Tula's principal rival in the highlands was probably Cholula, but this is difficult to verify in the absence of inscriptions. Sometime around AD 1150–1200 Tula violently collapsed, as indicated by signs of burning in the principal buildings; somewhat later, these same buildings were heavily looted. Many people still lived in outlying settlements, however, and the urban zone was later reoccupied, persisting as a small city subject to the Aztecs in the early 16th century. Carved and painted motifs in the later Aztec capital resemble those found at Tula, and some of Tula's sculpture might have been relocated there.

The Postclassic Maya

The Puuc Florescence Maya polities in the northern part of the Yucatán Peninsula weathered the collapse of the great southern kingdoms and in some ways might even have benefited from it (Sabloff and Andrews 1986; Milbrath and Peraza 2003). Early in the 8th century AD, population began to expand greatly in the Puuc region of northwest Yucatán (Prem 1994). Soils there were very fertile, but rainfall was comparatively low and the water table deep, so it was not until sophisticated water storage technology was developed that people began to live there in large numbers. They seem to have moved in from several directions, and many archaeologists think that the increasingly troubled southern Maya contributed some of the migrants.

Eventually the Puuc landscape was packed with imposing centers such as **Sayil**, **Kabah**, **Labna**, and, most famous of them all, **Uxmal**. Distinctive elements of Puuc architecture include columns and complicated mosaic sculptures of gods, humans, and geometric facade designs [**16.39**]. The House of the Governor and the Nunnery at Uxmal are among the most famous

16.40 *Reconstruction drawings showing how the site of Dos Pilas deteriorated dramatically from a flourishing regal-ritual center to a ruin with stockades for defense. However, the collapse was not a sudden event and not all ancient Maya were affected by it – the northern half of the Yucatán remained comparatively unscathed.*

Before AD 761

AD 761

of interacting factors was responsible, and that the single most important elements in this mix were overpopulation and a deteriorating agricultural landscape. These stresses triggered more savage warfare, population movements, famine, disease, and loss of confidence in the pretensions of rulers. Particular kingdoms were more or less vulnerable to specific subsets of causes, but the synergism among all these problems eventually undermined the larger system of civilization in the southern lowlands.

(and frequently visited) of all Maya buildings. Originally there might have been several autonomous Puuc polities, but by AD 875–900 Uxmal probably gained political ascendancy.

Puuc architectural influences extended onto the northern plains of Yucatán, and ceramics of the kind typical of Chichén Itzá have been found in the Puuc heartland sites. Puuc prosperity was as short-lived as it was impressive, however, and the Puuc centers collapsed and the countryside around them was heavily depopulated *c.* AD 1000 or a little later. Many people probably migrated to the northern plains of Yucatán, where there were related Puuc tradition settlements and where the next great regional power was shortly to appear.

Chichén Itzá According to Maya chronicles, Chichén Itzá was the greatest of all Postclassic capitals. It began its rise during the 8th century AD on the flat plains of northern Yucatán, about 130 km (80 miles) northwest of Uxmal, near a huge water-filled sinkhole, or *cenote*, that became a major pilgrimage center. At

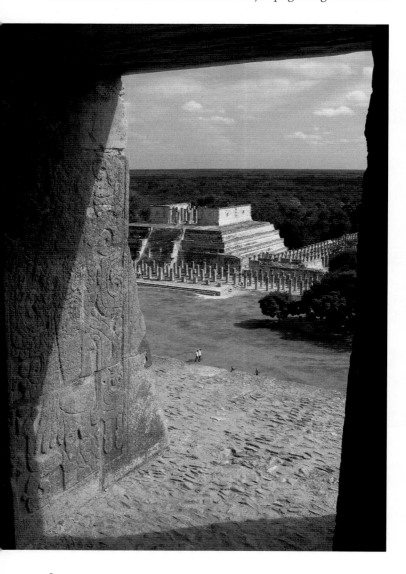

the core of this immense site are the Castillo Pyramid, the Monjas Palace, a gigantic ball court, and other impressive structures [**16.41**]. Many buildings in the southern part of Chichén Itzá show Puuc architectural affinities, but elsewhere the abundant painted and carved motifs are strikingly central Mexican – and more specifically Toltec – in character. Chichén Itzá's connections with Tula have long been debated, but native histories say that the Itzá founders of Chichén were succeeded by Mexican migrants led by a man called Kukulkan, meaning "Feathered Serpent" in Maya. Inevitably this myth has become associated with the expulsion of Quetzalcoatl (which also means "Feathered Serpent") and his followers from Tula.

Details of Chichén Itzá's culture history are obscure, because inscriptions and dates are confined to the 9th century AD. Warrior imagery celebrates conquest and sacrifice, and Chichén Itzá was undoubtedly embroiled in many conflicts that probably involved Uxmal and the other Puuc centers. After about AD 900, Chichén Itzá eclipsed its major Maya rival, Coba, a large site in northeastern Yucatán, and Mexican influences proliferated. For the next several centuries it was the capital of an expansive northern state, as well as a mercantile emporium that probably benefited from the trade in salt, among many other commodities.

Then sometime around AD 1200 or 1250, Chichén Itzá rapidly declined as a regional power. Maya histories blame debauched leaders and internal strife, and claim that one faction of the Itzá fled far to the south, where its members founded the last Maya kingdom to be conquered by the Spaniards. Chichén Itzá itself was never completely abandoned, however, and remained a famous pilgrimage center where sacrifices were made even after the Spaniards arrived.

Mayapan Power in the north shifted to nearby Mayapan, said to have been founded by a lord of the Cocom family. Mayapan's main buildings are small and shabby compared to those at Chichén Itzá (one is a diminutive replica of the Castillo), but it has a very distinctive settlement layout. A low stone defensive wall encloses a zone of about 4.2 sq. km (1.6 sq. miles), crowded with over 4000 structures, most of them residences. With a population estimated at 12,000, Mayapan approached the urban densities of the great central Mexican cities. Exactly who lived there is unclear, but many of its inhabitants were probably elites and their retainers, who resided there during at least part of the year. Like Chichén Itzá, Mayapan is said to have been the capital of a great confederacy, but it seems less convincing as a dominant power than its great predecessor. Several conflicting

16.41 *Chichén Itzá: a view of part of the Temple of the Warriors and the Group of the Thousand Columns, from the Castillo Pyramid, which dominated the main plaza at the site.*

Maya accounts say that Mayapan fell *c.* AD 1441, beset by drought, famine, and a rebellion of Xiu lords against the evil Cocom lineage – a kind of replay of what happened earlier at Chichén Itzá. Signs of burning have been found in the ruins of some elite households, and Mayapan was largely abandoned two or three generations before the Spaniards came.

Mesoamerica Discovered: What the Spaniards Found

In 1519 the Spaniard Hernan Cortés sailed with a small fleet to Yucatán, following up two previous expeditions that had reported impressive native cultures there. Best known for his conquest of the Aztec empire, Cortés also left accounts of the 16th-century Maya, who were the first Mesoamerican people he encountered (Cortés 1986).

The Maya of the Early 16th Century

No great power arose to replace Chichén Itzá and Mayapan in northern Yucatán. Instead, the landscape was fragmented into hundreds of small polities ruled by hereditary leaders called *batabs*, most of whom had only a few thousand subjects (Roys 1965). Larger but fragile coalitions united sets of *batabs* who shared the same lineage, or who made alliances for mutual benefit. War was common among, and even within, the little *batab*ships, many of whose noble families – such as the Xiu and Cocom – had been traditional enemies for centuries. Here and there a very powerful leader managed to dominate many local *batabs* and suppress their conflicts, in effect creating a petty kingdom that might number as many as 60,000 people.

Despite this lack of overall political integration, northern Maya societies were quite complex, and still retained their own versions of much older Classic patterns. The Spaniards were impressed by the large towns they saw, organized around temple pyramids, public plazas, and elaborate houses (Landa 1941). Priests officiated at community rituals, wrote in books, and tracked time using somewhat altered forms of the old Classic Maya calendars. Nobles bore illustrious family names, were rich in land, and claimed descent from foreigners. They were supported by the taxes of commoners, and engaged in long-distance trade in cloth, honey, gold, obsidian, slaves, and chocolate. Most people grew maize, fished, or produced special products such as salt. Lowest in rank were slaves, mainly war captives or debtors, who were house servants or field hands. Clearly, some watered-down version of ancient Classic civilization still thrived in northern Yucatán when the Spaniards arrived, and even after (Restall 1997). Following a few skirmishes with the Maya there and along the Gulf Coast, Cortés and his army moved on to their confrontation with the Aztecs, leaving the Maya two more decades of freedom.

The Aztecs and the Late Horizon: History and Myth

Early in the 16th century many native peoples believed that their ancestors had migrated to the Basin of Mexico in successive waves from the northern fringes of Mesoamerica. These movements began about the time that Tula collapsed, or perhaps a little earlier. Such migrations may have been caused by some combination of climatic change and political instability. Most important are the migration stories of those people we today call Aztecs, who were Nahuatl speakers.

The Nahuatl word for the people who lived on this northern frontier was Chichimec. The Aztecs envisioned some of them as savage hunter-gatherers, others as farmers who practiced irrigation, played the ball game, and built temples; and there was a last, even more sophisticated group, who were refugees from the disintegrating Toltec kingdom. Some archaeologists believe these wanderings first introduced Nahua speakers into the Basin of Mexico. (Nahua languages, of which Nahuatl is one, are members of the Uto-Aztecan linguistic family and had probably long been spoken in other parts of Mesoamerica.) Others think many of these migration accounts were "reconstructed history," made up later to justify events, and that Nahua speakers had colonized the region much earlier. If the glyphs recently detected at Teotihuacán turn out to record Nahuatl speech, this second position will be strengthened. At the very least, they would show that there were some Nahua speakers in the region already by Classic times.

Whatever their origins, none of the people Cortés encountered in the Basin of Mexico would have called themselves Aztecs; instead, they used more specific ethnic labels, such as Mexica-Tenochca (the founders of Tenochtitlán), Acolhua, Tepaneca, or Chalca. A number of related groups of this kind purportedly came from a mythical homeland called Aztlan, and historians collectively label them "Aztecs." One such band of tribal farmer-migrants adopted the name Mexica along their route, and eventually found themselves driven as despised refugees (or if one prefers, led by their patron god) onto a set of small islands in Lake Texcoco, part of the shallow lacustrine system on the floor of the Basin of Mexico (Durán 1994). This refuge was a sort of no-man's land claimed by the Tepanecs of nearby Atzcapotzalco, and surrounded by enemy polities. There in AD 1325 the Mexica founded their capital and named it Tenochtitlán, a place destined to become a Tollan in its own right and the greatest metropolis of the pre-Columbian New World [see box: Tenochtitlán: The Aztec Capital, pp. 634–35].

At the end of the 14th century there were several dozen independent, warring city-states in the Basin of Mexico (Hicks 1986; Hodge 1996). The Mexica-Tenochca enlisted as mercenaries in the service of the powerful and aggressive Tepanecs, and in return received a share of tribute from their combined military victories. About this time the Mexica elected their [–> p. 636]

KEY SITE Tenochtitlán: The Aztec Capital

From humble beginnings *c.* AD 1325, Tenochtitlán grew to be the largest and most complex city in the New World by the early 16th century – a worthy successor to Teotihuacán and Tula (Calnek 1972). When Hernan Cortés and his soldiers first explored it in 1519, the core of the city – essentially an artificial urban island reclaimed from the shallow lake by draining and infilling – covered a 12–15-sq. km (4.6–5.8-sq. mile) area near the western edge of Lake Texcoco. Because it was crisscrossed by a network of canals and attached to the mainland by 60 km (37 miles) of causeways and an aqueduct, it reminded the Spaniards of Venice.

About 125,000 people resided in this core zone, most of them in single-story adobe houses aligned along streets, alleyways, and canals. Around the edge of the city were many houses set on small *chinampas*, or artificial islands, which were used to grow flowers and other special crops for the urban markets.

Tenochtitlán was organized into approximately 80 *barrios*, or neighborhoods, each of which probably housed members of an urban unit that pursued special economic tasks. The city probably housed a far smaller proportion of farmers than Teotihuacán had.

16.42 *(Right) Tenochtitlán, the island capital of the Mexica (Aztecs), was linked to the mainland by a system of causeways and an aqueduct. The shallow lake to the west and south of the capital was transformed into a vast zone of chinampas and canals.*

16.43 *(Below left) Reconstruction of the Mexica capital of Tenochtitlán, showing the central ceremonial precinct and part of the surrounding island city.*

Much of the lakebed outside the city to the south and west had been transformed by state projects into thousands of hectares of *chinampas* and tree-lined canals (Coe 1964). Farmers lived on many of these artificial fields, and there were scores of towns on

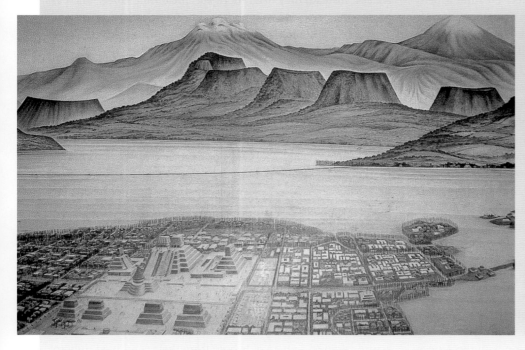

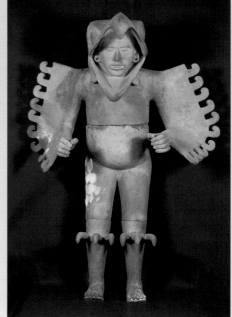

higher ground and along the shoreline. Enormous agricultural yields from the *chinampas*, coupled with efficient water transport, created a unique urban ecology that supported the large urban population.

There were other respectably sized cities in the Basin of Mexico as well, such as Texcoco on the eastern shore of the lake, but with an estimated population in the range of 30,000–40,000, even it was dwarfed by its powerful neighbor.

The Templo Mayor
At the center of Tenochtitlán was a great enclosure roughly 400 m (1300 ft) on a side. Recent discoveries suggest that its perimeter comprised a wide platform with smaller temples atop it, a design probably copied from the Ciudadela at Teotihuacán. Inside the enclosure were about 80 structures, including temples, dormitories for priests, schools for elite young men, dance platforms, ball courts, skull racks, and clubhouses for warrior societies.

Dominating all these was the 30-m (98-ft) high Templo Mayor or Great Temple, with its twin sanctuaries on the top dedicated to Tlaloc, the rain god, and Huitzilopochtli, the god of war and the sun. Some 7000 offerings, along with many human sacrifices, have been recovered from the fill of the Templo Mayor, which was rebuilt and enlarged seven times.

With this vast complex of buildings the Mexica created an architectural cosmogram – a model of the world, or at least the important elements of it – and they probably regarded Tenochtitlán as their own version of Tollan. It was at the Templo Mayor that the most extravagant human sacrifices took place, to ensure rain, energize the sun, and guarantee military success. Many other gods of the

Aztec pantheon were honored at lesser temples in the sacred enclosure; as among the Maya, the primary concern of ritual was to maintain balance in the universe and to suppress the forces of disorder that might destroy the world (Duran 1971).

The Palaces
Around the edges of the enclosure were the palaces of the highest nobles and officials, and grandest of all, the palaces of kings. One old royal palace was so large that it housed the entire Spanish army.

King Motecezuma's palace, located near the southeast corner of the sacred enclosure, was a labyrinthine complex of several hundred conjoined rooms and courtyards on varying levels. The upper levels housed the king and his household, and the palace contained armories, libraries, council rooms, and other facilities for governance and courtly functions.

There were workshops for attached artisans, and each day hundreds of noble warriors and other court officials attended the ruler and were fed by the royal kitchens. Royal facilities elsewhere in the city included

pleasure gardens, a zoo, and vast storehouses for food and the spoils of the empire.

The Central Market
About 1 km (0.62 mile) north of the sacred enclosure was the sprawling central market, where one could purchase virtually anything produced in the Basin of Mexico or brought to the city from elsewhere in the empire through tribute or trade. In this section of town were concentrated the houses of the *pochteca*, or professional merchants.

Destruction
Unfortunately, we must rely mainly on native and Spanish accounts for most of these details, because much of Tenochtitlán was destroyed in 1521 or later demolished by the colonial Spaniards. What is left mostly lies deep beneath the modern streets and houses of Mexico City. Large sections of the Templo Mayor zone have been excavated by Mexican archaeologists, however, and their findings correspond closely to written descriptions. The consolidated ruins of the Templo Mayor and its nearby museum are major tourist attractions today.

16.44 *(Opposite right) Ceramic statue of an Eagle Man, 1.8 m (c. 6ft) tall, found in the Hall of the Eagle Warriors.*

16.45 *(Right) Reconstruction of the Templo Mayor, the Great Temple, topped by twin shrines to Tlaloc, the rain god, and Huitzilopochtli, the god of war and the sun. The temple was rebuilt seven times, with each stage encased within the next.*

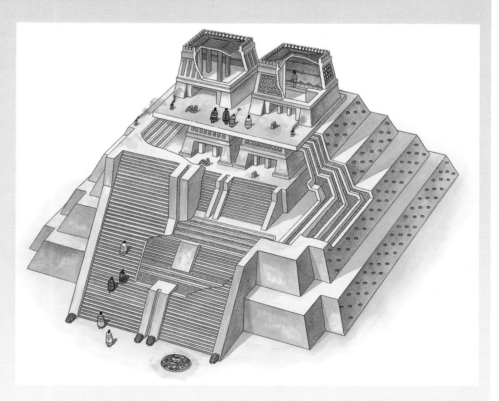

own king, who married into an exalted dynasty descended from the Toltecs. In response to a falling out with their Tepanec overlords in AD 1428, the Mexica rebelled, aided by two other allied states, Texcoco and Tlacopan. The overthrow of the Tepanecs vastly promoted the power of the Mexica king Itzcoatl and his fledgling dynasty, and helped to create a dominant class of nobles and a tradition of powerful kings, as well as promoting the Mexica tribal god.

At this juncture these emergent leaders, by their own account, burned their ancient books and proceeded to write "true" history (Duran 1971; 1994). All this set the stage for the dramatic explosion of empire under the Triple Alliance of Tenochtitlán, Texcoco, and Tlacopan over the next 91 years – an empire that was still expanding when the Spaniards arrived. This short interval of less than a century represents the third and last of the episodes of relative cultural unity in Mesoamerica – the so-called **Late Horizon**.

The Aztec Empire in 1519

By 1519 the mature Aztec empire [**16.46**] dominated some 400 previously independent polities over an area of about 200,000 sq. km (77,226 sq. miles), including the Gulf Coast, the Valley of Oaxaca, parts of western Mexico, and places as distant as the Pacific coast of Guatemala (Berdan et al. 1996). Its subjects numbered somewhere between 6 and 10 million people, and about 1 to 1.5 million of them lived in the Basin of Mexico, giving it demographic advantage over any outlying region; it was probably the most densely settled region of the entire pre-Columbian New World. The Basin of Mexico landscape was heavily transformed by terracing, irrigation systems, and artifi-

cially drained fields, and represented the most productive agrarian region of Mesoamerica in the early 16th century. Maize and beans were the most important staple crops, but others included amaranth, chia (both types of grain), and agave. The Aztecs also continued to use many wild resources, including waterfowl and a kind of blue-green algae that was skimmed from the surface of the lakes and made into high-protein cakes.

The empire was assembled through intimidation, alliance, and outright conquest. Conquered polities were grouped into 38 tributary provinces, from which tribute of all kinds [**16.47**] flowed into the Basin of Mexico (Anawalt and Berdan 1992). All this wealth disproportionately enriched the king of Tenochtitlán and his nobles, who effectively dominated their erstwhile partners in the Triple Alliance. Another set of strategic provinces consisted of polities that had joined the empire as military allies, and who paid only nominal tribute. Such allies were necessary because of the logistical problems in moving and feeding large armies without effective transport, making distant sources of loyal soldiers and staging areas necessary – and because there remained nearby powerful enemies to be contained.

Most formidable of these opponents were the **Tarascans**, who were vigorously building their own empire over some 75,000 sq. km (29,960 sq. miles) of western Mexico (Pollard 1993). By 1519 they controlled a population of about 1,500,000 people from their capital of **Tzintzuntzan**, on the shores of Lake Patzcuaro. With 20,000–25,000 inhabitants, Tzintzuntzan was much smaller than Tenochtitlán, but exercised highly centralized control over its empire. Fierce Tarascan warriors inflicted heavy defeats on Aztec armies in the late 15th century

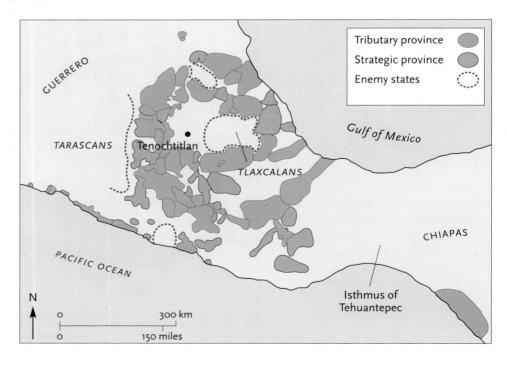

16.46 The Aztec empire: *map showing tributary and strategic provinces outside the Basin of Mexico in AD 1521. Note the discontinuous nature of the Aztec imperial territories, and the surviving enemy polities of the Tlaxcalans and Tarascans.*

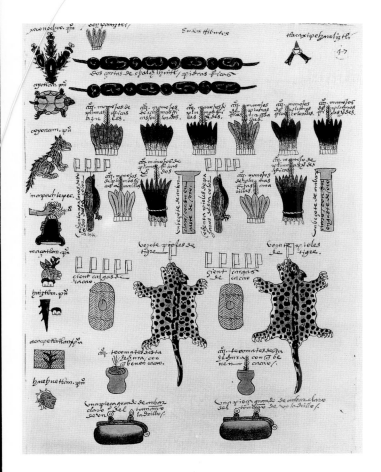

16.47 Aztec tribute: *this tribute list shows jaguar skins, gold, feathers, and other costly items that the Aztecs collected from tributary polities. It is part of a document called the* Codex Mendoza *commissioned by the Spaniards, but largely painted in pre-Columbian style.*

of Mexico were sometimes resettled as military colonists in sensitive frontier posts.

Aztec Society No matter what its rank in the imperial hierarchy, each city-state (*altepetl*) in the Basin of Mexico shared many common features with the others. Language, diet, technology, religion, and customs heavily overlapped, as did political organization. One or more hereditary king (*tlatoani*) ruled each *altepetl*. Kings and their families, along with other high nobles (collectively called *pipiltin*), comprised the hereditary upper class and were the primary beneficiaries of the tribute of empire. Kings and nobles were polygynous (having many wives or concubines), so their numbers grew rapidly, necessitating further resources and so additional conquests. Noble houses owned private lands, and their members were rewarded with further estates in return for military or governmental service.

While nobles were exempted from paying taxes, they were expected to serve the state in other ways. After receiving special education, the *pipiltin* monopolized the highest political and religious offices and formed the elite backbone of the army, which was otherwise conscripted. High *pipiltin* officers and warriors also attended the ruler every day at his palace [**16.48**] and participated in the extraordinary court life of the capital (Evans 1998).

Commoners, the largest component of society, owed both service and taxes to their own *tlatoani*, and often to his overlord. Most of these people were farmers or urban artisans, usually living together in communities or neighborhoods with their own leaders, schools, and temples, and owing collective obligations to the state; the most important of these were contributing corvée labor and serving in the army. Successful commoner warriors occasionally achieved quasi-noble rank and were rewarded with gifts, military titles, and land. Many of the most talented artisans, such as goldsmiths, also had high prestige because of their close associations with nobles. Richest among the commoners were the *pochteca*, or professional merchants, who led caravan-like trading expeditions to distant places both inside and outside the empire, their enterprises partly funded by nobles and even kings. Many of the valuable goods they brought back to Tenochtitlán or other towns found their way into the great markets, and the *pochteca* profited sufficiently to lead (at least in private) comparatively luxurious lives. Because they could afford to buy sacrificial victims, they also enjoyed limited upward social mobility since anyone who donated a sacrificial victim was honored and praised.

and forced a stalemate along their common border, which both sides fortified and garrisoned.

Closer at hand was the **Tlaxcalan confederation** to the east of the Basin of Mexico, whose people were culturally very similar to the Aztecs. Although surrounded by Aztec territory and allies, the Tlaxcalans retained their independence and ultimately became staunch supporters of the Spaniards.

For the most part, the members of the Triple Alliance managed to administer their provinces quite effectively, although an occasional rebellion had to be put down. Complaisant local rulers were left in place, and their offspring married into the royal families of Tenochtitlán, Texcoco, and Tlacopan. Sometimes, mainly in the imperial core territory, the Basin of Mexico, local dynasties were extinguished and replaced with royal governors, and their lands and peoples directly absorbed by the great rulers. Elsewhere, the Aztecs preferred to rule through the comparatively cheap expedients of intimidation and the frequent appearance of tax collectors.

Nevertheless, they found it necessary in some 20 places, such as in the Valley of Oaxaca and along the Tarascan frontier, to arrange more direct control through imperial governors and garrisons. On rare occasions they used very punitive measures against local communities, for example at some places along the Tarascan frontier, and groups of commoners from the Basin

16.48 Motecezuma's palace: *although schematic, this 16th-century drawing from the* Codex Mendoza *is the most complete surviving depiction of the palace of Motecezuma II, who is shown sitting in a chamber at the top. Members of the court, nobles or* pipiltin, *are seen in a lower room.*

Lower still in rank were the *mayeque*, who were tied to the land and who labored on the estates of kings and nobles, although they paid taxes only to their immediate lords. Many of these people were probably originally free commoners who had been relegated through conquest to a serflike condition. At the bottom of society were the *tlacotin*, who occupied a depressed economic status (the Spaniards called them "slaves"). These individuals owed service to others, and were demoted to this condition through debt or as a result of criminal acts. They could, however, own their own property, and buy their freedom, and their children were born free. Only if they proved recalcitrant were they mistreated, and consistently malcontent individuals could be sold or sacrificed.

The Spanish Conquest

In 1519 the Aztec empire showed no signs of serious weakness. Motecezuma II, the reigning king, worked to consolidate the gains of his predecessors, and had sent emissaries into the highlands of Guatemala to demand gifts, usually a prelude to absorption into the empire. Whether he would have been successful in subduing the highland Maya, whose Quiché and Cakchiquel kingdoms were themselves highly stratified and warlike (Sharer 2000), will never be known. A new and unexpected threat appeared in the form of Hernan Cortés and his little army, initially numbering only about 500 men (Diaz 1963; Hassig 1994). By coincidence, they landed on the shores of the empire on the very day that Aztec diviners prophesized the return of Quetzalcoatl, the hero-king of the Toltecs.

Having heard rumors on the Gulf Coast of Motecezuma's wealthy empire, Cortés and his men marched inland in August of 1519. The Tlaxcalans initially resisted the Spaniards, but they quickly realized that these aggressive newcomers could be used against their hated Aztec enemies. Accompanied by Tlaxcalan and other Indian allies, Cortés and his men finally entered Tenochtitlán in early November, where they were received amicably, if reluctantly, by Motecezuma and housed for six months in his father's palace. During this interlude (their host Motecezuma was placed under Spanish "house arrest" for most of it) they observed many details of Aztec life that contribute to the descriptions given above. Cortés and Motecezuma went on hunting trips together, and Spanish soldiers played games of chance with the Aztec monarch.

Eventually this amity broke down. Motecezuma was killed under mysterious circumstances during fighting that broke out in May 1520, precipitated by the desecration by the Spaniards of the main temple in the city. At this point the empire showed its weaknesses, as one by one, the allies of Tenochtitlán fell away; perhaps the most damaging defection occurred when Texcoco turned on its former imperial partner. After many months of fierce fighting, the Spaniards finally stood victorious amid the smoking ruins of Tenochtitlán in August 1521.

It would be convenient to end our story at this point, but there is one dramatic and poignant postscript. Most of Mesoamerica was firmly in Spanish hands by 1550, but the Itzá Maya held out deep in the forests of northern Guatemala for another 150 years (Jones 1998). According to Itzá traditions, their ancestors had migrated into these southern forests when Chichén Itzá fell. At their island capital of Nojpeten, located on a great lake near the long-abandoned ruins of Tikal, Itzá kings still sported the old Classic royal title of *ajaw*, built pyramids and temples, worshiped many of the old gods, and consulted painted books of prophecy. Not until 1697 was this last native kingdom finally brought under Spanish control, and with its conquest the rich independent tradition of Mesoamerican civilization that began 4000 years earlier ended, once and for all.

Summary and Conclusions

A few conspicuous New World societies – the Aztecs, Maya, and Incas – are widely known to the public, but the larger story of the rise of New World civilizations is not so familiar as that of their Old World counterparts in Egypt, Mesopotamia, China, and the Indus Valley. Nevertheless, the tradition of culture that emerged in Mesoamerica was every bit as complex and impressive. Nor is this a new perception, for when Europeans first embarked on the organized exploration of the Yucatán and Mexico in 1519, they encountered much that astounded them, but also much that they intuitively understood.

Hernan Cortés's letters to the Spanish king Charles V express his astonishment at what he and his little army saw on their march toward Tenochtitlán: people living in hierarchical, well-ordered, urban-centered, and literate societies, similar to those that the Spaniards knew from Europe, the Near East, and North Africa. Little of this complexity was evident in the Antilles or Panama, or in other parts of the New World that the Spaniards had previously explored. Cortés labeled these Mesoamerican people *gente de razón*, which was about as close as he could get to calling them civilized (the word "civilization" in its modern sense did not then exist in any European language). Indeed, one reason why Cortés so adroitly managed the conquest was because the general features and institutions of Mesoamerican society were comprehensible to him.

This familiarity fascinates anthropologists and archaeologists, who have long regarded the New World as a kind of vast anthropological laboratory from which comparative lessons can be drawn. We now know that New World civilizations evolved independently of Old World contacts, so the general patterns that Cortés saw and recognized are the result of convergence, a fact that strengthens our conviction that there are regularities in cultural evolution, one of the general themes of this book. Nevertheless, there was much that puzzled the Spaniards as well. How could Mesoamerican people be so prosperous without large domestic animals, or metal tools, or machines? How could merchants and markets thrive without sailing ships, or beasts of burden, or coinage? Most puzzling, how could these accomplished, sophisticated, and orderly people be ignorant of the Christian god, and even carry out horrific rituals that included human sacrifice? Ultimately, it is this contrast that is most fascinating of all. Over thousands of years, ancient Mesoamericans created a tradition of civilization that still strikes us as both familiar and strange.

In the next chapter we turn south to a second region of the Americas that witnessed the development of complex societies during the later Holocene. In South America (more particularly, in the Andean zone), a sequence of states and empires rose and fell from the late 1st millennium BC onwards. Yet

South America is a much larger landmass than Mesoamerica, and much of the continent lay beyond the reach of these changes. Social and cultural developments in less well-explored regions such as Amazonia are nevertheless significant, and contribute to an understanding of South America as a whole.

Further Reading and Suggested Websites

Clark, J. & Pye, M. (eds.). 2000. *Olmec Art and Archaeology in Mesoamerica*. Washington, D.C.: National Gallery of Art. Presents an overview of the Olmec by senior scholars, usefully supplemented by superb illustrations.

Coe, M.D. 2005. *The Maya.* (7th ed.). London & New York: Thames & Hudson. The most recent edition of this classic work.

Coe, M.D. & Koontz, R. 2002. (5th ed.). *Mexico: from the Olmecs to the Aztecs*. London & New York: Thames & Hudson. An up-to-date review of the cultures of ancient Mexico.

Diehl, R. 2004. *The Olmecs: America's First Civilization*. London & New York: Thames & Hudson. A recent synthesis.

Evans, S.T. 2004. *Ancient Mexico and Central America: Archaeology and Culture History*. London & New York: Thames & Hudson. Lavishly illustrated book presenting the most comprehensive and up-to-date overview of all things Mesoamerican.

Evans, S.T. & Webster, D. 2001. *Archaeology of Ancient Mexico and Central America*. New York: Garland. Encyclopedia in which entries by experts in the field provide information on virtually any subject mentioned in this chapter.

Handbook of Middle American Indians. 1965– . Austin: University of Texas Press. Ongoing multi-volume work with periodic supplements, edited by various scholars.

Marcus, J. & Flannery, K.V. 1996. *Zapotec Civilization*. London & New York: Thames & Hudson. Comprehensive source for one of the dynamic regional cultures of Mesoamerican civilization.

Miller, M. 2001. *The Art of Mesoamerica from Olmec to Aztec*. London & New York: Thames & Hudson. Review of monuments, architecture, and objects in their cultural contexts.

Miller, M. & Taube, K. 1993. *The Gods and Symbols of Ancient Mexico and the Maya*. London & New York: Thames & Hudson. Useful reference book for the religions and symbolic dimensions of ancient Mesoamerican culture.

Pohl, J.M. 1999. *Exploring Mesoamerica*. Oxford & New York: Oxford University Press. A handy and well-illustrated guidebook to the great places of ancient Mesoamerica.

Sanders, W.T., Parsons, J.R., & Santley, R.F. 1979. *The Basin of Mexico*. New York: Academic Press. A classic study of the most dynamic and culturally dominant region of Mesoamerica and the three great urban cultures that developed there.

www.famsi.org Website maintained by the Foundation for the Advancement of Mesoamerican Studies, with contributions by professional Mesoamericanists and many links to other good sources on almost any Mesoamerican topic.

www.doaks.org Website of Dumbarton Oaks Research Library and Collections, in Washington, D.C., which maintains one of the best on-line pre-Columbian research libraries and archives.

CHAPTER 17
FROM VILLAGE TO EMPIRE IN SOUTH AMERICA

Michael E. Moseley and Michael J. Heckenberger, University of Florida

Main Environmental Regions 641
The Andes 641
  • *The High Sierra* 641
  • *The Desert Coast* 641
Amazonia 642
  • *Coasts* 644
  • *Floodplains* 644
  • *Uplands* 644

Chronological Overview 645
The Andes and the Desert Coast 645
Amazonia and the Atlantic Coast 645

The Andean Preceramic, *c.* 3000–1800 BC 646
Early Mound Construction in Central and Northern Peru 646
Platforms and Sunken Courts along the Desert Coast 647
● **KEY CONTROVERSY** Maritime Foundations of Andean Civilization? 648
Mounds and their Builders at Caral and Paraiso 649
● **KEY SITE** Real Alto 650

Early Andean Civilization: The Initial Period and the Early Horizon 651
The Initial Period, c. 1800–400 BC 651
● **KEY SITE** Sechín Alto 652
Chavín and the Early Horizon, c. 400–200 BC 653
  • *Paracas* 654
  • *Pukara* 655

Andean Confederacies and States in the Early Intermediate Period, *c.* 200 BC–AD 650 655
Gallinazo, Moche, and the North Coast 655
● **KEY SITE** Sipán and the Presentation Theme 657
  • *The Temples of the Sun and the Moon* 658
Nazca and the South Coast 659
  • *The "Nazca Lines"* 660

The Rise and Fall of the Andean Empires 660
The Middle Horizon, c. AD 650–1000: Tiwanaku and Wari 660
The Late Intermediate Period, c. AD 1000–1470: Lambayeque and Chimor 662
  • *Lambayeque and Batan Grande* 662
  • *Chimor and Chan Chan* 663
The Late Horizon, 1476–1533: Cuzco and the Incas 665
  • *Origins and Expansion* 665
  • *Cuzco and the Trappings of Empire* 666
● **KEY SITE** The Sacred Valley of the Incas and Machu Picchu 667

Amazonia 668

The Amazonian Formative Period, *c.* 1000 BC–AD 500 668
The Linguistic Evidence 669
The Archaeological Evidence 669
● **KEY CONTROVERSY** The Rank Revolution 670

Regionalism and "Classic" Amazonia, *c.* AD 1–1500 670
The Lower Amazon 671
● **KEY CONTROVERSY** Amazonian Mound Builders 672
The Central Amazon 673
The Upper Amazon 674
The Orinoco and the Caribbean 674
● **KEY CONTROVERSY** Amazonian Urbanism? 675
The Southern Amazon 675

Summary and Conclusions 677

Further Reading and Suggested Websites 677

In this chapter we review the development of societies in South America from 3000 BC up to European contact in the 16th century AD. The earlier prehistory of the continent was covered in Chapter 9, which discussed the rise of the first agricultural communities in the moist tropics by 3000 BC and in the arid Andes Mountains by 1800 BC. The spread and refinement of the new food-producing economies sustained the rise of complex societies in many regions, and this chapter charts their development in two major geographical blocks: the Andes and Amazonia.

The mountainous Andes area is well known for its monumental stone architecture and elaborate terracing and irrigation systems. At the time of first European contact, the whole of this region had recently been brought under the control of a single political unit, the Inca empire; but this was only the final phase in a long process of formation, coalescence, and collapse of the Andean states. Amazonia is, in contrast, much less well studied, but there is now evidence that thriving communities and earthwork builders also existed here during the later Holocene period. Maize was introduced from Mesoamerica, but the primary staples in South America were root crops: the potato in the Andes and manioc in Amazonia. Fish were the principal protein source in both the Pacific and tropical lowlands, and along with farming formed the economic underpinning that allowed the emergence of complex societies in the southern continent of the Americas.

Main Environmental Regions

South America is characterized by global extremes in environmental conditions. It is home to the world's biggest river, largest tropical forest, driest desert, and longest mountain range, second only to the Himalayas in height and harshness. Great contrasts in the continent's habitats confronted native populations with markedly disparate conditions and resources. Over time, the descendants of Paleoindian colonists diverged, as people pursued various ways of making a living in one or another of the different environments. Whereas hunting, gathering, and foraging were enduring lifeways in the far south, the advent of agriculture fostered the rise of complex societies in the more northerly Amazonian tropics and Andes Mountains, which are the focus of this chapter. Because the highlands and lowlands of South America are characterized by great habitat diversity, which inevitably influenced the archaeological record, it is useful to summarize the subdivisions of the major environmental regions, beginning with the arid, mountainous Andes and concluding with the moist tropics of Amazonia [17.1].

The Andes

Where the Andean Range extends north from Ecuador to the Caribbean coast, the mountains are low, wet, and well vegetated, and supported human adaptations comparable with those of the tropical forest. Conditions change dramatically in northern Peru, as the Cordillera rises and divides into parallel eastern and western ranges; these bracket a longitudinal series of sierra basins, culminating in a vast mountain trough that holds Lake Titicaca at an altitude of 3805 m (12,500 ft). Then the parallel ranges grow progressively higher, wider, and drier, and split the continental climate. The lower, eastern mountain slopes are well watered, in contrast to the western high sierra. The Pacific coastlands are parched desert, and in Chile, arid conditions push up into the highlands, creating the driest region on earth. The actively growing Cordillera is subject to frequent earthquakes, and the climate suffers century-long swings in above- and below-normal rainfall and El Niño events (in which rising sea-surface temperatures in the western Pacific cause increased rainfall in Peru), which bring drought to the mountains and floods to the desert coast.

The High Sierra In the central Andes, the majority of people traditionally resided above 2500 m (8200 ft), because the sierra offers more farmland than the coast [17.2]. High altitudes have disadvantages, however, including steep, rugged terrain, high winds, elevated solar radiation, chronic erosion and poor soils, short growing seasons, aridity, erratic seasonal rainfall, frost, hail, cold, and hypoxia (shortage of oxygen in the air due to decreased barometric pressure). Low oxygen levels and cold temperatures exert constant stress on people, animals, and plants. Sierra societies depended on particularly hardy domesticates such as potatoes and llamas, because most crops and farm animals reproduce poorly at high elevations.

Farming and herding were generally pursued jointly, a practice called agropastoralism; animals provided fertilizer as well as transport and could graze on crop stubble after harvesting. Mountain ecological zones are stacked vertically atop one another in long, narrow bands, and people typically exploited a series of zones, from llama and alpaca pastures in high grasslands, with potato-growing areas lower down, to yet lower zones tolerated by other domesticates. Because the largest Andean populations resided at high altitudes, where the fewest types of crops grew, there was longstanding demand for products from the lowlands, where plant diversity was greater.

The Desert Coast Fishing is the oldest enduring profession in the Andes. The richest New World fishing grounds stretch

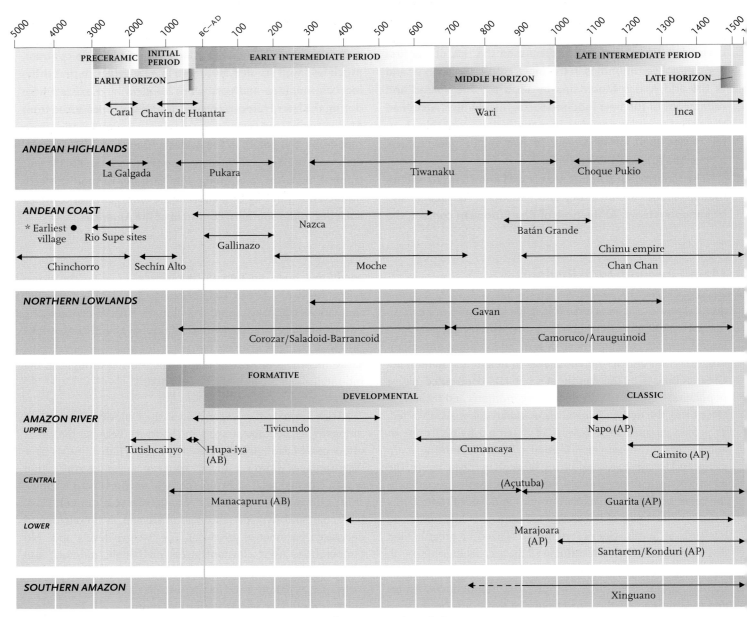

SOUTH AMERICA TIMELINE

* Real Alto (Valdivia)   AB Amazonian Barrancoid   AP Amazonian Polychrome

along the dry coasts of Peru and Chile, and local people began consuming seafood more than 11,000 years ago. Desert farming arose later, supported by the presence of widely spaced streams and rivers that carry seasonal runoff from the high sierra down to the sea. The runoff was diverted into canal systems and used to create irrigated valley oases, where a great variety of crops could grow year-round if scant water supplies endured. The largest irrigated valleys lie in northern Peru, which formed the demographic nexus of coastal civilization. Valleys decrease in size to the south and are small west of Lake Titicaca, which is the largest mountain basin and the demographic center of high-altitude civilization.

Amazonia

The moist Neotropics of South America, generally referred to as Amazonia, are dominated by the Amazon, Orinoco, and other large rivers [17.2]. The region, the largest major ecological zone of the continent, is predominantly high tropical rainforest, but is interspersed with diverse other forest types (seasonal deciduous forests, floodplain and gallery forests, the cloud or montaña forest), varied savannas and parklands, and a wide range of riparian (riverbank) settings and other wetlands (Moran 1993). The Amazon basin was once characterized as relatively homogeneous, with impoverished resources; it was thought to be hostile to human colonization and particularly inimical to the evolution of complex societies. Today, however, the discovery of large sedentary communities, expansive settlements encircled by massive earthworks, and long elevated causeways connecting far-flung sites is forcing critical re-examination of the multifaceted Amazonian environment. Nevertheless, the debate continues between those who doubt the capacity of the Amazonian rainforest to support dense human habitation, and those who believe in its richness (see Chapter 9, p. 346).

The primary ecological distinction recognized by anthropologists, following Julian Steward (1949), is that between river and uplands. Betty Meggers (1996) codified this distinction, using the Portuguese terms *várzea* (bottomlands or floodplain) and *terra firme* (uplands, "solid ground") as the key to the differential evolution of lowland peoples. The rich sediments deposited along major white-water tributaries (see below) were

seen to support the type of agricultural economy needed to sustain dense, sedentary populations, whereas the generally low fertility of soils in the so-called uplands (i.e., away from the major rivers) were assumed to have inhibited such economic and demographic developments. Research over the past few decades demonstrates far greater ecological and cultural diversity in Amazonia than expected, including the realization that much of what has been assumed to be natural is actually cultural in origin, the reflection of long-term human influences and/or the substantial impact of large late prehistoric polities on local ecology in some areas. The Amazon environment, far from being relatively homogeneous, harbors the greatest bio-

17.1 South America: *map showing the main regions and sites mentioned in the the text.*

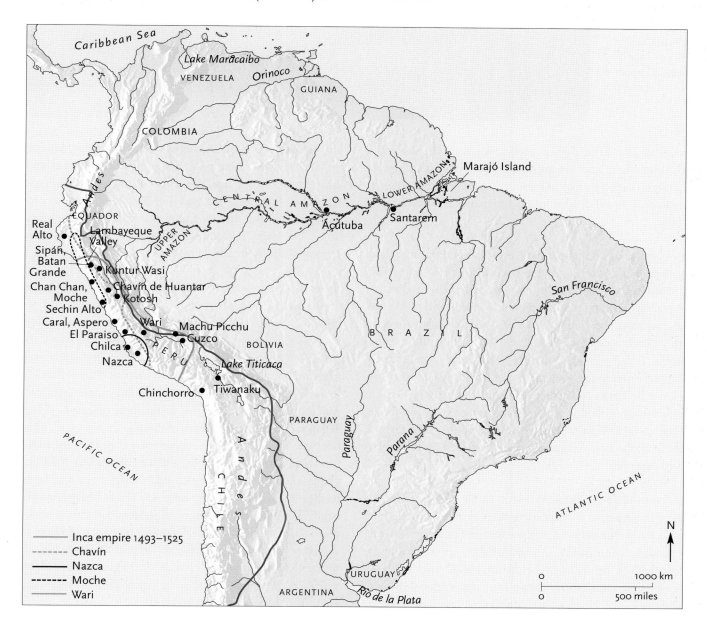

17.2 *Amazonia:* *the region is dominated by tropical forest and varied waterways, such as this oxbow lake on the Manu River of southeastern Peru, which has often compelled outside observers to characterize it as a fairly uniform and pristine "jungle" environment. Contemporary research documents the great variation within and between regions in the lowlands, phenomenal bio-diversity, and the tremendous impact of humans in many areas.*

diversity of any similar-sized geographic area in the world, which researchers now recognize is in part due to an equally complex and varied history of human culture. For convenience, the region can be subdivided into coasts, major floodplains, and uplands.

Coasts Coastal areas include the Caribbean and the mainland coasts from Maracaibo Bay in Colombia to the mouth of the Rio de la Plata in Uruguay. The massive estuary of the "mouth" of the Amazon, in Brazil, is dominated by the island of Marajó, wedged between the Pará River (south) and the lower Amazon (north). Human coastal adaptations throughout these areas, including Brazil's "Mata Atlantica" (the Atlantic rainforest), were diverse and long-lived, and the entire littoral was densely populated by large, regional polities, including so-called cir-cum-Caribbean chiefdoms, like the Arawak-speaking Taino, and the coastal Tupi; the latter included the cannibalistic Tupinamba, the first Amerindians encountered by Europeans in South America.

Floodplains Major floodplains occur along the Amazon and many of its principal tributaries, as well as along much of the Orinoco River. The *várzea* has come to signify the vast, season-ally flooded bottomlands of the Amazon and its primary Andean-derived tributaries, the "white-water" rivers. White-water rivers (actually muddy brown from suspended sediment) show significant ecological variety, although broad distinctions

can be made between the lower Amazon, below Manaus; the middle Amazon tributaries, including the Solimões and the lower Negro rivers; and the upper Amazonian tributaries in Colombia, Ecuador, Peru, and Bolivia. The floodplains of these major rivers were dominated by chiefdoms in late prehistoric times, but large, settled populations also lived in a variety of areas away from the annually rejuvenated *várzea*.

Uplands The uplands, or *terra firme*, constitute over 95 percent of Amazonia and are highly variable between and within regions, characterized by savannas, parkland or scrub forests, and closed or gallery (riverbank) tropical forests. True uplands, associated with the Guiana and Brazilian highlands and the Andean foothills, ring the Amazon basin and flank the Orinoco River, but much of Amazonia is essentially flat; thus, "interflu-vial" is a more appropriate designation of areas of human occupation throughout much of the region, referring to habita-tion on smaller rivers between major ones. The highland forests of Brazil and Guianas, and the sub-Andean foothills and plains show pronounced seasonal change, and the montaña forests from Bolivia to Ecuador are characterized by unique conditions of vertical change. All these upland areas have sup-ported a variety of cultural developments, including large, settled populations in many areas. Recent findings suggest sig-nificant environmental change throughout the Holocene within the general context of a highly diverse tropical forest environment (Colinvaux et al. 1998).

Chronological Overview

The Andes and the Desert Coast

Along the Pacific desert coast, people began exploiting marine resources by at least 9000 BC. In northern Chile, sedentary Chinchorro fishermen began mummifying their dead *c.* 6000 BC, while their counterparts in central Peru began erecting mounds around 3000 BC at sites such as Aspero, at the mouth of the Rio Supe. Inland economies mixing wild resources and limited farming supported sedentary communities whose people constructed platform mounds at valley sites such as Caral, and sierra settlements including Nanchoc and La Galgada on the upper Zana and Santa rivers. Thus, sedentary life had early origins in the Andes, where complex social organization began to arise before the adoption of intensive farming (Donnan 1985).

In the Andes [17.3], the long span of time when people relied principally on wild resources is called the Archaic (or Lithic) period. In Peru, it includes a late subdivision, the **Preceramic period** (c. 3000–1800 BC), when pre-pottery populations carried out large architectural projects. During the ensuing Ceramic period, people relied primarily on domesticated plants and animals. The spread of intensive farming and herding was generally accompanied by the production of pottery and by heddle-loom weaving. (The heddle loom is one with a series of warps or vertical threads; the heddle rods lift selected warps so that weft threads can be inserted between.) In northern Peru, this package of traits was adopted around 1800 BC. Moving south gradually, it entered the Lake Titicaca area *c.* 1400 BC, and appeared later still in the arid reaches of Chile. The agropastoral occupation of the Lake Titicaca region is subdivided into Ecuadorian Formative and Classic episodes, the latter associated with the Tiwanaku empire.

To the north, changing pottery styles in the coastal valley of Ica provide a chronological master sequence for dividing the prehistory of the region into units of time, with three periods and three interspersed horizons. The periods tend to correlate with episodes of coastal prosperity, beginning with the long **Initial period** (1800–400 BC, based on the latest radiocarbon dates), when the spread of coastal irrigation and sierra agropastoralism supported population growth and the construction of large monuments, such as at Sechín Alto. The Moche and Nazca cultures produced vibrant arts on the coast during the **Early Intermediate period** (200 BC–AD 650), and during the **Late Intermediate period** the lords of the Chimú empire (AD 1000–1476), ruling from the city of Chan Chan, consolidated much of the desert coast. Horizons, on the other hand, tend to correlate with expansions of sierra influence, beginning with the **Early Horizon** (400–200 BC), when Chavín religious ideology enveloped much of the northern Andes. The **Middle Horizon** (AD 650–1000) saw the spread of the Wari state from the central sierra and Tiwanaku from the Lake Titicaca region. Finally, the **Late Horizon** (1476–1533) was when the Incas exploded out of their mountain homeland to unite sierra and coast in the grandest of Native American empires.

Amazonia and the Atlantic Coast

Along South America's Atlantic coast, exploitation of shellfish and seafood allowed preceramic populations here to reside in one place throughout the year. Accumulated food debris and other refuse formed impressive mounds, called *sambaquis*, at various places; appearing as early as 4000–3000 BC, most date to between 2000 BC and AD 1. Although associated with refuse disposal and habitation activities, the mounds were also worked and sculpted into major ceremonial sites. Fluvial shell mounds (i.e., those made of river shells), some as impressive as the generally larger coastal *sambaquis* (e.g., the large mound at Taperinha), are spread throughout the middle to lower Amazon. Remarkably, the first ceramics from Taperinha and related Holocene occupations date to as early as 5500 BC, significantly

17.3 The Sacred Valley of the Incas: *this was carved by the Rio Urubamba, which had headwaters framing the imperial capitol of Cuzco. The Incas lavished great labor on canalizing the river, leveling the bottomlands, and terracing the hillsides, as seen downstream here.*

older than the much better-known coastal traditions of Ecuador, Colombia, and the northern Atlantic coast; these include the Mina tradition of brackish-water shell mounds (the *salgado*) of the lower Amazon, dating to *c.* 3500 BC (Roosevelt et al. 1991).

In Amazonia, the earliest semi-settled populations, including river and forest foragers and river folk with some form of incipient horticulture (Lathrap 1977; Roosevelt 1995), were present by middle Holocene times (c. 4000–2000 BC). By around 2000 BC, incipient agriculturalists were present in several areas, including the Ucayali, middle Orinoco, and lower Amazon rivers, as suggested by the widespread appearance of ceramics, particularly griddles, presumably for cooking manioc flatbread. Paleoethnobotanical studies in the moist lowlands are still extremely rare (Pearsall 1989; Piperno et al. 2000), but it appears that various plants, notably manioc, sweet potato, and squashes, may have been domesticated by *c.* 5000 BC (see Chapter 9).

After about 1000 BC, Amazonian prehistory can be divided into several loosely defined periods that describe common processes. The **Amazonian Formative** (1000 BC–AD 500), characterized by early settled agriculturalists, is notable for rapid population dispersals by the speakers of several major linguistic families. Subsequently, and partially overlapping the Formative, a **"Regional Developmental"** period (AD 1–1000) can be suggested, involving local co-evolution of human populations and their landscapes, giving rise to extended societies and interregional systems of interaction. Next, a broad regional **"Classic"** period (AD 1000–1500) can be described, which saw the emergence of full-blown political economies. Finally, native systems were eclipsed soon after the European arrival in the Caribbean in the 1490s and eastern Brazil in 1500, undergoing successive phases of collapse and reconstitution throughout the post-1492 period.

The Andean Preceramic, c. 3000–1800 BC

The survival of archaeological sites in the Andean region improves dramatically after 3000 BC, as glaciers ceased melting, sea levels stabilized, and the ecology of the Cordillera shifted into its current configuration. Although Preceramic people derived most of their food from the wild, they exhibited a trait more common in settled communities, that of erecting earthworks (Donnan 1985).

Early Mound Construction in Central and Northern Peru

As noted above, complex social institutions had already arisen in northern Chile, where sedentary **Chinchorro** fishermen began artificially mummifying their dead around 6000 BC (Arriaza 1995; and see The Chinchorro Mummies box, Chapter 9, pp. 338–39). Mound building never took hold in this

southerly region, but it did in central and northern Peru. At the site of Nanchoc in the lower sierra of the Rio Zaña, discussed in Chapter 9 (p. 334), two stone-faced platforms dating between 6000 and 5500 BC consisted of superimposed floors interspersed with artificial fill layers that gradually added height to the structures.

This building pattern, with alternating episodes of use and stages of construction, is typical of other, later platform structures, including the paired 6.5-m (21-ft) and 8-m (26-ft) high mounds at **Kotosh** [17.4–17.6] on the eastern Andean slopes, and two mounds at **La Galgada** on the western slopes. At both highland sites, platforms were surmounted by freestanding, one-room structures. Each roofed chamber had a single entrance that could be sealed, and a prominent central hearth; when the door was closed, air was fed to the fire by a sub-floor ventilator. Often embellished with wall niches, these little rooms characterize the so-called Kotosh religious tradition, which focused on burnt offerings made by small, secluded groups of devotees (Burger 1992). Significantly, during mound construction stages at La Galgada, older ritual chambers were used as mausoleums for elite interments, including those of females, and were then sealed and buried. There is scant evidence of elite Preceramic burials elsewhere, however.

The occupants of Nanchoc, Kotosh, and La Galgada are assumed to have relied on wild resources and, to some degree, on cultivated plants. Vegetable remains are well preserved only at La Galgada, located 70 km (44 miles) from the coast in the lower arid sierra, at a normally rainless elevation of 1000 m (3280 ft). Here, one maize cob was recovered in a large plant

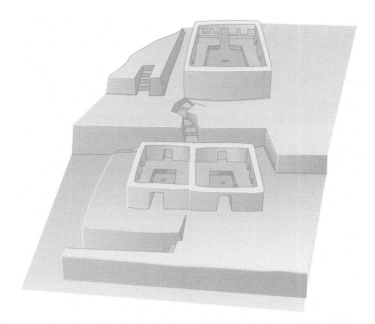

17.4–17.6 Kotosh: *the Preceramic masonry architecture at Kotosh (opposite) was characterized by single-room, single-entrance sanctuaries, with benches around a central hearth used to burn offerings, (reconstructed above). Interior walls often had niches, and the base of one was ornamented with a clay frieze of crossed hands (right).*

assemblage dominated by cotton remains, leading investigators to wonder if cotton seeds were not being rendered into oil for human consumption (Grieder et al. 1988). Indeed, the dearth of domesticated staples and the scarcity of adjacent farmland suggest that the estimated community of 2000 individuals that erected the Galgada monuments only congregated there for part of each year.

Platforms and Sunken Courts along the Desert Coast

The largest Preceramic monuments in the hemisphere were erected along the desert coast between the Chicama and Chillon rivers. Many sites with small and large architectural works are adjacent to the littoral including, from north to south, **Huaca Prieta**, **Salinas de Chao**, and **Los Morteros** by the Rio Chao shoreline; **Huaynuna** near Casma; **Aspero** at the Rio Supe mouth; **Culebras** and **Bandurria** near the Hurra Valley; **Rio Seco**

north of Chancay; and **El Paraiso** 2 km (1.25 miles) from the Chillon delta. Inland valley complexes are known in the Chillon Valley, and they are abundant in Supe drainages, where the sprawling mound center of **Caral** is now 20 km (12.5 miles) from the sea; yet they are absent in fully surveyed valleys from the Casma north, and have not been found south of Lima.

Most, but not all, public works emphasized elevated, flat-topped platforms with wide central staircases, which served as ritual display stages for audiences assembled in forecourts at ground level. Some mounds were steep-sided, whereas the fronts of others rose in wide terraces that supported courts and compartments, as did the mound summits. Hierarchical organization is indicated, because more people helped build the platforms than could be accommodated by the terrace-top and summit facilities. Such organization must have been enduring in order to build structures incrementally over generations, with multiple stages of construction separated by episodes of use. As in the highlands, many coastal sites have two platforms, which might reflect dual, or moiety, organization of communities. Other complexes, such as Aspero, Caral, and El Paraiso, have six or more mounds, suggesting more multifaceted institutions. The earthworks are called "civic-ceremonial" facilities because they probably served both secular and sacred purposes.

Although less common than platforms, stone-lined circular sunken courts formed a very distinctive type of structure, with oppositely aligned descending and ascending stairways. Modestly sized subterranean sanctuaries were commonly erected centrally in front of larger platforms, so that processions would descend into the earth before ascending skyward up the mound. Rites and beliefs associated with sunken courts, the so-called **Plaza Hundida tradition**, need not always involve an elevated mound, however; the sanctuaries were sometimes built without associated platforms, and in the case of the Caral "amphitheater," the subterranean plaza was far larger and more elaborate than the attendant mound. Religious notions about entering the earth endured but evolved over time; circular and rectangular sunken courts occur later at Chavín de Huantar, and rectangular forms atop platforms remained common in the Titicaca region through the Tiwanaku occupation (see below).

The civic-ceremonial facilities at **Rio Seco**, **Bandurria**, and **Huaynuna** consist of modest-sized mounds associated with residential midden deposits of sufficient size to suggest that the architectural works were built by the coastal communities. Well-preserved food remains indicate that residents were obtaining all of their protein, if not most of their calories, from the sea. Although these fishing communities were not located near arable land, cotton and gourd are the dominant domesticated plants, although chili peppers, beans, squash, tubers, and tree fruits were consumed in minor quantities. Some cultigens may have been traded, but at Huaynuna, if not other coastal

KEY CONTROVERSY Maritime Foundations of Andean Civilization?

This hypothesis proposes that the exceptionally rich, near-shore anchovy fishery of the South American Pacific coast, with its easily netted schooling fish and other prey, provided calories that sustained early sedentism, population growth, and the rise of complex social organization along the coast. Independently formulated by several American, Andean, and Soviet scholars in the 1960s, then synthesized in the mid-1970s (Moseley 1975), the evolving hypothesis now extends to both Peruvian and Chilean regions affected by the Humboldt Current.

Juxtaposition of the world's driest desert, with its scant resources, and the hemisphere's richest fishery, with its abundance, prompted early exploitation of the ocean in Chile (Llagostera 1992), where the bone chemistry of some Preceramic groups points to a diet of 90 percent seafood.

Mummification and Monuments

By 6000 BC, sedentary Chinchorro fishermen began artificially mummifying certain of their dead [see Chinchorro Mummies box, Chapter 9, pp. 338–39]. Most people did not receive special mortuary treatment, and the known sample of artificial mummies is less than 250 (Arriaza 1995). Significantly, the majority are neonates (new-borns) and children, who may have inherited special status and privileged mortuary entitlements from their parents.

Some mummies were interred as family groups with children and adults, and one group spanning three generations included infants, a mature couple of reproductive age, and an elderly person, probably a grandparent. Thus, it can be argued (although not everyone agrees) that maritime Chinchorro populations exhibit a hallmark of social complexity: elites who inherit their status.

At the northern, richer end of the anchovy fishery, one significant indicator of social complexity is mound and monument building. At Aspero, littoral people were erecting platforms well before the final construction stages of Huaca de los Idolos were laid down, and the 3055 BC radiocarbon result from this late building is centuries older than dates from inland Caral.

Intensification of Food Production

The maritime hypothesis is very specific about economic relationships of coastal and river valley resources. Because average yields of the northern anchovy fishery are around 100 metric tons per year, with isolated ones of 1000 tons, sustained Preceramic population growth required ever-greater net harvesting of small schooling fish. Although the sea could feed multitudes, and anchovy were dried, rendered into meal, and stored as a staple, the ocean did not provide fiber for line or net, nor floats essential to fishing tackle, nor reed or wood for watercraft, let alone materials for housing, clothing, and fuel.

Consequently, intensified fishing demanded increased production of terrestrial resources and ever increasing yields of industrial cultigens, dominated by cotton and gourd, but also including trees for wood. As demands increased, cultivation was pushed upstream into seasonally inundated river floodplains and easily irrigated lands at places such as Caral, where fishermen congregated periodically for planting and harvesting. Intriguingly, chili pepper, a condiment for marinating fish, is the most ubiquitous comestible at early desert sites, followed by beans and squash, which do not require constant tending. Although maize, manioc, and potatoes do appear sporadically at Preceramic sites, these crops are very infrequent in comparison to their presence in overlying (more recent) strata or at adjacent sites dating to the Initial period of ceramic use and intensive irrigation agriculture.

The proposition that rich marine resources sustained the rise of complex coastal societies and propelled incipient cultivation along uniquely industrial lines remains a refreshing, viable challenge to the traditional orthodoxy that only staple plants produced sufficient calories to underwrite the initial foundations of civilization.

sites, the common occurrence of cotton bolls and other unusable plant parts implies that residents made seasonal trips to arable land to sow and later harvest crops that were then brought back to the fishing village for processing. They may have stayed at valley mouth sites, such as Aspero and El Paraiso, to do their plant tending.

Aspero probably served, and drew labor from, a broader populace than lived at the site year round, having 11 smaller mounds 1–2 m (3.3–6.6 ft) high, and six major platforms surrounded by 15 ha (37 acres) of dark midden, implying occupation. Variable in their orientation, the larger freestanding mounds at Aspero rise up to 4 m (13 ft) or more in height. Excavations at one of these, Huaca de los Idolos, investigated the last three stages of construction, which were dated to 3055–2558 BC; basal dates on the earliest stages of the mound would certainly be far older. The summit had a large entry court with compartments and rooms behind it, and one chamber with an altar-like bench against the rear wall. Investigation of the last summit construction phase of another platform at Aspero, Huaca de los Sacrificios (with radiocarbon dates averaging 2857 BC) revealed an unusual child burial. Placed on its side, the two-month-old infant was wrapped in a cotton textile and had a cap adorned with 500 shell, clay, and plant beads. The corpse was placed in a basket that was wrapped first in textiles and then in a reed mat. The assemblage was then covered with an inverted, four-legged stone basin standing 9 cm (3.5 in) high. The burial was clearly important, but it is not apparent whether it was a sacrifice or an elite infant.

Mounds and their Builders at Caral and El Paraiso

The Supe Valley on Peru's desert coast has 17 Preceramic civic-ceremonial centers, ranging in size from 10 to more than 70 ha (25 to over 173 acres). Ruth Shady (1997) argues that high water-table conditions and numerous springs facilitated simple, extensive irrigation, which fostered an early symbiotic relationship between fishing and farming evident in her studies of **Caral**, a 50-ha (124-acre) mound and residential complex 20 km (12.5 miles) upstream from the Supe delta [see Caral box, Chapter 9, p. 345]. With storage facilities filled with anchovies and small fish, it is clear that the residents ate plentiful seafood, though no fishing tackle has yet been found at the site. In addition to abundant remains of cotton and gourd, recovered cultigens include the root crops achira and sweet potatoes, as well as squash and beans, and pacae and guayaba fruit. Intriguingly, such later agricultural mainstays as maize, manioc, and white potatoes are not in evidence, and lacking such staples people may have dispersed to fish during non-farming times. In addition to its "amphitheater" and other smaller circular sunken courts, Caral has six imposing mounds, including the Templo Mayor, the largest Preceramic platform excavated to date. Shady's excavations have also identified two classes of residential quarters. The most prevalent have walls and roofs of mats, reeds, and thatch. Others, presumably elite quarters, featured plastered floors and masonry walls with vertical wooden beams for large roofs and were erected adjacent to mounds and monuments.

Addressing the 17 Preceramic civic-ceremonial complexes in the lower Supe drainage as a whole, Shady proposes that they could not have been built and maintained without drawing upon human resources from outside the valley. This proposition could be framed in a broader hypothesis of seasonal dual residency and split subsistence activity, with Preceramic populations temporarily nucleating around arable land for planting and later harvesting, while dispersing during long intervening times to exploit natural resources [see box: Maritime Foundations of Andean Civilization?].

El Paraiso [17.7, 17.8], directly overlooking 150 ha (370 acres) of easily farmed low Rio Chillon floodplain, 2 km (1.25 miles) from the sea, is unique in its monumentality. More than 100,000 tons of quarried stone were used to erect nine grand architectural complexes, three stories high, that sprawl over 58 ha (143 acres) in which there is almost no surrounding midden or occupational debris. Analysis of what scant midden deposits and food remains there are indicates that protein came entirely from the sea, while cotton and gourd were ubiquitous in the domesticated plant assemblage, which closely parallels that of

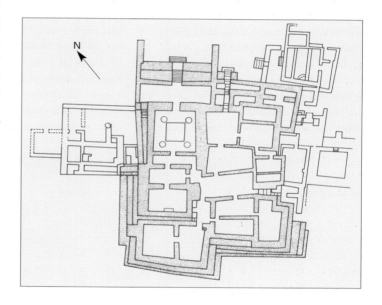

17.7, 17.8 El Paraiso: *a small restored section of the preceramic masonry complex of El Paraiso (left), is more than two stories high and about half the size of a football field. Seen in plan (above), entry stairs at the top lead to a court with four fire basins and a sunken central floor.*

KEY SITE Real Alto

Valdivia is a cultural phase widely spread throughout coastal Ecuador, named after the type site excavated in the 1950s by Betty Meggers, Clifford Evans, and Emilio Estrada (1965). It and the subsequent Machalilla phase represent the transition to settled village life and cultural elaboration in nearly every quarter, including ceramics, possible maize cultivation, figurative art, and village form: the Formative period.

Meggers and Evans (1978) suggested trans-Pacific influences at the time, specifically Japanese; according to James Ford (1969), these influences gave rise to the Formative throughout the Americas by means of the diffusion of the plaza village. Since the 1970s, Donald Lathrap and his students, working at Real Alto and other Valdivia sites, have suggested that the plaza village was a very early expression – if not the birthplace – of an autochthonous "tropical forest cosmology," a type of cosmic power that

lay at the root of all New World civilizations, giving rise to Olmec and Chavín alike (Lathrap 1985; Lathrap et al. 1977). The Valdivia phase has come to signify early ceramics, early agriculture, early maize, early plaza villages, and emergent social complexity. The type site of Valdivia, with its circular village plan, has become the site of one of the most fruitful experiments in broad ethnographic analogy.

Real Alto has produced a particularly complete record of development, extending from a small village c. 3500–3200 BC (though deposits at the site date to as early as 3800 BC) to a large, complex chiefdom in late prehistoric times. The site also appears to exhibit a basic element of social hierarchy in the notion of vertical stratification, with a founding dynast buried in the Charnel House; this was one of two ceremonial mounds at the site, the other being the Fiesta House, where feasting and drinking took

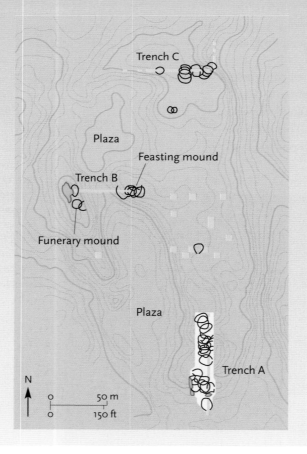

17.9 *Reconstruction of a Real Alto house, modeled after ethnographic Jivaro of the montana forests of eastern Ecuador.*

place. The mound under the Charnel House became the exclusive burial place of elite persons in the Valdivia II phase, c. 3000 BC, although the overall village apparently consisted of small, nuclear-family dwellings erected around a small circular plaza.

Some 200 years later, the next incarnation of this public space (Valdivia III) was as a great rectangular plaza. Lathrap (1985) saw this change as typical of the birth of social complexity from the tropical forest model. Mike Moseley (1975) also viewed the differentiation of public and ritual space as critical in the emergence of late Preceramic temple centers, particularly in the context of control over community labor.

By Valdivia IV, Real Alto was the center of a small settlement cluster (of four other villages), one of several along the southern coast of Ecuador. The leaders at Real Alto and other Valdivia clusters may have operated more like bigmen than hereditary chiefs (Zeidler 1991), but that would assume that competitive, incremental exchange in luxury goods (shells primarily) or staples were the basis of status.

Spondylus shells may well have served this end, but shamanistic knowledge and technique, and not economic goods, may have been the primary source of power that was appropriated by an emerging elite who controlled monuments such as ancestral tombs and icons (e.g. figurines). There is some evidence that the power holders, these early shaman-chiefs, were women more commonly than men (Zeidler 2000).

17.10 *Site plan of Real Alto, in the coastal lowlands of western Ecuador. Note the funerary mound (charnel house) and feasting mound (fiesta house) located in the rectangular plaza area; trenches A and C are located in residential areas.*

Trench C

Plaza

Feasting mound

Trench B

Funerary mound

Plaza

Trench A

N

0   50 m

0   150 ft

Caral. Here again, it seems that the multitudes that erected El Paraiso did not reside there for most of the year. Yet the grand monument presages things to come, because many of its radiocarbon dates fall after 1800 BC (the beginning of the Initial period), and its largest mounds give the complex a U-shaped configuration, foreshadowing the form of future civic-ceremonial complexes.

Early Andean Civilization: The Initial Period and the Early Horizon

In South America, agriculture spread along the path of least resistance, coming first to low, tropical, moist areas well before the more inhospitable desert coast and rugged arid sierra of the central Andean Cordillera (Piperno and Pearsall 1995). In Ecuador, where the mountains are low and well-watered, **Valdivia** people living along the coast and the western watershed were actively farming and producing pottery by 3000 BC. At sites such as **Real Alto**, they lived in circular houses arranged around a circular plaza, a village plan common in the Amazon [see box: Real Alto]. Yet, more than a millennium passed before aspects of this way of life pushed south into drier and higher environments.

The Initial Period, c. 1800–400 BC

Beginning about 1800 BC, the Initial period is marked in northern Peru by the adoption of pottery, weaving, intensive farming, and herding. These innovative economic adaptations opened new inland habitats to exploitation. Coastal and highland populations grew, and today are revealed in numerous archaeological sites, most representing modest-sized communities. Over the course of centuries there was a spate of large-scale construction, as each community of consequence seems to have erected its own civic and ceremonial facilities expressed as mounds, attendant sunken courts, and walled enclosures (Richardson 1996). Building monumental architecture requires hierarchical decision-making, and many archaeologists believe that early agricultural communities were kin groups organized by descent, and that social rank and leadership were inherited. La Galgada provides Initial period mortuary evidence of elites, but elsewhere those in power seem not to have taken recognizable insignia of rule and privilege to their graves, perhaps because distinctive symbols of rank were not particularly elaborate.

The site of **Cerro Sechín** in the Casma Valley has a square central mound faced with unique bas-relief stone carvings showing men with axe-like clubs parading among dismembered human bodies [17.11, 17.12]. This appears to foreshadow later Moche artistic themes of elite warrior combat, with losers being sacrificed and dismembered. The Sechín combatants are very simply attired, however, compared to the elaborate regalia and armaments of the Moche. Otherwise, early art and iconography emphasize metaphysical and "other-worldly" themes, perhaps due to the insecurities of farming in unpredictable habitats, and governance probably conducted in the name of the gods (Stone-Miller 1995).

17.11, 17.12 Cerro Sechín: *a monumental mosaic wall at the site depicts men carrying arms (below left), parading among dismembered body parts. Processions along each side of the wall converged on the entrance framed by tall stelae each with a carved banner (below right).*

KEY SITE Sechín Alto

Sechin Alto is a colossal U-shaped architectural complex, built on Peru's desert coast in multiple stages, interspersed with long episodes of use. Construction was underway by 1400 BC, and over the course of centuries the complex grew to be the largest monument ever built by early agriculturalists in the Western Hemisphere.

Measuring 300 x 250 m (985 x 820 ft), the main platform stands some 40 m (131 ft) high and was faced with masonry comprised of gigantic stone blocks covered with thick plaster. Traces of huge adobe friezes flank the central staircase that led to spacious courts and buildings on the summit. A row of three contiguous U-shaped platforms, each more than three stories high and 80 m (262 ft) wide, face the rear of the main structure, and to its left is a pair of similar large mounds.

In front of the principal edifice, low elongated wing mounds bracket a 1100-m (3600-ft) long succession of four vast rectangular plazas, each of which held two circular sunken courts with two centrally aligned stairs, one for descending access and the other for ascending egress (Williams 1980). With standing room for tens of thousands of viewers, the linearly aligned plazas could accommodate great ritual pageants that would have proceeded down their central axes, in and out of the subterranean courts and then up the towering stairway ascending to the summit of the enormous platform mound.

Facing inland to the mountain sources of irrigation water and the rising sun, the gigantic U was erected on the Rio Sechin branch of the Casma Valley, and anchored a 10-sq.-km (4-sq.-mile) sprawl of other large buildings and imposing mounds that comprise the Sechin Alto complex (Pozorski and Pozorski 1987).

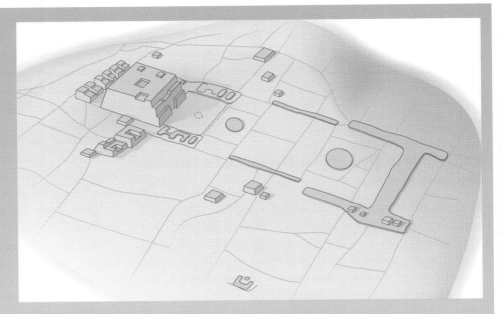

17.13 By 1200 BC the U-shaped ceremonial center of Sechín Alto was the largest architectural monument in the hemisphere, with four rectangular forecourts leading to a grand platform mound.

Pampa de los Llamas-Moxeke

The smaller, complementary Pampa de los Llamas-Moxeke complex of paired, aligned platforms 1 km (0.6 mile) apart, with aligned architectural structures, was built adjacent to the nearby Rio Casma. Here, the exterior of the main platform mound had a high facade with giant niches framing polychrome friezes in high relief. Two scenes depicted human-like faces, two showed forward-facing individuals in rich garb, and one portrayed a captive from the rear, with arms bound in rope at his back; prisoners are typically depicted this way in later Moche arts showing throat-cutting and physical dismemberment of enslaved warriors [see box: Sipán and the Presentation Theme, p. 657].

Cerro Sechín Temple

Dismembered body parts are the dominant motifs of a wall surrounding the Cerro Sechín temple, a uniquely ornate but modest-sized component of the Sechín Alto complex. The grand masonry mosaic is composed of large engraved stone blocks and elongated stelae.

The stelae depict a procession of well-garbed warriors, each holding vertically an axe-like staff or club. They converge from both sides of the temple upon its entrance, which is framed by large banners rendered on projecting monoliths. Between each of the weapon-bearing warriors are carved stones graphically depicting mutilated bodies: spilled intestines, severed arms, legs, heads, eyes, and vertebrae.

Although archaeologists have long debated the meaning of this macabre iconography, it clearly presages later artistic themes of combat between elite warriors, prisoner taking, sacrifice, and corpse dismemberment in order to appease the gods (Donnan 1993).

Whatever its basis, socio-political organization was certainly very complex, because more large monuments were erected in coastal valleys during the Initial period than at any other time. Most comprise big platform mounds built accretively over long periods. The most distinctive are U-shaped complexes with a high rear mound and two lower wings that frame a spacious central court (Williams 1980). Many were ornamented with monumental adobe friezes of supernatural beings, suggesting theocratic governance. U-shaped complexes occur in most valleys from the Rio Mala north. Beginning with numerous

17.14, 17.15 *Chavín de Huántar: the U-shaped New Temple section of Chavín de Huantar framed a rectangular sunken courtyard, while the contemporary Old Temple section held a circular sunken court. The latter was ornamented with stone carved depictions of fanged deities, as shown below right.*

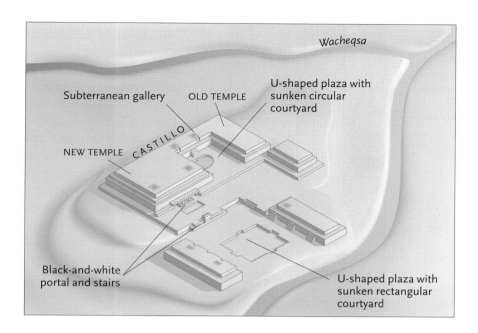

moderate-scale examples and grading through progressively larger complexes, the size hierarchy culminates in the Casma Valley with the vast site of Sechín Alto, the largest monument in the Americas for its time (Pozorski and Pozorski 1987) [see box: Sechín Alto]. After almost a millennium of agrarian expansion and prosperity, a pervasive abandonment of Sechín Alto and all other coastal monuments set in between 900 and 800 BC, spreading through much of the sierra (Burger 1992). Several centuries of drought were apparently among many potential factors contributing to this evolutionary turning point.

Chavín and the Early Horizon, c. 400–200 BC

Chavín de Huántar [**17.14**] is an impressive and uniquely ornate Andean monument situated high in the northern sierra between two streams that feed into the distant Amazon. The main complex of masonry building, called the Castillo, comprises two conjoined U-shaped platform mounds. Framing a circular sunken court, the smaller northern structure is called the Old Temple; to the south, a spacious rectangular sunken court fronts the larger New Temple. The platforms are not solid, but riddled with a multi-story labyrinth of long, narrow galleries roofed by great slabs of stone (Lumbreras 1989). Detailed study of gallery construction indicates that the Castillo was largely built as a single undertaking during the latter part of the Initial period, and the two temples, despite their assigned names, functioned together until their abandonment around 200 BC.

The Castillo was ornamented with splendid stone carvings, including three-dimensional, tenon-mounted heads of humans, birds, and canines, as well as numerous engraved wall plaques of felines, raptors, and supernatural composite beings, all frequently embellished with serpents [**17.15**]. The art drew inspiration from the Amazonian tropics in its prominent fea-

turing of the jungle's top predators, including harpy eagles and spotted jaguars; one stela had paired caymans. The paramount Chavín deity is depicted on a 4.5-m (15-ft) tall stela mounted in the central, mid-line gallery of the Old Temple. The low relief carving depicts a finely attired standing figure with claws, and bangled ear spools that frame a catlike face. Curled lips expose two tusklike canine teeth, while eyebrows and hair are rendered as snakes. The stela divinity is thought to have been an oracle that communed with supplicants through attendant priests.

17.16 (Right) **The richly garbed Chavín Staff God:** *a drawing of the supernatural being depicted on the Raimondi Stone, holding a ceremonial scepter in each hand.*

17.17, 17.18 (Below, left and right) **Mummy bundle:** *placed in a large basket in a seated position, Paracas elites were accompanied by finely embroidered garments and headgear, and ornaments of gold and shell. The basket, body, and grave goods were then wrapped in multiple layers of plain cloth to form a large mummy bundle.*

Called the Staff God, other renditions frequently depict a staff held vertically in each clawed hand (Rowe 1962) [**17.16**].

Characteristic of the Early Horizon, the Staff God cult and its supernatural raptorial birds and felines spread over much of northern and central Peru between 400 and 200 BC. These were times of drought, and under environmental stress the Chavín religious beliefs cut across old social boundaries and facilitated far-flung communication and interchange in the northern sphere of Andean civilization (Burger 1984). This era was marked by the spread of innovative technologies in many media. Cloth production was revolutionized as tapestry came into use, along with supplemental, discontinuous warps, tie dying, and batik. Metallurgical innovations included soldering, sweat welding, repoussé (raised relief), and alloying gold with silver or copper. This allowed the creation of bold three-dimensional gold and alloy artworks from pre-shaped metal sheets. Social changes were also underway. At several places, including Kuntur Wasi in the sierra and Paracas on the coast, rich grave goods point to elites who probably ruled in the name of the gods.

Paracas This peninsula jutting out of Peru's south-central coast contained a necropolis for elites from adjacent valleys. Subterranean vaults, in the form of large bell-shaped pits and rectangular masonry crypts, were used over generations and contained up to 40 mummy bundles, presumably family members and kin (Paul 1991). Nude corpses were prepared for burial by being placed in a flexed, seated position and bound with cords to maintain the pose, which is typical of interments in the south and the Titicaca region. The body was next wrapped in textiles and seated upright in a large shallow basket containing garments and other offerings. Then the basket, accompaniments, and corpse were swathed together in many layers of plain cotton cloth to create the final mummy bundle [**17.17, 17.18**]. Grave goods include exquisite fabrics in dazzling colors. Intricately embroidered mantles, tunics, and headgear depict mythical creatures and ornately garbed humans; these wear gold ornaments resembling cat whiskers, and carry human trophy heads and ornamental staves (Paul 1990). A preference for polychrome ornamentation extends to Paracas ceramics, and aligns the arts of this coastal society with southern traditions of highly colorful adornment.

Pukara In the Titicaca region, ornate polychrome pottery is typical of the Pukara style, which emerged around 400 BC and assumed regional prominence four centuries later (Stanish 2003) [**17.20**]. Situated 75 km (47 miles) northwest of Lake Titicaca, the type site is dominated by monumental structures erected on massive masonry terraces banked against the slopes of a lofty bedrock hill. Faced with boulders and rock slabs, the largest terrace had centrally positioned stairs leading to its summit, which was occupied by a large rectangular sunken court with well-made stone walls. The rear and two sides of the court were enclosed by a series of one-room masonry buildings that may once have contained ritual paraphernalia.

In the Andes, elite architecture emphasized freestanding one-room buildings for houses, warehouses, and offices. Although not as prolific as their Chavín counterparts, Pukara stone-carvers created flat-relief and three-dimensional works depicting felines, serpents, lizards, and anthropomorphic beings, often accompanied by trophy heads. Potters used incision to outline motifs, including birds, llamas, felines, and humans, which were then painted in red, yellow, and black. Well-decorated libation vessels, called *keros*, were a common vessel form later used by the Incas for ritual drinking.

Andean Confederacies and States in the Early Intermediate Period, *c.* 200 BC–AD 650

Dated to 200 BC–AD 650, the Early Intermediate period saw a marked change in the tenor of Andean life. Easily exploited habitats were now fully occupied, and recurrent long droughts curtailed unbridled prosperity. Sites with monumental structures decreased in frequency, and simple residential communities became the norm. In some coastal and sierra areas, fortified villages and hilltop bastions point to hostilities (Topic 1992). Earlier metaphysical interests gave way to much more earthly concerns. In the sierra highlands and along the desert coast, governance was now in the hands of a well-established elite class, whom the Spanish later called the *kuraka*. They ruled as divine intermediaries between heaven and earth, and inherited privileged rank by claiming special descent from sacred forebears. Noble status was carried to the grave and marked by uncommon mortuary treatment and rich grave goods (Dillehay 1995). The *kuraka* class monopolized the production of fine arts because valued objects, not currency, were used to reward service and finance the nobility. This resulted in vibrant "corporate" styles, reflecting the political, religious, and ethnic composition of elite sponsoring bodies. The Early Intermediate has also been called the Master Craftsmen and Regional Developmental period, due to the flourishing of patronized arts (Silverman 1996).

Gallinazo, Moche, and the North Coast

Moche is the most acclaimed art style to arise in desert valleys of the north, and it owes much to Gallinazo cultural developments which preceded it, including substantial expansion of coastal irrigation systems. Irrigation created silty soils suitable for producing mud-bricks, called adobes, and these became the hallmark of coastal monuments and elite quarters. Gallinazo builders had a penchant for erecting adobe platform mounds high up on steep hillsides or perched atop isolated valley peaks, as in the case of the Rio Santa's Castillo and the Rio Viru's Tomoval promontory. Near the mouth of the latter valley there is a vast sprawl of collapsed adobe buildings and quarters called the **Gallinazo Group**, which is estimated to contain some 30,000 rooms and compartments (Willey 1953). Some scholars believe that this was the capital of an ancient state or confederated realm stretching to the adjacent Moche and Santa valleys. Gallinazo remains extend further north into the Lambayeque region, however, and it is difficult to interpret their political implications, because the ceramic style and other arts are not uniform or homogeneous [**17.19**]. Still, the *kuraka* nobility across this region doubtless shared similar values and beliefs, and local strategic alliances probably strengthened during several centuries of drought, when sierra people encroached on valley canyon lands held by Gallinazo populations.

17.19 *(Right)* **A Gallinazo vessel:** *negative black painting decorates this Gallinazo vessel in the shape of a reed boat with a club-carrying warrior at one end wearing elite earspools.*

17.20 *(Far right)* **A Pukara-style incised polychrome vessel:** *this fragment is decorated with a feline head.*

Moche art and culture arose around AD 200, as dry times waned and the *kuraka* class adopted a new style that reflected somewhat standardized beliefs and governance. Fine arts were fully in the service of the political order, and expressed a brilliant, highly realistic iconography that rationalized an ideology of *kuraka* rule and ritual. Supernatural composite beings are commonly depicted, but so too are well-garbed humans (Donnan 1978). Archaeologists often portray the new order as the first native state to arise in the continent. This political characterization is most applicable in the south of the Moche realm, where the temples of the Sun and Moon (Huaca del Sol and Huaca de la Luna) in the Moche Valley (discussed below) anchored a seemingly integrated political dominion between the Chicama and Nepeña rivers. On the other hand, Moche-affiliated fiefdoms and principalities seem more typical of northern valleys, from the Rio Jetepeque to the Rio Lambayeque (Moseley 2001).

The Moche realm was united by a shared ideology expressed in iconography that survives largely in mural and ceramic arts. Ritual drinking vessels were made in multi-piece molds in the form of spouted globular bottles, some of them three-dimensional depictions of divinities, people [**17.21**], and animals. Others were ornamented with finely painted scenes pertaining to particular themes or

17.21 *(Left)* **Moche ceramics:** *Moche portrait head vessels depict elite who were generally warriors.*

17.22 *(Below)* **Moche art:** *this composite of three different fine-line drawing scenes shows fox hunting (top), combat between elite warriors (center), and a deity battling a fish monster.*

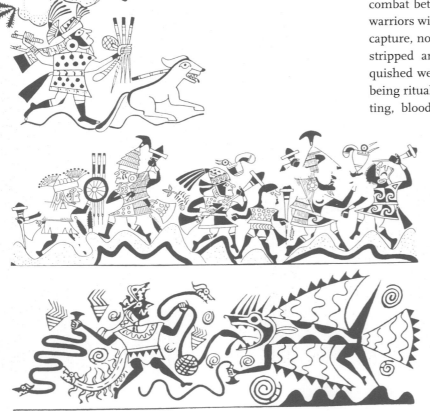

stories (Donnan 1993). Among the stories depicted, one relates to a battle between supernatural beings, another to the death and burial of a king. A common set of scenes depicts one-to-one combat between teams of richly garbed, well-armored *kuraka* warriors wielding clubs and shields [**17.22**]. Combatants aim to capture, not kill, opponents, whose attire and armor would be stripped and retained by the victor. Rope-bound, the vanquished were then paraded about in nude humiliation before being ritually sacrificed in a ceremony that entailed throat cutting, blood collecting, and body dismemberment [see box: Sipán and the Presentation Theme]. These ritual sacrifices probably took place at major Moche seats; scenes from the "warrior narrative" theme are depicted in murals and friezes at monumental centers in three separate valleys, and warrior accouterments accompany elite graves at other sites. Warrior combatants are almost always other Moche *kuraka*; some portrait vessels depict specific individuals attired for combat, while others show them later stripped, bound, and awaiting ceremonial execution. Thus ritual combat, the shedding of one's blood and life for the good of the gods and society, was clearly an honorable demise commemorated in the arts. It is unclear if battle losses extended beyond captured prisoners to territorial subjugation (Pillsbury 2001).

KEY SITE Sipán and the Presentation Theme

Moche iconography is often narrative, and revolves around themes or stories that justified and enhanced rule by the *kuraka*, or elite. Combat between richly garbed noble warriors is a frequent subject. The aim of armed conflict was to capture, but not kill, opponents, who are stripped of their armaments and finery, with the spoils going to the victor. After being paraded about, what happens next to the losers is portrayed in the so-called "Presentation Theme," which narrates an elaborate ceremony.

It begins with the nude, hands-bound captives having their throats slit by elaborately garbed figures wearing feline or fox masks. The masked sacrificers collect the victims' blood in a distinctive chalice shaped like a cup with an extended flaring base that serves as a handle. They then pass the chalice to much higher-ranking members of a supreme priesthood. The entourage often includes an important individual ornately bedecked as an owl, and it always includes a finely attired priestess adorned with sashes ending in serpent heads, and wearing a distinctive double-plumed headdress. Carefully carrying the chalice, she presents it to the paramount celebrant, the "warrior priest," who ritually consumes the sacrificial content. Generally accompanied by a spotted dog, the "warrior

17.23 *At the bottom of this fine-line drawing of the Presentation Theme captive warriors have their throats cut with blood collected in chalices. At the top priests and a priestess carry the chalices to a paramount "warrior priest" who consumes the content accompanied by a small spotted dog.*

priest" is uniquely costumed, crowned with a double-flared headdress and often carrying a war club.

Although the art and iconography of the Presentation Theme was long considered

fanciful, it is now clear that the story reveals ceremonies and social roles that Moche lords regularly enacted. Female tombs with priestess attire have been excavated at San Jose de Moro in the Jequetepeque Valley. Most importantly, at Sipán in the Lambayeque Valley, archaeologists have exposed the richly accompanied burial of a "warrior priest," replete with his special costume, headgear, sacrificial chalice, and accompanying spotted dog (Alva and Donnan 1993).

17.24 *In this reconstruction of one of the Sipán burials the richly attired warrior priest occupies the central coffin, and attendants lateral coffins. A small spotted dog also accompanied the tomb.*

17.25 *(Right)* ***Polychrome frieze from Huaca de la Luna:*** *a monstrous fanged deity dominated some painted friezes at Huaca de la Luna.*

17.26 *(Below)* ***Huaca del Sol and Huaca de la Luna:*** *seen from the air the heavily looted Huaca de la Luna sits at the base of the foreground hill. A teeming city occupied the plains stretching up to Huaca del Sol in the upper right which sits near the floodplain of the Rio Moche.*

The Temples of the Sun and the Moon Two enormous mounds, the Huaca del Sol (Temple of the Sun) and Huaca de la Luna (Temple of the Moon), standing some 500 m (1640 ft) apart, dominate the capital of the southern Moche realm, a few miles south of Trujillo [**17.26**]. Built on the flanks of a white hill, the smaller Luna complex consists of three platforms interconnected and enclosed by high adobe walls richly ornamented with polychrome friezes and murals [**17.25**]. The large central mound had spacious summit courts ornamented with huge depictions of the head of a supernatural being. The rayed face gazes forward with curled lips, exposing elongated, interlocking canine teeth. Other polychrome panels depict spider-like creatures, anthropomorphic beings, and the parading of warrior captives (Uceda and Morales 1997). To the south, a small platform was built over the upper side of a prominent rocky outcrop, leaving the high stony face exposed to viewers in an enclosing court below. The outcrop platform was apparently the sacramental stage for rituals depicted in Moche arts that show the mountaintop sacrifice of captive warriors, whose mutilated corpses were then flung downhill. Below the outcrop platform,

archaeologists excavated remains of more than 20 young males, who had been dispatched by blows to the head or other violent acts and then had their corpses dismembered. This, and discoveries of other mutilated male corpses, confirms that warrior narrative iconography was indeed acted out by the *kuraka* nobility.

The plains to the west of the Luna complex were occupied by walled adobe enclosures that flanked north–south avenues. Subdivided into open courts, hallways, and smaller roofed quarters, the rectangular enclosures were where extended families lived and worked. Some compounds housed skilled artisans who produced elite ceramics and fine arts; others were the residences of noble families.

Sovereigns apparently resided in opulent quarters atop the great platform of the Huaca del Sol. Measuring 340 x 160 m (1115 x 525 ft) and standing over 40 m (130 ft) high today, it is one of the three or four largest mounds ever erected in South America [**17.26**]. However, because in Spanish colonial times the Rio Moche was diverted to wash away the structure in order to mine it for treasure, less than half of the original monument survives. The river-cut profile indicates that the mound was erected in stages, each phase building over existing summit rooms and courts. Millions of mud-bricks were used in the construction, and before drying, many of the adobes had distinctive "makers' marks" impressed upon them. The marks identify different communities of workmen, each of which produced bricks, carried them to the building site, and then used them to build an assigned section of the project. Originally, the Huaca del Sol took the form of a cross that rose from the north in three successively higher tiers before descending to a fourth (lower) level, probably comprising servants' or retainers' quarters. The highest tier was the focus of colonial mining and looting, presumably because it contained royal tombs. Traces of courts and chambers, and refuse indicative of residential activities, survive on several lower tiers.

Reflecting the architectural and iconographic canons of the capital, provincial seats of Moche government were built in nearby valleys, including **Huancaco** in the Virú Valley, **Pampa de Los Incas** (Guadalupito) in the Santa Valley, **Pañamarca** in the Nepeña Valley, and **El Brujo** in the Chicama Valley. To the north, archaeologists believe that such monumental centers as **Dos Cabesas** in the Jetepeque Valley and Sipán in the Lambayeque Valley reflect more independent political development (Bawden 1996).

Natural disaster visited coastal Peru in the form of a massive El Niño flood, sand dune incursions, and a drought between AD 562 and 594. In the aftermath, Moche was recast and endured as but a remnant of the former order until it disappeared *c.* AD 700–800.

Nazca and the South Coast

Partially contemporary with Moche, the vivacious culture and style of Nazca flourished *c.* 200 BC–AD 650 in its namesake valley formed by small streams converging at the base of the mountains (Silverman and Prulx 2001). Maintaining earlier Paracas liking for polychrome decoration, Nazca weavers and potters produced vibrant arts, conveying a rich, often abstract iconography that was intelligible to its users but is elusive today [**17.27**]. There are recognizable depictions of plants, animals, people, and supernatural beings, but rarely are they portrayed in interactive scenes revealing of broader stories or rituals. Some supernatural creatures sprout feline-like whiskers and carry human heads, and some grave accompaniments include whiskered nose ornaments of gold or mummified human trophy skulls. Thus, aspects of the arts seem to capture certain hallmarks of *kuraka* ceremony.

With much of its arable land split among separate headwater streams, the Nazca drainage is small and sustained a dispersed prehistoric population of under 25,000 people, most of them living in simple farming communities. Nonetheless, ancient Nazca did have a central ceremonial place, **Cuachi**, with more than 40 small- to modest-sized mounds and a 20-m (66-ft) high Great Temple, made by encasing a natural hill in adobes (Silverman 1993). Platforms were fronted by plazas, where feasting and drinking generated refuse that was added to the mound tops, increasing their height, if not their total stature. A

17.27 Nazca vessel: *the Nazca were accomplished potters and produced vessels decorated in a wide range of imagery, often brightly colored. A whiskered feline being is depicted on this polychrome, double-spouted Nazca drinking vessel.*

paucity of residential quarters and domestic garbage indicates that Cuachi was used on ritual occasions by people who resided elsewhere, and the multitude of mounds suggests that every social group of consequence asserted its identity by erecting a separate platform-plaza complex.

The "Nazca Lines" Nazca is of course most famous for its desert ground drawings on the dry rocky plains between the river tributaries. Called "geoglyphs," lines and figures were created by removing the upper dark rocks and sediments to expose lower, lighter-colored surfaces. Sizable areas can be cleared with relatively little work, and while geoglyphs are found along much of the coastal desert, their greatest concentration is on the Nazca plains. There are more than 1000 km (620 miles) of straight lines of varying widths, and some lengths exceed 20 km (12 miles); many lines issue from isolated hills and end at other hills. In addition, there are more than 300 geometric figures, including trapezoids, triangles, zigzags, and spirals. Near the valley in one corner of the plains, some three dozen animal figures were etched in the desert, including numerous birds, several killer whales, a monkey, a spider, a fox or llama, one human, and several plants [17.28].

People have variously proposed that the glyphs were alien landing strips, guides for condors flying to the coast, maps of underground streams, or were surveyed from hot-air balloons as make-work projects to tire out Nazca men and prevent their siring too many children. Conservatively, it can be said that glyphs on hillsides were similar to billboards, while many on flat land were to be walked on, and others may have served still other purposes. Newer creations cross older ones in amazing profusion, indicating that the works were not integrated in an overall plan; rather, each geoglyph was separately created, used for a time and then forgotten (Aveni 1991).

The Rise and Fall of the Andean Empires

At its height in the early 16th century, the Inca empire stretched more than 6000 km (3730 miles) down the Andes Mountains to form the largest native state to arise in the Americas, as well as the largest ancient empire to develop south of the equator (Morris and Von Hagen 1992). By dint of conquest and concord, it enveloped the most rugged mountain chains in the hemisphere and the greatest ethnic diversity in the continent. The Incas themselves were a closed ethnic group founded by a venerated ancestor, called Manco Capac. They ruled as a great royal family of ten *kuraka* lineages, with kinship terminology serving as the idiom of social and political relationships.

Similar kin-based organization, revolving around revered ancestors and various descendant lineages of *kurakas* and commoners, characterized most Inca subject states societies, each of which scrupulously maintained its own separate ethnic identity. Hierarchy was deeply imbued in this type of organization by recognized differences between older and younger generations and siblings of different ages. Yet, heterogeneity was also imbued by separate competing *kuraka* families, lineages, kin, and ethnic groups. Consequently, there is debate about the degrees to which pre-Inca empires – Tiwanaku and Wari in the highlands, Chimor on Peru's north coast – were hierarchical and centralized, or heterogeneous and confederated.

The Middle Horizon, c. AD 650–1000: Tiwanaku and Wari

The Inca achievement had political antecedents in Middle Horizon times (c. AD 650–1000), when two great empires held sway over the Cordillera, with Wari ruling in the north and Tiwanaku in the south. Characterized as youthful, secular, militant, centralized, and hierarchical, Wari governed almost all of highland and coastal Peru from its upland capital in the sierra of Ayacucho (Schreiber 1992). Portrayed as mature, religious, proselytizing. heterogeneous, and more confederated, Tiwanaku dominated the mountains of southern Peru, Bolivia, and northern Chile from its metropolis on the plains of Lake Titi-

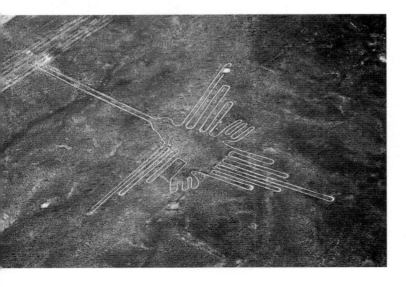

17.28 *(Left)* **The "Nazca Lines":** *this Nazca geoglyph, or desert drawing, depicts a long-beaked humming bird that cannot be made out on the ground because of its size. Such geoglyphs were created by removing dark rocks and sediments from the surface, thus revealing lighter surfaces below; but the exact purpose of the lines is not so certain.*

17.29 *(Opposite below)* **Tiwanaku:** *situated on the plains of Lake Titicaca, this site was the capital of a large empire and contained the largest platform mound in the southern Andes. A megalithic stairway leads up to the Kalasaya gateway which frames a large anthropomorphic stela in the background.*

caca (Kolata 1993). Although relatively flat, the lake's expansive high plains, the altiplano, lie above 3200 m (10,500 ft), where few domesticated plants thrive. The Ayacucho sierra is lower and receives more rain, but the topography is broken and very rugged. Among many other factors, distinct environments contributed to great differences between the continent's two nascent empires. Wari increased agricultural production by constructing large irrigated terrace systems on steep mountain slopes, where maize and other crops could be cultivated. Tiwanaku instead reclaimed flat terrain for farming potatoes and other high-altitude crops, while herding llama and alpacas in towering pasturelands (Albaracin-Jordan 1996; Kolata 1996). Both empires employed llama caravans to import resources from colonies and clients in distant provinces.

Great labor was lavished on monumental construction at both capitals, although very different forms of architecture were designed. At Tiwanaku the ruling *kuraka* stressed imposing temple mounds for ritual display visible to large audiences, and the largest platform mound in the southern Andes anchored the capital's monumental core (Manzanilla 1992). Atop the flat summit was a spacious rectilinear sunken ceremonial court, an arrangement typical of other, smaller, temple mounds [**17.29**]. Tiwanaku is renowned for its fine stonework, and mounds and courts were faced with well-cut masonry. Sunken courts housed numerous large stelae, some of anthropomorphic form, per-

17.30 Detail from the Gateway of the Sun: *perhaps harking back to the Chavín Staff God, a richly garbed, ray-headed deity standing atop a platform and holding two ceremonial scepters is the central figure depicted on the monolithic Gateway of the Sun at Tiwanaku.*

haps representing regents or deities. Portals were of great ritual significance, and finely carved lintels depicting converging figures were common. Occasionally, megalithic portals were hewn from a single block of stone. The most ornate is the Gateway of the Sun, with a lintel depicting rows of winged beings converging on a central figure standing atop a platform mound and holding a vertical staff in each hand [**17.30**].

Gateways, stelae, and temple mounds were eschewed by **Wari**, which employed fine-cut stonework only occasionally, for very special buildings (Isbell and McEwan 1991). The general norm was plaster-covered walls of fieldstones set in abundant mud mortar. Monumental architecture tended to be cloistered and compartmentalized, stressing grand compounds with high enclosing walls and interiors subdivided by clusters of one- and two-story hall-like buildings, called "galleries," arranged around open patios. Single-story D-shaped buildings with open, undivided interiors are thought to have been temples, although they were neither numerous nor capable of accommodating large audiences.

Architectural canons promulgated at each capital were followed when the states erected administrative centers in their hinterlands (Berman 1994; McEwan 1987). Although provincial centers served different functions, their monumental architecture provided graphic statements about the power of their respective capitals. The largest Wari center, **Pikillacta**, was a sprawling complex of courts, galleries, and chambers erected 40 km (25 miles) up the Rio Huantanay from the later Inca capital of Cuzco. To the south, a wide buffer zone typically separated the Wari and Tiwanaku empires, except in Peru's Moquegua Valley, where a provincial center of each state lay within distant eyesight of the other. Here, the Tiwanaku temple mound complex of **Omo** occupied mid-valley flatlands, while in the upper sierra an intrusive Wari complex perched atop the high, sheer-sided mesa and natural bastion of **Cerro Baul** (Goldstein 1993).

Several centuries of interaction may explain how Wari came to adopt Tiwanaku's paramount pantheon, depicted on the Gateway of the Sun. Holding two vertical staffs, the garbed divinity is a likely revitalization of the Chavín Staff God. Short rays issuing from the head terminate in feline heads or ovals (perhaps potatoes) in Tiwanaku renditions, whereas Wari added terminal corncobs, more appropriate for its maize-based economy. The secondary converging winged figures, called "angels," were similarly reinterpreted by Wari and then spread through its territory. Although central religious concepts were shared, diversity of view was probably as great as Christians or Muslims exhibit today. Faith in both religion and government was seemingly undermined after about AD 1050, when the climate turned drier for centuries. With economic stress exacerbating social tensions, Wari and Tiwanaku collapsed, each fragmenting into small polities (Stanish 1992; Hastorf 1993).

The Late Intermediate Period, AD 1000–1476: Lambayeque and Chimor

Governed from the Moche Valley metropolis of Chan Chan, Chimor was South America's second-largest native empire, as documented by both ethnohistorical accounts and archaeological remains. Established by a venerated ancestor called Taycanamu, Chan Chan's *kurakas* consolidated their hold over the Moche Valley by about AD 900, and then expanded their rule over societies up and down the coast. By 1450 Chimor encompassed a 1000-km (620-mile) swathe of the Pacific lowlands, reaching from the southern frontier of Ecuador to the Chillon Valley just north of Lima. The empire held two-thirds of all irrigated desert land and presumably two-thirds of the coastal population (Moseley and Day 1982). The core holdings were very large valleys that lay north of the Rio Moche.

Lambayeque and Batán Grande With massive canals extending laterally to drainages that crossed the coastal desert in more or less parallel courses, Lambayeque was the biggest and most powerful of Chimor's coastal opponents. After the Moche polities dissolved *c.* AD 800, the pre-eminent center in the Lambayeque region arose at **Batán Grande** in the northern lateral drainage of the Leche River. By about AD 1000 the civic core had grown to over 4 sq. km (1.5 sq. miles), and was dominated by a dozen enormous platform mounds surrounded by smaller monuments. Batán Grande was hallowed ground, with more than 10,000 interments. (It now looks like the cratered surface of the moon, due to the extensive looting that has produced much of the Andean goldwork in museums and private collections.) Indeed, as some scholars suggest, it may have been akin to a Vatican-like religious center, where multitudes from near and far were buried with their richest finery [**17.31**].

Although not specifically named, Batán Grande was probably one of the many Lambayeque sites that figure in oral traditions recorded by the Spanish. The historical lore recounts that a great lord and founding ancestor, called Naymlap, arrived by sea along with his wife and large entourage. The founder built his quarters at a place known as Chot, thought to be the monumental ruins of **Chotuna**. His son had 12 sons, each of whom founded or settled a major Lambayeque center, becoming its paramount *kuraka*. This story implies a heterogeneous political order with confederated city-states that reputedly endured for ten generations, at least figuratively. Then one of Naymlap's descendant lords invoked the gods' wrath, occasioning 30 days of disastrous rains, followed by pestilence, famine, and political collapse.

The rains were probably an exceptionally catastrophic El Niño event in AD 1100, which inundated Chotuna and flooded Batan Grande, leading to its abandonment. Prior to Chimor's conquest of the region, the oral traditions tell of a long interregnum following the flood. During this time **Tucume Viejo** became Lambayeque's major political center, retaining its importance after the region was conquered by Chimor and then the Incas. The Tucume complex has many large monuments, including Huaca Larga, one of the largest platform mounds ever erected in the Andes (Heyerdahl et al. 1995).

The minor nobility resided in 30 modest-sized compounds with relatively low adobe walls, while paramount rulers and their kin held court in enormous enclosures called *ciudadelas* ("citadels"), although none were fortified. Nine of these grand structures survive, along with traces of one or two others. The earliest versions were built by about AD 900; two centuries later they began to assume a standardized layout, being erected in east–west pairs (Moseley and Cordy-Collins 1990).

The last two compounds, Rivero and Tschudi, were built at the southern margin of the urban core shortly before the Incas subdued Chimor. Thick mud-brick walls towering three stories high enclosed both *ciudadelas*. Lacking battlements, the perimeter walls were for social seclusion of the potentates residing within, who probably ruled as god-kings. Other than royal families and servants, few people lived in the stately *ciudadelas*, even though the smallest, Rivero, is six times the size of a football field [**17.34**]. Access to the complex was through a single narrow gateway in the north. High curtain walls partitioned the interiors into northern, central, and southern sectors, and sometimes a fourth eastern sector; all contained palatial buildings except for the southern sector, where servants and retainers lived in humble cane quarters. The northern and central sectors each held large, centrally positioned entry courtyards, focal points for pomp and ceremony and often ornamented with carved friezes.

Each quadrangle had a southern mid-line ramp leading to an elevated rear complex of mazelike corridors connecting smaller courts with two types of interior buildings. One consisted of rows of cell-like rectangular rooms for storage of elite goods; warehouse courts were most common in the central sectors. Other courts, particularly in northern sectors, held important U-shaped rooms called *audiencias*. Ornamented with friezes and slightly elevated above the court floor, the structures are about 4 m (13 ft) square. Textiles, woodcarvings, and three-dimensional ceramic representations depict *audiencias* with richly attired figures standing in their centers, holding audience with people assembled in front of U-shaped structures; these have distant origins in the great U-shaped ceremonial centers of the Initial period, discussed above (Moore 1996).

Situated in spacious courts within the *ciudadelas*, single- or multi-storied burial platforms with numerous interior chambers are the largest buildings associated with Chan Chan's imperial compounds. Generally located in the central sector, the grand sepulchers were commercially looted for treasure in post-conquest times, and Spanish documents record inordinate

Chimor and Chan Chan Vaguely listing between nine and 11 pre-Inca rulers, the Spanish recorded only meager indigenous lore relating to Chimor. Its founder, Taycanamu, arrived alone by sea, saying that he was sent from afar to govern. After his son and grandson united the Moche Valley, there were supposedly two major stages of foreign political expansion. According to lore, the later stage was initiated by the ruler who battled with and lost to the Incas. However, to judge from archaeological data that place the incorporation of Lambayeque around 1370 and Chimor's subjugation by the Incas about a century later, expansion was a more gradual process.

Ethnohistorical sources say that prosperous coastal *kuraka* lords resided in spacious walled compounds with interior courts and facilities for receiving their subjects and entertaining *kuraka* elites. The grandest of these quarters were vast rectangular enclosures with towering adobe walls and an interior mortuary mound, such as comprise the dominant monuments of Chimor's imperial capital, **Chan Chan** [**17.32**, **17.33**]. The densely packed civic center of great enclosures and other buildings covered 6 sq. km (2.3 sq. miles). The metropolitan majority, totaling perhaps 29,000, were skilled craftspeople, particularly weavers and metalsmiths who lived and worked in humble quarters built of cane and thatch. Rulers and *kurakas* were the urban minority, numbering 6000 or less.

17.32, 17.33 *Chan Chan: an aerial view of metropolitan Chan Chan (above), capital of Chimor, with vast rectangular compounds reserved for the ruling elite. (Below) An adobe frieze in the Uhle Compound at Chan Chan depicts fish, sea birds, mythical creatures, and wave motifs reflecting worship of the sea.*

yields of precious metal artifacts. Excavating looters' dregs in plundered chambers produced copious remains of fine ceramics, ornate textiles, rich artworks, and bones of young women, all apparently accompaniments of the primary royal interment. Two relatively late, more-or-less intact mortuary platforms had rows of rectangular crypts surrounding a large, centrally positioned T-shaped chamber that apparently held the mortal remains of one *ciudadela*'s founding potentate.

In other *ciudadelas*, smaller platforms with T-shaped chambers that served subsequent royal heirs were abutted to the main mound. The mortuary structures are compatible with propositions that a dynasty of Chimor's potentates built *ciudadelas* to serve as palaces and then as family mausoleums, as the reins of power passed to subsequent generations. Particularly telling is the recent discovery of ancient wooden models of *ciudadela* entry courts mounted on cloth, with attached figures portraying entrance processions of priests and sanctified hunchbacks leading llamas and warrior captives to apparent sacrifice before cloth-bundled noble mummies occupying the rear of the court. It seems that the apex of rule in Chimor was maintained by royal corpses and ancestor veneration, much as was the case with the Incas.

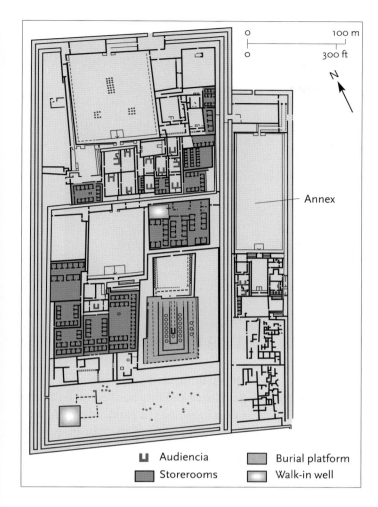

Audiencia
Storerooms
Burial platform
Walk-in well

17.34 *The Rivero Compound at Chan Chan:* serving a ruler and his kindred in life as well as death, this compound had U-shaped audiencia offices, store rooms for rich objects, and a burial platform mausoleum where royal mummies remained accessible to the living.

"imperial styles" of art and architecture that made it opulent and rich far beyond the spoils plundered from the Aztecs (Gasparini and Morgolies 1980). Yet the splendor of Inca imperial styles was relatively young; radiocarbon dates suggest that these uniquely Inca hallmarks of technique and fashion began to crystallize only shortly after 1375.

Origins and Expansion Although ethnohistorical accounts of Inca "history" are often contradictory, popular interpretations hold that a venerated ancestor, Manco Capac, who turned to stone, founded a ten-fold dynasty of rulers, and that Tawantinsuyu was largely the product of a three-generation "blitzkrieg" initiated by Pachacuti, the seventh potentate, and then furthered by his son and grandson (Cobo 1990; Zuidema 1986). The emerging archaeological record indicates that while the great expansion was indeed quite late, Inca origins stretch back to around AD 1000, when the collapse of Wari led to political fragmentation and the rise of the Incas.

There were more than a dozen different ethnic groups within a 100-km (62-mile) radius of Cuzco (Bauer 1992; Bauer and Covey 2002). Some groups allied themselves peacefully with the Incas, whose rulers often married noble women of other ethnic collectives to establish coalitions. Groups that did not resist Cuzco's early expansion were made "Inca by privilege" and given minor bureaucratic posts, while still paying tribute to the "Incas by birth." Some groups fiercely defended their independence, however. One of these was the Mohina, who lived upstream from Cuzco in the Lucre basin, where Wari formerly had its largest provincial center, Pikillacta. Upon abandonment it was replaced by a local metropolitan center, **Chokepukio**. Here, earlier traditions of monumental construction and ornate arts persisted in modified forms that were rather more elaborate and developed than those Cuzco was producing at the time. Repeated conflict between the Mohina and Incas led to the creation of a sparsely occupied buffer zone separating the forces of Cuzco and Chokepukio. When the Incas finally prevailed, many of the Mohina were exiled, and people loyal to the Incas were settled in the area.

With their homeland consolidated, the lords of Cuzco were well positioned both to create imperial-style art and architecture and to launch aggressive expansion further afield. Their initial foreign conquests were in the Titicaca basin; securing this high mountain "bread basket" in turn fueled northern expansion into the sierra and subjugation along the coast (Hyslop 1990; Marcus 1987).

The Late Horizon, 1476–1533: Cuzco and the Incas

At its height, the Inca empire – largest of the Native American empires – was composed of 80 political provinces, each embracing ethnically diverse and linguistically distinct subject populations. Indeed, with provincial people speaking so many different tongues, the Incas were compelled to impose a *lingua franca*, called Runa Simi, for conducting government business. The provinces were grouped into four geographical territories, known as *suyu*, and the Incas called their realm Tawantinsuyu, "Land of the Four Quarters" (D'Altroy 1992). Four lines creating the grand quadrants radiated out of the capital, **Cuzco**, as did four splendid all-weather highways uniting the empire, a configuration reinforcing the Incas' view that their metropolis was the navel of the known universe [see box: The Sacred Valley of the Incas and Machu Picchu, p. 667].

This *axis mundi* was truly spectacular: first-hand accounts by Spanish conquistadors say that Cuzco's splendor was unmatched in Europe (Cieza de Leon 1976). To judge from ethnohistorical and archaeological sources, what European invaders encountered and immediately sacked was a vibrant and growing "new city," largely built in the wake of earlier territorial expansion. Cuzco vividly expressed highly distinctive

17.35 *Inca masonry:* *at the royal Inca compound of Ollantaytambo massive polygonal blocks were individually carved into unique shapes to fit with similarly irregular adjacent blocks of stone.*

Cuzco and the Trappings of Empire Inca subjects were highland agropastoralists and coastal farmers and fishermen. Because currency was alien to the central Andes, the imperial economy was based on extracting three types of labor levies: agricultural taxation; textile tribute; and work draft. Commoners of both sexes were required to plow, plant, and harvest both government and state religious lands. Women were also obliged to weave textiles for the regime, while men were additionally drafted to work on building projects. Such incomes supported the "Incas by birth" in regal style, not simply in life but also in death. Deceased rulers and important officials were artificially mummified. Venerated as grand ancestors and religious objects, the mummies often continued to reside in their former quarters or in special sanctuaries, and were brought forth to attend major ritual events with the living. Viewing the landscape as sacrosanct and vibrant, the Incas revered mountains as sacred sources of rainfall and water, to be propitiated with peak-top sacrifices of highly valued goods, occasionally including young people of great purity.

With millions of male workers to draw upon, the Incas built and maintained a vast all-weather highway system, with 30,000–40,000 km (18,600–24,800 miles) of thoroughfares and trunk lines. Great labor was lavished on imperial construction (Niles 1987), and imperial-style buildings employed two notable forms of cut-rock masonry that did not use mortar (Frost 1989; Hemming and Ranney 1992). One of these, ashlar, employed rectangular stones hewn to the same size and was generally used for the freestanding walls of buildings. The other, polygonal [**17.35**], used for terraces and solid structures, employed large multi-sided rocks, each uniquely faceted and

sized to fit the angles of adjoining blocks. Both masonry forms went into the building of Cuzco and into transforming the surrounding hinterland into a monumental parkland replete with noble estates, imperial shrines, and royal sanctuaries. A rotating force of 20,000 corvée laborers reputedly worked for decades to erect Cuzco's largest monument, **Sacsahuaman**, interpreted as either a temple or a fort – a massive acropolis of cyclopean masonry terraces and summit buildings crowning the heights of the imperial capital [**17.37**].

The metropolis that sprawled out below was composed of high-walled enclosures called *kanchas*, each about the size of a city block, with a single entry. The thatched-roofed buildings inside were usually one-room structures known as *wasi*, generally built on three or four sides of a patio where daily life went on. *Kanchas* served as the residences of the ten royal lineages that lived in Cuzco when the Spanish arrived. The most opulent enclosure was the **Coricancha**, a great temple. It held the House of the Sun, a lavish, gold-bedecked *wasi*, while another temple richly adorned with silver served the moon, and still other sanctuaries were dedicated to other members of the imperial pantheon. The conquistador Cieza de Leon (1976) also describes a sacred Coricancha garden, with dirt clods and maize plants with cobs made of gold, as were 20 llamas and their attendant herders. He concludes by saying that if the other marvels he saw were described, he would not be believed.

The marvel that was the Inca imperium was decimated by a smallpox pandemic that killed the emperor and triggered a disastrous seven-year civil war between rival claimants to the throne. Then, just as one of them, Atahualpa, was marching south to claim Cuzco, he was intercepted, kidnapped, ransomed,

KEY SITE The Sacred Valley of the Incas and Machu Picchu

Two revered streams, the Huantanay and Tullumay, framed Cuzco, the center of the Inca universe. Straightened, canalized, and faced with fine masonry, the waterways converged at the base of the metropolis that they helped drain. Believing the waters to be therapeutic, people bathed in the streams, offered sacrifices to them, and used them to carry away the hallowed remains of numerous ceremonies, from the dregs of libation beverages and fine food, to the ashes of exquisite cloth and other burnt offerings. All of this conferred exceptional sanctity on these special waters that fed into Rio Urubamba, making equally sacred its often raging currents and steep valley.

The lords of Cuzco invested great labor in transforming the valley into an amazing imperial parkland (Bauer 1998). Hillsides were expertly terraced with stone masonry [17.22], and the fields irrigated from rock-lined canals. Audacious engineering and exceptional effort were devoted to canalizing the Rio Urubamba and then facing its vertical banks with well-cut stone walls, still visible today. A series of stunning sanctuaries and settlements were erected in the valley, one of which is Ollantaytambo, which initially served as a Versailles-like rural palace and estate for the emperor Pachacuti. His royal successors added to the complex of sumptuous residences and stately temples, which remain very well preserved. Remnants of the Inca royal court retreated to Ollantaytambo in defiance of the conquistadors, before being driven down the Urubamba and into the jungle fringes of the Andes.

The discoverer of Machu Picchu, Hiram Bingham, thought he had found this final jungle retreat in 1911. The forested hilltop sanctuary was not a retreat from European invaders, however, but rather a particularly spectacular example of the royal retreats that were built in the sacred valley well before the Spanish conquest. Whereas Ollantaytambo is in the sparsely vegetated sierra, Machu Picchu is downstream and lower, where the Rio Urubamba cascades down the Andean escarpment in a canyon-like valley entering the Amazonian rainforest (Reinhard 1991). Although the forested terrain is exceptionally rugged, the Incas terraced and farmed the pendulous slopes and perched Machu Picchu on a towering promontory overlooking a verdant agricultural landscape that is wilderness today. The origins and development of this highly complex undertaking span several generations of Inca potentates, who expended vast resources on transforming the mountain pinnacle into a verdant royal haven.

17.36 With the Sacred Valley below, Machu Picchu is a masterwork of Inca engineering and architecture that began with artificially leveling the hill-top and terracing the hill sides, and culminated in fine cut stone buildings frequented by the nobility and their retainers.

17.37 Sacsahuaman: *crowning the heights of the Inca capital at Cuzco, the fort-like temple of Sacsahuaman had three high ramparts of polygonal masonry with individual cut stones weighing tons which had been hauled in from great distances.*

and killed by Francisco Pizarro's forces as they dismembered the apex of indigenous political achievement and plundered the empire's cities. Consequently, centuries later archaeologists confront a uniquely difficult task in attempting to reconstruct the Inca achievement and that of their ancestors.

Amazonia

In the Amazon, adventurers searched for centuries for the "lost cities" of legend – the golden capital of El Dorado or the sunken city of Atlantis. Colonel Percy Fawcett, inspired by Hiram Bingham's discovery of Machu Picchu in 1911, was perhaps the last to go looking, and was lost in the Upper Xingu River in 1925. Today, regional specialists agree that some form of "civilization" existed in parts of Amazonia in 1492, including large, settled populations with sophisticated technology, elaborate built environments characterized by spectacular complexes of earthen mounds and enclosures, and complex, hierarchically organized societies.

As noted above, population movements dominated the Amazonian Formative period (*c.* 1000 BC–AD 500), which was overlapped and followed by the so-called Regional Developmental and Classic periods from AD 1 to 1500 throughout most of the area. These later periods were characterized by internal growth and diversification in technology, culture, and populations; they experienced the profound effects of regional and continental integration, and, later, incorporation into the European world system. By the time of European contact, *c.* 1500–1550, societies ranged from the large polities of the lower and middle Amazon,

ranked into regional hierarchies, and the equally large and powerful confederacies that lacked rigid hierarchies (e.g., the Tupinamba), to the small, egalitarian groups that sometimes preyed on the settled peoples.

The Amazonian Formative Period, *c.* 1000 BC–AD 500

Greatly exceeding the size of Europe, Amazonia was long ignored by archaeologists. Indeed, evidence of sizable sedentary communities, earthworks, and ancient social complexity has begun to emerge only recently and sporadically in disparate environmental settings. Because the prehistoric record is very poorly sampled, reconstructions of past cultural groups are often made from the much better investigated record of Amazonian languages. As is common in similarly large regions of the world, such as Oceania, equatorial Africa, and temperate Europe, archaeologists have turned to historical linguistics to model the origins and dispersals of ancient peoples who swept over the sprawling lowlands of eastern South America and colonized the Caribbean.

The Linguistic Evidence

The earliest European expeditions in the Americas, those of Christopher Columbus, Pedro Cabral, and others, encountered peoples descended from Amazonian populations. The Taino of the Greater Antilles and the coastal Tupi of Brazil were the endpoints of two great Amazonian linguistic radiations, the **Arawak** and **Tupiguarani** language groups. The speakers of both these languages expanded rapidly across much of the lowlands *c.* 1000–500 BC. These two linguistic diasporas, the largest in the Americas and on a par with those of Polynesia (the Austronesian languages; see Chapter 8) and Africa (the Niger-Congo/Bantu language family; see Chapter 10), define the Formative period throughout much of Amazonia. Other significant cultural radiations are documented by the current linguistic distribution and histories of Carib, Gê, and other language families.

The Tupian languages, particularly the Tupiguarani language family, which included the coastal Tupi and Guarani peoples, began dispersing from somewhere in southwestern Amazonia *c.* 3000–2000 BC. Other families of macro-Tupi also dispersed widely, but far less than speakers of Tupiguarani languages. Tupiguarani peoples in eastern Brazil and around the Paraguay River to the west were in place from at least around 2000 years ago; colonization of the Amazon basin and the land north of it occurred after *c.* AD 1500 (e.g. Kocama/Omagua and northern Amazonian languages) (Urban 1992).

Proto-Arawak languages also began to diverge by around 2000 BC or soon after, probably in northeast South America, in the area bordered by the Negro, upper Orinoco, and Amazon (called the Solimões River in Brazil) (Aihkenvald 1999). Proto-Arawak already had words for manioc, ceramics, cayman, and, perhaps, an older/younger sibling distinction, but great linguistic distance between sometimes even neighboring languages suggests that the divergences happened quickly in the remote past (Payne 1991).

Technological innovation is often seen as the root cause of both the Arawak and Tupiguarani diasporas, specifically related to the emergence of a developed system of root-crop agriculture that resulted in population growth and dispersal (Vansina 1990). Similar models are proposed for other tropical diasporas in Polynesia and Africa; but in Amazonia, agricultural origins go much deeper, perhaps several thousand years to *c.* 5000–6000 BC for the first cultivation of manioc and a variety of "core" crops (Oliver 2001; Piperno et al. 2000). Innovations in the swidden (slash-and-burn) agricultural system may have been at the heart of the early Amazonian diaspora *c.* 1000–500 BC (Lathrap 1970; 1977), but the small size of sites of this period, such as Trants and Osvaldo (see below), suggests that population pressure, narrowly defined as stress on the carrying capacity of the land, was not the principal cause.

Changes in social, political, and ideological forces, notably the emergence of hierarchical systems of prestige and value, including hereditary rank, a "founder's ideology," and rivalry between high-ranking individuals, may have been a primary stimulus for village break-up, expansion, and even long-distance migration (Heckenberger 2002).

The Archaeological Evidence

The Orinoco River of Venezuela and adjacent areas have long been a region of interest when looking into the ancient Arawak peoples, in part due to the fact that the "Nu-Arawak," the Aruaca and Maipure peoples, were first described here. Today, there is disagreement on the cultural affiliations or dating of initial ceramic industries (the La Gruta tradition), but there is some consensus that between *c.* 1000 and 500 BC, peoples called the Saladoid and the Barrancoid were established in the middle Orinoco floodplains and the Caribbean (Roosevelt 1997). Early **Saladoid** sites in the Lesser Antilles place initial occupation at *c.* 500 BC, slightly later in the Greater Antilles. These sites were apparently occupied by people who constructed villages characterized by circular plazas, and who transported their agricultural and fishing technologies, including domesticated and other managed plants (manioc, bananas, etc.) and animals (Petersen 1997). The colonization of much of the Caribbean seems to have occurred relatively quickly (*c.* 500–200 BC), and these earliest Saladoid peoples, who flourished *c.* 500 BC–AD 500, were the proto-typical societies of the Arawak peoples who were inhabiting the area in 1492. These are the indigenous societies, such as the Caquetio and Taino, that so impressed Americanists as "circum-Caribbean chiefdoms" (Steward and Faron 1959).

Research in the lower Rio Negro basin, dominated by Arawak peoples historically, suggests a correlation between central-plaza villages and "modeled-incised" or "Barrancoid" ceramics. The **Osvaldo** site (*c.* 170 BC–AD 850) has a central cleared area (plaza) and is dominated by diagnostic **Barrancoid** ceramics (Petersen et al. 2001). The **Açutuba** site, just above the confluence of the upper Amazon and the Rio Negro at Manaus, was occupied continually (if not continuously) from *c.* 500 BC until ethnohistoric times, with a large central-plaza village dominating the extensive site (Heckenberger et al. 1999; Neves 2001). The early portions of this sequence of occupation (beginning 920–360 BC, according to radiocarbon dates, and ending around AD 920) are dominated by a local variant of the Amazonian Barrancoid, whereas later ceramics, after *c.* AD 900, although showing clear continuity with earlier Barrancoid styles, represent a local variant of the Amazonian Polychrome tradition called Guarita; it was widespread throughout the floodplains of the Amazon and its major tributaries in late prehistoric times.

The Arawak peoples of the early diaspora, *c.* 500 BC–AD 500, most nearly fit the model of Formative peoples described for other parts of the Americas: agricultural, hierarchical, monument-building, theocratic "chiefdoms." These populations lived in large, settled, and sometimes fortified villages organized around central public spaces, elaborations of the circular plazas characteristic of the earlier Caribbean and Orinocan Arawaks. Although Tupiguarani (particularly coastal Tupi), Carib-speaking, and other groups developed into complex regional societies

KEY CONTROVERSY The Rank Revolution

Carneiro's Theory

In 1970, Robert Carneiro proposed an ecological theory for the origin of social complexity and the state, based on the divergent historical trajectories of Peru and Amazonia. Coined the circumscription theory, it suggests that states should emerge in areas where pronounced geographic barriers, such as the river valleys on the desert coast of Peru, tightly circumscribe agricultural lands. The theory also suggests that in some areas, such as along the fertile floodplains of the Amazon, resource concentration created an attenuated form of circumscription; nevertheless, the more "shallow ecological gradient" of Amazonia resulted in significant population movement as a valve for population pressure, competition, and conquest. Thus, social evolution quickly resulted in primary or "pristine" state development in Peru, whereas in the lowlands, chiefdoms arose.

On the coast of Peru, the exemplary case in Carneiro's model, the idea that initial social complexity – measured in terms of increasing functional variation between and within settlements, notably the construction of major temple centers – emerged without staple agriculture brought into question the validity of the theory [see box: Maritime Foundations of Andean Civilization?, p. 648]. In the late Preceramic, changes in the *relations* of production – the organization of communal labor – were at the root of initial complex societies, not fundamental changes in *mode* of production, i.e., cultivation. Moreover, in the Andean Initial period and Early Intermediate times, warfare and significant competition over agricultural lands and production were critical factors in early chiefdoms and states.

Recent Views

Most specialists today eschew monocausal "prime-mover" explanations for something as complicated as the rise of institutional social inequality and the bureaucratic state. Further research in the lowlands has shown far greater variability in the ecological and economic conditions associated with complex societies, and their distribution, than previously thought. By late prehistoric times, substantial social power was exercised in the large central plazas of major settlements and chiefs there had the means to command large labor projects. Both the Amazon and the Andes show that inherited social rank and chiefly status, as evidenced by the corporate organization of communities, architectural monuments, iconography, ideology, and mortuary practices, are critical elements in the emergence of complex societies.

Overview

The circumscription theory still holds important insights into South American cultural history. There is a recognizable tendency over several millennia for Andean societies to stratify into steep, complex, vertically controlled hierarchies, whereas lowland societies tended to ramify within broad regional social systems that, while often hierarchical, were not based on politico-economic exploitation or coercion. In Amazonia, only rarely and apparently late did true economic exploitation develop, comparable to that seen in Moche or Inca taxation, for instance, or in political coercion and conquest (Roosevelt 1999).

This points to an interesting contrast between the Andes and the Amazon. The landscape of the former is marked by dramatic, even awesome physical contrasts, its history by the rise and fall of precipitous vertical social hierarchies and the large-scale effects of natural disasters. Amazonia, conversely, is marked by gradual changes in the land and the humans that occupy it. One wonders what constitutes a natural disaster here, where there are no earthquakes, no flash floods, no tidal waves, and nothing like a catastrophic drought in the Peruvian sense. Here instead there is a measured development of complex societies and the expansive regional political economies that built up around them.

---

as well as the Arawak populations, such organization is almost ubiquitous among Arawak speakers throughout the historical period [see box: The Rank Revolution]. There is now a significant body of evidence for various pathways to early social complexity, based on hereditary social hierarchy or meritocracies, and for the probable presence in prehistoric Amazonia of peoples who chose to live in small communities, similar in several ways to many of the ethnographically known peoples of Amazonia.

Regionalism and "Classic" Amazonia,
c. AD 1–1500

Around 2000 years ago, the two great linguistic diasporas had expanded to nearly their maximum extent. As the integrating force of Chavín declined (see above), and distinctive regional polities emerged throughout Andean South America, the Amazon was also moving into an era marked by increasing regionalism.

The **Arawaks** had already spread from the Urubamba River in the west to the northern Atlantic coast, and from the Greater Antilles to the Paraguay River in the south. The **Tupiguarani** had likewise spread far from their homeland in the southern Amazon, throughout the Amazonian uplands and the tropical forests of the Brazilian Serra do Mar and the Paraguay River. By about AD 500, the era of large-scale population movements was largely over. Many of these peoples entered a new phase from AD 1 to 500, as both immigrants and established peoples settled into more deeply rooted societies, involving the development of discrete regional social systems: a regional development period.

Early examples of emergent social complexity are present, notably, in the areas transitional with the central Andes, the so-called montaña sites, such as Sangay in eastern Ecuador and Gran Pajetan, Peru. These small regional polities are characterized by small earth and stone domestic and ceremonial structures that date to as early as the mid-1st millennium BC (Salazar 1993), no doubt influenced by the remarkable events taking place just over the mountain peaks, at Chavín de Huantar, for example.

Deeper in the Amazon, the period from 1000 BC to AD 1 was equally fertile for cultural development. By *c.* 200 BC, the Barrancoid (probably Arawak) midden of Hupa-iya on the Ucayali extended for over 600 m (1970 ft) along the river, and was the home of a local population of manioc-farming fishermen (Lathrap 1970; Lathrap et al. 1985). Remnants of large Barrancoid middens were found at the Açutuba site, dating to *c.* 500 BC or earlier, and at the circular-plaza Osvaldo site, dating to *c.* 200 BC, some 20 km (12 miles) away. Earthworks in the northern Llanos de Moxos (Baures), Bolivia, also date to as early as *c.* AD 1 (Erickson 2003).

By AD 500–1000, large, densely populated regional polities, such as those described by early European expeditionary groups, became established along many of the primary rivers of Amazonia. These polities were tied into regional systems of interaction that, although competitive and even occasionally at war, clearly shared great cultural traditions across the broad region in late prehistoric times. There is evidence of trade in precious stones, metals, ceramics, and other objects. In fact, the late prehistoric period in greater Amazonia is remarkable for the largely shared ceramic tradition – the Polychrome Tradition – from Marajó to Peru.

The Lower Amazon

Marajó Island, in the vast Amazon estuary, has been the subject of archaeological research since the turn of the last century. The **Marajoara**, the pre-Columbian people who dominated the island from *c.* AD 400 to 1400, are particularly well known for their elaborate polychrome ceramics [**17.38**] and their large and spectacular platform mounds. Marajoara is the earliest expression of the widespread Polychrome Tradition, which by late prehistoric times can be divided into several major sub-traditions on the island, probably associated with individual small polities (Schaan 2001). These polities of Brazil (notably in the state of Amapa) and neighboring French Guiana have produced remarkable archaeological discoveries over the past century, including the elaborate painted and modeled anthropomorphized burial urns found in caves and shaft graves (Guapindaia 2001).

Initial construction of the Marajó mounds, which rise up to 10 m (33 ft) above the rivers, began *c.* AD 400; mound building apparently peaked in the period from AD 600 to 800, although the mounds continued to be occupied and used for ceremonial purposes until at least AD 1300, after which some apparently ceased to be maintained [see box: Amazonian Mound Builders, p. 672]. It was long assumed that these were mortuary mounds, given the presence of the huge, elaborate burial urns found in many. Recent excavations and geophysical survey, however, show that they were also occupational mounds, with cemetery features built into them. Great variations in size and composition suggest that regional ritual and political activity were concentrated on the big central mounds in some of the large mound groups. There seems also to have been significant functional variability between settlements, with large ceremonial mounds and numerous basic domestic occupation mounds, as well as non-mound sites, in savanna and forest environments over a very broad area. Burial urns are located in mounds of all sizes, and it appears that burial in the major mounds was reserved for elites, an assumption supported by the concentration of highly decorated burial urns in the large mounds (Roosevelt 1991; Schaan 1997).

Equally impressive, although later than the Marajoara, is the **Santarem**, or Tapajós culture; its capital was located some 500 km (310 miles) upstream, atop a large bluff just east of the mouth of the Tapajós River. The site consists of much of the area within and around the modern city of Santarem [**17.40**], which gets its name from the large, powerful Amerindian state

17.38 Replica of an urn from Marajoara archaeological culture, Marajó Island, Brazil: the urn (rim diameter 18 cm/7in) was made by traditional potters from pre-Columbian examples in the Museu Paraense Emílio Goeldi (Belém), the primary center of Amazonian archaeological research for over 100 years.

KEY CONTROVERSY Amazonian Mound Builders

Unlike Mesoamerica and the central Andes, where stone masonry was so critical, the Amazon, like the southeastern United States (Chapter 18), was dominated by earth mound-building peoples. Proto-Arawak peoples were settled riverine and maritime agriculturalists, who lived in villages organized around exclusive centralized "sacred" and public areas. An essential feature of their settlements is the central plaza, and the monuments and ceremonies attached to it. Indeed, the appearance of plazas and monuments represents the emergence of an architectural feature that lay at the root of power in many later pre-Columbian societies.

The earliest expression of mound building comes from Marajó Island. The single occupational mound of Teso dos Bichos, initiated around AD 400 and formed by accretion, ultimately reached a height of some 7 m (22 ft) by AD 1300. The large Camutins group contains some 40 mounds spread over about 6 km (3.75 miles) of the headwater tributary of the Anajas River (Schaan 2001). At Camutins, numerous small- and medium-sized mounds, generally only a few meters high, are located up- and downstream from the major paired mounds that face one another on either side of the river: Camutins itself, some 10 m (33 ft) high and several hectares in extent, and the slightly smaller Belém mound.

As is true in Peru, Egypt, and elsewhere, the initial period of mound building saw the major episode of construction, in this case c. AD 600–800. Camutins, Belém, and a third mound, circular and smaller (but still larger than most domestic mounds), comprise a central precinct, where elaborate urn burials, fine ceramic wares, and other prestige goods were concentrated, the result of ritual activity and public access to such broad communal areas.

Eastern Bolivia has also been long noted for its complex constructed landscapes, since the early work of Erland Nordenskiöld on occupation mounds and other earthworks, including raised fields, raised causeways and roads, fish weirs and ponds (e.g. Denevan 1966; 2001; Erickson 1995).

Major earthworks, including domestic or ritual structures and raised fields, are also known from the Orinoco, the Guiana coast, and the Caribbean. Along the Upper Xingu, massive and extensive earthworks in the form of banks and ditches that outline the primary features of landscape architecture – plaza enclosures, roads, and moats – create an integrated or even gridlike settlement pattern of broad straight roads and circular plaza nodes.

Massive plaza centers such as Açutuba, with its sculpted banks some 10 m (33 ft) above the floor of the huge (450 x 100 m, or 1475 x 328 ft) central plaza complex, with its ramparts and terminal barricade, make us pause and think: could this be a prehistoric Amazonian town, or, at least, a large town according to the measure of the day, c. AD 1000?

17.39 *Photograph looking south across the large, sunken "plaza" area at Açutuba. The plaza area, which extends over 400 m (1312 ft), is bisected by a ditch that delineates central precincts of the site. Traces of extensive agricultural activities are preserved primarily in areas of pronounced archaeological dark earth (terra preta).*

that was located there in the 16th and 17th centuries. It was initially reported by Francisco de Orellana and his expeditioners, the first Europeans to descend the Amazon, in 1541–42. Santarem is deservedly famous for its elaborate plastic arts, especially ceramics, suggesting craft specialization and far-flung trade in prestige goods (Gomes 2001; Roosevelt 1999). Unlike Marajoara, the Santarem culture survived well into the historical period. Friar Gaspar Cavajal, a priest who chronicled the first expedition down the Amazon in 1541, marveled at the "great white city" that lay just beyond the banks of the river.

Upstream from Santarem, the related **Konduri** ceramic style, clearly linked to Carib populations of the Guiana shield (the vast rainforest between the mouth of the Orinoco and the Amazon), indicates that the unique ceramic styles of the Santarem people [**17.42**], similar to the broad Polychrome Tradition located both up and downstream from Santarem/Konduri,

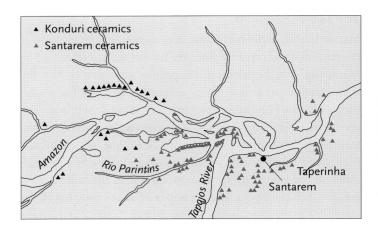

17.40 *The Santarem archaeological region of the Lower Amazon:* map showing the archaeological sites relating to the ceramic traditions of Konduri and Santarem.

17.41 Açutuba: *plan of the central portions of the site, near Manaus, Brazil, showing investigations 1995–99. Note concentrated fine-ware ceramics and raised mounds adjacent to the central plaza, suggesting high-ranking residential areas.*

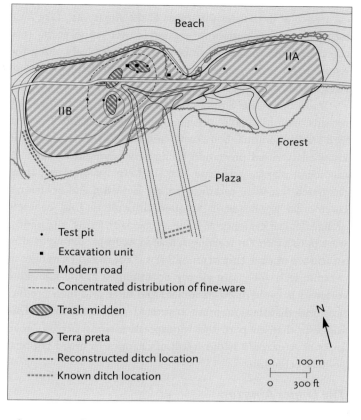

were the result of hybridization between Amazon populations and those to the north (Prous 1992).

Limited archaeological reconnaissance of black earth (*terra preta*) sites – i.e., those with evidence of settled occupation, including areas of ancient cultivation that lack artifacts – has demonstrated fairly dense settlement throughout the region, with sites commonly separated by only a few kilometers. In the broad Santarem region, *terra preta* sites include large non-domestic dark earths, the remnants of forest gardens and other manmade features; nearer to the city, local farmers still harvest the soils, which have some capacity to renew themselves (Woods and McCann 1999).

This brings up an important question in lowland archaeology: what do the frequent and often large expanses of dark earth mean? Are they simply palimpsests of long-term but small-scale occupation and gradual landscape modification, or do they represent, in part, the large-scale impact of major social formations in late prehistory? Preliminary survey indicates that the archaeological remains of Santarem may extend discontinuously over an area of some 25 sq. km (10 sq. miles) (Roosevelt 1999), which, if actually a reflection of the size of the Amerindian town, puts it well within the range of some of the larger pre-Columbian New World centers, such as Chan Chan (described above), Teotihuacán (Chapter 16), and Cahokia (Chapter 18). Archaeologists working in the Amazon generally agree that some very large and elaborate settlements were present in the region in 1492, which, if ranked according to the European standard of the day, could be characterized as towns [see box: Amazonian Urbanism?, p. 675].

17.42 Replica of an ornate effigy base: *Santarem (the "Tapajós" ethnohistoric polity), made by traditional potters, modeled after ceramics in the Museu Goeldi, Brazil (rim diameter 10 cm/3.9 in).*

The Central Amazon

The central Amazon played a critical role in discussions about Amazonian cultural history in the 1950s through 1970s, although no in-depth archaeological work was done in the region until the mid-1990s. Investigations in the Manaus area have focused on regional survey and on excavations and mapping at several sites, including the large Açutuba center (Heckenberger et al. 1998; 1999; Neves 2001; Petersen et al. 2001). At **Açutuba**, which extends over 30 ha (c. 75 acres), the central plaza is composed of a massive sunken amphitheater the size of four football fields, which is ramped by a sculpted slope over 10 m (33 ft) high on three sides and bisected by a lin-

ear trench at the western margins of the site [**17.41**]. Like Açutuba, the site of **Manacapuru** extends over some 50 ha (124 acres) or more on various lobes of the high bluffs along the Amazon; the recently discovered **Hatahara** site, lying just downriver, is over 10 ha (25 acres) in size.

Trade items are amply documented in the ethnohistoric records, including gold, precious gems, tropical forest woods, bird feathers, animal body parts, and salt, as well as shamanic knowledge, ritual prestation (obligatory payment or service), medicinal plants, pigments, etc. (Lathrap 1968). Apart from decorated fine-ware ceramics [**17.43**], however, and occasional ceremonial axe-heads, it is often difficult to find concrete archaeological evidence of trade in specialty items, since most were perishable. (In feasting refuse at Açutuba, dating to after AD 1000, a minute chip of amethyst was recovered.) Changes in ceramic technology are clearly documented at the site. Elite ceramics became more elaborated and finer, and their production and distribution more restricted and specialized. This suggests that, in part, the widespread sharing across broad areas of Amazonia is the result of changes in broad regional political economies.

The Upper Amazon

The upper Amazon has one of the better-known cultural sequences in Amazonia, due to the pioneering work of Clifford Evans and Betty Meggers (1968) on the Napo River in Ecuador and, particularly, Donald Lathrap (1970) and his students on the Ucayali River and its tributaries. In this region, the general processes of occupation – whereby immigrant tropical forest farmers had settled by c. 200 BC into fixed villages that grew into large riverbank towns in later periods – also involved cultural sharing, as established communities entered into relations with incoming peoples, sometimes involving warfare. As often as not, however, this resulted in cultural pluralism. The **Cumancaya peoples** (c. AD 800–1000), for example, the earliest Pano speakers in the region, became culturally and geographically intermixed with the **Caimito peoples**, bearers of the Polychrome Tradition in this area, giving rise to the modern Shipibo-Conibo style [**17.44**].

Lathrap was keenly aware of the complicated cultural pluralism and subtle historical twists in this part of Amazonia, strategically positioned between the Andes and the Amazon. In historic times, complicated systems of regional interaction are known, sometimes focused on major ceremonial centers controlled by chiefs, sharing power with equally powerful shamans and prophets (e.g. Santos Granero 1986). Still other groups remained small and "fugitive," perhaps as a form of resistance to the mighty Inca and later Spanish and American empires that were just over the mountains. Indeed, Scott Raymond (1972) found evidence for direct contact between highlanders, perhaps fleeing nobles, and Amazon peoples.

The Orinoco and Caribbean

Between 1000 and 500 BC, if not earlier, Saladoid-Barrancoid riverine agriculturalists, apparently Arawak speakers, came to dominate the middle and lower Orinoco (Boomert 2000; Roosevelt 1997; Rouse and Cruxent 1963). After c. AD 1, sequences of what appear to be complex regional societies from the northwestern plains and northern coastal areas of Colombia and Venezuela in the northern Andean piedmont are typically seen as the result of highland influence. However, cultural continuity between early populations (c. AD 300–500) and ethnohistoric

17.43 Upper portion of a burial urn: *the urn from the area of the Açutuba central plaza, related to the Guarita archaeological tradition (Amazonian Polychrome).*

17.44 Pottery from modern Shipibo (right) and Conibo (center) Panoan-speaking peoples of the Peruvian Amazon: *these ceramics show clear affinities with pre-Columbian ceramics of the Amazonian Polychrome, such as the Caimito sub-tradition also from the Ucayali River area where the Shipibo/Conibo live today.*

KEY CONTROVERSY Amazonian Urbanism?

In 1936, Gordon Childe proposed a model of the "urban revolution" (see Chapter 5, p. 196), in which cities were the product of surplus agricultural production and functioned as economic-administrative centers. Childe viewed the urban revolution according to common traits, such as writing, that were present in Europe and Southwest Asia. The Americas played only a very small part in his vision, but few today would deny that Inca Cuzco or Aztec Tenochtitlán merit the label "city," by any definition. Can one, however, detect pre-Columbian cities or towns – urbanism – in Amazonia? Regional specialists today agree that much of Amazonia was characterized by some form of "civilization" in 1492. Thus we are faced again with the old question: what would a city or town – urbanism – be like in the Amazon?

The ancient site of Santarem, seat of the paramount chief of the Tapajós polity, may have extended over an area as large as 25 sq. km (10 sq. miles), placing it within the range of many major American and Old World centers. At Açutuba, the sculpted banks rising above a huge 4.5 ha (10 acre) central plaza complex also suggest a very large settlement. It remains uncertain, however, whether the Amazonian polities existed at the same level demographically, economically, or politically as coastal Peruvian Chimor, or Cahokia on the Mississippi c. AD 1000 [see box: The Size and Influence of Cahokia, Chapter 18, p. 690].

The essential feature of the early American city is the central plaza, and the monuments and ceremony attached to it. These features have long been recognized as a key link between the lowlands and the highlands. In Amazonia, no pyramids stand high above the trees, as in the Maya lowlands, but the settlement patterns of the Upper Xingu indicate that the Amazon was every bit as socially complex. We may perhaps recognize a distinctive South American urbanism, in which the ceremonial center stood within a regional network, a pattern equally typical of the extensive Xingu polity and the Inca empire, where such a network linked the sacred center, Cuzco, to the administrative provinces. This Amazonian variant of the "theater state" would have been held together by impressive public rituals at a central ceremonial place.

Arawak groups in the area, such as Achagua and Caquetio, or related peoples (Oliver 1989), suggests that although localized interactions are clearly important, the scale of these populations and the basic orientation of these groups is fundamentally Amazonian.

The **Gaván-period** occupations (c. AD 300–1200) along the Meta River in Barinas state, Venezuela, provide a particularly well-documented case of initial colonization of the region c. AD 300, followed by significant in-filling by the small colonizing population, who over two centuries or so had developed into ranked polities located around regional centers (Spencer and Redmond 1992). These populations can be associated tentatively with Lokono, Achagua, and Caquetio Arawaks and related peoples, and their theocratic power structure was remarkably different from the militaristic chiefdoms of Colombia and Panama (Steward and Faron 1959).

Whatever settlement changes transpired in the Orinoco after c. 500 BC, it is clear that as Arawak peoples expanded, local in-filling in many regions resulted in growth and cultural elaboration of the pre-existing structures of the early diaspora. The various Arawak-speaking peoples that inhabited the Caribbean in 1492, generally called **Taino**, lived in large plaza settlements and were ruled by chiefs. As elsewhere in the Arawak diaspora, major plazas, causeways, and other ceremonial structures characterize the political core; these include the unique Greater Antillean ball courts, or *bateys*, as at Caguana in Puerto Rico (Oliver 1998), and circular plazas, such as En Bas Saline.

Caribbean prehistory is dominated by a settlement history of plazas and public precincts, ball courts, and sacred sites, from beginning to end of the cultural sequence. What, we might wonder, did the Taino elite feel for the ancestors, the founders who successfully bent tradition from a circle to a square in the form of a ball court – a clear indication of traffic with the Maya kingdoms, as well as a continuation of the widespread Arawak rubber ball game (Alegria 1983)? Regardless of shape, the enclosures are centers of power and operate as sacred focal points in regional landscapes; the concentration or "containment" of power, in social memory, was already part and parcel of the Arawak peoples as they migrated into the Caribbean.

The Southern Amazon

When Europeans first arrived in the southern peripheries of Amazonia in central Brazil and eastern Bolivia in the late 17th and early 18th centuries, they encountered numerous dense sedentary populations, many of which were Arawak. Early explorers, drawn by rumors of gold and precious gems, often remarked on the high level of engineering in the planned plaza villages that they saw, with "temples" (ceremonial houses), "idols," and an elaborate ritual life. Julian Steward and Louis Faron noted similarities across the lowlands: "the chiefdoms of Venezuela, the Greater Antilles, and eastern Bolivia consisted of a number of villages bound together through common religious worship" (Steward and Faron 1959, 2).

17.45, 17.46 *Contemporary Xinguano chiefs initiate a mortuary feast commemorating recently deceased chiefs: the direct genealogical connection between chiefs and immediate chiefly ancestors legitimizes social rank between community members through exclusive "ownership" of the ritual and related sacred objects, places, names, chants/songs, and body adornments, including blackwood bows, jaguar skin diadems, and body paints shown here. The wooden idol (far right) is the* kuarup *trunk, which embodies a recently deceased chiefly person and is erected on the day of the chief's funeral ceremony.*

The southern Amazonian chiefdoms largely comprised a related group of Arawak cultures, including Bauré, Pareci, Terêna, Xinguano, and other groups, which dominated many primary riverine areas in the southern Amazon, hugging the southern margins of the forested Amazonian lowlands just as they rise up into the high plateau lands of central Brazil, the Llanos de Moxos, and the Gran Chaco. These chiefdoms consisted of manioc farmers who supplemented their staple foods – manioc, fish, and fruits – with a wide range of secondary resources. (Fishing, including large-scale harvesting in weirs and ponds, is generally seen as the primary means of obtaining animal protein for large, settled groups in Amazonia (Erickson 2001).) These societies uniformly show characteristics commonly found in other late prehistoric polities: a regional, hierarchical organization, staple agricultural and fishing economies, central plaza space, and monumentality, among other things. Archaeological research conducted over the past decade or so has begun to reveal just how large and complex these southern Amazonian chiefdoms really were, perhaps rivaling much better-known areas of the Amazon floodplains, the Caribbean, and even much of the Andes.

The southern Amazon is important because it shows a pattern of complex multi-ethnic social formations, which while rooted in the Arawak diaspora took on an increasingly hybrid character over time. In much of this region, the sedentary chiefdoms were often surrounded by smaller, more mobile, and predatory Tupiguarani and Gê-speaking peoples of the uplands. Material culture also shows not only great diversity and internal consistency within evolving regional traditions, but also a great admixture of distinctive elements, particularly after AD 900.

The **Upper Xingu** region is particularly important, since cultural continuity between late prehistoric Arawak polities (*c.* AD 800 onwards) and contemporary Xinguano peoples [**17.45, 17.46**] can be demonstrated, due to conservatism in basic village organization (circular plaza villages), regional settlement locations, and material culture – notably ceramic technology, a late variant of the Amazonian Barrancoid (Heckenberger 1996). The Upper Xingu marks the eastern extent of Arawak peoples in southern Amazonia, and the sequence of settlement here recapitulates in some ways the general chronology of the diaspora: initial occupations by plaza agriculturalists, rapid and large-scale development of settlements, then the large, integrated regional polities of late prehistoric times. The late prehistoric polities of the Upper Xingu were organized in hierarchical clusters characterized by small- and medium-sized plaza communities between 5 and 30 ha (10–75 acres), linked to primary centers extending up to 40–50 ha (100 acres) or more. This, of course, was followed by post-European demographic collapse, but in the Upper Xingu the contemporary descendants of these ancient complex societies continue to practice their traditional lifeways.

17.47 Shell necklaces: *these are a critical element of personal adornment (as worn by the chiefs in 17.45), display and wealth, and an exchange item. As throughout much of Andean South America, shell objects were central to prestige-good political economies, much like metals, precious stones, and other rare commodities.*

Summary and Conclusions

This chapter has illustrated the enormous diversity of South American societies in the later Holocene period, a diversity that arose as people adapted to such environmental extremes as the world's largest river and longest mountain ranges, the latter second only to the Himalayas in height and harshness. Yet, there were commonalities and shared patterns of behavior across this vast and diverse area. Fish and seafood were typically the principal protein source for lowland peoples on both sides of the Andes, while llama and alpaca were critical in the mountains. Primary reliance on domesticated staples arose first in the moist, warm environments conducive to plant propagation, and spread later to the rugged Cordillera, which required irrigation and robust cultigens to mitigate aridity and high altitude. Nonetheless, root crops – not grains, as in other centers of cultivation – were the principal staples, with potatoes prevailing in the highlands and manioc in the lowlands. Although Mesoamerican maize was adopted, its role as a food source was generally secondary. It grows poorly or not at all at elevations above 2500 m (8200 ft), where the majority of Andean peoples resided, and it was valued principally for the production of beer, an essential ingredient of ritual ceremony.

Throughout prehistory, South American people organized themselves by kinship and descent, real and fictive. Kinship lineages structured by dual, or moiety, division were widespread, as was the superiority of senior generations and of older siblings to younger ones. The "rank revolution" separated commoners from chiefs, and Andean *kurakas* (elites) rationalized their privileged position and class by claims of descent from special ancestors and creators; ultimately, the Incas did nothing less than proclaim special descent from the sun. Significantly, the idioms of kinship dominance and subordination not only characterized the Inca court, but also conquered and subject polities and peoples, who were inducted into the mystical descent system as distant juniors, if not wayward kindred.

With standardized currency all but absent, people relied on labor to render tribute to their social collectives and leaders. This practice underwrote the earthwork enclosures of Amazonia, as well as the monumental masonry of the Andes. Peoples also rendered labor by producing arts and crafts that were standardized relative to linguistic, ethnic, and social milieus, culminating in the Amazonian ceramic horizon styles and Andean corporate styles, such as the distinctive architecture, costume, and utensils of the Incas. These patterns of behavior and organization are the keys for elucidating the archaeology of marvelous adaptations and great cultural achievements.

Thus South America, like Africa or South Asia, presents a complicated mosaic of diverse societies, separate though often interrelated. As we shall see in the next chapter, a very similar pattern of proximity and diversity is to be found also in the last region covered in this book: North America.

Further Reading and Suggested Websites

Burger, R. L. 1992. *Chavín and the Origins of Andean Civilization.* London & New York: Thames & Hudson. A thorough overview of the Initial period and Chavín horizon by a senior scholar, usefully supplemented by good illustrations.

Donnan, C. 2003. *Moche Portraits from Ancient Peru.* Austin: University of Texas Press. A lavishly illustrated, detailed study of Moche ceramic portraits.

Heckenberger, M. J. 2004. *The Ecology of Power: Culture, Place, and Personhood in the Southern Amazon, AD 1000–2000.* New York: Routledge. Overview of the archaeology, ethnohistory, and ethnography of the important Upper Xingu region and other areas of the southern Amazon.

McEwan, C., Barretto, C., & Neves, E. G. (eds.). 2001. *The Unknown Amazon.* London: British Museum Press. Excellent overview of recent research in areas along the Amazon River in Brazil.

Moseley, M. E. 2001. *The Incas and Their Ancestors: The Archaeology of Peru.* (2nd ed.). London & New York: Thames & Hudson. The most recent archaeological synthesis.

Roosevelt, A. C. 1992. *Moundbuilders of the Amazon: Geophysical Archaeology on Marajó Island.* San Diego: Academic Press. An overview of work by Roosevelt and others on the Marajoara culture from the mouth of the Amazon.

Rostworowski de Diez Canseco, M. 1999. *History of the Inca Realm.* Cambridge: Cambridge University Press. A thorough overview of the Inca realm, translated by H.B. Iceland.

Shady, R. & Leyva, C. (eds.). 2003. *La Ciudad Sagrada de Caral-Supe.* Lima: Instituto Nacional de Cultura. Stunning data documenting the Preceramic rise of Andean civilization.

http://www.marajoara.com Website maintained by Denise Pahl Schaan (Museu Goeldi, Brazil) about recent research on Marajoara culture.

http://www.angelfire.com/pe/contisuyo/MuseoE.html Website of the Museo Contisuyo, with information on the prehistory of the Moquegua area, a regional bibliography, and regional links.

http://inca.blogspot.com/ Website of Brian Bauer and other scholars, which discusses facts, recent research, and upcoming conferences relating to the Incas and the Andes.

http://www.huacas.com/page170.htm Website maintained by the Trujillo Museum and University, with information on the Moche Pyramids of the Sun and moon and related links.

CHAPTER 18
COMPLEX SOCIETIES OF NORTH AMERICA

George R. Milner, The Pennsylvania State University, and W. H. Wills, University of New Mexico

The Eastern Woodlands 681
Adena and Hopewell: The Early and Middle Woodland Period, c. 800 BC–AD 400 682
  • *Mounds and Earthworks* 682
  • *Exchange Systems and Cultural Ties* 683
  • *The Beginning of Food-producing Economies* 684
Settlement Patterns in the Late Woodland Period, c. AD 400–1000 684
● **KEY SITE** Hopewell 685
  • *Warfare, Maize and the Rise of Chiefdoms* 686
The Mississippian Period Mound Centers and Villages, AD 1000–15th/16th Century 687
  • *Mounds and Burials* 687
  • *Settlement Patterns and Food-procurement Strategies* 688
● **KEY SITE** Craig Mound 688
  • *Increased Tensions among Northern Tribes* 690
● **KEY CONTROVERSY** The Size and Influence of Cahokia 690

The Southwest 692
Preclassic and Classic Hohokam, c. AD 700–1450 692
● **KEY DISCOVERY** Hohokam Ball Courts 693
Pueblo Villages on the Colorado Plateau 695
  • *Agricultural Foundations* 695
● **KEY METHOD** Tree-ring Dating 696
Pueblo I Settlement Patterns, c. AD 750–900 696
Pueblo II: The Chaco Phenomenon, c. AD 900–1150 698
  • *The Chaco Phenomenon* 698

● **KEY CONTROVERSY** Chaco's Population During the Bonito Phase 698
  • *Population and Agriculture* 699
Pueblo III: Regional Population Shifts, c. AD 1150–1300 700
Pueblo IV: Abandonment of the Colorado Plateau, 14th and 15th Centuries AD 700
  • *Pottery Innovations* 702
● **KEY SITE** Pecos Pueblo 702
Population Decline 703

The Plains 703
Village Settlements 704
● **KEY SITE** Crow Creek: Scene of a Massacre 705
Exchange Systems 705

The Pacific Coast 706
Southern California 706
The Pacific Northwest 707
  • *Village Life* 708
  • *Warfare and Population Decline* 708
● **KEY SITE** Ozette 709

The Arctic and Subarctic 710
● **KEY SITE** L'Anse aux Meadows 710
The Dorset and Thule Cultures 711

The Collision of Two Worlds 712

Summary and Conclusions 713
● **KEY CONTROVERSY** Native American Population on the Eve of European Contact 714

Further Reading and Suggested Websites 715

When the first European explorers arrived in North America in the 16th century they entered a territory that was vast and varied both in terms of its landscape and its human societies. In Chapter 9 we covered the development of North American communities in the early Postglacial period, from the demise of the megafauna to the development of a rich diversity of regionally specific societies. By 2000 BC, some of these (notably in the Eastern Woodlands) had domesticated local plant species, though it is unlikely that any of these species alone could have supported entire communities and hunting and gathering remained important. During the centuries that followed, cultivation of more productive maize spread from Mesoamerica into parts of the Southwest and the Mississippi Valley and beyond, eventually reaching the Great Plains.

Further north, in the forests and tundra of Canada and Alaska, hunting and gathering remained the principal way of life. Some of these hunting and gathering communities developed sophisticated social structures; those of the Northwest Coast, for example, famous for their elaborately carved totem poles, were able to live in permanent villages by exploiting a rich combination of marine, riverine, and woodland resources. Further east, in the Eastern Woodlands, incipient agriculturalists known as Adena and Hopewell raised elaborate burial mounds over their dead and practiced elaborate mortuary rituals that involved the bringing of exotic raw materials over astonishing distances.

The introduction of maize agriculture led to demographic growth and the establishment of larger settlements, including Cahokia in the Mississippi Valley, which in the 11th and 12th centuries AD grew to become North America's largest town, with a population of perhaps 3000 or more people. The remains of the temple and burial mounds raised by these late prehistoric societies puzzled early European explorers. They attributed them to the mysterious "Moundbuilders" and did not at first recognize them as the work of the local indigenous populations. Further west, impressive remains of the late prehistoric period survive in the Pueblo ruins of the Colorado Plateau and in the cluster of sites in Chaco Canyon, New Mexico, possibly the center of a major regional cult. At the far edge of the continent, in Arctic North America, this same period (11th–12th centuries AD) saw the expansion of the Thule communities, skillful hunters of sea mammals, who were able to survive even the worsening climatic conditions of the Little Ice Age.

In this chapter we shall follow these developments region by region, beginning with the Eastern Woodlands, and the increasing elaboration of societies from the Adena and Hopewell to the chiefdoms of the Mississippian period. In the following section our attention turns to the Southwest, and the Hohokam and Pueblo developments of the arid zone that culminated in the so-called Chaco Phenomenon of the 11th to 13th centuries AD. The final part of the chapter deals with the north and the west: the hunter-gatherers and first farmers of the Great Plains; the rise of chiefdoms on the Pacific coast from California to British Columbia; and the specialized adaptations of the Arctic zone. Though none of these societies reached the level of organization seen in the cities and states of Mesoamerica (Chapter 16) and Andean South America (Chapter 17), a number of them merit the description of "complex." We can only speculate what the future might have held had these indigenous developments not been disrupted by the fateful impact of European contact.

When Europeans first established a permanent toehold on the North American continent in the 16th century, they found a remarkably diverse array of societies. Many Native Americans were living in settled communities numbering from a few hundred to a thousand or more people, living on what they could grow; this included plants that had originated in Mesoamerica, most importantly maize. Other groups hunted, fished, and foraged for whatever grew nearby, and some natural settings were so well endowed that they supported hunter-gatherer societies every bit as large and complex as those based on agriculture. Most of these non-agricultural societies, however, occupied regions where the distribution and reliability of wild foods was uncertain, and lived in small, mobile groups.

The people who occupied what are now the United States, Canada, and Greenland adapted successfully to a wide range of environmental settings, from the subtropics to the Arctic [18.1].

Some of the most productive areas were coastlines and river valleys, especially where there were large wetlands. Thick forests covered the eastern United States and southeast Canada (Eastern Woodlands), gradually giving way to the vast grasslands of the rolling plains west of the Mississippi River. The high Rocky Mountains form the western spine of the continent, beyond which lies the Pacific Coast, with its dense, wet forests stretching from northern California into southeastern Alaska. The southwest corner of the Unites States is a desert, although one with agricultural potential in places. Far to the north, much of Canada is covered by boreal forest, an area of relatively low productivity for prehistoric people, beyond which is tundra that extends to the Arctic Ocean and the icy wastes of Greenland.

North America is commonly divided into several overlapping cultural and environmental areas, among them the Eastern Woodlands, the Plains, the Southwest, California, the

NORTH AMERICA TIMELINE

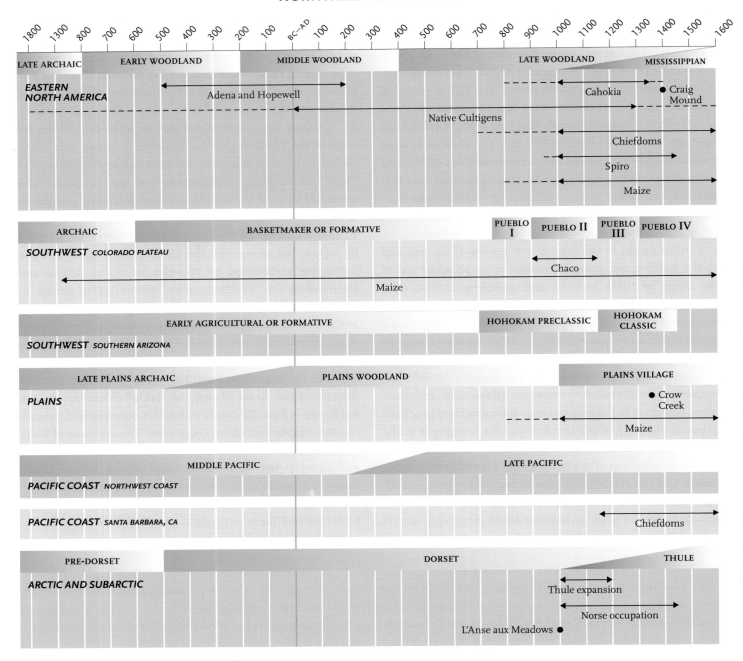

Northwest Coast, and the Arctic. Within these broadly defined areas there was considerable regional and local variation in the resources needed for survival, differences that had a profound effect on the distribution and density of human populations, as well as the diversity of their cultures.

The areas discussed in this chapter, while not covering the full range of North American societies, illustrate the great variation in how people lived. The largest and most organizationally complex societies developed in the Eastern Woodlands. The distinctive Southwestern pueblos, especially the cliff dwellings, are perhaps the most widely recognized evidence of prehistoric

life in the continent. The hunters of the far north are of particular interest because of their sophisticated adaptation to a frigid environment. They were the first to meet Europeans – small groups of Norse who sailed to North America 1000 years ago. Over 500 more years would pass before the other native peoples of the continent would find they were not alone in the world, in an encounter that would leave them reeling from devastating population loss, cultural disintegration, and forced migration.

In this chapter, the most organizationally complex societies in their respective culture areas are emphasized, those commonly referred to as tribes or chiefdoms (except the northern hunters). (For formal definitions of these and other social categories see Chapter 1.) These societies often left readily apparent evidence of their existence, including earth mounds, adobe and stone architecture, and finely crafted artifacts. Exactly what took place during the emergence of these societies, and why it did so, are matters of lively debate. What is clear is that the historic successors to these societies had roots that extended far into prehistory.

The Eastern Woodlands

Several important changes in how people lived can be dated to the 1st millennium BC, during the Early Woodland period (c. 800–200 BC). One sign of new social relationships is the appearance of numerous conical mounds in the middle Ohio Valley, referred to as Adena, a term applied to Early to Middle Woodland-period cultures in that area. By the Middle Woodland period (c. 200 BC–AD 400), mounds had become an important feature of a rich ceremonial life that included elaborate burials, graveside rituals, and aesthetically pleasing artifacts fashioned from rare materials. These mounds were not the earliest ones to be built – some are several thousand years older, such as those at Watson Brake in Louisiana (see Watson Brake and Poverty Point box, Chapter 9, p. 328) – but they were the first to appear in large numbers from the Great Lakes southward through the Southeast.

18.1 *North America: map showing sites mentioned in the text.*

18.2 *(Right) Grave Creek, West Virginia:* this postcard shows it as it appeared about a century ago. It is one of the largest Adena mounds.

18.3 *(Below) The Mount Horeb earthwork, Kentucky:* the earthwork consisted of an embankment, ditch, and wooden wall marked by a line of postmolds (stains in the soil where posts once stood).

Adena and Hopewell: The Early and Middle Woodland Period, c. 800 BC–AD 400

Mounds and Earthworks Mounds were rarely more than a few meters high (although there are exceptions, such as the 19-m (62-ft) Adena mound in West Virginia, known as **Grave Creek** [**18.2**]). Adena mounds were often built in ritually significant places, associated with earlier wooden structures or enclosures. Graves, including log-lined tombs for one or more people, were added to growing heaps of earth and periodically covered with caps of soil laid down to renew cemetery surfaces (Milner and Jefferies 1987). Most of these Adena mounds are poorly dated, although it is clear that some were still being used as late as Middle Woodland times in Kentucky and elsewhere.

Mounds became more common after Early Woodland times. Conical Middle Woodland mounds in Illinois often contained centrally located log-lined tombs for a few important people, accompanied by rare objects (Brown 1979; Buikstra 1976); surrounding these central tombs were simple graves with comparatively plain burial offerings. Some Middle Woodland, or Hopewell, mounds in Ohio covered wooden structures

containing, in places, the remains of over 100 people, along with many artifacts (Brown 1979; Greber 1983; Greber and Ruhl 1989; Konigsberg 1985). Rituals that extended beyond those directly connected to the disposal of bodies involved destroying artifacts by means of fire or burial. Interment in an Illinois log tomb or Ohio mortuary structure was probably as important for reaffirming group identity as it was a means of commemorating a person's life and disposing of a corpse. The demand on labor needed to build the often impressive mounds would have been well within the capacity of even small communities whose members only infrequently moved earth and chopped down trees for ceremonial structures and log-lined tombs.

In addition to mounds, numerous other types of earthworks were distributed from central Ohio southward into central Kentucky; a few were also built elsewhere. They form circles, squares, and other shapes, as well as irregular hilltop enclosures. Small circles typically enclosed no more than about 1 ha (2.5 acres) of ground, and either mounds or walls of vertical posts were sometimes located within them, as at **Mount Horeb** [**18.3**] in Kentucky (Webb 1941). Larger geometric earthworks of various shapes often covered a few tens of acres (although some were bigger), and several might be joined together. Enclosures of earth and stone partially or completely ringed hilltops, such as the enormous **Fort Ancient** earthwork in Ohio, which enclosed about 51 ha (125 acres) (Essenpreis and Moseley 1984). The Middle Woodland enclosures occasionally had wooden walls that enhanced the visual effect of earthen embankments (Riordan 1998). Openings in these walls were often partly obstructed by small mounds. At Fort Ancient, there were stone circles, ponds, and specially constructed walkways in addition to mounds, forcing people to pass through gaps in the walls that were blocked by symbolically significant obstacles and crossed by paths (Connolly 1998). Little is known about what actually

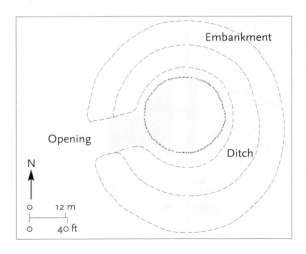

Embankment

Opening

Ditch

N

0 — 12 m
0 — 40 ft

took place within the enclosures, other than the burial of the dead, although several large wooden structures containing non-local materials, including mica, have been found at **Seip** in Ohio (Smith 1992).

Exchange Systems and Cultural Ties Adena and Middle Woodland societies are known for the many finely crafted artifacts that come from mounds and, to a lesser extent, from village sites, indicating a broadening and deepening of contacts among widely separated groups. Materials exchanged during this time include copper from the Great Lakes, mica from the southern Appalachians, colorful chert and pipestone from the Midwest, and marine shells, including whelks, from the south Atlantic and Gulf coasts (Griffin 1967). Most remarkable of all is obsidian from Yellowstone in Wyoming; the straight-line distance between the source and the **Hopewell** site, where most of the obsidian east of the Mississippi River has been found, is about 2300 km (1430 miles) [see box: Hopewell, p. 685].

Many more Middle Woodland objects made from non-local materials have been found in Ohio than elsewhere, for reasons unknown. Most of these items have been found in mounds, and were presumably passed from one individual to the next, probably during ceremonies requiring conspicuous displays of wealth or generosity. But the markedly uneven distribution of rare artifacts and non-local materials, most notably the great obsidian hoards at Hopewell, also raises the possibility that people occasionally traveled long distances to procure unusual, highly prized, and symbolically important objects (Griffin 1967). That this was a time of low inter-group hostilities is indicated by relatively few skeletons with purposeful injuries

(Milner 1999). Little serious conflict is consistent with social boundaries that were permeable enough to allow a few people to travel unscathed across long distances with valuable objects.

Local leaders must have played a critical role in maintaining contacts among neighboring communities, such as those at **Tunacunnhee** in northwest Georgia, who lived along a natural route through rugged country (Jefferies 1976). Perhaps kin groups participated in competitive displays to enhance their local reputations. Such events would account for the effort required to build mounds, construct elaborate mortuary facilities, and collect the materials, including fine objects, consumed in the ceremonies.

Key community members were singled out for special burial treatment with the finest objects, and the most important mortuary facilities in Early and Middle Woodland mounds in Kentucky, Illinois, and Ohio contained burials of both sexes and all ages (Buikstra 1976; Konigsberg 1985; Milner and Jefferies 1987). The range of people buried indicates that social group affiliation was an important consideration in securing access to elaborate mortuary areas. Some of the dead apparently took part in special rituals during life, in which they wore ceremonial paraphernalia that occasionally included masks, represented archaeologically by cut carnivore maxillae (jaw bones) (Milner 2004; Webb and Baby 1957). A small figurine from **Newark** in Ohio shows one such individual, a person partly covered with a robe made of a bear hide complete with head (Dragoo and Wray 1964) [**18.4, 18.5**]. Ersatz objects took the place of real ones when necessary, including mica-covered clay beads mixed with pearl beads, and points made from polished coal instead of rare obsidian (Mills 1907; Seeman 1995).

18.4, 18.5 *Newark earthworks, Ohio:* *(above) this stone figurine depicts a man, perhaps a shaman, covered by a bear robe (16 cm/6.3 in long). (Right) This circle and octagon are part of the Newark earthworks; mounds are located just inside the octagon's corners.*

Distinctive ways of decorating pottery used in special contexts, such as funerals, were widely shared during Middle Woodland times. Thus, there is archaeological evidence for a thin veneer of common beliefs and customs spread across many different societies with otherwise distinctive ways of life, pottery, and tools.

The Beginning of Food-producing Economies More is known about mounds than ordinary settlements, which tended to be small during this period (Milner 2004; Smith 1986; 1992). Most people lived in relative isolation in dispersed communities that consisted of houses scattered along the banks of lakes and creeks or other favorable spots (e.g. scattered near the big Ohio earthworks). Short-term camps for hunting, fishing, or collecting wild plants have also been detected archaeologically. The overall picture is one of a patchy distribution of people across even the best land during the Early and Middle Woodland.

One of the most important changes to take place in the mid-continent about 2000 years ago was a dramatic increase in the dietary significance of native cultigens (Smith 1989). The cultivation of plants such as goosefoot (or chenopod), maygrass, erect knotweed, marsh elder, sunflower, and squash boosted productivity near settlements, most notably through the addition of a readily storable harvest of nutritious seeds. By this time, the move toward a more settled existence, and diets based partly on native cultigens, had already spanned several thousand years, as described in Chapter 9. Yet when viewed in terms of consumption, the shift to a greater reliance on cultivated plants was more abrupt than gradual (Milner 2004). ("Abrupt" change refers to archaeological time; within any particular area it probably spanned several human lifetimes.) A point was at last reached at which far-reaching changes in the way people lived, including changes in social organization, mobility, and technology, were needed for further increases in reliable yields. While the appearance in the mid-continent of abundant carbonized seeds of several cultivated plants marks the beginning of food-producing economies, in peripheral areas another thousand years would pass before people switched from wild plants to cultivated ones, in this instance largely maize from Mesoamerica.

This change in diet occurred during a lengthy period of population expansion, although the general trend must mask shorter intervals of increase, stasis, and decline, along with considerable interregional variability in occupational histories. The numbers of sites, a crude reflection of numbers of people, indicate a growth rate exceeding that of most of the Archaic period (Milner 2004). This slow but eventually significant growth – an increase of about 0.06 percent annually, according to data from eight states – began in the Late Archaic, around the time when a few domesticated native plants first appeared, and it would continue through the rest of prehistory.

The appearance of pottery across much of eastern North America is a convenient marker for the Early Woodland period. Pottery began to be made by many Midwestern and Northeastern groups at the beginning of the 1st millennium BC, earlier in some places than in others, and surely related to changes in cooking and storing food. In the Southeast, pottery had been around for about two millennia in a few areas, but here too it became much more common and broadly distributed during Early Woodland times. New food-procurement practices must also have played a part in the ostentatious ceremonies, exchange of extraordinary objects, and harmonious relations that characterize the Adena and Hopewell societies. A heavier reliance on cultivated plants resulted in greater and more reliable food surpluses, which could have been deployed in ceremonies orchestrated by influential members of society. A cushion to blunt the effects of shortfalls in wild foods lessened uncertainty about the future and reduced the need to expand into land claimed by neighboring groups. The relaxation of inter-group tensions – which were higher among earlier, relatively sedentary, Archaic hunter-gatherers – would by Middle Woodland times have facilitated occasional trips across long distances with precious artifacts, as already noted.

Settlement Patterns in the Late Woodland Period, c. AD 400–1000

By the beginning of the Late Woodland period in the Midwest and Southeast (*c.* AD 400), the construction of elaborate burial mounds and exchanges of non-local objects had virtually ceased in most places. The overall population, however, continued to grow, as indicated by greater numbers of sites. By this time, sites in the Midwest and Southeast were often located along the upper reaches of tributary streams, in addition to the major rivers (Milner 2004; Smith 1986). Movement from mid-continental river valleys was facilitated by the cultivation of native plants, which increased the productivity and reliability of less desirable land, so that people were not as tightly tethered as they had been to the richest settings.

Settlements consisted of isolated buildings or small groups of structures. Large-scale excavations near East St. Louis in Illinois, particularly at the **Range** site, have uncovered a number of communities consisting of structures arrayed around open areas that often contained a post, several big pits, or a spacious building (Kelly 1990). This arrangement – houses encircling public spaces that contained special features – anticipates the layout of later Mississippian mound centers (see below). Most villages were inhabited for only several years by no more than a few dozen people, although dark middens indicate some lengthier occupations. By this time, dense forests in long-occupied places had been transformed into vegetation mosaics consisting of actively cultivated gardens, patches of shrubby

KEY SITE Hopewell

Some of the most extraordinary artifacts ever found in eastern North America were uncovered at the Middle Woodland Hopewell mound site in Ohio (Greber and Ruhl 1989; Shetrone 1926). Many of them were discovered while digging for artifacts to display at the 1893 World's Columbian Exposition in Chicago.

The site consists of a square embankment adjacent to a much larger and roughly rectangular enclosure that encompassed more than 40 ha (100 acres), along with over 40 mounds. Within this larger enclosure were two additional embankments, one of which surrounded the largest mound at the site, Mound 25. This mound was about 6.4 m (21 ft) high, with a base measuring as much as 58 x 168 m (189 x 550 ft).

Many remarkable artifacts, often buried together in single deposits, were discovered at Hopewell. Among the objects from Mound 25 were more than 100 obsidian bifaces and a cache of copper artifacts, including axes and breastplates. The obsidian points were

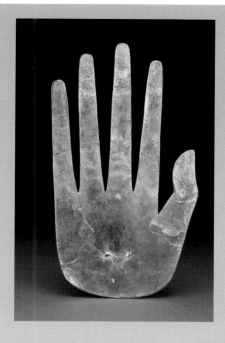

intended for display; many of them were so large – 30 cm (12 in) or more in length – that they could have had no practical use, and they were often curiously shaped. Other impressive hoards from the site's mounds included 136 kg (300 pounds) of obsidian

debris, several thousand sheets of mica, and over 8000 oval chert bifaces. The biface deposit consisted of small groups of artifacts, each covered with a little soil, seemingly having been laid down in separate bundles.

Although it is unclear exactly what the deposits signify, the symbolically potent objects were certainly used in various rituals, not all of which were directly associated with the burial of the dead.

18.6 *(Above left) This hand was one of a number of mica cut-outs that have been found at Hopewell (29 cm/11.4 in long). Mica is only one of the nonlocal materials found at this site.*

18.7 *(Above right) Many points made of Yellowstone obsidian were found in one of the Hopewell mounds. These particular specimens are large, the larger one shown here measures 24 cm (9.5 in), and well made.*

18.8 *(Left) Over a century ago, during excavations for the World's Columbian Exposition, a large cache of copper artifacts was found in one of the Hopewell mounds.*

growth, and mature stands of trees. Many edible plants and animals thrived in the overgrown clearings, and saplings filled a need for straight house poles.

Villages tended to be of similar size, although that situation began to change a few centuries before AD 1000, especially along the central and lower Mississippi River and its principal tributaries. Here, locally dominant centers with mounds developed, surrounded by smaller villages and isolated houses (Kidder 1998; Milner 1998; Rolingson 1998). The presence of mound centers and distinctions among sites in terms of size and internal layouts are thought to mark the emergence of chiefdoms. Of particular importance are platform mounds at lower Mississippi Valley sites collectively referred to as **Coles Creek**, such as Lake George in Mississippi (Williams and Brain 1983). The Mississippi Valley, however, was not the only place where mound centers appeared. The single most impressive site is **Toltec**, in the heart of Arkansas (Rolingson 1998) [18.9]. Here, 18 mounds, two plazas, and habitation areas were spread across 42 ha (104 acres). They were enclosed on one side by an abandoned river channel and on the others by a curved embankment and ditch. The two largest mounds, despite years of erosion, are still 15 m (49 ft) and 11.5 m (37.5 ft) high. They tower over the others, among which are rectangular platforms used in feasts that involved the consumption of numerous white-tailed deer, presumably organized by leading figures in this society.

Warfare, Maize, and the Rise of Chiefdoms A decline in the exchange of non-local materials is an indication of worsening inter-group relations following the Middle Woodland florescence, but it is not the only sign. Small arrowheads first appear

18.9 *Toltec in central Arkansas: with its mounds and plazas, this is one of the most impressive sites of the late 1st millennium AD.*

in large numbers during Late Woodland times, and whatever their value for hunting, bows and arrows were also weapons. People were dying as a result of fighting between communities (Milner 1999), and increased tensions eventually contributed to the formation of politically and militarily formidable groups, a process that was underway in some parts of the Midwest and Southeast by the end of the 1st millennium AD.

Somewhere between AD 800 and 1100 – the precise timing varied from place to place – maize became an essential part of diets throughout much of the Eastern Woodlands, as outlined in Chapter 9 (Fritz 1990; Milner 2004; Smith 1986; 1989). Charred maize is commonly found in excavations at village sites, and the stable carbon isotope signatures of human bones also indicate a change in diet. (For an explanation of this method of determining ancient dietary habits, see Chapter 2.) Within any particular region, the shift to a heavy reliance on maize took place over only a few centuries, even a few generations. This rapid shift was probably related to greater local population densities, hence pressure on resources, following the appearance of clusters of villages that were separated by stretches of infrequently used and perhaps bitterly contested land. The choice of this crop over native cultigens increased household efficiency and flexibility at harvest time, precisely when scheduling concerns were greatest.

Changes in economy, population, and inter-group relations were associated in poorly understood ways with the emergence of chiefdoms, which became widespread after AD 1000. Patchy distribution of the most productive land gave leaders of strong lineages in especially favorable locations an opportunity to expand their influence. During hard times, desperate people inevitably became indebted to situationally advantaged leaders, who were thus able to recruit and retain the most supporters. Dispersal from population pockets was limited not so much by the natural landscape, although fertile river bottoms were far better places to live than forested uplands, but by tense inter-group relations that made movement elsewhere a hazardous undertaking.

Chiefdoms – societies with permanent leadership positions firmly embedded in kinship relations – had become increasingly common across much of the Southeast and Midwest by the 11th century AD, the beginning of the Mississippian period. A northward expansion of these societies as far as southern Wisconsin coincided with the Medieval Warm Period of *c.* AD 1000–1300, when conditions were also more favorable for agriculture in Europe.

The Mississippian Period: Mound Centers and Villages, AD 1000–15th/16th Century

Most of the chiefdoms are considered part of the Mississippian culture (from AD 1000 to the 15th century in the Midwest, and to the 16th century in the Southeast) on the basis of distinctive artifacts and architecture. Mounds were critical elements of principal settlements. Most were rather small, but some were truly massive piles of earth; even these, however, could have been built by the local population. The largest mound of all, **Monks Mound** at **Cahokia** in Illinois, which is 30.5 m (100 ft) tall and covers 5.6 ha (13.8 acres) (Fowler 1997), greatly exceeds any other mound in the Eastern Woodlands [see **18.15**]. It contains as much earth as the more than 100 other mounds at Cahokia put together.

Mounds and Burials Many mounds were rectangular, flat-topped platforms intended to support wooden buildings [**18.12**], including houses of chiefs and their families, community buildings such as council houses, and charnel structures for the bones of important ancestors. These elevated buildings, often more spacious than structures elsewhere on these sites or in the surrounding villages, would have been effective reminders of the high social standing of the people associated with them. They were prominently placed, typically fronting plazas used for community-related events. Mississippian mounds were usually raised in a series of stages: the wooden buildings on them were destroyed, more soil was laid down, and new structures were erected. Adding earth to an existing mound yielded a more impressive platform than had existed before. More importantly, it maintained a tangible connection with the past that legitimized the positions of the living. Continuity at a socially or ritually significant spot sometimes stretched back to

a time before mound building commenced. At **Lubbub Creek** in Alabama, the orientation of a mound conformed to that of a series of rectangular structures and an enclosing fence that once stood on the original ground surface (Blitz 1993).

Charnel houses, bone deposits, and other burials are often found within the mounds. Objects fashioned from precious materials, including marine shell and copper, were buried with the dead; indeed, the finest objects available tended to end up in mounds, including those referred to collectively as belonging to the **Southern Cult** or **Southeastern Ceremonial complex**, which are particularly common in the 13th–14th centuries AD (Brown 1985; 1996; Knight et al. 2001). Artifacts of such rare materials as seashell and naturally occurring copper, including hammered copper plates, were often decorated with cosmic imagery and symbolic motifs such as weeping eyes, bird designs, and crosses within circles. While there was stylistic variation according to their place of origin, these artifacts are thought to indicate widely, but variably, shared beliefs. They probably did not hold precisely the same meanings in all places, but they were commonly used as a means of distancing important people from the rest. They highlighted the roles of leaders, reinforced the naturalness of the existing social order, and depicted supernatural beings. A few themes received disproportionate attention, particularly ancestors and war: human figurines of wood and stone have been found in mortuary contexts, as have whelk shells and copper plates decorated with warrior and bird-of-prey composites, some of whom clutch maces and severed heads. Occasionally, human sacrifice was involved in the burial rituals of highly ranked people, a practice that continued to historic times (Fowler et al. 1999).

Although some mounds held as many as 100 or more individuals, burial in mounds was enjoyed by only a small fraction of the local Mississippian population (Brown 1996; Fowler et al. 1999; Milner 1998). People of all ages and both sexes were interred, although adults are more frequently represented than juveniles. So while the significance of social group affiliation was reinforced by communal burial, access to these burial areas was for the most part restricted to people who had reached adulthood. The most obvious example of a connection to ancestors comes from the **Craig Mound** at **Spiro**, in Oklahoma (Brown 1996). Here old bones and artifacts assembled from earlier deposits are tangible evidence for an ancestry that might have been more fiction than fact [see box: Craig Mound, p. 688].

The mounds occupied prominent positions in major sites, but easy access was occasionally prevented by rows of posts around their bases or summits (Milner 2004). A charnel house built by the early historic Taënsa of the lower Mississippi Valley, for example, was surrounded by poles surmounted with skulls (Swanton 1911) – a clear warning that this sacred place should only be approached by the proper people on appropriate occasions.

Settlement Patterns and Food-procurement Strategies Mississippian settlements ranged from isolated farmsteads to villages and mound centers. Most of the principal sites had no more than a few mounds, often only one. These mounds, along with their associated wooden buildings for important people and special purposes, ringed a central plaza. In the historic period, various ceremonies were held in these centrally located open areas, and the same was probably true of prehistoric times. The plazas, while swept clean, were not necessarily empty. Mounds were located within them at **Moundville** in Alabama and at **Cahokia** in Illinois, and the remains of an enormous post were found in excavations at **Mitchell** in Illinois [**18.13**] (Fowler 1997; Knight 1998; Milner 1998). Ordinary people lived in houses that surrounded the plazas and accompanying mounds. Palisades were often built to protect villages; many of them were studded with bastions spaced within overlapping bow fire (Milner 1999). Local topography, along with the position and orientation of earlier architecture, influenced the overall layouts of major centers, though the use of space could change over time. A few hundred to several thousand people occupied the mound centers, although they rarely approached the upper end of the size range (Milner 1998; Muller 1997; Steponaitis 1998) [see box: The Size and Influence of Cahokia, pp. 690–91].

Mound centers were surrounded by innumerable smaller settlements, which were typically occupied for much shorter periods of time (Milner 2004; Kidder 1998; Muller 1997; Smith 1986). The specific configurations and locations of these settlements balanced the distribution of critical resources with labor demands and defensive requirements. Houses were often arranged in a regular fashion, around small plazas for example, to produce compact communities of several dozen or more dwellings. Widely scattered single-family houses were the norm elsewhere. In the Cahokia area, scattered dwellings were

KEY SITE Craig Mound

Looters tunneled into the Craig Mound at Spiro in eastern Oklahoma in the 1930s, nearly destroying one of the most extraordinary mortuary deposits in the United States (Brown 1996). They encountered a hollow chamber (the Great Mortuary) and expanded it, exposing a great number of human bones and artifacts. The objects found include those made of wood and basketry, which normally do not survive prolonged burial. Fortunately, the looters were stopped before completing their work, and subsequent controlled excavations clarified what was found.

The Great Mortuary, dating to *c.* AD 1400, was not the only burial feature in the Craig Mound, but because of its impressive collection of grave goods, it has received the most attention. It consisted of an 11 x 17-m (37 x 55-ft) floor on an earthen platform. Resting on this surface were broken artifacts and disarticulated bones, along with rows of baskets and cedar litters that held still more bones and artifacts. These remains and the objects with them apparently were removed from other locations before being buried here. Intact bodies were also laid out, probably primary interments. The artifacts found

18.10, 18.11 *(Above left) Several red cedar figurines were found in the Craig Mound at Spiro, Oklahoma. (Above right) Red cedar masks were also found in the Craig Mound. This one, with carved deer antlers and ear spools, had shell inserts accentuating the eyes and mouth.*

alongside the bones included engraved marine shell cups, tens of thousands of shell beads, and carved wooden figurines and masks.

Once the Great Mortuary was sealed with soil, its position was marked by cedar poles that were subsequently buried as the mound was enlarged. In this manner a visible connection with the buried deposit was maintained for long afterwards.

18.12 *(Left)* **Reconstructed building:** *this building reconstructed on a mound at Town Creek, North Carolina, shows what these mounds might have looked like in Mississippian times.*

18.13 *(Below)* **Mitchell, Illinois:** *during the early 1960s highway excavations at Mitchell, Illinois, the bottom end of a large bald cypress post was discovered. It had broken when an attempt was made to remove it many hundreds of years ago.*

part of dispersed communities that encompassed small groups of buildings, including residences and special structures of social or ritual significance, such as sweat lodges. These buildings, in which people gathered around specially built fires, were presumably used for personal rituals, much like in historic times, with the largest also serving as meeting places that fostered community cohesion through shared experience.

Mississippian chiefdoms were scattered along major stream valleys where wild foods and fertile soils were plentiful. Pockets of population extended for as little as 10 to over 100 km (6–60 miles) (Hally 1993; Milner 1998). Most of these settlement concentrations were toward the low end of the population range, with the largest situated in especially rich locations, such as the Mississippi Valley. Better survey coverage and chronological controls since the 1980s have shown that the geographical locations of these population and political centers changed over time (Anderson 1994; Hally and Rudolph 1986). Mound centers might be eclipsed by their neighbors, with periods of ascendancy lasting several generations up to a few centuries. Volatile socio-political and demographic landscapes were a result of factional competition within chiefdoms and outright warfare between neighboring societies.

While most Mississippian people cultivated plants, including maize, they also depended heavily on naturally occurring foods, particularly those from the wetlands of major river floodplains (Milner 1998; Smith 1986). In addition to maize, food plants included native cultigens such as squash, as well as the common bean, which was introduced to the Eastern Woodlands several centuries after maize-based agricultural practices were already in place (Chapter 9). In the most densely settled places, hunting pressure depleted local game, most importantly deer.

A mix of wild and cultivated foods gave subsistence strategies a certain resilience, but people still suffered from the effects of droughts and floods, even where fertile soils and productive wetlands were abundant. Nevertheless, individual households were self-sufficient in all but the worst of times.

Maize was central to many diets, but it was not grown everywhere (Fritz 1990; Kidder 1998; Marquardt 2001). Maize was not adopted in the lower Mississippi Valley until well after chiefdoms were established, and little of it was eaten in much of

peninsular Florida. The Calusa of southern Florida exemplify a society living in an area where wetland and near-shore resources were abundant, dependable, and concentrated, characteristics that mimicked those of agricultural fields elsewhere. Thus, agriculture was not a necessary prerequisite for the emergence of chiefdoms in the Southeast.

Increased Tensions among Northern Tribes During the last several hundred years of prehistory, agriculturist tribal societies were distributed in a broad band from the Midwest, through the Great Lakes, to the Atlantic Coast. Northern villages were often clustered together, sharing economic interests and social institutions, and populations moved from one place to another over time. Palisades, larger villages, and a shift to more defensible locations point to increasing conflicts in the centuries following AD 1000. A greater number and a broader distribution of palisaded settlements are evidence that skirmishes became more severe and widespread as climatic conditions deteriorated;

KEY CONTROVERSY The Size and Influence of Cahokia

A direct connection is commonly drawn between large mounds, huge populations, and great societies characterized by considerable political centralization and coercive power. That line of reasoning is nowhere more evident than at Cahokia, which, with over 100 mounds, including massive Monks Mound, is by far the largest and most impressive prehistoric site in the Eastern Woodlands. While a direct link between mounds and population/society has been assumed since the early 19th century, it is no longer tenable.

18.14 *Two large mounds are located at the southern end of a large plaza opposite Monks Mound at Cahokia, Illinois.*

Size and Population
In reference to the size of the mounds, the amount of earth moved at Cahokia was well within the limits of even the lowest population estimates for the site, assuming the work was spread out over the several-century occupation of the area. Different

estimates for Cahokia at its peak of development have been proposed, with the high end of the range, *c.* 40,000 people, being favored in popular descriptions of the site; this total exceeds the population of the largest cities in the United States in 1790 (Gregg 1975; Milner 1998). Estimates in the tens of thousands are based on structural

remains in some of the most heavily used parts of Cahokia, a badly biased sample of the entire site. Divergent views on the longevity of thatch-covered houses constructed of narrow poles also contribute to differences in population estimates. A broader range of excavation areas, along with reasonable estimates of house duration and occupancy,

18.15 *Monks Mound is the largest of the more than 100 mounds at Cahokia. About one half of the earth moved to build mounds at the site was used in the construction of this impressive monument.*

these changes culminated in the Little Ice Age, a period of low temperatures that began around 1400 (Milner 1999). Some groups suffered greatly, such as those at the leading edge of a population expansion into west-central Illinois. A village cemetery here, **Norris Farms #36**, contained victims from multiple ambushes that collectively resulted in the deaths of at least one-third of all adults, both men and women. These people had been shot with arrows, clubbed with axes, and mutilated by the removal of scalps, heads, and limbs.

In such difficult times, separate groups of people found it advantageous to forge alliances to dampen tensions between them and to present a more formidable face to their enemies. The most well-known historic alliance was the **League of the Iroquois**. It seems to have reached its Five Nations form by 1600, although close ties among its constituent groups date a century or more earlier (Kuhn and Sempowski 2001; Snow 1994). The League put the Iroquois in a good position for the turbulent times that followed the early 17th-century European colonization of the Northeast.

indicate that the site was more likely inhabited by several thousand people, roughly a tenth of the maximum estimate, a respectable figure for a chiefdom anywhere in the world.

State or Chiefdom?

The issue of political power is the most difficult to address, because incomplete archaeological data are only indirect measures of social and political organization and strength. (For another look at this problem, this time in South America, see

18.16 *The central part of Cahokia consisted of a plaza flanked by mounds, including Monks Mound (18.15) adjacent to swampy ground and, at the opposite end, two large paired mounds (18.14). A wooden palisade surrounded this area for part of the site's history.*

Amazonian Urbanism? box, Chapter 17, p. 675.) Cahokia has been characterized as a powerful state featuring considerable political centralization and economic specialization, which dominated groups throughout the mid-continent, in part because it needed to feed a huge local population (O'Brien 1989; 1990). Alternatively, it has been argued that it was a chiefdom, albeit an unusually large and strong one, structured along much the same lines as its contemporaries (Milner 1998; Muller 1997). The labor needed to build mounds was well within what a few thousand people could muster, and economic differentiation extended no farther than the occasional production of socially and ritually significant objects, such as precious

ornaments mostly worn by the highest-ranked people. Distinctions between leading figures and the rest of the population were surely present, but there is no evidence for a great gulf separating chiefs and their kin from common people.

The important issue here is not one of putting societies into a particular category, either chiefdom or state. It is, instead, one of determining how Cahokia was organized and arose, and whether this society was structured along lines fundamentally different from those of its smaller contemporaries elsewhere in the Eastern Woodlands. At this point, it is clear that Cahokia was much larger than its contemporaries, but it is not at all clear it was structurally much different from the others.

The Southwest

More than two million people live today in the metropolitan area of Phoenix, Arizona, which sprawls across a vast inland basin of the Sonoran Desert. This modern city flourishes in the desert because huge reservoirs in distant, wetter montane zones feed water to the city through massive aqueducts. A water control technology tapping into distant river systems allows Phoenix to defy local environmental constraints that would otherwise limit population to a tiny fraction of the current level. The prehistoric farmers of the Sonoran Desert also raised the carrying capacity of their environment by managing the flow of water that originated in faraway mountains. Indeed, the name Phoenix was chosen by pioneering Mormon settlers because their earliest farms were irrigated from abandoned canals originally constructed a thousand or more years ago – their community literally rose from the ashes of an older, indigenous agricultural society.

Recent archaeological excavations in southern Arizona indicate that canal irrigation for crop production (primarily maize and cotton) extends back to at least 1000 BC, and perhaps several centuries earlier (Mabry 2003) [**18.17**]. Not long ago, archaeologists thought it unlikely that water management was so ancient, since during this Early Agricultural, or Formative, period, farming was only associated with small family settlements located on river floodplains. These early agricultural sites were at extremely favorable locations for growing maize, and the first farmers in this region occupied these advantageous places repeatedly from one year to the next, though probably only during the growing season (Gregory and Diehl 2002). Investigations in other parts of the Southwest are revealing similar indications of crop irrigation in small settlements, and it is now certain that water-control technology preceded the development of large permanent villages (Damp et al. 2002). In the Sonoran Desert, this precocious technological innovation became the economic foundation for the emergence, after around AD 700, of the Hohokam cultural tradition, characterized by a coherent regional system of iconography, ritual, cremation mortuary programs, trade in exotics, and the creation of public architecture (Bayman 2001; Crown 1990).

Preclassic and Classic Hohokam, c. AD 700–1450

The relationship between irrigation management and the hallmarks of Hohokam society came together during the Preclassic period (c. AD 700–1150). Excavations at the large site of **Snaketown**, on the Gila River southeast of Phoenix, provide some of the best insights into this dynamic cultural interval (Haury 1976). Houses at Snaketown were single-room structures constructed of *jacal* (wattle and daub), with thatch roofs; three or four were arranged around small courtyards or plazas. Researchers tend to see these house groups as the physical remains of corporate descent groups. At Snaketown [**18.18**] and other large Preclassic settlements, these complexes with their courtyards were distributed around large central plazas containing ball courts [**18.19**] – large, oval, unroofed, semi-subterranean structures that suggest some degree of political integration among the resident descent groups [see box: Hohokam Ball Courts]. The Preclassic period apparently witnessed the formation of village social organization, with some settlements having peak populations of 1000–2000 people.

Hydrological conditions in the Gila River valley were favorable during the Preclassic for the development of extensive irrigation systems. The river's flow was perennial in a narrow channel that coursed through a broad floodplain, and regular seasonal flooding deposited fertile silt in fields (Waters and Ravesloot 2001). It would have been easy to divert stream flow into headgates and thence into feeder canals for fields. Large villages such as Snaketown had enough labor to construct and maintain elaborate water-control systems.

Scholars describe the Classic period (c. AD 1150–1450) as one of socio-economic reorganization initiated by the abandonment

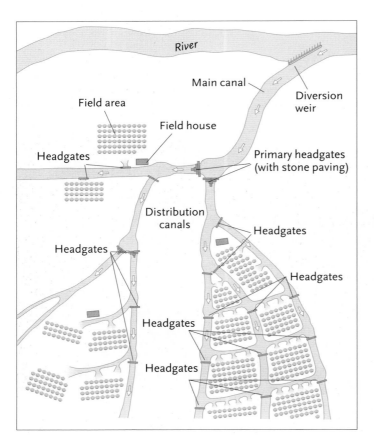

Field area
River
Main canal
Diversion weir
Field house
Headgates
Primary headgates (with stone paving)
Distribution canals
Headgates
Headgates
Headgates
Headgates
Headgates

18.17 Canal irrigation system: *plan of the Hohokam irrigation system which diverted water from the Salt and Gila rivers into a network of canals that provided water to individual fields.*

18.18 Snaketown: *aerial view of excavations at Snaketown during the 1960s. Numerous superimposed houses reflect the long occupation period between* c. AD 200 and 1200.

KEY DISCOVERY Hohokam Ball Courts

Excavations at Snaketown, directed by Emil Haury in 1934–35, uncovered a large, oval, earthen depression with high, banked sides and an unroofed floor. Haury described this structure as a ball court by analogy to similar masonry structures found throughout Mesoamerica, which were associated with a ritual game involving rubber balls [see box The Mesoamerican Ball Game, Chapter 16, p. 599]. Today there are more than 200 documented ball courts at 166 archaeological sites in Arizona; there are none elsewhere in the Southwest United States.

These clearly represent the northernmost expression of a typical form of public architecture in ancient Mexico, and Hohokam ball courts appear to have been very much like earthen ball courts found in the northern Mexican state of Chihuahua. The extent to which these features mimicked the social and ritual contexts of Mesoamerican ball courts is

debated. Some interpretations favor generalized communal events, while others suggest a Southwest version of the Mesoamerican ball game.

The earliest Hohokam ball courts date to about AD 700, and the last versions fell into disuse by AD 1250. Sizes range from about 20 to 85 m in length (65–280 ft), but most were between 30 and 40 m (100–130 ft). The ball

courts are universally interpreted as public architecture with ritual functions, but opinions vary as to the nature of the ritual. Whatever their physical function, most researchers probably agree with David Wilcox's (1991) argument that ball court sites were placed at fixed locations within a region as a way of promoting solidarity among a number of dispersed communities.

18.19 *The ball court at Snaketown was constructed between* AD 700 and 1000. *This unroofed structure measured 63 m (207 ft) in length and 32 m (105 ft) in width.*

of many settlements in peripheral areas and the compression of regional populations into the core portions of the Gila and Salt rivers. Adobe construction techniques became widespread and were used to build large walled enclosures, or compounds. Cremation burial was largely replaced by inhumation, and platform mounds replaced ball courts as the primary expression of public architecture (Bayman 2001; Crown 1990). Compounds containing platform mounds were probably the residences of distinct kin groups ranked hierarchically within larger settlements.

Platform mound settlements in the Phoenix, Tucson, and Tonto basins were organized in linear systems along major canals, often with the largest sites, such as **Las Colinas** and **Casa Grande**, at canal termini. Although there is considerable variability in the size and configuration of individual Hohokam platform mound compounds, the association of multiple compounds with single canal systems suggests discrete political units, or irrigation communities.

There is only limited evidence for aggrandizing leadership within these communities, but it is argued that Classic-period ritual and political events became increasingly centralized at larger villages and inaccessible to the overall Hohokam population, indicating "the concentration and consolidation of formerly disparate and competing sources of societal power" (Fish and Fish 2000, 167).

Some researchers feel that the Hohokam might have achieved a chiefdom level of social complexity during the Classic, perhaps similar to chiefdoms of the Mississippian period in the Eastern Woodlands; specialists in Hohokam archaeology, however, generally prefer to describe Hohokam polities simply as having evidence for social ranking and regional community integration. The common view is that platform compounds and irrigation communities reflect a hierarchical form of organization based on corporate control of land and water.

The Hohokam were skilled in a variety of **crafts**, including the manufacture of elaborately etched shell ornaments [**18.20**], but it does not appear that these were prestige goods in the sense of signifying elevated wealth or political status. Instead, unusual and imported objects, although widely dispersed among settlements, were probably used in ritual activities controlled by religious leaders. Many ritual items were obtained through long-distance exchange: shell from the Pacific Coast, and copper bells and parrots from Mesoamerica. As in the case of Hopewell societies in the eastern United States, rare items from very distant places may have had a prominent role in ceremonial life.

Irrigation agriculture was clearly central to Classic-period economies, but subsistence was based on a diversity of food-production strategies, combined with significant dietary contributions from wild resources. In addition to the core crops of maize, beans, and squash, Hohokam farmers also cultivated agave and made extensive use of such wild plants as mesquite, amaranth, chenopod, saguaro and prickly pear cactus, and tansy mustard. Canal irrigation was supplemented by floodwater farming on alluvial fans and floodplains.

Hohokam dependence on canal irrigation was affected by major changes in the hydrological dynamics of the Gila River at the beginning of the Classic period. Between AD 1020 and 1160 the main channel of the Gila experienced both deepening and widening, presumably in response to lowered water tables, intensified by irregular episodes of extremely large and destructive flooding (Waters and Ravesloot 2001). As a consequence of these two geomorphic processes, Hohokam farmers found it increasingly difficult to divert water from the Gila into canal headgates. The increased complexity of capturing stream flow for irrigation might have favored concentrated populations from which larger communal labor groups could be formed, as well as hierarchical organizational structures for managing large work groups over protracted periods. Irrigation communities emerged, with a platform mound administrative center exerting some degree of political control over integrated networks of villages.

The end of the Classic period, around AD 1450, is marked by the abandonment of most Hohokam settlements and a dramatic decline in the regional population. Explanations for this collapse vary, but most look to systemic problems in agricultural production that may have stemmed from regional changes in climate or the effects of prolonged human impact on local environments, such as salinization of fields. The region was thinly populated by Piman-speaking groups at the time of Spanish contact, although it is unclear whether these were Hohokam descendants.

18.20 Etched shell ornaments: *shells used as ornaments were imported into the Hohokam area from the Gulf of California and etched with naturalist designs. Fired clay figurines are a hallmark of the Hohokam tradition and may have had ritual functions.*

Pueblo Villages on the Colorado Plateau

The Colorado Plateau is a vast region of canyons and tablelands interspersed with rugged mountain ranges, occupying a large portion of the northern Southwest. Aridity is the dominant environmental factor in plateau country, but different elevations create distinctive vegetation zones over relatively short distances. For example, in most parts of the Colorado Plateau it is possible to move upward from grasslands through open woodlands and into heavily forested zones in no more than a few dozen kilometers.

Vertical vegetation zones result in complex spatial and temporal resource patterns, and equally complicated variation in factors affecting food production, especially precipitation and temperature. Higher elevations are wetter, which is good for agriculture, although they are also colder, which is not. Lower, warmer elevations have longer growing seasons but also higher evaporation rates, which hinder plant cultivation. So for prehistoric farmers on the Colorado Plateau and adjacent portions of the northern Southwest, subsistence strategies were predicated on finding the right balance of temperature and moisture. Because of changing climatic regimes, this equilibrium was never constant, resulting in a seemingly continual ebb and flow of human populations across the region.

Agricultural Foundations Maize was introduced to the Colorado Plateau by at least 2000 BC, and perhaps as early as 2500 BC. Although maize and other cultigens that were not indigenous to this area (beans and squash, both derived from Mexico) would eventually become the economic foundation for village life in the northern Southwest, the first two millennia of farming mostly involved family groups cultivating small agricultural plots in systems of frequently changing residential locales. These patterns are typical of long-fallow production systems, in which farmers move to new arable areas as soon as their fields experience diminished productivity. Rather than invest labor or additional resources in intensive production strategies that might offset declining soil fertility, long-fallow farmers simply pack up and move to places where they can continue cultivation at minimal cost. Shifting agriculture implies relatively low population densities, since farmers must find new or open spaces for their fields. Since good agricultural locations are limited in the arid Southwest, even in low-density situations, farmers will tend to reoccupy prime locations after local resources have recovered.

Shifting farming was characteristic of agricultural adaptations on the Colorado Plateau throughout the prehistoric period, although recent archaeological investigations in west-central New Mexico have identified small water-control systems associated with agricultural plots as early as 1000 BC (Damp et al. 2002). This is the only currently known example of small-scale irrigation in the northern Southwest that predates AD 1000, but it probably portends the discovery of more, which would dramatically alter conventional views of agricultural development in this region.

The use of water management tactics by farming populations organized in small, dispersed, and residentially fluid groups indicates that agricultural strategies were more complex than simple long fallowing. Rather than employing one type of production system, farmers altered their strategies to suit local ecological and demographic conditions. In fact, the archaeological record of agricultural development in the Southwest reveals enough temporal and spatial variability to support the idea that switching back and forth between farming and foraging was a likely economic option for many groups (Madsen and Simms 1998; Upham 1994).

For at least 2000 years the first farmers on the Colorado Plateau were organized in small, highly mobile kin groups that seldom formed settlements of more than a few families. During this long period prior to the adoption of pottery, the farming population appears to have been much like historically documented band societies, which are characterized by loosely integrated and fluid residential groups geared toward rapid economic adjustments to environmental variability (see Chapter 1, p. 32). When pottery became widespread in the northern Southwest between AD 100 and 400, economically autonomous households emerged as the fundamental unit of production (Wills 2001).

Households are corporate residential groups that cooperate in basic economic activities and retain control over land, surplus, and other resources by restricting sharing to household members. Intensive farming systems are typically structured around household production strategies because the ability to control labor and surplus provides households with incentives to work harder or invest more in production activities. The archaeological markers of household development shortly after the adoption of pottery include a dramatic increase in the size of domestic structures (pithouses), suggesting multiple family residential units; a shift to storage features located inside dwellings rather than outside in public areas; and technological innovations in food processing that reflect intensification, such as larger milling stones and ceramic manufacture. Heavy dietary dependence on maize had already occurred in the preceramic period, meaning that the emergence of household organization was probably linked to regional demographic and social factors promoting competition, rather than simply greater reliance on domesticated plants.

Archaeologists have traditionally referred to prehistoric farming settlements in the southern Colorado Plateau postdating the beginning of pottery manufacture as the "Anasazi" or "Ancestral Pueblo" cultural tradition, in recognition of

KEY METHOD Tree-ring Dating

Tree-ring dating, or dendrochronology, is based on the counting of growth rings in trees. In the American Southwest, coniferous species such as Ponderosa and Pinyon pine, and Douglas fir, are commonly used in dating because their physiological traits produce growth patterns that are tightly controlled by a few critical variables, such as moisture and temperature. These species grow for just part of the year, producing an annual growth ring that reflects any variability in environmental conditions experienced by the tree. Narrow rings tend to indicate poor growing conditions, and broader rings more favorable ones. Thus, individual rings provide an environmental history for the lifespan of the tree, especially with respect to climate.

Tree-ring dates can be extraordinarily precise; dendrochronologists are sometimes able to establish the calendar year a tree died and occasionally even the season of a specific year. The year a tree died or was felled, however, may not be the same date as the cultural event with which it is associated. Wood was a precious commodity in the arid Southwest, and ancient people often reused construction timber when building houses. So a tree-ring date might be considerably older than the structure in which it was discovered. Careful consideration of the wood's context is necessary to determine whether a tree-ring date is reliably associated with a particular construction episode. Multiple specimens of the same age found together provide a stronger chronological marker than single dated pieces of wood.

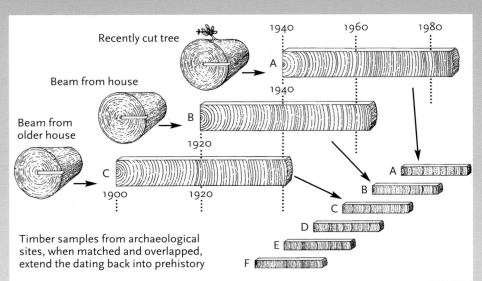

Timber samples from archaeological sites, when matched and overlapped, extend the dating back into prehistory

All tree-ring analysis in the Southwest is conducted by specialists at the University of Arizona in Tucson, who create sequences, or chronologies, by matching tree-ring growth patterns from living trees to ring patterns from dead trees. For example, a core sample taken from a living tree might extend back a hundred or more years, providing a record of growth marked by a series of rings varying in width according to annual amounts of moisture. Using wooden beams made from trees that were felled while the cored tree was growing (found, for example, in old buildings), dendrochronologists search for any overlap in the ring records, which will be marked by a sequence of similar ring widths. Overlapping rings allow the linking together of pieces of wood in a chain of increasingly

18.21 *Tree-ring chronologies provide the primary dating method for archaeological sites in the northern Southwest that are less than 2000 years old. Prehistoric settlements were usually located near sources of timber.*

older specimens, producing a composite, or master, tree-ring chronology for a particular species. Since trees growing in different localities may experience very different moisture regimes over time, reflected in varying ring widths, researchers must create chronologies from trees of the same species that grew in approximately the same place.

similarities in material culture to modern Pueblo people in the Southwest. However, a dramatic increase in field research during the past two decades associated with Cultural Resource Management has revealed many examples of prehistoric farming settlements in the Colorado Plateau and adjacent regions that do not fit easily into Pueblo patterns (e.g. Madsen and Simms 1998). Archaeologists still use the term "Ancestral Pueblo," but they do not attribute all agricultural sites to this tradition.

Pueblo I Settlement Patterns, c. AD *750–900*

Settlement patterns during the Pueblo I period (c. AD 750–900) consisted mostly of dispersed households, but in some parts of the Colorado Plateau, especially along the San Juan River in southwest Colorado and southeast Utah, aggregates of multiple households herald the formation of relatively permanent villages. **Alkalai Ridge** in southeast Utah and **McPhee Village** in southwest Colorado are examples of these first villages, with clusters of surface rooms and adjoining pithouses that indicate populations exceeding 100 residents. Rooms were usually wattle-and-daub (*jacal*) structures built with upright posts and mud plaster. There is little differentiation among domestic rooms or household room suites that might reflect status or wealth variation among residents, just as there is no evidence for status differences in mortuary patterns.

Some of the early northern villages included an exceptionally large building that archaeologists refer to as a "great kiva," probably an important focus of village life. In modern Pueblo villages a kiva is a multi-purpose room used for religious, political, and social functions, and there seems to be good continuity in kiva architecture over the past 1500 years. The largest known great kiva is at **Grass Mesa Pueblo**, a settlement of perhaps 200 or more inhabitants located on the Dolores River in southwestern Colorado; it was occupied between AD 700 and 920. A circular structure 22.5 m (74 ft) in diameter, with a floor area exceeding 400 sq. m (4300 sq. ft), the construction of this kiva must have been a major community undertaking, a task that Ricky Lightfoot (1988) estimates took more than two months to complete. The Grass Mesa great kiva undoubtedly served as a focal point in community politics and religion, but since great kivas are relatively rare in the Pueblo I period, researchers generally assume that these buildings served larger social groups spread out among several settlements.

Many of the early villages in the northern San Juan River system were stable for several generations, despite high levels of household movement between settlements (Varien 2002). Thanks to the excellent chronological resolution afforded by tree-ring dating in the northern Southwest [see box: Tree-ring Dating], we now know that the Pueblo I period was a time of occasional interregional migrations as entire villages were abandoned and then re-established in new locations. For example, Andrew Duff and Richard Wilshusen (2000) documented a major episode of depopulation in the **Mesa Verde** region between AD 800 and 950, associated with new village formation further south in New Mexico, as well as several shorter intervals

of demographic downturns. They argue that different cultural groups may have been present in the San Juan River system at different times, as a result of repeated episodes of immigration and resettlement after AD 575. It is striking that entire areas were depopulated synchronously; apparently, the conditions that prompted groups to leave their homes and fields were experienced by all the farmers in an area, not just individual communities. These periodic shifts must have been driven by climatic change that made agriculture difficult, or population movements cycled around systems of long-term fallowing (Stone and Downum 1999). In either case (or both in combination), residential mobility was apparently a response to the inability of food production strategies and technology to sustain local or regional populations.

After about AD 800, there is evidence for regional variation in ceramic designs that may signify the existence or increased importance of group boundaries. In addition to unpainted pots used for cooking and storage, many ceramic vessels were covered with a white slip and black-painted designs [**18.22**]. Stylistic variants in these painted wares tend to be geographically discrete and may therefore represent bounded social groups. Nonetheless, it appears that similarities in ceramic design were more pronounced than differences throughout the northern Southwest during this time, suggesting broadly shared cultural affinities and relatively high levels of interaction.

Farming was widespread over the Colorado Plateau during the Pueblo I period, yet settlement clustering in the San Juan River system and shifting population centers would have left much of the northern Southwest open to occupation by mobile groups with mixed economies that were not as closely tied to agriculture. There is substantial evidence for low-intensity farmers at this time in the Great Basin to the northwest of the San Juan River and along the eastern margins of the Southwest, as well as hunter-gatherers in the adjacent southern High Plains. The possibility that foraging groups moved into and out of portions of the Colorado Plateau during the Pueblo I period, and later as well, cannot be dismissed out of hand, although few archaeologists currently favor this idea.

18.22 Pueblo I ceramics: *two large storage jars (ollas), with black painted geometric decoration on a white slip ground, Pueblo I period.*

Pueblo II: The Chaco Phenomenon, c. AD 900–1150

Geographic shifts in regional population concentrations continued during the Pueblo II period (c. AD 900–1150), as small farming settlements expanded over an increasingly larger portion of the Colorado Plateau. Maize remained the principal food source, with wild plants and animals adding important nutritional components to local diets. Food production strategies were generalized enough that they could be transferred easily between different locales. Population growth rates during the 10th century seem to have been unusually high in the San Juan basin of northwestern New Mexico, possibly in response to the late 9th-century depopulation of the Mesa Verde area to the north (Dean et al. 1994).

The Chaco Phenomenon A truly remarkable transformation in settlement patterns occurred in the San Juan basin in the midst of these late 10th- and early 11th-century population shifts, with small household farmsteads giving way to aggregated communities centered on communal masonry buildings that are now called "great houses." These structures are found throughout the basin but are concentrated in **Chaco Canyon**, where several examples contained hundreds of rooms and reached four stories in height (Vivian 1990). The largest great house is **Pueblo Bonito**, with over 600 rooms covering 0.8 ha (2 acres) [**18.23**]. The entire episode of great house construction in Chaco, the Bonito phase (AD 900–1140), was obviously a time of immense cooperative effort. At least 200,000 wooden beams averaging 5 m (15 ft) long and 20 cm (8 in) in diameter were brought to the canyon from distances between 40 and 100 km (25–62 miles) away to build a dozen great houses, signifying a huge labor investment and a complex production process. The bulk of construction took place in the 11th century, but by AD 1140 it had ceased abruptly, after which there was a rapid decline in use of the great houses and apparent abandonment of the canyon in the 13th century.

For more than a century archaeologists have struggled to understand the circumstances surrounding the rise and collapse of Chacoan society – dubbed the Chaco Phenomenon by the National Park Service. In particular, research has focused on determining why such an apparently inhospitable place as Chaco, which today is extremely arid and has very short growing seasons, should have favored the concentration of labor that must have been required for such massive construction projects over brief periods of time. Until the 1970s, it was widely assumed that Chaco had been a forested oasis that attracted farmers who initially flourished but eventually fell victim to their own success and exuberance, as they denuded the canyon of trees and vegetation to build large great houses. In the 1980s this reconstruction was largely dismissed in response to evidence that there had never been a forest in Chaco, and that canyon soils had poor agricultural potential. As scientific interpretations about Chaco changed, explanatory models altered their focus from the attractiveness of the canyon for farmers to the position of the canyon within a regional network of dispersed agricultural communities.

The adoption of a regional perspective in explaining the Chaco Phenomenon was based in part on the discovery of formal trails connecting many of the great houses in Chaco, as

KEY CONTROVERSY Chaco's Population During the Bonito Phase

The most important clue to identifying the function of Chacoan great houses and the place of Chaco Canyon within a regional social network is the number of people who resided in these buildings and nearby canyon. If the number was relatively high, then explanations for the Bonito phase reside in conditions that made Chaco attractive to farmers. If the number was low, then accounting for the labor spent in construction requires a more complex explanation that involves non-residential work parties. Current population estimates are small relative to energy outlays, favoring explanations for social mechanisms such as pilgrimages that periodically brought workers to the canyon from outlying areas.

Demographic reconstructions for the Bonito phase, however, involve a great deal of uncertainty, regardless of whether the resulting numbers are large or small. Until the 1980s, most archaeologists familiar with Chaco estimated population by counting the total number of rooms and calculating overall site sizes. The numbers of residents at historical Pueblos were then used to extrapolate figures for the Bonito phase. This approach typically produced estimates of 6000–10,000 people.

In the mid-1980s, some archaeologists adopted a household-based estimation method, using either the number of fire pits in habitation rooms (one per household) or the number of room suites (one per household). These assumptions yielded estimates of around 2000–3000 people, and stunningly small numbers for some of the largest great houses (for example, fewer than 100 residents for Pueblo Bonito). The internal organization of great house architecture is very unlike historical Pueblos, so it may be that modern analogies are not reliable demographic guides. Until this issue is resolved, all population estimates for the Bonito phase will remain frustratingly speculative.

18.23 *Pueblo Bonito:* this is the largest Great House in Chaco Canyon, with more than 600 rooms. Its present form was reached in the middle AD 1100s, after a series of complex building and razing episodes that began in the AD 800s. The occupation of Pueblo Bonito continued through the 13th century but the canyon was probably completely abandoned during the 14th century.

well as linking the canyon to smaller great houses located throughout the San Juan basin; the latter are referred to as Chaco "outliers." These trails are densest around the concentration of great houses in the center of Chaco, and the canyon itself is roughly at the center of the basin. Consequently, the canyon occupies the geographical and social center of the network formed by the connecting trails. The current consensus view is that religion provides the fundamental explanation for this centrifugal pattern.

Archaeologists now describe Chaco during the Bonito phase as a location of high devotional expression, a rituality, and the pilgrimage center of a sacred landscape (Mills 2002). These descriptions emphasize aspects of the archaeological record presumed to be associated with ritual activity, including caches of turquoise beads and pendants, unusual ceramic vessels and wooden objects, several rooms with multiple human burials (some accompanied by extraordinary numbers of ornaments), and especially the large number of kivas found in great houses. Most of these indicators occur only at Pueblo Bonito, but archaeologists generally assume that all the great houses had a similar ritual function. In fact, some scholars have suggested that the great houses were temples rather than residences, although not all archaeologists agree with this interpretation (Mills 2002).

Population and Agriculture Biometric analysis (statistical analysis of size and shape) of human skeletons from Pueblo Bonito indicates that at least two genetically distinct groups were interred at this site; other archaeological information, such as variation in architectural style, may indicate co-residence in the canyon by groups with different geographical origins (Vivian 1990). At this point, specialists cannot say whether these groups were linguistically or ethnically distinct as well. The presence of different social groups in Chaco during the Bonito phase is consistent with regional patterns of demographic fluidity in the 10th and 11th centuries, and it may help to explain the considerable investment in communal architecture, if these buildings were important to creating social bonds within the community [see box: Chaco's Population during the Bonito Phase].

New geological field studies in Chaco have produced results that may require a significant reassessment of the assumption that the canyon was not a favorable agricultural setting. It appears that during the first half of the 11th century, during the extraordinary boom in construction, a large volume of water and suspended sediment flowed into the canyon (Force et al. 2002). A large natural lake may have existed at the western end of Chaco, near the biggest concentration of great houses. The presence of large quantities of water and, equally important, a source of sediment that replenished agricultural fields presumably made the canyon an extremely attractive place for newly arriving people from the northern San Juan River basin. The possibility that the Chaco Phenomenon was related to locally high carrying capacities during a period of regional demographic realignment suggests that earlier economic models may have been on the right track, and that continuing research will increasingly focus on agricultural production in addition to religious function (Wills 2000).

Pueblo III: Regional Population Shifts, c. AD 1150–1300

Whatever forces led to great house construction in Chaco and the widespread emulation of great architecture at smaller outlying communities, they apparently dissipated by the mid-12th century, when building ceased in the canyon. Political and social influence shifted northward again, first to a cluster of Chaco-like great houses along the Animas River near Aztec, New Mexico, then further north to settlements in the Mesa Verde region of southwestern Colorado. Although great houses at **Aztec** initially were similar to those in Chaco Canyon, the farming communities established during the 13th century in the northern portions of the San Juan River drainage adopted very different kinds of residential architecture than that found in Chaco. These developments define the Pueblo III period (c. AD 1150–1300), and they occurred within a context of extreme demographic change that preceded the complete abandonment of the northern Colorado Plateau by farming populations.

The population of southwestern Colorado increased slightly during the 12th and 13th centuries (Duff and Wilshusen 2000). Large settlements (those in excess of 50 rooms) in the Mesa Verde region during the 1200s were usually situated in defensible locations that also provided control over local water sources. The large villages included the famous cliff dwellings on **Mesa Verde** proper, situated along the rims of deep canyons [18.24]; pueblos in lowland settings, such as Sand Canyon Pueblo, enclosed canyon-head springs.

Cliff dwellings are visually impressive, sited in beautiful sandstone alcoves and rockshelters and often incorporating towers and other striking architectural elements. But compared to Chacoan great houses, cliff dwellings were quite small, rarely more than 100 rooms. They lacked the impressive communal features of Chacoan architecture, such as great kivas or large enclosed plazas, and only a small portion of the regional population resided in them. The densest concentrations of Pueblo III villages were in the **McElmo Creek** watershed northwest of Mesa Verde, where average village sizes ranged between 200 and 400 inhabitants. As the number of communities grew, their resource catchment areas began to overlap, presumably causing tension, if not overt conflict, between them (Varien et al. 2000).

Subsistence during the Pueblo III period in the northern San Juan region continued to focus on maize production and the extensive use of wild resources. Increased size and complexity in millstone technology suggests intensification of food-processing activities (Hard et al. 1996), but local environmental conditions probably placed significant limitations on the ability of farmers to intensify overall agricultural production through greater labor investment. Many researchers argue that farming communities at this time were forced to maintain continuous control over large tracts of arable land that were not in production because soils were unsuited for short-fallow cultivation. Such reserved land may have been indicated on the landscape by walls and other physical markers.

Tenure systems based on control of land held in reserve for future production reflect economic competition between groups, and there are striking indications of violence in the Mesa Verde area during the 13th century. Skeletal evidence for head and limb trauma consistent with battering and arrow wounds is widespread after AD 1000. This probably reflects low-level conflict such as ambushing isolated individuals (Stodder et al. 2002), but by the 12th century, mass killings were occurring that produced distinctive archaeological deposits of disarticulated and intentionally fragmented human remains, some of which may be byproducts of cannibalism. At **Castle Rock Pueblo** in southern Colorado, at least 41 people were killed in a single event that took place around AD 1280 (Kuckelman et al. 2002). Violent death is also evident in other parts of the Colorado Plateau during the Pueblo III period, evidence that competition between farming communities was significant.

Pueblo IV: Abandonment of the Colorado Plateau, 14th and 15th Centuries AD

The wholesale abandonment of the Colorado Plateau by farming groups by AD 1300 is often attributed to a severe drought that lasted from 1276 to 1299, but Carla Van West (1996) demonstrated that even during this episode, the agricultural carrying capacity could have sustained the regional population. It is unlikely, therefore, that climate change can fully explain this depopulation. One important additional factor may have been the increasing presence of hunter-gatherer groups in the region. Around AD 1150, small farming groups throughout the Great Basin to the northwest of the San Juan River began switching to full-time foraging, and by the late 13th century there were no longer any farmers in this huge region (Madsen and Simms 1998).

Assuming that these hunter-gatherers used larger areas for subsistence than agriculturalists, it is likely that some of them would have impinged on the territories of the Mesa Verde farmers, especially if the latter kept extensive areas fallow. A combination of drought and competition for wild resources

18.24 *Cliff Palace:* *the largest cliff dwelling at Mesa Verde, Colorado, with over 200 rooms. The settlement was built and abandoned during the 13th century. Rooms at Cliff Palace were much smaller than those at earlier Chaco great houses and there was no associated great kiva.*

could have severely impacted farmers' ability to manage subsistence risks that were high even in the best of times.

By the early 1300s, farming populations were increasing dramatically along the Rio Grande and Little Colorado rivers, presumably as a result of immigrants arriving from northern areas. These regions were not empty prior to the 14th century, but the local agricultural populations were organized in small settlements, generally consistent with extended household groups that probably moved frequently between patchy distributions of well-watered arable land. Extensive land-use systems are common in contexts of low population density, so it is not surprising that the influx of immigrants during the 1300s was accompanied by the development of more intensive economies

[see box: Pecos Pueblo, p. 702]. Archaeologists often refer to the 14th and 15th centuries, or the Pueblo IV period, as a time of socio-economic reorganization (Speilmann 1998).

Pueblo IV settlements were considerably larger than antecedent farming villages: many Rio Grande Valley pueblos exceeded 1000 rooms. Villages consisted of aggregates of domestic rooms arranged around extremely large plazas in which one or two kivas were generally located. In contrast to earlier Pueblo III sites, such as **Sand Canyon Pueblo**, which had many small household-size kivas, villages in the 14th and 15th centuries typically had just a few exceptionally large kivas. It may be that the replacement of many small integrative architectural structures with the more inclusive plaza and big kiva complex represents some loss of household autonomy in these large communities.

Subsistence economies continued to rely heavily on the ancient staples of maize, beans, and squash, and cotton production for textiles became extremely important in most areas. Curiously, there is no substantive evidence for stream irrigation agriculture during this interval, although early Spanish accounts refer to ditches in some places. Dry-farming methods, however, were widespread, including elaborate bordered fields, terraced slopes, diversion dams for rainfall runoff, reservoirs, and extensive arrays of cobble mulch and rock piles. This large-scale land modification for crop production points to communal production strategies, and may signal the control of land and labor by social units larger than the household.

Pottery Innovations In the early 14th century, a series of technological innovations made it possible for potters to create polychrome designs on ceramic vessels, some of which included lead glazing [**18.27**]. Glaze ware production was con-fined to a limited number of villages that may have specialized in manufacture for exchange, although the relative contribution of any single producing village to regional consumers varied through time. Some researchers (e.g. Spielmann 1998) have suggested that glaze wares were markers of status or coveted for use in ritual, and that demand for these types was driven by social rather than utilitarian demands.

Salado polychrome pottery appeared around AD 1275, and by the late 14th century became the most widely distributed ceramic style in Southwestern prehistory, cutting across traditional archaeological culture traditions. Patricia Crown (1994) studied hundreds of whole Salado polychrome vessels and discovered that these pots were manufactured locally, with little

KEY SITE Pecos Pueblo

The excavation from 1916 to 1922 of Pecos Pueblo in northern New Mexico, by Alfred V. Kidder, is considered one of the seminal archaeological investigations in the Southwest (for that matter, in the United States). The results of that work made archaeological history and set standards for all subsequent field studies in the region, including the establishment of detailed stratigraphic associations for recovered materials. These carefully recorded contextual relationships allowed Kidder to define a relative temporal sequence for changes in pottery styles that was the basis for ordering

18.25 *(Left) View of the reconstructed kiva at Pecos Pueblo.*

18.26 *(Below) Aerial view of Pecos Pueblo, northern New Mexico. The exposed walls are part of the 17th-century Spanish colonial mission complex.*

other unexcavated sites in the region (Kidder 1958). The basic elements of Kidder's regional chronology remain useful today.

In addition to the development of systematic field methods, Kidder was able to show continuity between the historical occupation of the Pueblo and deeply buried remains of a much earlier prehistoric village. In doing so, he demonstrated that Pueblo communities encountered by Spanish explorers in the mid-16th century had occupied the Rio Grande Valley for many hundreds of years. Some of these villages are among the oldest continuously occupied towns in North America.

18.27 Polychrome ceramic vessel: *painted jar (Four Mile polychrome) from west-central New Mexico,* c. AD 1325–1400.

variation in design composition. She interprets the Salado polychromes as one expression of a Southwest Cult that emerged during the regional population diasporas of the 14th and 15th centuries. The **Southwest Cult** was a pan-regional religious ideology tied to water control and agricultural fertility, with an emphasis on social inclusiveness. Thus it would have lessened social tensions caused during the formation of new villages, which were quite possibly made up of mixed ethnic and linguistic groups.

Population Decline

The Pueblo IV period has been called a Golden Age in recognition of its large villages, technological innovations, and the appearance of elaborate religious mechanisms for social cohesion. Nonetheless, this was also a time when the health of Pueblo villagers was declining due to malnutrition and the increased prevalence of disease. Some villages were intentionally destroyed, and warfare imagery became prominent in rock art. Moreover, the overall population of farmers in the Southwest was dropping precipitously, perhaps as much as 70 percent between AD 1300 and 1500. There was no shortage of agricultural land, nor would extreme climate conditions explain such a widespread failure of farming economies, and scholars have found this severe population decline baffling.

Although there is no apparent archaeological evidence for competition from non-farming groups during this period, this may still be the critical factor in demographic trends among agricultural peoples. By the 15th century, Athapaskan-speaking groups originating in western Canada entered areas of the Colorado Plateau abandoned by Pueblo farmers. Uto-Aztecan speakers from the Great Basin were also arriving from the west, and various Plains tribes occupied the eastern margins of the Southwest following a shift after AD 1450 from mixed farming economies to more mobile, hunting adaptations focused on bison. It is difficult to explain the clustering of rapidly diminishing farming populations in dense villages surrounded by vast areas of potential farmland unless access to those lands was somehow constrained; an exploding regional population of hunter-gatherers might plausibly be the reason.

From this perspective, the arrival of Spanish expeditions and colonizing groups in the 16th century may have been less dramatic than generally assumed. Historians often characterize the colonial period as a clash of two cultures, the dominant European and the subjugated Pueblo. Yet the archaeological record points to the 16th and 17th centuries as a time of great demographic flux. Spanish administrators and settlers may have fixed their attention on Pueblo villages, whose farming economies and compact settlements were familiar and easy to understand, but the Pueblos were undoubtedly already occupied with the tangled crush of new competitors and rapidly changing social networks.

Pueblo society almost disappeared in the turmoil of the Spanish Colonial period (1542–1821), as the combined effects of enforced labor, introduced disease, and raiding by non-Pueblo hunter-gatherers ravaged individual villages. By the late 19th century, the total Pueblo population was reduced to a few thousand people scattered in isolated clusters over an enormous area. Nonetheless, these resilient communities have slowly recovered, and now, at the beginning of the 21st century, are taking a major political role in local and national issues related to indigenous human rights and cultural patrimony.

The Plains

Two centuries have passed since Lewis and Clark's Corps of Discovery went up the Missouri River, meeting both village agriculturalists and nomadic bison hunters while crossing the Louisiana Purchase. Their journey took them through a vast grassland – tall-grass prairie was located to the east of drier short-grass prairie – that extended across the middle of the continent from Texas northward into Canada. This grassland was broken by deciduous forests in river and stream bottomlands. The best places to live were along these rivers, with their fertile, cultivable soils and mix of wild animals and plants.

Popular images of life on the Great Plains are often far removed from reality (Wood 1998). Nomadic equestrian bison hunters were a historic-period development, for example; it took until the early 18th century before large numbers of Spanish horses from the Southwest spread northward onto the Great Plains. Prior to that time, bison were hunted on foot, and dogs were used as beasts of burden. Furthermore, a sharp distinction is often made between village and nomadic peoples, which obscures some fundamental commonalities in ways of life. Groups such as the **Mandan** and **Arikara** lived in permanent villages consisting of large, earth-covered structures and grew crops including maize, but they also participated in annual bison hunts that took them far out onto the surrounding grassland. Villages were politically and economically autonomous, and nowhere were chiefs particularly powerful, even in the largest settlements.

Village Settlements

Pottery first became widespread across the Great Plains as early as 500 BC (Johnson and Johnson 1998). In addition to pottery, the appearance of substantial houses, burial mounds, and occasionally cultivated plants indicate that hunter-gatherer societies had begun to change during Plains Woodland times (which lasted to about AD 1000), showing a growing tendency for a more settled existence.

Some sites have yielded artifacts reminiscent of those found east of the Mississippi River in Middle Woodland societies (Chapman 1980; Johnson and Johnson 1998), the best known being a cluster of sites located near Kansas City on the Missouri River. Villages, some covering several acres, and camps have been identified, as have earthen mounds over tombs with walls made of stacked stones. Here, the relationship with groups to the east is mainly indicated by styles of pottery and projectile points, not by fine mortuary offerings.

Other sites with evidence for eastern connections include some in northeastern Oklahoma and adjacent Missouri, which have also produced pottery and projectile points similar to Middle Woodland forms, as well as mounds along the Missouri River near the North Dakota and South Dakota border (Bell 1984; Newman 1975). The mounds are of special interest because they contain tombs that mostly held disarticulated bones along with artifacts of marine shell and obsidian, as well as cut human, bear, canid (wolf/coyote/dog), and beaver maxillae and mandibles. The tombs and their contents indicate some form of contact with Eastern Woodlands peoples, specifically those in western Illinois, which must have involved the exchange of ideas, not just the occasional prized object that might have

crossed long distances by being passed from one group to another. The Missouri River sites are of special interest since Yellowstone obsidian from much farther upstream has been found at Midwestern sites, most notably Hopewell in Ohio (see above).

As in the Eastern Woodlands, maize was present in the Plains for several centuries before it became a significant component of diets in some regions late in the 1st millennium AD (Johnson and Johnson 1998). From about AD 1000 onward, a variety of agricultural societies in the central and eastern Plains, referred to by archaeologists as **Plains Village**, featured settlements consisting of structures – often earth-covered lodges –

18.28, 18.29 Village settlements: *settlements on the Great Plains varied in size. In this excavation of a site in Nebraska (above), postmolds outline a large square building, while the surface of this historic-period village in North Dakota (right) is pockmarked by depressions where earthlodges were once located.*

accompanied by commodious storage pits (Blakeslee 1994; Drass 1998; Johnson 1998). Wooden palisades and ditches sometimes surrounded compact villages, although the need for defensive structures varied over time and from one region to another. Plains Village people were successful farmers who worked their fields with bison-scapula hoes; they also sought out wild plants and animals, particularly from nearby forested bottomlands, and many groups engaged in long hunting trips for bison. The occupation of the forested rivers was spotty, and population distributions changed over time.

Settlements varied greatly in size, typically from a few houses to several tens of them [18.28, 18.29] (Brookes 1994; Steinacher and Carlson 1998; Winham and Calabrese 1998). Some Plains Village communities consisted of dispersed houses, while others comprised compact clusters of buildings, occasionally surrounded by a stout wall. Villages might be occupied by several hundred people, an example being the 14th-century **Crow Creek** site along the Missouri River in South Dakota, where there were 50 or more houses (Kivett and Jensen 1976; Willey and Emerson 1993). Although the buildings were not necessarily all contemporaneous, at least 500 people lived there, judging from the number killed in a devastating raid on the village [see box: Crow Creek: Scene of a Massacre]. This particular settlement was surrounded by a wooden palisade and ditch, which was replaced by a deep ditch alone when the settle-

ment expanded. Signs of a palisade have not been identified adjacent to the outer ditch, and it may be that the villagers had not completed their defenses when they were attacked.

Plains Village populations were unevenly distributed, even along the best river bottomlands. Movement from one place to another was undoubtedly caused by environmental and social concerns, including the need to forge alliances, aggregate for protection, and flee from enemy groups. Conflicts, indicated archaeologically by skeletal injury and by settlements protected by ditches and palisades, are more apparent among Plains Village populations than earlier Plains Woodland people, although the likelihood of localized warfare seems to have varied over time and space (Blakeslee 1994).

Exchange Systems

Pottery indicative of connections to contemporaneous Mississippian societies to the east, specifically Cahokia, occurs in the Kansas City area, the location of sites referred to as **Steed-Kisker** (Chapman 1980; O'Brien 1993; Steinacher and Carlson 1998). This relationship faded in the 13th century as Cahokia began its slide into obscurity, part of a general reduction of Mississippian influence through the eastern Plains.

Elsewhere in the Great Plains, wide-ranging exchange networks that extended to the Eastern Woodlands, the Southwest, and the Pacific Coast are indicated by rarely occurring trade

KEY SITE Crow Creek: Scene of a Massacre

In the late 1970s, human bones were discovered washing out of an eroded bank at the Crow Creek village in South Dakota (Willey and Emerson 1993). Upon excavation, it was found that the deposit included the remains of at least 486 people who had been massacred in the mid-14th century. Men, women, and children died in an attack that probably resulted in the deaths of most of the village's inhabitants. Skeletons bore evidence of injuries from clubs and arrows, and cut marks show that bodies were then scalped, decapitated, and dismembered. The remains were left scattered across the site long enough for bodies to decay, scavenging animals to feed on them, and skeletons to fall apart. Eventually people did return and collect the bones, gathering them in a 1.5-m (5-ft) high pile within a defensive ditch that surrounded the settlement. Soil eventually eroded into the

ditch, covering the deposit and preserving the bones. Earlier excavations at the site encountered charred structures and scattered human bones, indicating that the village was burned and that not all the human bones were picked up for burial in the ditch.

It is likely that the raid took place when the site's defenses were incomplete, leaving the villagers vulnerable. Interestingly, a few people had survived earlier attacks, as indicated by scalping trauma that had healed, evidence that the massacre was not an isolated event. Warfare among modern small-scale societies tends to consist of isolated ambushes punctuated by devastating raids on situationally weakened foes (Keeley 1996). That is precisely what seems to have happened at Crow Creek.

18.30 *House depressions are surrounded by a ditch at Crow Creek, South Dakota.*

wares, local pottery inspired by them, or seashells (Drass 1998; Steinacher and Carlson 1998).

European trade objects arrived on the Plains in the 17th century – new additions to an exchange of valued objects, including marine shell, that extended back into Archaic times (Johnson 1998). By the 17th century, Spanish missions had been established at Pueblos along the border of the southern High Plains, in a deliberate attempt to control trade between Southwestern farmers and Plains hunter-gatherers. These missions disrupted the social relationships that had previously characterized Plains-Pueblo interaction, leading to increased violence and the destruction of many villages by the late 17th century. Horses then arrived in great numbers by the 18th century, transforming life on the plains. By the early 19th century, equestrian nomadic peoples such as the Sioux, who had not long before been pushed onto the northern Plains from the woodlands to the east, had gained ascendancy on the Great Plains.

One reason for the decisive shift in the balance of power toward these mounted hunters was the greater vulnerability of settled villagers to newly introduced diseases, which had made their appearance by the late 18th century, if not earlier. Once a highly contagious disease such as measles or smallpox appeared in a village of several hundred people, everyone might become ill, and many would soon die. Village peoples remained strong into the 19th century, but they were decimated by a wide-ranging smallpox epidemic in the late 1830s, and never recovered their former position (Trimble 1994). Death tolls for nomadic equestrian groups, while still horrific, tended to be proportionately less, because these people lived in small, dispersed, highly mobile bands that only maintained irregular contact with one another. These were the people who survived in sufficient numbers to play such a prominent role in the Indian Wars of the mid-19th century.

The Pacific Coast

Several hundred years ago, California and the Pacific Northwest were home to a diverse array of hunting-gathering-fishing societies, including the organizationally complex societies of the Northwest Coast and the Santa Barbara Channel of California (Ames and Maschner 1999; Arnold et al. 2004). The northern societies, among them the **Haida**, **Kwakiutl**, and **Tlingit**, are well known, largely because many elements of traditional life continued into the 19th and early 20th centuries, when they were thoroughly described, sometimes in the works of early ethnologists (Suttles 1990; 1991). The **Chumash** of southern

California are not as widely recognized, although recent archaeological work has done much to augment the documentary record for these people, which is sparse in comparison to that of the Northwest Coast (Arnold 1992; 2001).

Southern California

The Santa Barbara Channel islands and shoreline in southern California were heavily populated when the Spanish mission system was established in the late 18th century (Grant 1978). The late prehistoric people of this area, known for their large plank canoes [**18.31**], relied heavily on what the sea could provide, including fish, shellfish, birds, and sea mammals (Arnold 1992). Up to a few hundred people might live in villages on the channel islands and the nearby mainland. Stable isotope analysis of human bones indicates that the islanders ate a diet consisting of more marine animals than the people of the mainland, including those along the coast (Lambert and Walker 1991).

The precise timing of the emergence of chiefdoms in the Santa Barbara area is hotly debated, but societies with some form of formal social ranking had certainly appeared by the late 12th century AD (Arnold 1992; 2001; Arnold and Green 2002). They had perhaps arisen as much as several centuries earlier, when distinctions in social positions, presumably based on kin affiliation, are indicated by unusually rich offerings (especially shell beads), buried with a few people in cemeteries mostly consisting of graves holding few, if any, artifacts (Gamble et al. 2001). The emergence of these societies, whatever the precise date of their appearance, followed several centuries of greater inter-community conflict, as indicated by skeletons with projectile points embedded in bones (Arnold 2001; Lambert and Walker 1991).

Much like what happened elsewhere in the continent, deteriorating relations roughly coincided with the earliest widespread use of the **bow and arrow**. After the establishment of chiefdoms throughout the Santa Barbara area, there is less

18.31 *A Chumash canoe: a reproduction of a wooden plank Chumash canoe, or tomol, in use. They were an essential part of late prehistoric life on the Pacific coast, being used when fishing and trading.*

18.32 Totem poles: *a village with totem poles and plank houses in the Queen Charlotte Islands, British Columbia, as they appeared in 1878.*

skeletal evidence of violent deaths, perhaps indicating a decline in the frequency of inter-group conflicts.

In the Santa Barbara area, an accentuation of social inequalities and the appearance of hereditary positions of authority took place during a period of pressure on locally available resources, principally food, when marine productivity declined. This situation provided aspiring leaders, particularly those on islands where serious shortfalls were likely to occur, with opportunities to promote the production of surpluses of food and valued objects. To do so reduced the threat of famine through the mobilization and exchange of goods under the sponsorship of chiefs.

Chiefs were behind the production of great numbers of marine shell beads and the construction of plank canoes (Arnold 1992; 2001; Arnold et al. 2004). Most of the shell beads were made on the islands, as were many chert microblades used to work the shell. While everyone provided for their own basic subsistence needs, there was some variation from one vil-lage to the next in what people produced, as shown by an uneven distribution of beads and microblades throughout the region, including the islands. Seaworthy canoes from driftwood logs originating in more northerly forests were difficult to make, so only high-ranking people possessed the wherewithal to see the job through to completion. Canoes facilitated deep-water fishing, hence an increase in fish such as swordfish, as well as trade in various goods, including food, among coastal communities. Great effort went into the construction of these canoes [see **18.31**], which were both economically useful and conspicuous markers of high status.

The Pacific Northwest

Societies along the Pacific Coast from northern California to southeastern Alaska are undoubtedly the best-known North American examples of complex hunter-gatherer-fishers. Here, late 18th-century explorers, including Captain James Cook, found permanent villages consisting of substantial plank houses and a rich artistic tradition that in many places included tall totem poles [**18.32**]. Museums around the world are filled with remarkable everyday and ritually significant objects from that period onward, and aesthetically pleasing items have also

18.33 *Signs of social status:* *this Northwest Coast woman from the late 18th century is wearing a large labret, a sign of her social status.*

been found in archaeological excavations. The preservation of ancient objects can be excellent, as shown by those from the mud-covered **Ozette** site in northwest Washington state [see box: Ozette]. Archaeological materials dating back several thousand years indicate a strong continuity between prehistoric people and those of more recent times.

Village Life The basic outline of Northwest Coast life in historic times – plank houses, permanent villages, and social inequalities – had begun to emerge in the 2nd millennium BC during the **Middle Pacific** period, from around 1800 BC to as late as AD 500 (Ames 2003; Ames and Maschner 1999). Rectangular buildings consisting of planks covering a framework of posts provided secure housing for large households and abundant storage space for food. Salmon were hung overhead to dry, and other items, including food, were stored in watertight bentwood boxes. Stone celts suggest that wooden canoes were being made, and net weights, toggle harpoons, and weirs underscore the critical role of fishing over the last several thousand years. By the 1st millennium AD, in the **Late Pacific** period (*c.* AD 500–1775), these social and technological changes had coalesced in societies that closely approximated those of early historic times.

Middle to Late Pacific people relied heavily on what could be obtained from the sea and coastal rivers, ranging from whales in the open ocean to salmon caught while swimming upriver to spawn. Diets varied along the coast according to the considerable local differences in marine and terrestrial settings. Of special importance were salmon runs up coastal streams, which produced a plentiful and predictable source of food. Fishing, however, could only be done for a short period, required coordinated labor, and resulted in an abundant catch that had to be preserved before it spoiled. So, much like agricultural societies elsewhere in North America, the Northwest Coast people had fixed territories and lived in sedentary communities that permitted the periodic mobilization of considerable labor and the storage of substantial amounts of food.

Despite the overall richness of this environment, communities suffered from occasional mortality crises stemming from unpredictable shortfalls in essential foods. Households were buffered from hardship by access to neighboring territories and exchange networks that in historic times typically involved interactions among highly ranked people. Exchange among prehistoric communities is indicated by finds of copper, obsidian, nephrite (a type of stone) for celts, and *dentalium* shell from distant places. Even iron from Asia, obtained through trade or

from debris that washed ashore, occurs rarely in prehistoric contexts.

Villages, which varied widely in size, consisted of large plank houses in rows near shorelines, consistent with the principal focus of their subsistence economies (Ames 2003; Ames and Maschner 1999; Archer 2001). In the historic period, a household's social standing was based on rights to various ceremonial privileges and natural resources, hence its productive capacity and wealth. Social status was marked by the size of houses and their location within villages. Communities with a few noticeably larger houses had appeared in some places early in the 1st millennium AD, a reason for believing that ranked households were already in existence by that time.

Artifacts and debris scattered across house floors indicate that the part-time specialization of household members also extended deep into prehistory. Some people were even marked in life by artificial cranial deformation and lip or cheek plugs, known as labrets [18.33]. These practices, which leave an indelible mark on the body, date back several thousand years. Mortuary practices varied geographically and temporally, but also according to an individual's social standing. Thus archaeologically detectable differences existed among people in life as well as in death.

Warfare and Population Decline The appearance of Northwest Coast societies in the Middle Pacific period was accompanied by warfare that, in general, increased in intensity later in time. By the 1st millennium AD, hilltop fortifications had appeared in many places, as did the bow and arrow. A skeletal collection from Prince Rupert Harbour in British Columbia provides an indication of the difficulties these people faced (Cybulski 1999). About one-third of the men and half as many women experienced some form of cranial fracture, many of which had healed. While a number of the injuries could have resulted from accidents or altercations within villages, many, if not the majority, probably came from attacks by enemy groups. Several people who were decapitated were almost certainly victims of such attacks. In the historic period, the unfortunate people captured in raids were enslaved, as was probably true in the past (Ames and Maschner 1999).

The region's population may have peaked 1000 years ago, and it certainly plummeted rapidly in the 19th century (Ames and Maschner 1999). This precipitous decline, coupled with unprecedented economic opportunities and an abundance of newly introduced goods, resulted in many changes during the 19th century. These included an elaboration of the **"potlatch,"** a competitive ceremony accompanied by a feast, where many items were distributed and destroyed to enhance the prestige of the individuals who sponsored it (Suttles 1991).

It has even been argued that the region's most widely recognized aspect of material culture – the elaborately carved and painted totem poles [see **18.32**] – date back no further than the 18th century, when metal tools first became widely available. Identifying their presence in earlier times, however, would be difficult except under exceptional circumstances of preservation.

KEY SITE Ozette

A most remarkable excavation came about when parts of houses and other artifacts began to wash out of a bank after a storm struck Washington's Olympic Peninsula coast in 1970 (Ames and Maschner 1999; Samuels and Daugherty 1991). Part of the village, which was 250–450 years old, had been destroyed by a mudslide that paradoxically also preserved it for the future. This village – one of several built at this particular spot over many centuries – had belonged to the ancestors of the present-day Makah tribe, which still occupies the area today. The tribe runs an outstanding museum, where many of the Ozette artifacts can be seen.

Up to 3 m (10 ft) of clay had to be laboriously removed by water pumped through hoses to reach the house remnants and artifacts. The suddenness of the disaster and the depth of burial meant that everyday objects were left behind and survived to modern times. Over 55,000 artifacts were discovered, including wooden tools, clubs, bowls, and boxes, along with basketry containers, hats, and cords used for various purposes. These discoveries indicate just how much is missed at Northwest Coast sites because items made from plant materials are normally poorly preserved. The house planks were western red cedar (a good choice

because of its resistance to decay); many support posts had been snapped when the mudslide hit. Shellfish, along with the bones of fish and sea mammals – especially northern fur seals but also whales – indicate a heavy reliance on what the ocean could

18.34 *Elaborately carved clubs were among the well-preserved materials from Ozette.*

provide. The largest of the three completely excavated houses had several carved panels and was cleaner than the others. There were also some differences in the proportions of the many animal bones in refuse associated with these buildings. Such variation, along with the distance of houses to the shore, probably reflects the social standing of different households in the community.

18.35 *The Ozette excavations were remarkable for the abundance of materials preserved by the mudslide that covered the village, including wooden objects that normally decay in archaeological sites.*

The Arctic and Subarctic

Life in the far north required a special set of skills, but people nevertheless proved remarkably adept at occupying dense boreal forests, open tundra, and, especially, coasts, where good use was made of offshore resources. Indeed, the earliest colonizers of the Americas were already adapted to a cold environment as they crossed Beringia, the landmass connecting Siberia and Alaska that was exposed when sea levels dropped as water became locked up in massive ice sheets during the last Ice Age (Chapter 4).

People occupying the barren coasts of Greenland and Labrador southward to the grassy and wooded shorelines of Newfoundland were the first in the New World to set eyes on Europeans. They did so about 1000 years ago, when the **Norse**, who had spread across the North Atlantic during the Medieval Warm Period, reached Greenland and the North American mainland, the outermost fringe of their westward expansion [see box: L'Anse aux Meadows]. The Norse called the natives they encountered *skraelings*.

The Norse remained in Greenland through the Medieval period, but their settlements died out less than a century before Columbus's "discovery" of the Americas. At roughly the same time, the Thule Inuit, or Eskimo, were pushing eastward along the treeless Arctic coast. Inuit and Norse cultures were not equally well adapted to the harsh conditions of the far north. Inuit fishing and hunting ultimately proved more successful than Norse farming, which became increasingly difficult as the North Atlantic slipped into the colder and more unpredictable weather of the Little Ice Age.

KEY SITE L'Anse aux Meadows

In 1960, a 1000-year-old settlement where Vikings, most famously Leif Eriksson, had briefly lived was found only 100 m (328 ft) from a shallow bay on the Newfoundland coast (Wallace 2000). Here at long last was the much sought-after Vinland of Norse sagas. The discovery of L'Anse aux Meadows, as the site is now known, is all the more remarkable because no other evidence of a Norse presence has been found on nearby shorelines, despite intensive searches. The Norse were not content to stay at L'Anse aux Meadows, but instead used it as a base for further exploration. Their journeys must have taken them to the south, where they obtained butternuts, which do not grow near the site.

When first identified, the remnants of house walls were visible as raised areas in thick grass. Subsequent excavations have revealed eight buildings much like those built elsewhere in the North Atlantic. They ranged from spacious multi-roomed structures to small buildings, all of which had sod walls supported by wooden frameworks. They were used as both living quarters and workshops, including smithies, and might have accommodated as many as 70–90 people. Iron nails and scrap indicate that long ships, critical to survival on distant shores, were repaired where they were pulled up on the beach. Excavations have shown that the first iron smelting in North America took place at this site.

The settlement had a rather short life, and it was picked clean by its occupants (mostly men but some women as well) when they left for good. There were too few people and insufficient economic incentives to make the kind of concerted effort needed for the successful European colonization of North America. That would only take place many centuries later, during which time the Norse achievement had passed into obscurity, only to be recognized again by the discovery of L'Anse aux Meadows.

18.36 *Excavation at L'Anse aux Meadows where the remains of Norse buildings were still visible almost a thousand years after the settlement was abandoned.*

The Dorset and Thule Cultures

When the Norse arrived, small groups of people were spread thinly across the breadth of the Arctic, as they had been for 3000 or more years (Dumond 1987; Maxwell 1985; McGhee 1996). The inhabitants of the eastern Arctic at that time are known as **Dorset** [**18.37, 18.38**], a term that refers to a way of life that had emerged by 500 BC. Diets varied from one place to another, although musk ox, caribou, and sea mammals often fell victim to intrepid hunters who pursued different prey throughout the year. Dorset winter settlements consisted of several small houses heated by oil burned in soapstone lamps. These sites were located in especially favorable places for hunting sea mammals, including seals and walrus, from the shore or the edge of the sea-ice. Dwellings at this time are thought to have included snow-block houses, perhaps similar to later igloos, based on the presence of long bone and antler snow knives. Late Dorset sites occasionally included elongated enclosures defined by stones, which can be up to several tens of meters long, and nearby hearths. They must have held some ritual or social significance for the people who gathered in these resource-rich places.

The **Thule** expansion eastwards across Arctic Canada, usually said to have begun around AD 1000, coincided with the Medieval Warm Period, although ancestral cultures in eastern Siberia and Alaska date back as much as 2000 years. The Thule originated as one of the cultures that focused on rich marine resources along the North Pacific Rim. These skillful hunters of sea mammals, including bowhead whales, possessed a sophisticated technology that included specialized harpoons and skin-covered boats. A capacity for open-water whale hunting became increasingly important as the ice pack receded during this comparatively warm period. Bones found at Thule sites show that small bowhead whales were targeted, especially yearlings, where whales were abundant (Savelle and McCartney

1994). Thule winter communities consisted of houses built of stone, sod, driftwood, and whale bones [**18.39**], with specific house-construction techniques varying across the Arctic. Sometimes there were also buildings for special ritual and social purposes (Fitzhugh 1994).

At one settlement, and presumably others as well, a nearby freshwater pond and the immediately surrounding area were enriched by enough nutrients from decaying whale carcasses to promote greater moss growth (Douglas et al. 2004). Thus, even hunter-gatherers in the thinly populated Arctic could leave a lasting imprint on the landscape.

Life was hard for the Thule, as it had been for earlier Arctic peoples. Essential sources of food were often widely and unpredictably distributed, and available for only short periods of time. Severe shortages must have frequently resulted in the reduction or extinction of entire communities as well as families. One such event took place at **Ukkuqsi** in Alaska, where a young girl's frozen body was recently found eroding out of an empty meat-cache pit (Zimmerman et al. 2000). Already weakened by chronic illness, she had died of starvation, and before her death she had been reduced to eating gravel, sand, and animal hair, all of which were found in her gastrointestinal tract.

Despite problems related to life in harsh conditions, a specialized technology for hunting whales enhanced the availability of critical resources for larger groups (Dumond 1987; McGhee 1996; Sutherland 2000). The Thule, therefore, gained a demographic edge over thinly scattered Dorset people. Bows in the hands of the Thule would have also put them in an advantageous position in any fighting that broke out between these two groups of people, who were competing for many of the same resources.

Within a few hundred years of the Thule arrival in the eastern Arctic islands, during the 11th or 12th century, the Dorset groups and Norse colonies had disappeared forever. The last generations of the Dorset were quite likely the earlier, vaguely described people in Inuit traditions who were said to have been pushed off their land. By the 15th century, there were no more Norse in Greenland, and climatic deterioration surely played a

18.37, 18.38 Dorset culture: *the people of the Arctic made heavy use of elaborately carved tools, such as these Dorset harpoons and needles (left), that were often aesthetically pleasing as well as functional. This polar bear carving out of ivory (below), which measures 15 cm (6 in), is an excellent example of Dorset carving skills.*

part in their demise. The abandonment of their settlements, however, need not have involved anything other than a return to Iceland of a trickle of people over several generations, part of the population redistribution that followed great losses of life from repeated plague epidemics that began to strike Europe, including Iceland, in the mid-14th century (Lynnerup 1996).

Physical traces of Norse and *skraeling* contact are limited to a small number of artifacts, including those of wood and iron, at Dorset and Thule sites (McGhee 1996; Sutherland 2000; Schledermann 1993). The artifacts are consistent with Norse sagas that tell of sporadic encounters and often uneasy relations with native peoples. This early contact had no lasting effect on the native societies of Greenland southward to Newfoundland. That would change, however, starting in the 16th century, when Europeans returned to the Arctic to search for a passage to Asia, a global economic interest quite different from the local concerns of Norse settlers, who maintained only a precarious existence on the outer edge of their world.

The Collision of Two Worlds

All native cultures were irrevocably changed or disappeared entirely within a few centuries of the establishment of a permanent European presence in North America during the 16th century. In some places – most commonly along coastlines and in the arid Southwest – it is possible to move from archaeological sequences to historically documented groups with relative ease. In others, including most of the continental interior, demonstrating continuity across the prehistoric to historic interface is much more difficult, if not impossible. When a century or more elapsed between the European arrival in North America and their first contacts with Native Americans, the chance of bridging the gap between the archaeological record and historically documented groups diminishes precipitously. This is because appalling population losses were coupled with group movement, amalgamation, and dramatic cultural change, which included the adoption of European trade goods along with the alteration or abandonment of traditional crafts. These profound changes in ways of life took place on time-scales measured by generations, not centuries.

Europeans began to explore the North American coastline in earnest shortly after Columbus's arrival in the Caribbean in AD 1492. It did not take long before several expeditions penetrated deep into the continental interior. Two of the best-known and longest expeditions were undertaken simultaneously in the mid-16th century: Hernando De Soto's in the Southeast, and Francisco Vasquez de Coronado's through the Southwest into the central Plains. While these early adventurers were for the most part unsuccessful, in marked contrast to their counterparts in Mesoamerica and Peru (chapters 16 and 17), by the end of the

18.39 Whale bone houses: whale bones were used as roof supports on Thule houses, such as seen in this reconstruction.

century Spanish colonies had finally been established in Florida and far to the west in New Mexico. In the early 17th century, the English successfully colonized parts of the eastern seaboard, and the French did the same in eastern Canada. In the 18th and 19th centuries, the Spanish established missions in California, the Americans pushed their way westward across the continent, the British moved deep into Canada, and the Russians made inroads into Alaska and the Pacific Northwest. Relations with Native Americans varied greatly, but there were some general tendencies in how interactions played out, primarily because of differences in the economic objectives of European nations. The Spanish wanted to organize native labor for their various enterprises and to protect their interests from other Europeans; the French and Russians were principally intent on trading with Native Americans, most notably for furs; and the English and, later, Americans wanted above all else land for themselves, which meant pushing the original inhabitants off it.

Native Americans suffered greatly from wars, mistreatment, and forced relocations. Even natural settings were altered for better or worse by newly introduced plants and animals. But the greatest declines in Native American populations – which set the stage for the loss of a continent – were surely caused by diseases, aggravated by the social and economic disruptions that followed in their wake. The major culprits were acute, highly contagious, fever-producing diseases including smallpox and measles. Records are poor, but the reduction in the native population began in some places, such as around England's Lost Colony at Roanoke, immediately upon the European arrival in the 16th century [see box: Native Population on the Eve of European Contact, p. 714]. Here the newly contacted inhabitants of the North Carolina coast "began to die very fast, and many in short space; in some townes about twentie, in some fourtie, in some sixtie, & in one six score" (Harriot 1972 [1590], 28).

Horrific losses of life from disease were just the beginning of the problems Native Americans faced. Critical knowledge vanished, viable households and communities had to be reconstructed from shattered remnants, and famine from unfinished subsistence-related tasks had to be averted. Suddenly weakened groups became irresistible targets for traditional enemies, resulting in even more deaths and forced movement. Matters were not helped by involvement in the affairs of the European countries and the United States, which were intent on expanding their economic and political spheres of influence.

The plight of the surviving Native Americans only became a matter of widespread concern in the late 19th century, when most groups were already confined to the poorest land. Their numbers rose once again in the 20th century, despite great problems with health, education, and economic opportunities. These people survive as the rightfully proud descendants of cultural traditions that extend back for thousands of years.

Summary and Conclusions

Over the past century, the broad outline of human settlement in North America during prehistoric times has been worked out through the considerable effort of numerous archaeologists. It is now clear that across much of this vast and environmentally diverse continent, people began to settle down in villages over the past few thousand years, doing so earlier in some places than in others. On the other hand, some areas were never home to settled village peoples, including inhospitable parts of the arid West and frigid Arctic. While far-flung groups maintained some form of intermittent contact with one another – a relatively few objects ended up far from their points of origin – each major cultural area, such as the Southwest, had its own cultural trajectory. Thus, to explain what unfolded over time in any particular part of North America, we must look to local and regional social, technological, and environmental conditions, not to new ways of life introduced wholesale from distant parts of the continent.

In some parts of North America, social inequalities in the form of ranked households or larger descent groups with fixed leadership positions eventually emerged in village-based societies. The nature of these societies has been the subject of increasing attention over the past several decades. Too much attention, however, has been directed toward merely pigeonholing ancient societies into categories such as chiefdoms. It is more important to document how individual societies were organized, to identify the reasons for geographical and temporal variation among them, to chart their development and dissolution over time, and to explain why such changes took place.

Despite heated debates over these issues, it is nonetheless clear that new technologies and diets, greater sedentism, and more conspicuous differences among burials, houses, and settlements did not appear in lockstep, or change at the same rate. In the Eastern Woodlands, for example, archaeologically visible distinctions among people in Middle Woodland societies are mostly confined to burial contexts; in Mississippian societies, they are noticeable in both habitation and mortuary sites. Moreover, there was neither a unidirectional shift toward more elaborate burials nor an ever-increasing distinction between the richest and plainest graves. Populations, likewise, did not increase steadily in various parts of North America, as shown most clearly by the abundant and tightly dated Southwestern sites.

Where there is sufficient information, it seems clear that the emergence of larger and more complex societies often took place in the context of increasing conflicts among communities that relied on spatially fixed resources. This is true of Mississippian societies, as well as those of the Pacific Northwest and

KEY CONTROVERSY Native American Population on the Eve of European Contact

No one doubts that Native American populations plummeted after AD 1500, but the magnitude and timing of this decline are hotly debated. The issue of population loss is closely tied to estimates of the number of people who occupied the Americas 500 years ago. Authoritative pre-contact population estimates for the United States and Canada range from 2 to 18 million. Most of the other researchers who have made a stab at this subject provide estimates that fall somewhere between these extremes. Any such figure, of course, will have a wide margin of error. Data on population numbers are indirect, incomplete, and often badly biased. It seems to us, however, that the range is unacceptably broad, and that the work of innumerable archaeologists should be able to contribute something to this issue.

Low and High Estimates

The low end of the range is based on admittedly crude census information – numbers of warriors and the like – taken from various historical documents (Ubelaker 1988). Even if it is accepted that the original counts are, within reason, generally correct, it is certain that much of this information postdates great losses from epidemics. Thus the 2 million figure can be viewed as conservative: it is unlikely that the true number of people would have been any lower.

The high end, in contrast, was calculated by extrapolating from population density and resource productivity estimates (Dobyns 1983). The information used for this purpose can be charitably characterized as sketchy, and the resource yield as overly optimistic. The 18 million figure was supported by a pre-contact estimate for a group in Florida, the Timucua. This population was ratcheted upward in a series of steps to account for losses from postulated 16th-century pandemics.

18.40 *This 1567 illustration shows an Inuit woman and child. Groups in many parts of the New World were at that time reeling from the effects, intended or not, of contact with Europeans.*

Contacts and Disease

In order for the upper end of the range to be correct, it must be assumed that devastating epidemics appeared early, happened frequently, and spread uniformly across the continent. Looking at the possibility that high-mortality epidemics occurred repeatedly during the 16th century, the issue is not whether horrifyingly large numbers of people died when epidemics struck – that, no doubt, took place. The problem lies with the claim that great killers like smallpox and measles frequently swept across vast areas, striking everyone in their path.

Groups of people were more unevenly distributed across even the best land than was recognized when the high estimates were

proposed in the early 1980s, as indicated by better data on site locations and more refined chronological controls. Furthermore, contacts among these population pockets, while they certainly took place, appear to have been more sporadic than continuous. Such a conclusion stems in part from the unrelenting hostilities that existed between many neighboring groups, which were only recognized in the 1990s as having been a pervasive element of late prehistoric life.

The issue of contact among geographically isolated populations is important, because highly contagious diseases such as smallpox and measles must often have burned themselves out in small groups before they could be passed on to the next cluster of villages. It is undoubtedly true that such epidemics spread with devastating effect beyond face-to-face contact with sick Europeans, but they did not extend as widely and uniformly as needed for the high estimates to be correct. In short, there is no reason to believe that the Timucua example, based as it is on an absence of direct information, accurately depicts what happened across all of 16th-century North America.

Overview

No one knows how many people occupied North America 500 years ago. Perhaps we will never have the data needed for a reasonably accurate estimate, but the issue is important enough that we should not give up on it. Our guess – and it is only that – is that a total somewhere in the bottom end of the range would not be wide of the mark. It is likely that there were over 2 million people, although probably not more than two or three times that number.

Santa Barbara coast, but not of Middle Woodland groups in the Eastern Woodlands. While conflicts certainly occurred among hunter-gatherers throughout North America, it is nevertheless true that complex societies consisting of settled villages were particularly prone to conflict, which waxed and waned over time. The existence of warfare can be recognized by the skeletons of injured and mutilated people, settlements with defensive structures, sites in inaccessible places, and, occasionally, actual weapons or depictions of them. Increases in late prehistoric conflicts appear to have been accompanied in at least some places by the adoption of the bow and arrow, a critical change in technology that probably had as much to do with killing human enemies as it did with hunting game.

Most of the villagers scattered across North America relied heavily on agriculture based on a variable mix of native and introduced crops, most importantly maize, which came ultimately from Mesoamerica. People even proved remarkably adept at farming in the arid Southwest, where their cultural achievements include impressive sites such as Chaco. Yet nowhere on the continent did farmers move entirely away from their hunting-and-gathering roots.

Archaeologists quite naturally tend to focus on the development of agricultural economies – after all, their appearance marks a major watershed in cultural evolution – but this emphasis is somewhat misplaced. What is of importance is the productivity and reliability of geographically fixed and unevenly distributed resources, regardless of what form they took. Relatively complex sedentary societies arose in various parts of North America where people could make use of highly productive freshwater and brackish wetlands, shallow coastal lagoons, or the open sea. They include the late prehistoric peoples of southern peninsular Florida, the Pacific Northwest, the Santa Barbara Channel, and the lower Mississippi River valley. Even the populations of agricultural chiefdoms along the major rivers of the Eastern Woodlands – such as Cahokia, the largest of them all – relied heavily on food from wetlands, especially fish. The contribution of aquatic resources to the subsistence economies of tribal- to chiefdom-scale societies in North America deserves as much attention as agriculture has traditionally received.

Long-established ways of life were forever changed in the several centuries following the first sustained contact with Europeans in the 16th century; earlier encounters with the Norse in the western North Atlantic had only limited local impact, principally on the inhabitants of the eastern Arctic. Great population loss and movement accompanied by major alterations in ways of life often make it difficult for archaeologists to associate prehistoric sequences with historic groups, particularly in the interior of the continent. Where that can be done, the connections drawn between historic and prehistoric groups greatly enrich our understanding of the latter.

Knowledge about the people who once inhabited all of North America – those of both prehistoric and historic times – is increasing rapidly. Much of this new information has come about through innumerable projects undertaken at sites threatened with destruction in both the United States and Canada. A recent, and welcome, development in many places is a greater involvement of Native Americans in the management and study of their past. In the Southwest, for example, different groups operate their own archaeological and historic preserva-

tion programs. Their involvement in defining research questions and methods is now felt at every level of field research in the Southwest. There is no question that the future of archaeology will be an increasingly collaborative process among Native Americans, scientists, and historians.

Further Reading and Suggested Websites

Ames, K. M. & Maschner, H.D.G. 1999. *Peoples of the Northwest Coast: Their Archaeology and Prehistory*. London & New York: Thames & Hudson. Outstanding and well-illustrated review of the prehistoric societies of the Northwest Coast, with archaeological information augmented by detailed information on life during early historic times.

Cordell, L. S. 1997. *Archaeology of the Southwest*. San Diego: Academic Press. Comprehensive review covering prehistoric Southwestern societies.

Fagan, B. M. 2005. *Ancient North America*. (4th ed.) London & New York: Thames & Hudson. A wide-ranging introduction to North American prehistory.

McGhee, R. 1996. *Ancient People of the Arctic*. Vancouver: University of British Columbia. An engaging book covering the prehistoric societies of the Arctic.

Milner, G. R. 2004. *The Moundbuilders*. London & New York: Thames & Hudson. This overview of Eastern Woodlands prehistory emphasizes ancient societies in the Midwest and Southeast from the Middle Archaic through the Mississippian period.

Plog, S. 1998. *Ancient Peoples of the American Southwest*. London & New York: Thames & Hudson. Well-illustrated book introducing the last few thousand years of Southwestern prehistory.

Wood, W. R. (ed.). 1998. *Archaeology on the Great Plains*. Lawrence: University Press of Kansas. Includes chapters by regional experts on prehistoric Plains societies, divided by time period and geographical area.

http://medicine.wustl.edu/~mckinney/cahokia/cahokia.html The website of the Cahokia Mounds State Historic Site, with events, visitor information, related links, and other features.

http://archive.ncsa.uiuc.edu/Cyberia/RiverWeb/Projects/Ambot/entry.html This website of the Illinois State Museum examines Native and European American culture and history in the American Bottom, the floodplain of the Mississippi River near St. Louis, Missouri.

http://www.cr.nps.gov/ The National Park Service "Links to the Past" website.

http://www.ibiblio.org/dig/ Excellent coverage of the excavations at Occaneechi Town, an 18th-century Indian village in North Carolina; created by the Research Laboratories of Archaeology at the University of North Carolina at Chapel Hill.

http://www2.sfu.ca/archaeology/museum/ Website of the Museum of Archaeology and Ethnology, Simon Fraser University, in British Columbia, Canada.

CHAPTER 19
THE HUMAN PAST: RETROSPECT AND PROSPECT

Chris Scarre, University of Cambridge

Demographic Increase 717
Intensification and Degradation 718
Biological Exchange 719
Climate Change and Human Society 720

In this book we have described the development of human societies over the past 2.5 million years, from the invention of pebble tools to the growth of cities and empires. The evidence on which this account is based has been drawn from archaeology – the study of the material remains – supplemented by written records for more recent periods. The period of written records falls conventionally within the domain of history, but archaeology does not stop when writing appears. It continues to inform us about the material conditions of life, and about social practices, up to the present day. More significantly, it allows us to view recent events in the perspective of the long-term development of humanity.

How then do developments over the past 2000 years or so fit within the huge diversity of human societies that we have illustrated in the foregoing chapters? A brief answer can be presented under four specific themes.

Demographic Increase

At the end of the last Ice Age, world population numbered perhaps only a few million. Today that population stands at 6 billion, and is set to grow further as better medicine and nutrition increase longevity and reduce infant mortality. The dramatic growth in human numbers (especially rapid since AD 1500) has been the product of a combination of factors, including the relative stability of postglacial climate and the ability of humans as a species to develop social and economic mechanisms that are capable of supporting high population densities. If the key challenge to human societies during the glacial periods was to cope with hostile and unpredictable or rapidly fluctuating environmental conditions, the challenge since the last Ice Age has been to develop ways of extracting more food from the environment to feed the growing numbers of people. This process began with the development of increasingly sophisticated strategies of hunting and gathering. In several regions these were sufficiently productive to allow the establishment of modest-sized sedentary settlements, as can be seen, for example, in the Jomon societies of Japan, the Natufian of Southwest Asia, or the peoples of the Northwest Coast of North America. It is a mistake to envisage all hunter-gatherers in the image of the small mobile societies of the Kalahari and Australian deserts, or of the Arctic, even though many may have been of this kind.

Whatever the successes of hunter-gatherers, the crucial innovation in human demographic history was without question the development of agriculture. Hitherto, all human communities, even the most sophisticated, had been limited in size by the ceiling imposed by the availability of wild resources. Once agriculture was introduced, that ceiling was lifted so that populations could grow dramatically. The process was gradual, with early farming methods dependent on plants and animals that were locally available and on rain-fed cultivation with a

19.1, 19.2 *Population increase:* *rising human numbers since the end of the last Ice Age have been accompanied by radical changes in the character and scale of human settlements. The small impermanent camps of nomadic hunter-gatherers such as the Kalahari San (left, photographed in around 1927) now account for only a tiny fraction of the world's population; most people today live in dense urban environments such as Udaipur, in India (right).*

technology of hoes and digging sticks. Many, but not all, of these farming societies also had domestic animals (in addition to the dog), though these were kept for a variety of purposes – often for traction and transport, for milk or wool, or as wealth on the hoof, rather than as a routine meat source. Farming was not a single pattern-book strategy that was the same wherever it was adopted, but a series of parallel adaptations based on the availability of particular species and on factors of soils and climate. It did, however, result everywhere in the spread of sedentary settlements that ultimately became the usual human residence pattern.

Agriculture also had its down side. Many studies have shown that the health of early farming populations was poorer than that of their hunter-gatherer predecessors. This may not always have been the case, and contrary examples must have been common; but the reliance on a narrower range of foods that characterizes farming communities inevitably brought its own problems. The risk of an unbalanced diet or of dietary deficiencies necessarily increased. Furthermore, where grinding of cereals to flour was the standard practice, increased tooth wear became an issue, owing to the fragments of grit that found their way into the food. Farmers were also constantly at the mercy of the weather, and as population levels grew, the impact of occasional crop failures became all the more severe.

One further negative consequence of farming would have been the increased incidence of infectious disease. Demographic growth provided a much larger reservoir of human hosts, and the crowding of people together in larger communities created ideal conditions for epidemics. Living in proximity to domestic animals, and in particular cattle and pigs, also allowed the mutation of animal diseases into human-related forms, especially in the Old World, where close associations between domestic animals and humans were common. Thus, human tuberculosis may have been derived from bovine tuberculosis. The process continues to the present day: the 1918 epidemic of Spanish flu that killed 18 million people worldwide probably crossed to humans from pigs.

Though these consequences have had a damaging effect, in long-term perspective they are greatly overshadowed by the profile of demographic growth that agriculture has made possible. That growth continues today, supported by industrialized farming in the developed world and by increasingly intensive methods in other regions.

Intensification and Degradation

Intensification and complexity have become especially significant during the past 10,000 years. As human population levels began to rise, taking advantage of the greater food resources provided by cultivation, new ways had to be found to feed the growing numbers. This was achieved by adjustments to agriculture: breeding new, more productive varieties of crops or livestock, or devising new methods and technologies of cultivation. The use of fertilizer (manure) or the shortening of fallow periods are two of these new methods; so too were irrigation and terracing.

With higher agricultural productivity and larger populations came growing social and economic complexity. Inequalities of wealth and status led to the rise of hierarchical societies, including the state societies or "civilizations" of the ancient world. Large, centralized polities such as these made it possible for ever more complex economic systems to develop. Communities and individuals became more specialized; it was no longer necessary for everyone to be engaged in primary subsistence activities. Specialist metalworkers in an early state society, for example, could depend on a network of others to support their needs and enable them to focus on their craft: miners and traders to provide the raw materials; farmers and administrators to organize and supply their food; market sellers, perhaps, to furnish other needed commodities; scribes, maybe, to record disbursements of food and materials on the one hand and productivity (in terms of finished metal products) on the other.

Complexity of this kind relied on intensification of primary agricultural production, and though that intensification allowed more food to be produced per unit area, it also rendered human populations considerably more vulnerable. The unprecedented size and food requirements of early urban populations placed very heavy demands on agricultural systems. These, in turn, were often in fragile environmental settings, vulnerable either to over-exploitation by the farmers themselves, or to climatic irregularities. Some climatic events were on such a scale that they would have overwhelmed even low-density farming communities, and the scope for human catastrophe was made all the greater by the dependence on fragile irrigation systems. The problem of achieving long-term environmental sustainability is one that has haunted complex societies for over 4000 years. Mesopotamian records of the late 3rd millennium BC refer to salination and the loss of fertility (perhaps only temporary) caused by excessive irrigation. Clearance of forest to increase the amount of agricultural land might have been a natural response to rising food demand in the short term, but in the medium or long term the removal of vegetation may have provoked erosion and the loss of the very soil that the farmers were seeking to exploit. These problems are still with us today, despite advances in agricultural and environmental science. The intensive agriculture on which modern urban populations depend continues to place pressure on the world environment, with a consequent pay-off in terms of degradation as rainforest is lost to logging, for example, or river flows are crippled by the waters drawn from them for irrigation schemes.

Biological Exchange

Thousands of years ago, early farmers may have been directly familiar with only a limited geographical area around their settlements, never traveling far, and relying on traders or down-the-line exchange to bring raw materials from distant sources. The materials may have traveled thousands of miles, passing from hand to hand, but few individuals made long journeys or had extensive geographical knowledge.

This is not to discount the importance of human movement in the peopling of the world, nor the subsequent colonization events that carried individuals and entire communities over spectacular distances. Much of this long-distance connectivity, however, lapsed once the initial movement was complete. Easter Island, perhaps the most impressive example of human colonization, quickly became isolated from the rest of the Polynesian islands. Other colonization movements, however, most notably within the past 2000 years, have opened up patterns of contact that have remained active, and which have become increasingly global in scope in recent decades.

One consequence of these growing connections has been biological exchange. Domestic plant and animal species, in particular, have been transported to new areas and become globally widespread. Thus Eurasian cattle and sheep first domesticated in Southwest Asia 9000 or 10,000 years ago are now a mainstay of livestock farming in places as distant as South Africa, New Zealand, and North America, while the Mesoamerican domesticate maize is grown extensively in Europe and sub-Saharan Africa. Indeed, maize is now the third most important crop on earth, in terms of the quantity produced. This pattern of biological exchange accelerated with the European voyages of exploration (followed by European colonization) in the 15th and 16th centuries. These brought New World crops such as potato and tobacco to Europe, and European cereals, cattle, and sheep to the Americas.

The newly imported crops benefited some agricultural systems while damaging others and disrupting local ecosystems. Much deadlier, however, was the exchange of human diseases that accompanied these contacts. We have already noted the contribution of domestic animals to infectious diseases in humans. The ever-growing size of human communities during the later Holocene period has made them increasingly vulnerable to such disease, a vulnerability that advances in medical knowledge and hygiene have only partly been able to counterbalance. Ancient

historians tell of disease epidemics such as the outbreak that struck Athens during the Peloponnesian War in 430 BC, or the plague that afflicted the Byzantine empire in the 6th century AD. Another cycle of epidemic disease, usually identified as bubonic plague, ravaged Eurasian populations recurrently from the 14th to the 17th centuries AD. These epidemics appear to have spread widely through long-distance contact; it is significant, for example, that 14th-century bubonic plague, originating perhaps in China, hit Sicily and the great Italian seafaring cities (Pisa, Genoa, Venice) before spreading thence to the rest of Europe. Around one quarter of Europe's population may have died in the Black Death that followed (1346–1352).

The most tragic of all such biological exchanges, however, was the series of epidemic diseases spread by European invaders to the native peoples of the Americas in the wake of Christopher Columbus's first transatlantic crossing in 1492. European diseases, of which smallpox was the most lethal, are estimated to have killed up to 95 percent of the pre-European population of the Americas during the following 150 years. Conversely, native American diseases appear to have had little impact on Europe. Syphilis is one of the few that may have traveled in the opposite direction, and even for that, the evidence is disputed; it may simply have arisen coincidentally in Europe at the end of the 15th century. The imbalance of the "Columbian exchange" is one of the major factors that have shaped human history during the last 500 years. Its explanation may lie in the origins of the epidemic diseases concerned. The domestic livestock kept by Eurasian farmers were the source of these new diseases, but domestic livestock played a much smaller part in the farming systems of the New World. In addition, some diseases need very large, dense population reservoirs, and these

19.3 The fallen statues of Easter Island: *deforestation, land exhaustion, and over-population on this isolated island led to hunger and warfare, in which the statues of the ancestors were obvious targets for hostile groups. The statues were still standing when the first Europeans visited the island in 1722; 50 years later, they had been toppled.*

19.4 *European exploration and colonization: in the 16th and 17th centuries violent conflict arose with many native populations, fueled by incomprehension on both sides. In this drawing by John White, English explorer Sir Martin Frobisher's expedition of 1577 to discover the fabled North-West Passage is attacked by a party of Inuit.*

were much less common in the New World. Thus it was among Eurasian populations that the lethal epidemic diseases developed, but those same populations through exposure to these diseases developed a certain level of immunity. No such immunity protected the native Americans when Europeans first arrived on their shores.

Climate Change and Human Society

The rapid growth in human numbers over the past 12,000 years illustrates how successfully human societies have adapted to the postglacial environment and the opportunities it has offered. Postglacial climate has been characterized both by significantly more clement conditions than those of the last Ice Age, and by a much greater stability. There has, however, been at least one significant deviation within this pattern. At around 6200 BC, evidence from the Greenland ice core shows that global climate went into a sharp cold phase that persisted for around 200 years. The cause is thought to have been the sudden emptying of Lake Agassiz, a vast freshwater lake that had formed west of the present Great Lakes area on the US/Canadian border, fed by meltwater from the Canadian ice sheets. Around 6200 BC, Lake Agassiz broke through to the North Atlantic, the sudden access of cold fresh water halting the Gulf Stream and bringing two centuries of severe cold to global climate.

A more recent, less severe excursion occurred during the period known as the Little Ice Age, *c.* 1300–1850. The climate of

western Europe and eastern North America was marked during these centuries by severe winters, there was higher rainfall in parts of tropical Africa, and there were impacts too on the monsoon regimes of the Indian Ocean.

What caused the Little Ice Age is uncertain, but it is clear that human society is still subject to changes in climate that can be gradual, but which may also be sudden and unpredictable. There is no reason to believe that the mechanism that lies behind the long-term cycle of ice ages has ceased to operate. The periodicity of the ice ages, which recur every 100,000 years, is generally attributed to subtle changes in the pattern of the earth's orbit around the sun. Thus it may be technically correct to label the present warm phase an interglacial, rather than calling it the postglacial. Whether or when another ice age may ensue is highly uncertain. One argument holds that human interference with the environment, by raising temperatures, may already have forestalled the onset of a new ice age. Others worry that global warming threatens to halt the Gulf Stream once again within a few decades, causing climatic change that may be rapid and catastrophic. What is clear above all, however, is that human societies remain at the mercy of the climatic changes – both for good and ill – for which their own activities may be partly responsible. Coping with such changes has been a key feature of the human past; it will remain so into the foreseeable future.

19.5 *Global warming: one of the greatest challenges to human society during the 21st century, the break-up of the ice sheets could release sufficient meltwater to flood many coastal regions and cities, but the possibility that rising temperatures will disrupt world climate systems is an even greater threat. Adaptability to such changes has been one of the keys to human survival and success over the past 3 million years, but as archaeology shows, that survival has not been achieved without cost.*

GLOSSARY

achene seed surrounded by hard, dry fruit coat, or shell

adaptive radiation in which a set of related species radiate and branch out to occupy and adapt to a range of diverse environmental niches

adobe dried mud, often mixed with straw to form mud-bricks

aeolian dust wind-borne deposits

agency theory approach to the study of past societies in reference to the individuals operating within them as agents of change

agora ancient Greek marketplace and city center

agropastoralism the combined activity of farming and animal herding

ahu stone platforms on which *moai* were erected (Easter Island)

alleles variants of a gene

altiplano high altitude grasslands in the central Andes

amphitheater oval or roughly circular arena surrounded by seating, in which wild animal or gladiatorial contests were held during the Roman Republic and Empire

amphora (pl. amphorae) large Classical vase-form, used for carrying water or wine and other commodities

AMS radiocarbon dating accelerator mass spectrometer dating, a highly accurate form of radiocarbon dating

anthropology the study of humanity, commonly subdivided into cultural, biological, and linguistic anthropology, and **archaeology**

arboreal tree-dwelling

archaeology a subdiscipline of anthropology involving the study of the human past through its material remains

archaeomagnetic dating see **paleomagnetic dating**

arroyo rocky ravine or dry watercourse

artifact any portable object made, used, or modified by humans

assemblage a group of artifacts recurring together at a particular time and place, representing the sum of human activities in that respect

atlatl spearthrower

aurochs Paleolithic species of wild bovine

backing the deliberate blunting of a stone tool by means of steeply-angled removals, presumably to facilitate insertion into a haft

baetyl sacred stone

Bamboo Annals a history of China up to 298 BC

band small group of 25–60 individuals related through marriage or family ties; typically mobile hunter-gatherer groups

basilica large rectangular columned hall used as a law court during the Roman empire

bed stratigraphic unit

biface flat cobble flaked over both surfaces to produce a sharp edge around the entire periphery; also called a hand axe

bipedal walking on two legs

bipolar technique the production of flakes by resting the core on an anvil and splitting it with a hammerstone

Bodhisattva follower of the Buddha who chooses not to attain nirvana, but to stay on earth and help others

bola stones two or more stones strung together and thrown so as to entangle an animal; used in Archaic Central and South America

braincase the part of the skull that encases the brain

breccia type of rock formed of sediments and small rocks cemented together

burin stone flake or blade with chisel-like edges

caitya barrel-vaulted Buddhist shrine

calvarium skull cap

causewayed camp a Neolithic enclosure characteristic of southern Britain, with one or more circuits of ditches interrupted by undug areas, or causeways

chiefdom a society of several thousand individuals organized on institutionalized lines of hierarchical lineages ruled over by a chief

chinampa gardens constructed in a shallow lakebed, exemplified by the Aztec fields of Tenochtitlán

chryselephantine made of gold and ivory

Chunqiu "Spring and Autumn Annals," history of the state of Lu during the Warring States period in China, by Confucius

ciudadela Spanish term meaning "citadel," applied for example to the unfortified royal complexes of the Chimu empire, Peru

clade group with a common ancestor, i.e., a single evolutionary branch

coalescence the appearance of specific genotypes in **mitochondrial DNA**

codex (pl. codices) accordion-fold books used by Mesoamerican peoples, made of bark paper or animal parchment pages sized with washes of lime plaster and enclosed in wooden covers

cognitive archaeology the study of past ways of thought and symbolic structures from material remains

colluvial slope one in which the soil has been washed down to its base

cong ceremonial jade tube with square or circular cross-section, often elaborately carved

corbeled vaulting roofing technique wherein each higher level of stones slightly overhangs the previous one, eventually meeting at the top under a capstone

cordillera system of mountain ranges, often consisting of more or less parallel chains; used often to refer to the Andean range

core parent rock from which flakes are detached

cultural ecology an approach to the study of human society which argues that change results in large part from the response of human societies to the challenges and opportunities of their environments

cuneiform a form of script used in Southwest Asia during the Bronze Age and Early Iron Age; literally, "wedge-shaped"

cupellation method of obtaining silver ore involving the blowing of air across a crucible of molten silver-bearing lead, first developed in the 3rd millennium BC in the Cycladic islands of Greece

cupule cup-shaped vegetal wrapping that holds the kernels of an ear of maize

cyclopean masonry style of building characteristic of Mycenaean sites, using massive, roughly cut stones, uncoursed, the interstices randomly filled with smaller stones

debitage flakes and fragments detached from a rock core

democracy system of government based on the enfranchisement of all citizens; literally, "rule of the people"

demography the study of human populations, in particular their size, composition, and distribution

demotic script used in the Late and Greco-Roman periods of ancient Egypt for everyday writing

denticulate stone flake or blade retouched to produce a saw-tooth edge

diffusion the spread of materials, ideas and innovations from one society to another

diurnal daytime (as opposed to nocturnal, night-time)

DNA deoxyribonucleic acid, a molecule that carries genetic instructions from parents to offspring

doab tongue of land between two rivers (India)

domestication the human propagation of selected species

dolmen a megalithic tomb type, usually consisting of upright stone slabs, on which rests a large capstone or capstones

Doric order Archaic and Classical Greek architectural style, with unadorned columns topped by a simple capital, and with a **triglyph** and **metope** pattern decorating its external upper **entablature**, above the columns

dry farming farming without the use of irrigation, in areas in which normal rainfall is sufficient for cultivation

ecotone an area forming the boundary between contrasting environmental regions

electron spin resonance dating (ESR) dating method that measures trapped electrons in bone and shell, the number of such electrons indicating the age of the specimen

encephalization enlargement of the brain

entablature horizontal element high up on the facade of a Classical building between the column capitals and the pediment or roof; see also **Doric order**

eustatic rise rise in sea level as a result of glacial melting

experimental archaeology in which tasks or objects from the past are replicated and compared with the archaeological remains

femur (pl. femora) thigh bone

fibula (pl. fibulae) smaller of two lower leg bones (with **tibia**)

flowstone stalagmite or stalactite

foramen magnum hole in the base of the skull through which the spinal column and associated nerves and muscles pass to join the head

foraminifera skeletons of shelled protozoa, also called forams

formation stratigraphic unit comprising several members

formation processes the processes that have affected the survival of materials from the past, and the formation of the archaeological record

forum (pl. fora) Roman marketplace and city center, equivalent to the Greek **agora**

frontal bone forehead

ge Chinese ceremonial jade halberd, an axe-like weapon

gender archaeology an approach emphasizing in particular the role of females in past societies, arising out of feminist critiques of male-dominated science

gene flow the introduction of new genes into regional populations

genome complete genetic component of a cell; nuclear **DNA** and **mitochondrial DNA** each comprise a single genome

genotype a complete set of genes possessed by an individual

genus group of closely related **species**

geomorphology study of the development of land forms

GIS Geographical Information Systems

glacial period an Ice Age

glottochronology statistical study of vocabulary to determine the degree of relationship between particular languages, and the chronology of their independent development

glume the sterile bract, hull, or husk that encloses the grain of grasses such as rice

GPS Global Positioning System

gradualism model of human evolution in which major changes are the result of a slow and steady accumulation of small changes

gui Chinese bronze vessel in the form of a low-footed bowl

Guiana shield the vast rainforest between the mouth of the Orinoco and the Amazon

half-life the time it takes for half the quantity of a radioactive isotope in a sample to decay

hand axe see **biface**

haniwa models of houses, people, and animals that encircled elite Yamato tombs in Japan

Han Shu "History of the Former Han," early Chinese history by Ban Biao and Ban Gu

haplotype see **clade**

heddle loom loom with a series of vertical cords, each with a loop in the middle to receive a warp thread

heiau Hawaiian religious structures comprising terraced platforms and walled enclosures

heröon Greek shrine or temple dedicated to a legendary hero

hieratic cursive form of Egyptian hieroglyphic script that was used for writing on papyrus

holotype type specimen

Hou Han Shu "History of the Later Han," an early Chinese history

humerus (pl. humeri) upper arm bone

iconography artistic representations that usually have overt religious or ceremonial significance; the study of such images

interglacial period of warmer, wetter climate between two Ice Ages or glacials

Ionic order Greek architectural style of the Classical period and later, with volute-headed column capitals (like rams' horns) and a continuous (often sculpted) frieze on the external **entablature**

isostatic uplift the rise of landmasses once the weight of the ice sheets has been removed

isozyme variant of an individual enzyme

jacal wattle-and-daub, used in the construction of buildings in the Southwest United States

jia Chinese bronze tripod vessel

kancha high-walled enclosure of the Incas, the size of a city block, containing **wasi**

karstic region an irregular limestone region with sinkholes, underground streams, and caverns

kero libation vessel used by the Incas and earlier Andean cultures

kiva multi-purpose room used for religious, political, and social functions in Pueblo villages on the Colorado Plateau

kofun burial mounds of the Yamato kings of Japan

Kojiki history of the Yamoto kingdom of Japan, compiled in the early 8th century AD

kore (pl. korai) statue of a clothed young woman, common in the Greek Archaic period

kouros statue of a nude standing youth, common in the Greek Archaic period

krater ancient Greek mixing bowl with wide mouth and two handles

Kufic an early angular form of the Arabic alphabet

kuraka Andean elite class who claimed descent from sacred ancestors

kurgan mound-covered Scythian tomb from the second half of the 1st millennium BC

labret lip or cheek plug

lahar volcanic mudflow

langi coral, slab-terraced earthen burial mound built for the nobility of Tonga

laterite a clay formed by weathering of rocks in the tropics, used for bricks

latte stone pillar foundation for a chiefly house with raised floors, built in the Mariana Islands, Micronesia

lens thin stratigraphic layer

Levallois technique method of stone flaking associated with Mousterian in which the core pebble was shaped in advance so that it would provide a flake of predetermined size and shape

lexicostatistics a method of core vocabulary comparison between related languages

lingam phallus-shaped rock symbolizing the god Shiva

Li Yul Tibetan text with details of Khotanese history

loess fine, wind-blown silt

lost-wax method method of casting metal, in which a wax original is replaced by molten metal in a clay mold

luminescence dating dating method that relies indirectly on radioactive decay, employing heat or light to release trapped electrons; related to **electron spin resonance dating**

lunate crescent-shaped microlith

mandible lower jawbone

marai Polynesian shrine/temple platforms

Mata Atlantica the Atlantic rainforest of coastal Brazil

maxilla (pl. maxillae) upper jawbone

megaron the central unit of a Mycenaean palace, composed of a linear arrangement of three rooms: porch, anteroom, and interior room with a hearth and throne

member stratigraphic unit comprising several **beds** related spatially and in terms of their rock type

menhir single standing stone found in Neolithic and Bronze Age Europe, sometimes decorated

mesa a high, flat-topped hill

metope square panel, often sculpted, that alternated with the **triglyph** to form a frieze that decorated buildings of the Greek **Doric order**

microliths small, standardized stone flakes, originally set into composite tools or weapons

midden a concentration of cultural debris; in places where fishing is a primary subsistence strategy, they are often made up primarily of shell

Middle Range Theory conceptual framework linking raw archaeological data with higher-level generalizations and conclusions about the past that can be derived from this evidence

mitochondrial DNA genetic instructions inherited through the maternal line

moai massive stone statues characteristic of Easter Island

mobiliary art portable art produced during the Upper Paleolithic

monocephaly having only a single flower

montane mountain-dwelling

morphology physical structure or form

necropolis (pl. necropoleis) cemetery; literally "city of the dead"

New Archaeology approach advocated in the 1960s, which argued for an explicitly scientific framework of archaeological method and theory, with hypotheses rigorously tested; it promoted an emphasis on culture process, understanding how and why change occurred, rather than simple description; also called processual archaeology

Nihongi history of the Yamoto kingdom of Japan, compiled in the early 8th century AD

nosed-end scraper stone tool with a protruding working end

notch denticulate tool with single indentation

occipital region back of the head, as seen in profile

ocher the iron oxide minerals hematite (for red ocher), limonite and goethite (for brown, yellow, and black ochers), used as pigments for painting and pottery slips

olfaction sense of smell

oligarchy system of government based on rule by a limited elite group; literally, "rule of the few"

oppidum (pl. oppida) Iron Age European fortified site, often with timber-framed defensive circuit

oracle bones animal **scapulae** and turtle carapaces deliberately pitted on the underside, to which heat was applied in order to form cracks for divination purposes; script detailing these oracles forms the earliest evidence for Chinese writing

orthostat large upright wall stone

oxygen isotope analysis analysis of the ratio of two oxygen isotopes (^{18}O and ^{16}O) in materials; when studied in sediments from the deep-sea floor, differences in ratios can be equated with glacial and interglacial intervals recorded on land; the assignment of terrestrial deposits to a particular glacial (or interglacial) interval allows archaeological sites to be dated by extrapolation from the deep-sea record

pa Maori earthwork enclosures on New Zealand

paleoanthropology study of earliest humans from fossil remains

paleobotany study of fossil plants

paleomagnetic dating method of dating baked clay structures (ovens, kilns, hearths) based on correlating the magnetic direction of the enclosed iron particles to known variations in the earth's magnetic direction; also known as archaeomagnetic dating

paleontology study of fossils

palynology the study of pollen and spores

pan ritual bronze serving vessel

papyrus an aquatic plant native to Egypt, from whose stems a type of paper was made

páramo high-altitude grasslands of the northern Andes

passage grave a type of chamber tomb in which the burial chamber is reached via a long passage from the edge of the covering mound

pediment the triangular area below the roof pitch at either end of a building

peer-polity interaction the full range of interchanges – diffusion, emulation, warfare, interaction, material exchange – that take place between different societies, generally within the same geographical area; sometimes responsible for secondary state formation

peripteral temple one in which the central chamber is surrounded on all four sides by a colonnade

phalange finger or toe bone

phenotype a set of genes possessed by a particular group

phylogeny an evolutionary pedigree, or family tree

phytoliths minute particles of silica derived from the cells of plants, able to survive after the organism has decomposed or been burned; common in ash layers, pottery, and even on stone tools

piece-mold technique bronze-casting method in which the vessel was cast in sections, which were then joined with mortises and tenons

pithos (pl. pithoi) large Greek storage jar

postcranium the skeleton below the head

postprocessual archaeology an approach which questions the rigidly scientific methods of archaeology in favor of a variety of "individualist" approaches and multiple interpretations

potlatch a competitive and feasting ceremony common among Northwest Coast peoples of North America

prehistory the period of human history before the invention of writing

processual archaeology see **New Archaeology**

prognathic having a projecting jaw

pseudomorphs the space left by decayed organic objects within brecciated sediments

puna high-altitude grasslands in the Andes; in the central Andes they are referred to as wet puna, whereas in the southern Andes they are called the dry or salt puna

punctuated equilibrium model of human evolution in which periods of rapid, dramatic change occur over short periods of time, separated by longer periods of little change

quadrupedal walking on four legs

rachis tiny joining stalk that connects the grain to the ear in such plants as maize, wheat, and other cereals

radiometric dating the determination of age relative to a specific (often calendrical) timescale; also referred to as absolute or chronometric dating

radius (pl. radii) one of two lower arm bones (with **ulna**)

refitting putting stone flakes back together to recreate the original core, thus giving insights into the knapper's craft

relative dating determination of chronological sequence without reference to a fixed time scale

retouched flakes those whose edges were further modified by the striking off of tiny chips to reshape or sharpen the edge

rhyton Greek ceremonial vessel for pouring libations

sagittal crest bony ridge running along the top midline of the cranium

Sahul Land the continuous landmass formed by Australia and New Guinea in periods of low sea level

salgado brackish water shell mound of the lower Amazon

sambaqui shell mound common along the Atlantic coast of Amazonia

scapula (pl. scapulae) shoulder blade

seal stone object carved with a design that was impressed into a lump of clay to form a **sealing**; the design might be carved into the flattened surface of the stone (a stamp seal) or around the surface of a cylindrical stone (a cylinder seal)

sealing lump of clay impressed with a **seal**, used for administrative purposes to seal jars, documents, and other objects

sedentism a residence pattern of permanent, year-round settlement

sexual dimorphism difference in size between male and female of a species

Shi Ji "Records of the Grand Historian," a history of early Chinese states by Sima Qian

Shu Jing "Book of History," an early Chinese history edited by Confucius

sigloi Persian bent bar coins

skraelings Norse name for the people of the eastern North American arctic regions, from the coasts of Greenland and Labrador south to Newfoundland

species distinct populations of plants or animals that can and do interbreed and produce fertile offspring

state a society of high population and complexity, in which centralized and institutionalized control overrides kinship ties, and in which wealth and rank hierarchies are protected and fostered

stela (pl. stelae) freestanding carved stone monument

stoa Greek long, shallow building open on one long side, fronted by a colonnade

strangulated blade one in which the mid-region has been thinned to provide two concave edges, forming a "waist"

stratigraphy the successive deposition of superimposed layers of either natural or cultural material

stupa domed building often containing Buddhist relics

subduction the process of one part of the earth's crust moving beneath another along plate boundaries, resulting in chains of volcanoes and parallel formations of uplifted sedimentary rock

Sundaland the continuous landmass formed by island Indonesia and Borneo during periods of low sea level

sutra Buddhist text

swidden land made cultivable by cutting and/or burning off the vegetative cover

taphonomy study of processes that affect organic materials after deposition

taxon (pl. taxa) unit of zoological classification, such as **genus**, **species**, family

tektite small, glassy objects that result from an ancient asteroid impact; can be dated by potassium-argon and fission-track dating methods

tell artificial mound characteristic of Southwest Asian settlement sites, created by the accumulation of centuries of disintegrated mud-brick walls and domestic debris

temper material added to clay to improve the firing qualities of pottery, preventing excessive shrinking and cracking

teosinte wild maize, from which the domesticated species evolved

tephra volcanic ash

terra firma in South America a Portuguese term referring to the Amazonian uplands, away from the rivers

terra preta in South America a Portuguese term ("black earth") referring to occupation-related (settlement) sediments; also includes ancient cultivation areas that lack artifacts

thalassocracy system of government based on sea-borne power; literally, "rule by sea"

thermoluminescence dating see **luminescence dating**

tholos tomb (pl. tholoi) Greek circular tomb with a domed or conical roof, also called a beehive tomb

Three Age System classification system for the sequence of technological periods (Stone, Bronze, Iron) in Old World prehistory

tibia (pl. tibiae) shin bone

tophet in ancient Carthaginian religion, a sacred enclosure in which child sacrifices took place

transhumance seasonal movement of human groups with their livestock, such as sheep, between mountain and lowland pastures

tribe group of a few hundred to a few thousand individuals, commonly settled farmers or pastoralist herders, usually descended from a common ancestor; loosely organized without central control or strongly developed hierarchy

triglyph a tripartite grooved element that alternated with the **metope** to form a frieze that decorated buildings of the Greek **Doric order**

tumulus (pl. tumuli) earthen or stone mound, usually covering a burial or burials

tuff deposit made of compacted volcanic ash

ulna (pl. ulnae) one of two lower arm bones (with **radius**)

uranium-series dating dating method based on the radioactive decay of isotopes of uranium

várzea Portuguese term referring to the bottomlands or floodplains of Amazonia

wasi one-roomed residential structure characteristic of the Incas

world system economic unit articulated by trade networks extending beyond the boundaries of individual political units and linking them together in a larger functioning unit

xiaozhuan "small seal script," a form of standardized writing instituted under the Qin Dynasty in China

yazhang Chinese ceremonial jade blade

yoni representation in stone of the female vagina, symbol of the goddess Sakti

zun Chinese ritual bronze serving vessel

BIBLIOGRAPHY

CHAPTER 1: INTRODUCTION: THE STUDY OF THE HUMAN PAST

Bahn, P. G. (ed.). 1996. *The Cambridge Illustrated History of Archaeology*. Cambridge: Cambridge Univ. Press.

Binford, L. R. 1972. *An Archaeological Perspective*. New York: Seminar Press.

Bowler, P. J. 1990. *Charles Darwin: The Man and his Influence*. Oxford: Blackwell.

Buchli, V. 2000. *An Archaeology of Socialism*. Oxford & New York: Berg.

Butzer, K. W. 1989. Cultural ecology, in *Geography in America*. Gaile, G. L. & Willmott, C. J. (eds.). 92–208. Columbus: Merrill.

Clarke, D. L. 1968. *Analytical Archaeology*. London: Methuen.

Daniel, G. E. 1975. *150 Years of Archaeology*. London: Duckworth.

Daniel, G. E. & Renfrew, C. 1988. *The Idea of Prehistory*. Edinburgh: Edinburgh Univ. Press.

Dobres, M.-A. & Robb, J. (eds.). 2000. *Agency in Archaeology*. London: Routledge.

Grayson, D. K. 1983. *The Establishment of Human Antiquity*. Orlando: Academic Press.

Hodder, I. 1998. *The Archaeological Process: Towards a Reflexive Methodology*. Oxford: Blackwell.

Johnson, M. 1999. *Archaeological Theory: An Introduction*. Oxford: Blackwell.

Jones, M. K. 2001. *The Molecule Hunt*. London: Allen Lane, and New York: Arcade Publishing (2002).

Layton, R. (ed.). 1989. *Conflict in the Archaeology of Living Traditions*. London: Unwin Hyman.

Little, B. J. (ed.). 1992. *Text-Aided Archaeology*. Boca Raton, Ann Arbor, & London: CRC Press.

Mithen, S. J. 1996. *The Prehistory of the Mind*. London & New York: Thames & Hudson.

Moser, S. 1998. *Ancestral Images: The Iconography of Human Origins*. Ithaca: Cornell Univ. Press.

Rappaport, R. A. 1968. *Pigs for the Ancestors: Ritual in the Ecology of a New Guinea People*. New Haven: Yale Univ. Press.

Rathje, W. L. & Murphy, C. 1992. *Rubbish! The Archaeology of Garbage*. New York: HarperCollins.

Renfrew, C. & Bahn, P. G. 2004. *Archaeology: Theories, Methods and Practice*. (4th ed.). London & New York: Thames & Hudson.

Renfrew, C. & Cherry, J. F. (eds.). 1982. *Peer-Polity Interaction and Socio-Political Change*. Cambridge: Cambridge Univ. Press.

Renfrew, C. & Scarre, C. (eds.). 1998. *Cognition and Material Culture*. Cambridge: McDonald Institute for Archaeological Research.

Schiffer, M. B. 1987. *Formation Processes of the Archaeological Record*. Albuquerque: Univ. of New Mexico Press.

Service, E. R. 1962. *Primitive Social Organization*. New York: Random House.

Steward, J. H. 1955. *Theory of Culture Change*. Urbana: Univ. of Illinois Press.

Trigger, B. G. 1980. *Gordon Childe: Revolutions in Archaeology*. London & New York: Thames & Hudson.

—. 1989. *A History of Archaeological Thought*.

Cambridge: Cambridge Univ. Press.

White, L. A. 1959. *The Evolution of Culture*. New York: McGraw Hill.

Willey, G. R. & Sabloff, J. A. 1993. *A History of American Archaeology*. (3rd ed.). New York: Freeman.

CHAPTER 2: AFRICAN ORIGINS

Aiello, L. C. & Wheeler, P. 1995. The expensive-tissue hypothesis: the brain and digestive system in human and primate evolution. *Current Anthropology* 36 (2), 199–221.

Asfaw, B., Beyene, Y., Semaw, S., Suwa, G., White, T., & WoldeGabriel, G. 1991. Fejej: a new paleoanthropological research area in Ethiopia. *Journal of Human Evolution* 21, 37–43.

Asfaw, B., White, T., Lovejoy, O., Latimer, B., Simpson, S., & Suwa, G. 1999. *Australopithecus garhi*: a new species of early hominid from Ethiopia. *Science* 284 (23 April), 629–35.

Barsky, D., Cauche, D., Celiberti, V., Pleurdeau, D., Beyene, Y., & de Lumley, H. In press. Les industries lithiques archaïques du site de Fejej FJ-1 en Éthiopie. XIVème Congrès de l'U.I.S.P.P. Liège.

Bellomo, R. V. 1994. Methods of determining early hominid behavioral activities associated with the controlled use of fire at FxJj 20 main, Koobi Fora, Kenya. *Journal of Human Evolution* 27, 173–95.

Biberson, P. 1961. *Le Paléolithique Inférieur du Maroc Atlantique*. Rabat: Service des Antiquités du Maroc.

Bilsborough, A. 1992. *Human Evolution*. Glasgow: Blackie Academic & Professional.

Binford, L. R. 1981. *Bones: Ancient Men and Modern Myths*. New York: Academic Press.

Blumenschine, R. J. 1986. *Early Hominid Scavenging Opportunities*. Oxford: British Archaeological Reports.

—. 1987. Characteristics of an early hominid scavenging niche. *Current Anthropology* 28 (4), 383–407.

Blumenschine, R. J. & Peters, C. R. 1998. Archaeological predictions for hominid land use in the Paleo-Olduvai Basin, Tanzania, during lowermost bed II times. *Journal of Human Evolution* 34, 565–607.

Brain, C. K. 1981. *The Hunters or the Hunted?* Chicago: Univ. of Chicago Press.

Brain, C. K. & Sillen, A. 1988. Evidence from the Swartkrans Cave for the earliest use of fire. *Nature* 336, 464–66.

Bunn, H. T. & Kroll, E. M. 1986. Systematic butchery by Plio-Pleistocene hominids at Olduvai Gorge, Tanzania. *Current Anthropology* 27, 431–52.

Campbell, B. G. & Loy, J. D. (eds.). 1996. *Humankind Emerging*. (7th ed.). Rhode Island: HarperCollins College Publishers.

Chavaillon, J. 1970. Découverte d'un niveau oldowayen dans la Basse Vallée de l'Omo (Éthiopie). *Bulletin de la Société Préhistorique Française* 67, 7–11.

—. 1976. Evidence for the technical practices of early Pleistocene hominids, Shungura Formation,

Lower Omo Valley, Ethiopia, in *Earliest Man and Environments in the Lake Rudolf Basin*. Coppens, Y., Howell, F. C., Isaac, G. Ll., & Leakey, R. E. (eds.). 565–73. Chicago: Univ. of Chicago Press.

Clark, J. D. 1991. Stone artifact assemblages from Swartkrans, Transvaal, South Africa. *Cultural Beginnings: Approaches To Understanding Early Hominid Life-Ways in the African Savanna* 19, 137–58.

Clark, J. D. & Harris, J. W. K. 1985. Fire and its roles in early hominid lifeways. *The African Archaeological Review* 3, 3–27.

Clark, J. D., Cole, G. H., Isaac, G. Ll., & Kleindienst, M. R. 1966. Precision and definition in African archaeology. *South African Archaeological Bulletin* XXI (83), 114–21.

Conroy, G. C. 1990. *Primate Evolution*. New York: W. W. Norton & Co.

Dart, R. A. 1925. *Australopithecus africanus*: the man-ape of South Africa. *Nature* 115, 195–99.

Day, M. H. 1986. *Guide to Fossil Man*. Chicago: Univ. of Chicago Press.

Deacon, T. W. 1997. *The Symbolic Species: The Co-Evolution of Language and the Brain*. New York: W. W. Norton & Co.

de Heinzelin, J. 1994. Rifting: a long-term African story, with considerations on early hominid habitats, in *Integrative Paths to the Past: Paleoanthropological Advances in Honor of F. Clark Howell*. Corruccini, R. S. & Ciochon, R. L. (eds.). 313–20. New Jersey: Prentice Hall.

de la Torre, I., Mora, R., Dominguez-Rodrigo, M., de Luque, L., & Alcala, L. 2003. The Oldowan industry of Peninj and its bearing on the reconstruction of the technological skills of Lower Pleistocene hominids. *Journal of Human Evolution* 44, 203–24.

Delson, E., Tattersall, I., Van Couvering, J. A., & Brooks, A. S. 2000. A brief introduction to human evolution and prehistory, in *Encyclopedia of Human Evolution and Prehistory*. (2nd ed.). Delson, E., Tattersall, I., Van Couvering, J. A., & Brooks, A. S. (eds.). xvii–xxii. New York: Garland.

de Menocal, P. B. & Bloemendal, J. 1995. Plio-Pleistocene climatic variability in subtropical Africa and the paleoenvironment of hominid evolution: a combined data-model approach, in *Paleoclimate and Evolution, with Emphasis on Human Origins*. Vrba, E. S., Denton, G. H., Partridge, T. C., & Burckle, L. H. (eds.). 262–88. New Haven: Yale Univ. Press.

Ditchfield, P., Hicks, J., Plummer, T., Bishop, L. C., & Potts, R. 1999. Current research on the Late Pliocene and Pleistocene deposits north of Homa Mountain, Southwestern Kenya. *Journal of Human Evolution* 36, 123–50.

Dominguez-Rodrigo, M. 2002. Hunting and scavenging in early humans: the state of the debate. *Journal of World Prehistory* 16, 1–56.

Dominguez-Rodrigo, M. & Pickering, T. 2003. Early hominid hunting and scavenging: a zooarchaeological view. *Evolutionary Anthropology* 12 (6), 275–82.

Dominguez-Rodrigo, M., de la Torre, I., de Luque,

L., Alcala, L., Mora, R., Serralonga, J., & Medina, V. 2002. The ST site complex at Peninj, West Lake Natron, Tanzania: implications for early hominid behavioral models. *Journal of Archaeological Science* 29, 639–65.

Falk, D. 2000. *Primate Diversity*. New York: W. W. Norton & Co.

Field, A. S. 1999. An analytical and comparative study of the earlier Stone Age archaeology of the Sterkfontein Valley. Unpublished M. A. thesis, Univ. of Witwatersrand, Johannesburg.

Fleagle, J. G. 1988. *Primate Adaptation and Evolution*. New York: Academic Press.

Goodall, J. 1986. *The Chimpanzees of Gombe: Patterns of Behavior*. Cambridge, MA: The Belknap Press of Harvard Univ. Press.

Gowlett, J. A. J., Harris, J. W. K., Walton, D., & Wood, B. A. 1981. Early archaeological sites, hominid remains and traces of fire from Chesowanja, Kenya. *Nature* 294, 125–29.

Harris, J. W. K. & Capaldo, S. D. 1993. The earliest stone tools: their implications for an understanding of the activities and behavior of Late Pliocene hominids, in *The Use of Tools by Human and Non-Human Primates*. Berthelet, A. & Chavaillon, J. (eds.). 196–220. Oxford: Clarendon Press.

Harris, J. W. K. & Gowlett, J. A. J. 1980. Evidence of early stone industries at Chesowanja, Kenya, in *Pre-Acheulean and Acheulean Cultures in Africa*. Leakey, M. D. and Harris, J. W. K. (eds.), 208–12. Nairobi: The International Louis Leakey Memorial Institute for African Prehistory.

Harris, J. W. K., Williamson, P. G., Verniers, J., Tappen, M. J., Steward, K., Helgren, D., de Heinzelin, J., Boaz, N. T., & Bellomo, R. V. 1987. Late Pliocene hominid occupation in Central Africa: the setting, context, and character of the Senga 5A site, Zaire. *Journal of Human Evolution* 16, 701–28.

Howell, F. C., Haesaerts, P., & de Heinzelin, J. 1987. Depositional environments, archaeological occurrences and hominids from Members E and F of the Shungura Formation (Omo Basin, Ethiopia). *Journal of Human Evolution* 16, 665–700.

Isaac, G. Ll. 1976. Plio-Pleistocene artifact assemblages from East Rudolf, Kenya, in *Earliest Man and Environments in the Lake Rudolf Basin: Stratigraphy, Paleoecology, and Evolution*. Coppens, Y., Howell, F. C., Isaac, G. Ll., & Leakey, R. E. F. 552–64. Chicago: Univ. of Chicago Press.

—. 1978. The food-sharing behavior of protohuman hominids. *Scientific American* 238 (4), 90–108.

—. 1984. The archaeology of human origins: studies of the Lower Pleistocene in East Africa 1971–1981. *Advances in World Archaeology* 3, 1–87.

Isaac, G. Ll. & Harris. J. W. K. 1980. A method for determining the characteristics of artefacts between sites in the Upper Member of the Koobi Fora Formation, East Lake Turkana, in Proceedings of the 8th Panafrican Congress of Prehistory and Quaternary Studies, Nairobi, September 1977, 19–22. Leakey, R. E. & Ogot, B. A. (eds.). Nairobi: The International Louis Leakey Memorial Institute for African Prehistory.

Isaac, G. Ll. & Isaac, B. (eds.). 1997. *Koobi Fora Research Project*. Vol. 5: Plio-Pleistocene archaeology. Oxford: Clarendon Press.

Johanson, D. & Edey. M. 1981. *Lucy: The Beginnings of Humankind*. New York: Simon & Schuster.

Johanson, D. & Edgar, B. 1996. *From Lucy to Language*. New York: Simon & Schuster.

Kaufulu, Z. M. & Stern, N. 1987. The first stone artifacts to be found *in situ* within the Plio-Pleistocene Chiwondo Beds in Northern Malawi. *Journal of Human Evolution* 16, 729–40.

Keeley, L. H. 1980. *Experimental Determination of Stone Tool Uses*. Chicago: Univ. of Chicago Press.

Keeley, L. H. & Toth, N. 1981. Microwear polishes on early stone tools from Koobi Fora, Kenya. *Nature* 293, 464–65.

Kibunjia, M. 1994. Pliocene archaeological occurrences in the Lake Turkana Basin. *Journal of Human Evolution* 27, 159–71.

Kibunjia, M., Roche, M. H., Brown, F. H., & Leakey, R. E. 1992. Pliocene and Pleistocene archaeological sites west of Lake Turkana, Kenya. *Journal of Human Evolution* 23, 431–38.

Kimbel, W. H., Walter, R. C., Johanson, D. C., Reed, K. E., Aronson, J. L., Assefa, Z., Marean, C. W., Eck, G. G., Bobe, R., Hovers, E., Rak. Y., Vondra, C., Yemane, T., York, D., Chen, Y., Eversen, N. M., & Smith, P. E. 1996. Late Pliocene *Homo* and Oldowan tools from the Hadar Formation (Kada Hadar Member), Ethiopia. *Journal of Human Evolution* 31, 549–61.

Klein, R. G. 1999. *The Human Career*. (2nd ed.). Chicago: Univ. of Chicago Press.

Kuman, K. 1994. The archaeology of Sterkfontein – past and present. *Journal of Human Evolution* 27, 471–95.

Kuman, K., Field, A. S., & Thackeray, J. F. 1997. Discovery of new artefacts at Kromdraai. *South African Journal of Science* 93, 187–93.

Leakey, M. D. 1971. *Olduvai Gorge*. Vol. 3: Excavations in Beds I and II, 1960–1963. New York: Cambridge Univ. Press.

—. 1975. Cultural patterns in the Olduvai Sequence, in *After the Australopithecines: Stratigraphy, Ecology, and Culture Change in the Middle Pleistocene*. Butzer, K. W. & Isaac, G. Ll. (eds.). 477–93. The Hague: Mouton.

Leakey, M. D. & Harris, J. M. 1987. *Laetoli: A Pliocene Site in Northern Tanzania*. Oxford: Clarendon Press.

Lee-Thorpe, J. A., van der Merwe, N. J., & Brain, C. K. 1994. Diet of *Australopithecus robustus* at Swartkrans from stable carbon isotopic analysis. *Journal of Human Evolution* 27, 361–72.

McGrew, W. C. 1992. *Chimpanzee Material Culture: Implications for Human Evolution*. New York: Cambridge Univ. Press.

Merrick, H. V. 1976. Recent archaeological research in the Plio-Pleistocene deposits of the Lower Omo, Southwestern Ethiopia, in *Human Origins: Louis Leakey and the East African Evidence*. Isaac, G. Ll. & McCown, E. R. (eds.). 461–81. Menlo Park, CA: W. A. Benjamin, Inc.

Peters, C. R. & Blumenschine, R. 1995. Landscape perspectives on possible land use patterns for Early Pleistocene hominids in the Olduvai Basin, Tanzania. *Journal of Human Evolution* 29, 321–62.

Plummer, T., Bishop, L. C., Ditchfield, P., & Hicks, J. 1999. Research on Late Pliocene Oldowan sites at Kanjera South, Kenya. *Journal of Human Evolution* 36, 151–70.

Potts, R. 1988. *Early Hominid Activities at Olduvai*. New York: Aldine De Gruyter.

Raynal, J.-P., Sbihi Alaoui, F. Z., Magoga, L., Mohib, A., & Zouak, M. 2002. Casablanca and the earliest occupation of North Atlantic Morocco.

Quarternaria 13 (1), 65–77.

Roche, H. 1989. Technological evolution in early hominids. *OSSA* 4, 97–98.

Roche, H. & Kibunjia, M. 1994. Les sites archéologiques Plio-Pléistocènes de la formation de Nachukui, West Turkana, Kenya. *Comptes Rendus de l'Académie des Sciences, Paris* 318 (Série II), 1145–51.

Roche, H., Brugal, J.-P., Delagnes, A., Feibel, C., Harmand, S., Kibunjia, M., Prat, S., & Texier, P.-J. 2003. Les sites archéologiques plio-pléistocènes de la formation de Nachukui, Ouest-Turkana, Kenya: bilan synthétique 1997–2001. *Comptes Rendus Palevol.* 2, 663–73.

Roche, H., Brugal, J.-P., Delagnes, A., Feibel, C., Kibunjia, M., Mourre, V., & Texier, P.-J. 1999. Early hominid stone tool production and technical skill 2.34 Myr Ago in West Turkana, Kenya. *Nature* 399, 57–60.

Sahnouni M. & de Heinzelin, J. 1998. The site of Ain Hanech revisited: new investigations at this Lower Pleistocene site in Northern Algeria. *Journal of Archaeological Science* 25, 1083–101.

Sahnouni M., de Heinzelin, J., Brown, F., & Saoudi, Y. 1996. Récentes recherches dans le gisement oldowayen d'Ain Hanech, Algérie. *Comptes Rendus de l'Académie des Sciences, Paris*, 323, série II a, 639–44.

Sahnouni M., Hadjouis, D., van der Made, J., Derradji, A., Canals, A., Medig, M., Balahrech, H., Harichane, Z., & Rabhi, M. 2002. Further research at the Oldowan site of Ain Hanech, northeastern Algeria. *Journal of Human Evolution* 43, 925–37.

Sahnouni M., Schick, K., & Toth, N. 1997. An experimental investigation into the nature of faceted limestone 'spheroids' in the Early Palaeolithic. *Journal of Archaeological Science* 24, 1–13.

Schick, K. D. 1986. *Stone Age Sites in the Making: Experiments in the Formation and Transformation of Archaeological Occurrences*. Oxford: British Archaeological Reports International Series 319.

—. 1987. Modeling the formation of early Stone Age artifact concentrations. *Journal of Human Evolution* 16, 789–807.

Schick, K. D. & Toth, N. 1993. *Making Silent Stones Speak: Human Evolution and the Dawn of Technology*. New York: Simon & Schuster.

—. 1994. Early Stone Age technology in Africa: a review and case study into the nature and function of spheroids and subspheroids, in *Integrative Paths to the Past: Paleoanthropological Advances in Honor of F. Clark Howell*. Corrucine, R. S. & Ciochon, R. L. (eds.). 429–50. Englewood Cliffs: Prentice Hall.

—. 2001. Paleoanthropology at the millennium, in *Archaeology at the Millennium: A Sourcebook*. Feinman, G. & Price, D. (eds.). 39–108. New York: Kluwer Academic/Plenum Publishers.

Schick, K. D., Toth, N., Garufi, G., Savage-Rumbaugh, E. S., Rumbaugh, D., & Sevcik, R. 1999. Continuing investigations into the stone tool-making and tool-using capabilities of a Bonobo (*Pan paniscus*). *Journal of Archaeological Science* 26, 821–32.

Semaw, S. 2000. The world's oldest stone artefacts from Gona, Ethiopia: their implications for understanding stone technology and patterns of human evolution between 2.6–1.5 million years ago. *Journal of Archaeological Science* 27, 1197–214.

Semaw, S., Renne, P., Harris, J. W. K., Feibel, C. S., Bernor, R. L., Fesseha, N., & Mowbray, K. 1997. 2.5-million-year-old stone tools from Gona, Ethiopia. *Nature* 385, 333–36.

Semenov, S. A. 1964. *Prehistoric Technology*. Transl. Thompson, M. W. London: Cory, Adams & Mackay.

Senut, B., Pickford, M., Ssemmanda, I., Elepu, D., & Obwona, P. 1987. Découverte du premier homininae (*Homo* sp.) dans le Pléistocene de Nyabusosi (Ouganda Occidental). *Comptes Rendus de l'Academie des Sciences, Paris*, 305, série II, 819–22.

Sillen, A., Hall, G., & Armstrong, R. 1995. Strontium calcium ratios (Sr/Ca) and strontium isotope ratios (Sr-87/Sr-86) of *Australopithecus robustus* and *Homo* sp. from Swartkrans. *Journal of Human Evolution* 28, 277–85.

Susman, R. L. 1994. Fossil evidence for early hominid tool use. *Science* 265, 1570–73.

Toth, N. 1985. The Oldowan reassessed: a close look at early stone artifacts. *Journal of Archaeological Science* 12, 101–20.

Toth, N. & Schick, K. D. 1986. The first million years: the archaeology of protohuman culture. *Advances in Archaeological Method and Theory* 9, 1–96.

Toth, N., Schick, K. D., Savage-Rumbaugh, E. S., Sevcik, R. A., & Rumbaugh, D. M. 1993. Pan the tool-maker: investigations into the stone tool-making and tool-using capabilities of a Bonobo (*Pan paniscus*). *Journal of Archaeological Science* 20, 81–91.

Wrangham, R. W. 1987. The significance of African apes for reconstructing human social evolution, in *The Evolution of Human Behavior: Primate Models*. Kinzey, W. G. (ed.). 51–71. Albany: State Univ. of New York Press.

Wynn, T. & McGrew, W. C. 1989. An ape's view of the Oldowan. *Man* 24, 383–98.

CHAPTER 3: HOMININ DISPERSALS IN THE OLD WORLD

Abbate, E., Albianell, A., Azzaroli, A., Benvenuti, M., Tesfamariam, B., Bruni, P., Cipriani, N., Clarke, R. J., Piccarelli, G., Macchiarelli, R., Napeoleone, G., Papini, M., Rook, L., Sagri, M., Tecle, T. M., Toree, D., & Villa, I. 1998. A one-million-year-old *Homo* cranium from the Danakil (Afar) Depression of Eritrea. *Nature* 393, 458–60.

Andrews, P. 1984. On the characters that define *Homo erectus*. *Courier Forschungsinstitut Senckenberg* 69, 167–78.

Arsuaga, J. L., Carbonell, E., & Bermúdez de Castro, J. M. 2003. *Treasures from the Hills of Atapuerca*. New York: Junta de Castilla y León.

Asfaw, B., Beyene, Y., Suwa, G., Walter, R. C., White, T. D., WoldeGabriel, G., & Yemane, T. 1992. The earliest Acheulean from Konso-Gardula. *Nature* 360, 732–35.

Asfaw, B., Gilbert, W. H., Beyene, Y., Hart, W. K., Renne, P. R., WoldeGabriel, G., Vrba, E. S., & White, T. D. 2002. Remains of *Homo erectus* from Bouri, Middle Awash, Ethiopia. *Nature* 416, 317–20.

Bar-Yosef, O. & Belfer-Cohen, A. 2001. From Africa to Eurasia – early dispersals. *Quaternary International* 75, 19–28.

Barham, L. S. 2002. Systematic pigment use in the Middle Pleistocene of South-Central Africa. *Current Anthropology* 43, 181–90.

Binford, L. R. 1985. Human ancestors: changing views of their behavior. *Journal of Anthropological Archaeology* 4, 292–327.

Binford, L. R. & Ho, C. K. 1985. Taphonomy at a distance: Zhoukoudian, "the cave home of Beijing Man"? *Current Anthropology* 26, 413–42.

Bischoff, J. L., Shamp, D. D., Aramburu, A., Arsuaga, J. L., Carbonell, E., & Bermúdez de Castro, J. M. 2003. The Sima de los Huesos hominids date to beyond U/Th equilibrium (> 350 kyrs) and perhaps to 400–500 kyrs: new radiometric dates. *Journal of Archaeological Science* 30, 275–80.

Bonifay, E., Bonifay, M.-F., Panattoni, R., & Tiercelin, J.-J. 1976. Soleihac (Blanzac, Haute-Loire): nouveau site préhistorique du début du Pléistocène moyen. *Bulletin de la Société Préhistorique Française* 73, 293–304.

Bordes, F. H. 1968. *The Old Stone Age*. New York: McGraw Hill.

Brown, F. H. & McDougall, I. 1993. Geologic setting and age, in *The Nariokotome Homo erectus Skeleton*. Walker, A. & Leakey, R. (eds.). 9–20. Cambridge, MA: Harvard Univ. Press.

Callow, P., Walton, D., & Shell, C. A. 1986. The use of fire at La Cotte de St. Brelade, in *La Cotte de St. Brelade, Jersey: Excavations by C. B. M. McBurney 1961–1978*. 193–95. Norwich: Geo Books.

Calvin, W. H. 2002. *A Brain for all Seasons: Human Evolution and Abrupt Climate Change*. Chicago: Univ. of Chicago Press.

Carbonell, E., García-Anton, M. D., Mallol, C., Mosquera, M., Ollé, A., Rodríguez, J. P., Sahnouni, M., Sala, R., & Vergès, J. M. 1999. The TD6 level lithic industry from Gran Dolina, Atapuerca (Burgos, Spain): production and use. *Journal of Human Evolution* 37, 655–93.

Chase, P. G. 1988. Scavenging and hunting in the Middle Paleolithic: the evidence from Europe, in *Upper Pleistocene Prehistory of Western Asia*. Dibble, H. L. & Montet-White, A. (eds.). 225–32. Philadelphia: Univ. Museum, Univ. of Pennsylvania.

Clark, J. D. & Harris, J. W. K. 1985. Fire and its roles in early hominid lifeways. *African Archaeological Review* 3, 3–27.

Clark, J. D. & Kurashina, H. 1979. Hominid occupation of the east-central highlands of Ethiopia in the Plio-Pleistocene. *Nature* 282, 33–39.

Clarke, R. J. 1990. The Ndutu cranium and the origin of *Homo sapiens*. *Journal of Human Evolution* 19, 699–736.

—. 1994. The significance of the Swartkrans *Homo* to the *Homo erectus* problem. *Courier Forschungsinstitut Senckenberg* 171, 185–93.

Cruz-Uribe, K., Klein, R. G., Avery, G., Avery, D. M., Halkett, D., Hart, T., Milo, R. G., Sampson, C. G., & Volman, T. P. 2003. Excavation of buried late Acheulean (Mid-Quaternary) land surfaces at Duinefontein 2, Western Cape Province, South Africa. *Journal of Archaeological Science* 30, 559–75.

Cuenca-Bescós, G., Laplana, C., & Canudo, J. I. 1999. Biochronological implications of the Arvicolidae (Rodentia, Mammalia) from the Lower Pleistocene hominid-bearing level of Trinchera Dolina 6 (TD6, Atapuerca, Spain). *Journal of Human Evolution* 37, 353–73.

d'Errico, F. 2003. The invisible frontier: a multiple species model for the origin of behavioral modernity. *Evolutionary Anthropology* 12, 188–202.

d'Errico, F. & Nowell, A. 2000. A new look at the Berekhat Ram figurine: implications for the origins of symbolism. *Cambridge Archaeological Journal* 10, 123–67.

De Lumley, H. 1975. Cultural evolution in France in its paleoecological setting during the Middle Pleistocene, in *After the Australopithecines*. Butzer, K. W. & Isaac, G. Ll. (eds.). 745–808. The Hague: Mouton.

de Vos, J., Sondaar, P., & Swisher, C. C. 1994. Dating hominid sites in Indonesia. *Science* 266, 1726–27.

Dean, C., Leakey, M. G., Reid, D., Schrenk, F., Schwartz, G. T., Stringer, C. B., & Walker, A. C. 2001. Growth processes in teeth distinguish modern humans from *Homo erectus* and earlier hominins. *Nature* 414, 628–31.

Diez, J. C., Fernández-Jalvo, Y., Rosell, J., & Cáceres, I. 1999. Zooarchaeology and taphonomy of Aurora Stratum (Gran Dolina, Sierra de Atapuerca, Spain). *Journal of Human Evolution* 37, 623–52.

Falguères, C., Bahain, J.-J., Yokoyama, Y., Arsuaga, J. L., Bermúdez de Castro, J. M., Carbonell, E., Bischoff, J. L., & Dolo, J.-M. 1999. Earliest humans in Europe: the age of TD6 Gran Dolina, Atapuerca, Spain. *Journal of Human Evolution* 37, 343–52.

Feathers, J. K. 1996. Luminescence dating and modern human origins. *Evolutionary Anthropology* 5, 25–36.

Fernández-Jalvo, Y., Diez, J. C., Cáceres, I., & Rosell, J. 1999. Human cannibalism in the Early Pleistocene of Europe (Gran Dolina, Sierra de Atapuerca, Burgos, Spain). *Journal of Human Evolution* 37, 591–622.

Franciscus, R. G. & Trinkaus, E. 1988. Nasal morphology and the emergence of *Homo erectus*. *American Journal of Physical Anthropology* 75, 517–27.

Freeman, L. G. 1994. Torralba and Ambrona: a review of discoveries, in *Integrative Paths to the Past: Paleoanthropological Advances in Honor of F. Clark Howell*. Corruccini, R. S. & Ciochon, R. L. (eds.). 597–637. Englewood Cliffs: Prentice Hall.

Gabunia, L., Vekua, A., & Lordkipanidze, D. 2000. The environmental contexts of early human occupation of Georgia (Transcaucasia). *Journal of Human Evolution* 38, 785–802.

Gaudzinski, S. & Turner, E. 1996. The role of early humans in the accumulation of European Lower and Middle Palaeolithic bone assemblages. *Current Anthropology* 37, 153–56.

Goren-Inbar, N. & Peltz, S. 1995. Additional remarks on the Berekhat Ram figure. *Rock Art Research* 12, 131–32.

Groves, C. P. 1996. Hovering on the brink: nearly but not quite getting to Australia. *Perspectives in Human Biology* 2, 83–87.

Grün, R. 1993. Electron Spin Resonance dating in paleoanthropology. *Evolutionary Anthropology* 2, 172–81.

Harris, J. W. K. 1983. Cultural beginnings: Plio-Pleistocene archaeological occurrences from the Afar, Ethiopia. *African Archaeological Review* 1, 3–31.

Henshilwood, C. S., d'Errico, F., Yates, R. J., Jacobs, Z., Tribola, C., Duller, G. A. T., Mercier, N., Sealy, J. C., Valladas, H., Watts, I., & Wintle, A. G. 2002. Emergence of modern human behavior: Middle

Stone Age engravings from South Africa. *Science* 295, 1278–80.

Hofreiter, M., Serre, D., Poinar, H. N., Kuch, M., & Pääbo, S. 2001. Ancient DNA. *Nature Reviews Genetics* 2, 353–59.

Hou, Y., Potts, R., Yuan, B., Guo, Z., Deino, A., Wei, W., Clark, J., Zie, G., & Huang, W. 2000. Mid-Pleistocene Acheulean-like stone technology of the Bose Basin, South China. *Science* 287, 1622–26.

Hovers, E., Ilani, S., Bar-Yosef, O., & Vandermeersch, B. 2003. An early case of color symbolism: ochre use by modern humans in Qafzeh Cave. *Current Anthropology* 44, 491–522.

Howell, F. C. 1986. Variabilité chez *Homo erectus*, et problème de la présence de cette espèce en Europe. *L'Anthropologie* 90, 447–81.

Hublin, J.-J. 1996. The first Europeans. *Archaeology* 49 (1), 36–44.

Isaac, G. Ll. 1977. *Olorgesailie*. Chicago: Univ. of Chicago Press.

Jelinek, A. J. 1977. The Lower Paleolithic: current evidence and interpretations. *Annual Review of Anthropology* 6, 11–32.

Jones, P. R. 1980. Experimental butchery with modern stone tools and its relevance for Palaeolithic archaeology. *World Archaeology* 12, 153–75.

Klein, R. G. 1979. Stone age exploitation of animals in southern Africa. *American Scientist* 67, 151–60.

—. 1987. Problems and prospects in understanding how early people exploited animals, in *The Evolution of Human Hunting*. Nitecki, M. H. & Nitecki, D. V. (eds.). 11–45. New York: Plenum Press.

—. 1994. Southern Africa before the Iron Age, in *Integrative Paths to the Past: Paleoanthropological Advances in Honor of F. Clark Howell*. Corruccini, R. S. & Ciochon, R. L. (eds.). 471–519. Englewood Cliffs: Prentice Hall.

Kohn, M. & Mithen, S. 1999. Handaxes: products of sexual selection? *Antiquity* 73, 518–26.

Langbroek, M. & Roebroeks, W. 2000. Extraterrestrial evidence on the age of the hominids from Java. *Journal of Human Evolution* 38, 595–600.

Larick, R., Ciochon, R. L., Zaim, Y., Sudijono, S., Rizal, Y., Aziz, F., Reagan, M., & Heizler, M. 2001. Early Pleistocene $^{40}Ar/^{39}Ar$ ages for Bapang Formation hominins, Central Jawa, Indonesia. *Proceedings of the National Academy of Sciences (USA)* 98, 4866–71.

Leakey, L. S. B. 1961. New finds at Olduvai Gorge. *Nature* 189, 649–50.

Leinders, J. J. M., Aziz, F., Sondaar, P. Y., & de Vos, J. 1985. The age of the hominid-bearing deposits of Java: state of the art. *Geologie en Mijnbouw* 64, 167–73.

Levine, M. 1983. Mortality models and the interpretation of horse population structure, in *Hunter-Gatherer Economy in Prehistory*. Bailey, G. (ed.). 23–46. Cambridge: Cambridge Univ. Press.

Mania, D. & Mania, U. 1988. Deliberate engravings on bone artefacts of *Homo erectus*. *Rock Art Research* 5, 91–107.

Mania, D., Mania, U., & Vlcek, E. 1994. Latest finds of skull remains of *Homo erectus* from Bilzingsleben (Thuringia). *Naturwissenschaften* 81, 123–27.

Mania, U. 1998. A special aspect of the cultural evolution, the tools from organic material of the

Middle Pleistocene *Homo erectus*, in *The First Europeans: Recent Discoveries and Current Debate*. Carbonell, E., Bermudéz de Castro, J., Arsuaga, J. L., & Rodriguez, X. P. (eds.). 151–67. Burgos: Aldecoa.

Mason, R. J. 1962. *Prehistory of the Transvaal*. Johannesburg: Univ. of the Witwatersrand Press.

Mayr, E. 1950. Taxonomic categories in fossil hominids. *Cold Spring Harbor Symposia on Quantitative Biology* 15, 109–18.

McHenry, H. M. 1996. Sexual dimorphism in fossil hominids and its socioecological implications, in *The Archaeology of Human Ancestry: Power, Sex and Tradition*. Steele, J. & Shennan, S. (eds.). 91–109. London: Routledge.

Milo, R. G. 1998. Evidence for hominid predation at Klasies River Mouth, South Africa, and its implications for the behaviour of early modern humans. *Journal of Archaeological Science* 25, 99–133.

Morwood, M. J., O'Sullivan, P. B., Aziz, F., & Raza, A. 1998. Fission-track ages of stone tools and fossils on the East Indonesian island of Flores. *Nature* 392, 173–76.

Movius, H. L. 1948. The Lower Palaeolithic cultures of southern and eastern Asia. *Transactions of the American Philosophical Society* 38, 329–420.

O'Connell, J. F., Hawkes, K., & Blurton Jones, N. G. 1999. Grandmothering and the evolution of *Homo erectus*. *Journal of Human Evolution* 36, 461–85.

Oakley, K. P. 1964. The problem of man's antiquity: an historical survey. *Bulletin of the British Museum (Natural History) Geology* 9, 86–155.

Parés, J. M. & Pérez-González, A. 1999. Magnetochronology and stratigraphy at Gran Dolina section, Atapuerca (Burgos, Spain). *Journal of Human Evolution* 37, 325–42.

Pei, W. & Zhang, S. 1985. A study on lithic artifacts of *Sinanthropus* (in Chinese with an English summary on pp. 259–77). *Palaeontologia Sinica* 168 (n. s.), 1–277.

Pope, G. G. 1993. Ancient Asia's cutting edge. *Natural History* 102 (5), 54–59.

Potts, R., Behrensmeyer, A. K., Deino, A. L., Ditchfield, P., & Clark, J. 2004. Small mid-Pleistocene hominin associated with East African Acheulean technology. *Science* 305, 75–78.

Rightmire, G. P. 1990. *The Evolution of Homo erectus: Comparative Anatomical Studies of an Extinct Human Species*. Cambridge: Cambridge Univ. Press.

Roche, H. & Kibunjia, M. 1994. Les sites archéologiques plio-pléistocènes de la Formation de Nachukui, West Turkana, Kenya. *Comptes Rendus de l'Académie des Sciences* 318, série II, 1145–51.

Roebroeks, W. 2001. Hominid behaviour and the earliest occupation of Europe: an exploration. *Journal of Human Evolution* 41, 437–61.

Roebroeks, W. & van Kolfschoten, T. 1994. The earliest occupation of Europe: a short chronology. *Antiquity* 68, 489–503.

Ruff, C. B. & Walker, A. 1993. Body size and body shape, in *The Nariokotome Homo erectus Skeleton*. Walker, A. & Leakey, R. (eds.). 234–63. Cambridge, MA: Harvard Univ. Press.

Ruff, C. B., Trinkaus, E., & Holliday, T. W. 1997. Body mass and encephalization in Pleistocene *Homo*. *Nature* 387, 173–76.

Schick, K. D. & Toth, N. 1993. *Making Silent Stones*

Speak: Human Evolution and the Dawn of Technology. New York: Simon & Schuster.

Schwarcz, H. P. 1992. Uranium series dating in paleoanthropology. *Evolutionary Anthropology* 1, 56–62.

Scott, K. 1989. Mammoth bones modified by humans: evidence from La Cotte de St. Brelade, Jersey, Channel Islands, in *Bone Modification*. Bonnichsen, R. & Sorg, M. H. (eds.). 335–46. Orono, Maine: Center for the Study of the First Americans, Univ. of Maine.

Sémah, F., Saleki, H., & Falguères, C. 2000. Did early man reach Java during the Late Pliocene? *Journal of Archaeological Science* 27, 763–69.

Shapiro, H. L. 1974. *Peking Man*. New York: Simon & Schuster.

Smith, B. H. 1993. The physiological age of KNM-WT 15000, in *The Nariokotome Homo erectus Skeleton*. Walker, A. & Leakey, R. (eds.). 195–220. Cambridge, MA: Harvard Univ. Press.

Stiner, M. C. 1994. *Honor Among Thieves: A Zooarchaeological Study of Neanderthal Ecology*. Princeton: Princeton Univ. Press.

Storm, P. 2001. The evolution of humans in Australasia from an environmental perspective. *Palaeogeography, Palaeoclimatology, Palaeoecology* 171, 363–83.

Swisher, C. C., Curtis, G. H., Jacob, T., Getty, A. G., Suprijo, A., & Widiasmoro. 1994. Age of the earliest known hominids in Java, Indonesia. *Science* 263, 1118–21.

Swisher, C. C., Rink, W. J., Antón, S. C., Schwarcz, H. P., Curtis, G. H., Suprijo, A., & Widiasmoro. 1996. Latest *Homo erectus* of Java: potential contemporaneity with *Homo sapiens* in southeast Asia. *Science* 274, 1870–74.

Theunissen, B. 1989. *Eugène Dubois and the Ape-Man from Java: The History of the First "Missing Link" and its Discoverer*. Dordrecht: Kluwer Academic.

Theunissen, B., de Vos, J., Sondaar, P. Y., & Aziz, F. 1990. The establishment of a chronological framework for the hominid-bearing deposits of Java: a historical survey. *Geological Society of America Special Paper* 242, 39–54.

Thieme, H. 1997. Lower Palaeolithic hunting spears from Germany. *Nature* 385, 807–10.

Tryon, C. A. & McBrearty, S. 2002. Tephrostratigraphy and the Acheulean to Middle Stone Age transition in the Kapthurin Formation, Kenya. *Journal of Human Evolution* 42, 211–35.

Turner, E. 1986. The 1981–83 excavations in the Karl Schneider Quarry, Ariendorf, West Germany, in *Chronostratigraphie et faciés culturels du Paléolithique inférieur et moyen dans l'Europe du Nord-Ouest*. Tuffreau, A. & Sommé, J. (eds.). 35–42. Paris: Supplement au Bulletin de l'Association Française pour l'Étude du Quaternaire.

Vekua, A., Lordkipanidze, D., Rightmire, G. P., Agustí, J., Ferring, C. R., Maisuradze, G., Mouskhelishivili, A., Nioradze, M., Ponce de León, M. S., Tappen, M., Tvalchrelidze, M., & Zollikofer, C. P. E. 2002. A new skull of early *Homo* from Dmanisi, Georgia. *Science* 297, 85–89.

Villa, P. 1976. Sols et niveaux d'habitat du Paléolithique inférieur en Europe et au Proche Orient. *Quaternaria* 19, 107–34.

Villa, P. & d'Errico, F. 2001. Bone and ivory points in the Lower and Middle Paleolithic of Europe.

Journal of Human Evolution 41, 69–112.

Villa, P. & Soressi, M. 2000. Stone tools in carnivore sites: the case of Bois Roche. *Journal of Anthropological Research* 56, 187–215.

Volman, T. P. 1984. Early prehistory of southern Africa, in *Southern African Prehistory and Paleoenvironments*. Klein, R. G. (ed.). 169–220. Rotterdam: A. A. Balkema.

von Koenigswald, G. H. R. 1975. Early man in Java: catalogue and problems, in *Paleoanthropology, Morphology and Paleoecology*. Tuttle, R. H. (ed.). 303–09. The Hague: Mouton.

von Koenigswald, G. H. R. & Weidenreich, F. 1939. The relationship between *Pithecanthropus* and *Sinanthropus*. *Nature* 144, 926–29.

Walker, A. C. & Leakey, R. 1993a. Perspectives on the Nariokotome discovery, in *The Nariokotome Homo erectus Skeleton*. Walker, A. & Leakey, R. (eds.). 411–30. Cambridge, MA: Harvard Univ. Press.

—. 1993b. The skull, in *The Nariokotome Homo erectus Skeleton*. Walker, A. & Leakey, R. (eds.). 63–94. Cambridge, MA: Harvard Univ. Press.

Walker, A. C. & Ruff, C. B. 1993. The reconstruction of the pelvis, in *The Nariokotome Homo erectus Skeleton*. Walker, A. & Leakey, R. (eds.). 221–33. Cambridge, MA: Harvard Univ. Press.

Walker, A. C., Zimmerman, M. R., & Leakey, R. E. F. 1982. A possible case of hypervitaminosis A in *Homo erectus*. *Nature* 296, 248–50.

Weiner, S., Xu, Q., Goldberg, P., Liu, J., & Bar-Yosef, O. 1998. Evidence for the use of fire at Zhoukoudian, China. *Science* 281, 251–53.

Wendorf, F. E. & Schild, R. 1980. *Prehistory of the Eastern Sahara*. New York: Academic Press.

Wrangham, R. W., Jones, J. H., Laden, G., Pilbeam, D., & Conklin-Brittain, N. 1999. The raw and the stolen: cooking and the ecology of human origins. *Current Anthropology* 40, 567–94.

Wu, R. & Lin, S. 1983. Peking Man. *Scientific American* 248 (6), 86–95.

Wu, X. & Poirier, F. E. 1995. *Human Evolution in China: A Metric Description of the Fossils and a Review of the Sites*. New York: Oxford Univ. Press.

Wynn, T. 1995. Handaxe enigmas. *World Archaeology* 27, 10–24.

Zhu, R. X., Hoffman, K. A., Potts, R., Deng, C. L., Pan, Y. X., Guo, B., Shi, C. D., Guo, Z. T., Yuan, B. Y., Hou, Y. M., & Huang, W. W. 2001. Earliest presence of humans in northeast Asia. *Nature* 413, 413–17.

Zhu, R. X., Potts, R., Xie, F., Hoffman, K. A., Deng, C. L. et al. 2004. New evidence on the earliest human presence at high northern latitudes in northeast Asia. *Nature* 431: 559–62.

CHAPTER 4: THE RISE OF MODERN HUMANS

Adovasio, J. M. & Pedler, D. R. 1997. Monte Verde and the antiquity of humankind in the Americas. *Antiquity* 71, 573–80.

Adovasio, J. M., Pedler, D. R., Donahue, J., & Stuckenrath, R. 1998. Two decades of debate on Meadowcroft rockshelter. *North American Archaeologist* 19 (4), 317–41.

Adovasio, J. M., Soffer, O., & Klíma, B. 1996. Upper Paleolithic fibre technology: interlaced woven finds from Pavlov I, Czech Republic, *c.* 26,000 BP. *Antiquity* 70, 526–34.

Aiello, L. 1993. The fossil evidence for modern human origins in Africa: a revised view. *American Anthropologist* 95, 73–96.

Akazawa, T. & Muhesen, S. 2002. *Neanderthal Burials: Excavations of the Dederiyeh Cave, Afrin, Syria*. Kyoto: International Research Centre for Japanese Studies.

Akazawa, T., Muhesen, S., Ishida, H., Kondo, O., & Griggo, C. 1999. New discovery of a Neanderthal child burial from the Dederiyeh Cave in Syria. *Paléorient* 25/2, 129–42.

Albert, R. M., Weiner, S., Bar-Yosef, O., & Meignen, L. 2000. Phytoliths in the Middle Paleolithic deposits of Kebara Cave, Mt. Carmel, Israel: study of the plant materials used for fuel and other purposes. *Journal of Archaeological Science* 27, 931–47.

Allen, J. & Holdaway, S. 1995. The contamination of Pleistocene radiocarbon determinations in Australia. *Antiquity* 69, 101–12.

Ambrose, S. 1998. Late Pleistocene human population bottlenecks, volcanic winter, and differentiation of modern humans. *Journal of Human Evolution* 34, 623–51.

Bahn, P. 1984. *Pyrenean Prehistory*. Warminster: Aris and Phillips.

Barker, G., Barton, H., Beavitt, P., Bird, M., Daly, P., Doherty, C., Gilbertson, D., Hunt, C., Krigbaum, J., Lewis, H., Manser, J., McLaren, S., Paz, V., Piper, P., Pyatt, B., Rabett, R., Reynolds, T., Rose, J., Rushworth, G., & Stephens, M. 2002. Prehistoric foragers and farmers in south-east Asia: renewed investigations at Niah Cave, Sarawak. *Proceedings of the Prehistoric Society* 68, 147–64.

Barnosky, A. D., Koch, P. L., Feranec, R. S., & Scott, L. 2004. Assessing the causes of Late Pleistocene extinctions on the continents. *Science* 306: 70–75.

Barton, N. 2000. Mousterian hearths and shellfish: late Neanderthal activities on Gibraltar, in *Neanderthals on the Edge: Papers from a Conference Marking the 150th Anniversary of the Forbes' Quarry Discovery, Gibraltar*. Stringer, C. B., Barton, R. N. E., & Finlayson, J. C. (eds.). 211–20. Oxford: Oxbow.

Bar-Yosef, O. 1993. The role of western Asia in modern human origins, in *The Origin of Modern Humans and the Impact of Chronometric Dating*. Aitken, M. J., Stringer, C. B., & Mellars, P. A. (eds.). 132–47. Princeton: Princeton Univ. Press.

—. 2002. The Upper Paleolithic revolution. *Annual Review of Anthropology* 31, 363–93.

Berger, T. D. & Trinkaus, E. 1995. Patterns of trauma among the Neanderthals. *Journal of Archaeological Science* 22, 841–52.

Binford, L. R. 1984. *Faunal Remains from Klasies River Mouth*. New York: Academic Press.

Binford, L. R. & Binford, S. R. 1966. A preliminary analysis of functional variability in the Mousterian of Levallois facies. *American Anthropologist* 68, 238–95.

Bocherens, H., Billiou, D., Mariotti, A., Patou-Mathis, M, Bonjean, D., & Toussaint, M. 1999. Palaeoenvironmental and palaeodietary implications of isotopic biogeochemistry of Last Interglacial Neanderthal and mammal bones in Scladina Cave (Belgium). *Journal of Archaeological Science* 26, 599–607.

Boëda, E., Geneste, J.-M., Griggo, C., Mercier, N., Muhesen, S., Reyss, J. L., Taha, A., & Valladas, H. 1999. A Levallois point embedded in the vertebra of a wild ass (*Equus africanus*): hafting, projectiles and Mousterian hunting weapons. *Antiquity* 73, 394–402.

Bordes, F. & de Sonneville-Bordes, D. 1970. The significance of variability in Paleolithic assemblages. *World Archaeology* 2, 61–73.

Bortolini, M. C., Salzano, F. M., Thomas, M. G., & Ruiz-Linares, A. 2003. Y-chromosome evidence for differing ancient demographic histories in the Americas. *American Journal of Human Genetics* 73, 524–39.

Bräuer, G. 1989. The evolution of modern humans: a comparison of the African and non-African evidence, in *The Human Revolution: Behavioural and Biological Perspectives in the Origins of Modern Humans*. Mellars, P. A. & Stringer, C. B. (eds.). 123–54. Edinburgh: Edinburgh Univ. Press.

Bräuer, G. & Leakey, R. E. 1986. The ES-11693 cranium from Eliye Springs, West Turkana, Kenya. *Journal of Human Evolution* 15, 289–312.

Brown, P. 1981. Artificial cranial deformation: a component in the variation in Pleistocene Australian aboriginal crania. *Archaeology in Oceania* 16, 156–67.

—. 2001. Chinese Middle Pleistocene hominids and modern human origins in east Asia, in *Human Roots: Africa and Asia in the Middle Pleistocene*. Barham, L. & Robson-Brown, K. (eds.). 135–47. Bristol: Western Academic & Specialist Press.

Brown, P., Sutikna, T., Morwood, M. J., Soejono, R. P., Jatmiko, Wayhu Saptomo, E., & Due, R. A. 2004. A new small-bodied hominin from the Late Pleistocene of Flores, Indonesia. *Nature* 431, 1055–61.

Callow, P. & Cornford, J. M. 1986. *La Cotte de St. Brelade 1961–1978: Excavations by C. B. M. McBurney*. Norwich: Geo Books.

Cann, R. L., Stoneking, M., & Wilson, A. 1987. Mitichondrial DNA and human evolution. *Nature* 325, 31–36.

Castro-Curel, Z. & Carbonell, E. 1995. Wood pseudomorphs from Level I and Abric Romaní (Barcelona, Spain). *Journal of Field Archaeology* 22, 376–84.

Chase, P. G. 1986. *The Hunters of Combe Grenal: Approaches to Middle Paleolithic Subsistence in Europe*. Oxford: British Archaeological Reports International Series 286.

Chatters, J. C. 2000. The recovery and first analysis of an early Holocene human skeleton from Kennewick, Washington. *American Antiquity* 65 (2), 291–316.

Chauvet, J.-M., Brunel Deschamps, E., & Hillaire, C. 1996. *Dawn of Art. The Chauvet Cave: the Oldest Known Paintings in the World*. Trans. Bahn, P. G. New York: Abrams. Published as *Chauvet Cave: the Discovery of the World's Oldest Paintings*. London: Thames & Hudson.

Churchill, S. E. & Smith, F. H. 2000. The makers of the early Aurignacian of Europe. *American Journal of Physical Anthropology* 43, 61–115.

Clark, J. D., Beyene, Y., WoldeGabriel, G., Hart, W. K., Renne, P. R., Gilbert, H., Defleur, A., Suwa, G., Katoh, S., Ludwig, K. R., Boisserie, J.-R., Asfaw, B., & White, T. D. 2003. Stratigraphic, chronological and behavioural contexts of Pleistocene *Homo sapiens* from Middle Awash, Ethiopia. *Nature* 423, 747–52.

Clottes, J. 1998. The 'three Cs': fresh avenues towards European Paleolithic art, in *The Archaeology of Rock Art*. Chippindale, C. & Taçon, P. S. C. (eds.). Cambridge: Cambridge Univ. Press.

—. 2003. *Chauvet Cave: the Art of Earliest Times*. Trans. Bahn, P. G. Salt Lake City: University of Utah Press. Published as *Return to Chauvet Cave. Excavating the Birthplace of Art: The First Full Report*. London: Thames & Hudson.

Condemi, S. 2000. The Neanderthals: *Homo neanderthalensis* or *Homo sapiens neanderthalensis*? Is there a contradiction between the paleogenetic and paleoanthropological data?, in *Neanderthals and Modern Humans: Discussing the Transition*. Orscheidt, J. & Weniger, G.-C. (eds.). 287–95. Mettmann: Neanderthal Museum.

Conroy, G. C., Weber, G. W., Seidler, H., Recheis, W., Zur Nedden, D., & Haile Mariam, J. 2000. Endocranial capacity of the Bodo cranium determined from three-dimensional computed tomography. *American Journal of Physical Anthropology* 113, 111–18.

Crow, T. J. 2002. Sexual selection, timing and an X-Y homologous gene: did *Homo sapiens* speciate on the Y chromosome?, in *The Speciation of Modern Homo sapiens*. Crow, T. (ed.). 197–216. London: The British Academy.

Davies, S. W. G. 2001. A very model of a modern human industry: new perspectives on the origins and spread of the Aurignacian in Europe. *Proceedings of the Prehistoric Society* 67, 195–217.

Day, M. H. 1986. *Guide to Fossil Man*. (4th ed.). London: Cassell.

Deacon, H. J. 1989. Late Pleistocene palaeoecology and archaeology in the southern Cape, South Africa, in *The Human Revolution: Behavioural and Biological Perspectives on the Origin of Modern Humans*. Mellars, P. & Stringer, C. (eds.). 547–64. Edinburgh: Edinburgh Univ. Press.

D'Errico, F. & Laroulandie, V. 2000. Bone technology at the Middle to Upper Paleolithic transition. The case of worked bone from Buran-Kaya III level C (Crimea, Ukraine), in *Neanderthals and Modern Humans: Discussing the Transition*. Orscheidt, J. & Weniger, G.-C. (eds.). 227–42. Mettmann: Neanderthal Museum.

Dillehay, T. D. 2000. *The Settlement of the Americas: A New Prehistory*. New York: Basic Books.

Evins, M. A. 1982. The fauna from Shanidar Cave: Mousterian wild goat exploitation in Northeastern Iraq. *Paléorient* 8/1, 37–58.

Franciscus, R. G. 2003. Internal nasal floor configuration in *Homo* with special reference to the evolution of Neanderthal facial form. *Journal of Human Evolution* 44, 701–29.

Gale, R. & Carruthers, W. 2000. Charcoal and charred seed remains from Middle Paleolithic levels at Gorham's and Vanguard Caves, in *Neanderthals on the Edge: Papers from a Conference Marking the 150th Anniversary of the Forbes' Quarry Discovery, Gibraltar*. Stringer, C. B., Barton, R. N. E., & Finlayson, J. C. (eds.). 207–10. Oxford: Oxbow.

Gamble, C. S. 1982. Interaction and alliance in Paleolithic society. *Man* 17, 92–107.

—. 1991. The social context for European Paleolithic art. *Proceedings of the Prehistoric Society* 57 (1), 3–16.

Gaudzinski, S. 1999a. The faunal record of the Lower and Middle Paleolithic of Europe: remarks on human interference, in *The Middle Paleolithic Occupation of Europe*. Roebroeks, W. & Gamble, C. (eds.). 215–33. Leiden: Leiden Univ. Press.

—. 1999b. Middle Paleolithic bone tools from the open-air site of Salzgitter-Lebenstedt (Germany).

Journal of Archaeological Science 26, 125–41.

Goldberg, P. & Arpin, T. 1999. Micromorphological analysis of sediments from Meadowcroft rockshelter, Pennsylvania: implications for radiocarbon dating. *Journal of Field Archaeology* 26, 325–42.

González, S., Jiménez-López, J. C., Hedges, R., Huddart, D., Ohman, J. C., Turner, A., & Pompa y Padilla, J. A. 2003. Earliest humans in the Americas: new evidence from Mexico. *Journal of Human Evolution* 44, 379–87.

González-José, R., González-Martin, A., Hernández, M., Pucciarelli, H. M., Sardi, M., Rosales, A., & van der Molen, S. 2003. Craniometric evidence for Paleoamerican survival in Baja California. *Nature* 425, 62–65.

Grayson, D. K. & Meltzer, D. J. 2002. Clovis hunting and large mammal extinction: a critical review of the evidence. *Journal of World Prehistory* 16 (4), 313–51.

Greenberg, J., Turner, C., & Zegura, S. 1986. The settlement of the Americas: a comparison of the linguistic, dental and genetic evidence. *Current Anthropology* 27, 477–97.

Grine, F. E. & Klein, R. G. 1985. Pleistocene and Holocene human remains from Equus Cave, South Africa. *Anthropology* 8, 55–98.

Groves, C. P. 1997. Thinking about evolutionary change: the polarity of our ancestors, in *Conceptual Issues in Modern Human Origins Research*. Clark, G. A. & Willermet, C. M. (eds.). 319–26. New York: Aldine de Gruyter.

Grün, R. & Beaumont, P. 2001. Border Cave revisited: a revised ESR chronology. *Journal of Human Evolution* 40, 467–82.

Grün, R., Brink, J. S., Spooner, N. A., Stringer, C. B., Franciscus, R. G., & Murray, A. S. 1996. Direct dating of the Florisbad hominid. *Nature* 382, 500–01.

Guthrie, R. D. 1990. *Frozen Fauna of the Mammoth Steppe*. Chicago: Univ. of Chicago Press.

Gvozdover, M. 1995. *Art of the Mammoth Hunters: The Finds from Avdeevo*. Oxford: Oxbow.

Harpending, H. C., Batzer, M. A., Gurven, M., Jorde, L. B., Rogers, A. R., & Sherry, S. T. 1998. Genetic traces of ancient demography. *Proceedings of the National Academy of Sciences (USA)* 95, 1961–67.

Haynes, G. 2002. *The Early Settlement of North America*. Cambridge: Cambridge Univ. Press.

Hennesy, R. J. & Stringer, C. B. 2002. Geometric morphometric study of the regional variation of modern human craniofacial form. *American Journal of Physical Anthropology* 117, 37–48.

Henshilwood, C. S., d'Errico, F., Vanhaeren, M., van Niekert, K. & Jacobs, Z. 2004. Middle Stone Age shell beads from South Africa. *Science* 304, 404.

Henshilwood, C. S., d'Errico, F., Yates, R., Jacobs, Z., Tribolo, C., Duller, G. A. T., Mercier, N., Sealy, J. C., Valladas, H., Watts, I., & Wintle, A. G. 2002. Emergence of modern human behaviour: Middle Stone Age engravings from South Africa. *Science* 295, 1278–80.

Hoffecker, J. F., Baryshnikov, G. & Potapova, O. 1991. Vertebrate remains from the Mousterian site of Il'skaya I (Northern Caucasus, U.S.S.R.): new analysis and interpretation. *Journal of Archaeological Science* 18, 113–47.

Howells, W. W. 1976. Explaining modern man: evolutionists versus migrationists. *Journal of*

Human Evolution 5, 477–96.

Hublin, J.-J. 1993. Recent human evolution in Northwestern Africa, in *The Origin of Modern Humans and the Impact of Chronometric Dating*. Aitken, M. J., Stringer, C. B., & Mellars, P. A. (eds.). 118–31. Princeton: Princeton Univ. Press.

—. 2000. Modern/Non Modern human interactions: a Mediterranean perspective, in *The Geography of Neanderthals and Modern Humans in Europe and the Greater Mediterranean*. Bar-Yosef, O. & Pilbeam, D. (eds.). 157–82. Harvard: Peabody Museum Bulletin 8.

—. 2001. Northwestern African Middle Pleistocene hominids and their bearing on the emergence of *Homo sapiens*. Comparison of Middle Pleistocene hominids from Africa and Asia, in *Human Roots: Africa and Asia in the Middle Pleistocene*. Barham, L. & Robson-Brown, K. (eds.). 99–121. Bristol: Western Academic & Specialist Press.

Keates, S. G. 2001. An examination of culture and evolution in Middle Pleistocene Chinese hominids, in *Human Roots: Africa and Asia in the Middle Pleistocene*. Barham, L. & Robson-Brown, K. (eds.). 159–85. Bristol: Western Academic & Specialist Press.

King, M. L. & Slobodin, S. B. 1996. A fluted point from the Uptar site, Northeastern Siberia. *Science* 273, 634–36.

Kipnis, R. 1998. Early hunter-gatherers in the Americas: perspectives from central Brazil. *Antiquity* 72, 581–92.

Klein, R. G. 1973. *Ice Age Hunters of the Ukraine*. Chicago: Univ. of Chicago Press.

—. 1995. Anatomy, behavior and modern human origins. *Journal of World Prehistory* 9 (2), 167–98.

—. 1999. (2nd ed.). *The Human Career: Human Biological and Cultural Origins*. Chicago: Univ. of Chicago Press.

Kolen, J. 1999. Hominids without homes: on the nature of Middle Paleolithic settlement in Europe, in *The Middle Paleolithic Occupation of Europe*. Roebroeks, W. & Gamble, C. (eds.). 139–76. Leiden: Leiden Univ. Press.

Krings, M., Capelli, C., Tschentscher, F., Geisert, H., Meyer, S., von Haeseler, A., Grossschmidt, K., Possnert, G., Paunovic, M., & Pääbo, S. 2000. A view of Neanderthal genetic diversity. *Nature Genetics* 26, 144–46.

Krings, M., Stone, A., Schmitz, R. W., Krainitzki, H., Stoneking, M., & Pääbo, S. 1997. Neanderthal DNA sequences and the origin of modern humans. *Cell* 90, 19–30.

—. 1999. DNA sequence of the DNA hypervariable region II from the Neanderthal type specimen. *Proceedings of the National Academy of Sciences (USA)* 96, 5581–85.

Kuhn, S. L. 1995. *Mousterian Lithic Technology: An Ecological Perspective*. Princeton: Princeton Univ. Press.

Kuhn, S. L., Stiner, M. C., Reese, D. S., & Gülec, E. 2001. Ornaments of the earliest Upper Paleolithic: new insights from the Levant. *Proceedings of the National Academy of Sciences (USA)* 98 (13), 7641–46.

Lahr, M. M. & Foley, R. A. 1994. Multiple dispersals and modern human origins. *Evolutionary Anthropology* 3, 48–60.

Leroi-Gourhan, A. 1968. *The Art of Prehistoric Man in Western Europe*. London: Thames & Hudson.

Lieberman, D. E. & Shea, J. J. 1994. Behavioral differences between archaic and modern humans in the Levantine Mousterian. *American Anthropologist* 96 (2), 300–32.

Lieberman, P. 2002. On the nature and evolution of the neural bases of human language. *Yearbook of Physical Anthropology* 45, 36–62.

Lorblanchet, M. 1995. *Les Grottes Ornées de la Préhistoire: Nouveaux Regards*. Paris: Editions Errance.

Martin, P. S. 1984. Prehistoric overkill: the global model, in *Quaternary Extinctions: A Prehistoric Revolution*. Martin, P. S. & Klein, R. G. (eds.). 354–403. Tucson: Univ. of Arizona Press.

McBrearty, S. & Brooks, A. S. 2000. The revolution that wasn't: a new interpretation of the origin of modern human behaviour. *Journal of Human Evolution* 39, 453–563.

McDermott, L. 1996. Self-representation in Upper Paleolithic female figurines. *Current Anthropology* 37 (2), 227–75.

Meignen, L., Bar-Yosef, O., Goldberg, P., & Weiner, S. 2001. Le feu au Paléolithique Moyen: recherches sur les structures de combustion et le statut des foyers. L'exemple du Proche-Orient. *Paléorient* 26 (2), 9–22.

Mellars, P. A. 1969. The chronology of Mousterian industries in the Périgord region of south-west France. *Proceedings of the Prehistoric Society* 35, 134–71.

—. 1989. Major issues in the emergence of modern humans. *Current Anthropology* 30, 349–85.

—. 1993. Archaeology and the population-dispersal hypothesis of modern human origins in Europe, in *The Origin of Modern Humans and the Impact of Chronometric Dating*. Aitken, M. J., Stringer, C. B., & Mellars, P. A. (eds.). 196–216 Princeton: Princeton Univ. Press.

—. 1994. The Upper Palaeolithic revolution, in *The Oxford Illustrated History of Europe*. Cunliffe, B. (ed.). 42–78. Oxford: Oxford Univ. Press.

—. 1999. The Neanderthal problem continued. *Current Anthropology* 40, 341–50.

Meltzer, D. J., Adovasio, J. M., & Dillehay, T. D. 1994. On a Pleistocene human occupation at Pedra Furada, Brazil. *Antiquity* 68, 695–714.

Mitchell, P. 2002. *The Archaeology of Southern Africa*. Cambridge: Cambridge Univ. Press.

Morwood, M. J., Soejono, R. P., Roberts, R. G., Sutikna, T., Turney, C. S. M., Westaway, K. E., Rink, W. J., Zhao, J.-X., van den Bergh, G. D., Due, R. A., Hobbs, D. R., Moore, M. W., Bird, M. I., & Fifield, L. K. 2004. Archaeology and age of a new hominin from Flores in eastern Indonesia. *Nature* 431, 1087–91.

Mulvaney, J. & Kamminga, J. 1999. *Prehistory of Australia*. Washington D.C.: Smithsonian Institution Press.

Mussi, M. 1999. The Neanderthals in Italy: a tale of many caves, in *The Middle Paleolithic Occupation of Europe*. Roebroeks, W. & Gamble, C. (eds.). 49–80. Leiden: Leiden Univ. Press.

Oakley, K. P. 1964. The problem of man's antiquity: an historical survey. *Bulletin of the British Museum (Natural History) Geology* 9, 86–155.

Ovchinnikov, I. V., Gotterstrom, A., Romanova, G. P., Kharitonov, V. M., Liden, K., & Goodwin, W. 2000. Molecular analysis of Neanderthal DNA from the northern Caucasus. *Nature* 404, 490–93.

Pettitt, P. B. 2002. The Neanderthal dead: exploring mortuary variability in Middle Paleolithic Eurasia. *Before Farming* 1, 1–26.

Pettitt, P. B. & Bahn, P. 2003. Current problems in dating Paleolithic cave art: Candamo and Chauvet. *Antiquity* 77, 134–41.

Politis, G. G., Prado, J. L., & Beukens, R. P. 1995. The human impact in Pleistocene-Holocene extinctions in South America: the Pampean case, in *Ancient Peoples and Landscapes*. Johnson, E. (ed.). 187–205. Lubbock: Museum of Texas Publications.

Pope, G. G. 1995. The influence of climate and geography on the biocultural evolution of the far eastern hominids, in *Paleoclimate and Evolution, with Emphasis on Human Origins*. Vrba, E. S., Denton, G. H., Partridge, T. C., & Burckle, L. H. (eds.). 493–506. New Haven: Yale Univ. Press.

Relethford, J. H. 2001. *Genetics and the Search for Modern Human Origins*. New York: Wiley-Liss.

Rice, P. 1981. Prehistoric Venuses: symbols of motherhood or womanhood? *Journal of Anthropological Research* 37, 402–14.

Richards, D. A. & Beck, J. W. 2001. Dramatic shifts in atmospheric radiocarbon during the Last Glacial Period. *Antiquity* 75, 482–85.

Richards, M. P., Pettitt, P. B., Stiner, M., & Trinkaus, E. 2001. Stable isotope evidence for increasing dietary breadth in the European mid-Upper Paleolithic. *Proceedings of the National Academy of Sciences (USA)* 98 (11), 6528–32.

Richards, M. P., Pettitt, P. B., Trinkaus, E., Smith, F. H., Paunovic, M., & Karavanic, I. 2000. Neanderthal diet at Vindija and Neanderthal predation: the evidence from stable isotopes. *Proceedings of the National Academy of Sciences (USA)* 97 (13), 7663–66.

Rightmire, G. P. 1989. Middle Stone Age humans from Eastern and Southern Africa, in *The Human Revolution: Behavioural and Biological Perspectives in the Origins of Modern Humans*. Mellars, P. A. & Stringer, C. B. (eds.). 109–22. Edinburgh: Edinburgh Univ. Press.

—. 1998. Human evolution in the Middle Pleistocene: the role of *Homo heidelbergensis*. *Evolutionary Anthropology* 6 (6), 218–27.

—. 2001. Comparison of Middle Pleistocene hominids from Africa and Asia, in *Human Roots: Africa and Asia in the Middle Pleistocene*. Barham, L. & Robson-Brown, K. (eds.). 123–33. Bristol: Western Academic & Specialist Press.

Rightmire, G. P. & Deacon, H. J. 2001. New human teeth from Middle Stone Age deposits at Klasies River, South Africa. *Journal of Human Evolution* 41, 535–44.

Ripoll López, S. & Municio González, L. J. 1999. *Domingo García: Arte Rupestre Paleolítico al Aire Libre en la Meseta Castellana*. Salamanca: Junta de Castilla y León.

Roebroeks, W., Mussi, M., Svoboda, J., & Fennema, K. (eds.). 2000. *Hunters of the Golden Age: The Mid Upper Paleolithic of Eurasia 30,000–20,000 BP*. Leiden: Leiden Univ. Press.

Seielstad, M. 2003. A novel Y-chromosome variant puts an upper limit on the timing of the first entry into the Americas. *American Journal of Human Genetics* 73, 700–05.

Singer, R. & Wymer, J. 1982. *The Middle Stone Age at Klasies River Mouth in South Africa*. Chicago: Univ. of Chicago Press.

Smith, F. H., Simek, J. F., & Harrill, M. S. 1989. Geographic variation in supraorbital torus reduction during the later Pleistocene (*c.* 80,000 to 15,000 BP), in *The Human Revolution: Behavioural and Biological Perspectives in the Origins of Modern Humans*. Mellars, P. A. & Stringer, C. B. (eds.). 172–93. Edinburgh: Edinburgh Univ. Press.

Smith, F. H., Trinkaus, E., Pettitt, P. B., Karavanic, I., & Paunovic, M. 1999. Direct radiocarbon dates for Vindija G1 and Velika Pecina Late Pleistocene hominid remains. *Proceedings of the National Academy of Sciences (USA)* 96, 12281–86.

Soffer, O. 1985. *The Upper Palaeolithic of the Central Russian Plain*. Orlando: Academic Press.

Soffer, O., Adovasio, J. M., & Hyland, D. C. 2000. The 'Venus' Figurines: textiles, basketry, gender and status in the Upper Paleolithic. *Current Anthropology* 41 (4), 511–37.

Speth, J. D. & Tchernov, E. 2002. Middle Paleolithic tortoise use at Kebara Cave, Israel. *Journal of Archaeological Science* 29, 471–83.

Steele, J. 2002. When did directional asymmetry enter the record?, in *The Speciation of Modern Homo sapiens*. Crow, T. (ed.). 153–68. London: The British Academy.

Stiner, M. 1994. *Honor Among Thieves: A Zooarchaeological Study of Neandertal Ecology*. Princeton: Princeton Univ. Press.

Stoneking, M. & Cann, R. L. 1989. African origin of human mitochondrial DNA, in *The Human Revolution: Behavioural and Biological Perspectives in the Origins of Modern Humans*. Mellars, P. A. & Stringer, C. B. (eds.). 17–30. Edinburgh: Edinburgh Univ. Press.

Storm, P. 2001. An environmental approach to the fate of *Homo erectus* in Australia, in *Human Roots: Africa and Asia in the Middle Pleistocene*. Barham, L. & Robson-Brown, K. (eds.). 203–15. Bristol: Western Academic & Specialist Press.

Stringer, C. B. 2001. Modern human origins – distinguishing the models. *African Archaeological Review* 18 (2), 67–75.

Stringer, C. B. & Andrews, P. 1988. Genetic and fossil evidence for the origin of modern humans. *Science* 239, 1263–68.

Stringer, C. B. & Gamble, C. S. 1993. *In Search of the Neanderthals: Solving the Puzzle of Human Origins*. London & New York: Thames & Hudson.

Templeton, A. R. 2002. Out of Africa again and again. *Nature* 416, 45–51.

Théry, I., Gril, J., Vernet, J. L., Meignen, L., & Maury, J. 1996. Coal used for fuel at two prehistoric sites in Southern France: Les Canalettes (Mousterian) and Les Usclades (Mesolithic). *Journal of Archaeological Science* 23, 509–12.

Thorne, A. G. 1971. Mungo and Kow Swamp: morphological variation in Pleistocene Australians. *Mankind* 8, 85–89.

Thorne, A. G. & Wolpoff, M. H. 1981. Regional continuity in Australasian Pleistocene hominid evolution. *American Journal of Physical Anthropology* 55, 337–49.

—. 1992. The multiregional evolution of humans. *Scientific American* (April), 28–33.

Trinkaus, E. 1981. Neanderthal limb proportions and cold adaptation, in *Aspects of Human Evolution*. Stringer, C. B. (ed.). 187–224. London: Taylor & Francis.

—. 1987. The Neanderthal face: evolutionary and functional perspectives on a recent hominid face. *Journal of Human Evolution* 16, 429–43.

—. 1988. The evolutionary origins of the Neanderthals or, why were there Neanderthals?, in *L'homme de Néandertal*, 3: *L'anatomie*. Liège: Etudes et Recherches Archéologiques de l'Université de Liège 30, 11–30.

Tyler-Smith, C. 2002. What can the Y chromosome tell us about the origin of modern humans?, in *The Speciation of Modern Homo sapiens*. Crow, T. (ed.). 217–29. London: The British Academy.

Vacquero, M. & Pastó, I. 2001. The definition of spatial units in Middle Paleolithic sites: the hearth-related assemblages. *Journal of Archaeological Science* 28, 1209–20.

Vermeersch, P. M., Paulissen, E., Stokes, S., Charlier, C., Van Peer, P., Stringer, C., & Lindsay, W. 1998. A Middle Paleolithic burial of a modern human at Taramsa Hill, Egypt. *Antiquity* 72, 475–84.

Ward, R. 1999. Language and genes in the Americas, in *The Human Inheritance: Genes, Language and Human Evolution*. Sykes, B. (ed.). 135–57. Oxford: Oxford Univ. Press.

Ward, R. & Stringer, C. 1997. A molecular handle on the Neanderthals. *Nature* 388, 225–26.

Weidenreich, F. 1947. Facts and speculations concerning the origin of Homo sapiens. *American Anthropologist* 49 (2), 187–203.

White, T. D. 1986. Cutmarks on the Bodo cranium: a case of prehistoric defleshing. *American Journal of Physical Anthropology* 69, 503–09.

White, T. D., Asfaw, B., DeGusta, D., Gilbert, H., Richards, G. D., Suwa, G., & Clark Howell, F. 2003. Pleistocene *Homo sapiens* from Middle Awash, Ethiopia. *Nature* 423, 742–47.

Wilson, A. C. & Cann, R. L. 1992. The recent African genesis of humans. *Scientific American* (April), 68–73.

Wolpoff, M. H. 1989. Multiregional evolution: the fossil alternative to Eden, in *The Human Revolution: Behavioural and Biological Perspectives in the Origins of Modern Humans*. Mellars, P. A. & Stringer, C. B. (eds.). 62–108. Edinburgh: Edinburgh Univ. Press.

Wolpoff, M. H. & Caspari, R. 1997a. *Race and Human Evolution*. New York: Simon & Schuster.

—. 1997b. What does it mean to be modern?, in *Conceptual Issues in Modern Human Origins Research*. Clark, G. A. & Willermet, C. M. (eds.). 28–44. New York: Aldine de Gruyter.

Yellen, J. E., Brooks, A. S., Cornelissen, E., Mehlman, M. J., & Stewart, K. 1995. A Middle Stone Age worked bone industry from Katanda, upper Semliki Valley, Zaire. *Science* 268, 553–56.

Zilhão, J. 2000. The Ebro frontier: a model for the late extinction of Iberian Neanderthals, in *Neanderthals on the Edge*. Stringer, C. B., Barton, R. N. E., & Finlayson, J. C. (eds.). 21. Oxford: Oxbow.

Zilhão, J. & Trinkaus, E. (eds.). 2002. *Portrait of the Artist as a Child: The Gravettian Human Skeleton from the Abrigo do Lagar Velho and its Archaeological Context*. Lisbon: Instituto Português de Arqueologia.

Züchner, C. 1996. The Chauvet Cave: radiocarbon versus archaeology. *INORA* 13, 25–27.

CHAPTER 5: THE WORLD TRANSFORMED: FROM FORAGERS AND FARMERS TO STATES AND EMPIRES

Adams, R. M. 1966. *The Evolution of Urban Society*. Chicago: Aldine.

Bellwood, P. & Renfrew, C. (eds.). 2003. *Examining the Language/Farming Dispersal Hypothesis*. Cambridge: McDonald Institute for Archaeological Research.

Bender, B. 1978. Gatherer-hunter to farmer: a social perspective. *World Archaeology* 10, 204–22.

Binford, L. R. 1968. Post-Pleistocene adaptations, in *New Perspectives in Archaeology*. Binford, S. R. & Binford, L. R. (eds.). 313–42. Chicago: Aldine.

Blanchon, P. & Shaw, J. 1995. Reef drowning during the last deglaciation: evidence for catastrophic sea-level rise and ice sheet collapse. *Geology* 23, 4–8.

Boserup, E. 1965. *The Conditions of Agricultural Growth: The Economics of Agrarian Change under Population Pressure*. New York: Aldine.

Braidwood, R. J. 1960. The agricultural revolution. *Scientific American* 203, 130–41.

Braidwood, R. J. & Howe, B. 1960. *Prehistoric Investigations in Iraqi Kurdistan*. Chicago: Univ. of Chicago Press.

Braidwood, R. J. & Willey, G. 1962. Conclusions and afterthoughts, in *Courses Toward Urban Life*. Braidwood, R. J. & Willey, G. (eds.). 330–59. Chicago: Aldine.

Butzer K. W. 1976. *Early Hydraulic Civilization in Egypt: A Study in Cultural Ecology*. Chicago: Univ. of Chicago Press.

Carneiro, R. 1970. A theory of the origin of the state. *Science* 169, 733–38.

Childe, V. G. 1936. *Man Makes Himself*. London: Watts.

—. 1950. The urban revolution. *The Town Planning Review* 21, 3–17.

Coles, B. J. 1998. Doggerland: a speculative survey. *Proceedings of the Prehistoric Society* 64, 45–81.

Daniel, G. E. & Renfrew, C. 1988. *The Idea of Prehistory*. Edinburgh: Edinburgh Univ. Press.

Diamond, J. 1997. *Guns, Germs and Steel: A Short History of Everybody for the Last 13,000 Years*. New York: W. W. Norton; London: Jonathan Cape.

Flannery, K. V. 1999. Process and agency in early state formation. *Cambridge Archaeological Journal* 9, 3–21.

Flannery, K. V. & Marcus, J. 2003. The origin of war: new ^{14}C dates from ancient Mexico. *Proceedings of the National Academy of Sciences (USA)* 100, 11801–05.

Grayson, D. K. & Meltzer, D. J. 2003. A requiem for North American overkill. *Journal of Archaeological Science* 30, 585–93.

Hanotte, O., Bradley, D. G., Ochieng, J. W., Verjee, Y., Hill, E. W., & Rege, J. E. O. 2002. African pastoralism: genetic imprints of origins and migrations. *Science* 296, 336–39.

Harlan, J. R. 1967. A wild wheat harvest in Turkey. *Archaeology* 20, 197–201.

Hayden, B. 1990. Nimrods, piscators, pluckers and planters: the emergence of food production. *Journal of Anthropological Archaeology*, 31–69.

—. 1995. A new overview of domestication, in *Last Hunters, First Farmers*. Price, T. D. & Gebauer, A. B. (eds.). 273–99. Santa Fe: School of American Research.

—. 2003. Were luxury foods the first domesticates? Ethnoarchaeological perspectives from Southeast Asia. *World Archaeology* 34, 458–69.

Hooker, J. T. (ed.). 1990. *Reading the Past: Ancient Writing from Cuneiform to the Alphabet*. London: British Museum Press.

Jones, M. K. 2001. *The Molecule Hunt*. London: Allen Lane; New York: Arcade Publishing (2002).

Keightley, D. N. 1996. Art, ancestors and the origins of writing in China. *Representations* 56, 68–95.

Larsson, L. 1989. Late Mesolithic settlements and cemeteries at Skateholm, southern Sweden, in *The Mesolithic in Europe*. Bonsall, C. (ed.). 367–78. Edinburgh: John Donald.

Leach, H. M. 2003. Human domestication reconsidered. *Current Anthropology* 44, 349–68.

Lee, R. B. 1968. What hunters do for a living, or, how to make out on scarce resources, in *Man the Hunter*. Lee, R. B. & De Vore, I. (eds.). 30–48. Chicago: Aldine.

Marcus, J. 1998. The peaks and valleys of ancient states, in *Archaic States*. Feinman, G. M. & Marcus, J. (eds.). 60–94. Santa Fe: School of American Research.

McIntosh, R. J. 1991. Early urban clusters in China and Africa: the arbitration of social ambiguity. *Journal of Field Archaeology* 18, 191–212.

Morrison, K. D. 2001. Sources, approaches, definitions, in *Empires: Perspectives from Archaeology and History*. Alcock, S. E., D'Altroy, T. N., Morrison, K. D., & Sinopoli, C. M. (eds.). 1–9. Cambridge: Cambridge Univ. Press.

Oppenheimer, S. 1998. *Eden in the East: The Drowned Continent of Southeast Asia*. London: Weidenfeld & Nicolson.

Pennisi, E. 2002. A shaggy dog history. *Science* 298, 1540–42.

Pollock, S. 1999. *Ancient Mesopotamia: The Eden That Never Was*. Cambridge: Cambridge Univ. Press.

Postgate, N., Wang, T., & Wilkinson, T. 1995. The evidence for early writing: utilitarian or ceremonial? *Antiquity* 69, 459–90.

Price, T. D. & Gebauer, A. B. 1995. New perspectives on the transition to agriculture, in *Last Hunters, First Farmers*. Price, T. D. & Gebauer, A. B. (eds.). 3–19. Santa Fe: School of American Research.

Rathje, W. L. 1971. The origin and development of Lowland Classic Maya civilization. *American Antiquity* 36, 275–85.

Renfrew, C. 2003. 'The emerging synthesis': the archaeogenetics of farming/language dispersals and other spread zones, in *Examining the Farming/Language Dispersal Hypothesis*. Bellwood, P. & Renfrew, C. (eds.). 3–16. Cambridge: McDonald Institute for Archaeological Research.

Renfrew, C. & Boyle, K. (eds.). 2000. *Archaeogenetics: DNA and the Population Prehistory of Europe*. Cambridge: McDonald Institute for Archaeological Research.

Richerson, P. J., Boyd, R., & Bettinger, R. L. 2001. Was agriculture impossible during the Pleistocene but mandatory during the Holocene? A climate change hypothesis. *American Antiquity* 66, 387–411.

Rindos, D. 1984. *The Origins of Agriculture: An Evolutionary Perspective*. Orlando: Academic Press.

Roberts, N. 1998. *The Holocene: An Environmental History*. (2nd ed.). Oxford: Blackwell.

Sahlins, M. D. 1968. Notes on the original affluent society, in *Man the Hunter*. Lee, R. B. & De Vore, I. (eds.). 85–89. Chicago: Aldine.

Savolainen, P., Zhang, Y.-P., Luo, J., Lundeberg, J., & Leitner, T. 2002. Genetic evidence for an East Asian origin of domestic dogs. *Science* 298, 1610–13.

Smith, B. D. 2001. Low-level food production. *Journal of Anthropological Research* 9, 1–43.

Steward, J. H. 1949. Cultural causality and law: a

trial formulation of the development of early civilizations. *American Anthropologist* 51, 1–27.

Thomas, R. 1992. *Literacy and Orality in Ancient Greece*. Cambridge: Cambridge Univ. Press.

Trigger, B. G. 2003. *Understanding Early Civilizations*. Cambridge: Cambridge Univ. Press.

Troy, C. S., MacHugh, D. E., Bailey, J. F., Magee, D. A., Loftus, R. T., Cunningham, P., Chamberlain, A. T., Sykes, B. C., & Bradley, D. G. 2001. Genetic evidence for Near-Eastern origins of European cattle. *Nature* 410, 1088–91.

Vartanyan, S. L., Garutt, V. E., & Sher, A. V. 1993. Holocene dwarf mammoths from Wrangel Island in the Siberian Arctic. *Nature* 362, 337–40.

Vilà, C., Savolainen, P., Malonaldo, J. E., Amorim, I. R., Rice, J. E., Honeycutt, R. L., Crandall, K. A., Lundeberg, J., & Wayne, R. K. 1997. Multiple and ancient origins of the domestic dog. *Science* 276, 1687–89.

Wilson, P. J. 1988. *The Domestication of the Human Species*. New Haven: Yale Univ. Press.

Wittfogel K. A. 1957. *Oriental Despotism: A Comparative Study of Total Power*. New Haven: Yale Univ. Press.

Yen, D. E. 1989. The domestication of the environment, in *Foraging and Farming: The Evolution of Plant Domestication*. Harris, D. R. & Hillman, G. C. (eds.). 55–75. London: Unwin Hyman.

CHAPTER 6: FROM FORAGERS TO COMPLEX SOCIETIES IN SOUTHWEST ASIA

Bar-Yosef, O. 1986. The walls of Jericho: an alternative interpretation. *Current Anthropology*, 27/2, 157–62.

Bar-Yosef, O. & Belfer-Cohen, A. 1989. The Levantine 'PPNB' Interaction Sphere, in *People and Culture in Change*. Hershkovitz, I. (ed.). Vol. I, 59–72.

Bar-Yosef, O. & Valla, F. R. 1991. The Natufian culture: an introduction, in *The Natufian Culture in the Levant*. Bar-Yosef, O. & Valla, F. R. (eds.). 1–10. International Monographs in Prehistory, Archaeological Series vol. 1. Ann Arbor: Univ. of Michigan Press.

Bar-Yosef, O., Gopher, A., Tchernov, E., & Kislev, M. E. 1991. Netiv Hagdud: an Early Neolithic village site in the Jordan valley. *Journal of Field Archaeology* 18, 405–24.

Belfer-Cohen, A. 1995. Rethinking social stratification in the Natufian culture, in *The Archaeology of Death in the Ancient Near East*. Campbell, S. & Green, A. (eds.). 9–16. Oxford: Oxbow.

Binford, L. R. 1980. Willow smoke and dogs' tails: hunter-gatherer settlement systems and archeological site information. *American Antiquity* 45, 4–20.

—. 1983. *In Pursuit of the Past: De-Coding the Archaeological Record*. London & New York: Thames & Hudson.

—. 1990. Mobility, housing and environment: a comparative study. *Journal of Anthropological Research* 46, 119–52.

Boyd, B. 1995. Houses and hearths, pits and burials: Natufian mortuary practices at Mallaha (Eynan), Upper Jordan Valley, in *The Archaeology of Death in the Ancient Near East*. Campbell, S. & Green, A. (eds.). 17–23. Oxford: Oxbow.

Braidwood, R. J. 1960. The agricultural revolution. *Scientific American* 203, 130–41.

Braidwood, R. J. & Howe, B. 1960. *Prehistoric Investigations in Iraqi Kurdistan*. Chicago: Univ. of Chicago Press.

Byrd, B. 2000. Households in transition: Neolithic social organization within Southwest Asia, in *Life in Neolithic Farming Communities: Social Organization, Identity, and Differentiation*. Kuijt, I. (ed.). 63–98. New York: Kluwer Academic/Plenum Publishers.

Cauvin, J. 1977. Les fouilles de Mureybet (1971–1974) et leur signification pour les origines de la sédentarisation au Proche-Orient. *Annual of the American Schools of Oriental Research* 44, 19–48.

—. 2001. *The Birth of the Gods and the Beginnings of Agriculture*. Cambridge: Cambridge Univ. Press. Transl. Watkins, T. from *Naissance des Divinités, Naissance de l'Agriculture: la révolution des symboles au Néolithique*. (2nd ed.). Paris: CNRS.

Childe, V. G. 1936. *Man Makes Himself*. London: Watts.

Colledge, S. 1991. *Plant Exploitation on Epipalaeolithic and Early Neolithic sites in the Levant*. Oxford: British Archaeological Reports International Series 986.

—. 1998. Identifying pre-domestication cultivation using multivariate analysis, in *The Origins of Agriculture and Crop Domestication: The Harlan Symposium*. Damania, A. B., Valkoun, J., Willcox, G., & Qualset, C. O. (eds.). 121–30. Aleppo, Syria: ICARDA, IPGRI, FAO & Univ. of California, GRCP.

Flannery, K. V. 1969. The origins and ecological effects of early domestication in Iran and the Near East, in *The Domestication and Exploitation of Plants and Animals*. Ucko, P. J. & Dimbleby, G. W. (eds.). 73–100. London: Duckworth; Chicago: Aldine.

Garrard, A. 1998. Environment and culture adaptations in the Azraq Basin: 24,000–7,000 BP, in *The Prehistoric Archaeology of Jordan*. Henry, D. O. (ed.). 139–48. Oxford: British Archaeological Reports International Series 705.

—. 1999. Charting the emergence of cereal and pulse domestication in South-west Asia. *Environmental Archaeology* 4, 67–86.

Garrard, A., Betts, A., Byrd, B., Colledge, S., & Hunt, C. 1988. Summary of palaeoenvironmental and prehistoric investigations in the Azrq basin, in *The Prehistory of Jordan*. Garrard, A. & Gebel, H. (eds.). 331–37. Oxford: British Archaeological Reports International Series 356, vol. 1.

Garrod, D. A. E. 1932. A new Mesolithic industry: the Natufian of Palestine. *Journal of the Royal Anthropological Institute* 62, 257–70.

Goring-Morris, N. 1987. *Beyond the Edge*. Oxford: British Archaeological Reports International Series 361.

Guilaine, J. & Briois, F. 2001. Parekklisha Shillourokambos: an Early Neolithic site in Cyprus, in *The Earliest Prehistory of Cyprus: From Colonization to Exploitation*. Swiny, S. (ed.). Cyprus American Archaeological Research Institute Monograph Series, vol. 2: 37–54. Boston: American Schools of Oriental Research.

Harlan, J. R. 1967. A wild wheat harvest in Turkey. *Archaeology* 20/3, 197–201.

Harris, D. R. (ed.). 1996. *The Origins and Spread of Agriculture and Pastoralism in Eurasia*. London: Univ. College London Press.

Hauptmann, H. 1993. Ein Kult Gebäude in Nevali Çori, in *Between the Rivers and Over the Mountains*.

Frangipane, M., Hauptmann, H., Liverani, M., Matthiae, P., & Mellink. P. (eds.). 37–69. Rome: Università di Roma La Sapienza.

—. 1999. The Urfa Region, in *Neolithic in Turkey, the Cradle of Civilization: New Discoveries*. Özdogan, M. & Basgelen, N. (eds.). 65–86. Istanbul: Arkeoloji ve Sanat Yayinlari.

Henry, D. O. 1989. *From Foraging to Agriculture: The Levant at the End of the Ice Age*. Philadelphia: Univ. of Pennsylvania Press.

—. 1995. *Prehistoric Cultural Ecology and Evolution: Insights from South Jordan*. New York: Plenum Press.

Hillman, G. C. 1996. Late Pleistocene changes in wild plant-foods available to hunter-gatherers of the northern Fertile Crescent: possible preludes to cereal cultivation, in *The Origins and Spread of Agriculture and Pastoralism in Eurasia*. Harris, D. J. (ed.). 159–203. London: Univ. College London Press.

Hodder, I. 2004. Women and men at Çatalhöyük. *Scientific American* (January), 77–83.

—. (ed.). 1996. On the surface: Çatalhöyük 1993–1995. McDonald Institute for Archaeological Research/British Institute of Archaeology at Ankara Monograph No. 22.

Hole, F. & Flannery, K. V. 1967. The prehistory of southwestern Iran: a preliminary report. *Proceedings of the Prehistoric Society*. 147–70.

Hopf, M. 1983. Jericho plant remains, in *Excavations at Jericho*, vol. 5, 576–621. Kenyon, K. & Holland, T. (eds.). London: British School of Archaeology in Jerusalem.

Kaufman, D. 1989. Observations on the geometric Kebaran: a view from Neve David, in *Investigations in South Levantine Prehistory*. Bar-Yosef, O. & Vandermeersch, B. (eds.). 275–86. Oxford: British Archaeological Reports.

Kenyon, K. M. 1957. *Digging up Jericho*. London: Ernest Benn.

Köhler-Rollefson, I. 1992. A model for the development of nomadic pastoralism on the Transjordan plateau, in *Pastoralism in the Levant: Archaeological Materials in Anthropological Perspective*. Bar-Yosef, O. & Khazanov, A. (eds.). 11–18. Madison: Prehistory Press.

Kuijt, I. 2000a. People and space in early agricultural villages: exploring daily lives, community size, and architecture in the Late Pre-Pottery Neolithic. *Journal of Anthropological Archaeology* 19, 75–102.

—. 2000b. Keeping the peace: ritual, skull caching and community integration in the Levantine Neolithic, in *Life in Neolithic Farming Communities: Social Organization, Identity, and Differentiation*. Kuijt, I. (ed.). 137–62. New York: Kluwer Academic/Plenum Publishers.

Legge, A. J. & Rowley-Conwy, P. 1987. Gazelle killing in Stone Age Syria. *Scientific American* 257 (2), 76–83.

Mellaart, J. 1967. *Çatal Hüyük: A Neolithic Town in Anatolia*. London: Thames & Hudson.

Molleson, T. 1994. The eloquent bones of Abu Hureyra. *Scientific American* 271, 70–75.

Molleson, T. & Jones, K. 1991. Dental evidence for dietary change at Abu Hureyra. *Journal of Archaeological Science* 18, 525–39.

Moore, A. M. T., Hillman, G. C., & Legge, A. J. 2001. *Village on the Euphrates*. Oxford: Oxford Univ. Press.

Nadel, D. & Hershkovitz, I. 1991. New subsistence

data and human remains from the earliest Levantine Epipalaeolithic. *Current Anthropology* 32, 631–35.

Nadel, D. & Werker, E. 1999. The oldest ever brush hut plant remains from Ohalo II, Jordan Valley, Israel (19,000 BP). *Antiquity* 73, 755–64.

Özdoğan, A. 1999. Çayönü, in *Neolithic in Turkey, the Cradle of Civilization: New Discoveries*. Özdoğan, M. & Başgelen, N. (eds.). 35–63. Istanbul: Arkeoloji ve Sanat Yayınları.

Özdoğan, M. & Özdoğan, A. 1990. Çayönü, a conspectus of recent work, in *Préhistoire du Levant: processus des changements culturels*. Aurenche, O., Cauvin, M.-C., & Sanlaville, P. (eds.). 68–77. Paris: CNRS.

Peltenberg, E. 2000. Agro-pastoralist colonization of Cyprus in the 10th millennium BP: initial assessments. *Antiquity* 74, 844–53.

Renfrew, C. 1986. Introduction: peer polity interaction and social change, in *Peer Polity Interaction and Social Change*. Renfrew, C. & Cherry, J. (eds.). 1–18. Cambridge: Cambridge Univ. Press.

—. 1998. Mind and matter: cognitive archaeology and external symbolic storage, in *Cognition and Material Culture: The Archaeology of Symbolic Storage*. Renfrew, C. & Scarre, C. (eds.). 1–6. Cambridge: McDonald Institute for Archaeological Research.

Renfrew, C. & Bahn, P. 2004. *Archaeology: Theories, Methods and Practice*. (4th ed.). London & New York: Thames & Hudson.

Renfrew, C. & Dixon, J. E. 1976. Obsidian in West Asia: a review, in *Problems in Economic and Social Archaeology*. de Sieveking, G. et al. (eds.). 137–50. London: Duckworth.

Renfrew, C., Dixon, J. E., & Cann, E. R. 1968. Further analyses of Near Eastern obsidians. *Proceedings of the Prehistoric Society* 34, 319–31.

Rollefson, G. O. 1990. The aceramic neolithic of the southern Levant: the view from Ain Ghazal, in *Préhistoire du Levant: processus des changements culturels*. Aurenche, O., Cauvin, M.-C., & Sanlaville, P. (eds.). Part 2, 138–43. (Also published as the two fascicules of *Paléorient* for the same year.)

—. 1998. Ain Ghazal (Jordan): ritual and ceremony III. *Paléorient* 24/1, 43–58.

—. 2000. Ritual and social structure at Neolithic 'Ain Ghazal, in Kuijt, I. (ed.). *Life in Neolithic Farming Communities*. 165–90. New York: Kluwer Academic/Plenum Publishers.

Rosenberg, M., Nesbitt, R. M., Redding, R., & Peasnall, B. L. 1998. Hallan Çemi, pig husbandry, and post-Pleistocene adaptations along the Taurus-Zagros arc (Turkey). *Paléorient* 24/11, 25–42.

Sanlaville, P. 1997. Les changements dans l'environnement au Moyen Orient de 20,000 à 6,000 BP. *Paléorient* 23/2, 249–62.

Schirmer, W. 1990. Some aspects of the building in the 'aceramic neolithic' settlement at Çayönü Tepesi. *World Archaeology* 21/3, 363–87.

Schmidt, K. 1998. Frühneolitische Tempel: ein Forschungs bericht zum präkeramischen Neolithikum Obermesopotamiens. *Mitteilungen der Deutschen Orientgesellschaft zu Berlin* 130, 17–49.

—. 2000. Göbekli Tepe, Southeastern Turkey: a preliminary report on the 1995–1999 excavations. *Paléorient* 26, 45–54.

Simmons, A. 2001. The first humans and last pygmy hippopotomoi of Cyprus, in *The Earliest Prehistory of Cyprus: From Colonization to Exploitation*. Swiny, S. (ed.). Cyprus American Archaeological Research Inst. Monograph, vol. 2, 1–18. Boston: American Schools of Oriental Research.

Smith, B. D. 1995. *The Emergence of Agriculture*. New York: Scientific American Library.

Solecki, R. L. 1981. *An Early Village Site at Zawi Chemi Shanidar*. Biblioteca Mesopotamica, vol. 13. Malibu: Undena Publications.

Solecki, R. L. & Solecki, R. S. 1983. Late Pleistocene – Early Holocene cultural traditions in the Zagros and the Levant, in *The Hilly Flanks and Beyond: Essays on the Prehistory of Southwestern Asia*. Young, T. C., Smith, P. E. L., & Mortensen, P. (eds.). 123–37. Chicago: Oriental Institute of the Univ. of Chicago.

Stordeur, D. 1999. Organisation de l'espace construit et organisation sociale dans le Néolithique de Jerf el Ahmar (Syrie, Xe–IXe millénaire avant J.-C.), in *Habitat et Société, XIXe Rencontres internationales d'archéologie et d'histoire d'Antibes*. Braemer F., Cleuziou, S., & Coudart A. (eds.). 131–49. Antibes: APDCA.

Stordeur, D., Brenet, M., der Aprahamian, G., & Roux, J.-C. 2000. Les bâtiments communautaires de Jerf el Ahmar et Mureybet, horizon PPNA (Syrie). *Paléorient* 26/1, 29–44.

Stordeur, D., Helmer, D., & Willcox, G. 1997. Jerf-el Ahmar: un nouveau site de l'horizon PPNA sur le moyen Euphrate Syrien. *Bulletin de la Société Préhistorique Française* 94/2, 282–85.

Testart, A. 1982. The significance of food storage among hunter-gatherers: residence patterns, population densities and social inequalities. *Current Anthropology* 23, 523–37.

Valla, F. R. 1991. Les Natoufiens de Mallaha et l'espace, in *The Natufian Culture in the Levant*. Bar-Yosef, O. & Valla, F. (eds.). 111–22. Oxford: Oxbow.

Van Zeist, W. & Bottema, S. 1982. Vegetational history of the Eastern Mediterranean and the Near East during the last 20,000 years, in *Palaeoclimates, Palaeoenvironments and Human Communities in the Eastern Mediterranean Region in Later Prehistory*. Bintliff, J. L. & van Zeist, W. (eds.). 277–321. Oxford: British Archaeological Reports International Series 133.

—. 1991. *Late Quaternary Vegetation of the Near East*. Beihefte zum Tübinger Atlas des Vorderen Orients, Reihe A18. Wiesbaden: Dr L. Reichert Verlag.

Watkins T. 1990. The origins of house and home. *World Archaeology* 21/3, 336–47.

—. 1992a. The beginning of the Neolithic: searching for meaning in material culture change. *Paléorient*, 18/1, 63–75.

—. 1992b. Pushing back the frontiers of Mesopotamian prehistory. *Biblical Archaeologist*, vol. 55, No. 4 (December 1992), 176–81.

—. 2004. Architecture and 'theatres of memory' in the Neolithic of southwest Asia, in *Rethinking Materiality: The Engagement of Mind with the Material World*. Renfrew, C., de Marrais, E., & Gosden, C. (eds.). Cambridge: McDonald Institute for Archaeological Research.

—. (ed.). 1995. *Qermez Dere, Tel Afar; Interim Report No. 3*. Edinburgh, Department of Archaeology, Univ. of Edinburgh, Project Paper No. 14.

Wilson, P. J. 1988. *The Domestication of the Human Species*. New Haven: Yale Univ. Press.

Woodburn, J. 1982. Egalitarian societies. *Man* 17, 431–45. Reprinted in, *Limited Wants, Unlimited Means: A Reader on Hunter-Gatherer Economics and the Environment*. 1998. Gowdy, J. (ed.). Washington D.C.: Island Press.

Wright, G. A. 1978. Social differentiation in the early Natufian, in *Social Archaeology: Beyond Subsistence and Dating*. Redman, C. L., Berman, M. J., Curtin, E. V., Laghorne, W. T., Versaggin, H., & Wanser, J. C. (eds.). 201–23. New York: Academic Press.

Wright, K. 1994. Ground-stone tools and hunter-gatherer subsistence in south-west Asia: implications for the transition to farming. *American Antiquity* 59/2, 238–63.

Zohary, D. 1996. The mode of domestication of the founder crops of Southwest Asian agriculture, in *The Origins and Spread of Agriculture and Pastoralism in Eurasia*. Harris, D. J. (ed.). 142–58. London: Univ. College London Press.

Zohary, D. & Hopf, M. 2000. *The Domestication of Plants in the Old World: The Origin and Spread of Cultivated Plants in West Asia, Europe and the Nile Valley*. (3rd ed.). Oxford: Oxford Univ. Press.

CHAPTER 7: EAST ASIAN AGRICULTURE AND ITS IMPACT

Agelarakis, A. 1997. Some reconstructions of human bio-cultural conditions during the 3rd and 2nd millennia B.C. in South-East Asia, in *South-East Asian Archaeology 1992*. Ciarla, R. & Rispoli, F. (eds.). 99–117. Rome: Istituto Italiano per l'Africa e l'Oriente.

Au Ka-Fat. 1993. An introduction to the spread of various ancient cultures from the middle and lower Yangtze River area to the Guangdong region, in *Collected Essays on the Culture of the Ancient Yue People in South China*. Chau Hing-Wah (ed.). 24–33. Hong Kong: Hong Kong Museum of History.

Barnes, G. L. 1993. *China, Korea and Japan: The Rise of Civilization in East Asia*. London & New York: Thames & Hudson.

Bar-Yosef, O. & Meadow, R. H. 1995. The origins of agriculture in the Near East, in *Last Hunters – First Farmers: New Perspectives on the Prehistoric Transition to Agriculture*. Price, T. D. & Gebauer, A. B. (eds.). 39–94. Santa Fe: American School of Prehistoric Research.

Bing Su & Li Jin. 2000. Origins and prehistoric migrations of modern humans in East Asia, in *Genetic, Linguistic and Archaeological Perspectives on Human Diversity in Southeast Asia*. Li Jin, Seiestad, M., & Chunjie Xiao (eds.). 107–32. New Jersey: World Scientific.

Cavalli-Sforza, L. L. & Cavalli-Sforza, F. 1996. *The Great Human Diasporas: The History and Diversity of Evolution*. Wokingham: Addison-Wesley.

Ciarla, R. 1992. The Thai-Italian Lopburi regional archaeological project: preliminary results, in *Southeast Asian Archaeology 1990*. Glover, I. C. (ed.). 111–28. Hull: Centre for Southeast Asian Studies, Univ. of Hull.

Crawford, G. W. & Takamiya, H. 1990. The origins and implications of late prehistoric plant husbandry in northern Japan. *Antiquity* 64, 889–911.

Diffloth, G. 1994. The lexical evidence for Austric, so far. *Oceanic Linguistics* 33, 309–22.

Fontaine, H. 1972. Deuxième note sur le

'néolithique' du bassin inférieur du Dong-Nai. *Archives géologiques du Viet-Nam* 15, 123–29.

Gorman, C. F. 1972. Excavations at Spirit Cave, northern Thailand: some interim impressions. *Asian Perspectives* 13, 79–107.

Greenland, D. J. 1997. *The Sustainability of Rice Farming*. New York: CAB International.

Hagelberg, E. 2000. *Genetics in the Study of Human History: Problems and Opportunities*. Amsterdam: 21st Kroon Lecture.

He Jiejun. 1995. Early Neolithic relics in Hunan, in *Archaeology in Southeast Asia*. Yeung Chun-tong & Li Wai-ling (eds.). 371–78. Hong Kong: Univ. Museum and Art Gallery.

—. 1999. Excavations at Chengtoushan in Li County, Hunan Province, China. *BIPPA* 18, 101–03.

Higham, C. F. W. & Kijngam, A. 1984. *Prehistoric Excavations in Northeast Thailand: Excavations at Ban Na Di, Ban Chiang Hian, Ban Muang Phruk, Ban Sangui, Non Noi and Ban Kho Noi*. Oxford: British Archaeological Reports International Series 231 (i–iii).

Higham, C. F. W. & Lu, T. L.-D. 1998. The origins and dispersal of rice cultivation. *Antiquity* 72, 867–77.

Higham, C. F. W. & Thosarat, R. 1994. *Khok Phanom Di: Prehistoric Adaptation to the World's Richest Habitat*. Fort Worth: Harcourt Brace Jovanovich.

Kealhofer, L. 1996. The human environment during the terminal Pleistocene and Holocene in Northeastern Thailand: phytolith evidence from Lake Kumphawapi. *Asian Perspectives* 35 (2), 229–54.

—. 1997. Evidence for cultural impact on the environment during the Holocene: two phytolith sequences from the Lopburi region, Central Thailand, in *South-East Asian Archaeology 1992*. Ciarla, R. & Rispoli, F. (eds.). 9–28. Rome: Istituto Italiano per l'Africa e l'Oriente.

Leong, S. H. 1991. Jenderam Hilir and the mid-Holocene prehistory of the west coast plain of Peninsular Malaysia. *Bulletin of the Indo-Pacific Prehistory Association* 10, 150–60.

Li Jin, Seiestad, M., & Chunjie Xiao (eds.). 2001. *Genetic, Linguistic and Archaeological Perspectives on Human Diversity in Southeast Asia*. New Jersey: World Scientific.

Loofs-Wissowa, H. H. E. 1967. The Thai-British archaeological expedition: a preliminary report on the work of the first season, 1965–66. *Journal of the Siam Society* lv (2), 237–62.

Lu, T. Lie Dan. 1999. *The Transition from Foraging to Farming and the Origin of Agriculture in China*. Oxford: British Archaeological Reports International Series 774.

Luce, G. H. 1985. *Phases in Pre-Pagan Burma*. Oxford: Oxford Univ. Press.

Mahdi, W. 1998. Linguistic data on transmission of Southeast Asian cultigens to India and Sri Lanka, in *Archaeology and Language*. Vol. II: Correlating archaeological and linguistic hypotheses. Blench, R. & Spriggs, M. (eds.). 390–415. London: Routledge.

Malleret, L. 1959–63. *L'Archéologie du Delta du Mékong*. Paris: EFEO.

Mudar, K. M. 1995. Evidence for prehistoric dryland farming in Mainland Southeast Asia: results of regional survey in Lopburi Province, Thailand. *Asian Perspectives* 34, 157–94.

Nelson, S. 1993. *The Archaeology of Korea*. Cambridge: Cambridge Univ. Press.

—. 1999. Megalithic monuments and the introduction of rice into Korea, in *The Prehistory of Food*. Gosden, C. & Hather, J. (eds.). 147–63. London: Routledge.

Nishimura, M. 2002. Chronology of the Neolithic Age in southern Vietnam. *Journal of Southeast Asian Archaeology* 22, 25–57.

Norman, J. & Mei, T. 1976. The Austroasiatics in ancient South China: some lexical evidence. *Monumenta Serica* 32, 274–301.

Pei Anping. 1998. Notes on new advancements and revelations in the agricultural archaeology of early rice domestication in the Dongting Lake region. *Antiquity* 72, 878–85.

Pejros, I. & Shnirelman, V. 1998. Rice in Southeast Asia: a regional interdisciplinary approach, in *Archaeology and Language*. Vol. II: Correlating archaeological and linguistic hypotheses. Blench, R. & Spriggs, M. (eds.). 379–89. London: Routledge.

Penny, D., Grindrod, J., & Bishop. P. 1996. Holocene palaeoenvironmental reconstruction based on microfossil analysis of a lake sediment core, Nong Han Kumphawapi, Udon Thani, Northeast Thailand. *Asian Perspectives* 35 (2), 209–28.

Pham Duc Manh. 2000. Some recent discoveries about the pre- and protohistory of the southeastern part of Vietnam, in *Southeast Asian Archaeology 1998*. Lobo, W. & Reimann, S. (eds.). 139–48. Hull: Centre for South-East Asian Studies, Univ. of Hull & Ethnologisches Museum, Staatliche Museum zu Berlin.

Pigott, V. C., Weiss, A. D., & Natapintu, S. 1997. The archaeology of copper production: excavations in the Khao Wong Prachan Valley, Central Thailand, in *South-East Asian Archaeology 1992*. Ciarla, R. & Rispoli, F. (eds.). 119–57. Rome: Istituto Italiano per l'Africa e l'Oriente.

Reid, L. A. 1994. Morphological evidence for Austric. *Oceanic Linguistics* 33, 323–44.

Renfrew, C. 1987. *Archaeology and Language. The Puzzle of Indo-European Origins*. London: Jonathan Cape.

Rispoli, F. 1997. Late 3rd–2nd millennium B.C. pottery traditions in Central Thailand: some preliminary observations in a wider perspective, in *South-East Asian Archaeology 1992*. Ciarla, R. & Rispoli, F. (eds.). 59–97. Rome: Istituto Italiano per L'Africa e L'Oriente.

Sagart, L. 1993. Chinese and Austronesian: evidence for a genetic relationship. *Journal of Chinese Linguistics* 21, 1–62.

—. 1994. Old Chinese and Proto-Austronesian: evidence for a genetic relationship. *Oceanic Linguistics* 33, 271–308.

Schauffler, W. 1976. Archaeological survey and excavation of Ban Chiang culture sites in Northeast Thailand. *Expedition* 18, 27–37.

Shoocondej, R. 1996. Working towards an anthropological perspective on Thai prehistory. *BIPPA* 14, 119–32.

Sørensen, P. 1972. The Neolithic cultures of Thailand (and North Malaysia) and their Lungshanoid relationship, in *Early Chinese Art and its Possible Influence in the Pacific Basin*. Barnard, N. (ed.). 459–506. New York: Intercultural Arts Press.

Sørensen, P. & Hatting, T. 1967. *Archaeological Investigations in Thailand*. Vol. II: Ban Kao. Part 1: The archaeological materials from the burials. Copenhagen: Munksgard.

Tayles, N. G. 1999. *The Excavation of Khok Phanom Di: A Prehistoric Site in Central Thailand*. Vol. V: The people. London: Reports of the Research Committee of the Society of Antiquaries of London No. LXI.

Tsutsumi, T. 1999. The oldest pottery in Japan archipelago. Newsletter of the Grant-in-Aid Program for COE Research Foundation of the Ministry of Education, Science, Sports and Culture in Japan 2 (1), 4–5.

Underhill, P. & Roseman, C. C. 2000. The case for an African rather than an Asian origin of the human Y-chromosome Yap insertion, in *Genetic, Linguistic and Archaeological Perspectives on Human Diversity in Southeast Asia*. Li Jin, Seiestad, M., & Chunjie Xiao (eds.). 43–56. New Jersey: World Scientific.

Watson, W. 1979. Kok Charoen and the early metal age of Central Thailand. *Early South East Asia*, 53–62.

White, J. C. 1997. A brief note on new dates for the Ban Chiang cultural tradition. *BIPPA* 16, 103–06.

Winkler, M. G. & Wang, P. K. 1993. The late Quaternary vegetation and climate of China, in *Global Climates Since the Last Glacial Maximum*. Wright, H. E., Kutzbach, J. E., Webb, T., Ruddiman, W. F., Street-Perrott, F. A., & Bartlein, P. J. (eds.). 221–64. Minneapolis: Univ. of Minnesota Press.

Yan Wenming. 1991. China's earliest rice agriculture remains. *BIPPA* 10, 118–26.

Yoshizaki, M. 1997. Domesticated plants of the Jomon Period. *Quaternary Research* 36, 343–46.

Yuan Jairong & Zhang Chi. 1999. The origins of pottery and rice cultivation in China. *Newsletter of the Grant-in-Aid Program for COE Research Foundation of the Ministry of Education, Science, Sports and Culture in Japan* 2 (1), 3–4.

Zhao, Z. 1998. The Middle Yangtze region in China is one place where rice was domesticated: phytolith evidence from the Diaotonghuan Cave, Northern Jiangxi. *Antiquity* 72, 885–97.

Zide, A. R. K. & Zide, N. H. 1976. Proto-Munda cultural vocabulary: evidence for early agriculture, in *Austroasiatic Studies*. Jenner, P. N., Thompson, L. C., & Starosta, S. (eds.). II, 1295–334. Honolulu: Oceanic Linguistics special publication.

CHAPTER 8: AUSTRALIA AND THE AUSTRONESIANS

Adelaar, K. A. 1995. Borneo as a cross-roads for comparative Austronesian linguistics, in *The Austronesians: Historical and Comparative Perspectives*. Bellwood, P., Fox, J., & Tryon, D. (eds.). 75–95. Canberra: Department of Anthropology, RSPAS, Australian National Univ.

Allen, H. 1979. Left out in the cold: why the Tasmanians stopped eating fish. *The Artefact* 4, 1–10.

Allen, J. & Gosden, C. (eds.). 1992. *Report of the Lapita Homeland Project*. Canberra: Department of Prehistory, Research School of Pacific Studies, Occasional Papers in Prehistory 20.

Ambrose, W. 1997. Contradictions in Lapita pottery, a composite clone. *Antiquity* 71, 525–38.

Anderson, A. 1989. *Prodigious Birds*. Cambridge: Cambridge Univ. Press.

—. 1995. Current approaches in East Polynesian colonization research. *Journal of the Polynesian*

Society 104, 110–32.

—. 2001. Towards the sharp end: the form and performance of prehistoric Polynesian voyaging canoes, in *Pacific 2000*. Stevenson, C., Lee, G., & Morin, F. (eds.). 29–36. Los Osos, CA: Easter Island Foundation.

Ardika, I. W. & Bellwood, P. 1991. Sembiran: the beginnings of Indian contact with Bali. *Antiquity* 65, 221–32.

Barker, B. C. 1991. Nara Inlet 1: coastal resource use and the Holocene marine transgression in the Whitsunday Islands, central Queensland. *Archaeology in Oceania* 26 (3), 102–09.

—. 1996. Maritime hunter-gatherers on the tropical coast: a social model for change, in *Australian Archaeology 95*. Ulm, S., Lilley, I., & Ross, A. (eds.). 31–43. Tempus 6, Anthropology Museum, Univ. of Queensland.

Bayliss-Smith, T. 1996. People-plant interactions in the New Guinea highlands, in *The Origins and Spread of Agriculture and Pastoralism in Eurasia*. Harris, D. (ed.). 499–523. London: Univ. College London Press.

Bayliss-Smith, T. & Golson, J. 1992. A Colocasian revolution in the New Guinea Highlands? *Archaeology in Oceania* 17, 1–21.

Bellwood, P. 1978. *Man's Conquest of the Pacific*. Auckland: Collins.

—. 1987. *The Polynesians*. (2nd ed.). London: Thames & Hudson.

—. 1991. The Austronesian dispersal and the origin of languages. *Scientific American* 265 (1), 88–93.

—. 1996a. The origins and spread of agriculture in the Indo-Pacific region, in *The Origins and Spread of Agriculture and Pastoralism in Eurasia*. Harris, D. (ed.). 465–98. London: Univ. College London Press.

—. 1996b. Hierarchy, founder ideology and Austronesian expansion, in *Origin, Ancestry and Alliance*. Fox, J. & Sather, C. (eds.). 18–40. Canberra: Department of Anthropology, Comparative Austronesian Project, Australian National Univ.

—. 1997. *Prehistory of the Indo-Malaysian Archipelago*. (Rev. ed.). Honolulu: Univ. of Hawaii Press.

—. 2000. Formosan prehistory and Austronesian dispersal, in *Austronesian Taiwan*. Blundell, D. (ed.). 337–65. Berkeley: Phoebe A. Hearst Museum of Anthropology.

—. 2001. Polynesian prehistory and the rest of mankind, in *Pacific 2000*. Stevenson, C., Lee, G., & Morin, F. (eds.). 11–25. Los Osos, CA: Easter Island Foundation.

Blust, R. A. 1993. Central and Central-Eastern Malayo-Polynesian. *Oceanic Linguistics* 32, 241–95.

—. 1995. The prehistory of the Austronesian-speaking peoples: a view from language. *Journal of World Prehistory* 9, 453–510.

—. 2000. Chamorro historical phonology. *Oceanic Linguistics* 39/1, 83–122.

Bowdler, S. 1981. Hunters in the Highlands: Aboriginal adaptations in the eastern Australian uplands. *Archaeology in Oceania* 16, 99–111.

—. 1988. Tasmanian Aborigines in the Hunter Islands in the Holocene: island resource use and seasonality, in *The Archaeology of Prehistoric Coastlines*. Bailey, G. & Parkington, J. (eds.). 42–52. Cambridge: Cambridge Univ. Press.

Bowdler, S. & Lourandos, H. 1982. Both sides of Bass Strait, in *Coastal Archaeology in Eastern Australia*. Bowdler, S. (ed.). 121–32. Canberra: Department of Prehistory, Research School of Pacific Studies, Australian National Univ.

Burley, D. et al. 2001. Lapita on the periphery. *Archaeology in Oceania* 36, 89–104.

Burley, D. & Dickinson, W. 2001. Origin and significance of a founding settlement in Polynesia. *Proceedings of the National Academy of Sciences (USA)* 98, 11829–31.

Butlin, N. G. 1983. *Our Original Aggression: Aboriginal Populations of Southeastern Australia 1788–1850*. Sydney: Allen & Unwin.

Chang, K. C. 1995. Taiwan Strait archaeology and the Protoaustronesians, in *Austronesian Studies Relating to Taiwan*. Jen-kuei Li, P., Cheng-hwa Tsang, Ying-Kuei Huang, Dah-an Ho, & Chiu-yu Tseng (eds.). 161–84. Taipei: Institute of History and Philology, Academia Sinica.

Clark, G., Anderson, A., & Vunidilo, T. (eds.). 2001. *The Archaeology of Lapita Dispersal in Oceania*. Canberra: Pandanus Books.

Clarke, A. 1994. Romancing the stones: the cultural construction of an archaeological landscape in the Western District of Victoria. *Archaeology in Oceania* 29, 1–15.

Craib, J. 1999. Colonization of the Mariana Islands, in *The Pacific from 5000 to 2000 Years Ago*. Galipaud, J.-C. & Lilley, I. (eds.). 477–86. Paris: Institut de Recherche pour le Développement.

David, B. 1991. Fern Cave, rock art and social formations: rock art regionalisation and demographic models in southeastern Cape York Peninsula. *Archaeology in Oceania* 26, 41–57.

David, B. & Cole, N. 1990. Rock art and inter-regional interaction in northeastern Australian prehistory. *Antiquity* 64, 788–806.

Denham, T., Haberle, S. et al. 2003. Origins of agriculture at Kuk Swamp in the Highlands of New Guinea. *Science* 301: 189–93.

Dewar, R. & Wright, H. 1993. The culture history of Madagascar. *Journal of World Prehistory* 7, 417–66.

Diamond, J. 1989. Express train to Polynesia. *Nature* 336, 307–08.

Dickinson, W. & Shutler, J. R. 2000. Implications of petrographic temper analysis for Oceanian prehistory. *Journal of World Prehistory* 14, 203–66.

Dye, T. & Komori, E. 1992. A pre-censal population history of Hawai'i. *New Zealand Journal of Archaeology* 14, 113–28.

Dyen, I. 1965. *A Lexicostatistical Classification of the Austronesian Languages*. International Journal of American Linguistics Memoir 19.

Finney, B. et al. 1989. Wait for the west wind. *Journal of the Polynesian Society* 98, 261–302.

Flenley, J. & Bahn, P. 2002. *The Enigmas of Easter Island*. Oxford: Oxford Univ. Press.

Fullagar, R. & David, B. 1997. Investigating changing attitudes towards an Australian Aboriginal Dreaming Mountain over >37,000 years of occupation via residue and use wear analyses of stone artifacts. *Cambridge Archaeological Journal* 7, 139–44.

Goldman, I. 1970. *Ancient Polynesian Society*. Chicago: Univ. of Chicago Press.

Golson, J. 1977. No room at the top, in *Sunda and Sahul*. Allen, J., Golson, J., & Jones, R. (eds.). 601–38. London: Academic Press.

Green, R. C. 1979. Early Lapita art from Polynesia and Island Melanesia, in *Exploring the Visual Art of Oceania*. Mead, S. M. (ed.). 13–31. Honolulu: Univ. of Hawaii Press.

—. 1991a. Near and Remote Oceania, in *Man and a Half*. Pawley, A. (ed.). 484–91. Auckland: Polynesian Society Memoir No. 48.

—. 1991b. The Lapita Cultural Complex: current evidence and proposed models. *Bulletin of the Indo-Pacific Prehistory Association* 11, 295–305.

—. 1998. Rapanui origins prior to European contact, in *Easter Island and East Polynesian Prehistory*. Vargas Casanova, P. (ed.). 87–110. Santiago: Universidad de Chile.

Haberle, S. G. & Lusty, A. C. 2000. Can climate influence cultural development? A view through time. *Environment and History* 6, 349–69.

Hagelberg, E. 2001. Genetic affinities of the principal human lineages in the Pacific, in *The Archaeology of Lapita Dispersal in Oceania*. Clark, G., Anderson, A., & Vunidilo, T. (eds.). 167–76. Canberra: Pandanus Books.

Heyerdahl, T. 1952. *American Indians in the Pacific*. London: Allen & Unwin.

—. 1997. A reappraisal of Alfred Métraux's search for extra-island parallels to Easter Island culture elements. *Rapa Nui Journal* 11/1, 12–20.

Heyerdahl, T. & Ferdon, E. (eds.). 1961. *Archaeology of Easter Island*. Santa Fe: School of American Research.

Hiscock, P. 1994. Technological responses to risk in Holocene Australia. *Journal of World Prehistory* 8, 267–92.

—. 2001. Late Australian. *Encyclopedia of Prehistory*, vol. III. 132–49. New York: Plenum Press.

—. 2002. Pattern and context in the Holocene proliferation of backed artefacts in Australia, in *Thinking Small: Global Perspectives on Microlithization*. Kuhn, S. & Elston, R. (eds.). Anthropological Papers of the American Anthropological Assoc. (AP3A) no. 12, 163–77.

—. 2003. Prehistoric Populations: Australia and the Pacific, in *Encyclopedia of Population*. Demeny, P. & McNicoll, G. (eds.). 796–98. Vol. 2. New York: Macmillan Reference USA.

Hiscock, P. & Mitchell, S. 1993. *Stone Artifact Quarries and Reduction Sites in Australia: Towards a Type Profile*. Australian Heritage Commission. Australian Government Publishing Service.

Hunter-Anderson, R. 1998. Human vs. climatic impacts at Rapa Nui, in *Easter Island in Pacific Context*. Stevenson, C. M., Lee, G., & Morin, F. J. (eds.). 85–99. Santa Barbara: Easter Island Foundation.

Hurles, M. E. et al. 2002. Y chromosomal evidence for the origins of Oceanic-speaking peoples. *Genetics* 160, 289–303.

Irwin, G. 1992. *The Prehistoric Exploration and Colonization of the Pacific*. Cambridge: Cambridge Univ. Press.

Ipoi, D. & Bellwood, P. 1991. Recent research at Gua Sireh (Serian) and Lubang Angin (Gunung Mulu National Park), Sarawak. *Bulletin of the Indo-Pacific Prehistory Association* 11, 386–405.

Jones, R. 1977. The Tasmanian paradox, in *Stone Tools as Cultural Markers: Change, Evolution and Complexity*. Wright, R. V. S. (ed.). 189–204. Canberra: Australian Institute of Aboriginal Studies.

—. 1978. Why did the Tasmanians stop eating fish?, in *Explorations in Ethnoarchaeology*. Gould, R. (ed.). 11–48. Albuquerque: Univ. of New Mexico Press.

Kirch, P. V. 1984. *The Evolution of the Polynesian Chiefdoms*. Cambridge: Cambridge Univ. Press.

—. 1985. *Feathered Gods and Fishhooks*. Honolulu: Univ. of Hawaii Press.

—. 1989. Second millennium BC arboriculture in Melanesia. *Economic Botany* 43, 225–40.

—. 1990. The evolution of sociopolitical complexity in prehistoric Hawaii. *Journal of World Prehistory* 4, 311–46.

—. 1994. *The Wet and the Dry*. Chicago: Univ. of Chicago Press.

—. 1997. *The Lapita Peoples*. Oxford: Blackwell.

—. 2000. *On the Road of the Winds*. Berkeley: Univ. of California Press.

—. (ed.). 2001. *Lapita and its Transformations in Near Oceania*. Berkeley: Univ. of California, Archaeological Research Facility.

Kirch, P. V. & Green, R. C. 2001. *Hawaiki, Ancestral Polynesia*. Cambridge: Cambridge Univ. Press.

Kirch, P. V. & Hunt, T. (eds.). 1997. *Historical Ecology in the Pacific Islands*. New Haven: Yale Univ. Press.

Kirch, P. V. & Yen, D. 1983. *Tikopia*. Honolulu: Bishop Museum Bulletin 238.

Lebot, V. 1999. Biomolecular evidence for plant domestication in Sahul. *Genetic Resources and Crop Evolution* 46, 619–28.

Levison, M., Ward, R. G., & Webb, J. 1973. *The Settlement of Polynesia*. Minneapolis: Univ. of Minnesota Press.

Lewis, D. 1994. *We, the Navigators*. (2nd ed.). Honolulu: Univ. of Hawaii Press.

Lien, C. 1993. Pei-nan: a Neolithic village, in *People of the Stone Age*. Burenhult, G. (ed.). 132–33. San Francisco: Harper.

Lourandos, H. 1980. Change or stability? Hydraulics, hunter-gatherers and population in temperate Australia. *World Archaeology* 11, 245–66.

—. 1983. 10,000 years in the Tasmanian highlands. *Australian Archaeology* 16, 39–47.

—. 1987. Swamp managers of southwestern Victoria, in *Australians to 1788*. Mulvaney, D. J. & White, J. P. (eds.). 292–307. Sydney: Fairfax, Syme & Weldon.

Matthews, P. & Gosden, C. 1997. Plant remains from waterlogged sites in the Arawe Islands. *Economic Botany* 51, 121–33.

Meehan, B., Brockwell, S., Allen, J., & Jones, R. 1985. The wetlands sites, in *Archaeological Research in Kakadu National Park*. Jones, R. (ed.). 103–54. Canberra: Australian National Parks and Wildlife Special Publication 13.

Merriwether, D. et al. 1999. Mitochondrial DNA variation is an indicator of Austronesian influence in Island Melanesia. *American Journal of Physical Anthropology* 110, 243–70.

Mitchell, S. 1994. Stone exchange network in north-western Arnhem Land, in *Archaeology in the North*. Sullivan, M., Brockwell, S., & Webb, A. (eds.). 188–200. Darwin: North Australia Research Unit, Australian National Univ.

Mulvaney, D. J. & Joyce, E. B. 1965. Archaeological and geomorphological investigations on Mt. Moffit Station, Queensland, Australia. *Proceedings of the Prehistoric Society* 31, 147–212.

Nunn, P. 1994. *Oceanic Islands*. Oxford: Blackwell.

—. 2000. Environmental catastrophe in the Pacific Islands around AD 1300. *Geoarchaeology* 15, 715–40.

Oppenheimer, S. & Richards, M. 2001. Fast trains, slow boats, and the ancestry of the Polynesian islanders. *Science Progress* 84, 157–81.

Pardoe, C. 1988. The cemetery as symbol. The distribution of prehistoric Aboriginal burial grounds in southeastern Australia. *Archaeology in Oceania* 23, 1–16.

Pawley, A. 1996. On the Polynesian subgroup as a problem for Irwin's continuous settlement hypothesis, in *Oceanic Culture History*. Davidson, J. M., Irwin, G., Leach, F., Pawley, A., & Brown, D. (eds.). 387–410. Dunedin: New Zealand Journal of Archaeology Special Publication.

—. 1999. Chasing rainbows: implications of the rapid dispersal of Austronesian languages, in *Selected Papers from the Eighth International Conference on Austronesian Linguistics*. Zeitoun, E. & Li, P. J.-K. (eds.). 95–138. Taipei: Institute of Linguistics, Academia Sinica.

—. 2003. The Austronesian dispersal: languages, technologies and people, in *Examining the Farming/Language Dispersal Hypothesis*. Bellwood, P. & Renfrew, C. (eds.). 251–74. Cambridge: McDonald Institute for Archaeological Research.

Phelps, S. 1975. *Art and Artefacts of the Pacific, Africa and the Americas*. London: Hutchinson.

Pietrusewsky, M. 1994. Pacific-Asian relationships: a physical anthropological perspective. *Oceanic Linguistics* 33, 407–30.

Porter, D. 1823. *A Voyage in the South Seas*. London: Sir Richard Phillips.

Rainbird, P. 1994. Prehistory in the northwest tropical Pacific. *Journal of World Prehistory* 8, 293–349.

—. 2002. A message for our future? *World Archaeology* 33, 436–51.

Richardson, N. 1992. Conjoin sets and stratigraphic integrity in a sandstone shelter: Kenniff Cave (Queensland, Australia). *Antiquity* 66, 408–18.

Rolett, B., Wei-chun Chen, & Sinton, J. 2000. Taiwan, Neolithic seafaring and Austronesian origins. *Antiquity* 74, 54–61.

Sahlins, M. 1958. *Social Stratification in Polynesia*. Seattle: Univ. of Washington Press.

Sand, C. 2001. Evolutions in the Lapita cultural complex. *Archaeology in Oceania* 36, 65–76.

Sharp, A. 1963. *Ancient Voyagers in Polynesia*. Auckland: Paul's.

Sheppard, P. & Green, R. C. 1991. Spatial analysis of Nenumbo (SE-RF-2) Lapita site. *Archaeology in Oceania* 26, 89–101.

Sim, R. 1994. Prehistoric human occupation in the King and Furneaux Island regions, Bass Strait, in *Archaeology in the North*. Sullivan, M., Brockwell, S., & Webb, A. 358–74. Darwin North Australian Research Unit.

Skjolsvold, A. 1994. *Archaeological Investigations at Anakena, Easter Island*. Oslo: Kon-Tiki Museum Occasional Papers 3.

—. 1996. Age of Easter Island settlement, *Ahu* and monolithic sculpture. *Rapa Nui Journal* 10/4, 104–09.

Spriggs, M. 1989. The dating of the Island Southeast Asian Neolithic. *Antiquity* 63, 587–612.

—. 1996. What is southeast Asian about Lapita?, in *Prehistoric Mongoloid Dispersals*. Akazawa, T. & Szathmary, E. (eds.). 324–48. Oxford: Oxford Univ. Press.

—. 1997a. *The Island Melanesians*. Oxford: Blackwell.

—. 1997b. Landscape catastrophe and landscape enhancement, in *Historical Ecology in the Pacific Islands*. Kirch, P. & Hunt, T. (eds.). 105–23. New Haven: Yale Univ. Press.

—. 2003. Chronology of the Neolithic transition in Island Southeast Asia and the western Pacific. *Review of Archaeology* 24/2: 57–80.

Spriggs, M. & Anderson, A. 1993. Late colonization of Eastern Polynesia. *Antiquity* 67, 200–17.

Steadman, D. 1997. Extinctions of Polynesian birds, in *Historical Ecology in the Pacific Islands*. Kirch, P. & Hunt, T. (eds.). 105–23. New Haven: Yale Univ. Press.

—. 1999. The prehistoric extinction of South Pacific birds, in *The Pacific from 5000 to 2000 Years Ago*. Galipaud, J.-C. & Lilley, I. (eds.). 375–86. Paris: Institut de Recherche pour le Développement.

Summerhayes, G. 2001a. *Lapita Interaction*. Vol. 15. Canberra: ANH Publications, Terra Australis.

—. 2001b. Defining the chronology of Lapita in the Bismarck Archipelago, in *The Archaeology of Lapita Dispersal in Oceania*. Clark, G., Anderson, A., & Vunidilo, T. (eds.). 25–38. Canberra: Pandanus Books.

Swadling, P. 1997. Changing shorelines and cultural orientations in the Sepik-Ramu, Papua New Guinea. *World Archaeology* 29, 1–14.

Swadling, P., Araho, N., & Ivuyo, B. 1991. Settlements associated with the inland Sepik-Ramu Sea. *Bulletin of the Indo-Pacific Prehistory Association* 11, 92–112.

Taçon, P. S. C. 1993. Regionalism in the recent rock art of western Arnhem Land, Northern Territory. *Archaeology in Oceania* 28, 112–20.

Taçon, P. S. C. & Chippindale, C. 1994. Australia's ancient warriors: changing depictions of fighting in the rock art of Arnhem Land, N.T. *Cambridge Archaeological Journal* 4, 211–248.

Taçon, P. S. C., Wilson, M., & Chippindale, C. 1996. Birth of the Rainbow Serpent in Arnhem Land rock art and oral history. *Archaeology in Oceania* 31, 103–24.

Thomas, N. 1990. *Marquesan Societies*. Oxford: Clarendon Press.

Thomas, N., Guest, H., & Dettelbach, M. (eds.). 1996. *Observations Made During a Voyage Round the World* (by Johann Reinhold Forster). Honolulu: Univ. of Hawaii Press.

Tsang Cheng-hwa. 1992. *Archaeology of the P'eng-hu Islands*. Taipei: Academia Sinica, Institute of History & Philology.

Vanderwal, R. & Horton, D. 1984. *Coastal Southwest Tasmania*. Canberra: Department of Prehistory, RSPAS, Australian National Univ.

Vérin, P. & Wright, H. 1999. Madagascar and Indonesia: new evidence from archaeology and linguistics. *Bulletin of the Indo-Pacific Prehistory Association* 18, 35–42.

Walters, I. 1989. Intensified fishery production at Moreton Bay, southeast Queensland, in the late Holocene. *Antiquity* 63 (239), 215–24.

—. 1992. Farmers and their fires, fishers and their fish: production and productivity in pre-European south-east Queensland. *Dialectical Anthropology* 17, 167–82.

Weisler, M. 1998. Hard evidence for prehistoric interaction in Polynesia. *Current Anthropology* 39, 521–31.

Welch, D. 2002. Archaeological and paleoenvironmental evidence of early settlement in Palau. *Bulletin of the Indo-Pacific Prehistory Association* 22. The Melaka Papers, vol. 6.

Wilson, J. (ed.). 1987. *From the Beginning: The Archaeology of the Maori*. Auckland: Penguin.

CHAPTER 9: ORIGINS OF FOOD-PRODUCING ECONOMIES IN THE AMERICAS

Adovasio, J. M., Hyland, D. C., Andrews, R. L., & Illingworth, J. S. 2002. Wooden artifacts, in *Windover: Multidisciplinary Investigations of an Early Archaic Florida Cemetery*. Doran, G. H. (ed.). 166–90. Gainesville: Univ. Press of Florida.

Aldenderfer, M. S. 1991. Continuity and change in ceremonial structures at Late Preceramic Asana, Southern Peru. *Latin American Antiquity* 2 (3), 227–59.

—. 1993. Cronología y definición de fases arcaicas en Asana, Sur del Perú. *Chungara* 24/25, 13–35.

—. 2000. Cronología y conexiones: evidencias preceramicas de Asana, in *El Periodo Arcaico en El Perú: hacia una definición de los orígenes*. Kaulicke, P. (ed.). 375–92. Lima: Pontificia Universidad Católica del Perú, Boletín de Arqueología No. 3.

—. 2001. An archaeological perspective on the human use of cold montane environments in Andean South America. *Revista de Arqueología Americana* 17/18/19, 75–96.

—. 2002. Late Andean hunting-collecting, in *Encyclopedia of Prehistory*. Vol. 7: South America. Peregrine, P. N. & Ember, M. (eds.). 200–16. New York: Kluwer Academic/Plenum Publishers.

Andrews, R. L., Adovasio, J. M., Humphrey, B., Hyland, D. C., Gardner, J. S., & Harding, D. G. 2002. Conservation and analysis of textile and related perishable artifacts, in *Windover: Multidisciplinary Investigations of an Early Archaic Florida Cemetery*. Doran, G. H. (ed.). 121–65. Gainesville: Univ. Press of Florida.

Arriaza, B. T. 1995. *Beyond Death: The Chinchorro Mummies of Ancient Chile*. Washington D.C.: Smithsonian Institution Press.

Asch, D. L. 1994. Aboriginal specialty-plant cultivation in Eastern North America: Illinois prehistory and a post-contact perspective, in *Agricultural Origins and Developments in the Midcontinent*. Green, W. (ed.). 25–86. Iowa City: Univ. of Iowa, Office of the State Archaeologist, Report 19.

Asch Sidell, N. 1999. Prehistoric plant use in Maine: Paleoindian to Contact Period, in *Current Northeast Paleoethnobotany*. Hart, J. P. (ed.). 191–223. New York: New York State Museum Bulletin No. 494. State Univ. of New York.

Beck, C. & Jones, G. T. 1997. The terminal Pleistocene/Early Holocene archaeology of the Great Basin. *Journal of World Prehistory* 11, 161–236.

Benfer, Jr., R. A. 2000. Proyecto de excavaciones en Paloma, Valle de Chilca, Perú, in *El Periodo Arcaico en El Perú: hacia una definición de los orígenes*. Kaulicke, P. (ed.). 213–38. Lima: Pontificia Universidad Católica del Perú, Boletín de Arqueología No. 3

Benz, B. B. 2001. Archaeological evidence of teosinte domestication from Guila Naquitz, Oaxaca. *Proceedings of the National Academy of Sciences (USA)* 98, 2103–06.

Benz, B. B. & Long, A. 2000. Prehistoric maize evolution in the Tehuacan Valley. *Current Anthropology* 41, 459–65.

Berry, M. S. 1985. The age of maize in the greater Southwest: a critical review, in *Prehistoric Food Production in North America*. Ford, R. I. (ed.). 279–308. Ann Arbor: Museum of Anthropology, Univ. of Michigan, Anthropological Papers No. 75.

Bever, M. 2001. An overview of Alaskan late Pleistocene archaeology: historical themes and current perspectives. *Journal of World Prehistory* 15, 125–91.

Blake, M., Clark, J. E., Chisholm, B., & Mudar, K. 1992. Non-agricultural staples and agricultural supplements: Early Formative subsistence in the Soconusco Region, Mexico, in *Transitions to Agriculture in Prehistory*. Gebauer, A. B. & Price, T. D. (eds.). 133–51. Madison: Prehistory Press.

Bohrer, V. L. 1962. Nature and interpretation of ethnobotanical materials from Tonto National Monument, in *Archaeological Studies of Tonto National Monument, Arizona*. Steen, C. R., Pierson, L. M., Bohrer, V. L., & Kent, K. P. 75–114. Globe: Southwestern Monuments Association Technical Series vol. 2.

—. 1970. Ethnobotanical aspects of Snaketown, a Hohokam village in Southern Arizona. *American Antiquity* (4), 413–30.

Bonavia, D. 1999. The domestication of Andean camelids, in *Archaeology in Latin America*. Politis, G. G. & Alberti, B. (eds.). 130–47. London: Routledge.

Breitburg, E. 1993. The evolution of turkey domestication in the Greater Southwest and Mesoamerica, in *Culture and Contact: Charles Di Peso's Gran Chichimeca*. Woosley, A. I. & Ravesloot, J. C. (eds.). 153–72. Dragoon: Amerind Foundation.

Browman, D. L. 1989. Origins and development of Andean pastoralism: an overview of the past 6000 years, in *The Walking Larder: Patterns of Domestication, Pastoralism, and Predation*. Clutton-Brock, J. (ed.). 256–68. London: Unwin Hyman.

Brown, J. & Vierra, R. 1983. What happened in the Middle Archaic: introduction to an ecological approach to Koster Site archaeology, in *Archaic Hunters and Gatherers in the American Midwest*. Phillips, J. & Brown, J. (eds.). 165–95. New York: Academic Press.

Bruhns, Olsen, K. 1994. *Ancient South America*. New York: Cambridge Univ. Press.

Caldwell, J. 1965. Primary Forest Efficiency. Southeastern Archaeological Conference Bulletin 3, 66–69.

Cardich, A. 1958. Los yacimientos de Lauricocha: nuevas interpretaciones del prehistoria peruana. *Acta Prehistórica* 2, 1–65.

—. 1966. Lauricocha: fundamentos para una prehistoria de los Andes Centrales. *Acta Prehistórica* 8/10, 3–171.

Chapman, J. 1994. *Tellico Archaeology: 12,000 Years of Native American History*. (2nd ed.). Knoxville: Univ. of Tennessee.

Chapman, J. & Adovasio, J. 1977. Textile and basketry impressions from Icehouse Bottom, Tennessee. *American Antiquity* 42, 620–25.

Chapman, J. & Shea, A. 1981. The archeobotanical record: Early Archaic to Contact in the Lower Little Tennessee River Valley. *Tennessee Anthropologist* VI, 64–84.

Chapman, J., Delcourt, P., Cridlebaugh, P., Shea, A., & Delcourt, H. 1982. Man-land interaction: 10,000 years of American Indian impact on native ecosystems in the Lower Little Tennessee River Valley, Eastern Tennessee. *Southeastern Archaeology* 1, 115–21.

Chartkoff, J. L. & Chartkoff, K. K. 1984. *The Archaeology of California*. Stanford: Stanford Univ. Press.

Chauchat, C. 1988. Early hunter-gatherers on the Peruvian coast, in *Peruvian Prehistory: An Overview of Pre-Inca and Inca Society*. Keatinge, R. W. (ed.). 41–66. Cambridge: Cambridge Univ. Press.

Cordell, L. 1997. *Archaeology of the Southwest*. (2nd ed.). San Diego: Academic Press.

Crawford, G. W. 1982. Late Archaic plant remains from West-Central Kentucky: a summary. *Midcontinental Journal of Archaeology* 7, 205–24.

Crawford, G. W., Smith, D. G., & Bowyer, V. E. 1997. Dating the entry of corn (*Zea mays*) into the Lower Great Lakes Region. *American Antiquity* 62, 112–29.

Crothers, G., Faulkner, C., Simek, J., Watson, P. J., & Willey, P. 2002. Woodland cave archaeology in Eastern North America, in *The Woodland Southeast*. Anderson, D. & Mainfort, R. (eds.). 502–24. Tuscaloosa: Univ. of Alabama Press.

Damp, J. E., Hall, S. A., & Smith, S. J. 2002. Early irrigation on the Colorado Plateau near Zuni Pueblo, New Mexico. *American Antiquity* 67, 665–76.

Decker-Walters, D. S., Walters, T. W., Cowan, C. W., & Smith, B. D. 1993. Isozymic characterization of wild populations of *Cucurbita pepo*. *Journal of Ethnobiology* 13, 55–72.

Delcourt, P. A., Delcourt, H. R., Ison, C. R., Sharp, W. E., & Gremillion, K. J. 1998. Prehistoric human use of fire, the Eastern agricultural complex, and Appalachian oak-chestnut forests: paleoecology of Cliff Palace Pond, Kentucky. *American Antiquity* 63, 163–78.

Diamond, J. & Bellwood, P. 2003. Farmers and their languages: the first expansions. *Science* 300, 597–603.

Dillehay, T. D. 1992. Widening the socio-economic foundations of Andean civilization: prototypes of early monumental architecture. *Andean Past* 3, 55–66.

—. 2000. *The Settlement of the Americas: A New Prehistory*. New York: Basic Books.

Dillehay, T. D. & Rossen, J. 2002. Plant food and its implications for the peopling of the New World: a view from South America, in *The First Americans: The Pleistocene Colonization of the New World*. Jablonski, N. (ed.). Memoirs of the California Academy of Sciences 27, 237–53.

Doebley, J. F. 2004. The genetics of maize evolution. *Annual Review of Genetics* 38: 37–59.

Doebley, J. F., Goodman, M. M., & Stuber, C. 1986. Exceptional genetic divergence of Northern Flint corn. *American Journal of Botany* 73, 64–69.

Doran, G. H. (ed.). 2002. *Windover: Multidisciplinary Investigations of an Early Archaic Florida Cemetery*. Gainesville: Univ. Press of Florida.

Doran, G. H., Dickel, D., & Newsom, L. A. 1990. A 7,290-year-old bottle gourd from the Windover Site, Florida. *American Antiquity* 55, 354–59.

Ellis, C. J. & Deller, D. B. 1997. Variability in the archaeological record of northeastern early Paleoindians: a view from southern Ontario. *Archaeology of Eastern North America* 25, 1–30.

Ellis, C. J., Goodyear, A., Morse, D., & Tankersley, K. 1998. Archaeology of the Pleistocene-Holocene transition in Eastern North America. *Quaternary International* 49/50, 151–66.

Engel, F. A. 1976. *An Ancient World Preserved: Relics and Records of Prehistory in the Andes*. Transl. Gordon, R. K. New York: Crown Publishers.

Fish, S. K., Fish, P. R., Miksicek, C., & Madsen, J. 1985. Prehistoric agave cultivation in Southern

Arizona. *Desert Plants* 7, 107–13.

Flannery, K. V. 1986. *Guilá Naquitz: Archaic Foraging and Early Agriculture in Oaxaca, Mexico.* New York: Academic Press.

Ford, R. I. 1981. Gardening and farming before A.D. 1000: patterns of prehistoric cultivation north of Mexico. *Journal of Ethnobiology* 1, 6–27.

Frison, G. C. 1991. *Prehistoric Hunters on the High Plains.* (2nd ed.). New York: Academic Press.

Fritz, G. J. 1990. Multiple pathways to farming in Precontact Eastern North America. *Journal of World Prehistory* 4, 387–435.

—. 1994. In color and in time: prehistoric Ozark agriculture, in *Agricultural Origins and Development in the Midcontinent.* Green, W. (ed.). 105–26. Iowa City: Univ. of Iowa, Office of the State Archaeologist, Report 19.

—. 1997. A three-thousand-year-old cache of crop seeds from Marble Bluff, Arkansas, in *People, Plants, and Landscapes: Studies in Paleoethnobotany.* Gremillion, K. (ed.). 42–62. Tuscaloosa: Univ. of Alabama Press.

—. 1999. Gender and the early cultivation of gourds in Eastern North America. *American Antiquity* 64, 417–29.

Fritz, G. J. & Smith, B. D. 1988. Old collections and new technology: documenting the domestication of *Chenopodium* in Eastern North America. *Midcontinental Journal of Archaeology* 13, 3–28.

Fritz, G. J., Drywater Whitekiller, V., & McIntosh, J. W. 2001. Ethnobotany of Ku-Nu-Che: Cherokee hickory nut soup. *Journal of Ethnobiology* 21, 1–27.

Gaspar, M. D. 1998. Considerations of the sambaquis of the Brazilian coast. *Antiquity* 72, 592–615.

Gasser, R. E. & Kwiatkowski, S. M. 1991. Food for thought: recognizing patterns in Hohokam subsistence, in *Exploring the Hohokam: Prehistoric Desert Peoples of the American Southwest.* Gumerman, G. J. (ed.). 417–60. Albuquerque: Univ. of New Mexico Press.

Gibson, J. L. 2000. *Ancient Mounds of Poverty Point: Place of Rings.* Gainesville: Univ. Press of Florida.

Gnecco, V. C. & Mora, S. 1997. Early occupations of the tropical forest of northern South America by hunter-gatherers. *Antiquity* 71, 683–90.

Goodyear, A. 1989. A hypothesis for the use of cryptocrystalline raw materials among Paleoindian groups of North America, in *Eastern Paleoindian Lithic Resource Use.* Ellis, C. J. & Lothrop, J. (eds.). 1–9. Boulder: Westview Press.

Gremillion, K. J. 2002. The development and dispersal of agricultural systems in the Woodland Period Southeast, in *The Woodland Southeast.* Anderson, D. G. & Mainfort, Jr., R. C. (eds.). 483–501. Tuscaloosa: Univ. of Alabama Press.

Hard, R. J. & Roney, J. R. 1998. A massive terraced village complex in Chihuahua, Mexico, 3000 years before present. *Science* 279, 1661–64.

—. 1999. An archaeological investigation of Late Archaic *Cerros de Trincheras* sites in Chihuahua, Mexico. San Antonio: Univ. of Texas, Center for Archaeological Research, Special Report 25.

Hart, J. P. 1999. Maize agriculture evolution in the eastern woodlands of North America: an evolutionary perspective. *Journal of Archaeological Method and Theory* 6, 137–80.

Hart, J. P. & Asch Sidell, N. 1997. Additional evidence for early cucurbit use in the northern eastern woodlands of the Allegheny Front. *American Antiquity* 62, 523–37.

Hart, J. P., Asch, D. L., Scarry, C. M., & Crawford, G. W. 2002. The age of the common bean (*Phaseolus vulgaris* L.) in the northern eastern woodlands of North America. *Antiquity* 76, 377–85.

Heiser, Jr., C. B. 1985. Some botanical considerations of the early domesticated plants north of Mexico, in *Prehistoric Food Production in North America.* Ford, R. I. (ed.). 57–72. Ann Arbor: Museum of Anthropology, Univ. of Michigan, Anthropological Papers No. 75.

Hesse, B. 1980. Archaeological evidence for muscovy duck in Ecuador. *Current Anthropology* 21 (1), 139–40.

Hill, J. H. 2001. Proto-Uto-Aztecan: a community of cultivators in Central Mexico? *American Anthropologist* 103, 913–34.

Huckell, B. B. 1996. The Southwestern Archaic: scale and perception of Preceramic hunter-gatherers, in *Interpreting Southwestern Diversity: Underlying Principles and Overarching Patterns.* Fish, P. R. & Reid, J. J. (eds.). 7–16. Tucson: Arizona State Univ., Anthropological Research Papers No. 48.

Hurt, W. 2002a. Early East Brazilian uplands, in *Encyclopedia of Prehistory.* Vol. 7: South America. Peregrine, P. N. & Ember, M. (eds.). 98–107. New York: Kluwer Academic/Plenum Publishers.

—. 2002b. Late East Brazilian uplands, in *Encyclopedia of Prehistory.* Vol. 7: South America. Peregrine, P. N. & Ember, M. (eds.). 228–34. New York: Kluwer Academic/Plenum Publishers.

Jackson, H. E. 1989. Poverty Point adaptive systems in the Lower Mississippi Valley: subsistence remains from the J. W. Copes site. *North American Archaeologist* 10, 173–204.

Jones, G., Beck, C., Jones, E., & Hughes, R. 2003. Lithic source use and Paleoarchaic foraging territories in the Great Basin. *American Antiquity* 68, 5–38.

Kadwell, M., Fernandez, M., Stanley, H. F., Baldi, R., Wheeler, J. C., Rosadio, R., & Bruford, M. W. 2001. Genetic analysis reveals the wild ancestors of the llama and the alpaca. *Proceedings of the Royal Society of London*, Series B, 268, 2575–84.

Kaplan, L. & Lynch, T. F. 1998. *Phaseolus* (Fabaceae) in archaeology: AMS radiocarbon dates and their significance for pre-Columbian agriculture. *Economic Botany* 53 (3), 261–72.

Keefer, D. K., DeFrance, S. D., Moseley, M. E., Richardson III, J. B., Satterlee, D. R., & Day-Lewis, A. 1998. Early maritime economy and El Niño events at Quebrada Tacahuay, Peru. *Science* 281, 1833–35.

Kessler, M., Gualy, M., Frese, C., & Hiendleder, S. 1996. DNA studies on South American camelids, in *Second European Symposium on South American Camelids, Camerino, August 30–September 2, 1995.* Gerken, M. & Renieri, C. (eds.). 269–78. Matelica, Italy: Università degli studi di Camerino.

King, F. B. 1985. Early cultivated cucurbits in Eastern North America, in *Prehistoric Food Production in North America.* Ford, R. I. (ed.). 73–98. Ann Arbor: Museum of Anthropology, Univ. of Michigan, Anthropological Papers No. 75.

Kipnis, R. 1998. Early hunter-gatherers in the Americas: perspectives from central Brazil. *Antiquity* 72, 581–592.

Kuznar, L. A. 1989. The domestication of camelids in southern Peru: models and evidence, in *Ecology, Settlement and History in the Osmore*

Drainage, Peru. Rice, D. S., Stanish, C., & Scarr, P. R. (eds.). 167–82. Oxford: British Archaeological Reports International Series 545, Part 1.

—. 2002. Late Highland Andean Archaic, in *Encyclopedia of Prehistory.* Vol. 7: South America. Peregrine, P. N. & Ember, M. (eds.). 235–52. New York: Kluwer Academic/Plenum Publishers.

Lathrap, D. 1970. *The Upper Amazon.* London: Thames & Hudson.

—. 1977. Our father the cayman, our mother the gourd: Spinden revisited or a unitary model for the emergence of agriculture in the New World, in *Origins of Agriculture.* Reed, C. A. (ed.). 713–51. The Hague: Mouton.

Lavallée, D. 1987. *Telarmachay: chasseurs et pasteurs préhistoriques des Andes.* Paris: Editions Recherche sur les Civilisations.

—. 1990. La domestication animale en Amérique du Sud: le point des connaissances. *Bulletin de l'Institut Français d'Etudes Andines* 19 (1), 25–44.

—. 2000. *The First South Americans: The Peopling of a Continent from the Earliest Evidence to High Culture.* Transl. Bahn, P. G. Salt Lake City: Univ. of Utah Press.

Leonard, J. A., Wayne, R. K., Wheeler, J., Valdez, R., Guillen, S., & Vila, C. 2002. Ancient DNA evidence for the Old World origin of New World dogs. *Science* 298, 1613–16.

Lepper, B. T. 1999. Pleistocene peoples of midcontinental North America, in *Ice-Age People of North America: Environments, Origins, and Adaptations.* Bonnichsen, R. & Turnmire, K. (eds.). 362–94. Corvallis: Center for the Study of the First Americans.

Lewis, T. M. N. & Lewis, M. K. 1961. *Eva: An Archaic Site.* Knoxville: Univ. of Tennessee Study in Anthropology.

Llagostera, A. 1992. Early occupations and the emergence of fishermen on the Pacific coast of South America. *Andean Past* 3, 87–111.

Long, A., Benz, B. F., Donahue, D. J., Jull, A. J. T., & Toolin, L. J. 1989. First direct AMS dates on early maize from Tehuacán, Mexico. *Radiocarbon* 31 (3), 1035–40.

Lopinot, N. H. 1994. A new crop of data on the Cahokian polity, in *Agricultural Origins and Developments in the Midcontinent.* Green, W. (ed.). 127–53. Iowa City: Univ. of Iowa, Office of the State Archaeologist, Report 19.

—. 1997. Cahokian food production reconsidered, in *Cahokia: Domination and Ideology in the Mississippian World.* Pauketat, T. R. & Emerson, T. E. (eds.). 52–68. Lincoln: Univ. of Nebraska Press.

Lopinot, N. H., Fritz, G. J., & Kelly, J. E. 1991. The archaeological context and significance of *Polygonum erectum* achene masses from the American Bottom Region. St. Louis: Paper presented to the 14th Annual Meeting of the Society of Ethnobiology.

Lynch, T. F. 1980. *Guitarrero Cave: Early Man in the Andes.* New York: Academic Press.

—. 1991. Paleoindians in South America: a discrete and identifiable cultural stage?, in *Clovis: Origins and Adaptations.* Bonnichsen, R. & Turnmire, K. (eds.). 255–59. Corvallis: Center for the Study of the First Americans.

—. 1999. The earliest South American lifeways, in *The Cambridge History of the Native Peoples of the Americas.* Vol. 3, part 1: South America. Salomon, F. & Schwartz, S. B. (eds.). 188–263. Cambridge: Cambridge Univ. Press.

Lynott, M. J., Boutton, T. W., Price, J. E., & Nelson, D. E. 1986. Stable carbon isotopic evidence for maize agriculture in Southeast Missouri and Northeast Arkansas. *American Antiquity* 51, 51–65.

Mabry, J. B. 1999. Las Capas and early irrigation farming. *Archaeology Southwest* 13 (1), 14.

McClung de Tapia, E. 1992. The origins of agriculture in Mesoamerica and Central America, in *The Origins of Agriculture: An International Perspective*. Wesley Cowan, C. & Watson, P. J. (eds.). 143–71. Washington D.C.: Smithsonian Institution Press.

MacNeish, R. S. 1971. Speculation about how and why food production and village life developed in the Tehuacan Valley, Mexico. *Archaeology* 24 (4), 307–315.

MacNeish, R. S., Garcia Cook, A., Lumbreras, L. G., Vierra, R. K., & Nelken-Terner, A. 1981. *Prehistory of the Ayacucho Basin, Peru*. Vol. 2: Excavations and chronology. Ann Arbor: Univ. of Michigan Press.

MacNeish, R. S., Patterson, T. C., & Browman, D. L. 1975. *The Central Peruvian Prehistoric Interaction Sphere*. Andover: Papers of the Robert S. Peabody Foundation for Archaeology, vol. 7.

MacNeish, R. S., Vierra, R. K., Nelken-Terner, A., Lurie, R., & Garcia Cook, A. 1983. *Prehistory of the Ayacucho Basin, Peru*. Vol. 4: The Preceramic way of life. Ann Arbor: Univ. of Michigan Press.

Mangelsdorf, P. C., Dick, H. W., & Camara-Hernandez, J. 1967a. Bat Cave revisited. Harvard Univ., Botanical Museum Leaflets, 22 (1), 1–19.

Mangelsdorf, P. C., MacNeish, R. S., & Galinat, W. C. 1967b. Prehistoric wild and cultivated maize, in *The Prehistory of the Tehuacan Valley. Vol. 1: Environment and Subsistence*. Byers, D. (ed.). 178–200. Austin: Univ. of Texas Press.

Marquardt, W. H. & Watson, P. J. 1983. The shell mound archaic of Western Kentucky, in *Archaic Hunters and Gatherers in the American Midwest*. Phillips, J. & Brown, J. (eds.). 323–39. New York: Academic Press.

—. 2005. *Archaeology of the Middle Green River Region, Kentucky*. Gainesville: Institute of Archaeology and Paleoenvironmental Studies, Univ. of Florida.

Matson, R. G. 1999. The spread of maize to the Colorado Plateau. *Archaeology Southwest* 13 (1), 10–11. Tucson: Center for Desert Archaeology.

Matsuoka, Y., Vigouroux, Y., Goodman, M., Jesus Sanchez G., Buckler, E., & Doebley, J. 2002. A single domestication for maize shown by multilocus microsatellite genotyping. *Proceedings of the National Academy of Sciences (USA)* 99, 6080–84.

Meggers, B. J. 1977. Vegetational fluctuation and prehistoric cultural adaptations in Amazonia: some tentative correlations. *World Archaeology* 8 (3), 287–303.

—. 1987. The early history of man in Amazonia, in *Biogeography and Quaternary History in Tropical America*. Whitmore, T. & Prance, G. (eds.). 151–74. Oxford: Clarendon Press.

—. 1995. Judging the future by the past: the impact of environmental instability on prehistoric Amazonian populations, in *Indigenous Peoples and the Future of Amazonia: An Ecological Anthropology of an Endangered World*. Sponsel, L. E. (ed.). 15–43. Tucson: Univ. of Arizona Press.

—. 1996. *Amazonia: Man and Culture in a Counterfeit Paradise*. (Revised ed.) Washington D.C.: Smithsonian Institution Press.

Meggers, B. J. & Miller, E. T. 2003. Hunter-gatherers in Amazonia during the Pleistocene-Holocene transition, in *Under the Canopy: The Archaeology of Tropical Rain Forests*. Mercader, J. (ed.). 291–316. New Brunswick: Rutgers Univ. Press.

Meltzer, D. J. 1999. Human responses to Middle Holocene (Altithermal) climates on the North American Great Plains. *Quaternary Research* 52, 404–16.

—. 2002. What do you do when no one's been there before? Thoughts on the exploration and colonization of new lands, in *The First Americans: The Pleistocene Colonization of the New World*. Jablonski, N. (ed.). Memoirs of the California Academy of Sciences 27, 25–56.

Messerli, B., Grosjean, M., Hofer, T., Nunez, L., & Pfister, C. 2000. From nature-dominated to human-dominated environmental changes. *Quaternary Science Reviews* 19, 459–79.

Miksicek, C. H. 1987. Late Sedentary-Early Classic Period Hohokam agriculture: plant remains from the Marana community complex, in *Studies in the Hohokam Community of Marana*. Rice, G. E. (ed.). 197–216. Tempe: Arizona State Univ. Anthropological Field Studies No. 15.

Milanich, J. 1994. *Archaeology of Precolumbian Florida*. Gainesville: Univ. Press of Florida.

Minnis, P. E. 1992. Earliest plant cultivation in the desert borderlands of North America, in *The Origins of Agriculture: An International Perspective*. Cowan, C. W. & Watson, P. J. (eds.). 121–42. Washington D.C.: Smithsonian Institution Press.

Mora, S. & Gnecco, C. 2003. Archaeological hunter-gatherers in tropical forests: a view from Colombia, in *Under the Canopy: The Archaeology of Tropical Rain Forests*. Mercader, J. (ed.). 271–90. New Brunswick: Rutgers Univ. Press.

Morse, D. 1997. *Sloan: A Paleoindian Dalton Cemetery in Arkansas*. Washington D.C.: Smithsonian Institution Press.

Moseley, M. E. 2001. *The Incas and their Ancestors: The Archaeology of Peru*. (Rev. ed.). London & New York: Thames & Hudson.

Nabhan, G. P. & Felger, R. 1984. Teparies in Southwestern North America: a biogeographical and ethnohistorical study of *Phaseolus acutifolius*. *Economic Botany* 32, 2–19.

Newsom, L. A., Webb, D., & Dunbar, J. S. 1993. History and geographic distribution of *Cucurbita pepo* gourds in Florida. *Journal of Ethnobiology* 13, 75–97.

Niederberger, C. 1979. Early sedentary economy in the Basin of Mexico. *Science* 203, 131–42.

Núñez, L. 1992. Ocupación arcaica en la puna de Atacama: secuencia, movilidad y cambio, in *Prehistoria Sudamericana: Nuevas Perspectivas*. Meggers, B. J. (ed.). 283–308. Washington D.C.: Taraxacum.

—. 1998. Archaic adaptation on the South-Central Andean coast, in *Pacific Latin America in Prehistory: The Evolution of Archaic and Formative Culture*. Blake, M. (ed.). 199–211. Pullman: Washington State Univ. Press.

Núñez, L., Grosjean, M., & Cartagena, I. 2002. Human occupations and climate change in the Puna de Atacama, Chile. *Science* 298, 821–24.

Pearsall, D. M. 1980. Pachamachay ethnobotanical report: plant utilization at a hunting base camp, in *Prehistoric Hunters of the High Andes*. Rick, J. W. (ed.). 191–231. New York: Academic Press.

Piana, E. L. 2002. Magellan-Fuegan, in *Encyclopedia of Prehistory*. Vol. 7: South America. Peregrine, P. N. & Ember, M. (eds.). 255–71. New York: Kluwer Academic/Plenum Publishers.

Piperno, D. R. & Flannery, K. V. 2001. The earliest archaeological maize from highland Mexico: new accelerator mass spectrometry dates and their implications. *Proceedings of the National Academy of Sciences (USA)* 98, 2101–03.

Piperno, D. R. & Pearsall, D. M. 1998. *The Origins of Agriculture in the Lowland Neotropics*. San Diego: Academic Press.

Piperno, D. R. & Stothert, K. E. 2003. Phytolith evidence for early Holocene *Cucurbita* domestication in Southwest Ecuador. *Science* 299 (5609), 1054–57.

Piperno, D. R., Ranere, A., Holst, I., & Hansell, P. 2000. Starch grains reveal early root crop horticulture in the Panamanian tropical forest. *Nature* 407, 894–97.

Politis, G. 1991. Fishtail projectile points in the southern cone of South America: an overview, in *Clovis: Origins and Adaptations*. Bonnichsen, R. & Turnmire, K. (eds.). 287–301. Corvallis: Center for the Study of the First Americans.

Pope, K. O., Pohl, M. E., Jones, J. G., Lentz, D. L., von Naby, C., Vega, F. J., & Quitmyer, I. R. 2001. Origin and environmental setting of ancient agriculture in the lowlands of Mesoamerica. *Science* 292, 1370–73.

Prous, A. 1992. *Arqueologia Brasileira*. Brasilia: Editora PnB.

Purdy, B. (ed.). 1988. *Wet Site Archaeology*. Caldwell: Telford.

Ranere, A. & Cooke, R. 1991. Paleoindian occupation in the Central American tropics, in *Clovis: Origins and Adaptations*. Bonnichsen, R. & Turnmire, K. (eds.). 237–53. Corvallis: Center for the Study of the First Americans.

—. 2003. Late glacial and early Holocene occupation of Central American tropical forests, in *Under the Canopy: The Archaeology of Tropical Rain Forests*. Mercader, J. (ed.). 219–38. New Brunswick: Rutgers Univ. Press.

Richardson III, J. B. 1992. Early hunters, fishers, farmers and herders: diverse economic adaptations in Peru to 4500 B.P. *Revista de Arqueología Americana* 6, 71–90.

—. 1999. Looking in the right places: pre-5,000 b.p. maritime adaptations in Peru and the changing environment. *Revista de Arqueología Americana* 15, 33–56.

Rick, J. W. 1980. *Prehistoric Hunters of the High Andes*. New York: Academic Press.

Rick, J. W. & Moore, K. M. 2000. El preceramico de la punas de Junín: el punto de vista desde Panaulauca, in *El Periodo Arcaico en El Perú: hacia una definición de los orígenes*. Kaulicke, P. (ed.). 263–96. Lima: Pontificia Universidad Católica del Perú, Boletín de Arqueología No. 3.

Riley, T. J., Walz, G. R., Bareis, C. J., Fortier, A. C., & Parker, K. E. 1994. Accelerator Mass Spectrometry (AMS) dates confirm early *Zea mays* in the Mississippi River Valley. *American Antiquity* 59 (3), 490–98.

Rivera, M. A. 1995. The preceramic Chinchorro mummy complex of Northern Chile: context, style, and purpose, in *Tombs for the Living: Andean Mortuary Practices*. Dillehay, T. D. (ed.). 43–77. Washington D.C.: Dumbarton Oaks Research Library & Collection.

Roney, J. R. & Hard, R. J. 2000. *Una investigación arqueológica de los sitios cerros con trincheras del Arcaico Tardio en Chihuahua, México: Las investigaciones de campo de 1999*. México, D.F.: Informe al Consejo de Arqueología, Instituto Nacional de Antropología e Historia, Univ. of Texas at San Antonio, Center for Archaeological Research, Special Report 26-S.

Roosevelt, A. C. 2000. The Lower Amazon: a dynamic human habitat, in *Imperfect Balance: Landscape Transformations in the Precolumbian Americas*. Lentz, D. L. (ed.). Ch. 15. New York: Columbia Univ.

—. 2002a. Early Amazonia, in *Encyclopedia of Prehistory*. Vol. 7: South America. Peregrine, P. N. & Ember, M. (eds.). 75–77. New York: Kluwer Academic/Plenum Publishers.

—. 2002b. Old Amazonian collecting-hunting, in *Encyclopedia of Prehistory*. Vol. 7: South America. Peregrine, P. N. & Ember, M. (eds.). 289–92. New York: Kluwer Academic/Plenum Publishers.

Roosevelt, A. C., Douglas, J., & Brown, L. 2002. The migrations and adaptations of the first Americans: Clovis and pre-Clovis viewed from South America, in *The First Americans: The Pleistocene Colonization of the New World*. Jablonski, N. (ed.). Memoirs of the California Academy of Sciences 27, 159–235.

Roosevelt, A. C., Housley, R., Imazio da Silveira, M., Maranca, S., & Johnson, R. 1991. Eighth millennium pottery from a prehistoric shell midden in the Brazilian Amazon. *Science* 254 (5038), 1621–24.

Roosevelt, A. C., Lima de Costa, M., Lopes Machado, C., Michab, M., Mercier, N., Valladas, H., Feathers, J., Barnett, W., Imazio da Silveira, M., Henderson, A., Sliva, J., Chernoff, B., Reese, D. S., Holman, J. A., Toth, N., & Shick, K. 1996. Paleoindian cave dwellers in the Amazon: the peopling of the Americas. *Science* 272 (5260), 373–84.

Rossen, J. & Dillehay, T. D. 2000. La colonización y el asentamiento del norte del Perú: innovación, tecnología y adaptación en el valle de Zaña, in *El Periodo Arcaico en El Perú: hacia una definición de los orígenes*. Kaulicke, P. (ed.). 121–40. Lima: Pontificia Universidad Católica del Perú, Boletín de Arqueología No. 3.

Rossen, J., Dillehay, T. D., & Ugent, D. 1996. Ancient cultigens or modern intrusions? Evaluating plant remains in an Andean case. *Journal of Archaeological Science* 23 (3), 391–407.

Russo, M. 1996. Southeastern Archaic Mounds, in *Archaeology of the Mid-Holocene Southeast*. Sassaman, K. E. & Anderson, D. G. (eds.). 259–87. Tuscaloosa: Univ. of Alabama Press.

Sandweiss, D. H., McInnis, H., Burger, R. L., Cano, A., Ojeda, B., Paredes, R., Sandweiss, M. del C., & Glascock, M. D. 1998. Quebrada Jaguay: early South American maritime adaptations. *Science* 281, 1830–32.

Sandweiss, D. H., Richardson III, J. B., Reitz, E. J., Hsu, J. T., & Feldman, R. A. 1989. Early maritime adaptations in the Andes: preliminary studies at the Ring Site, Peru, in *Ecology, Settlement and History in the Osmore Drainage, Peru*. Rice, D. S., Stanish, C. & Scarr, P. R. (eds.). 35–84. Oxford: British Archaeological Reports International Series 545, Part 1.

Sassaman, K. E. 2002. Woodland ceramic beginnings, in *The Woodland Southeast*.

Anderson, D. G. & Mainfort, Jr., R. C. (eds.). 398–420. Tuscaloosa: Univ. of Alabama Press.

Saunders, J. W., Mandel, R. D., Saucier, R. T., Thurman Allen, E., Hallmark, C. T., Johnson, J. K., Jackson, E. H., Allen, C. M., Stringer, G. L., Frink, D. S., Feathers, J. K., Williams, S., Gremillion, K. J., Vidrine, M. F., & Jones, R. 1997. A mound complex in Louisiana at 5400–5000 years before the present. *Science*. 277, 1796–99.

Schmitz, P. I. 1987. Prehistoric hunters and gatherers of Brazil. *Journal of World Prehistory* 1 (1), 53–126.

—. 1998. Peopling of the seashore of Southern Brazil, in *Explorations in American Archaeology: Essays in Honor of Wesley R. Hurt*. Plew, M. G. (ed.). 193–220. Lanham: Univ. Press of America.

Schulderein, J. 1996. Geoarchaeology and the mid-Holocene landscape history of the greater Southeast, in *Archaeology of the Mid-Holocene Southeast*. Sassaman, K. & Anderson, D. (eds.). 3–27. Gainesville: Univ. Press of Florida.

Shady Solís, R. & López Trujillo, S. 2000. Ritual de enterramiento de un recinto en el Sector Residencial A en Caral-Supe, in *El Periodo Arcaico en El Perú: Hacia una Definición de los Orígenes*. Kaulicke, P. (ed.). 187–212. Lima: Pontificia Universidad Católica del Perú, Boletín de Arqueología No. 3.

Shady Solís, R., Haas, J., & Creamer, W. 2001. Dating Caral, a preceramic site in the Supe valley on the central coast of Peru. *Science* 292 (5517), 723–26.

Smith, B. D. 1997a. The initial domestication of *Cucurbita pepo* in the Americas 10,000 years ago. *Science* 276, 932–34.

—. 1997b. Reconsidering the Ocampo Caves and the era of incipient cultivation in Mesoamerica. *Latin American Antiquity* 8, 342–83.

—. 2000. Guilá Naquitz revisited: agricultural origins in Oaxaca, Mexico, in *Cultural Evolution: Contemporary Viewpoints*. Feinman, G. M. & Manzanilla, L. (eds.). 15–60. New York: Plenum Press.

Smith, B. D., Cowan, C. W., & Hoffman, M. D. 1993. Is it an indigene or a foreigner?, in *Rivers of Change: Essays on Early Agriculture in Eastern North America*. Smith, B. (ed.). 67–100. Washington D.C.: Smithsonian Institution Press.

Staller, J. E. 2003. An examination of the palaeobotanical and chronological evidence for an early introduction of maize (*Zea mays L.*) into South America. *Journal of Archaeological Science* 50 (3), 373–80.

Stanford, D. J. 1999. Paleoindian archaeology and late Pleistocene environments of the Plains and southwestern United States, in *Ice-Age People of North America: Environments, Origins, and Adaptations*. Bonnichsen, R. & Turnmire, K. (eds.). 281–339. Corvallis: Center for the Study of the First Americans.

Stanley, H. F., Kadwell, M., & Wheeler, J. 1994. Molecular evolution of the family Camelidae: a mitochondrial DNA study. *Proceedings of the Royal Society of London, Series B*, 256, 1–6.

Stothert, K. E. 1988. *La Prehistoria Temprana de la Península de Santa Elena, Ecuador: Cultura Las Vegas*. Quito: Miscelánea Antropológica Ecuatoriana, Serie Monográfica 10.

—. 1992. Early economics of coastal Ecuador and the foundations of Andean civilization. *Andean Past* 3, 43–54.

Tagg, M. D. 1996. Early cultigens from Fresnal Shelter, Southeast New Mexico. *American Antiquity* 61, 311–24.

Todd, L. C. 1991. Seasonality studies and Paleoindian subsistence strategies, in *Human Predators and Prey Mortality*. Stiner, M. (ed.). 217–38. Boulder: Westview Press.

Wagner G. E. 2000. Tobacco in prehistoric Eastern North America, in *Tobacco Use by Native North Americans*. Winter, J. C. (ed.). 185–201. Norman: Univ. of Oklahoma Press.

Walker, R. B. & Morey, D. F. 2002. Canid skeletons from the 2002 season of excavations at Dust Cave, Alabama. Abstracts of the 59th Annual Meeting. *Southeastern Archaeological Conference Bulletin* 45, 40.

Walthall, J. 1998. Rockshelters and hunter-gatherer adaptation to the Pleistocene/Holocene transition. *American Antiquity* 63, 223–38.

Watson, P. J. (ed.). 1969. *The Prehistory of Salts Cave, Kentucky*. Springfield: Illinois State Museum Reports of Investigations No. 16.

—. (ed.). 1974. *Archeology of the Mammoth Cave Area*. New York: Academic Press.

Watts, W. A., Grimm, E. C., & Hussey, T. C. 1996. Mid-Holocene forest history of Florida and the coastal plain of Georgia and South Carolina, in *Archaeology of the Mid-Holocene Southeast*. Sassaman, K. & Anderson, D. (eds.). 28–40. Gainesville: Univ. Press of Florida.

Wheat, J. B. 1972. The Olsen-Chubbuck site: a Paleoindian bison kill. *American Antiquity Memoir* 26.

Willig, J. 1991. Clovis technology and adaptation in far western North America: regional pattern and environmental context, in *Clovis: Origins and Adaptations*. Bonnichsen, R. & Turnmire, K. (eds.). 91–118. Corvallis: Center for the Study of the First Americans.

Wills, W. H. 1988. *Early Prehistoric Agriculture in the American Southwest*. Santa Fe: School of American Research Press.

—. 1990. Cultivating ideas: the changing intellectual history of the introduction of agriculture to the American Southwest, in *Perspectives on Southwestern Prehistory*. Minnis, P. E. & Redman, C. L. (eds.). 319–32. Boulder: Westview Press.

—. 1995. Archaic foraging and the beginning of food production in the American Southwest, in *Last Hunters, First Farmers*. Price, T. D. & Gebauer, A. B. (eds.). 215–42. Santa Fe: School of American Research Press.

—. 2001. Pithouse architecture and the economics of household formation in the prehistoric American Southwest. *Human Ecology* 29 (4), 477–500.

Wise, K. 1999. Archaic Period maritime adaptations in Peru, in *Pacific Latin America in Prehistory: The Evolution of Archaic and Formative Cultures*. Blake, M. (ed.). 189–98. Pullman: Washington State Univ. Press.

Yarnell, R. A. 1969. Contents of human paleofeces, in *The Prehistory of Salts Cave, Kentucky*. Watson, P. J. (ed.). 41–54. Springfield: Illinois State Museum, Reports of Investigations No. 16.

—. 1974a. Intestinal contents of the Salts Cave mummy and analysis of the initial Salts Cave flotation series, in *Archaeology of the Mammoth Cave Area*. Watson, P. J. (ed.). 109–12. New York: Academic Press.

—. 1974b. Plant food and cultivation of the Salts Cavers, in *Archaeology of the Mammoth Cave Area*. Watson, P. J. (ed.). 113–22. New York: Academic Press.

—. 1978. Domestication of sunflower and sumpweed in Eastern North America, in *The Nature and Status of Ethnobotany*. Ford, R. A. (ed.). 289–99. Ann Arbor: Museum of Anthropology, Univ. of Michigan, Anthropological Papers 67.

CHAPTER 10: HOLOCENE AFRICA

Aubet, M. E. 2001. *The Phoenicians and the West: Politics, Colonies and Trade*. (2nd ed.). Cambridge: Cambridge Univ. Press.

Baines, J. & Malek, J. 2000. *Cultural Atlas of Ancient Egypt*. (Rev. ed.). New York: Checkmark Books.

Baker, S. W. 1866. *The Albert N'yanza, Great Basin of the Nile, and Explorations of the Nile Sources*. 2 vols. London: Macmillan.

Bard, K. A. 2000. The emergence of the Egyptian state (*c.* 3200–2686 BC), in *The Oxford History of Ancient Egypt*. Shaw, I. (ed.). 61–88. Oxford: Oxford Univ. Press.

Barnett, T. 1999. *The Emergence of Food Production in Ethiopia*. Oxford: British Archaeological Reports International Series 763.

Bernal, M. 1985. *Black Athena: The Afroasiatic Roots of Classical Civilisation*. Vol. I: *The Fabrication of Ancient Greece*. London: Free Association Press.

Bisson, M. S. 2000. Precolonial copper metallurgy: sociopolitical context, in *Ancient African Metallurgy: The Sociocultural Context*. Vogel, J. O. (ed.). 83–145. Walnut Creek: AltaMira Press.

Blench, R. 1993. Ethnographic and linguistic evidence for the prehistory of African ruminant livestock, horses and ponies, in *The Archaeology of Africa: Food, Metals and Towns*. Shaw, T., Sinclair, P., Andah, B., & Okpoko, A. (eds.). 71–103. London & New York: Routledge.

Brett, M. & Fentress, E. 1997. *The Berbers*. Oxford: Blackwell.

Breunig, P. 1996. The 8000-year-old dugout canoe from Dufuna (NE Nigeria), in *Aspects of African Archaeology: Papers from the 10th Congress of the PanAfrican Association for Prehistory and Related Studies*. Pwiti, G. & Soper, R. (eds.). 461–68. Harare: Univ. of Zimbabwe Publications.

Breunig, P. & Neumann, K. 2002. From hunters and gatherers to food producers: new archaeological and archaeobotanical evidence from the West African Sahel, in *Droughts, Food and Culture: Ecological Change and Food Security in Africa's Later Prehistory*. Hassan, F. A. (ed.). 123–55. New York: Kluwer Academic/Plenum Publishers.

Brothwell, D. & Shaw, T. 1971. A Late Upper Pleistocene proto-West African negro from Nigeria. *Man* (New Series) 6 (2), 221–27.

Casey, J. 2000. *The Kintampo Complex: The Late Holocene on the Gambaga Escarpment, Northern Ghana*. Oxford: British Archaeological Reports International Series 906.

Chippindale, C., Smith, B., & Taçon, P. S. C. 2000. Visions of dynamic power: archaic rock-paintings, altered states of consciousness and "clever men" in western Arnhem Land (NT), Australia. *Cambridge Archaeological Journal* 10 (1), 63–101.

Chittick, N. 1974. *Kilwa: An Islamic Trading City on the East African Coast*. 2 vols. Nairobi: British Institute in Eastern Africa, Memoir 5.

Clark, J. D. 1971. A re-examination of the evidence for agricultural origins in the Nile Valley. *Proceedings of the Prehistoric Society* 37 (2), 34–79.

—. 1975–77. Interpretations of prehistoric technology from Ancient Egyptian and other sources. Part 2: Prehistoric arrow forms in Africa as shown by surviving examples of the traditional arrows of the San Bushmen. *Paléorient* 3, 127–50.

Clark, J. D., Phillips, J. L., & Staley, P. S. 1974. Interpretations of prehistoric technology from Ancient Egyptian and other sources. 1: Ancient Egyptian bows and arrows and their relevance for African prehistory. *Paléorient* 2 (2), 323–88.

Clutton-Brock, J. 1993. The spread of domestic animals in Africa, in *The Archaeology of Africa: Food, Metals and Towns*. Shaw, T., Sinclair, P., Andah, B., & Okpoko, A. (eds.). 61–70. London & New York: Routledge.

Connah, G. 2001. *African Civilizations: An Archaeological Perspective*. (2nd ed.). Cambridge: Cambridge Univ. Press.

D'Andrea, A. C., Klee, M., & Casey, J. 2001. Archaeobotanical evidence for pearl millet (*Pennisetum glaucum*) in sub-Saharan West Africa. *Antiquity* 75, 341–48.

Dark, P. J. C. 1973. *An Introduction to Benin Art and Technology*. Oxford: Clarendon Press.

Davidson, B. 1966. *Africa: History of a Continent*. New York: Macmillan.

Davies, V. & Friedman, R. 1998. *Egypt*. London: British Museum Press.

De Langhe, E., Swennen, R., & Vuylsteke, D. 1996. Plantain in the early Bantu world, in *The Growth of Farming Communities in Africa from the Equator Southwards*. *Azania* special vol. 29–30. Sutton, J. E. G. (ed.). 147–60. Nairobi: The British Institute in Eastern Africa.

De Maret, P. 1996. Shum Laka (Cameroon): human burials and general perspectives, in *Aspects of African Archaeology: Papers from the 10th Congress of the PanAfrican Association for Prehistory and Related Studies*. Pwiti, G. & Soper, R. (eds.). 275–79. Harare: Univ. of Zimbabwe Publications.

—. 1997. Savanna states, in *Encyclopedia of Precolonial Africa: Archaeology, History, Languages, Cultures, and Environments*. Vogel, J. O. (ed.). 496–501. Walnut Creek: AltaMira Press.

Deacon, H. J. 1976. *Where Hunters Gathered: A Study of Holocene Stone Age People in the Eastern Cape*. Claremont: South African Archaeological Society Monograph Series No. 1.

Deacon, H. J. & Deacon, J. 1999. *Human Beginnings in South Africa: Uncovering the Secrets of the Stone Age*. Walnut Creek: AltaMira Press.

Dowson, T. A. 1997. Southern African rock art, in *Encyclopedia of Precolonial Africa: Archaeology, History, Languages, Cultures, and Environments*. Vogel, J. O. (ed.). 373–79. Walnut Creek: AltaMira Press.

Eggert, M. K. H. 1997. Equatorial African Iron Age, in *Encyclopedia of Precolonial Africa: Archaeology, History, Languages, Cultures, and Environments*. Vogel, J. O. (ed.). 429–35. Walnut Creek: AltaMira Press.

Ehret, C. 2002. *The Civilizations of Africa: A History to 1800*. Oxford: James Currey.

Fagan, B. M. & Van Noten, F. L. 1966. Wooden implements from Late Stone Age sites at Gwisho hot-springs, Lochinvar, Zambia. *Proceedings of the Prehistoric Society* (New Series) 32, 246–61.

—. 1971. *The Hunter-Gatherers of Gwisho*. Tervuren: Musée Royal de l'Afrique Centrale.

Fletcher, R. 1998. African urbanism: scale, mobility and transformations, in *Transformations in Africa: Essays on Africa's Later Past*. Connah, G. (ed.). 104–38. London & Washington: Leicester Univ. Press.

Garlake, P. 1973. *Great Zimbabwe*. London: Thames & Hudson.

—. 1995. *The Hunter's Vision: The Prehistoric Art of Zimbabwe*. Harare: Zimbabwe Publishing House.

Hassan, F. A. 2000. Climate and cattle in North Africa: a first approximation, in *The Origins and Development of African Livestock: Archaeology, Genetics, Linguistics and Ethnography*. Blench, R. M. & MacDonald, K. C. (eds.). 61–86. London: Univ. College London Press.

—. 2002. Palaeoclimate, food and culture change in Africa: an overview, in *Droughts, Food and Culture: Ecological Change and Food Security in Africa's Later Prehistory*. Hassan, F. A. (ed.). 11–26. New York: Kluwer Academic/Plenum Publishers.

Hendrickx, S. & Vermeersch, P. 2000. Prehistory: from the Palaeolithic to the Badarian culture (*c.* 700,000–4000 BC), in *The Oxford History of Ancient Egypt*. Shaw, I. (ed.). 17–43. Oxford: Oxford Univ. Press.

Holl, A. F. C. 2000. Metals and precolonial African society, in *Ancient African Metallurgy: The Sociocultural Context*. Vogel, J. O. (ed.). 1–81. Walnut Creek: AltaMira Press.

Horton, M. 1996. *Shanga: The Archaeology of a Muslim Trading Community on the Coast of East Africa*. London: British Institute in Eastern Africa, Memoir 14.

Horton, M. & Middleton, J. 2000. *The Swahili: The Social Landscape of a Mercantile Society*. Oxford: Blackwell.

Hourani, G. F. 1995. *Arab Seafaring: In the Indian Ocean in Ancient and Early Medieval Times*. Revised and expanded by Carswell, J. Princeton: Princeton Univ. Press.

Insoll, T. & Shaw, T. 1997. Gao and Igbo-Ukwu: beads, interregional trade, and beyond. *African Archaeological Review* 14 (1), 9–23.

Kemp, B. J. 1989. *Ancient Egypt: Anatomy of a Civilization*. London & New York: Routledge.

Kendall, T. 1997. *Kerma and the Kingdom of Kush 2500–1500 BC: The Archaeological Discovery of an Ancient Nubian Empire*. Washington D.C.: Smithsonian Institution Press.

Kirkman, J. S. 1964. *Men and Monuments on the East African Coast*. London: Lutterworth Press.

Kusimba, C. M. 1999. *The Rise and Fall of Swahili States*. Walnut Creek: AltaMira Press.

Lehner, M. 1997. *The Complete Pyramids*. London & New York: Thames & Hudson.

Lewis-Williams, J. D. 1981. *Believing and Seeing: Symbolic Meanings in Southern San Rock Paintings*. London & New York: Academic Press.

—. 1983. *The Rock Art of Southern Africa*. Cambridge: Cambridge Univ. Press.

—. 1995. Seeing and construing: the making and "meaning" of a southern African rock art motif. *Cambridge Archaeological Journal* 5 (1), 3–23.

—. 2001. Southern African shamanistic rock art in its social and cognitive contexts, in *The Archaeology of Shamanism*. Price, N. (ed.). 17–39. London: Routledge.

—. 2002. *The Mind in the Cave: Consciousness and the Origins of Art*. 136–62. London & New York: Thames & Hudson.

—. 2003. Putting the record straight: rock art and

shamanism. *Antiquity* 77 (295), 165–70.

Lonsdale, J. 1981. States and social processes in Africa: a historiographical survey. *The African Studies Review* 24 (2 and 3), 139–225.

Macdonald, K. C. 1998. Before the Empire of Ghana: pastoralism and the origins of cultural complexity in the Sahel, in *Transformations in Africa: Essays on Africa's Later Past*. Connah, G. (ed.). 71–103. London & Washington: Leicester Univ. Press.

—. 2000. The origins of African livestock: indigenous or imported?, in *The Origins and Development of African Livestock: Archaeology, Genetics, Linguistics and Ethnography*. Blench, R. M. & MacDonald, K. C. (eds.). 2–17. London: Univ. College London Press.

Marean, C. W. 1992. Hunter to herder: large mammal remains from the hunter-gatherer occupation at Enkapune Ya Muto rock-shelter, Central Rift, Kenya. *African Archaeological Review* 10, 65–127.

Marshall, F. 2000. The origins and spread of domestic animals in East Africa, in *The Origins and Development of African Livestock: Archaeology, Genetics, Linguistics and Ethnography*. Blench, R. M. & MacDonald, K. C. (eds.). 191–221. London: Univ. College London Press.

Mbida, C. M., Van Neer, W., Doutrelepont, H., & Vrydaghs, L. 2000. Evidence for banana cultivation and animal husbandry during the first millennium BC in the forest of southern Cameroon. *Journal of Archaeological Science* 27, 151–62.

McIntosh, S. K. (ed.). 1995. *Excavations at Jenné-Jeno, Hambarketolo, and Kaniana (Inland Niger Delta, Mali): The 1981 Season*. Berkeley & Los Angeles: Univ. of California Press.

Midant-Reynes, B. 2000. The Naqada Period (*c.* 4000–3200 BC), in *The Oxford History of Ancient Egypt*. Shaw, I. (ed.). 44–60. Oxford: Oxford Univ. Press.

Miller, J. I. 1969. *The Spice Trade of the Roman Empire, 29 BC to AD 641*. Oxford: Oxford Univ. Press.

Mitchell, P. J. 1997. Southern African advanced foragers, in *Encyclopedia of Precolonial Africa: Archaeology, History, Languages, Cultures, and Environments*. Vogel, J. O. (ed.). 341–46. Walnut Creek: AltaMira Press.

—. 2002. *The Archaeology of Southern Africa*. Cambridge: Cambridge Univ. Press.

Muzzolini, A. 2000. Livestock in Saharan rock art, in *The Origins and Development of African Livestock: Archaeology, Genetics, Linguistics and Ethnography*. Blench, R. M. & MacDonald, K. C. (eds.). 87–110. London: Univ. College London Press.

Neumann, K. 1999. Early plant food production in the West African Sahel: new evidence, in *The Exploitation of Plant Resources in Ancient Africa*. van der Veen, M. (ed.). 73–80. New York: Kluwer Academic/Plenum Publishers.

O'Connor, D. 1993. *Ancient Nubia: Egypt's Rival in Africa*. Philadelphia: Univ. of Pennsylvania Press.

Phillipson, D. W. 1993a. *African Archaeology*. (2nd ed.). Cambridge: Cambridge Univ. Press.

—. 1993b. The antiquity of herding and cultivation in Ethiopia, in *The Archaeology of Africa: Food, Metals and Towns*. Shaw, T., Sinclair, P., Andah, B., & Okpoko, A. (eds.). 344–57. London & New York: Routledge.

—. 1998. *Ancient Ethiopia. Aksum: Its Antecedents and Successors*. London: British Museum Press.

Pikirayi, I. 2001. *The Zimbabwe Culture: Origins and Decline in Southern Zambezian States*. Walnut Creek: AltaMira Press.

Purseglove, J. W. 1976. The origins and migrations of crops in tropical Africa, in *Origins of African Plant Domestication*. Harlan, J. R., de Wet, J. M. J., & Stemler, A. B. L. (eds.). 291–309. The Hague: Mouton.

Rawlins, D., Pickering, K., & Spence, K. 2001. Astronomical orientation of the pyramids. *Nature* 412, 699–700.

Reid, A. 1996. Ntusi and the development of social complexity in southern Uganda, in *Aspects of African Archaeology: Papers from the 10th Congress of the PanAfrican Association for Prehistory and Related Studies*. Pwiti, G. & Soper, R. (eds.). 621–27. Harare: Univ. of Zimbabwe Publications.

Robbins, L. H. 1997. Eastern African advanced foragers, in *Encyclopedia of Precolonial Africa: Archaeology, History, Languages, Cultures, and Environments*. Vogel, J. O. (ed.). 335–41. Walnut Creek: AltaMira Press.

Robertshaw, P. 1994. Archaeological survey, ceramic analysis, and state formation in western Uganda. *African Archaeological Review* 12, 105–31.

Rossel, G. 1996. *Musa* and *Ensete* in Africa: taxonomy, uses and nomenclature, in *The Growth of Farming Communities in Africa from the Equator Southwards*. *Azania* special vol. 29–30. Sutton, J. E. G. (ed.). 130–46. Nairobi: The British Institute in Eastern Africa.

Rossignol-Strick, M. 2002. Holocene climatic changes in the Eastern Mediterranean and the spread of food production from Southwest Asia to Egypt, in *Droughts, Food and Culture: Ecological Change and Food Security in Africa's Later Prehistory*. Hassan, F. A. (ed.). 157–69. New York: Kluwer Academic/Plenum Publishers.

Shaw, I. 2001. Were the ancient Egyptians black Africans?, in *The Seventy Great Mysteries of the Ancient World: Unlocking the Secrets of Past Civilizations*. Fagan, B. M. (ed.). 147–50. London & New York: Thames & Hudson.

—. (ed.). 2000. *The Oxford History of Ancient Egypt*. Oxford: Oxford Univ. Press.

Shaw, T. 1970. *Igbo-Ukwu: An Account of Archaeological Discoveries in Eastern Nigeria*. 2 vols. London: Faber & Faber.

Shaw, T. & Daniels, S. G. H. 1984. Excavations at Iwo Eleru, Ondo State, Nigeria. *West African Journal of Archaeology* 14, 1–269.

Smith, M. C. & Wright, H. T. 1988. The ceramics from Ras Hafun in Somalia: notes on a classical maritime site. *Azania* 23, 115–41.

Spence, K. 2000. Ancient Egyptian chronology and the astronomical orientation of pyramids. *Nature* 408, 320–24.

Summers, R. (ed.). 1959. *Prehistoric Rock Art of the Federation of Rhodesia and Nyasaland*. Salisbury, Southern Rhodesia: National Publications Trust.

Sutton, J. E. G. 1991. The international factor at Igbo-Ukwu. *African Archaeological Review* 9, 145–60.

—. 2001. Igbo-Ukwu and the Nile. *African Archaeological Review* 18 (1), 49–62.

—. (ed.). 1996. *The Growth of Farming Communities in Africa from the Equator Southwards*. *Azania* special vol. 29–30. Nairobi: The British Institute in Eastern Africa.

van der Veen, M. 1999. Introduction, in *The Exploitation of Plant Resources in Ancient Africa*. van der Veen, M. (ed.). 1–10. New York: Kluwer Academic/Plenum Publishers.

Vinnicombe, P. 1976. *People of the Eland: Rock Paintings of the Drakensberg Bushmen as a Reflection of their Life and Thought*. Pietermaritzburg: Univ. of Natal Press.

Vogel, J. O. 1997. Bantu expansion, in *Encyclopedia of Precolonial Africa: Archaeology, History, Languages, Cultures, and Environments*. Vogel, J. O. (ed.). 435–38. Walnut Creek: AltaMira Press.

Welsby, D. A. 1996. *The Kingdom of Kush: The Napatan and Meroitic Empires*. London: British Museum Press; Princeton: Markus Wiener.

Welsby, D. A. 2002. *The Medieval Kingdoms of Nubia: Pagans, Christians and Muslims along the Middle Nile*. London: British Museum Press.

Wendorf, F., Schild, R., & Associates. 2001. *Holocene Settlement of the Egyptian Sahara*. Vol. 1: *The Archaeology of Nabta Playa*. New York: Kluwer Academic/Plenum Publishers.

Wheatley, P. 1975. Analecta Sino-Africana recensa, in *East Africa and the Orient: Cultural Syntheses in Pre-Colonial Times*. Chittick, H. N. & Rotberg, R. I. (eds.). 76–114. New York & London: Africana Publishing Company.

Whitelaw, G. 1997. Southern African Iron Age, in *Encyclopedia of Precolonial Africa: Archaeology, History, Languages, Cultures, and Environments*. Vogel, J. O. (ed.). 444–55. Walnut Creek: AltaMira Press.

Willett, F. 1967. *Ife in the History of West African Sculpture*. London: Thames & Hudson.

—. 2002. *African Art: An Introduction*. (New ed.). London & New York: Thames & Hudson.

Woodhouse, J. 1998. Iron in Africa: metal from nowhere, in *Transformations in Africa: Essays on Africa's Later Past*. Connah, G. (ed.). 160–85. London & Washington: Leicester Univ. Press.

CHAPTER 11: HOLOCENE EUROPE

Albrethsen, S. E. & Brinch Petersen, E. 1976. Excavation of a Mesolithic cemetery at Vedbaek, Denmark. *Acta Archaeologica* 47, 1–28.

Alföldy, G. 1974. *Noricum*. London: Routledge & Kegan Paul.

Ammerman, A. J. & Cavalli-Sforza, L. 1971. Measuring the rate of spread of early farming in Europe. *Man* 6, 674–88.

—. 1984. *The Neolithic Transition and the Genetics of Population in Europe*. Princeton: Princeton Univ. Press.

Anati, E. 1972. *I Massi di Cemmo*. Capo di Ponte: Centro Camuno di Studi Preistorici.

—. 1984. *Valcamonica Rock Art: A New History for Europe*. Capo di Ponte: Edizioni del Centro.

Andersen, N. H. 2002. Neolithic enclosures of Scandinavia, in *Enclosures in Neolithic Europe*. Varndell, G. & Topping, P. (eds.). 1–10. Oxford: Oxbow.

Arias, P. 1999. The origins of the Neolithic along the Atlantic coast of Continental Europe: a survey. *Journal of World Prehistory* 13, 403–64.

Arnold, B. 1986. *Cortaillod-Est: Un village du Bronze Final I. Fouille subaquatique et photographie aérienne*. Sainte-Blaise: Ruau.

Bailey, D. W. 2000. *Balkan Prehistory: Exclusion, Incorporation and Identity*. London: Routledge.

Barfield, L. & Chippindale, C. 1997. Meaning in the later prehistoric rock-engravings of Mont Bégo,

Alpes-Maritimes, France. *Proceedings of the Prehistoric Society* 63, 103–28.

Barnett, W. K. 2000. Cardial pottery and the agricultural transition in Mediterranean Europe, in *Europe's First Farmers*. Price, T. D. (ed.). 93–116. Cambridge: Cambridge Univ. Press.

Bennike, P., Ebbesen, K., & Jørgensen, L. B. 1986. Early Neolithic skeletons from Bolkilde bog, Denmark. *Antiquity* 60, 199–209.

Benoît, F. 1975. The Celtic oppidum of Entremont, Provence, in *Recent Archaeological Excavations in Europe*. Bruce-Mitford, R. (ed.). 227–59. London: Routledge & Kegan Paul.

Bentley, R. A. et al. 2002. Prehistoric migration in Europe: strontium isotope analysis of Early Neolithic skeletons. *Current Anthropology* 43, 799–804.

Beyneix, A. 2003. *Traditions funéraires néolithiques en France méridionale (6000–2200 avant J.-C.)*. Paris: Errance.

Binder, D. 2000. Mesolithic and Neolithic interaction in southern France and northern Italy: new data and current hypotheses, in *Europe's First Farmers*. Price, T. D. (ed.). 117–43. Cambridge: Cambridge Univ. Press.

Boardman, J. 1999. *The Greeks Overseas: Their Early Colonies and Trade*. (4th ed.). London & New York: Thames & Hudson.

Bogucki, P. 2000. How agriculture came to north-central Europe, in *Europe's First Farmers*. Price, T. D. (ed.). 197–218. Cambridge: Cambridge Univ. Press.

Bogucki, P. & Grygiel, R. 1993. The first farmers of Europe: a survey article. *Journal of Field Archaeology* 20, 399–426.

Boric, D. 2002. The Lepenski Vir conundrum: reinterpretation of the Mesolithic and Neolithic sequences in the Danube Gorges. *Antiquity* 76, 1026–39.

Bradley, R. 1990. *The Passage of Arms: An Archaeological Analysis of Prehistoric Hoards and Votive Deposits*. Cambridge: Cambridge Univ. Press.

—. 1998. *The Significance of Monuments: On the Shaping of Human Experience in Neolithic and Bronze Age Europe*. London: Routledge.

—. 2000. *An Archaeology of Natural Places*. London: Routledge.

—. 2001. Orientations and origins: a symbolic dimension to the long house in Neolithic Europe. *Antiquity* 75, 50–56.

—. 2002. *The Past in Prehistoric Societies*. London: Routledge.

Broodbank, C. & Strasser, T. F. 1991. Migrant farmers and the Neolithic colonisation of Crete. *Antiquity* 65, 233–45.

Cassen, S. & Pétrequin, P. 1999. La chronologie des haches polies dites de prestige dans la moitié ouest de la France. *European Journal of Archaeology* 2, 7–33.

Chapman, J. 1997. The origins of tells in eastern Hungary, in *Neolithic Landscapes*. Topping, P. (ed.). 139–64. Oxford: Oxbow.

—. 2000. *Fragmentation in Archaeology: People, Places and Broken Objects in the Prehistory of South-Eastern Europe*. London & New York: Routledge.

Chapman, R. 1990. *Emerging Complexity: The Later Prehistory of South-east Spain, Iberia and the West Mediterranean*. Cambridge: Cambridge Univ. Press.

Chernykh, E. N. 1978. Ai Bunar, a Balkan copper mine of the IVth millennium BC. *Proceedings of the Prehistoric Society* 44, 203–18.

Cherry, J. F. 1990. The first colonization of the Mediterranean islands: a review of recent research. *Journal of Mediterranean Archaeology* 3, 145–221.

Chikhi, L., Nichols, R., Barbujani, G., & Beaumont, M. A. 2002. Y genetic data support the Neolithic diffusion model. *Proceedings of the National Academy of Sciences (USA)* 99, 11008–13.

Chippindale, C. 2004. *Stonehenge Complete*. (Rev. ed.). London & New York: Thames & Hudson.

Clark, J. G. D. 1954. *Excavations at Star Carr: An Early Mesolithic Site at Seamer near Scarborough, Yorkshire*. Cambridge: Cambridge Univ. Press.

—. 1972. *Star Carr: A Case Study in Bioarchaeology*. Addison-Wesley module in anthropology 10. Reading, MA: Addison-Wesley.

Cleal, R. M. J., Walker, K. E., & Montague, R. 1995. *Stonehenge in its Landscape*. London: English Heritage.

Coles, B. J. 1998. Doggerland: a speculative survey. *Proceedings of the Prehistoric Society* 64, 45–81.

Collis, J. 1984. *The European Iron Age*. London: Batsford.

—. 2003. *The Celts: Origins, Myths and Inventions*. Stroud: Tempus.

Cooney, G. 2000. *Landscapes of Neolithic Ireland*. London: Routledge.

Copley, M. S. et al. 2003. Direct chemical evidence for widespread dairying in prehistoric Britain. *Proceedings of the National Academy of Sciences (USA)* 100, 1524–29.

Cunliffe, B. 1988. *Greeks, Romans and Barbarians: Spheres of Interaction*. London: Batsford.

—. 2001. *Facing the Ocean: The Atlantic and its Peoples, 8000 BC–AD 1500*. Oxford: Oxford Univ. Press.

Dickson, J. H. 1978. Bronze Age mead. *Antiquity* 52, 108–13.

Dronfield, J. 1995. Subjective vision and the source of Irish megalithic art. *Antiquity* 69, 539–49.

—. 1996. Entering alternative realities: cognition, art and architecture in Irish passage-tombs. *Cambridge Archaeological Journal* 6, 37–72.

Fisher, A. 1982. Trade in Danubian shaft-hole axes and the introduction of Neolithic economy in Denmark. *Journal of Danish Archaeology* 1, 7–12.

Fitzpatrick, A. P. 2003. The Amesbury Archer. *Current Archaeology* 184, 146–52.

Fowler, B. 2000. *Iceman: Uncovering the Life and Times of a Prehistoric Man found in an Alpine Glacier*. London: Macmillan.

Gkiasta, M., Russell, T., Shennan, S., & Steele, J. 2003. Neolithic transition in Europe: the radiocarbon record revisited. *Antiquity* 77, 45–62.

Gronenborn, D. 1999. A variation on a basic theme: the transition to farming in southern Central Europe. *Journal of World Prehistory* 13, 123–210.

Guerrero Ayuso, V. M. 2001. The Balearic Islands: prehistoric colonization of the furthest Mediterranean islands from the mainland. *Journal of Mediterranean Archaeology* 14, 136–58.

Harding, A. F. 2000. *European Societies in the Bronze Age*. Cambridge: Cambridge Univ. Press.

James, S. 1999. *The Atlantic Celts: Ancient People or Modern Invention?* London: British Museum Press.

Jochim, M. 2000. The origins of agriculture in south-central Europe, in *Europe's First Farmers*. Price, T. D. (ed.). 183–96. Cambridge: Cambridge Univ. Press.

Keeley, L. H. & Cahen, D. 1989. Early Neolithic forts and villages in NE Belgium: a preliminary report. *Journal of Field Archaeology* 16, 157–76.

King, R. & Underhill, P. A. 2002. Congruent distribution of Neolithic painted pottery and ceramic figurines with Y-chromosome lineages. *Antiquity* 76, 707–14.

Kristiansen, K. 1998. *Europe before History*. Cambridge: Cambridge Univ. Press.

Larsson, L. 1989. Late Mesolithic settlements and cemeteries at Skateholm, southern Sweden, in *The Mesolithic in Europe*. Bonsall, C. (ed.). 367–78. Edinburgh: John Donald.

Livadie, C. A. 2002. A first Pompeii: the Early Bronze Age village of Nola-Croce del Papa (Palma Campania phase). *Antiquity* 76, 941–42.

Liversage, D. 1992. *Barkaer: Long Barrows and Settlements*. Copenhagen: Akademisk Forlag, Universitetsforlag I København.

Lüning, J. 1982. Research in the Bandkeramik settlement of the Aldenhovener Platte in the Rhineland. *Analecta Praehistorica Leidensia* 15, 1–30.

Madsen, T. 1979. Earthen long barrows and timber structures: aspects of the early Neolithic mortuary practice in Denmark. *Proceedings of the Prehistoric Society* 45, 301–20.

Manning, W. H. 1995. Ironworking in the Celtic world, in *The Celtic World*. Green, M. J. (ed.). 310–20. London: Routledge.

Megaw, J. V. S. & Megaw, M. R. 1996. Ancient Celts and modern ethnicity. *Antiquity* 70, 175–81.

Mellars, P. A. & Dark, S. P. 1998. *Star Carr in Context*. Cambridge: McDonald Institute for Archaeological Research.

Meskell, L. 1995. Goddesses, Gimbutas and 'New Age' archaeology. *Antiquity* 69, 74–86.

Midgley, M. 1992. *TRB Culture: The First Farmers of the North European Plain*. Edinburgh: Edinburgh Univ. Press.

Modderman, P. J. R. 1988. The Linear Pottery Culture: diversity in uniformity. *Berichten van te Rijksdienst voor het Oudheidkundig Bodemonderzoek* 38, 63–139.

Müller, W., Fricke, H., Halliday, A. N., McCulloch, M. T., & Wartho, J.-A. 2003. Origin and migration of the Alpine Iceman. *Science* 302, 862–66.

Niewiarowski, W., Noryskiewicz, B., Piotrowski, W., & Zajaczkowski, W. 1992. Biskupin fortified settlement and its environment in the light of new environmental and archaeological studies, in *The Wetland Revolution in Prehistory*. Coles, B. (ed.). 81–92. Exeter: The Prehistoric Society.

O'Brien, W. 2001. New light on Beaker metallurgy in Ireland, in *Bell Beakers Today: Pottery, People, Culture, Symbols in Prehistoric Europe*. Nicolis, F. (ed.). 561–76. Trento: Officio Beni Culturali.

O'Shea, J. & Zvelebil, M. 1984. Oleneostrovski Mogilnik: reconstructing the social and economic organisation of prehistoric foragers in northern Russia. *Journal of Anthropological Archaeology* 3, 1–40.

Ottaway, B. 1973. Earliest copper ornaments in northern Europe. *Proceedings of the Prehistoric Society* 39, 294–331.

Özdogan, M. 1997. The beginning of Neolithic economies in southeastern Europe: an Anatolian perspective. *Journal of European Archaeology* 5 (2), 1–33.

Pauli, L. 1984. *The Alps: Archaeology and Early History*. London: Thames & Hudson.

Perlès, C. 2001. *The Early Neolithic in Greece: The First Farming Communities in Europe*. Cambridge: Cambridge Univ. Press.

Price, T. D. 2000. The introduction of farming in northern Europe, in *Europe's First Farmers*. Price, T. D. (ed.). 260–318. Cambridge: Cambridge Univ. Press.

Rajewski, Z. 1980. *Biskupin: A Fortified Settlement Dating from 500 BC*. Poznan: Wydawnictwo Poznanskie.

Rankin, H. D. 1987. *Celts and the Classical World*. London: Croom Helm.

Reeder, E. D. 1999. *Scythian Gold*. New York: Abrams.

Richards, M. P., Macaulay, V., Hickey, E., et al. 2000. Tracing European founder lineages in the Near Eastern mtDNA pool. *American Journal of Human Genetics* 67, 1251–76.

Richards, M. P., Price, T. D., & Koch, E. 2003. Mesolithic and Neolithic subsistence in Denmark: new stable isotope data. *Current Anthropology* 44, 288–95.

Roberts, N. 1998. *The Holocene: An Environmental History*. (2nd ed.). Oxford: Blackwell.

Rolle, R. 1989. *The World of the Scythians*. London: Batsford.

Ruggles, C. 1999. *Astronomy in Prehistoric Britain and Ireland*. New Haven: Yale Univ. Press.

Ruiz-Taboada, A. & Monetro-Ruiz, I. 1999. The oldest metallurgy in western Europe. *Antiquity* 73, 897–903.

Scarre, C. 2002. Contexts of monumentalism: regional diversity at the Neolithic transition in north-west France. *Oxford Journal of Archaeology* 21, 23–61.

Schulting, R. J. 1996. Antlers, bone pins and flint blades: the Mesolithic cemeteries of Téviec and Hoëdic. *Antiquity* 70, 335–50.

Schulting, R. J. & Richards, M. P. 2002. The wet, the wild and the domesticated: the Mesolithic-Neolithic transition on the west coast of Scotland. *European Journal of Archaeology* 5, 147–89.

Shackleton, J. C. & van Andel, T. H. 1980. Prehistoric shell assemblages from Franchthi cave and evolution of the adjacent coastal zone. *Nature* 288, 357–59.

Sherratt, A. S. 1981. Plough and pastoralism: aspects of the secondary products revolution, in *Pattern of the Past*. Hodder, I., Isaac, G., & Hammond, N. (eds.). 261–305. Cambridge: Cambridge Univ. Press.

Skeates, R. 2002. The Neolithic enclosures of the Tavoliere, south-east Italy, in *Enclosures in Neolithic Europe*. Varndell, G. & Topping, P. (eds.). 51–58. Oxford: Oxbow.

Spindler, K. 1994. *The Man in the Ice*. London: Weidenfeld & Nicolson.

Stehli, P. 1989. Merzbachtal: Umwelt und Geschichte einer bandkeramischen Siedlungskammer. *Germania* 67, 51–76.

Thomas, J. 1999. *Understanding the Neolithic*. London: Routledge.

Thorpe, I. J. 1996. *The Origins of Agriculture in Europe*. London: Routledge.

—. 2001. Danish causewayed enclosures: temporary monuments?, in *Neolithic Enclosures in Atlantic Northwest Europe*. Darvill, T. & Thomas, J. (eds.). 190–203. Oxford: Oxbow.

Tilley, C. 1996. *An Ethnography of the Neolithic: Early Prehistoric Societies in Southern Scandinavia*. Cambridge: Cambridge Univ. Press.

van Andel, T. H. & Runnels, C. N. 1995. The earliest farmers in Europe. *Antiquity* 69, 481–500.

van der Sanden, W. 1996. *Through Nature to Eternity: The Bog Bodies of Northwest Europe*. Amsterdam: Batavian Lion International.

Vencl, S. 1999. Stone age warfare, in *Ancient Warfare: Archaeological Perspectives*. Carman, J. & Harding, A. (eds.). 57–72. Stroud: Sutton.

Wahl, J. & König, H. G. 1987. Anthropologisch-traumatologische Untersuchung der menschlichen Skelettreste aus dem bandkeramischen Massengrab bei Talheim, Kreis Heilbronn. *Fundberichte aus Baden-Württemberg* 12, 65–193.

Wasny, T. 1993. Dendrochronological dating of the Lusatian culture settlement at Biskupin, Poland: first results. *Newswarp* 14, 3–5.

Waterbolk, H. 1964. The Bronze Age settlement of Elp. *Helinium* 4, 97–131.

Wells, P. 1980. *Culture Contact and Culture Change. Early Iron Age Central Europe and the Mediterranean World*. Cambridge: Cambridge Univ. Press.

—. 1995. Settlement and social systems at the end of the Iron Age, in *Celtic Chiefdom, Celtic State: The Evolution of Complex Social Systems in Prehistoric Europe*. Arnold, B. & Gibson, D. B. (eds.). 88–95. Cambridge: Cambridge Univ. Press.

Whittle, A. 1996. *Europe in the Neolithic: The Creation of New Worlds*. Cambridge: Cambridge Univ. Press.

Zilhão, J. 2000. From the Mesolithic to the Neolithic in the Iberian peninsula, in *Europe's First Farmers*. Price, T. D. (ed.). 144–82. Cambridge: Cambridge Univ. Press.

Zvelebil, M. & Dolukhanov, P. 1991. The transition to farming in eastern and northern Europe. *Journal of World Prehistory* 5, 233–78.

CHAPTER 12: THE RISE OF CIVILIZATION IN SOUTHWEST ASIA

Adams, R. McC. 1981. *Heartland of Cities: Surveys of Ancient Settlement and Land Use on the Central Floodplain of the Euphrates*. Chicago: Univ. of Chicago Press.

Akkermans, P. M. M. G. & Duistermaat, K. 1997. Of storage and nomads: the clay sealings from Late Neolithic Sabi Abyad, Syria. *Paléorient* 22, 2, 17–44.

Al-Ansary, A. R. T. 2000. Editorial. *Adumatu* 2, 4–6.

Albright, W. F. 1949. *The Archaeology of Palestine*. Harmondsworth: Penguin.

Algaze, G. 1993. *The Uruk World System: The Dynamics of Expansion of Early Mesopotamian Civilization*. Chicago: Univ. of Chicago Press.

Aruz, J. (ed.). 2003. *Art of the First Cities: The Third Millennium B.C. from the Mediterranean to the Indus*. New York: Metropolitan Museum of Art.

Bahrani, Z. 1998. Conjuring Mesopotamia: imaginative geography and a world past, in *Archaeology Under Fire: Nationalism, Politics and Heritage in the Eastern Mediterranean and Middle East*. Meskell, L. (ed.). 159–74. London: Routledge.

Bass, G. F. 1995. Sea and river craft in the ancient Near East, in *Civilizations of the Ancient Near East*. Sasson, J. M. (ed.). 1421–31. New York: Scribner.

Beaulieu, P.-A. 1989. *The Reign of Nabonidus, King of Babylon: 556–539 BC*. New Haven: Yale Univ. Press.

Bittel, K. 1970. *Hattusha, the Capital of the Hittites*. New York: Oxford Univ. Press.

Boehmer, R. M. 1999. *Uruk früheste Siegelabrollungen*. Ausgrabungen in Uruk-Warka Endberichte 24. Mainz am Rhein: Philipp von Zabern.

Bottéro, J. 1992. *Mesopotamia: Writing, Reasoning, and the Gods*. Chicago: Univ. of Chicago Press.

Briant, P. 1995. Social and legal institutions in Achaemenid Iran, in *Civilizations of the Ancient Near East*. Sasson, J. M. (ed.). 517–28. New York: Scribner.

Brusasco, P. 1999–2000. Family archives and the social use of space in Old Babylonian houses at Ur. *Mesopotamia* 34–35, 1–173.

Bryce, T. 1998. *The Kingdom of the Hittites*. Oxford: Oxford Univ. Press.

Buccellati, G. & Kelly-Buccellati, M. 1997. Urkesh, the first Hurrian capital. *Biblical Archaeologist* 60, 80–82.

Bunimovitz, S. 1995. On the edge of empires – Late Bronze Age (1500–1200 BCE), in *The Archaeology of Society in the Holy Land*. Levy, T. E. (ed.). 320–31. London: Leicester Univ. Press.

Collon, D. 1987. *First Impressions: Cylinder Seals in the Ancient Near East*. London: British Museum Press.

Crawford, H. 1998. *Dilmun and its Gulf Neighbours*. Cambridge: Cambridge Univ. Press.

—. 2004. *Sumer and the Sumerians*. (2nd ed.). Cambridge: Cambridge Univ. Press.

Curtis, J. E. 1989. *Ancient Persia*. London: British Museum Press.

Curtis, J. E. & Reade, J. E. 1995. *Art and Empire: Treasures from Assyria in the British Museum*. London: British Museum Press.

Dalley, S. (ed.). 1998. *The Legacy of Mesopotamia*. Oxford: Oxford Univ. Press.

Damerow, P. & Englund, R. K. 1989. *The Proto-Elamite Texts from Tepe Yahya*. Cambridge: Peabody Museum of Archaeology & Ethnology.

Dolce, R. 1998. The palatial Ebla culture in the context of north Mesopotamian and north Syrian main powers, in *About Subartu: Studies Devoted to Upper Mesopotamia*. Lebeau, M. (ed.). 67–81. Turnhout: Brepols.

Dothan, M. 1967. *Ashdod I: The First Season of Excavations, 1962*. Jerusalem: Department of Antiquities.

Dothan, T. 1995. The 'Sea Peoples' and the Philistines of ancient Palestine, in *Civilizations of the Ancient Near East*. Sasson, J. M. (ed.). 1267–79. New York: Scribner.

Dothan, T. & Gitin, S. 1993. Miqne, Tel Ekron, in *The New Encyclopedia of Archaeological Excavations in the Holy Land*, vol. 3. Stern, E. (ed.). 1051–59. Jerusalem: Israel Exploration Society.

Englund, R. K. 1998. Texts from the Late Uruk Period, in *Mesopotamien: Späturuk-Zeit und Frühdynastische Zeit. Annäherungen 1*. Bauer, J., Englund, R. K., & Krebernik, M. 15–233. Freiburg: Universitätsverlag Freiburg Schweiz.

Finkelstein, I. & Silberman, N. A. 2001. *The Bible Unearthed*. New York: Touchstone.

Frangipane, M. 2001. Centralization processes in Greater Mesopotamia: Uruk 'expansion' as the climax of systemic interactions among areas of the Greater Mesopotamian region, in *Uruk Mesopotamia and its Neighbors: Cross-Cultural Interactions in the Era of State Formation*. Rothman, M. (ed.). 307–47. Santa Fe: School of

American Research Press.

Frankel, D. 1979. *Archaeologists at Work: Studies on Halaf Pottery.* London: British Museum Press.

Groube, L. 1996. The impact of diseases upon the emergence of agriculture, in *The Origins and Spread of Agriculture and Pastoralism in Eurasia.* Harris, D. R. (ed.). 101–29. London: Univ. College London Press.

Harden, D. B. 1980. *The Phoenicians.* (3rd ed.). Harmondsworth: Penguin.

Hawkins, J. D. 1995. Karkamish and Karatepe: Neo-Hittite city-states in north Syria, in *Civilizations of the Ancient Near East.* Sasson, J. M. (ed.). 1295–1307. New York: Scribner.

Henrickson, E. & Thuesen, I. (eds.). 1989. *Upon this Foundation—the 'Ubaid Reconsidered.* Copenhagen: Museum Tusculanum Press.

Holladay, Jr., J. S. 1995. The kingdoms of Israel and Judah: political and economic centralization in the Iron IIA–B (ca. 1000–750 BCE), in *The Archaeology of Society in the Holy Land.* Levy, T. E. (ed.). 368–98. London: Leicester Univ. Press.

Ilan, D. 1995. The dawn of internationalism – the Middle Bronze Age, in *The Archaeology of Society in the Holy Land.* Levy, T. E. (ed.). 297–319. London: Leicester Univ. Press.

Isserlin, B. S. J. 1998. *The Israelites.* London & New York: Thames & Hudson.

Jansen, H. G. 1995. Troy: legend and reality, in *Civilizations of the Ancient Near East.* Sasson, J. M. (ed.). 1121–34. New York: Scribner.

Klein, J. 1995. Shulgi of Ur: king of a neo-Sumerian empire, in *Civilizations of the Ancient Near East.* Sasson, J. M. (ed.). 842–857. New York: Scribner.

Kohl, P. L. 1989. The material culture of the modern era in the ancient Orient: suggestions for future work, in *Domination and Resistance.* Miller, D., Rowlands, M., & Tilley, C. 240–45. London: Unwin Hyman.

Lamberg-Karlovsky, C. C. 1997. Tepe Yahya, in *The Oxford Encyclopedia of Archaeology in the Near East* (Volume 5). Meyers, E. M. (ed.). 187–88. New York: Oxford Univ. Press.

Larsen, M. T. 1989. Orientalism and Near Eastern archaeology, in *Domination and Resistance.* Miller, D., Rowlands, M., & Tilley, C. (eds.). 229–39. London: Unwin Hyman.

—. 1996. *The Conquest of Assyria: Excavations in an Antique Land, 1840–1860.* New York: Routledge.

Liverani, M. 1987. The collapse of the Near Eastern regional system at the end of the Bronze Age: the case of Syria, in *Centre and Periphery in the Ancient World.* Rowlands, M., Larsen, M. T., & Kristiansen, K. (eds.). 66–73. Cambridge: Cambridge Univ. Press.

—. 1990. *Prestige and Interest: International Relations in the Near East ca. 1600–1100 BC.* Padua: Sargon.

—. 1993. Akkad: an introduction, in *Akkad: The First World Empire.* Liverani, M. (ed.). 1–10. Padua: Sargon.

Lumsden, S. 2001. Power and identity in the Neo-Assyrian world, in *The Royal Palace Institution in the First Millennium BC.* Nielsen, I. (ed.). 33–51. Aarhus: Aarhus Univ. Press.

Margueron, J.-C. 1995. Mari: a portrait in art of a Mesopotamian city-state, in *Civilizations of the Ancient Near East.* Sasson, J. M. (ed.). 885–99. New York: Scribner.

Markoe, G. E. 2000. *The Phoenicians.* London: British Museum Press.

Matthews, R. 1993. *Cities, Seals and Writing: Archaic Seal Impressions from Jemdet Nasr and Ur.* Berlin: Gebr. Mann.

—. 2000. *The Early Prehistory of Mesopotamia 500,000 to 4,500 BC.* Turnhout: Brepols.

—. 2001. From Kuwait to Ras al-Khaimah: Ubaid connections in the Gulf, in *Études mésopotamiennes: recueil de textes offert à Jean-Louis Huot.* Breniquet, C. & Kepinski, C. (eds.). 347–61. Paris: ERC.

Matthiae, P. 1980. *Ebla: An Empire Rediscovered.* London: Hodder & Stoughton.

Moran, W. L. 1992. *The Amarna Letters.* Baltimore: Johns Hopkins Univ. Press.

Morandi Bonacossi, D. 2003. Tell Mishrifeh/Qatna 1999–2002: a preliminary report of the Italian component of the joint Syrian-Italian-German project. *Akkadica* 124, 65–120.

Nissen, H. J. 2002. Uruk: key site of the period and key site of the problem, in *Artefacts of Complexity: Tracking the Uruk in the Near East.* Postgate, J. N. (ed.). 1–16. Warminster: British School of Archaeology in Iraq.

Nissen, H. J., Damerow, P., & Englund, R. K. 1993. *Archaic Bookkeeping: Early Writing and Techniques of Economic Administration in the Ancient Near East.* Chicago: Univ. of Chicago Press.

Oates, J. 1979. *Babylon,* London & New York: Thames & Hudson.

Oates, J. & Oates, D. 2001. *Nimrud: An Assyrian Imperial City Revealed.* London: British School of Archaeology in Iraq.

Postgate, J. N. 1979. The economic structure of the Assyrian empire, in *Power and Propaganda: A Symposium on Ancient Empires.* Larsen, M. T. (ed.). 193–221. Copenhagen: Akademisk Forlag.

—. 1992. *Early Mesopotamia: Society and Economy at the Dawn of History.* London: Routledge.

—. 1994. How many Sumerians per hectare? Probing the anatomy of an early city. *Cambridge Archaeological Journal* 4, 47–65.

—. 2003. Learning the lessons of the future: trade in prehistory through a historian's lens. *Bibliotheca Orientalis* 60/1–2, 5–26.

—. (ed.). 2002. *Artefacts of Complexity: Tracking the Uruk in the Near East.* Warminster: British School of Archaeology in Iraq.

Potts, D. T. 1999. *The Archaeology of Elam.* Cambridge: Cambridge Univ. Press.

Pulak, C. M. 1998. The Uluburun shipwreck: an overview. *International Journal of Nautical Archaeology* 27/3, 188–224.

Reade, J. E. 1998. *Assyrian Sculpture.* London: British Museum Press.

Roaf, M. 1989. Social organization and social activities at Tell Madhhur, in *Upon this Foundation – the 'Ubaid Reconsidered.* Henrickson, E. F. & Thuesen, I. (eds.). 91–146. Copenhagen: Museum Tusculanum Press.

—. 2000. Nineve-5-Kultur (Ninevite 5). *Reallexikon der Assyriologie und Vorderasiatischen Archäologie* 9, 5/6, 434–39.

Rothman, M. S. (ed.). 2001. *Uruk Mesopotamia and its Neighbors: Cross-Cultural Interactions in the Era of State Formation.* Santa Fe: School of American Research Press.

Safar, F., Mustafa, M. A., & Lloyd, S. 1981. *Eridu.* Baghdad: State Org. of Antiquities & Heritage.

Saggs, H. W. F. 1984. *The Might that was Assyria.* London: Sidgwick & Jackson.

Sams, G. K. 1995. Midas of Gordion and the Anatolian kingdom of Phrygia, in *Civilizations of the Ancient Near East.* Sasson, J. M. (ed.). 1147–59. New York: Scribner.

Seeher, J. 1995. Forty years in the capital of the Hittites. *Biblical Archaeologist* 58 (2), 63–67.

Silberman, N. A. 1998. Whose game is it anyway? The political and social transformation of American biblical archaeology, in *Archaeology Under Fire: Nationalism, Politics and Heritage in the Eastern Mediterranean and Middle East.* Meskell, L. (ed.). 175–88. London: Routledge.

Snell, D. C. 1997. *Life in the Ancient Near East 3100–332 B.C.E.* New Haven: Yale Univ. Press.

Sommerfeld, W. 1995. The Kassites of ancient Mesopotamia: origins, politics, and culture, in *Civilizations of the Ancient Near East.* Sasson, J. M. (ed.). 917–30. New York: Scribner.

Stager, L. E. 1993. Ashkelon, in *The New Encyclopedia of Archaeological Excavations in the Holy Land,* vol. 1. Stern, E. (ed.). 103–12. Jerusalem: Israel Exploration Society.

—. 1995. The impact of the Sea Peoples in Canaan (1185–1050 BCE), in *The Archaeology of Society in the Holy Land.* Levy, T. E. (ed.). 332–48. London: Leicester Univ. Press.

Stein, D. 1997. Hurrians, in *The Oxford Encyclopedia of Archaeology in the Near East* (Vol. 3). Meyers, E. M. (ed.). 126–30. New York: Oxford Univ. Press.

Stein, G. 1999. *Rethinking World Systems: Diasporas, Colonies, and Interaction in Uruk Mesopotamia.* Tucson: Univ. of Arizona Press.

Stone, E. C. & Zimansky, P. 2004. *The Anatomy of a Mesopotamian City: Survey and Soundings at Mashkan-Shapir.* Winona Lake: Eisenbrauns.

Tolstikov, V., Treister, M., Antonova, I. et al. 1996. *The Gold of Troy: Searching for Homer's Fabled City.* New York: Abrams; London: Thames & Hudson.

Traill, D. A. 1995. *Schliemann of Troy: Treasure and Deceit.* London: John Murray.

Van De Mieroop, M. 2003. Reading Babylon. *American Journal of Archaeology* 107, 257–75.

—. 2005. *King Hammurabi of Babylon.* Oxford: Blackwell.

Van Soldt, W. H. 1995. Ugarit: a second-millennium kingdom on the Mediterranean coast, in *Civilizations of the Ancient Near East.* Sasson, J. M. (ed.). 1255–66. New York: Scribner.

Veenhof, K. R. 1995. Kanesh: an Assyrian colony in Anatolia, in *Civilizations of the Ancient Near East.* Sasson, J. M. (ed.). 859–71. New York: Scribner.

Voigt, M. M. 1997. Gordion, in *The Oxford Encyclopedia of Archaeology in the Near East* (Volume 2). Meyers, E. M. (ed.). 426–31. New York: Oxford Univ. Press.

Watson, P. J. 1983. The Halafian culture: a review and synthesis, in *The Hilly Flanks and Beyond: Essays on the Prehistory of Southwestern Asia Presented to Robert J. Braidwood.* Young, T. C., Smith, P. E. L., & Mortensen, P. 231–50. Chicago: Oriental Institute of the Univ. of Chicago.

Weiss, H. 2000. Beyond the Younger Dryas, in *Environmental Disaster and the Archaeology of Human Response.* Bawden, G. & Reycraft, R. M. (eds.). 75–98. Albuquerque: Maxwell Museum of Anthropology.

Wilhelm, G. 1989. *The Hurrians.* Warminster: Aris & Phillips.

—. 1995. The kingdom of Mitanni in second-millennium Upper Mesopotamia, in *Civilizations of the Ancient Near East.* Sasson, J. M. (ed.). 1243–54. New York: Scribner.

Yener, K. A. 2002. Excavations in Hittite heartlands: recent investigations in Late Bronze Age Anatolia, in *Recent Developments in Hittite Archaeology and History*. Yener, K. A. & Hoffner, H. A. (eds.). 1–9. Winona Lake: Eisenbrauns.

Zettler, R. & Horne, L. (eds.). 1998. *Treasures from the Royal Tombs of Ur*. Philadelphia: Univ. of Pennsylvania Museum.

Zimansky, P. E. 1985. *Ecology and Empire: The Structure of the Urartian State*. Chicago: Univ. of Chicago Press.

—. 1995. Urartian material culture as state assemblage: an anomaly in the archaeology of empire. *Bulletin of the American Schools of Oriental Research* 299/300, 103–15.

CHAPTER 13: THE MEDITERRANEAN WORLD

Alcock, S. E. 1993. *Graecia Capta: The Landscapes of Roman Greece*. Cambridge: Cambridge Univ. Press.

—. 1998. Environment, in *The Cambridge Illustrated History of Ancient Greece*. Cartledge, P. (ed.). 13–34. Cambridge: Cambridge Univ. Press.

Alcock, S. E., Cherry, J. F., & Davis, J. L. 1994. Intensive survey, agricultural practice and the classical landscape of Greece, in *Classical Greece: Ancient Histories and Modern Archaeologies*. Morris, I. (ed.). 137–70. Cambridge: Cambridge Univ. Press.

Allison, P. M. 1992. Artefact assemblages: not the Pompeii Premise, in *Papers of the Fourth Conference on Italian Archaeology, London 1990*, vol. 3.1. Herring, E., Whitehouse, R., & Wilkins, J. (eds.). 49–56. London: Accordia Research Centre.

Andronikos, M. 1994. *Vergina: The Royal Tombs and the Ancient City*. Athens: Ekdotiki Athenon.

Ashmole, B. 1972. *Architect and Sculptor in Classical Greece*. London: Phaidon.

Aubet, M. E. 1993. *The Phoenicians and the West: Politics, Colonies and Trade*. Cambridge: Cambridge Univ. Press.

Barker, G. (ed.). 1995. *A Mediterranean Valley: Landscape Archaeology and Annales History in the Biferno Valley*. London: Leicester Univ. Press.

Barker, G. & Mattingly, D. (eds.). 1999–2000. *The Archaeology of Mediterranean Landscapes*. 5 vols. Oxford: Oxbow.

Barker, G. & Rasmussen, T. 1998. *The Etruscans*. Oxford: Blackwell.

Beard, M. 2003. *The Parthenon*. Cambridge, MA: Harvard Univ. Press.

Beard, M. & Crawford, M. 1985. *Rome in the Late Republic*. Ithaca: Cornell Univ. Press.

Beard, M. & Henderson, J. 1995. *Classics: A Very Short Introduction*. Oxford: Oxford Univ. Press.

Ben-Yehuda, N. 1995. *The Masada Myth: Collective Memory and Mythmaking in Israel*. Madison: Univ. of Wisconsin Press.

Bernal, M. 1985. *Black Athena: The Afroasiatic Roots of Classical Civilisation*. Vol. I: *The Fabrication of Ancient Greece*. London: Free Association Press.

Binford, L. R. 1981. Behavioral archaeology and the 'Pompeii premise'. *Journal of Anthropological Research* 37.3, 195–208.

Boardman, J. 1978. *Greek Sculpture: The Archaic Period*. London: Thames & Hudson.

—. 1999. *The Greeks Overseas: Their Early Colonies and Trade*. (4th ed.). London & New York: Thames & Hudson.

Bonfante, L. 1986. Daily life and afterlife, in *Etruscan Life and Afterlife*. Bonfante, L. (ed.). 232–78. Detroit: Wayne State Univ. Press.

—. 1990. *Reading the Past: Etruscan*. London: British Museum Press.

—. 1994. Excursus: Etruscan women, in *Women in the Classical World: Image and Text*. Fantham, E., Foley, H. P., Kampen, N. B., Pomeroy, S. B., & Shapiro, H. A. (eds.). 243–59. New York & Oxford: Oxford Univ. Press.

Bosworth, A. B. 1988. *Conquest and Empire: The Reign of Alexander the Great*. Cambridge: Cambridge Univ. Press.

Branigan, K. 1970. *The Tombs of Mesara: A Study of Funerary Architecture and Ritual in Southern Crete, 2800–1700 BC*. London: Duckworth.

Braudel, F. 1966. *La Méditerranée et le Monde Méditerranéen à l'époque de Philippe II* (1st ed. 1949; 2 vols.). Paris: Colin.

Broodbank, C. 2000. *An Island Archaeology of the Early Cyclades*. Cambridge: Cambridge Univ. Press.

Brown, S. 1991. *Late Carthaginian Child Sacrifice and Sacrificial Monuments in their Mediterranean Context*. Sheffield: JSOT Press.

Bruit Zaidman, L. & Schmitt Pantel, P. 1992. *Religion in the Ancient Greek City*. Transl. Cartledge. P. A. Cambridge: Cambridge Univ. Press.

Camp, J. M. 1992. *The Athenian Agora: Excavations in the Heart of Classical Athens*. (2nd ed.). London & New York: Thames & Hudson.

—. 2001. *The Archaeology of Athens*. New Haven & London: Yale Univ. Press.

Carter, J. C. 2005. *Discovering the Greek Countryside at Metaponto*. Ann Arbor: Univ. of Michigan Press.

—. (ed.). 1998. *The Chora of Metaponto: The Necropoleis*. 2 vols. Austin: Univ. of Texas Press.

Cartledge, P. A. 1993. *The Greeks: A Portrait of Self and Others*. Oxford & New York: Oxford Univ. Press.

—. 2003. *The Spartans: The World of the Warrior-Heroes of Ancient Greece, from Utopia to Crisis and Collapse*. New York: Overlook Press.

Chadwick, J. 1958. *The Decipherment of Linear B*. Cambridge: Cambridge Univ. Press.

—. 1976. *The Mycenaean World*. Cambridge: Cambridge Univ. Press.

Cherry, J. F. 1983. Evolution, revolution and the origins of complex society in Minoan Crete, in *Minoan Society*. Kryszkowska, O. & Nixon, L. (eds.). 33–45. Bristol: Bristol Classical Press.

—. 1986. Polities and palaces: some problems in Minoan state formation, in *Peer Polity Interaction and Sociopolitical Change*. Renfrew, C. & Cherry, J. F. (eds.). 19–45. Cambridge: Cambridge Univ. Press.

—. 2003. Archaeology beyond the site: regional survey and its future, in *Theory and Practice in Mediterranean Archaeology: Old World and New World Perspectives*. Leventhal, R. & Papadopoulos, J. (eds.). 137–60. Los Angeles: Cotsen Institute of Archaeology, Univ. of California at Los Angeles.

Cherry, J. F. & Davis, J. L. 2001. Under the scepter of Agamemnon: the view from the hinterlands of Mycenae, in *Urbanism in the Aegean Bronze Age*. Branigan, K. (ed.). 141–59. Sheffield: Sheffield Academic Press.

Cherry, J. F., Davis, J. L., & Mantzourani, E. 1991. *Landscape Archaeology as Long-Term History: Northern Keos in the Cycladic Islands from Earliest Settlement to Modern Times* (Monumenta Archeologica 16). Los Angeles: Institute of Archaeology, Univ. of California at Los Angeles.

Childe, V. G. 1925. *The Dawn of European Civilization*. New York: Knopf.

Coleman, K. 2000. Entertaining Rome, in *Ancient Rome: The Archaeology of the Eternal City*. Coulston, J. & Dodge, H. (eds.). 210–58. (Oxford Univ. School of Archaeology Monograph 54.) Oxford: Oxford Univ. School of Archaeology, Institute of Archaeology.

Cornell, T. 1995. *The Beginnings of Rome: Italy and Rome from the Bronze Age to the Punic Wars (c. 1000–264 BC)*. London: Routledge.

—. 2000. The city-states in Latium, in *A Comparative Study of Thirty City-State Cultures: An Investigation Conducted by the Copenhagen Polis Centre*. Hansen, M. H. (ed.). 209–28. Copenhagen: Royal Danish Academy of Sciences & Letters.

Cornell, T. & Matthews, J. F. 1982. *Atlas of the Roman World*. Oxford: Phaidon.

Davidson, J. 1997. *Courtesans and Fishcakes: The Consuming Passions of Classical Athens*. New York: St. Martin's Press.

Davies, P. J. E. 2000. *Death and the Emperor: Roman Imperial Funerary Monuments, from Augustus to Marcus Aurelius*. Cambridge: Cambridge Univ. Press.

Davis, E. N. 1995. Art and politics in the Aegean: the missing ruler, in *The Role of the Ruler in the Prehistoric Aegean* (Aegaeum 11). Rehak, P. (ed.). 11–22. Liège: Université de Liège.

de Polignac, F. 1995. *Cults, Territory and the Origins of the Greek City-State*. Transl. Lloyd, J. Chicago: Univ. of Chicago Press.

Dench, E. 1995. *From Barbarians to New Men: Greek, Roman and Modern Perceptions of the Central Apennines*. Oxford: Clarendon Press.

Doumas, C. 1983. *Thera. Pompeii of the Ancient Aegean: Excavations at Akrotiri, 1967–79*. New York: Thames & Hudson.

Driessen, J. & Farnoux, A. (eds.). 1997. *La Crète Mycénienne: Actes de la Table Ronde Internationale organisée par l'École française d'Athènes*. Paris: De Boccard.

Duchêne, H. 1996. *Golden Treasures of Troy: The Dream of Heinrich Schliemann*. New York: Abrams; London: Thames & Hudson.

Elia, R. J. 2001. Analysis of the looting, selling, and collecting of Apulian red-figure vases: a quantitative approach, in *Trade in Illicit Antiquities: The Destruction of the World's Archaeological Heritage*. Brodie, N., Doole, J., & Renfrew, C. (eds.). 145–53. Cambridge: McDonald Institute for Archaeological Research.

Elsner, J. 1995. *Art and the Roman Viewer: The Transformation of Art from the Pagan World to Christianity*. Cambridge: Cambridge Univ. Press.

—. 1997. The origins of the icon: pilgrimage, religion and visual culture in the Roman East as 'resistance' to the Center, in *The Early Roman Empire in the East*. Alcock, S. E. (ed.). 179–99. Oxford: Oxbow.

Empereur, J.-Y. 2002. *Alexandria: Jewel of Egypt*. New York: Abrams; London: Thames & Hudson.

Etienne, R. 1992. *Pompeii: The Day A City Died*. New York: Abrams; London: Thames & Hudson.

Evans, A. 1921–35. *The Palace of Minos at Knossos*. 4 vols. London: Macmillan.

Favro, D. 1996. *The Urban Image of Augustan Rome*. Cambridge: Cambridge Univ. Press.

Finley, M. I. 1973. *The Ancient Economy*. London: Chatto & Windus.

Finley, M. I. & Pleket, H. W. 1976. *The Olympic Games: The First Thousand Years*. New York: Viking Press.

Fraser, P. M. 1996. *Cities of Alexander the Great*. Oxford: Clarendon Press.

Garnsey, P. 1988. *Famine and Food Supply in the Graeco-Roman World: Responses to Risk and Crisis*. Cambridge: Cambridge Univ. Press.

Getz-Preziosi, P. 1987. *Sculptors of the Cyclades: Individual and Tradition in the Third Millennium BC*. Ann Arbor: Univ. of Michigan Press.

Gill, D. W. J. & Chippindale, C. 1993. Material and intellectual consequences of esteem for Cycladic figures. *American Journal of Archaeology* 97, 601–59.

Gillings, M., Mattingly, D., & van Dalen, J. 1999. *Geographical Information Systems and Landscape Archaeology*. Oxford: Oxbow.

Goitein, S. D. 1967–1993. *A Mediterranean Society: The Jewish Communities of the Arab World as Portrayed in the Documents of the Cairo Geniza*. 6 vols. Berkeley: Univ. of California Press.

Goodison, L. & Morris, C. 1998. Beyond the 'Great Mother': the sacred world of the Minoans, in *Ancient Goddesses: The Myths and the Evidence*. Goodison, L. & Morris, C. (eds.). 113–32. London: British Museum Press.

Graepler, D. & Mazzei, M. 1993. *Fundort— Unbekannt: Raubgrabungen zerstoren das Archäologische Erbe*. Heidelberg: Univ. of Heidelberg.

Green, P. 1990. *Alexander to Actium: The Hellenistic Age*. London: Thames & Hudson.

Green, R. & Handley, E. 1995. *Images of the Greek Theatre*. London: British Museum Press.

Greene, K. 1986. *The Archaeology of the Roman Economy*. London: Batsford.

Hägg, R. (ed.). 1997. *The Function of the 'Minoan Villa': Proceedings of the Eighth International Symposium at the Swedish Institute at Athens, 6–8 June 1992*. Stockholm: Paul Åströms Förlag.

Hansen, M. H. (ed.). 2000. *A Comparative Study of Thirty City-State Cultures: An Investigation Conducted by the Copenhagen Polis Centre*. Copenhagen: Royal Danish Academy of Sciences & Letters.

Hellenkemper Salies, G. 1994. *Das Wrack: Die Antike Schiffsfund von Mahdia I–II*. Cologne: Rheinland.

Herz, N. & Waelkens, M. (eds.). 1988. *Classical Marble: Geochemistry, Technology and Trade*. (NATO Advanced Research Workshop on Marble in Ancient Greece and Rome: Geology, Quarries, Commerce, Artifacts [1988: Lucca, Italy].) Boston: Kluwer Academic Publishers.

Hingley, R. 2000. *Roman Officers and English Gentlemen: The Imperial Origins of Roman Archaeology*. London: Routledge.

—. (ed.). 2001. *Images of Rome: Perceptions of Ancient Rome in Europe and the United States in the Modern Age*. (*Journal of Roman Archaeology* Supplementary Series 44.) Portsmouth, RI: Journal of Roman Archaeology.

Hodkinson, S. 2000. *Property and Wealth in Classical Sparta*. London & Swansea: Duckworth & Classical Press of Wales.

Hoffman, G. 1997. *Imports and Immigrants: Near Eastern Connections with Iron Age Crete*. Ann Arbor: Univ. of Michigan Press.

Hopkins, K. 1980. Taxes and trade in the Roman Empire (200 BC–AD 400). *Journal of Roman Studies* 70, 101–25.

Horden, P. & Purcell, N. 2000. *The Corrupting Sea: A Study of Mediterranean History*. Oxford: Blackwell.

Houby-Nielsen, S. 1995. 'Burial language' in Archaic and Classical Kerameikos. *Proceedings of the Danish Institute at Athens* 1, 129–91.

Hoyos, D. 2003. *Hannibal's Dynasty: Power and Politics in the Western Mediterranean, 247–183 BC*. London: Routledge.

Hurwit, J. M. 1985. *The Art and Culture of Early Greece, 1100–480 BC*. Ithaca: Cornell Univ. Press.

—. 1999. *The Athenian Acropolis: History, Mythology and Archaeology from the Neolithic Era to the Present*. Cambridge: Cambridge Univ. Press.

Isaac, B. 1990. *The Limits of Empire: The Roman Army in the East*. Oxford: Clarendon Press.

Jacob, C. & de Polignac, F. (eds.). 2000. *Alexandria, Third Century BC: The Knowledge of the World in a Single City*. Alexandria: Harpocrates.

Jones, J. E. 1982. The Laurion silver mines: a review. *Greece and Rome* n.s. 29, 169–83.

Keay, S. 1988. *Roman Spain*. London: British Museum Press.

Kennedy, D. & Riley, D. 1990. *Rome's Desert Frontier from the Air*. Austin: Univ. of Texas Press.

King, A. 1990. *Roman Gaul and Germany*. London: British Museum Press.

Knapp, A. B. 1993. Thalassocracies in Bronze Age Eastern Mediterranean trade: making and breaking a myth. *World Archaeology* 24, 332–47.

La Riche, W. 1997. *Alexandria: The Sunken City*. London: Weidenfeld & Nicolson.

Lawrence, D. H. 1960. *Mornings in Mexico and Etruscan Places*. (Originally published 1927 and 1932.) Harmondsworth: Penguin.

Lefkowitz, M. R. & Rogers, G. M. (eds.). 1996. *Black Athena Revisited*. Chapel Hill: Univ. of North Carolina Press.

Lewthwaite, J. G. 1983. Why did civilization not emerge more often? A comparative approach to the development of Minoan Crete, in *Minoan Society*. Kryszkowska, O. & Nixon, L. (eds.). 171–83. Bristol: Bristol Classical Press.

Lilliu, G. 1985. *Origini della Civiltà in Sardegna*. Torino: ERI.

Lissarrague, F. 1989. The world of the warrior, in *A City of Images: Iconography and Society in Ancient Greece*. Bérard, C., Bron, C., Durand, J.-L., Frontisi-Ducroux, F., Lissarrague, F., Schnapp, A., & Vernant, J.-P. 39–51. Princeton: Princeton Univ. Press.

Loraux, N. 1986. *The Invention of Athens: The Funeral Oration in the Classical City*. Transl. Sheridan, A. Cambridge, MA: Harvard Univ. Press.

Lyons, C. L. & Papadopoulos, J. K. (eds.). 2002. *The Archaeology of Colonialism*. Los Angeles: Getty Research Institute.

MacGillivray, J. A. 2000. *Minotaur: Sir Arthur Evans and the Archaeology of the Minoan Myth*. New York: Hill & Wang.

Manning, S. W. 1999. *A Test of Time: The Volcano of Thera and the Chronology and History of the Aegean and East Mediterranean in the Mid-Second Millennium BC*. Oxford: Oxbow.

Marinatos, N. 1993. *Minoan Religion: Ritual, Image, and Symbol*. Columbia: Univ. of South Carolina Press.

Mathers, C. & Stoddart, S. (eds.). 1994. *Development and Decline in the Mediterranean Bronze Age* (Sheffield Archaeological Monographs 8). Sheffield: J. R. Collis Publications.

Mattingly, D. & Aldrete, G. 2000. The feeding of Imperial Rome: the mechanics of the food supply system, in *Ancient Rome: The Archaeology of the Eternal City*. Coulston, J. & Dodge, H. (eds.). 142–65. (Oxford Univ. School of Archaeology Monograph 54.) Oxford: Oxford Univ. School of Archaeology, Institute of Archaeology.

Millett, P. 1998. Encounters in the Agora, in *Kosmos: Essays in Order, Conflict and Community in Classical Athens*. Cartledge, P. A., Millett, P., & von Reden, S. (eds.). 203–28. Cambridge: Cambridge Univ. Press.

Moatti, C. 1993. *The Search for Ancient Rome*. New York: Abrams; London: Thames & Hudson.

Moreland, J. 2001. The Carolingian empire: Rome reborn?, in *Empires: Perspectives from Archaeology and History*. Alcock, S. E., D'altroy, T. N., Morrison, K. D., & Sinopoli, C. M. (eds.). 392–418. Cambridge: Cambridge Univ. Press.

Morris, I. 1987. *Burial and Ancient Society: The Rise of the Greek City-State*. Cambridge: Cambridge Univ. Press.

—. 1992. *Death-Ritual and Social Structure in Classical Antiquity*. Cambridge: Cambridge Univ. Press.

—. 1994. Introduction, in *Classical Greece: Ancient Histories and Modern Archaeologies*. Morris, I. (ed.). 8–47. Cambridge: Cambridge Univ. Press.

Morris, S. P. 1992. *Daidalos and the Origins of Greek Art*. Princeton: Princeton Univ. Press.

Moscati, S. (ed.). 1988. *The Phoenicians*. Milan: Bompiani.

Neils, J. 1992. *Goddess and Polis: The Panathenaic Festival in Ancient Athens*. Princeton: Princeton Univ. Press.

Nevett, L. 1999. *House and Society in the Ancient Greek World*. Cambridge: Cambridge Univ. Press.

Nichols, D. L. & Charlton, T. H. (eds.). 1997. *The Archaeology of City-States: Cross-Cultural Approaches*. Washington D.C.: Smithsonian Institution Press.

Niemeyer, H. G. 2000. The early Phoenician city-states on the Mediterranean: archaeological elements for their description, in *A Comparative Study of Thirty City-State Cultures: An Investigation Conducted by the Copenhagen Polis Centre*. Hansen, M. H. (ed.). 89–115. Copenhagen: Royal Danish Academy of Sciences & Letters.

Osborne, R. 1986. 'Pots, trade, and the Archaic Greek economy.' *Antiquity* 70: 31–44.

—. 1987. *Classical Landscape with Figures*. London: George Philip.

—. 1996. *Greece in the Making, 1200–479 BC*. London: Routledge.

—. 1998. *Archaic and Classical Greek Art* (Oxford History of Art). Oxford: Oxford Univ. Press.

Packer, J. E. 2001. *The Forum of Trajan in Rome: A Study of the Monuments in Brief*. Berkeley: Univ. of California Press.

Parker, A. J. 1992. *Ancient Shipwrecks of the Mediterranean and the Roman Provinces*. Oxford: British Archaeological Reports International Series 580.

Peacock, D. P. S. & Maxfield, V. A. (eds.). 1997. *Mons Claudianus: Survey and Excavation, 1987–1993*. Vol. 1: Topography and quarries. Cairo: Institut français d'archéologie orientale.

Perticarari, L. 1986. *I Segreti di un Tombarolo.* Milan: Rusconi Editore.

Pollitt, J. J. 1972. *Art and Experience in Classical Greece.* Cambridge: Cambridge Univ. Press.

—. 1986. *Art in the Hellenistic Age.* Cambridge: Cambridge Univ. Press.

Popham, M. R., Sackett, L. H., & Themelis, P. G. 1993. *Lefkandi II.2. The Protogeometric Building at Toumba: The Excavation, Architecture and Finds.* London: British School at Athens.

Potter, T. W. & Johns, C. 1992. *Roman Britain.* London: British Museum Press.

Powell, B. B. 1992. Homer and the origin of the Greek alphabet. *Cambridge Archaeological Journal* 2, 115–26.

Prag, A. W. & Neave, R. 1997. *Making Faces: Using Forensic and Archaeological Evidence.* London: British Museum Press.

Pugliese Carratelli, G. (ed.). 1996. *The Western Greeks.* London: Thames & Hudson.

Price, S. 1984. *Rituals and Power: The Roman Imperial Cult in Asia Minor.* Cambridge: Cambridge Univ. Press.

Raschke, W. J. (ed.). 1988. *The Archaeology of the Olympics: The Olympics and Other Festivals in Antiquity.* Madison: Univ. of Wisconsin Press.

Rehak, P. & Younger, J. G. 1998. Review of Aegean Prehistory VII: Neopalatial, Final Palatial, and Postpalatial Crete. *American Journal of Archaeology* 102, 91–173.

Renfrew, C. 1972. *The Emergence of Civilisation.* London: Methuen.

—. 1979. Systems collapse as social transformation: catastrophe and anastrophe in early state societies, in *Transformations: Mathematical Approaches to Culture Change.* Renfrew, C. & Cooke, K. L. (eds.). 481–506. New York: Academic Press.

—. 1986. Varna and the emergence of wealth in prehistoric Europe, in *The Social Life of Things.* Appadurai, A. (ed.). 141–68. Cambridge: Cambridge Univ. Press.

—. 1991. *The Cycladic Spirit: Masterpieces from the Nicholas P. Goulandris Collection.* New York: Abrams; London: Thames & Hudson.

Robinson, A. 2002. *The Man Who Deciphered Linear B. The Story of Michael Ventris.* London & New York: Thames & Hudson.

Saprykin, S. J. 1994. *Ancient Farms and Land-Plots on the Khora of Khersonesos Taurike: Research in the Herakleian Peninsula, 1974–1990.* Amsterdam: J. C. Gieben.

Sarris, A. & Jones, R. E. 2000. Geophysical and related techniques applied to archaeological survey in the Mediterranean: a review. *Journal of Mediterranean Archaeology* 13, 3–75.

Scarre, C. 1995a. *The Penguin Historical Atlas of Ancient Rome.* Harmondsworth: Penguin.

—. 1995b. *Chronicle of the Roman Emperors.* London & New York: Thames & Hudson.

Scheidel, W. & von Reden, S. (eds.). 2002. *The Ancient Economy.* Edinburgh Univ. Press.

Schiffer, M. B. 1987. *Formation Processes of the Archaeological Record.* Albuquerque: Univ. of New Mexico Press.

Scobie, A. 1986. Slums, sanitation and mortality in the Roman world. *Klio* 68, 399–433.

Shanks, M. 1995. *Classical Archaeology of Greece: Experiences of the Discipline.* London: Routledge.

Shaw, J. W. 1987. The Early Helladic II Corridor House: development and form. *American Journal of Archaeology* 91, 59–79.

—. 1989. Phoenicians in southern Crete. *American Journal of Archaeology* 93, 165–83.

Sherratt, A. 1993. What would a Bronze-Age world system look like? Relations between temperate Europe and the Mediterranean in later prehistory. *Journal of European Archaeology* 1 (2), 1–58.

Sherratt, A. & Sherratt, S. 1998. Small worlds: interaction and identity in the ancient Mediterranean, in *The Aegean and the Orient in the Second Millennium: Proceedings of the 50th Anniversary Symposium, Cincinnati, 18–20 April 1997 (Aegaeum 18).* Cline, E. H. & Harris-Cline, D. (eds.). 329–34. Liège: Université de Liège, Histoire de l'art et archéologie de la Grèce antique; Austin: Univ. of Texas at Austin, Program in Aegean Scripts and Prehistory.

Shotyk, W., Weiss, D. J., Appleby, P. G., Cheburkin, A. K., Frei, R., Gloor, M., Kramers, J. D., Reese, S., & van der Knaap, O. W. 1998. History of atmospheric lead deposition since 12,370 14C yr BP from a peat bog, Jura Mountains, Switzerland. *Science* 281, 1635–40.

Smith, C. J. 1996. *Early Rome and Latium: Economy and Society c. 1000 to 500 BC.* Oxford: Clarendon Press.

Smith, R. R. R. 1991. *Hellenistic Sculpture.* London & New York: Thames & Hudson.

Snodgrass, A. M. 1977. *Archaeology and the Rise of the Greek State.* Cambridge: Cambridge Univ. Press.

—. 1980. *Archaic Greece: The Age of Experiment.* Berkeley: Univ. of California Press.

—. 1987. *An Archaeology of Greece: The Present State and Future Scope of a Discipline.* Berkeley: Univ. of California Press.

Spivey, N. 1997. *Etruscan Art.* London & New York: Thames & Hudson.

—. 1991. Greek vases in Etruria, in *Looking at Greek Vases.* Rasmussen, T. & Spivey, N. (eds.). 31–50. Cambridge: Cambridge Univ. Press.

Spivey, N. & Stoddart, S. 1990. *Etruscan Italy: An Archaeological History.* London: Batsford.

Stambaugh, J. E. 1988. *The Ancient Roman City.* Baltimore & London: The Johns Hopkins Univ. Press.

Stewart, A. F. 1993. *Faces of Power: Alexander's Image and Hellenistic Politics.* Berkeley: Univ. of California Press.

—. 1997. *Art, Desire and the Body in Ancient Greek Culture.* Cambridge: Cambridge Univ. Press.

Swain, S. 1996. *Hellenism and Empire: Language, Classicism and Power in the Greek World, AD 50–250.* Oxford: Clarendon Press.

Torelli, M. 2000. The Etruscan city-state, in *A Comparative Study of Thirty City-State Cultures: An Investigation Conducted by the Copenhagen Polis Centre.* Hansen, M. H. (ed.). 189–208. Copenhagen: Royal Danish Academy of Sciences & Letters.

Tsetskhladze, G. R. & De Angelis, F. (eds.). 1994. *The Archaeology of Greek Colonisation.* Oxford: Oxford Univ. Committee for Archaeology, Institute of Archaeology.

Van Andel, T. H. & Runnels, C. 1987. *Beyond the Acropolis: A Rural Greek Past.* Stanford: Stanford Univ. Press.

Van Dommelen, P. 1998. *On Colonial Grounds: A Comparative Study of Colonialism and Rural Settlement in First Millennium BC West Central Sardinia.* Leiden: Faculty of Archaeology, Univ. of Leiden.

Vickers, M. & Gill, D. 1994. *Artful Crafts: Ancient Greek Silverware and Pottery.* Oxford: Clarendon Press.

Walbank, F. W. 1992. *The Hellenistic World.* (Rev. ed.). Cambridge, MA: Harvard Univ. Press.

Walker, S. 1985. *Memorials to the Roman Dead.* London: British Museum Press.

Walker, S. & Burnett, A. 1981. *The Image of Augustus.* London: British Museum Press.

Walker, S. & Higgs, P. 2001. *Cleopatra of Egypt: From History to Myth.* Princeton: Princeton Univ. Press.

Webster. G. S. 1996. *A Prehistory of Sardinia: 2300–500.* Sheffield: Sheffield Academic Press.

Wells, P. S. 1980. *Culture Contact and Culture Change: Early Iron Age Central Europe and the Mediterranean World.* Cambridge: Cambridge Univ. Press.

Whitelaw, T. M. 1983. The settlement at Fournou Koriphi Myrtos and aspects of Early Minoan social organisation, in *Minoan Society.* Kryszkowska, O. & Nixon, L. (eds.). 323–45. Bristol: Bristol Classical Press.

Whitley, J. 2001. *The Archaeology of Ancient Greece.* Cambridge: Cambridge Univ. Press.

Whittaker, C. R. 1994. *Frontiers of the Roman Empire: A Social and Economic Study.* Baltimore & London: The Johns Hopkins Univ. Press.

Wiencke, M. H. 2000. *Lerna, a Preclassical Site in the Argolid IV: The Architecture, Stratification, and Pottery of Lerna III.* Princeton: Princeton Univ. Press.

Wiseman, T. P. 1995. *Remus: A Roman Myth.* Cambridge: Cambridge Univ. Press.

Woolf, G. 1998. *Becoming Roman: The Origins of Provincial Civilization in Gaul.* Cambridge: Cambridge Univ. Press.

Wycherley, R. E. 1978. *The Stones of Athens.* Princeton: Princeton Univ. Press.

Xenakis, D. K. & Chryssochoou, D. N. 2001. *The Emerging Euro-Mediterranean System.* Manchester & New York: Manchester Univ. Press.

Yadin, Y. 1966. *Masada: Herod's Fortress and the Zealot's Last Stand.* New York: Random House.

Yener, K. A. 2000. *The Domestication of Metals: The Rise of Complex Metal Industries in Anatolia (Culture and History of the Ancient Near East 4.).* Leiden: Brill.

Zanker, P. 1988. *The Power of Images in the Age of Augustus.* Ann Arbor: Univ. of Michigan Press.

—. 1998. *Pompeii: Public and Private Life.* Transl. Schneider, D. L. Cambridge, MA: Harvard Univ. Press.

—. 2000. The city as symbol: Rome and the creation of an urban image, in *Romanization and the City: Creation, Transformations and Failures (Journal of Roman Archaeology Supplementary Series 38).* Fentress, L. (ed.). 25–41. Portsmouth, RI: Journal of Roman Archaeology.

CHAPTER 14: SOUTH ASIA: FROM EARLY VILLAGES TO BUDDHISM

Agrawal, D. P. 1982. *The Archaeology of India.* London: Curzon Press.

Agrawal, D. P., Kharrakwal, J., Kusumgar, S., & Yadava, M. G. 1995. Cist burials of the Kumaun Himalayas. *Antiquity* 69, 550–54.

Ali, I., Batt, C. M., Coningham, R. A. E., & Young, R. L. 2002. New exploration in the Chitral valley, Pakistan: an extension of the Gandharan grave culture. *Antiquity* 76, 647–53.

Ali, T., Coningham, R. A. E., Durrani, M. A., & Khan, G. R. 1998. Preliminary report of two seasons of archaeological investigations at the Bala Hisar of Charsadda, NWFP, Pakistan. *Ancient Pakistan* 12, 1–34.

Allchin, B. & Allchin, F. R. 1968. *The Birth of Indian Civilisation.* Harmondsworth: Penguin.

—. 1982. *The Rise of Civilisation in India and Pakistan.* Cambridge: Cambridge Univ. Press.

Allchin, F. R. 1963. *Neolithic Cattle-Keepers of South India.* Cambridge: Cambridge Univ. Press.

—. 1982. How old is the city of Taxila? *Antiquity* 56, 8–14.

—. 1995a. The end of Harappan urbanisation and its legacy, in *The Archaeology of Early Historic South Asia.* Allchin, F. R. (ed.). 26–40. Cambridge: Cambridge Univ. Press.

—. 1995b. The Mauryan state and empire, in *The Archaeology of Early Historic South Asia.* Allchin, F. R. (ed.). 187–221. Cambridge: Cambridge Univ. Press.

—. 1995c. Mauryan architecture and art, in *The Archaeology of Early Historic South Asia.* Allchin, F. R. (ed.). 222–73. Cambridge: Cambridge Univ. Press.

Allchin, F. R. & Joshi, J. P. 1995. *Excavations at Malvan.* New Delhi: Archaeological Survey of India.

Allchin, F. R. & Norman, K. R. 1985. Guide to Asokan inscriptions. *South Asian Studies* 1, 43–50.

Bandaranayake, S. D. 1974. *Sinhalese Monastic Architecture.* Leiden: E. J. Brill.

Bechert, H. (ed.). 1995. *When Did the Buddha Live? The Controversy on the Dating of the Historical Buddha.* New Delhi: Sri Satguru Publications.

Begley, V. 1996. *The Ancient Port of Arikamedu: New Excavations and Researches 1989–1992.* Paris: École française d'Extrême-Orient.

Bernard, P. 1994. The Greek kingdoms of Central Asia, in *History of Civilisations of Central Asia.* Vol. II: The development of sedentary and nomadic civilisations: 700 BC to AD 250. Harmatta, J. (ed.). 99–130. Paris: UNESCO.

Bisht, R. S. 1989. A new model of Harappan town planning as revealed at Dholavira in Kutch, in *History and Archaeology: Professor H.D. Sankalia Felicitation Volume.* Chatterjee, B. (ed.). 265–72. New Delhi: Ramanand Vidya Bhavan.

Casal, J.-M. 1949. *Fouilles de Virampatnam-Arikamedu.* Paris: Imprimerie Nationale.

—. 1961. *Fouilles de Mundigak.* Paris: Memoires de la Delegation Archéologique Française en Afghanistan.

—. 1964. *Fouilles d'Amri.* Paris: Commission des Fouilles Archéologiques.

Chakrabarti, D. K. 1995. Post-Mauryan states of mainland south Asia, in *The Archaeology of Early Historic South Asia.* Allchin, F. R. (ed.). 274–326. Cambridge: Cambridge Univ. Press.

—. 1999. *India: An Archaeological History.* New Delhi: Oxford Univ. Press.

Coningham, R. A. E. 1995a. Dark age or continuum? An archaeological analysis of the second emergence of urbanism in South Asia, in *The Archaeology of Early Historic South Asia.* Allchin, F. R. (ed.). 54–72. Cambridge: Cambridge Univ. Press.

—. 1995b. Monks, caves and kings: a reassessment of the nature of early Buddhism in Sri Lanka. *World Archaeology* 27, 222–42.

—. 1999. *Anuradhapura.* Vol. I: The site. Oxford: Archaeopress.

—. 2001. The archaeology of Buddhism, in *Archaeology and World Religion.* Insoll, T. (ed.). 61–95. London: Routledge.

—. 2002a. Beyond and before the imperial frontiers: Early historic Sri Lanka and the origins of Indian Ocean trade. *Man and Environment* 27, 99–108.

—. 2002b. Deciphering the Indus script, in *Indian Archaeology in Retrospect.* Vol. II: Protohistory: archaeology of the Harappan civilisation. Settar, S. & Korisettar, R. (eds.). 81–103. New Delhi: Indian Council of Historical Research.

Coningham, R. A. E. & Sutherland, T. 1998. Dwellings or granaries? The pit phenomenon of the Kashmir-Swat Neolithic. *Man and Environment* XXII, 29–34.

Coningham, R. A. E., Allchin, F. R., Batt, C. M., & Lucy, D. 1996. Passage to India? Anuradhapura and the early use of the Brahmi script. *Cambridge Archaeological Journal* 6, 73–97.

Constantini, L. 1984. The beginnings of agriculture in the Kachi plain: the evidence from Mehrgarh, in *South Asian Archaeology 1981.* Allchin, B. (ed.). 29–33. Cambridge: Cambridge Univ. Press.

Dales, G. F. 1964. The mythical massacre at Mohenjo-daro. *Expedition* 6, 36–43.

—. 1965. Civilisation and floods in the Indus valley. *Expedition* 7, 10–19.

—. 1979. The Balakot project: summary of four years of excavations in Pakistan, in *South Asian Archaeology 1977.* Taddei, M. (ed.). 241–74. Naples: Istituto Universitario Orientale.

Dani, A. H. 1966. Shaikhan Dheri excavations. *Ancient Pakistan* 3, 121–82.

—. 1967. Timargha and the Gandharan grave culture. *Ancient Pakistan* 3, 1–407.

—. 1986. *The Historic City of Taxila.* Paris: UNESCO.

—. 1992. Pastoral-agricultural tribes of Pakistan in the post-Indus Period, in *History of Civilisations of Central Asia.* Vol. I: The dawn of civilisation: earliest times to 700 BC. Dani, A. H. & Masson, V. M. (eds.). 395–419. Paris: UNESCO.

De Silva, K. M. 1981. *A History of Sri Lanka.* Berkeley: Univ. of California Press.

Deraniyagala, S. U. 1992. *The Prehistory of Sri Lanka.* Colombo: Archaeological Survey Department.

Dhavalikar, M. K. 1995. *Cultural Imperialism: Indus Civilisation in Western India.* New Delhi: Books & Books.

—. 1996. *Kuntasi: A Harappan Emporium on West Coast.* Pune: Deccan College.

Dhavalikar, M. K., Sankalia, H. D., & Ansari, Z. D. 1988. *Excavations at Inamgaon.* Pune: Deccan College.

Dikshit, K. N. 1982. Hulas and the late Harappan complex of western Uttar Pradesh, in *Harappan Civilisation: A Contemporary Perspective.* Possehl, G. L. (ed.). 339–52. New Delhi: Oxford & IBH.

Durrani, F. A. 1988. Excavations in the Gomal valley: Rehman Dheri excavation report no. 1. *Ancient Pakistan* 6, 1–232.

Erdosy, G. 1987. *Urbanisation in Early Historic India.* Oxford: British Archaeological Reports.

—. 1995a. The prelude to urbanisation: ethnicity and the rise of late Vedic chiefdoms, in *Early Historic South Asia: The Emergence of Cities and States.* Allchin, F. R. (ed.). 75–98. Cambridge: Cambridge Univ. Press.

—. 1995b. City states of north India and Pakistan at the time of the Buddha, in *Early Historic South Asia: The Emergence of Cities and States.* Allchin, F. R. (ed.). 99–122. Cambridge: Cambridge Univ. Press.

Fairservis, W. 1971. *The Roots of Ancient India.* London: George, Allen & Unwin.

—. 1986. Cattle and the Harappan chiefdoms of the Indus valley. *Expedition* 28, 43–50.

Fuller, D. Q. & Madella, M. 2002. Issues in Harappan archaeobotany: retrospect and prospect, in *Indian Archaeology in Retrospect.* Vol. II: Protohistory: archaeology of the Harappan civilisation. Settar, S. & Korisettar, R. (eds.). 317–90. New Delhi: Indian Council of Historical Research.

Glover, I. C. & Higham, C. F. W. 1996. New evidence for early rice cultivation in South, Southeast and East Asia, in *The Origins and Spread of Agriculture and Pastoralism in Eurasia.* Harris, D. R. (ed.). 413–41. London: Univ. College London Press.

Hackin, J. 1939. *Recherches archéologiques à Begram.* Paris: Memoires de la Delegation Archéologique Française en Afghanistan.

Halim, M. A. 1972. Excavations at Sarai Khola. *Pakistan Archaeology* 7, 23–89.

Hegde, K. T. M., Bhan, K. K., Sonawane, V. S., Krishnan, K., & Shah, D. R. 1992. *Excavations at Nageshwar, Gujarat: A Harappan Shell-Working Site on the Gulf of Kutch.* Baroda: Univ. of Baroda.

Helms, S. W. 1982. Excavations at the 'city and the most famous fortress of Kandahar, the foremost place in all of Asia'. *Afghan Studies* 3 & 4, 1–24.

Jansen, M. 1993. *Mohenjo-Daro: City of Wells and Drains.* Bergisch Gladbach: Frontinus Society.

Jarrige, C., Jarrige, J.-F., Meadow, R. H., & Quivron, G. 1995. *Mehrgarh 1974–1985: From Neolithic Times to the Indus Civilisation.* Karachi: Government of Sindh.

Jarrige, J.-F. 1984. Chronology of the earlier periods of the greater Indus as seen from Mehrgarh, Pakistan, in *South Asian Archaeology 1981.* Allchin, B. (ed.). 21–28. Cambridge: Cambridge Univ. Press.

Jarrige, J.-F. & Hassan, M. U. 1989. Funerary complexes in Baluchistan at the end of the third millennium, in *South Asian Archaeology 1985.* Frifelt, K. & Sorenson, P. (ed.). 150–66. London: Curzon Press.

Jarrige, J.-F. & Santoni, M. 1979. *Fouilles de Pirak.* Paris: Commission des Fouilles Archéologiques.

Joshi, R. V. 1978. *Stone Age Culture of Central India: Report on Excavations of Rock Shelters at Adamgarh, Madhya Pradesh.* Pune: Deccan College.

Karve-Corvinus, G. & Kennedy, K. A. R. 1964. Preliminary report on Langhnaj excavations 1963. *Bulletin of the Deccan College Research Institute* XXIV, 44–57.

Kennedy, K. A. R. 2002. The search for fossil man in south Asia: retrospect and prospect, in *Indian Archaeology in Retrospect.* Vol. III: Archaeology and interactive disciplines. Settar, S. & Korisettar, R. (eds.). 87–92. New Delhi: Indian Council of Historical Research.

Kennedy, K. A. R., Lukacs, J. R., Pastor, R. F., Johnston, T. L., Lovell, N. C., Pal, J. N., Hemphill, B. E., & Burrow, C. B. 1992. *Human Skeletal Remains from Mahadaha: A Gangetic Mesolithic Site.* Ithaca: Cornell Univ. Press.

Kenoyer, J. M. 1998. *Ancient Cities of the Indus*

Valley Civilisation. Karachi: Oxford Univ. Press.

Khan, F. A. 1965. Excavations at Kot Diji. *Pakistan Archaeology* 2, 11–85.

—. 1973. Excavations at Zarif Karuna. *Pakistan Archaeology* 9, 1–94.

Khanna, G. S. 1992. Patterns of mobility in the Mesolithic of Rajasthan, in *South Asian Archaeology 1989.* Jarrige, C. (ed.). 153–60. Madison: Prehistory Press.

Korisettar, R. & Rajaguru, S. N. 1988. Quaternary stratigraphy, palaeoclimate and the lower Palaeolithic of India, in *Early Human Behaviour in Global Context: The Rise and Diversity of the Lower Palaeolithic Record.* Petraglia, M. D. & Korisettar, R. (eds.). 304–342. London: Routledge.

Korisettar, R., Venkatasubbaiah, P. C., & Fuller, D. Q. 2002. Brahmagiri and beyond: the archaeology of the southern Neolithic, in *Indian Archaeology in Retrospect.* Vol. I: Prehistory: archaeology of South Asia. Settar, S. & Korisettar, R. (eds.). 151–237. New Delhi: Indian Council of Historical Research.

Kulke, H. & Rothermunde, D. 1986. *A History of India.* London: Routledge.

Lahiri, N. (ed.). 2000. *The Decline and Fall of the Indus Civilisation.* New Delhi: Permanent Black.

Lal, B. B. 1955. Excavations at Hastinapura and other explorations in the upper Ganga and Sutlej basins. *Ancient India* 11, 5–151.

—. 1979. Kalibangan and the Indus valley civilisation, in *Essays in Indian Protohistory.* Agrawal, D. P. & Chakrabarti, D. K. (eds.). 65–97. New Delhi: B. R. Publishing.

—. 1993. A glimpse of the social stratification and political set-up of the Indus civilisation. *Harappan Studies* 1, 63–71.

Lal, M. 1984. *Settlement History and Rise of Civilisation in the Ganga-Yamuna Doab from 1500 BC–300 AD.* New Delhi: B. R. Publishing.

Lambrick, H. T. 1967. The Indus flood plain and the 'Indus' civilisation. *Geographical Journal* 133, 483–95.

Lukacs, J. R., Misra, V. N., & Kennedy, K. A. R. 1983. *Bagor and Tilwara: Late Mesolithic Cultures of Northwest India.* Vol. I: Human skeletal remains. Pune: Deccan College.

Mackay, E. J. H. 1943. *Chanhu-daro Excavations 1935–1936.* New Haven: American Oriental Society.

Marshall, J. H. 1912. Excavations at Bhita. *Annual Report of the Archaeological Survey of India* 1911–1912, 29–94.

—. 1931. *Mohenjo-daro and the Indus Civilisation.* London: Arthur Probsthain.

—. 1951. *Taxila: An Illustrated Account of Archaeological Excavations.* Cambridge: Cambridge Univ. Press.

Mathpal, Y. 1984. *Prehistoric Rock Art of Bhimbetka, Central India.* New Delhi: Abhinav.

McIntosh, J. 1985. Dating the South Indian megaliths, in *South Asian Archaeology 1983.* Schotsmans, J. & Taddei, M. (eds.). 467–93. Naples: Istituto Universitario Orientale.

—. 2001. *A Peaceful Realm: The Rise and Fall of the Indus Civilisation.* Oxford: Westview Press.

McNicoll, A. & Ball, W. 1996. *Excavations at Kandahar 1974 and 1975.* Oxford: British Archaeological Reports.

Meadow, R. H. 1984. Notes on faunal remains from Mehrgarh, in *South Asian Archaeology 1981.* Allchin, B. (ed.). 34–40. Cambridge: Cambridge Univ. Press.

—. (ed.). 1991. *Harappa Excavations 1986–1990: A Multidisciplinary Approach to Third Millennium Urbanisation.* Madison: Prehistory Press.

Meadow, R. H. & Kenoyer, J. M. 1997. Excavations at Harappa 1994–1995: new perspectives on the Indus script, craft activities and city organisation, in *South Asian Archaeology 1995.* Allchin, B. (ed.). 139–72. New Delhi: Oxford & IBH.

Meadow, R. H. & Patel, A. K. 2002. From Mehrgarh to Harappa and Dholavira: prehistoric pastoralism in north-west south Asia through the Harappan period, in *Indian Archaeology in Retrospect.* Vol. II: Protohistory: archaeology of the Harappan civilisation. Settar, S. & Korisettar, R. (eds.). 391–408. New Delhi: Indian Council of Historical Research.

Miller, D. 1985. Ideology and the Harappan civilisation. *Journal of Anthropological Archaeology* 4, 34–71.

Misra, V. N. 1973. Bagor: a Mesolithic settlement in northwest India. *World Archaeology* 5, 92–110.

—. 2002. The Mesolithic age in India, in *Indian Archaeology in Retrospect.* Vol. I: Prehistory: archaeology of South Asia. Settar, S. & Korisettar, R. (eds.). 111–25. New Delhi: Indian Council of Historical Research.

Mughal, M. R. 1990. Further evidence of the Early Harappan culture in the Greater Indus Valley. *South Asian Studies* 6, 175–200.

—. 1997. *Ancient Cholistan: Archaeology and Architecture.* Lahore: Feroz Sons.

Paddayya, K. 1973. *Investigations into the Neolithic of the Shorapur Doab, South India.* Leiden: E. J. Brill.

Parpola, A. 1994. *Deciphering the Indus Script.* Cambridge: Cambridge Univ. Press.

Piggott, S. 1950. *Prehistoric India to 1000 BC.* Harmondsworth: Penguin.

Possehl, G. L. 1979. Pastoral nomadism in the Indus civilisation: a hypothesis, in *South Asian Archaeology 1977.* Taddei, M. (ed.). 537–51. Naples: Istituto Universitario Orientale.

—. 1980. *Indus Civilisation in Saurashtra.* New Delhi: B. R. Publishing.

—. 1993. The date of the Indus urbanization: a proposed chronology for the pre-urban and urban Harappan phases, in *South Asian Archaeology 1991.* Gail, A. J. & Mevissen, G. J. R. (eds.). 231–49. Stuttgart: Franz Steiner.

Possehl, G. L. & Raval, M. H. 1989. *Harappan Civilisation and Rojdi.* New Delhi: Oxford & IBH.

Puri, B. N. 1994. The Kushans, in *History of Civilisations of Central Asia.* Vol. II: The development of sedentary and nomadic civilisations: 700 BC to AD 250. Harmatta, J. (ed.). 247–64. Paris: UNESCO.

Raikes, R. L. 1967. The Mohenjo-daro floods: further notes. *Antiquity* 41, 64–66.

Rajan, K. 1994, *Archaeology of Tamilnadu (Kongu country).* New Delhi: Book India Publishing.

Rao, S. R. 1973. *Lothal and the Indus Civilisation.* New York: Asia Publishing.

Ratnagar, S. 2000. *The End of the Great Harappan Tradition.* New Delhi: Monhar.

Rendell, H. M., Dennell, R. W., & Halim, M. A. 1989. *Pleistocene and Palaeolithic Investigations in the Soan Valley, Northern Pakistan.* Oxford: British Archaeological Reports.

Renfrew, A. C. 1987. *Language and Archaeology.* London: Jonathan Cape.

Rissman, P. 1988. Public displays and private values: a guide to buried wealth in Harappan

archaeology. *World Archaeology* 20, 209–28.

Robinson, F. (ed.). 1989. *The Cambridge Encyclopedia of India, Pakistan, Bangladesh, Sri Lanka, Nepal, Bhutan and the Maldives.* Cambridge: Cambridge Univ. Press.

Rosenfield, J. M. 1967. *The Dynastic Art of the Kushans.* Berkeley: Univ. of California Press.

Sahni, M. R. 1956. Biogeological evidence bearing on the decline of the Indus valley civilisation. *Journal of the Palaeontological Society of India* 1, 101–07.

Sankalia, H. D. 1965. *Excavations at Langhnaj 1944–1963, part 1: Archaeology.* Pune: Deccan College.

—. 1974. *Prehistory and Protohistory of India and Pakistan.* Pune: Deccan College.

Santoni, M. 1984. Sibri and the south cemetery of Mehrgarh: third millennium connections between the northern Kachi plain (Pakistan) and central Asia, in *South Asian Archaeology 1981.* Allchin, B. (ed.). 52–60. Cambridge: Cambridge: Univ. Press.

Sarcina, A. 1979. The private house at Mohenjo-daro, in *South Asian Archaeology 1977.* Taddei, M. (ed.). 433–62. Naples: Istituto Universitario Orientale.

Seneviratne, S. 1981. Kalinga and Andhra: the process of secondary state formation in early India, in *The Study of the State.* Claessen, H. J. M. & Skalnik, P. (eds.). 317–38. The Hague: Mouton.

Shaffer, J. M. 1978. *Prehistoric Baluchistan.* New Delhi: B. R. Publishing.

—. 1992. Indus valley, Baluchistan and the Helmand, in *Chronologies in Old World Archaeology,* vol. 1. Ehrich, R. W. (ed.). 441–46. Chicago: Univ. of Chicago Press.

—. 1993. Reurbanisation: the eastern Punjab and beyond, in *Urban Form and Meaning in South Asia: The Shaping of Cities from Prehistoric to Precolonial Times.* Spodek, H. & Srinivasan, D. M. (eds.). 53–67. Washington D.C.: National Gallery of Art.

Shaffer, J. M. & Thapar, B. K. 1992. Pre-Indus and early Indus cultures of Pakistan and India, in *The History of Civilisations of Central Asia.* Vol. I: The dawn of civilisation: earliest times to 700 BC. Dani, A. H. & Masson, V. M. (eds.). 247–83. Paris: UNESCO.

Sharif, M. & Thapar, B. K. 1992. Food-producing communities in Pakistan and northern India, in *The History of Civilisations of Central Asia.* Vol. I: The dawn of civilisation: earliest times to 700 BC. Dani, A. H. & Masson, V. M. (eds.). 127–52. Paris: UNESCO.

Sharma, A. K. 1982. Excavations at Gufkral 1981. *Puratattva* 11, 19–25.

Sharma, G. R. 1973. Mesolithic lake culture in the Ganga valley. *Proceedings of the Prehistoric Society* 39, 129–46.

Sharma, G. R. & Clark, J. D. 1983. *Palaeoenvironments and Prehistory in the Middle Son Valley.* Allahabad: Abinash Prakashan.

Sharma, G. R., Misra, V. D., Mandal, D., Misra, B. B., & Pal, J. N. 1980. *Beginnings of Agriculture: Excavations at Chopani-Mando, Mahadaha and Mahagara.* Allahabad: Abinash Prakashan.

Singh, G. 1964. A preliminary survey of post-glacial vegetation history of Kashmir. *Palaeobotanist* 12, 72–108.

Singh, P. 2002. The Neolithic cultures of northern and eastern India, in *Indian Archaeology in*

Retrospect. Vol. I: Prehistory: archaeology of South Asia. Settar, S. & Korisettar, R. (eds.). 127–50. New Delhi: Indian Council of Historical Research.

Srivastava, K. M. 1984. The myth of the Aryan invasion of Harappan towns, in *Frontiers of the Indus Civilisation*. Lal, B. B. & Gupta, S. P. (eds.). 437–43. New Delhi: Books & Books.

Stacul, G. 1969. Discovery of protohistoric cemeteries in the Chitral valley (West Pakistan). *East and West* 19, 92–99.

—. 1977. Dwelling and storage-pits at Loebanr III, Swat, Pakistan. *East and West* 27, 227–53.

—. 1987. *Prehistoric and Protohistoric Swat, Pakistan (c. 3000–1400 BC)*. Rome: Istituto Italiano per il Medio ed Estremo Oriente.

—. 1989. Continuity of forms and traditions at Birkot-ghundai, Swat, in *South Asian Archaeology 1985*. Frifelt, K. & Sorenson, P. (eds.). 321–26. London: Curzon Press.

—. 1994. Neolithic inner Asian traditions in northern Indo-Pakistani valleys, in *South Asian Archaeology 1993*. Parpola, A. & Koskikallio, P. (eds.). 707–14. Helsinki: Suomalainen Tiedeakatemia.

Thapar, R. 1961. *Asoka and the Decline of the Mauryans*. Oxford: Oxford Univ. Press.

Thomas, K. D. 1997. Review of Kennedy et al. 1992. Human skeletal remains from Mahadaha: a Gangetic Mesolithic site. *South Asian Studies* 13, 323–25.

Tosi, M. (ed.). 1983. *Prehistoric Sistan*. Rome: Istituto Italiano per il Medio ed Estremo Oriente.

Varma, R. K., Misra, V. D., Pandey, J. N., & Pal, J. N. 1985. A preliminary report on the excavations at Damdama. *Man and Environment* IX, 45–65.

Wakankar, V. S. & Brooks, R. R. R. 1976. *Stone Age Paintings in India*. Bombay: Taraporewala and Sons.

Weber, S. A. 1991. *Plants and Harappan Subsistence: An Example of Stability and Change from Rojdi*. New Delhi: Oxford & IBH.

—. 1999. Seeds of urbanisation: palaeoethnobotany and the Indus civilisation. *Antiquity* 73, 813–26.

Wheeler, R. E. M. 1946. Arikamedu: an Indo-Roman trading-station on the east coast of India. *Ancient India* 2, 17–124.

—. 1947. Harappan Chronology and the Rigveda. *Ancient India* 3, 78–82.

—. 1953. *The Indus Civilisation*. Cambridge: Cambridge Univ. Press.

—. 1954. *Rome Beyond the Imperial Frontiers*. Harmondsworth: Pelican.

—. 1959. *Early India and Pakistan to Ashoka*. London: Thames & Hudson.

—. 1962. *Charsada: A Metropolis on the Northwest Frontier*. London: British Academy.

—. 1968. *Flames over Persepolis*. London: Weidenfeld & Nicolson.

—. 1976. *My Archaeological Mission to India and Pakistan*. London: Thames & Hudson.

CHAPTER 15: COMPLEX SOCIETIES OF EAST AND SOUTHEAST ASIA

Anthony, D. W. 1998. The opening of the Eurasian steppe at 2000 BCE, in *The Bronze Age and Early Iron Age Peoples of Eastern Central Asia*. Mair, V. H. (ed.). 94–113. Philadelphia: Institute for the Study of Man and the Univ. of Pennsylvania Museum Publications.

Aston, W. G. 1995. *Nihongi: Chronicles of Japan from the Earliest Times to A.D. 697*. Rutland, Vermont, & Tokyo: Tuttle.

Bagley, R. W. 1977. P'an-lung-ch'eng: a Shang city in Hupei. *Artibus Asiae* 39, 165–219.

—. 1990. A Shang city in Sichuan Province. *Orientations* 21, 52–67.

—. 1993. An early Bronze Age tomb in Jiangxi Province. *Orientations* 24, 20–36.

—. 1999. Shang archaeology, in *The Cambridge History of Ancient China*. Loewe, M. & Shaughnessy, E. L. (eds.). 124–231. Cambridge: Cambridge Univ. Press.

—. (ed.). 2001. *Ancient Sichuan*. Seattle & Princeton: Seattle Art Museum.

Bailey, H. 1970. Saka-studies: the ancient kingdom of Khotan. *Iran* 8, 65–72.

Barnes, G. 1988. *Prehistoric Yamato: Archaeology of the First Japanese State*. Ann Arbor: Univ. of Michigan Press.

—. 2001. *State Formation in Korea*. London: Curzon Press.

Bielenstein, H. 1954. The restoration of the Han Dynasty. *BMFEA* 26, 9–20.

Brown, D. M. 1993. *The Cambridge History of Japan*. Cambridge: Cambridge Univ. Press.

Brown, R. L. 1996. The Dvaravati wheels of the law and Indianisation in Southeast Asia. *Studies in Asian Art and Archaeology* 18. Leiden: Brill.

Cœdès, G. 1966. *Angkor: An Introduction*. Hong Kong: Oxford Univ. Press.

—. 1968. *The Indianized States of Southeast Asia*. Honolulu: Univ. of Hawaii Press.

Dematte, P. 1999. Longshan-era urbanism: the role of cities in predynastic China. *Asian Perspectives* 38, 119–53.

Donovan, D. G., Kukui, H., & Itoh, T. 1998. Perspective on the Pyu landscape. *Southeast Asian Studies* 36, 19–126.

Fitzgerald-Huber, L. G. 1995. Qijia and Erlitou: the question of contacts with distant cultures. *Early China* 20, 17–58.

Gao Dalun. 2001. Bronze ritual artifacts of the Shu culture: a preliminary survey. *Orientations* 32, 45–51.

Gaucher, J. 2002. Archaeology and town planning in Southeast Asia: new archaeological data on the urban space of the capital city of Angkor Thom, in *Fishbones as Glittering Emblems*. Karlström, A. & Källén, A. (eds.). 233–42. Stockholm: Museum of Far Eastern Antiquities.

Glover, I. C. & Yamagata, M. 1998. Excavations at Tra Kieu, Vietnam, 1993, in *Southeast Asian Archaeology 1994*, vol. 1. Manguin, P.-Y. (ed.). 75–94. Hull: Centre for Southeast Asian Studies.

Groslier, B. P. 1958. Angkor et le Cambodge au XVIᵉ Siècle d'après les Sources Portugaises et Espagnoles. *Annales du Musée Guimet* 63.

Guillon, E. 2001. *Cham Art*. London: Thames & Hudson.

Guo Da-Shun. 1995. Lower Xiajiadian Culture, in *The Archaeology of Northeast China Beyond the Great Wall*. Nelson, S. (ed.). 171–81. London: Routledge.

Gutman, P. 2001. *Burma's Lost Kingdoms: Splendours of Arakan*. Bangkok: Orchid Press.

Higham, C. F. W. 2001. *The Civilization of Angkor*. London: Weidenfeld & Nicholson.

Hsu Cho-Yun. 1980. *Han Agriculture: The Formation of Early Chinese Agrarian Economy*. Seattle: Univ. of Washington Press.

Hsu Cho-Yun & Linduff, K. M. 1988. *Western Zhou Civilization*. New Haven: Yale Univ. Press.

Huang Xuanpei, Song Jian, & Sun Weichang. 1992.

Gems of the Liangzhu Culture. Hong Kong: Hong Kong Museum of History.

Hyung Il Pai. 2000. *Constructing Korean Origins*. Cambridge, MA: Harvard Univ. Press.

Jay Xu. 2001. Reconstructing Sanxingdui imagery: some speculations. *Orientations* 32, 32–44.

Keightley, D. N. 1978. *Sources of Shang History: The Oracle Bones of Bronze Age China*. Berkeley: Univ. of California Press.

Kiyotari, T. (ed.). 1987. *Recent Archaeological Discoveries in Japan*. Tokyo: Centre for East Asian Cultural Studies.

Lewis, M. E. 1999. Warring states: political history, in *The Cambridge History of Ancient China*. Loewe, M. & Shaughnessy, E. L. (eds.). 587–650. Cambridge: Cambridge Univ. Press.

Li Xueqin. 1985. *Eastern Zhou and Qin Civilizations*. New Haven: Yale Univ. Press.

Loewe, M. 1982. *Chinese Ideas of Life and Death*. London: Allen & Unwin.

Lubotsky, A. 1998. Tocharian loanwords in Old Chinese: chariots, chariot gear, and town building, in *The Bronze Age and Early Iron Age Peoples of Eastern Central Asia*. Mair, V. H. (ed.). 379–90. Philadelphia: Institute for the Study of Man and the Univ. of Pennsylvania Museum Publications.

Maspero, M. G. 1928. *Le Royaume de Champa*. Paris & Brussels: Librairie Nationale d'Art et d'Histoire.

Nelson, S. M. 1993. *The Archaeology of Korea*. Cambridge: Cambridge Univ. Press.

—. 1995. Ritualized pigs and the origins of complex society: hypotheses regarding the Hongshan Culture. *Early China* 20, 1–16.

Nienhauser, W. H. (ed.). 1994. *The Grand Scribe's Records*. Vol. 1: The basic annals of Pre-Han China by Ssu-ma Ch'ien. Bloomington & Indianapolis: Indiana Univ. Press.

Pearson, R. J. (ed.). 1986. *Windows on the Japanese Past: Studies in Archaeology and Prehistory*. Ann Arbor: Univ. of Michigan Press.

Portal, J. 2000. *Korea: Art and Archaeology*. London: British Museum Press.

Pottier, C. 2000. Some evidence of an inter-relationship between hydraulic features and rice field patterns at Angkor during ancient times. *Journal of Sophia Asian Studies* 18, 99–120.

Puett, M. 1998. China in early Eurasian history: a brief review of recent scholarship on the issue, in *The Bronze Age and Early Iron Age Peoples of Eastern Central Asia*. Mair, V. H. (ed.). 699–715. Philadelphia: Institute for the Study of Man and the Univ. of Pennsylvania Museum Publications.

Rawson, J. 1989. Statesmen or barbarians? The Western Zhou as seen through their bronzes. *Proceedings of the British Academy* 75, 71–95.

—. 1999. Western Zhou archaeology, in *The Cambridge History of Ancient China*. Loewe, M. & Shaughnessy, E. L. (eds.). 352–449. Cambridge: Cambridge Univ. Press.

Rhie, M. M. 1999. *Later Han, Three Kingdoms and Western Chin in China and Bactria to Shan-shan*. Leiden: Brill.

Sage, S. F. 1992. *Ancient Sichuan and the Unification of China*. Albany: SUNY Press.

Sedov, L. A. 1978. Angkor: society and state, in *The Early State*. Claessen, H. J. M. & Skalník, P. (eds.). 111–30. The Hague: Mouton.

Shaughnessey, E. L. 1986. On the authenticity of the Bamboo Annals. *Harvard Journal of Asiatic Studies* 46, 149–80.

—. 1991. *Sources of Western Zhou History*. Berkeley: Univ. of California Press.

Skilling, P. 2003. Dvaravati: recent revelations and research, in *Dedications to Her Royal Highness Princess Galyani Vadhana Krom Luang Naradhiwas Rajanagarindra on her 80th Birthday*. 87–112. Bangkok: Siam Society.

Southworth, W. 2000. Notes on the political geography of Campa in Central Vietnam during the late 8th and early 9th century, in *Southeast Asian Archaeology 1998*. Lobo, W. & Reimann, S. (eds.). 237–44. Hull: Centre for South-East Asian Studies, Univ. of Hull & Ethnologisches Museum, Staatliche Museum zu Berlin.

Stargardt, J. 1990. *The Ancient Pyu of Burma*. Vol. 1: Early Pyu cities in a man-made landscape. Cambridge: PACSEA Cambridge and ISEAS Singapore.

Stein, A. 1907. *Ancient Khotan*. Oxford: Clarendon Press.

Totman, C. 2000. *A History of Japan*. Oxford: Blackwell.

Twitchet, D. & Loewe, M. (eds.). 1986. *The Cambridge History of China*. Vol. I: The Ch'in and Han empires, 221 B.C.–A.D. 220. Cambridge: Cambridge Univ. Press.

Underhill, A. 1994. Variation in settlements during the Longshan Period of northern China. *Asian Perspectives* 33, 197–228.

Vickery, M. 1998. *Society, Economics and Politics in Pre-Angkor Cambodia*. Tokyo: Centre for East Asian Cultural Studies for Unesco.

von Falkenausen, L. 1999. The waning of the Bronze Age: material and social developments, 770–481 B.C., in *The Cambridge History of Ancient China*. Loewe, M. & Shaughnessy, E. L. (eds.). 450–544. Cambridge: Cambridge Univ. Press.

Wang Zhongshu. 1982. *Han Civilization*. New Haven: Yale Univ. Press.

Wu Hung. 1992. Art in its ritual context: rethinking Mawangdui. *Early China* 17, 111–45.

—. 1995. *Monumentality in Early Chinese Art and Architecture*. Stanford: Stanford Univ. Press.

Zheng Zhenxiang. 1996. The royal consort Fu Hao and her tomb, in *Mysteries of Ancient China*. Rawson, J. (ed.). 240–47. New York: Braziller.

Zhou Baquan, Hu Youyan, & Lu Benshan. 1988. Ancient copper mining and smelting at Tonglushan, Daye, in *The Beginning of the Use of Metals and Alloys*. Maddin, R. (ed.). 125–9. Cambridge, MA: MIT Press.

CHAPTER 16: MESOAMERICAN CIVILIZATION

Alva, W. & Donnan, C. 1993. *Royal Tombs of Sipan*. Los Angeles: Fowler Museum of Culture History, Univ. of California.

Anawalt, P. 1997. Traders of the Ecuadorian littoral. *Archaeology* 50, 48–52.

Anawalt, P. & Berdan, F. 1992. *The Codex Mendoza: Scientific American* (June), 71–79.

Ball, J. & Taschek, J. 2003. Reconsidering the Belize Valley Preclassic. *Ancient Mesoamerica* 14 (2), 179–218.

Beekman, C. 2000. The correspondence of regional patterns and local strategies in Formative to Classic Period West Mexico. *Journal of Anthropological Archaeology* 18, 385–412.

Benson, E. & de la Fuente, B. (eds.). 1996. *Olmec Art of Ancient Mexico*, Washington D.C.: National Gallery of Art.

Berdan, F. F., Blanton, R. E., Boone, E. H., Hodge, M. G., Smith, M. E., & Umberger, E. 1996. *Aztec Imperial Strategies*. Washington D.C.: Dumbarton Oaks.

Berrin, K. & Pasztory, E. (eds.). 1993. *Teotihuacán: Art from the City of the Gods*. New York & London: Thames & Hudson.

Blake, M. 1991. An emerging early formative chiefdom at Paso de la Amada, Chiapas, Mexico, in *The Formation of Complex Society in Southeastern Mesoamerica*. Fowler, W. L. (ed.). 27–46. Boca Raton: CRC Press.

Blanton, R. E., Kowalewski, S. A., Feinman, G., & Finsten, L. 1993. *Ancient Mesoamerica*. New York: Cambridge Univ. Press.

Boone, E. H. 2000. *Stories in Red and Black*. Austin: Univ. of Texas Press.

Calnek, E. 1972. The internal structure of Tenochtitlán, in *The Valley of Mexico*. Wolf, E. (ed.). 287–303. Santa Fe: School of American Research Press.

Clark, J. E. & Pye, M. E. 2000. *Olmec Art and Archaeology in Mesoamerica*. Washington D.C.: National Gallery of Art.

Coe, M. 1964. The chinampas of Mexico. *Scientific American* 211 (1), 90–98.

—. 1992. *Breaking the Maya Code*. London & New York: Thames & Hudson.

—. 2004. *The Maya*. (7th ed.). London & New York, Thames & Hudson.

Cortés, H. 1986. *Letters From Mexico*. Ed. & transl. Pagden, A. New Haven: Yale Univ. Press.

Cyphers, A. 1996. Reconstructing Olmec life at San Lorenzo, in *Olmec Art of Ancient Mexico*. Benson, E. & de la Fuente, B. (eds.). 61–72. Washington D.C.: National Gallery of Art.

Dahlin, B. 2000. The barricade and catastrophic abandonment of Chinchucmil, Yucatan, Mexico. *Latin American Antiquity* 11 (3), 282–98.

de Landa, D. Ed. & annotated Tozzer, A. 1941. *Relacion de las Cosas de Yucatán*. Papers of the Peabody Museum of Archaeology and Ethnology, vol. 18. Cambridge, MA: Harvard Univ. Press.

Diaz, B. 1963. *The Conquest of New Spain*. Baltimore: Penguin.

Diehl, R. 1996. The Olmec world, in *Olmec Art of Ancient Mexico*. Benson, E. & de la Fuente, B. (eds.). 29–34. Washington D.C.: National Gallery of Art.

—. 2000. The precolumbian cultures of the Gulf Coast, in *The Cambridge History of the Native Peoples of the Americas*, vol. 2, part 1. Adams, R. E. W. & Murdo, M. (eds.). 156–96. New York: Cambridge Univ. Press.

Durán, D. 1971. (1st ed. 1579). *The History of the Indies of New Spain*. Transl. & ed. Heyden, D. & Horcasitas, F. Norman: Univ. of Oklahoma Press.

—. 1994. (1st ed. 1579). *Book of the Gods and Rites and the Ancient Calendar*. Transl. & ed. Heyden, D. & Horcasitas, F. Norman: Univ. of Oklahoma Press.

Evans, S. T. 1998. Sexual politics in the Aztec palace: public, private, and profane. *RES* 33, 167–83.

—. 2004. *Ancient Mexico and Central America: Archaeology and Culture History*. London & New York: Thames & Hudson.

Flannery, K. V. & Marcus, J. 2003. The origin of war: new 14C dates from ancient Mexico. *Proceedings of the National Academy of Sciences (USA)* 100, 11801–05.

Fowler, W. R. 1989. *The Cultural Evolution of Ancient Nahua Civilization: The Pipil-Nacarao of Central America*. Norman: Univ. of Oklahoma Press.

García Cook, A. & Carrión, B. L. M. 1998. Cantona: Urbe prehispánica en el altiplano central de Mexico. *Latin America Antiquity* 9, 191–216.

Gill, R. 2000. *The Great Maya Droughts*. Albuquerque: Univ. of New Mexico Press.

Gonzales Lauck, R. 1996. La Venta: an Olmec capital, in *Olmec Art of Ancient Mexico*. Benson, E. & de la Fuente, B. (eds.). 73–82. Washington D.C.: National Gallery of Art.

Grove, D. 1984. *Chalcatzingo*. London: Thames & Hudson.

—. 2000. The preclassic societies of the central highlands of Mesoamerica, in *The Cambridge History of the Native Peoples of the Americas*, vol. 2, part 1. Adams, R. E. W. & Murdo, M. (eds.). 122–55. New York: Cambridge Univ. Press.

Grube, N. (ed.). 2001. *Maya: Divine Kings of the Rain Forest*. Cologne: Könemann.

Hammond, N. 1999. The genesis of hierarchy: mortuary and offertory ritual in the Pre-Classic at Cuello, Belize, in *Social Patterns in Pre-Classic Mesoamerica*. Grove, D. & Joyce, R. 49–66. Washington D.C.: Dumbarton Oaks.

Harrison, P. 1999. *The Lords of Tikal*. London & New York: Thames & Hudson.

Hassig, R. 1985. *Trade, Tribute and Transportation*. Norman: Univ. of Oklahoma Press.

—. 1994. *Mexico and the Spanish Conquest*. New York: Longman.

Hicks, F. 1986. Prehispanic background of colonial political and economic organization in central Mexico, in *Handbook of Middle American Indians Supplement 4*, 35–54. Austin: Univ. of Texas Press.

Hill, W. D., Blake, M., & Clark, J. 1998. Ball court design dates back 3,400 years. *Nature* 392, 878–79.

Hirth, K. 2000. *Ancient Urbanism at Xochicalco*, vols. 1–2. Salt Lake City: Univ. of Utah Press.

Hodge, M. 1996. Political organization of the central provinces, in *Aztec Imperial Strategies*. Berdan, F. F., Blanton, R. E., Boone, E. H., Hodge, M. G., Smith, M. E., & Umberger, E. 17–46. Washington D.C.: Dumbarton Oaks.

Hosler, D. 1988. Ancient west Mexican metallurgy: a technological chronology. *Journal of Field Archaeology* 15, 191–217.

—. 1994. *The Sounds and Colors of Power: The Sacred Metallurgical Technology of Ancient West Mexico*. Cambridge, MA: MIT Press.

Houston, S., Chinchilla M., O., & Stuart, D. (eds.). 2001. *The Decipherment of Ancient Maya Writing*. Norman: Univ. of Oklahoma Press.

Houston, S., Robertson, J., & Stuart, D. 2000. The language of Classic Maya inscriptions. *Current Anthropology* 41 (3), 344–45.

Iltis, H. H. 2000. Homeotic sexual translocations and the origin of maize (*Zea mays*, Poaceae): a new look at an old problem. *Economic Botany* 54 (1), 7–42.

Inomata, T. & Houston, S. (eds.). 2001. *Royal Courts of the Classic Maya*, vols. 1–2. Boulder: Westview Press.

Jones, G. D. 1998. *The Conquest of the Last Itzá Kingdom*. Stanford: Stanford Univ. Press.

Lecthman, H. N. 1984. Pre-Columbian surface metallurgy. *Scientific American* 250 (6), 56–63.

Marcus, J. 1992. *Mesoamerican Writing Systems*. Princeton: Princeton Univ. Press.

Marcus, J. & Flannery, K. 1996. *Zapotec Civilization*.

London & New York: Thames & Hudson.

Martin, Simon, & Grube, N. 1995. Maya superstates. *Archaeology* 48 (6), 41–46.

—. 2000. *Chronicle of the Maya Kings and Queens.* London & New York: Thames & Hudson.

Mastache, A. G., Cobean, R., & Healan, D. 2002. *Ancient Tollan: Tula and the Toltec Heartland.* Boulder: Univ. of Colorado Press.

Matheny, R. 1986. Investigations at El Mirador, Peten, Guatemala. *National Geographic Research* 2, 332–53.

Matsuoka, Y., Vigouroux, Y., Goodman, M. M., Sanchez G. J., Buckler, E., & Doebley, J. 2002. A single domestication for maize shown by multilocus microsatellite genotyping. *Proceedings of the National Academy of Sciences (USA)* 99 (9), 6080–84.

McVicker, D. 1985. The 'Mayanized' Mexicans. *American Antiquity* 50, 82–101.

Milbrath, S. & Peraza Lope, C. 2003. Revisiting Mayapan. *Ancient Mesoamerica* 14 (1), 1–46.

Miller, M. & Martin, S. (eds.). 2004. *Courtly Art of the Ancient Maya.* London & New York: Thames & Hudson.

Millon, R. 1988. The last years of Teotihuacán dominance, in *The Collapse of Ancient States and Civilizations.* Yoffee, N. & Cowgill, G. (eds.). 102–64. Tucson: Univ. of Arizona Press.

Newsome, E. A. 2001. *Trees of Paradise and Pillars of the World: The Serial Stela Cycle of "18-Rabbit-God K," King of Copán.* Austin: Univ. of Texas Press.

Pasztory, E. 1998. *Precolumbian Art.* New York: Cambridge Univ. Press.

Piperno, D. R. & Flannery, K. V. 2001. The earliest archaeological maize (Zea mays) from highland Mexico: new accelerator mass spectrometry dates and their implications. *Proceedings of the National Academy of Sciences (USA)* 98, 2101.

Pohl, M. E. D., Pope, K. O., Jones, J. G., Jacob, J., Piperno, D., de France, S., Lentz, D. L., Gifford, J., Danforth, M., & Josserand, J. K. 1996. Early agriculture in the Maya lowlands. *Latin American Antiquity* 7 (4), 355–72.

Pollard, H. P. 1993. *Tariacuri's Legacy: The Prehispanic Tarascan State.* Norman: Univ. of Oklahoma Press.

Pope, K. O., Pohl, M. E. D., Jones, J. G., Lentz, D. L., von Nagy, C., Varga, F. J., & Quitmyer, I. R. 2001. Origin and environmental settings of ancient agriculture in the lowlands of Mesoamerica. *Science* 292, 1370–73.

Prem, H. J. (ed.). 1994. *Hidden Among the Hills.* Mockmuhl: Verlag von Flemming.

Restall, M. 1997. *The Maya World.* Stanford: Stanford Univ. Press.

Roys, R. 1965. Lowland Maya native society at Spanish contact, in *Handbook of Middle American Indians*, vol. 3, 659–78. Austin: Univ. of Texas Press.

Sabloff, J., Andrews, E., & Wyllys, V. (eds.). 1986. *Late Lowland Maya Civilization.* Santa Fe: School of American Research.

Sanders, W. T. 1972. Population, agricultural history, and societal evolution in Mesoamerica, in *Population Growth: Anthropological Implications.* Spooner, B. (ed.). 101–53. Cambridge: MIT Press.

Sanders, W. T. & Webster, D. 1988. The Mesoamerican urban tradition. *American Anthropologist* 90 (3), 521–46.

Sanders, W. T., Mastache, G. & Cobean, R. (eds.). 2003. *Urbanism in Mesoamerica*, vol. 1. Mexico City: Instituto Nacional de Antropologia e Historia & Pennsylvania State Univ.

Sanders, W. T., Parsons, J. R., & Santley, R. F. 1979. *The Basin of Mexico.* New York: Academic Press.

Santley, R. S. 1994. The economy of ancient Matacapan. *Ancient Mesoamerica* 5, 243–66.

Sharer, R. 1994. *The Ancient Maya.* Stanford: Stanford Univ. Press.

—. 2000. The Maya highlands and the adjacent Pacific coast, in *The Cambridge History of the Native Peoples of the Americas*, vol. 2, part 1. Adams, R. E. W. & Murdo, M. (eds.). 449–99. New York: Cambridge Univ. Press.

Sheets, P. 1990. *The Cerén Site.* Fort Worth: Harcourt Brace Jovanovich.

Smith, M. 1989. Cities, towns, and urbanism: comment on Sanders and Webster. *American Anthropologist* 91 (2), 454–60.

Smith, M. & Berdan, F. (eds.). 2003. *The Postclassic Mesoamerican World.* Salt Lake City: Univ. of Utah Press.

Stuart, D. 2000. The arrival of strangers, in *Mesoamerica's Classic Heritage: From Teotihuacán to the Aztecs.* Carrasco, D., Jones, L., & Sessions, S. (eds.). 465–513. Boulder: Univ. of Colorado Press.

Sugiyama, S. 1998. Termination programs and prehistoric looting at the Feathered Serpent Pyramid in Teotihuacán, Mexico, in *The Sowing and the Dawning.* Mock, S. B. (ed.). 147–64. Albuquerque: Univ. of New Mexico Press.

Taube, K. 1996. The Olmec maize god: the face of corn in formative Mesoamerica. *RES* vols. 29–30, 39–82.

—. 2000. *The Writing System of Teotihuacán.* Washington D.C.: Center for Ancient American Studies.

Webster, D. 2000. The not so peaceful civilization: a review of Maya war. *Journal of World Prehistory* 14 (1), 65–117.

—. 2002. *The Fall of the Ancient Maya.* London & New York: Thames & Hudson.

Weigand, P. C. 2001a. West Mexico, in *Archaeology of Ancient Mexico and Central America.* Evans, S. T. & Webster, D. (eds.). 818–24. New York: Garland Publishing.

—. 2001b. Teuchitlan tradition, in *Archaeology of Ancient Mexico and Central America.* Evans, S. T. & Webster, D. (eds.) 738–41. New York: Garland Publishing.

Whitmore, T. & Turner II, B. L. 1992. Landscapes of cultivation in Mesoamerica on the eve of the conquest. *Annals of the Association of American Geographers* 82 (3), 386–402.

Whittington, E. M. (ed.). 2001. *The Sport of Life and Death.* London & New York: Thames & Hudson.

CHAPTER 17: FROM VILLAGE TO EMPIRE IN SOUTH AMERICA

Aihkenvald, A. 1999. The Arawak language family, in *The Amazonian Languages.* Dixon, R. W. & Aikhenvald, A. (eds.). 65–106. Cambridge: Cambrdige Univ. Press.

Albarracin-Jordan, J. 1996. *Tiwanaku: Arqueología Regional y Dinamica Segmentaria.* La Paz: Editores Plural.

Alegría, R. E. 1983. *Ball Courts and Ceremonial Plazas in the West Indies.* New Haven: Yale Univ. Publications in Anthropology 79.

Alva, W. & Donnan, C. B. 1993. *Royal Tombs of Sipan.* Los Angeles: Univ. of California Press.

Arriaza, B. 1995. *Beyond Death: The Chinchorro Mummies of Ancient Chile.* Washington D.C.: Smithsonian Institution Press.

Aveni, A. (ed.). 1991. *The Lines of Nazca.* Philadelphia: American Philosophical Society.

Bauer, B. 1992. *The Development of the Inca State.* Austin: Univ. of Texas Press.

—. 1998. *The Sacred Landscape of the Inca: The Cuzco Ceque System.* Austin: Univ. of Texas Press.

Bauer, B. & Covey, A. 2002. Processes of state formation in the Inca heartland (Cuzco Peru). *American Anthropologist* 104 (3), 846–64.

Bawden, G. 1996. *The Moche.* Cambridge: Blackwell.

Berman, M. 1994. *Lukurmata: Household Archaeology in Prehispanic Bolivia*: Princeton: Princeton Univ. Press.

Boomert, A. 2000. *Trinidad, Tobago and the Lower Orinoco Interaction Sphere: An Archaeological/Ethnohistorical Study.* Alkmaar: Cairi Publications.

Burger, R. 1984. *The Prehistoric Occupation of Chavin de Huantar, Peru.* Berkeley: Univ. of California Press.

—. 1992. *Chavin and the Origins of Andean Civilization.* London & New York: Thames & Hudson.

Carneiro, R. L. 1970. A theory of the origin of the state. *Science* 169, 733–38.

Cobo, B. 1990. *Inca Religion and Customs [1653].* Transl. Hamilton, R. Austin: Univ. of Texas Press.

Colinvaux, P. 1998. Ice-age Amazon and the problem of diversity: new interpretations of Pleistocene Amazonia. *Review of Archaeology* 19, 1–10

D'Altroy, T. N. 1992. *Provincial Power in the Inka Empire.* Washington D.C.: Smithsonian Institution Press.

de Cieza de Leon, P. 1976. *The Incas of Pedro Cieza de Leon* [Part 1, 1553 & Part 2, 1554]. Transl. de Onis, H. Norman: Univ. of Oklahoma Press.

Denevan, W. 1966. The aboriginal cultural geography of the Llanos de Mojos of Bolivia. *Ibero-americana* no. 48. Berkeley: Univ. of California Press.

—. 2001. *The Cultivated Landscapes of South America.* Oxford: Oxford Univ. Press.

Dillehay, T. (ed.). 1995. *Tombs for the Living: Andean Mortuary Practices.* Washington D.C.: Dumbarton Oaks.

Donnan, C. 1978. *Moche Art of Peru.* Los Angeles: Univ. of California.

—. 1993. *Ceramics of Ancient Peru.* Los Angeles: Fowler Museum of Cultural History, Univ. of California at Los Angeles.

—. (ed.). 1985. *Early Ceremonial Architecture in the Andes.* Washington D.C.: Dumbarton Oaks.

Erickson, C. 1995. Archaeological methods for the study of landscapes of the Llanos de Mojos in the Bolivian Amazon, in *Archaeology in the Lowland American Tropics: Current Analytical Methods and Applications.* Stahl, P. (ed.). 66–95. Cambridge: Cambridge Univ. Press.

—. 2000. An artificial landscape-scale fishery in the Bolivian Amazon. *Nature* 408 (9 November), 190–93.

Evans, C. & Meggers, B. 1968. *Archaeological Investigations in the Rio Napo, Eastern Ecuador.* Washington D.C.: Smithsonian Contributions to Anthropology, No. 6. Smithsonian Institution.

Ford, J. A. 1969. *A Comparison of Formative Cultures in the Americas: Diffusion or the Psychic Unity of Man.* Washington D.C.: Smithsonian Institution Press.

Frost, P. 1989. *Exploring Cuzco*. Lima: Nuevas Imagenes, S.A.

Gasparini, G. & Margolies, L. 1980. *Inca Architecture*. Transl. Lyon, P. J. Bloomington: Indiana Univ. Press.

Goldstein, P. 1993. Tiwanaku temples and state expansion: a Tiwanaku sunken-court temple in Moquegua, Peru. *Latin American Antiquity* 4 (1), 22–47.

Gomes, D. 2001. Santarém: symbolism and power in the tropical forest, in *The Unknown Amazon: Culture in Nature in Ancient Brazil*. McEwan, C., Neves, E., & Barreto, C. (eds.). 134–55. London: British Museum Press.

Grieder, T. A., Bueno, A., Smith, C., & Molina, R. 1988. *La Galgada, Peru: A Preceramic Culture in Transition*. Austin: Univ. of Texas Press.

Guapindaia, V. 2001. Encountering the ancestors: the Maracá urns, in *The Unknown Amazon: Culture in Nature in Ancient Brazil*. McEwan, C., Neves, E., & Barreto, C. (eds.). 156–75. London: British Museum Press.

Hastorf, C. A. 1993. *Agriculture and the Onset of Political Inequity Before the Inca*. Cambridge: Cambridge Univ. Press.

Heckenberger, M. J. 2002. Rethinking the Arawakan diaspora: hierarchy, regionality, and the Amazonian Formative, in *Comparative Arawakan Histories: Rethinking Culture Area and Language Group in Amazonia*. Hill, J. & Santos-Granero, F. (eds.). 99–121. Urbana: Univ. of Illinois Press.

Heckenberger, M. J., Neves, E. G., & Petersen, J. B. 1998. Onde surgem os modelos? As Origens e Expansões Tupi na Amazônia Central. *Revista de Antropologia* (São Paulo) 41, 69–96.

Heckenberger, M. J., Petersen, J. B., & Neves, E. G. 1999. Village permanence in Amazonia: two archaeological examples from Brazil. *Latin American Antiquity* 10, 535–76.

Hemming, J. & Ranney, E. 1992. *Monuments of the Inca*. Albuquerque: Univ. of New Mexico Press.

Heyerdahl, T., Sandweiss, D., & Navaez, A. 1995. *Pyramids of Tucume: The Quest for Peru's Forgotten City*. London & New York: Thames & Hudson.

Hyslop, J. 1990. *Inka Settlement Planning*. Austin: Univ. of Texas Press.

Isbell, W. & McEwan, G. (ed.). 1991. *Huari Administrative Structure: Prehistoric Monumental Architecture and State Government*. Washington D.C.: Dumbarton Oaks.

Kolata, A. L. 1993. *The Tiwanaku: Portrait of an Andean Civilization*. Oxford: Blackwell.

—. (ed.). 1996. *Tiwanaku and its Hinterland: Archaeology and Paleoecology of an Andean Civilization*. Vol. 1: Agroecology. Washington D.C.: Smithsonian Institution Press.

Llagostera, A. 1992. Fishermen on the Pacific Coast of South America. *Andean Past* (3), 87–109.

Lathrap, D. W. 1968. The 'hunting' economies of the tropical forest zone of South America: an attempt at historical perspective, in *Man the Hunter*. Lee, R. B. & DeVore, I. (eds.). 23–29. Chicago: Aldine.

—. 1970. *The Upper Amazon*. London: Praeger.

—. 1977. Our father the cayman, our mother the gourd: Spinden revisited, or a unitary model for the emergence of agriculture in the New World, in *Origins of Agriculture*. Reed, C. A. (ed.). 713–51. The Hague: Mouton.

—. 1985. Jaws: the control of power in the early nuclear American ceremonial center, in *Early Andean Ceremonial Centers*. Donnan, C. (ed.). 241–67. Washington D.C.: Dumbarton Oaks.

Lathrap, D. W., Gebhart-Sayer, A., & Mester, A. M. 1985. Roots of the Shipibo art style: three waves at Imariacocha or there were 'Incas' before the 'Inca.' *Journal of Latin American Lore* 11, 31–119.

Lathrap, D. W., Marcos, J. G., & Zeidler, J. 1977. Rio Alto: an ancient ceremonial center. *Archaeology* 30, 2–13.

Lumbreras, L. 1989. *Chavin de Huantar en el Nacimiento de la Civilización Andina*. Lima: Instituto Andino de Estudios Arqueológicos.

Manzanilla, L. 1992. *Akapana: Una Pirámide en el Centro del Mundo*. Mexico City: Instituto de Investigaciones Antropológicas.

Marcus, J. 1987. *Late Intermediate Occupation at Cerro Azul, Peru*. Ann Arbor: Museum of Anthropology, Univ. of Michigan.

McEwan, G. F. 1987. *The Middle Horizon in the Valley of Cuzco, Peru: The Impact of the Wari Occupation of the Lucre Basin*. Oxford: British Archaeological Reports.

Meggers, B. J. 1996. *Amazonia: Man and Culture in a Counterfeit Paradise*. (2nd ed.). Washington D.C.: Smithsonian Institution Press.

Meggers, B. J. & Evans, C. 1978. Lowland South America and the Antilles, in *Ancient South Americans*. Jennings, J. (ed.). 543–91. San Francisco: W. H. Freeman.

Meggers, B. J., Evans, C., & Estrada, E. 1965. *The Early Formative Period of the Coast of Ecuador: The Valdivia and Machalilla Phases*. Washington D.C.: Smithsonian Contributions to Anthropology.

Moore, J. 1996. *Architecture and Power in the Ancient Andes: The Archaeology of Public Buildings*. Cambridge: Cambridge Univ. Press.

Moran, E. F. 1993. *Through Amazonian Eyes: The Human Ecology of Amazonian Populations*. Iowa City: Univ. of Iowa Press.

Morris, C. & Von Hagen, A. 1992. *The Inka Empire and its Andean Origins*. New York: American Museum of Natural History.

Moseley, M. E. 1975. *The Maritime Foundations of Andean Civilization*. Menlo Park: Cummings Publications.

—. 2001. (Rev. ed.). *The Incas and their Ancestors*. London & New York: Thames & Hudson.

Moseley, M. E. & Cordy-Collins, A. (eds.). 1990. *The Northern Dynasties: Kingship and Statecraft in Chimor*. Washington D.C.: Dumbarton Oaks.

Moseley, M. E. & Day, K. (eds.). 1982. *Chan Chan: Andean Desert City*. Albuquerque: Univ. of New Mexico Press.

Neves, E. G. 2001. Indigenous historical trajectories in the Upper Rio Negro Basin, in *The Unknown Amazon: Culture in Nature in Ancient Brazil*. McEwan, C., Neves, E., & Barreto, C. (eds.). 266–86. London: British Museum Press.

Niles, S. A. 1987. *Callachaca: Style and Status in an Inca Community*. Iowa City: Univ. of Iowa Press.

Oliver, J. R. 1998. *El Centro Ceremonial Caquana, Puerto Riso: Simbolismo Iconográfico, cosmovisión y el Poderío Caciquil Taíno de Borínquen*. Oxford: British Archaeological Reports International Series 727.

—. 2001. The archaeology of forest foraging and agricultural production in Amazonia, in *The Unknown Amazon: Culture in Nature in Ancient Brazil*. McEwan, C., Neves, E., Barreto, C. (eds.). 50–85. London: British Museum Press.

Paul, A. 1990. *Paracas Ritual Attire: Symbols of Authority in Ancient Peru*. Norman: Univ. of Oklahoma Press.

—. (ed.). 1991. *Paracas: Art and Architecture, Object and Context in South Coastal Peru*. Iowa City: Univ. of Iowa Press.

Payne, D. L. 1991. A classification of Maipuran (Arawakian) languages based on shared lexical retentions, in *Handbook of Amazonian Languages*. Derbyshire, D. C. & Pullum, G. K. (eds.). 355–499. The Hague: Mouton.

Pearsall, D. M. 1989. *Paleoethnobotany: A Handbook of Procedures*. San Diego: Academic Press.

Petersen, J. B. 1997. Taino, island Carib, and prehistoric Amerindian economies in the West Indies: tropical forest adaptations to island environments, in *The Indigenous People of the Caribbean*. Wilson, S. M. (ed.). 118–30. Gainesville: Univ. Press of Florida.

Petersen, J. B., Neves, E. G., & Heckenberger, M. J. 2001. Gift from the past: Terra Preta and prehistoric Amerindian occupations in Amazonia, in *The Unknown Amazon: Culture in Nature in Ancient Brazil*. McEwan, C., Barreto, C., & Neves, E. G. (eds.). 86–105. London: British Museum Press.

Pillsbury, J. (ed.). 2001. *Historiographic Guide to Andean Sources in Art History and Archaeology*. Oklahoma: Univ. of Oklahoma Press.

Piperno, D. R. & Pearsall, D. M. 1998. *The Origins of Agriculture in the Lowland Neo Tropics*. San Diego: Academic Press.

Piperno, D. R., Ranere, A. J., Holst, I., & Hansell, P. 2000. Starch grains reveal early root crop horticulture in the Panamanian tropical forest. *Nature* 407, 894–97.

Pozorski, S. & Pozorski, T. 1987. *Early Settlement and Subsistence in the Casma Valley, Peru*. Iowa City: Univ. of Iowa Press.

Prous, A. 1992. *Arqueologia Brasileira*. Brasilia: Editora Universidade de Brasilia.

Reinhard, J. 1991. *Machu Picchu: The Sacred Center*. Lima: Nuevas Imagenes.

Richardson, J. 1996. *People of the Andes*. Washington D.C.: Smithsonian Institution Press.

Roosevelt, A. C. 1991. *Moundbuilders of the Amazon: Geophysical Archaeology on Marajo Island, Brazil*. New York: Academic Press.

—. 1995. Early pottery in the Amazon: twenty years of scholarly obscurity, in *The Emergence of Pottery: Technology and Innovation in Ancient Societies*. Barnet, W. K. & Hoopes, J. (eds.). 115–31. Washington D.C.: Smithsonian Institution Press.

—. 1997. *The Excavations at Corozal, Venezuela: Stratigraphy and Ceramic Seriation*. New Haven: Yale Univ. Publications in Anthropology, 83.

—. 1999. The development of prehistoric complex societies: Amazonia, a tropical forest, in *Complex Societies in the Ancient Tropical World*. Bacus, E. A. & Lucero, L. J. (eds.). 13–34. Archaeological Papers of the American Anthropological Association, Number 9.

Roosevelt, A. C., Houseley, R. A., Imazio da Silveira, M., Maranca, S., & Johnson, R. 1991. Eighth millennium pottery from a prehistoric shell midden in the Brazilian Amazon. *Science* 24, 1621–24.

Rostain, S. 1994. L'occupation amérindienne ancienne du littoral de Guyane. 2 vols. Paris: ORSTOM.

Rouse, I. & Cruxent. J.-M. 1963. *Venezuelan Archaeology*. New Haven: Yale Univ. Press.

Rowe, J. 1962. *Chavin Art: An Inquiry into its Form and Meaning*. New York: Museum of Primitive Art.

Salazar, E. 1993. Traces of the past: archaeology and ethnohistory of Ecuador's Amazon region, in *Amazon Worlds: Peoples and Cultures of Ecuador's Amazon Region*. Patmal, N. & Sosa, C. (eds.). 18-–43. Quito: Sinchi Sacha Foundation.

Santos-Granero, F. 1986. Power, ideology, and the ritual of production in lowland South America. *Man* 21 (4), 657–79.

Schaan, D. P. 1997. *A linguagem Iconográfica de Cerâmica Marajoara. Um estudo de arte pré-histórica na Ilha de Marajó (400–1300 AD)*. Porto Alegre: Edipucrs.

—. 2001. Into the labyrinths of Marajoara pottery: status and cultural identity in prehistoric Amazonia, in *Unknown Amazon: Culture in Nature in Ancient Brazil*. McEwan, C., Barreto, C., Neves, E. (eds.). 108–33. London: British Museum Press.

Schreiber, K. 1992. *Wari Imperialism in Middle Horizon, Peru*. Ann Arbor: Univ. of Michigan Museum of Anthropology.

Shady, R. S. 1997. *La Ciudad Sagrada de Caral-Supe en Los Albones de la Civilización en El Peru*. Lima: Universidad Nacional Mayor de San Marcos.

Silverman, H. 1993. *Cahuachi in the Ancient Nasca World*. Iowa City: Univ. of Iowa Press.

—. 1996. *Ancient Peruvian Art: An Annotated Bibliography*. New York: G. K. Hall & Co.

Silverman, H. & Proulx, D. 2001. *The Nazca*. London: Blackwell.

Spencer, C. S. & Redmond, E. M. 1992. Prehispanic chiefdoms of the western Venezuelan Llanos. *World Archaeology* 24, 134–57.

Stanish, C. 1992. *Ancient Andean Political Economy*. Austin: Univ. of Texas Press.

—. 2003. *Ancient Titicaca*. Berkeley: Univ. of California Press.

Steward, J. H. 1949. South American cultures: an interpretative overview, in *Handbook of South American Indians*. Vol. 5: The comparative ethnology of South American Indians. Steward, J. H. (ed.). 669–772. Bureau of American Ethnology, Bulletin 143. Washington D.C.: Smithsonian Institution Press.

Steward, J. H. & Faron, L. 1959. *Native Peoples of South America*. New York: McGraw Hill.

Stone-Miller, R. 1995. *Art of the Andes: From Chavin to Inca*. London & New York: Thames & Hudson.

Topic, J. 1992. Las huacas de Huamachuco: precisiones en torno a una imagen indígena de un paisaje andino, in *La Persecución del Demonio: Crónica de los Primeros Augustinos en el Norte del Perú*. Deeds, T. V. R. E., Millones, L., Topic, J., & González, J. (eds.). Málaga: Algazara.

Uceda, S., Mujica, E., & Morales, R. (eds.). 1997. *Proyecto Arqueologico Huacas de Sol y de la Luna: Investigaciones en la Huaca de la Luna 1995*. Trujillo: Universidad Nacional de la Libertad.

Urban, G. 1992a. História da cultura Brasileira segundo as línguas nativas, in *História dos Índios do Brasil*. carneiro da Cunha, M. (ed.). 87–102. São Paulo: Companhia das Letras.

Vansina, J. 1990. *Paths in the Rainforest: Towards a History of Political Tradition in Equatorial Africa*. Madison: Univ. of Wisconsin.

Willey, G. 1953. *Prehistoric Settlement Patterns in the Viru Valley, Peru*. Washington D.C.: Smithsonian Institution Press.

Williams Leon, C. 1980. Complejos piramides con planta en U, patron arquitectonico de la costa central. *Revista del Museo Nacional* (1978–80) 44, 95–110.

Woods, W. & McCann, J. 1999. The anthropogenic origin and persistence of Amazonian dark earths. *Yearbook: Conference of Latin American Geographers* 25, 7–14.

Zeidler, J. A. 1991. Maritime exchange in the Early Formative Period of coastal Ecuador: geopolitical origins of uneven development. *Research in Economic Anthropology* 13, 247–68.

—. 2000. Gender, status, and community in Early Formative Valdivia society, in *The Archaeology of Communities: A New World Perspective*. Canuto, M. A. & Yaeger, J. (eds.). 161–81. London: Routledge.

Zuidema, R. T. 1986. *La Civilisation Inca au Cuzco*. Paris: Presses Universitaires de France, College de France.

CHAPTER 18: COMPLEX SOCIETIES OF NORTH AMERICA

Ames, K. M. 2003. The Northwest Coast. *Evolutionary Anthropology* 12, 19–33.

Ames, K. M. & Maschner, H. D. G. 1999. *Peoples of the Northwest Coast: Their Archaeology and Prehistory*. London & New York: Thames & Hudson.

Anderson, D. G. 1994. *The Savannah River Chiefdoms: Political Change in the Late Prehistoric Southeast*. Tuscaloosa: Univ. of Alabama Press.

Archer, D. J. W. 2001. Village patterns and the emergence of ranked society in the Prince Rupert area, in *Perspectives on Northern Northwest Coast Prehistory*. Cybulski, J. S. (ed.). 203–22. Mercury Series 160. Hull, Quebec: Canadian Museum of Civilization.

Arnold, J. E. 1992. Complex hunter-gatherer-fishers of prehistoric California: chiefs, specialists, and maritime adaptations of the Channel Islands. *American Antiquity* 57, 60–84.

—. 2001. Social evolution and the political economy in the northern Channel Islands, in *The Origins of a Pacific Coast Chiefdom: The Chumash of the Channel Islands*. Arnold, J. E. (ed.). 287–96. Salt Lake City: Univ. of Utah Press.

Arnold, J. E. & Green, T. M. 2002. Mortuary ambiguity: the Ventureño Chumash case. *American Antiquity* 67, 760–71.

Arnold, J. E., Walsh, M. R., & Hollimon, S. E. 2004. The archaeology of California. *Journal of Archaeological Research* 12, 1–73.

Bayman, J. M. 2001. The Hohokam of southwest North America. *Journal of World Prehistory* 15, 257–311.

Bell, R. E. 1984. *Prehistory of Oklahoma*. Orlando: Academic Press.

Blakeslee, D. J. 1994. The archaeological context of human skeletons in the northern and central Plains, in *Skeletal Biology in the Great Plains*. Owsley, D. W. & Jantz, R. L. (eds.). 9–32. Washington D.C.: Smithsonian Institution Press.

Blitz, J. H. 1993. *Ancient Chiefdoms of the Tombigbee*. Tuscaloosa: Univ. of Alabama Press.

Brookes, R. L. 1994. Southern Plains cultural complexes, in *Skeletal Biology in the Great Plains*. Owsley, D. W. & Jantz, R. L. (eds.). 33–50. Washington D.C.: Smithsonian Institution Press.

Brown, J. A. 1979. Charnel houses and mortuary crypts: disposal of the dead in the Middle Woodland period, in *Hopewell Archaeology*. Brose,

D. S. & Greber, N. (eds.). 211–19. Kent: Kent State Univ. Press.

—. 1985. The Mississippian period, in *Ancient Art of the American Woodland Indians*. 93–146. New York: Abrams.

—. 1996. *The Spiro Ceremonial Center*, 2 vols. Memoir 29. Ann Arbor: Museum of Anthropology, Univ. of Michigan.

Buikstra, J. E. 1976. *Hopewell in the Lower Illinois Valley*. Scientific Papers 2. Evanston: Northwestern Univ. Archeological Program.

Chapman, C. H. 1980. *The Archaeology of Missouri, II*. Columbia: Univ. of Missouri Press.

Connolly, R. P. 1998. Architectural grammar rules at the Fort Ancient hilltop enclosure, in *Ancient Earthen Enclosures of the Eastern Woodlands*. Mainfort, Jr., R. C. & Sullivan, L. P. (eds.). 85–113. Gainesville: Univ. Press of Florida.

Crown, P. L. 1990. The Hohokam of the American Southwest. *Journal of World Prehistory* 4, 223–55.

—. 1994. *Ceramics and Ideology: Salado Polychrome Pottery*. Albuquerque: Univ. of New Mexico Press.

Cybulski, J. S. 1999. Trauma and warfare at Prince Rupert harbour. *The Midden* 31, 5–7.

Damp, J. E., Hall, S. A., & Smith, S. J. 2002. Early irrigation on the Colorado Plateau near Zuni Pueblo, New Mexico. *American Antiquity* 67, 665–76.

Dean, J. S., Doelle, W. H., & Orcutt, J. D. 1994. Adaptive stress: environment and demography, in *Themes in Southwest Prehistory*. Gumerman, G. (ed.). 53–86. Santa Fe: School of American Research Press.

Dobyns, H. F. 1983. *Their Number Become Thinned*. Knoxville: Univ. of Tennessee Press.

Douglas, M. S. V., Smol, J. P., Savelle, J. M., & Blais, J. M. 2004. Prehistoric Inuit whalers affected Arctic freshwater ecosystems. *Proceedings of the National Academy of Sciences (USA)* 101, 1613–17.

Dragoo, D. W. & Wray, C. F. 1964. Hopewell figurine rediscovered. *American Antiquity* 30, 195–99.

Drass, R. R. 1998. The Southern Plains villagers, in *Archaeology on the Great Plains*. Wood. W. R. (ed.). 415–55. Lawrence: Univ. Press of Kansas.

Duff, A. I. & Wilshusen, R. H. 2000. Prehistoric population dynamics in the northern San Juan region, A.D. 950–1300. *Kiva* 65, 167–90.

Dumond, D. E. 1987. *The Eskimos and Aleuts*. (Rev. ed.). London: Thames & Hudson.

Essenpreis, P. S. & Moseley, M. E. 1984. Fort Ancient: citadel or coliseum? *Field Museum of Natural History Bulletin* 55, 5–10, 20–26.

Fish, S. K. & Fish, P. R. 2000. The institutional contexts of Hohokam complexity and inequality, in *Alternative Leadership Strategies in the Prehispanic Southwest*. Mills, B. (ed.). 154–67. Tucson: Univ. of Arizona Press.

Fitzhugh, W. W. 1994. Staffe Island 1 and the northern Labrador Dorset-Thule succession, in *Threads of Arctic Prehistory: Papers in Honour of William E. Taylor, Jr*. Morrison, D. & Pilon, J.-L. (eds.). 239–68. Mercury Series 149. Hull, Quebec: Canadian Museum of Civilization.

Force, E. R., Vivian, R. G., Windes, T. C., & Dean, J. S. 2002. *Relation of 'Bonito' Paleo-Channels and Base-Level Variations to Anasazi Occupation, Chaco Canyon, New Mexico*. Arizona State Museum Archaeological Series 194. Tucson: Univ. of Arizona.

Fowler, M. L. 1997. *The Cahokia Atlas: A Historical*

Atlas of Cahokia Archaeology. (Revised ed.). Illinois Transportation Archaeological Research Program. Urbana: Univ. of Illinois.

Fowler, M. L., Rose, J., Vander Leest, B., & Ahler, S. R. 1999. *The Mound 72 Area: Dedicated and Sacred Space in Early Cahokia.* Reports of Investigations 54. Springfield: Illinois State Museum.

Fritz, G. J. 1990. Multiple pathways to farming in precontact eastern North America. *Journal of World Prehistory* 4, 387–435.

Gamble, L. H., Walker, P. L., & Russell, G. S. 2001. An integrative approach to mortuary analysis: social and symbolic dimensions of Chumash burial practices. *American Antiquity* 66, 185–212.

Grant, C. 1978. Chumash: Introduction, in *California.* Handbook of North American Indians, vol. 8. Heizer, R. F. (ed.). 505–08. Washington D.C.: Smithsonian Institution Press.

Greber, N. 1983. *Recent Excavations at the Edwin Harness Mound.* MCJA Special Paper 5. Kent: Kent State Univ. Press.

Greber, N. & Ruhl, K. C. 1989. *The Hopewell Site: A Contemporary Analysis Based on the Work of Charles C. Willoughby.* Boulder: Westview Press.

Gregg, M. L. 1975. A population estimate for Cahokia, in *Perspectives in Cahokia Archaeology.* 126–36. Bulletin 10. Urbana: Illinois Archaeological Survey.

Gregory, D. A. & Diehl, M. W. 2002. Duration, continuity, and intensity of occupation at a Late Cienega phase settlement in the Santa Cruz River floodplain, in *Traditions, Transitions, and Technologies: Themes in Southwestern Archaeology.* Schlanger, S. H. (ed.). 220–23. Boulder: Univ. of Colorado Press.

Griffin, J. B. 1967. Eastern North American archaeology: a summary. *Science* 156, 175–91.

Hally, D. J. 1993. The territorial size of Mississippian chiefdoms, in *Archaeology of Eastern North America: Papers in Honor of Stephen Williams.* Stoltman, J. B. (ed.). 143–68. Archaeological Report 25. Jackson: Mississippi Department of Archives and History.

Hally, D. J. & Rudolph, J. L. 1986. *Mississippi Period Archaeology of the Georgia Piedmont.* Laboratory of Archaeology Report 24. Athens: Univ. of Georgia.

Hard, R. J., Mauldin, R. P., & Raymond, G. R. 1996. Mano size, stable carbon isotope ratios, and macrobotanical remains as multiple lines of evidence of maize dependence in the American Southwest. *Journal of Archaeological Method and Theory* 3, 253–318.

Harriot, T. 1972. *A Briefe and True Report of the New Found Land of Virginia.* New York: Dover.

Haury, E. W. 1976. *The Hohokam, Desert Farmers and Craftsmen: Excavations at Snaketown, 1964–1965.* Tucson: Univ. of Arizona Press.

Jefferies, R. W. 1976. *The Tunacunnhee Site: Evidence of Hopewell Interaction in Northwest Georgia.* Anthropological Papers 1. Athens: Univ. of Georgia.

Johnson, A. M. & Johnson, A. E. 1998. The Plains Woodland, in *Archaeology on the Great Plains.* Wood, W. R. (ed.). 201–34. Lawrence: Univ. Press of Kansas.

Johnson, C. M. 1998. The Coalescent tradition, in *Archaeology on the Great Plains.* Wood, W. R. (ed.). 308–44. Lawrence: Univ. Press of Kansas.

Keeley, L. H. 1996. *War Before Civilization.* New York: Oxford Univ. Press.

Kelly, J. E. 1990. Range site community patterns and the Mississippian emergence, in *The Mississippian Emergence.* Smith, B. D. (ed.). 67–112. Washington D.C.: Smithsonian Institution Press.

Kidder, A. V. 1958. *Pecos, New Mexico: Archaeological Notes.* Papers of the Robert S. Peabody Foundation for Archaeology, vol. 5. Andover: Phillips Academy.

Kidder, T. R. 1998. Mississippi period mound groups and communities in the Lower Mississippi Valley, in *Mississippian Towns and Sacred Spaces.* Lewis, R. B. & Stout, C. (eds.). 123–50. Tuscaloosa: Univ. of Alabama Press.

Kivett, M. F. & Jensen, R. E. 1976. *Archeological Investigations at the Crow Creek Site (39 BF 11).* Publications in Anthropology 7. Lincoln: Nebraska State Historical Society.

Knight, Jr., V. J. 1998. Moundville as a diagrammatic ceremonial center, in *Archaeology of the Moundville Chiefdom.* Knight, Jr., V. J. & Steponaitis, V. P. (eds.). 44–62. Washington D.C.: Smithsonian Institution Press.

Knight, Jr., V. J., Brown, J. A., & Lankford, G. E. 2001. On the subject matter of Southeastern Ceremonial Complex art. *Southeastern Archaeology* 20, 129–41.

Konigsberg, L. W. 1985. Demography and mortuary practice at Seip Mound One. *Midcontinental Journal of Archaeology* 10, 123–48.

Kroeber, A. L. 1939. *Cultural and Natural Areas of Native North America.* Berkeley: Univ. of California Press.

Kuckelman, K. A., Lightfoot, R. R., & Martin, D. 2002. The bioarchaeology and taphonomy of violence at Castle Rock and Sand Canyon pueblos, Southwestern Colorado. *American Antiquity* 67, 486–513.

Kuhn, R. D. & Sempowski, M. L. 2001. A new approach to dating the League of the Iroquois. *American Antiquity* 66, 301–14.

Lambert, P. M. & Walker, P. L. 1991. Physical anthropological evidence for the evolution of social complexity in coastal southern California. *Antiquity* 65, 963–73.

Lightfoot, R. R. 1988. Roofing an early Anasazi Great Kiva: analysis of an architectural model. *The Kiva* 53, 253–72.

Lynnerup, N. 1996. Paleodemography of the Greenland Norse. *Arctic Anthropology* 33, 122–36.

Mabry, J. B. 2003. Diversity in early southwestern farming systems and optimization models of transitions to agriculture, in *Early Agricultural Period Environment and Subsistence.* Diehl, M. (ed.). Anthropological Papers No. 34. Tucson: Center for Desert Archaeology.

Madsen, D. B. & Simms, S. R. 1998. The Fremont complex: a behavioral perspective. *Journal of World Prehistory* 12, 255–336.

Marquardt, W. H. 2001. The emergence and demise of the Calusa, in *Societies in Eclipse.* Brose, D. S., Cowan, C. W., & Mainfort, Jr., R. C. (eds.). 157–71. Washington D.C.: Smithsonian Institution Press.

Maxwell, M. S. 1985. *Prehistory of the Eastern Arctic.* Orlando: Academic Press.

McGhee, R. 1996. *Ancient People of the Arctic.* Vancouver: Univ. of British Columbia.

Mills, B. 2002. Recent research on Chaco: changing views on economy, ritual, and society. *Journal of Archaeological Research* 10, 45–117.

Mills, W. C. 1907. Explorations of the Edwin Harness Mound Ohio. *Archaeological and Historical Quarterly* 16, 5–85.

Milner, G. R. 1998. *The Cahokia Chiefdom: The Archaeology of a Mississippian Society.* Washington D.C.: Smithsonian Institution Press.

—. 1999. Warfare in prehistoric and early historic eastern North America. *Journal of Archaeological Research* 7, 105–51.

—. 2004. *The Moundbuilders.* London & New York: Thames & Hudson.

Milner, G. R. & Jefferies, R. W. 1987. A reevaluation of the WPA excavation of the Robbins Mound in Boone County, Kentucky, in *Current Archaeological Research in Kentucky,* vol. 1. Pollack, D. (ed.). 33–42. Frankfort: Kentucky Heritage Council.

Muller, J. 1997. *Mississippian Political Economy.* New York: Plenum Press.

Newman, R. W. 1975. *The Sonota Complex and Associated Sites on the Northern Great Plains.* Publications in Anthropology 6. Lincoln: Nebraska State Historical Society.

O'Brien, P. J. 1989. Cahokia: the political capital of the 'Ramey' state? *North American Archaeologist* 10, 275–92.

—. 1991. Early state economics: Cahokia, capital of the Ramey state, in *Early State Economics.* Claessen, H. J. M. & van de Velde, P. (eds.). 143–75. Political and Legal Anthropology 8. London: Transaction.

—. 1993. Steed-Kisker: the western periphery of the Mississippian tradition. *Midcontinental Journal of Archaeology* 18, 227–47.

Riordan, R. V. 1998. Boundaries, resistance, and control: enclosing the hilltops in Middle Woodland Ohio, in *Ancient Earthen Enclosures of the Eastern Woodlands.* Mainfort, Jr., R. C. & Sullivan, L. P. 68–84. Gainesville: Univ. Press of Florida.

Rolingson, M. A. 1998. *Toltec Mounds and Plum Bayou Culture: Mound D Excavations.* Research Series 54. Fayetteville: Arkansas Archeological Survey.

Samuels, S. R. & Daugherty, R. D. 1991. Introduction to the Ozette archaeological project, in *Ozette Archaeological Project Research Reports.* Vol. 1: House structure and floor midden. Samuels, S. R. (ed.). 1–27. Department of Anthropology Reports of Investigations 63. Pullman: Washington State Univ.

Savelle, J. M. & McCartney, A. P. 1994. Thule Inuit bowhead whaling: a biometrical analysis, in *Threads of Arctic Prehistory: Papers in Honour of William E. Taylor, Jr..* Morrison, D. & Pilon, J.-L. (eds.). 281–310. Mercury Series 149. Hull, Quebec: Canadian Museum of Civilization.

Schledermann, P. 1993. Norsemen in the High Arctic?, in *Viking Voyages to North America.* Clausen, B. L. (ed.). 54–66. Roskilde: Viking Ship Museum.

Seeman, M. F. 1995. When words are not enough: Hopewell interregionalism and the use of material symbols at the GE Mound, in *Native American Interactions: Multiscalar Analyses and Interpretations in the Eastern Woodlands.* Nassaney, M. S. & Sassaman, K. E. 122–43. Knoxville: Univ. of Tennessee Press.

Shetrone, H. C. 1926. Explorations of the Hopewell group of prehistoric earthworks. *Ohio Archaeological and Historical Publications* 35, 5–227.

Smith, B. D. 1986. The archaeology of the

southeastern United States: from Dalton to de Soto 10,500–500 B.P. *Advances in World Archaeology* 5, 1–92.

—. 1989. Origins of agriculture in eastern North America. *Science* 246, 1566–71.

—. 1992. Hopewellian farmers of eastern North America, in *Rivers of Change: Essays on Early Agriculture in Eastern North America*. Smith, B. D. 201–48. Washington D.C.: Smithsonian Institution Press.

Snow, D. R. 1994. *The Iroquois*. Oxford: Blackwell.

Spielmann, K. A. (ed.). 1998. *Migration and Reorganization: The Pueblo IV Period in the American Southwest*. Anthropological Research Paper 51. Tempe: Arizona State Univ.

Steinacher, T. L. & Carlson, G. F. 1998. The Central Plains tradition, in *Archaeology on the Great Plains*. Wood, W. R. (ed.). 235–68. Lawrence: Univ. Press of Kansas.

Steponaitis, V. P. 1998. Population trends at Moundville, in *Archaeology of the Moundville Chiefdom*. Knight, Jr., V. J. & Steponaitis, V. P. (eds.). 26–43. Tuscaloosa: Univ. of Alabama Press.

Stodder, A. L., Martin, D. L., Goodman, A. H., & Reff, D. T. 2002. *The Backbone of History: Health and Nutrition in the Western Hemisphere*. Steckel, R. & Rose, J. (eds.). 481–505. New York: Cambridge Univ. Press.

Stone, G. D. & Downum, C. E. 1999. Non-Boserupian ecology and agricultural risk: ethnic politics and land control in the arid Southwest. *American Anthropologist* 101, 113–28.

Sutherland, P. D. 2000. The Norse and native North Americans, in *Vikings: The North Atlantic Saga*. Fitzhugh, W. W. & Ward, E. I. (eds.). 238–47. Washington D.C.: Smithsonian Institution Press.

Suttles, W. (ed.). 1990. *Northwest Coast*. Handbook of North American Indians, vol. 7. Washington D.C.: Smithsonian Institution Press.

—. 1991. Streams of property, armor of wealth: the traditional Kwakiutl potlatch, in *Chiefly Feasts: The Enduring Kwakiutl Potlatch*. Jonaitis, A. (ed.). 71–134. Seattle: Univ. of Washington Press.

Swanton, J. R. 1911. *Indian Tribes of the Lower Mississippi Valley and Adjacent Coast of the Gulf of Mexico*. Bulletin 43. Washington D.C.: Bureau of American Ethnology.

Trimble, M. K. 1994. The 1837–1838 smallpox epidemic on the Upper Missouri, in *Skeletal Biology in the Great Plains*. Owsley, D. W. & Jantz, R. L. (eds.). 81–89. Washington D.C.: Smithsonian Institution Press.

Ubelaker, D. H. 1988. North American Indian population size, A.D. 1500 to 1985. *American Journal of Physical Anthropology* 77, 289–94.

Upham, S. 1994. Nomads of the desert west: a shifting continuum in prehistory. *Journal of World Prehistory* 8, 113–67.

Van West, C. 1996. Agricultural potential and carrying capacity in southwestern Colorado, A.D. 901 to 1300, in *The Prehistoric Pueblo World A.D. 1150–1350*. Adler, M. (ed.). 214–27. Tucson: Univ. of Arizona Press.

Varien, M. D. 2002. Persistent communities and mobile households: population movement in the central Mesa Verde region, A.D. 950–1290, in *Seeking the Center Place: Archaeology and Ancient Communities in the Mesa Verde Region*. Varient, M. & Wilshusen, R. (eds.). 163–202. Salt Lake City: Univ. of Utah Press.

Varien, M. D., Van West, C. R., & Patterson, G. S. 2000. Competition, cooperation, and conflict: agricultural production and community catchments in the central Mesa Verde region. *Kiva* 66, 45–66.

Vivian, R. G. 1990. *The Chacoan Prehistory of the San Juan Basin*. San Diego: Academic Press.

Wallace, B. L. 2000. The Viking settlement at L'Anse aux Meadows, in *Vikings: The North Atlantic Saga*. Fitzhugh, W. W. & Ward, E. I. (eds.). 208–16. Washington D.C.: Smithsonian Institution Press.

Waters, M. R. & Ravesloot, J. C. 2001. Landscape change and the cultural evolution of the Hohokam along the Middle Gila River and other river valleys in south-central Arizona. *American Antiquity* 66, 285–300.

Webb, W. S. 1941. *Mt. Horeb Earthworks and the Drake Mound*. Reports in Anthropology 5 (2). Lexington: Department of Anthropology, Univ. of Kentucky.

Webb, W. S. & Baby, R. S. 1957. *The Adena People No. 2*. Columbus: Ohio Historical Society.

Wilcox, D. R. 1991. The Mesoamerican ballgame in the American Southwest, in *The Mesoamerican Ballgame*. Scarborough, V. & Wilcox, D. (eds.). 101–128. Tucson: Univ. of Arizona Press.

Willey, P. & Emerson, T. E. 1993. The osteology and archaeology of the Crow Creek massacre. *Plains Anthropologist* 38, 227–69.

Williams, S. & Brain, J. P. 1983. *Excavations at the Lake George Site, Yazoo County, Mississippi, 1958–1960*. Papers of the Peabody Museum of Archaeology and Ethnology 74. Cambridge: Harvard Univ. Press.

Wills, W. H. 2000. Political leadership and the construction of Chacoan great houses, A.D. 1020–1140, in *Alternative Leadership Strategies in the Prehispanic Southwest*. Mills, B. (ed.). 19–44. Tucson: Univ. of Arizona Press.

—. 2001. Pithouse architecture and the economics of household formation in the prehistoric American Southwest. *Human Ecology* 29, 477–99.

Winham, R. P. & Calabrese, F. A. 1998. The Middle Missouri tradition, in *Archaeology on the Great Plains*. Wood, W. R. (ed.). 269–307. Lawrence: Univ. Press of Kansas.

Wood, W. R. 1998. Introduction, in *Archaeology on the Great Plains*. Wood, W. R. (ed.). 1–15. Lawrence: Univ. Press of Kansas.

Zimmerman, M. R., Jensen, A. M., & Sheehan, G. W. 2000. Agnaiyaaq: The autopsy of a frozen Thule mummy. *Arctic Anthropology* 37, 52–59.

SOURCES OF ILLUSTRATIONS

p. 1 National Museum Bucharest; **p. 3** British Tourist Authority; **p. 21** American Museum of Natural History, New York; 1.1 © Justin Kerr; 1.2 Griffith Institute, Ashmolean Museum, Oxford; 1.4 Bridgeman Art Library; 1.5 British Museum, London; 1.6 British Museum, London; 1.7 Trustees of Sir John Soane's Museum, London; 1.8 Science Photo Library; 1.9 Science Photo Library; 1.10 Science Photo Library; 1.11 Chris Scarre; 1.12 Gordon Willey; 1.13 British Museum, London; 1.14 Liverpool Museums; 1.15 Courtesy of Lewis Binford, painting by Ray Smith; 1.16 Werner Forman Archive; 1.17 © BBC; 1.19 John Swogger/Çatalhöyük Research Project; 1.20 Semitour Périgord/Jean Grelet; **p. 44** Ministère de la culture et de la communication, Direction régionale des affaires culturelles de Rhône-Alpes, Service regional de l'archéologie; 2.1 Ben Plumridge, after Fagan, B. (2004), *People of the Earth*, p. 38; 2.2 Kathy Schick and Nicholas Toth; 2.3 ML Design; 2.4 Science Photo Library; 2.5 Ben Plumridge; 2.6 Rowena Alsey, after R. Klein; 2.7 Science Photo Library; 2.8 Science Photo Library; 2.9 Science Photo Library; 2.10 Science Photo Library; 2.11 Science Photo Library; Table 3 Richard Klein/Kathy Schick and Nicholas Toth; 2.12–2.14 Kathy Schick and Nicholas Toth; 2.15 M.H. Day; 2.16 Mary Jelliffe/Ancient Art and Architecture Collection; 2.17 Peter Bull Art Studio; 2.18–2.26 Kathy Schick and Nicholas Toth; 2.27, 2.28 Michael Rogers; 2.29 Richard Klein; 2.30, 2.31 Kathy Schick and Nicholas Toth; 3.1 ML Design; 3.2 Science Photo Library; 3.3 National Museums of Kenya; 3.4 Science Photo Library;

Table 1 Richard Klein; 3.5 Landsamt Heidelberg; 3.6 Rowena Alsey, after Richard Klein; 3.7 Peter Bull Art Studio; 3.8 © Photo RMN; 3.9 *Archaeologia*, 1800; 3.10 Richard Klein; 3.11 Richard Klein; 3.12 Pamela Willoughby; 3.13 Peter Bull Art Studio; 3.14 © Photo RMN; 3.15 NHM, Leiden, The Netherlands; 3.16 Science Photo Library; 3.17 Science Photo Library; 3.18 Richard Klein; 3.19 Science Photo Library; 3.20 Richard Klein; 3.21 Drazen Tomic, after Richard Klein; 3.22 Drazen Tomic after Richard Klein; 3.23 Richard Klein; 3.24 David Lordkipanidze; 3.25 Richard Klein; 3.26 David Lordkipanidze; 3.27 David Lordkipanidze; 3.28 Richard Klein; 3.29 Drazen Tomic, after R. Foley; 3.30 Richard Klein 3.31 ML Design, after Parés and Pérez-González, The Pleistocene Site of Gran Dolina, *Journal of Human Evolution* 37, p. 317; 3.32 Madrid Scientific Films; 3.33 Giorgio Manzi; 3.34, 3.35 Madrid Scientific Films; 3.36 Richard Klein; 3.37, 3.38 Dr Hartmut Thieme; 3.39 Drazen Tomic after Richard Klein; 3.40 © John Sibbick; 3.41 Steve Weiner; 3.42 Courtesy Francesco d'Errico, CNRS; 3.43, 3.44 Photo: Juraj Lipták, Landesamt für Archäologie; 3.45 Jeremy Percival; 3.46 Drazen Tomic after Richard Klein; 4.1 after Richard Klein; 4.2 ML Design; 4.4 Morning Glory Publishers, Beijing; 4.5 Dr Graeme Barker; 4.6 Natural History Museum, London; 4.7 Kenneth Garrett/National Geographic Image Collection; 4.8 National Museum, Bloemfontein; 4.9 Peter Mitchell; 4.10 Richard Klein; 4.11c M.H. Day; 4.11l&r Richard Klein; 4.12 Chris Stringer; 4.13 Richard Klein; 4.14 Science Photo Library; 4.15 Geoff Penna, after Fagan, B. (2004), *People of the Earth*, p. 105; **4.16** Ben Plumridge; **4.17–4.20** Courtesy of Chris Henshilwood; **4.21** Igor Astrologo, after Krings et al., Neanderthal DNA sequences and the origin of modern humans, *Cell* 90 (1997); **4.22** after Giovanni Caselli; **4.23, 4.24** ML Design; **4.25** Richard Klein; **4.26** Paul Pettitt; **4.27** John Sibbick; **4.28, 4.29** John Shea; **4.30** Drs Steven Kuhn and Mary Stiner; **4.31** ML Design; **4.32** Peter Brown; **4.33** John Sibbick; **4.34** C. Groves, ANU; **4.35** Paul Pettitt; **4.36–4.38** Photo by Hilde Jensen, Institut für Ur-und Frühgeschichte und Archäologie des Mittelalters, Eberhard-Karls-Universität, Tübingen; **4.39** Courtesy Cidália Duarte, Instituo Portugues de Arquelogia; **4.40** Musée de l'Homme, Paris; **4.41** Ministère de la culture et de la comminication, Direction régionale des affaires culturelles de Rhone-Alpes, Service regional de l'archéologie; **4.42** Rowena Alsey; **4.43** Peter Bull Art Studio; **4.44** © Photo RMN – R.G. Ojede; **4.45** Dr Ninel'Leonidovna Kornietz; **4.46** ML Design; **4.47** Weinstadt Museum, Krems an der Donau; **4.48** John Freeman; **4.49** akg-images; **4.50** ML Design; **4.51** Courtesy J.M. Adovasio, Department of Anthropology, University of Pittsburgh; **4.52, 4.53** Thomas Dillehay; **4.54** Smithsonian Institution, Washington D.C.; **4.55** Drazen Tomic, after Davis, S. (1987), *The Archaeology of Animals*; **p. 174** Michael D. Coe; **5.1** after S. Mithen (2003), *After the Ice*, p. 12; **5.2** after Oppenheimer, S. (1998), *Eden in the East*, p. 30; **5.3** ML Design, after Oppenheimer, S. (1998), *Eden in the East*, p. 82; **5.4** ML Design, after Coles, B. J. *Proceedings of the Prehistoric Society* 64 (1998); **5.5** ML Design, after LeQuellec (2003); **5.6** after Troy, C. S. et al. *Nature* 2001; **5.7** from Brothwell, D. and P., *Food in Antiquity* (1969), pl. 23; **5.8** ML Design; **5.9** The National Museum of Denmark; **5.10** ML Design, after Sherratt, A. (1997), p. 239; **5.11** ML Design; insets (left to right): Peabody Museum of Archaeology and Ethnology, Harvard University; The Art Institute of Chicago; Acropolis Museum, Athens; Staatliche Museen zu Berlin; British Museum, London; National Museum, Karachi; Qin Terracotta Museum, Lintong, Shaanxi Province; **5.12** ML Design; insets (left to right): Sachische Landesbibliothek Dresden; Scala; British Museum, London; Iraq Museum, Baghdad; National Museum, Karachi; Institute of Archaeology, CASS, Beijing; **6.1, 6.2** ML Design; **6.3** Trevor Watkins; **6.4–6.6** Dr Daniel Nadel, University of Haifa; **6.7, 6.8** Ofer Bar-Yosef; **6.9–6.11** Peter Bull Art Studio; **6.12** Trevor Watkins; **6.13** Gordon Hillman; **6.14** ML Design; **6.15** Trevor Watkins; **6.16** A.M.T. Moore; **6.17** Zev Radovan; **6.18–6.20** Danielle Stordeur; **6.21** Prof. Harald Hauptmann, Heidelberg University; **6.22–6.24** DAI Berlin; **6.25** British School of Archaeology, Jerusalem; **6.26** Photo by Yusif Zoubi, courtesy Dr. Gary Rollefson; **6.27** Courtesy Kathryn Tubb, Institute of Archaeology; **6.28–6.29** Çatalhöyük Research Project; **6.30–6.31** ML Design, after Çatalhöyük Research Project; **6.32** Drazen Tomic; **6.33** ML Design; **6.34** Trevor Watkins; **6.35–6.36** Alan Simmons; **7.1** ML Design, after Charles Higham; **7.2** Tracey Lu; **7.3, 7.4** Institute of Archaeology, CASS, Beijing; **7.5, 7.6** CPAM of Kaifeng Prefecture; **7.7** Morning Glory Publishers, Beijing; **7.8** Drazen Tomic, after Charles Higham; **7.9** Tracey Lu; **7.10** Robert Harding Picture Library; **7.11** Charles Higham; **7.12** Historical Museum, Beijing; **7.13** Morning Glory Publishers, Beijing; **7.14** Drazen Tomic; **7.15, 7.16** Morning Glory Publishers, Beijing; **7.17** ML Design, after Charles Higham; **7.18–7.21** Charles Higham; **7.22, 7.23** Per Sørensen; **7.24** Dr Helmut Loofs-Wissowa; **7.25, 7.26** Charles Higham; **7.27** Drazen Tomic, after Charles Higham; **7.28** Vince Piggot; **7.29** Kim Gwon-gu, Curator, National Folk Museum, Korea; **7.30** ML Design, after Charles Higham; **7.31** Peter Bull Art Studio; **7.32** Courtesy Museum of Fine Arts, Boston; **7.33, 7.34** National Museum Tokyo; **7.35** Yoshinogari Historical National Government Park Office; **8.1** ML Design; **8.2** Peter Hiscock; **8.3** ML Design, after Jenny Sheehan in the Cartography Unit, Research School of Pacific and Asian Studies, Australian National University; **8.4** Peter Hiscock; **8.5** D. J. Mulvaney; **8.6, 8.7** Peter Hiscock; **8.8** Photo ©Tom Till; **8.9** ML Design, after Jenny Sheehan in the Cartography Unit, Research School of Pacific and Asian Studies, Australian National University; **8.10** Photo Jack Golson; **8.11** E.C. Harris, 1977, used with permission of Jack Golson; **8.12, 8.13** ML Design, after Jenny Sheehan in the Cartography Unit, Research School of Pacific and Asian Studies, Australian National University; **8.14, 8.15** Peter Bellwood; **8.16** ML Design, after Jenny Sheehan in the Cartography Unit, Research School of Pacific and Asian Studies, Australian National University; **8.17** a) Courtesy Yang Yaolin, Shenzhen Museum; b) Courtesy Yoji Aoyagi; c) Courtesy Department of Anthropology, Taiwan National University; d) courtesy Tsang Chengohwa, Academia Sinica, Taipei; e) courtesy Glenn Summerhayes; f) courtesy Social Science Research Institute, University of Hawaii; g) courtesy Glenn Summerhayes; h) courtesy Christophe Sand; **8.18** Courtesy Lien Chao-mei, Taiwan National University; **8.19** National Museum of Prehistory, Taidong; **8.20** Courtesy Lien Chao-mei, National Taiwan University; **8.21** Peter Bellwood; **8.22** ML Design, after Jenny Sheehan in the Cartography Unit, Research School of Pacific and Asian Studies, Australian National University; **8.23** Courtesy Roger Green, redrawn by ML Design; **8.24** Courtesy Patrick Kirch; **8.25, 8.26** Peter Bellwood; **8.27** National Maritime Museum, Greenwich, London; **8.28** Peter Bellwood; **8.29** Annick Boothe; **8.30** Robert Harding Picture Library; **8.31** Peter Bellwood; **8.32** Courtesy Paul Wallin, Kon-Tiki Museum, Oslo; **8.33** Peter Bellwood; **8.34** Courtesy Tarisi Vunidilo; **8.35, 8.36** Peter Bellwood; **8.37** Whites Aviation; **8.38** Robert Harding Picture Library; **8.39, 8.40** Peter Bellwood; **8.41** Courtesy Derek Reid; **8.42** Peter Bellwood; **9.1** David Meltzer; **9.2** ML Design; **9.3** Joe Ben Wheat, University of Colorado Museum; **9.4, 9.5** David Meltzer; **9.6, 9.7** Science Photo Library; **9.8** Gayle Fritz; **9.9** Peter Bull Art Studio; **9.10** Michael D. Coe; **9.11, 9.12** Adriel Heisey; **9.13** Kirti Mathura, Desert Botanical Garden Horticulturist; **9.14, 9.15** Gayle Fritz; **9.16** Photo courtesy Glen Doran; **9.17** Frank H. McClung Museum, The University of Tennessee; **9.18, 9.19** Center for American Archaeology, Kampsville Archeological Center; **9.20** Courtesy of the W.S. Webb Museum of Anthropology, University of Kentucky; **9.21** Courtesy Dept. of Library Services, American Museum of Natural History, New York; **9.22** Peter Bull Art Studio; **9.23** Cave Research Foundation; photo William T. Austin; **9.24** Peter Bull Art Studio; **9.25** Head-Smashed-In Bison Jump, Alberta; **9.26–9.29** University Museum of Archaeology and Ethnology, Cambridge; **9.30** ML Design; **9.31** Peter Bull Art Studio, after Lavallée, D. (2000), *The First South Americans: The Peopling of a Continent from the Earliest Evidence to High Culture*, fig. 18; **9.32** Lucinda Rodd, after C. Donnan; **9.33** Peter Bull Art Studio; **9.34** Peter Bull Art Studio, after Bernardo Arriaza; **9.35** Bernardo Arriaza; **9.36** Drazen Tomic, after M. E. Moseley; **9.37** Thomas Lynch; **9.38** Peter Bull Art Studio, after Lynch, T. F. (1980), *Guitarrero Cave: Early Man in the Andes*; **9.39** ©Michael Langford 2003; **9.40** Peter Bull Art Studio; **9.41** Peter Bull Art Studio, after Shady Solis, R. et al. (2001), Dating Caral, a preceramic site in the Supe Valley on the Central Coast of Peru, *Science* 292, fig. 3; **9.42** George Steinmetz; **9.43** Edithe Pereira; **9.44** Peter Bull Art Studio, after Lavallée, D. (2000), *The First South Americans: The Peopling of a Continent from the Earliest Evidence to High Culture*, fig. 22; **10.1** ML Design, after Iliffe, J. (1995), *Africans: The History of a Continent*, fig. 1; **10.2** Graham Connah, after Hassan, F.A. (2002), fig. 2.2; **10.3** ML Design, Iliffe, J. (1995), *Africans: The History of a Continent*, fig. 1; **10.4, 10.5** Peter Bull Art Studio, after Sampson, C.G. (1974), *The Stone Age Archaeology of Southern Africa*, fig. 105; **10.5** Peter Bull Art Studio, after Fagan, B. M. and Van Noten, F. L. (1966), Wooden implements from Late Stone Age sites at Gwisho hot-springs, Lochinvar, Zambia. *Proceedings of the Prehistoric Society* (New Series) 32, fig. 4; **10.6** Gordon Hillman; **10.7** Peter Bull Art Studio, after Phillipson, D. W. (1982), The Later Stone Age in Sub-Saharan Africa, in *The Cambridge History of Africa*, Vol. 1, fig. 6.8; **10.8, 10.9** Rock Art Research Institute, University of Witwatersrand; **10.10** Graham Connah, after Vernet, R. (2002), in *Droughts, Food and Culture: Ecological Change and Food Security in Africa's Later Prehistory* (F. A. Hassan ed.), fig. 4.5; **10.11** ML Design, Iliffe, J. (1995), *Africans: The History of a Continent*, fig. 1; **10.12** akg-images/Erich Lessing; **10.13** Graham Connah; **10.14** Peter Bull Art Studio, after Shaw, T. (1980), Agricultural origins in Africa, in *The Cambridge encyclopedia of Archaeology* (A Sherratt, ed.), fig. 25.6; **10.15** ML Design, after Iliffe, J. (1995), *Africans: The History of a Continent*, fig. 1, and fig. 1.1 in Holl, A.F.C. (2000), Metals and precolonial African society, in *Ancient African Metallurgy: the Sociocultural Context* (J. O. Vogel ed.); **10.16** Werner Forman Archive; **10.17** Peter Bull Art Studio, after Phillipson, D. W. (1977), The spread of the Bantu language. *Scientific American* 236(4), p. 112; **10.18** Peter Bull Art Studio, after Haaland, R. (1985), Iron production, its socio-cultural context and ecological implications, in *African Ironworking – Ancient and Traditional* (R. Haaland and P. Shinnie, eds.), fig. 3; **10.19** ML Design, Iliffe, J. (1995), *Africans: The History of a Continent*, fig. 1; **10.20** ML Design; **10.21** Petrie Museum of Egyptian Archaeology, University College London; **10.22** Jürgen Liepe; **10.23** Photo Heidi Grassley, © Thames & Hudson Ltd, London; **10.24** Jürgen Liepe; **10.25** John Ross; **10.26** G. Eliot Smith, *The Royal Mummies*, 1901; **10.27** John Ross; **10.28** after Kemp, B. J. (1991), *Ancient Egypt: Anatomy of a Civilization*, fig. 98; **10.29** Egyptian Museum, Cairo; **10.30** Jeremy Stafford-Deitsch; **10.31** Courtesy of the Mission archéologique de l'Université de Genève au Soudan; **10.32** Tracy Wellman; **10.33** Werner Forman Archive; **10.34** British Museum, London; **10.35** Graham Connah; **10.36** ML Design, after Connah, G. (2001), *African Civilizations: An Archaeological Perspective*, fig. 4.4; **10.37** National Museum, Lagos; **10.38** British Museum, London; **10.39** Graham Connah; **10.40** Peter Bull Art Studio, after Bisson, M. S. (2000), Precolonial copper metallurgy: sociopolitical context, in *Ancient African Metallurgy: The Sociocultural Context* (J. O. Vogel ed.), fig. 2.12; **10.41** Peter Bull Art Studio, after Connah, G. (2001), *African Civilizations: An Archaeological Perspective*, fig. 7.5; **10.42** Graham Connah; **10.43** National Museum, Lagos; **11.1** ML Design; **11.2** Annick Boothe, after Shackleton and van Andel (1980), fig. 1; **11.3** Peter Bull Art Studio, after Gurina, N. N. (1956), fig. 22; **11.4** British Museum, London; **11.5** Museum of Archaeology and Anthropology, University of Cambridge; **11.6** after Gkiaska, M. et al., *Antiquity* 77, 2003, fig. 1; **11.7, 11.8** ML Design; **11.9** Peter Bull Art Studio; **11.10** Professor Alexander Fol; **11.11** R. J. Rodden, An Early Neolithic Village in Greece, *Scientific American*, 212; **11.12** Archaeological Museum, Varna, Bulgaria; **11.13** Pitt Rivers Museum, Oxford; **11.14** Peter Bull Art Studio; **11.15** Museo Arqueologico, Barcelona; **11.16, 11.17** Photo Drag. Kazié, Belgrade; **11.18** Peter Bull Art Studio; **11.19** ©Frank Spooner Pictures. Photo: Henry Paul; **11.20** Drazen Tomic and Tracy Wellman; **11.21** The National Museum of Denmark, Copenhagen; **11.22** Pequart, S. J. et al. (1937), *Téviec, Station-Necropole mésolithique du Morbihan*, fig. 15; **11.23** Courtesy Landesdenmalamt Baden-Württemberg – Archäologisches Denkmalpflege; **11.24** Peter Bull Art Studio, after Wahl, K. and Köhnig, H. G., *Fundberichte aus Baden-Württemberg* 12, 1987; **11.25** Peter Bull Art Studio; **11.26** ML Design; **11.27** Michael Jenner; **11.28** The Trustees of the National Museums of Scotland, Edinburgh; **11.29** ML Design, after *Bulletin de la Société Préhistorique Française*, 1998, fig. 3; **11.30** Philip Winton; **11.31** ML Design, after Cleal et al. (1995), *Stonehenge in its Landscape*, fig. 256; **11.32** ML Design, after Souden, D. (1997), *Stonehenge: Mysteries of the Stones and Landscape*, p. 124; **11.33** Mike Pitts; **11.34** ML Design, after S. Andersen; **11.35** Niels Andersen; **11.36** The Trustees of the National Museums of Scotland, Edinburgh; **11.37** ML Design, after Benz, M. and Stadelbacher, A. (1995), *Das Glockenbecher-Phänomen*, p. 14; **11.38** Wessex Archaeology; **11.39** Photo: D.Sommer, Brandenburgisches Landsamt für Denkmalpflege und Archäologisches

Landesmuseum; 11.40 Landsamt für Denkmalpflege und Archäologie Sachsen-Anhalt. Photo Juraj Lipták; 11.41 Kit Weiss, The National Museum of Denmark; 11.42 Giovanni Lattanzi; 11.43 Neuchâtel Archaeological Society; 11.44 akg-images/Erich Lessing; 11.45 Simon James; 11.46 Warsaw State Archaeological Museum; 11.47 Centro Camuno de Studi Preistorici, Capo di Ponte, Italy; 11.48 Werner Forman Archive; 11.49 ML Design; 11.50 Centre Camille Julian, CNRS; 11.51 Drents Museum; 11.52 Musée cantonal d'archéologie, Neuchâtel; 12.1, 12.2 ML Design; 12.3 Professor Merpert; 12.4 Peter Bull Art Studio; 12.5 Iraq Museum, Baghdad; 12.6 British Museum, London; 12.7, 12.8 Peter Bull; 12.9 Rowena Alsey, after Roaf, M. *Cultural Atlas of Mesopotamia and the Ancient Near East*; 12.10, 12.11 Iraq Museum, Baghdad; 12.12 akg-images/Erich Lessing; 12.13 ML Design; 12.14, 12. 15 Roger Matthews; 12.16 University of Pennsylvania Museums, Philadelphia; 12.17 Roger Matthews; 12.18 Peabody Museum of Archaeology and Ethnology, Harvard University, Cambridge; 12.19 Peter Bull Art Studio; 12.20 © Photo RMN – Chuzeville; 12.21 Philip Winton; 12.22 Iraq Museum, Baghdad; 12.23 Musée du Louvre, Paris; 12.24 Drawing by Lloyd Townsend; 12.25 Pushkin State Museum of Fine Arts, Moscow; 12.26 Philip Winton; 12.27 Paolo Matthaie; 12.28 © Photo RMN – Arnaudet; 12.29 Hirmer; 12.30 ML Design; 12.31, 12.32 Roger Matthews; 12.33 Bildarchiv Preussicher Kulturbesitz, Berlin; 12.34 British Museum, London; 12.35 Zev Radovan; 12.36 Peter Bull Art Studio, after Margueron, J. C. (2000), 207; 12.37 ML Design; 12.38 Institute of Nautical Archaeology, College Station, Texas; 12.39 British Museum, London; 12.40 ML Design; 12.41 Michael Roaf; 12.42 © Photo RMN – D.Chenot; 12.43 Zev Radovan; 12.44, 12. 45 Roger Matthews; 12.46 Roger Matthews; 12.47 akg-images; 12.48 ML Design; 13.1 ML Design; 13.2 British Museum, London; 13.3 Courtesy Emma Blake, 13.4 Ashmolean Museum, Oxford; 13.5, after Hutchinson, R. W., *Prehistoric Crete*; 13.6 Judith Newcomer, in Hodges, H. (1970), *Technology in the Ancient World*, p. 118; 13.7 after Griffiths Pedley, J. (1993), *Greek Art and Archaeology*, fig. 1.16; 13.8 John F. Cherry; 13.9 Ancient Art & Architecture Collection; 13.10 Scala; 13.11 after S. Iakovidis; 13.12 Scala; 13.13 after Chadwick, J. (1976), *The Mycenaean World*, fig. 12; 13.14 Camera Press; 13.15 Courtesy of Tiryns Project, German Archaeological Institute, J.Maran/photo by J.W. Myers; 13.16 Drazen Tomic, after Whitley, J. (2001), *The Archaeology of Greece*, fig. 5.3; 13.17 Michael Jenner; 13.18 Drazen Tomic, after Carter, J. C. (1998), *The Chora of Metaponto: The Necropolis*, Vol. I, fig. 5A.7; 13.19 akg-images/Erich Lessing; 13.20 akg-images; 13.21 T. Okamura; 13.22 Nigel Spivey; 13.23, 12.24 British Museum, London; 13.25 Drazen Tomic, after *An Historical Guide to the Sculptures of the Parthenon, London* (1962), fig. 8; 13.26 Heidi Grassley; 13.27 Research Library, Getty Research Institute, Los Angeles; 13.28 Archaeological Receipts Fund, Athens; 13.29 American School of Classical Studies, Athens; 13.30 Sonia Halliday; 13.31 John F. Cherry; 13.32 British Museum, London; 13.33 Scala; 13.34 Drazen Tomic, after Andronicos, M. (1984), *Vergina; The Royal Tombs and the Ancient City*, fig. 55; 13.35 Scala; 13.36 Bibliothèque Nationale de France, Paris; 13.37 Stephane Compoint; 13.38 Bildarchiv Preussicher Kulturbesitz, Berlin; 13.39 Somerset County Museum; 13.40 Museo Capitolino, Rome; 13.41 akg-images/Erich Lessing; 13.42 Fototeca Unione; 13.43 John Ross; 13.44 By permission of John Burge, John Clarke, and James Packer; 13.45 ML Design; 13.46 Unit for Landscape Modelling, University of Cambridge; 13.47 Courtesy J. Hartnett; 13.48 S. Sidebotham; 13.49 Sally Nicholls; 13.50 Zev Radovan; 13.51 after Parker, A. J. (1992), *Ancient Shipwrecks of the Mediterranean and the Roman Provinces*, fig. 3; 13.52 Bardo Museum, Tunis; 13.53 Emily Lane; 13.54 British Museum, London; 13.55 Sally Nicholls; 13.56 Hirmer; 14.1 ML Design; 14.2, 14.3 © C. Jarrige; 14.4 Archaeological Survey of India; 14.5 ML Design; 14.6 Robin Coningham; 14.7 Georg Helmes; 14.8 Courtesy of Drs F. R. & B. Allchin; after the later Dr F. Durrani (CUP, 1982); 14.9 ML Design; 14.10 Georg Helmes; 14.11 National Museum, Karachi; 14.12 ML Design; 14.13 ©Taisei Corporation, ©NHK; 14.14 ML Design; 14.15 Georg Helmes; 14.16 ML Design; 14.17 J. M. Kenoyer, Courtesy Dept. of Archaeology and Museums, Govt. of Pakistan; 14.18 Courtesy Museum of Fine Arts, Boston; 14.19 Georg Helmes; 14.20 Robin Coningham; 14.21 Peter Bull Art Studio; 14.22 DAI, Tehran; 14.23–14.28 Robin Coningham; 14.28 Archaeological Survey of India; 14.29 Robin Coningham; 14.30 British Museum, London; 14.31 Courtesy D.A.F.A.; 14.32, 14.33 ML Design; 14.34 British Museum, London; 14.35 Robin Coningham; 14.36 Archaeological Survey of India; 15.1 Zhejian Provincial Institute of Archaeology, Hanzhou; 15.2, 15.3 Institute of Archaeology, CASS, Beijing; 15.4 ML Design, after Charles Higham; 15.5 ML Design, after Chang, K.-C. (2000), *The Archaeology of Ancient China*, p. 311; 15.6, 15.7 Institute of Archaeology, CASS, Beijing; 15.8, 15.9 Morning Glory Publishers, Beijing; 15.10 Peter Bull Art Studio, after Barnes, G. (1999), *The Rise of Civilization in East Asia*, fig. 57; 15.11 ML Design; 15.12 Institute of Archaeology, CASS Beijing; 15.13 Jiangxi Provincial Museum, Nanchang; 15.14 Zhou Yuan Administrative Office of Cultural Relics, Fufeng, Shanxi Province; 15.15, 15.16 Sanxingdui Museum, Guanghan, Sichuan Province; 15.17 ML Design; 15.18 Sanxingdui Museum, Guanghan, Sichuan Province; 15.19 Drazen Tomic; 15.20 Morning Glory Publishers, Beijing; 15.21 Hubei Provincial Museum, Wuhan; 15.22 ML Design; 15.23 Qin Terracotta Museum, Lintong, Shaanxi Province; 15.24 ML Design; 15.25 Peter Bull Art Studio, after Barnes, G. (1999), *The Rise of Civilization in East Asia*, fig. 66; 15.26 Institute of Archaeology, CASS Beijing; 15.27 Morning Glory Publishers, Beijing; 15.28 Institute of Archaeology, CASS Beijing; 15.29 Werner Forman Archive; 15.30, 15.31 National Museum of Korea; 15.32 Ministry of Culture, Seoul; 15.33 ML Design, after Charles Higham; 15.34 Orion Press, Tokyo; 15.35 ML Design; 15.36 National Museum Tokyo; 15.37–15.39 Edward Kidder; 15.40 ML Design; 15.41 Peter Bull Art Studio; 15.42 Michael Freeman; 15.43 Charles Higham; 15.44, 15.45 Sally Nicholls; 15.46 Robert Harding Picture Library; 15.47 Museum of Cham Sculpture, Danang; 15.48 French Association of Friends of the Orient; 16.1, 16.2 ML Design; 16.3 © Justin Kerr; 16.4 David Drew; 16.5 Drazen Tomic, after Marcus, J. and Flannery, K. V. (1996); 16.6 Joyce Marcus and Kent V. Flannery; 16.7 Michael Blake; 16.8 Photo Irmgard Groth-Kimball © Thames and Hudson Ltd; 16.9 Drazen Tomic, after Gonzalez Lauck, R. (1996), La Venta: an Olmec capital, in *Olmec Art and Archaeology* (Benson, E. P. and de la Fuente, B. eds.), fig. 1; 16.10 National Geographic Society Image Collection; 16.11 Evans, S. T. and Webster, D. (2001), *Archaeology of Ancient Mexico and Central America: An Encyclopedia*, p. 725 16.12 after Newsome, E. A. (2001), *Trees of Paradise and Pillars of the World: The Serial Stela Cycle of "18-Rabbit-God K," King of Copán*, p. 3; 16.13 after R. Diehl; 16.14 Joyce Marcus and Kent V. Flannery; 16.15 drawing George Stuart; 16.16 Photo Irmgard Groth-Kimball © Thames & Hudson Ltd; 16.17 Drazen Tomic, after Newsome, E. A. 2001. *Trees of Paradise and Pillars of the World: The Serial Stela Cycle of "18-Rabbit-God K," King of Copán*, p. 25; 16.18 Photo Irmgard Groth-Kimball © Thames & Hudson Ltd; 16.19 Drazen Tomic; 16.20 Archivio White Star; 16.21 Photo Irmgard Groth-Kimball © Thames & Hudson Ltd; 16.22 Corbis; 16.23 Ruben Cabrera Castro; 16.24 Drazen Tomic, after Cabrero Castro, R. (1996), Figuras glificas de La Ventilla, Teotihuacan, *Arqueologia* 15, fig. 8; 16.25 Drazen Tomic; 16.26 ffotograff; 16.27 Drazen Tomic, after Stone, D. (1976); 16.28 Drazen Tomic; 16.29 Photo Irmgard Groth-Kimball © Thames & Hudson Ltd; 16.30 from Hirth, K. (2000), *Ancient Urbanism at Xochicalco*, p. 255; 16.31 ffotograff; 16.32 © Justin Kerr; 16.33 Philip Winton, courtesy of Simon Martin; 16.34 ©Nicholas Hellmuth, courtesy FLAAR; 16.35 Philip Winton after Carr and Hazard; 16.36 ©Stephan Gore/Ancient Art & Architecture Collection; 16.37 Drazen Tomic; 16.38 Jeremy A. Sabloff; 16.39 ©Dr S. Coyne/Ancient Art & Architecture Collection; 16.40 National Geographic Society Image Collection; 16.41 Simon Nicholls; 16.42 ML Design; 16.43 from Boone, E. (1994), *The Aztec World*; 16.44 Great Temple Project, Mexico City; 16.45 Philip Winton; 16.46 ML Design, after Berdan, F. et al. (1996), *Aztec Imperial Strategies*, fig. II.1; 16.48 Bodleian Library, Oxford; 17.1 ML Design; 17.2, 17.3 © Michael Langford 2003; 17.4 Yoshio Onuki, Archaeological Mission of the University of Tokyo; 17.5 Drazen Tomic; 17.6 Yoshio Onuki, Archaeological Mission of the University of Tokyo; 17.7 from Moseley, M. E. (2001), *The Incas and their Ancestors*, fig. 54; 17.8 Michael E. Moseley; 17.10 ML Design, after Zeidler 1998; 17.11, 17.12 © Philip Baird/www.anthroarcheart.org; 17.13, 17.14 Drazen Tomic; 17.15 Adriana von Hagen; 17.16 from Anton, F. (1972), *The Art of Ancient Peru*; 17.17 Archivio Museo de America, Photo Joaquin Otero; 17.18 Drazen Tomic; 17.19 Michael E. Moseley; 17.20 Rafael Larco-Hoyle; 17.21 Bildarchiv Preussicher Kulturbesitz, Berlin; 17.23 Fowler Museum of Cultural History, University of California, Los Angeles; 17.24 Carlos Angel/Katz Pictures Ltd.; 17.25 Adriana von Hagen; 17.26 Courtesy Dept. of Library Services, American Museum of Natural History; 17.27 Fowler Museum of Cultural History, University of California, Los Angeles; 17.28 Photo © Tom Till; 17.29 from Anton, F. (1972), *The Art of Ancient Peru*; 17.30 © Michael Langford 2003; 17.31 Sicán Archaeological Project, photo Y.Yoshii; 17.32 Courtesy Dept. of Library Services, American Museum of Natural History; 17.33 Hans Mann; 17.34 ML Design; 17.35–17.37 © Michael Langford 2003; 17.38, 17.39 Michael Heckenberger; 17.40, 17.41 ML Design, after M. Heckenberger; 17.42–17.47 Michael Heckenberger; 18.1 ML Design; 18.2 Postcard; 18.3 S. Hammerstedt after Webb, W. S. (1941), *Mt. Horeb Earthworks and the Drake Mound*. Reports in Anthropology 5 (2), figs 5 and 11; 18.4 J. Cooper after the Ohio Historical Society P396, B6, F1, E7; 18.5 Courtesy of the Ohio Historical Society; 18.6 Photo Dirk Bakker © 1985 The Detroit Institute of Arts/Ohio Historical Society; 18.7 Photo G. Milner (Field Museum of Natural History, Illinois, 56784, 56797); 18.8 Courtesy of the Ohio Historical Society; 18.9 Courtesy of the Arkansas Archaeological Survey; 18.10 Photo Dirk Bakker © 1985 The Detroit Institute of Arts/Ohio Historical Society; 18.11 Courtesy of the National Museum of the American Indian, Smithsonian Institution, New York; 18.12 George Milner; 18.13 Courtesy of the Center for Archeological Investigations, Southern Illinois University, and J. Porter; 18.14 George Milner; 18.15 Photo © Tom Till; 18.16 Richard Schlecht, National Geographic Society Image Collection; 18.17 Peter Bull Art Studio, after Masse, W. B. (1991), The quest for subsistence sufficiency and civilization in the Sonoran desert, in *Chaco and Hohokam* (Crown, P. L. and Judge, W. J. eds.), fig. 9.2; 18.18, 18.19 Arizona State Museum, University of Arizona, photo Helga Teiwes; 18.20 Amy Elizabeth Grey, after Gladwin, H. S. et al. (1938), *Excavations at Snaketown: Material Culture*; 18.21 Simon S. S. Driver; 18.22 University of Colorado Museum, Boulder; 18.23 Photo © Tom Till; 18.24 Werner Forman Archive; 18.25 Photo © Tom Till; 18.26 Photo Fred Mang Jr., National Parks Service, US Department of the Interior; 18.27 Photo Dirk Bakker © 1985 The Detroit Institute of Arts; 18.28 University of Nebraska; 18.29 Russ Hanson, Courtesy National Parks Service; 18.30 Larry J. Zimmerman; 18.31 Photo Peter Howorth, courtesy Santa Barbara Museum of Natural History; 18.32 Photo Collection, Royal Anthropological Institute, London; 18.33 Oregon Historical Society; 18.34, 18.35 Richard D. Daugherty; 18.36 Parks Canada/H.01.11.06.02 (1); 18.37 Newfoundland Museum, NFM 1dcq-22; 18.38 Canadian Museum of Civilization; 18.39 Bryan and Cherry Alexander; 18.40 Dept. of Prints and Drawings, Zentralbibliothek, Zurich; 19.1 Africana Museum, Johannesburg; 19.2 Sally Nicholls; 19.3 Peter Bellwood; 19.4 British Museum, London; 19.5 Science Photo Library.

INDEX

Illustrations are indexed by illustration number

Abric Romaní 152
Abri Jean-Cros 404
Abu Hureyra 203, 204, 208, 214–15, 217, 218, 226, 230, 231, 232; 6.13–6.16
Abu Salabikh 444; 12.15
Abydos 371, 373, 373
Acanceh 619
Accelerator Mass Spectrometer (AMS) 157, 1.10
Achaemenids 434, 469, 471, 540, 541, 544, 584; 12.48; 14.22
Achagua 675
Acheulean 57, 66, 67, 70, 72, 73, 83, 85, 93–96, 101, 102, 104, 105, 107, 110, 112, 113, 114, 117, 118, 119, 121, 133, 135, 150, 151; 2.6, 2.14, 3.6, 3.7, 3.8, 3.9, 3.10, 3.11, 3.12, 3.20, 3.21, 3.39, 3.42, 3.46
Achilleion 401
Achilles Painter 13.32
achira 341, 344, 649; 9.40
Acolhua 633
acorns 149, 324, 329, 331, 333
acropolis: Athens 494, 496, 497, 511; 13.26; Mycenae 482, 485; 13.11; Sirkap 545; Tikal 626, 627
Actium, battle of 474, 507
Açutuba 669, 671, 674; 17.39, 17.41, 17.43
Adad-nirari I, King 460
Adamgarh 522–23
Adams, Robert 438
adaptive radiation 49
Adelaar, Alexander 286
Adena 679, 681, 682, 683, 684
Admiralty Islands 287, 288
adobe 345, 612, 615, 618, 629, 634, 652, 655, 658, 659, 663; 17.33
Adrar Bous 362
Adulis 382
adzes 252, 253, 254, 256, 288, 292, 311, 363, 411; 7.21, 8.21, 8.25, 9.5
Aedui 428, 11.49
Aegean 196, 394, 400, 450, 459, 463, 464, 476, 477–80, 482, 510
Aeneas 503, 13.39
aerial photography 34
Aegyptopithecus 51
Afalou 137
Afanasievo culture 582
Afar Rift 68
Afghanistan 453, 476, 500, 502, 519, 531, 532, 539, 540, 546, 547, 550; 14.31; 14.32
Africa 28, 30, 75, 720; Acheulean tools 57, 66, 70, 83, 93–96, 101, 110; agriculture 186, 187, 190, 192, 351, 356, 361–65; 10.11, 10.15; animal evolution 75; Bantu 28, 37, 188, 366; behavioral modernity 146; cattle 185, 358, 361, 362, 363, 364, 365, 367, 371, 382; 10.12; chronology 182; cities and states 380–91; climate 55–57, 127, 178, 188, 351–53, 365; 5.5, 10.1, 10.2; contacts with the outside world 387–90; dispersion of *Homo* from 101–06, 104, 121, 153; 3.22; domestication of plants 10.14; goats 362, 363, 364, 365, 369, 371, 382, 387; Holocene 351–91; and *Homo sapiens* 85, 107, 121, 125, 126, 128, 129, 132–40, 146, 155; human origins in 34, 47–83, 85–96, *see also* human fossils; ironworking 365–68, 10.18; Late Stone Age 141; Masai 33; Middle Stone Age 141, 142; 4.16; Oldowan tools 61–83; 2.12, 2.13, 2.14, 2.16; pigment fragments 118; primates 51–54,

69; rock art 358–59; 10.8, 10.9; state formation and trade 389, 389–90; 10.19; Stone Age 75, 93, 125, 126; urbanization 380–87, *see also individual regions and countries*
African Rift Valley 53, 55, 75, 101
Afroasiatic languages 363
Agadez 368
Agamemnon 482; 13.10
agate 584; beads 585; 8.40; ornaments 247
Agate Basin points 9.1
agave 315, 320, 321, 636; 9.13
Agelarakis, Anagnosti 256
agency theory 35–36
Age of Reptiles 50
Agia Irini 478
Agia Triada 484
agora 496, 497, 506; 13.29, 13.30
agriculture 28, 40, 717–18; Africa 351, 356, 361–65; alternatives to in North America 330–34; Amazonia 643; Americas 349; Andes 343–44, 641; archaeological traces 184; beginnings 182–91, 183; China 570; consequences 190–93; in Cyprus 229; definition 183; desert farming 642; East Africa 364–65; East Asia 235–63; Egypt 361, 371; Europe 396–400, 419–20; Greece 498; and hunter-gatherers 33, 183–84, 186, 187, 188, 190, 235, 256, 361, 404, 407, 595–96, 718; intensification 718; Mesoamerica 313–19, 595, 598–601, 626; New Guinea 186, 277–78; Nile Valley 363; and nomadism 448; North America 317–30, 348, 349, 694, 695, 699, 700, 715; plowing 410, 419; reasons for adoption of 186–89; and sedentism 260, 314; South America 186, 193, 343–44, 646; South Asia 524–26; Southwest Asia 201–33, 434–36, 438, 448; spread 107–90; and state formation 195, 196, 198–99; West Africa 363–64
"A Group" 363
Ahmose 377
ahu 295, 297, 301; 8.30; Vinapu 297, 8.31
Ai Bunar 402
Aiello, Leslie 78, 129
Ai Khanoum 501, 546; 14.31, 14.32
'Ain Ghazal 217, 222–23, 230, 231; 6.26, 6.27
Ain Hanech 73; 2.21
'Ain Mallaha *see* Eynan
Ainu 260
Akan states 384
Akhenaten 378, 456, 459, 460; 10.27, 10.28
Akkadian 446, 466; 12.34
Akkadian empire 434, 445–47, 448, 452
Akrotiri (Cyprus) 229; 6.35
Akrotiri (Thera) 482, 510
Aksum 196, 382, 388; 10.34, 10.35
Alabama 326, 688
Alacahöyük 445
Alalakh 458–59, 460; 12.39
Alaric the Visigoth 516
Alaska 38, 166, 167, 178, 310, 331, 710, 711, 713
alcohol 389
Aldenderfer, Mark 342
Aleppo 451, 452, 454, 456, 459
Alexander the Great 378, 469, 473, 474, 500–01, 503, 544, 546; 13.36, 14.31, 14.32
Alexandria 474, 502, 549; 13.37
al-Fustat (old Cairo) 383, 388, 390
algarroba 337
Algeria 73, 119, 358, 362, 383; 2.21
Al-Hiba 444; 12.14

Aligrama 539
Ali Kosh 203, 228–29, 230, 232, 525
Allen, Harry 156, 272, 291
Almería 405
alpacas 341, 343, 349, 641, 661
Alpine rock carvings 406
Alps 393, 408
Altamira 126, 163
Alta Vista 619
Altun Ha 619
alum 384
Amanus Mountains 446
amaranth 315, 320, 636
Amaravati 591
Amarna 377, 378, 434, 456, 458; 10.28, 12.34; Letters 456, 458, 460, 461; 12.34
Amazon 312, 346–47, 348, 644, 669; 9.43, 17.2
Amazonia 178, 642–44, 645, 668–77
amber 420, 422; 11.36
Ambrona 119; 3.46
Ambrose, Stan 140, 288, 289
Amenemhet I 377
Amenhotep II 377
Amenhotep III 460, 461
Americas 195, 199, 313, 389, 719; agriculture 187, 192; colonization of 125, 166–71; domestication in 184; Formative period 650; languages 669; Native Americans 30; 1.5; tools 30, *see also* Mesoamerica; North America; South America
Amerindians 166, 167, 644, 672
"Amesbury archer" 421, 11.38
Ammermann, Albert 398
Amorites 434, 448, 449, 451, 461
Amri 520, 530
Amud, 149, 154
Anajas River 672
Anak 574
Analects 567
Anandacandra, King 590
Anapchi Lake 577
Anaro 287
Anati, Emmanuel 426–27
Anatolia 203, 224, 228, 398, 400, 434, 436, 443, 445, 448, 453–55, 457, 458, 459, 460, 467–68, 476, 486
Anawratha of Pagan, King 590
ancestor veneration 223, 286, 598, 666
anchovies 345, 649
Andarayan 262
Anderson, Atholl 293
Andes 194, 195, 196, 312, 326, 338–46, 348, 610, 641–42, 645, 646–51, 679; 9.36
Andrews, Peter 92, 127, 322
Andronovo culture 557
Angkor 195, 554, 585, 586, 587, 589, 590; 15.41, 15.42, 15.44, 15.45
Angola 356, 367, 385
animals: in art 287, 346, 356, 358, 364, 426, 481, 504, 523, 526, 554, 562, 573, 574, 576, 584, 605, 655, 659, 660; 10.8, 10.12, 11.41, 11.47; foods 119–21; migration 523; remains 119, 143, 228, 229, 231, 239, 247, 251, 336, 355, 370, 522, 523, 525, 526, 546, 556, 558, 562, 564, 709; in the Roman amphitheaters 508
annatto 315
An, sky god 439
Anangula 331
Antalya 209
Antarctic 204

anteaters 347
anthropologyand archaeology 25–26; biological 25; cultural 25; linguistic 25
Antigonids 501, 506
Antilles 676
antler 140, 151, 152, 157, 158, 162, 164, 321, 323, 396, 397, 426, 427, 523; 4.43, 4.44, 11.4
antler knives 711
Anuradhapura 520, 523, 545–46, 548, 550, 551; 14.29
Anu temple area, Uruk 439, 440
Anyang 236, 554, 558, 560–61, 562
Apa 424
"Ape Men" 59
apes 52–53, 56, 79
Aphrodite, goddess 507
Apollo, god 501
Apollo II Cave 356
Appalachians 325, 683
Arabian Gulf 539
Arabian Sea 521
Arabs 383, 384, 388, 448, 585
Arago 148
Arakan coast 590
Aramaeans 434, 448, 461
Aramaic 464, 541, 547; 14.33
Arawak 669, 670–71, 675, 676
archaeology: and anthropology 25–26; and chronology 25–26, 30, 31; and computers 25, 38; definition of 25; of Greece and Rome 475–76; and history 25, 28–34; of the Industrial Revolution 26; linguistic 668–69; and modern techniques 33–34; in the 19th century 31–32; relevance of 27–28; in the Renaissance 28–30; and the sciences 25, 34; scope of 25, 26; in the 17th and 18th centuries 30; theories of change 35–42; and written records 27
Archaic 182, 332; Mexico 313, 316; North America 317–21; South America 645
Archanes 480
architecture 382, 385, 516, 612; Chichén Itzá 632; Egyptian 379; 10. 30; Great Zimbabwe 10.42; Greek 488, 494, 499, 504; of Hattusa 455; Maya 611; Meroitic 10.33; Olmec 605; Puuc 631, 632; Teotihuacán 619, 16.28; Wari 662
Arch of Titus 512; 13.49
Arctic 204, 679, 717
Ardika 296, 302
Ardipithecus ramidus 62
Argissa 400
argon-argon dating 75
Argos 487
Arikamedu 520, 550, 14.36
Arikara people 703
Aristotle 29
Arizona 317, 318, 320, 680, 692, 693, 696; 9.11
Arkansas 322, 326, 686; 18.9
armadillos 347
Armenia 561
Armenoi 484
armor 563, 574
arm rings 252
Arnhem Land 267, 271, 274, 275; 8.2, 8.8
aromatics 351
Arpachiyah 435, 436
arrowroot 340, 343, 344, 348
arrows/arrowheads 164, 213, 238, 355, 370, 522, 561, 576, 585
Arslantepe 442, 445
art 26, 41, 79, 117, 122, 141, 143–46; 1.20; Hellenistic 503; mobiliary art 163–64; Neolithic 213, 215, see also carving; cave art; rock art; sculpture

Artemis (goddess) 515
Arthasastra 547
Arverni 428; 11.49
Aryans 519, 538, 541
Asa Koma 364
Asana 341, 342
Asfaw, Berhane 68, 71, 105
Ashdod 463
Ashkelon 464
ashlar masonry 666
ash mounds 527–28; 14.6
Ashur 434, 449, 453, 459, 460, 461
Ashurnasirpal I, King 461; Ashurnasirpal II 465, 466; 12.45
Ashuruballit, King 460
Asia: agriculture 186, 188; cattle 185; climate change 178, 179, 186; as cradle of humankind 59, 139; early pottery 260; hand axe tradition 101, 110; Homo erectus 92, 97–106, 106, 121; 3.15, 3.16, 3.17, 3.18, 3.19; Homo sapiens 128, 130–31, 153, 154, 155; human fossils sites 86; Lower Paleolithic 93; Mousterian 96; pigment fragments 118; source for early Americans 167, 168; tools 114, see also individual regions and countries
Asoka. Emperor 519, 541, 542, 545, 547; 14.33
Aspero 345, 645, 647, 648
Assyria 196, 453, 460, 460–61, 463, 464, 465–67
Astarte, goddess 504
astronomy 416–17, 11.40
Asuka 580, 582; 15.37, 15.38, 15.39
Aswan 356
Atahualpa 668
Atapuerca 90, 102, 108, 111, 149; 3.31, 3.32, 3.34, 3.35; see also Gran Dolina; Sima de los Huesos
Aten (god) 377
Aterian 141
Athapaskan people 703
Athena (goddess) 484, 494, 495, 497, 498; 13.38
Athens 198, 473, 487, 488, 492, 494, 495, 496, 499, 500, 506, 511, 512, 513, 719; 13.27, 13.30
atlatl 162, 163, 165; 322, 333; 9.31, 9.44
Atranjikhera 540
Attica 487, 495, 513
Attila 516
Atzcapotzalco 633
Aubrey, John 30
Aucilla River 322
Auckland Isthmus 299
Augustus 474, 507; 13.43
Au Ka-fat 248
Aurignac 126, 154, 156, 157–58
aurochs 150, 395
Australia 102, 130, 131, 155, 156, 173, 181; Aborigines 184, 265–75; climate changes 265, 267–68; Homo sapiens 128, 130–31, 139, 153, 155, 156; and hunter-gatherers 183; landscape 266–67, 271–72; Pleistocene coastline 8.3; rock art 192, 267, 271–72; 8.2, 8.7, 8.8; and Southeast Asia 269; Tasmania 270–71; trade and foreign contacts 273–75
Australopithecines 33, 60–61, 68, 82; 2.6, 2.11; Australopithecus: aethiopicus 61, 64, 68, 82; afarensis 57, 62; 2.4; africanus 57, 61, 62, 68, 82, 98; 2.8, 2.11; anamensis 62; boisei 61, 64, 67, 68, 71, 82, 95; garhi 61, 62, 69, 82; robustus 72, 73, 82; 2.11; and Homo (genus) 70, 78, 88, 92
Austria 164, 407, 411, 419, 428
Austro-Asiatic 262; 7.17
Austronesian 187, 279, 280–83, 591
Austronesians 265, 270, 277; dispersal 279–83, 284; 8.12, 8.13; origins 282–83; social organization 303
Avdeevo 165

Avebury 30
avocado 344
awls 257, 333, 582, 610
axes 347, 360, 363, 403, 409, 419, 421, 422, 524, 526, 527, 539, 555, 582; 3.8, 8.6. 9.44, 11.28, 11.29, 11.39, 11.48
Ayacucho 341, 661
Ayanis 467; 12.46
Azilian 165
Aztecs 196, 349, 595, 596, 608, 610, 613, 617, 618, 620, 622, 633; empire 636–38, 16.46; social organization 637; see also Tenochtitlán
Aztlan 633

Baal 457, 505; Baal Hammon 504
Babel-el-Mandeb Strait 102
Babylon/ia 434, 448, 449, 450, 452, 454, 460, 461, 463, 468–69; 12.47, 14.30
Bac Bo 236
Bacho Kiro 156
Bacon Bend 326
Bactria 446, 548, 549, 557
Badakshan 536
Bad Cannstatt 119
Bagor 520, 522, 523, 536
Bahrain 438, 446, 462
Baijia 236, 238
Bailey, Douglass 403
Baines, John 373
Baiyangcun 236, 249. 250
Baja California 166, 168
Bakheng Hill 587
Bala Hisar 541, 542; 14.24
Balakot 528, 530, 535
Balkans 393, 400–02, 500; agriculture 397, 398, 399; 11.7, 11.8
ball court 597, 598, 601, 604, 605, 611, 612, 613, 618, 620, 622, 624, 628, 629, 632, 635, 693; 16.4, 16.37, 18.19
ball game 595, 598, 599, 601, 604, 675, 693; 16.3, 16.4
Balloy 418
Balsas River 599
Baluchistan 520, 524, 528, 529, 530, 532, 536, 538
Bambandyanalo 388
Bambata people 369
bamboo artifacts 113–14
bamboo slips 559; 15.8
bananas 365, 369, 523
Banaue 304; 8.42
Ban Biao 555
Banbo 245; 7.13, 7.14
Ban Chiang 236, 251, 254
Bandkeramik culture 394, 398, 407–13, 418; 11.8, 11.23, 11.24, 11.25, 11.26
Ban Don Ta Phet 236
bands (human society) 32
Bandurria 647
Bangkok 252
Bangladesh 547; 14.35
Bang Pakong River 252
Ban Gu 555
Ban Kao 248, 252; 7.23
Ban Khu Muang 591
Ban Lum Khao 251
Ban Na Di 236
Ban Non Wat 250; 7.19, 7.20
Ban Phak Top 251
Ban Prasat 236
Banteay Choeu 586
Bantu 28, 37, 366–67
Baoshan 559

Baradostian 203
Bard 372, 375
Barhut 548
Barinas 675
Barkaer 418
barkcloth beaters 284, 287
Barlambidj 275
barley 184, 185, 205, 226, 227, 261, 351, 362, 363, 365, 371, 388, 433, 436, 525, 526, 536; 6.32, 14.3
Barrancoid 669, 671, 675
Barton Gulch 331
Bar-Yosef, O. 153, 217, 227, 230, 233, 242
Bashidang 242, 243, 244
baskets 311, 322, 333, 340, 525, 553, 688, 709
Bass Strait 181, 267, 270
Basta 217
Ba system 566
Batadomba Lena 523
Batanes Islands 283, 285, 289
Batan Grande 642, 662; 17.31
Bat Cave 317
batons 165
battleaxes 419, 557
Bau Du 236
Bavaria 420, 424, 428
beads 154, 253, 254, 287, 356, 390, 403, 522, 525, 550, 585, 688, 699, 707; 4.30, 8.40, 10.7
Beaker pottery 408, 419, 420–21, 424; 11.36, 11.37, 11.38
beans 186, 205, 226, 314, 315, 320, 321, 340, 344, 349, 636, 647, 649, 689, 701
Becán 611, 620
Beck, Warren 157, 311
bees 371
Begho 384
Begram 540, 549
behavioral patterns 49, 78, 130, 140–46, 162–63
Behustun 541
Beijing 99, 563
Beikthano 590
Beinan 286–87; 8.18, 8.19, 8.20
Belém mound 672
Belfer-Cohen, Anna 209, 230
Belgium 148
Belize 611, 619, 630
Bell beakers see Beaker pottery
bells 555, 562, 563, 568, 582, 597, 610
bell-shaped pits 526; 14.4
Bel'sk 428
belts 211, 576, 585
Bengal 521
Benin City 352, 384; 10.38
Berber 383
Berekhat-Ram 117, 118; 3.42
Beringia 166, 169, 710
Bering Strait 166, 179
Bernal, Martin 375, 475, 490
Beydar 452
Bhimbetka 520, 523
Bhir Mound 544; 14.24, 14.26
Bhita 548
Bhokardan 549
Bible 28, 31, see also Old Testament
Bidatsu, Emperor 580
Bien Ho 252
big-game extinctions and hunters 171, 172, 312, 339; 4.55
Bigo 386
Bilzingsleben 112, 114, 115, 116, 117, 119, 126, 148; 3.36, 3.43, 3.44
Binford, Lewis 70, 75, 120, 143, 144, 152, 189, 212, 510; 1.15
Bingham, Hiram 667

biostratigraphy 75
bipedal walking 47, 49, 52, 56, 61, 83; 2.5
birdman figures 297, 301; 8.32, 8.33
birds 296, 339, 358, 706
Birimi 364
Bir-kotghundai 539
Birnin 384
Biskupin 394, 425; 11.46
Bismarck Archipelago 291
bison 150, 166, 172, 307–08, 309, 331, 703; butchering 309; 9.3, 9.4, 9.24, 9.25
bitumen 525; 14.23
Bituriges 428; 11.49
Black Death 719
black earth sites 673
Black Sea 393, 402, 403, 406, 453, 486, 488; cities 420, 427
Blackwater Draw 171
Blegen, Carl 484
Blombos Cave 126, 141, 142, 143; 4.17, 4.18, 4.19, 4.20
Blumenschine, Robert 74, 75, 81, 82
Blust, Robert 280, 290
boar 527
boats 102, 246, 247, 275, 358, 553
Bodhgaya 542
Bodo 132, 133, 141
Boeotia 484, 488
Boğazköy 454, 455
Bohemia 424, 430
Boii 430
bolas 347
Boldkilde 418
Bolivia 297, 644, 660, 671, 672, 676; Moundbuilding cultures 642
Bonampak 625
bone artifacts 112, 115, 118, 120, 122, 142, 143, 144, 158, 239, 526, 530, 546; 3.36, 3.43, 3.44, 4.19, 4.35; arrowheads 561; awls 257, 333; beads 154; butchering tools 309–10; dating of 142; fishhooks 253, 292; hairpins 561; harpoons 292, 357, 363, 396; hoes 705; knives 246, 711; needles 158, 247, 333; 4.35; ornaments 561; pendant 356; points 272, 523, 525; 8.21; reels 292; shuttles 247; spades 247, 556; 7.15; spatulas 272; spindle whorls 247
bone dwelling: Mezhirich 4.45; Thule 18.39
bonobos 52, 53, 69
Border Cave 132
Bordes, François 152
Borneo 155, 276, 278, 279, 284, 285, 286, 289, 291
Borobudur 302, 303, 304; 8.26, 8.38
Boserup, Ester 186
Botswana 142, 369
bottle gourds see gourd
bow and arrow 163, 706
Bowdler, Sandra 270, 271, 272
Boxgrove 119
Boyd Hawes, Harriet 482
bracelets 211, 254, 259, 287, 403, 582
Bradley, Richard 412, 427
Brahmans 542
Brahui 521, 532
Braidwood, Robert 188, 201, 212, 216, 226
brains 50, 52, 61, 78, 81, 89–90, 110, 121–22; and language 146
brass 10.37, 10.38
Bräuer, Gunter 129, 135, 139
Brazil 169, 312, 347, 644, 646, 669, 671, 676
breadfruit 523
Bresinchen 422; 11.39
Breton 430
Britain 394, 398, 420, 421, 427, 430; Fosse Way 13.46; Hadrian's Wall 514; 13.53; Magdalenian 163;

postglacial 179, 394; Roman 511; Star Carr 396–97, 415; 11.4, 11.5, 11.6; Stonehenge 414, 416
British Columbia 167, 260, 331, 679
Britons 30
Brittany 414, 420, 427; 11.22, 11.29; farming 394
broad-spectrum economies 142, 144
Broederstroom 369
Broken Hill 132, 133, 134
bronze 351, 390, 393, 419–20. 421, 424, 476, 540, 562, 565, 571; axes 422, 582; 11.39; bells 555, 582; 7.32; belts 585; breastplates 425; ceremonial vessels 561; daggers 422, 582; earrings 582; figure of a man 565; 15.18; figurines 565, 590; helmets 425; hoard 422, 11.39; knives 582; krater 424, 427, 490; 11.44; mirrors 578; 13.23; neckrings 11.39; ornaments 557, 559, 575; ritual vessels 559, 568; shoes 576; spearheads 582; swords 425, 576; vessels 560, 562, 566, 576; 10.43, 15.12, 15.13, 15.14
Bronze Age 31, 236; Aegean 394, 450, 463, 476, 477–80, 482, 510; China 582; Europe 420, 426, 473; 11.23; Jericho 216; Korea 554; Mediterranean 476–80; Scandinavia 394, 426; South Asia 534, 537; Southeast Asia 554; Southwest Asia 433, 434, 442–63; Syria 231; Thailand 250
bronze casting 582
bronzeworking 302, 419, 420, 557, 565–66, 568, 583
Brooks, Allison 141, 143, 144
Brown, Peter 87, 131
Bruce-Foote, Robert 522
Brudevaelte 422
bubonic plague 719
Budakalasz 410
Buddha 540, 542, 590; 15.32
Buddhism 280, 302, 303, 519, 548, 549; Borobudur 303, 304; 8.26, 8.38; Cambodia 589; China 575, 576, 577, 585; Japan 580, 581, 582; Mohenjo-daro 534; South Asia 545, 548, 549, 550; Thailand 591; 15.46
buffalo 142, 522, 523
Buganda 385
Bug River 427, 488
Buhen 374
Buia 105
Bulgaria 402; Karanovo 401; 11.10
burial jars 303
burials 113, 141, 152–53, 162, 165, 249; of ashes 425, 590; in cairns 365; children buried alive 561; child wrapped in cotton textile 648; cist burial 544; 14.28 ; in cruciform pattern 256; with deer antlers 11.22; detached skulls 223; of dogs 323, 326, 561; 9.19; in family group 489; funerary feasts 410; Ganges plain 523; of horse 539; jar burials 575; kofun, Japan 578; 15.34, 15.35; lion and leopard cub, Uruk 440; Middle Paleolithic 26, 141; Native Americans 30; Neolithic practices 418–19; in peat deposits, Florida 322; of pigs 556; pit graves in hillsides 574; in pottery vessels 250; 7.19; in raised precincts at Yaoshan 553; and ritual enclosures 428–29; ritual treatment 341; shell mounds 9.19; Sipán 657; 17.24; skull caching 221; Southwest Asia 436; stone-lined pits 539; under houses 222, 223, 225, 286; Upper Paleolithic 26; urn 671; in vessels 537; Windover, Florida 322
burins 311
Burkina Faso 364
Burley, David 288
Burma 302, 590
Burnaburiash II, King 460
Burnt House, Arpachiyah 436
Burundi 365, 367, 368

Burzahom 520, 526, 531; 14.4
Bushmen 355, 358; 10.9
butchering tools 309–10
butterflies 628
Butzer, Karl 35, 43, 134
Byblos 434, 453
Byzantine empire 516, 719

Cabeço da Arruda 397
Cabral, Pedro 669
Cacaxtla 596, 621, 622, 624
cactus 331, 334, 337, 343
Cactus Hill, USA 168, 169
Cagayan Valley 285, 289
Cagny l'Épinette 119
Cahokia 330, 673, 680, 688–89, 690–91, 705; 18.14, 18.15, 18.16
Cai Beo 236
Caimito 642, 674, 17.44
cairns 414
calabash tree gourds 315
Calakmul 623, 624, 626, 627
Caldwell, Joseph 311
calendars 37, 595; Mesoamerica 37, 606–07; 1.14, 16.12, 16.13, 16.14
California 330, 331, 333, 334, 679, 706, 713
Calmadana 584
Calusa 689
Cambodia 195, 252, 302, 586, 593; see also Angkor
camelids 326, 336, 339, 341, 342, 343
Cameron, Judith 262
Cameroon 360, 364, 365, 367, 369
campsites, early 70, 110, 154, 162, 206, 208, 212, 314, 324–25, 333, 334, 338, 341, 342, 396–97; 9.17
Camutins people 672
Canaan 456
Canada 166, 171, 310, 679, 703, 712, 714, 715
canals 570, 620, 634, 694; irrigation
Cancuen 628
Caneiro, Robert 197
Cannae 504
cannibalism 108, 120, 700
Cann, Rebecca 137, 139
canoes 275, 292, 293, 332, 338, 358, 383, 597, 706, 707, 708; 8.27
Cantona 620, 621
Cape Dinh 591
Cape of Good Hope 30, 355, 359, 369, 370
Cape Nay 591
Cape York 273
Capitoline Hill 506
Cappadocia 453
Capsian industries 358
capybara 347
Caquetio 669, 675
Caracol 623
Caral 344, 348, 642, 645, 648, 649; 9.41, 9.42
carbon-14 see dating methods: radiocarbon
Carchemish 456, 460, 464
Carib 669
Caribbean 30, 644, 672, 675
caribou 711
Carib people 673
Cariguela de Piñar 404
Carlston Annis 326; 9.20
Carnac 414–15
Carneiro, Robert 670
carnelian 442, 536, 540; beads 390, 550, 585; 8.40
Caroline Islands 290, 292, 294, 296; 8.34
Carpathians 393, 406
carpets 504
Cartailhac, Emile 252
Carter, Howard 27

Carter, Joe 489
Carthage 388, 427, 473, 474, 490, 500, 516; empire 503; ironworking 368; and Rome 383; Tophet, child sacrifice 504. 505; 13.41
carving 26, 118, 152, 162–63, 216; 3.43, 3.44; bas-reliefs of animals 220; Celtic 11.50; Cerro Sechín 651; 17.11, 17.12; Chavín de Huántar 653; 17.15; Hittite 455; Monte Albán 608, 612; 16.18; monument from San José Mogote 16.14; Olmec 605; 16.8, 16.10; Plumed Serpent Pyramid, Xochicalco 622; Pukara 655
Casa Grande 694
Casas Grandes 631
Casma Valley 647, 651, 652, 653
Caspian Sea 583
Castel di Guido 112
Castle Rock Pueblo 700
Çatalhöyük 40, 203, 217, 218, 223, 224–25, 230, 231–32, 439, 476; 1.19, 6.28, 6.29. 6.30, 6.31
Catalonia 398
Catfish Cave 357
Cato "the Censor" 504
cattle: Africa 358, 361, 362, 363, 364, 365, 367, 371, 382; 10.12; China 556; domestication 184, 227, 228, 229, 362; 5.6, 5.7; Europe 414, 419; North America 719; Philistines 464; "Sanga" 369; South Asia 519, 522, 523, 526, 528, 530
Caucasus Mountains 106, 155, 449
Cau Sat 252
Cauvin, Jacques 208, 212, 230, 233
Cavajal, Friar Gaspar 672–73
Cavalli-Sforza, Luca 187, 398
cave art 158, 160–61, 163; 1.20, 4.41
Cave of Hearths 116, 132, 137
caves 312, 322, 332, 340, 395
Çayönü 203, 218, 220, 228, 476
Celts 394, 420, 424, 428–29, 430, 488
cemeteries: Balkans 402; Banditaccia, Cerveteri 492, 13.22; Bandkeramik 407; Bronze Age 250, 251; Cambodia 253; Carthage 505; Central Africa 386; Chengzi 555; Chile 334; China 242, 247; Chisandong 575; Craig Mound 688; Cyclades 479; Dadianzi 556–57; El Kurru 381; Eridu 437; Eynan 211; Fangshan 563; Greek 496; Gumogu 582; Harappa 537, 538; Karakdong 575; Kerma 380; Khok Phanom Di 254–55; 7.26, 7.27; Kyongju 576; Metapontum 489; 13.18; Mochlos 479; Naju 575; Norris Farms 691; Nuri 381; Oleneostrovski Mogilnik (Deer island Cemetery) 11.3; Peiligang, China 7.5, 7.6; Pokchongdong 574; Rome 509; Sarai Khola, Taxila 539; Scandinavia 418; Sumer 444; Susa 437; Taosi 555; Tarquinia 492; Téviec, Brittany 410; 11.22; Tiszapolgor-Basatanya 406; Ur 444; urnfields 425; Varna 403; 11.12; Xincun 563, see also burials; grave goods; tombs
Cemetery H culture (Late Harrappan) 537, 538
cenotaphs 403
Cenozoic era 50
Centaurs 499
Central Africa 355–56, 385–86
Ceprano 108, 110; 3.33
ceramics 245, 246, 247, 346–47, 388, 524, 525, 526, 527, 530, 564, 616, 645, 654, 663, 669, 671, 674, 697, 699
cereals 205, 222, 226, 229, 367, 525, 718
Cernunnos 427
Cerro Baul 662
Cerro Juanaqueña 318; 9.12
Cerros 611
Cerro Sechín 651; 17.11, 17.12
Cerveteri 491, 492; 13.22
Chaco 679, 680, 698–700, 715; 18.23

Chad 56, 59, 362
Chaeronea 474, 500
Chagar Bazar 436
Chalandriani 479
Chalca 633
Chalcatzingo 596, 600, 605
Chalchuapa 605
Chalcolithic period 229, 231, 427, 442, 528, 543, 551
Chaldeans 468
chalice 539
Cham 591–92
Champa 592; 15.47, 15.48
Chancay 647
Chan Chan 642, 645, 662, 663, 673; 17.32, 17.33, 17.34
Chandragupta 551
Chang'an 569
Changbin 284
Chang Chu 590
Changjiang culture 562–63
Changsha 572
Chania 480, 484
Chao Phraya River 252, 591
chariots 425, 560, 564, 566
Charklik 584
Charlemagne 516
charnel houses 687
Charsadda 520, 541, 542, 546, 548, 549
chat 365
Chatters, James 168
Chau Can 236
Chauvet 158, 160–61; 4.41
Chaves 404
Chavin de Huantar 642, 645, 650, 653–55, 671; 17.14, 17.15, 17.16
Chengbeixi culture 248
Chengdu 562
Chengtoushan 236, 246, 553, 562
Chengziyai 555, 558
Chenla 554
chenopod 321, 328, 330, 335, 348
Cherchen 584
chert 536, 683; microblades 707
Chersonesus 488
chia 315, 636
Chiapa de Corzo 605
Chibuene 388
Chicama Valley 647, 656, 659
Chichén Itzá 596, 610, 632, 638; 16.41
Chichimec 633
chickens 239, 242, 369, 387
chickpeas 365, 371
chiefdoms 32–33, 290, 298–9, 300–01, 380, 540, 670, 676, 703, 707; North America 680, 680–81, 686–87, 691
Chifumbaze 367; 10.17
Chihuahua 318, 319, 693; 9.12
Chijiayngzi 556
Chilca 336, 337, 344; 9.32
Childe, V. Gordon 32, 188, 196, 205, 217, 477–78, 675
Chile 167, 168, 169, 312, 342, 641, 645, 646, 648, 660; Chilean coast 336–38; Chinchorro mummies 336, 337, 338–39; 9. 9.34, 9.35; Monte Verde 170
chili peppers 315, 340, 344, 647, 648
Chillon River 647, 649
Chimor 662, 663, 664, 675
chimpanzees 52, 53, 61, 69, 79; chimpanzee-human divergence 54; compared with Homo sapiens and Homo neanderthalensis 4.21
Chimú empire 297, 645; 8.32

China 26, 126, 187, 194, 195, 198, 235, 245–49, 248, 259, 261, 277, 280, 384, 388, 549, 719; agriculture 187, 235, 238, 240–44, 570; Chinese script 558–59; complex societies 553–74; Eastern Zhou Dynasty 566–68; Han Dynasty 569–74; *Homo erectus* 99–101, 116, 119, 130, 155; 3.19; *Homo sapiens* 130; and Japan 580; Longshan 555–56; Lower Xiajiadian culture 556–57; metallurgy 582; pottery and hunter-gatherers 260; Qin Dynasty 568; religion 571–73; Shang Dynasty 558–63; and Southeast Asia 302; and Southeast Asian islands 302; Western Zhou Dynasty 563–66; Yellow River Valley 245–49; *see also* individual sites

chinampas 620, 628, 634, 635
Chinchorro 336, 337, 338–39, 642, 645, 646, 648; mummies 336, 337, 338–39; 9. 9.34, 9.35
Chinchukmil 628
Chinpari 574
Chirand 527
chisels 249, 288, 403, 582; 8.21
Chitamni 257
Chitral 539
chlorite 446; 12.18
Chobshi 339
Chogha Zanbil 434
Chokepukio 665
Cholistan Desert 530, 531
Cholula 620, 622, 631
Chopani Mando 527
Chotuna 662
Christianity 28, 29, 382, 388, 475, 515; and Darwinism 31, 32
chronology 182; and archaeology 25–26; sequences 31; stratigraphy 30; *see also* dating methods
Chu 236, 563, 566, 571, 572
Chuangbanlin 248
Chuera 445, 452
Chulmun culture 236, 256
Chumash 706; 18.31
Chu-mei Ho 254
Chunchucmil 619
Chupacigarro, Caral 345; 9.42
Cieza de Leon 666
Cilicia 457
cinnabar 616
Circeo 149
Cishan 236, 238, 239
citadels 534, 615, 616, 663
cities 193–97, 380–82, 420, 426, 530, 610–11, 624, 628; and citizen ideal 487; city-states 394, 456, 486, 488, 490, 491, 516; Egypt 372, 378, 379; Indus 529, 537–38; Phoenicians 490; Southwest Asia 438–71; urban abandonment 448; urban spread 624
citrus fruit 369
ciudadelas 615, 616, 663, 664
civilization 33, 193, 196, 438, 471, 476, 528–29, 531, 639, 648, 718; Amazon 675; Mesoamerica 598, 604; South America 651, 668
Clacton-on-Sea 114
Clark, Desmond 68, 70, 78
Clarke, David 38
Clark, Graham 396
Classic Kisalian tradition 387
clay: building 401; figures 401–02, 554; 11.11, 12.3, 12.5, 12.6; house models 401; models 573; seals 436
clay tablets 440, 441, 452, 453, 454, 455, 466; 12.10, 12.19, 12.33, 12.34; Ebla 452; 12.26; Ugarit 457
Cleopatra VII 507
climate 40, 55–57, 127, 172, 177–83, 393, 474, 633; Africa 353; 10.2; change 718, 720; and collapse of

empires in Mesopotamia 448; Europe 393, 474; and extinction of animals 178; North America 317; post glacial changes 177–83, 204, 206, 242, 244, 265, 267, 307, 394; 5.1, 7.11; South America 641; South Asia 521
Cloaca Maxima, Rome 506; 13.42
clothes 158, 272, 322, 355, 408, 574, 610, 654; 11.20
Clottes, Jean 160
Cloudsplitter 327
Clovis period 126, 168, 169, 170, 171, 172, 178, 307, 331; points 307, 333; 4.54, 9.1
clubs 709
Côa Valley, Portugal 160
coastal landscape 267, 641–42, 644; 8.2
Coba 630, 632
coca 335, 344
cocoa 315
Cocom 633
coconut 369
Codex Fejérváry-Mayer 1.14
Cody 307; 9.1
coffee 365
coffins 553, 557, 575, 576, 578
cognitive archaeology 26
Cohuna 131
coins and currency 382, 385, 387, 388, 428, 584; 1.13, 10.34; cowrie shells 562; of Alexander the Great 13.36, 14.30; Mauryan 548, 14.34; Mexico 610; "owl" of Athens 495, 13.24; Persian 544; Vesali 590
Cold Oak 327
Coles Creek 686
Colima 604
Colledge, Sue 226, 227
Co Loa 249
Colombia 334, 339, 347, 597, 610, 644, 646, 675
Colorado 309, 318, 319, 679, 696, 697
Colorado Plateau 695, 696, 697, 700; abandonment 700
Colosseum 508
Colossus of Rhodes 503
Columbia River 332
Columbus, Christopher 669, 710, 712, 719
Columnata 358
columns and archaeology 25
Con Co Ngua 236
Confucianism 566, 567, 574, 580, 581; 15.20
Congo 355, 385
cong tubes 248, 553, 555; 7.16
Constantine 515, 13.55
Constantinople 516
Constantini, Lorenzo 525
cooking 223, 239, 247, 259, 260, 261, 327, 357, 684, 697; 6.29; mounds 274; Neanderthal 152; vessels 242, 288
Cook Islands 292, 294, 296, 300
Cook, James 280, 282, 292, 298, 301, 707
Copán 596, 619, 623, 624, 625, 628
Copeland Island 275
Coppens, Yves 60
copper 192, 256, 326, 343, 351, 363, 368, 371, 384, 387, 390, 403, 405, 419, 459, 467, 490, 510, 525, 540, 546, 562, 598, 610, 654; artifacts 409, 685; awls 582; axes 403, 409, 421, 539; beads 525; bells 597; bracelets 582; chisels 403, 582; currency 10.40; daggers 406, 420, 421; earrings 582; hairpin 582; hammered copper plates 687; hammers 403; hoard 408, 11.21; ingots 459; 12.38; knives 421, 582; ornaments 409; tools 536
Copper Age 231, 394, 402, 406, 476
copper alloy 384
copper mining 419–20, 510, 571; 15.25
copperworking 394

cordage 322, 333, 340
corded ware beakers 419
Cordillera 312, 641, 646, 651; 9.36
Coren del Valento 427
Corinth 474, 504
cormorants 335
Cornwall 420, 430
Corozar 642
Corsica 404, 477
Cortaillod-Est 394, 423; 11.43
Cortés, Hernan 598, 633, 634, 638
Cosquer Cave 160
Costa Rica 610
Cotahuasi 336
cotton 320, 343, 344, 345, 348, 525, 616, 628, 647, 649, 701; 9.6
counting systems 440–41, 446, 595, 606
Cousteau, Yves 512
Coveta del'Or 404
cowpeas 364, 369
cowrie shells 384, 561, 562, 564
Coxcatlán 316
Craig Mound 687, 688; 18.10, 18.11
cremation 26, 425, 504, 590, 694
Creswellian 163
Crete 394, 400, 473, 474, 476, 477, 479, 486, 490; agriculture 11.8; *see also* Minoans
Crimea 427
Croatia 126, 140, 149, 150, 158, 400, 508
Croce del Papa 394, 423; 11.42
Crow Creek 680, 705; 18.30
crowns 575, 576
Cuachi 659
Cubilan 339
cucumbers 536
Cueva del Medio 168
Cu Lao Rua 252
Culebras 647
cultivation 183, 184, 213, 214, 347, 351, 362, 684; Mexico 314–15; North America 689
cultural anthropology 25
cultural ecology 32, 35–36
Cultural Resource Management 696
Cumancaya 642, 674
Cunningham, Sir Alexander 544
Cunzierton 11.28
cushaw squash 314, 315, 320; 9.8
Cuzco 662, 665, 666, 667, 668, 675
Cybele cult 224
Cycladic Islands 196, 476, 479, 482, 487; 13.4, 13.5
Cyclopean masonry 482, 485
cylinder seals 441, 442, 459; 12.11
Cyprus 203, 228, 229, 456, 457, 459, 477, 486; colonization 229; 6.34, 6.35; Troödos Mountains 476
Cyrene 383
Cyrus the Great 468, 469
Czech Republic 116, 160, 162

Dabenkeng 262, 283–84; 8.15
Dacian wars 508
Dadianzi 557; 15.6
Dadiwan 238
Dadunzi 236, 249
daggers 406, 420, 421, 422, 479, 564, 582; 11.21, 11.39
Dagon, god 457
Dahezuang 582
Dahshur 374
Daima 363; 10.13
Dainzu 613
Dakhleh Oasis 358
Dakhlet el Atrous 383

Dali 126, 130; 4.4
Dalmatia 400
Dalton 9.5
Dalverzin-tepe 549
Damdama 522
dance 26, 359; in art 359; 10.9
Danger Cave 326, 332; 9.26, 9.27, 9.28, 9.29
Danube 393, 402, 406, 430, 508; 11.8, 11.16, 11.17
Daode jing 559
Daoism 559, 580
Dardanelles 450
Dar-es-Soltan 132, 137
Darius I, King 469, 487; 14.22
Darius III, King 500; 13.35
Dark Age, Greek 486
Dart, Raymond 97; 2.8
dart shafts 333
Darwin, Charles 31, 43, 47–48, 53, 59; 1.9
Dasas 538
dates (fruit) 362, 384
dating: of artifacts 100; of bone artifacts 142;
    Electron Spin Resonance (ESR) 106, 107; of
    fossils of early hominins 74–75, 98; Homo erectus
    in Java 97–99; Homo ergaster at Dmanisi 103–04
dating methods: argon-argon 75; biostratigraphy 75;
    fission-track 75, 98, 102; luminescence dating
    119; paleomagnetism 74, 104; potassium-argon
    75, 89, 98; radiocarbon dating 33–34, 36, 74, 156,
    157, 602; 1.10; stratigraphy 30, 74, 98; tree-ring
    dating 696; 18.21; tuff correlations 74, 98;
    Uranium-Series 111
David, King 464
Dawenkou 236, 245–46
Daxi culture 236, 246, 553
Dayan Cave 260
Deacon, Terrence 79–80
Dead Sea 512
Debert 171
Debra damo 388
Deccan 521, 527, 536, 548, 549; 14.6, 14.21
Dederiyeh 149, 150, 154
deep-sea diving 337
deer 172, 225, 227, 311, 331, 338, 339, 342, 347, 395,
    522, 523, 525; antler frontlet 396, 397; 11.4
Deer Island Cemetery 11.3
defensive walls 559
Delian League 487
Delphi 430, 499, 501, 546
Democratic Congo 72, 126, 142, 356, 359, 367, 386
demographic theories of agriculture 188–89
Denham, Tim 278
Denmark 179, 415, 417, 418, 425, 429; 11.34, 11.35;
    Bygholm 409; 11.21; metalworking 422;
    Trundholm sun chariot 422; 11.41
Dennell, Robin 522
Deraniyagala, S. U. 523
deserts 178, 181, 312, 317, 320, 353, 641–42, 645,
    647, 648, 649, 655, 660, 662; Great Basin
    Desert Archaic 322–23; see also Sahara
devil's claw 321
Devil's Tower 149
Dhanyawadi 590
Dhar Tichitt 362
Dhar Tichitt-Walata 383
Dhayakataka 549
Dholavira 520, 533; 14.12, 14.13
Diamabad 540
Diaotonghuan 236, 241, 242; 7.8
Dickinson, William 288
Dido, Queen 503; 13.39
Die Kelders 132, 137, 143, 369
diet 78, 118–19, 150–51, 162, 207, 214, 684; and
    bone chemistry 81–82; Paleoindian 310, 311, 313

diffusion 36
digging stick weights 356
Di, god 562, 571
Dillehay, Thomas 167, 168, 169, 170, 173, 312, 313,
    334, 335
Dillingen 407
Dilmun 446
Dinggong 555, 558
Diocletian, Emperor 508, 516
Dionysos, god 498
Dir Valley 539, 542
diseases 706, 713, 714, 718, 719; spread of 275
ditches 274, 278, 570, 702
Diuktai culture 166
divination 557, 562
Divostin 406
Dixon, Jim 230
Djibouti 364
Djoser, King 373; 10.23
Dmanisi 57, 102, 103, 104; 3.23, 3.24; 3.25, 3.26,
    3.27
DNA 32, 34, 53, 54, 125, 128, 137–38; 4.21; and
    Austronesians 283; and colonization of the
    Americas 166–67; analysis of human remains
    322; and domestication 184, 185; and European
    population 398; and language 146; and maize
    316; mtDNA genealogy 138–40, 235, 398; 4.15
Dnieper 393, 488
Dniester 393
Dodecanese 486
Do Dimi 365, 368
Doggerland 179; 5.4
dogs 183, 252, 288, 298, 363, 423, 523, 556, 610,
    703, 718; burial, Green River, Kentucky 326; 9.19;
    for hunting 369; Mexico 314; remains 284
dolmen tombs 257; 7.29
Dolní Věstonice 162, 164
Dolores River 697
dolphins 346, 347
domesticated animals 183–86, 188, 189, 718, 719;
    Africa 361–62, 369; 10.11; Andes 343–44;
    Austronesians 283; Egypt 369; Europe 397, 402,
    414, 419, 477; Sahara 361–62; South America
    342, 645, 647; South Asia 519, 523, 524, 526;
    Southwest Asia 212, 227, 228, 229, 230, 435, 436;
    6.33
domesticated plants 184, 185, 188, 189, 719; Africa
    364, 369; 10.14; Americas 314, 324–25; Andes
    343–44; East Asia 241–42; Europe 397, 402, 414,
    477; Mesoamerica 596, 598–99; South America
    645, 647; South Asia 519, 524; Southwest Asia
    214, 226–27, 228, 229, 230; in the tropical
    rainforest 348
domestication and DNA 185; 5.6
Domingo Garcia 160
Dominguez-Rodrigo, Manuel 75
Dong Dau 236
Dong Lakhon 591
Dong Nai Valley 252
Dongodien 365
Dongola Reach 380
Dong Shou 574
Dong Si Mahosod 591
Dong Son 236, 302
donkeys 369, 453
Dorians 486
Dorset culture 711; 18.37, 18.38
Dos Cabesas 659
Dos Pilas 16.40
Dourgne 404
drains 620, 628, 634
Drakensberg Mountains 358
Dravidian 521–22, 532, 538

drills 249, 323, 333
drums 302, 555
Dryas see Younger Dryas
Dryopithecus 51
dry-stone masonry 385
Dubois, Eugène 59, 97; 3.16
ducks 371
Duff, Andrew 697
Dufuna 358
Duinefontein 117, 119
Dura Europus 515
Durango 320
Durankulak 403
Dur Kurigalzu 461; 12.41
Dust Cave 326
Duvensee 395
Dvan Candra, King 590
Dvaravati 554, 590–91
dye, purple 464, 504

Eanna precinct, Uruk 439, 440; 12.7, 12.8
Early Archaic, Americas 322, 331, 334, 339, 342, 346
Early Khartoum 357, 358; 10.7
early non-lithic tools 79, 112, 113, 114, 122; 3.37, 3.38
earrings 287, 582
earth movement 276
earthworks 327, 329, 626, 647, 671, 672, 682;
    Mesoamerica 626; North America 327, 329, 682;
    18.5; South America 647, 671, 672
East Africa 351, 352, 359, 369, 388; agriculture
    364–65; human fossils 34, 61; iron 365; trade
    10.39
East Asia 139, 553; agriculture 235–63, 351
Easter Island (Rapa Nui) 108, 187, 265, 280, 290,
    293, 295–96, 299, 719; ahu and moai 301; 8.29,
    8.30, 19.2; social organization 300, 301; and
    South America 297; 8.31, 8.32, 8.33
Eastern Agricultural Complex 328, 330; 9.15
Eastern Han 554
Eastern Mebon, Angkor 588
Eastern Zhou dynasty 563, 566–68
East St Louis 684
East Turkana 77, 78, 82, 104; 2.19
Ebla 434, 445, 446, 447, 451, 452; 12.26, 12.26
Eburran 359
Ecuador 297, 334, 343, 348, 610, 641, 644, 646,
    651, 671, 674; 17.10
Edict of Milan 515
Edith Shahr 520, 536
Edo 384
eels 274
eggs 343
eggshells 356
Egypt 370–80; and Achaemenids 469; agriculture
    361; Akhenaten 377, 378, 459; 10.27; and
    Alexander the Great 500, 549; Alexandria 502;
    13.37; Amarna 378–79; 10.28; and Arabs 383;
    arrows 355; building 374, 376, 379; carnelian
    beads 390; chronology 371; decline of power
    378–79; domesticated animals 369; Early
    Dynastic period 372, 373, 477; faience tiles 10.24;
    First and Second Intermediate periods and and
    Middle Kingdom 376–77; fishing 357;
    hieroglyphs 372, 381, 382; and Hittites 456, 460;
    human fossils 132, 137; hunter-gatherers 356;
    10.6; Hypostyle Hall 10.30; iron 292, 365;
    irrigation 192; Mons Claudianus quarry 13.48;
    mounds 672; mummies 377; 10.26; and
    Mycenaeans 486; New Kingdom 377–79; and
    Nubia 380; Old Kingdom 374, 376, 447, 448; and
    the Old Testament 466; as part of Africa 375;
    pharaohs 375; Predynastic period 363, 371–73,
    477; 10.21; Ptolemaic dynasty 501, 503, 507;

pyramids 374, 376; 10.23, 10.25, 10.32; ships 292; Narmer palette 10.22; states 194, 195; Step Pyramid 10.25; Tutankhamun's tomb 26, 379; 1.2, 10.29; urban life 10.28; Valley of the Kings 377; 1.2, 10.29; writing 197, 198
Ehringsdorf 126, 148
Eisack Valley 409
Ekron 464
El Abra 339
Elam 447, 449, 461, 462, 536
eland 142, 144, 359; 10.8
Elandsfontein 119, 132, 133–34
Elbe River 393
El Bujo 659
El Castillo 156
El Chayal 619
Electron Spin Resonance (ESR) 106, 107
elephants 150, 522, 564
Eleusis 484
Eliye Springs 134, 135
elk 311, 396, 397
elk antlers 396
El-Kherba, 73
Elmenteitan 365
El Mirador 611, 623, 624
El Morro 9.45
El Niño 641, 659, 662
Eloaua 291
Elp 423
El Paraiso 647, 648, 649, 651; 17.7, 17.8
El Porton Monument 1 609
El Salvador 595, 605
El Tajín 596, 620, 621; 16.29
Elymians 490
Emar 459
empires 193, 198, 302, 445, 453, 471, 660; collapse in Southwest Asia 447, 448, 456, 463
emulation 36
Endere 584
Endröd 406
Engel 337
Engis 148
England 30, 94, 107, 114, 119; Amesbury archer 421; 11.38; Boxgrove 119; Grimes Graves 415; Lindow Man 429; Low Ham 13.39; Star Carr 396–97; 11.4, 11.5; Stonehenge 30, 416–17; 11.30, 11.31, 11.32, 11.33; Swanscombe 147; see also individual sites
English Channel 5.4
Enkapune Ya Muto 365
Enlil, god 443
Enneri Bardagué 362
ensete 365; 10.14
Entremont 428; 11.30
Eocene epoch 50, 51
Ephesus 515
Epigravettian 163
Epi-Olmec 596
Epipaleoloithic 201, 203, 204, 205, 206, 207, 208, 209, 210, 212, 214, 221, 226, 227, 229, 232
equids 227
Equus cave 132, 137
Erbil 460, 461
Erdosy, George 527
Erech see Uruk
Eridu 436–37, 449, 470; 12.4, 12.5, 12.6
Eriksson, Leif 710
Eritrea 364, 382, 388
Erlitou 571
Eros 507
Er Shi Huangdi 568
Ertebølle-Ellerbek culture 415–16

Esarhaddon, King 464
Esh Shaheinab 363
Eskimo-Aleut 166, 167
Eskimos 710; see also Inuit
Estrada, Emilio 650
Estremadura 412
Ethiopia 352, 388; 10.35; cattle 364; Chistianity 382; colonization by Homo ergaster 101; Daka 105; Gona 69, 71, 82; Herto 126, 135, 141; Konso 94, 95; Melka Kunturé 114; Middle Awash Valley 61, 132, 135; Omo Valley 68, 71; states 380; see also Aksum
Ethiopian Plateau 351, 382
ethnicity and identity 39
Etruscans 394, 420, 427, 474, 490, 491–93, 493, 506; 13.20, 13.21, 13.22, 13.23
Euphrates 195, 201, 208, 214, 229, 232, 433, 436, 438, 442, 443, 450, 452, 461, 468, 532
Eurasia: agriculture 187, 192; Homo sapiens 85; primates 51
Europe 160, 720; Acheulean hand axes 101, 104, 105, 110; 3.8, 3.9, 3.21; agriculture 188, 193, 393, 396–400, 419–20; 11.8; Atlantic Europe 410–15; Aurignacian tools 157; Bronze Age 11.39, 11.42, 423; Central 406–10; chronology 182; climate change 177, 179, 181; colonist farmers 11.7, 11.8; Corded Ware culture 419; 11.37; dispersal of Homo sapiens in 153, 155, 156, 204; DNA studies of population 398; 11.6; domestication 185; farming settlements 402; fire 116–17; Gravettian 161–62; hand axe tradition 110; Holocene 394–431; Homo antecessor 108; Homo heidelbergensis 85, 106–07, 108; Homo neanderthalensis 107, 110–12, 117, 125; Homo sapiens 141, 156–58, 159, 161–66; Ice Age 178; Lower Paleolithic 93; Magdalenian 163–65; Mediterranean 402, 404–06, 473–517; Mesolithic 395, 396–97; metallurgy 192; Mousterian 96; non-lithic tools 114, 141; Northern 415–19; pigment fragments 118; post-glacial environment 393–95; Solutrean 161, 162; Southeastern 400–02; see also individual sites and countries
Eva 323
Evans, Arthur 477, 480, 484, 536
Evans, Clifford 650, 674
evolution 31–32, 43, 50–51; and agriculture 189; models of evolutionary change 48–49, see also Darwin, Charles; human evolution; primates, evolution of
evolutionary ecology 32
excavations 30; 1.11; Al-Hiba 12.14; Arikamedu 550; 14.36; Ban Kao 7.23; Ban Non Wat 7.24; Daima 10.13; Dmanisi 3.26, 3.27; Icehouse Bottom 9.17; Koster site 9.18; Star Carr 11.5
experimental archaeology 38, 76, 80–81; 1.16, 2.23, 2.24, 2.25, 2.26
exploration 29–30, 273
extinct mammals 172, 178; 4.55
Eyasi 132
Eynan 203, 208, 209, 210–11

faience 10.24
Fairservis, Walter 537
Faiz Muhammad 528
false banana 365; 10.14
Fan-Wen 592
Faron, Louis 676
Fawcett, Colonel Percy 668
Fa Xi' 585
Fayum Depression 363
feathers 603, 616
Fejej 71
Feldhoffer Cave 148; 1.8

feminist archaeology 39
Fengpitou 262
Fengxia 556
Fen River 237, 238
Fenshanbao, 246
Ferghana 583
Fertile Crescent 188, 201, 216, 226, 433
fibers 311, 320, 322, 323, 327, 328, 330, 333, 343, 536, 616; 9.1, 9.16, 9.27
Fiedel, Stuart 170
figs 362
figures/figurines 117, 158, 216, 223, 401, 542, 565, 590, 604, 687, 688; 3.42, 6.27, 11.11, 15.8, 18.10; Cycladic 478; 13.4; Halaf 436; 12.3; Ubaid 437; 12.5, 12.6; "Venus" 163, 164–65; 4.46, 4.47, 4.48, 4.49
Fiji 276, 296, 301
Finney, Ben 293
Fiorelli, Giuseppe 1.17
fire 78, 116–17, 122, 143, 144, 152, 169; 2.27, 2.28, 3.40, 3.41
fish 142, 144, 162, 163, 257, 275, 346, 347, 522
fishhooks 253, 256, 275, 292, 336, 337, 363; 9.31
fishing 142–43, 163, 312, 336, 357, 530, 676, 707; Africa 354, 357, 363; 10.3; Australia 270, 274; Egypt 357; Lepenski Vir 406; 11.16, 11.17; North America 324; salmon 333; South Africa 144; South America 338, 345, 641–42, 645; in Tasmania 271, 272
fishing gear 347; 9.31
fishing nets 311
fishing spears 247
fission-track dating 75
Five Hegemonies 566
Flannery, Kent 197, 205, 210, 228, 232, 314, 316
Flavian dynasty 508
flax 363, 371
Fleagle, John 51, 134
Flinders Ranges 273
flint 73, 94, 96, 108, 116, 163, 200, 396, 397, 403, 404, 415; 1.11; arrowheads 408, 421; 11.36; blades 211; knife 408; 11. 20; and luminescence dating 119; scatters 395, 396; working 38, 163, 230
Flomborn 407
floodplains 644, 692
Flores 102, 155, 277; 8.8; Homo floresiensis 155; 4.32
Florida 181, 260, 322, 327, 348, 349, 689, 712, 714, 715; 9.16
Florisbad 126, 134; 4.8, 4.9
Foley, Robert 129
Folsom 126, 168, 307, 309; 9.1
Fontaine, Henri 252
Fontana Ranuccio 112
food remains 254, 395
food storage 204, 205, 211, 212, 214, 217, 218, 219, 224, 239, 325, 327; meat 331; pits 319, 324
foraging 269, 270, 271, 274, 275, 313, 346, 355, 519, 646, 684; and farming 407
forams 254
Forbe's Quarry 148
Ford, James 320, 650
forests 181, 311; clearance 223, 365, 526, 684, 686, 718; North America 311–12; in Southwest Asia 6.1
formation processes 38
Forster, Johann Reinhold 280, 282, 292
Fort Ancient 682
Fort Myers 327
fortresses 576
Fort Rock Cave 333; 9.29
Forum Romanum 506
Forum of Trajan 508; 13.44
Fosse way 13.46

fossils 72, 74–75; African species in Israel 102; cut marks on fossil bones 74, 78, 82, 110; 2.22; dwarf mammoth 178; footprints 60; 2.10; isotopic studies 81–82; *Stegdon trigonocephalus* 102
Fossum 11.48
Fourth Cataract 381
fowl 288
fowling 324
foxes 227
France 30, 148; Acheulean hand axes 94, 119; Aurignac 156; burial mounds 418; caves 115; Celts 430; Chauvet Cave 44, 160, 161; 4.41; cities 420, 428; Entremont 429; 11.50; farming 11.7; Gravettian 162; hunter-gatherers 150; La Lazaret 115; 3.39; Mousterian 151; Neolithic 413–14; tin mining 420; Vix 427; 11.44; *see also individual sites*
Franchthi cave 395, 400; 11.2
Fraser River 332
Frere, John 94
frieze 494, 495, 612; 16.18; Moche, Huaca de la Luna 658; 17.25; Sechín Alto 652
fruits, as containers 324
Fubin 250
Fu Hao 562
Fujian 248, 284, 296
Fujiwara 582, 583
Funan 554, 585, 586
Funnel beaker (TRB) groups 394
furnace remains 368
furniture 464
furs 326, 574
Fushun 574
Futuna 290, 301

Gabon 365, 368
Gadir 490
Galatas 480
Galgenberg 164; Venus 4.47
Galicia 420, 427
Galigai 539
Gallinazo 642, 655; 17.19
Gama, Vasco da 30
Gamble, Clive 165
Gandhara 39, 541, 544, 546, 584; 14.22
Gandharan Grave culture 539, 541, 542, 545; 14.20, 14.24
Ganges, River 519, 520, 521, 522, 523, 524, 527, 539, 542, 543, 546, 547, 548
Ganges-Yamuna Doab 539–40, 543
Ganj Dareh 228
Gan River 248
Gansu 245, 570, 582
Ganweriwala 533, 537
Gao 384
Garden of Eden hypothesis 127
Garrard, Andrew 231
Garrod, Dorothy 208
Gate Basin 307; 9.1
Gaucher, Jacques 587
Gaudzinski, Sabine 150, 152
Gaugamela 500
Gaul 430, 506
Gaván period 642, 675
Gavrinis 414
Gaza 464
Gazargamo 384
gazelle 214, 215, 227, 525, 530; 6.15
Gê 669, 676
Gedi 384; 10.39
geese 371
ge (halberd) 249
Geissenklösterle 158, 164
gender archaeology 28

Genmei, Empress 580, 582
Geographical Information Systems (GIS) 25, 34, 476
geological eras 50–51
geomagnetic prospection 34
Georgia 57, 102, 103, 104, 106, 327, 683; 3.23, 3.24, 3.25, 3.26, 3.27
Germany 112, 126, 140, 148, 398; Bad Canstatt 119; Bandkeramik 407, 412–13; 11.23, 11.24, 11.26, 11.27; Bilzingsleben 114, 115, 116, 117, 118; 3.36, 3.43, 3.44; burial mounds 418; cave art 63, 164; Feldhoffer Cave 148; 1.8; Heuneburg hilltop enclosure 424; 11.45; hunter-gatherers 150, 152, 158, 415; Ice Age 5.4; Langweiler 412; Mauer jaw 92; 3.5; mounded burials 425; Neander Valley 128; Nebra sky-disk 422; 11.40; Schöningen wooden spears 114, 116; 3.37, 3.38; Talheim Death Pit 411; 11.23, 11.24; warfare 192; *see also individual sites*
Gesher Benot Ya'aqov, Israel 114, 116, 119
Ghaggar 528
Ghaggar-Hakra River 195, 533, 534, 536, 538
Ghagharia 523
Ghana 364, 380, 384
Ghats 521
giant deer 395
giant elk 178
Gibbon, Edward 516
gibbons 52, 53, 55
Gibraltar 149, 150; 4.26, 4.27
Gila river 692, 694
giraffe 359
Girsu 449
GIS (Geographic Information Systems) 25, 34, 476
Giza 292, 374, 376; 10.25
Gla 485
glass 382, 387, 390, 459, 464; beads 576, 584
goats 184; Africa 362, 363, 364, 365, 369, 371, 382, 387; China 556; Europe 423, 436; Mediterranean 494; South Asia 522, 526, 527, 530; Southwest Asia 223, 227, 228, 229, 231
Göbekli Tepe 203, 220; 6.22, 6.23, 6.24
Godin Tepe 442
Gogo Falls 365
Gokomere tradition 367
gold 192, 371, 382, 384, 403, 424, 442, 444, 457, 490, 510, 536, 540, 562, 564, 568, 574, 577, 597, 598, 610, 654; Andean 662; 17.31; beads 403; belts 576; bowl and spoon 568; 15.21 bracelets 403; chalice 575, 576; 15.31; crowns 575, 576; from Troy 451; 12.25; masks 482; 13.10; ornaments 403, 576, 585, 659; pectoral 610; pendants 539; penis sheath 403; rings 403, 576; Varna 402, 403; 11.12
Goldman, Irving 301
Golson, Jack 278
Go Mun 236
Gondophares 549
Gongwangling 130
Gontzy 163
goosefoot 325, 684; *see also* chenopod
Gordion 468, 469
Gordon, Chester 243
Goring-Morris, Nigel 206
Gorham's Cave 149; 4.26
gorillas 52, 53, 69
Gorman, Chester 243
Goshen 307; projectile points 9.1
Goulandris Master 478
gourds 314, 315, 322, 323, 324, 325, 326, 334, 340, 342, 344, 348, 647, 648, 649; 9.15, 9.38; bottle 314, 315, 319, 326, 328, 334, 335, 336, 337, 341, 343, 344; *see also* squash
Gournia 482

GPS (Global Positioning Systems) 34
gradualism (evolution) 48
graffiti 529, 531
Gran Chaco 676
Gran Dolina 102, 104, 108–09; 3.31. 3.32; *see also* Atapuerca; Sima de los Huesos
Grand Pressigny 415
Granikos River 500
Gran Pajetan 671
grapes 362, 494
graphite decoration 402
Grass Mesa Pueblo 697
Grauballe Man 429
Grave Creek 682; 18.2
grave goods 245, 246, 251, 323, 396, 522; adzes 253, 256; agate beads 585; agate ornaments 247; antlers 523; armor 574; arrowheads 522, 576; axes 555; bangles 585; baskets 688; battleaxes 419, 557; beads 253, 287, 522; belts 211; bone ornaments 561; bone points 523; bracelets 211, 287; bronze 424, 563; bronze bells 555; bronze belts 585; bronze figures 565; bronze ornaments 557, 575; bronze shoes 576; bronze swords 576; bronze vessels 560, 576; burnt rice 585; carnelian beads 585; ceramic vessels 553, 557, 585; ceremonial parapernalia 683; *cong* tubes 553, 555; copper 403, 405; corded ware beakers 419; cowrie shells 561; daggers 479; earrings 287; fabrics 654; figurines 401, 604; figurines of dogs 604; garters 211; gold 403, 424, 444; gold belts 576; gold crowns 575, 576; gold masks 482; gold nose ornaments 659; gold ornaments 576, 585; gold rings 576; Greek painted vases 492; headdress 211; headgear 654; helmets 560, 574, 576; hoes 585; images of animal masks and birds 553; iron armor 574; iron knives 585; iron spears 576; iron swords 576, 579; ivory 405; jade 287, 553, 561; jade axes 555; jade blades 565; jade faces 563; jade figures 561; jade figurines of turtles, frogs and monsters 561; jade ornaments 247, 557, 560, 576; jade pendants 553; jade rings 553, 555; lacquerware 557; lapis lazuli 444; limbs of pigs 557; mantles 654; masks 683; metal goods 11.12; mirrors 575, 576; 13.23; models of houses 604; mortuary vessels 15.6; necklaces 211; ocher 523; ostrich eggshell 405; pendants 256, 522; pigs' mandibles 555; quivers 575; riding accoutrements 576; rings 585; sealstones 479; shell beads 688; shell cups 688; shell jewelry 256; 7.26; shields 575; sickles 585; silver 444; silver ornaments 585; spades 585; spearheads 560; stone figure 683; swords 575; tools and ornaments 356; trophy heads 604; trophy skulls 659; tunics 654; vessels 254, 256; weapons 604; wine and food vessels 561; wooden drums 555; wooden figurines 688; wooden masks 688
gravers 311
graves: "Amesbury archer" 421; 11.38; Beaker 421; graves circles at Mycenae 482; 13.10, 13.11; St.Michel-du-Touch 405; Téviec 410; 11.22; *see also* burials; grave goods; tombs
Gravettian 126, 161–63; art 163, 164–65
Grayson, Donald 31, 172, 178
Great Basin 311, 330, 332, 333, 697, 703; 9.26, 9.27, 9.28, 9.29
Great Lake 586
Great Lakes 683
Great Orme 419
Great Plains 324, 330–31, 679, 703, 704, 705, 706
Great Salt Desert 332
Great Silla 554, 577
Great Temple of Amun-Re 10.30
Great Wall of China 568, 570; 15.24

Great Zimbabwe 385, 386–87, 388; 10.41, 10.42
Greece 149, 198, 378, 394, 422, 426, 427, 448, 450, 466, 474, 475; Archaic Period 486–87; cities 420, 486–87, 488, 494–500; Classical Period 487–88; colonization 488, 490, 506; countryside 498; culture 499, 501, 546; Dark Age 486; festivals 499; Franchthi cave 395, 400; 11.2; and India 544; Mycenean 482–86; Nea Nikomedeia 400; 11.9, 11.11; Neolithic 400–02, 404; Roman 511
Greenberg, Joseph 167
Greenland 204, 417, 511, 679, 710, 712, 720; 5.1
Greenlawdean 11.28
Green River 322, 323, 326; 9.19, 9.20
Green, Roger 297
Gremillion 328, 330
Grimes Graves 415
grindstones 208, 209, 246, 249, 343, 356, 526, 616; 6.7, 6.8
Gröbern 150
Grotta de Fumane 156
Grotta dell'Uzzo 404
Grotte Capeletti 362
Grotte du Pape 164
Grotte du Renne 148, 159; 4.40
Grotte Gazel 404
guanaco 338
Guangdong 248, 284, 296
Guarita 642
Gua Sireh 284
Guatemala 595, 601, 603, 605, 611, 616, 619, 638
Guattari 126, 148
guavas 315, 337, 344
guayaba 649
Gufkral 526
Guiana 644, 672
Guilá Naquitz 312, 314, 316, 599
guinea pigs 326, 342, 343
Guitarrero Cave 168, 312, 340, 341, 344; 9.37, 9.38
Gujarat 522, 532, 535, 536, 539, 550
Gulf of Antalya 203
Gulf of Honduras 597
Gulf of Mexico 324, 326, 327, 602
Gulf States 201
Gulf Stream 395, 720
Gulf of Thailand 235, 260
Gupta empire 551
Guta do Caldeirao 151
Gutenberg, Johannes 29
Guti 449
Gwisho hot springs 355; 10.5

Habuba Kabira 442
Habur plains 448
Hacınebi Tepe 442
Hadar 60, 71, 75, 89
Hadrian 511
Hadrian's Wall 514, 515; 13.53
Hadza 359
Haft Tepe 462
Hagelberg, Erika 235, 283
Haida 706
hairpins 561, 582
Hajdusamson 424
Hajji Muhammed 436
Hakra 530
Halaf 433–36, 470; 12.2
halberds 563; 11.39
Haldi, god 467
Haleakala 298
Halin 590
Hallan Çemi 203, 212, 218
Hallstatt 394, 490
Hallur 528

Hamburg 415
hammers 403, 526
Hammurabi, King 448, 449, 450; Law Code 434, 449; 12.23
hands 49, 52, 61
Han Dynasty 236, 302, 560, 566, 567, 569–70, 569–74, 584, 585
Hanging Gardens of Babylon 468
Hangzhou River 246–47
Hannibal 504
Han Shu 555
Han Songchram 253
Harappa 530, 531, 532, 533, 535, 536, 537, 551; 14.16, 14.17
Harappan 195, 196, 519, 520, 528, 529, 530, 531, 532, 533, 534–35, 536, 537, 539, 540, 551; script 519; *see also* Harappa; Indus civilization
hares 227, 522
Hariharalaya 588; 15.43
Hariti, god 545
Harlan, Jack 184, 205
Harpocrates 545
harpoons 142, 275, 292, 334, 357, 363, 396, 708; 9.31, 10.7, 18.37
Hastinapura 520, 540, 543
Hatay 458
Hathial ridge 542, 545; 14.25
hats 332, 709
Hattusa 434, 454, 455; 12.31, 12.32
Hattusili, King 454, 456
Hauah Fteah 132
Haury, Emil 693
Hawai'i 33, 187, 279, 290
Hawaiian Islands 296, 300, 301; 8.35; and New Zealand 298–99
Hayden, Bryan 187
Hayonim 209
Hazor 453, 463
headdress 211
Head-Smashed-In buffalo jump 331; 9.24, 9.25
hearths 143, 144, 152, 161
Hebat, sun goddess 455
Hebei 237, 238, 242, 556, 568
heddle-loom weaving 645
heiau 298; Mo'okini 8.35
Heidelberg 92
Heijo-kyo 583
Hellenistic culture 501, 503
Hell Gap 307; 9.1
Helmer, Daniel 228
helmets 560, 574, 576
Hemedu 243, 246, 247; 7.15
hemp 571
Henan 558, 559, 566
Henry, Don 206, 233
Hephaisteion 497
Hephthalite Huns 585
Herakleopolis 376
Herakles 501; 13.33
Herat 502
herding 183, 213, 222, 342, 343, 351, 364, 596, 641, 645, 661
Hermes 545
Herodotus 375, 387, 428, 430, 467, 469, 486, 493
Herold's Bay caves 142
Heröon 487
Herto 126, 135, 141
Heuneburg 424; 11.45
Hexian 130
Heyerdahl, Thor 293, 297
hickory nuts 322, 328
hides 343, 396, 504, 536
Hierakonpolis 371; 10.21

hierarchy 345, 553, 556, 576, 604, 625–27, 647, 650, 670, 708, 713, 718; Aztecs 637–38; and landscape 670; of settlement 532–35
hieroglyphs 199, 371, 381, 382, 454
Hilly Flanks Hypothesis 188
Himalayas 526, 539
Hinduism 302, 303, 550, 585; temple of Candi Lorojonggrang, Prambanan 8.39
Hindu Kush 521
Hiscock, Peter 268, 269, 270, 273
Hissarlık 450, 451, 482
history and archaeology 28; and prehistory 25, 26–27, 28; and written records 27, 28
Hittites 450, 454, 454–56, 458, 461; 10.24, 12.31, 12.32; and Egypt 456, 460; texts 454; 12.33
Hmong Mien 262
Hoabinhian 236, 249, 277
Hodder, Ian 39, 217, 224
Hodges, William 292, 301; 8.27
Hoedjies Punt 126, 132, 142
hoes 340, 556, 570, 585, 705; 7.31
Hogup Cave 332
Hohle Fels 158
Hohokam 318, 320, 348, 596, 680, 692, 693, 694; 18.17, 18.20
Hokkaido 259
Hoko River 332
Hole, Frank 210, 228, 232
Holocene 130, 165, 168, 177, 178, 179, 181, 185, 186, 195, 212, 229, 231, 719; 5.8; Africa 351–91; 10.1; Americas 307–49; Australia and Austronesians 265–305; Europe 393–431; hunter-gathers 265, 274; Sahara Desert 10.10; South America 644, 645, 646; South Asia 519–51, 527; Southeast Asia 276, 296
Homer 450, 451, 482
hominins 47, 53, 56–57, 61, 66, 68, 69, 70, 74, 75, 76, 77, 79, 80, 81, 82, 92, 98, 100, 102, 105, 121, 124, 126, 130, 133, 134, 146, 153, 155, 171
Homo (genus) 47, 61, 71, 73, 82, 153, 522; and Australopethecines 70, 78, 92
Homo antecessor 108–10
Homo erectus 33, 57, 58, 59, 61, 68, 70, 82, 85, 97–106, 121, 127, 136, 276, 277; 3.18, 3.19, 3.20, 3.40; in China 99–101, 120, 155; in Java 97–99, 105–06, 131, 155; 3.15, 3.16, 3.17; and other hominins 92, 99, 107, 110, 130
Homo ergaster 57, 61, 68, 70, 72, 82, 83, 95, 97, 98, 108, 118, 119, 133; anatomy of 85–92, 93, 135; 3.3; dispersion from Africa 101–05, 104; 3.22; and *Homo sapiens* 128, 133; and other hominins 92, 99, 105, 107, 121; *see also* Turkana Boy
Homo floresiensis 155; 4.32
Homo habilis 57, 61, 64, 67, 68, 72, 78, 79, 82, 85, 87, 88, 92, 104, 121
Homo heidelbergensis 85, 94, 102, 105, 106–07, 108, 110, 111, 125, 132, 133, 147; 3.5, 3.30; and other hominins 128, 147
Homo helmei 132, 134
Homo leakeyi 132, 133
Homo neanderthalensis 85, 92, 105, 106, 107, 108, 120, 121, 136; 3.29; anatomy 147, 149; 4.22; art 118; behavior 152–54; and DNA evidence 140; 4.21; evolution in Europe 110–12, 140; and *Homo sapiens* 125, 147, 159–60; extinction of 16–61; hunting, gathering and scavenging 149–50; Mousterian industry 150–51; and rodeo riders 149; 4.24; transitional industries 158–59
Homo rhodesiensis 133
Homo rudolfensis 61, 64, 68, 71, 72, 82, 85, 92, 104
Homo sapiens 25, 85, 92, 106, 107, 108, 121, 136, 522; 2.7, 3.29; anatomy 130–32, 137; art 143–46, 158; behavior 140–47, 153; dispersal from Africa

125, 153, 155, 204; earliest 133–34; genetic evidence 137–39; and *Homo neanderthalensis* 125, 147, 159–61; hunting and diet 142–43; language 146; origins of 127–40; and other hominins 125, 128, 133; transitional 134–37

Hongshan culture 554–55

Honshu 258, 259, 260

Hopewell 679, 682, 683, 684, 685, 694, 704; 18.6, 18.7, 18.8

Horace 511

Horr's Island 327

horse beans 365

horse riding equipment 581

horses 166, 172, 384, 425, 522, 527, 546, 576, 703, 706; and chariots 560, 564

Horus, god 374

Houli culture 240

houses 114–15, 143–44, 162, 170, 207, 210, 214, 224, 246, 553; 1.19, 6.29; around plazas, North America 688–89; Bandkeramik 407, 412–13; 11.18, 11.25; cane and matting huts 337; 9.32, 9.33; cedar wood 709; Chaco Canyon "great houses" 698–99; 18.23; circular 338, 556; clay daub 401; cliff dwellings 700, 701; 18.34; compound houses in Teotihuacán 615; House of Tiles 479; 13.7; dry-stone walls 286, 405; Ecuador 334; elite, Andes 655; elite *kuraka* 663; elite two-storied 457; elite wooden, North America 688; L'Anse aux Meadows 710; longhouses 332, 412; mud-brick 214, 222, 380, 400, 401, 525, 530, 531, 534; mammoth bone 163; 4.45; pit houses 239, 320; with plastered floors and masonry walls 649; platform structures 646; Real Alto 650; 17.9; rectangular, adobe, Tula 629; snow block 711; stilt-houses 288, 291; 8.24; stone and stamped earth 556; storage areas 218, 219, 239, 704; Tell Madhhur 437; thatched, Cahokia 690; Thule 711, 18.39; underground pits 526; villas in Crete 482; with walls and roofs of mats 649; wattle and daub 600, 692, 696; whale bone 711; 18.39

Howieson's Poort 141, 144, 354; 4.16

Hoxne 94, 119

Huaca de los Idolos 648

Huaca de los Sacrificios 648

Huaca Prieta 647

Huai River 237, 239, 240

Huanaco Valley 659

Huanbei 560, 562

Huang He 195, 235

Huangniangniangtai 582

Huan River 558

Huantanay 667

Hua Xia 566

Huaynuna 647–48

Hubei 562, 571

Huckell, Bruce 317, 319

Huizilopochtli, god 635

Hujiawuchang 246

human fossils 32, 59, 60, 68–69, 110; 1.8; 2.4, 2.7, 3.33; the Americas 167–71; at Oldowan sites 71, 73, 83; in Australasia 155, 156; Australia 130–31, 155; Daka 105; 3.28; dating 33, 34, 106, 107, 111; "Deep Skull" 155; Dmanisi discoveries 102–04; 3.23, 3.24, 3.25; Florisbad skull 134; 4.8; *Homo antecessor* (TD6) 108–10; *Homo erectus* in China 100, 130; 4.4; *Homo erectus* in Java 106, 130; 3.15, 3.17, ; *Homo heidelbergensis* 3.30; *Homo neanderthalensis* 147–49; *Homo sapiens* 128, 132–38; Kennewick Man 168; KNM-ER 104, 119; 3.3; Laetoli hominid skull 135; 4.12; Lucy skeleton 60, 87, 89; 2.4; major sites (maps and tables) 62–65, 86, 90–91, 132, 148, 149; 2.3, 2.6, 3.1 3.6; Mauer Jaw 92; Omo skulls 135; 4.10. 4.11; Qafzeh

skeleton 137; 4.14; Rhodesian Man 133; 4.6; Saldanha skull 133; 4.7; Sima de los Huesos 108, 111–13; 3.34, 3.35; Turkana Boy 86–92; 3.2, 3.4

human origins 32; anatomical and genetic evidence 51–56, 59; and climate 55–57; dating 74–75; earliest hominins 57–83; evolution models 4.3; and primates 49–57; spine diagram 2.1; timeline chart 48, *see also* australopithecines; *Homo* (genus and individual species); human fossils

human remains 206, 207, 219, 523; 6.5, 6.18, 7.26; bog bodies, Yde Girl 428; 11.51; Crow Creek massacre 705; detached skulls 221, 223; 6.25; in ditch enclosures 402; evidence of violence 356, 411, 418, 683, 700; 11.23, 11.24; frozen body of girl in Alaska 711; Iceman 408–09; 4.19; Mohenjaro-daro massacre 538; 14.19; skulls on poles 687; Talheim 411; 11.23, 11.24; West Africa 360, *see also* burials; cemeteries; tombs

human sacrifice: Africa 380; Carthage 503, 505; China 555, 559, 561, 575; Mesoamerica 595, 599, 611; North America 687; South America 656, 658–59; Southwest Asia 444

Humboldt 333

Humboldt Current 336, 648

Hunamni 236, 257

Hunan 242, 244, 246, 572

Hungary 119, 149, 160, 401, 402, 406, 410, 424, 425; Bandkeramik 407; fire deposits 116; Neanderthal art 152

Huns 516

Hunter-Anderson, Rosalind 296

hunter-gatherers 33, 74–76, 118, 119, 150–51, 214, 238, 241, 717; 19.1; Africa 354, 355–56; 10.3; and agriculture 183–84, 186, 187, 188, 190, 235, 256, 361, 404, 407, 595–96, 718; Andes 339, 342; China 235, 237, 238, 241, 242, 248, 554; "complex" 410, 412; Egypt 356; 10.6; England 396–97; Europe 393; 11.7; and farmers 369–70; in the Holocene epoch 181, 183–84; Japan 258–59, 554; Korea 554; Mesoamerica 595, 598, 631; North America 312, 313, 314, 317, 319, 323, 326, 330–31, 679, 684; Paleoindian 313; and pottery 260; Sahara 358; seasonal mobility 523; and sedentism 160; South America 334; South Asia 519, 522–23; Southwest Asia 205, 206, 214; West Africa 359–60

hunting 120–21, 142–43, 150–51, 324, 436, 530; Africa 354; 10.3; and agriculture in Africa 370; Amazon 347; for big-game 122–23, 172, 178, 205, 312; bison 309, 331, 703; 9.3, 9.4, 9.24, 9.25; camelids 342; North America 679, 680; rainforest animals 347; Sahara 358; sea mammals 711; South Asia 522, 523; whales 711

Huoshaogou 582

Hupa-iya 642

Hurles, Matthew 283

Hurra Valley 647

Hurrians 434, 448, 455, 456, 458–59

Husuni Kubwa 385

Huxley, T.H. 53

Hwangsong-dong 576

hydraulic hypothesis of civilization 196–97

Hyksos 377

Hypostyle Hall 10.30

Iban 291

Iberia 156, 165, 397, 404; farming enclaves 394, *see also* Portugal; Spain

Ibo people 384

Ice Ages 40, 41, 51, 57, 116, 120, 125, 127, 136, 162, 163, 165, 265, 393, 710, 717; Last Glacial Maximum 177–83, 201, 202, 203, 204, 205, 206, 207, 209, 232, 238, 307; 5.3, 5.4, 6.1

Icehouse Bottom, 323; 9.17

"Iceman" 406, 408–09; 11.19, 11.20

Iddins 326

Idrimi, King 459; 12.39

Ife 384; 10.37

Igbo-Ukwu 388, 390; 10.43

Ilion 450

Illinois 323, 326, 330, 682, 684, 688, 704; Koster 324–25; 9.18

Illinois River 324, 325

Il'skaya 151

Inamgaon 520; 14.21

Inanna, goddess 439

Inariyama 580

Incas 297, 343, 349, 608, 660, 663, 665–68, 675; conquest by Spaniards 666, 668; Sacred Valley 667; *see also* individual sites

India 262, 363, 369, 519, 521, 522–23, 524, 527–28, 533, 546; and Greece 544; and Southeast Asia 302, 302–03, 303, 585; rock art 523

Indian Knoll 326

Indian Ocean 351, 388–89, 550, 720

indigo 315

Indo-European 189, 454, 521–22, 532, 538

Indonesia 97, 100, 102, 140, 155, 265, 266, 276, 283, 285, 302; 8.1; Bronze-Iron Age 302; tombs 304

Indra, god 538

Indratataka 588

Indus civilization 532–40; script 532; 14.11

Indus Valley 194, 195, 446, 447, 449, 519, 520, 521, 525, 528, 529, 530, 549; 14.8

inhaling tubes 339

Inland Sea 578

Inner Mongolia 554, 556

innovation 36

Inter-Tropical Convergence Zone 181

Inuit 88, 167, 710, 711; 18.40; 19.3

Iolkos 485

Ipoi 284

Iran 203, 210, 227, 228–29, 232, 433, 434, 441, 442, 443, 445, 458, 469, 519, 541; *see also* individual sites

Iraq 149, 150, 152, 154, 201, 203, 213, 216, 217, 232, 433, 435, 458, 466, 470, 500; *see also* individual sites

Iraq ed-Dubb 227

Ireland 394, 414, 416; 11.27; Celts 430; *see also* individual sites

iron 351, 365, 383, 386, 467, 522, 546, 710; armor 574; arrowheads 370, 585; furnace 10.18; hoes 570; knives 585; plows 570; points 370; scythes 570; sickles 570; spades 570; spears 576; swords 576, 579; tools 292, 366, 540; weapons 578

Iron Age 31, 231, 250, 279, 394, 528; Europe 420, 425; Korea 554; South Asia 539, 540, 551; Southeast Asia 554, 585, 587; Southwest Asia 433, 434, 450, 455, 456, 463

iron casting 567

iron ore 576

ironworking 302, 365–68; 10.18; and farmers 367, 369

irrigation 35, 192, 196, 246; Americas 345, 348; 9.11, 18.17; China 570; Egypt 192; Mesoamerica 612; North America 692, 694; 18.17; Peru 642; Southeast Asia 587; Southwest Asia 232, 433, 436, 438, 443

Irtysh Valley 582

Iruka 581

Irwin, Geoffrey 293, 305

Isaac, Glynn 61, 70, 82, 83, 96

Isernia la Pineta 119

Ishanapura 586

Ishtar Gate 468–69; 12.47
Ishtar, goddess 451; 12.28
Isimila 95
Isin 449, 450
Isin-Larsa 434
Isis 502, 515
Islam 303, 304, 383, 384, 516
Isle de la Tortue 252
Isong Sansong 575
Israel 57, 102, 103, 114, 116, 117, 118, 119, 126, 132, 136, 137, 149, 150, 154, 203, 204, 205, 206, 208, 226, 434, 514; 4.14, 4.28, 4.29; see also individual sites
Israelites 464, 465, 466
Issus 500
Isthmia 499
Italy 107, 108, 110, 112, 119, 126, 148, 149, 150, 151, 156, 160, 163, 394, 397, 404, 406, 422, 423, 486, 489, 491–93, 512, 516, 719; cities 420, 426, 427; Copper Age 394; Croce del Papa 423; rock art 426; Tavoliere 402; 11.13; Valcamonica valley 426, 11.47; see also individual sites
Itazuke 259
ivory 158, 162, 164, 351, 382, 384, 459, 464, 540, 562; 18.38
Iwo Eleru 359, 360, 364

jack beans 320, 344
jade 250, 287, 553, 561, 562, 583, 595, 601; axes 555; beads 526; blades 564, 565; 15.7; carvings 556, 603; cong 248; 7.16; jewelry 287; ornaments 246, 247, 248, 557, 560, 576; pendants 553; plaque 553, 15.1; rings 553, 555; suit 573; 15.28
Jade Gate 570, 583, 584
jadeite axes 415; 11.28, 11.29
Jalisco 604
Japan 160, 235, 236, 256, 258, 259–62, 261, 567, 574, 575, 578–83; Ainu 260; and China 580; hunter-gatherers 554; and Korea 581, 583; see also individual sites
Jarmo 203, 216
Jarrige, Jean-François 524
jasper 578
Java 59, 98, 106, 130, 155, 276, 286, 296, 303; 8.26, 8.38; Buddhism 303; 8.26, 8.38; Hinduism 8.39; Homo erectus 33, 97–99, 105–06, 130, 155; trade with India 302; see also individual sites
Javanese 279, 280
Jayavarman II 585, 586, 587, 588; IV 588; V 587, 588; VII 587, 589; 15.41; see also Angkor
Jebel Aruda 442
Jebel Barkal 381
Jebel et Tomat 363
Jebel Irhoud 126, 132, 134, 135, 137
Jebel Sahaba 356
Jebel Sinjar 232
Jefferson, Thomas 30
Jemdet Nasr 442
Jenderam Hilir 254
Jenné-jeno 364, 383, 384; 10.36
Jequetepeque Valley 657
Jerf el Ahmar 203, 217, 218
Jericho 203, 213, 216–17, 221, 227, 230, 231, 525; 6.17, 6.25
Jersey 116, 120, 121, 150; 3.45
Jerusalem 465, 468, 512
Jetepeque Valley 659
jewelry 192, 254, 256, 284, 464, 504, 616; 7.26
Jews 512, 514
Jhukhar 520, 539
Jiahu 236, 239, 558
Jian 574
Jiangsu 553

Jiangxi 242, 562
jicama 344
Jin 563, 566
Jingdi, Emperor 573
Jinniushan 126, 130
Jinyanggang 555
Jiroft 446
Jito, Empress 582
Jivaro 17.9
Johanson, Donald 57, 83, 123; 2.9
Jomei, Emperor 581
Jomon 235, 236, 258–59, 260, 717; pottery 258; 7.33, 7.34
Jones, Rhys 272
Jordan 201, 203, 205, 206, 217, 222–23, 230, 466; see also individual sites
Jordan Valley 226, 227
Jos Plateau 366; 10.16
Judaea 512, 514
Judah 465, 466
jujube fruit 525
Julius Caesar 30, 430, 506, 507; 11.49
Juno, goddess 506
Jupiter, god 506
Jutland 418

Kabah 631
Kachi 528
Kadai 262
Kadero 363
Kahun 372
Kairouan 383
Kalahari 189, 359, 717
Kalako-deray 520, 526
Kalambo Falls 95, 114, 119
Kalhu 465
Kalibangan 195, 520, 529, 530, 531, 533–34, 534, 538, 551; 14.9
Kamares Cave 481; 13.8
Kamehameha 290
Kaminaljuyu 609, 611, 619, 620; 16.27
Kanchanaburi 252, 253
kanchas 666
Kandahar 540, 541, 546
Kanem 384
Kanesh 434, 453
Kangaroo Island 267
Kanjera 72
Kano 384
Kapilavastu 542
Kapthurin 117
Kapwirimbwe 367
Kara 544
Karakoram 521, 526
Karanovo 401; 11.10
Karatepe 12.44
Karelia 396, 415
Karkarichinkat 363
Karkov 428
Karnak 10.27, 10.30
Kar-Tukulti-Ninurta 460
Kashka tribes 455
Kashmir 526, 531, 549; 14.4
Kashmir-Swat Valley 524, 526–27
Kassites 434, 450, 461, 461–62
Kastri 479
Katanda 126, 141, 142
Katongo 386
Kato Zakros 481; 13.9
Kattwinkel, Wilhelm 67
Kausambi 520, 542
Kaya 554, 574–75, 575
Kealhofer, Lisa 250, 252

Kebara Cave, Israel 150, 154
Kechi Beg 528
Keeley, Lawrence 81
Keilor Lake 130
Keitai 580
Kennewick Man 166, 168
Kenniff Cave 268, 269; 8.5
Kenoyer, Mark 533, 536
Kentucky 322, 330; Green River 323, 326, 327; 9.19, 9.20; Salts Cave, Mammoth Cave 328; 9.23; Mount Horeb 682; 18.3
Kenya 56, 117, 119, 134, 135, 359, 365, 367; Gedi 384; 10.39; Koobi Fora 77, 78, 82, 116; 2.19, 2.27, 2.28; Olorgesailie 95, 96, 105, 114; 3.12; Turkana 71–72, 85, 86, 89, 94, 104, 359
Kenyapithecus 51
Kenyon, Kathleen 216–17, 221, 227, 230
Keos 487
Kerak 434
Kerma 380; 10.31
Keros-Syros culture 478; 13.4
Kesh 442
kettledrums 302
Khabur River 458
Khafre 374
Khami 386
Kharga Oasis 358
Kharoshthi 302, 584
Khartoum 375
Kheit Qasim 437
Khiam points 213
Khirbet 434, 445
Khmer 585, 590
Khodjend 502
Khoisan 355
Khok Charoen 254
Khok Phanom Di 236, 243, 252, 254–56, 260; 7.25, 7.26, 7.27
Khorammabad Valley 210, 232
Khorat Plateau 251, 252
Khorramabad Valley 203
Khorsabad 466
Khotamna 584
Khotan 554, 583–84
Khufu 292, 374, 376
Khwae Noi River 252
Kibiro 386
Kidder, Alfred V. 702
Kiik-Koba 149
Kikulu 386
Kili Gul Mohammad 520, 524, 525, 528
Kilwa 384, 387
Kimeu, Kamoya 89
kingdoms 443, 444, 449, 543, 610–11, 624; Mycenaean 485
King Island 267
kings 450, 451, 460, 480, 623, 624, 630; Aztec 637; Korea 575–76; Maya 625, 630; in Rome 504
K'inich Janaab' Pakal 624, 625; 16.33
Kirch, Patrick 291, 301
Kish 446, 449
Kislev, Mordecai 227
Kissonerga-Mylouthkia 229
Kitugala 523
kivas 696, 698; 18.25
Klasies River 126, 132, 137, 141, 142, 143, 144, 355
Klein, Richard 133, 141, 142, 145
knives 246, 253, 261, 284, 311, 313, 323, 582, 585, 711
Knossos 400, 474, 477, 480, 481, 482, 484; 13.13
knotweed 348, 684
Knowth 394, 414
Koguryo 554, 574, 581; 15.29
Koh Ker 588

Kohn, Marek 95
Koldihawa 527
Kommos 490
Kom Ombo 357
Konduri 642
Kongju 575
Kongo 385
Kong Qiu 567
Konqi River 582
Konso 94, 95
Kon-Tiki 293, 297
Koobi Fora 71, 77, 79, 82, 86, 104, 116, 119; 2.19, 2.27, 2.28, 3.3
Koptos 371
Korea 236, 256, 259, 574–77, 580; hunter-gatherers 554; and Japan 581, 583; *see also* Koguryo; Paekche; Great Silla, Silla; *and individual sites*
Koryo 554, 577
Kostenki 162, 165
Koster 183, 323, 324–25, 326; 9.18
Kot Diji 520, 528, 529, 531; 14.7
Kotosh 646; 17.4, 17.5, 17.6
Koumbi Saleh 384
Kow Swamp 130, 131, 155
Krapina 126, 148, 150
krater 424, 427, 490; Vix 424; 11.24
Kromdraai 59, 73
Kroran 584
Ksaesong 577
Ksar Akil 126, 154
Ku Bua 591
Kudatini 527
Kufic 388
Kuhn, Steven 150
Kuk 278; 8.10, 8.11
Kukulkan 632
Kulen Hills 586
Kultepe-Kanesh 453, 455
Kumsong 577
!Kung 33, 186
Kunlun Range 583
Kuntasi 535
kuraka 661, 663, 655, 656, 657, 659, 660
Kurdistan 188
Kurigalzu, King 461
Kursakata 364
Kuruk Darya River 584
Kusakli 454
Kushans 302, 545, 549
Kusinagara 542
Kwakiutl 706
Kwale ware 367, 369
Kyongju 576
Kyushu 259, 578, 580

La Baume Bonne 115
Labna 631
Labrador 710
labrets 708; 18.33
La Chaise 126, 148
La Chapelle-aux-Saints 148
Lachish 463
La Cocina 404
La Cotte de St. Brelade, Jersey 116, 120, 121, 150; 3.45
lacquerware 553, 557, 564
La Draga 404
Laetoli 57, 89, 135; 2.10, 4.12
La Ferrassie 126, 148, 152
La Galgada 642, 645, 646, 647, 651
Lagar Velho boy 126, 159; 4.39
Lagash 444; 12.14

La Gravette 161
La Gruta tradition 669
Lahr, Marta Mirazón 129, 131
Lakes: Agassiz 720; Besaka 364; Chad 363; Dongting 244, 246; Edward 359; Eyre 274; George 686; Great Lake 586; Huleh, Israel 204, 210; Kumphawapi 250; Lisan 207; Longquan 240; Lop Nur 584; Moondarra 273; Mungo 126, 131, 156; 4.33, 4.34; Neuchâtel 424; 11.43, 11.52; Pickering 396; Tai 247; Texcoco 633, 634; Titicaca 642, 645; Turkana 71, 71–72, 85, 86, 89, 94, 359, 365; Urmia 467; Van 436, 467; Victoria 365, 367; Zeribar 209
Lakota Indians 331
Lalibela Cave 365
La Madeleine 163
Lamanai 611, 630
Lambayeque Valley 657, 659, 662, 663
Lamet 262
La Moderna 312
landscape 267, 296; and Australian aborigines 271–72; and social hierarchy 670
landscape archaeology 82
Langnaj 522
Lang Rongrien rockshelter 253
languages 42, 79–80, 130, 146, 235, 262; and agriculture 187–90, 261–62; in the Americas 166–67; Austroasiatic 262; 7.17; Austronesian 262, 280–83; linguistic archaeology 668–69
Langweiler 412–13
L'Anse aux Meadows 710; 18.36
Lantian 100, 130
Laos 250
La Paloma 336, 337; 9.33
lapis lazuli 442, 444, 462, 536, 539, 550
Lapita 287–89, 290, 292; 8.16, 8.22, 8.23
La Polledrara, 112, 119
La Quemada 622
La Quina, 148, 152
Larsa 442, 449, 450
Las Bela 536
Las Capas 317, 318; 9.11
Lascaux 126, 163; 1.20
Las Colinas 694
Las Vegas, Ecuador 334
Latamne 114
Late Archaic 314, 318, 319, 323–24, 326, 327, 334, 336, 343, 347, 684; 9.11, 9.19, 9.20
La Tène 424, 430; 11.52
Late Stone Age 141, 143, 152, 155
Lathrap, Donald 346, 650, 674
Latium 151, 491
Laugerie Haute 163
Laurentide ice sheet 166
Lauricocha 340
Laurion 495
Lavallée 312, 313, 338, 341, 343, 347, 349
La Venta 596, 602, 603, 604, 605, 613, 628; 16.9, 16.10
Lawrence, D.H. 493
Lchashen 560
Leakey, Louis 61, 127
Leakey, Maeve 89
Leakey, Mary 60, 61, 67, 70, 72, 83
Leakey, Richard 89
leather 340, 355, 384, 576
Lebanon 126, 201, 203, 228, 374, 433, 464, 490
Leche River 662
Lee, Richard 186
Lefkandi 486; 13.16
legumes 222, 226, 229, 315, 433
Lehringen 152
Lelang 236, 554, 574

Le Lazaret Cave 114, 115; 3.39
Le Moustier 126, 148, 151
Lemovices 11.49
lemurs 52, 53
Lengyel 408
lentils 205, 226, 371, 436, 526
Leong Sau Heng 254
Lepenski Vir 394, 406; 11.16, 11.17
Leptis Magna 383, 511
leren 340, 344, 348
Lerna 474, 479; 13.7
Leroi, Gourhan André 165
Les Canalettes 152
Lesser Antilles 669
Lesser Sundas 276, 303, 304
Leucate 404
Levallois technique 96, 150, 152, 153, 160; 3.13, 3.14; Levant 201, 204, 212, 213, 231, 434, 451, 453, 460, 486, 490; 12.35; 'Ain Ghazal 222–23; Early Epipaleolithic 205–09; Israel and Judah 465; Later Bronze Age 456–58
Levantine Corridor 153
Lewis, David 293
Lewis-Williams, David 359
L'Hortus 148
Liangzhu 236, 247, 248, 553, 555, 558; 7.16, 15.1
Liaoning 554, 556
Libby, Willard 33, 157, 333
Libya 132, 362, 383, 511
Li Cang 572, 573
Lieberman, Daniel 153
Lightfoot, Ricky 697
Lima 337, 662
lima beans 337, 344
lime processing 335
Limpopo 385
Lindow Man 429
Linearbandkeramik *see* Bandkeramik culture
Linear Pottery Culture *see* Bandkeramik culture
linen 457
Lingnan 236, 249
Lingones 11.49
linguistic anthropology 25
Linyi 592
Linzi 568
Lipari 404
Lithuania 417
Little Colorado River 701
Little Ice Age 710, 720
Little Salt Spring 322
Little Tennessee River 323, 326; 9.17
Liulin 245
Liu Sheng, Prince 573; 15.28
Liyang 244, 247
Llagostera, Agustin 336
llamas 341, 343, 349, 641, 661; 9.39
Llanos de Moxos 671, 676
Loango 385
Loebanr 526, 539
Lokalalei site 71
Lokono 675
Loma Alta 334
Longnan 553
Longshan 236, 246, 554, 555–56, 582; 15.2
Loofs-Wissowa, Helmut 254
Lopburu 591
lorises 52, 53
Los Gavinales 335
Los Millares 405, 477; 11.15
Los Morteros 647
Lothal 534; 14.14
Louisiana 327, 328, 329, 681; 9.15
Loulan 584

Lourandos, Harry 270, 272, 274, 305
Low Ham 13.39
Lu 566, 567
Lualaba River 286
Luba 286
Lubbub Creek 687
Luce, Gordon 262
"Lucy" 57, 60, 87, 89; 2.4, 2.5
Lukenya Hill 359
Lu, Lie Dan 241
Lumbini 542; 14.23
luminescence dating 119
Lung Hoa 236, 249
Luojiajiao 246
Luoyang 566, 569, 584
Lusaka 367
Luwian 464
Luzon 193, 283, 289; 8.42
Lydia 434, 468, 493
Lynch, Thomas 339
Lysimachos 13.36

Maba 126, 130
McArthur Creek 274
Macassan fishermen 275
McBrearty, Sally 141, 143, 144
McDermott, LeRoy 165
Macedo 9.44
Macedonia 379, 400, 488, 500, 501, 541
McElmo Creek 700
Machang 582; 7.12
Machu Picchu 667, 668; 17.36
McPhee Village 696
Madagascar 265, 280, 286, 369; 8.26
Ma Dong 259
Maeklong River 591
Magan 446
Magapit 285; 8.17
Magdalenian 126, 163, 164, 165–66; 4.44
Magdalensberg 428
Maghreb 383
Maglemosian culture 395
Magna Graecia 488
Mahadaha 522
Mahagara 527; 14.5
Mahasthan 548; 14.35
Mahcalilla phase 650
Mahdia Shipwreck 512–13; 13.52
Mahdi, Waruno 262
Mahidharapura 589
Maipure people 669
Maitum 303
maize 186, 317, 318, 319, 320, 330, 348, 349, 626,
   661, 662; 9.9, 9.10; Aztecs 636; domestication
   of 314, 315, 316; 9.9; in Ecuador 334;
   Mesoamerica 599–600; North America 680,
   686, 689, 689–90, 692, 695, 698, 700, 701,
   704
Majiabang 247
Majiayao culture 582
Makah tribe 709
Makkran coast 530, 532
Malagrotta 112
Malakunanja 156
malaria 435, 538
Malawi 72, 356, 367
Malay 279, 280
Malay Peninsula 265, 277, 286, 303
Malaysia 179, 254, 265
Maldive Islands 521
Málek, Jaromir 373
Malemba Nkulu 386
Mali 362, 364, 383, 384, 388, 390; 10.36

Malleret, Louis 252
Mallia 480, 484
Malta 404
Malvan 540
Malwattu River 523
Mammoth Cave National Park 328; 9.23
mammoths 150, 164, 166, 172, 178, 395
Manacapuru 642
manatees 346
Manaus 644, 674
Manching 420, 428
Manco Capac 660, 665
Mandan people 703
Manetho 379
Mangaia 301
Mangareva 295, 297
Mangelsdorf 314, 317
Mangia 300
Manila 282
Manilla 282
manioc 335, 343, 344, 646, 669, 676
Mantai 523
mantles 683
Manx 430
Maori pa 299; 8.37
Maoris 290, 294, 296, 298, 299
Mapuche 167, 170
Mapungubwe 388
Maracaibo Bay 644
Marajó 644, 671, 672; 17.38
Marajoara 642
Marathon 474, 487, 495
marble 388, 494, 511
Marble Bluff 327
Marduk, god 461, 463, 468
Margala Pass 544
Mari 434, 445, 449, 450, 451, 452, 453;; 12.28, 12.29
Mariana Islands 283, 288, 290, 292, 298
maritime ecoonomies 334, 335, 336, 337
Mark Antony 507
marmosets 347
Marne 424
Marquesas 292, 294, 296, 300, 301
Marquis of Zeng 571; 15.21
Marshall, Sir John 529, 534, 536, 544, 545
marsh elder 684
Martin, Paul 172
Masada 512, 514; 13.50
Masai 33
Masat 454
Mashkan-shapir 450
masks 482, 562, 688; 13.10, 18.11
Massilia 394, 427, 430, 488
Masso di Cemmo 426; 11.47
mastadons 172
Matacapan 596, 619
Mata Menge 102
material culture 25–26; and chimpanzees 61, 79
Matupi Cave 355
Mauer 92, 146, 148; 3.5
Maui 293
Mauna Kea 298
Mauran 150
Mauritania 362, 368, 383
Mauryan empire 302, 519, 547–48; 14.33, 14.34,
   14.35
mausoleum 587
Mawangdui 559, 572, 573; 15.26
Maxentius 515
Maya 476, 595, 596, 597, 610–13, 617, 623–33,
   625–26, 675; art 26; bloodletting 1.1; calendar
   606–07; 16.12; collapse 630–31; 16.40;
   kingdoms 610–11; language 607, 617; society
   625–27; states 195, 196, 197, 198; writing 617

Mayapan 596, 628, 632–33
maygrass 321, 328, 330, 348, 684
Mbanza Kongo 385
Meadowcroft 126, 168–69; 4.51
Meadow, Richard 525, 533
measles 706, 714
meat storage 274, 309, 331
Medes 434, 468
medicine 558, 629
medicine wheels 331
Mediterranean 102, 193, 194, 205, 206, 212, 231,
   375, 378, 383, 387, 393, 402, 404–06, 459; 13.1;
   archaeology of 475–76; Bronze Age 476–80; city
   states 420, 426; civilizations 473–517; diversity of
   473, 517; farming enclaves 399
Meggers, Betty 346, 347, 643, 650, 674
Megiddo 434, 453; 12.35
Mehmet II 516
Mehrgarh 519, 520, 524–25, 525, 526, 528, 529, 551;
   14.2, 14.3
Meishan 582
Mekong 236, 251, 252, 585, 586
Melanesia 265, 266, 279, 282, 283, 288, 289, 298;
   8.1
Melid 464
Melka Kunturé 95, 114, 132
Melkart, god 504
Melkhoutboom Cave 355
Mellaart, James 216, 217, 224, 225
Mellars, Paul 146, 151, 160
melons 536
Melos 400
Meltzer, David 172
Melville, Herman 502
Memphis (Egypt) 373, 377
Mendel, Gregor 31
Menelaion 485
Menez-Dregan 116
"menhirs" 414
Menjiaquan 238
Mentuhotep 376
Merenptah 466
Merimde 363
Meroë 197, 365, 368, 375, 381–82, 388; 10.32, 10.33;
   and Egypt 382
Merv 502
Merzbach Valley 412; 11.26
Mesa complex 310
Mesa Verde 697, 700; 18.24
Mesoamerica 166, 187, 193, 194, 196, 197, 198, 312,
   312–13, 595–639, 679, 712; agriculture 313–17,
   313–19, 595, 595–96, 598–601, 626; arrival of
   Spaniards 595–98; calendars 606–07; 16.12;
   Classic period 616–21; crops 315; 9.6, 9.7, 9.8;
   culture 598, 604; domesticated plants 596; Early
   Horizon 602, 604; Epiclassic period 621–22;
   hunter-gatherers 595; hunting 312; language 595,
   607; Late Horizon 633; metallurgy 598, 604,
   605, 610; Middle Horizon 616; Postclassic
   627–33; Preclassic 598–615; religion 595; and the
   Spaniards 633–39; topography 598; writing
   607–10; see also Aztecs; Maya; Olmecs; and
   individual regions and sites
Mesolithic 165, 179, 181, 182, 523; Europe 393, 397,
   400, 404, 416, 418; South Asia 522
Mesopotamia 230, 433, 434, 436, 437, 441, 442,
   446, 449–53, 458, 466, 471, 529, 536, 718;
   agriculture 192, 193; Early Dynastic period 443;
   states and "civilization" 194, 195, 197, 198, 438,
   439, 441, 448; writing 372
Mesozoic era 50
metal 351, 387, 393, 530, 671; axes 275; early use in
   Europe 393, 394, 402; lip plugs 610; tools 192

metallurgy 192, 351, 365, 368, 371, 405, 419, 421, 556, 654; 10.15; in China 582; Mesoamerica 598, 604, 605, 610; South America 654; spread in Europe 394, 476–77; *see also* bronze; copper; iron
Metapontum 474, 488, 489
Meta River 675
Mexica 635, 636; 16.42
Mexica-Tenocha 633
Mexico 348, 612, 693; agriculture 184, 186, 314–15, 316, 318, 320, 330, 599; Archaic period 313–14; arrival of Spaniards 595, 598; Aztec empire 636–38; metallurgy 610; Paso de la Amada 601; 16.7; social organization 604; states development 195; Teotihuacán 616, 619, 620; 16.25, 16.26, 16.28; Tula 629, 631; *see also* Aztecs, Maya, Olmecs *and individual regions and sites*
Mexico City 635
Mezhirich 163; 4.45
Mezin 163
Mezmaiskaya Cave 140
mica 683; cut out hand 685; 18.5
Michelsberg 408
Michigan 326
microblades 707
microliths 141, 166, 205, 207, 208, 213, 277, 354–55, 356, 363, 522, 523, 524, 530; 6.3, 10.4, 10.7
Micronesia 266, 276, 283, 285, 288, 290; 8.1
Midas, King 467
middens 314, 317, 330, 344, 522, 523, 526, 647, 648, 649, 671, 684; shell 142, 257, 275, 296, 322, 325, 336, 347, 410, 412, 415; 9.44, 11.34
Middle Archaic 322, 327, 331, 332, 334, 336, 341, 342, 343, 347
Middle Awash 61, 68, 126, 132, 134, 135
Middle Range Theory 38
Middle Stone Age 118, 132, 133, 143, 144; Africa 141, 142, 173
Miesenheim 119
migration 36–37, 294
Milagro 317
Milan 474
milk 410, 718; hickory nut 327
Miller, Danny 537
millet 185, 235, 236, 238–40, 245–46, 257, 362, 364, 367, 369, 528, 536, 553, 562, 582; 7.2, 10.14
milling slabs 333
Milo 121
Milvian Bridge, battle of the 515
Mindanao Island 303
Minerva, goddess 506
mines/mining 402, 419, 510–11, 571; 15.25
Ming dynasty 560
Minisink 126
Minoans 36, 196, 458, 474, 477, 479, 484; 13.9, 13.10; palace period 480–82; religion 481; writing 484
Minos, King 482
Miocene epoch 51, 56, 83
Miran 584
mirrors 575, 576, 578, 603; 13.23
Mississippi 311, 321, 324, 330, 679, 683, 686, 687–91, 688–89, 694, 715
Missouri 312, 321, 324, 330, 703, 704
Mitchell (Illinois) 688
Mithen, Steven 95
Mithraism 515; 13.54
Mittani 434, 456, 457, 458, 459, 460
Mitterberg 419
Mixe-Zoque 595, 601, 607
Mixtec 595, 596, 598, 607, 608, 617
moai 295–96; 8.29, 8.30
mobiliary art 163, 165; 4.44
moccasins 333

Moche 645, 651, 655, 656, 658, 659, 662; 17.21, 17.22, 17.23, 17.25, 17.26
Moche Valley 343, 656, 662, 663; 17.26
Modjokerto 57
Modoc 312, 323
Mogador 387
Mogollon highlands 317
Mohenjo-daro 520, 529, 533, 534–35, 536, 537, 539; 14.15; massacre 538; 14.19; weight system 537, 538; 14.18; *see also* Indus civilization; Indus Valley
Mohina 665
Moita da Sebastião 397, 410
Mojokerto 97
Moldavia 160, 407
Moluccas 276, 277, 288, 289, 302
Mon 590
Mongchon 575
Mongolia 167
monitor lizards 523
monkeys 49, 51, 52, 54, 55, 56, 523; 2.2; New World monkeys 51, 52, 53, 54, 55
Mon-Khmer 262
Monks Mound 690–91; 18.14, 18.15, 18.16
Mons Claudianus 511; 13.48
Monsu 334
Montagu Cave 116
Montana 331
Mont Bégo 406
Mont Beuvray 428
Monte Albán 174, 596, 606, 607, 612–13, 613, 618, 619, 621, 624; 16.25, 16.26
Monte Verde 126, 168, 169, 170, 312; 4.52, 4.53
Mont Lassois 11.44
Moorea 292
Moore, Andrew 214
Moquegua Valley 662
Morava Valley 400, 406
Moravia 162, 165
Moreton Bay 268
Morgan, Lewis Henry 32, 177, 193
Morocco 73, 126, 132, 134, 135, 137, 141
mortars and pestles 205, 206, 348; 6.7, 6.8
mortuary jars 249
mosaic: Dido and Aeneas 13.39; House of the Faun, Pompeii 13.35; masonry, Sechín Alto 652
Moscow 419
Moseley, M. 650
Moselle 424
Motagua River 603
Motecezuma II 635, 638; 16.48
mounds 347, 348, 393, 414, 418, 524, 646, 647, 648, 661, 671, 672; 18.2, 18.5; around sacred stones 554; Cahokia 690–91; 18.14, 18.15, 18.16; Hopewell 685; 18.8; Jenné-jeno 383; Mississippian 686, 687, 688–89; North America 679, 681, 687, 694, 704
Moundville 688
Mount Cameron 271
Mount Carmel 206, 208
Mount Hagen 278
Mount Horeb 682; 18.3
Mount Isa 273
Mount Iuktas 481
Mount Meru 587, 588
Mount Miwa 578, 580
Mount P'along 577
Mount Pangaion 500
Mount Pentele 496, 513
Mouseion 502
Mousterian 96, 116, 118, 120, 126, 150–51, 152, 154; 3.45, 4.13, 4.25

Movius, Hallam L. 101, 114; 3.21
Mozambique 367, 384, 388
Mozu 579
Mrauk-U 590
Muang Phra Rot 591
Mudar, Karen 252
mud-bricks 214, 219, 222, 225, 228, 230, 231, 232, 373, 380, 381, 383, 400, 401, 424, 436, 439, 443, 451, 519, 525, 526, 530, 531, 533, 534, 536, 655, 659, 663; 6.16, 11.10, 12.14, 14.2, 14.8, 14.14, 14.15
Mughal, Rafique 530, 531, 537
Mugharet el Aliyeh 132
mulberry trees 571
multi-regional evolution hypothesis 127, 128, 129, 130–31, 138, 139, 172; 4.3
multivocality 39
Mulvaney, John 268, 269, 270, 305; 8.5
Mumba 132, 141
mummies 336, 337, 645; Ramesses II 10.26; South America 336, 338–39, 645, 646, 648, 654, 666; 9.34, 9.35, 17.17, 17,18; *see also* Chinchorro
Munda 262
Mundigak 528, 539
Mun Valley 585
murals 616, 658; 16.22; *see also* wall painting
Murray River 274
Mursili I, King 454
Muryong, King 575
Musasir 467
muscovy ducks 326, 343
musk ox 711
Mussau Island 288
Mussi 150
Mussolini, Benito 504
Mustang Spring 331
Mwene Mutapa 386
Mwimbi 72
Mycenae 196, 422, 450, 456, 458, 463, 474, 482, 484, 485–86, 498; 12.43, 13.10, 13.11, 13.12; acropolis 482, 485; 13.11; and Egypt 486; Lion Gate 482; 13.12; Treasury of Atreus 485
Myrtos 479

Nabta Playa 361, 362
Nachukui Formation 71
Na Dene 166, 167
Nageshwar 535
Nahua 607, 617, 633
Nahuatl 608, 613, 629
nails 710
Nakbé 611, 623, 624
Nakhon Pathom 591
Naktong River 574
Nal 528
Namibia 356, 369
Namu 331
Nanchoc 334, 645, 646
Nanguanli 284
Naniwa 581
Nan Madol 298; 8.34
Napata 381
Napir-Asu 462; 12.42
Naples 491, 510
Napo River 642, 674
Naqada 371
Nara 578, 580, 582, 583
Naram-Sin 446, 463; 12.20
"Narmada Man" 522
Narmer Palette 372; 10.22
Narofkim Communal House, Moscow 27
Natal 367
National American Graves Protection and Repatriation Act 168

Native Americans 30, 167, 348, 715; 1.6; burial 30; and Europeans 712–13, 714; languages 166
Natufian 187, 202, 206, 208–09, 210–11, 216, 217; 6.7, 6.8
natural selection 31–32, 43, 47
Nausharo 525, 529
naviform core method 230
navigation 292–94
Naymlap 662
Nazca 642, 645, 659 17.27; "Nazca Lines" 660; 17.28
Nazlet Khater 137
Ndorwa 385
Ndutu 132, 133
Neanderthals see Homo neanderthalensis
Neander Valley 31, 32, 128; 1.8
Nea Nikomedeia 400; 11.9, 11.11
Nebra sun-disk 422; 11.40
Nebuchadnezzar 468
necklaces 211; 17.47
neckrings 11.39
necropolis 496, 560; Etruscan 492; 13.22; Pantanello, Metapontum 489; 13.18; Shizhaishan 570; Xin'gan 562
needles 158, 239, 247, 333, 610; 4.35
Nefertiti 459
Negev Desert 205
Negro River 644, 669
Nemea 499
Neo-Assyrian Empire 434
Neo-Elamite 434
Neo-Hittites 434, 464; 12.44
Neolithic 31, 181, 182, 188; Austronesian 283–87; China 235, 238–63, 554, 555, 556, 582; East Asia 235, 245–48, 251, 253; Europe 395, 396, 399, 400–10, 413, 418, 476; Jericho, tower 6.17; Korea 554; South Asia 519, 523, 524–28; Southeast Asia 554; Southwest Asia 201, 203, 209, 212–32
Neolithic Revolution 188, 197, 243
Neon U-Loke 585
Nepeña Valley 656, 659
nephrite bracelets 249
Nero, Emperor 507, 515
Netherlands 179, 419, 423; Yde girl 429; 11.51
Netiv Hagdud 227
net floats 314, 324, 348; sinkers 256, 287; weights 253, 708
nets 239, 247, 332, 333, 337, 648; 9.27; see also fishing
Nevalı Çori 220
Neve David 203, 206
New Archaeology 38
New Britain 288, 289
Newfoundland 710, 712
Newgrange 414, 416; 11.27
New Guinea 35, 126, 131, 139, 155, 173, 265, 266, 276, 289, 298, 302; agriculture 186, 277, 278; 8.10, 8.11; dispersal of Homo sapiens 153
New Mexico 679, 698, 700, 712; agriculture 317, 318, 319, 695; Pecos Pueblo 702; 18.25, 18.26
New Stone Age 182
Newt Kash 327
New Zealand 187, 265, 290, 294, 296, 300; colonization of 298; and Hawaiian Islands 298–99; Maori pa 300; 8.37; social organization 301; stone adzes 8.25
Ngaloba 126, 134, 135
Ngandong 106, 130
Ngarrabulgan 273
Ngobe 167
Niah Cave 126, 131, 155, 277; 4.5
Nicobar Islands 262

Niger 362, 365, 368, 383, 390
Niger-Congo languages 279
Nigeria 358, 359, 364, 365, 366, 368, 390; brass head 384; 10.37
Nihewan Basin 100
Ni Kham Haeng 236
Nile Valley 201, 352, 365, 374, 375, 380, 381, 382, 387, 501; 10.20, 10.25; agriculture 351, 363, 365; hunter-gatherers 356, 358; irrigation 192; metallurgy 368; Napata 381; predyastic cultures 363; seasonal floods 371; state development 195, 197; 10.19
Niling 248
Nimrud 460, 465
Nindowari 536
Nineveh 434, 445, 449, 460, 461, 466; 12.45
Nippur 438, 443, 447, 461
Nishida 259
Nishimura, Masanari 252
Niuheliang 554–55
Niya 584
Njoro River Cave 365
Nkang 364, 369
Nkope 367
Noah's Ark hypothesis 127
Noen U-Loke 236
Nok 366; 10.16
nomads 452, 703
Nong Chae Sao 253
Nong Nor 152, 236, 260
Non Kao Noi 251
Non Mak La 256
Non Nok Tha 236, 251
Non Pa Wai 236, 254, 256, 262
Nordenskiöld, Erland 672
Norfolk Islands 296
Noricum 428
Norman conquest 37
Norse 710, 711, 712; 18.36
North Africa 351, 383, 388, 459, 488, 490, 491, 500, 511, 516; climate 358; Mediterranean 473; transition to agriculture 356; urbanization 383–84; see also individual countries and sites
North America 166, 307, 313, 679–714, 720; agriculture 186, 190, 317–30, 348, 349, 694, 695, 699, 700, 715; alternatives to agriculture 330–34; Archaic 317–21, 706; Arctic 710–12; and arrival of Europeans 712–13; arrival of Spaniards 703, 706; Atlantic coast 645–46, 690; bison hunting 307–11; 9.3, 9.4; chronology 183; climate 177, 179, 181, 317, 695; complex societies 680; dogs 326; Early Woodland 328–29, 684; eastern 321; Eastern Woodland 679, 680, 681–91, 694, 704, 715; environments 695; Great Lakes 681, 690; Great Plains 324, 330–31, 679, 703, 704, 705, 706; Little Ice Age 691; Midwest 690; Pacific coast 679, 694, 706–09; Pacific Northwest 715; Plains 307–11, 703–06; primates 51; projectile points 307; 9.1; Southeast 684; Southern cult 687; Southwest 321, 692–706, 702, 715; see also individual sites
North China Plain 238
North Sea 179, 181, 393, 394, 395, 396, 415; 5.4
Ntusi 386
Nubia 375, 377, 378, 380–82; 10.20, 10.24, 10.31, 10.32, 10.33
Nunamiut 38
Núñez, Lautaro 336, 343
Nunn, Patrick 296
Nuu-Chah-Nulth 167
Nuzi 458, 460
Nyerup, Rasmus 25

Oakhurst Complex 355
oasis theory of agriculture 188
Oaxaca 312, 314, 316, 595, 599, 600, 606, 608, 610, 612, 617, 618, 636; 16.5
obsidian 230, 334, 336, 337, 359, 436, 600, 601, 603, 613, 616, 619; jewelry 436; points 685; 18.7
Ob Valley 582
oca 337, 342, 344
Oceania 276, 277, 279, 280, 290, 292; colonization 287–88; see also individual regions and sites
Oc Eo 585, 586
ocher 141, 143, 144, 152, 160, 163, 165, 356, 523; 4.17, 4.39
Ockov 425
Octavian 507; see also Augustus
Ohalo II 203, 206, 207; 6.4, 6.5, 6.6
Ohio 330, 682, 704; 18.4, 18.5
Ohio Valley 322, 326, 681
oil 647
oil palms 269, 364; 10.14
oilseed 536
Ojin 578
Okiek 188, 359
Oklahoma 687, 688, 704; 18.10, 18.11
Okunevo culture 582
Olbia 427, 488
Old Assyrian Trade 434
Old Mon 262
Oldowan 61–83, 95; 2.12, 2.13, 2.16, 2.17, 2.19; stone tool uses 74–77, 81, 82; 2.23, 2.24, 2.25, 2.26
Old Oyo 384
Old Testament 434, 466, 503
Olduvai Gorge, 61, 67, 70, 72, 75, 79, 82, 83, 92, 102, 104, 105, 132; 2.15, 2.29
Oleneostrovski Mogilnik 396; 11.3
olives 457, 494; 13.2
Ollantaytambo 666, 667; 17.35
Olmeca-Xicalanca 624
Olmecs 196, 596, 601, 602–05, 604, 605, 613, 650; 16.8, 16.9, 16.10, 16.11; as "Mother Culture" 604, 605
Olorgesailie 95, 96, 105, 114, 116, 119; 3.12
Olsen-Chubbuck 309; 9.3
Olympia 499, 500
Olympic Games 474, 499
Oman 438, 446, 449
Omo 71, 126, 132, 134, 135; 4.10, 4.11
One Tree Hill 8.37
Ongagawa ware 260
Ontario 330
O'odham 320
Oppenheimer, Stephen 179, 283
oracle bones 555, 558–59, 564; 15.9
orangutans 53, 55
Orchomenos 484, 485
Oregon 331, 333; 9.29
Orellana, Francisco de 672
Orgnac 115
Orinoco River 644, 646, 669, 672, 675
ornaments 209, 210, 246, 247, 248, 403, 409, 557, 559, 560, 575, 576, 585, 694; 18.20
Orrorin tugenensis 63
Ortaköy 454, 458
Osaka 579
Osanni 236, 256
Osiris, god 374
Osmore Valley 341
Ostia 504
Osvaldo 669, 671
Otsu 582
Otumbi 368

Ötzi see "Iceman"
Out of Africa hypothesis 127, 128, 129, 138–39
Owens Valley 184
Oxus 532
oygen isotope studies 56, 115, 127; 4.1
Ozark highlands 330
Ozette 332, 708, 709; 18.34, 18.35

Pachacuti, Emperor 665, 667
Pachamachay 312, 341
Pachuca 619
Paekche 554, 574, 575, 578, 581
Paekchonni 574
Pagnolo d'Asolo 150
Paijan complex 312, 313, 334
Painted Stoa 496
Pakal , 195, 624; 16.33
Pakistan 519, 521, 524–26, 528, 529, 534, 541, 544, 549; see also individual sites
palaces: Assyrian palace 466; 12.45; Babylonian Summer Palaces 468; Chichén Itzá 632; Ebla 452; 12.26, 12.27; Fengchu 564–65; Jian 574; Kato Zakros, Crete 481; 13.8; Kyomihara 582; Linzi 568; Maya 611; Minoan 480–81; 13.8; Mycenae 485; of Nestor, Pylos 484, 485; Olmec Red Palace 602; palace industries 484; Tenochtitlán 635; Ugarit 457; 12.36, Zhengzhou 559; of Zimri-Lim, Mari 450–51; 12.28
Palatine Hill 506
Palau Island 290
Palawan 284
Palenque 195, 624, 625; 16.33, 16.34
Paleocene epoch 50
Paleoindian period 182, 307–13, 322, 331, 348; 9.1
Paleolithic 31, 41, 125, 126, 182, 190, 197, 208, 395, 397; South Asia 522
paleomagnetism 74
Paleozoic era 50
Palestine 201, 203, 213, 377, 466; see also individual sites
Palmarola 404
palm nuts 347
palms 340
Palo Blanco 320
Palung-Wa 262
Pamir 521
Pampa de los Fósiles 334
Pampa de los Llamas Moxeke 652
Pampas 312, 313
Panama 167, 312, 348, 597, 610, 675
Pañamarca 659
Panathenaic: procession 495; Way 497
Panaulauca 341
Panduranga 591
Panlongcheng 562
Panticapaeum 427
Panwolsong 576
papaya 315
paper 574
Paphos 229
Papuan-speaking people 265
papyrus 373, 464
Paracas 654
Paraguay River 669
parchment 464
Pareci 676
Parekklishia-Shillourkambos 229
Parpola, Asko 526
Parthenon 474, 494–95, 511, 513; 13.25, 13.26, 13.27
Parthians 507, 549
Pasemah Plateau 303; 8.41
Paso de la Amada 601, 604, 605; 16.7
Passo di Corvo 402; 11.13

Patagonia 312, 338
Pataliputra 520, 541, 547, 548
Pauli, Ludwig 427
Pavlov 162
peak sanctuaries, Minoan 481
peanuts 335, 344
Pearl River 235, 248, 256
Pearsall, Deborah 348
peas 205, 226, 436
peccaries 347
Pech de l'Azé 116
Pech Merle 163
Pediada plain 480
Pedra Furada 126, 168, 169
Pedra Pintada 171, 312, 347
Peiligang 236, 238, 239; 7.3, 7.4, 7.5, 7.6
"Peking Man" 99; 3.19
Pella 500
Peloponnese 474, 485, 487, 489, 719
Peltenburg, Edgar 229
Pena Roja 340
pendants 273, 356, 539, 553, 699
Penghu Islands 284, 296
Pengtoushan 242, 244, 246, 248
Peninj 72, 94, 95
penis sheath 403
Pennsylvania 171, 324
pepo gourds see gourd
pepper 384
Pergamon 503, 506; Great Altar 503; 13.38
Perrot, Jean 208
Persepolis 541; 14.22
Persia 515
Persian Gulf 201, 232, 388, 438, 443, 446, 449, 462, 532, 536
Persians 378, 387, 469, 487, 488, 495, 500, 501, 540, 541; 13.35; see also Achaemenids
Perthes, Jacques Boucher de 94
Peru 168, 192, 195, 197, 297, 312, 337, 340, 344, 348, 610, 641, 644, 645, 646, 648, 649, 651, 652, 659, 660, 662, 670, 671, 712; coast 334–36; mounds 646–47, 672; see also individual sites
Pestera cu Oase 159
pestles 246, 247, 261, 323; 6.7, 7.7
Petralona 107, 148; 3.30
Petras 480
petroglyphs 8.36
Phaistos 481, 484; 13.8
Pham Duc Manh 252
Pham Van Kinh 252
pharaohs of Egypt 372, 374, 375, 376; 10.26, 10.27, 10.28, 10.29
Pharos 502
Phia Diem 249
Philip II, of Macedon 428, 500; 1.13, 13.34
Philippines 187, 193, 262, 265, 266, 276, 277, 284, 290, 303; 8.9, 8.42
Philistines 434, 463–64; 12.43
Phillips Spring 324
Phnom Rung 586
Phoenicians 387, 420, 426, 427, 434, 464, 474, 486, 490, 503, 505; trading ship 13.19; see also Carthage
Phoenix 692, 694
Phrygia 434, 455, 463, 467, 468
Phu Lon 236
Phung Nguyen 236, 249; 7.18
phytoliths 34, 241–42, 244, 257, 340, 344
Pickering, Travis 75
Pictish warrior 1.5
Piedras Negras 623
pigeons 371

Piggot, Stuart 537
pigment 117–18, 337
Pigott, Vincent 256
pigs 212, 227, 228, 229, 277, 288, 363, 371, 419, 522, 523, 718; China 556; and Philistines 464
Pikillacta 662
Pikimachay 168
Piltdown Man 59
Piman-speaking groups 694
Piperno, Dolores 348
Piraeus 496, 512
Pirak 520, 539
pistachio nuts 149
Pitcairn Islands 188, 294, 296
Pithecanthropus erectus 97, 100
Pizarro, Francisco 668
Plains Village people 704, 705
Plainview 307; 9.1
plantains 369
plants: in diet 118–19, 150–51, 170, 214, 239, 310, 311, 347, 355, 356, 361, 395, 523; as medicine 170, 328; remains 119, 170, 244, 254, 284, 288, 291, 326, 330, 334, 335, 340, 344, 355, 523, 525, 528, 646; as utensils 324, 348
platforms 647, 648, 652, 653, 659, 664, 671, 694; 17.29
plaza 329, 334, 335, 613, 617, 618, 620, 624, 628, 633, 647, 650, 651, 652, 659, 660, 669, 670, 671, 672, 673, 675, 676, 688; 16.35, 16.41, 17.10, 17.39, 17.41, 17.43
Plaza Hundida tradition 647
Pleistocene epoch 51, 57, 61, 72, 73, 75, 153, 163, 165, 170, 172, 173, 178, 179, 182, 186, 188, 189, 204, 205, 212, 229, 235, 237, 240, 243, 348; Africa 356; Australia 265, 268, 270; 8.3; East and Southeast Asia 260, 261–62, 276, 277; North America 308, 312, 321, 333; South America 348
Pliocene 51, 57, 61, 72, 73, 75, 146
plows/plowing 183, 184, 192–93, 394, 410, 419, 570; 5.10
Plutarch 502
Pohnpei 298; 8.34
points 213, 249, 272, 284, 307–08, 311, 312, 313, 323, 333, 370, 523, 525, 704; 6.12, 8.21, 9.1, 9.5; Dalton 9.5; North American Paleoindian 307; 9.1; Western Stemmed 311
Poland 160, 418, 425; see also individual sites
polar bear, carving of 18.38
pollen 181, 204, 238, 257, 367, 409
Polynesia 181, 187, 235, 266, 276, 277, 279, 282, 288, 669; 8.1; contact with Europeans 300, 301; settlement of 290–94; social organization 300–01; and South America 297
Pompeii 509, 510; 1.17, 13.35, 13.47
Pompey the Great 506
Po Nagar 592
pongids 52
population: and agriculture 228; changes 274, 700; decline 342, 706, 715; dispersion 101–05, 154; genetics of Europeans 398; 11.6, 11.7; growth 25, 40–41, 192, 223, 274, 294, 333, 370–71, 395, 400, 553, 613, 698, 717; 1.18, 8.28; movement 463, 488, 490, 570, 693–94, 715, 719; of Native Americans 714
Porc Epic 132
porcupines 331, 523
Porter, David 296
Portonaccio 474, 492, 506; 13.20
Portugal 149, 151, 397, 405, 410, 412, 414, 427, 490, 510; Côa Valley 160; see also individual sites
Poseidon, god 484
Possehl, Greg 533
postprocessual archaeology 39

potassium-argon dating 75
potatoes 185, 338, 342, 344, 348, 661
potter's wheel 246
pottery 192, 231, 232, 239, 246, 524; 7.12, 7.13;
   Açutuba 674; Amazonia 346–47; Andes and
   Desert coast 645; Asuka 580; Athenian 493; Attic
   black figure 13.2; Baluchistan 528; Bambata cave
   370; Bandkeramik 407; Bell Beaker 420–22;
   11.36, 11.37; Burnished Red ware 541, 542, 545;
   Cardial ware 404; 11.14; ceremonial 259;
   Chicanel 616; Chifumbaze, Africa 367; 10.17;
   Classic Kisalian 387; Corded Ware 419; 11.37; with
   crushed shell tempers 288; Dabenkeng 284;
   8.15; dentate stamped 289; 8.22, 8.23; Early
   Transcausian 445; eastern North America 684;
   Eridu 436; Ertebølle-Ellerbek 415; in the form of a
   cow 256; Four Mile 18.27; Gandharan Grave
   culture 539, 541, 542; 14.20; Ganges-Yamuna
   Doab 540; glaze ware 702; Great Plains 704;
   Greek vases in Etruscan tombs 493; Greek vases
   traded with Europe 424; griddles 646; Halaf sites
   435; Hastinapura 543; and hunter-gatherers 260;
   incised 250, 254, 256, 285; with incised
   longboats, Cyclades 479; 13.5; Indian 302; Jomon
   259; 7.33, 7.34; Kamares ware, Crete 481; Khirbet
   Kerak ware 445; Konduri 17.42; Kot Diji 519,
   530; 14.10; Kwale ware 367; Lapita 285, 287, 288,
   290, 291; 8.16, 8.22, 8.23; Marajó 671; 17.38;
   Matola ware 367; Maya 623; 16.3, 16.32; Meroë
   382]; in Mesoamerica 600; Moche 656; 17.21;
   Mycenaean 451, 485–86; Nazca 659; 17.27;
   Ninevite 5 445; 12.17; North America 327, 684,
   695; Northern Black Polished ware 543; Painted
   Gray ware 543; Paracas 654; pedestalled bowls
   252; Peru 651; Philistine 463; 12.43; polychrome
   655, 673, 674; Pueblo 697; 18.22; Pukara 655;
   17.20; Red-figure 493, 499; 13.32; red-slipped
   284, 285, 287; 8.17; red-ware 257; Salado
   polychrome 702–03; saucerboat type 479; serving
   bowls, Paso de la Amada 601; Shipibo-Conibo
   674; 17.44; Silver Leaves 369; Sokchondong 575;
   South Asia 524; Southeast Asian Neolithic 7.20;
   "tattooed" 289; thin-walled, Hungary 402; trade
   in Saudi Arabia 438; Trichterbecher 408–09;
   Ubaid period 438; Urewe 367; West Africa 360;
   wheel-thrown 530
Potts, Richard 70
Po Valley 406
Poverty Point 328–29; 9.21, 9.22
Prambanan 303; 8.39
Pratisthana 549
Preah Ko 588; 15.43
prehistory and history 25, 26–27, 28
Prei Khmeng 586
Pre-Pottery Neolithic A and B (PPNA, PPNB) 212,
   216, 217, 222, 230, 231
Pre Rup 588
Prestwich, Joseph 94
Pretoria 369
Prezletice 116
prickly pear 315; 9.7
Prima Porta Augustus 507; 13.43
primates, evolution of 49–57; anatomy and
   genetics 53–56; anthropoids 50, 51, 52;
   classification of 52–53, 54; ; modern, as
   toolmakers 69; 2.18 prosimians 50, 51, 52, 54;
   spine 2.1; see also under individual species
printing press 29, 36
prismatic blades 600
processual archaeology 38
Proconsul 51; 2.7
"progress" 32–33, 43, 193
Proto-Arawak people 672

Proto-Elamite 434, 442, 445, 446
Provence 428
Ptolemaic kingdom 501
Ptolemy I 501, 502
Puebla 314, 316, 348, 605, 620, 624
Puebla-Tlaxcala region 613, 621
Pueblo 679, 680
Pueblo Bonito 698–99; 18.23
pueblos 680, 695–703; Pecos Pueblo 702; 18.25,
   18.26; population changes 700; population
   decline 703
Puerto Hormigo 334
Puget Sound 332
Pukara 642, 655; 17.20
pulses 205, 528, 536
pumpkins 315, 319, 322
Punapau crater 295
punctuated equilibrium (evolution) 48–49
Pungnamni 575
Punic Wars 383
Punjab 533, 536, 537, 548, 549
Punt, Land of 388
Puripica 342, 343
Pushyamitra Sunga 548
Puuc 596, 631–32
Pu'uloa petroglyphs 8.36
Pylos 484, 485
Pyongyang 574
pyramids 373, 613; Caral, Peru 345; Castillo,
   Chichén Itzá 632; Egypt 374; 10.23, 10.25; La
   Venta 605; of the Niches, El Tajín 16.29; Meröe
   381; 10.32; Plumed Serpent, Xochicalco 622;
   16.30, 16.31; Teotihuacán 613, 614, 615; 16.19,
   16.20; Tula 629; 16.37, 16.38
Pyrenees 393, 404
Pyu 554, 590

Qadan 356
Qadesh, battle of 456; 12.33
Qafzeh 126, 136, 137, 152, 153, 154; 4.14
Qasr Ibrim 363
Qatar 438
Qatna 451, 453, 460
Qermez Dere 203, 217, 218
Qi 566
Qija culture 582
Qin 302, 554, 567, 568, 571
Qinghai 245, 582
Qin Shi Huangdi 26, 568, 572, 593; 15.22, 15.23
Quebrada Jaguay 335, 336
Quebrada Las Conchas 336, 337
Quebrada Tacahuay 335
Queensland 269, 273
Quelcatani 342
querns 205, 215, 522, 523, 527
Quetta 528, 539
Quetzalcoatl, god 628
Quiché 638
Quiha 365
quinoa 341, 344, 349
Quiriguá 625
quiver 408, 575; 11.20
Qujialing 236

rabbits 311, 331
radiocarbon dating 33–34, 36, 74, 157
Rai Arnon 253
Rainbird, Paul 296
Rainbow Serpent 271, 272, 273; 8.8
rainforests 178, 346–47, 364, 369, 644, 674
Rajasthan 522
Rajendravarman II 588
Rajghir 542

Rakhigarhi 533
Ralegh, Walter 29
Ramapithecus 54
Ramesses II 377, 456; 10.26; III 10.24
Rana Ghundai 525, 539
Range site 684
Rann Chuang River 590
Rann of Kutch 533
Rano Raraku 295
Rapa Nui see Easter Island
Rappaport, Roy 35
Rarotonga 8.25
Ras Hafun 388
Ra, sun god 374
Rathje, William 27, 197
Rawson, Jessica 566
Raymond, Scott 674
Real Alto 334, 650, 651
Reck, Hans 67
red deer 395, 397
Red River 249, 570
Red Sea 102, 209, 351, 382, 388
reels 292
Regardou 148
Rehman Dheri 528, 530–31, 551; 14.8
Reid, Laurence 262, 386
religion 26, 345, 558, 628–29, 647; Amazonia 676;
   ceremonial enclosures 635; 11.35; China 571–73;
   Crete 481; Egypt 374, 376, 377; enclosures 666;
   Olmec 602; Roman 515; South America 652,
   653–54, 662, 667; Southwest Asia 436
Remedello 406
Rendell, Helen 522
Renfrew, Colin 189, 230, 231, 479
repoussé 654
reservoirs 587, 588, 589
Revadiml 119
rhea 338
Rhine 407, 414, 421, 430
rhinoceros 522, 523
rhizomes 528
Rhodes 482, 503
Rhône 393, 488
rice 185, 187, 235, 236, 240–42, 246, 284, 364, 369,
   527, 536, 553; 7.8, 7.9, 7.10; expansion into Korea
   and Japan 257–62; expansion into Southeast Asia
   248–56, 261–62; 7.17; hillside terraces 8.42; in
   Thailand 250; wild rice to cultivated rice 241–42,
   243; 7.8
Rice, Patricia 165
Richards, David 157
Richards, Martin 283
Rick, John 341
Rightmire, Philip 133, 134, 135
Rigveda 538
Rim-Sin 449
Rindos, David 189
rings 403, 522, 523, 553, 555, 576
Ring Site 335
Rio: Camana 336; Caquetá 340; Casas Grandes 318;
   Chao 647; de la Plata 644; Grande 701, 702;
   Huantanay 662; Jetepeque 656; Lambayeque
   656; Mala 652; Santa 655; Sechín 652; Seco 647;
   Supe 642, 645, 647; Tinto 510; Urubamba 667;
   Viru 655; Zaña 646
Rispoli, Fiorella 256
Rissman, Paul 537
ritual 26, 42, 418, 553, 599, 652, 657, 659, 661, 671,
   681; enclosures 418; 11.35; mounds 327; North
   America 694, 699; pits 564; vessels 559, 568
Rivero Compound 663; 17.34
Roanoke, Virginia 1.5, 1.6
Robinson, Edward 466

Roc de Marsal 148
Roche, Hélène 71
rock art 192, 267, 271–72, 342, 346, 396, 406, 414, 523; 8.7, 8.8, 9.43, 10.12, 11.47, 11.48; Africa 356, 358–59; 10.8, 10.9, 10.12; symbols 358; see also cave art
rockshelters 270, 284, 289, 312, 314, 322, 326–27, 328, 332, 333, 344, 395, 404, 523; 9.26, 9.27, 9.28, 9.29
Rocky Cape South 272
Rocky Mountains 166, 331
rodents 339
roe deer 397
Rohri Hills 536
Rollefson, Gary 223; 6.26
Romania 159, 425
Romans 383, 393, 420, 475, 491, 500, 503, 549; army 514–15; and Carthage 503–04; Colosseum 1.4; conquest of Gaul 394; conquest of Italy 394; empire 28, 30, 379, 388, 420, 429, 473, 474, 507–16; 13.45; expansion 394, 506–07; Republic 506–07; roads 509; 13.46; Rome 508–09; 13.42; 13.44; in South Asia 550; trade 550; unification of Italy 394
Romulus and Remus 504; 13.40
Roosevelt, Anna 346, 347
Rosenberg, Michael 212
Rössen 408
Ross Island 421
Rudna Glava 402
Rumbaugh, Duane 69
Russia 151, 162, 163, 165, 257, 396, 425; pottery and hunter-gatherers 260; see also individual sites
Rwanda 365, 367, 368, 385
rye 203, 214, 226; 6.1

Sabah 283, 284
Sabaña de Bogatá 339
saber-toothed cats 178
Sabi Abyad 460
Saccopastore 126, 148, 149
Sacred Cenote, Chichén Itzá 610
sacrifice 558, 559, 628, see also human sacrifice
Sacsahuaman 297; 17.37
Sagart, Laurent 262
Sahara 56, 127, 181, 185, 188, 351, 352, 356, 358, 388, 390; 5.5, 10.12; cattle 362; 10.12; climate 358, 360; 5.5; Holocene 360; 10.10; ironworking 365; "mobile elites" 380
Sahel 390
Sahelanthropus tchadensis 63
Sahlins, Marshall 301
Sahndong 558
Sahnouni 73, 80
Sahul Land 131, 152, 155, 173; 4.31, 5.3, 8.9
Saigon 591
Saint Acheul 94; 3.8
St Césaire 126, 148
St Louis 321
Sai Yok 253
Saka 584
Sakas 549
Saki 578
Sakitima 580
Saladoid 669, 675
Saladoid-Barrancoid 642
Salama Valley 605
Salambo 505
Salamis 487
Salé 134
Salinas de Chao 647
salmon 708
salt 351, 384, 386, 387, 457, 585, 632

Salts Cave 328; 9.23
Salzgitter-Lebenstedt 152
Samaria 465
sambaquis 347, 645; 9.44
Sambungmacan 90, 106
Samnites 491
Samoa 290, 294, 300, 301
Samrong Sen 252
San Bushmen 355, 356; 19.1
Sanam 381
San Andrés 314, 316
Sanchi 548
sandals 333; 9.29
Sandawe 359
Sand Canyon Pueblo 700
Sanders, William 616
Sané 388
Sanga 386; 10.40
Sangankallu 528
Sangay 671
Sanggan 238
Sangiran 97, 130; 3,17
San Isidoro 339
San Jacinto 334
San Jose de Moro 657
San José Mogote 596, 600, 607, 608, 612; 16.5, 16.6, 16.14
San Juan River 696, 697, 698, 699, 700
San Lorenzo 596, 602–03, 605; 16.8
San Marcos 316
Sannati 549
San Pedro 317, 318, 342
Sanskrit 585, 586
Santa Barbara 706, 707, 715
Santa Cruz 288
Santa Elena 343
Santarem 346, 642, 672–73, 673, 675; 17.40, 17.42
Santa Rosa 333
Sanxingdui 562, 564–65; 15.15, 15.16, 15.17, 15.18, 15.19
sapota 315
Saqqara 373; Step Pyramid 373; 10.23
Sarai Khola 526, 530, 539
Sarai Nahar Rai 522, 523
Sarawak 131, 155, 277, 284
Sardinia 404, 477, 486, 491, 505; 13.3
Sardis 469
Sargon II 465, 466, 467; 12.40
Sargon of Akkad 445, 446, 452; 12.22
Sarnarth 542
Sarup 11.35
Sasanian empire 470, 549
Satanikota 549
Satavahanas 549
Saudi Arabia 363
Saushtatar, King 460
Savage-Rumbaugh, Sue 69
Savannah River 327
Sava valley 400
saws 249
Sayil 631
Scandinavia 30, 398, 399, 417, 418, 425, 427; Bronze Age 394; 11.48; burials 418; 11.21; see also individual countries and sites
scavenging 120, 121, 143, 150–51
scepters 539
Schauffler, Richard 251
Schick, Kathy 69, 74
Schliemann, Heinrich 450, 480, 482
Schmidt, Klaus 220
Schöningen 114, 116, 119; 3.37, 3.38
Schwetzingen 407
Scordisci 430

Scotland 430; 11.28
scrapers 61, 66, 72, 73, 80, 112, 150, 157, 268, 311, 313, 323, 341; 2.12, 2.13, 4.25, 8.4, 9.38, 9.44; end-scraper 162
sculpture: Akhenaten 10.27; Alalakh 12.39; Altar of Zeus at Pergamon 503; 13.38; Assyrian palace relief 465; 12.45; Benin 384; 10.38; Buddha 586; 15.32; bull leaping, Crete 481; Champa 15.47; Constantine 515; 13.55; Cycladic figures 478, 479; 13.4; Etruscan Apollo 492; Mahdia shipwreck 513; 23.52; Ife 384; 10.37; kouros and kore, Merenda 13.28; Herakles 13.33; Mari 12.29; Mithras 515; 13.54; Napir-Asu 462; 12.42; Neo-Hittite relief, Karatepe 12.44; Nok 366; 10.16; Olmec 603, 604; 16.8, 16.10; Parthenon 494–95; Prima Porta Augustus 507, 515; 13.43; Ptolemy I 502; 13.37; "Ram in a Thicket", Ur 445, 12.16; relief of Gandharans bearing tribute 14.22; relief of Phoenician ship 13.19; Sanxingdui bronzes 565; 15.18; she-wolf 13.40
scythes 570
Scythians 420, 427, 428, 488
seafood 160, 331–32, 334, 346, 414, 494, 647, 649, 706
sea level changes 131, 143, 155, 166, 177, 178, 179, 181, 237, 240, 241, 252, 266, 268, 272, 276, 394; 4.31, 5.2, 5.3, 5.4, 8.2, 8.3, 8.9, 11.2, 11.34
seals/sealing 142, 160, 338, 347, 438, 441, 442, 459, 480, 529, 544, 566, 584, 709; 12.11, 14.11
sea mammals 336, 706, 711
Sea Peoples 434, 458, 463, 486
seasonal mobility 523
Sechín Alto 642, 645, 652–53, 653; 17.13
secondary state formation 36
Seddin 425
sedentism 183, 190–91, 192, 205, 274, 348, 645, 717; and agriculture 260, 314, 348; in Mesoamerica 313; North Africa 358
seed drill 571
Selassie, Johannes Haile 68
Seleucid Empire 501, 506
Sémah 98
Sembiran 302
Semenov, Sergei 81
Semitic 443, 448; languages 363, 446, 452, 458
Semliki River 142
Senga 72
Sennacherib, King 465, 466, 468
sense of smell 49
Senwosret I 377; III 377
Septimius Severus 511
Sequani 428; 11.49
Serapis 502, 515
Serra da Lua 9.43
Serra do Mar 671
Service, Elman 32
sesame 371
Sety I 377; 10.30
sexual dimorphism 57, 78
Shaanxi 238, 245, 563, 564, 573
Shady, Ruth 649
Shaffer, Jim 519, 528, 532, 551
Shahr-i Sokhta 520, 529, 530, 536
Shaikhan Dheri 548, 549
Shalmaneser I, King 460; II 468
shamanism/shamans 245, 260, 334, 409, 576, 595, 598, 603, 605, 650, 674; 7.12, 7.13, 15.36, 18.4
Shamash, god 449; 12.23
Shandong 555, 567, 568
Shang 196, 236, 240, 553, 554, 555, 557, 558–63, 571, 582; 15.9
Shanga 384

Shangdong 245, 555
Shanggan Valley 238
Shanidar 149, 150, 152, 154, 211
Shanshan 584–85
Shao Tuo, tomb of 559
Sharma, G.R. 523, 527
Sharp, Andrew 293
Sharruma, god 12.32
Shawnee 126
Shawnee Minisink, 171
Shea, John 154, 326
Shechem 465
sheep 211–12, 214–15, 228, 229, 230, 363, 364, 365, 369, 371, 382, 387, 419, 436, 494, 522, 526, 527, 530, 719; 6.33, 6.34; China 556; Ebla 452
shellfish 254, 334, 335, 336, 338, 346, 347, 395, 523, 645, 706, 709; 11.2
shell middens 142, 257, 275, 296, 322, 325, 336, 347, 410, 412, 415; 9.44, 11.34; see also midden
shell mounds 274, 326, 347, 645, 646; 9.19
shells 337, 525, 536, 540, 616, 650, 683, 687; 8.21; adzes 288; beads 254, 688, 707; fishhooks 363; 9.31; jewelry 254, 256, 284; 7.26; knives 253, 284; necklaces 17.47; ornaments 209, 210, 694; 18.20; pendants 273, 356; decorated pottery 404; 11.14
Shichishito sword 578
shields 575
Shi Ji 553, 555, 558, 562
Shikala 458
Shinzhaishan 236
ships 292, 459, 482, 512–13, 710; 8.26, 11.48, 13.19; see also boats
shipwrecks 459, 512–13; 12.37, 12.38, 13.51, 13.52
Shi Qiang 563
Shiva, god 538, 588
Shixia 248
Shizitan 238
shoes 576
Shona 387
Shoocondej, Rasmi 253
Shotoku, Prince 567, 580, 581
Shu 565
Shum Laka 360, 364
Shuppiluliuma I, King 456, 460
Shutruk-Nahhunte 463
shuttles 247
siamangs 52
Siberia 158, 166, 167, 168, 173, 178, 582, 710, 711
Sichuan 562, 564
Sicily 404, 477, 486, 488, 490, 505, 719
sickles 208, 244, 253, 525, 526, 556, 570, 585; 7.4, 14.3
Sidi Abderahman 132
Sidon 464
Sidun 553
Sierra Nevadas 333
Sifendi 556
Sikels 490
silk 261, 553, 572, 574, 576; 15.26
Silk Road 261, 549, 571, 583–85; 15.40
Silla 554, 574, 575–77, 580; 15.31; Great Silla 554, 577
Sillen, Andrew 82
silver 371, 427, 442, 444, 457, 467, 490, 495, 510, 574, 598, 610, 654; from Troy 451; ornaments 585
Silver Leaves 269
Sima de los Huesos 108, 111–13, 149; 3.31, 3.34, 3.35; see also Atapuerca; Gran Dolina
Sima Qian 553, 558, 562
Simmons, Alan 229
Sinanthropus pekinensis 99, 100
Sindh 531, 535, 536, 539

Singa 126, 132, 134, 136
Sino-Tibetan 262
Siouan 330
Sioux 706
Sipán 610, 657, 659; 17.24; Presentation Theme 657; 17.23
Sirkap 544–45, 548, 549; 14.26
Sirsukh 544, 545, 549; 14.27
site formation/modification 81, 114, 142
Siteia 480
Sivapithecus 51
Siwah 501
Siyaj K'ak 616, 619
Skåne 415
Skagit River 332
Skateholm 183, 416
skull shape 51, 57, 59, 61, 86, 87, 89, 92, 97, 100, 102, 103, 106, 107, 108, 110, 111; 2.7, 2.11, 3.2, 3.3, 3.15, 3.17, 3.18, 3.25, 3.28
slate hoes 257
slaves 351, 384, 389, 442, 495, 499, 510
sling stones 313
Sloan 312; 9.5
sloth 171, 172
Slovakia 162, 409, 425
Slovenia 410
smallpox 706, 714
smelting, iron 350, 365, 367, 368, 369
Smith, Bruce 228, 314
Smith, Fred 129
snails 358
Snaketown 320, 692, 693; 18.18
Snodgrass, Antony 487
Snofru 374
Snohomish River 332
snuff trays 339
Sørensen, Per 248, 254; 7.23
Soane, Sir John 1.7
social complexity 191, 670; Amazonia 676; Andes 652; China 553–54; Maya 633; Mesoamerica 598, 605; South America 641, 645
social evolution 32, 78
social exchange and networking 230–31
social organization 217, 232, 245, 300–01, 444, 567–68, 604, 615, 647, 670, 718; Aztecs 637; Egypt 374; Indus 519, 537; Maya 625–27
social status markers 332
societies and individuals 35; types 32–33, 193
Society Islands 296, 300
Soga no Imako 580, 581
Sogdiana 584
Sokchondong 575
Soleihac 114
Solomon Islands 276, 277, 279, 287, 288, 291, 296
Solomon, King 464
Solutrean 161, 163, 166
Solutré 163
Somalia 364, 384, 388
Somme River 94
song 26; 10.9
Songhai 384
Songungon 257
Songze 247
Sonora 319, 320, 692
Son Valley 523
Sopohang 257
sorghum 361, 364, 367, 369; 10.14
Soto, Hernando de 712
soursop 315
South America 31, 166, 170, 312–13, 367, 648; 9.30; agriculture 186, 193, 343–44, 646; Amazonia

642–44, 668–77; Amazonian Lowlands 346–47; Andean empires 660–68; Andes 195, 312, 326, 338–46, 348, 610, 641–2; Archaic 645; 9.31, 9.43; Atlantic Lowlands 347–48; Early Intermediate period 655–60; and Easter Island 297; environments 641; Holocene 644, 645, 646; hunting 312; Pacific Lowlands 334–38; primates 51; see also individual countries and sites
South Asia 302; climate 521; foundations 522–23; Holocene 519–51; language 519, 521–22; topography 521; see also individual countries and sites
South Carolina 327
South Dakota 704, 705; 18.30
Southeast Asia 276, 292, 369, 585–93; and Australia 269, 275, 276; Bronze Age 554; contacts with China, India, and Europe 302–04; early settlers 277; and India 585; language 261–62; Neolithic 286, 554; trade 301–04; see also individual countries and sites
Southern Africa 59, 61, 68, 70, 116, 117, 119, 126, 133–34, 141, 142, 143, 144, 352; Equus cave 132, 137; rock art 356, 358–59; 10.8, 10.9
Southwest Asia 197, 375, 397, 402, 433, 434, 450, 455, 456, 463, 717; agriculture 201–33, 434–36, 438; Bronze Age 433, 434, 442–63; Chalcolithic 433, 435; environment 201–04; Halaf 433–36; 12.2; influence on Mediterranean 477–78; "International Age" 12.30; Iron Age 433, 434, 450, 455, 456, 463; language 440, 443; and Mediterranean 473; and present-day scholarship 470; topography 433; Ubaid period 434, 436–38; 12.2; Uruk period 438–42
soybeans 571
spades 238, 239, 243, 244, 246, 247, 470, 556, 585; 7.15, 7.31
Spain 102, 104, 107, 119, 148, 149, 150, 152, 156, 160, 388, 412, 427, 430, 490, 491, 510; cities 420; farming enclaves 11.7; Roman 511; tin mining 420; see also individual sites
Spanish flu 718
Sparta 473, 485, 487, 488, 499
spatulas 272, 339
spearheads 560, 582
spears 322, 576, 585
spearthrowers 162, 322; see also atlatl
Spice Islands 276
spices 384, 464
spindle whorls 246, 247, 261, 284, 287
Spirit Cave 168, 243
spiro 680, 687, 688; 18.10, 18.11
Spondylus shell 337
Spring and Autumn period 566
Spy 148
squash 186, 314, 315, 319, 320, 321, 322, 324, 335, 338, 341, 344, 348, 536, 646, 647, 649, 684, 701
Sravasti 542
Sri Ksetra 590
Sri Lanka 519, 520, 521, 522, 523, 545, 546, 548, 551, 590; see also individual sites
Sri Thep 591
stable isotope analysis 82, 150, 154, 162, 171
Staller, John 334
Stallings Island 327
stamp seals 449
Star Carr 394, 395–97, 415; 11.4, 11.5
Starcevo Grad 406
states 33, 193–98, 196, 248, 380, 420, 453, 471, 691; 5.11; in Africa 351, 380; 10.19; archaeological features 195–96; Egypt 194, 195; in Europe 420, 426; 11.49; geography of state formation 195; Greece 486; Sumerian city-states 443–44
steatite 334, 536; beads 525

Stehli, Petar 413
Stein, Aurel 583
Steinheim 126, 148
stelae 382, 406; Aksum 382; 10.35; Chavín de
  Huántar 653–54; 17.16; Hammurabi 449; 12.23;
  Hauberg 611; 16.17; La Mojarra 608, 609; 16.15;
  Merenptah 466; Monte Albán 607; Naram-Sin
  446; 12.20; Olmec 603; Tiwanaku 661;
  Xochicalco 622
Stellmoor 163, 415
Step Pyramid 373; 10.23
Sterkfontein 59, 68, 72
Steward, Julian 35, 196, 643, 675
Stillbay points 143; 4.16
Stone Age 31, 41, 67, 73, 126; Africa 75, 93, 96
stone artifacts 192, 238, 239, 241, 356, 364, 526,
  527; axes for display 419; bangles 253; barkcloth
  beaters 284, 287; beads 254; 10.7; bolas 347;
  bracelets 254; butchering 309–10; digging stick
  weights 356; drills 323; early Australian 268–70,
  270; 8.4, 8.6; figurines 687; fishhooks 256;
  gravers 311; grinding stones 526, 616; hammers
  526; harpoons 334; hoes 556; knives 261, 311, 323;
  mano and metate 9.26; mortar and pestles 261,
  323; 6.7, 6.8; prismatic blades 600; querns 522,
  523, 527; rings 522, 523; rings/weights 522;
  scepters 539; sickles 253, 525, 526, 556; 7.4, 14.3;
  weights 256, see also stone tools
Stonehenge 38, 394, 414, 416–17; 1.7, 1.16, 11.30,
  11.31, 11.32, 11.33
stone quarries 496, 511, 602; 13.48
stone tools 26, 30, 32, 41, 47, 60, 89, 100–01, 536;
  2.18, 2.30, 2.31; Acheulean hand axes 57, 66, 70,
  73, 85, 93–96, 101, 104, 105, 112, 113; 3.7, 3.8, 3.9,
  3.10, 3.11, 3.12; adzes 252, 253, 254, 288, 292, 311,
  411; 7.21, 8.21, 8.25, 9.5; in the Americas 168–71;
  4.53, 4.54; Aurignacian tools 126, 154, 156,
  157–58; axes 347, 360, 363, 524, 526, 527; 3.8, 8.6,
  9.44; and behavioral patterns 49, 141; blades 151,
  160, 161, 525; burins 162, 311; chisels 288; 8.21;
  dating 100, 101; experimental studies 76–77,
  2.23, 2.24, 2.25, 2.26; flakes 100, 101, 102, 104,
  109, 151, 181, 268, 277; 3.20; microliths 141, 166,
  205, 207, 208, 213, 277, 354–55, 356, 363, 522,
  523, 524, 530; 6.3, 10.4, 10.7; Gravettian 161–62;
  Kebaran 205; Levallois technique 96, 150, 152,
  153, 160; 3.13, 3.14; microliths 205, 213, 522, 523;
  microscopic analysis 2.22; Mousterian 150–52,
  154; 4.25; Natufian 205; Oldowan 61–83, 2.12,
  2.13, 2.16, 2.17, 2.23, 2.24, 2.25, 2.26; pebble tools
  277; points 145, 213, 268, 307–08, 311, 312, 313,
  323; 4.18, 6.12, 9.1, 9.5; scraper 61, 66, 72, 73, 80,
  112, 150, 157, 268, 311, 313, 323, 341; 2.12, 2.13,
  4.25, 8.4, 9.38, 9.44; and seasonal mobility 523;
  South Asia 522; and symbols 80; transitional
  industries 160; use 74–77, 81, 82; 2.23, 2.24,
  2.24, 2.26; see also stone artifacts
storage pits 211, 238, 239, 245, 259, 319, 556, 582,
  705
Stordeur, Danielle 217, 218, 219
Storm, Paul 131
Strait of Gibraltar 102, 427, 490
Strait of Malacca 179; 5.3
Straits of Hormuz 446
stratigraphy 30, 74
Strato III, King 548
Stringer, Chris 127, 129
stucco: images 591; ornamentation 584
Stukeley, William 416
Subartu 449
Sudan 126, 132, 134, 363, 365, 368, 388; 10.18
Suetonius 507
sugarcane 369

Sui dynasty 580, 581
Suiko, Empress 580, 581
Sujin 578
Sulawesi 276
Sumatra 179, 275, 276, 279, 285, 296, 303, 304; 5.3,
  8.31
Sumerians 434, 443–44, 445, 446, 452; language
  447
sumpweed 321, 325, 326, 328
Sunazawa 260
sun circles 331
Sunda Islands 276, 277, 302, 303
Sundaland 155, 178, 179, 276; 5.3, 8.9
sunflower 321, 325, 326, 328, 330, 348, 684
Sunga dynasty 548
Sunget 287
Sungir' 162
sunken courts 647, 649, 652, 661
Suogang 284
Supe Valley 345, 649
Surkh Kotal 549
Surkotada 528, 535
Suryavarman 588, 589
Susa 434, 437, 442, 445, 446, 447, 449, 462, 469;
  12.23, 12.42
Sushun 580
Sussmann, Randall 70
Swanscombe 111, 146, 148
Swartkrans 59, 68, 70, 72, 78, 116; 2.20
Swat 526–27, 530, 539, 542, 546
Sweden 418
sweet potatoes 277, 297, 298, 338, 343, 344, 646,
  649
swidden agriculture 626
Switzerland 410, 423; 11.43
swordfish 707
swords 425, 563, 576, 579
Sybaris 488
symbols 41–42, 49, 79, 80, 141, 356, 396; in rock
  art 358, 397
syphilis 719
Syracuse 488, 505
Syr Darya Valley 583
Syria 114, 117, 118, 149, 150, 154, 201, 203, 205, 208,
  226, 227, 228, 229, 230, 433, 445, 451, 454, 456,
  460, 466, 501; 12.36; Habur plains 448; Jebel
  Aruda 442; see also individual sites
Syros 479
Szigetszentmarton 410

Tabasko 316
Tabon 277
Tabun 152, 153; 4.28, 4.29
Tacitus 30, 428
Taçon 192, 267, 272, 273
Taedong River 574
Taënsa 687
Taesongdong 574
Taforalt 137
Tagales 282
Tagus 394, 412, 413
Tahiti 282, 292, 301; 8.27
Tai 262
Taieb, Maurice 60
Taihang Mountains 237
Taima-Taima 168
Taino 644, 669, 675
Taipei basin 284
Taiwan 187, 247, 262, 265, 266, 280, 281, 283,
  283–84, 284, 289, 290
Tajikistan 501, 502
Ta Keo 587
Taklamakan Desert 583, 584

Talaud Islands 284; 8.40
Talepakemalai 291; 8.24
Talheim 192, 411; 11.23, 11.24
Tal-i Iblis 442
Tamaulipas 314
Tang dynasty 574, 575, 577, 581, 582, 583, 585
Tanit, god 504, 505
Tanshishan 248, 249
Tanzania 57, 70, 72, 75, 79, 83, 94, 95, 126, 132, 133,
  134, 141, 188, 356, 359, 365, 367; see also Olduvai
  Gorge and individual sites
Taosi 582
Tapajós River 672
Taperinha 346, 645
tapestry 654
Taramsa 132, 137
Tarascans 595, 598, 610, 636
Tarentum 506; 11.44
Tarim basin 582, 583
Tarquinia 491, 492; 13.21
Tarquinius Superbus 504
tarsiers 52
Tartessos 427
Taruga 365, 366, 368
tarwi 342, 344
Tasmania 126, 131, 155, 156, 181, 266, 267; 8.7;
  environmental changes 270–71
Tassili 10.12
Tata 152
tattooing 288, 289
Taung 2.8
Taurus Mountains 201, 232, 433, 453, 476
Tavoliere 394, 402; 11.13
Taxila 520, 526, 540, 541, 544–45, 546, 548, 549;
  14.25, 14.26, 14.27
Taycanamu 662, 663
teeth 52, 61, 137, 523; and diet 82; extractions 287
Tehuacán Valley 314, 316, 320, 335, 600
Tehuantepec 605, 610, 621
Tekkalakota 528
tektites 98
Telarmachay 341
Tell Abadeh 437
Tell al-Ubaid 436
Tell Awayli 436
Tell Beydar 445, 452
Tell Brak 445, 458, 459; 12.17
Tell el-Amarna see Amarna
Tell el-Far'ah South 463
Tell el-Oueili 436
Tell es-Sultan see Jericho
Tell Halaf 433
Tell Leilan 445, 448, 452
Tell Madhhur 437
Tell Mardikh see Ebla
Tell Miqne (Ekron) 463
Tell Mozan 458
Tell Mureybit 208
Tell Qasile 463
Tell Sheikh Hamad 460
tells 401, 419, 524; 11.10
Temara 132
Temnata 156
temples 438; Baal and Dagon 457; Alexandria 502;
  Angkor 587; 15.42, 15.44; Anyang 562; Asuka-
  dera 581; Babylon 468; Buddhist 576; Capitoline
  Triad 506; Champa 592; 15.48; Coricancha 666;
  Egypt 374, 377; 10.30; Enlil, Nippur 463; Eridu
  436; 12.4; Etruscan at Veii 492; 13.20; Greek
  499; Greek colonies 488; Guatemala 605; Haldi
  at Musasir 467; 12.46; Hariharalaya 588; 15.43;
  Hemasringagiri 588; Hephaisteion 497; Hera I
  and II, Paestum 488; 13.17; Hittites 455; Jebel

Barkal 381; Jerusalem 512; Kamun-sa 577; Karnak, Thebes 10.30; Moche, Sun and Moon 656, 658–59; 17.25, 17.26; Neak Pean 589; Nippur 443; Niuheliang 554–55; 15.3; Olympia 499; Pagan 590; 15.46; Palenqeue, Temple of the Inscriptions 16.33, 16.34; Parthenon 494–95; 13.26, 13.27; Phimeanakas 588; Roma and Augustus 511; Rome 506; Shitenno-ji, Osaka 581; Sokkuram Buddha 577; 15.32; Ta Prohm 589; Templo Mayor, Tenochtitlán 633, 635; 16.45; Teotihuacán 615; 16.19, 16.20; Tepe Gawra 437; Tikal 627; Tiwanaku, Gateway of the Sun 661, 662; 17.29; Ur, ziggurat 447; 12.21; Uruk 439–40, 442; 12.8

Tenji, emperor 581
Tenmu, emperor 581, 582
Tennessee 322, 323, 326, 330
Tenochtitlán 596, 597, 628, 633, 634–35, 636, 637, 638, 639, 675; 16.42, 16.43; Eagle Warrior 16.44
Ten Thousand Chariot states 566
Teopantecuanitlan 16.11
teosinte 314, 316, 600; 9.9; see also maize
Teotihuacán 195, 596, 606, 613, 614–15, 616, 618, 619, 620–21, 623, 624, 628, 633; 16.19, 16.20, 16.21, 16.22; La Ventilla 617; Street of the Dead 614, 615; writing 609, 617; 16.23, 16.24
teparies 320
tepee 331
Tepe Gawra 437, 470
Tepe Hissar 442
Tepeneca 633
Tepe Sialk 442
Tepe Yahya 434, 446; 12.18
Tepti-ahar, king 462
Tequendam 339
Ter 549
Terêna 676
Termez 502
Ternifine 119
Terra Amata 114, 116
terracing 193; rice 303; 18.42
terracotta 384; army 568; 15.23; figurines 526, 530, 548, 583–84; humans 366, 369
Teshik-Tash 149
Teshub, god 12.31
Teso dos Bichos 672
Testart, Alain 212
Teuchitlan 604, 619, 620
Téviec 394, 410; 11.22
Texas 703
Texcoco 635, 636, 637, 638
textiles 192, 238, 261, 340, 343, 452, 616, 654, 663, 664; 17.17; see also silk
Tezcatlipoca, god 629
Thailand 243, 250, 252, 254, 260, 286, 302, 585; see also individual sites
Tha Kae 252, 254
Thar Desert 521
theater 498, 506
Theater of Dionysos 498
Thebes 376, 377, 484, 485, 487, 488, 500; 10.24, 10.27, 10.29, 10.30
Theodosius I 516
Thera 474, 482, 510
Thessaly 394, 400, 401; agriculture 11.8
Third Cataract, Nile 380; 10.31
Tholos, Athens 496; 13.29
tholos tombs see tombs
Thomas, Nicholas 301
Thorne, Alan 127, 131
Thrace 400, 401
thrones 605
Thule 679, 680, 710, 711; 18.39
Thutmose I 377

Tiaho Code 582
Tianna Qucun 563
Tiber 504
Tiberius 507
Tierra del Fuego 167, 312, 338
Tiger Warrior infantry 563
Tighenif 132
Tiglath-pileser, King 461, 464, 468
Tigris 195, 201, 232, 436, 438, 443, 459, 460
Tikal 596, 611, 616, 619, 620, 623, 624, 626–27, 628, 630; 16.35, 16.36
Tikopia 296
Tilcajete 195
Tiliviche 336, 337
Tilkitepe 436
Timargarha 520, 542
timber 464, 467, 504
Timbuktu 384
Timgad 383
Timor 288
Timucua 714
tin 419, 420, 427, 450, 453, 476, 490, 536, 562; mining 420
Ti-n-akof 364
Tiryns 451, 484, 485, 486; 13.15
Tisza Valley 406
Titicaca 342, 654, 655, 660
Tivicundo 642
Tiwanaku 297, 642, 645, 660–62; 17.29, 17.30
Tlacopan 636, 637
Tlaloc, god 635
Tlaxcallan 637, 638
Tlingit 706
Toalian 277
tobacco 330, 344, 389, 390
Toba volcano 140
Tollan 613, 622
Tolteca-Chichimeca people 629
Toltec (Arkansas) 686; 18.9
Toltecs 628–29, 631, 633, 636; see also Tula
tomatillos 315
tomatoes 344
tombs 261, 304, 418; Anyang 560, 562; 15.10, 15.12; beehive tombs, Crete 479; chambered Neolithic monuments 414; complex of King Tepti-ahar 462; dolmen, Korea 257; 7.29; Etruscan 492, 493; 13.21, 13.22; of Fu Hao, Anyang 561; 15.12; Gold Crown, Kyongju 576; 15.31; Great Plains 704; Heavenly Horse, Kyongju 576; 15.30; Jingdi 573; Kaminaljuyu 16.27; kings of Shu 565; K'inich Janaab' Pakal 624; 16.33; Koguryo 574; 15.29; Lintong 568; Liu Sheng 573; 15.28; Mawangdui 572–73; 15.26; Meroë 381; models 573; 15.27; Monte Albán 610, 618; Muryong, Kongju 575; Mycenae 485; Nan Douwas 8.34; Newgrange 414; 11.27; Nintoku, 579; 15.34, 15.35; Paekche 575; passage graves 414; Philip at Vergina 500; 13.34; Qin Shi Huangdui 568; 15.22, 15.23; Real Alto 650; ritual enclosures 418; Teotihuacán 16.19; tholos 479, 485; Tomb of the Dancers, Jian 574; of Tutankhamun 26, 377; 1.2, 10.29; vertical shaft in Mexico 604; Warring States period 558; Xin'gan 563; 15.13
Tomizawa 260
Tonga 276, 288, 290, 294, 296, 300, 301
Tongapatu 301
Tonglushan 571; 15.25
Tongsamdong 256–57
Tonto National Monument 320
Toolondo 274
Toprakkale 467
Toro 261
Torralba 119; 3.46

tortoises 150, 323, 522
Torwa 386
totem poles 707; 18.32
Toth, Nicholas 69
Toulouse 405
Toumra 10.18
Toutswe 369
towns 184, 196, 246, 372
trade 193, 195, 197, 273, 301–04, 351, 382, 383, 384, 385, 388, 390, 435, 438, 444, 449, 471, 719; 10.36; and African state formation 389; Aksum 382, 388; Amazonia 671; Ashur and Kültepe 453; Assyrian 455, 461; Aztec 637; Babylonia 462; Carthage 504; China 557, 586; Egyptian 377, 380, 388; expansion in Uruk 442; Indian Ocean 384, 388–89, 550; Indus Valley 536; Korea and China 574; Levant 450, 457; Mauryans 548; Mycenae 486; North America and Europeans 706; Old Assyrian 453; Persian Gulf 449; Philistines 464; Phoenicians 464; slave 351, 389; Southwest Asia 438, 443; Sumerian city-states 443; Tenochtitlan 635; Teotihuacán 616; Toltec 631; Ugarit 457; Uluburun shipwreck 459; Uruk 442
Trajan 474, 508, 509, 511; Column 508; 13.44; Forum 508; 13.44
Trang Kenh 249
transhumance 409, 528
Transvaal 367, 369
treasure: Troy 451; 12.25; Uluburun shipwreck 459
Treasury of Atreus 485
tree ring dating 696; 18.21
Tres Zapotes 602; 16.13
tribes 32, 680
Trichtebecher culture 408–09, 416
Trier 516
Trigger, Bruce 194
Trinil 59, 106, 130; 3.15, 3.16
Troödos Mountains 476
Troy 185, 434, 450–51, 476, 479, 480, 482, 500; 12.24, 12.25
Trujillo 658
Trundholm sun chariot 394, 422; 11.41
Tsang Cheng-hwa 284, 296
Tshitolian industry 356
Tsushima Strait 583
Tsutsumi 259
Tuamotus 296
tuberculosis 718
tubers 528, 647
Tucson 27, 317, 694, 696
Tucumé 297; Viejo 663
Tudhaliya, King 455, 456; 12.32
tuff correlations 74
tuff jewelry 578
Tukulti-Ninurta I, King 460, 461
Tula 596, 622, 628–29, 631, 633; 16.37, 16.38
Tula Chico 629
Tulan 342
Tularosa 320
Tullumay 667
Tunacunnhee 683
tundra 181
Tunisia 368, 383, 427, 490, 512
Tupi 644, 669
Tupiguarani 669, 671, 676
Tupinamba 644
Turkana Boy 86–92; 3.2, 3.4
Turkey 126, 154, 184, 196, 201, 209, 212, 226, 227, 229, 398, 433, 436, 446, 449, 458, 503, 585; Hittites 450, 454–56; 12.31, 12.32; Uluburun shipwreck 459; 12.37, 12.38; see also individual sites
turkeys 320, 326

Turner, Christy 167
turquoise 525, 597; beads 699
turtles 323, 550
turtle shells 558, 562; 15.9
Tuscany 406
Tushpa 467
Tushratta, King 460
Tutankhamun 26, 377; 1.2, 10.29
Tutishcainyo 642
Tuttul 449
Tuxtla Mountains 620
tweezers 610
Twin Rivers 117, 118
Tylissos 482
Tylor, Edward 32, 177, 193
Tynemouth 396
Tyre 464, 500
Tzintzuntzan 636

Uan Muhuggiag 362
Ubeidiya 57, 102, 103
Üçagizli 126, 152; 4.30
Ucayali River 646, 674
Udayadityavarman 589
Uganda 72, 365, 367, 386
Ugarit 434, 453, 456, 457, 460, 463; 12.36
Ukkuqsi 711
Ukraine 149, 152, 393, 396, 407
ullucu 341, 342, 344, 348
Uluburun shipwreck 459, 474, 476, 486, 513; 12.37, 12.38
Umm el Tlel 150, 154
Unguja Ukuu 388
Untash-Napirisha, King 462; 12.42
Upemba Depression 386
Upper Paleolithic period 141, 152, 154, 155, 156, 158, 159, 160, 161, 162, 164, 165, 166, 191, 201, 203, 205, 209, 393, 398, 400
Upper Xingu River 668, 672, 676–77
Uptar 166
Ur 442, 444, 447, 448, 449, 450, 461; 12.16; Royal Cemetery 444; 12.16; Ziggurat 447, 12.21
uranium-series dating 111
Urartu 434, 449, 463, 467; 12.46
urban development 502, 506, 508–09, 533, 534, 535, 568, 615, 629
urbanism: Amazon 675; Egypt 377–78; Mesoamerica 628
urbanization 380–87, 613; 10.19, 10.36
Urban Revolution 188, 196
Urewe 367
Urubamba River 671
Uruguay 644
Uruk 434, 438–42, 446, 470; 12.7, 12.8, 12.11; Warka Vase 441; 12.12
Utah 317, 326, 696; 9.26, 9.27, 9.28
U-Thong 590, 591
Utnur 520, 528; 14.6
Uto-Aztecan people 319, 703
Uttar Pradesh 539
Uxmal 631, 632; House of Governors 631; 16.39
Uzbekistan 149, 549

Valcamonica 426; 11.47
Valdivia 650, 651
Vale of Peshawar 539, 542
Valley Farms 317, 318
Valley of the Kings 377; 10.29
Vall, François 210
Vandals 516
Vanguard Cave, Gibraltar 150; 4.26, 4.27
van Heemskerk, Maerten 1.4
vanilla 315

Varna 394, 402, 403, 476; 11.12
Vasilievka III 396
Vasiliki 479
Vasques de Coronado, Francisco 712
Vathypetro 482
Vatsa 543
Vedbaek 416
Veii 474, 491, 492, 500, 506; 13.20
Venezuela 168, 669, 675, 676
Ventris, Michael 484; 13.14
Vera Cruz 608, 621
Vergina 500; 13.34
Vértesszöllös 116, 119
Vesali 590
Vespasian 508
Vesuvius 474, 510; 1.17
Via Appia 509
Viet Khe 236
Viet-Muong 262
Vietnam 235, 236, 249, 249–50, 262, 265, 302, 303, 570, 586, 591–92; see also individual sites
Vijaya Sambhava 584
Vikings 710
village farming 212–13, 216, 477
villages/settlements: aceramic Neolithic 218; Bandkeramik 412–13; 11.25, 11.26; Bronze Age Greece 479; "central place" for religious practices 220; with central plaza 334, 335; in central and western Europe 423; community buildings 218–19; 6.20; conflict between, North America 690–91; Eastern Woodlands, North America 684; Ecuador 334; Egypt 371; farming villages 525, 600–01; fortified 425–26, 428; Great Plains 704–05; Halaf communities 435; Hawaiian 298; Hofplatz 412; kin groups, Colorado 695; Late Woodland period, North America 684, 686; with longhouses 412–13; Mesoamerica 600–01; Minoan Crete 482; Mississippian 688–89; with moats 585; Neolithic in South Asia 524–28, 526; Nile Valley 363; Northwest, North America 708; outside the Greek cities 498; with palisades and ditches 688, 705; pithouse 320; Plains Village 705; planned settlements 530, 531; 14.8; with plazas 675, 676, 692; pueblos 680, 696–97, 701; and rice cultivation 242; with sacred enclosures 672; "settlement cells" 413; in South Asia 519; stamped earth enclosures 556; with stilt houses 288; stockades and pens 527, 528; stone, sod, driftwood 711; subterranean buildings 217; 6.18; Wohnplatz 412
Villanova Iron Age 493
Vinca 406
Vindhyan escarpment 521, 522, 523
Vindija 126, 140, 148
Vinland 710
Vinnicombe, Patricia 358
Vinschgau 409
Virgil 503
Virú Valley 35, 659; 1.12
Vishnu, god 589
Vistula 393
Vix 424, 427, 490; 11.44
Vogelherd 158; 4.35, 4.36, 4.37, 4.38
volcanic eruption 39, 482, 508, 613; 1.15
voyages of discovery 30

Wadi en-Natuf 208; see also Natufians
Wadi Kubbaniya 356; 10.6
Wales 419, 430
Walker, Alan 89
Wallacea 155, 276
Wallace, Alfred 47
Wallace Line 283

wall frescoes/paintings 201, 224, 440, 451, 461, 574, 605, 619; 6.28, 10.21, 12.28, 15.29, 16.22, 17.25; Etruscan 492; 13.21
walls for defense 564, 611, 688; Great Wall of China 570; 15.24
Ward, Ryk 167
warfare 192, 197, 298, 536, 604, 611, 623, 627, 656, 705; and Confucianism 567; North America 686, 705; Northwest, North America 708
Wari 645, 660, 661, 662, 665
Warka see Uruk
Warka Vase 441; 12.12
Warring States period 560, 566, 567–68, 570
warriors 604, 612, 622, 624, 625, 629, 630, 635, 636, 637, 656, 658–59, 687, 714; 13.32, 16.30, 16.36, 16.41; Eagle Warrior 16.45
Washington 332, 708, 709; Kennewick Man 168
wasi 666
water buffalo 536
waterlogged sites 395, 396, 406, 425; 11.5
Watson Brake 328–29, 681
Watson, William 254
weapons 158, 162–63, 163, 322, 436, 562, 563, 566, 568, 574, 576, 604; clay sling missiles 436; swords 424, 425, 427; 11.52; wrist guards for archers 436
weaving 238, 242, 243, 247, 248, 249, 251, 261, 262, 281, 290, 651, 659; 9.39
Wei 566, 567, 585
Weidenreich, Franz 99, 127; 3.18
Wei River, China 237, 238
Weiss, Andrew 256
Wei Valley 563
Wei zhi 260
Wendi, Emperor 580
West Africa 351, 352, 362, 364, 383–84, 383; agriculture 363–64; hunter-gatherers 359–60; iron 366
Western Deffufa 380
Western Han 554
Western Jin 584
Western Zhou dynasty 563–66
West Virginia 682; 18.2
whales 337, 709; whale bone houses 18.39
whale-tooth pendants 292
wheat 184, 185, 205, 226–27, 261, 351, 362, 363, 388, 433, 436, 525, 525, 526, 536; China 571; Egypt 371
Wheat, Joe Ben 309
Wheeler, Sir Mortimer 78, 524, 529, 537, 538, 541, 550; 14.36
wheels 410
White, John 30; 1.5, 1.6, 19.3
White, Leslie 35
White Paintings Shelter 142
White, Tim 68
Whitsunday Island 268
Wilcox, David 693
wild ass 227
wild cattle 527, 528
wild pigs 395
Wilgie Mia 273
Willandra Lakes 130, 131, 156
Willendorf 164; Venus of 4.49
Willey, Gordon 30, 188; 1.12
Wilshusen, Richard 697
Windmiller Tradition 333
Windover 322; 9.21
wine 427, 428, 430, 457, 490, 498
Wittfogel, Karl 196
Wolpoff, Milford 127
wolves 183
Wonderwerk Cave 356

wood: bows and arrows 355; containers 576; digging sticks 355; 10.5; drums 555; figurines 687, 688; 18.10, 18.11; fire-making tools 340; masks 688; 18.11; models of entry courts, Chimor 664–65; objects 699; paddle 396; pegs 355; shelves 452; sickle 363; spears 114; 3.37, 3.38; tools 246, 709; 7.31, 10.4, 10.5; wedges 355
Woodburn, James 212
woodcarving 366, 663
wool 343, 452, 536, 576, 718
wool garments 457
woolly rhinoceros 150, 178, 395
workshops 629
World's Columbian Exposition 685; 18.8
Wrangel Island 178
Wrangham, Richard 78
Wright, Gary 209
writing 27, 196–98, 197, 372, 375, 379, 382, 440–41, 456; 5.12, 12.11; alphabetic script 458, 464, 490; Chinese 558–59; 15.8; cuneiform 440–41, 442, 443, 452, 454, 455, 466; 12.9, 12.10; Egypt 197, 198; glyphs 607, 608, 609, 617, 629, 660; 16.23, 16.24; Harappan script 519; hieroglyphs 458, 464, 484; Indian Brahmi script 584; Indus script 532; 14.11; Kharoshthi script 302, 584; Linear A 480, 481, 482, 484; Linear B 480, 482, 484, 485; 13.13, 13.14; Maya 607–10; 16.15, 16.17; Mesoamerica 597, 598, 607–10; Proto Elamite script 445; small seal script, China 568; Teotihuacán 609, 617; 16.23, 16.24
writing board 459
written records 27, 198, 260, 471; Amarna Letters 378, 456, 458, 460, 461; 12.34; and archaeology 27; Assyria 460, 461, 466; Bamboo Annals 562; bamboo slips 559, 566; 15.8; bilingual texts at Hattusa 458; bronze vessel, China 15.14; Champa 592; Codex Fejérváry-Mayer 1.14; Codex Mendoza 16.47; Confucian 15.20; Dvaravati 590–91; Ebla 452, 453; 12.26, 12.27; Hittites 454; Hittite treaty with Egypt 12.33; Ipsongni inscription 574; Kültepe-Kanesh 453, 455; letters from Egypt to Amarna 458, 460; 12.34; Mai zun 563; Mauryan empire 547; Mauryans, edicts 14.33; Maya 632; Maya inscriptions 611, 623; 16.15, 16.17; Minoan Crete 484; 13.13; Nuzi, Mittani stat 458; Old Testament 465; Shanshan 584; Shattiwaza Treaty 460; Shi Ji 553, 555, 558; Shitthaung Pagoda 590; on silk 559, 566; Tibetan Li Yul annals 584; Ugarit 458; Urartu 467; Yamato kingdom of Japan 578; Yucatán 623; Zhou 562; Zimri-Lim 451
Wucheng 562
Wudi, Emperor 570, 573
Wu Ding 560, 562
Wu, Emperor 120, 566, 585
Wuhan 571
Wu Hung 573
Wynn, Thomas 69
Wyoming 683

Xeguan 238
Xerxes, King 487
Xi 559

Xiachuan 236, 238
Xiadu 568
Xia dynasty 236, 553, 554, 556, 557, 570, 582, 571; 15.5, 15.7
Xiajiadian culture 556–57, 557
Xi'an 573
Xi'ang 560
Xiang River 248
Xianrendong 236, 241, 242, 243
Xiaotoun 558
Xiashu 240
Xibaimaying 238
Xincun 248
Xin'gan 562
Xinguano 642, 676; 17.45, 17.46
Xinjiang 582
Xin Zhui 572
Xiongnu 584
Xiu 633
Xochicalco 596, 622; 16.30, 16.31
Xochitecatl 621
Xom Ren 236
Xon Con 252
Xuan Lu 236
Xueguan 238
Xuejiaganglu 247
Xujiayo 126, 130

Yalu River 574
Yamashiro, Prince 581
Yamato 554, 567, 578–83
Yamhad 451, 453, 454, 459
Yamnaya culture 582
yams 185, 364, 369; 10.14
Yan 563, 566, 568
Yangshao 236, 245, 555; 7.12, 7.13
Yangzi Valley 235, 236, 240–42, 244, 246–48, 250, 261, 262, 280, 553, 558, 562, 566; social complexity 554
Yan Wenming 242
Yaoshan 553; 15.1
Yarim-Lim, King 451
Yarim Tepe 436; 12.3
Yashovarman 587, 588
Yasmah-Adad, King 451
Yaxchilán 625
Yayoi culture 236, 258–59, 260–61, 554, 578; 7.31, 7.32
Yazılıkaya 455; 12.32
Yde Girl 429; 11.51
Yellow Emperor 559
Yellow River 195, 235, 237, 238, 238, 239, 240, 553, 561, 562, 570
Yellowstone 683; 18.7
Yenesi Valley 582
Yi Jing 572
Yi Jiu 566
Yinshanling 236
Yomei 580
Yoruba 384
Yoshinogari 260; 7.35
Yotkan 583

Younger Dryas 178, 178, 186, 203, 204, 206, 214, 227, 237, 242; 6.1
Yuan 241
Yuanmou 130
Yuanshan 284; 8.17
Yucatán 595, 610, 619, 623, 628, 630, 632
Yuchan 236, 241
Yue 566
Yunnan 236, 248–49, 251, 570
Yunxian 130
Yuryaku 578

Zagros Mountains 188, 201, 203, 209, 210, 216, 228, 433, 442, 465
Zaire see Democratic Congo
Zambezi River 144
Zambia 95, 114, 117, 118, 119, 132, 133, 134, 355, 356, 367; 10.5
Zambujal 405
Zana River 645
Zanzibar 388
Zapotec 196, 595, 596, 598, 601, 607, 612, 618; 16.14
Zarzian culture 203, 210, 211
Zawi Chemi 211
zebra 142
zebu cattle 185, 364, 369, 387, 525
Zegura, Stephen 167
Zeus, god 484, 499, 501; 13.36; Altar at Pergamon 503; 13.38
Zhangnao 241
Zhao 566, 567
Zhejiang 247, 553
Zheng 566
Zhengdi, Emperor 571
Zheng Han 566
Zhengzhou 236, 559, 561, 562
Zhishanyan 284
Zhob 528
Zhong Ding 561
Zhongyuan 236
Zhou 236, 555, 559
Zhoukoudian 99, 116, 117, 119, 130; 3.41; animal bones 120; skull of Homo erectus 3.19; stone tools 100–01; 3.20
Zhuangbai 564; 15.14
Zide, Arlene 262
Zide, Norman 262
ziggurat: Al Untash-Napirisha 463; Dur Kurigalzu 12.41; of Ur 447; 12.21
Zimbabwe 351, 356, 367, 369, 384, 386
Zimri-Lim 450; 12.28
Zinchecra 362
Zincirli 464
Zinjanthropus site 67
Ziwa tradition 367
Zohapilco 316
Zongzhou 563
zoomorphic monuments 605
Zuni Pueblo 318
Zurla 427